Key to map symbols

III

(22a)	**Motorway** with junction number
	Primary route – dual/single carriageway
	A road – dual/single carriageway
	B road – dual/single carriageway
	Minor road – dual/single carriageway
	Other minor road – dual/single carriageway
	Road under construction
	Tunnel, covered road
	Rural track, private road or narrow road in urban area
	Gate or obstruction to traffic (restrictions may not apply at all times or to all vehicles)
	Path, bridleway, byway open to all traffic, road used as a public path
	Pedestrianised area
DY7	**Postcode boundaries**
	County and unitary authority boundaries
	Railway, tunnel, railway under construction
	Tramway, tramway under construction
	Miniature railway
Walsall	**Railway station**
	Private railway station
	London Underground station
	Tram stop, tram stop under construction
	Bus, coach station

◆	**Ambulance station**
◆	**Coastguard station**
◆	**Fire station**
◆	**Police station**
✚	**Accident and Emergency entrance to hospital**
H	**Hospital**
+	**Place of worship**
i	**Information Centre** (open all year)
P	**Parking**
P&R	**Park and Ride**
PO	**Post Office**
⋏	**Camping site**
⊞	**Caravan site**
▶	**Golf course**
⊠	**Picnic site**
Prim Sch	**Important buildings, schools, colleges, universities and hospitals**
River Medway	**Water name**
	River, weir, stream
	Canal, lock, tunnel
	Water
	Tidal water
	Woods
	Built up area
Church	**Non-Roman antiquity**
ROMAN FORT	**Roman antiquity**
◀ 87 / 228	**Adjoining page indicators and overlap bands** The colour of the arrow and the band indicates the scale of the adjoining or overlapping page (see scales below)

Abbr	Full	Abbr	Full	Abbr	Full
Acad	**Academy**	Inst	**Institute**	Recn Gd	**Recreation Ground**
Allot Gdns	**Allotments**	Ct	**Law Court**		
Cemy	**Cemetery**	L Ctr	**Leisure Centre**	Resr	**Reservoir**
C Ctr	**Civic Centre**	LC	**Level Crossing**	Ret Pk	**Retail Park**
CH	**Club House**	Liby	**Library**	Sch	**School**
Coll	**College**	Mkt	**Market**	Sh Ctr	**Shopping Centre**
Crem	**Crematorium**	Meml	**Memorial**	TH	**Town Hall/House**
Ent	**Enterprise**	Mon	**Monument**	Trad Est	**Trading Estate**
Ex H	**Exhibition Hall**	Mus	**Museum**	Univ	**University**
Ind Est	**Industrial Estate**	Obsy	**Observatory**	Wks	**Works**
IRB Sta	**Inshore Rescue Boat Station**	Pal	**Royal Palace**	YH	**Youth Hostel**
		PH	**Public House**		

■ The small numbers around the edges of the maps identify the 1 kilometre National Grid lines

■ The dark grey border on the inside edge of some pages indicates that the mapping does not continue onto the adjacent page

The scale of the maps on the pages numbered in blue is 5.52 cm to 1 km • 3½ inches to 1 mile • 1: 18103	0 ¼ ½ ¾ 1 mile 0 250 m 500 m 750 m 1 kilometre
The scale of the maps on pages numbered in red is 11.04 cm to 1 km • 7 inches to 1 mile • 1: 9051.4	0 220 yards 440 yards 660 yards ½ mile 0 125 m 250 m 375 m ½ kilometre

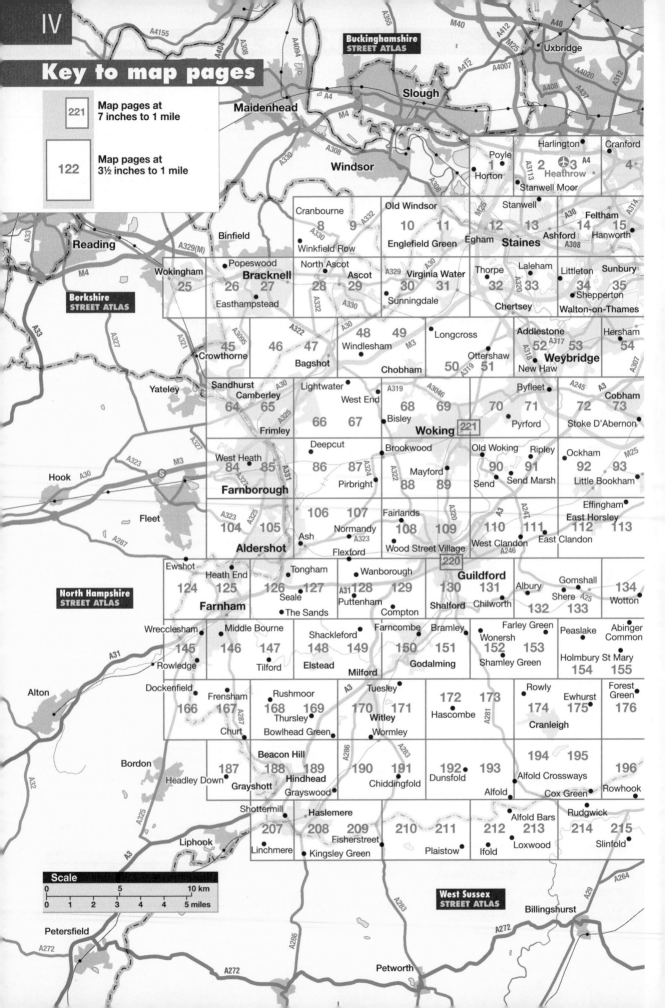

IV

Key to map pages

221	Map pages at 7 inches to 1 mile
122	Map pages at 3½ inches to 1 mile

Buckinghamshire STREET ATLAS

Uxbridge

Slough

Maidenhead

Windsor

Harlington Cranford

Poyle **1** Horton **2** ✈**3** **A4** **4**
Heathrow
Stanwell Moor

Stanwell

Reading

Binfield

Cranbourne **8** **9** Old Windsor **10** **11** **12** **13** **14** Feltham **15** Hanworth
Winkfield Row Englefield Green Egham Staines Ashford

Berkshire STREET ATLAS

Wokingham

Popeswood **25** North Ascot **26** **27** Bracknell **28** Ascot **29** **30** Virginia Water **31** Thorpe **32** Laleham **33** Littleton **34** Sunbury **35**
Easthampstead Sunningdale Chertsey Shepperton Walton-on-Thames

45 Crowthorne **46** **47** **48** **49** Windlesham Longcross Addlestone **52** **53** Weybridge Hersham **54**
Bagshot Chobham **50** Ottershaw **51** New Haw

Yateley

Sandhurst Lightwater West End Byfleet Cobham
Camberley **64** **65** **66** **67** **68** **69** Bisley **70** **71** **72** **73** Stoke D'Abernon
Frimley Woking **221** Pyrford

Hook

Deepcut Brookwood Old Woking Ripley Ockham
West Heath **84** **85** **86** **87** **88** **89** Mayford **90** **91** Send Marsh **92** **93** Little Bookham
Farnborough Pirbright Send

Fleet

Effingham
104 **105** **106** **107** Fairlands **108** **109** **110** **111** **112** East Horsley **113**
Aldershot Ash Normandy Wood Street Village West Clandon East Clandon
Flexford **220**

North Hampshire STREET ATLAS

Ewshot Tongham Wanborough Guildford Gomshall
124 Heath End **125** **126** **127** **128** **129** **130** **131** Albury Shere **134**
Farnham Seale Puttenham Shalford Chilworth **132** **133** Wotton
The Sands Compton

Alton

Wrecclesham Middle Bourne Shackleford Farncombe Bramley Farley Green Peaslake Abinger Common
145 **146** **147** **148** **149** **150** **151** Wonersh **152** **153** **154** **155** Holmbury St Mary
Rowledge Tilford Elstead Godalming Shamley Green
Milford

Dockenfield Tuesley Rowly Forest Green
166 Frensham **167** **168** **169** **170** **171** **172** **173** **174** Ewhurst **175** **176**
Churt Thursley Bowlhead Green Witley Hascombe Cranleigh
Wormley

Bordon

Beacon Hill **194** **195**
187 **188** **189** **190** **191** **192** **193** Alfold Crossways **196**
Headley Down Grayshott Hindhead Chiddingfold Dunsfold Alfold Cox Green Rowhook
Grayswood

Shottermill Haslemere Alfold Bars Rudgwick
207 **208** **209** **210** **211** **212** **213** **214** **215**
Linchmere Fisherstreet Plaistow Ifold Loxwood Slinfold
Liphook Kingsley Green

Scale

0 ——— 5 ——— 10 km
0 1 2 3 4 4 5 miles

West Sussex STREET ATLAS

Billingshurst

Petersfield

Petworth

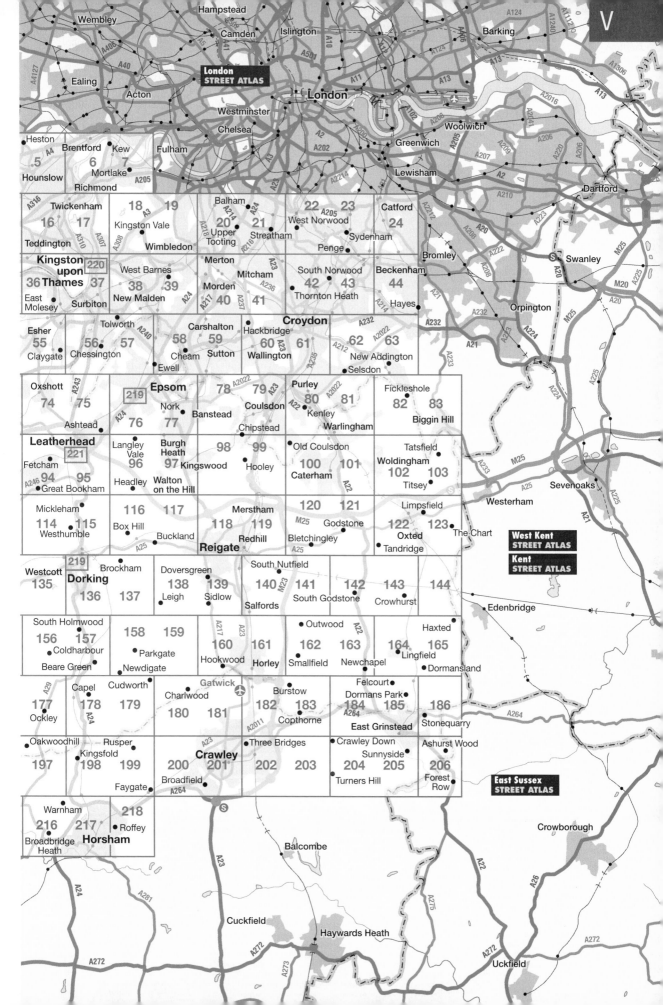

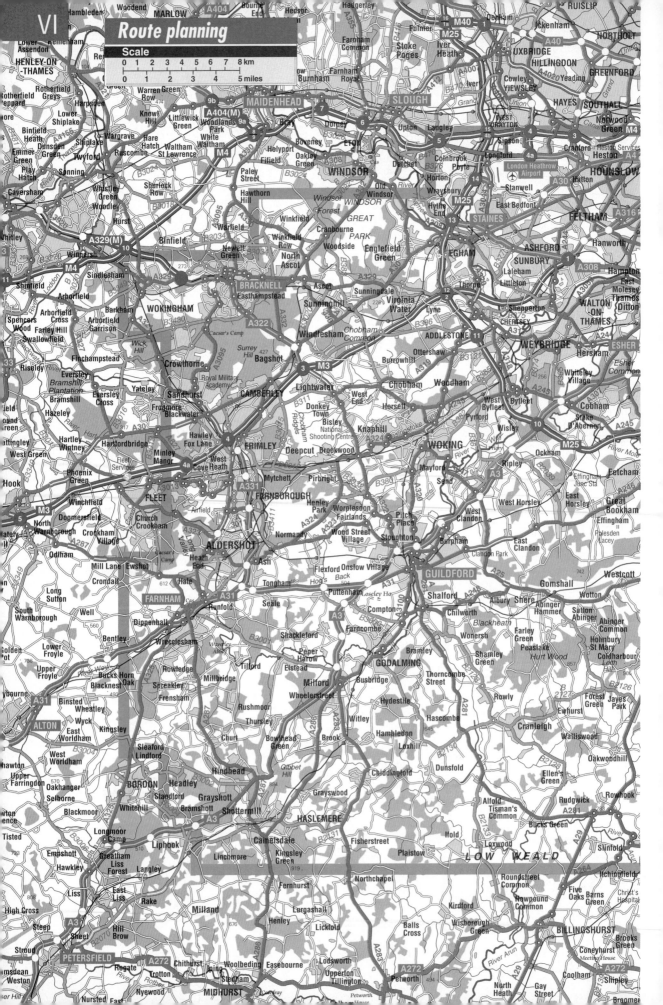

Route planning

Scale

0 1 2 3 4 5 6 7 8 km
0 1 2 3 4 5 miles

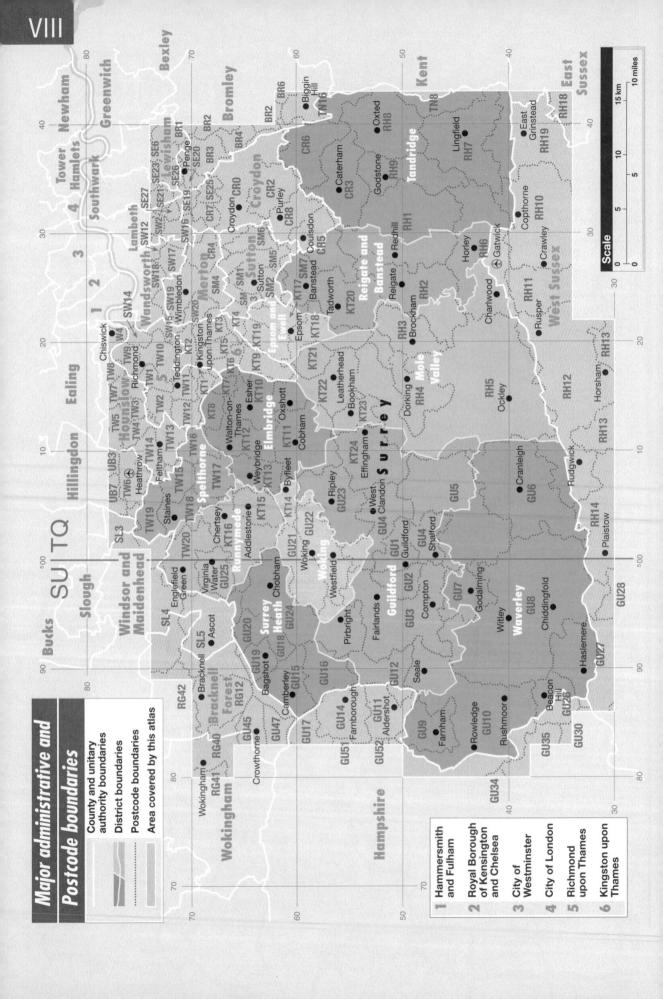

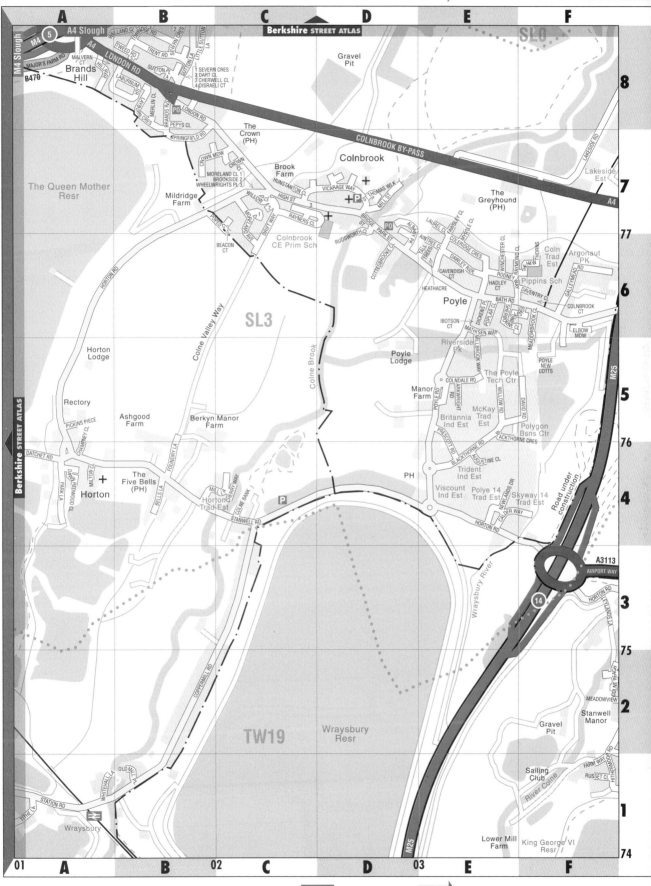

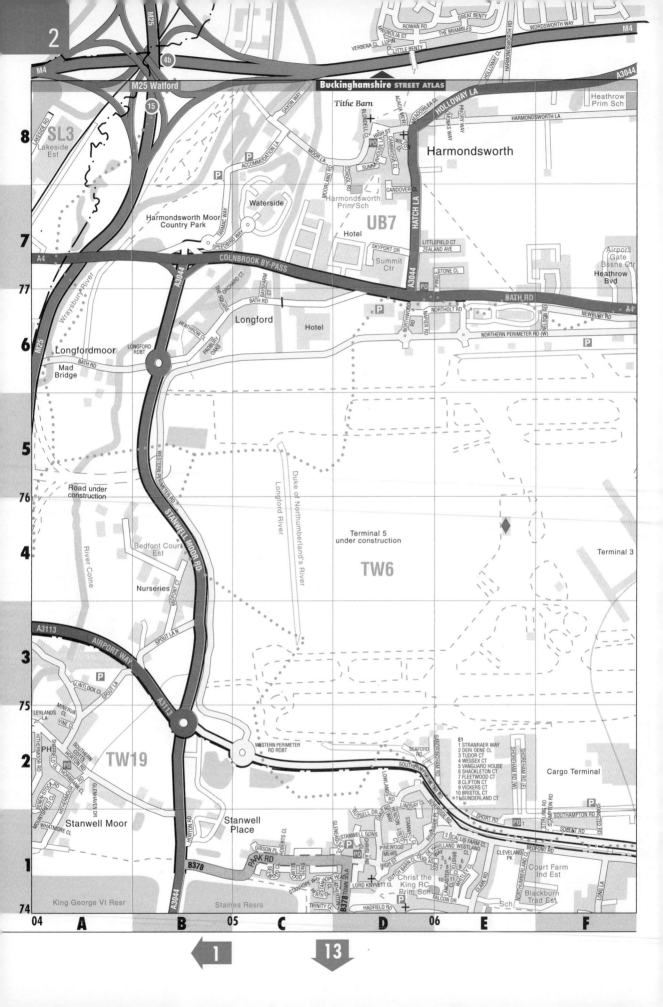

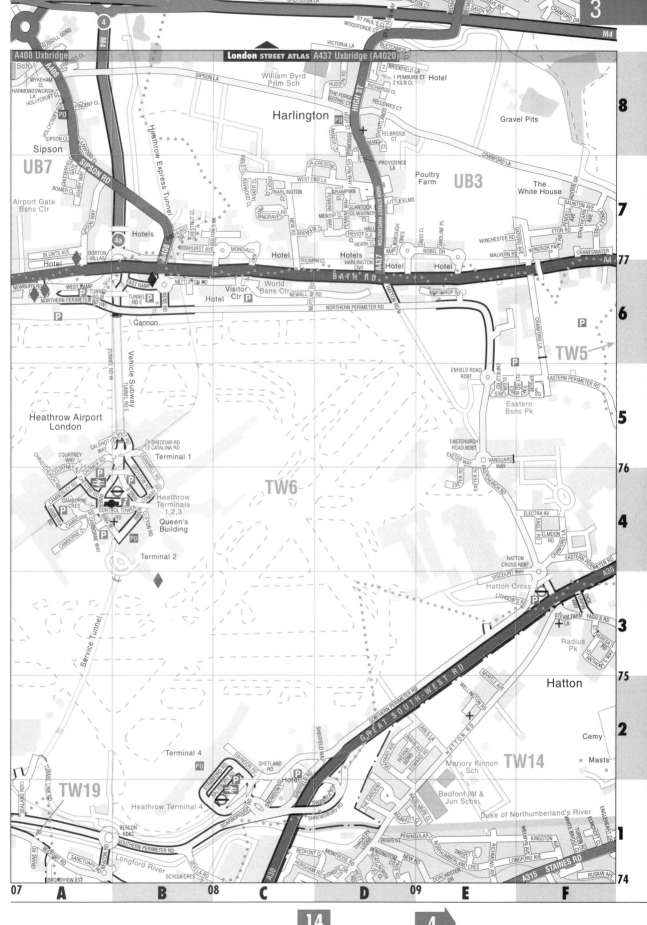

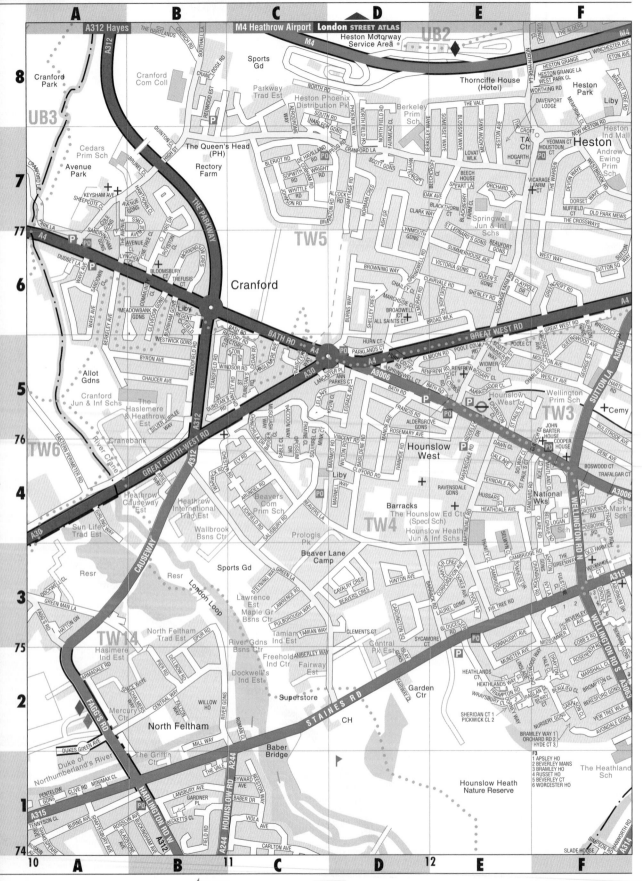

A312 Hayes

A   B   C   D   E   F

UB2

8 Cranford Park   Cranford Com Coll   Sports Gd   Heston Motorway Service Area   Thorncliffe House (Hotel)   Heston Grange   Heston Park

UB3   Parkway Trad Est   Heston Phoenix Distribution Pk   Berkeley Prim Sch   Heston Ind Mall   Heston

Cedars Prim Sch   The Queen's Head (PH)   Andrew Ewing Prim Sch

7 Avenue Park   Rectory Farm   TA Ctr   Heston

Keysham Ave   Sheepcote La

77   Springwell Jun & Inf Schs

6 Cranford   TW5   The Crossways

Liby

Great West Rd

5 Allot Gdns   The Haslemere & Heathrow Est   Hounslow West   Wellington Prim Sch   TW3   Cemy

Cranford Jun & Inf Schs   John Barter House   Cooper House

76 TW6   Cranebank   Hounslow West   PO

River Crane   Great South-West Rd   Liby   National Wks   St Mark's Sch

4 Heathrow Causeway Est   Heathrow International Trad Est   Beavers Com Prim Sch   Barracks   The Hounslow Ed Ctr (Specl Sch)   Logan Sch   A3006

Sun Life Trad Est   Wallbrook Bsns Ctr   Prologis Pk   TW4   Hounslow Heath Jun & Inf Schs   The Greenway

Resr   Beaver Lane Camp

3 Green Man La   London Loop   Sports Gd   Wellington Rd S

Resr   A315

TW14   Lawrence Est Maple Gr Bsns Ctr   North Feltham Trad Est   River Gdns Bsns Ctr

75 Haslemere Ind Est   Tamian Ind Est   Central Pk Est   Heathlands   The Heathland Sch

Freehold Ind Ctr   Fairway Est   Garden Ctr

Dockwell's Ind Est

2 Mercury Ctr   Willow Ho   Superstore   CH   F3
  1 APSLEY HO
  2 BEVERLEY MANS
  3 BRAMLEY HO
  4 RUSSET HO
  5 BEVERLEY CT
  6 WORCESTER HO

North Feltham   SHERIDAN CT 1 PICKWICK CL 2   BRAMLEY WAY 1 ORCHARD RD 2 HYDE CT 3

Duke of Northumberland's River   The Griffin Ctr   Baber Bridge

1 A315   Hounslow Heath Nature Reserve

74

10   A   11   B   C   12   D   E   F

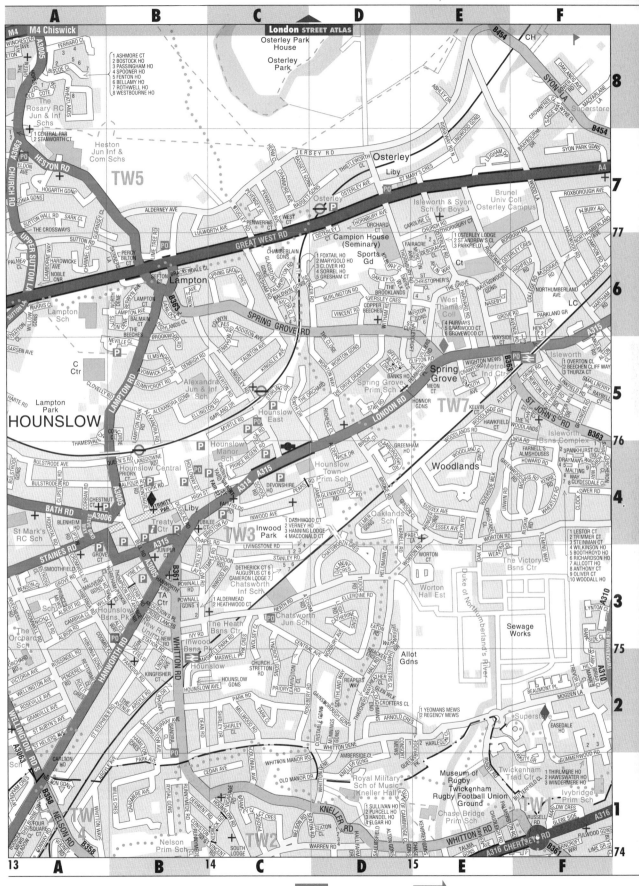

D8
1 BROCKSHOT CL
2 WESTBURY PL
3 BROOK LA N
4 Brook La Bns Ctr
5 BREAMAR CT
6 BROOK CT
7 CLIFDEN HO
8 CEDAR CT
9 CRANBROOK CT
10 ALEXANDRA RD
11 BERKELEY HO
12 WATERMANS CT

E8
1 FERRY SQ
2 WATERMANS CT
3 WILKES RD
4 ALBANY PAR
5 CHARLTON HO
6 ALBANY RD
7 ALMA HOUSE
8 GRIFFIN CT
9 CRESSAGE HO
10 TUNSTALL WLK
11 TRIMMER WLK
12 RUNNING HORSE YD
13 MISSION SQ
14 DISTILLERY WLK
15 COATES WLK
16 PERRAN CT

Map of Brentford, Isleworth, Richmond, Kew (TW7, TW8, TW9, TW1, TW10). London Street Atlas.

Grid index panels (within map):

D7
1 GALBA CT
2 SERVIUS CT
3 MAURICE CT
4 LEO CT
5 OTHO CT
6 ROMULUS CT

F6
1 PRIMROSE HO
2 LAWMAN CT
3 ROYSTON CT
4 GARDEN CT
5 CAPEL LODGE
6 DEVONSHIRE CT
7 CELIA CT
8 ROSSLYN HO
9 BRANSTONE CT
10 KEW LODGE
11 DUNRAVEN HO
12 STONELEIGH LODGE
13 TUNSTALL CT
14 VOLTAIRE

(White Lodge area)
1 WHITE LODGE CE
2 FERNEY MEADE WAY
3 TOWN FIELD WAY
4 TECK CL
5 THACKERAY CL

A4
1 Brewery Mews Bsns Ctr
2 TOLSTON HO
3 PERCY GDNS
4 WYNNE CT
5 WISDOM CT
6 SWANN CT
7 SHREWSBURY WLK
8 KING'S TERR

D2
1 GARRICK CL
2 OLD PALACE YD
3 THE WARDROBE
4 MAIDS OF HONOUR ROW
5 HUNTERS CT
6 QUEENSBERRY HO
7 THE GREEN
8 OLD PALACE TERR
9 PAVED CT
10 GOLDEN CT
11 BREWERS LA
12 THE SQUARE
13 LOWER GEORGE ST
14 ST JAMES'S COTTS
15 CHURCH WLK
16 VICTORIA PL
17 CASTLE YD
18 LEWIS RD
19 WAKEFIELD RD
20 CHURCH TERR
21 WARRINGTON RD
22 ORMOND AVE
23 ST HELENA TERR
24 WHITTAKER PL
25 HERON SQ
26 NORTHUMBERLAND PL

E3
1 ST JOHN'S GR
2 MICHEL'S ROW
3 MICHELSDALE DR
4 BLUE ANCHOR ALLEY
5 CLARENCE ST
6 SUN VALLEY
7 THAMES LINK HO

F3
1 THE TOWERS
2 LONGS CT
3 SOVEREIGN CT
4 ROBINSON CT
5 CALVERT CT
6 BEDFORD CT
7 HICKEY'S ALMSHOUSES
8 CHURCH ALMSHOUSES

(Gateways area)
THE GATEWAYS
1 FITZWILLIAM HO
2 PORTLAND TERR
3 PEMBROKE VILLAS

Bottom index:

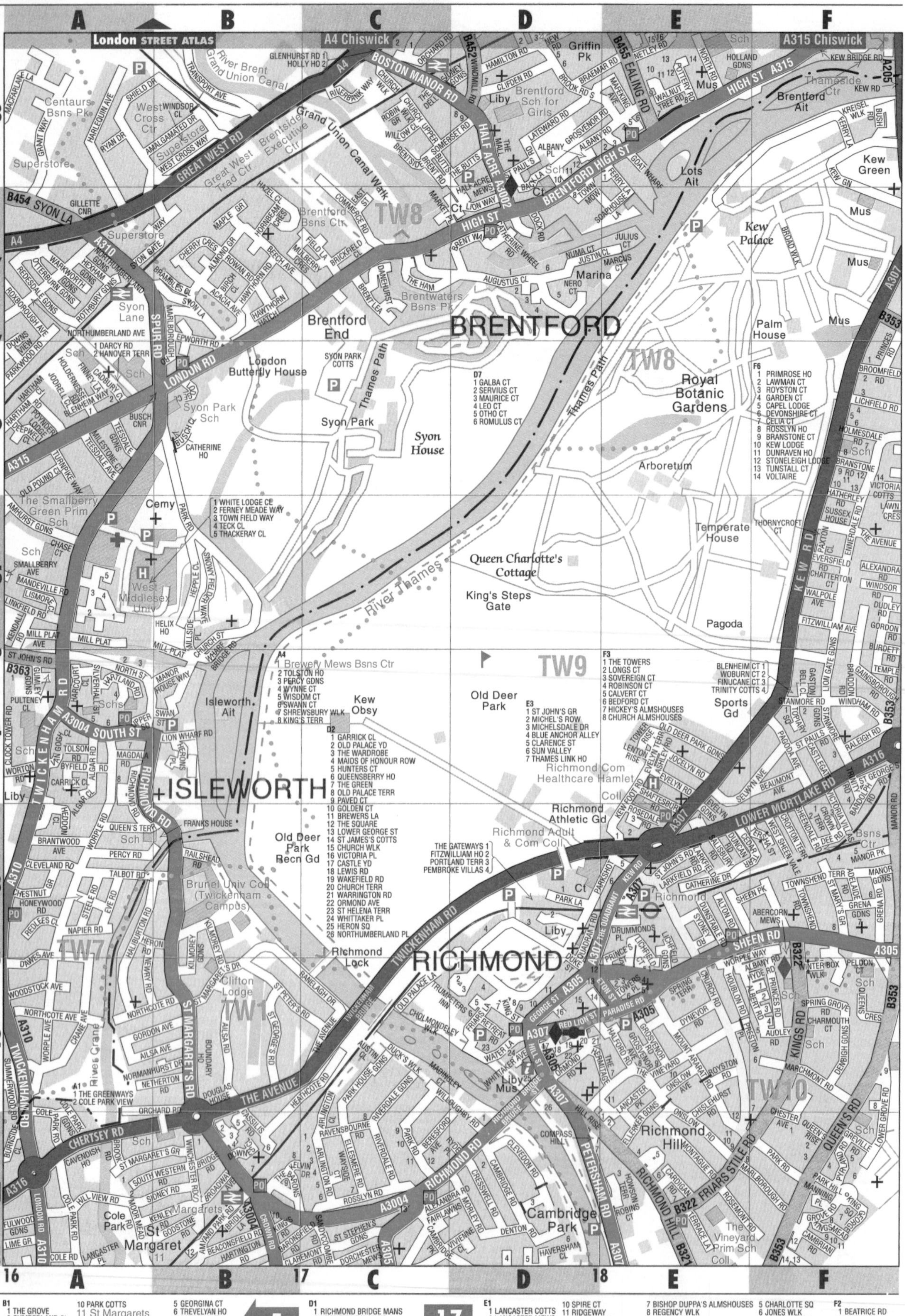

B1
1 THE GROVE
2 CUMBERLAND CL
3 WESTMORLAND CL
4 SUSSEX CL
5 NORFLK CL
6 NICOL CL
7 OLD LODGE PL
8 KELVIN CT
9 ST MARGARET'S CT
10 PARK COTTS
11 St Margarets Bsns Ctr

C1
1 HOWMIC CL
2 SEFTON CL
3 RAVENSBOURNE
4 ARLINGTON CT
5 GEORGINA CT
6 TREVELYAN HO
7 CARADON CT
8 GREEN HEDGES
9 OLD HOUSE GDNS
10 QUEENS KEEP
11 BERESFORD CT
12 LANGHAM CT
13 POPLAR CT

D1
1 RICHMOND BRIDGE MANS
2 HEATHERDENE MANS
3 AROSA RD
4 ROSELEIGH CL
5 RICHMOND HILL CT
6 GLENMORE HO
7 HILLBROW
8 HEATHSHOT
9 FRIARS STILE PL
10 SPIRE CT
11 RIDGEWAY
12 MATTHIAS CT

E1
1 LANCASTER COTTS
2 LANCASTER MEWS
3 BROMWICH HO
4 PRIORS LODGE

E2
1 LICHFIELD TERR
2 UNION CT
3 CARRINGTON LODGE
4 WILTON CT
5 EGERTON CT
6 BEVERLEY LODGE
7 BISHOP DUPPA'S ALMSHOUSES
8 REGENCY WLK
9 TEMPLE CT
10 ONSLOW AVENUE MANS
11 MICHELS ALMSHOUSES

F1
1 CHESTER CL
2 GROSVENOR CT
3 QUEEN'S CT
4 RUSSELL WLK
5 CHARLOTTE SQ
6 JONES WLK
7 HILDITCH HOU
8 ISABELLA CT
9 DAMER HO
10 ELIOT HO
11 FITZHERBERT HO
12 REYNOLDS CT
13 CHISHOLM RD
14 HOBART PL

F2
1 BEATRICE RD
2 LORNE RD
3 YORK RD
4 CONNAUGHT RD
5 ALBANY TERR
6 KINGSWOOD CT
7 SELWYN CT
8 BROADHURST CL
9 GROVE RD

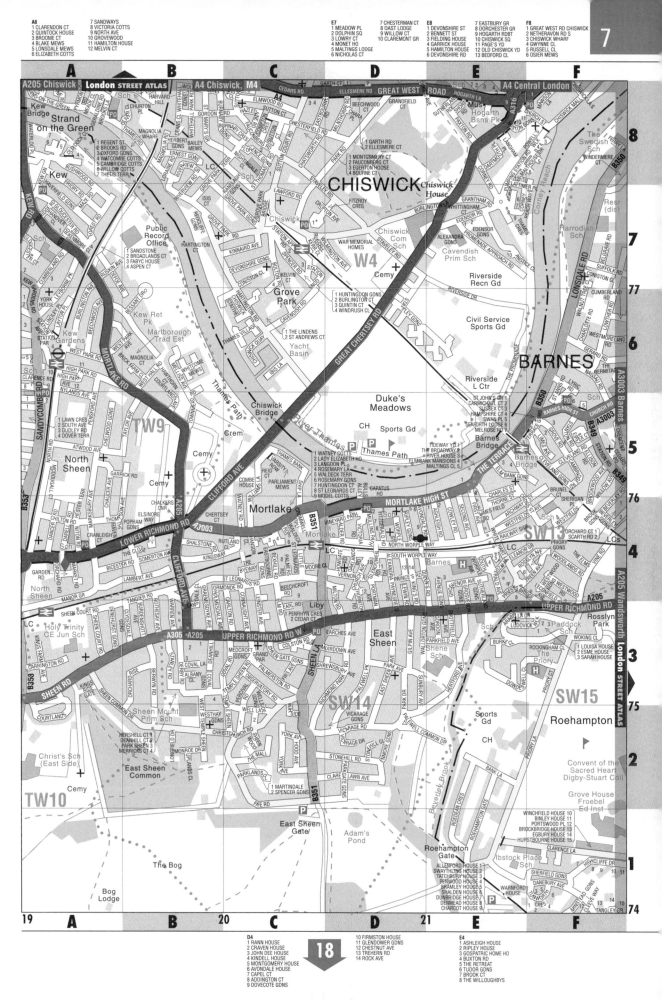

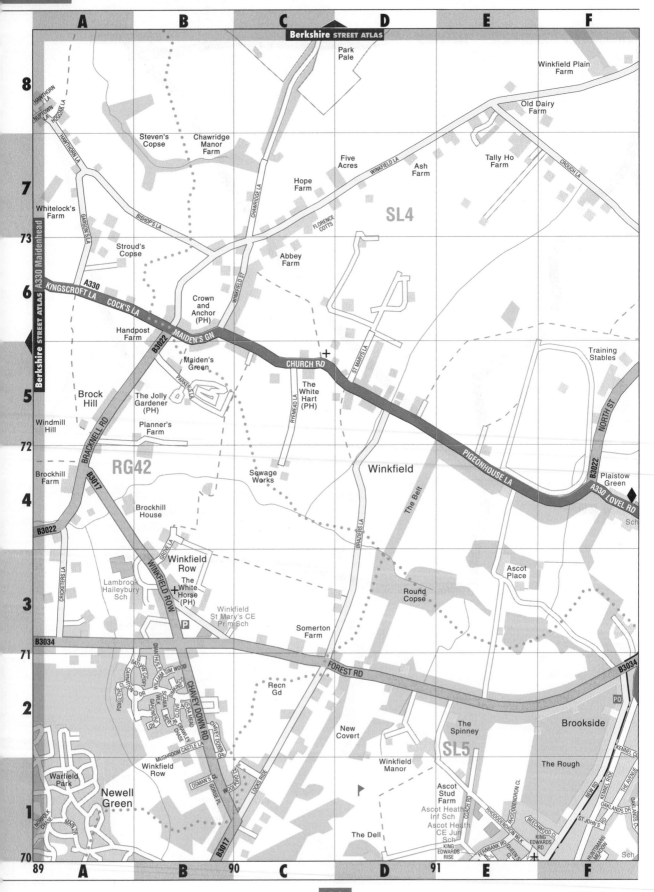

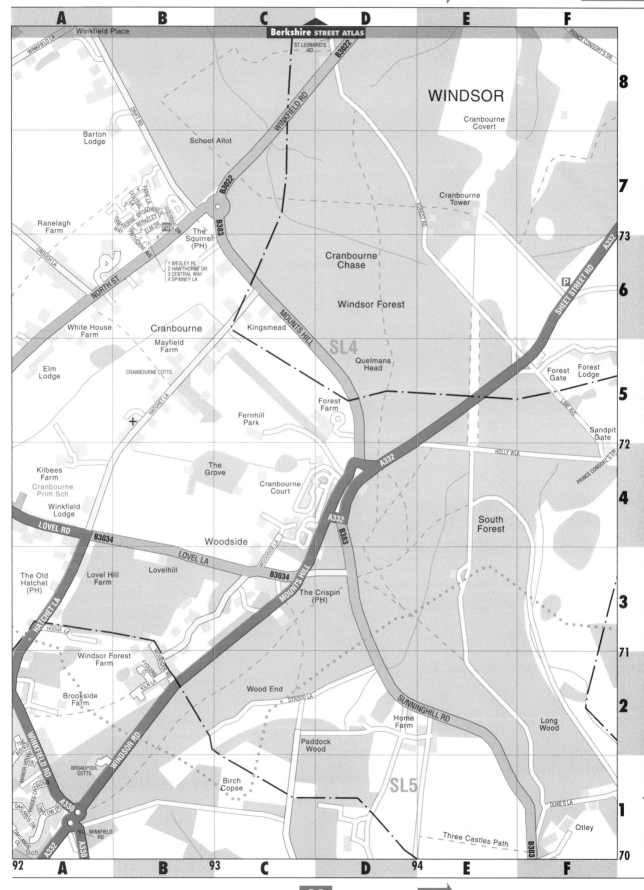

Berkshire STREET ATLAS

WINDSOR

A332 Windsor (A308)

Berkshire STREET ATLAS

Flemish Farm

Pickleherring Pond

Ranger's Lodge

Beehive Hill

Russel's Pond

Fiddle Covert

Seymours Plantation

Battle Bourne

The Gallop

Prince of Wales Pond

Rush Pond

Bear's Rails

Bear's Rails Pond

Cemy

PRINCE CONSORT'S DR

Richardson's Lawn Cotts

THE VILLAGE

QUEEN ANNE'S CL

Richardson's Lawn

The Village

PO

Isle of Wight Pond

SL4

Statue

Snow Hill

Deepstrood

Three Castles Path

Spring Hill

Cookes Hill

BISHOPSGATE RD

The Fox & Hounds (PH)

Poets Lawn

Queen Anne's Ride

Royal Lodge

Windsor Great Park

Dark Wood

The Royal Fst Sch

Cow Pond

Bishopsgate

Chapel Wood

PARK CLOSE COTTS

BROCKENHURST RIDE

WICK LA

The Sun (PH)

Park Close

MEZEL HILL COTTS

CUMBERLAND LODGE

Mezel Hill

Hilton's Covert

DUKES LA

Wilderness

The Savill Gardens

Parkside House

Square Covert

Slans Hill

Leiper Hill

Great Meadow Pond

Temple Hill

TW20

P

SL5

Norfolk Plantation

Norfolk Farm

Mill Pond

Statue

Smith's Lawn

Obelisk

Rosy Bottom

Obelisk Pond

Polo Gds

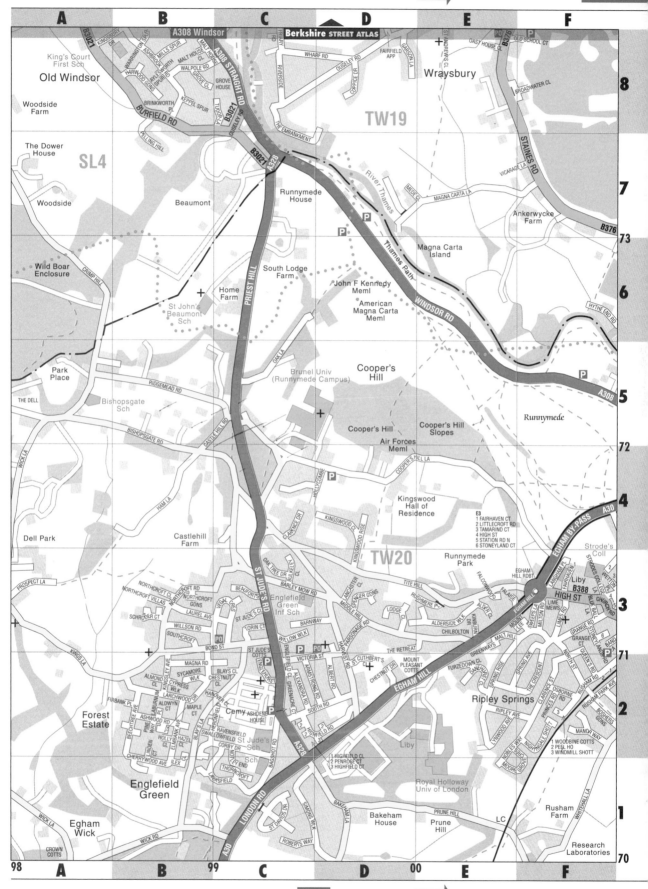

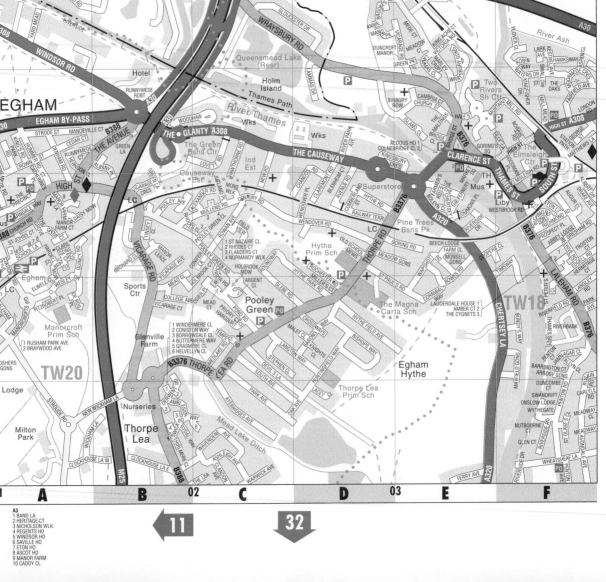

A B C D E F

8
7
73
6
5
72
4
3
71
2
1
70

01 A B 02 C D 03 E F

Wraysbury Resr

TW19

Bone Head

River Colne

Wks
RUNNYMEDE COTTS

Staines Moor

Bonehead Ditch

Sailing Club

Colne Brook

B376
STAINES RD
SARSBY DR
FEATHERS LA

Hythe End
BELL WEIR
COLNE WAY
FERRY LA

B376
13

Coline Valley Way

STAINES

The Moor
YEOVENEY CL
BERKELEY CL
Church Lammas

STAINES BY-PASS

A30
River Ash

WINDSOR RD
HYTHE END RD
RIVERSIDE
YARD MEAD

A308
A30

WRAYSBURY RD
GLOUCESTER DR
Queensmead Lake (Resr)
LAMMAS DR

ANNIE MANOR PK
MEDE CT
KING ACRE CT
VICARAGE RD
MEADOW
VICTORIA RD
GREEN PL
DUNCROFT MANOR
MABLEY CROFT
MARKET CL

LARK AVE
KESTREL AVE
HAWKSWAY
ROBIN WAY
WATERS DR
SWALLOW
THE OAKS
KINGFISHER
FAIRFIELD AVE

EGHAM
Hotel
RUNNYMEDE RDBT

Holm Island
Thames Path
WOODHAW
River Thames
Wks

BINBURY ROW
CAMBRIA CT
CHURCH ST
ISLAND CL
THE MALTINGS
HALE ST
BRIDGE ST
B376
GORING'S SQ

Two Rivers Sh Ctr
MUSTARD MILL RD
NORRIS RD
HIGH ST
A308
LONDON RD
PO
ST GEORGE
Station

A30
EGHAM BY-PASS
STRODE ST
MANDEVILLE CT
CEDAR CT
THE AVENUE
GREEN LA
ALBANY
THE GLANTY
A308
The Green Bsns Ctr
LOVETT RD
Causeway Est
Ind Est
THE CAUSEWAY

CHANDOS RD
NEW RD
KINGSBURY CRES
Superstore

ALDOUS HO 1
COLNEBRIDGE CL 2
RIVER PARK AVE
CLARENCE ST
Elmsleigh Ctr
TH
Mus
Liby
Westbrook Rd
MARKET PL
THAMES ST
SOUTH ST
P
P
MATTHEWS CL

MANOR FARM CT
HIGH ST
LC
VICARAGE RD CRES
PORTLAND RD
MONS WLK
CLAREMONT RD
BLEINGEM CT
AVENUE CL
HYTHE RD
B376
A320
RIVERSIDE DR
B376

The Precinct
MARDALE WAY
MANOR FARM
Mus
B388 CHURCH RD
ST JOHNS CT
CLARE GDNS
CLARE CRES
SCHOOL LA
DAISY MDW
ORCHARD CL
POOLEY AVE
RHODES RD
CENTURY RD
POOLEY GREEN RD
ALEXANDER WAY
FIELD VIEW
WENDOVER RD
1 ST NAZAIRE CL
2 RHODES CT
3 FLANDERS CT
4 NORMANDY WLK

Hythe Prim Sch
OLD SCHOOL LA
GORING RD
RAILWAY TERR
MEADOW GDNS
BEECH LODGE
FARM CL
MONSELL GDNS
Pine Trees Bsns Pk

PROSPECT PL
ABBEY LODGE
GRESHAM RD
BENTLEY RD
EDGELL RD
HERMITAGE
TROSTON RD

Egham
Sports Ctr
VICARAGE RD
MANOR LEAZE
VICARAGE CT
COLLEGE AVE
VICARAGE CT
MEAD CT
POND RD
PRIORY GDNS

Pooley Green
PO

CORNWALL WAY
BONDS RD
ST PAUL'S RD
WAPSHOT RD
COOPERS CL

The Magna Carta Sch
LAUDERDALE HOUSE 1
AMBER CT 2
THE CYGNETS 3

TW18
CHERTSEY LA
LALEHAM RD
TIMSWAY
SHEFFIELD
LANGLEY
PARK AVE
B376

Manorcroft Prim Sch
1 RUSHAM PARK AVE
2 BRAYWOOD AVE
Glenville Farm
1 WINDERMERE CL
2 CONISTON WAY
3 BORROWDALE CL
4 BUTTERMERE WAY
5 GRASMERE CL
6 HELVELLYN CL

MALET CL
LANGTON WAY
THE KNIGHTS
HYTHE FIELD AVE
BISHOPS WAY
Egham Hythe

RIVERFIELD RD
THAMES SIDE
RIVERBANK
BARRINGTON CT
ARGOSY GDNS
DUNCOMBE CT
SWANDRIFT
ONSLOW LODGE
WYTHEGATE

TW20
Lodge
Milton Park
STRODE RD
NEW WICKHAM LA
WICKHAM LA
Nurseries
Thorpe Lea
B3376 THORPE LEA RD
OVENDEN RD
CLOCKHOUSE LA W
CLOCKHOUSE LA E
B388
WARWICK AVE

CROSSWAYS
DEVIL'S LA
SOUTH AVE
PARK AVE
STEPHEN CL
OAK AVE
LACEY CL

Thorpe Lea Prim Sch

Mead Lake Ditch

NUTBOURNE CT
GLEN CT
MEADWAY
WHEATSHEAF LA
AVONDALE AVE
PO
FERRY AVE
RIVERSIDE DR
PENTON AVE
A320

M25

A3
1 BAND LA
2 HERITAGE CT
3 NICHOLSON WLK
4 REGENTS HO
5 WINDSOR HO
6 SAVILLE HO
7 ETON HO
8 ASCOT HO
9 MANOR FARM
10 CADDY CL

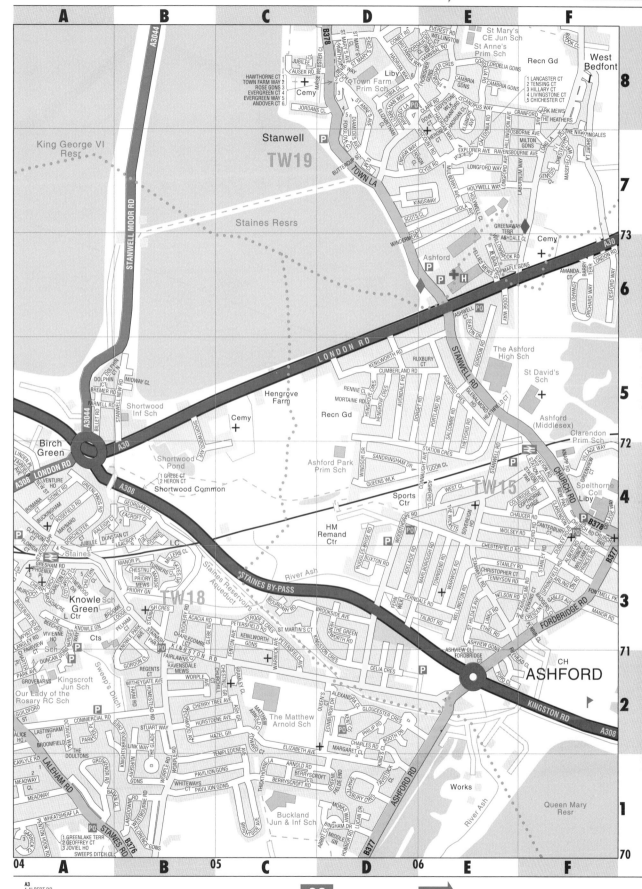

A3
1 ALBERT DR
2 BEACH'S HO
3 GRESHAM CT
4 PULLMANS PL
5 GRANGE CT

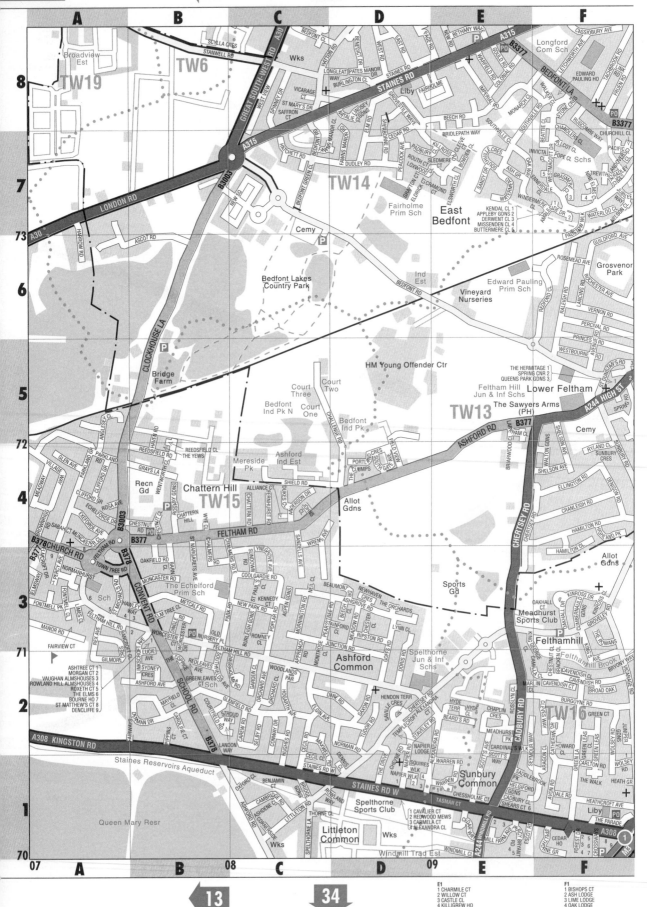

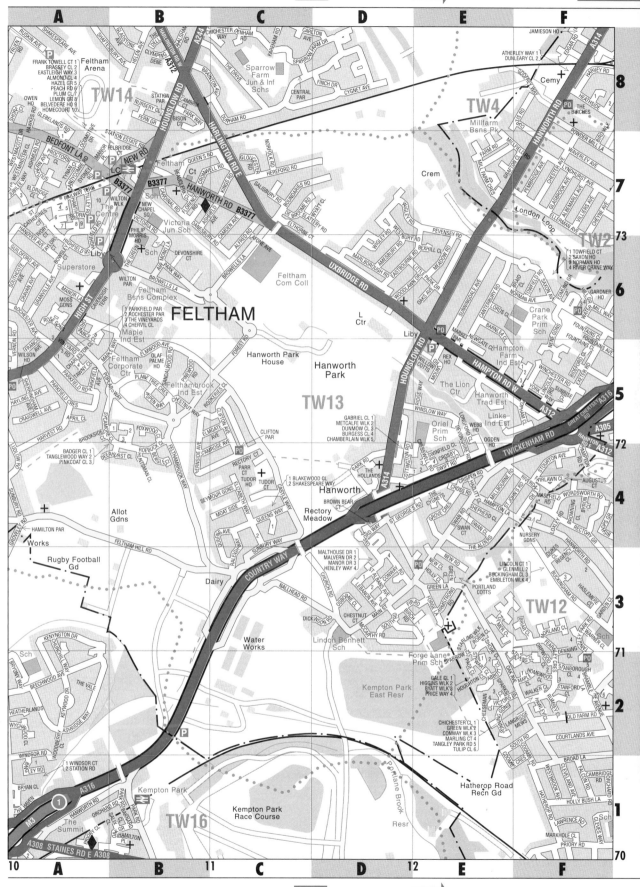

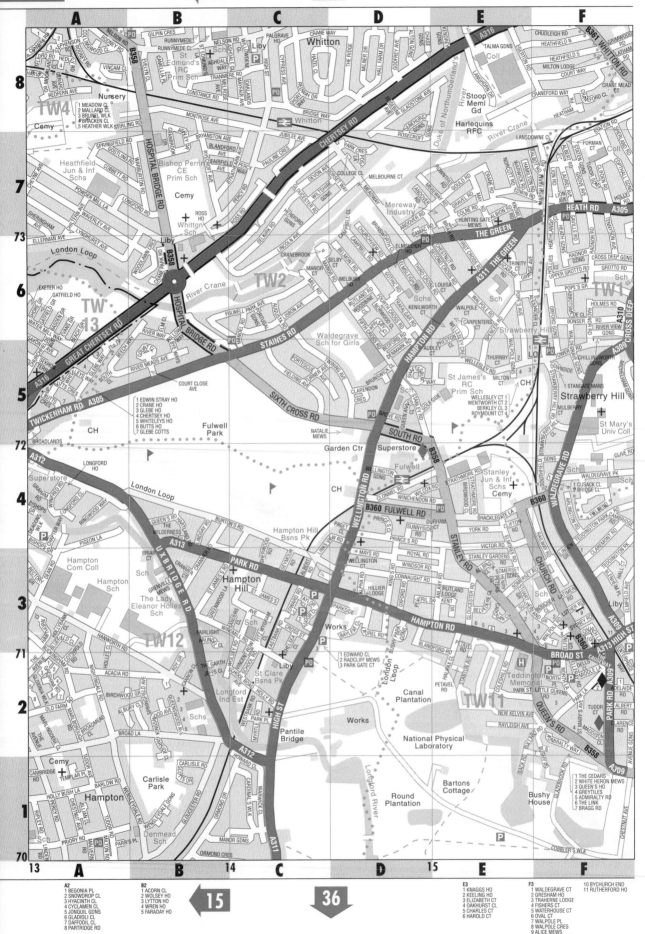

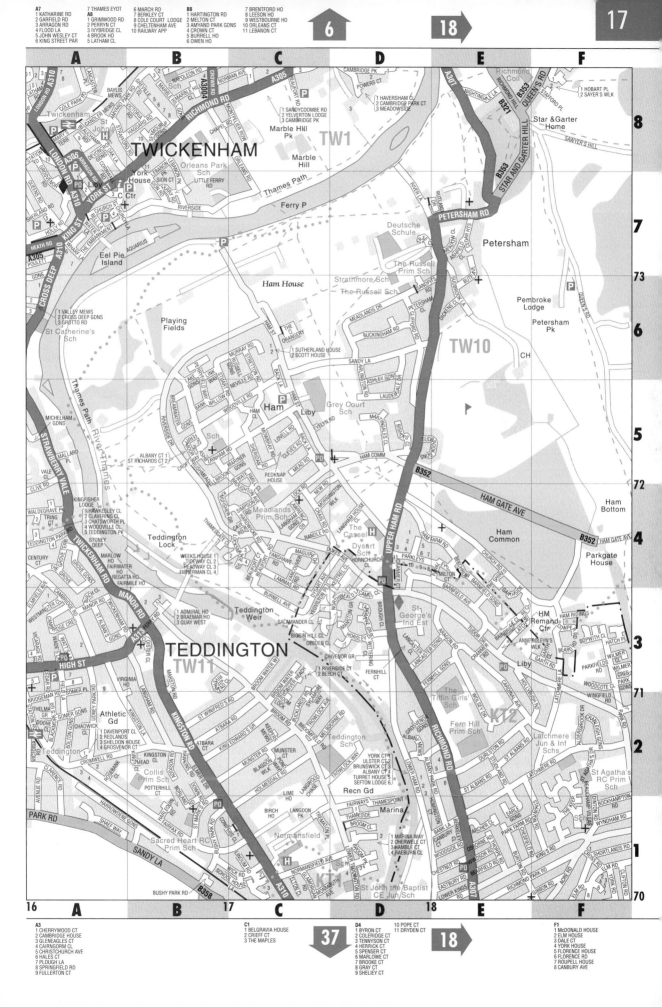

A B C D E F

8 7 73 6 5 72 4 3 71 2 1 70

Bog Lodge

SW14

Polo Field

Old House

Sawyer's Hill

Saw Pit Plantation

CLEEVE WAY 1
FINCHDEAN HOUSE 2
HOLMSLEY HOUSE 3
OVERTON HOUSE 4
TANGLEY GR 5
REDENHAM HOUSE 6
MOUNT ANGELUS RD 7

Sidmouth Wood

White Lodge
The Royal Ballet Sch

SW15

Beverley Brook

Deer Park

Pen Ponds

TW10

Spankers Hill Wood

Pond Plantation

Pond Slade

Richmond Park

FLORENCE TERR 1
EBOR COTTS 2

ROEHAMPTON VALE

Kingston Univ
Roehampton Vale Ctr

FRIARS AVE

STAG FRESHAM DR

STROUD CRES

War Meml

Robin Hood Gate

BEVERLEY COTTS

KINGSTON VALE

ROBIN HOOD RDBT

Hamcross Plantation

Liby

Playing Fields

Kingston Vale

Isabella Plantation

High Wood

VALE CRES

ADELAIDE RD

ROBIN HOOD LA

GRASMERE AVE

ULLSWATER CL

ULLSWATER CRES

Walkden Hall
(Hall of Residence)

WINDERMERE CRES

Sch

ROBIN HOOD WAY (KINGSTON BY PASS)

Combe Martin Coll

Combe Hurst

Kingston Univ

RYDAL GDNS

KESWICK AVE

COOMBE PK

Thatched House Lodge

King Clump

SW19

B2
1 GODSTONE HOUSE
2 HAMBLEDON HOUSE
3 KINGSWOOD HOUSE
4 LEIGH HOUSE
5 MILTON HOUSE
6 NEWDIGATE HOUSE
7 FARLEIGH HOUSE
8 OCKLEY HOUSE
9 EFFINGHAM HOUSE
10 DUNSFOLD HOUSE
11 RIBRIGHT HOUSE
12 CLANDON HOUSE
13 RIPLEY HOUSE

KINGSTON HILL

Mill Corner

Warren House
THE WATERGARDENS

WARREN PK

KT2

COOMBE RIDINGS

RANDOLPH CL

COOMBE WOOD RD

PAGET PL

CORSCOMBE CL

WARREN RD

WARREN CUTTING

HIGH COOMBE

SW20

THE LEIGH

Park Gdns

Queen's Rd

Cumberland House

MORECOMBE CL

RENFREW RD

STOKE RD

GEORGE RD

CRESCENT RD

Holy Cross Prep Sch

THE DRIVE

Schs

Coombe

COOMBE NEVILLE

EDGECOMBE CL

COOMBE END

GOLF CLUB DR

COOMBE HILL RD

BEVERLEY

COOMBE HILL GLADE

CH

Kingston

COOMBE LA W

A238 B283 A238

A308 B351

PO

ELM RD NEW RD

A1
1 QUEEN'S CT
2 ST GEORGES RD
3 PARK ROAD HOUSE
4 DAGMAR RD
5 TAPPING CL
6 ARTHUR RD
7 BOROUGH RD
8 BELVEDERE CT
9 BRAYWICK CT
10 DEAN CT
11 ROWAN CT
12 RICHMOND CT
13 SUNNINGDALE CT
14 HAWKER CT
15 CROMWELL CT
16 KINGS CT

B1
1 BRAMLEY HOUSE
2 ABINGER HOUSE
3 THURSLEY HOUSE
4 RIDGE HOUSE
5 THE CLONE
6 MOUNT CT
7 HILLSIDE CT
8 HILL CT
9 ROYAL CT
10 LAKESIDE
11 HIGH ASHTON

A B 20 C D 21 E F

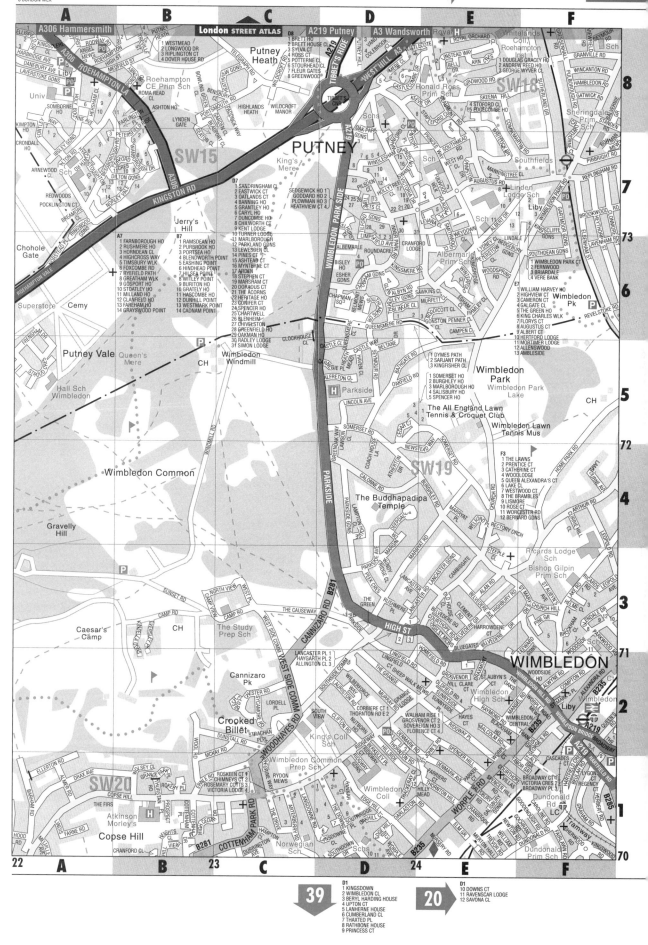

A8
1 WOODCOTT HO
2 LYNDHURST HO
3 WHEATLEY HO
4 NEPEAN ST
5 ALLBROOK HO
6 BORDON WLK
7 CHILCOMBE HO
8 LYNDHURST HO
9 SHAWFORD CT
10 EASTLEIGH WLK
11 KINGS CT

London STREET ATLAS

A306 Hammersmith

A219 Putney   **A3 Wandsworth**

D8
1 BRETT HO
2 BRETT HO
3 SYLVA CT
4 ROSS CT
5 POTTERNE CL
6 STOURHEAD CL
7 FLEUR GATES
8 GREENWOOD

Putney
Heath

D7
1 SANDRINGHAM CL
2 EASTWICK CT
3 OATLANDS CT
4 BANNING HO
5 GRANTLEY HO
6 CARYL HO
7 DUNCOMBE HO
8 CHILWORTH CT
9 KENT LODGE
10 TURNER LODGE
11 MARLBOROUGH
12 PARKLAND GDNS
13 LEWESDEN CL
14 PINES CT
15 ASHTEAD CT
16 MYNTERNE CT
17 ARDEN
18 STEPHEN CT
19 MARSHAM CT
20 DORADOUS CT
21 THE ACORNS
22 HERITAGE HO
23 CONIFER CT
24 SPENCER HO
25 CHARTWELL
26 BLENHEIM
27 CHIVESTON
28 GREENFIELD HO
29 OAKMAN HO
30 RADLEY LODGE
31 SIMON LODGE

SEDGEWICK HO 1
GODDARD HO 2
PLOWMAN HO 3
HEATHVIEW CT 4

A7
1 FARNBOROUGH HO
2 RUSHMERE HO
3 HORNDEAN CL
4 HIGHCROSS WAY
5 TIMSBURY WLK
6 FOXCOMBE HO
7 RYEFIELD PATH
8 GREATHAM WLK
9 GOSPORT HO
10 STOATLEY HO
11 MILLAND HO
12 CLANFIELD HO
13 FAREHAM HO
14 GRAYSWOOD POINT

B7
1 RAMSDEAN HO
2 PUREBROOK HO
3 PORTSEA HO
4 BLENDWORTH POINT
5 EASHING POINT
6 HINDHEAD POINT
7 HILSEA POINT
8 WITLEY POINT
9 BURITON HO
10 GRATELY HO
11 HASCOMBE HO
12 DUNHILL POINT
13 WESTMARK POINT
14 CADNAM POINT

SW15

PUTNEY

SW18

E7
1 WILLIAM HARVEY HO
2 HIGHVIEW CT
3 CAMERON CT
4 GALGATE CL
5 THE GREEN HO
6 KING CHARLES WLK
7 FLORYS CT
8 AUGUSTUS CT
9 ALBERT CT
10 HERTFORD LODGE
11 MORTIMER LODGE
12 ALLENSWOOD
13 AMBLESIDE

1 WIMBLEDON PARK CT
2 FERNWOOD
3 BRIARDALE
4 VERE BANK

1 DYMES PATH
2 SARJANT PATH
3 KINGFISHER CL

1 SOMERSET HO
2 BURGHLEY HO
3 MARLBOROUGH HO
4 SALISBURY HO
5 SPENCER HO

Wimbledon
Park

Wimbledon Park
Lake

The All England Lawn
Tennis & Croquet Club

Wimbledon Lawn
Tennis Mus

F3
1 THE LAWNS
2 PRENTICE CT
3 CATHERINE CT
4 WOODLODGE
5 QUEEN ALEXANDRA'S CT
6 LAKE CL
7 WESTWOOD CT
8 THE BRAMBLES
9 LISMORE
10 ROSE CT
11 WORCESTER RD
12 BERNARD GDNS

SW19

The Buddhapadipa
Temple

Ricards Lodge
Sch

Bishop Gilpin
Prim Sch

Wimbledon
Windmill

Parkside

Putney Vale

Wimbledon Common

Gravelly
Hill

Caesar's
Camp

The Study
Prep Sch

Cannizaro
Pk

Crooked
Billet

Lancaster Pl 1
Haygarth Pl 2
Allington Cl 3

HIGH ST

WIMBLEDON

King's Coll
Sch

Wimbledon Common
Prep Sch

Wimbledon
High Sch

Wimbledon
Central

Wimbledon
Coll

SW20

Atkinson
Morley's

Copse Hill

Dundonald
Prim Sch

D1
1 KINGSDOWN
2 WIMBLEDON CL
3 BERYL HARDING HOUSE
4 UPTON CT
5 LANHERNE HOUSE
6 CUMBERLAND CL
7 THAXTED PL
8 RATHBONE HOUSE
9 PRINCESS CT

D1
10 DOWNS CT
11 RAVENSCAR LODGE
12 SAVONA CL

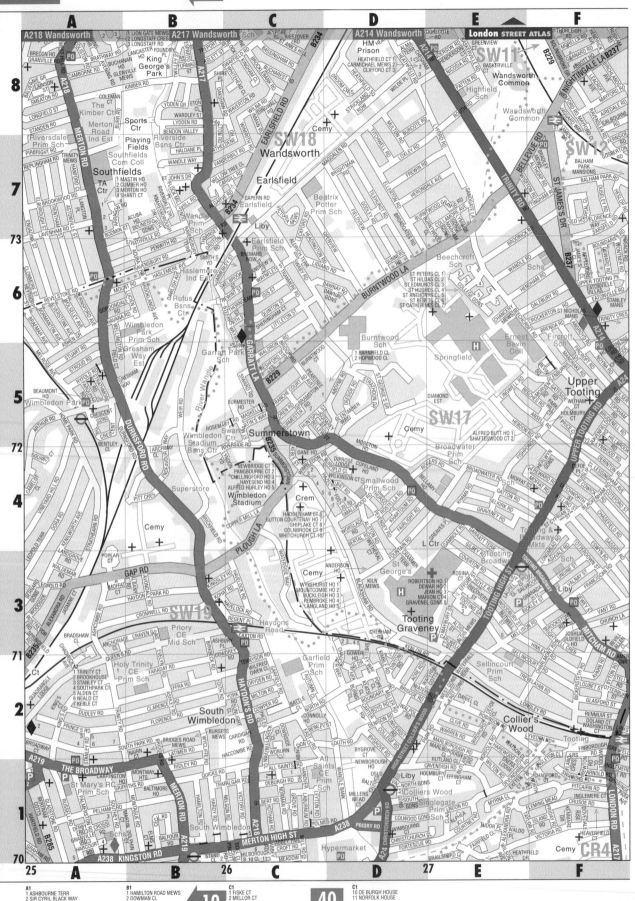

A1
1 ASHBOURNE TERR
2 SIR CYRIL BLACK WAY
3 DOWNING HO
4 PALMERSTON GR
5 GLADSTONE CT

B1
1 HAMILTON ROAD MEWS
2 DOWMAN CL

C1
1 FISKE CT
2 MELLOR CT
3 OLIVE RD
4 ALLERTON HOUSE
5 VICTORY ROAD MEWS
6 WILL MILES CT
7 VANGUARD HOUSE
8 MYCHELL HOUSE
9 MERTON PL

C1
10 DE BURGH HOUSE
11 NORFOLK HOUSE

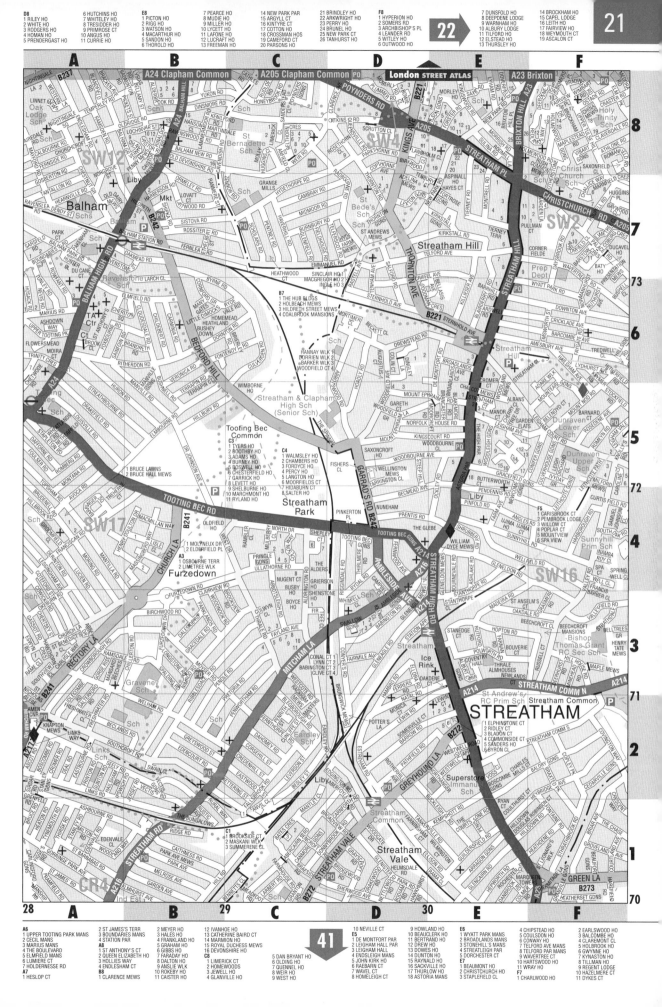

SE24
SE22
SE21
Tulse Hill
Dulwich Village
Dulwich Park
Knight's Hill
West Dulwich
Dulwich
West Norwood
SE27
SE19
Norwood New Town
Norwood Grove
Upper Norwood
Crystal Palace Par
SW2
SW16
Crown Dale
Westow Hill
Central Hill

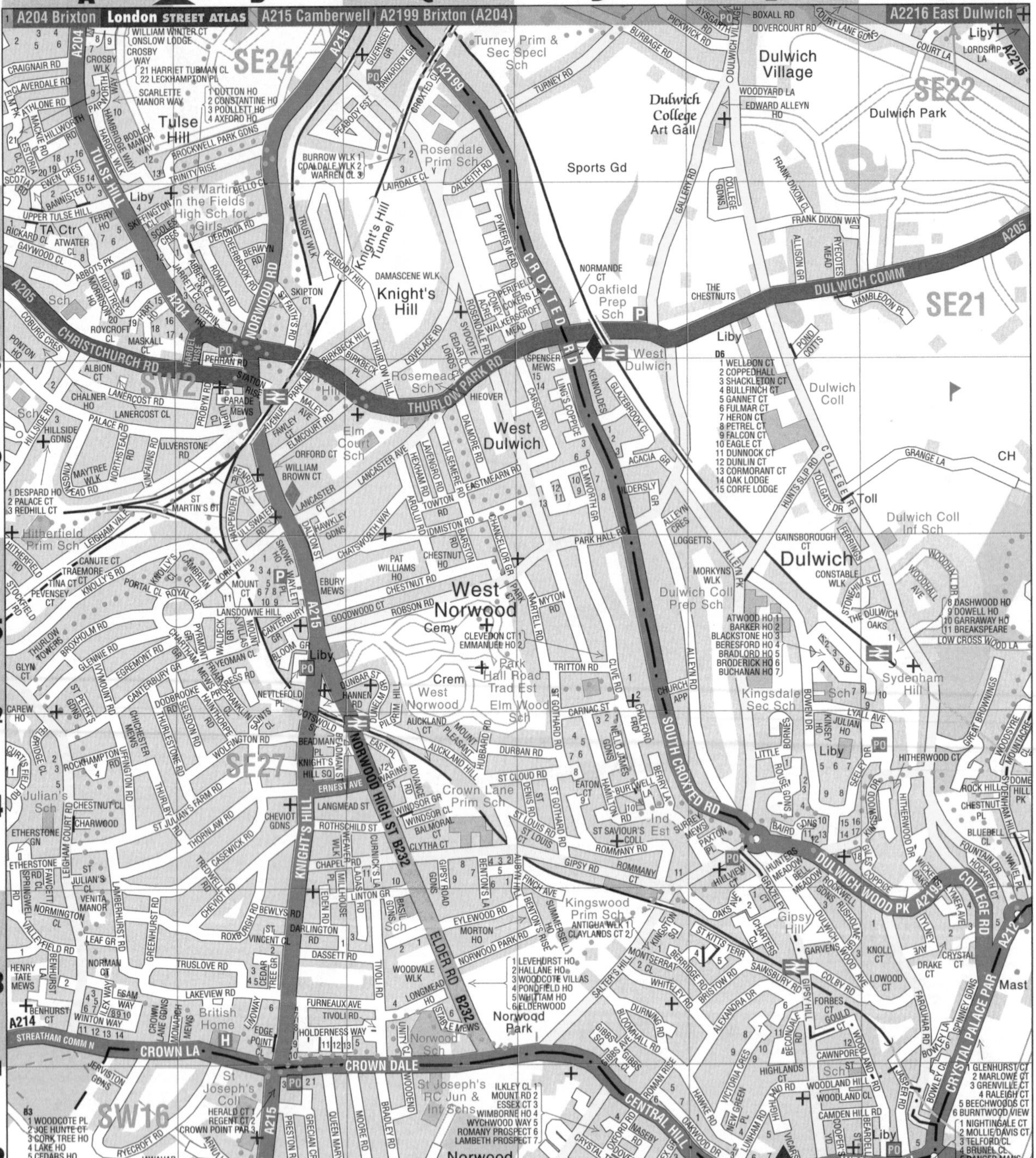

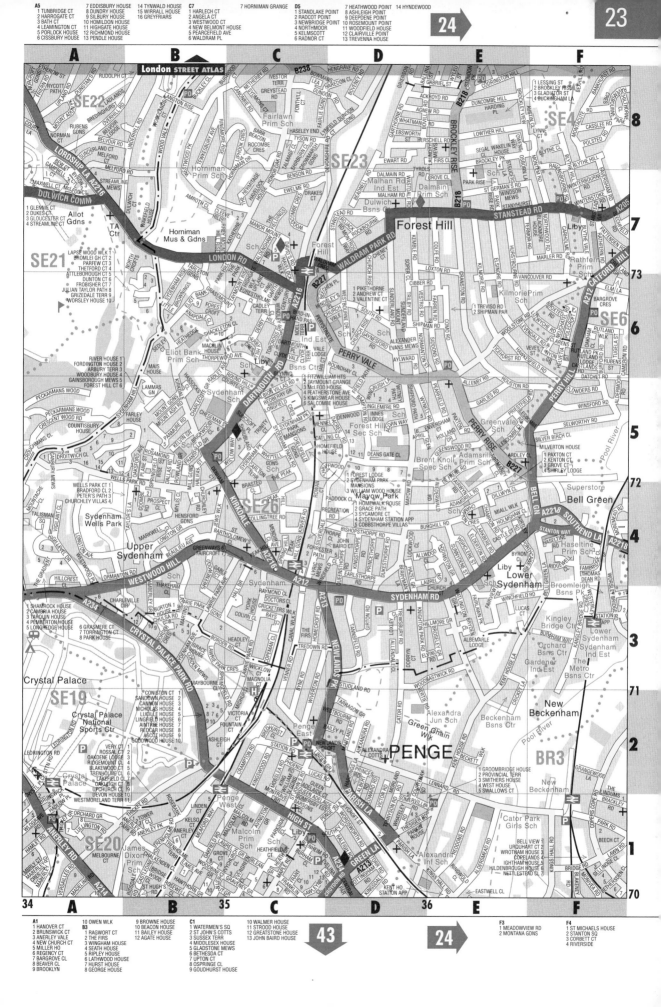

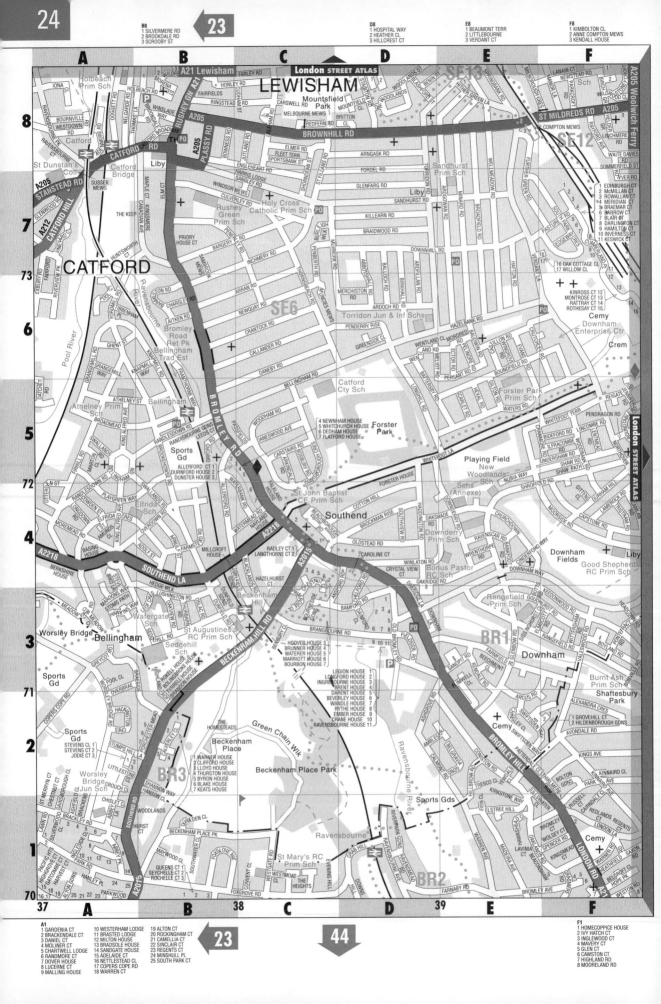

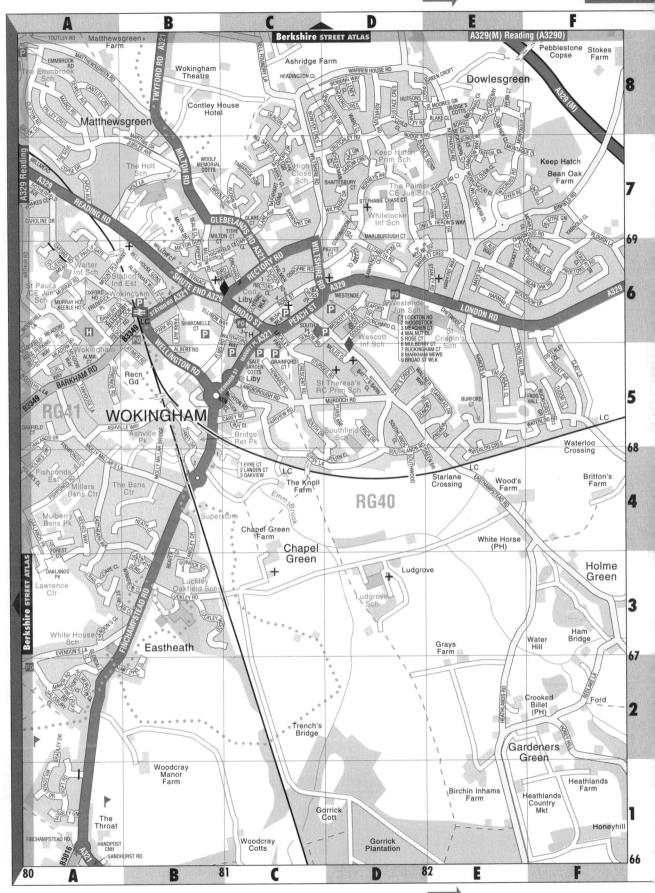

A329(M) Reading (A3290)

Dowlesgreen

Pebblestone Copse

Stokes Farm

Keep Hatch

Bean Oak Farm

Matthewsgreen Farm

TOUTLEY RD

Wokingham Theatre

Contley House Hotel

Ashridge Farm

Matthewsgreen

The Emmbrook Sch

The Holt Sch

WOOLF MEMORIAL COTTS

High Close Sch

Keep Hatch Prim Sch

The Palmer CE Jun Sch

Whitelocke Inf Sch

Stephanie Chase Ct

St Paul's CE Jun Sch

Walter Inf Sch

Station Ind Est

Wokingham

Coll

Liby

Westende

Westende Jun Sch

St Crispin's Sch

Wescott Inf Sch

1 LOCKTON HO
2 WOODSTOCK
3 MEACHEN CT
4 WALNUT CL
5 ROSE CT
6 MULBERRY CT
7 BUCKINGHAM CT
8 MARKHAM MEWS
9 BROAD ST WLK

RG41

WOKINGHAM

Recn Gd

Wokingham Alma Ct

Ashville Pk

Bridge Ret Pk

Sale Garden Cotts

Liby

St Theresa's RC Prim Sch

Southfield Sch

Waterloo Crossing

Britton's Farm

1 EYRE CT
2 LANDEN CT
3 OAKVIEW

The Knoll Farm

Starlane Crossing

Wood's Farm

RG40

Superstore

Chapel Green Farm

White Horse (PH)

Holme Green

Oaklands Pk

Lawrence Ctr

Fishponds Es!

Millers Bsns Ctr

The Bsns Ctr

Mulberry Bsns Pk

Luckley Oakfield Sch

Chapel Green

Ludgrove

Ludgrove Sch

Grays Farm

Water Hill

Ham Bridge

Crooked Billet (PH)

Ford

White House Sch

Eastheath

Trench's Bridge

Gardeners Green

Heathlands Farm

Woodcray Manor Farm

The Throat

HANDPOST CNR

SANDHURST RD

Woodcray Cotts

Gorrick Cott

Gorrick Plantation

Birchin Inhams Farm

Heathlands Country Mkt

Honeyhill

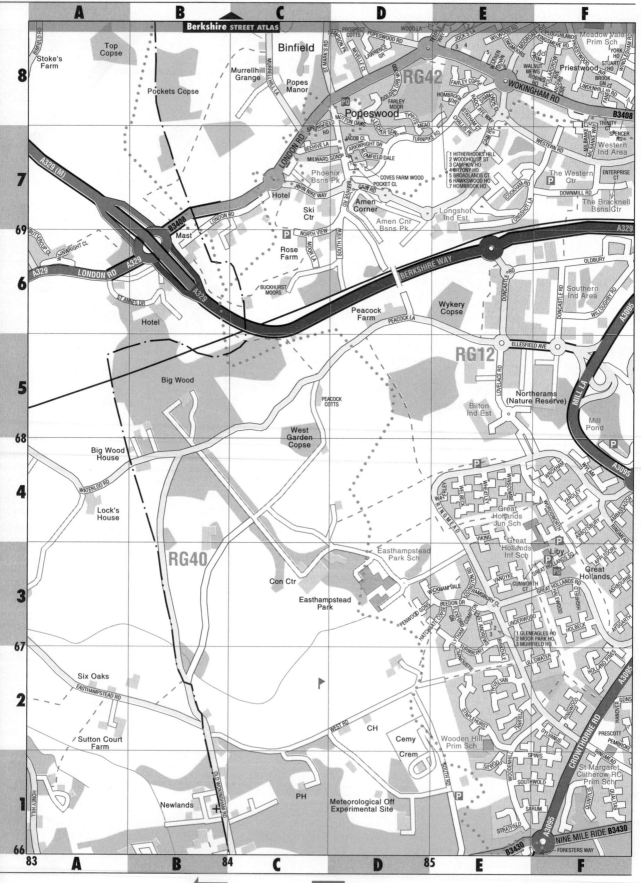

Berkshire STREET ATLAS

Binfield

RG42

Popeswood

Stoke's
Farm

Top
Copse

Pockets Copse

Murrellhill
Grange

Popes
Manor

Meadow Vale
Prim Sch

Priestwood

WOKINGHAM RD

B3408

The Western
Ctr

Enterprise
Ct

1 HITHERHOOKS HILL
2 WOODHOUSE ST
3 CAMPION HO
4 BRYONY HO
5 BROADLANDS CT
6 HAWKSWOOD HO
7 HOMBROOK HO

Western
Ind Area

Phoenix Bsns Pk

Hotel

Ski
Ctr

Amen
Corner

Amen Cnr
Bsns Pk

Longshot
Ind Est

The Bracknell
Bsns Ctr

DOWNMILL RD

A329

Mast

Rose
Farm

NORTH VIEW

Buckhurst
Moors

A329

LONDON RD

Hotel

ST ANNES DR

Berkshire Way

Oldbury

Southern
Ind Area

A329 (M)

Peacock
Farm

PEACOCK LA

Wykery
Copse

RG12

Mill
Pond

Big Wood

Peacock
Cotts

West
Garden
Copse

Northerams
(Nature Reserve)

Bilton
Ind Est

Mill
Pond

Big Wood
House

WATERLOO RD

Lock's
House

RINGMEAD

Great
Hollands
Jun Sch

Great
Hollands
Inf Sch

Liby

Great
Hollands

RG40

Con Ctr

Easthampstead
Park Sch

Wickham Vale

1 GLENEAGLES HO
2 MOOR PARK HO
3 MUIRFIELD HO

Easthampstead
Park

Six Oaks

EASTHAMPSTEAD RD

WEST RD

CH

Cemy

Crem

Wooden Hill
Prim Sch

St Margaret
Clitherow RC
Prim Sch

Sutton Court
Farm

OLD WOKINGHAM RD

PH

Newlands

Meteorological Off
Experimental Site

CROWTHORNE RD

A3095

NINE MILE RIDE B3430

B3430

Foresters Way

HONEY HILL

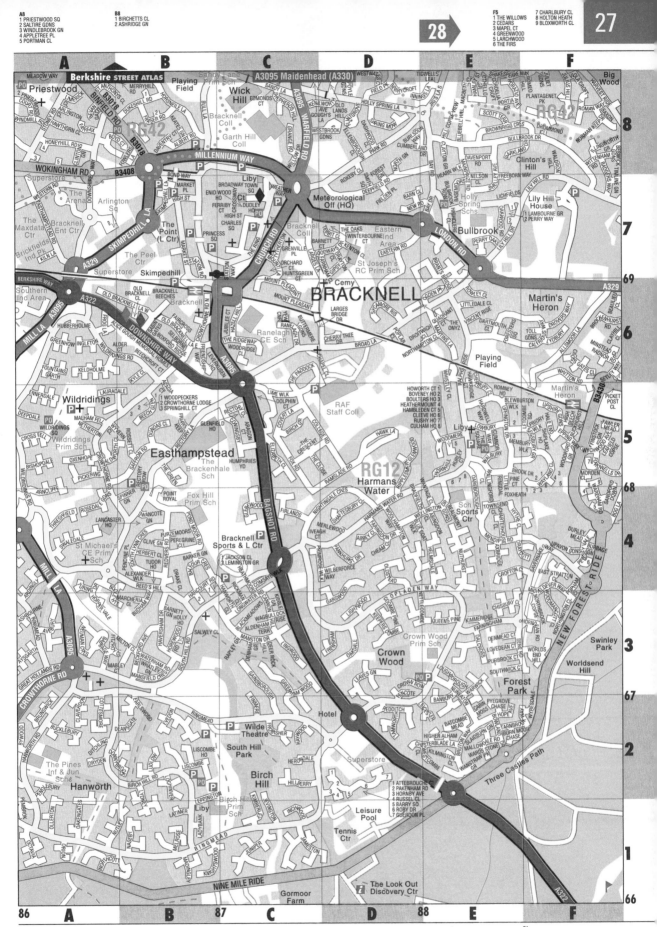

A8
1 PRIESTWOOD SQ
2 SALTIRE GDNS
3 WINDLEBROOK GN
4 APPLETREE PL
5 PORTMAN CL

B8
1 BIRCHETTS CL
2 ASHRIDGE GN

28 ▶

F5
1 THE WILLOWS
2 CEDARS
3 MAPEL CT
4 GREENWOOD
5 LARCHWOOD
6 THE FIRS

7 CHARLBURY CL
8 HOLTON HEATH
9 BLOXWORTH CL

27

F4
1 MULBERRY CT
2 ROWAN
3 LINDEN
4 LYTCHET MINSTER CL
5 STOKEFORD CL
6 FROXFIELD DOWN

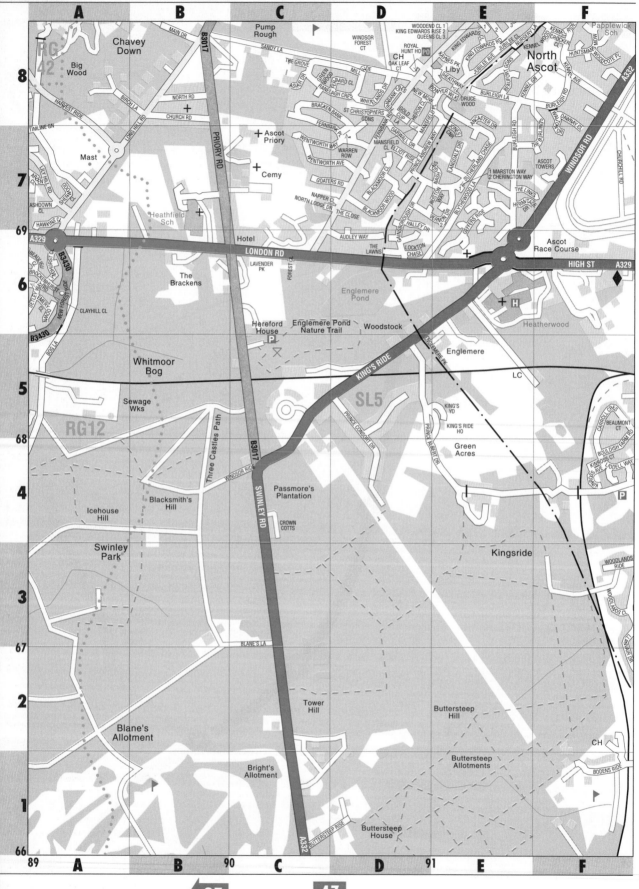

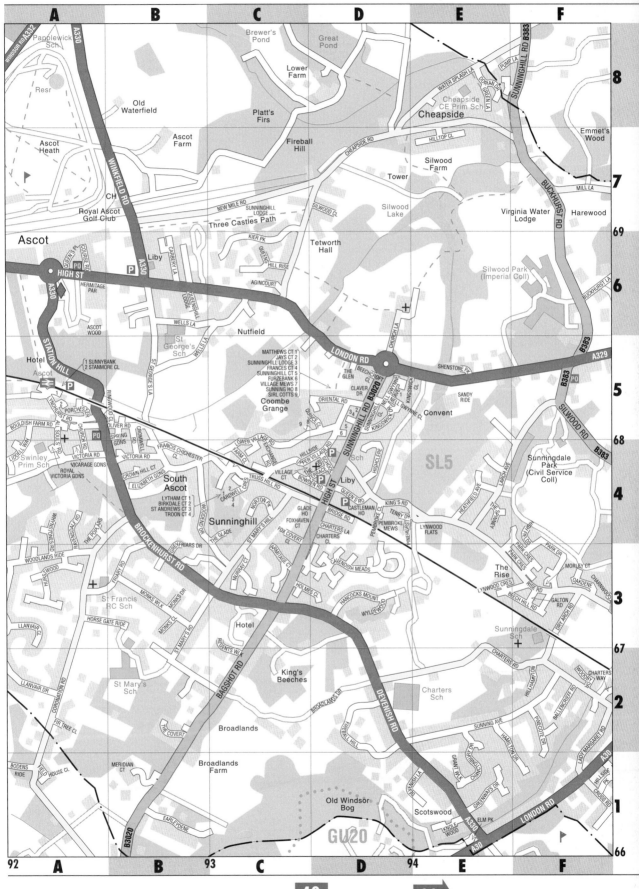

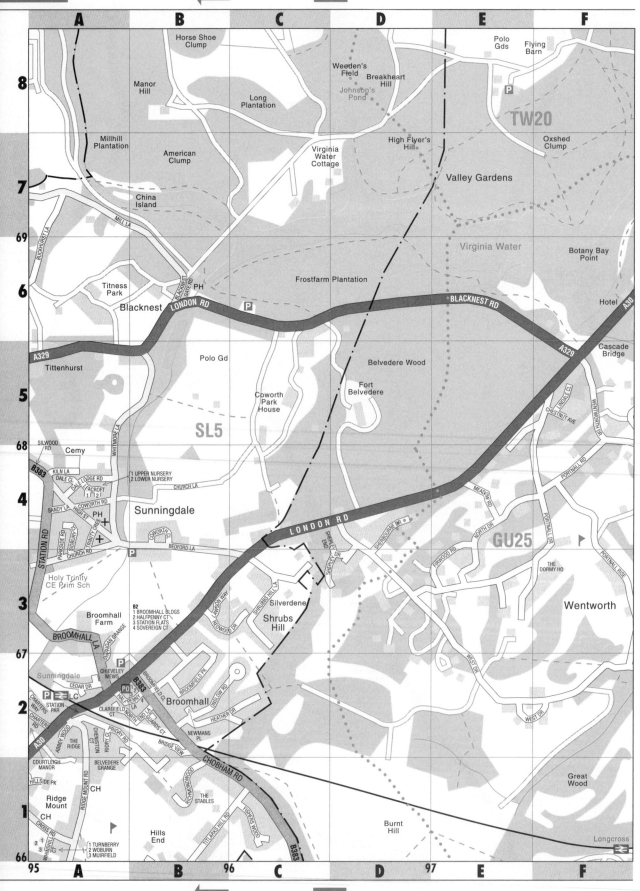

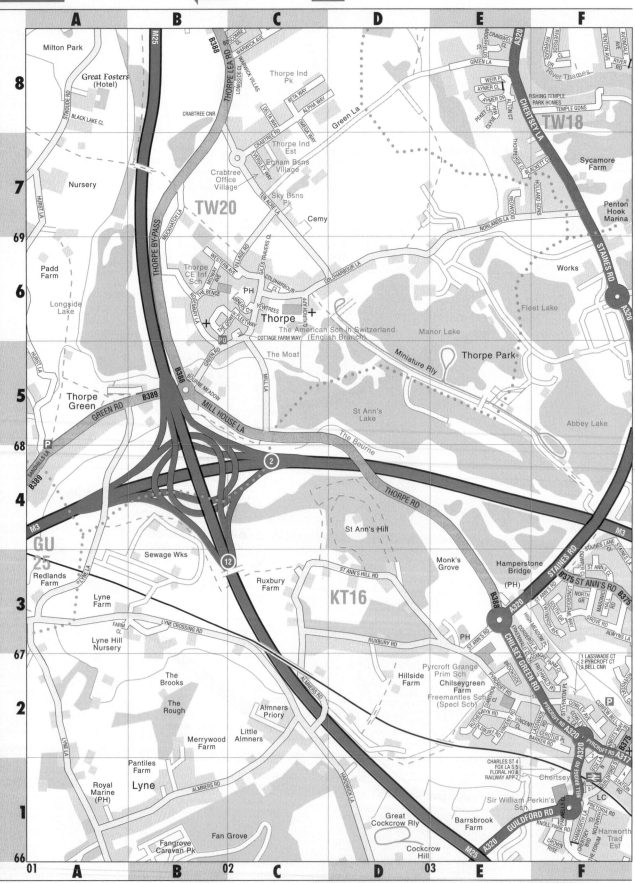

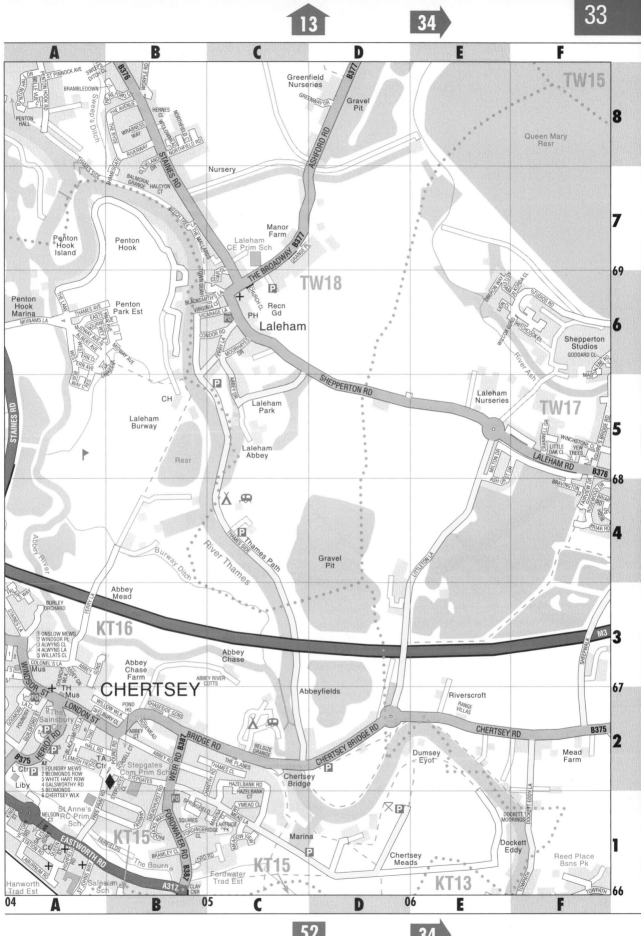

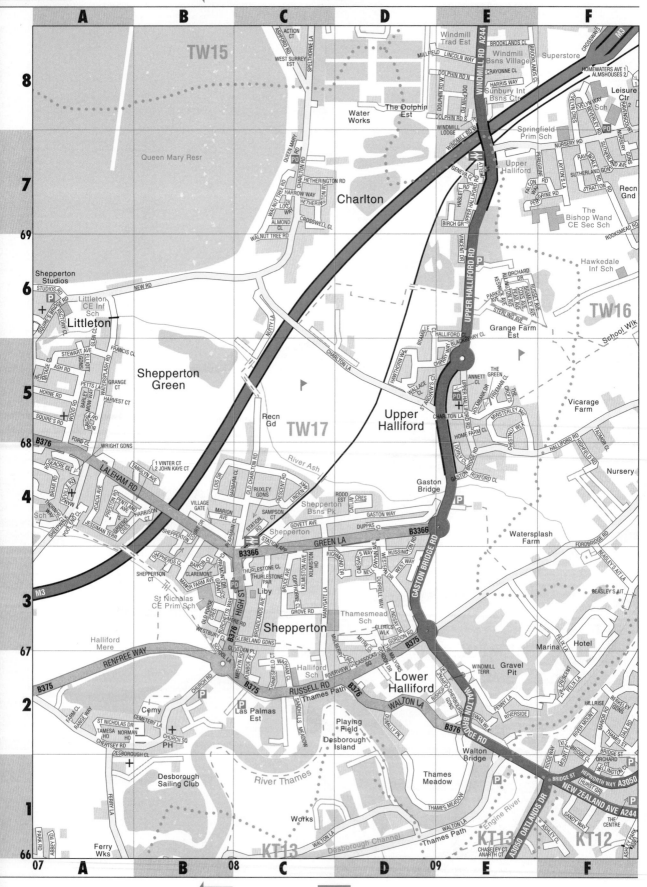

A B C D E F

8

7

69

6

5

68

4

3

67

2

1

66

TW15

Queen Mary Resr

Charlton

Shepperton Studios

Littleton

Shepperton Green

TW17

Recn Gd

Upper Halliford

TW16

Grange Farm Est

Vicarage Farm

Nursery

River Ash

Shepperton Bsns Pk

Gaston Bridge

Watersplash Farm

Beasley's Ait

Marina

Hotel

Gravel Pit

St Nicholas CE Prim Sch

Shepperton

Halliford Mere

Thamesmead Sch

Lower Halliford

Windmill Terr

Hillrise

Las Palmas Est

Halliford Sch

Playing Field

Walton Bridge

Desborough Island

Thames Meadow

Desborough Sailing Club

River Thames

Works

Desborough Channel

Ferry Wks

KT13

Thames Path

KT13

KT12

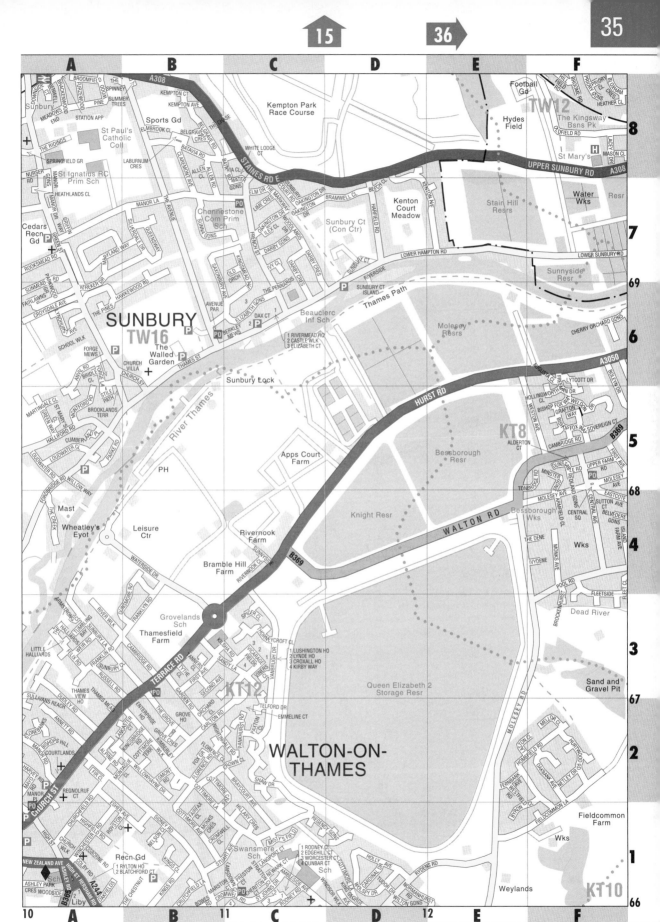

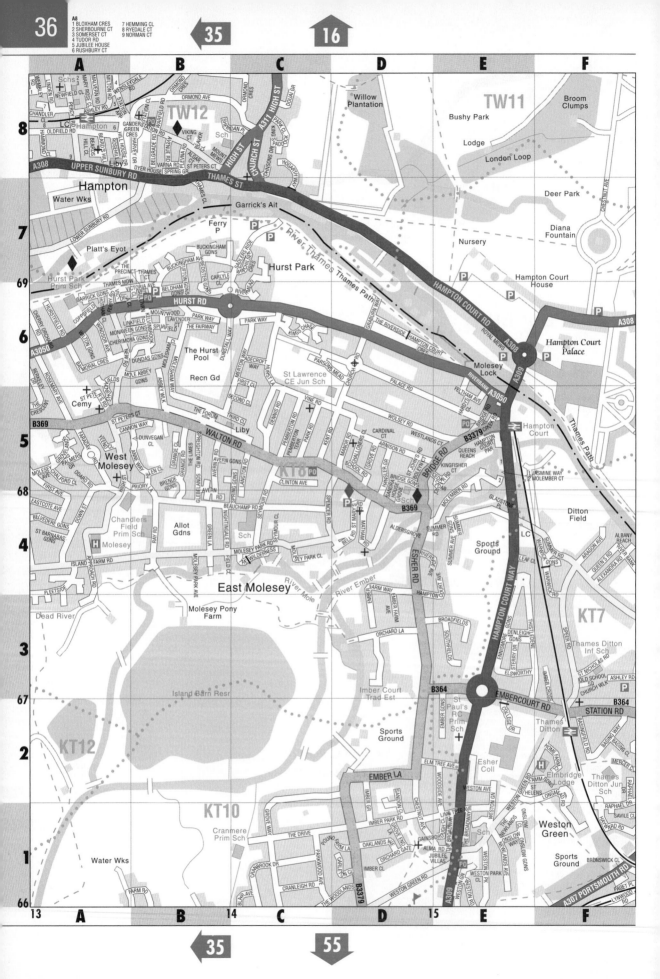

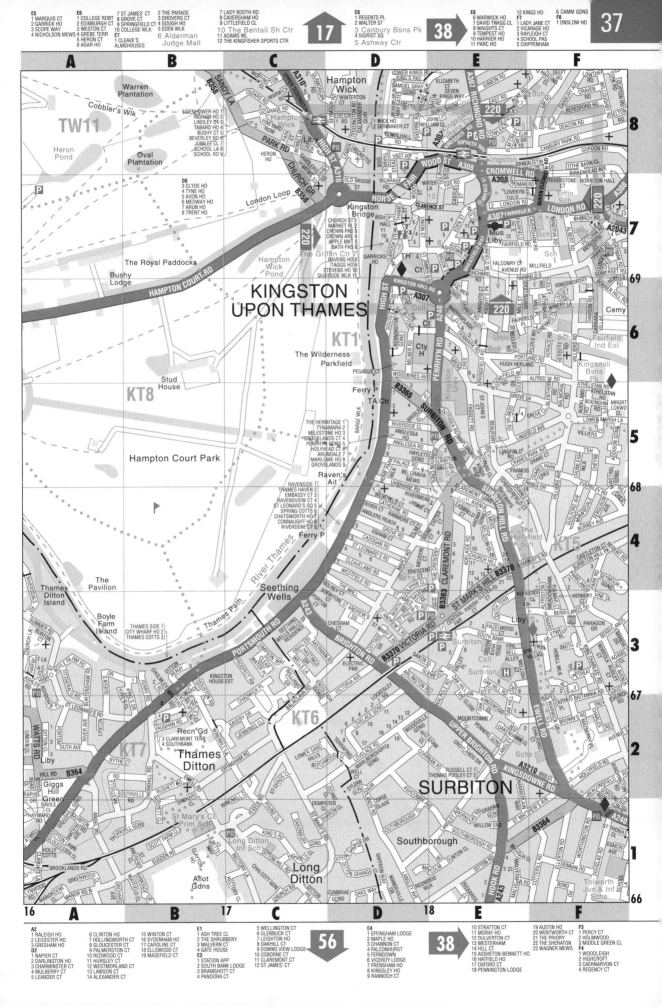

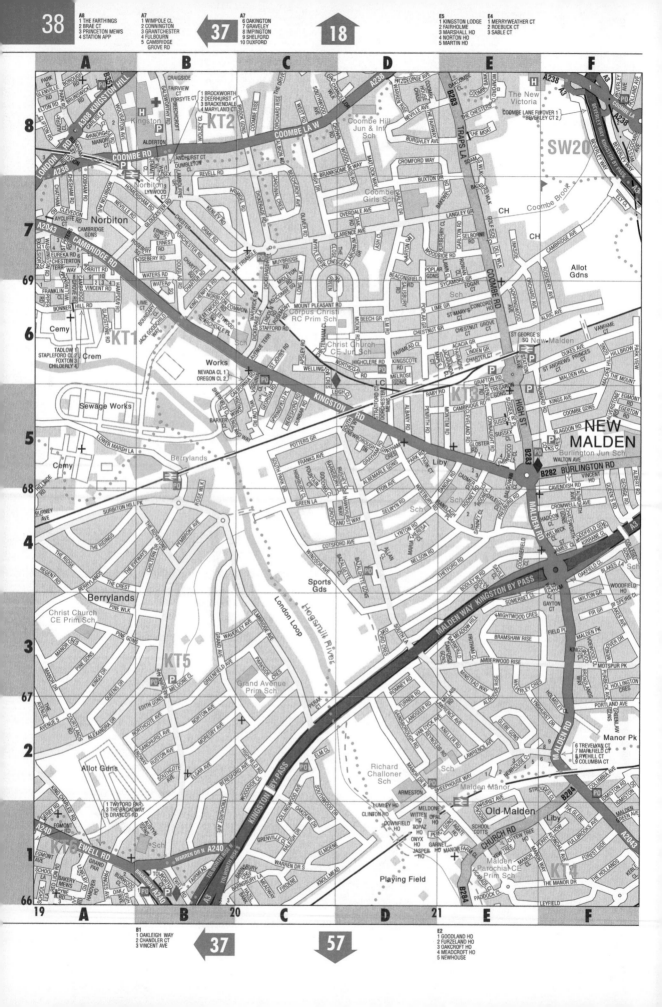

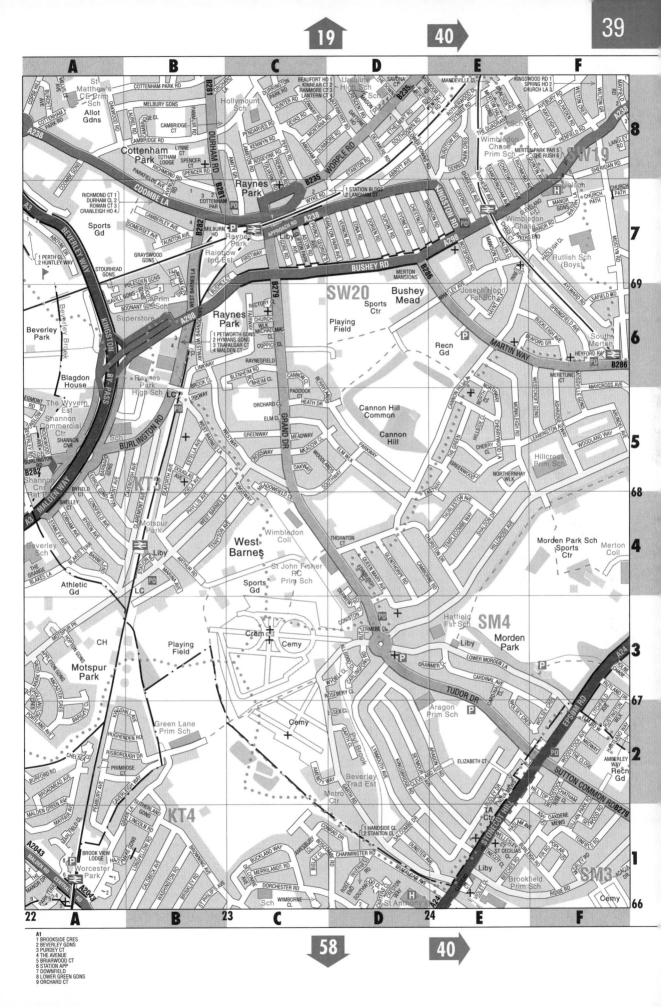

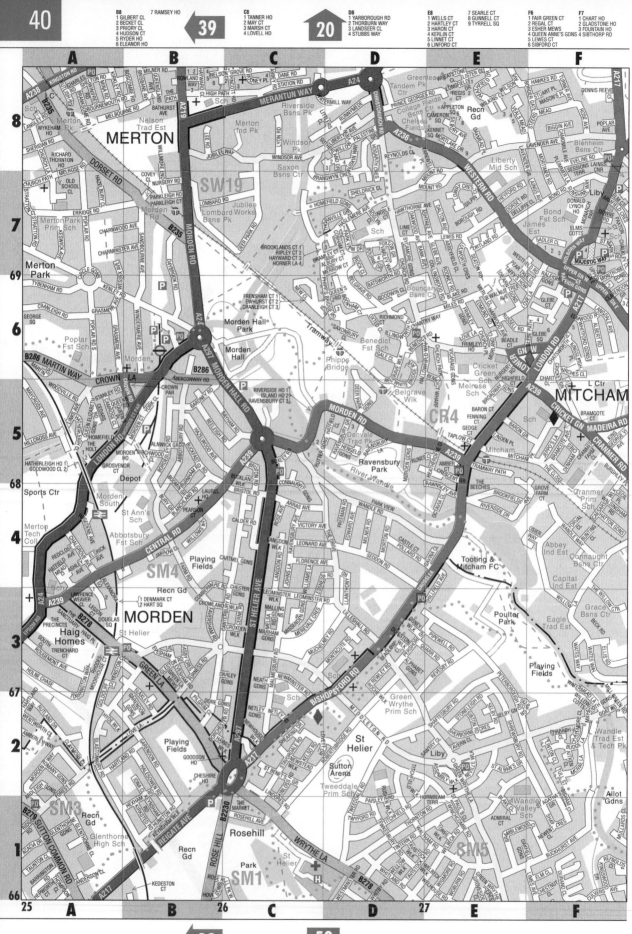

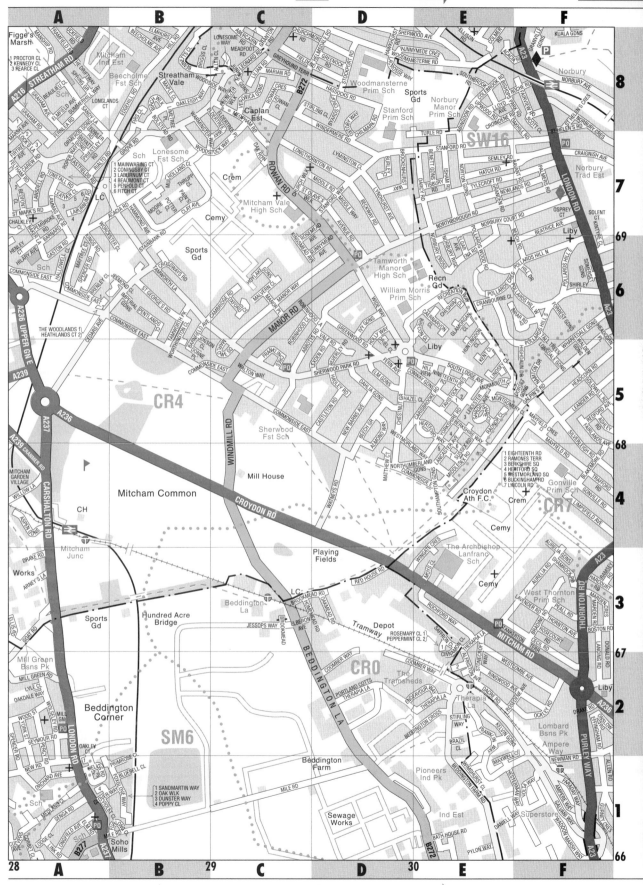

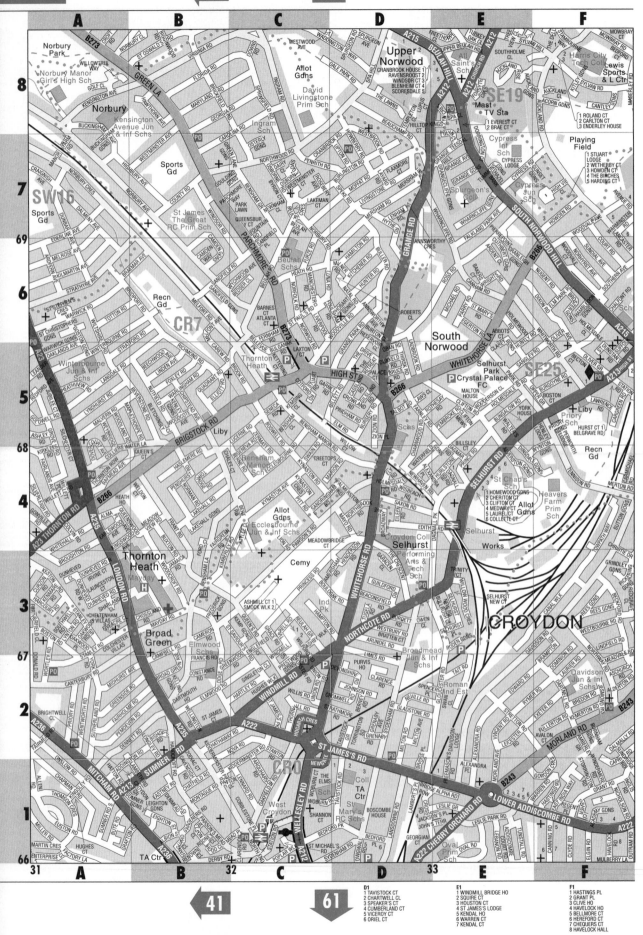

D1
1 TAVISTOCK CT
2 CHARTWELL CL
3 SPEAKER'S CT
4 CUMBERLAND CT
5 VICEROY CT
6 ORIEL CT

E1
1 WINDMILL BRIDGE HO
2 SQUIRE CT
3 HOUSTON CT
4 ST JAMES'S LODGE
5 KENDAL HO
6 WARREN CT
7 KENDAL CT

F1
1 HASTINGS PL
2 GRANT PL
3 CLIVE HO
4 HAVELOCK HO
5 BELLMORE CT
6 HEREFORD CT
7 CHEQUERS CT
8 HAVELOCK HALL

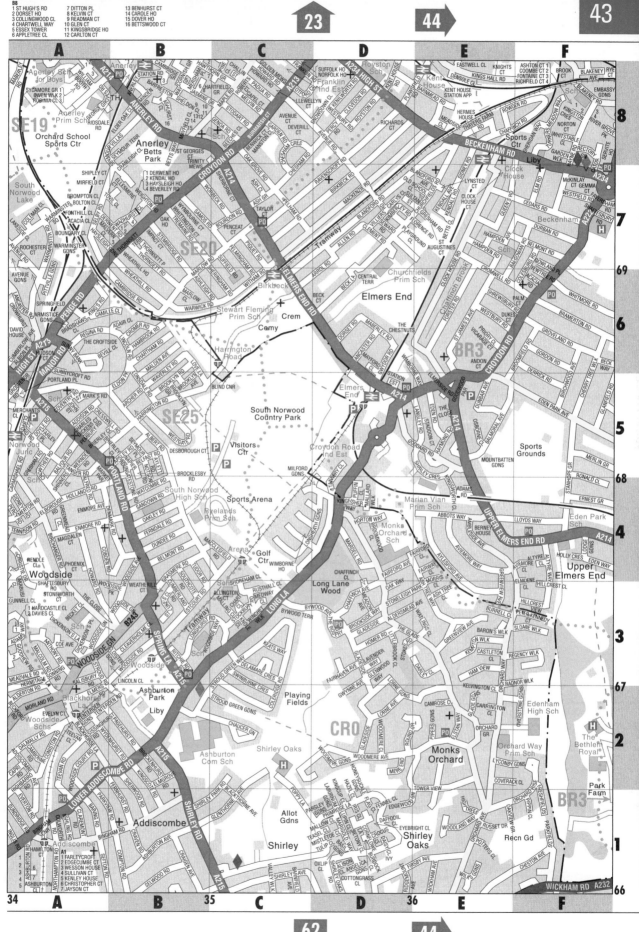

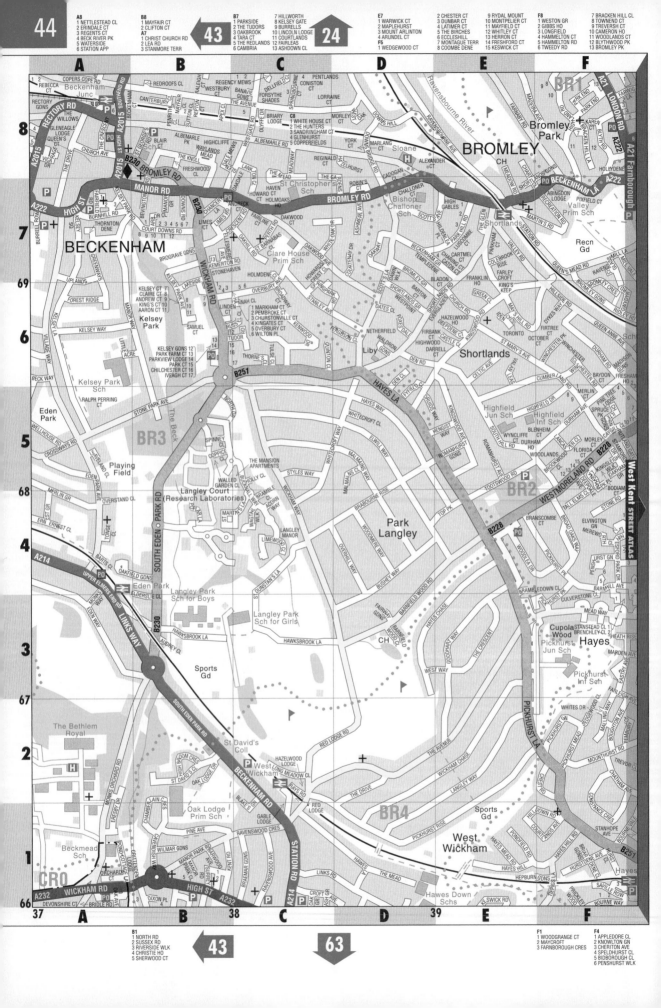

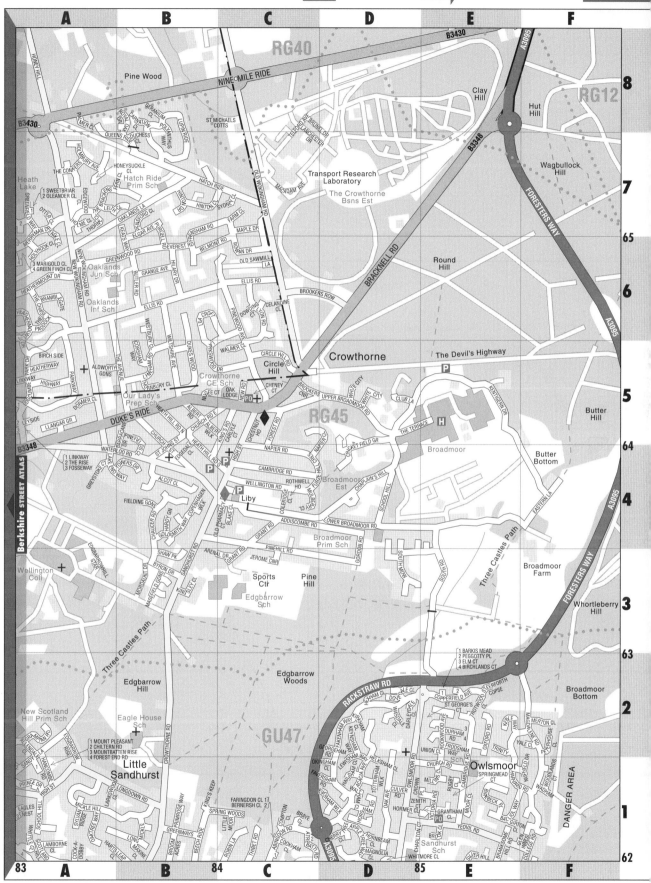

A B C D E F

8
7
65
6
5
64
4
3
63
2
1
62

RG40
B3430
PINE WOOD
NINE MILE RIDE
B3430
Heath Lake
Clay Hill
Hut Hill
RG12
Wagbullock Hill
ST MICHAELS COTTS
Transport Research Laboratory
The Crowthorne Bsns Est
Hatch Ride Prim Sch
Oaklands Jun Sch
Oaklands Inf Sch
Round Hill
Crowthorne
The Devil's Highway
Butter Hill
Crowthorne CE Sch
Our Lady's Prep Sch
Circle Hill
RG45
Broadmoor
Butter Bottom
DUKE'S RIDE
B3348
Liby
Broadmoor Est
Broadmoor Prim Sch
Three Castles Path
Broadmoor Farm
Whortleberry Hill
Wellington Coll
Sports Ctr
Edgbarrow Sch
Pine Hill
FORESTERS WAY
Broadmoor Bottom
Three Castles Path
Edgbarrow Hill
Edgbarrow Woods
1 BARKIS MEAD
2 PEGGOTTY PL
3 ELM CT
4 BIRCHLANDS CT
RACKSTRAW RD
New Scotland Hill Prim Sch
Eagle House Sch
GU47
St George's
Owlsmoor
DANGER AREA
Little Sandhurst
Sandhurst Sch
A3095

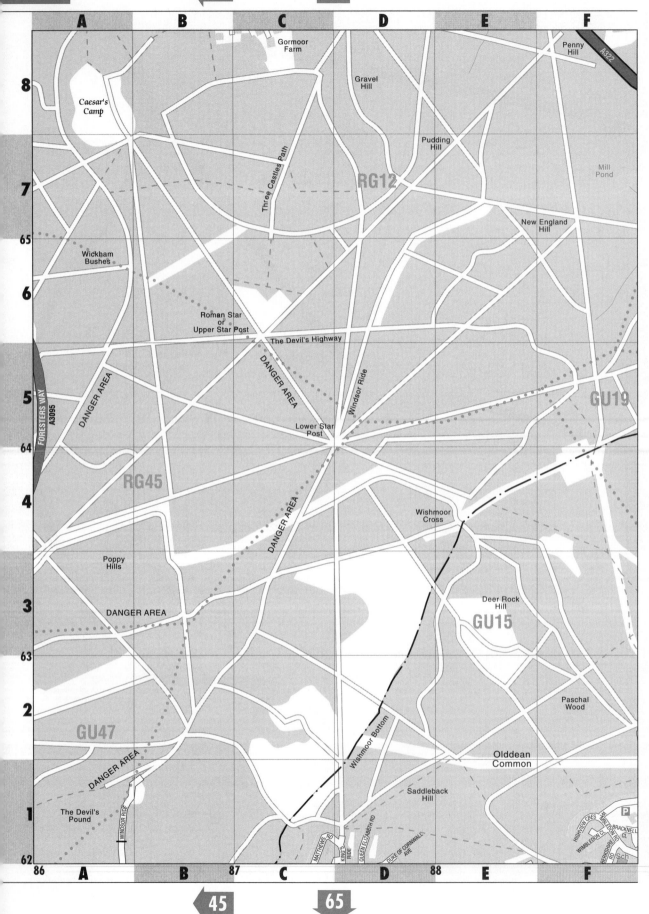

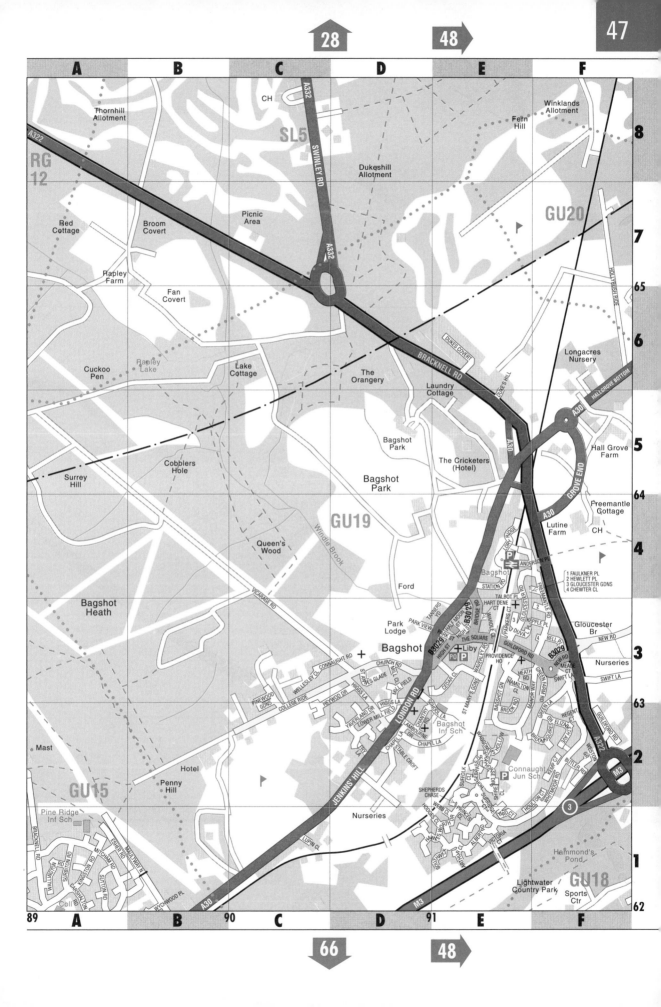

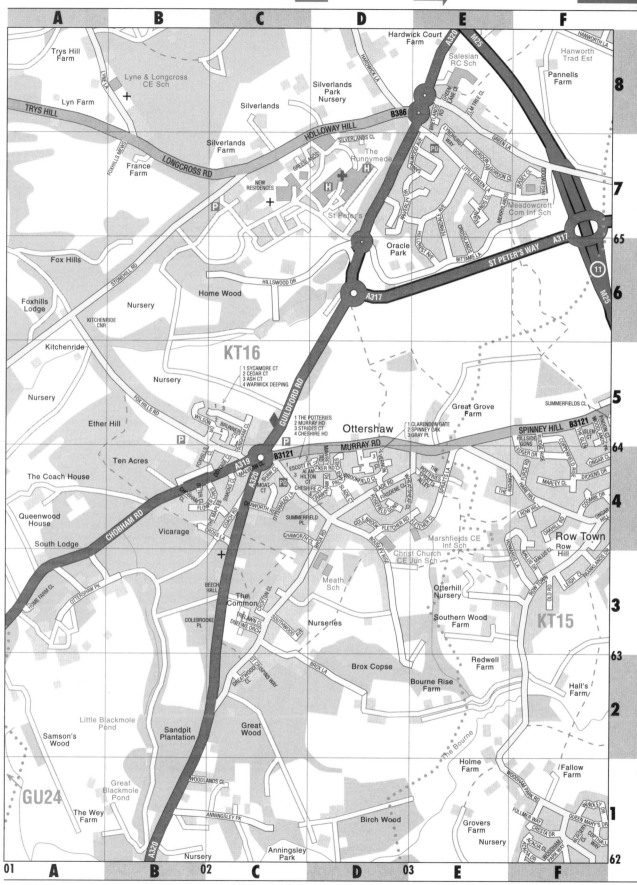

A B C D E F

8

7

65

6

5

64

4

3

63

2

1

62

Trys Hill Farm

Lyn Farm

TRYS HILL

LYNE LA

Lyne & Longcross CE Sch

FOXHILLS MEWS

France Farm

LONGCROSS RD

Silverlands Farm

Silverlands

Silverlands Park Nursery

GREENLANDS

HOLLOWAY HILL

SILVERLANDS CL

The Runnymede

Hardwick Court Farm

HARDWICK LA

B386

Salesian RC Sch

M25

A320

GREEN LANE CL

BRENLANDS RD

LYNWOOD AVE

ELM TREE CL

GREEN LA

Hanworth Trad Est

HANWORTH LA

Pannells Farm

New Residences

St Peter's

PO

LYTCHHURST WAY

PAVERLEY DR

HILLCREST AVE

FERNDALE AVE

GORDON DR

LITTLE GREEN LA

GORDON CL

JERSEY CL

FERNLANDS CL

MERRY LANDS

CROSSLANDS RD

GREEN LA

INGLEWOOD

Meadowcroft Com Inf Sch

Fox Hills

STONEHILL RD

Home Wood

HILLSWOOD DR

Oracle Park

BITTAMS RD

ST PETER'S WAY

A317

A317

A320

65

11

M25

Foxhills Lodge

KITCHENRIDE CNR

Nursery

KT16

Kitchenride

Nursery

Nursery

Ether Hill

FOX HILLS RD

GUILDFORD RD

1 SYCAMORE CT
2 CEDAR CT
3 ASH CT
4 WARWICK DEEPING

1 THE POTTERIES
2 MURRAY HO
3 STRIDES CT
4 CHESHIRE HO

Ottershaw

MURRAY RD

1 CLARENDON GATE
2 SPINNEY OAK
3 GRAY PL

Great Grove Farm

SUMMERFIELDS CL

SPINNEY HILL

B3121

HILLSIDE GDNS

RUDGE RISE

COPPERFIELD RISE

WOODLANDS CL

THE GLEN

GLEN CT

The Coach House

Ten Acres

WILSON DR

BRUNNER CT

TRINGHAM CL

A319

MALVERN CL

A320

B3121

SIMONS CL

COTTAGE CL

SHAW CL

MOAT CT

PO

ESCOTT PL

ALAN HILTON CT

CHESHIRE CL

CRAWS

VERNON RD

BROOKFIELD CL

MAYBRIDGE RD

PARKER RD

PANS RD

SIDE CL

SLADE RD

FINSCENE CL

ROSEFIELD GDNS

THE POTTERIES

SPRATT'S ALLEY

SPRATTS LA

WHEATSHEAF CL

HILLSIDE

LOZIER DR

ONGAR RD

SOMHIN

MARLEY CL

COMBE DR

DICKENS DR

OAKHILL RD

ONGAR HILL

JARE HILL

THE THORNS

ROW HILL

Row Town

Row Hill

KT15

Queenwood House

South Lodge

CHOBHAM RD

Ottershaw PK

Home Farm CL

FLOWERS CL

THE MAPLES

COACH RD

CROSS LA

CHOBHAM CL

OTTER CL

Vicarage

CHAWORTH RD

SUMMERFIELD PL

CHAWORTH RD

BROX RD

COLE BROOK

FLETCHER RD

FLETCHER CL

Marshfields CE Inf Sch

Christ Church CE Jun Sch

HOWARDS LA

MALLIS RD

LEIGH CL

ROW TOWN

FRANKLANDS DR

OLD RD

ROW HILL

BEECH HALL

CROFTON CL

The Common

SOUTHWOOD AVE

TRELAWN CL

DUFFINS ORCH

COLEBROOKE PL

Meath Sch

Nurseries

BROX LA

Brox Copse

Otterhill Nursery

Southern Wood Farm

Redwell Farm

Hall's Farm

ST CRISPINS WAY

GREATWOOD CL

Bourne Rise Farm

The Bourne

Holme Farm

Fallow Farm

Little Blackmole Pond

Samson's Wood

Sandpit Plantation

Great Wood

Birch Wood

Grovers Farm

Nursery

WOODHAM PARK RD

FULLMER WAY

WENDLEY DR

CRESTA DR

ACACIA CL

KAZAN CL

WOODHAM

Queen Mary's Dr

COWLEY WAY

WOODHAM PARK WAY

GU24

The Wey Farm

A320

Great Blackmole Pond

WOODLANDS CL

ANNINGSLEY PK

Nursery

Anningsley Park

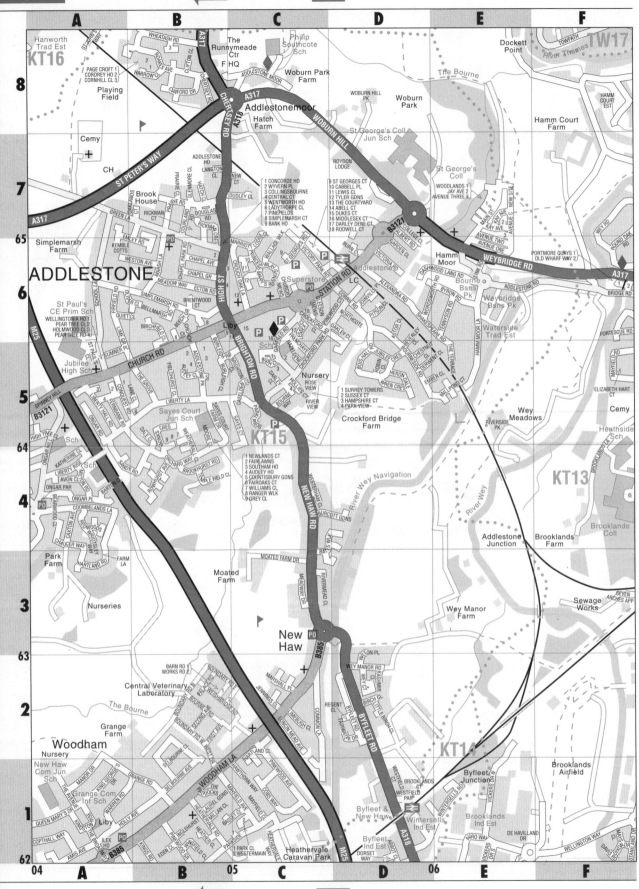

A B C D E F

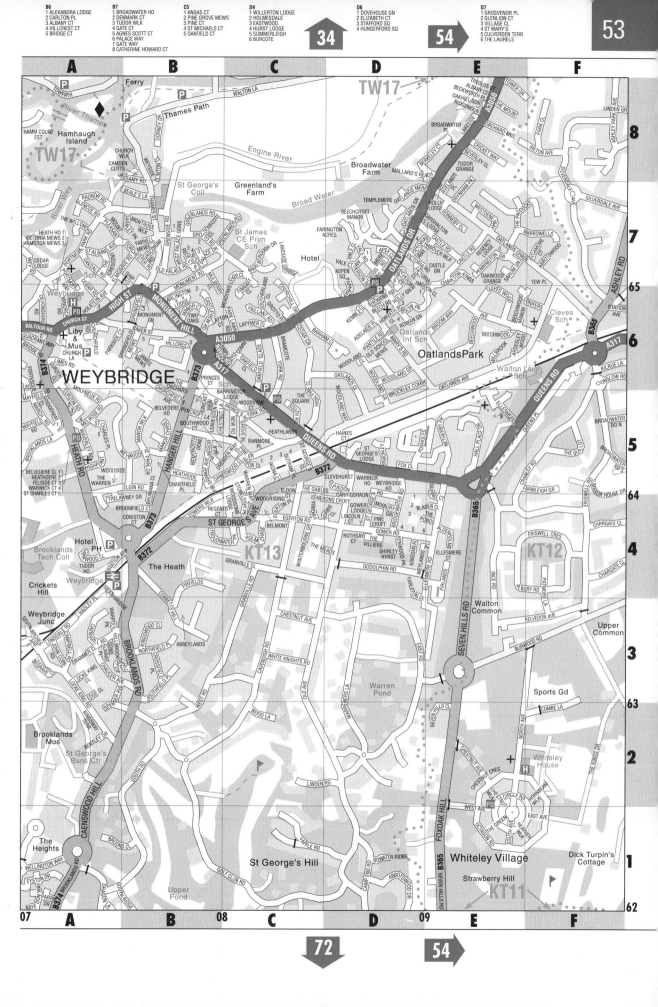

34
54

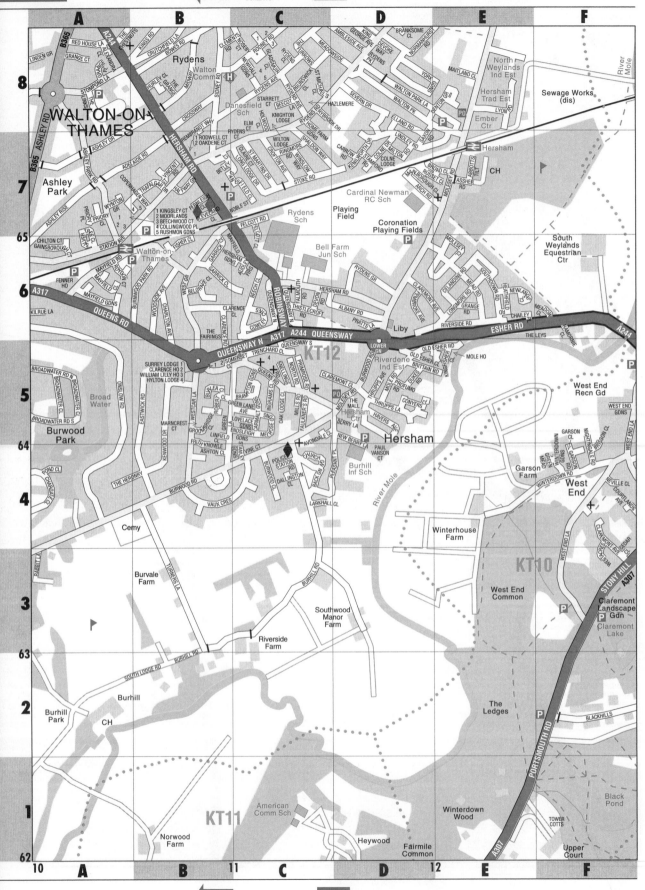

53

35

C8
1 INWOOD CT
2 WORCESTER CT
3 RODNEY GN
4 ST CHRISTOPHER'S CT
5 ORLEAN CT

53

73

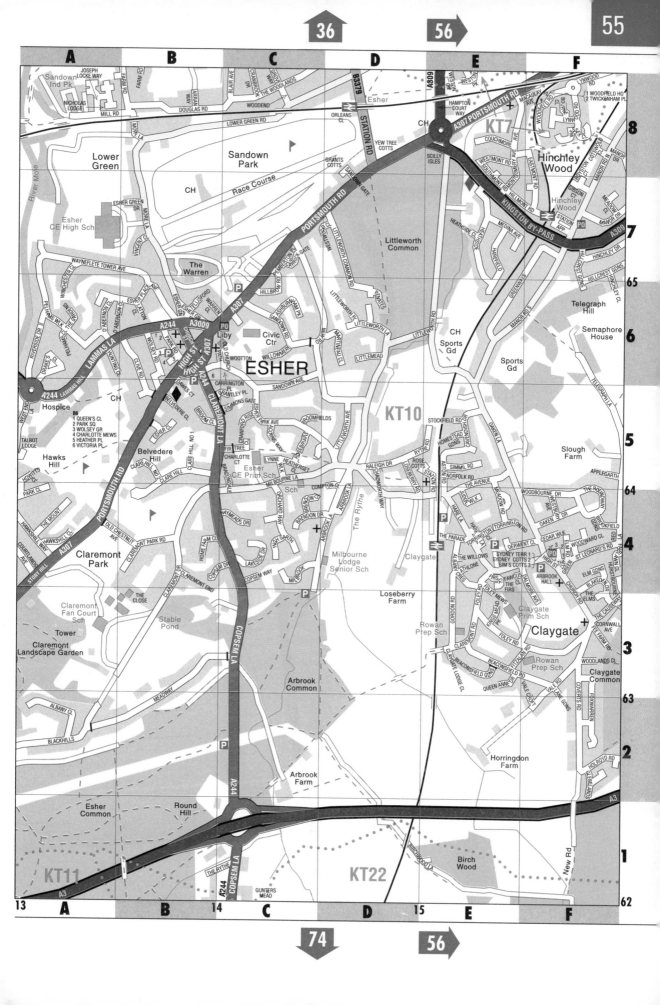

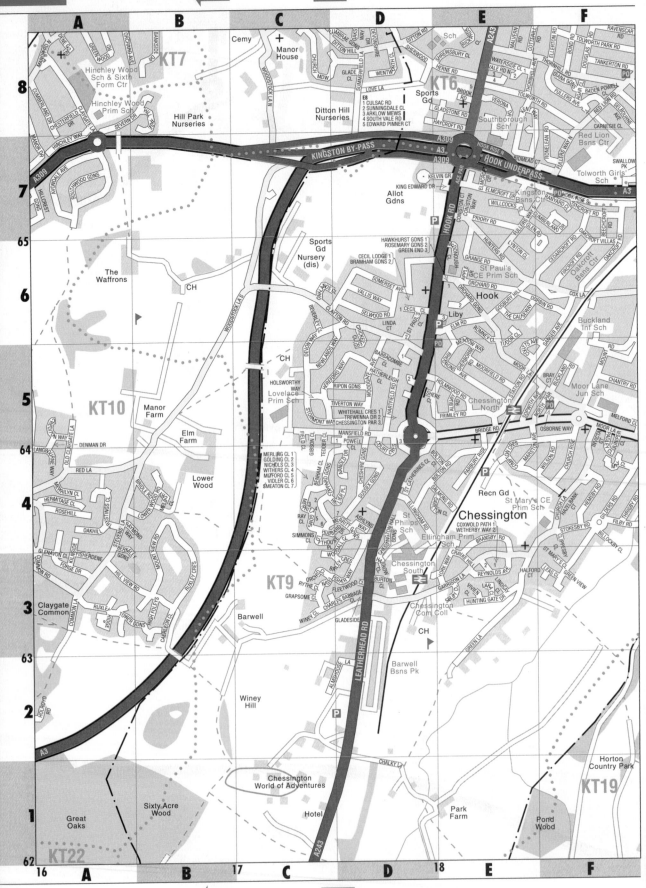

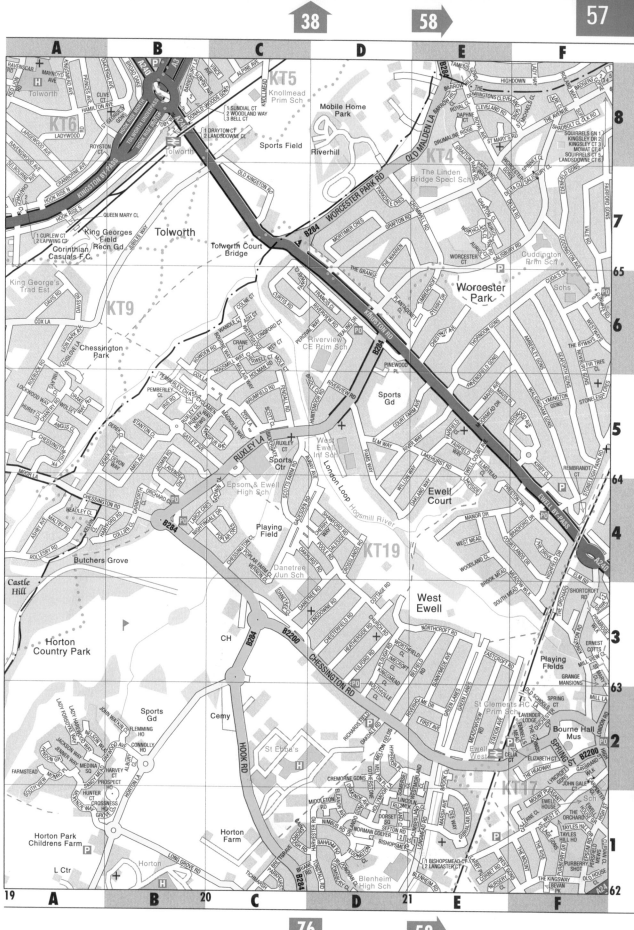

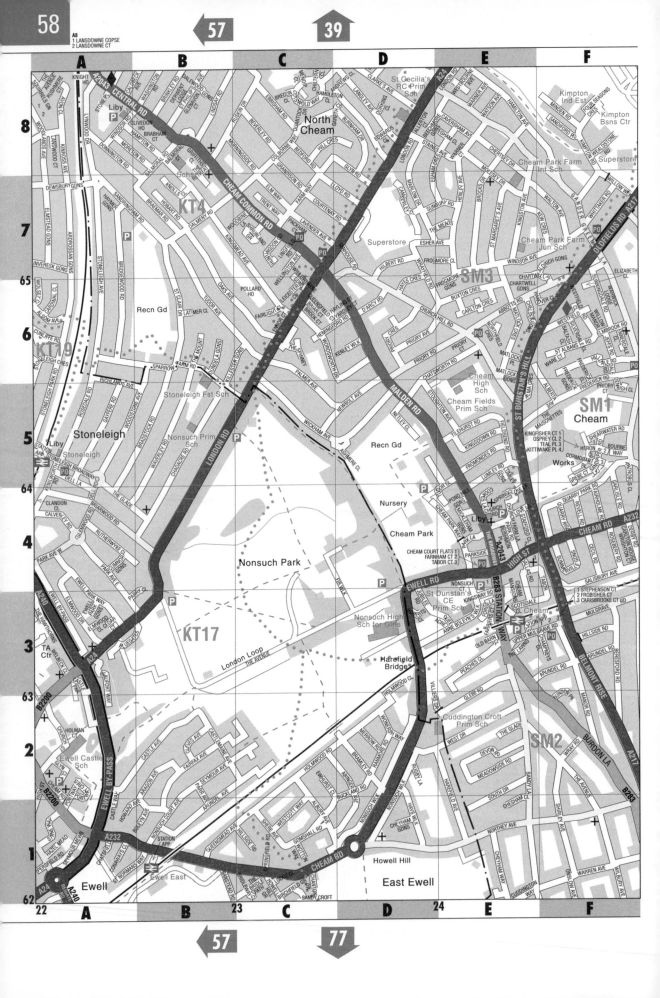

B7
1 ELMSLEIGH CT
2 ANGEL HILL CT
3 OAKHILL LODGE
4 ALVERNIA LODGE

C5
1 GOOSSENS CL
2 CLIFFE WLK
3 MARLINS CL
4 SHOTT CL
5 ELEONORA TERR
6 CLOWSER CL

C6
1 OAKWOOD CT
2 OCKLEY CT
3 ARNDELL HO
4 ADAM CT
5 THICKET CT

7 MONTANA GDNS

6 CHESTERTON HO
7 CLEVEDON HO
8 FERNHEAD
9 STANCLIFFE HO
10 DENEWOOD HO
11 NEWLYN HO
12 GLENROSE HO

C6
13 MANOR CT
14 OAK LODGE
15 BIRTWAY CT

D5
1 HOGARTH HO
2 GILLRAY HO

D5
3 CRAMHURST HO
4 RINGSTEAD CT
5 RAVENSBURY CT
6 YEOMAN CT
7 WELDON CT

E7
1 PARK TERR
2 CRICKETERS TERR
3 KINGS PAR
4 WATERLOO COTTS
5 ST ANDREW'S CT
6 LABURNUM AVE

40   60   **59**

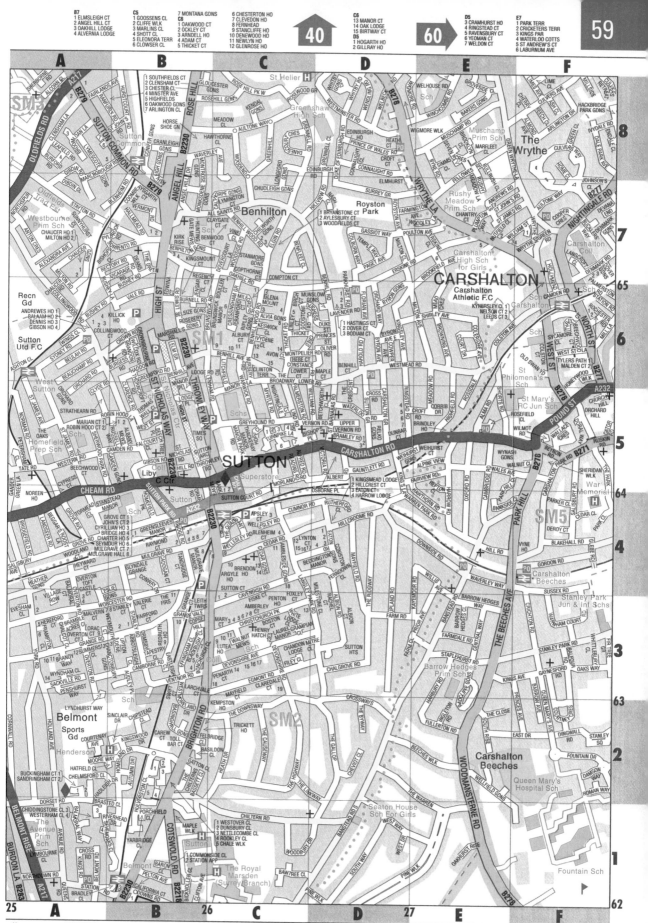

A3
1 LANCASTER CT
2 REDCLYFFE CT
3 CASTLE HO
4 HOLLY CT
5 KENILWORTH TERR
6 LINCOLN TERR
7 CLAREMONT HO
8 KINGSWOOD MANS
9 CAMILLA CT

10 GARDEN CT
11 ASHWOOD PK
12 LYNDHURST CT
13 BANBURY CT
14 MIDSUMMER APARTMENTS

B3
1 HADRIAN CT
2 SANDOWN CT
3 MAGNOLIA CT
4 ALFORD CT

5 BROCKHAM CT
6 BERRYLANDS CT
7 CAMBERLEY CT
8 DUNSFOLD CT
9 CAMBORNE HO
10 COURTLANDS
11 KINGSLEE CT

C4
1 BEAUCLERE HO
2 MELFORD CT

3 PARK MANOR
4 WOOD CREST
5 ELMHURST LODGE
6 DARSENA HO
7 DENVEGAN HO
8 MANSARD MANOR
9 NEW TREE CT
10 NEW TREE CT
11 SAVIN LODGE
12 BEECHCROFT LODGE

13 TRANMERE CT
14 DEVONSHIRE HO
15 HIDCOTE HO
16 MUNSTEAD CT
17 LODDEN LODGE
18 LEGMONT HO
19 STEETLEY CT

C4
1 BANK HO
2 WATERMEAD HO

C4
3 VANBOROUGH CT
4 CEDAR CT
5 TUDOR CT
6 STATION PAR
7 GROSVENOR CT
8 REGENT PAR
9 SUTHERLAND HO
10 FOREST DENE CT
11 ASHDOWN CT

C4
12 BEDFORD TERR
13 VUMBA HO
14 GRASMERE CT
15 NETHERLANDS CT
16 WINWARD HO
17 WILMOT HO
18 SHERBOURNE CT

78   60

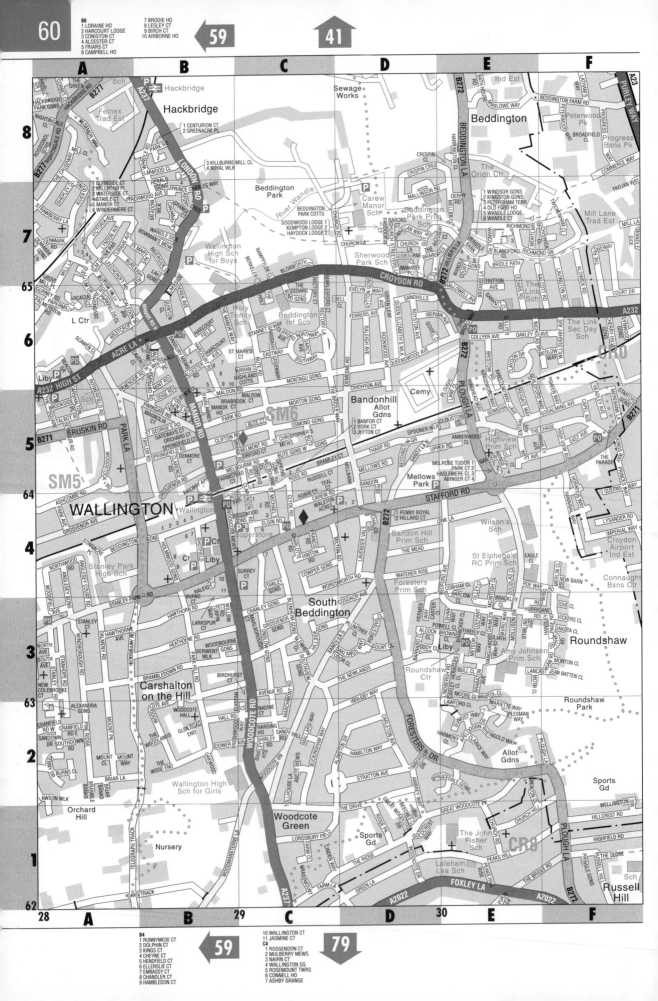

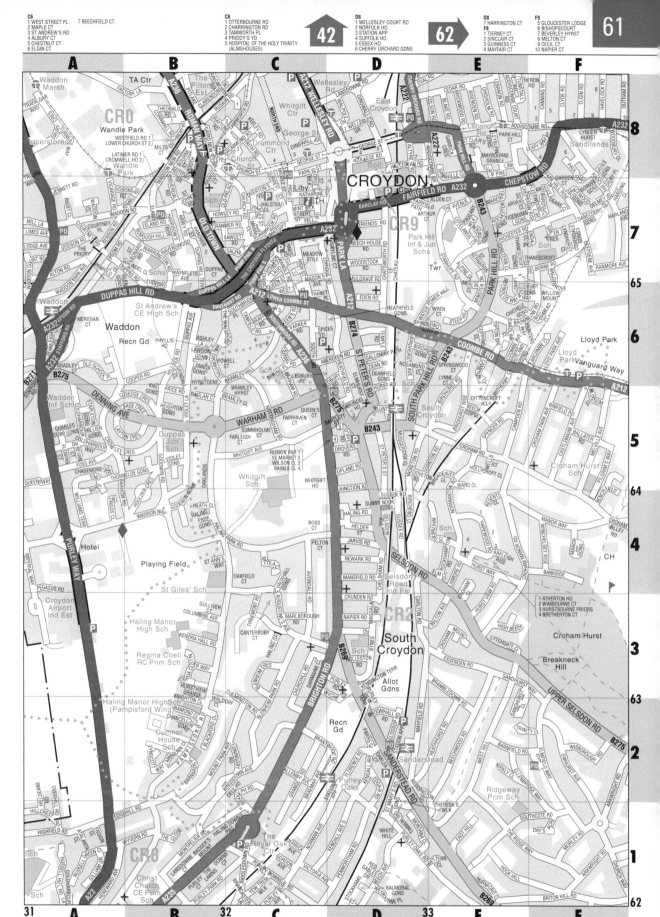

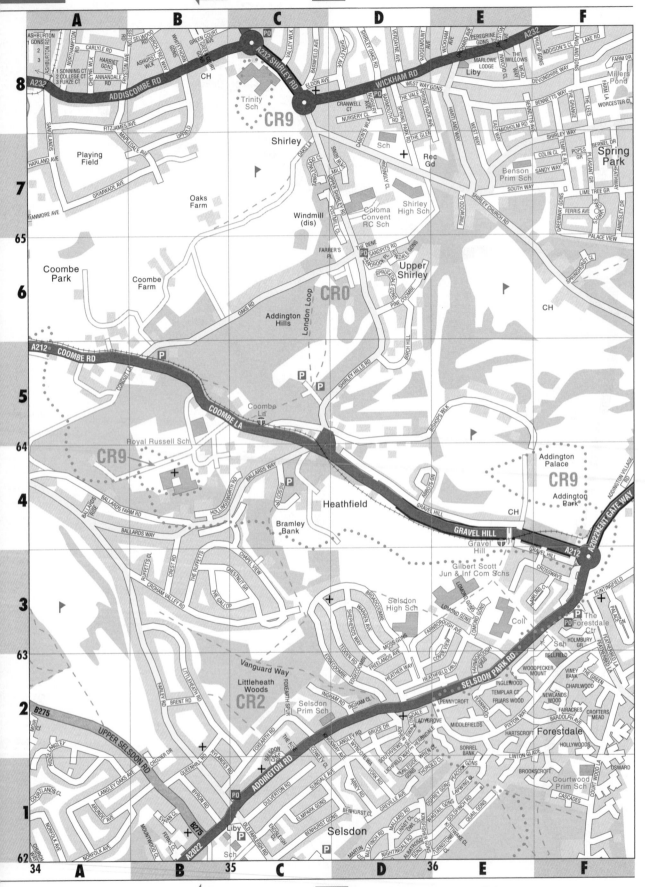

A B C D E F

8 A232 Addiscombe Rd A232 Shirley Rd Wickham Rd A232

CR9

Shirley

7 Playing Field Oaks Farm Windmill (dis)

65

6 Coombe Park Coombe Farm CR0 Addington Hills Upper Shirley

5 A212 Coombe Rd Coombe La

64 CR9 Royal Russell Sch

4 Heathfield Gravel Hill CR9 Addington Palace Addington Park

Bramley Bank Gravel Hill A212

3 Selsdon High Sch Gilbert Scott Jun & Inf Com Schs A202 Kent Gate Way

63 Vanguard Way Selsdon Park Rd Forestdale

2 Littleheath Woods CR2 Selsdon Prim Sch B275 Upper Selsdon Rd Addington Rd

1 B275 Liby Selsdon

62
34 A 35 B C 36 D E F

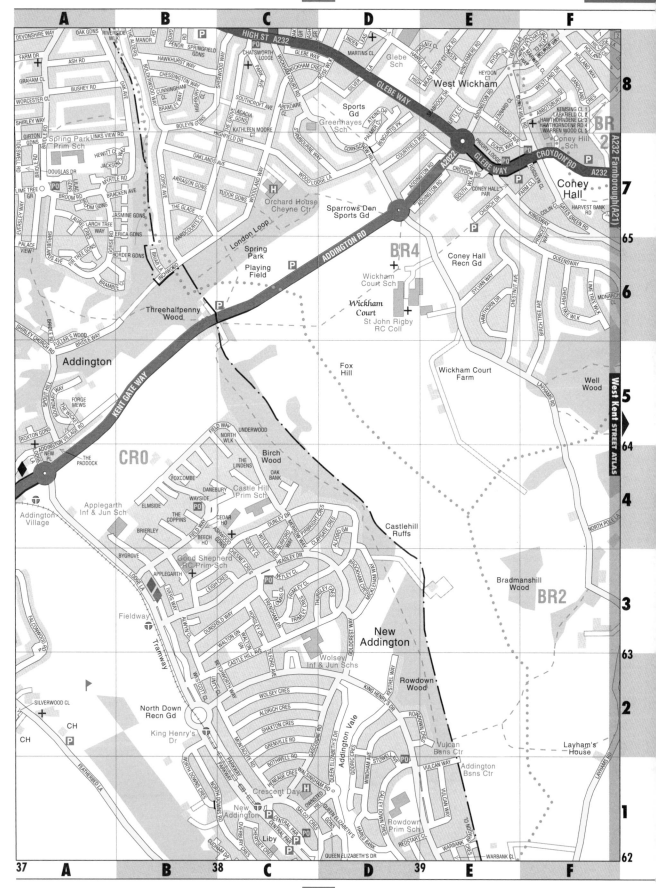

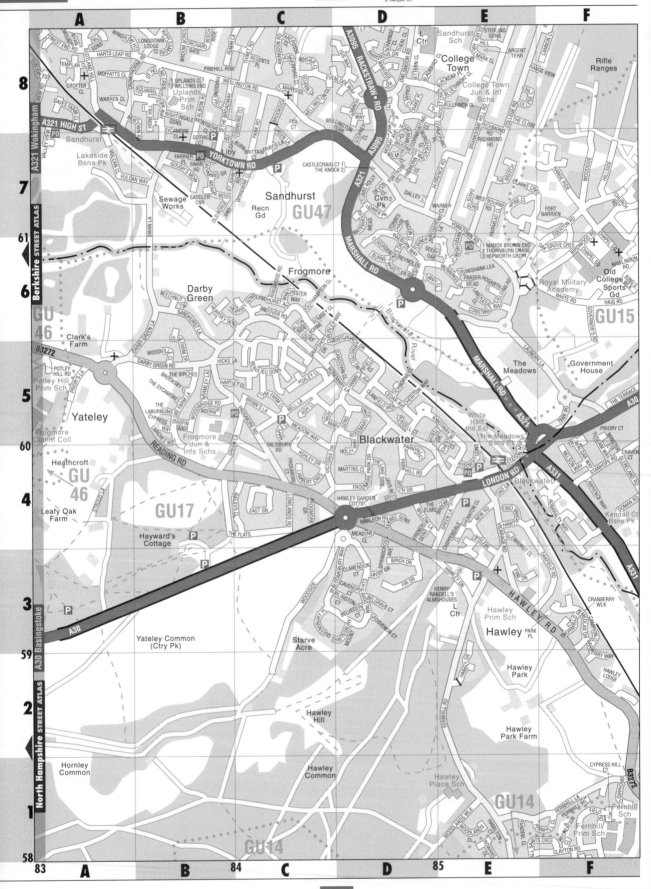

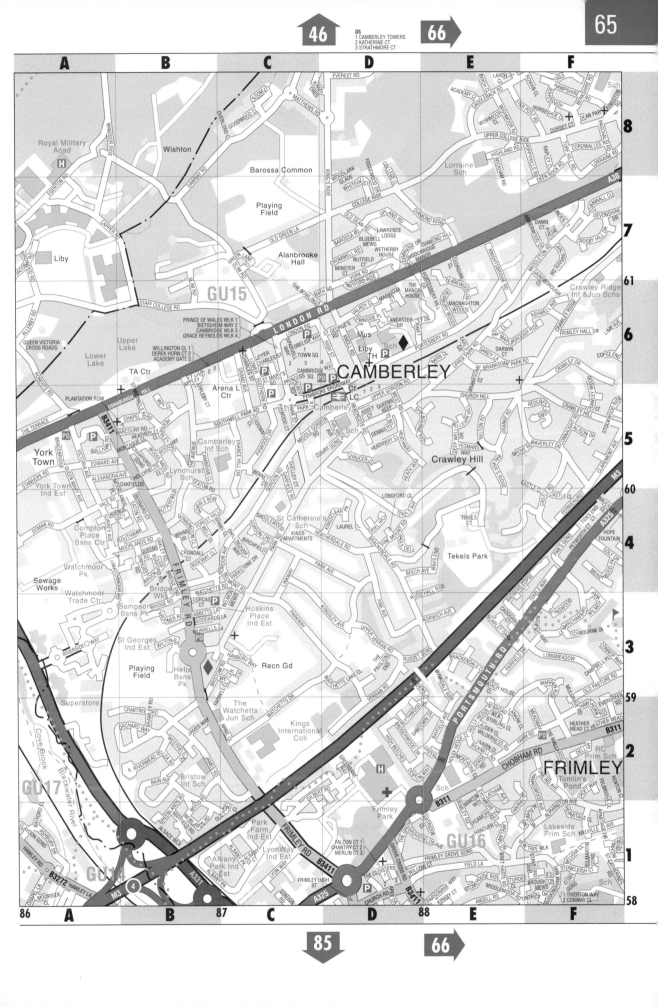

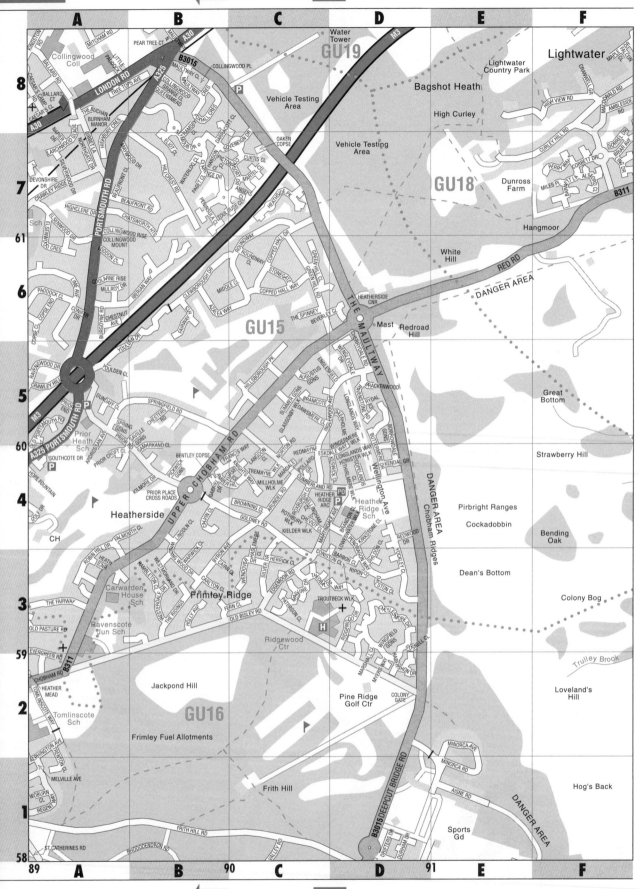

65
47

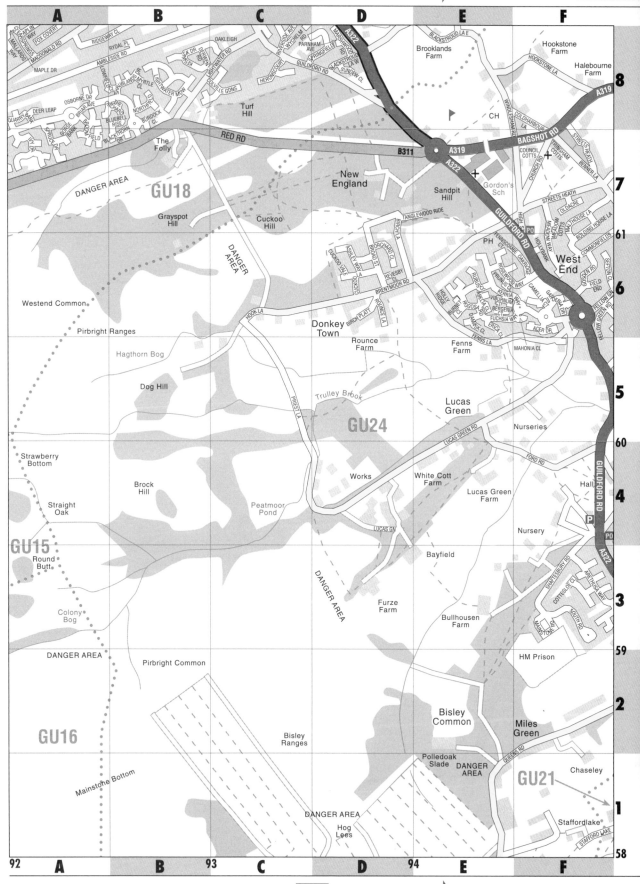

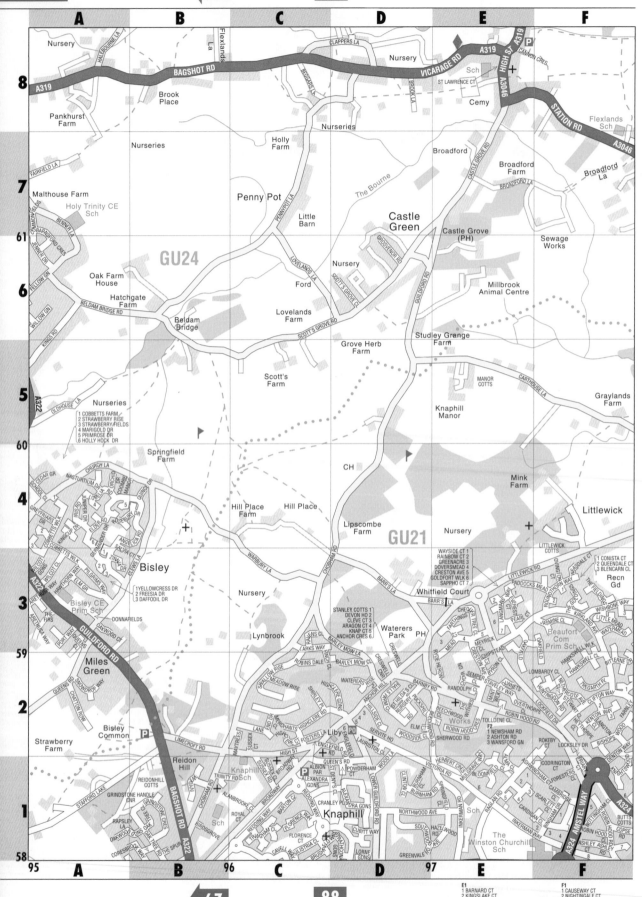

A B C D E F

8
Nursery
BAGSHOT RD
A319
CLAPPERS LA
Nursery
VICARAGE RD
A319
St
A319
HIGH ST
P
CANNON CRES.
A3046
STATION RD
Brook Place
Sch
ST LAWRENCE CT
Flexlands Sch
Pankhurst Farm
Cemy
A3046

7
Nurseries
Fairfield La
Nurseries
Holly Farm
Broadford
Broadford Farm
Broadford La
Broadford La
Malthouse Farm
Holy Trinity CE Sch
Penny Pot
The Bourne
Castle Green
Castle Grove (PH)
CASTLE GROVE RD
Sewage Works

61
Benner La
BARNSFORD CRES
JENNET GN
YELLOW GN
GU24
Little Barn
PENNYPOT LA
Nursery
GUILDFORD RD
SCOTT'S GROVE CL

6
WILLOW GN
KINGS RD
Oak Farm House
Hatchgate Farm
BELDAM BRIDGE RD
Beldam Bridge
LOVELANDS LA
Ford
Lovelands Farm
SCOTT'S GROVE RD
Grove Herb Farm
Studley Grange Farm
Millbrook Animal Centre

5
A322
OLDHOUSE LA
Nurseries
1 COBBETTS FARM
2 STRAWBERRY RISE
3 STRAWBERRY FIELDS
4 MARIGOLD DR
5 PRIMROSE DR
6 HOLLY HOCK DR
Scott's Farm
MANOR COTTS
CARTHOUSE LA
Knaphill Manor
Graylands Farm

60
Springfield Farm
CH
Mink Farm

4
CEDAR GR
CHURCH LA
NASTURTIUM DR
ORCHID
COOMBS
MANOR
QUINCE DR
GREYFRIARS DR
JUNIPER DR
ELDER RD
ROSE DR
ANGELICA RD
SALVIA CT
ZINNIA
Hill Place Farm
Hill Place
Lipscombe Farm
GU21
Nursery
Littlewick
WAYSIDE CT 1
RAINBOW CT 2
GREENACRE 3
DOVERSMEAD 4
CRESTON AVE 5
GOLDFORT WLK 6
Littlewick Cotts
1 CONISTA CT
2 QUEENDALE CT
3 BLENCARN CL
Recn Gd

3
ARETHUSA WAY
A322
COBBETTS WLK
KINGSUP RD
WILLOT GDNS
WILLCO CL
HAWTHORN WAY
ELM GR
PILGRIMS WAY
Bisley
1 YELLOWCRESS DR
2 FREESIA DR
3 DAFFODIL DR
WARBURY LA
Nursery
Bisley CE Prim Sch
DONNAFIELDS
OAKWOOD RD
GUILDFORD RD
THE FIRS
CROBHAM RD
BARR'S LA
BARR'S LA
Whitfield Court
STANLEY COTTS 1
DEVON HO 2
CLEVE CT 3
ARAGON CT 4
KNAP CT 5
ANCHOR CRES 6
Waterers Park PH
CHEDDER TREE CL
FARTHINGS
MEYRICK
CHIPSTEAD
PADDOCKS MEAD
RUNNINGBROOK
Beaufort Com Prim Sch
WISHBONE WAY
LITTLE MEAD
WATERMEAD

59
PORT WAY
RYDERS
Miles Green
Lynbrook
RAVENS CL
BARLEY MOW LA
CRESSWELL
Bisley Common
QUEENS WAY
SNOWDON WAY
CHATTON ROW
LIMECROFT RD
BAGSHOT RD
SWALLOW RISE
MEADOW RISE
SHIRLEY PL
ROBINS DALE
BARLEY MOW CT
HIGHCLERE GDNS
WATERERS
BARNBY RD
RYDE HERON
RANDOLPH CL

2
Strawberry Farm
A322
Reidon Hill
MATTRESS
SUSSEX LANE
END OR
MERCHANTS
HIGHCLERE RD
FOSTERS CT
ANCHOR HILL
ST HILDA'S CL
ROBIN HOOD LA
HILLSIDE
NURSERY
BEECHWOOD
Works
RANDOLPH CL
OVERTHORPE
ROBIN HOOD RD
LOCKFIELD DR
Liby
PO
WOODSIDE CL
SHERWOOD RD
F2
1 NEWSHAM RD
2 ASHTON RD
3 WANSFORD GN
ROKEBY CT
LOCKSLEY DR
BISHOPS WAY

1
GRINDSTONE HANDLE CNR
REIDONHILL COTTS
Stafford Lake
RAPSLEY LA
OAKWOOD
TREE HO
CORESBROOK WAY
BAGSHOT RD
A322
CHOBHAM RD
ALANBROOKE
Sch
ROYAL CT
Trinity Rd
REDDING WAY
BARTON CL
FLORENCE CT
FLORENCE CT
CAVELL RD
Alexandra Par
P
Alexandra Gdns
BROADWAY
RIDING WAY
CRANLEY PL
Alexandra Gdns
Knaphill
LOWER GUILDFORD RD
Queen's Rd
POWDERHAM RD
CLINTON RD
BURNHAM
ALEXANDRA GDNS
CUBITT WAY
NORTHWOOD AVE
SOUTH
HAZEL WOOD
GREENVALE RD
HERBERT CRES
VICTORIA RD
ALMA RD
BLOOMFIELD RD
INKERMAN WAY
Sch
RAGLAN RD
CARDIGAN RD
The Winston Churchill Sch
CODRINGTON CT
FORESTERS
WYNDHAM CT
SWINDON RD
SCARLETT CL
NOTTINGHAM CL
ROBIN HOOD RD
BUTTS COTTS
COPSE RD
ASHLEY RD
A324 AINSTEL WAY
A324
DENTON WAY

58
95 A 96 B C 97 D E F

E1
1 BARNARD CT
2 KINGSLAKE CT
3 WILLIAM RUSSELL CT
4 SAYER CT
5 ROBERTSON CT
6 WELLINGTON TERR

F1
1 CAUSEWAY CT
2 NIGHTINGALE CT
3 MOYNE CT
4 GUINNESS CT
5 NOTTINGHAM CT
6 CRANFIELD CT
7 CAPSTANS WHARF
8 BARRACK PATH

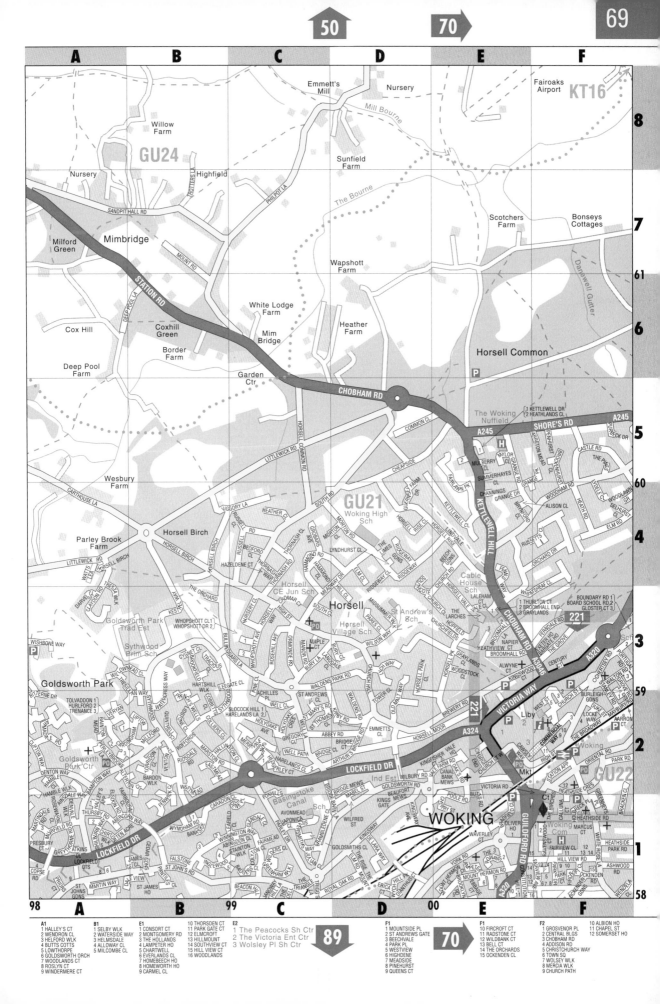

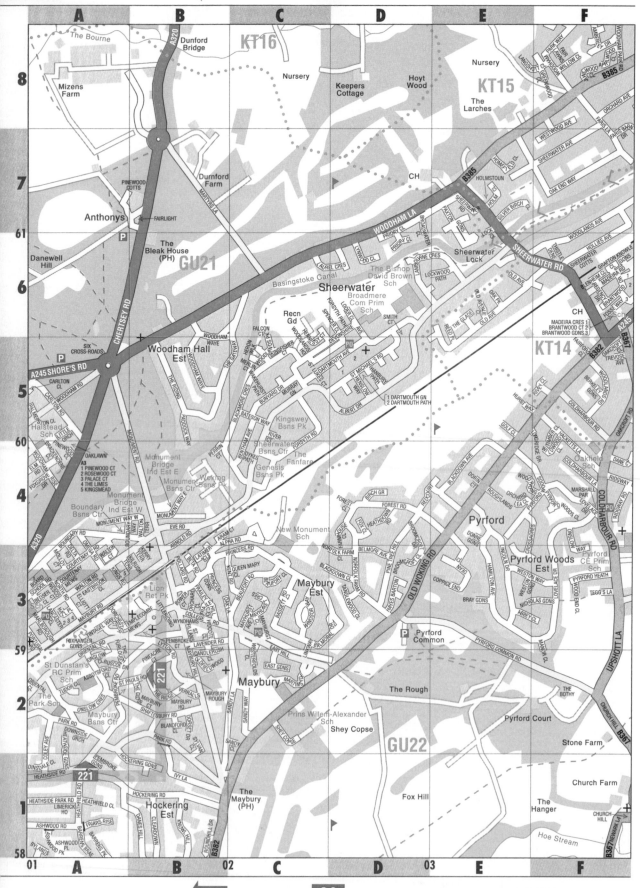

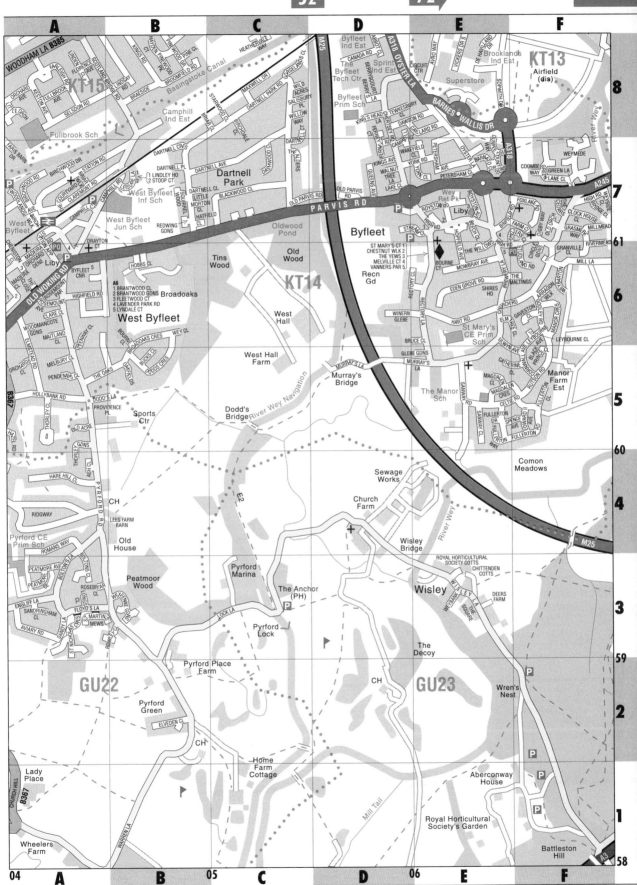

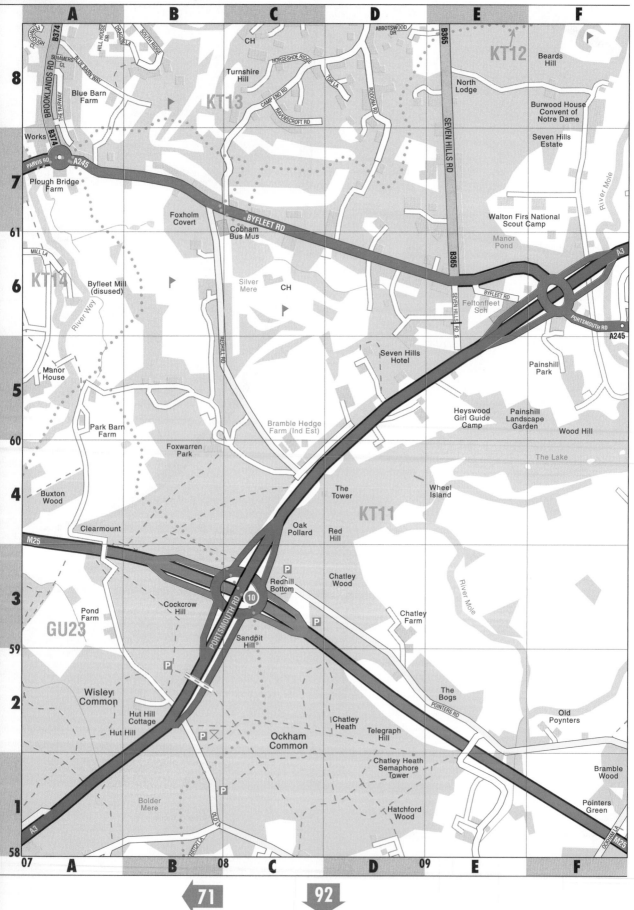

A B C D E F

8

KT12

Beards Hill

CH

Turnshire Hill

Horseshoe Ridge

North Lodge

Burwood House Convent of Notre Dame

KT13

Camp End Rd

Ravenscroft Rd

Tor La

Rodina Rd

Abbotswood Dr

B365

Seven Hills Estate

Works

B374

7

Plough Bridge Farm

Parvis Rd

A245

Byfleet Rd

Foxholm Covert

Cobham Bus Mus

Seven Hills Rd

Walton Firs National Scout Camp

River Mole

61

Mill La

KT14

Byfleet Mill (disused)

Silver Mere

CH

Byfleet Rd

Feltonfleet Sch

Manor Pond

B365

A3

6

River Wey

Seven Hills Rd S

Portsmouth Rd

A245

Manor House

Seven Hills Hotel

Painshill Park

5

Park Barn Farm

Bramble Hedge Farm (Ind Est)

Heyswood Girl Guide Camp

Painshill Landscape Garden

Wood Hill

60

Foxwarren Park

The Lake

4

Buxton Wood

The Tower

Wheel Island

Clearmount

KT11

M25

Oak Pollard

Red Hill

River Mole

3

Pond Farm

Cockcrow Hill

P

Redhill Bottom

Chatley Wood

Chatley Farm

GU23

Portsmouth Rd

10

Sandpit Hill

P

59

Wisley Common

P

The Bogs

Pointers Rd

Old Poynters

2

Hut Hill Cottage

Hut Hill

P

Ockham Common

Chatley Heath

Telegraph Hill

Bramble Wood

1

Bolder Mere

P

Old La

Chatley Heath Semaphore Tower

Hatchford Wood

Pointers Green

A3

Hatchf La

M25

Ockham La

58

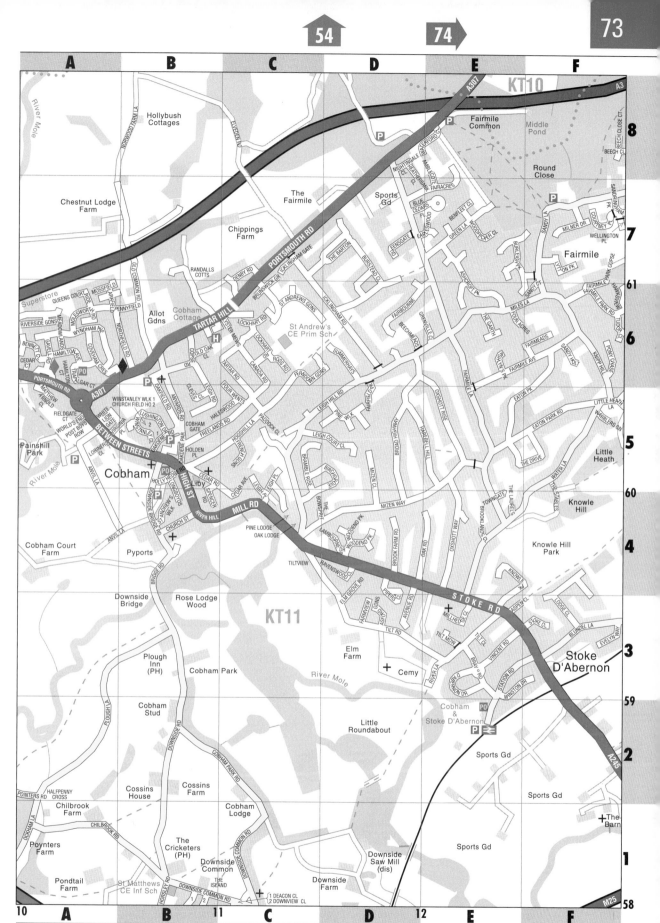

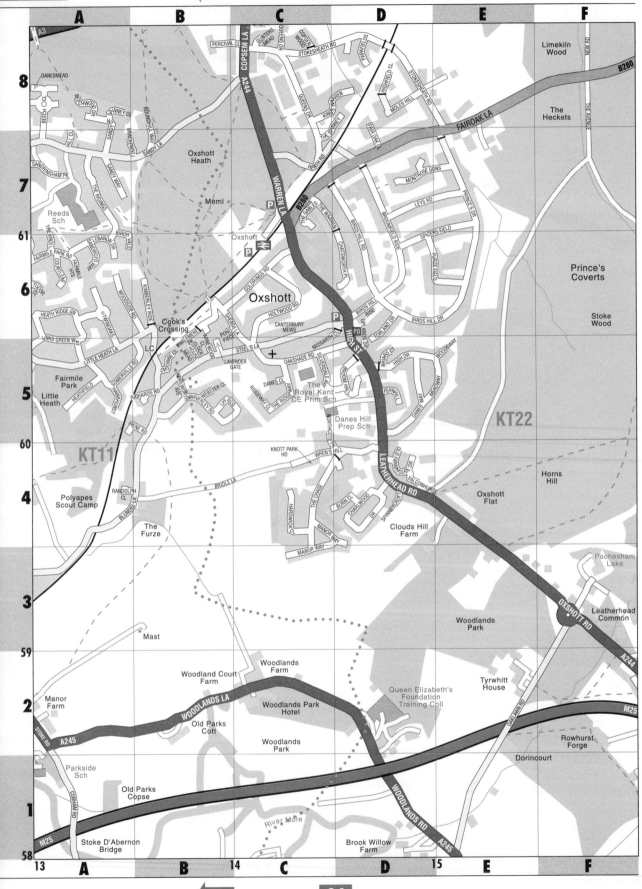

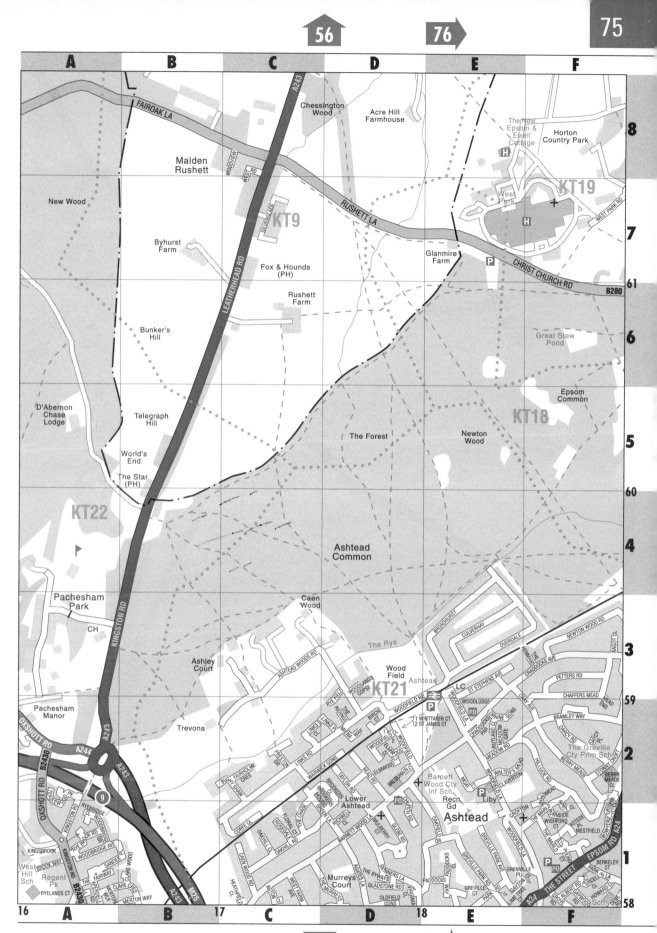

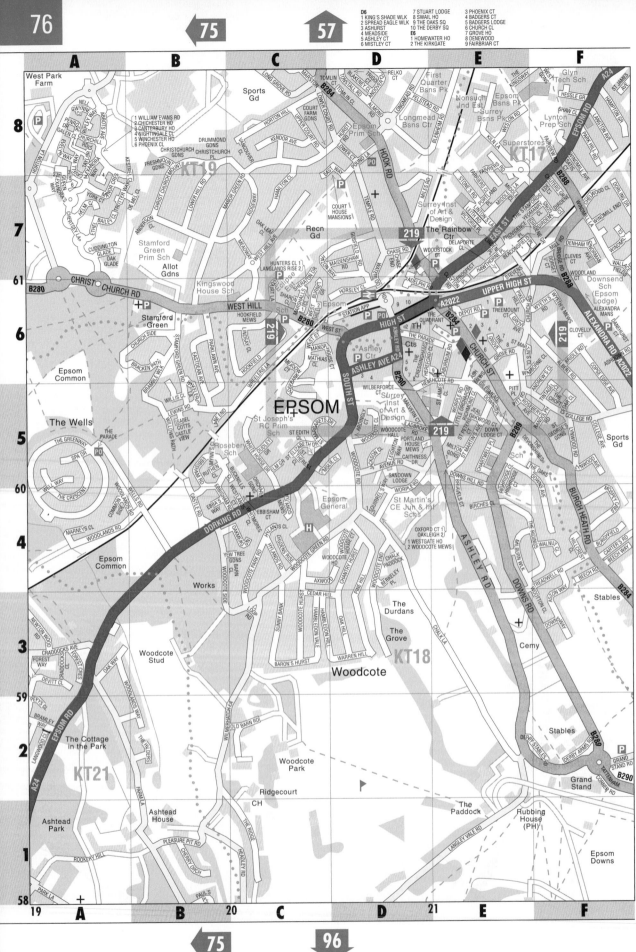

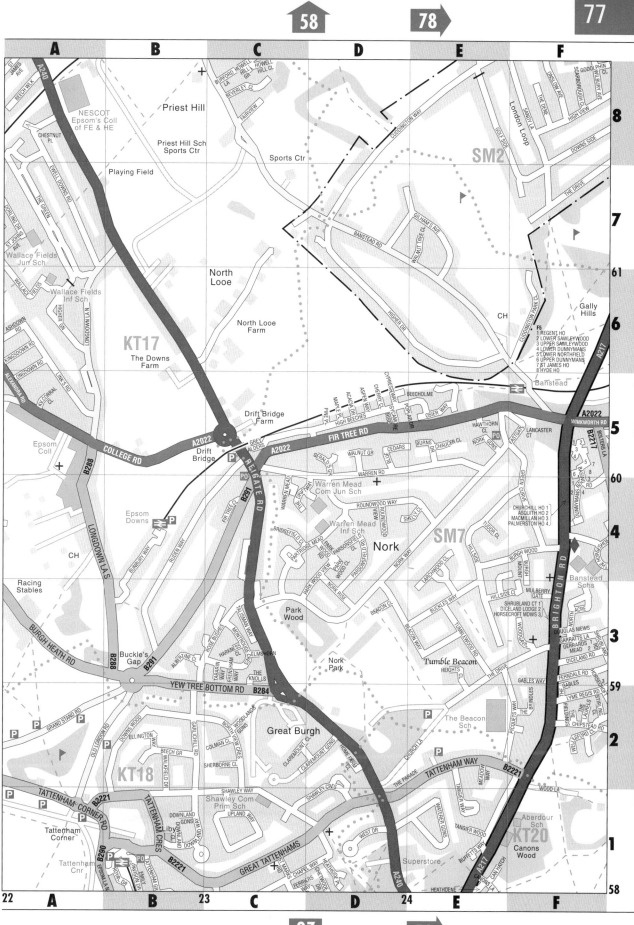

58
78

Priest Hill

NESCOT
Epsom's Coll
of FE & HE

Priest Hill Sch
Sports Ctr

Sports Ctr

Playing Field

SM2

North
Looe

KT17

North Looe
Farm

The Downs
Farm

Gally
Hills

CH

F5
1 REGENT HO
2 LOWER SAWLEYWOOD
3 UPPER SAWLEYWOOD
4 LOWER DUNNYMANS
5 LOWER NORTHFIELD
6 UPPER DUNNYMANS
7 ST JAMES HO
8 HYDE HO

Banstead

Wallace Fields
Jun Sch

Wallace Fields
Inf Sch

Drift Bridge
Farm

BEECHOLME

A2022
WINKWORTH RD

FIR TREE RD

COLLEGE RD

A2022

Drift
Bridge

Epsom
Coll

Warren Mead
Com Jun Sch

WARREN RD

Nork

SM7

CHURCHILL HO 1
ASQUITH HO 2
MACMILLAN HO 3
PALMERSTON HO 4.

Epsom
Downs

Warren Mead
Inf Sch

Racing
Stables

CH

Park
Wood

Banstead
Schs

BRIGHTON RD

Buckle's
Gap

Tumble Beacon

SHRUBLAND CT 1
DICELAND LODGE 2
HORSECROFT MDWS 3

Nork
Park

Tumble Beacon
HEIGHTS

The
Knolls

Douglas Mews

GARRATTS LA
GERRARDS
MEAD 2
DICELAND RD

YEW TREE BOTTOM RD

B284

The Beacon
Sch

GABLES WAY

THE GABLES

FERNDALE RD
LYME REGIS RD
THE
LAURELS

KT18

Great Burgh

TATTENHAM WAY

B2221

Shawley Com
Prim Sch

THE PARADE

WOOD LA

Aberdour
Sch

KT20

Canons
Wood

Tattenham
Corner

TATTENHAM CRES

GREAT TATTENHAMS

B2221

Superstore

A240

Tattenhams
Cnr

HEATHDENE

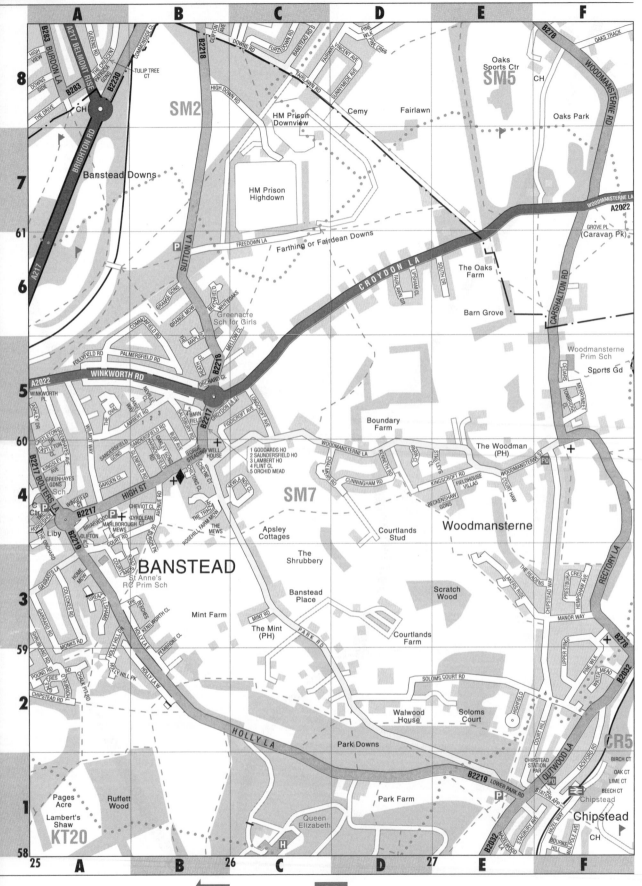

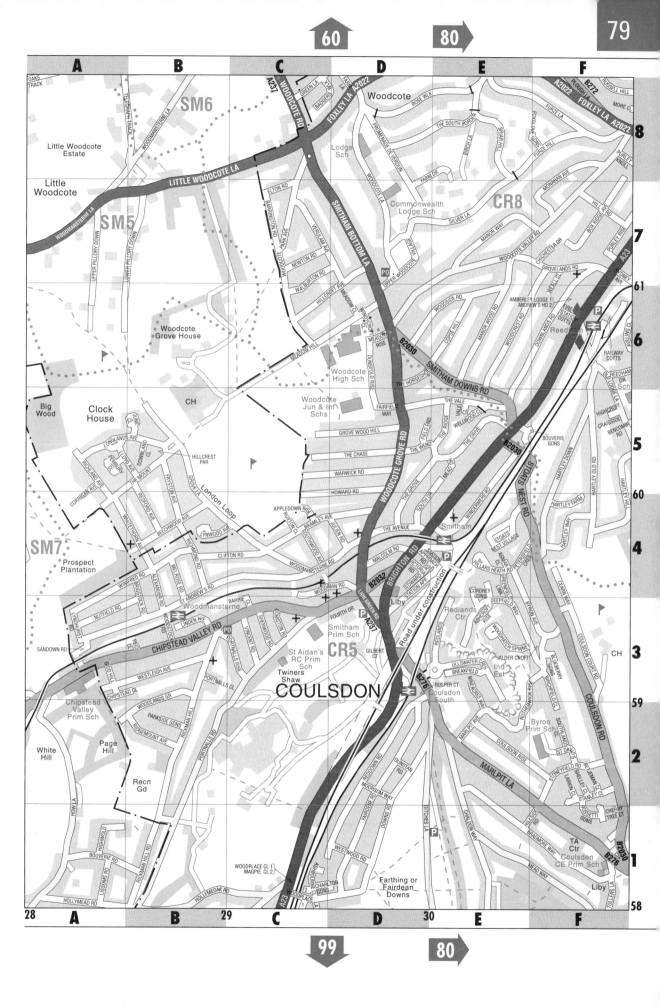

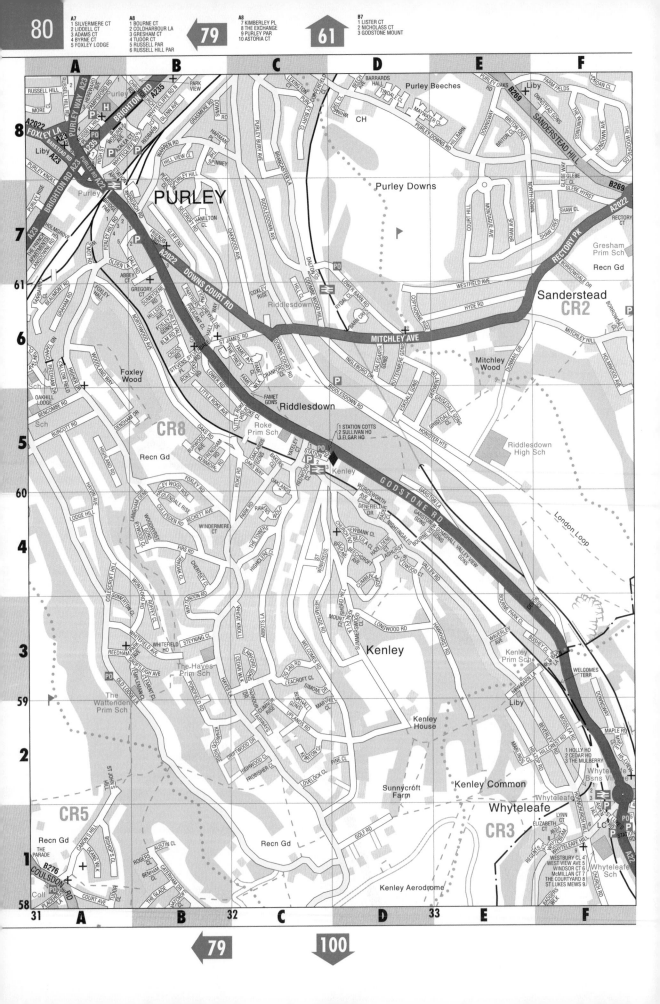

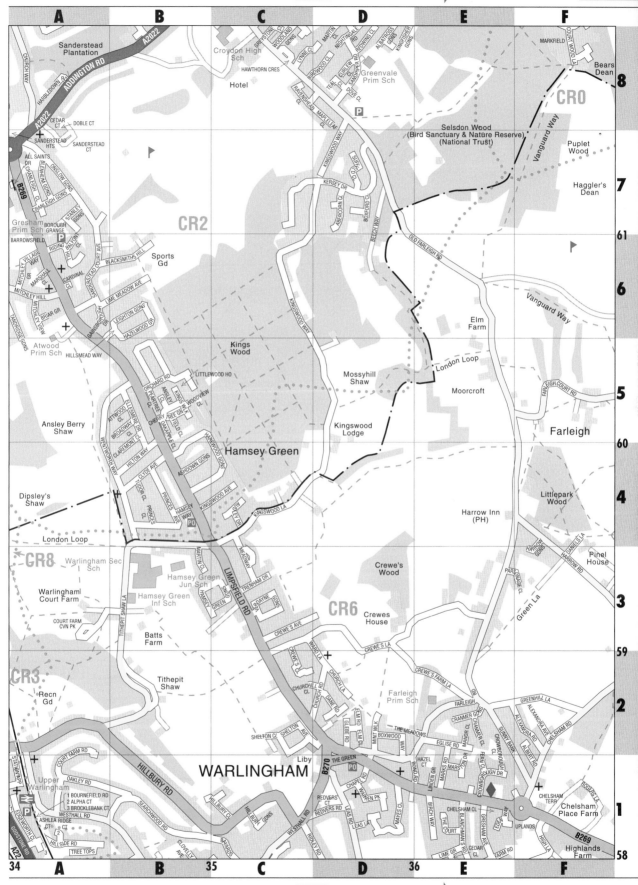

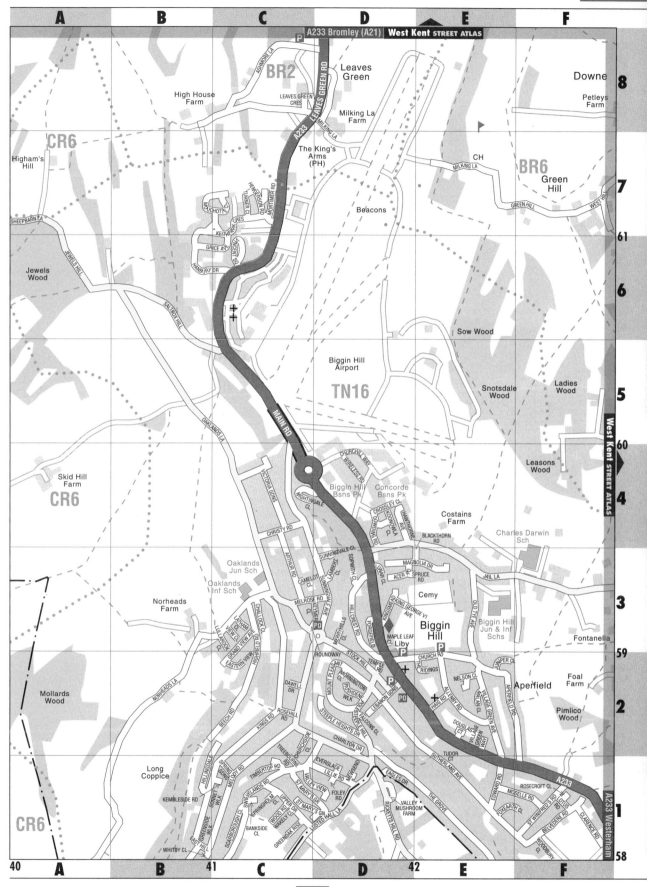

A233 Bromley (A21)   **West Kent** STREET ATLAS

BR2

Leaves Green

High House Farm

LEAVES GREEN CRES

Milking La Farm

8

CR6

Downe

Petleys Farm

Higham's Hill

A233

The King's Arms (PH)

CH

MILKING LA

BR6

Green Hill

7

SHEEPBARN LA

Beacons

GREEN HILL

WEST HILL

61

Jewels Wood

JEWELS HILL

Sow Wood

6

SALT BOX HILL

MAIN RD

Biggin Hill Airport

TN16

Snotsdale Wood

Ladies Wood

5

OAKLANDS LA

Skid Hill Farm

CR6

CHURCHILL WAY
WIRELESS RD

Biggin Hill Bsns Pk

Concorde Bsns Pk

Leasons Wood

West Kent STREET ATLAS

60

4

VICTORIA GDNS

NIGHTINGALE CL

CROSSLEY CL
KOONOWLA CL

HAWTHORNE

Costains Farm

Charles Darwin Sch

CHRISTY RD

DOWNING RD

BLACKTHORN RD

MAGNOLIA DR

ACER CL
SPRUCE RD

LILAC RD

Cemy

Oaklands Jun Sch

ARTHUR RD

SUNNINGVALE CL

LAMBERT CL
SOPWITH CL

KINGSMEAD KING GEORGE VI AVE

JAIL LA

Biggin Hill Jun & Inf Schs

3

Oaklands Inf Sch

CAMELOT CL

SUNNINGVALE AVE

HILCREST RD

MELROSE RD

MERRYWILLS

FORGEFIELD

Biggin Hill

Liby

CHURCH RD

Fontanella

Norheads Farm

CHALLOCK CL

LILLARDUR
GRAND VIEW AVE
EASTERN VIEW

ROUNDAWAY

STOCK HILL

TEMPLE RD

MAPLE LEAF CL

THE RIDINGS

NELSON CL

JUNIPER CL

OLD TYE AVE

VILLAGE GREEN WAY

APERFIELD RD

Aperfield

Foal Farm

59

BEECH RD

KINGS RD

ROSEHILL RD

DAWELL DR

MOUNT PLEASANT

MORNINGTON RD

ASHDENE

LEBANON GDNS

STEEPLE HEIGHTS DR

MILAN CL

DOUGLAS TERR

2

Mollards Wood

NORHEADS LA

Long Coppice

HILLINGDALE

SPOTTING

NELSON CL
TIMBERTOP RD

VALLEY VIEW

LILLIE RD

FOLEY RD

MENDIP RD

CHARLTON DR

EVERGLADE

EAGLES DR

THE GROVE

SUTHERLAND AVE

TUDOR CT

EDWARD RD

MOSELLE RD

ROSECROFT CL

A233

Pimlico Wood

KEMBLESIDE RD

SCARBOROUGH CL

SWEETLANDS CL

ST MARY'S GR

ST MARY'S GDN HALL LA

VALLEY MUSHROOM FARM

RICKETTS HILL RD

FOXEARTH CL

ST WINIFRED'S RD

BELVEDERE RD

LOTUS RD

CLARENCE RD

WOODBURY

A233 Westerham

1

CR6

GREENSIDE
SPRINGHILL
SPRINGOAK RISE
UPPER SR
WAKELY CL

BANKSIDE CL

GREENOAK RISE

58

WHITBY CL

EAST HILL

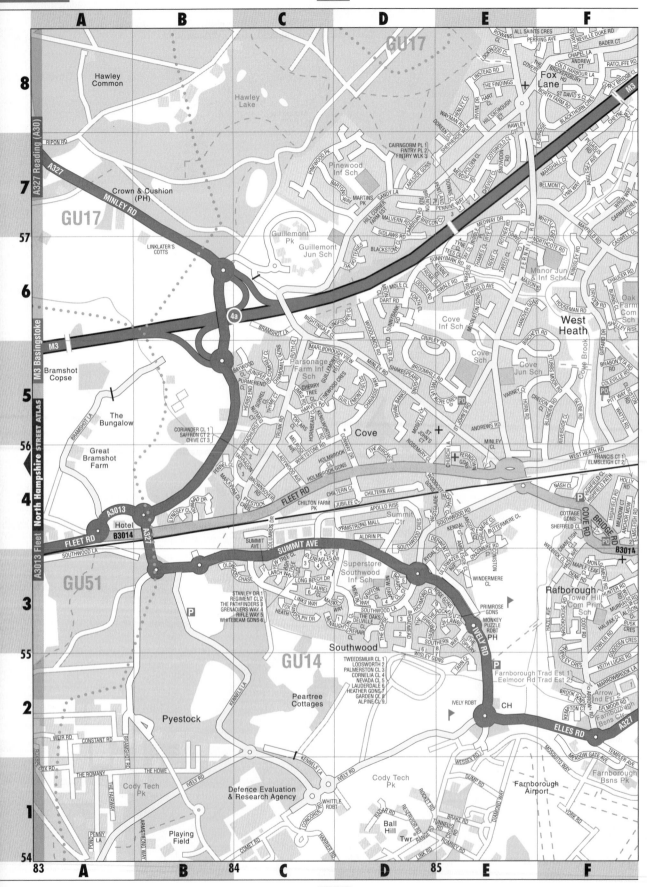

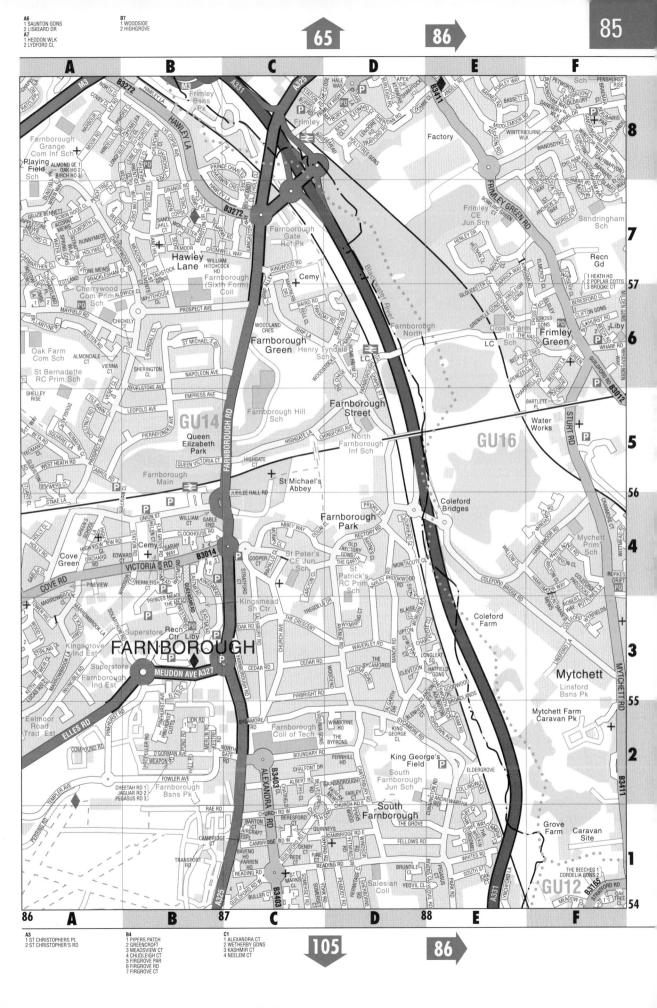

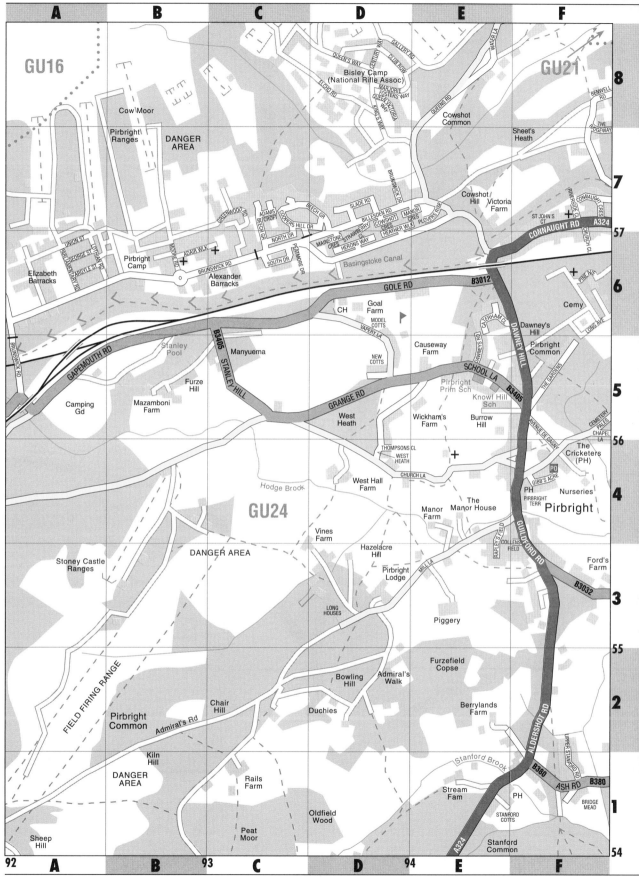

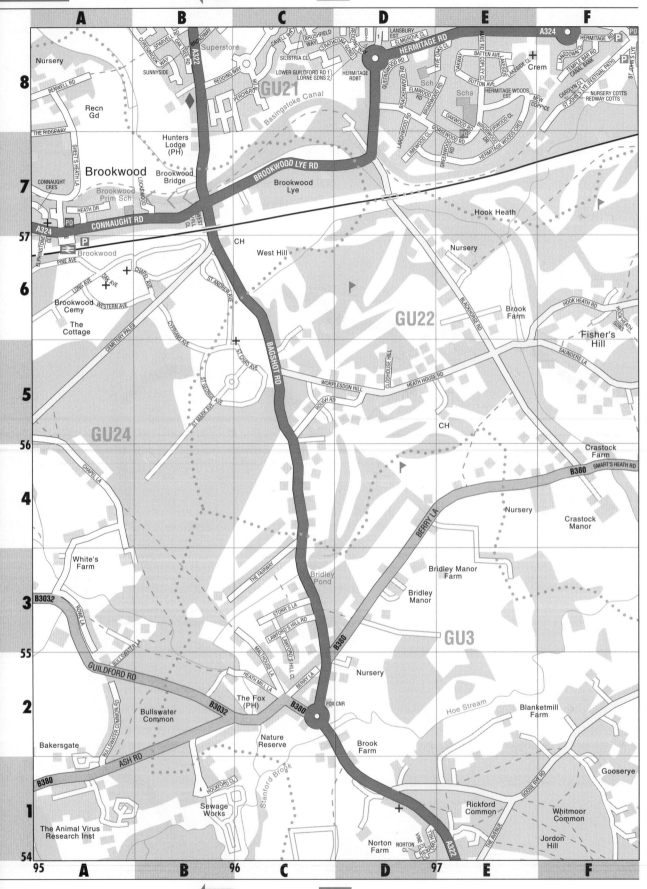

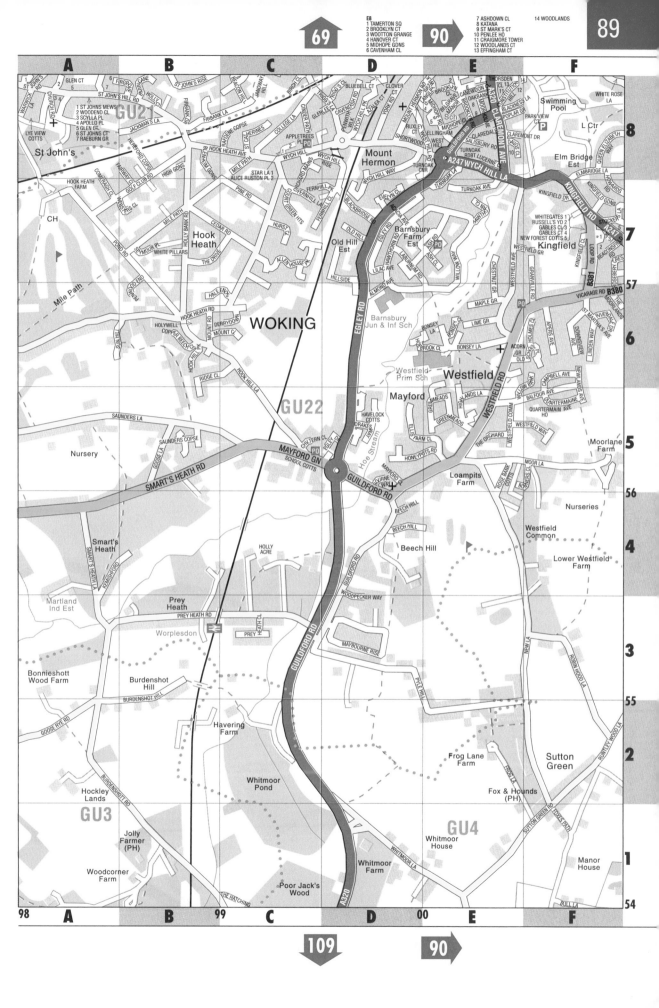

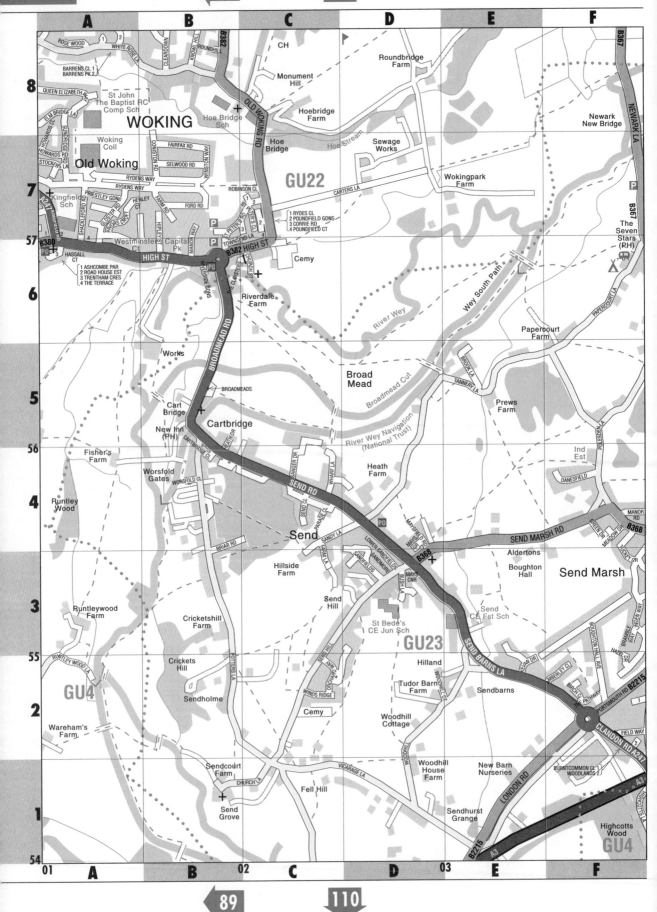

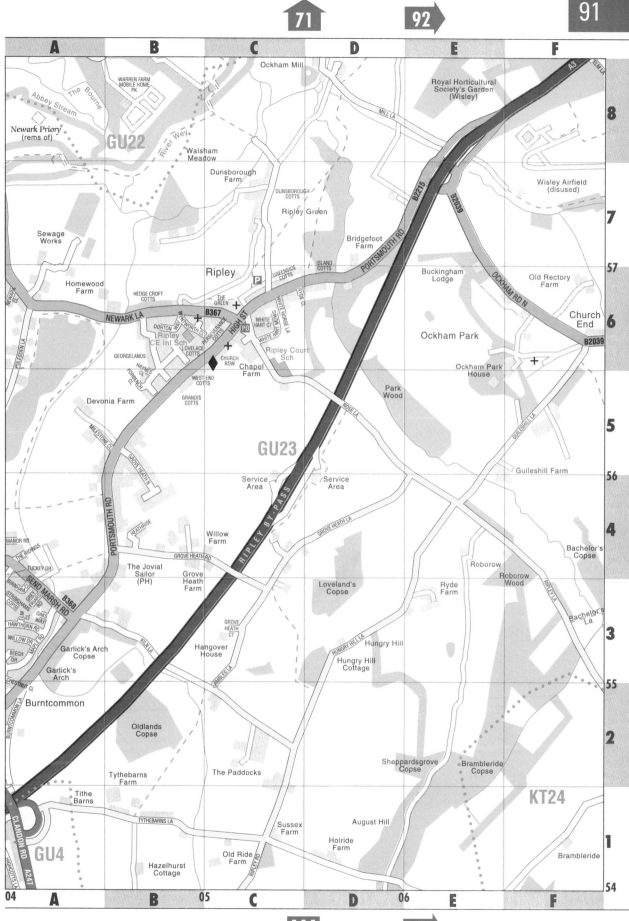

A B C D E F

8

7

57

6

5

56

4

55

2

1

54

Ockham Mill

Warren Farm
Mobile Home
Pk

The Bourne

Abbey Stream

Newark Priory
(rems of)

GU22

River Wey

Walsham
Meadow

Dunsborough
Farm

Dunsborough
Cotts

Ripley Green

Royal Horticultural
Society's Garden
(Wisley)

A3
ELM LA

Wisley Airfield
(disused)

MILL LA

B2215

B2039

Sewage
Works

Homewood
Farm

Ripley

Bridgefoot
Farm

Greenside
Cotts

Island
Cotts

Portsmouth Rd

Buckingham
Lodge

Ockham Rd N

Old Rectory
Farm

Church
End

B2039

NEWARK CL

POT ESSEX LA

NEWARK LA

Hedge Croft
Cotts

The Green

B367

Wentworth Cl

Dorton
Ct

Ripley
CE Inf Sch

Lovelace
Cotts

Georgelands

Haynes
Cl

Forbench
Cl

West End
Cotts

Grandis
Cotts

High St

Perseverance
Cotts

White Hr

White Horse La

White
Hart Ct

Simons La

Ryde Cl

Ripley Court
Sch

Chapel
Farm

Church
Row

Ockham Park

Ockham Park
House

Devonia Farm

Milestone Cl

Grove Heath N

Portsmouth Rd

Rose La

Park
Wood

Guileshill La

Guileshill Farm

GU23

Service
Area

Service
Area

Ripley By-Pass

Grove Heath La

Roborow

Roborow
Wood

Bachelor's
Copse

Heathrise

Willow
Farm

Grove Heath Rd

Ryde
Farm

Ripley La

Bachelor's
La

Manor Rd

The Ridings

Tuckey Gr

Send Marsh Rd

B368

The Jovial
Sailor
(PH)

Grove
Heath
Farm

Loveland's
Copse

Hungry Hill La

Hungry Hill

Birnham
Cl

Struthams
Cl

Grey
House
Cl

Copse
Cl

Oaks
Way

Hawthorn Rd

Willow Dr

Male Rd

Beech
Dr

Chestnut Cl

Kiln La

Grove
Heath
Ct

Gambles La

Hangover
House

Hungry Hill
Cottage

Garlick's Arch
Copse

Garlick's
Arch

Burntcommon

Oldlands
Copse

Sheppardsgrove
Copse

Brambleride
Copse

KT24

Burntcommon La

Tythebarns
Farm

The Paddocks

August Hill

Clandon Rd

A247

GU4

Tithe
Barns

Tythebarns La

Ripley Rd

Sussex
Farm

Holride
Farm

Brambleride

Highcotes La

Hazelhurst
Cottage

Old Ride
Farm

91 72

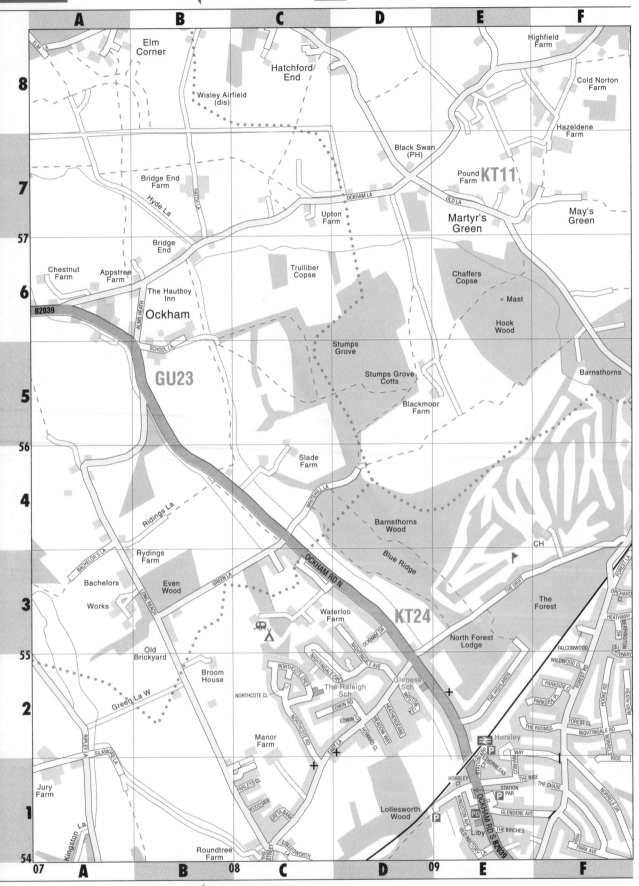

91 112

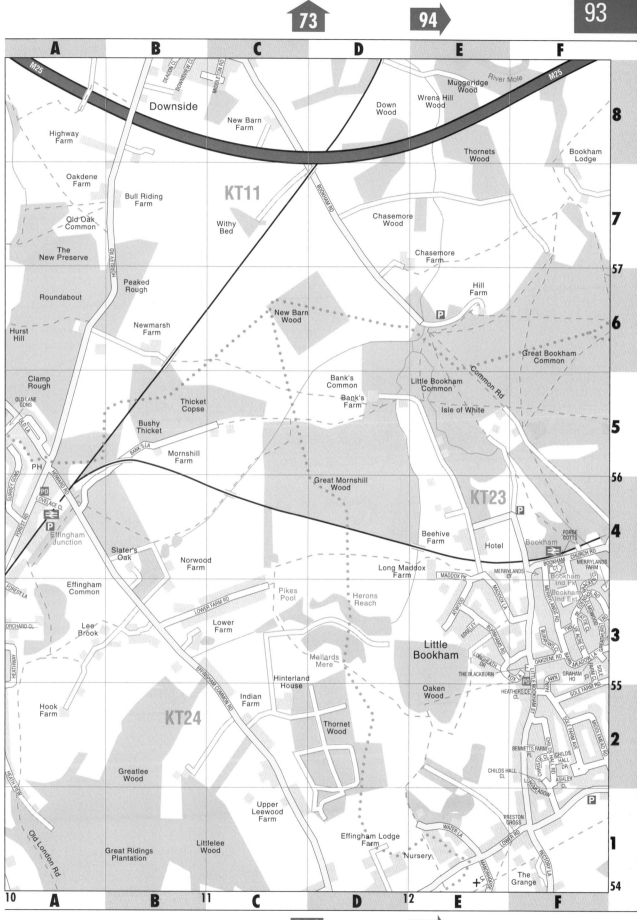

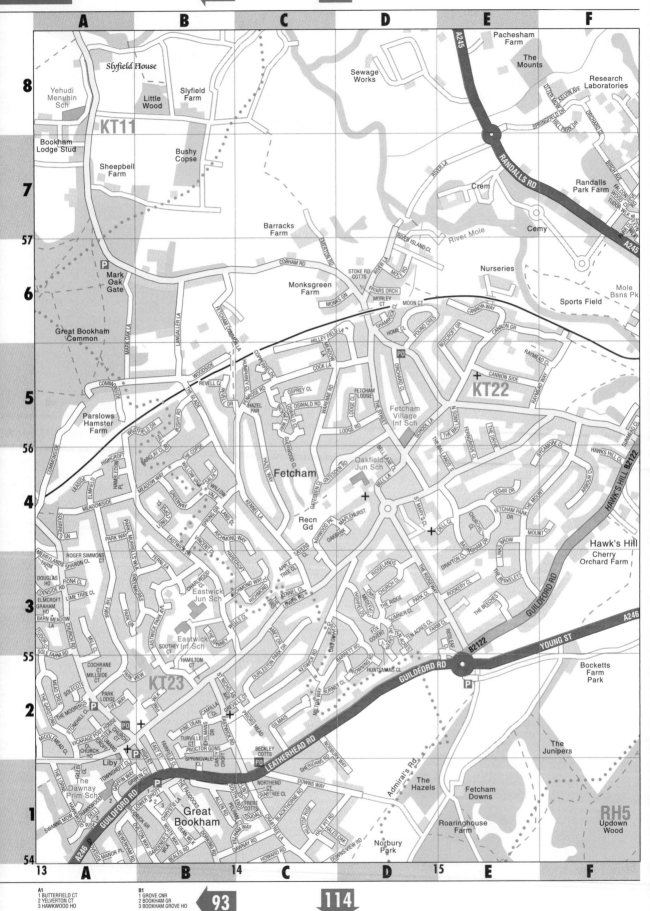

A1
1 BUTTERFIELD CT
2 YELVERTON CT
3 HAWKWOOD HO

B1
1 GROVE CNR
2 BOOKHAM GR
3 BOOKHAM GROVE HO

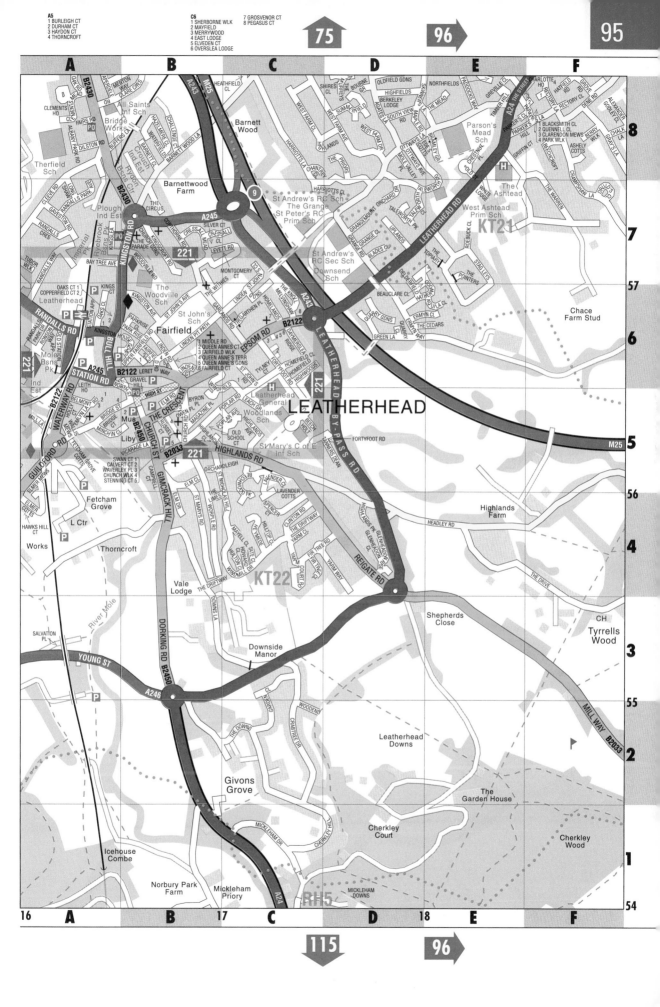

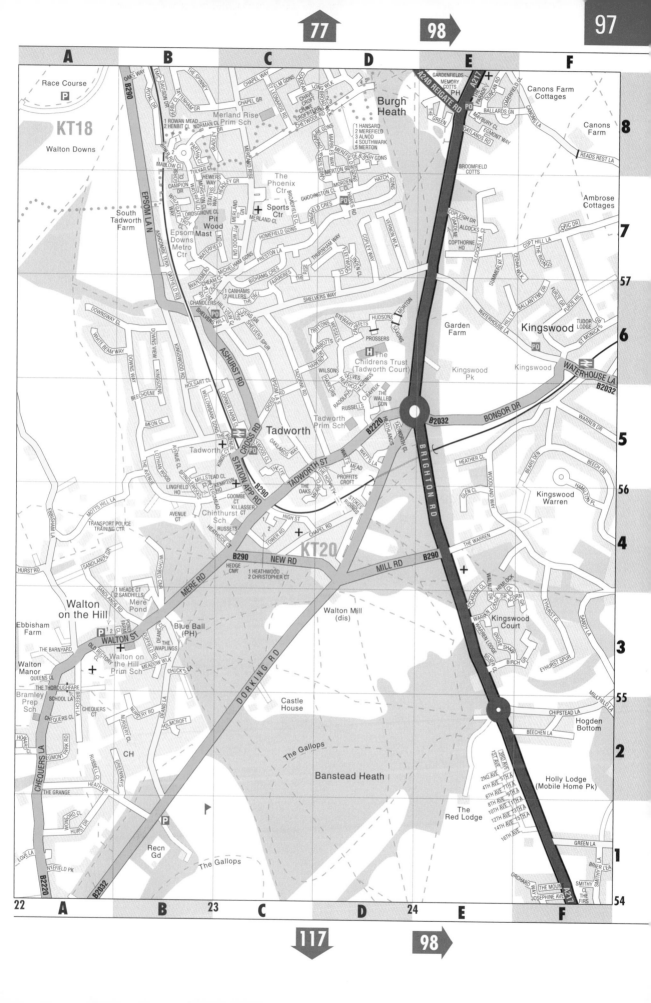

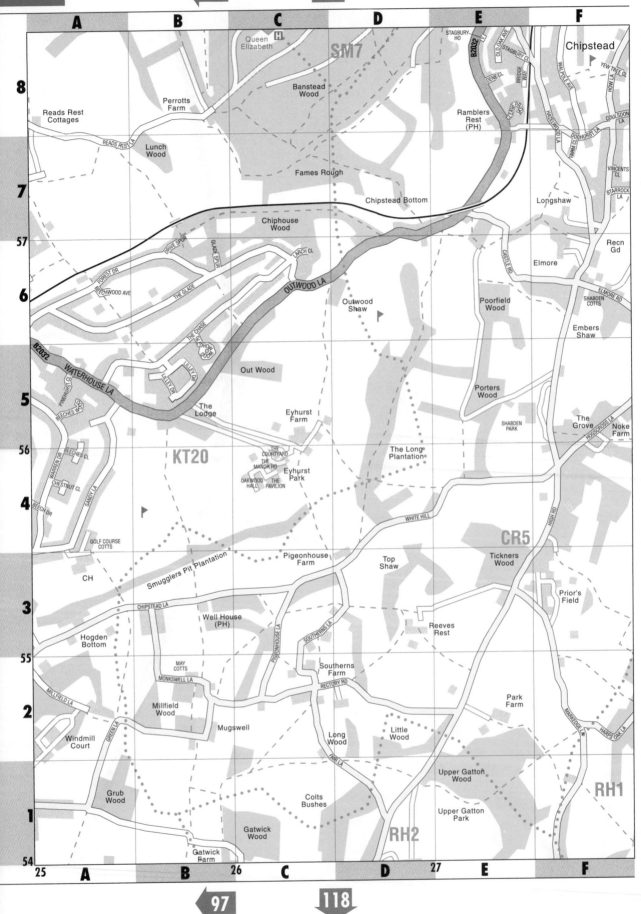

A B C D E F

8

Reads Rest
Cottages

Perrotts
Farm

Queen
Elizabeth H

SM7

Banstead
Wood

STAGBURY
HO

B2032

OLD OAK AVE

STAGBURY CL

Chipstead

YEW TREE CL

DENE CL

BRIDGE WAY

HAZELWOOD LA

DOGHURST LA

HOW LA

COULSDON LA

WALPOLE AVE

7

READS REST LA

Lunch
Wood

Fames Rough

Chipstead Bottom

Ramblers
Rest
(PH)

Longshaw

VINCENTS
CL

STARROCK
LA

57

DRIVE SPUR

GLADE SPUR

Chiphouse
Wood

LARCH CL

OUTWOOD LA

CASTLE RD

Recn
Gd

Elmore

ELMORE RD

SHABDEN
COTTS

6

FOREST DR

BEECHWOOD AVE

THE GLADE

THE CHASE

Outwood Shaw

Poorfield
Wood

Embers
Shaw

B2032

WATERHOUSE LA

BEECHWOOD CL

LILLEY DR

Out Wood

5

PINEHURST CL

BEECHES WY

The
Lodge

Eyhurst
Farm

Porters
Wood

SHABDEN
PARK

The
Grove

HORSECROSS LA

Noke
Farm

56

WARREN DR

BEECHES CL

SANDY LA

KT20

THE
COURTYARD

THE
MANOR HO

OAKWOOD
HALL

THE
PAVILION

Eyhurst
Park

The Long
Plantation

4

BEECH DR

CHESTNUT CL

WHITE HILL

CR5

HIGH RD

Tickners
Wood

Prior's
Field

GOLF COURSE
COTTS

CH

Smugglers Pit Plantation

Pigeonhouse
Farm

Top
Shaw

Reeves
Rest

3

CHIPSTEAD LA

Well House
(PH)

PIGEONHOUSE LA

SOUTHERNS LA

55

MILLFIELD LA

MAY
COTTS

MONKSWELL LA

RECTORY RD

Southerns
Farm

Park
Farm

MARKEDGE LA

HARPS OAK LA

2

GREEN LA

Millfield
Wood

Mugswell

Long
Wood

Little
Wood

Windmill
Court

PARK LA

Upper Gatton
Wood

RH1

1

Grub
Wood

Colts
Bushes

Upper Gatton
Park

Gatwick
Wood

RH2

Gatwick
Farm

54

25 A B 26 C D 27 E F

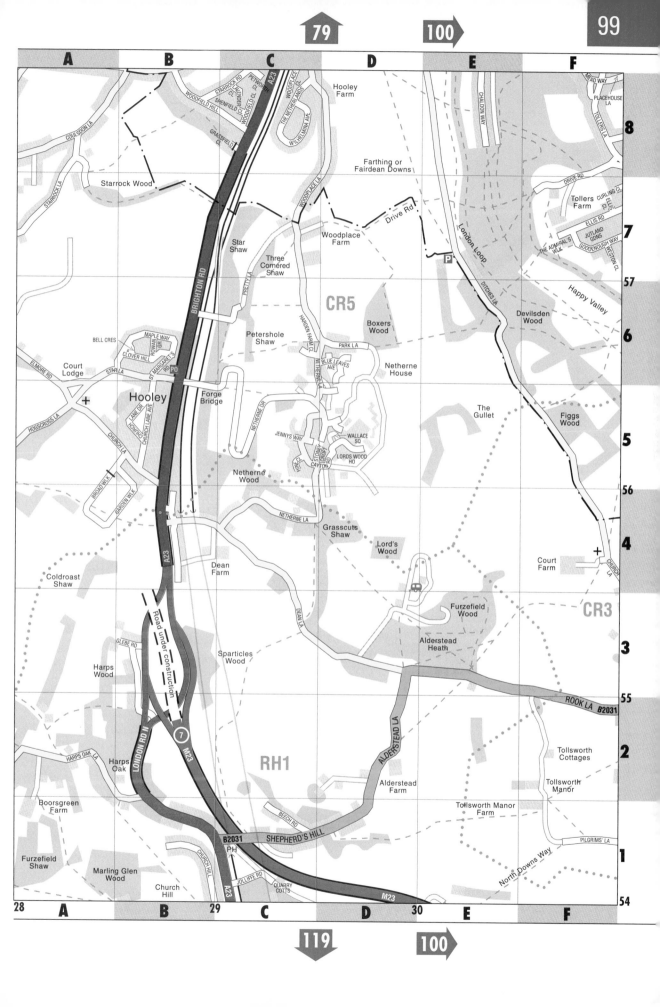

A   B   C   D   E   F

8

MEAD WAY
PLACEHOUSE LA
COULSDON LA
WOODFIELD HILL
STARROCK RD
LAVENDER CL
SHENFIELD CL
WOODFIELD CL
GRASSFIELD CL
PETWORTH CL
A23
THE NETHERLANDS
WOODPLACE
WILHELMINA AVE
Hooley Farm
TOLLERS LA
DRIVE RD
Tollers Farm
CURLING CL
ELLIS CL

Starrock Wood
STARROCK LA
Farthing or Fairdean Downs
WOODPLACE LA
Drive Rd
THE ADMIRAL'S WLK
ELLIS RD
JUTLAND GDNS
GOODENOUGH WAY
WESTON CL

7

London Loop
CR5
57

Star Shaw
Woodplace Farm
Three Cornered Shaw
PRETORIA
BRIGHTON RD
Happy Valley

6

Petershole Shaw
HARDEN FARM CL
Boxers Wood
PARK LA
DITCHES LA
Devilsden Wood

BELL CRES
MAPLE WAY
ROWAN GR
CLOVER HILL
ST MARGARET'S
STAR LA
NETHERNE LA
BLUE LEAVES AVE
Netherne House

ELMORE RD
Court Lodge
PO
NETHERNE DR
The Gullet
Figgs Wood

5

Hooley
Forge Bridge
CHURCH LA
LANE GR
CHURCH LANE AVE
JENNYS WAY
STONEY CROFT
HINCH CL
WALLACE SQ
LORDS WOOD HO
CAYTON
56

BROAD WLK
GARDEN WLK
Netherne Wood
NETHERNE LA
Grasscuts Shaw
Lord's Wood

4

HOGSCROSS LA
Dean Farm
Court Farm
CHURCH LA

Coldroast Shaw
A23
Furzefield Wood
CR3

3

DEAN LA
Alderstead Heath

Harps Wood
Road under construction
GLEBE RD
Sparticles Wood
ROOK LA
B2031
55

LONDON RD N
7
M23
RH1
ALDERSTEAD LA
Tollsworth Cottages

2

HARPS OAK LA
Harps Oak
Alderstead Farm
Tollsworth Manor

Boorsgreen Farm
BEECH RD
Tollsworth Manor Farm
PILGRIMS' LA

1

Furzefield Shaw
Marling Glen Wood
Church Hill
CHURCH HILL
JOLLIFFE RD
QUARRY COTTS
B2031
SHEPHERD'S HILL
PH
A23
M23
North Downs Way

28   29   30
A   B   C   D   E   F

99

C6
1 NEWLANDS CT
2 HUNTSMANS CT
3 ALMA CT

80

D5
1 LE PERSONNE HOMES
2 THE FIRS
3 CHATFIELD CT
4 CHRISTIE WLK

A   B   C   D   E   F

Kenley Aerodrome

CR8

Coxes Wood

Keston Schs
Coulsdon Coll
THE CROSSWAYS
Old Coulsdon
Coulsdon High Sch

Blize Wood

CR5

COULSDON RD

Coulsdon Common

London Loop
The Fox (PH)

Audley Prim Sch
St Francis RC Prim Sch
Sunnydown Sch
de Stafford Coll

BANSTEAD RD

Dean Hill

Broad Wood
Piles Wood

TOWNEND
The Raglan Prec

Liby

CHALDON RD
Prim Sch
CATERHAM

Fryern Farm
Fryern Broom Wood

CH

The Rookery

ROOK LA
Rook Farm
Chaldon

Caterham Dene
St Mary's Mount
Cemy
Queen's Park

CHURCH HILL

B2031
St Peter & St Paul CE Inf Sch

CR3

Uplands Farm
Six Brother's Field

Hill-Top Farm

Oakhyrst Grange Sch

Beech Hanger

Caterham Prep Sch

Mast
W Twr
PILGRIMS LA
North Downs Way
Willey Park Farm

RH1

31   A   32   B   C   D   33   E   F

99

120

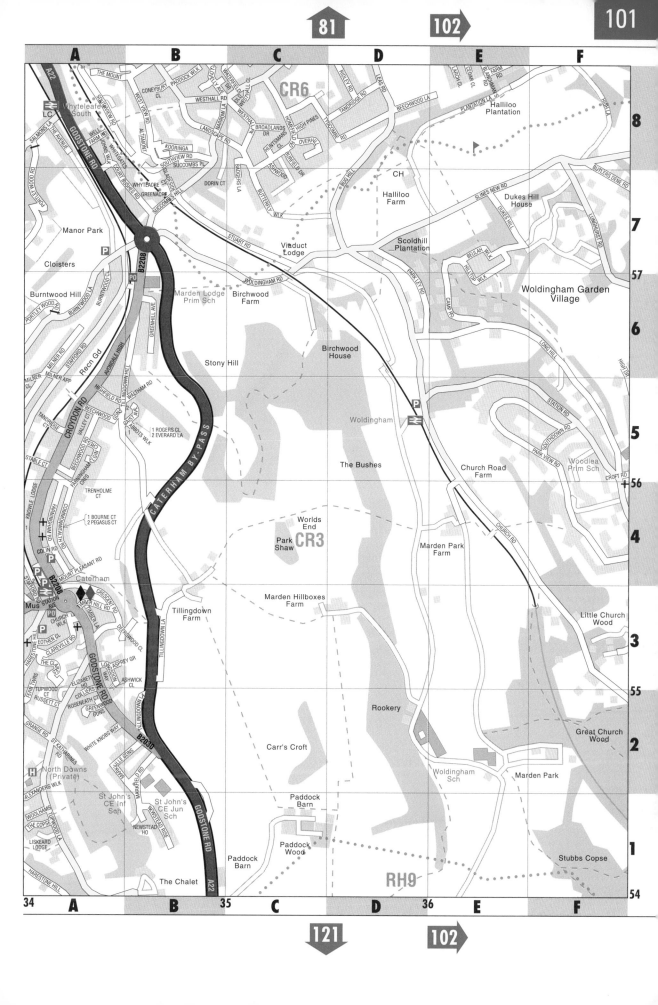

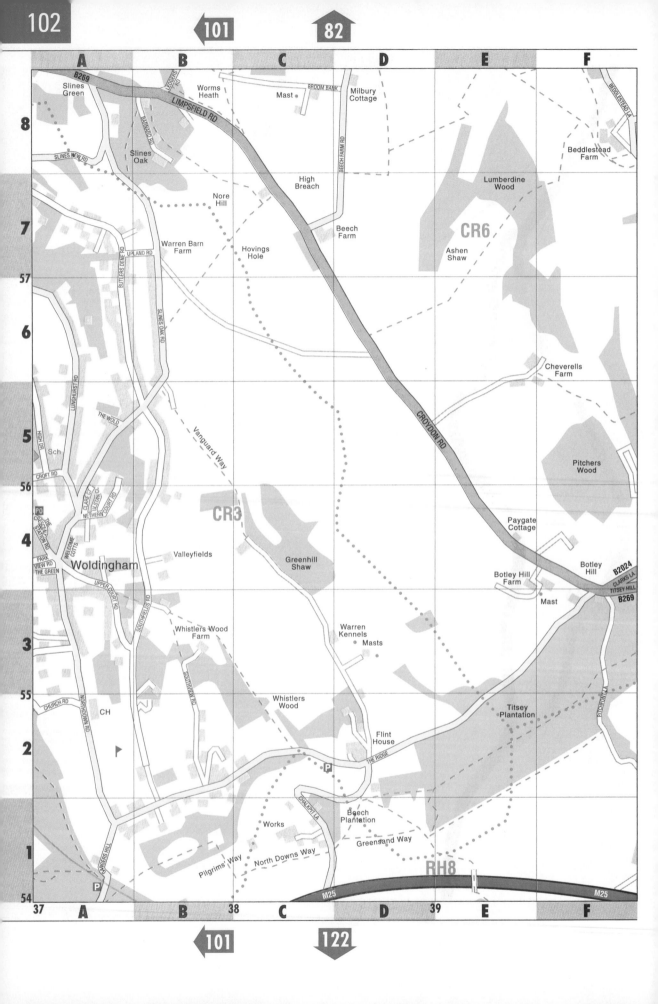

101
82

A B C D E F

8

7

57

6

5

56

4

3

55

2

1

54

37 38 39

A B C D E F

101
122

B269
Slines Green
Slines Oak
LEDGERS RD
Worms Heath
LIMPSFIELD RD
Mast
BROOM BANK
Milbury Cottage
BARNARD RD
BEECH FARM RD
High Breach
Lumberdine Wood
Beddlestead Farm
BEDDLESTEAD LA
Nore Hill
Slines New Rd
Warren Barn Farm
UPLAND RD
BUTLERS DENE RD
Hovings Hole
Beech Farm
CR6
Ashen Shaw
SLINES OAK RD
LUNGHURST RD
THE WOLD
Vanguard Way
CROYDON RD
Cheverells Farm
Pitchers Wood
HIGH DR
Sch
CROFT RD
CR3
Paygate Cottage
CLARE CT
V STN CT
NETHERN COURT RD
THE CRESCENT
PO
STATION RD
WELCOME COTTS
PARK VIEW RD
THE GREEN
Woldingham
Valleyfields
Greenhill Shaw
Botley Hill Farm
Botley Hill
B2024
CLARKS LA
TITSEY HILL
B269
UPPER COURT RD
SOUTHFIELDS RD
Whistlers Wood Farm
Warren Kennels
Masts
Mast
CHURCH RD
NORTHDOWN RD
CH
SOUTH VIEW RD
Whistlers Wood
Titsey Plantation
PITCHFONT LA
Flint House
THE RIDGE
P
Flint House
Beech Plantation
Greensand Way
RH8
CHALKPIT LA
Works
North Downs Way
Pilgrims Way
CANGERS HILL
P
M25
M25

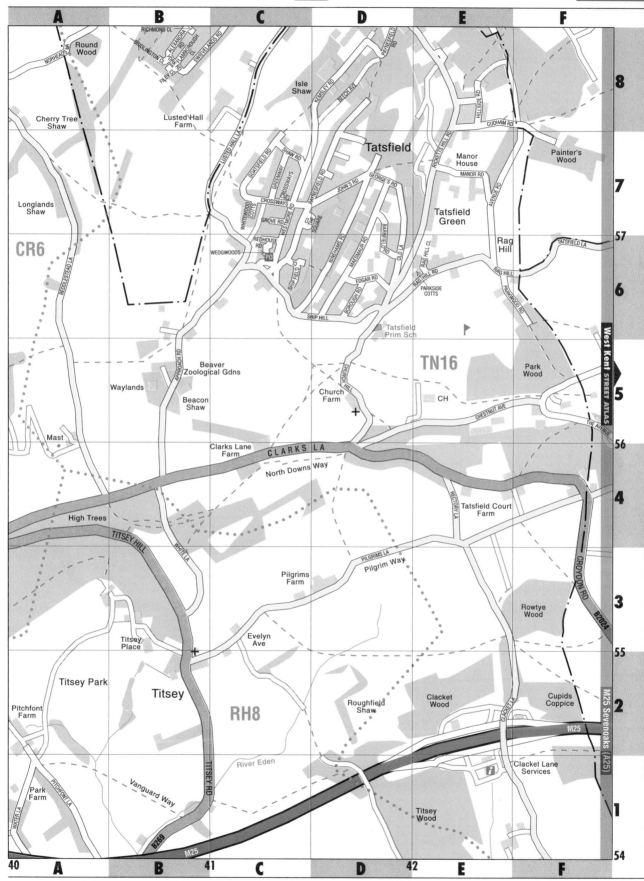

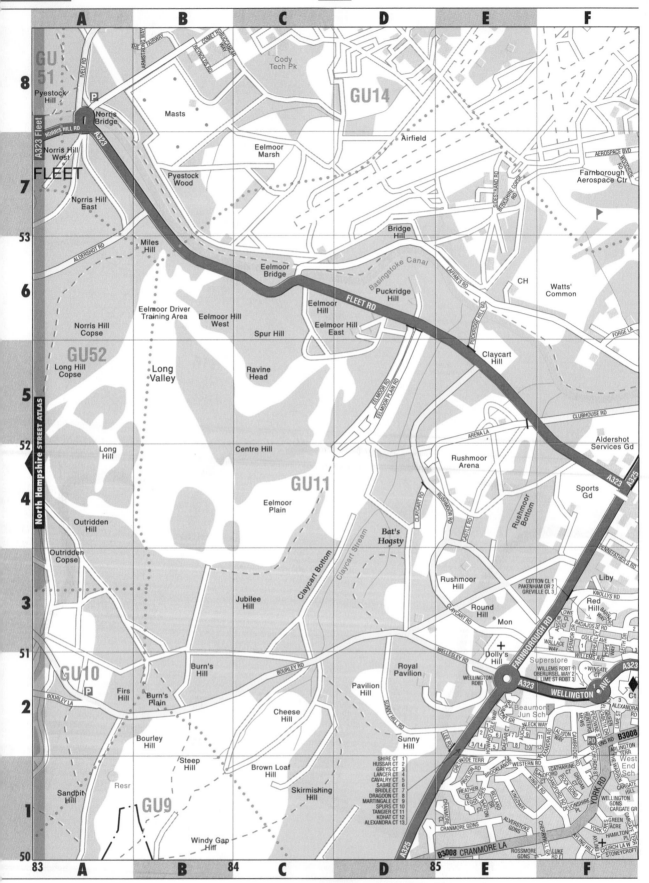

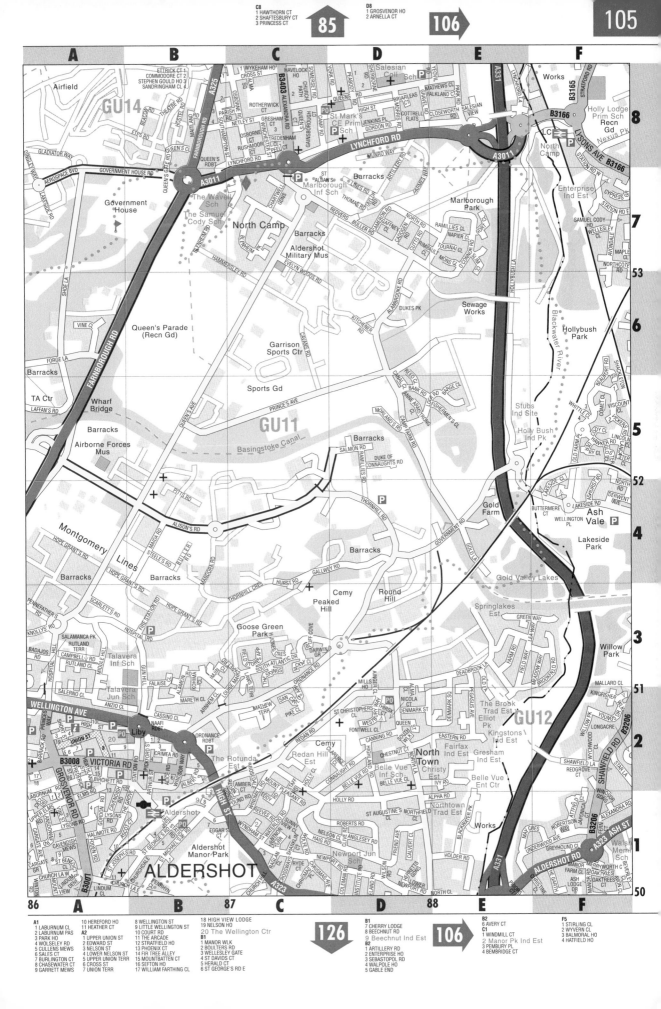

105
86

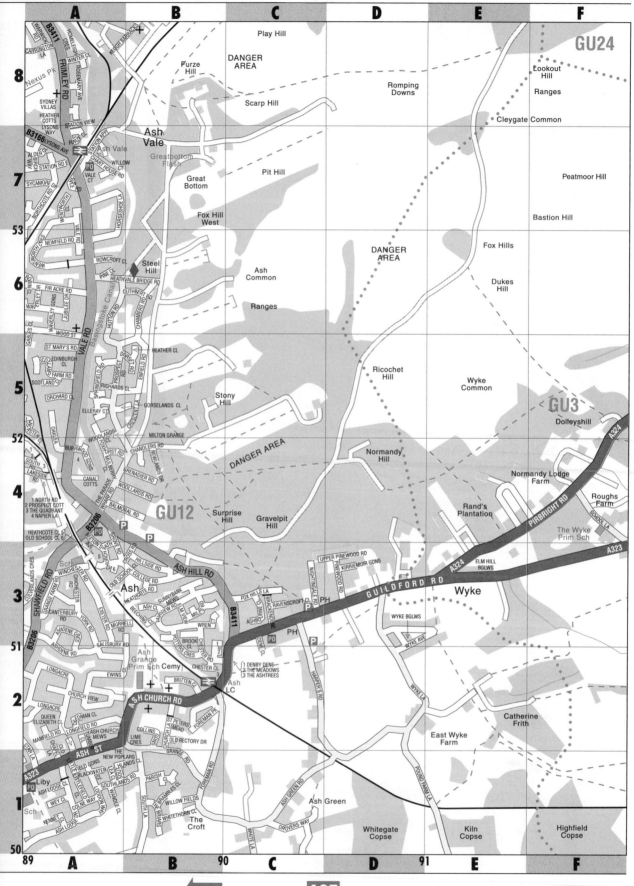

105
127

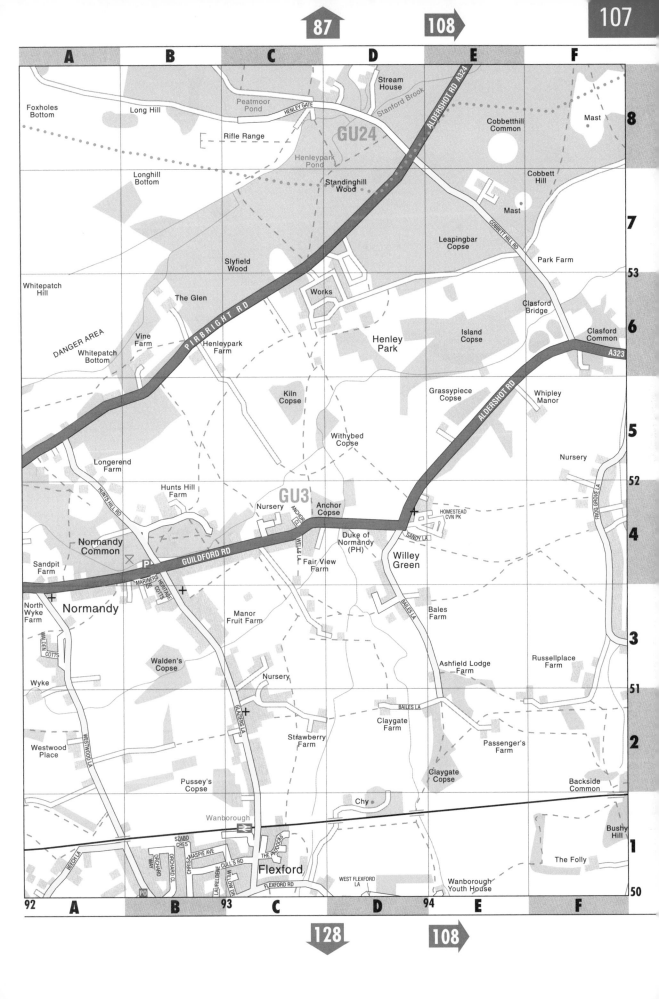

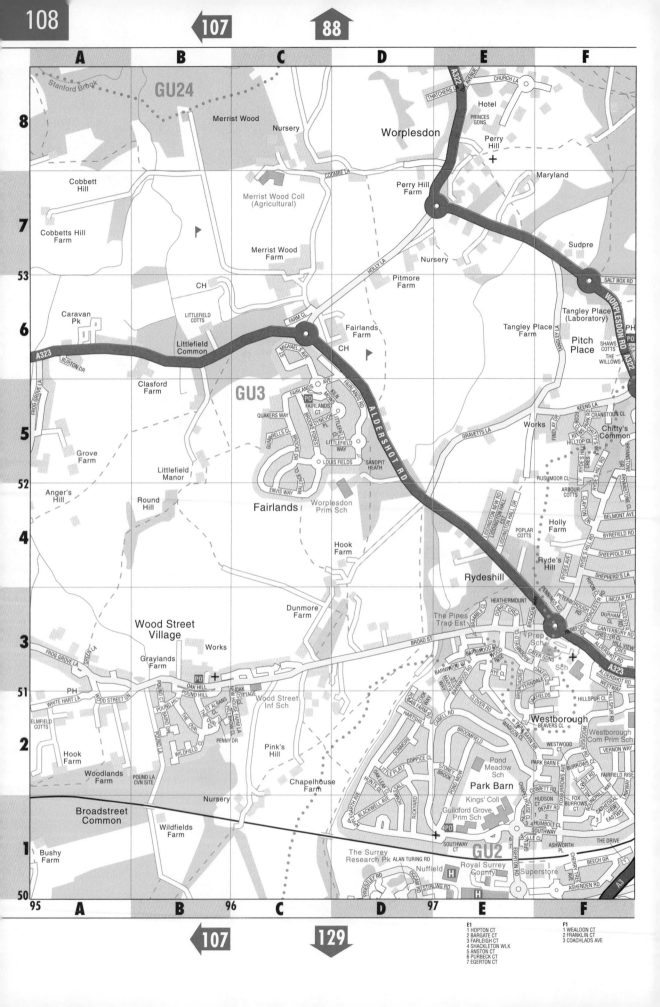

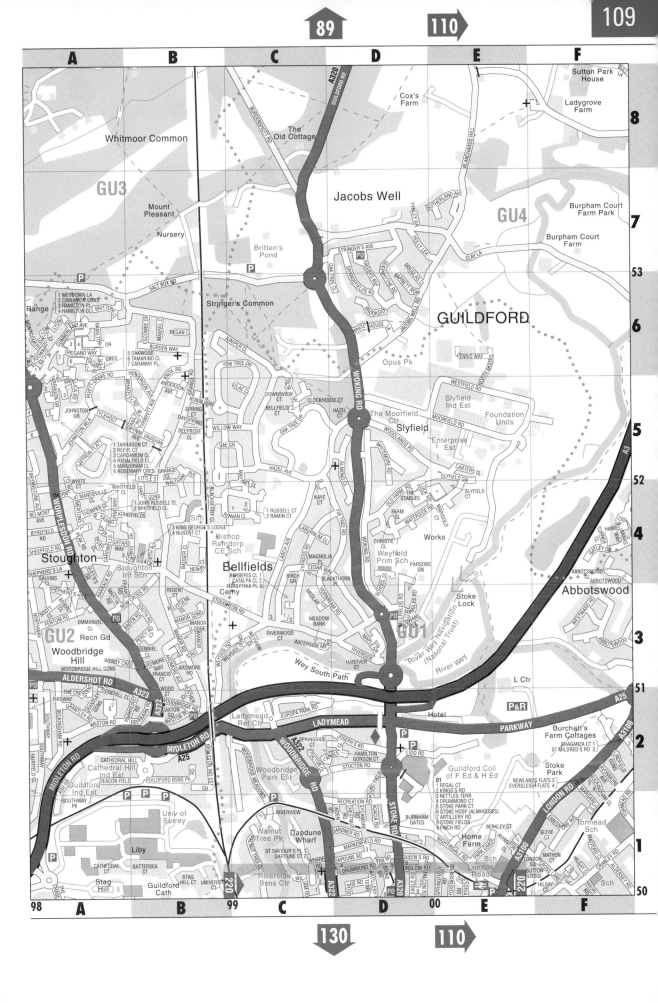

A B C D E F

8

Sutton Park

Sutton Boxes

GU23

Three Fords

Nutbourne Fruit Farm

B2215 A3

Sutton Place

Whitehouse Farm

Nuthill Farm

River Wey Navigation

7

Broadoak Bridge

Way South Path

River Wey

Frithys Wood

Guernsey Cl 1
Watersmeet Cl 2
Bowers Cl 3
Churchfields 4
Abinger Way 5
Tythebarn Gr 6
Whipley Cl 7
Newark Cl 8
Shetland Cl 9

53

6

Bowers Mill

Clay La

Bowers Mill

A3100

Cotts Wood

Gosden Hill Farm House

Dillon Cottages

P

Burpham Prim Sch
Howard Bldgs
Howard Ridge

Clay La

Burpham
Superstore

A3100

Oak Hill

Mead Way

Great Oaks Pk

Oak Tree Cl

Merrow La

5

A3

Sutherland
Abbots Ho
Burpham La

Orchard Rd

GU4

52

Alford Cl
Climmas Cl

Marlins Cl

Paddocks Rd

The Cedars

West Ct

London Rd

B2234

PO

New Inn La

Grosvenor Rd

Merrow Bsns Ctr

Merrow Depot

Keepers Cl

4

Hodson
Elver Cl
Colburn

Bladfield Cl
Colburn
Cres

Sutherland Rd

Darfield Rd

P

Highclere

Conners Way

Willow Ms

Thyme Ct

Windgates

Pitzjohn

Harms Cl

Miller Rd

Mourne Dr

Old Merrow St

Perram Wks Bridge Pk

Merrow Common

1 Platt Meadow
2 Burlingham Cl
3 Danses Cl
4 Kimber Cl
5 Mulberry Ct

Merrow Common Rd

Thrift Vale

Merrow Common

Clandon Park

3

Abbotswood

George Abbot Sch

Bishop
Bromhurst

Merrow Woods

Dene Cl

Little Dyke

Ledger Cl

Littlehide

Greenwill La

Ashburton
Highgrove Ho
Hillcrest Ho

Four Acres

Friars Croft

Foxglove Gdns

Greenside Cl

Collier Way

Kingfisher Rectory

Park La

Temple Court

51

A3100

A25

Caxtons Ct

Eaton Ct

Collingwood Cres

Howard Gdns

Brockway Cl

Woodlands Rd

Bushy Hill Dr

Finches Rise

Three Oaks

Chatfield Dr
Woodruffe Cl

Bushy Hill

Tansy Cl

Dunlin Rise

Lapwing Sch

Curlew Gdns

Merrow St

Field Cl

Goldfinch Gdns

Kestrel Cl

Linnet Ct

B2234

A25

Epsom Rd

1 Pond Ho
2 Paddock Ho
3 Stile Ho
4 Mares Field Ho
5 Meadow Ho
6 Poyle Ho
7 Browell Ho
8 Orchard Ho
9 Merrow Ho

2

Elgin Gdns

Robshott
Gdns

Duncan Dr

Nelson Gdns

Beatty Ho

PO

Admiral Napier Ct

Holmesdale Dr

Grasmere Cl

St Peter's RC Comp Sch

Hall Dene Cl

Wykeham Rd

Sadlers Cl

P

PO

Hedgers Almshouses

Merrow Way

Abbot's Way

GUILDFORD

Three Pears Rd

1

Tormead Rd

The Shimmings

Willow La

The Greenwood

Lansdown

Culver Ho

Boxgrove Prim Sch

Boxgrove Rd

Green La

Merrow Croft

GU1

Pengilly Ho
Fairlawns

Epsom Rd

Merrow Grange

Roke Ho

Levylsdene

Fairway

Levylsdene Ct

Down's La

50

A246

Hillier Rd
Mews
Hillier Ho

Guildcott Rd

Avon

Safeways

A246

A25

Orchard

Down Rd

Dartnell Cl

Carroll Ave

Elles Ave

High Path Rd

Grove Rd

Longford

Merrow Chase

Merrow Ct

Brantford Dr

Swayne's La

01 A B 02 C D 03 E F

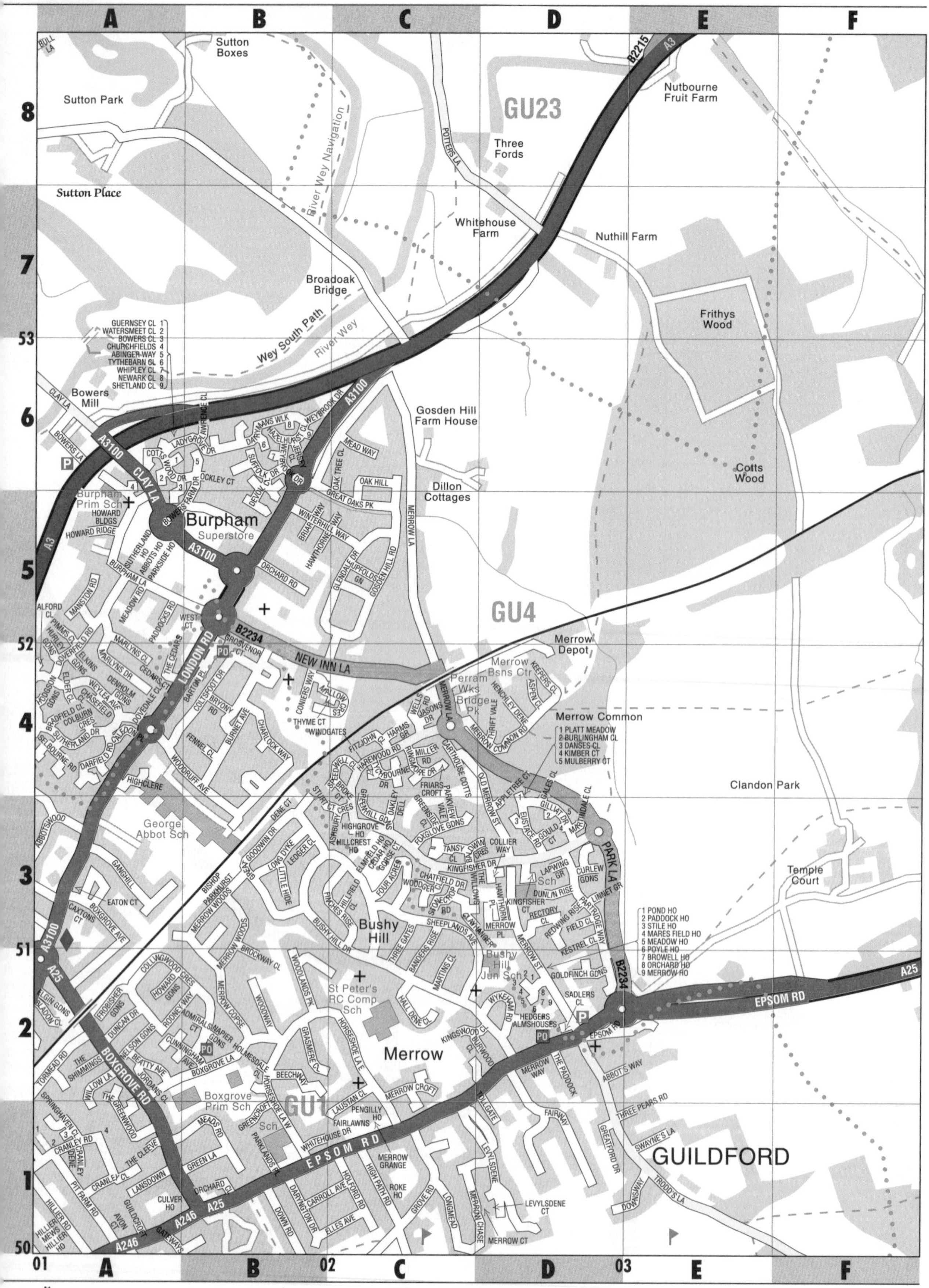

A1
1 Pine Ct
2 Shawfields
3 Fielders Gr
4 Cranley Manor

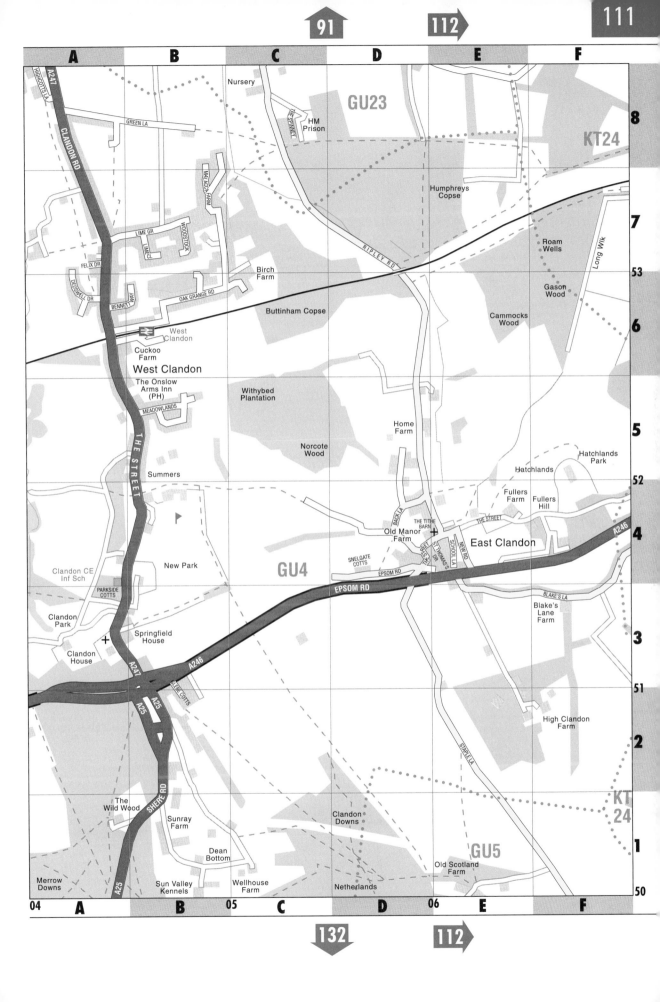

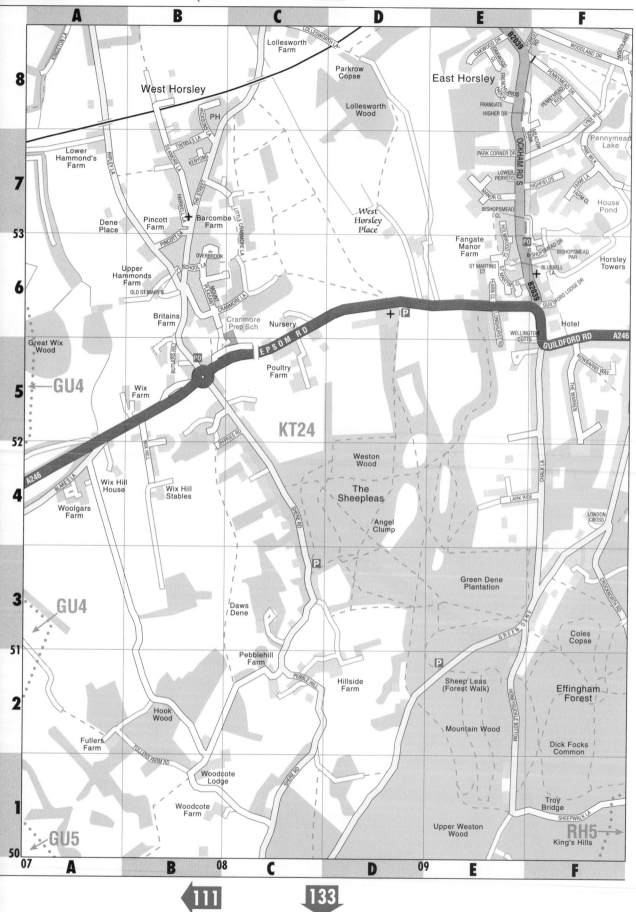

A   B   C   D   E   F

8

7

53

6

5
GU4

52

4
A246

3
GU4

51

2

1

50
GU5

07   A   B   08   C   D   09   E   F

West Horsley
East Horsley
KT24
RH5

Lollesworth La
Lollesworth Farm
Parkrow Copse
Lollesworth Wood

Lower Hammond's Farm
Kingston La
Ripley La
PH
Ricksons La
St Maure La
Tintells La
Kenyons
The Street
Fairwell La
Little Cranmore La

Dene Place
Pincott Farm
Barcombe Farm
Pincott La
School La
Mount Pleasant
Crammore La
Overbrook
Old St Mary's

Upper Hammonds Farm
Britains Farm
Cranmore Prep Sch
Nursery

West Horsley Place

Butlers Hill
PO
EPSOM RD
Poultry Farm

Great Wix Wood

Wix Farm
Wix Hill
Jeffries Rd

Wix Hill House
Wix Hill Stables
Shere Rd

Woolgars Farm
Blake's La
A246

Weston Wood

The Sheepleas

Angel Clump

Daws Dene

Pebblehill Farm
Pebble Hill
Hillside Farm

Hook Wood

Fullers Farm
Fullers Farm Rd

Woodcote Lodge
Shere Rd

Woodcote Farm

King's Hills

Green Dene Plantation

Sheep Leas (Forest Walk)
Honeysuckle Bottom
Green Dene

Mountain Wood

Coles Copse

Effingham Forest

Dick Focks Common

Troy Bridge
Sheepwalk La

Upper Weston Wood

Oakwood Dr
Oakwood Cl
B2039
Forest Rd
Woodland Dr
Woodland Cl

Frenchlands Hatch
Pennymead Dr
Pennymead Rise
Lynx Hill
Pennymead Lake

Frangate
Higher Dr
Meadow Bank
Park Walk
Pine Wlk
House Pond

Park Corner Dr
Lower Peryers
Highfields
Farm La
Farm Rd
OCKHAM RD S

Manor Cl
Bishopsmead Cl
Holmwood Cl
St Martins Ct
Fern Cl
St Martins Cl
PO
Bishopsmead Dr
Bishopsmead Par
Bluebell La
Horsley Towers

Fangate Manor Farm

B2039
Guildford Lodge Dr
Longhurst Rd

Hotel
Wellington Cottis
GUILDFORD RD
A246
Rowbarns Way
The Warren
Chalk La
Lark Rise
London Cross
Crocknorth Rd

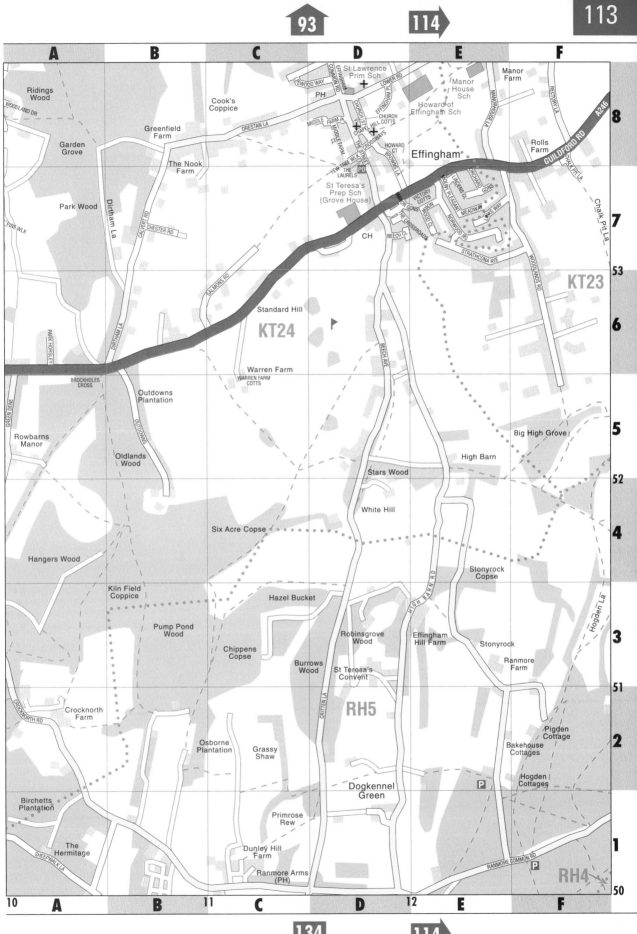

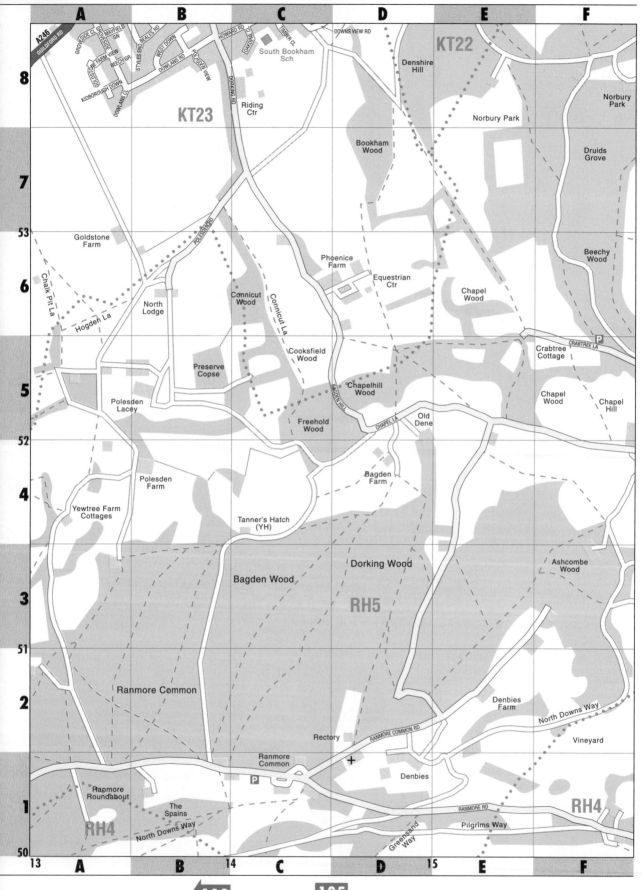

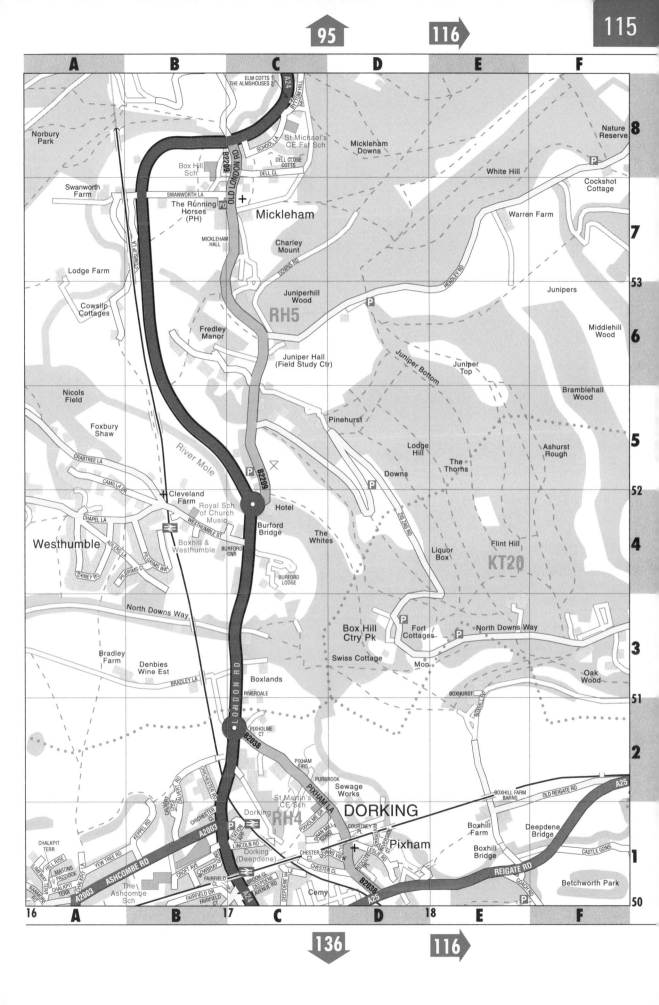

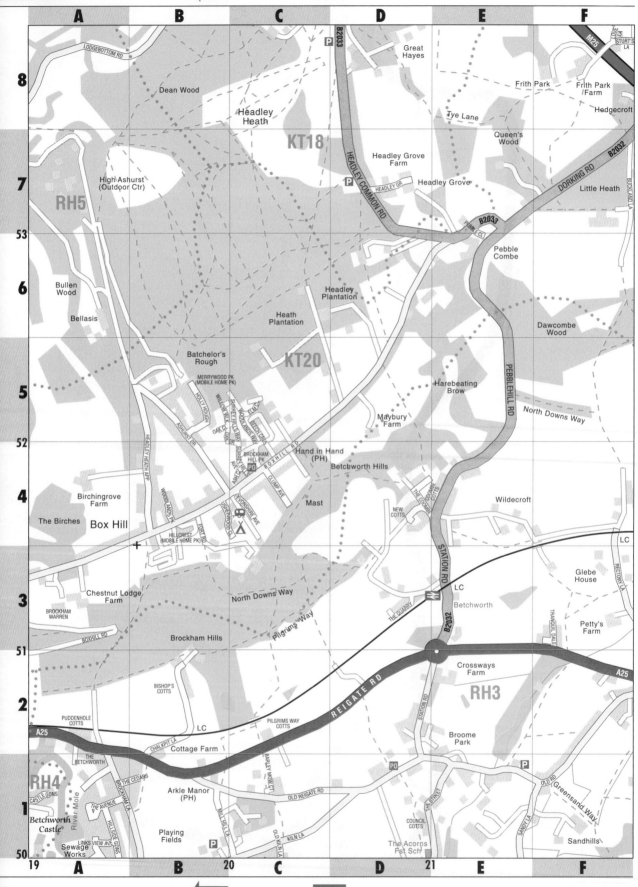

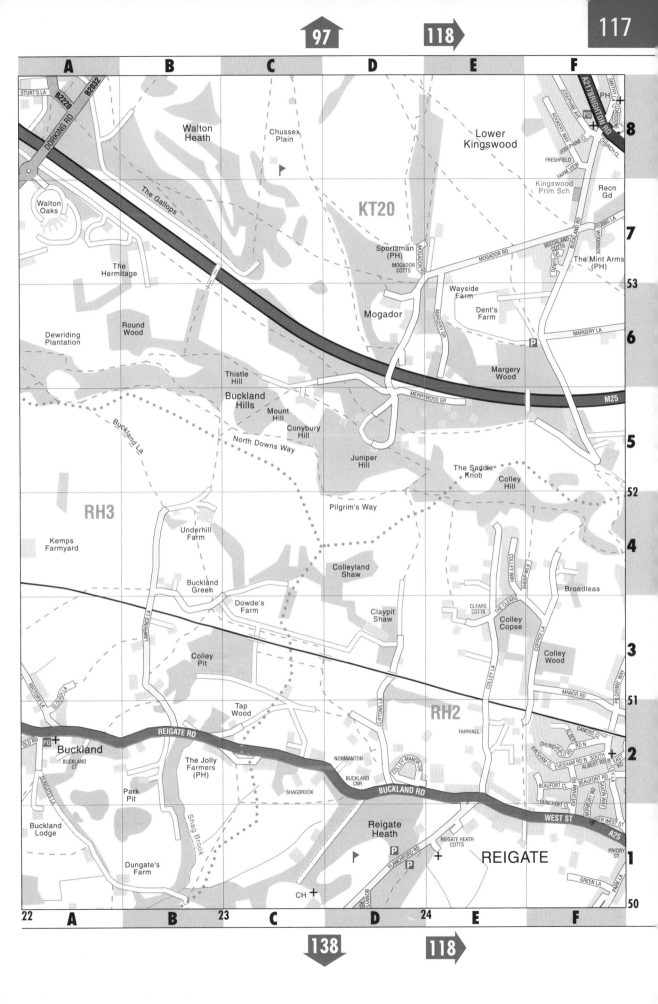

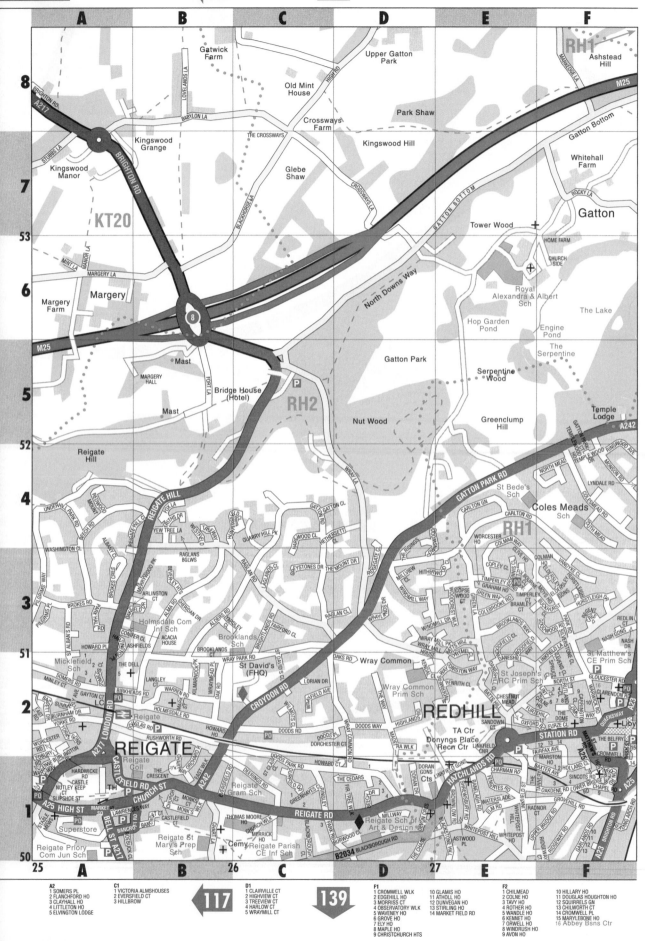

99
120
140
120

A2
1 PRINCESS HOUSE
2 LADBROKE COTTS
3 QUEENS CT
4 DIAMOND CT
5 ST ANNES WAY
6 CLEEVES CT
7 ST ANNES MOUNT
8 NIGHTINGALE CT
9 GABLE CT

10 HATHAWAY CT
11 BOLEYN CT
12 TUDOR CT
13 LENNOX CT
14 BRONTE CT
15 OAKLEY CT
16 STUART CT
17 CLYDE CT
18 LANCELOT HO
19 GIUNEVERE HO

20 GALAHAD HO
21 KNIGHTS PL
22 WARWICK QUADRANT

A3
1 ALTON HOUSE
2 SWALE HOUSE
3 BOVEY HOUSE
4 FRENCHES CT
5 PENRYN HOUSE
6 NASH DR

7 LADBROKE CT
8 PEBWORTH CT
9 BARFIELD CT

A4
1 RINGWOOD LODGE
2 DOWNS CT
3 LYNDALE CT
4 VICTORIA ALMSHOUSES
5 SPEEDWELL HOUSE
6 CAMPION HOUSE

← 119   100

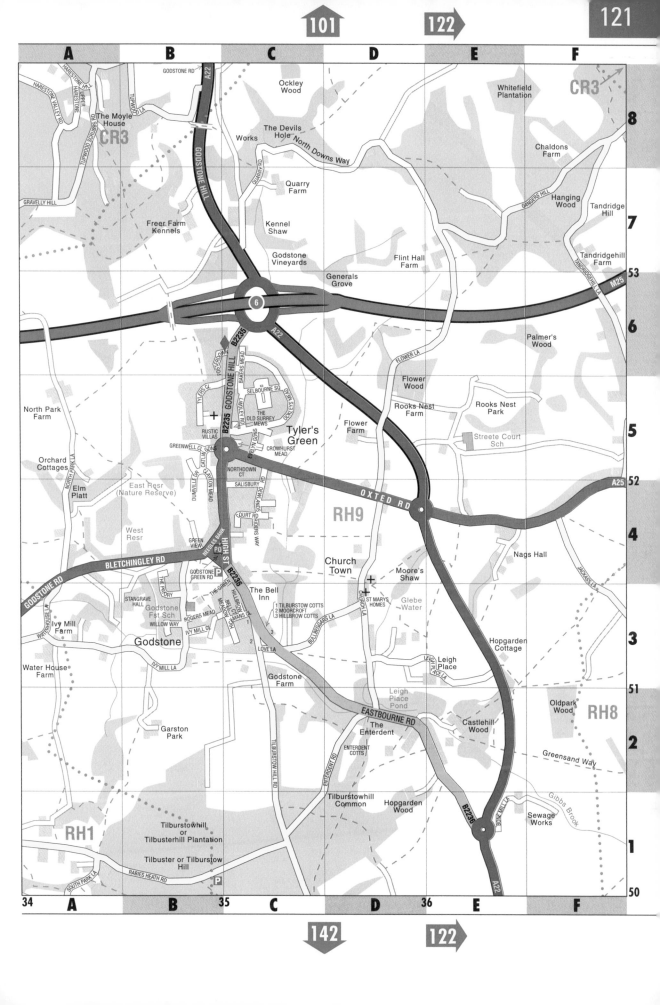

A B C D E F

M25

8

South Hawke

CR3

North Downs Way

GANGERS HILL

Lodge Wood

Chalkpit Wood

Five Acre Shaw

CHALKPIT LA

HAMFEY CL

WEST LANDS WAY

CENTRAL WAY

OAKSHAW

BARNETT'S SHAW

GREEN ACRES

SULKIN RD

EASTLANDS WAY

CHALKPIT

DOWNS WAY

Oxted & Limpsfield

FIELD WAY

GORDONS WAY

WOODLAND CT

H

Downs Way Sch

St Mary's CE Jun Sch

Oxted Sch

Greensand Way

PARK RD

7

Barrow Green Court

Robins Grove Wood

HOG TROUGH LA

Cemy

CHICHELE RD

Laverock Sch

STATION APP

MASTER

STATION RD W

CRAB WOOD

Oxted

BEATRICE RD

AMY RD

ELLICE RD

NEW LODGE DR

PARK CL

GRESHAM CL

GRANVILLE RD

BLUEHOUSE LA

53

M25

The Abbeys

Barrow Green Farm

BARROW GREEN RD

The Mount

The Bogs

St Mary's CL

OAKLEIGH CT

SYCAMORE CT

THE HOSKINS

Ct

HOSKINS RD

STATION RD E

Oxted

PO

THE COURTYARD

P

JOINSDALE

SNATTS HILL

Liby

P

A25

WESTERHAM RD

6

RH9

Priory Shaw

SANDY LA

Townland Pond

WHEELER AVE

Ct

CHURCH LA

EAST HILL RD

P

L Ctr

HILLCREST

ABBEYFIELD HO

EAST HILL

EAST HILL CT

BURWOOD

CALDER RD

OLD LA

BRASSEY RD

UVEDALE RD

5

TANDRIDGE HILL LA

The Priory

MEADOWBROOK

BROOK HILL

HIGH ST

West Hill Bank

WEST HILL

Oxted

FARLEY PK

WILDERNESS RD

FARLEY PK MEWS

WOODHURST PK

WOODLAND RISE

ROCKFIELD RD

QUARRY CL

QUARRY RD

52

A25 OXTED RD

GODSTONE RD

BUSHY CROFT

SPRINGFIELD

ST CLAIR CL

BEADLES LA

CH

NEB LA

Mill Barn

SPRING LA

Oxted Mill

PARKLANDS

ICEHOUSE WOOD

MYNNS LOW PK

ROCKFIELD RD

4

The Birches

BROADHAM PL

River Eden

Stonehall Farm

The Maltings

THE WALDRONS

LAUREL DR

QUEST RD

PADDOCK CL

3

JACKASS LA

Little Court Farm

Beechwood Hill

Oxted Place

Broadham Green

TAN HOUSE RD

The Haycutter (PH)

Tanhouse Farm

CHURCH WAY

Hurst Green

HURST GREEN RD

GREENHURST LA

MELDRUM CL

Hurst Green

Moor House Sch

51

TANDRIDGE LA

TANDRIDGE CT

Tandridge Court Farm

SOUTHLANDS

Perrysfield Farm

BROADHAM GREEN RD

HILL SHAW

HURSTLANDS

COLLINGWOOD

MILL LA

2

Tandridge

WEST VIEW COTTS

THE PACK

Greensand Way

Tandridge Park

Perrysfield

Mill Pond

GODSTONE RD

1

DEAN SHAW COTTS

Barley Mow (PH)

Reddings Wood

GIBBS BROOK LA

Stockett's Manor

Coltsford Mill

WARREN LA

Sewage Works

St Peters CE Inf Sch

Tandridge Hall

SOUTHLANDS LA

Southlands Wood

Rose Farm

FOREST LA

Stockett's Manor Farm

50

37 A 38 B C D 39 E F

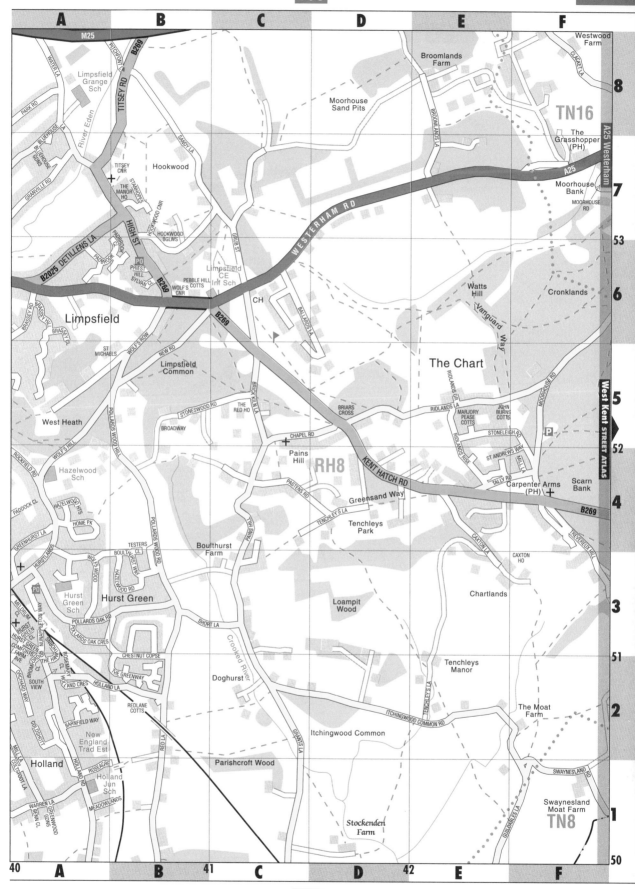

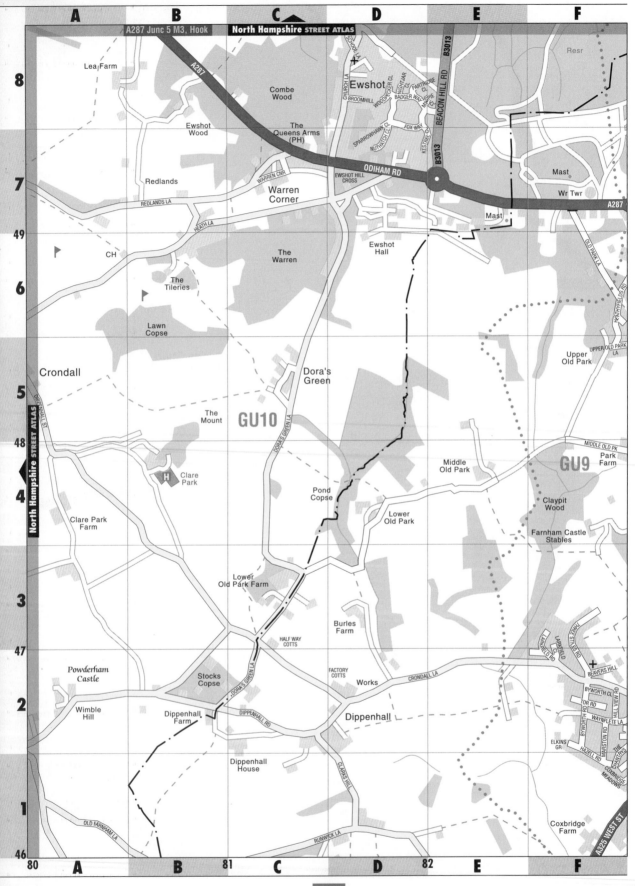

A287 Junc 5 M3, Hook

North Hampshire STREET ATLAS

Lea Farm

Combe Wood

SCHOOL LA

Ewshot

CHURCH LA

NIGHTJAR CL
PARTRIDGE CL
BROOMHILL
WOODPECKER CL
BADGER WAY MAGPIE

B3013

BEACON HILL RD

Resr

Ewshot Wood

The Queens Arms (PH)

SPARROWHAWK CL
NUTHATCH CL
FOX WAY
KESTREL CL

B3013

Mast

Wr Twr

Redlands

WARREN CNR

Warren Corner

ODIHAM RD

EWSHOT HILL CROSS

Mast

A287

REDLANDS LA

HEATH LA

Ewshot Hall

Mast

CH

The Warren

OLD PARK LA

HEATHFIELD RD

The Tileries

Lawn Copse

Dora's Green

Upper Old Park

UPPER OLD PARK

Crondall

DORA'S GREEN LA

GU10

The Mount

MIDDLE OLD PK

Park Farm

H Clare Park

Pond Copse

Middle Old Park

GU9

Claypit Wood

Clare Park Farm

Lower Old Park

Farnham Castle Stables

Lower Old Park Farm

HALF WAY COTTS

Burles Farm

Powderham Castle

Stocks Copse

DORA'S GREEN LA

FACTORY COTTS

Works

CRONDALL LA

HIGH STILES RD
LARKFIELD
LARKFIELD RD

BEAVERS HILL

Wimble Hill

Dippenhall Farm

DIPPENHALL RD

Dippenhall

BYWORTH CL
TOR RD
BYWORTH RD
HAZELL RD
MARSTON RD
HILL VIEW RD
WAYNFLETE LA

DIPPENHALL ST

North Hampshire STREET ATLAS

Dippenhall House

CLARKS HILL

ELKINS GR

THE CHANTRYS

COXBRIDGE MEADOWS

Coxbridge Farm

OLD FARNHAM LA

RUNWICK LA

A325 WEST ST

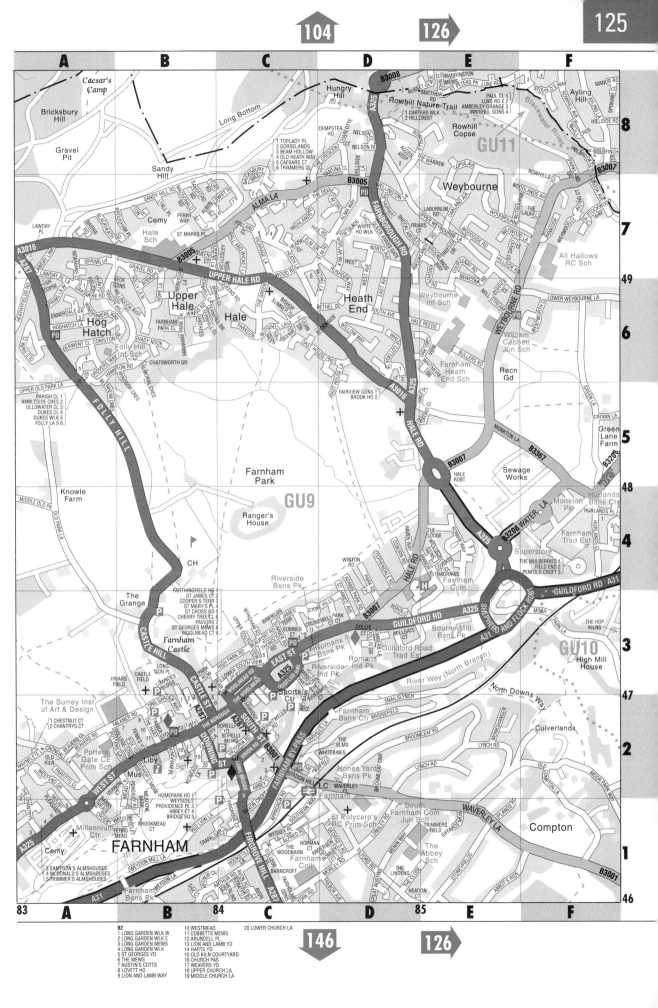

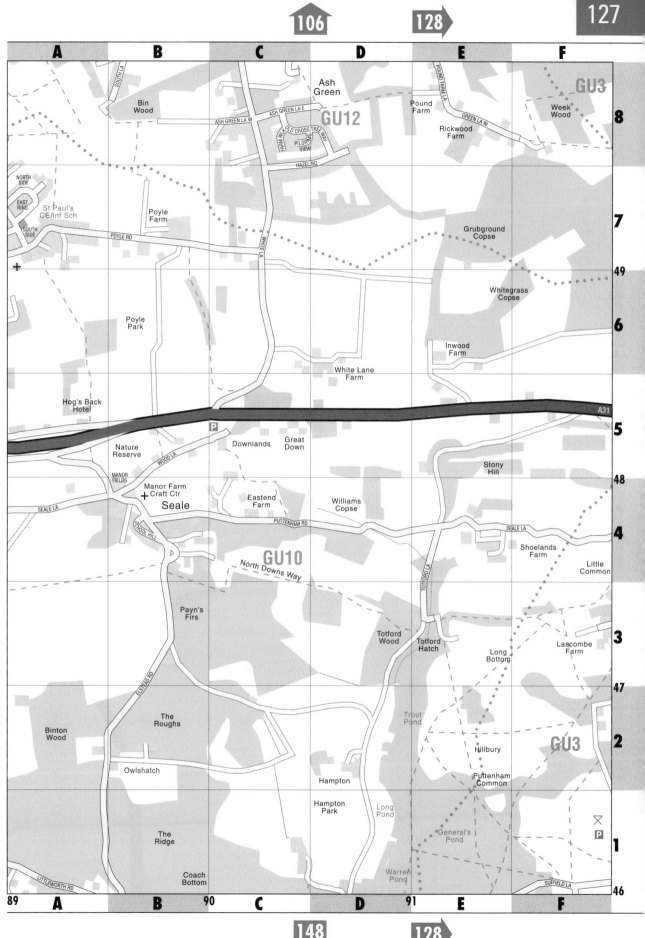

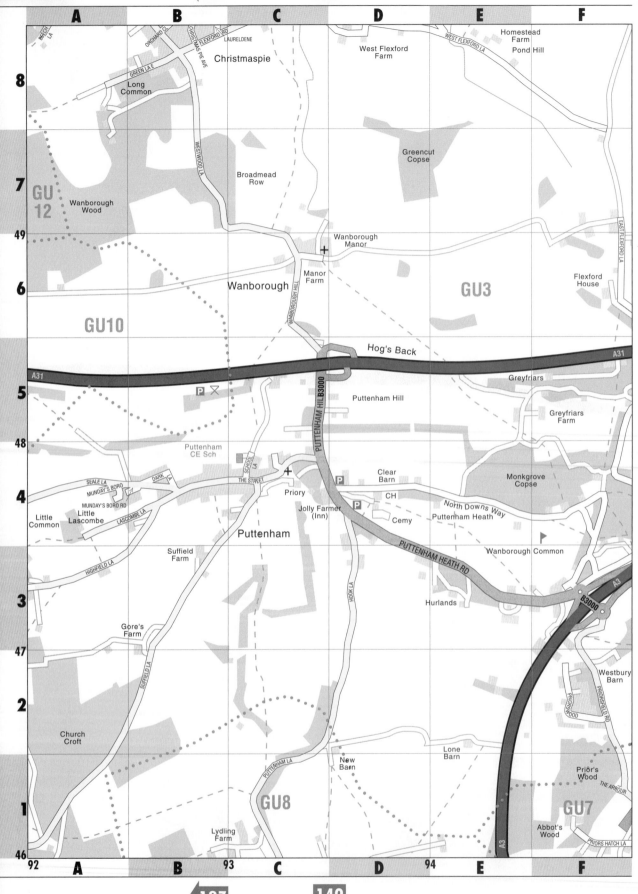

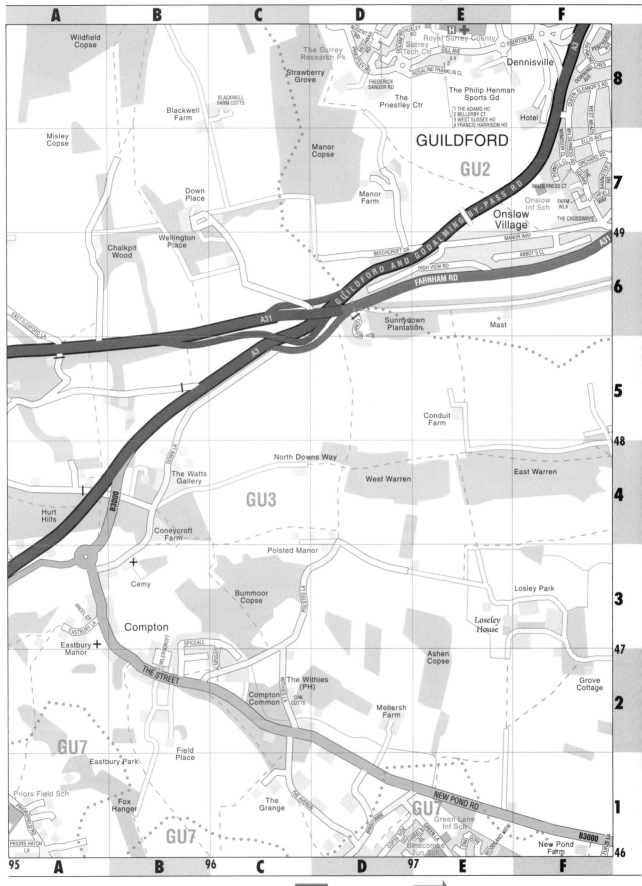

129
109

C8
1 MANGLES CT
2 BAYLISS CT
3 BEDFORD HO
4 FRIARY HO
5 THE FRIARY
6 THE MALL
7 Wey Ct

D7
1 WHITE LION WLK

E8
1 WILLIAM SWAYNE HO
2 DENEHYRST CT
3 EASTGATE HO
4 PROSPECT CT
5 CHANTRY PL
6 HILLSIDE CT
7 SYCAMORE CT
8 HARVEY LODGE

F8
1 FRESHBOROUGH CT
2 TELFORD CT
3 SHELDON CT
4 BEECH CT
5 GRAYLANDS CT
6 EDGEBOROUGH CT
7 COMPTON CT
8 GROSVENOR HO
9 ST LUKE'S SQ
10 KNIGHTSBRIDGE HO
11 CADOGAN HO
12 ALEXANDRA LODGE
13 LYNNE CT
14 CHESHAM MEWS

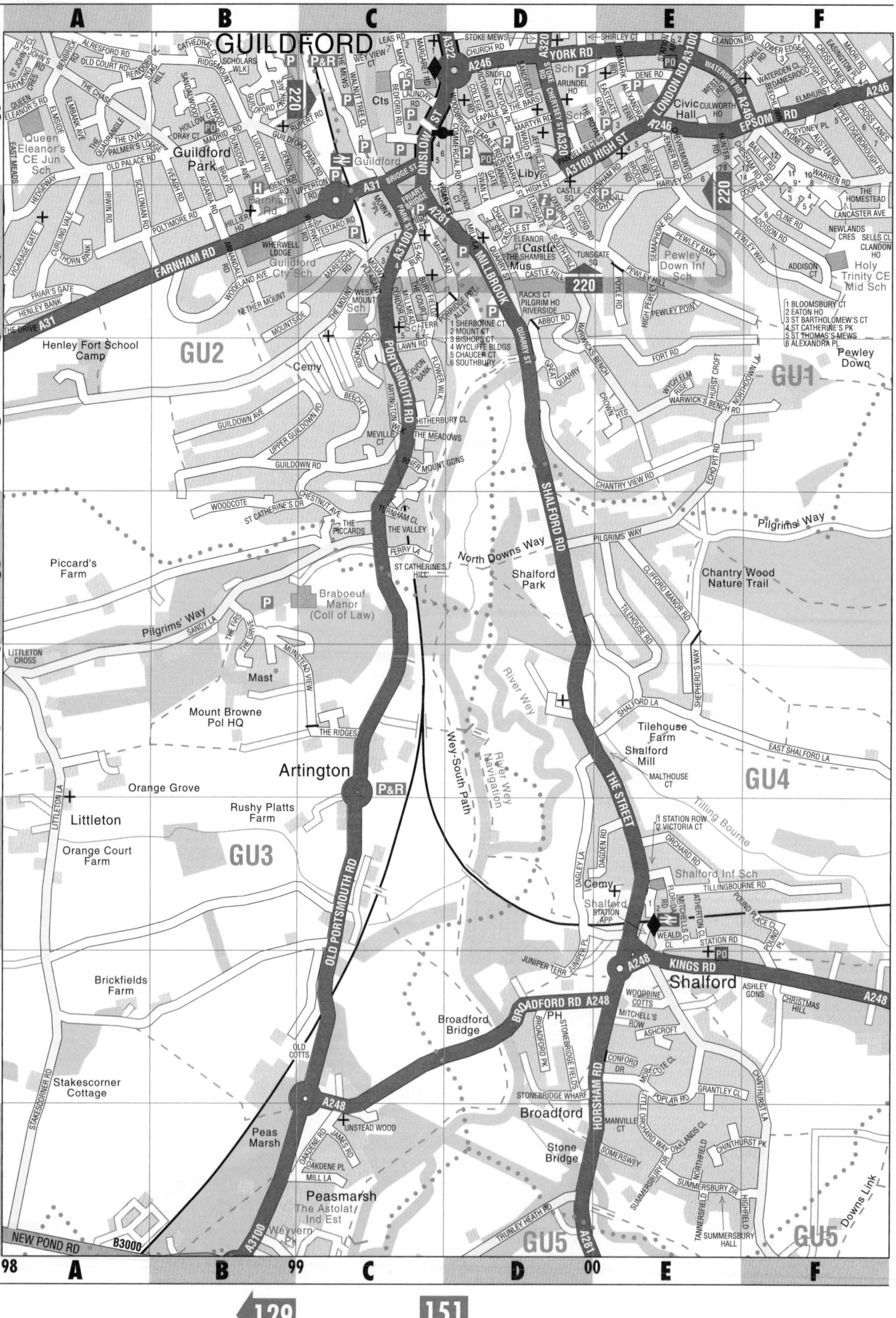
A B C D E F
8 7 6 5 4 3 2 1
49 48 47 46
98 99 00
GUILDFORD
Guildford Park
Queen Eleanor's CE Jun Sch
Farnham Rd
Guildford Cty Sch
Wherwell Lodge
FARNHAM RD
A31
BRIDGE ST
ONSLOW ST
YORK RD
LONDON RD
EPSOM RD
A3100 HIGH ST
Civic Hall
Liby
Castle
Mus
Pewley Down Inf Sch
Holy Trinity CE Mid Sch
Pewley Down
GU1
GU2
GU3
GU4
GU5
Henley Fort School Camp
Cemy
PORTSMOUTH RD
MILLBROOK
QUARRY ST
SHALFORD RD
North Downs Way
Pilgrims' Way
Shalford Park
Chantry Wood Nature Trail
Piccard's Farm
Braboeuf Manor (Coll of Law)
Mast
Mount Browne Pol HQ
River Wey
Wey-South Path
River Wey Navigation
Tilehouse Farm
Shalford Mill
Artington
Orange Grove
Rushy Platts Farm
Littleton
Orange Court Farm
THE STREET
Tilling Bourne
Shalford Inf Sch
Shalford
KINGS RD
A248
OLD PORTSMOUTH RD
BROADFORD RD
Broadford Bridge
Brickfields Farm
Stakescorner Cottage
Peas Marsh
Peasmarsh
The Astolat Ind Est
Broadford
Stone Bridge
HORSHAM RD
Downs Link
NEW POND RD
B3000
A3100
A281
1 SHERBORNE CT
2 MOUNT CT
3 BISHOPS CT
4 WYCLIFFE BLDGS
5 CHAUCER CT
6 SOUTHBURY
1 BLOOMSBURY CT
2 EATON HO
3 ST BARTHOLOMEW'S CT
4 ST CATHERINE'S PK
5 ST THOMAS'S MEWS
6 ALEXANDRA PL
1 STATION ROW
2 VICTORIA CT

129
151

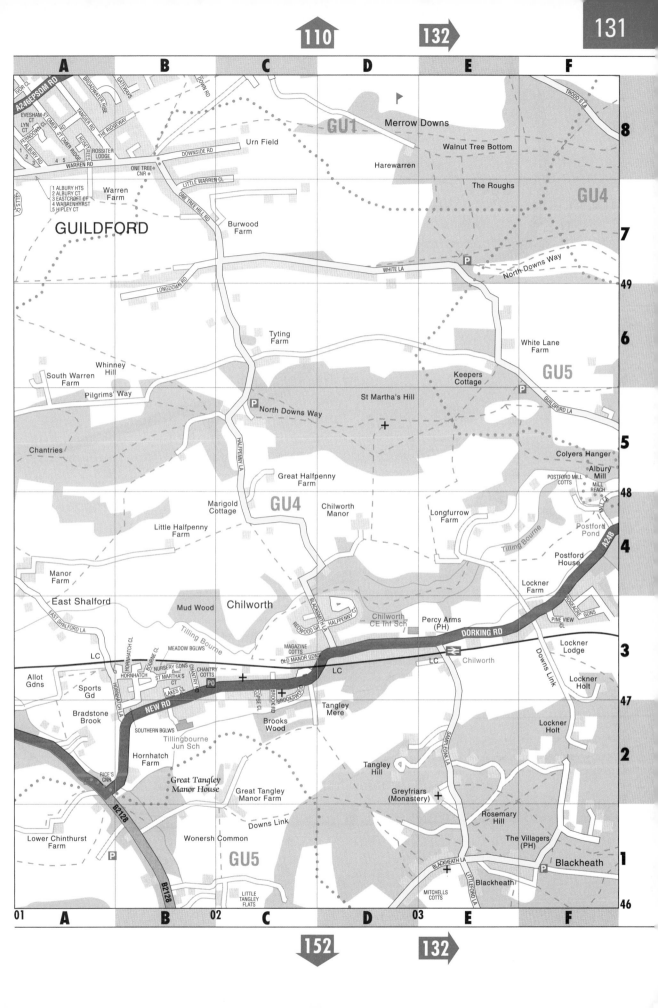

110
132

A B C D E F

8
7
49
6
5
48
4
3
47
2
1
46

GU1
Merrow Downs
Walnut Tree Bottom
Harewarren
The Roughs
GU4

A246 EPSOM RD
EVESHAM CT
ST OMER CT
LYN CT
FERNDOWN CT
HALLBURY RD
IVOR CL
ST OMER RISE
BROADWATER RISE
TANGIER RD
ROSE TREES
THE RIDGEWAY
GATEWAYS
DOWN RD
ROSSITER LODGE
WARREN RD
DOWNSIDE RD
Urn Field
ONE TREE CNR
LITTLE WARREN CL
ONE TREE HILL RD

1 ALBURY HTS
2 ALBURY CT
3 EASTCROFT CT
4 WARRENHYRST
5 HIPLEY CT

Warren Farm
Burwood Farm

GUILDFORD

TRODD'S LA

WHITE LA
North Downs Way

BELLS CT
LONGDOWN RD

Tyting Farm

White Lane Farm

GU5

Keepers Cottage
St Martha's Hill
North Downs Way
Whinney Hill
South Warren Farm
Pilgrims' Way
Chantries
HALFPENNY LA

Great Halfpenny Farm
Marigold Cottage
GU4
Chilworth Manor
Longfurrow Farm
Colyers Hanger
Albury Mill
POSTFORD MILL COTTS
MILL REACH
MILL LA

Little Halfpenny Farm

Manor Farm
East Shalford
Mud Wood
Chilworth
Tilling Bourne
BLACKSMITH LA
REDWOOD GR
HALFPENNY CL
Chilworth CE Inf Sch
Percy Arms (PH)
DORKING RD
Chilworth
Postford Pond
Postford House
A248
Lockner Farm
PINE VIEW CL
ROSEACRE GDNS
Tilling Bourne
Lockner Lodge
Downs Link
Lockner Holt
Lockner Holt

EAST SHALFORD LA
LC
Allot Gdns
Sports Gd
Bradstone Brook
HORNHATCH CL
BOURNE CL
MEADOW BGLWS
NURSERY GDNS
ST MARTHA'S CT
HORNHATCH
HORNHATCH LA
LAKES CL
CHANTRY COTTS
CHANTRY RD
PO
COPSE CL
BROOK RD
BROOKSWOOD
MAGAZINE COTTS
OLD MANOR GDNS
LC
LC
NEW RD
SOUTHERN BGLWS
Tillingbourne Jun Sch
Hornhatch Farm
Brooks Wood
Tangley Mere

Tangley Hill
SAMPLEOAK LA
Greyfriars (Monastery)
Rosemary Hill
The Villagers (PH)
Blackheath
BLACKHEATH LA
LITTLEFORD LA

RICE'S CNR
B2128
Lower Chinthurst Farm
Great Tangley Manor House
Great Tangley Manor Farm
Downs Link
Wonersh Common
GU5
LITTLE TANGLEY FLATS
Blackheath
MITCHELLS COTTS

152
132

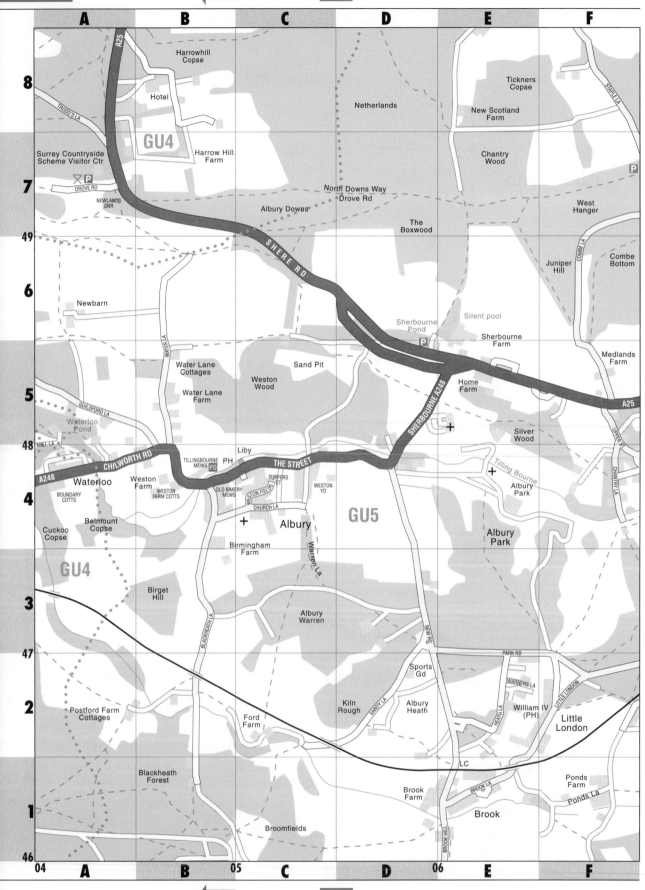

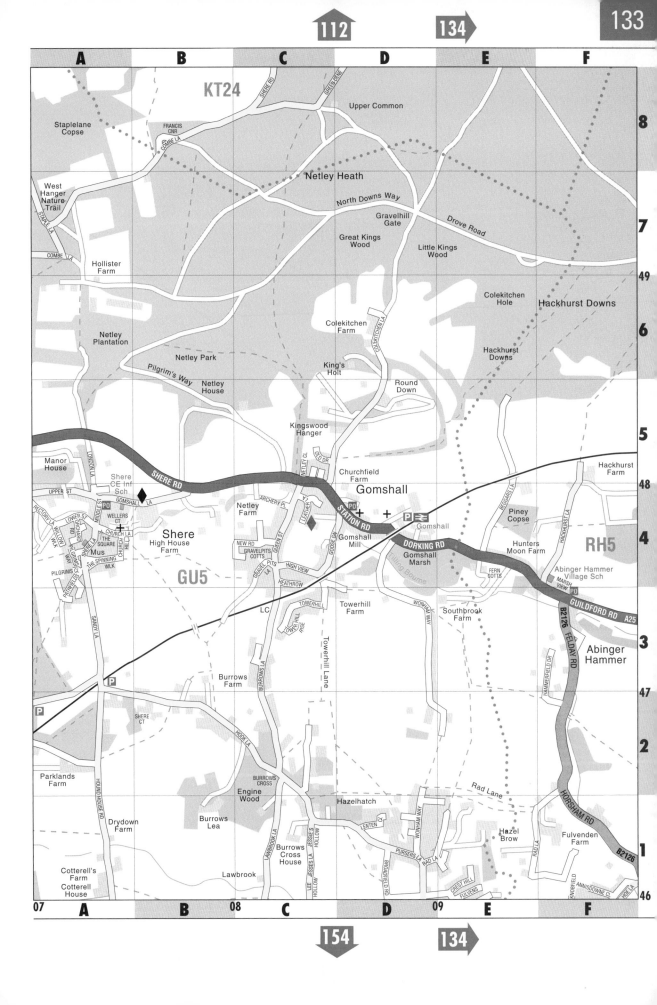

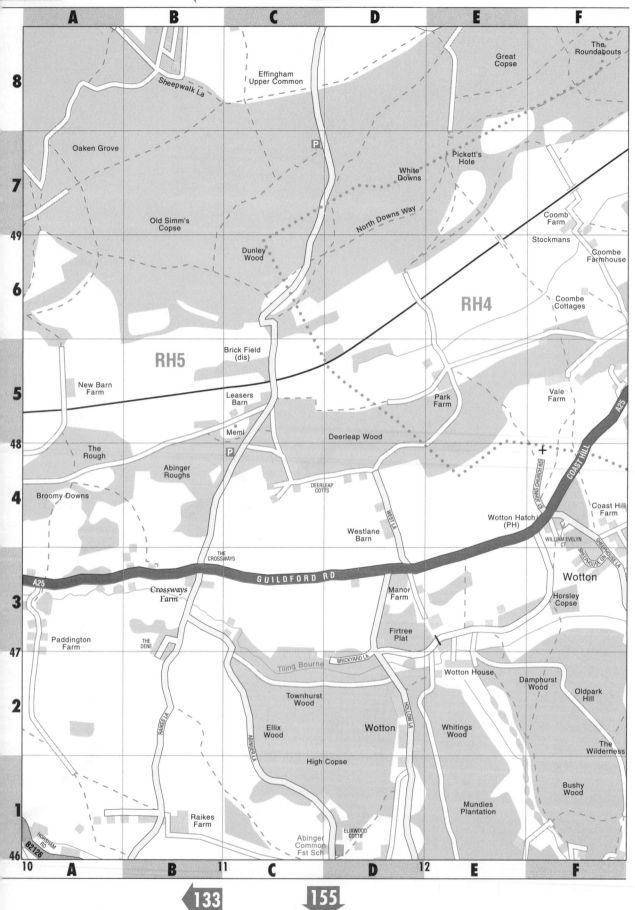

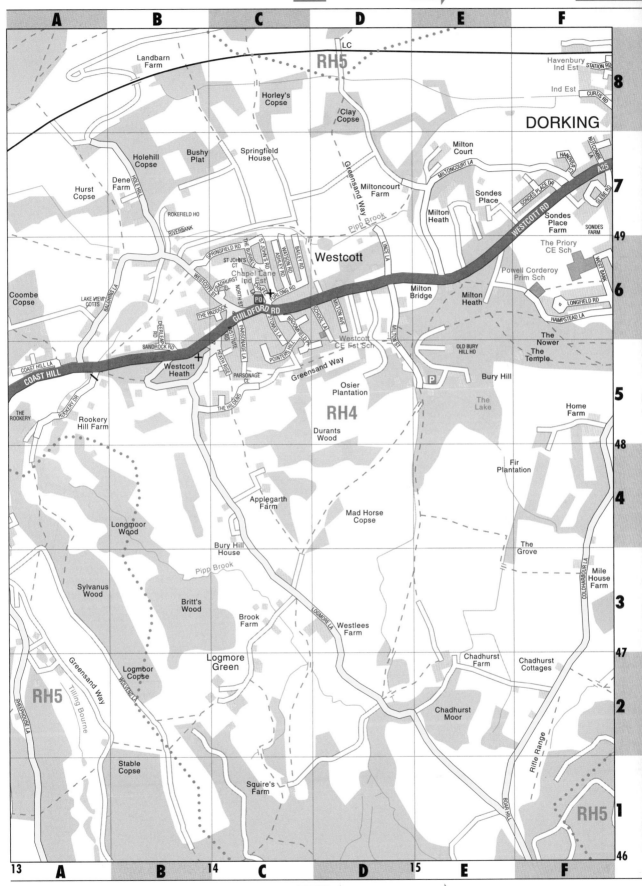

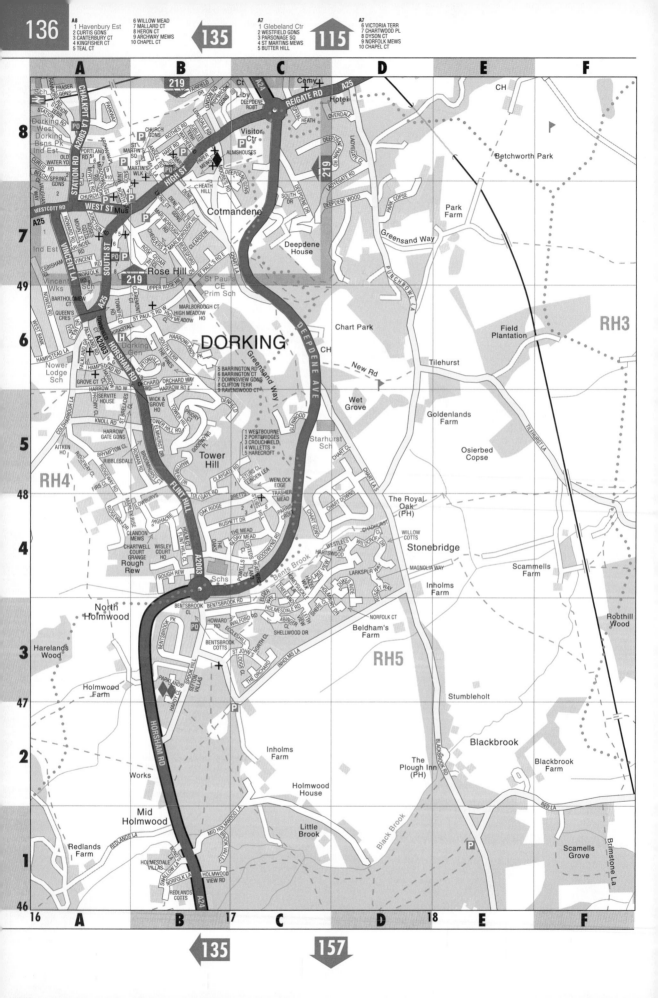

A8
1 Havenbury Est
2 CURTIS GDNS
3 CANTERBURY CT
4 KINGFISHER CT
5 TEAL CT

6 WILLOW MEAD
7 MALLARD CT
8 HERON CT
9 ARCHWAY MEWS
10 CHAPEL CT

135

A7
1 Glebeland Ctr
2 WESTFIELD GDNS
3 PARSONAGE SQ
4 ST MARTINS MEWS
5 BUTTER HILL

115

A7
6 VICTORIA TERR
7 CHARTWOOD PL
8 DYSON CT
9 NORFOLK MEWS
10 CHAPEL CT

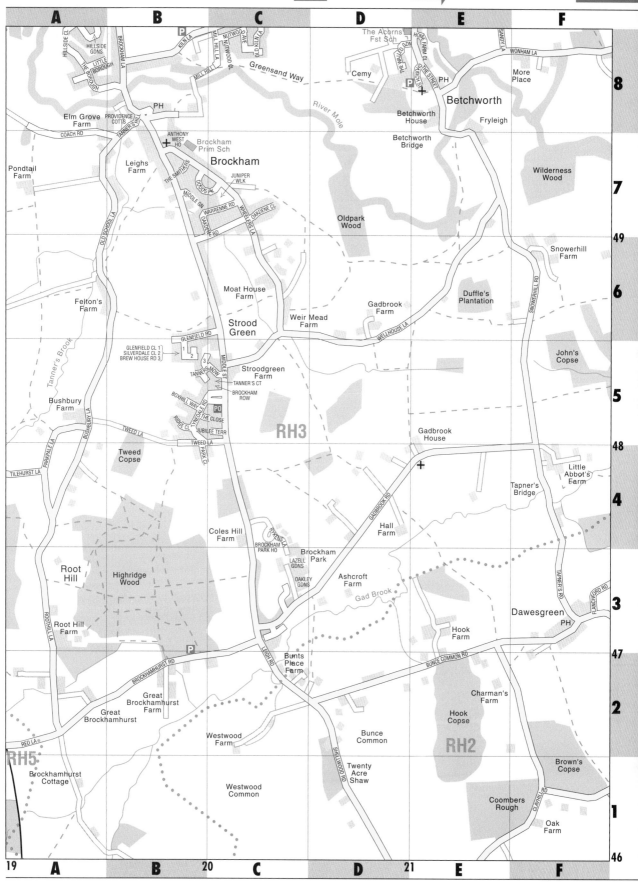

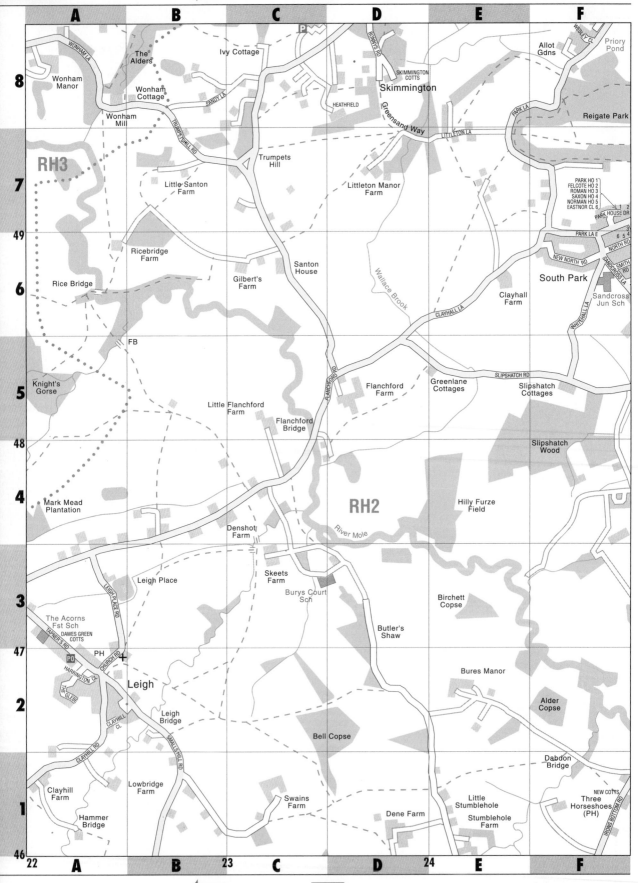

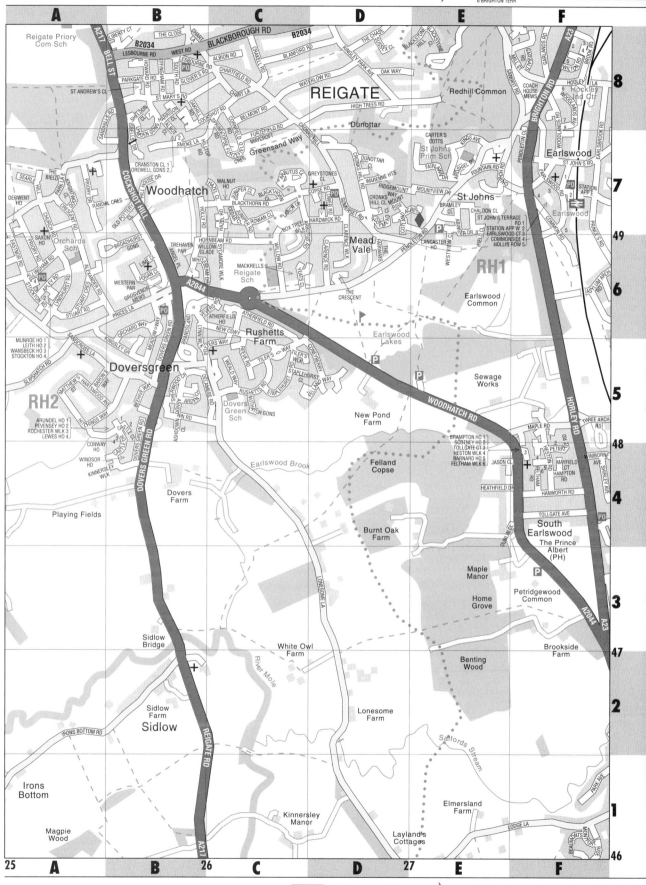

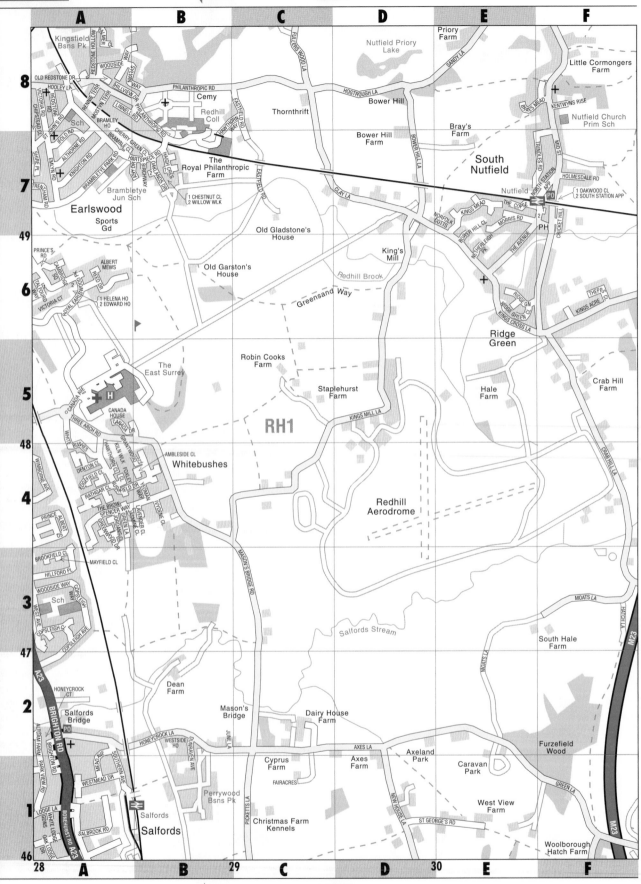

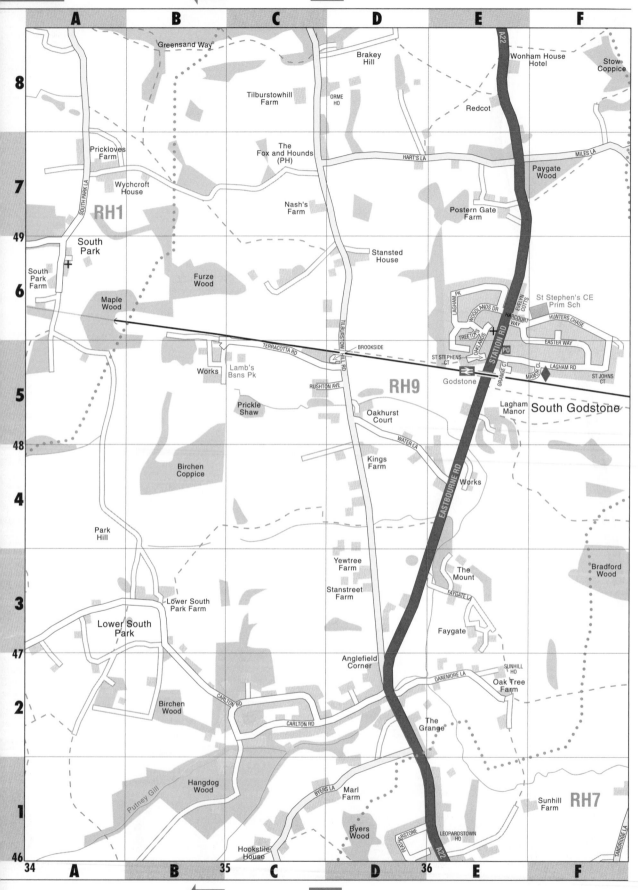

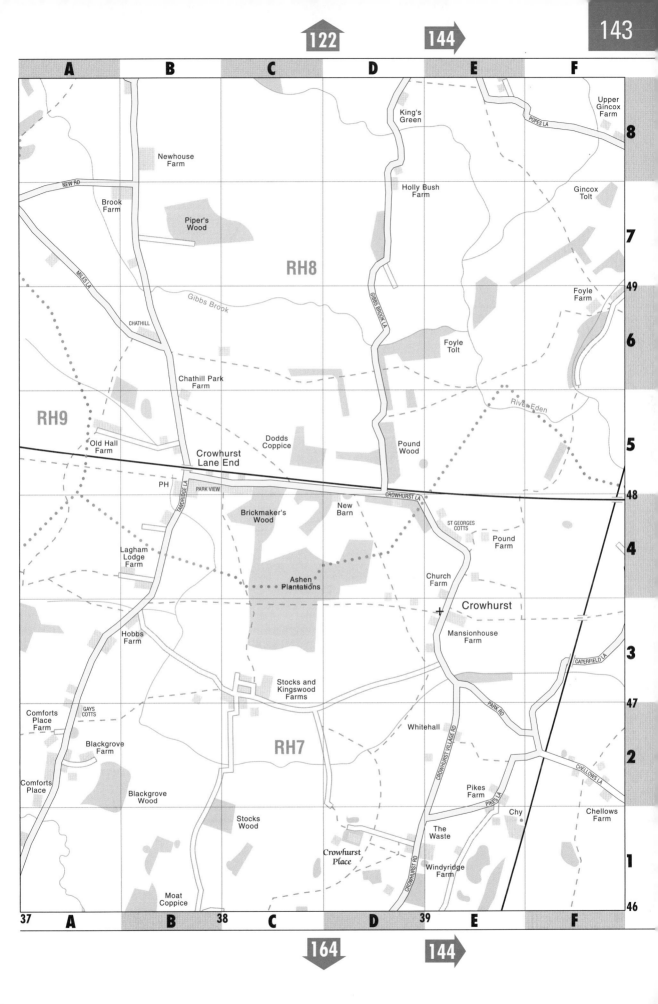

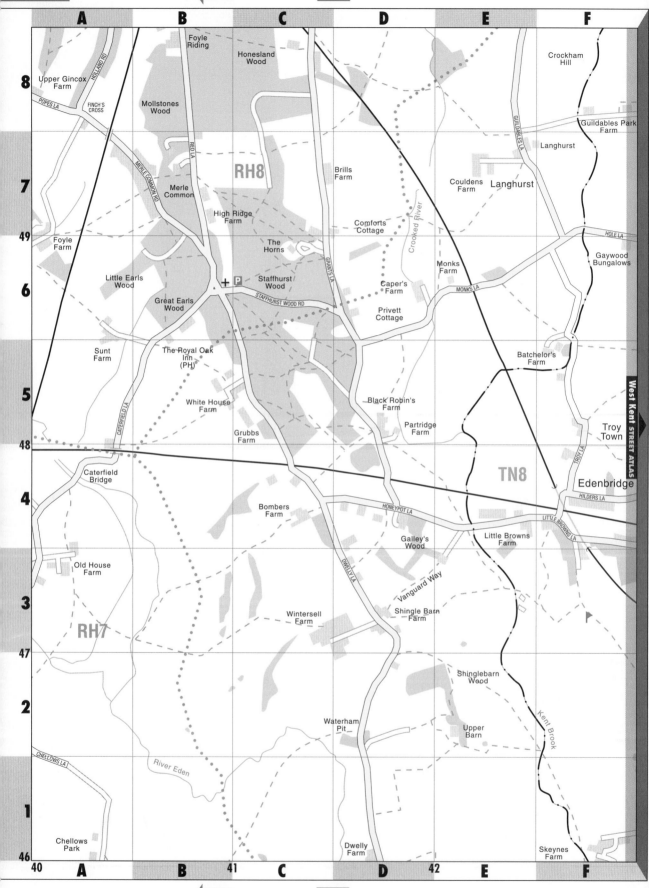
A B C D E F

8 Upper Gincox Farm
Foyle Riding
Honesland Wood
Crockham Hill

POPES LA
FINCH'S CROSS
Mollstones Wood
Guildables Park Farm

Langhurst

HOLLAND RD
RED LA
MERLE COMMON RD

7 Merle Common
Brills Farm
Couldens Farm
Langhurst

RH8
High Ridge Farm

Crooked River

49 Foyle Farm
The Horns
Comforts Cottage
Monks Farm
HOLE LA

Little Earls Wood
Staffhurst Wood
Caper's Farm
Gaywood Bungalows

6 Great Earls Wood
STAFFHURST WOOD RD
Privett Cottage
MONKS LA

GRANTS LA

Sunt Farm
The Royal Oak Inn (PH)
Batchelor's Farm

5
CATERFIELD LA
White House Farm
Black Robin's Farm
Troy Town

Partridge Farm
TROY LA

48 Grubbs Farm

Caterfield Bridge
TN8
Edenbridge
HILDERS LA

4 Bombers Farm
HONEYPOT LA
Little Browns Farm
LITTLE BROWNS LA

Galley's Wood

Old House Farm
Vanguard Way
Shingle Barn Farm

3 RH7
Wintersell Farm
Shinglebarn Wood

47

DWELLY LA

Kent Brook

2 Waterham Pit
Upper Barn

River Eden

1

46 Chellows Park
Dwelly Farm
Skeynes Farm

CHELLOWS LA

40 A 41 B C 42 D E F

West Kent STREET ATLAS

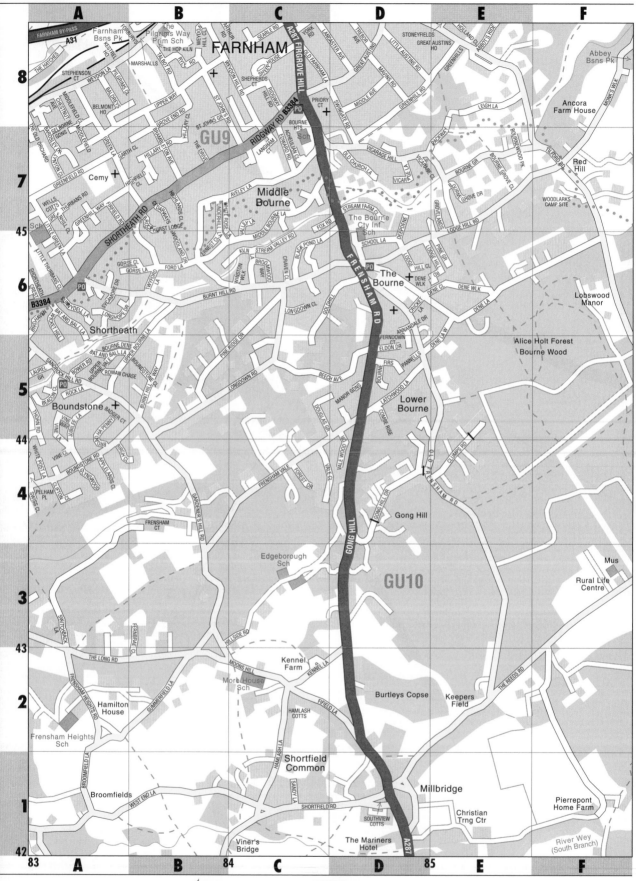

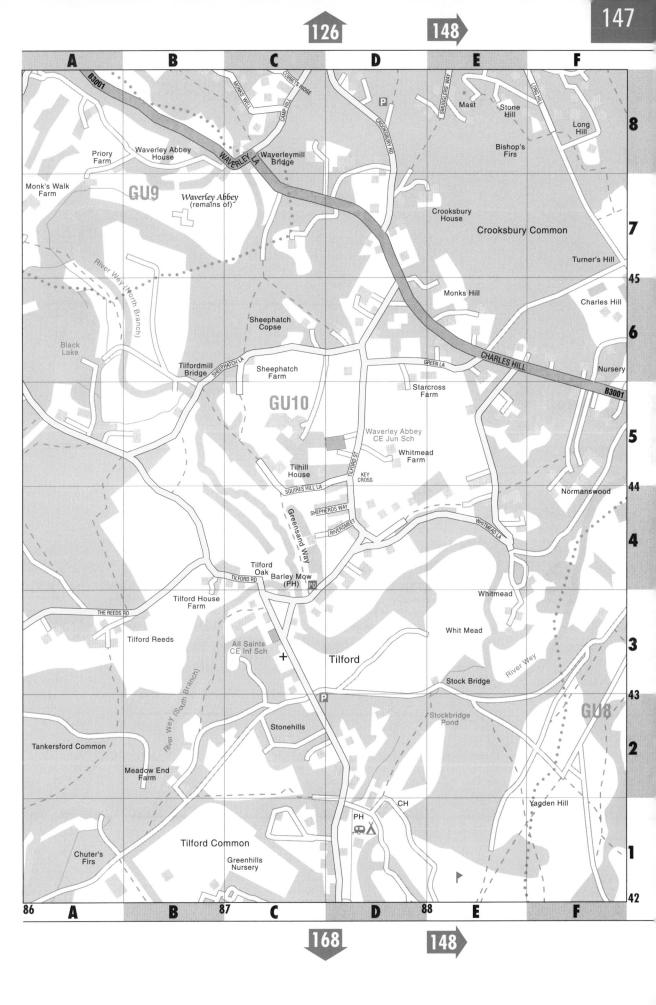

147   127

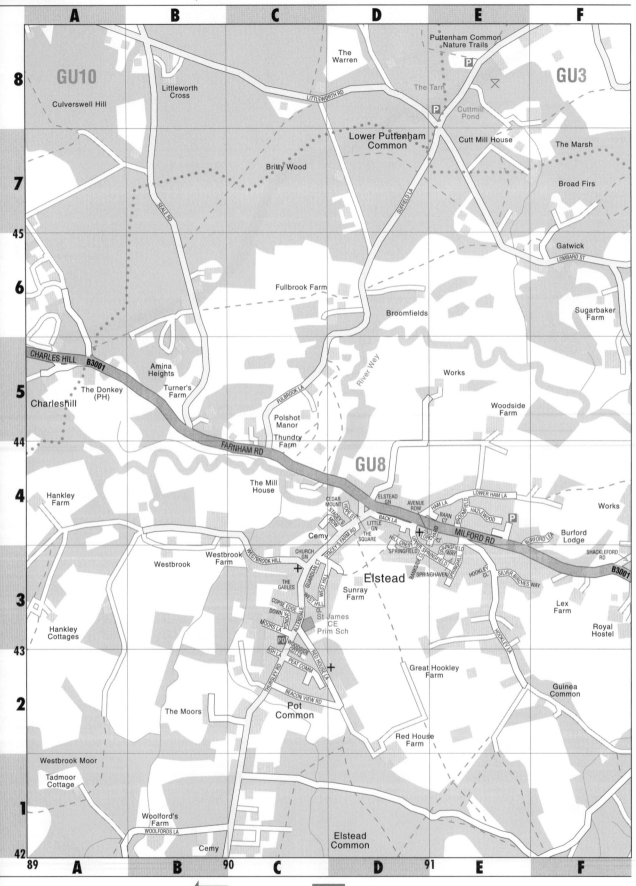

	A	**B**	**C**	**D**	**E**	**F**

8

GU10

Culverswell Hill

Littleworth Cross

The Warren

Puttenham Common Nature Trails

P

The Tarn

LITTLEWORTH RD

Cuttmill Pond

GU3

7

SEALE RD

Britty Wood

Lower Puttenham Common

Cutt Mill House

The Marsh

SHEEFIELD LA

Broad Firs

45

Gatwick

LOMBARD ST

6

Fullbrook Farm

Broomfields

Sugarbaker Farm

River Wey

Works

Woodside Farm

5

CHARLES HILL   B3001

The Donkey (PH)

Charleshill

Amina Heights

Turner's Farm

FULBROOK LA

Polshot Manor

44

Thundry Farm

FARNHAM RD

GU8

4

Hankley Farm

The Mill House

CEDAR MOUNT

STACEY'S MEW

HOYLE'S

ELSTEAD GN

BACK LA

AVENUE ROW

HAM LA

BARN CT

LOWER HAM LA

BROOMFIELD

HAZLEWOOD

P

Works

Westbrook

Westbrook Farm

WESTBROOK HILL

Cemy

STACEY'S FARM RD

LITTLE GN

THE SQUARE

MILFORD RD

Burford Lodge

BURFORD LA

SHACKLEFORD RD

B3001

3

CHURCH GN

GUARDIAN CT

WEST HILL

WEST HILL CL

HILL CREST

Springfield

UPPER SPRINGFIELD

BANKSIDE

SPRINGFIELD CL

SPRINGFIELD WAY

SPRINGHILL

Springhaven

HOOKLEY CL

SILVER BIRCHES WAY

Lex Farm

Elstead

THE GABLES

COPSE EDGE

DOWN AVENUE

ALLENDALE

Sunray Farm

St James CE Prim Sch

Royal Hostel

MOORS LA

Hankley Cottages

HORSLEY RD

ASH LA

PO

Woodside Cotts

PEAT COMM

RED HOUSE LA

Great Hookley Farm

HOOKLEY LA

43

Westbrook

BEACON VIEW RD

Pot Common

Guinea Common

2

The Moors

Red House Farm

1

Westbrook Moor

Tadmoor Cottage

Woolford's Farm

WOOLFORDS LA

Elstead Common

42

Cemy

89	**A**		**B**	**90**	**C**		**D**	**91**	**E**		**F**

147   169

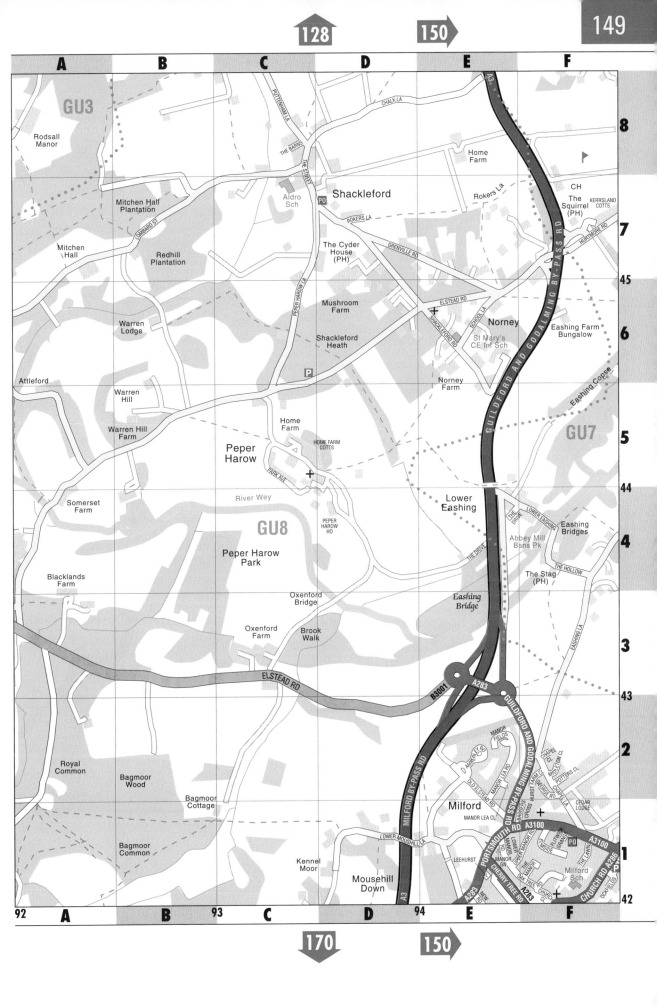

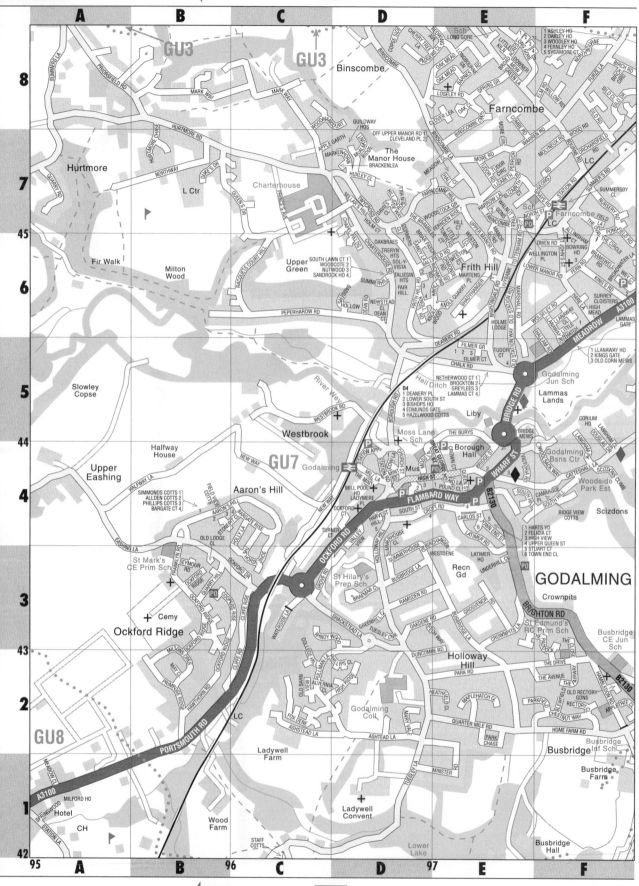

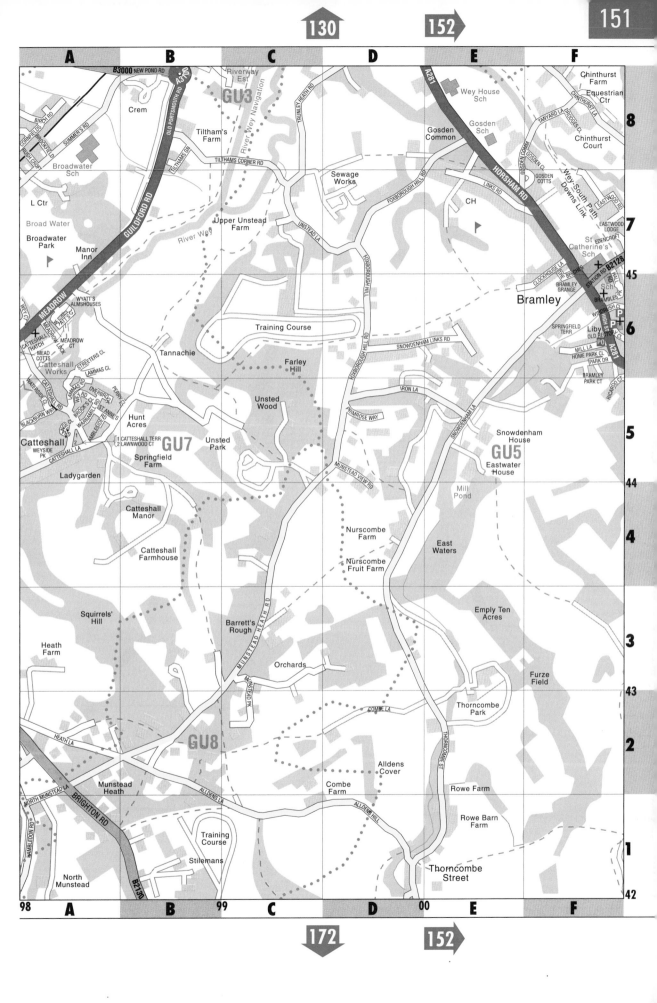

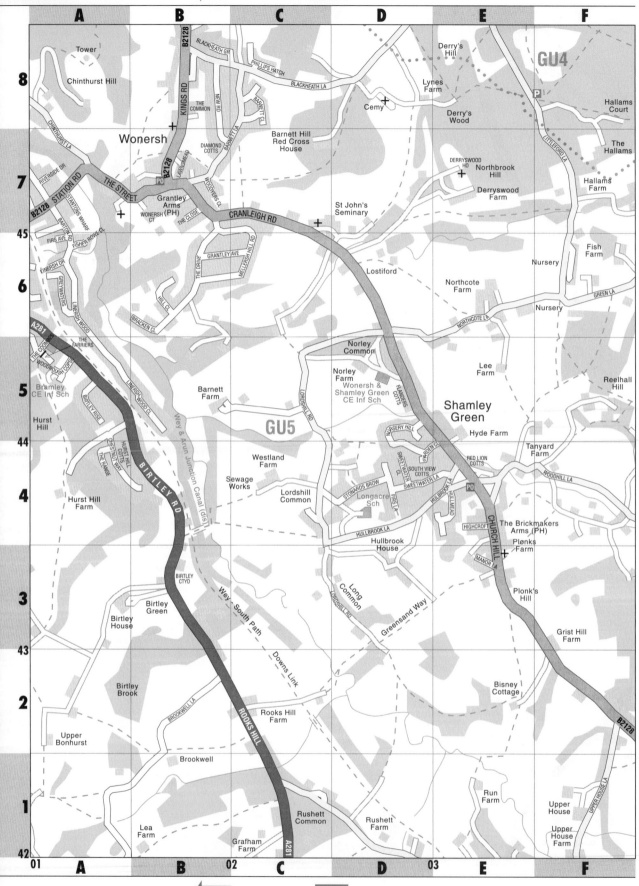

151
131

A B C D E F

8

GU4

Tower

Chinthurst Hill

Derry's
Hill

Lynes
Farm

Hallams
Court

BLACKHEATH GR

KINGS RD

PHILLIPS HATCH

THE
COMMON

NEW RD

BLACKHEATH LA

Cemy

Derry's
Wood

The
Hallams

B2128

Wonersh

BARNETT CL

Barnett Hill
Red Cross
House

DERRYSWOOD
HO

Northbrook
Hill

LITTLEFORD LA

Hallams
Farm

7

RIVERSIDE DR

CHINTHURST LA

THE STREET

B2128

PO

LAWNSMEAD

DIAMOND
COTTS

Derryswood
Farm

STATION RD

WOODVERS CL

Grantley
Arms
(PH)

St John's
Seminary

Fish
Farm

45

B2128

STANTONS WHARF

WONERSH
CT

THE CLOSE

CRANLEIGH RD

Lostiford

GREEN LA

Nursery

FIRS AVE

FISHER ROWE CL

THE DRIVE

MELLERSH HILL RD

GRANTLEY AVE

Northcote
Farm

Nursery

6

LINERSH DR

GREYWATERS

HILL CL

BRACKEN CL

NORTHCOTE LA

A281

LINERSH WOOD

Norley
Common

Lee
Farm

Reelhall
Hill

THE FARRIERS

Norley
Farm

Wonersh &
Shamley Green
CE Inf Sch

FLANDERS
COTTS

5

WOODROUGH COPSE

THE STOCK SHED

BIRTLEY RISE

LINERSH WOOD CL

Barnett
Farm

LORDSHILL RD

Shamley
Green

Hyde Farm

Tanyard
Farm

Bramley
CE Inf Sch

Wey & Arun Junction Canal (dis)

GU5

NURSERY HILL

RED LION
COTTS

WOODHILL LA

44

Hurst
Hill

HURST HILL
COTTS

CHESTNUT WAY

THE RANGE

Westland
Farm

SWEETWATER
CL

SOUTH VIEW
COTTS

GARDEN CL

PO

4

Hurst Hill
Farm

BIRTLEY RD

Sewage
Works

Lordshill
Common

STONARDS BROW

Longacre
Sch

FIRS LA

SWEETWATER LA

HULLBROOK LA

HULLMEAD

The Brickmakers
Arms (PH)

HIGHCROFT

CHURCH HILL

Plønks
Farm

Hullbrook
House

MANOR LA

3

Birtley
Green

BIRTLEY
CTYD

Wey South Path

Long
Common

Greensand Way

Plonk's
Hill

Birtley
House

LORDSHILL RD

Grist Hill
Farm

43

Birtley
Brook

BROOKWELL LA

Downs Link

Bisney
Cottage

2

ROOKS HILL

Rooks Hill
Farm

B2128

Upper
Bonhurst

Brookwell

Run
Farm

Upper
House

UPPER HOUSE LA

1

Lea
Farm

Grafham
Farm

A281

Rushett
Common

Rushett
Farm

Upper
House
Farm

42

01 A B 02 C D 03 E F

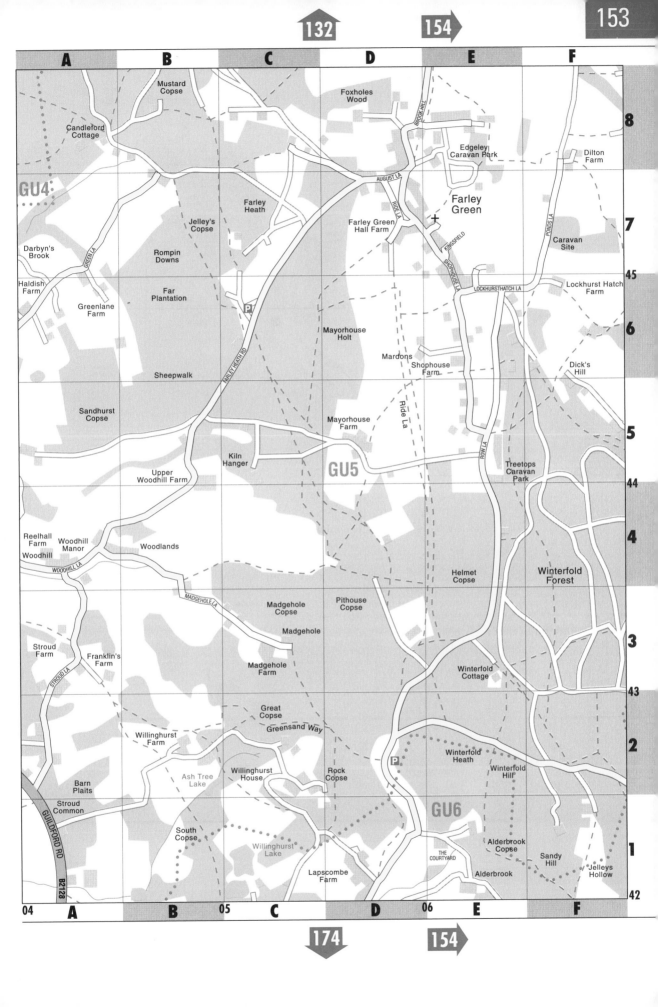

A   B   C   D   E   F

8

Dilton
Copse

Lane End
Farm

Broadfield Rd

Pursers La

Sweet La

Hoe La

St Martha's
Cotts

Horse
Shoes
Farm

Knobfield

Sutton Pl

Westfield

Hoe
Cotts

Pursers
Farm

Hoe

Hoe La

7

Jesse La

Lawbrook La

Pond La

Burchets Hollow

Hazel
Hall

Smoky
Hole

Hoe
Farm

Mackies Hill

Peaslake
Sch

Franksfield

Tenpingshook
Wood

RH5

45

Peaslake La

Colmans Hill

Hurtwood
Chase

Knowle
Farm

Hound
House
Farm

Hound
House

Peaslake

Colman's
Hill
Riding
Bottom

6

Hound House Rd

Kiln Platt
Cottage

Wickham's
Copse

The
Hurtwood
Inn

P

P

PO

Plaws Hill

Spurfold
Copse

Riding
Copse

Walking Bottom

Ridge
Hill

P

Cemy

GU5

5

Peaslake
House

Bentlys

44

Hurt Wood

P

Gasson
Farm

Radnor Rd

P

4

Gasson
Copse

Ewhurst Rd

Coverwood

3

Coverwood
Farm

43

Lake
House

Duke of Kent
Sch

Greensand Way

GU6

2

Ewhurst
Windmill

P

Pitch
Hill

P

Woolpit
Wood

Holt Copse

RH5

P

P

P

P

Reynards
Hill

The Warren

Ride Way

Windmill
Inn
(PH)

Woolpit
Farm

Isemongers
Farm

Sherborne La

1

Hurtwood
Edge

42

07   A   B   08   C   D   09   E   F

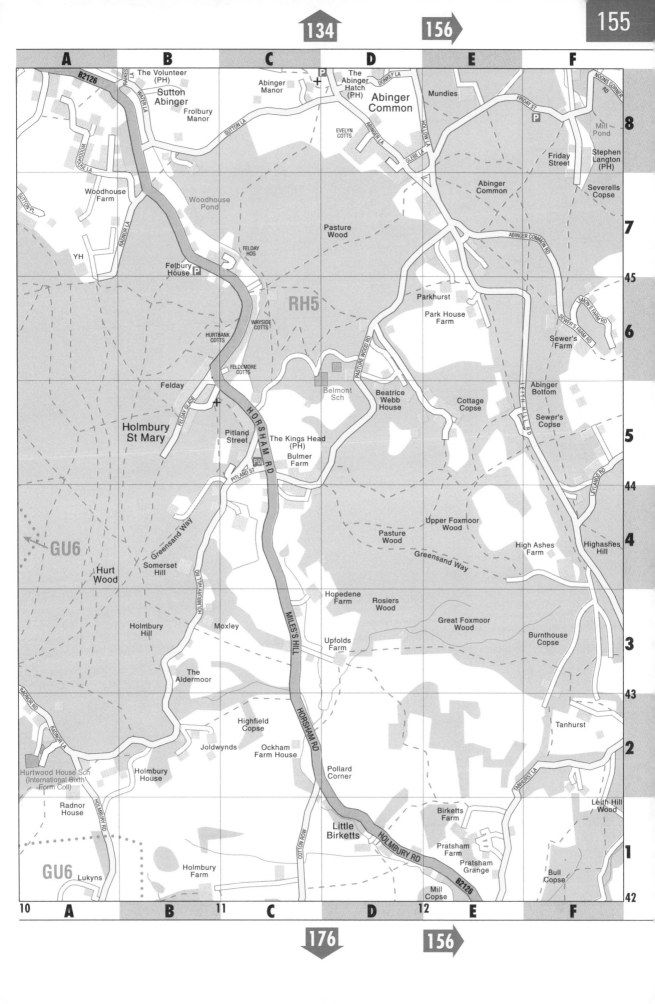

8

The Volunteer (PH)
Sutton Abinger
Frolbury Manor
Abinger Manor
The Abinger Hatch (PH)
Abinger Common
Mundies
Friday Street
Stephen Langton (PH)
Evelyn Cotts
Severells Copse
Woodhouse Farm
Abinger Common
7
YH
Pasture Wood
Woodhouse Pond
Felday Hos
Felbury House
45
RH5
Parkhurst
6
Wayside Cotts
Park House Farm
Sewer's Farm
Hurtbank Cotts
Feldemore Cotts
Belmont Sch
Beatrice Webb House
Abinger Bottom
Felday
Cottage Copse
Sewer's Copse
Holmbury St Mary
Pitland Street
The Kings Head (PH)
Bulmer Farm
5
Pitland St
PO
44
Upper Foxmoor Wood
4
Greensand Way
Pasture Wood
High Ashes Farm
Highashes Hill
GU6
Somerset Hill
Greensand Way
Hurt Wood
Hopedene Farm
Rosiers Wood
Great Foxmoor Wood
Burnthouse Copse
3
Holmbury Hill
Moxley
Upfolds Farm
The Aldermoor
43
Highfield Copse
Tanhurst
Joldwynds
Ockham Farm House
2
Hurtwood House Sch (International Sixth Form Coll)
Holmbury House
Pollard Corner
Radnor House
Birketts Farm
Leith Hill Wood
Little Birketts
Pratsham Farm
Pratsham Grange
Bull Copse
1
GU6
Lukyns
Holmbury Farm
Mill Copse
B2126
42

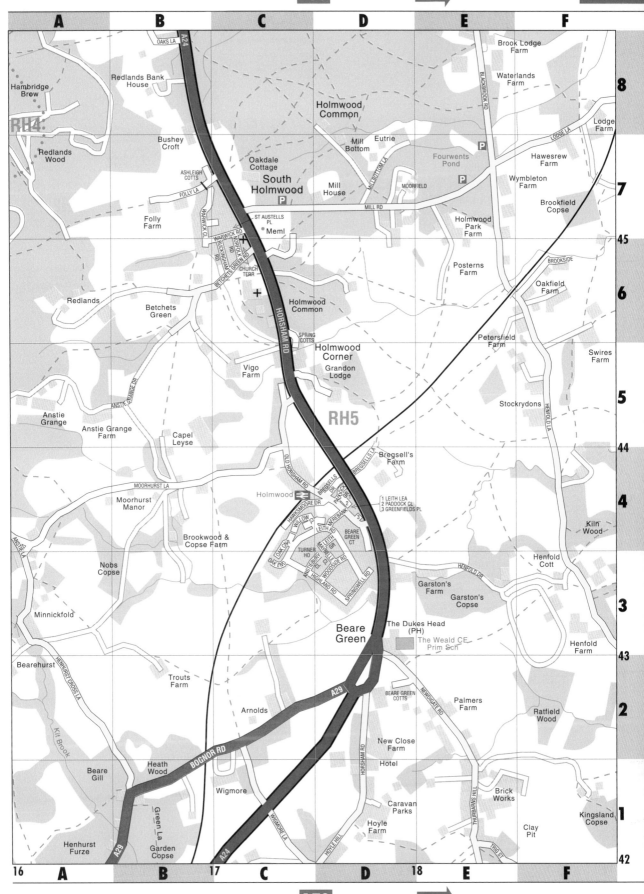

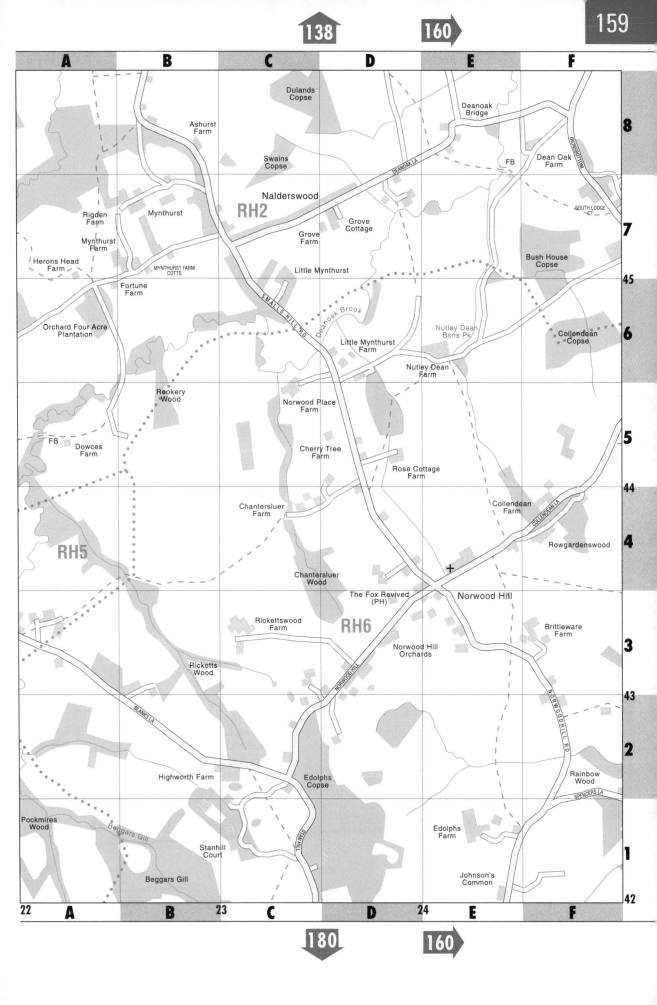

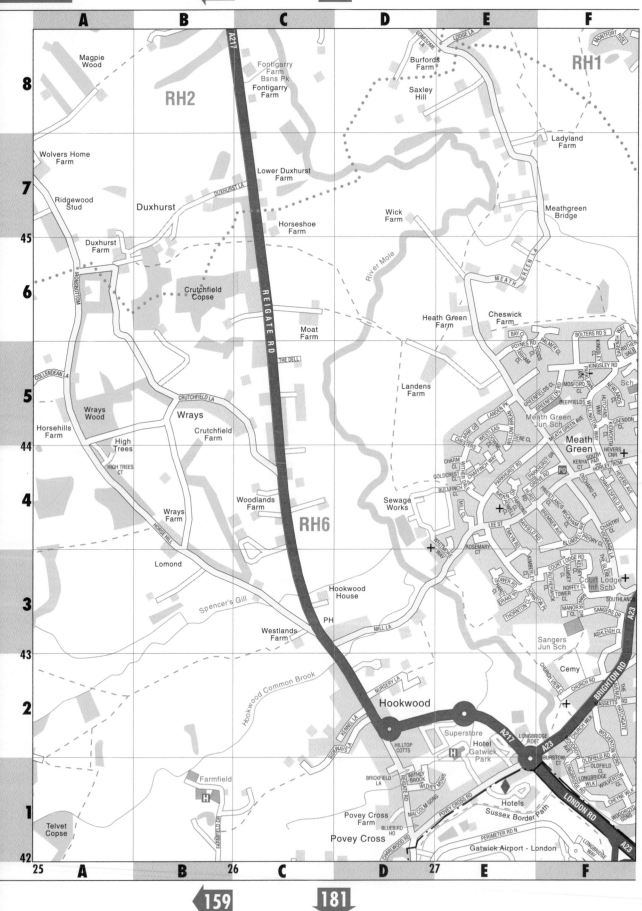

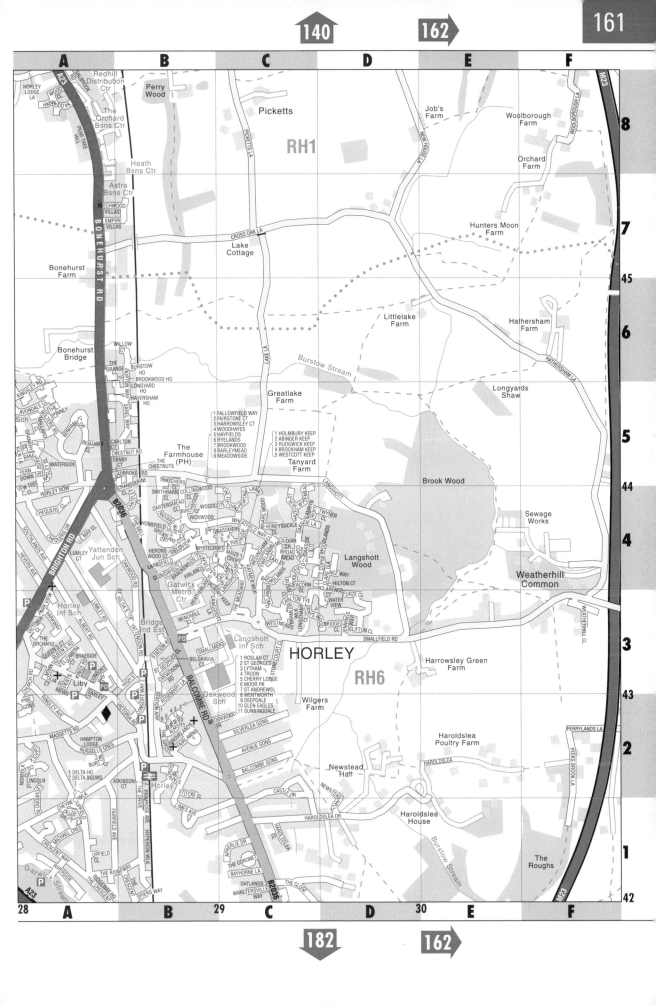

A B C D E F

8

Greenmeads Farm

Wasp Green Farm

The Bell Inn

Gay House

GAYHOUSE LA

Windmill

7

M23

The Castle (PH)

MILLERS COPSE

Wasp Green

Brightleigh Farm

RH1

Marl House

Copsley Court

Hornecourt Wood

Hornecourt Manor Farm

HORNECOURT HILL

LITTLE COLLINS

Outwood

45

Rookery Farm

Drivers Green

ROOKERY HILL

BELLWETHER LA

DAYSEY'S HILL

6

Old Hall Farm

Wilmot's Farm

NORMAN'S RD

SCOTT'S HILL

WILMOT'S LA

Horne Grange

Church Farm

Horne

5

Burstow Lodge Farm

Burstow Lodge

Hollesley Farm

CHURCH RD

Horne House Farm

44

Little Abbots Farm

COGMAN'S LA

CROYDONBARN LA

4

Weatherhill

WEATHERHILL COTTS

HAYES WLK

THE CRAVENS

CHARLOTTE CR

HATHERSHAM LA

CHAPEL RD

RH6

Short Acre Farm

SMALLFIELD RD

THE CRAVENS

CAREY'S WOOD

FIELD WLK

THISTLE WAY

RALEIGH DR

THE WOODLANDS

TUDOR CL

WEATHERHILL RD

GRANGEWAY

DYER'S RD

CHURCHILL RD

ORCHARD RD

CLOVELLY WAY

HEATHER WLK

MEADOW VIEW

3

COOPER CL 1
LARKFIELD CL 2
GRASSLANDS 3

GRANGE RD

WOODSIDE CRES

THE OAKS

NEW RD

The Plough (PH)

Smallfield Place

Rough Beech

Bysshe Court Farm

ALBERTA

VANCOUVER

QUEBEC CL

DR

ONTA

TORON

Burstow Prim Sch

THE ACORNS

PO

KINGS MEAD

PLOUGH RD

43

WHEELERS LA

BRIDGEHAM WAY

Smallfield

Rough Beech Farm

PERRYLANDS LA

REDEHALL RD

Green Farm

Triddles Farm

DOWLANDS LA

2

BROADBRIDGE LA

Bridgeham Grange

Redehall Prep Sch

Saconnex Farm

LABURNUM CT (CVN PK)

Broadmead Farm

GEA

THE HOMESTEAD

Dowlands Wood

Roughbeech Wood

1

Broadbridge Cottages

Broadbridge Farm

LONE OAK

Homestead Farm

PARK RD

CHITHURST LA

Chithurst Farm

42

CROSS LA

31 A B 32 C D 33 E F

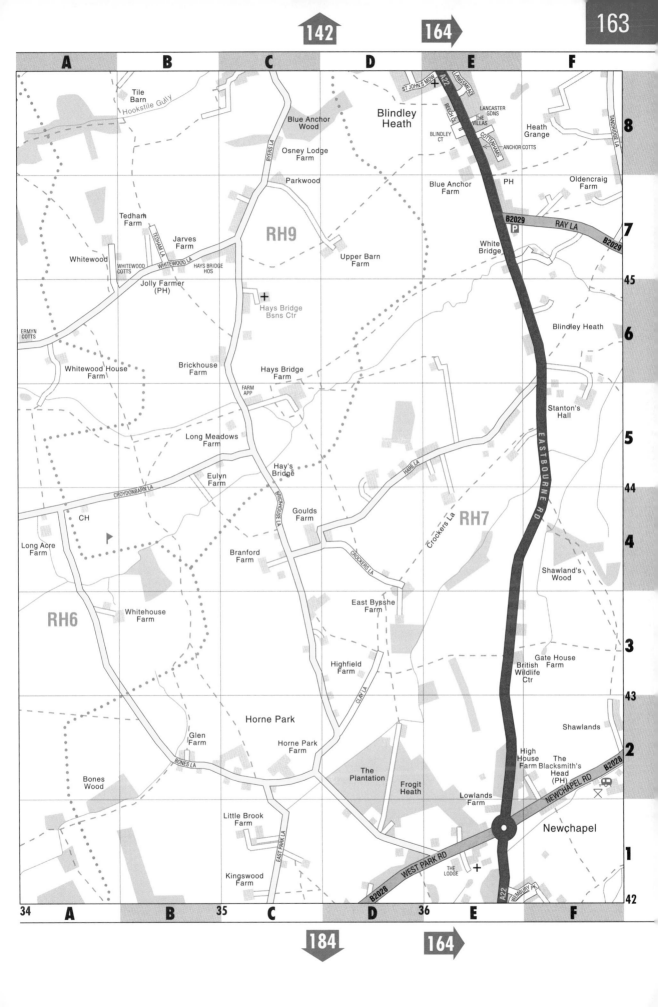

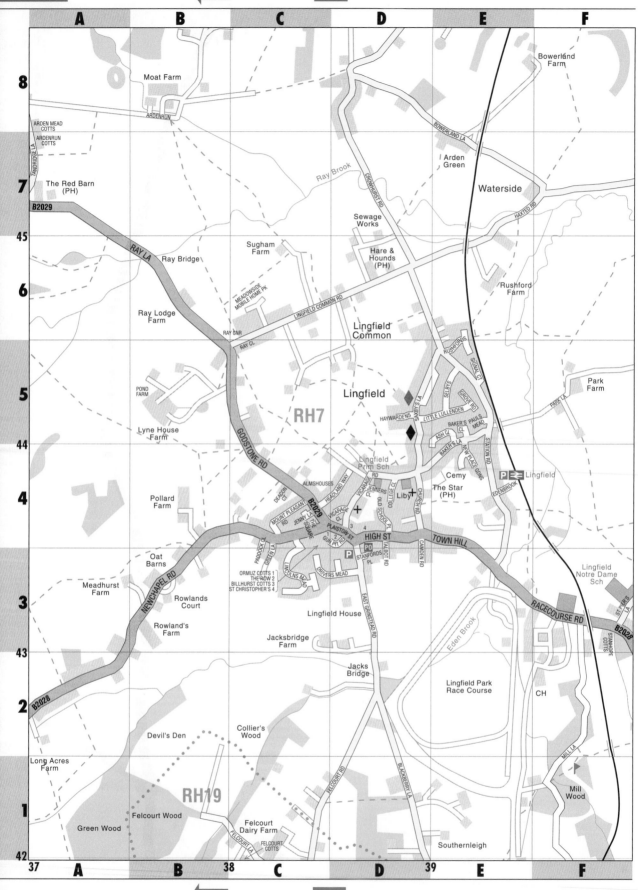

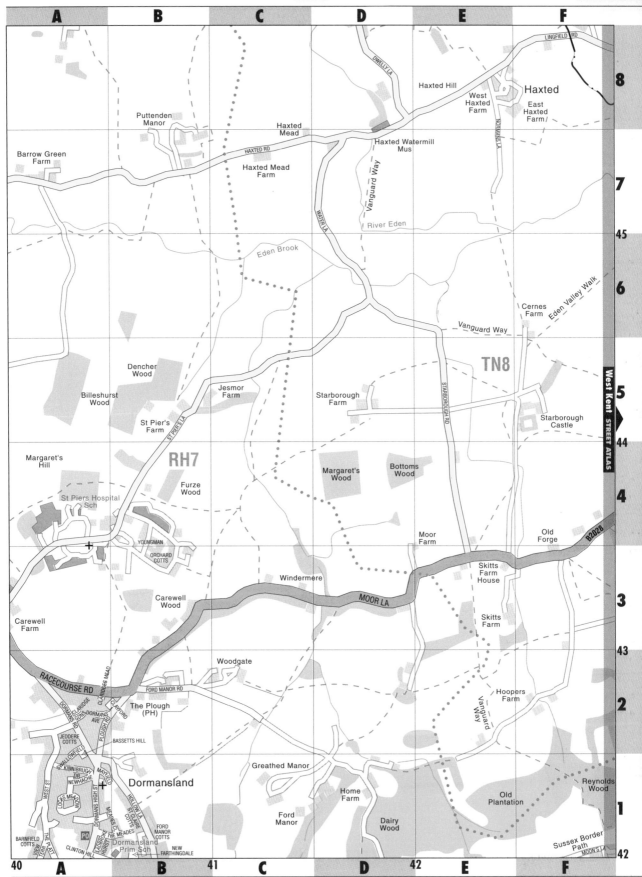

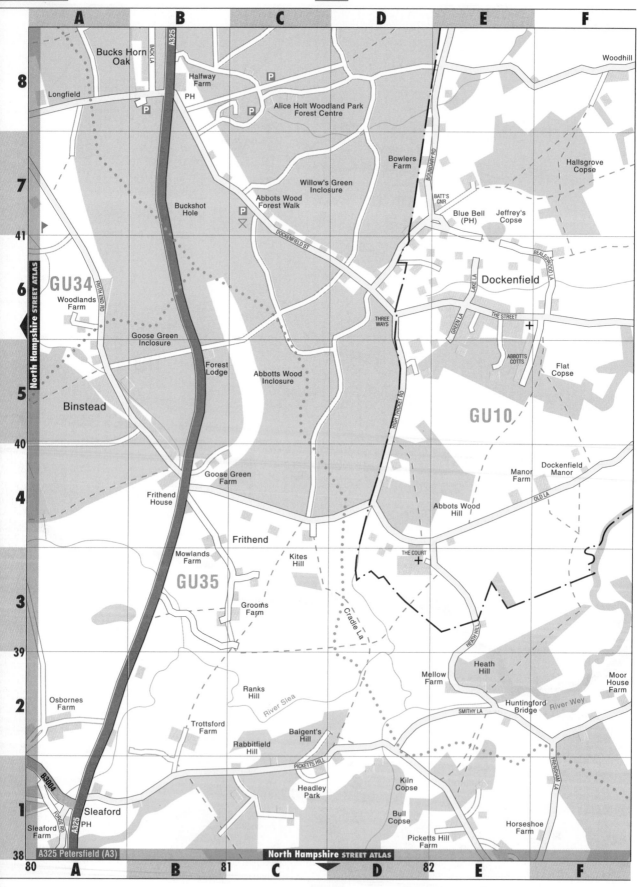

A   B   C   D   E   F

8

Bucks Horn
Oak

Longfield

BACK LA

Halfway
Farm

A325

PH

P

P

P

Alice Holt Woodland Park
Forest Centre

Woodhill

Bowlers
Farm

BOUNDARY RD

Hallsgrove
Copse

7

41

GU34

Buckshot
Hole

Willow's Green
Inclosure

Abbots Wood
Forest Walk

DOCKENFIELD ST

P

BATT'S
CNR

Blue Bell
(PH)

Jeffrey's
Copse

Dockenfield

BEALESWOOD LA

6

Woodlands
Farm

FRITH END RD

Goose Green
Inclosure

THREE
WAYS

GREEN LA

LAKE LA

THE STREET

5

Binstead

Forest
Lodge

Abbotts Wood
Inclosure

HIGH THICKET RD

ABBOTTS
COTTS

Flat
Copse

GU10

40

Goose Green
Farm

4

Frithend
House

Frithend

Mowlands
Farm

GU35

Kites
Hill

Abbots Wood
Hill

Manor
Farm

Dockenfield
Manor

OLD LA

THE COURT

3

Grooms
Farm

Cradle La

HEATH HILL

39

Mellow
Farm

Heath
Hill

Moor
House
Farm

2

Osbornes
Farm

Trottsford
Farm

Ranks
Hill

Rabbitfield
Hill

River Slea

Baigent's
Hill

PICKETTS HILL

SMITHY LA

Huntingford
Bridge

River Wey

FRENSHAM LA

B3004

Headley
Park

Kiln
Copse

Bull
Copse

Horseshoe
Farm

1

Sleaford
Farm

FORGE LA

A325

Sleaford
PH

Picketts Hill
Farm

38

North Hampshire STREET ATLAS

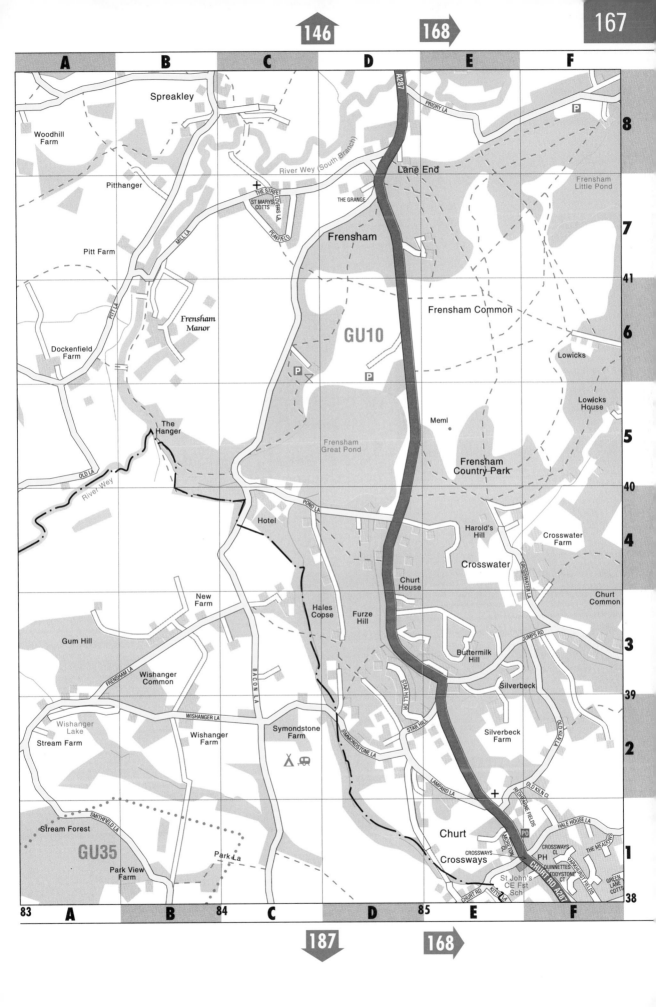

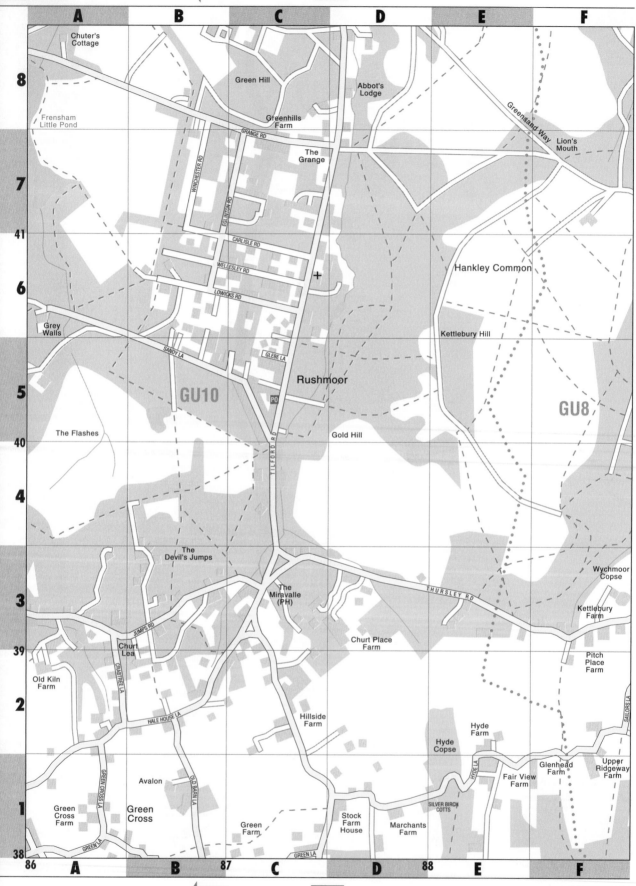

167
147

A **B** **C** **D** **E** **F**

8

Chuter's
Cottage

Green Hill

Abbot's
Lodge

Greenhills
Farm

Frensham
Little Pond

GRANGE RD

The Grange

Greensand Way

Lion's
Mouth

7

WINCHESTER RD

EGLINTON RD

41

CARLISLE RD

Hankley Common

6

WELLESLEY RD

LOWICKS RD

Grey
Walls

SANDY LA

Kettlebury Hill

GLEBE LA

Rushmoor

GU10

PO

GU8

5

TILFORD RD

The Flashes

40

Gold Hill

4

The Devil's Jumps

Wychmoor
Copse

3

The
Miravalle
(PH)

THURSLEY RD

Kettlebury
Farm

JUMPS RD

Churt Place
Farm

39

Churt
Lea

CRABTREE LA

Pitch
Place
Farm

Old Kiln
Farm

Hyde
Farm

SAILORS LA

2

HALE HOUSE LA

Hillside
Farm

Hyde
Copse

HYDE LA

Glenhead
Farm

Upper
Ridgeway
Farm

Avalon

OLD BARN LA

GREEN CROSS LA

Fair View
Farm

1

Green
Cross
Farm

Green
Cross

Green
Farm

Stock
Farm
House

Marchants
Farm

SILVER BIRCH
COTTS

38

GREEN LA

GREEN LA

86   **A**   **B**   87   **C**   **D**   88   **E**   **F**

167
188

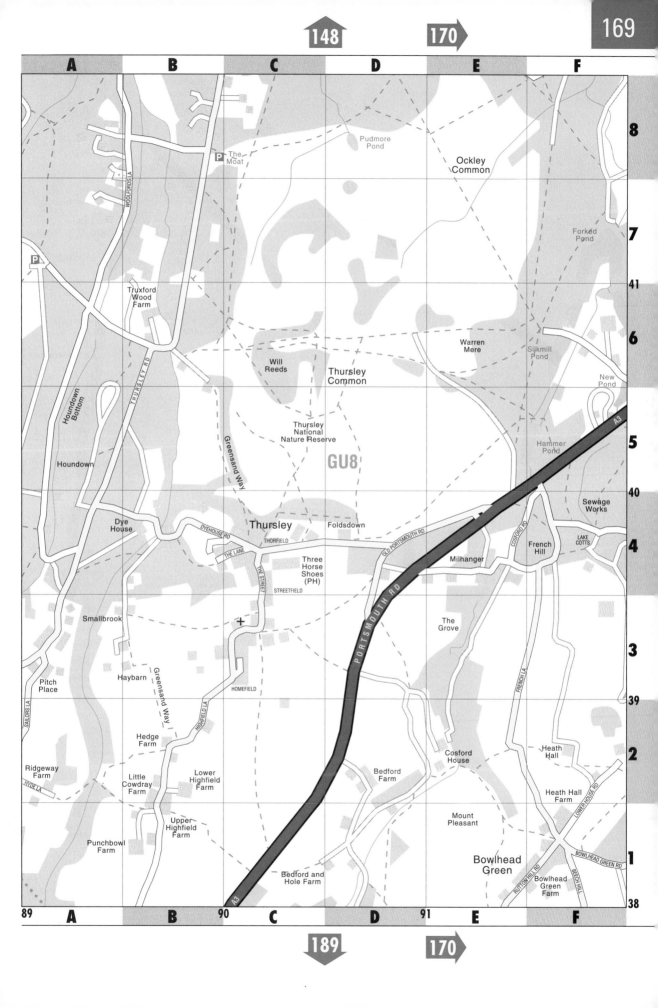

A B C D E F

Pudmore Pond

Ockley Common

The Moat

WOOLFORDS LA

P

Forked Pond

Truxford Wood Farm

THURSLEY RD

Warren Mere

Silkmill Pond

New Pond

A3

Will Reeds

Thursley Common

Houndown Bottom

Greensand Way

Hammer Pond

Houndown

Thursley National Nature Reserve

GU8

Dye House

DYEHOUSE RD

Thursley

Foldsdown

Old Portsmouth Rd

Sewage Works

COSFORD RD

French Hill

LAKE COTTS

THORFIELD

THE LANE

Three Horse Shoes (PH)

Milhanger

PORTSMOUTH RD

Smallbrook

THE STREET

STREETFIELD

The Grove

FRENCH LA

+

Haybarn

Greensand Way

HIGHFIELD LA

HOMEFIELD

Pitch Place

SAILORS LA

Hedge Farm

Heath Hall

Ridgeway Farm

HYDE LA

Little Cowdray Farm

Lower Highfield Farm

Bedford Farm

Cosford House

Heath Hall Farm

LOWER HOUSE RD

Upper Highfield Farm

Mount Pleasant

Bowlhead Green

RUTTON HILL RD

Punchbowl Farm

Bedford and Hole Farm

Bowlhead Green Rd

Bowlhead Green Farm

BEECH HILL

A3

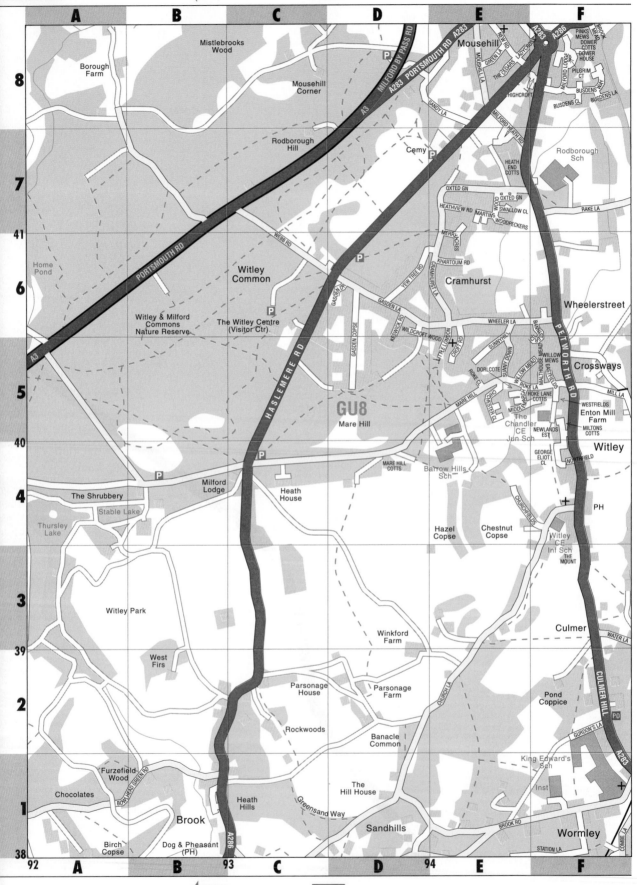

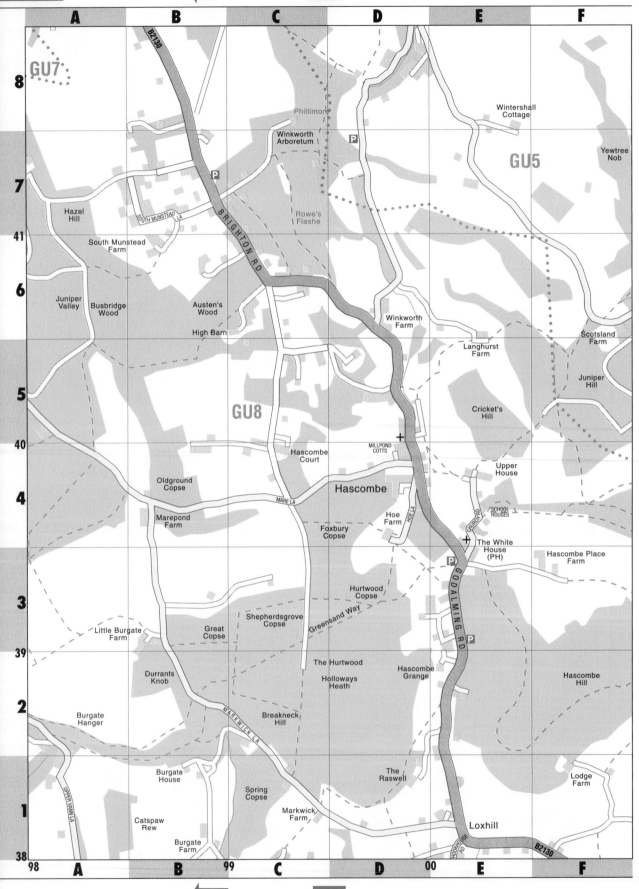

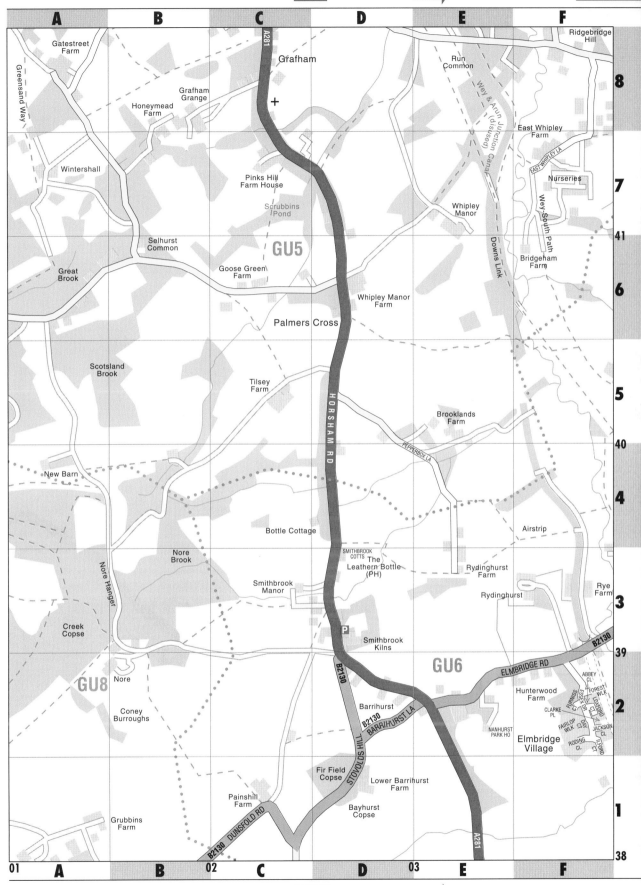

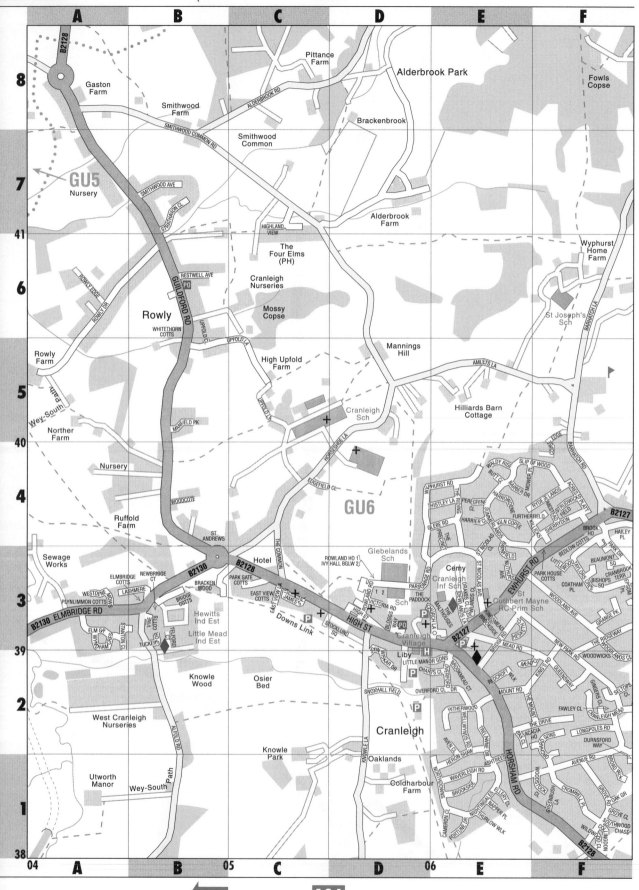

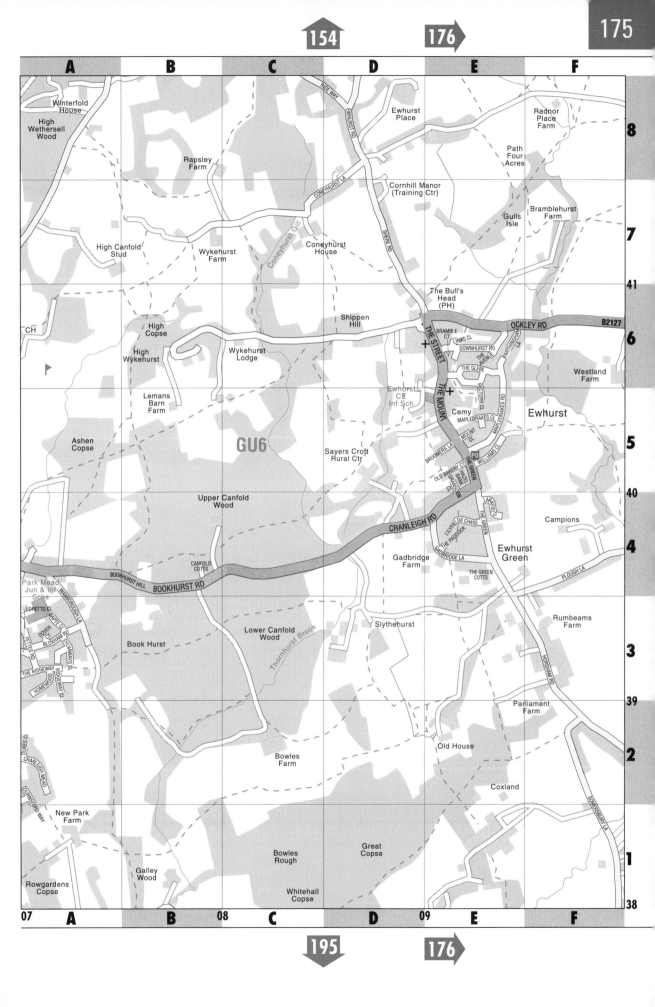

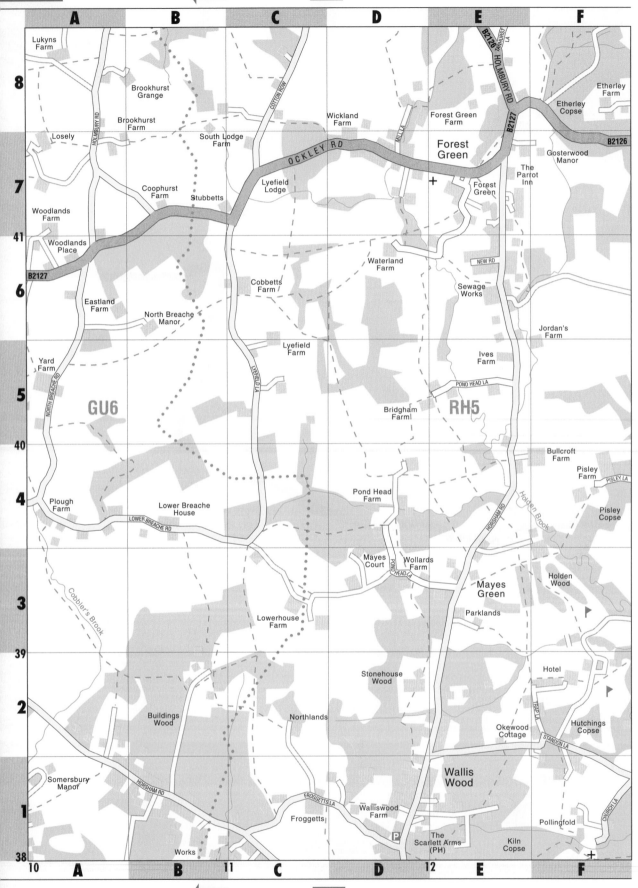

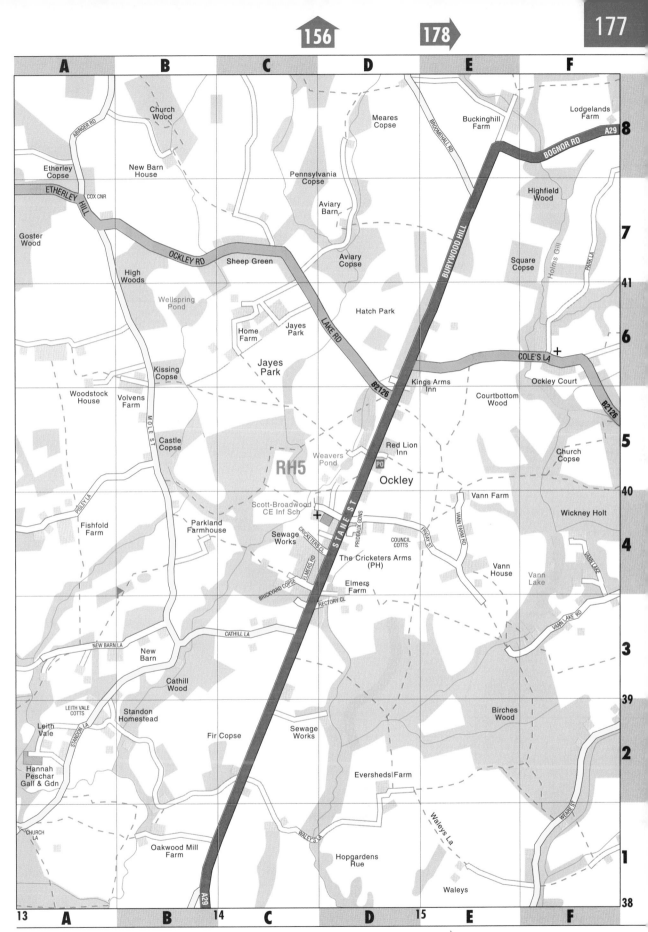

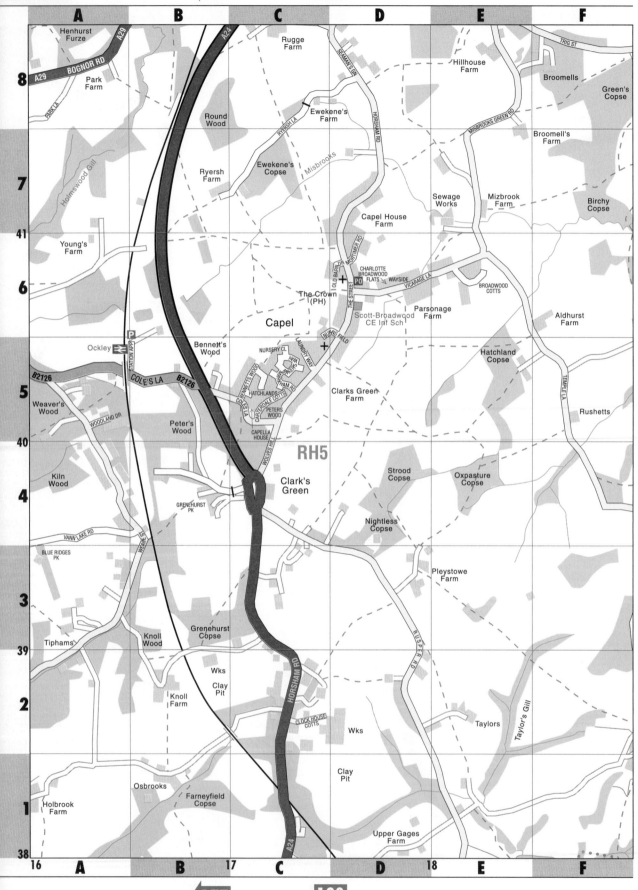

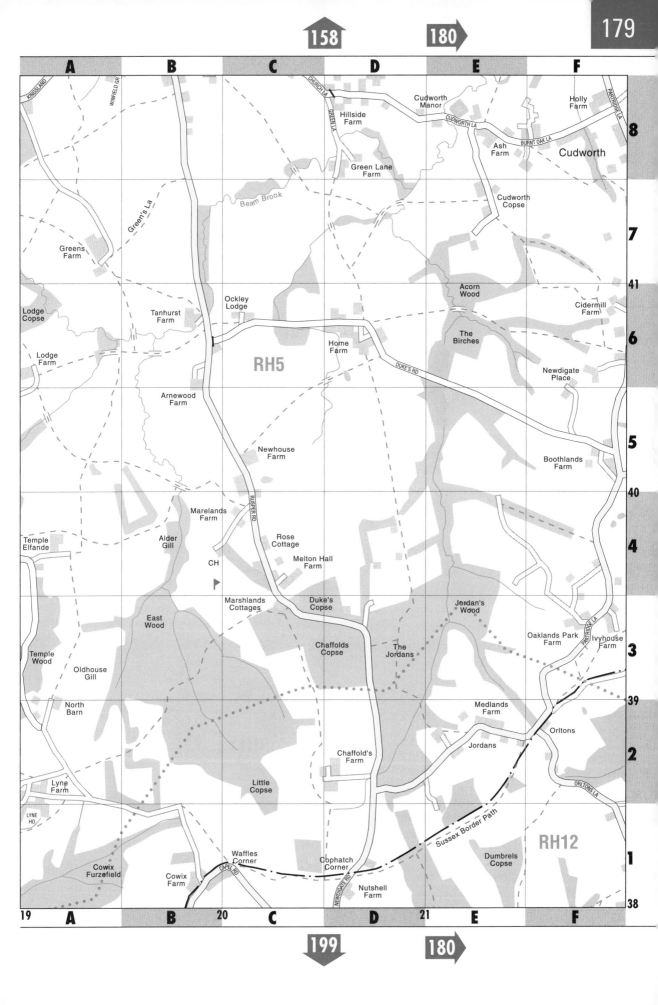

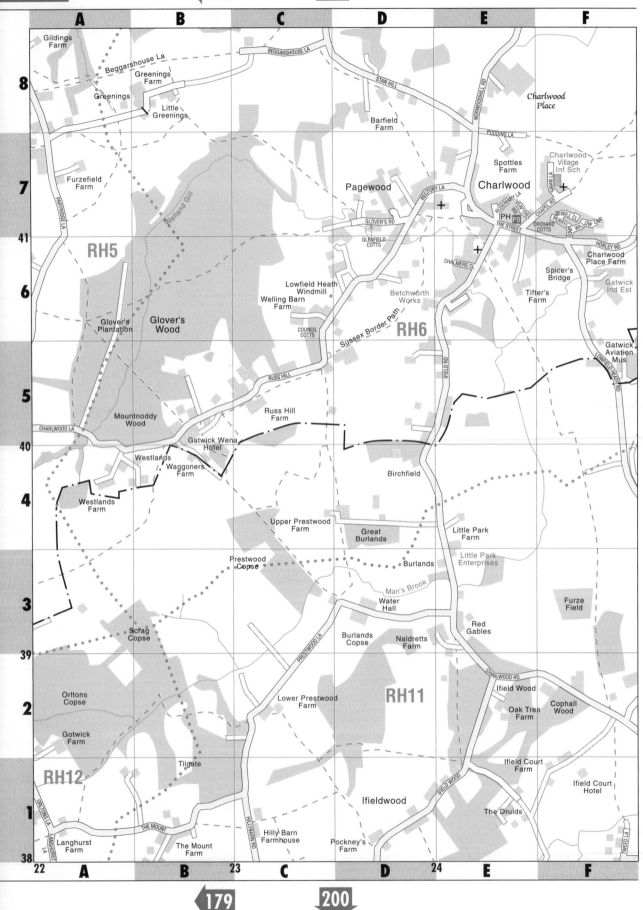

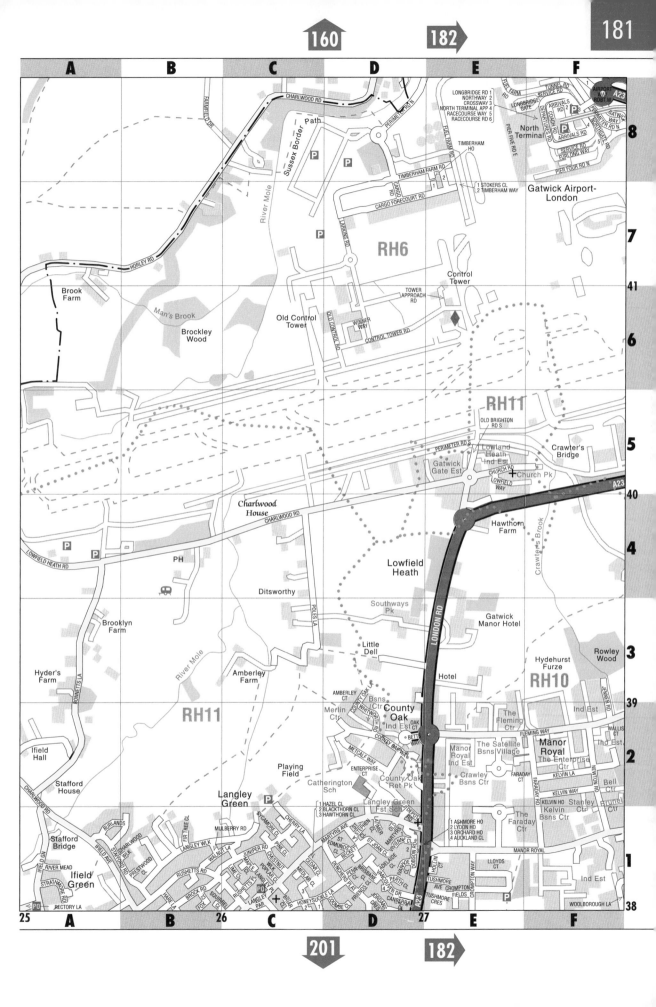

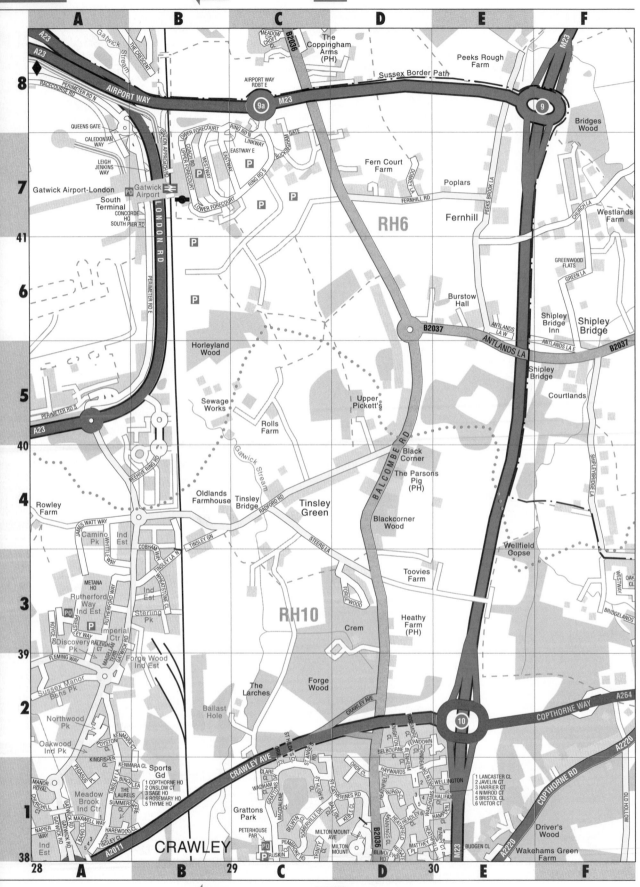

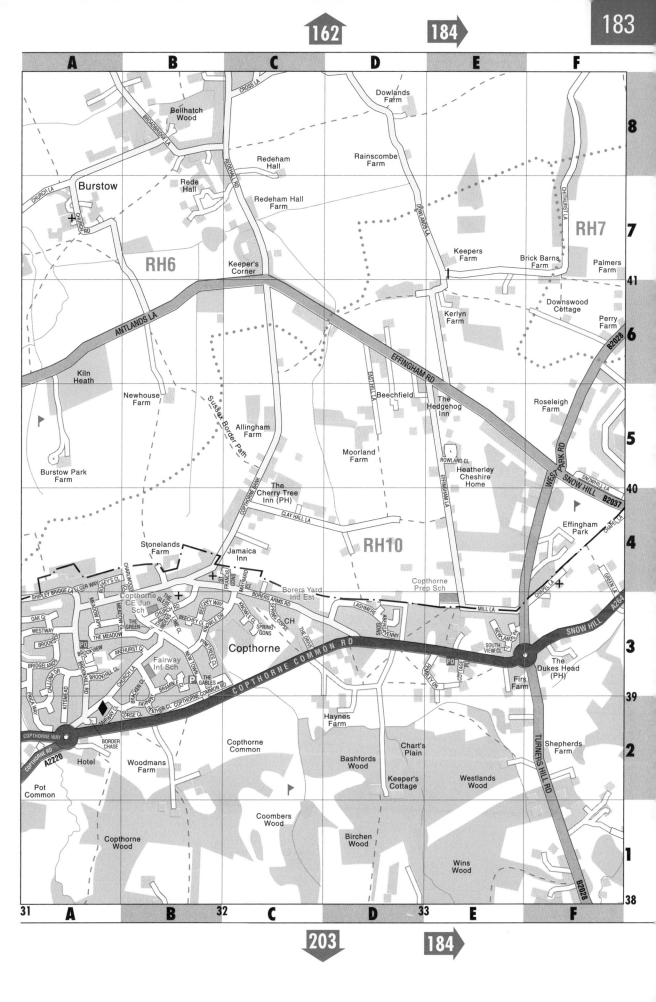

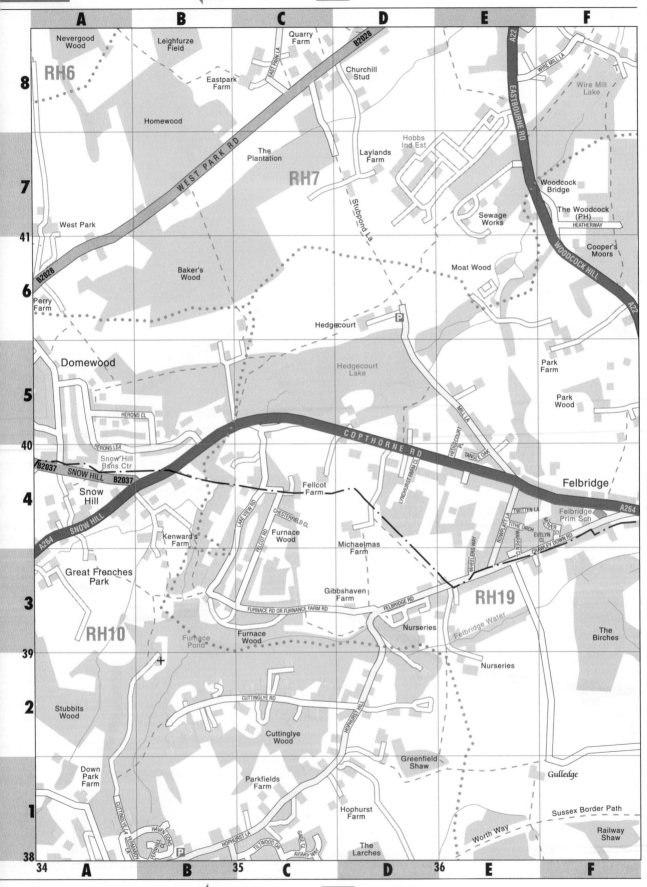

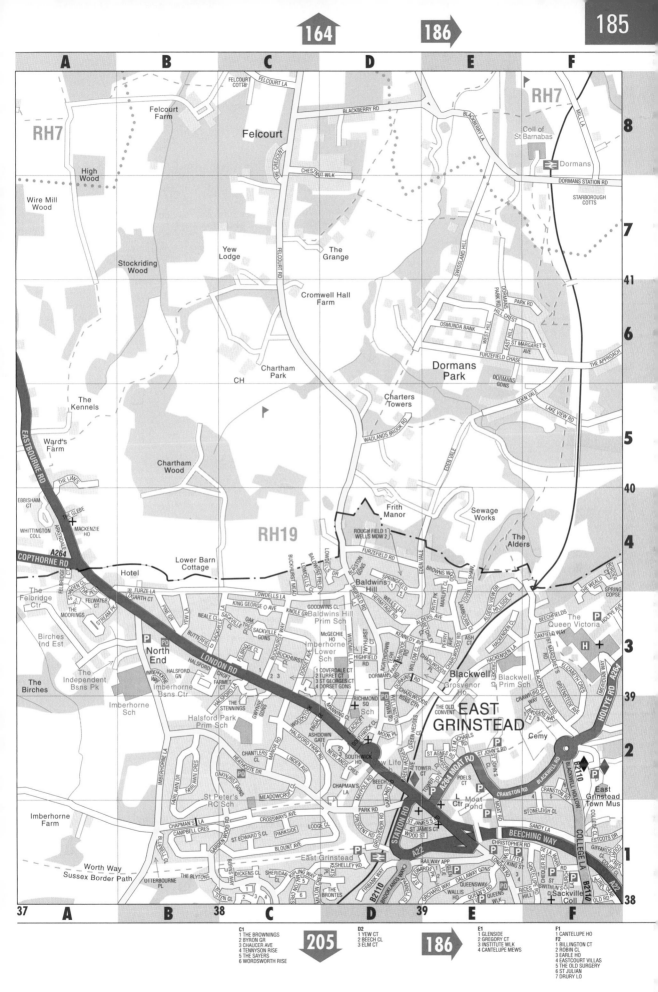

RH7

RH7

Coll of St Barnabas

Dormans

DORMANS STATION RD

STARBOROUGH COTTS

Felcourt Farm

FELCOURT COTTS

FELCOURT LA

BLACKBERRY RD

Felcourt

High Wood

Wire Mill Wood

THE CRESCENT

CHESTNUT WLK

FELCOURT RD

Yew Lodge

The Grange

Stockriding Wood

SWISSLAND HILL

DORMANS PARK RD

PARK RD

HILL CREST

OSMUNDA BANK

WEST HILL

ST HILL

ST MARGARET'S AVE

FURZEFIELD CHASE

Cromwell Hall Farm

Dormans Park

DORMANS GDNS

THE APPROACH

Chartham Park

CH

Charters Towers

EDEN VALE

LAKE VIEW RD

The Kennels

WADLANDS BROOK RD

EDEN VALE

Ward's Farm

Chartham Wood

RH19

Frith Manor

Sewage Works

The Alders

EBBISHAM CT

THE LIMES

THE GLEBE

MACKENZIE HO

WHITTINGTON COLL

A264

EASTBOURNE RD

COPTHORNE RD

FELBRIDGE CT

ARUNDALE

STANDEN CT

THE PLAT

ROUGH FIELD 1
WELLS MDW 2

FURZEFIELD RD

BROWNS WD

EDEN VALE

THE WEALD

BORDER

SPRING COPSE

Lower Barn Cottage

The Felbridge Ctr

The MOORINGS

FURZE LA

HOGARTH CT

FELWATER CT

STREAM PK

PINE GR

YEW LA

LOWDELLS LA

BUCKHURST MEAD

LOWDELLS DR

BALDWINS FIELD

LOWDELLS

LOWDELLS

BASTON GDNS

LINGFIELD RD

SPRINGFIELD RD

Baldwins Hill

HERMITAGE RD

WELLS LEA

FRITH PK

FRITH AVE

MARIPIT CT

OVERTON SHAW

ALDERS VIEW RD

HILLSIDE CT

HACKENDEN CL

BEECHFIELDS

HOLTYE AVE

The Queen Victoria

H

Birches Ind Est

North End

P PO

IMBERHORNE WAY

HALSFORD GN

HALSFORD WAY

LONDON RD

BUTTERFIELD

SAGE CL

HALSFORD CROFT

NEALE CL

SACKVILLE LA

OAK TREE CL

SACKVILLE GDNS

KING GEORGE AVE

KNOLE GR

GOODWINS CL

Baldwins Hill Prim Sch

McGECHIE HO

Imberhorne Lower Sch

WINDMILL LA

TWHURST AVE

HIGHFIELD

NORTHDOWN RD

KENNEDY AVE

WILLOW CL

PERRY HILL

ASH CL

CHARLWOODS RD

HACKENDEN LA

CRICKET CT

BLACKWELL FARM RD

GREENSTEDE AVE

ELIZABETH CRES

MERIDIAN WAY

The Birches

The Independent Bsns Pk

Imberhorne Bsns Ctr

Imberhorne Sch

1 COVERDALE CT
2 TURRET CT
3 ST GEORGES CT
4 DORSET GDNS

1 2 3

4

DORSET AVE

BUCKHURST WAY

FARMET CT

GWYNNE GDNS

HALSFORD LA

Halsford Park Prim Sch

The Stennings

CHANTLERS CT

MANOR RD

LINDEN AVE

HEATHCOTE DR

OAKHURST GDNS

MEADOWCROFT CL

ASHDOWN GATE

WOODSTOCK

MANNING CL

RICHMOND SQ

Sch

DORMANS

HIGHFIELD

Blackwell Grosvenor Ho

Blackwell Prim Sch

CRAWFURD WAY

RODGERS WAY

1 2 3

EAST GRINSTEAD

Cemy

B2110

East Grinstead Town Mus

P

CHARLWOODS RD

CHARLWOODS BSNS CTR

PO

The Old Convent

ST MICHAELS RD

ST AGNES RD

ST JOHN'S RD

St MICHAELS

ST JOHN'S

POELS CT

A264 MOAT RD

CRANSTON RD

MOAT RD

STONELEIGH CL

BLACKWELL RD

BLACKWELL HOLLOW

East Grinstead

Imberhorne Farm

FAIRLAWN LA

FAIRLAWN CRES

Chapman's La

CHAPMAN'S LA

St Peter's RC Sch

GARDEN WOOD RD

CAMPBELL CRES

BURNS CL

CROSSWAYS AVE

ST EDWARD'S CL

PARKSIDE

LODGE CL

BLOUNT AVE

PARK RD

HALSFORD PARK RD

SOUTHWICK HO

SOUTHWICK

New Life Sch

CHAPMAN'S LA

MAYPOLE RD

BEECH RD

GARLAND RD

CRESCENT RD

GROSVENOR RD

WOOD ST

ST JAMES'S RD

ST JAMES

STATION RD

A22

MOOR PL

Moat Ctr Pond

L

CRANSTON RD

4 5

1 2 3

SANDY LA

BEECHING WAY

COLLEGE LA

A22

A264

HOLTYE RD

B2110

GIFFARDS DR

ESTCOTS DR

Worth Way
Sussex Border Path

OTTERBOURNE PL

THE BLYTONS

DICKENS CL

SHERIDAN

KIPLING WAY

KEATS

SHELLEY RD

East Grinstead

RAILWAY APP

FIRBANK WAY

BROOKLANDS WAY

B2110

ST LEONARDS

ORCHARD WAY

WALLIS RD

QUEENS RD

QUEENSWAY

DALLAWAY GDNS

QUEEN'S RD

RICES HILL

SWITHUN'S CL

LONDON RD

LITTLE KING ST

CHRISTOPHER RD

DE LA WARR RD

CANTELUPE RD

CHEQUER RD

ROBIN CL

1 2 3

P

P

P

P

P

P

P

P

P

Sackville Coll

A22

OLD RD

THE BRONTES

1 2 3

5 6

A   B   C   D   E   F

8   7   41   6   5   40   4   3   39   2   1

37   38   39   38

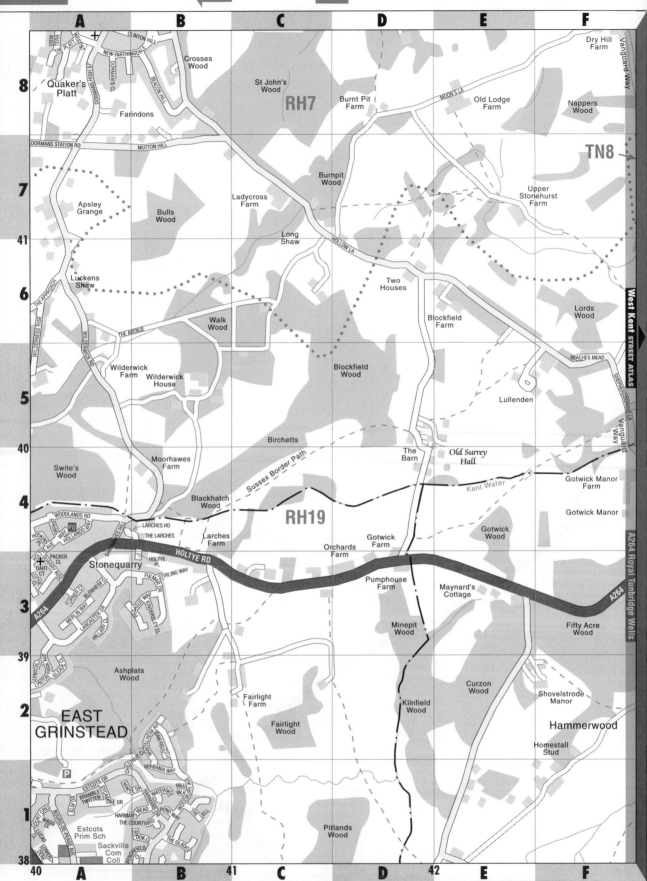

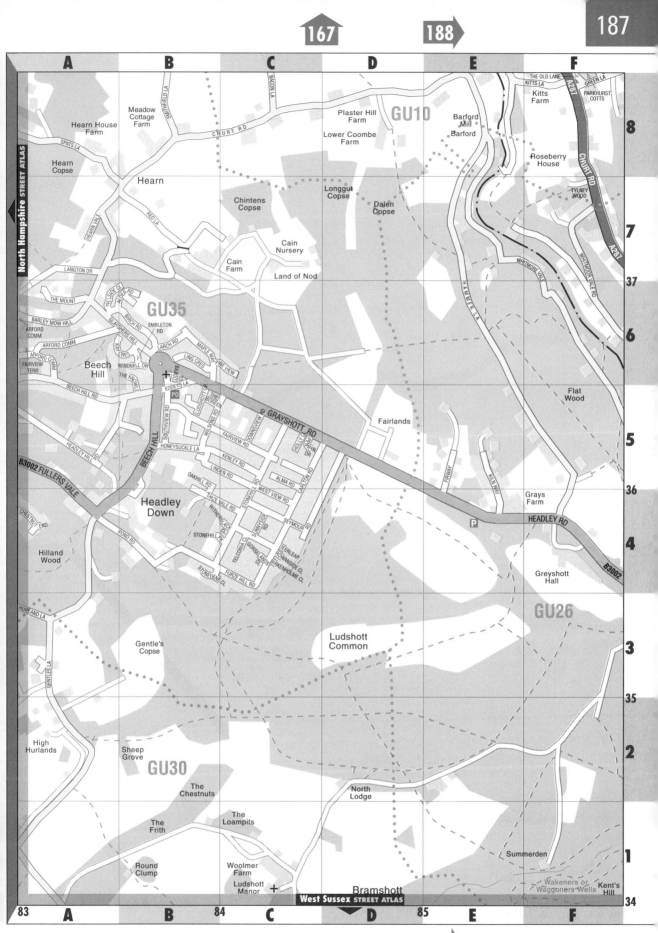

A | B | C | D | E | F

North Hampshire STREET ATLAS

8

THE OLD LANE
KITTS LA
Kitts Farm
GREEN LA
PARKHURST COTTS

Meadow Cottage Farm
SMITHFIELD LA
Plaster Hill Farm
GU10
Barford Mill
Barford
A287

Hearn House Farm
CHURT RD
Lower Coombe Farm
Roseberry House

SPATS LA
Hearn Copse
Hearn

Longgut Copse
Dalen Copse
TYLNEY WOOD
CHURT RD

7

Chintens Copse
A287

HEARN VALE
Cain Nursery
WHITMORE VALE
WHITMORE VALE RD

LANGTON DR
RED LA
Cain Farm
Land of Nod
HAMMER LA

37

THE MOUNT
GU35
6
Flat Wood

BARLEY MOW HILL
WILSIDE CT
ELDER RD
BIRCH RD
EMBLETON RD
ARFORD COMM
GLAYSHERS HILL
LARCH RD
MAPLE WAY
PINE VIEW
ARFORD COMM
KAY CRES
WINDMILL DR
LING CRES

FAIRVIEW TERR
Beech Hill
THE KNOWLE
EDDEYS
LUDSHOTT GR
THE BOREEN
GRAYSHOTT RD
Fairlands

5
BEECH HILL RD
PO
SOUTHVIEW RD
WILSONS RD
FAIRVIEW RD
DOWNSVIEW RD
HOLLY CL
GLYN DR
FIRWAY
KILN WAY

B3002 FULLERS VALE
HEADLEY HILL RD
BEECH HILL
HONEYSUCKLE LA
KENLEY RD
CARLTON RD
Grays Farm

36
CHESTNUT END
Headley Down
OAKHILL RD
LINDEN RD
STONEHILL RD
WEST VIEW RD
ALMA RD
P
HEADLEY RD

Hilland Wood
POND RD
PRICE VALE RD
WITHERSLACK CL
SUNNYSIDE RD
SEYMOUR RD
B3002
4
STONEHILL RD
TELFORD CL
GORSELANDS CL
DEERLEAP
ROWANSIDE CL
BIRKENHOLME CL
FURZE HILL RD
STONEDENE CL
Greyshott Hall

HURLAND LA
GU26
3
Gentle's Copse
Ludshott Common

GENTLES LA
35

High Hurlands
Sheep Grove
2
GU30
The Chestnuts
North Lodge

The Frith
The Loampits
Summerden

Round Clump
Woolmer Farm
Ludshott Manor
Bramshott
Wakeners or Waggoners Wells
Kent's Hill
1

34

83 | A | B | 84 | C | D | 85 | E | F

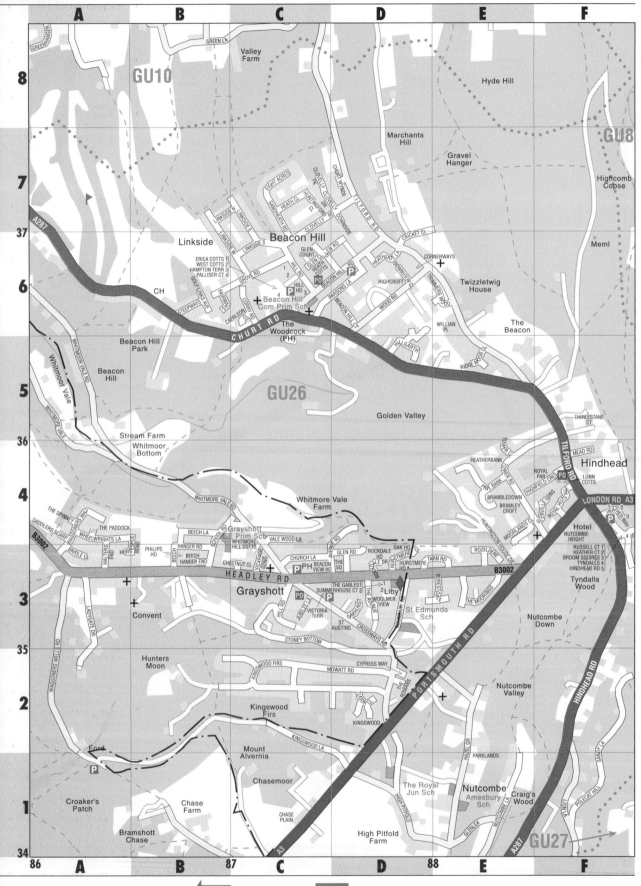

GU10

Valley
Farm

Hyde Hill

GU8

Highcomb
Copse

Marchants
Hill

Gravel
Hanger

Linkside

Beacon Hill

Meml

ERICA COTTS 1
WEST COTTS 2
HAMPTON TERR 3
PALLISER CT 4

CH

CORNERWAYS

Twizzletwig
House

GLEN
COURT

HIGHCROFT

CHURT RD

The
Woodcock
(PH)

Beacon Hill
Com Prim Sch

WOOD RD

WILLIAN
PL

The Beacon

Beacon Hill
Park

RIDGE MOOR CL

Beacon
Hill

GU26

Golden Valley

THIRLESTANE
CT

Whitmoor Vale

Stream Farm

Whitmoor
Bottom

MEAD RD

Hindhead

HEATHERBANK

Whitmore Vale
Farm

LONDON RD A3

The Spinney

The Paddock

Grayshott
CE Prim Sch

Whitmore
Hill Cotts

Vale Wood La

BRAMBLEDOWN

BRAMLEY
CROFT

MOORLANDS

Hotel
NUTCOMBE
HEIGHT

SADDLERS SCARP

WHEELWRIGHTS LA

BEECH LA

PHILIPS
HO

HANGER RD

SCHOOL RD

RUSSELL CT 1
HEATHER CT 2
BROOM SQUIRES 3
TYNDALLS 4
HINDHEAD RD 5

BEECH

BIRDLE CL

HALTERS
END

BEECH
HANGER END

CHESTNUT CL

CHURCH LA

PH

BEACON
VIEW HO

GLEN RD

THE
SQ

ROCKDALE
HO

OAK HO

ROZELDENE

HEADLEY RD

B3002

Tyndalls
Wood

Grayshott

THE GABLES 1
SUMMERHOUSE CT 2

Liby

HURSTMERE
HO

TARN RD

PORTSMOUTH RD

Nutcombe
Down

VICTORIA
TERR

WOOLMER
VIEW

St Edmunds
Sch

Convent

ST
AUSTINS

CROSSWAYS RD

Hunters
Moon

STONEY BOTTOM

Nutcombe
Valley

HINDHEAD RD

KINGSWOOD FIRS

MOWATT RD

CYPRESS WAY

Kingswood
Firs

Kingswood

KINGSWOOD LA

Ford

Mount
Alvernia

The Royal
Jun Sch

PARKLANDS

Nutcombe

Craig's
Wood

Chasemoor

Amesbury
Sch

Croaker's
Patch

Chase
Farm

CHASE
PLAIN

High Pitfold
Farm

GU27

Bramshott
Chase

A3

A287

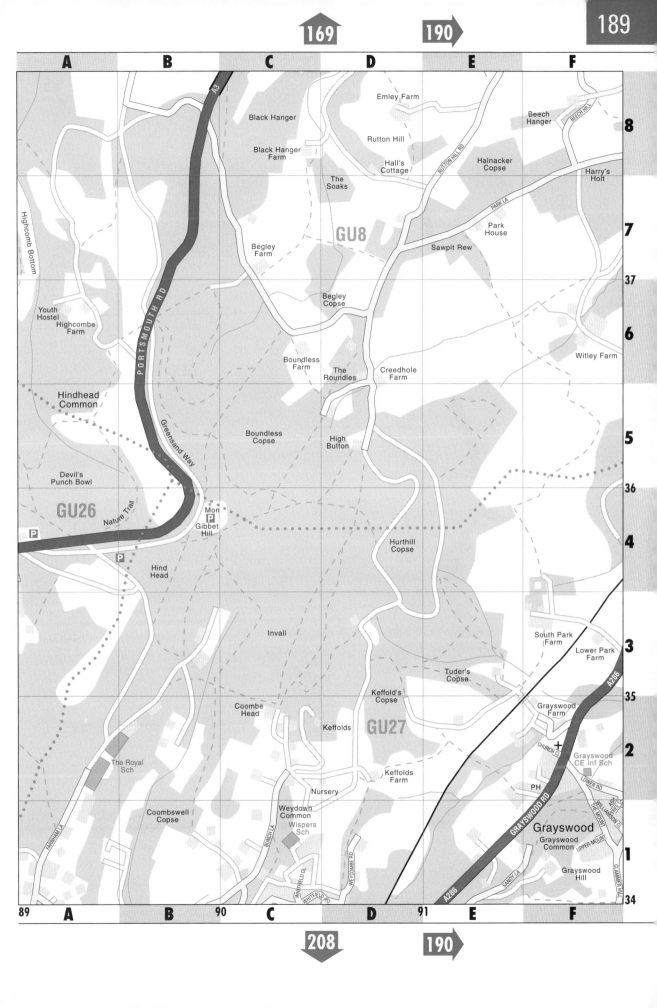

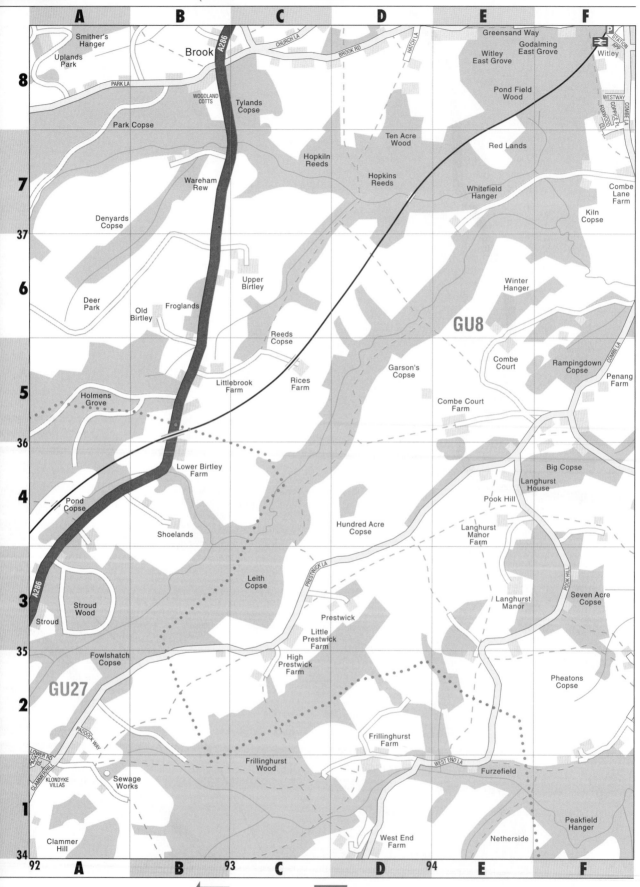

189
170

A B C D E F

8

7

37

6

5

36

4

3

35

2

1

34

Smither's Hanger

Uplands Park

Brook

A286

Church La

Brook Rd

Hatch La

Greensand Way

Witley East Grove

Godalming East Grove

Witley

Park La

Woodland Cotts

Tylands Copse

Westway

Coppice Pl

Foxwood Cl

Combe La

Park Copse

Pond Field Wood

Wareham Rew

Hopkiln Reeds

Ten Acre Wood

Red Lands

Combe Lane Farm

Denyards Copse

Hopkins Reeds

Whitefield Hanger

Kiln Copse

Deer Park

Old Birtley

Froglands

Upper Birtley

Winter Hanger

GU8

Reeds Copse

Littlebrook Farm

Rices Farm

Garson's Copse

Combe Court

Rampingdown Copse

Penang Farm

Combe La

Holmens Grove

Combe Court Farm

Big Copse

Langhurst House

Lower Birtley Farm

Pook Hill

Pond Copse

Shoelands

Hundred Acre Copse

Langhurst Manor Farm

Pook Hill

Seven Acre Copse

A286

Stroud Wood

Leith Copse

Prestwick La

Prestwick

Langhurst Manor

Stroud

Little Prestwick Farm

Fowlshatch Copse

High Prestwick Farm

Pheatons Copse

GU27

Paddock Way

Frillinghurst Farm

West End La

Furzefield

Lower Rd

Park Pl

Clammer Hill

Klondyke Villas

Sewage Works

Frillinghurst Wood

West End Farm

Netherside

Peakfield Hanger

Clammer Hill

92 A 93 B C 94 D E F

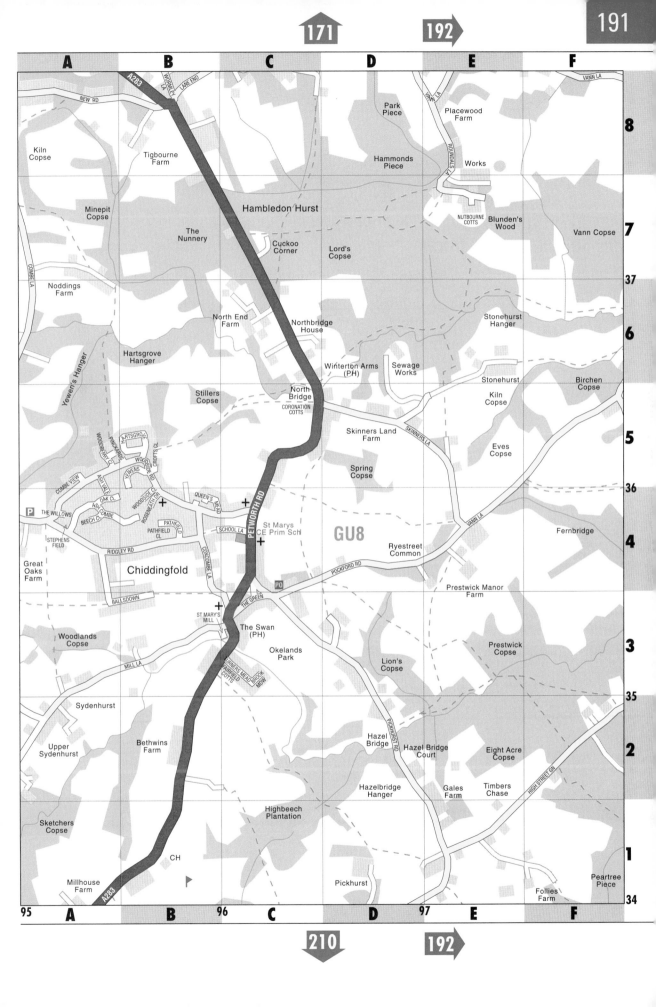

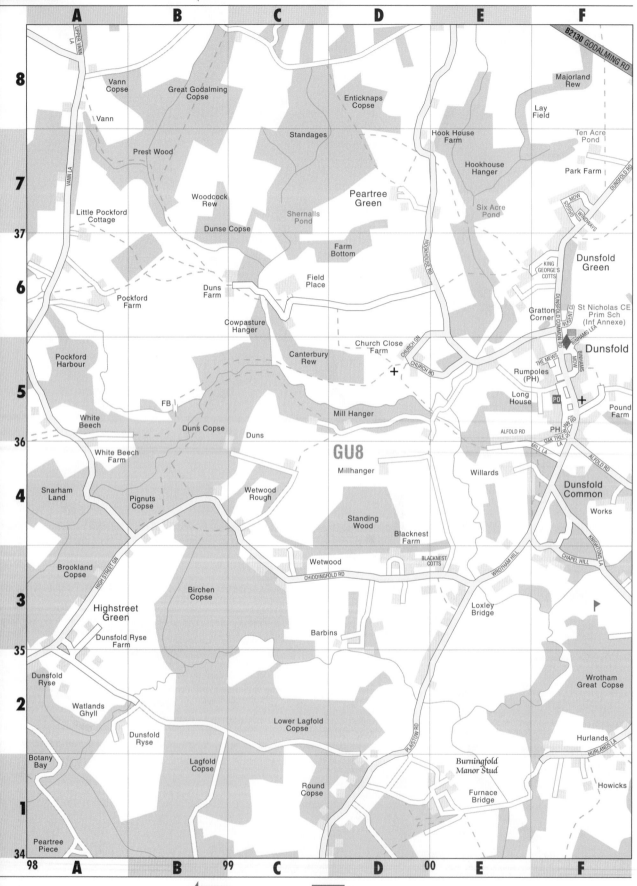

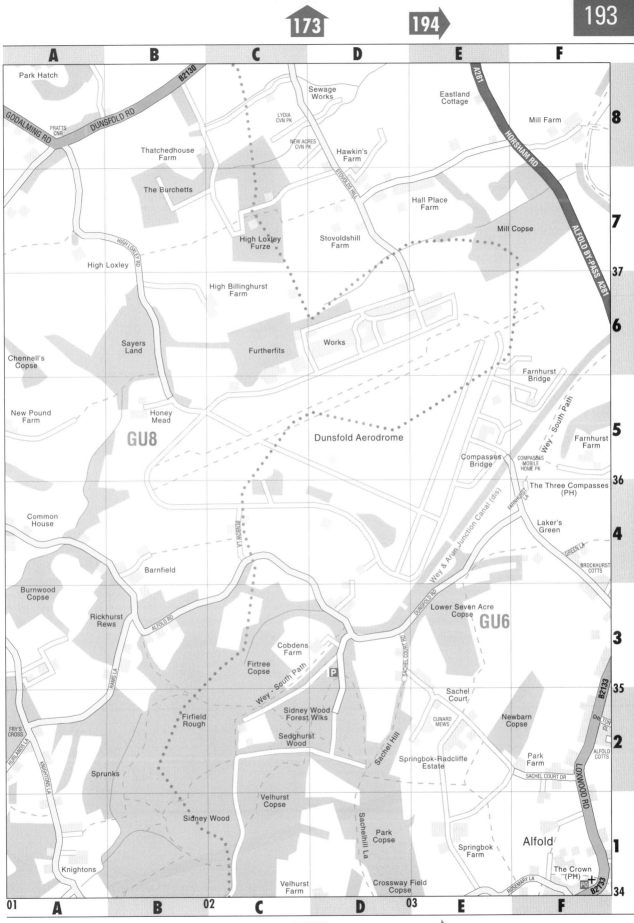

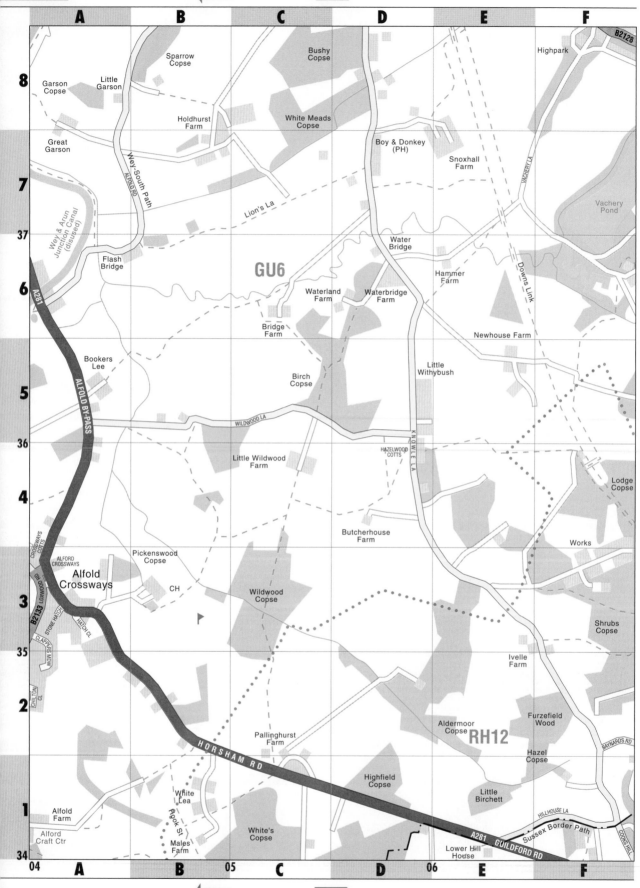

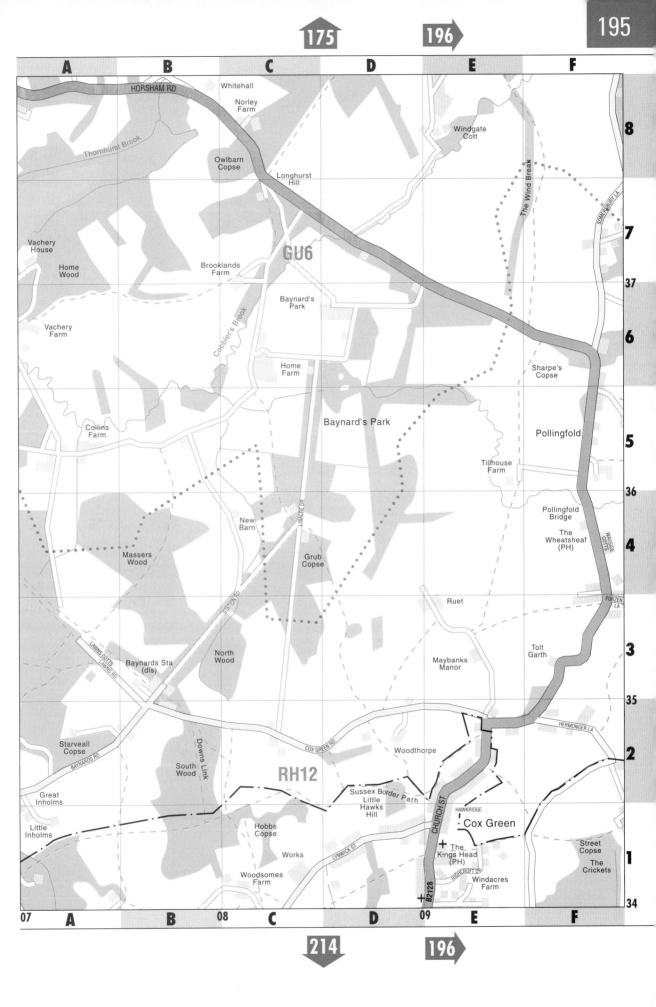

A B C D E F

8

GU6

Somersbury Wood

Abrahams

OAKFIELDS

Recn Gd

Chapel House

Rose Hill Farm

Oakwood Hill

HORSHAM RD

7

Nags Wood

Clay Pit

Works

Smokejack Farm

SMOKEJACK HILL

Wet Wood

37

Hillhouse Farm

RH5

6

Hoopwick Farm

Exfold Furze Field

Broadstone Farm

HONEYWOOD LA

Pound House

Pollingfold Copse

Pink Hurst

Pinkhurst Farm

MONKS MANOR

MONKS LA

5

Sansomes Copse

Honeybush Farm

36

Furzen Cottage

HORSHAM RD

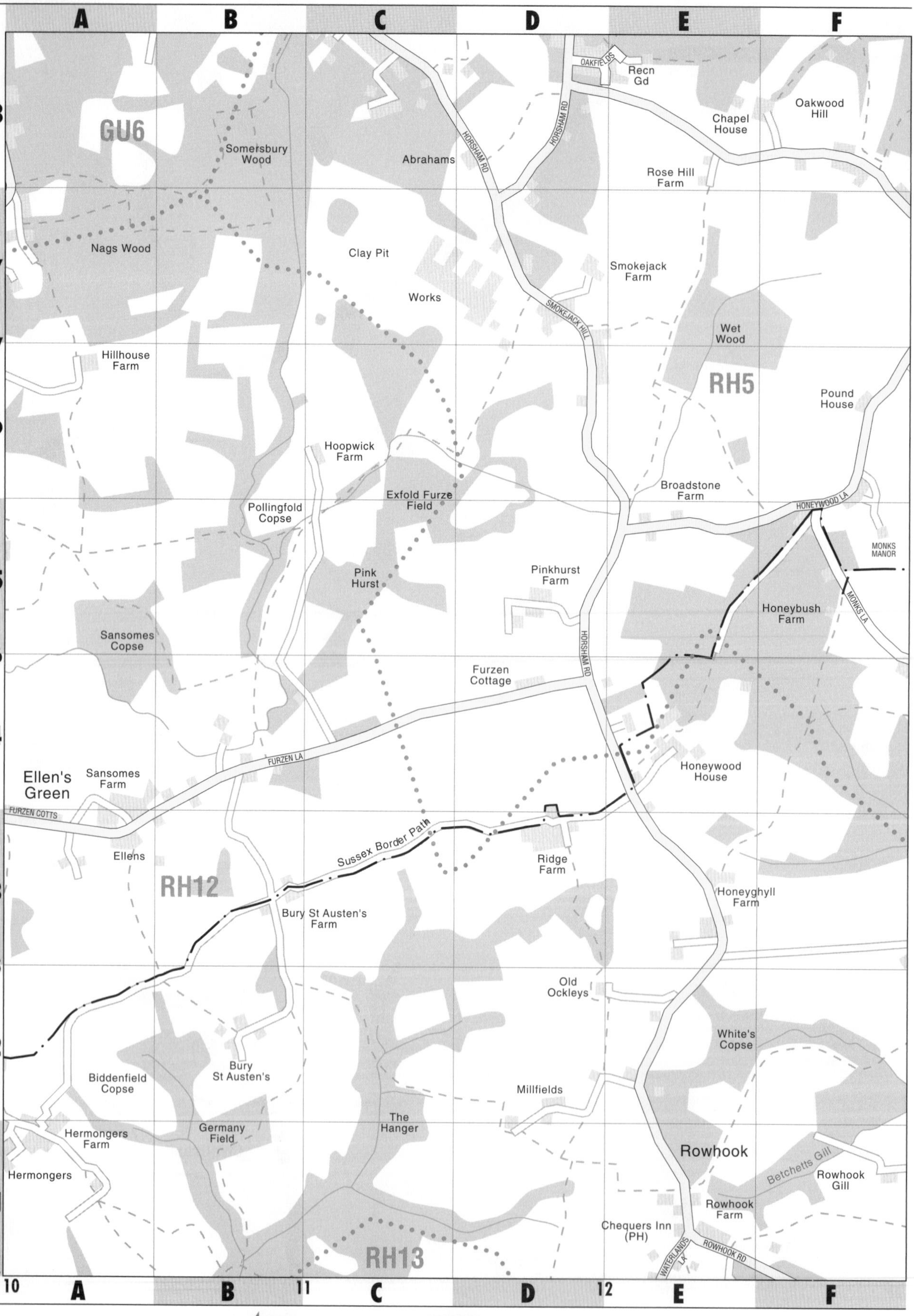

4

FURZEN LA

Honeywood House

Ellen's Green

Sansomes Farm

FURZEN COTTS

Ellens

Sussex Border Path

Ridge Farm

Honeyghyll Farm

RH12

Bury St Austen's Farm

3

35

Old Ockleys

White's Copse

2

Biddenfield Copse

Bury St Austen's

Millfields

The Hanger

Rowhook

Germany Field

Betchetts Gill

Rowhook Gill

Hermongers Farm

Rowhook Farm

Hermongers

1

Chequers Inn (PH)

WATERLANDS LA

ROWHOOK RD

34

RH13

10 A B 11 C D 12 E F

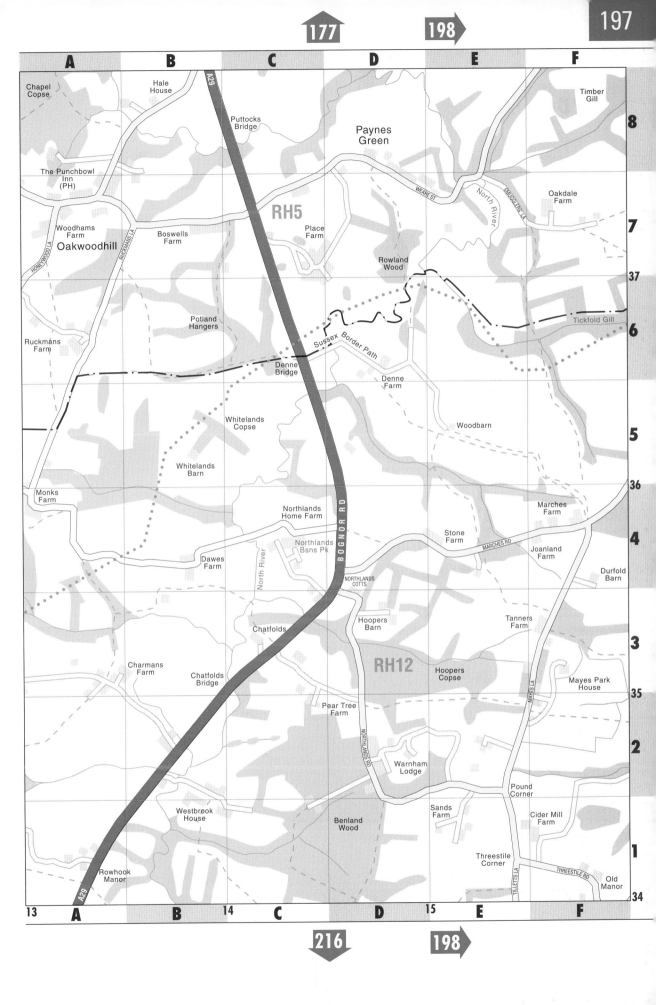

197
178

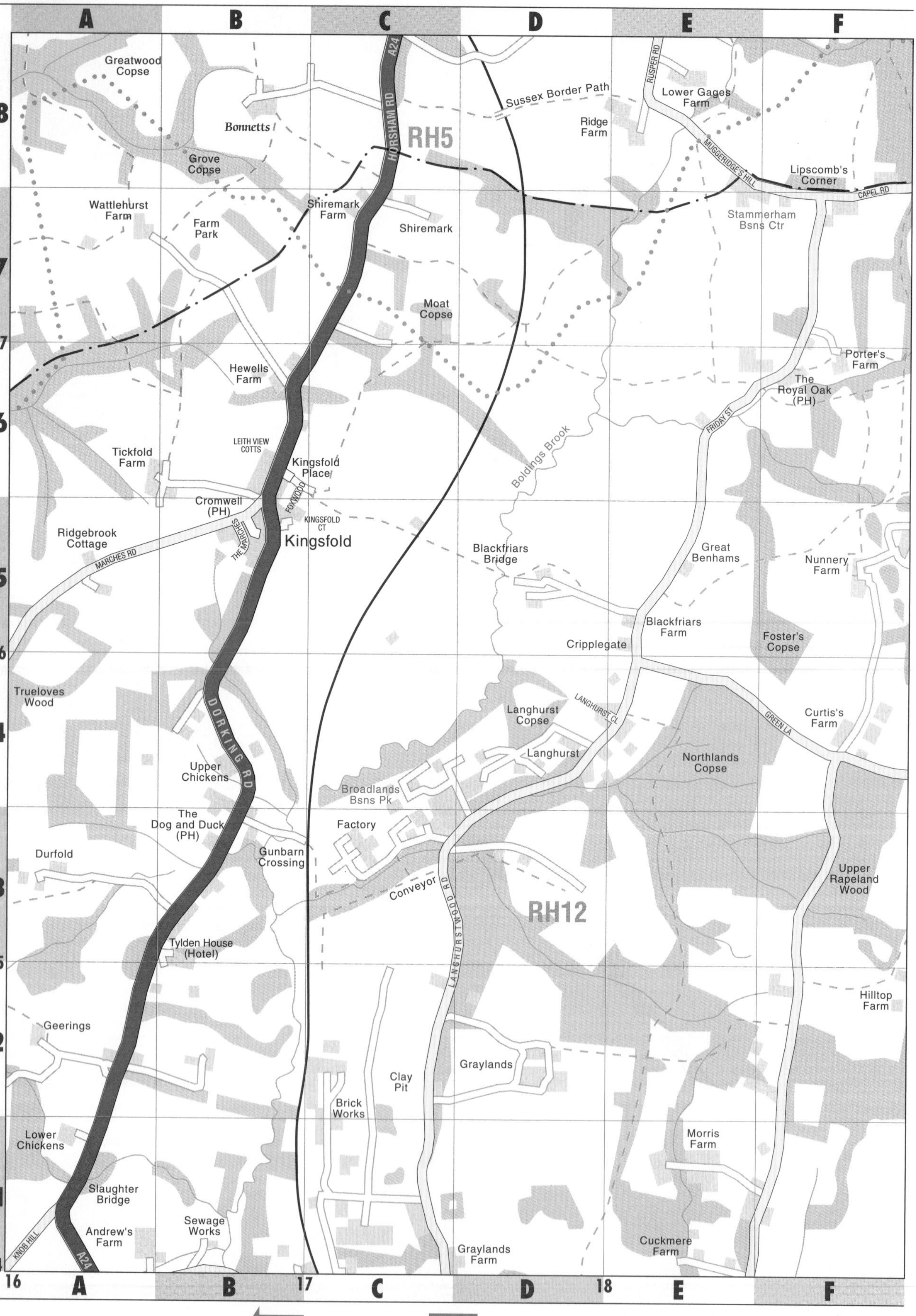

A **B** **C** **D** **E** **F**

8

Greatwood Copse

Bonnetts

Grove Copse

RH5

Sussex Border Path

Lower Gages Farm

Ridge Farm

Lipscomb's Corner

CAPEL RD

Wattlehurst Farm

Farm Park

Shiremark Farm

Shiremark

Stammerham Bsns Ctr

7

HORSHAM RD

RUSPER RD

MUGGERIDGE'S HILL

37

Hewells Farm

Moat Copse

Porter's Farm

The Royal Oak (PH)

6

LEITH VIEW COTTS

Tickfold Farm

Kingsfold Place

Boldings Brook

FRIDAY ST

Cromwell (PH)

KINGSFOLD CT

Kingsfold

Blackfriars Bridge

Great Benhams

Nunnery Farm

Ridgebrook Cottage

FOXHOLD

THE MARCHES

5

MARCHES RD

Blackfriars Farm

Foster's Copse

36

Cripplegate

Trueloves Wood

DORKING RD

LANGHURST CL

Curtis's Farm

GREEN LA

4

Upper Chickens

Langhurst Copse

Langhurst

Northlands Copse

Broadlands Bsns Pk

The Dog and Duck (PH)

Factory

Upper Rapeland Wood

3

Durfold

Gunbarn Crossing

Conveyor

RH12

LANGHURSTWOOD RD

Tylden House (Hotel)

35

Hilltop Farm

2

Geerings

Clay Pit

Graylands

Morris Farm

Brick Works

Lower Chickens

1

Slaughter Bridge

Sewage Works

Graylands Farm

Cuckmere Farm

KNOB HILL

34

Andrew's Farm

A24

16 **A** **B** **17** **C** **D** **18** **E** **F**

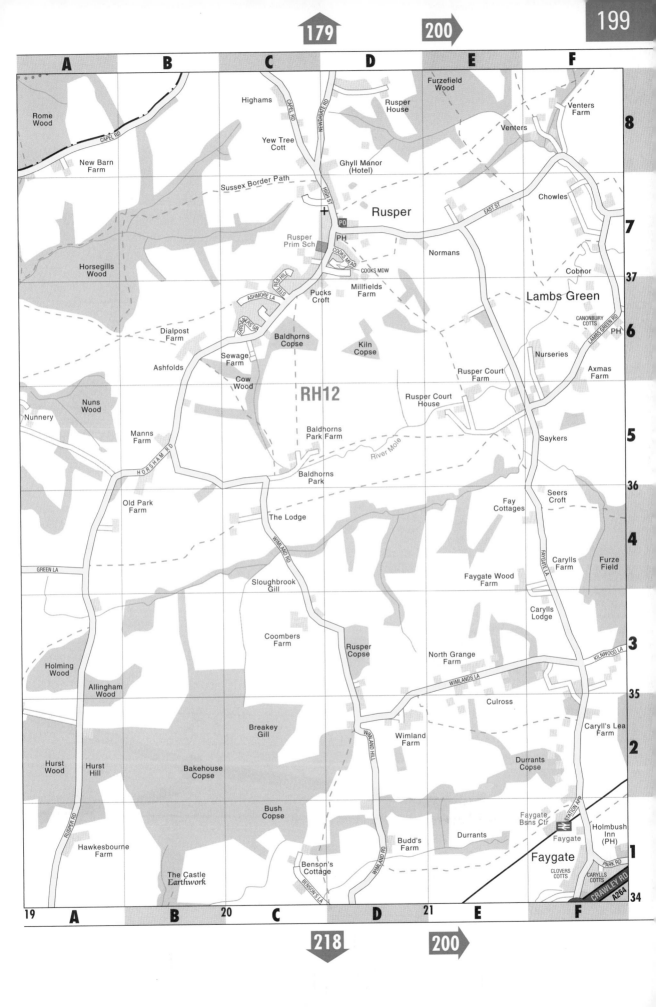

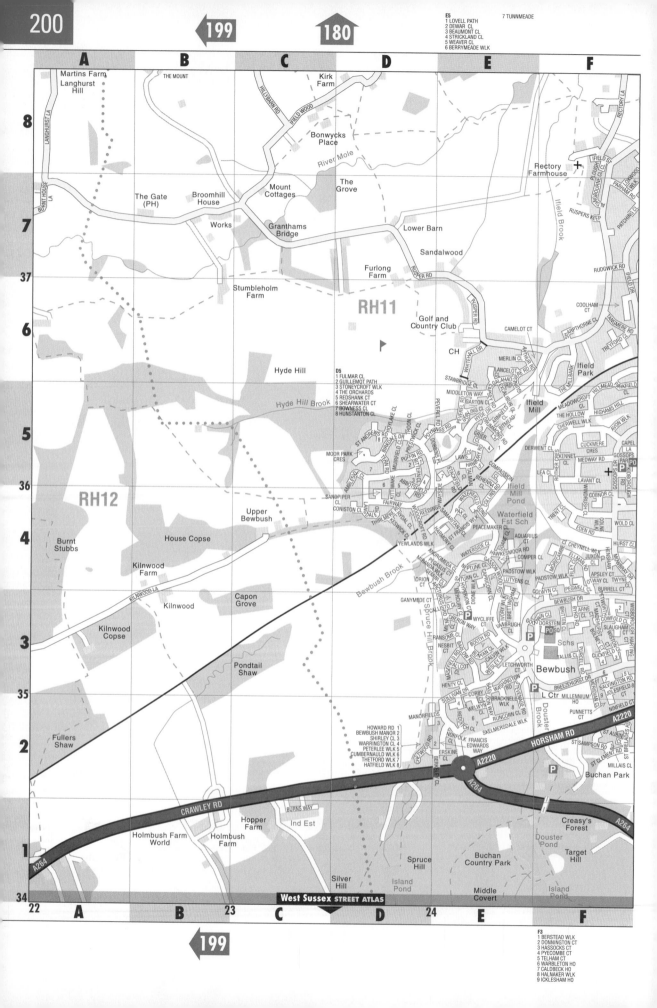

E5
1 LOVELL PATH
2 DEWAR CL
3 BEAUMONT CL
4 STRICKLAND CL
5 WEAVER CL
6 BERRYMEADE WLK

7 TUNNMEADE

D5
1 FULMAR CL
2 GUILLEMOT PATH
3 STONEYCROFT WLK
4 THE ORCHARDS
5 REDSHANK CT
6 SHEARWATER CT
7 BOWNESS CL
8 HUNSTANTON CL

HOWARD RD 1
BEWBUSH MANOR 2
SHIRLEY CL 3
WARRINGTON CL 4
PETERLEE WLK 5
CUMBERNAULD WLK 6
THETFORD WLK 7
HATFIELD WLK 8

F3
1 BERSTEAD WLK
2 DONNINGTON CT
3 HASSOCKS CT
4 PYECOMBE CT
5 TELHAM CT
6 WARBLETON HO
7 CALDBECK HO
8 HALNAKER WLK
9 ICKLESHAM HO

181 →

D5
1 THE COURTYARD
2 WALSTEAD HO
3 RAVENDENE CT
4 WILLOWFIELD
5 ASHWOOD
6 PARISH HO

202 →

7 PERRYFIELD HO
8 HANDSWORTH HO
9 GLENDON HO
10 ALEXANDRA CT

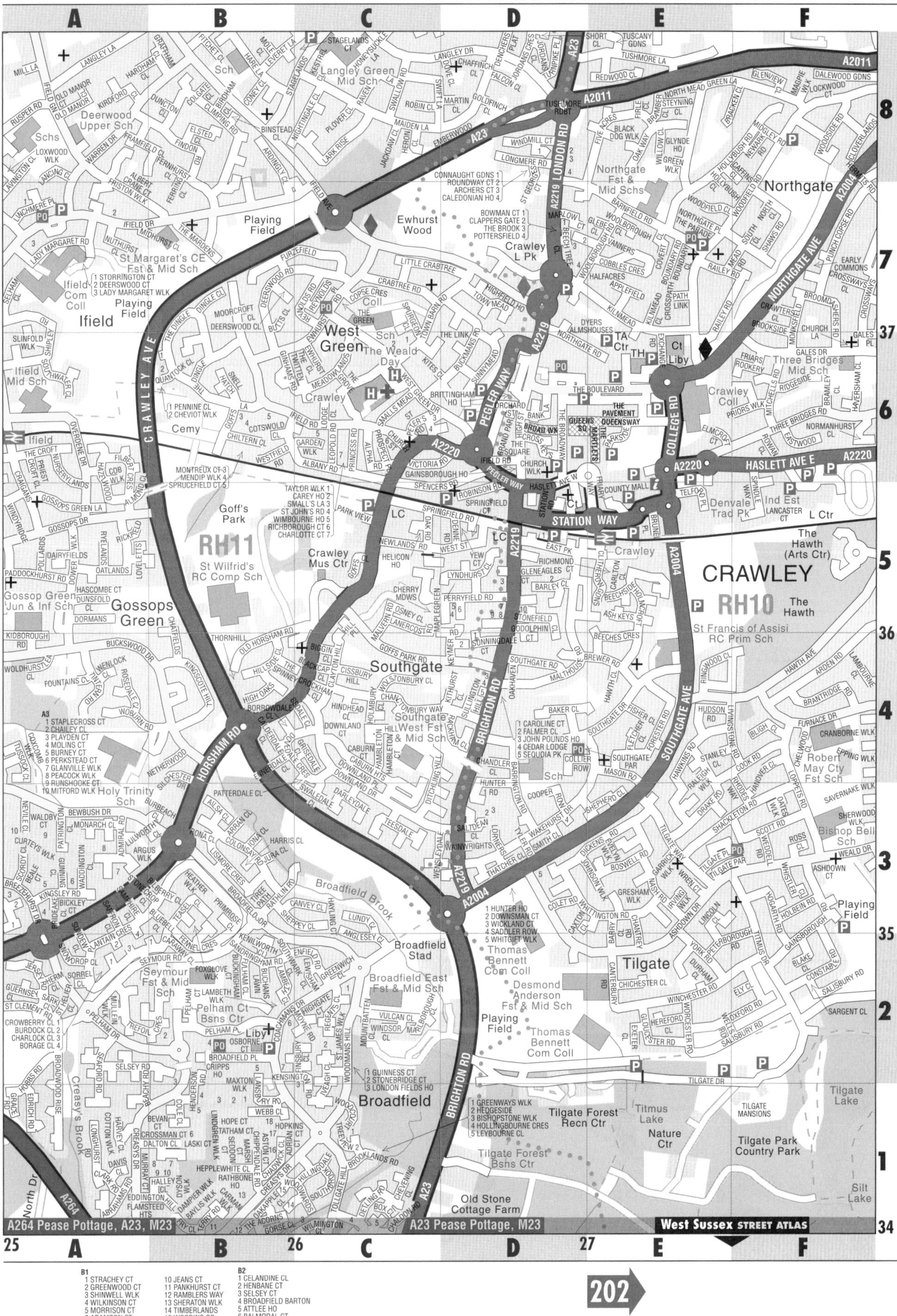

201

A | B | C | D | E | F

8

MILL LA
LANGLEY LA
Deerwood Upper Sch
Schs
LOXWOOD WLK
WARREN CT

STAGELANDS CT
Langley Green Mid Sch
LANGLEY DR

A2011
A2011

TUSHMORE LA
TUSHMORE RDBT
A2011
Northgate
NORTHGATE AVE
A2004

7

PO
St Margaret's CE Fst & Mid Sch
1 STORRINGTON CT
2 DEERSWOOD CT
3 LADY MARGARET WLK
Playing Field
Ifield Com Coll
Ifield
Playing Field

Ewhurst Wood
Crawley L Pk

Northgate Fst & Mid Schs
The Parade

37

Ifield Mid Sch
West Green
The Weald Day
H
Crawley
Cemy
1 PENNINE CL
2 CHEVIOT WLK

Coll
The Green
TOWN MEAD
NORTHGATE RD
PO TA Ctr
TH
DYERS ALMSHOUSES

Ct Liby
Crawley Coll
Three Bridges Mid Sch
GALES DR
CHURCH

6

Ifield
THE CROFT
PRIEST WLK
CRAWLEY AVE
Crawley
1 MONTREUX CT
3 MENDIP WLK
5 SPRUCEFIELD CT
PEGLER WAY
A2220
BROAD WLK
QUEENS SQ
THE PAVEMENT
QUEENSWAY
A2220
HASLETT AVE E
A2201
Three Bridges
NORMANHURST

GOSSOPS GREEN LA
Goff's Park
RH11
St Wilfrid's RC Comp Sch
Crawley Mus Ctr
1 TAYLOR WLK
2 CAREY HO
3 ST JOHN'S LA
4 WIMBOURNE HO
5 RICHBOROUGH CT
6 CHARLOTTE CT
PARK VIEW
SPENCERS RD
GAINSBOROUGH HO
ROBINSON CT
VICTORIA RD
SPRINGFIELD RD
LC
STATION WAY
Crawley
A2004
The Hawth (Arts Ctr)

5

Gossop Green Jun & Inf Sch
Gossops Green
HASCOMBE CT
DUNSFOLD CT
THORNHILL
CHERRY MDWS
PERRYFIELD RD
GLENEAGLES
LYNDHURST
HELICON HO
STONEFIELD
GODOLPHIN
LC
A2219
RICHMOND
BARLEY CL
CRAWLEY
RH10
The Hawth
St Francis of Assisi RC Prim Sch

36

KIDBOROUGH
WOLDHURST LEA
FOUNTAINS CL
BUCKSWOOD DR
OLD HORSHAM RD
BISGIN
CLAPTON HILL
CISSBURY
Southgate
WOLSTONBURY CL
SOUTHGATE RD
Southgate Fst & Mid Sch
BEECHES CRES
St

4

A3
1 STAPLECROSS CT
2 CHAILEY CL
3 PLAYDEN CT
4 MOLINS CT
5 BURNEY CT
6 PERKSTEAD CT
7 GLANVILLE WLK
8 PEACOCK WLK
9 HOOKE CT
10 MITFORD WLK
Holy Trinity Sch
HORSHAM RD
NETHERWOOD
HIGH OAKS
BORROWDALE
PATTERDALE CL
HINDHEAD
DOWNLAND
CABURN CL
DOWNLAND DR
DARLEYDALE
TEESDALE
CONYBURY WAY
Southgate West Fst & Mid Sch
SOUTHGATE DR
CHANDLER
HUNTER
COOPER
1 CAROLINE CT
2 FALMER CL
3 JOHN POUNDS HO
4 CEDAR LODGE
5 SEQUOIA DR
COLLIER ROW
MASON RD
SOUTHGATE PAR
HAWKINS RD
Robert May Cty Fst Sch
CRANBORNE WLK
FURNACE DR
EPPING WLK

3

WALDBY CT
BEWBUSH DR
KINGSLEY RD
BICKLEY
ARGUS WLK
LISMORE CRES
HARRIS CL
WENTS FIELD
WAINWRIGHTS
Broadfield Brook
A2219
A2004
1 HUNTER HO
2 DOWNSMAN CT
3 WICKLAND CT
4 SADDLER ROW
5 WHITGIFT WLK
Thomas Bennett Com Coll
GRESHAM WLK
IRVING WLK
BOSWELL RD
TILGATE PL
Playing Field
Bishop Bell Sch
WEALD DR
ASHDOWN CT

35

Seymour Fst & Mid Sch
FOXGLOVE WLK
Pelham Ct Bsns Ctr
Broadfield Stad
Broadfield East Fst & Mid Sch
Desmond Anderson Fst & Mid Sch
Tilgate
CHICHESTER CL
Thomas Bennett Com Coll

2

CROWBERRY CL
1 BURDOCK CL
2 CHARLOCK CL
3 BORAGE CL
Liby
PO
BROADFIELD PL
1 GUINNESS CT
2 STONEBRIDGE CT
3 LONDON FIELDS HO
Broadfield
Playing Field
SALISBURY RD
SARGENT CL
P

1

North Dr
A264
Creasy's Brook
1 GREENWAYS WLK
2 HEDGESIDE
3 BISHOPSTONE WLK
4 HOLLINGBOURNE CRES
5 LEYBOURNE CL
Tilgate Forest Recn Ctr
Titmus Lake
Nature Ctr
Tilgate Park Country Park
Tilgate Lake
Silt Lake

Old Stone Cottage Farm
Tilgate Forest Bshs Ctr

34

B1
1 STRACHEY CT
2 GREENWOOD CT
3 SHINWELL WLK
4 WILKINSON CT
5 MORRISON CT
6 ADAMSON CT
7 KEIR HARDIE HO
8 SILKIN WLK
9 HERSCHEL WLK
10 JEANS CT
11 PANKHURST CT
12 RAMBLERS WAY
13 SHERATON WLK
14 TIMBERLANDS
15 WOODING GR
16 THOMPSON CT
17 RICHARDSON CT
18 RAMSEY CT

B2
1 CELANDINE CL
2 HENBANE CT
3 SELSEY CT
4 BROADFIELD BARTON
5 ATTLEE HO
6 BALMORAL CT
7 ISLINGTON HO

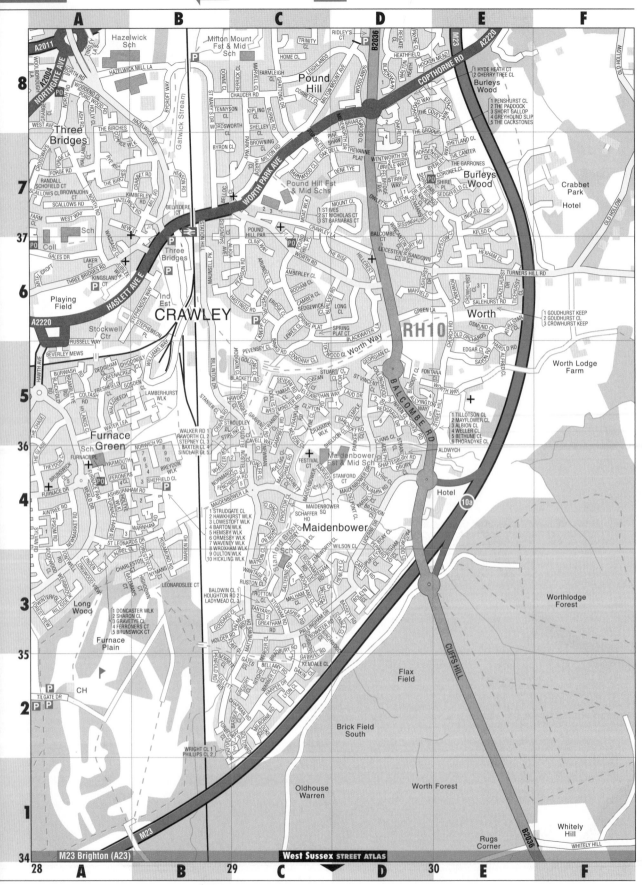

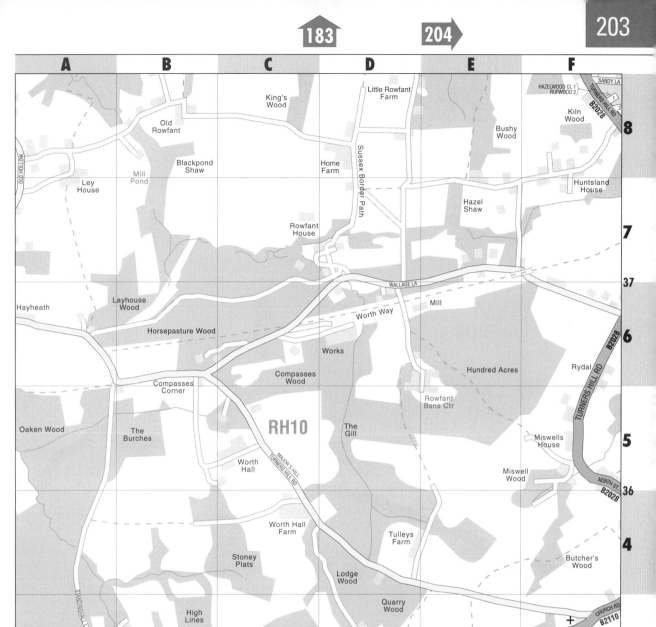

A B C D E F

SANDY LA

HAZELWOOD CL 1
RUFWOOD 2

TURNERS HILL RD

B2028

8

Little Rowfant
Farm

King's
Wood

Kiln
Wood

Old Hollow

Old
Rowfant

Home
Farm

Bushy
Wood

Ley
House

Blackpond
Shaw

Mill
Pond

Sussex Border Path

Huntsland
House

Hazel
Shaw

7

Rowfant
House

37

Hayheath

Layhouse
Wood

WALLAGE LA

Mill

Worth Way

Horsepasture Wood

Works

Hundred Acres

B2028

Rydal

TURNERS HILL RD

6

Compasses
Corner

Compasses
Wood

Rowfant
Bsns Ctr

Miswells
House

Oaken Wood

RH10

The
Burches

The
Gill

Miswell
Wood

NORTH ST
B2028

5

Worth
Hall

MAJOR'S HILL
TURNERS HILL RD

36

Worth Hall
Farm

Tulleys
Farm

Butcher's
Wood

Stoney
Plats

STANDINGHALL LA

Lodge
Wood

4

High
Lines

Quarry
Wood

CHURCH RD
B2110

Standinghall
Farm

Grove
Farm

3

The
Grove

35

Coldharbour
Farm

Rough
Wood

Grove
Farmhouse

Threepoint Gill

Brickkiln
Wood

PADDOCKHURST RD

South Hill

2

Bulls
Copse

MOUNT
NODDY

STONE
COTTS

BACK LA

Grove
Wood

Threepoint
Wood

Worth Sch

Worth
Abbey

RH17

1

B2110

34

West Sussex STREET ATLAS

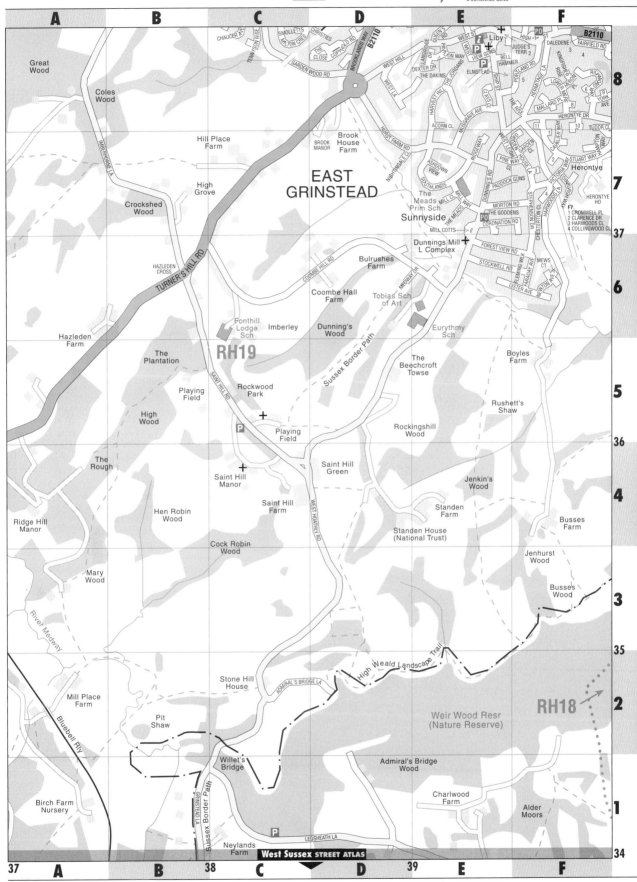

F8
1 MIDDLE ROW
2 FOREST LODGE
3 SACKVILLE CT
4 GREAT HOUSE CT
5 PORTLAND HOUSE
6 CORNWALL GDNS

7 NORMANDY CL
8 WILLOW MEAD
9 KINGS COPSE
10 REGAL DR
11 BECKETT WAY

Great Wood

Coles Wood

Crockshed Wood

Hill Place Farm

High Grove

Brook Manor

Brook House Farm

EAST GRINSTEAD

CHAUCER AVE
MILTON CRES
SMOLLETTS
THE CLOSE
CHRISTIES
COPPTHORNE RD
B2110
GARDEN WOOD RD
TENNYSON RISE
WEST HILL
WEST LA
HURST FARM RD
NIGHTINGALE CL
BROOKLANDS WAY

PO
B2110
DALEDENE
FAIRFIELD RD
Liby
WEST ST
HIGH ST
WEST HILL
DICKEN'S CL
HARVEST HILL
LANGRIDGE
MUSGRAVE AVE
ASHDOWN VIEW
ACORN CL
DEXTER DR
THE DAKINS
LDN WAY
THE JORDANS
JUDGE'S TERR
BELL HAMMER
ELMSTEAD
VIEW GDNS
SHIP ST
CLASS CL
PORTLAND RD
HERMITAGE LA
KINGFISHER RISE
CAVALIER WAY
LOWER MERE
HERON
MALLARD PL
YORK AVE
TUDOR CL
HERONTYE DR

RIDGEWAY
PINE WAY CL
DUNNING'S RD
WEST LEIGH
PADDOCK GDNS
GARDEN WOOD
VICTORIA WAY
STUART WAY
Herontye
HERONTYE HO

The Meads Prim Sch
Sunnyside
SOUTHLANDS
MILL WAY
MORTON RD
STEPHENSON DR
THE GODDENS
CORONATION RD
HARDOCKS CL
COLLINGWOOD CL
CHESTERTON DR

The Meads
MILL LA
THE MEADS
PO
MILL COTTS

Dunnings Mill L Complex
FOREST VIEW RD
FLEMING WLK
FARADAY AVE
LISTER AVE
STOCKWELL RD
MEWS CT
MEWTOWN CL

F7
1 CROMWELL PL
2 CLARENCE DR
3 HARWOODS CL
4 COLLINGWOOD CL

Bulrushes Farm

Coombe Hall Farm

COOMBE HILL RD

Tobias Sch of Art

MEDWAY DR

Eurythmy Sch

Hazleden Cross

TURNER'S HILL RD

Hazleden Farm

The Plantation

Fonthill Lodge Sch

Imberley

Dunning's Wood

Sussex Border Path

The Beechcroft Towse

Boyles Farm

RH19

Rockwood Park

Playing Field

High Wood

SAINT HILL RD

Rushett's Shaw

Rockingshill Wood

The Rough

Playing Field

Saint Hill Green

Jenkin's Wood

Saint Hill Manor

Saint Hill Farm

Hen Robin Wood

WEST HOATHLY RD

Standen Farm

Standen House (National Trust)

Busses Farm

Cock Robin Wood

Jenhurst Wood

Mary Wood

Ridge Hill Manor

Busses Wood

River Medway

High Weald Landscape Trail

RH18

Mill Place Farm

Bluebell Rly

Stone Hill House

ADMIRAL'S BRIDGE LA

Weir Wood Resr (Nature Reserve)

Pit Shaw

Willet's Bridge

Admiral's Bridge Wood

GRINSTEAD LA

Sussex Border Path

Charlwood Farm

Alder Moors

Birch Farm Nursery

Neylands Farm

LEGSHEATH LA

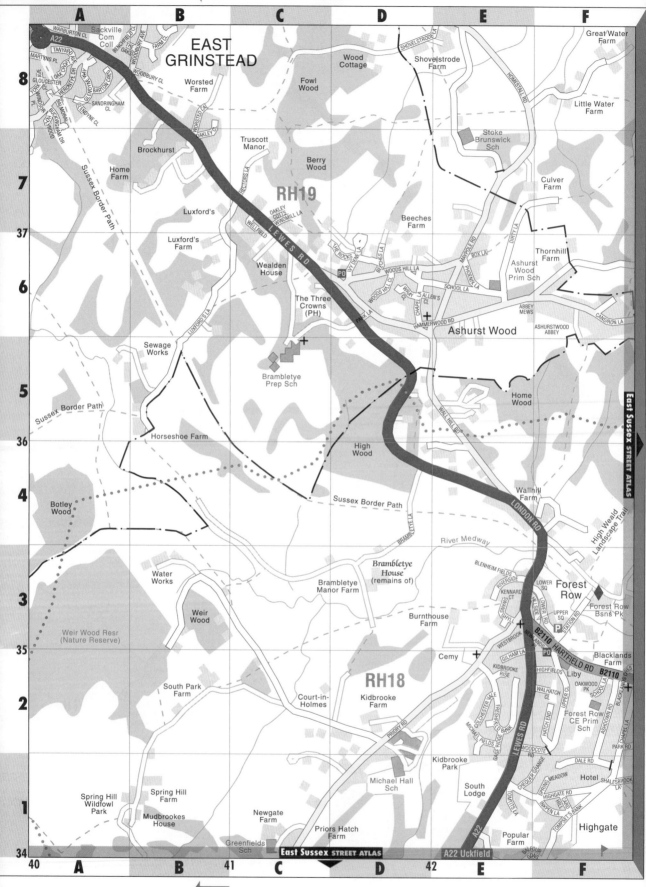

A B C D E F

8

7

37

6

5

36

4

3

35

2

1

34

40 A B 41 C D 42 E F

EAST GRINSTEAD

Sackville Com Coll

WARBURTON CL
A22
MARTYNS PL
TANYARD
AVE
GLOUCESTER
YORK
WINDSOR
PL
BALMORAL
BUCKINGHAM DR
GLENDYNE CL
HEDGERCROFT AVE
OAKCROFT AVE
WOODBURY AVE
FARM CL
THE OAKLEYS
BENCHFIELD CL
SANDRINGHAM CL
BARTON CL
WOODBURY CL

Worsted Farm

Brockhurst

WORSTED LA
OAKLEY
HECTORS LA

Truscott Manor

Fowl Wood

Wood Cottage

Shovelstrode Farm

SHOVELSTRODE LA

Great Water Farm

Little Water Farm

Home Farm

Luxford's

Luxford's Farm

Berry Wood

RH19

Beeches Farm

Stoke Brunswick Sch

Culver Farm

Sussex Border Path

LEWES RD
OAKLEY COTTS
WINDMILL LA
WELLFIELD

Wealden House

The Rocks
IVYDENE LA
PO
WOODS HILL LA
BEECHES LA
MAYPOLE RD
BOX LA
DIRTY LA

Thornhill Farm

Ashurst Wood Prim Sch

The Three Crowns (PH)

PARK LA

WOODS HILL LA
CHAPEL LA
WAY
ALLEN'S CL
PHOENIX LA
SCHOOL LA

ABBEY MEWS

Sewage Works

Brambletye Prep Sch

HAMMERWOOD RD

Ashurst Wood

ASHURSTWOOD ABBEY

CANSIRON LA

Horseshoe Farm

LUXFORD'S LA

High Wood

WALL HILL RD

Home Wood

Sussex Border Path

Botley Wood

Sussex Border Path

BRAMBLETYE LA

River Medway

Wallhill Farm

LONDON RD

High Weald Landscape Trail

Water Works

Weir Wood

Brambletye Manor Farm

Brambletye House (remains of)

BLENHEIM FIELDS

RIVERSIDE

LOWER SQ

Forest Row

Forest Row Bsns Pk

Weir Wood Resr (Nature Reserve)

Burnthouse Farm

KENNARD CT
SWANS GHYLL
LOWER RD
UPPER SQ
STATION RD
P
B2110 HARTFIELD RD
PO
B2110

Blacklands Farm

Liby

Cemy

WESTBROOK
NEWLANDS
GILHAM LA
HIGHFIELDS
KIDBROOKE RISE

OAKWOOD PK
ASHDOWN RD
CHAPEL LA
BLACKLANDS DR
PARK RD

South Park Farm

Court-in-Holmes

PRIORY RD

Kidbrooke Farm

RH18

COLCHESTER VALE
FRESHFIELD BANK
MICHAEL FIELDS
GAGE RIDGE
WALHATCH CL
UPPER RD
HATCH END

Forest Row CE Prim Sch

LEWES RD
WOODCOTE RD
CHEQUERS GRANGE
SPRING MEADOW
HIGHGATE RD
CARD
IMPEN LA
DALE RD

Hotel

SHALESBROOK LA

Spring Hill Wildfowl Park

Spring Hill Farm

Mudbrookes House

Newgate Farm

Priors Hatch Farm

Michael Hall Sch

Kidbrooke Park

South Lodge

A22

TOMSETT'S BANK
BALFOUR GDNS

Popular Farm

Highgate

Greenfields Sch

East Sussex STREET ATLAS

A22 Uckfield

East Sussex STREET ATLAS

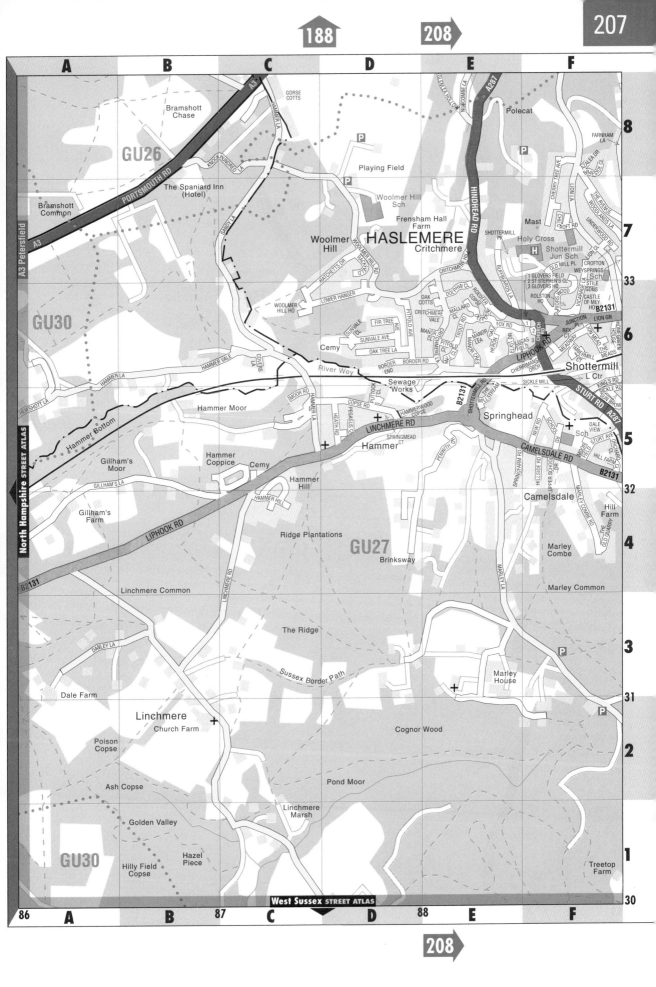

North Hampshire STREET ATLAS

A B C D E F

8
7
33
6
5
32
4
3
31
2
1
30

GU26
GU30
GU27
GU30

Bramshott Chase
Gorse Cotts
The Spaniard Inn (Hotel)
Bramshott Common
Playing Field
Woolmer Hill Sch
Frensham Hall Farm
Woolmer Hill
HASLEMERE
Critchmere
Polecat
FARNHAM LA
Mast
Holy Cross
Shottermill Pk
Shottermill Jun Sch
1 GLOVERS FIELD
2 ST STEPHEN'S CL
3 GLOVERS HO
Woolmer Hill HO
Lower Hanger
Cemy
Oak Cotts
Critchmere Vale
Manor Lea
River Wey
Border End
Border Rd
Sewage Works
Shottermill
L Ctr
Springhead
Sickle Mill
Hammer Moor
Hammer Coppice
Cemy
Hammer Hill
LINCHMERE RD
Hammer
Springmead Ct
Sch
Dale View
Camelsdale
CAMELSDALE RD
Gillham's Moor
GILLHAM'S LA
Gillham's Farm
LIPHOOK RD
Hammer Bottom
HAMMER LA
Marley Combe
Marley Common
Hill Farm
Ridge Plantations
GU27
Brinksway
Linchmere Common
DANLEY LA
The Ridge
Marley House
Dale Farm
Sussex Border Path
Linchmere
Church Farm
Cognor Wood
Poison Copse
Ash Copse
Pond Moor
Linchmere Marsh
Golden Valley
Hazel Piece
Hilly Field Copse
Treetop Farm

A3 Petersfield
PORTSMOUTH RD
KNOCK HUNDRED LA
HAMMER LA
SANDY LA
WOOLMER HILL RD
HATCHETTS DR
BLACK RD
HINDHEAD RD
A287
B2131
STURT RD
LINCHMERE RD
B2131

86 87 88

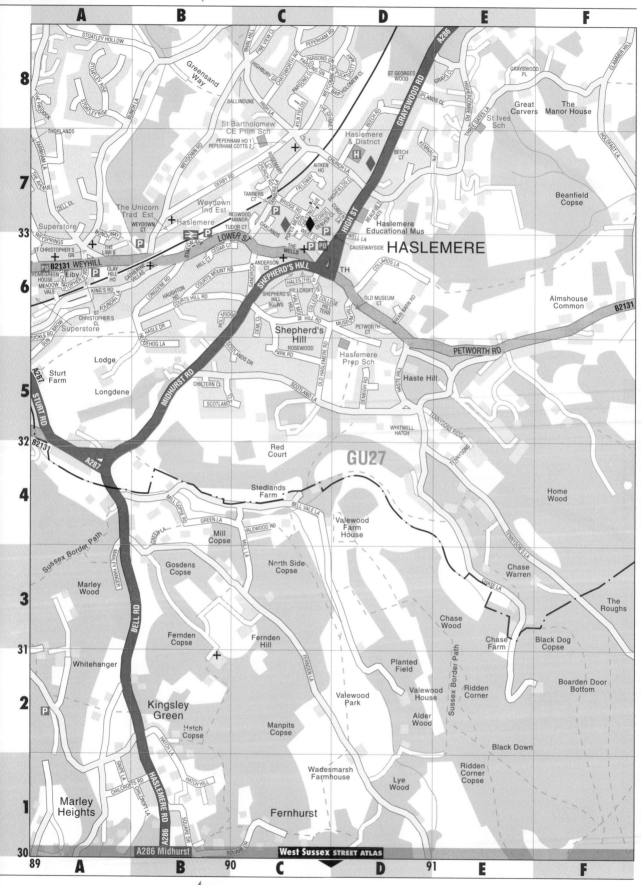

207
189

HASLEMERE

GU27

207

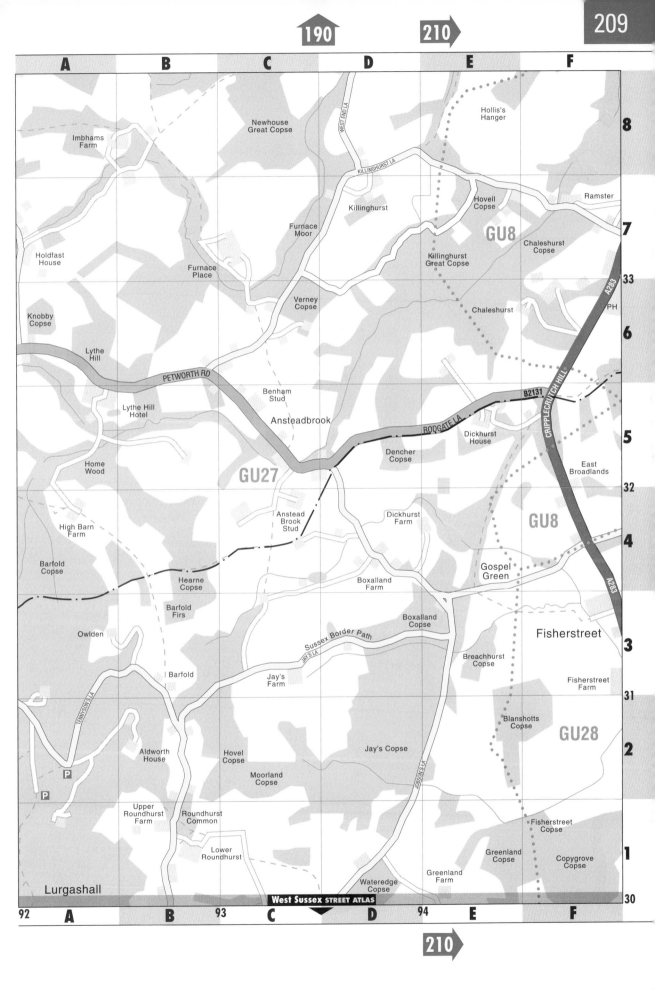

8

7

33

6

32

5

4

31

3

2

1

30

Imbhams Farm

Newhouse Great Copse

WEST END LA

Hollis's Hanger

KILLINGHURST LA

Killinghurst

Ramster

Hovell Copse

GU8

Chaleshurst Copse

Holdfast House

Furnace Moor

Killinghurst Great Copse

Furnace Place

Chaleshurst

A283

PH

Knobby Copse

Verney Copse

Lythe Hill

PETWORTH RD

Benham Stud

B2131

CRIPPLECRUTCH HILL

Lythe Hill Hotel

Ansteadbrook

RODGATE LA

Dickhurst House

East Broadlands

Home Wood

GU27

Dencher Copse

GU8

Anstead Brook Stud

Dickhurst Farm

High Barn Farm

Gospel Green

Barfold Copse

Hearne Copse

Boxalland Farm

Fisherstreet

A283

Barfold Firs

Boxalland Copse

Owlden

Sussex Border Path

JAY'S LA

Breachhurst Copse

Fisherstreet Farm

Barfold

Jay's Farm

TENNYSON'S LA

Blanshotts Copse

GU28

Aldworth House

Hovel Copse

Jay's Copse

P

Moorland Copse

JOBSON'S LA

P

Upper Roundhurst Farm

Roundhurst Common

Fisherstreet Copse

Copygrove Copse

Lower Roundhurst

Greenland Copse

Greenland Farm

Wateredge Copse

Lurgashall

92   A   B   93   C   D   94   E   F

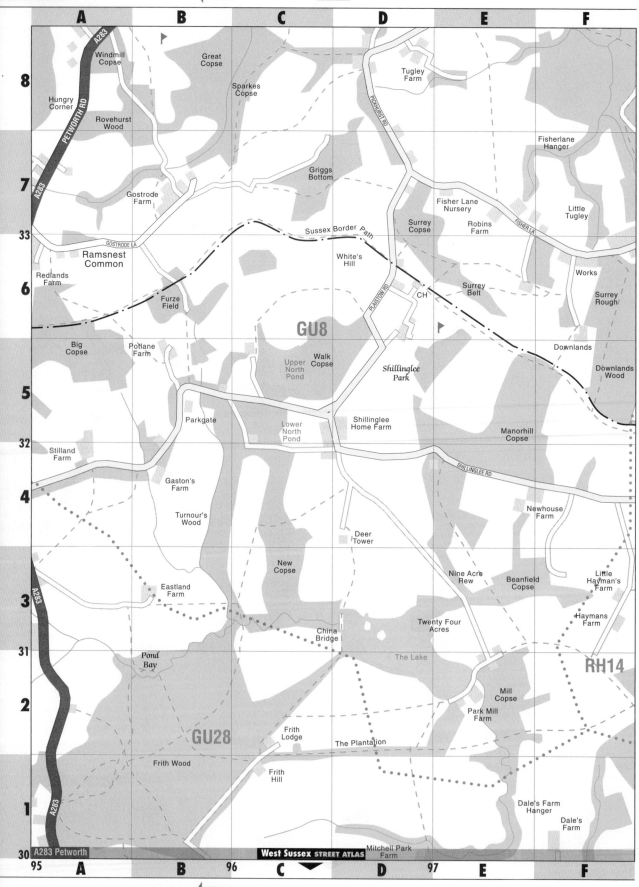

A283

Windmill Copse

PETWORTH RD

Hungry Corner

Rovehurst Wood

A283

Great Copse

Sparkes Copse

Tugley Farm

PICKHURST RD

Fisherlane Hanger

Griggs Bottom

Gostrode Farm

Fisher Lane Nursery

FISHER LA

Little Tugley

Sussex Border Path

Surrey Copse

Robins Farm

GOSTRODE LA

Ramsnest Common

White's Hill

Works

Redlands Farm

Furze Field

PLASTOW RD

CH

Surrey Belt

Surrey Rough

GU8

Downlands

Big Copse

Potlane Farm

Walk Copse

Downlands Wood

Upper North Pond

Shillinglee Park

Parkgate

Lower North Pond

Shillinglee Home Farm

Manorhill Copse

Stilland Farm

SHILLINGLEE RD

Gaston's Farm

Newhouse Farm

Turnour's Wood

A283

Deer Tower

New Copse

Nine Acre Rew

Beanfield Copse

Little Hayman's Farm

Eastland Farm

Haymans Farm

China Bridge

Twenty Four Acres

Pond Bay

The Lake

RH14

Mill Copse

Park Mill Farm

GU28

Frith Lodge

The Plantation

Frith Wood

Frith Hill

Dale's Farm Hanger

Dale's Farm

A283

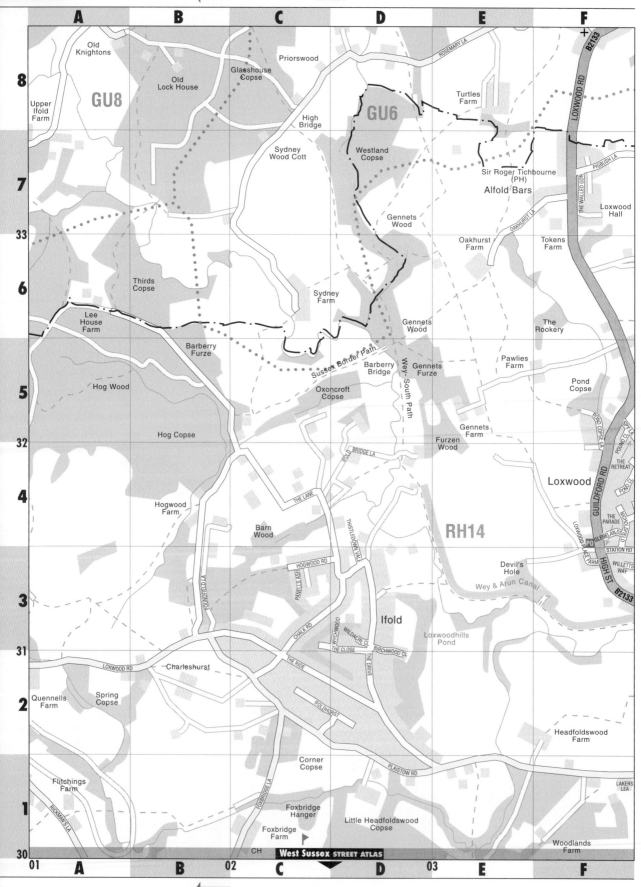

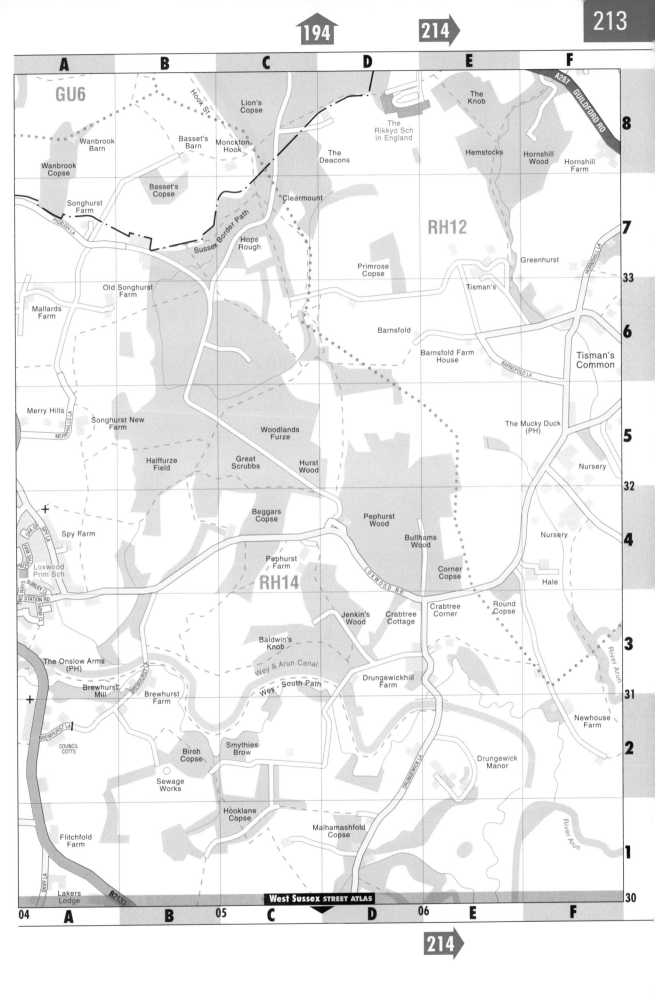

213
195

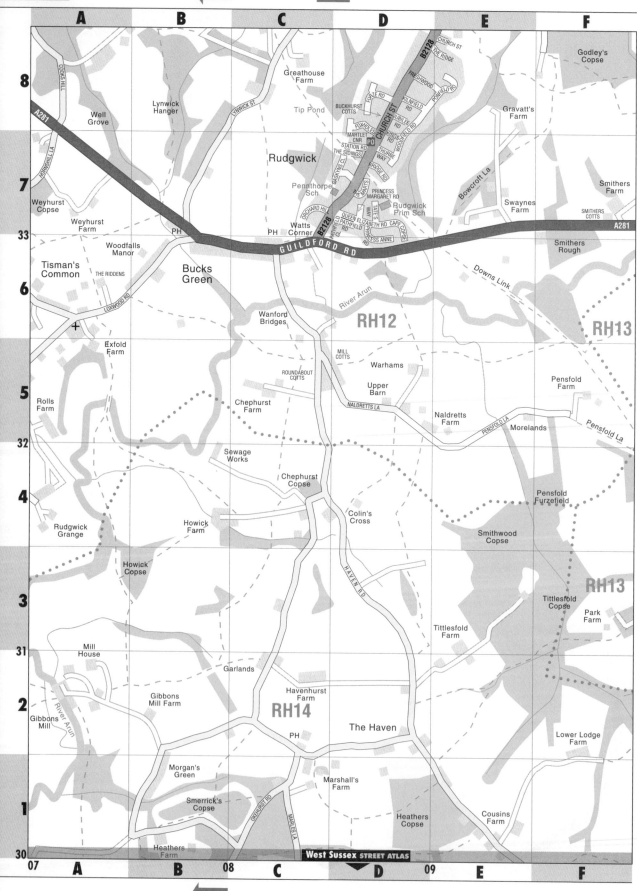

213

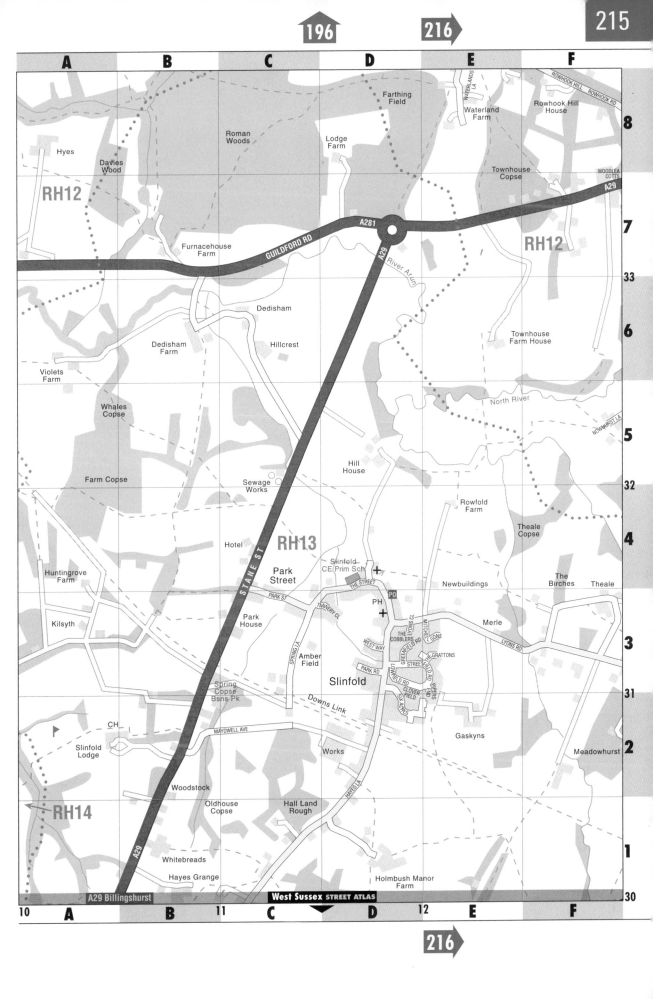

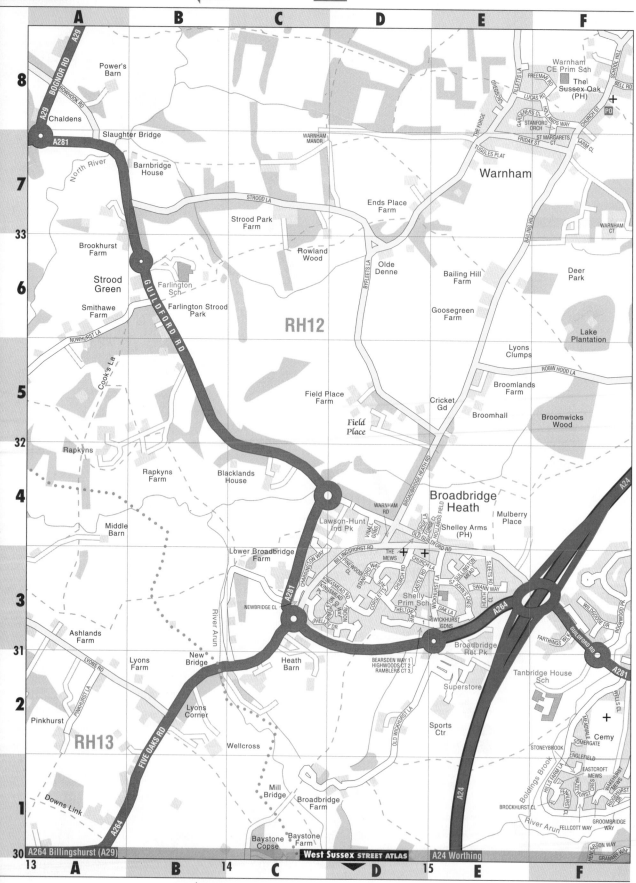

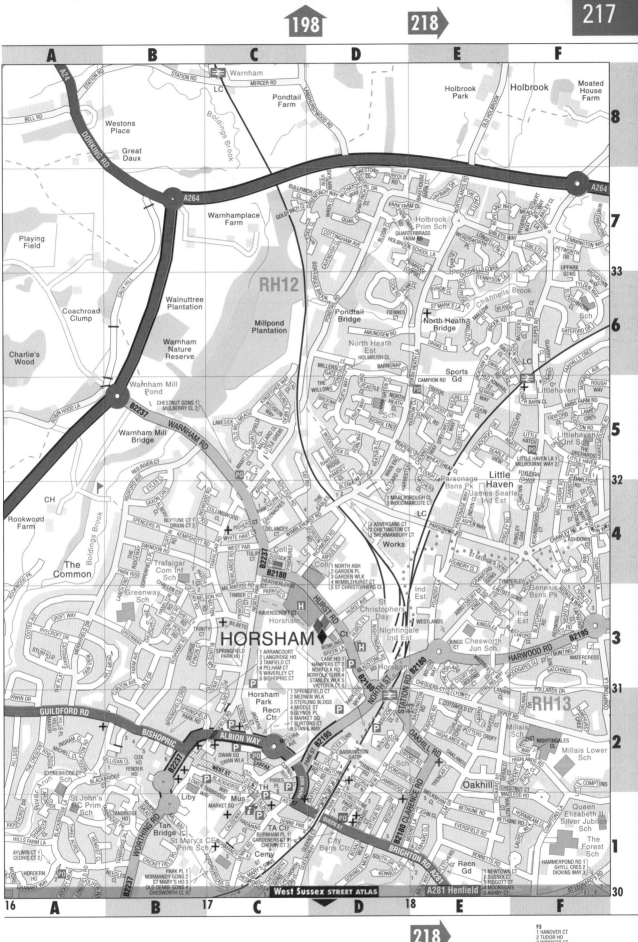

A B C D E F

8

RH12

7

33

6

Castle
Copse

Bush La

Benson's
Farm

Owlscastle
Farm

Cow
Barn

Channells Brook

The Cherry
Tree (PH)

A264

Dobsongill
Pond

Rookfield
Pond

Beechwood

Middle
Hill

Faygate
Forest

Dobson Gill

TOWER RD

LC

CRAWLEY RD

OLD CRAWLEY RD

CLOVERS WAY

ROSE
COTTS

Roffey Place
(Christian Training Ctr)

Roffey
Park

Newhouse
Farm

BROOK LA

WIMLAND RD

1 BUTTERMERE CL
2 GRASMERE GDNS

B2195

Moorhead
Farm

The Birches

NEW MOORHEAD DR

Roffey
Park

Roffey
Hurst

High
Wood

BEDDINGWOOD DR

Beddingwood

Roffey Park
Inst

HORSHAM

Woodside
Farm

Stonelodge
Plain

FOREST RD

CRAWLEY RD

6

Sch

Greenfields
Gr

Roffey

Cemy

5

32

4

3

31

2

1

30

Highbirch
Hill

Knights
Strength

THE
COURTYARD

Owlbeech
Wood

Leechpool & Owlbeech
Woods
Nature Reserve

Forest Grange
Manor

Whitevane
Hill

Playing
Fields

Whitevane
Pond

Race
Hill

Dogkennel
Pond

HARWOOD RD

B2195

P

MILLAIS

Leechpool
Wood

Townhouse
Copse

St Leonard's
Park

St Leonard's
Park Ho

Home
Farm

Greenbroom
Hill

HAMPER'S LA

Sandpit
Clump

Dry
Pond

Stew
Pond

Turf
Plain

RH13

High Weald Landscape Trail

Lily Beds

COMPTONS LA

HAMPER'S LA

BENS ACRE

GREBE CRES

HERON WAY

BRAMLING RD

Heron Way
Cty Prim
Sch

Scragged Oak
Hill

Sheepwash
Wood

Scragged
Oak

Sheepwash Gill

Inholme Gill

Mick's
Cross

Greenslade
Wood

The
Glen

Sunoak
Plantation

DOOMSDAY GDN

BRAMBLING RD

19 A 20 B C 21 D E F

West Sussex STREET ATLAS

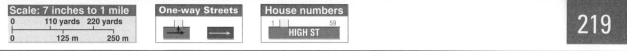

Scale: 7 inches to 1 mile

| 0 | 110 yards | 220 yards |
| 0 | 125 m | 250 m |

One-way Streets

House numbers
1 ─────── 59
HIGH ST

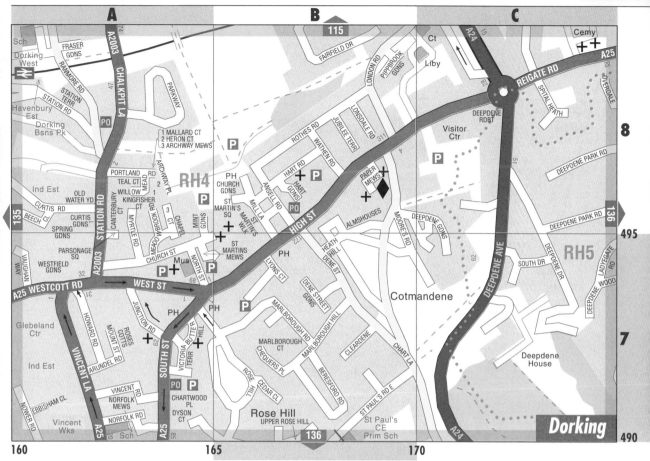

Dorking

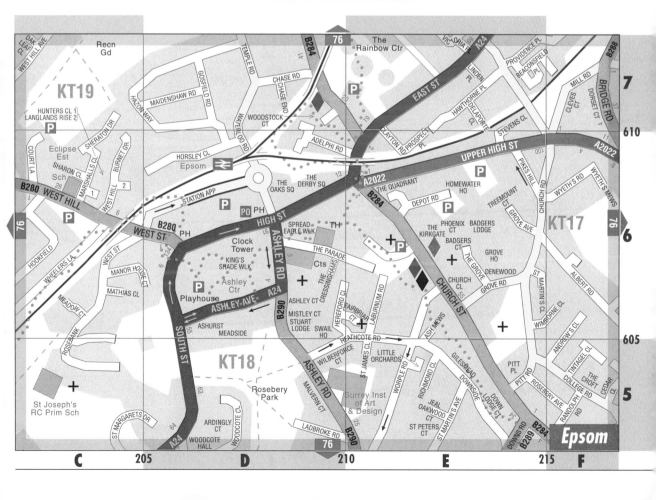

Epsom

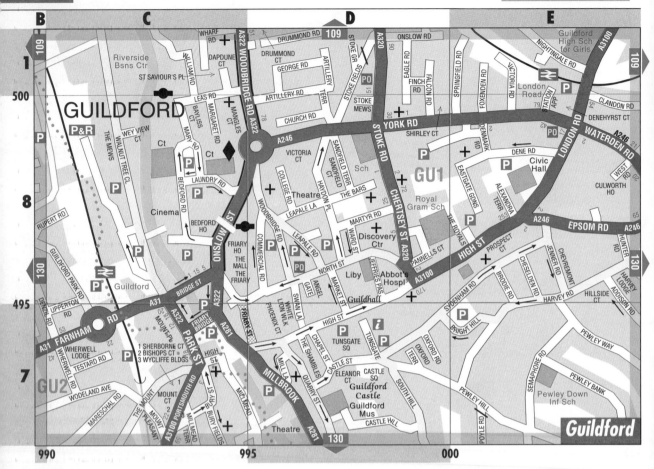

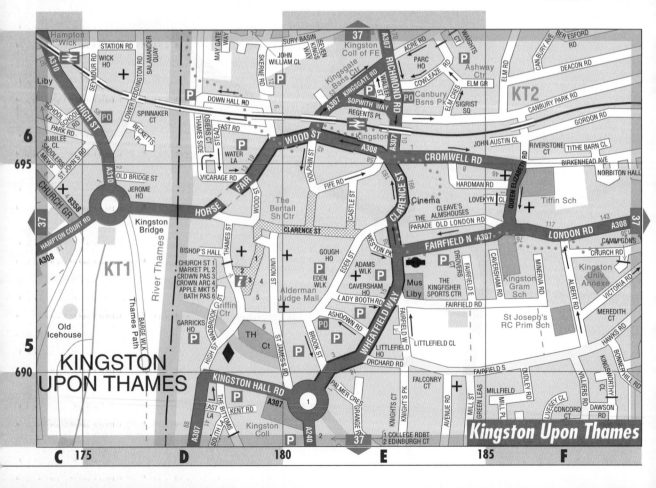

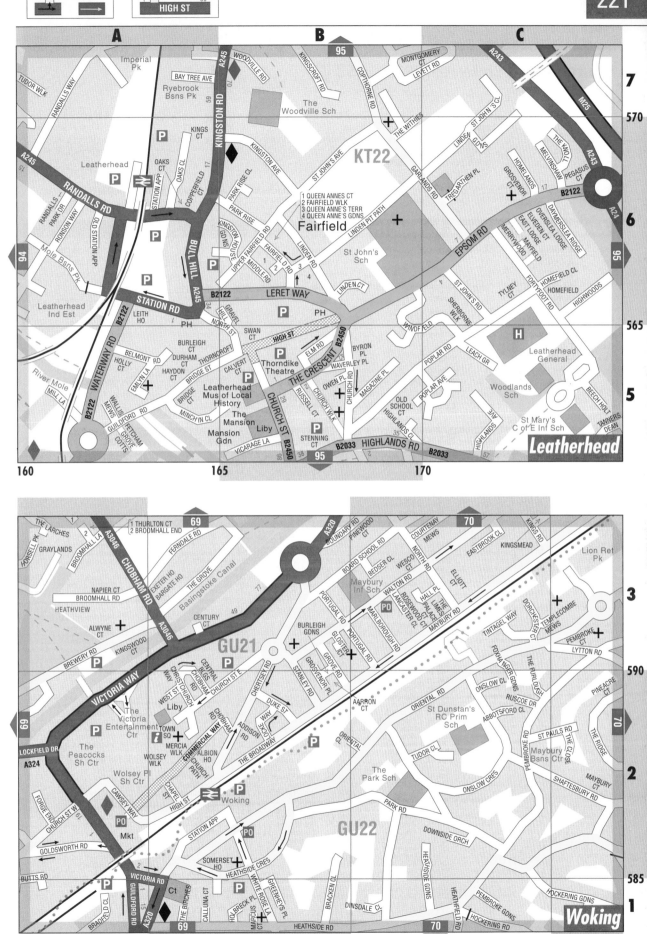

Leatherhead

Woking

Index

Church Rd **6** Beckenham BR2..........**53** C6

Place name	Location number	Locality, town or village	Postcode district	Page and grid square
May be abbreviated on the map	Present when a number indicates the place's position in a crowded area of mapping	Shown when more than one place has the same name	District for the indexed place	Page number and grid reference for the standard mapping

Public and commercial buildings are highlighted in magenta   **Places of interest** are highlighted in blue with a star ★

Abbreviations used in the index

Acad	**Academy**	Comm	**Common**	Gd	**Ground**	L	**Leisure**	Prom	**Prom**
App	**Approach**	Cott	**Cottage**	Gdn	**Garden**	La	**Lane**	Rd	**Road**
Arc	**Arcade**	Cres	**Crescent**	Gn	**Green**	Liby	**Library**	Recn	**Recreation**
Ave	**Avenue**	Cswy	**Causeway**	Gr	**Grove**	Mdw	**Meadow**	Ret	**Retail**
Bglw	**Bungalow**	Ct	**Court**	H	**Hall**	Meml	**Memorial**	Sh	**Shopping**
Bldg	**Building**	Ctr	**Centre**	Ho	**House**	Mkt	**Market**	Sq	**Square**
Bsns, Bus	**Business**	Ctry	**Country**	Hospl	**Hospital**	Mus	**Museum**	St	**Street**
Bvd	**Boulevard**	Cty	**County**	HQ	**Headquarters**	Orch	**Orchard**	Sta	**Station**
Cath	**Cathedral**	Dr	**Drive**	Hts	**Heights**	Pal	**Palace**	Terr	**Terrace**
Cir	**Circus**	Dro	**Drove**	Ind	**Industrial**	Par	**Parade**	TH	**Town Hall**
Cl	**Close**	Ed	**Education**	Inst	**Institute**	Pas	**Passage**	Univ	**University**
Cnr	**Corner**	Emb	**Embankment**	Int	**International**	Pk	**Park**	Wk, Wlk	**Walk**
Coll	**College**	Est	**Estate**	Intc	**Interchange**	Pl	**Place**	Wr	**Water**
Com	**Community**	Ex	**Exhibition**	Junc	**Junction**	Prec	**Precinct**	Yd	**Yard**

Index of localities, towns and villages

Abinger Common .155 D8
Abinger Hammer .133 F3
Addington 63 A5
Addlestone 52 A6
Albury 132 C4
Aldershot 105 B1
Alfold 193 F1
Alfold Crossways .194 A3
Artington 130 C4
Ascot 29 A6
Ash 106 B3
Ashford 13 F2
Ashtead 75 E1
Ashurst Wood ..206 E6
Ash Vale 106 B7
Bagshot 47 D3
Balham 21 A7
Banstead 78 B3
Barnes 7 F6
Beacon Hill ...188 C6
Beare Green ...157 D3
Beckenham 44 A7
Belmont 59 A2
Bentley 145 A7
Betchworth 137 E8
Biggin Hill 83 E3
Binstead 166 A5
Bisley 68 B3
Blackwater 64 D5
Bletchingley ..120 D2
Blindley Heath ..163 D8
Bowlhead Green .169 E1
Box Hill 116 A4
Bracknell 27 D6
Bramley 151 F6
Brands Hill 1 A8
Brentford 6 D7
Broadbridge
  Heath 216 E4
Brockham 137 C7
Bromley 44 E8
Brook 170 B1
Brookwood 88 A7
Buckland 117 A2
Burgh Heath 97 D8
Burrowhill 49 E3
Burstow 183 A7
Byfleet 71 D7
Camberley 65 D6
Capel 178 C6
Carshalton 59 E6
Caterham 100 F4
Catford 24 A7
Charlton 34 D7
Charlwood 180 E7
Cheam 58 F5

Chelsham 82 A2
Chertsey 33 B2
Chessington 56 E4
Chiddingfold ..191 B4
Chilworth 131 C3
Chipstead 78 F1
Chiswick 7 D7
Chobham 49 F2
Church 167 E1
Claygate 55 F3
Cobham 73 B5
Coldharbour ...156 E4
Colnbrook 1 D7
Compton 129 B3
Coney Hall 63 F7
Copthorne 183 C3
Coulsdon 79 D3
Cranford 4 C6
Cranleigh 174 D2
Crawley 201 F5
Crawley Down ..204 C7
Crondall 124 A5
Crowhurst 143 E3
Crowthorne 45 D5
Croydon 61 D7
Cudworth 179 E3
Dockenfield ...166 E6
Domewood 184 A5
Dorking 136 C6
Dormansland ..165 B1
Dormans Park ..185 E6
Downside 93 B8
Dulwich 22 E5
Dunsfold 192 F5
East Bedfont ...14 E7
East Clandon ..111 E4
East Ewell 58 D1
East Grinstead ..185 E2
East Horsley ..112 E8
East Molesey ...36 C4
Edenbridge 144 F4
Effingham 113 B2
Egham 12 A4
Ellen's Green ..196 A4
Elstead 148 D3
Englefield Green ..11 B1
Enton Green ...171 B5
Epsom 76 C5
Esher 55 C6
Ewell 58 A1
Ewhurst 175 F5
Fairlands 108 C4
Farley Green ..153 E7
Farnborough 85 B3
Farncombe 150 E8
Farnham 125 B1

Faygate 199 F1
Felbridge 184 F4
Felcourt 185 C8
Feltham 15 B6
Fetcham 94 C4
Fickleshole 82 E5
Fisherstreet ..209 F3
Fleet 104 A7
Flexford 107 C1
Forest Green ..176 E7
Forest Hill 23 D7
Forest Row 206 F3
Frensham 167 D7
Frimley 65 F2
Gatton 118 F7
Godalming 150 F3
Godstone 121 B3
Gomshall 133 D4
Grayshott 188 C3
Grayswood 189 F1
Great Bookham ..94 B1
Guildford 130 B8
Hackbridge 60 B8
Hale 125 C6
Hambledon 171 D2
Hampton 36 A7
Hamsey Green ...81 C4
Harlington 3 C8
Harmondsworth ...2 E8
Hascombe 172 D4
Haslemere 208 D6
Hatton 3 F2
Haxted 165 F8
Hayes 44 F3
Headley 96 C2
Headley Down ..187 B4
Heath End 125 D6
Hersham 54 D5
Heston 4 F7
Hinchley Wood ..55 F8
Hindhead 188 F4
Holmbury St Mary
  ....155 B5
Hookwood 160 D2
Hooley 99 B5
Horley 161 C3
Horne 162 F5
Horsham 217 C3
Horton 1 A4
Hounslow 5 A5
Hydestile 171 E6
Ifold 212 D3
Isleworth 6 B4
Kenley 80 D3
Kingsfold 198 B5
Kingsley Green .208 B2

Kingston Upon
  Thames 37 C6
Kingswood 97 F6
Knaphill 68 D1
Laleham 33 C6
Lambs Green ...199 F6
Langley Vale ...96 D8
Leatherhead 95 D5
Leigh 138 B2
Lewisham 24 C8
Lightwater 66 F8
Limpsfield 123 A6
Linchmere 207 B2
Lingfield 164 D5
Little Bookham ..93 93
Littleton 34 A6
Longcross 50 A7
Long Ditton 37 C1
Lower Halliford ..34 D2
Lower Kingswood .118 E8
Loxwood 212 F4
Lurgashall 209 A1
Lyne 32 B1
Martyr's Green ..92 E7
Merstham 119 D7
Merton 40 B8
Mickleham 115 C7
Milford 149 E1
Mitcham 40 F5
Morden 40 B3
Mortlake 7 C4
Mytchett 85 F3
New Addington ..63 D3
Newchapel 163 F1
Newdigate 158 B1
Newell Green 8 A1
New Haw 52 C3
New Malden 38 F5
Normandy 107 A3
North Ascot 28 E8
North Cheam 58 C8
Nutfield 120 F2
Oatlands Park ..53 E6
Ockham 92 B6
Ockley 177 D5
Old Windsor 11 A8
Old Woking 90 A7
Ottershaw 51 D5
Outwood 162 B7
Oxshott 74 C6
Oxted 122 E5
Parkgate 158 D4
Peaslake 154 D6
Penge 23 D2
Peper Harow ...149 C5
Pirbright 87 F4

Plaistow 211 F2
Poyle 1 E6
Purley 80 B7
Putney 19 C7
Puttenham 128 C4
Pyrford 70 E4
Redhill 118 E2
Reigate 118 B2
Richmond 6 D2
Ripley 91 C6
Roehampton 7 F2
Rowhook 196 E1
Rowledge 145 F3
Rowly 174 B6
Rudgwick 214 C7
Rushmoor 168 C5
Rusper 199 D7
Salfords 140 B1
Sanderstead 80 F6
Sandhurst 64 C7
Seale 127 B4
Selsdon 62 D1
Send 90 C4
Send Marsh 90 F3
Shackleford ...149 D7
Shalford 130 E2
Shamley Green .152 E5
Sheerwater 70 D6
Shepperton 34 C3
Shere 133 B4
Sidlow 139 B2
Slinfold 215 D3
Smallfield 162 B2
South Croydon ..61 D3
South Godstone .142 F5
South Holmwood .157 C7
South Norwood ..42 E5
South Nutfield .140 E7
Staines 12 E6
Stanwell 13 C7
Stoke D'Abernon .73 F3
Stoneleigh 58 A5
Streatham 21 E2
Sunbury 35 B6
Sunningdale 30 B4
Surbiton 37 E2
Sutton 59 C5
Tadworth 97 C5
Tandridge 122 A2
Tatsfield 103 D7
Teddington 17 B3
Thames Ditton ..37 B2
The Chart 123 E5
The Sands 126 E2
Thornton Heath ..42 B3
Thorpe 32 C6

Thorpe Lea 12 B1
Thursley 169 C4
Tilford 147 D3
Titsey 103 B2
Tolworth 57 B7
Tongham 126 F6
Turners Hill ..204 A4
Twickenham 17 B8
Tyler's Green .121 C5
Upper Halliford ..34 D5
Upper Tooting ..20 F5
Virginia Water ..31 C6
Wallington 60 A4
Wallis Wood ..176 E1
Walton-On-
  Thames 35 C2
Walton on the Hill .97 A3
Wandsworth 20 C7
Warlingham 81 C1
Warnham 216 E7
Wentworth 30 F3
West Barnes 39 C4
West Byfleet ...71 B6
West Clandon ..111 B6
Westcott 135 D6
West End 67 F6
West Ewell 57 E3
West Hoathly ..204 D1
West Horsley ..112 B8
Westhumble 115 A4
West Norwood ...22 C5
West Wickham ...44 E1
Weybridge 53 A6
Whiteley Village ..53 E1
Whyteleafe 80 E1
Wimbledon 19 F2
Windlesham 48 C4
Windsor 9 E8
Winkfield 8 D4
Wisley 71 E3
Witley 170 F4
Woking 69 E1
Wokingham 25 B5
Woldingham ...102 A4
Wonersh 152 B7
Woodham 52 A2
Woodmansterne ..78 E4
Wood Street
  Village 108 B3
Worcester Park ..57 C6
Wormley 170 F1
Worplesdon ...108 D8
Wotton 134 F3
Wraysbury 11 E8
Wrecclesham ..145 E6
Yateley 64 A5

1

10th Ave KT20 . . . . .97 E1
11th Ave KT20 . . . . .97 F1
12th Ave KT20 . . . . .97 F1
13th Ave KT20 . . . . .97 F1
14th Ave KT20 . . . . .97 F1
15th Ave KT20 . . . . .97 F1
16th Ave KT20 . . . . .97 F1
1st Ave KT20 . . . . .97 E2

2

2nd Ave KT20 . . . . .97 E2

3

3rd Ave KT20 . . . . .97 E2

4

4th Ave KT20 . . . . .97 E2

5

5th Ave KT20 . . . . .97 E2

6

6th Ave KT20 . . . . .97 E2

7

7th Ave KT20 . . . . .97 F2

8

8th Ave KT20 . . . . .97 E2

9

9th Ave KT20 . . . . .97 F2

A

A C Ct KT7 . . . . .37 A3
Aaron Ct BR3 . . . . .44 B6
Aaron's Hill GU7 . . . . .150 B4
Aarron Ct GU21 . . . . .69 F2
Abbess Cl SW2 . . . . .22 B7
Abbetts La GU15 . . . . .65 B3
Abbey Bsns Ctr 16 RH1 . . .118 F2
Abbey Cl Bracknell RG12 . . .27 D4
  Crawley GU6 . . . . .173 F2
  Pyrford GU22 . . . . .70 E3
  Wokingham RG40 . . . . .25 C7
Abbey Ct
  Camberley GU15 . . . . .65 D5
  Chertsey KT16 . . . . .33 B2
  Farnham GU9 . . . . .125 C2
  Purley CR8 . . . . .80 B7
Abbey Dr Laleham TW18 . . .33 C5
  Upper Tooting SW17 . . . . . .21 A3
Abbey Gdns KT16 . . . . .33 A3
Abbey Gn KT16 . . . . .33 B3
Abbey Ind Est CR4 . . . . .40 F4
Abbey La BR3 . . . . .24 A1
Abbey Lodge TW18 . . . . .12 F3
Abbey Mews RH19 . . . . . . .206 E6
Abbey Mill Bsns Pk GU7 149 F4
Abbey Par SW19 . . . . .20 C1
Abbey Pk BR3 . . . . .24 A1
Abbey Rd Chertsey KT16 . . .33 B2
  Croydon CR0,CR9 . . . . .61 B7
  Lower Halliford TW17 . . . . . .34 A1
  Merton SW19 . . . . .40 C8
  Selsdon CR2 . . . . .62 D1
  Virginia Water GU25 . . . . . .31 D5
  Woking GU21 . . . . .69 D2
Abbey River Cotts
  KT16 . . . . .33 C3
Abbey Sch The GU9 . . . . . .125 D1
Abbey St GU9 . . . . .125 C2
Abbey Way GU14 . . . . .85 C4
Abbey Wlk KT8 . . . . .36 B5
Abbey Wood SL5 . . . . .30 A2
Abbeyfield Cl CR4 . . . . .40 E7
Abbeyfield Ho RH8 . . . . . . .122 E5
Abbeylands KT13 . . . . .53 B3
Abbot Cl Byfleet KT14 . . . . . .71 D8
  Staines TW18 . . . . .13 D1
Abbot Rd GU1 . . . . .130 D7
Abbot's Cl GU2 . . . . .129 F6
Abbot's Ride GU9 . . . . .125 E1
Abbot's Way GU1 . . . . .110 D2
Abbots Ave KT19 . . . . .76 A8
Abbots Cl GU1 . . . . .110 D2
Abbots Ct SE25 . . . . .42 E6
Abbots Dr GU25 . . . . .31 C5
Abbots Gn CR0,CR2 . . . . . . .62 D4
Abbots Ho GU4 . . . . .110 A5
Abbots La CR8 . . . . .80 C3
Abbots Pk SW2 . . . . .22 A7
Abbots Way
  Beckenham BR3 . . . . .43 E4
  Chertsey KT16 . . . . .32 F2
Abbots Wlk CR3 . . . . .101 B5
Abbots Wood Forest Wlk★
  GU10 . . . . .166 C7

Abbotsbury RG12 . . . . .26 F4
Abbotsbury Ct RH13 . . . . . .217 E3
Abbotsbury Fst Sch SM4 .40 B4
Abbotsbury Rd
  Coney Hall BR2,BR4 . . . . . .63 F8
  Morden SM4,SW19 . . . . . . .40 B5
Abbotsfield Rd RH11 . . . . . .200 D4
Abbotsford Cl GU22 . . . . . . .70 A2
Abbotshall Rd SE6 . . . . .24 D6
Abbotsleigh Cl SM2 . . . . . . .59 B3
Abbotsleigh Rd SW16 . . . . .21 C3
Abbotsmede Cl TW1 . . . . . . .16 F6
Abbotswood
  Guildford GU1 . . . . .109 F3
  Walton-on-T KT13 . . . . .53 F7
Abbotswood Cl GU1 . . . . . .109 F4
Abbotswood Dr KT13 . . . . . .53 C6
Abbotswood Rd SW16 . . . . .21 D5
Abbott Ave SW20 . . . . .39 D8
Abbott Cl TW12 . . . . .15 E2
Abbott Ho SW12 . . . . .20 F8
Abbotts Cotts GU10 . . . . . .166 E5
Abbotts Rd
  Cheam SM1,SM3 . . . . .58 E6
  Mitcham CR4,SW16 . . . . . . .41 C5
Abbotts Rise RH1 . . . . .119 C3
Abbotts Tilt KT12 . . . . .54 E7
Abelia Cl GU24 . . . . .67 E6
Abell Ct KT15 . . . . .52 C6
Abercairn Rd SW16 . . . . . . .21 C1
Aberconway Rd SM4 . . . .40 B5
Abercorn Cl CR2 . . . . .81 D7
Abercorn Mews TW10 . . . . . .6 E3
Abercorn Way GU21 . . . . . . .69 A1
Aberdare Cl BR4 . . . . .63 C8
Aberdeen Rd CR0 . . . . .61 D6
Aberdour Sch KT20 . . . . .77 F1
Aberfoyle Rd SW16 . . . . . . .21 D2
Abergavenny Gdns
  RH10 . . . . .183 D3
Abingdon Cl
  Bracknell RG12 . . . . .27 E4
  Merton SW19 . . . . .20 C2
  Woking GU21 . . . . .69 C1
Abingdon Lodge BR2 . . . .44 F7
Abingdon Rd
  Sandhurst GU47 . . . . .45 C1
  Thornton Heath SW16 . . . . .41 E8
Abinger Ave SM2 . . . . .58 D2
Abinger Cl Dorking RH5 .136 C3
  Wallington SM6 . . . . .60 E5
Abinger Common Fst Sch
  RH5 . . . . .134 D1
Abinger Common Rd
  RH5 . . . . .155 F7
Abinger Ct SM6 . . . . .60 E5
Abinger Dr RH1 . . . . .139 E7
Abinger Gdns TW7 . . . . .5 E4
Abinger Hammer Village Sch
  RH5 . . . . .133 F4
Abinger Ho 2 KT2 . . . . . . .18 B1
Abinger Keep RH6 . . . . . . .161 C4
Abinger La RH5 . . . . .134 C2
Abinger Rd RH5 . . . . .156 C3
Abinger Way GU4 . . . . .110 B6
Aboyne Dr SW20 . . . . .39 A7
Aboyne Rd SW17 . . . . .20 D5
Abrahams Rd RH11 . . . . . . .201 A1
Acacia Ave
  Brentford TW8 . . . . .6 B7
  Littleton TW17 . . . . .34 A4
  Sandhurst GU47 . . . . .45 C1
  Woking GU22 . . . . .89 D7
Acacia Cl Penge SE20 . . . . .43 A7
  Woodham KT15 . . . . .51 F1
Acacia Ct Bracknell RG12 . . .27 B6
  6 West Norwood SW16 . . . .22 A3
Acacia Dr Banstead KT17 . . .77 D5
  Cheam SM3 . . . . .40 A1
  Woodham KT15 . . . . .51 F1
Acacia Gdns BR4 . . . . .63 C8
Acacia Gr Dulwich SE21 . . .22 D6
  Kingston u T KT3 . . . . .38 E6
Acacia Ho Cranleigh GU6 .174 E2
  Reigate RH2 . . . . .118 A3
Acacia Mews UB7 . . . . .2 D8
Acacia Rd
  Beckenham BR3 . . . . .43 F6
  Guildford GU1 . . . . .109 D1
  Hampton TW12 . . . . .16 A2
  Mitcham CR4 . . . . .41 B7
  South Norwood SW16 . . . . .41 E8
  Staines TW18 . . . . .13 B3
Academy Cl GU15 . . . . .65 E8
Academy Gate GU15 . . . . . .65 B6
Academy Gdns CR0 . . . . . . .42 F1
Accommodation La UB7 . .2 D8
Accommodation Rd KT16 .50 E6
Ace Par KT9 . . . . .56 E7
Acer Dr GU24 . . . . .67 E6
Acer Rd TN16 . . . . .83 D3
Acheulian Cl GU9 . . . . .146 C2
Achilles Pl GU21 . . . . .69 C2
Ackroyd Rd SE23 . . . . .23 E8
Acorn Cl
  East Grinstead RH19 . . . . .205 E8
  1 Hampton TW12 . . . . .16 B2
  Horley RH6 . . . . .161 C4
Acorn Gdns SE19 . . . . .42 F8
Acorn Gr Harlington UB3 . . .3 F7
  Kingswood KT20 . . . . .97 F3
  Woking GU22 . . . . .89 C6
Acorn Keep GU9 . . . . .125 D3
Acorn Mews GU14 . . . . .85 A7
Acorn Rd GU17 . . . . .64 B5
Acorn Way
  Beckenham BR3 . . . . .44 C4

Acorn Way continued
  Forest Hill SE23 . . . . .23 D5
Acorns RH13 . . . . .218 A4
Acorns Fst Sch The
  Betchworth RH3 . . . . .116 D1
  Leigh RH2 . . . . .138 A3
Acorns The
  Crawley RH11 . . . . .201 B1
  21 Putney SW19 . . . . .19 D7
  Smallfield RH6 . . . . .162 B3
Acorns Way KT10 . . . . .55 C5
Acre La SM5 . . . . .60 A6
Acre Rd Kingston u T KT2 . .37 E2
  Mitcham SW19 . . . . .20 D2
Acres Gdns KT20 . . . . .97 D8
Acres Platt GU6 . . . . .174 F4
Action Ct TW15 . . . . .34 C8
Acuba Ho SW18 . . . . .20 B7
Acuba Rd SW18 . . . . .20 B6
Adair Cl SE25 . . . . .43 B6
Adair Gdns CR3 . . . . .100 C6
Adair Wlk GU24 . . . . .87 B6
Adam Ct 4 SM1 . . . . .59 C6
Adams Cl KT5 . . . . .37 F3
Adams Croft GU24 . . . . .87 C7
Adams Ct 3 CR8 . . . . .80 A7
Adams Ho 3 SW16 . . . . . . .21 C3
Adams Ho The GU2 . . . . . .129 E8
Adams Rd BR3 . . . . .43 E4
Adams Way SE25,CR0 . . . . .43 A3
Adams Wlk 1 KT1 . . . . .37 E7
Adamson Ct 6 RH11 . . . . .201 B1
Adamsrill Prim Sch SE26 23 E4
Adamsrill Rd SE23,SE26 . . .23 E4
Adare Wlk SW16,SW2 . . . . .21 F5
Addington Ave SE26 . . . . . . .23 E4
Addington Bsns Ctr GU11 .63 E1
Addington Ct 8 SW14 . . . . .7 D4
Addington Gr SE26 . . . . .23 E4
Addington High Sch CR0 82 E7
Addington Rd
  Sanderstead CR2 . . . . .81 A8
  Selsdon CR2 . . . . .62 C1
  Thornton Heath CR0 . . . . . .42 A1
  West Wickham BR4,CR0 . . .63 D6
Addington Village Rd
  CR0 . . . . .63 A5
Addiscombe Ave CR0 . . . . .43 A2
Addiscombe Court Rd
  CR0,CR9 . . . . .61 E8
Addiscombe Rd
  Crowthorne RG45 . . . . .45 C4
  Croydon CR0,CR9 . . . . .61 E8
  South Croydon CR0 . . . . . . .61 E8
Addison Ave TW3 . . . . .5 C6
Addison Cl CR3 . . . . .100 D5
Addison Ct GU1 . . . . .130 F7
Addison Gdns KT5 . . . . .37 F5
Addison Rd
  Caterham CR3 . . . . .100 D6
  Croydon SE25 . . . . .43 A5
  Farnborough GU16 . . . . . . .85 E8
  Guildford GU1 . . . . .130 F7
  Teddington TW11 . . . . .17 B2
  4 Woking GU21 . . . . .69 F2
Addison's Cl CR0 . . . . .62 F8
Addlestone Ho KT15 . . . . . .52 B7
Addlestone Moor KT15 . . . .52 B8
Addlestone Pk KT13,KT15 52 E6
Addlestone Sta KT15 . . . . . .52 D6
Adecroft Way KT8 . . . . .36 C6
Adela Ave KT3 . . . . .39 B5
Adelaide Cl
  Crawley RH11 . . . . .181 D1
  Horsham RH12 . . . . .217 F4
Adelaide 15 BR3 . . . . .24 A1
Adelaide Pl KT13 . . . . .53 D6
Adelaide Rd
  Ashford TW15 . . . . .13 D3
  Heston TW5 . . . . .4 E6
  Kingston u T KT6 . . . . .37 E4
  Richmond TW9 . . . . .7 A4
  Teddington TW11 . . . . .16 F2
  Walton-on-T KT12 . . . . .54 B7
Adelina Mews SW12 . . . . . .21 D7
Adelphi Cl RH10 . . . . .202 D4
Adelphi Rd KT17 . . . . .76 D6
Adenmore Rd SE6 . . . . .24 A8
Adlers La RH5 . . . . .115 A4
Adlington Pl GU14 . . . . .85 E2
Admiral Ct SM5 . . . . .40 E1
Admiral Ho TW11 . . . . .17 B3
Admiral Rd RH11 . . . . .201 A3
Admiral's Bridge La
  RH19 . . . . .205 C2
Admiral's Wlk The CR5 . . . .99 F7
Admirals Ct GU1 . . . . .110 B2
Admiralty Rd TW11 . . . . .16 F2
Admiralty Way
  Camberley GU15 . . . . .64 F4
  Teddington TW11 . . . . .16 F2
Adolf St SE6 . . . . .24 B4
Adrian Ct RH11 . . . . .201 B1
Advance Rd SE27 . . . . .22 C4
Adversane Ct RH12 . . . . . .217 D4
Aerodrome Way TW5 . . . . . . .4 C8
Aerospace Bvd GU14 . . . .105 A7
Agar Cl KT6 . . . . .56 F8
Agar Ho 6 KT1 . . . . .37 E6
Agate Rd New Malden KT4 .38 A1
  12 Penge SE26 . . . . .23 B3
Agate La RH12 . . . . .217 F5
Agates La KT21 . . . . .95 D8
Agincourt SL5 . . . . .29 C6
Agnes Scott Ct 5 KT13 . . .53 B7
Agnew Rd SE23 . . . . .23 D8
Agraria Rd GU2 . . . . .130 B7

Ailsa Ave TW1 . . . . .6 B2
Ailsa Cl RH11 . . . . .201 B3
Ailsa Rd TW1 . . . . .6 B2
Ainger Cl GU12 . . . . .105 D2
Ainsdale Way GU21 . . . . . . .69 A1
Ainsworth Rd CR0,CR9 . . . .61 B8
Aintree Cl SL3 . . . . .1 E6
Aintree Ho SE26 . . . . .23 B2
Aintree Rd RH10 . . . . .202 A4
Air Forces Meml★ TW20 11 D4
Air Park Way TW13 . . . . .15 B6
Airborne Forces Mus★
  GU11 . . . . .105 A5
Airborne Ho 10 SM6 . . . . . .60 B6
Aircraft Espl GU14 . . . . .85 C1
Airedale Rd SW12 . . . . .20 F8
Airport Gate Bsns Ctr UB7 3 A7
Airport Way Horley RH6 . . .182 B8
  Stanwell TW19 . . . . .2 A3
Airport Way Rdbt E
  RH6 . . . . .182 C8
Airport Way Rdbt W
  RH6 . . . . .181 F8
Aisne Rd GU16 . . . . .66 E1
Aitken Cl CR4 . . . . .40 F2
Aitken Ho Dorking RH4 . . . .136 A5
  Haslemere GU27 . . . . .208 C7
Aitken Rd SE6 . . . . .24 B6
Akabusi Cl SE25 . . . . .43 A3
Akehurst Cl RH10 . . . . .183 B3
Akehurst St SW15 . . . . .19 A8
Akerman Rd KT6 . . . . .37 C3
Alamein Rd GU11 . . . . .105 B3
Alan Hilton Ct KT16 . . . . . . .51 D4
Alan Rd SW19 . . . . .19 E3
Alan Turing Rd GU2 . . . . . .108 D1
Alanbrooke Cl GU21 . . . . . .68 C1
Alanbrooke Rd GU11 . . . .105 D6
Albain Cres TW15 . . . . .13 E6
Albans Cl SW16 . . . . .21 E5
Albany Cl Esher KT10 . . . . . .55 A2
  Mortlake SW14 . . . . .7 B3
  Reigate RH2 . . . . .118 A3
Albany Cres KT10 . . . . .55 E4
Albany Ct Frimley GU16 . . . .65 C1
  Kingston u T KT2 . . . . .17 E2
  Oatlands Park KT13 . . . . . . .53 E8
  Richmond TW10 . . . . .17 B5
  3 Weybridge KT13 . . . . . . .53 B6
Albany Ho 6 TW8 . . . . .6 E8
Albany Mews
  Kingston u T KT2 . . . . .17 D2
  Sutton SM1 . . . . .59 B5
Albany Par 4 TW8 . . . . .6 E8
Albany Park Ind Est
  GU15 . . . . .65 C1
Albany Park Rd
  Kingston u T KT2 . . . . .17 D2
  Leatherhead KT22 . . . . .95 A8
Albany Pk Frimley GU15 . . .65 C1
  Poyle SL3 . . . . .1 D7
Albany Pl Brentford TW8 . . . .6 E8
  Egham TW20 . . . . .12 B4
Albany Rd Brentford TW8 . . .6 D8
  Crawley RH11 . . . . .201 C6
  Hersham KT12 . . . . .54 D6
  New Malden KT3 . . . . .38 D5
  Richmond TW10 . . . . .6 E2
  Wimbledon SW19 . . . . .20 B3
Albany Reach KT7 . . . . .36 F4
Albany Terr 5 TW10 . . . . . . .6 F2
Albatross Gdns CR2 . . . . . . .81 D8
Albemarle SW19 . . . . .19 D6
Albemarle Ave TW2 . . . . . . .15 F7
Albemarle Gdns KT3 . . . . . .38 D5
Albemarle Lodge SE26 . . . .23 E3
Albemarle Pk BR3 . . . . .44 B8
Albemarle Rd BR2, BR3 . . . .44 C8
Albemarle Prim Sch
  SW19 . . . . .19 E6
Albemarle Prim Sch
  (Annexe) SW19 . . . . .19 E7
Albert Ave KT16 . . . . .33 A6
Albert Carr Gdns SW16 . . .21 E3
Albert Crane Ct RH11 . . . .201 A8
Albert Ct 9 SW19 . . . . .19 E1
Albert Dr Putney SW19 . . . . .19 E6
  Sheerwater GU21,KT14 . . . .70 D5
  1 Staines TW18 . . . . .13 A4
Albert Gr SW20 . . . . .39 D8
Albert Mews RH1 . . . . .140 A4
Albert Rd Addlestone KT15 52 D6
  Aldershot GU11 . . . . .105 B2
  Ashford TW15 . . . . .13 F3
  Ashstead KT21 . . . . .75 F1
  Bagshot GU19 . . . . .47 E1
  Bracknell RG42 . . . . .27 B8
  Camberley GU15 . . . . .65 C5
  Carshalton SM1 . . . . .59 D5
  Crowthorne RG45 . . . . .45 B5
  Croydon CR0,SE25 . . . . . . .43 B5
  Englefield Green TW20 . . . .11 D2
  Epsom KT17 . . . . .76 F6
  Farnborough GU14 . . . . . . .85 C2
  Hampton TW12 . . . . .16 B3
  Horley RH6 . . . . .161 B4
  Hounslow TW3 . . . . .5 A3
  Kingston u T KT1 . . . . .37 F7
  Merstham RH1 . . . . .119 C6
  Mitcham CR4 . . . . .40 D7
  New Malden KT3 . . . . .38 F5
  Penge SE20 . . . . .23 D2
  Richmond TW10 . . . . .6 E2
  Teddington TW11 . . . . .16 F2
  Twickenham TW1 . . . . .16 F7
  Warlingham CR6 . . . . .81 E1
  Wokingham RG40 . . . . .25 B5
Albert Rd N RH2 . . . . .117 F2

Albert Wlk RG45 . . . . .45 B5
Alberta Ave SM1 . . . . .58 F5
Alberta Dr RH6 . . . . .162 A3
Albertine Cl KT17 . . . . .77 B3
Albery Cl RH12 . . . . .217 B4
Albion Cl RH10 . . . . .202 D5
Albion Ct Streatham SW2 . . .22 A6
  Sutton SM2 . . . . .59 D3
Albion Ho 10 GU21 . . . . . . .69 F2
Albion Par GU21 . . . . .68 C2
Albion Pl SE25 . . . . .43 A6
Albion Rd Hounslow TW3 . . . .5 A3
  Kingston u T KT2 . . . . .38 C8
  Reigate RH2 . . . . .139 C8
  Sandhurst GU47 . . . . .64 B8
  Sutton SM2 . . . . .59 D3
  Twickenham TW2 . . . . .16 E7
Albion St CR0,CR9 . . . . .42 B1
Albion Villas Rd SE26 . . . . .23 C5
Albury Ave East Ewell SM2 58 C1
  Hounslow TW7 . . . . .5 F7
Albury Cl Epsom KT19 . . . . .57 B2
  Hampton TW12 . . . . .16 B2
  Longcross KT16 . . . . .50 A7
Albury Ct 4 Croydon CR0 . .61 C6
  Guildford GU1 . . . . .131 A8
  Mitcham CR4 . . . . .40 D7
  Sutton SM1 . . . . .59 C6
Albury Hts GU1 . . . . .131 A8
Albury Keep RH6 . . . . .161 B4
Albury Lodge 10 SW2 . . . . .21 F8
Albury Pl RH1 . . . . .119 C6
Albury Rd Chessington KT9 56 E5
  Guildford GU1 . . . . .131 A8
  Hersham KT12 . . . . .53 F4
  Merstham RH1 . . . . .119 C6
Alcester Ct 4 SM6 . . . . .60 B6
Alcester Rd SM6 . . . . .60 B6
Alcock Cl SM6 . . . . .60 D3
Alcock Rd TW5 . . . . .4 D7
Alcocks Cl KT20 . . . . .97 E7
Alcocks La KT20 . . . . .97 E7
Alcorn Cl SM3 . . . . .59 A8
Alcot Cl RG45 . . . . .45 B4
Alden Ct
  South Croydon CR0 . . . . . . .61 D7
  5 Wimbledon SW19 . . . . . .20 A2
Aldenham Terr RG12 . . . . . .27 C3
Aldenholme KT13 . . . . .53 F4
Alder Cl Ash Vale GU12 . . .106 A7
  Crawley Down RH10 . . . . . .204 B8
  Englefield Green TW20 . . . .11 E3
Alder Croft CR5 . . . . .79 F3
Alder Ct Bracknell RG12 . . . .27 B6
  4 West Norwood SW16 . . .22 A3
Alder Rd
  Headley Down GU35 . . . . . .187 B6
  Mortlake SW14 . . . . .7 D4
Alderbrook Prim Sch
  SW12 . . . . .21 B8
Alderbrook Rd
  Balham SW12 . . . . .21 B8
  Cranleigh GU6 . . . . .174 C8
Aldercombe La CR3 . . . . . .100 E1
Aldergrove Gdns TW4 . . . . . .4 E5
Alderman Judge Mall 6
  KT1 . . . . .37 E7
Alderman Willey Cl RG41 25 B6
Aldermead TW3 . . . . .5 B3
Aldermoor Rd SE6 . . . . .23 F7
Alderney Ave TW5 . . . . .5 B7
Alders Ave RH19 . . . . .185 C3
Alders Rd RH2 . . . . .118 B3
Alders The
  Aldershot GU9 . . . . .126 B6
  Feltham TW13 . . . . .15 E4
  Heston TW5 . . . . .4 F8
  Streatham SW16 . . . . .21 C4
  West Byfleet KT14 . . . . .71 C7
  West Wickham BR4 . . . . . . .63 B8
Alders View Dr RH19 . . . . .185 C3
Aldersbrook Dr KT2 . . . . . . .17 F2
Aldersey Rd GU1 . . . . .109 F1
Aldersgrove KT8 . . . . .36 D4
Aldershot Military Mus★
  GU11 . . . . .105 C7
Aldershot Rd Ash GU12 . . .105 F1
  Fairlands GU3 . . . . .108 D5
  Fleet GU14,GU52 . . . . . . .104 A6
  Pirbright GU24 . . . . .87 F2
  Wood St V GU3 . . . . .107 E5
Aldershot Sta GU11 . . . . . .105 B1
Alderside Wlk TW20 . . . . . . .11 E3
Aldersmead Ave CR0 . . . . . .43 D3
Aldersmead Rd BR3 . . . . . . .23 E1
Alderstead La RH1 . . . . .99 D2
Alderton KT2 . . . . .38 B8
Alderton Ct KT8 . . . . .35 F5
Alderton Rd CR0 . . . . .43 A2
Alderwick Dr TW3 . . . . .5 D4
Alderwood Cl CR3 . . . . .100 E2
Aldingbourne Cl RH11 . . . .200 F7
Aldis Mews SW17 . . . . .20 E3
Aldis St SW17 . . . . .20 E3
Aldous Ho TW18 . . . . .12 E4
Aldren Rd SW17 . . . . .20 C5
Aldrich Cres CR0 . . . . .63 C2
Aldrich Gdns SM3 . . . . .58 F7
Aldrich Terr SW18 . . . . .20 C6
Aldridge Rise KT3 . . . . .38 E3
Aldrin Pl GU14 . . . . .84 F2
Aldrington Rd SW16 . . . . . . .21 C4
Aldro Sch GU8 . . . . .149 C7

Aldwick Cl GU14 ....85 A6
Aldwick Rd CR0 ....60 F6
Aldworth Cl RG12 ....27 A5
Aldworth Gdns RG45 ....45 A5
Aldwych Cl RH10 ......202 D4
Aldwyn Ct TW20 ....11 B2
Alexander Cl TW2 ....16 F6
Alexander Cres CR3 ....100 C6
Alexander Ct
Beckenham BR2 ....44 D8
14 Surbiton KT6 ....37 D2
Alexander Evans Mews
SE23 ....23 D6
Alexander Godley Cl
KT21 ....95 F8
Alexander Rd
Coulsdon CR5 ....79 B4
Egham TW20 ....12 C3
Reigate RH2 ....139 A6
Alexander Wlk RG12 ....27 B4
Alexanders Wlk CR3 ...101 A1
Alexandra Ave
Camberley GU15 ....65 A5
Sutton SM1 ....59 A7
Warlingham CR6 ....81 F2
Alexandra Cl
Ashford TW15 ....14 D1
Staines TW18 ....13 D2
Walton-on-T KT12 ....54 A8
Alexandra Cotts SE20 ...23 D2
Alexandra Cres BR1 .....24 F2
Alexandra Ct
Aldershot GU11 ....104 E1
Ashford TW15 ....14 D2
10 Crawley RH10 ....201 D5
1 Farnborough GU14 .....85 C1
Alexandra Dr Surbiton KT5 38 A2
West Norwood SE19 ......22 E3
Alexandra Gdns
Chiswick W4 ....7 E7
Hounslow TW3 ....5 B5
Knaphill GU21 ....68 D1
Wallington SM5 ....60 A2
Alexandra Inf Sch
Kingston u T KT2 ....18 A1
Penge BR3 ....23 D1
Alexandra Jun & Inf Sch
TW3 ....5 B5
Alexandra Jun Sch SE26 .23 D2
Alexandra Lodge
12 Guildford GU1 ....130 F8
1 Weybridge KT13 ....53 B6
Alexandra Mans KT17 ...76 F6
Alexandra Pl Croydon CR0 42 E1
Guildford GU1 ....130 F7
South Norwood SE25 .....42 D4
Alexandra Rd
Addlestone KT15 ....52 D6
Aldershot GU11 ....104 F2
Ash GU12 ....105 F1
Ashford TW15 ....14 E2
Biggin Hill TN16 ....103 B8
10 Brentford TW8 ....6 D8
Croydon CR0 ....42 E2
Englefield Green TW20 ....11 C2
Epsom KT17 ....76 F6
Farnborough GU14,GU11 ..85 C1
Hounslow TW3 ....5 B5
Kingston u T KT2 ....18 A1
Mitcham SW19 ....20 E1
Mortlake SW14 ....7 D4
Penge SE26 ....23 D2
Richmond TW9 ....6 F5
Thames Ditton KT7 ....36 F4
Twickenham TW1 ....6 C1
Warlingham CR6 ....81 F2
Wimbledon SW19 ....20 A3
Alexandra Sq SM4 ......40 A4
Alexandra Terr GU1 .....130 E8
Alexandra Way KT19 ....76 A8
Alexandra Wlk 8 SE19 ...22 E3
Alfold By-Pass
Alfold GU6 ....193 F7
Alfold Crossways GU6 ...194 A5
Alfold Cotts GU6 ....193 F2
Alfold Rd Cranleigh GU6 .194 B7
Dunsfold GU8 ....192 F4
Dunsfold GU8 ....193 B3
Alfonso Cl GU12 ....126 C8
Alford Cl GU4 ....110 A4
Alford Craft Ctr GU6 ...194 A1
Alford Crossways GU6 .194 A3
Alford Ct 4 SM2 ....59 B3
Alford Gn CR0 ....63 D4
Alfred Butt Ho SW17 ....20 F5
Alfred Cl RH10 ....202 E5
Alfred Hurley Ho SW17 ..20 C4
Alfred Rd Croydon SE25 ..43 A4
Farnham GU9 ....125 C1
Feltham TW13 ....15 C6
Kingston u T KT1 ....37 E6
Sutton SM1 ....59 C5
Alfreton Cl SW19 ....19 D5
Alfriston KT5 ....37 F3
Alfriston Ave CR0 ....41 E2
Alfriston Cl KT5 ....37 F3
Alfriston Rd GU16 ....86 C7
Algar Cl TW7 ....6 A4
Algar Ct TW12 ....36 B8
Algar Rd TW7 ....6 A4
Algarve Rd SW18 ....20 B7
Alice Gough Meml Homes
RG12 ....27 B6
Alice Ho TW18 ....13 A2
Alice Holt Woodland Park
Forest Ctr* GU10 ....166 C8
Alice Mews 9 TW11 .....16 F3
Alice Rd GU11 ....105 B2
Alice Ruston Pl GU22 ...89 C8
Alice Way TW3 ....5 B3
Alicia Ave RH10 ....202 C6
Alington Gr SM6 ....60 D2
Alison Cl Croydon CR0 ...43 D1
Farnborough GU14 ....84 F3
Woking GU21 ....69 E4
Alison Dr GU15 ....65 F5
Alison Way GU11 ....104 F2
Alison's Rd GU11 ......105 B4
All England Lawn Tennis &
Croquet Club The*
SW19 ....19 E5
All Hallows RC Sch GU9 125 F7
All Saint's CE Jun Sch
SE19 ....42 E8
All Saints Carshalton CE Prim
Sch SM5 ....60 A5
All Saints CE Inf Sch
GU10 ....147 C3
All Saints CE Prim Sch
Horsham RH12 ....217 F6
Merton SW19 ....20 C1
All Saints Cl RG40 ......25 C7
All Saints Cres GU14 ....64 E1
All Saints Ct TW5 ....4 D6
All Saints Dr CR2 ....81 A7
All Saints Inf Sch KT22 ..95 A8
All Saints Rd
Lightwater GU18 ....48 C1
Merton SW19 ....20 C1
Sutton SM1 ....59 C7
All Saints' Benhilton CE Prim
Sch SM1 ....59 B7
All Souls' Rd SL5 ....29 A5
Allan Cl KT3 ....38 D4
Allbrook Cl TW11 ....16 E3
Allbrook Ho 5 SW15 ....19 A8
Allcard Cl RH12 ....217 D4
Allcot Cl Crawley RH11 ..200 E3
East Bedfont TW14 ....14 F7
Allcott Ho TW7 ....5 F4
Allden Ave GU12 ....126 D7
Allden Cotts GU7 ....150 B4
Allden Gdns GU12 ......126 D7
Alldens Hill GU5,GU8 ...151 D1
Alldens La GU8 ....151 B1
Allder Way CR2 ....61 B3
Allen Cl Streatham CR4 ...41 C8
Sunbury TW16 ....35 B8
Allen House Pk GU22 ....89 C7
Allen Rd
Great Bookham KT23 .....94 B1
Penge BR3 ....43 D7
Sunbury TW16 ....35 B7
Thornton Heath CR0 ......42 A1
Allen's Cl RH19 ....206 D6
Allenby Ave CR2 ....61 C2
Allenby Rd
Biggin Hill TN16 ....83 E2
Forest Hill SE23 ....23 E5
Sandhurst GU15 ....65 A6
Allendale GU8 ....148 C3
Allendale Cl
Forest Hill SE26 ....23 D3
Sandhurst GU47 ....45 A2
Allenford Ho SW15 ....7 F1
Allenswood 12 SW19 ....19 E7
Allerford Ct SE6 ....24 B5
Allerford Rd SE6 ....24 B4
Allerton Ct SM3 ....58 D8
Allerton Ho 4 SW19 .....20 C1
Alleyn Cres SE21 ....22 D6
Alleyn Pk SE21 ....22 E5
Alleyn Rd SE21 ....22 E5
Allgood Cl SM4 ....39 D3
Alliance Ct TW15 ....14 C4
Allingham Ct GU7 ......150 F7
Allingham Gdns RH12 ..218 B5
Allingham Rd RH2 ......139 A6
Allington Ave TW17 ......34 E6
Allington Cl SW19 ....19 D3
Allington Ct CR0 ....43 C3
Allison Gr SE21 ....22 E7
Alloway Cl 4 GU21 ......69 B1
Allsmoor La RG12 ....27 F6
Allum Gr KT20 ....97 B6
Allwood Cl SE26 ....23 D4
Allyington Way RH10 ...202 D5
Allyn Cl TW18 ....12 F2
Alma Cl Aldershot GU12 .105 D2
Knaphill GU21 ....68 E1
Alma Cres SM1 ....58 E5
Alma Ct
3 Caterham CR3 ....100 C6
Wokingham RG41 ....25 A5
Alma Gdns GU16 ....86 E8
Alma Ho 7 TW8 ....6 E8
Alma La GU9 ....125 C7
Alma Pl Penge SE19 .....22 F1
Thornton Heath CR7 .....42 A4
Alma Rd Carshalton SM5 ..59 E5
Headley Down GU35 ....187 C5
Reigate RH2 ....118 B3
Thames Ditton KT10, KT7 ..36 E1
Alma Sq GU14 ....105 C8
Alma Terr SW18 ....20 D8
Alma Way GU9 ....125 D7
Almer Rd SW20 ....19 A1
Almners Rd Chertsey KT16 32 C2
Lyne KT16 ....32 B1
Almond Ave
Carshalton SM5 ....59 F8
Woking GU22 ....89 D6
Almond Cl Charlton TW17 .34 C7
Crawley RH11 ....201 A5
Englefield Green TW20 ....11 B2
Feltham TW13 ....15 A7
Guildford GU1 ....109 D5
Almond Gr TW8 ....6 B7
Almond Rd KT19 ....76 D8
Almond Way CR4 ....41 D5
Almondale Ct GU14 ......85 A6
Almorah Rd TW5 ....4 D6
Alms Heath GU23 ....92 B6
Almsgate GU3 ....129 C2
Almshouse La KT9 ....56 D2
Almshouses Dorking RH4 136 B8
Lingfield RH7 ....164 C4
Sunbury TW16 ....34 F8
Almshouses The RH5 ...115 C8
Alnod KT18 ....97 D8
Alnwick Gr SM4 ....40 B5
Alpha Ct CR6 ....81 A1
Alpha Rd Aldershot GU12 105 E1
Chobham GU24 ....49 F1
Crawley RH11 ....201 C6
Croydon CR0 ....42 E1
Surbiton KT5 ....37 F3
Teddington TW11 ....16 D3
Woking GU22 ....70 C4
Alpha Way TW20 ....32 C8
Alphabet Gdns SM5 .....40 D3
Alphea Cl SW19 ....20 E1
Alphington Ave GU16 ....65 F1
Alphington Gn GU16 .....65 F1
Alpine Ave KT5 ....57 C8
Alpine Cl
Farnborough GU14 ....84 D3
South Croydon CR0 ....61 E7
Alpine Rd Redhill RH1 ...119 A4
Walton-on-T KT12 ....35 A2
Alpine View SM5 ....59 E5
Alresford Rd GU2 ......130 A8
Alric Ave KT3 ....38 F6
Alsace Wlk GU15 ....65 B1
Alsford Cl GU18 ....66 F7
Alsom Ave KT19,KT4 .....58 A6
Alston Cl KT7 ....37 B2
Alston Rd SW17 ....20 D4
Alt Gr SW19 ....19 E1
Altdam Farm RH1 ......140 A2
Alterton Cl GU21 ....69 A2
Althorne Rd RH1 ....140 A7
Althorp Rd SW17 ....20 F7
Alton Cl TW7 ....5 F5
Alton Ct
19 Beckenham BR3 ....24 A1
Egham TW18 ....32 E8
Alton Gdns
Beckenham BR3 ....24 A1
Twickenham TW2 ....16 D8
Alton Ho 1 RH1 ....119 A3
Alton Rd Croydon CR0,CR9 .61 A7
Farnham GU10,GU9 .....145 D7
Richmond TW10,TW9 ......6 E3
Roehampton SW15 ....19 A7
Alton Ride GU17 ....64 C6
Altyre Cl BR3 ....43 F4
Altyre Rd CR0,CR9 ......61 D8
Altyre Way BR3 ....43 F4
Alvernia Cl GU7 ....150 C2
Alvernia Lodge 4 SM1 ...59 B7
Alverstoke Gdns GU11 ..104 E1
Alverston Gdns SE25 ....42 E4
Alverstone Ave SW18,
SW19 ....20 A6
Alverstone Rd KT3 ....38 F5
Alvia Gdns SM1 ....59 C6
Alway Ave KT19 ....57 D5
Alwin Pl GU9 ....125 B7
Alwyn Cl CR0 ....63 B3
Alwyne Ct GU21 ....69 E3
Alwyne Rd SW19 ....19 F2
Alwyns Cl KT16 ....33 A3
Alwyns La KT16 ....33 A3
Amalgamated Dr TW8 ....6 B8
Amanda Ct TW15 ....13 F6
Ambassador RG12 ....26 F4
Ambassador Cl TW3 ....4 E5
Amber Ct Aldershot GU12 105 C2
Mitcham CR4 ....40 E5
Staines TW18 ....12 F3
Amber Hill GU15 ....66 B4
Ambercroft Way CR5 ...100 B8
Amberley Cl
Crawley RH10 ....202 C6
Horsham RH12 ....218 A6
Send Marsh GU23 ....90 F2
Amberley Ct SM2 ....59 C3
Amberley Dr KT15 ......70 F8
Amberley Gdns KT19 ....57 F6
Amberley Gr Croydon CR0 .42 F2
Forest Hill SE26 ....23 B3
Amberley Grange GU11 .125 F8
Amberley Lodge CR8 ....79 F6
Amberley Rd
Horsham RH12 ....218 A6
Milford GU8 ....149 E2
Amberley Way Heston TW4 .4 C2
Morden SM4 ....39 F2
Amberside Cl TW2 ....5 D1
Amberwood Cl SM6 .....60 E5
Amberwood Dr GU15 .....65 F7
Amberwood Rise KT3 ....38 E3
Amblecote KT11 ....73 E7
Ambleside Catford BR1 ...24 D2
Godalming GU7 ....151 A5
13 Putney SW19 ....19 E7
Ambleside Ave
Beckenham BR3 ....43 E4
Streatham SW16 ....21 D4
Ambleside Ave continued
Walton-on-T KT12 ....35 C1
Ambleside Cl
Crawley RH11 ....200 D5
Farnborough GU14 ....84 E3
Mytchett GU16 ....86 A2
Redhill RH1 ....140 B4
Ambleside Cres GU9 ...125 A6
Ambleside Dr TW14 .....14 F7
Ambleside Gdns
Selsdon CR2 ....62 D1
Streatham SW16 ....21 D3
Sutton SM2 ....59 C4
Ambleside Jun Sch KT12 35 C1
Ambleside Rd GU18 ......67 B8
Ambleside Way TW20 ....12 B1
Ambrey Way CR8,SM6 ....60 D2
Amen Cnr SW17 ....21 A2
Amen Corner Bsns Pk
RG12 ....26 D7
Amenity Way SM4 ....39 C2
American Com Sch
TW20 ....31 C7
American Comm Sch
KT11 ....54 C1
American Magna Carta
Meml* TW20 ....11 D6
American Sch in Switzerland
(English Branch) The
TW20 ....32 C6
Amersham Rd CR0 ......42 D3
Amesbury Ave SW2 ......21 F6
Amesbury Cl KT4 ....39 C1
Amesbury Rd TW13 ......15 D6
Amesbury Sch GU26 ...188 E1
Amey Dr KT23 ....94 C3
Amhurst Gdns TW7 ....6 A5
Amis Ave
Chessington KT19 ....57 B5
Woodham KT15 ....52 A1
Amis Rd GU21 ....88 E8
Amity Gr SW20 ....39 C8
Amlets La GU6 ....174 E5
Ampere Way CR0,CR9 ....41 F1
Amroth Cl SE23 ....23 B7
Amstel Way GU21 ....68 F1
Amundsen Rd RH12 ....217 D6
Amy Johnson Prim Sch
SM6 ....60 E3
Amy Rd RH8 ....122 E6
Amyand Cotts 12 TW1 ....6 B1
Amyand Park Gdns 3
TW1 ....17 B8
Amyand Park Rd TW1 ...17 A8
Anarth Ct KT13 ....34 E1
Ancaster Cres KT3 ......39 A3
Ancaster Dr SL5 ....28 E8
Ancaster Rd BR3 ....43 D6
Anchor Cl GU3 ....107 C4
Anchor Cotts RH7 ......163 E8
Anchor Cres GU21 ....68 D2
Anchor Hill GU21 ....68 D2
Anchor Mdw GU14 ....84 F4
Anchorage Cl SW19 .....20 A3
Anders Cnr RG42 ....26 F8
Anderson Ave GU2 .....109 B5
Anderson Cl Cheam SM3 .40 A1
Epsom KT19 ....76 B7
Anderson Ct GU27 .....208 C6
Anderson Dr TW15 ......14 C4
Anderson Ho
Farnham GU9 ....125 D1
Upper Tooting SW17 ......20 D3
Anderson Pl GU19 ....47 E4
Anderson Rd KT13 ....53 D7
Anderson's Pl TW3 ....5 B3
Andhurst Ct KT2 ....38 B8
Andon Ct BR3 ....43 E6
Andover Cl
East Bedfont TW14 ....14 F7
Epsom KT19 ....76 D8
Andover Ct TW19 ....13 D8
Andover Rd
Blackwater GU17 ....64 C6
Twickenham TW2 ....16 D7
Andover Way GU11 .....126 B7
Andreck Ct BR3 ....44 C7
Andrew Cl RG40 ....25 E5
Andrew Ct Beckenham BR3 44 B6
Farnborough GU14 ....84 F8
Forest Hill SE23 ....23 D6
Andrew Ewing Prim Sch
TW5 ....4 F7
Andrew Reed Ho SW18 ..19 E8
Andrew's Cl KT17 ....76 F6
Andrew's Ho CR8 ....79 F6
Andrewartha Rd GU14 ...85 E2
Andrewes Ho SM1 ....59 A6
Andrews Cl KT4 ....58 D8
Andrews Rd GU14 ....84 E5
Andromeda Cl RH11 ....200 E4
Anerley Ct SE20 ....23 B1
Anerley Gr SE19 ....22 F1
Anerley Hill SE19 ....22 F2
Anerley Park Rd SE20 ....23 B1
Anerley Pk SE20 ....23 B1
Anerley Prim Sch SE20 ..43 A8
Anerley Rd SE20,SE19 ....43 B8
Anerley Sch for Boys
SE20 ....43 A8
Anerley Sta SE20 ....43 B8
Anerley Station Rd SE20 .43 B8
Anerley Vale 3 SE19 .....23 A1
Anfield Cl SW12 ....21 C8
Angas Ct 1 KT13 ....53 C5
Angel Ct GU3 ....129 A3
Angel Gate GU1 ....130 D8
Angel Hill SM1 ....59 B7
Angel Hill Ct 2 SM1 .....59 B7
Angel Hill Dr SM1 ....59 B7
Angel Mews SW15 ....19 A8
Angel Pl RH2 ....139 B6
Angel Rd KT7 ....37 A1
Angela Ct 2 SE23 ....23 C7
Angelfield TW3 ....5 B2
Angelica Gdns CR0 ......43 D1
Angelica Rd Bisley GU24 ..68 A4
Guildford GU2 ....109 A5
Angell Cl RH10 ....202 C5
Angers Cl GU15 ....66 C7
Anglers Reach KT6 ......37 D4
Angles Rd SW16 ....21 E4
Anglesea Ho KT1 ....37 D5
Anglesea Rd KT1 ....37 D5
Anglesey Ave GU14 ......84 F7
Anglesey Cl Ashford TW15 14 A5
Crawley RH11 ....201 C2
Anglesey Court Rd SM5 .60 A4
Anglesey Gdns SM5 .....60 A4
Anglesey Rd GU12 ......105 D1
Angus Cl Chessington KT9 .57 A5
Horsham RH12 ....217 D4
Angus Ho 12 SW12 ....21 D8
Anlaby Rd TW11 ....16 E3
Ann Parkes Ct TW5 ....4 D5
Annandale Dr GU10 ....146 D6
Annandale Rd
Croydon CR0 ....62 A8
Guildford GU2 ....130 B7
Anne Armstrong Cl
GU11 ....105 D5
Anne Boleyn's Wlk
Cheam SM2,SM3 ....58 E3
Kingston u T KT2 ....17 E3
Anne Compton Mews 2
SE12 ....24 F8
Anne Way KT8 ....36 B5
Anne's Wlk CR3 ....100 E7
Anners Cl TW20 ....32 C6
Annesley Dr CR0 ....62 F7
Annett Cl TW17 ....34 E5
Annett Rd KT12 ....35 A2
Annie Brookes Cl TW18 .12 D5
Anningsley Pk KT16 .....51 C1
Annisdowne Cl RH5 ....133 F1
Annsworthy Ave CR7,
SE25 ....42 D6
Annsworthy Cres CR7 ...42 D7
Ansell Gr SM5 ....41 A1
Ansell Rd Dorking RH4 ..136 B8
Frimley GU16 ....65 E1
Upper Tooting SW17 ......20 F5
Anselm Cl CR0 ....61 F7
Ansford Rd BR1,SE6 .....24 D4
Ansley Cl CR2 ....81 B5
Anslie Wlk 9 SW12 ......21 B8
Anson Cl Aldershot GU11 .104 F3
Caterham CR8 ....100 D7
Anstice Cl W4 ....7 E7
Anstie Grange Dr RH5 ..157 B5
Anstie La RH5 ....156 F4
Anstiebury Cl RH5 .....157 C3
Anston Ct 5 GU2 ....108 E1
Anthony Ct TW7 ....5 F4
Anthony Rd CR0,SE25 ....43 A3
Anthony West Ho RH3 ..137 B7
Antigua Wlk SE19 ....22 D3
Antlands La Burstow RH6 183 B6
Crawley RH6 ....182 E5
Antlands La E RH6 ....182 F5
Antlands La W RH6 ....182 E6
Anton Cres SM1 ....59 A7
Antrobus Cl SM1 ....58 F5
Anvil Cl SW16 ....21 C1
Anvil La KT11 ....73 A5
Anvil Rd TW16 ....35 A6
Anyards Rd KT11 ....73 B5
Anzio Cl GU11 ....105 A2
Apeldoorn Dr SM6 ....60 E2
Aperdele Rd KT22 ....75 A1
Aperfield Rd TN16 ....83 E2
Apers Ave GU22 ....89 F6
Apex Cl Beckenham BR3 ...44 B8
Oatlands Park KT13 ......53 D7
Apex Dr GU16 ....65 D1
Apley Rd RH2 ....139 A6
Aplin Way Hounslow TW7 ...5 E6
Lightwater GU18 ....48 A1
Apollo Pl GU21 ....89 A8
Apollo Rise GU14 ....84 D4
Apperlie Dr RH6 ....161 C1
Apple Garth GU7 ......150 C7
Apple Gr KT9 ....56 E6
Apple Mkt KT1 ....37 D7
Apple Tree Cl KT23 ......94 C3
Apple Tree Way GU47 ....45 D1
Appleby Cl TW2 ....16 D6
Appleby Ct GU15 ....65 B6
Appleby Gdns TW14 .....14 F7
Appledore RG12 ....26 F3
Appledore Cl
1 Hayes BR2 ....44 F4
Upper Tooting SW12,SW17 .20 F6
Appledore Mews GU14 ..85 A7
Appledown Rise CR5 .....79 C4
Applefield RH10 ....201 E7
Applegarth Claygate KT10 .55 F5
New Addington CR0 ......63 B3
Applegarth Ave GU2 ...108 D1
Applegarth Inf & Jun Sch
CR0 ....63 B4
Applelands Cl GU10 ....146 A4
Appleton Gdns KT3 .....39 A3
Appleton Sq CR4 ....40 E8
Appletree Cl
Godalming GU7 ....150 F2

Appletree Cl *continued*
6 Penge SE20 .... 43 B8
Appletree Ct GU4 .... 110 D3
Appletree Pl 4 RG42 .... 27 A8
Appletrees Pl GU22 .... 89 C8
Appley Dr GU15 .... 65 B6
Approach Rd
Ashford TW15 .... 14 C2
East Molesey KT8 .... 36 A4
Farnham GU9 .... 125 C1
Merton SW20 .... 39 C7
Purley CR8 .... 80 B7
Tatsfield CR6,TN16 .... 103 B5
Approach The RH19 .... 185 F6
April Cl Ashstead KT21 .... 75 F1
Camberley GU15 .... 65 C2
Feltham TW13 .... 15 A5
Horsham RH12 .... 217 C4
April Glen SE23 .... 23 D5
Aprilwood Cl KT15 .... 70 F8
Apsley Ct Crawley RH11 .... 200 F4
Sutton SM2 .... 59 C4
Apsley Ho TW4 .... 4 F3
Apsley Rd Croydon SE25 .... 43 B5
Kingston u T KT3 .... 38 C6
Aquarius TW1 .... 17 B7
Aquarius Ct RH11 .... 200 E4
Aquila Cl KT21 .... 95 E6
Arabella Dr SW15 .... 7 E3
Aragon Ave Ewell KT17 .... 58 B2
Thames Ditton KT7 .... 36 F4
Aragon Cl Ashford TW16 .... 14 F1
New Addington CR0 .... 63 E1
Aragon Ct Bracknell RG12 .... 27 C5
Knaphill GU21 .... 68 D2
Aragon Prim Sch SM4 .... 39 D2
Aragon Rd
Kingston u T KT2 .... 17 E3
West Barnes SM4 .... 39 E2
Aram Ct GU22 .... 70 B4
Arbor Cl BR3 .... 44 B7
Arborfield Cl SW2 .... 21 F7
Arbour Cl KT22 .... 94 F4
Arbour Cotts GU2 .... 108 F5
Arbour The GU7 .... 128 F1
Arbrook Hall KT10 .... 55 F4
Arbrook La KT10 .... 55 D4
Arbury Terr SE26 .... 23 B5
Arbutus Cl RH1 .... 139 C7
Arbutus Rd RH1 .... 139 C6
Arcacia Cl SM5 .... 60 A6
Arcade The 11 GU11 .... 105 A2
Arch Rd KT12 .... 54 D7
Archbishop Lanfranc Sch The
CR0 .... 41 E3
Archbishop Tenison's CE Sch
CR0 .... 61 F7
Archbishop's Pl 3 SW2 .... 21 F8
Archdale Pl KT3 .... 38 B6
Archdeacon Cambridge's CE
Prim Sch TW2 .... 16 E6
Archer Cl KT2 .... 17 E1
Archer Rd SE25 .... 43 B5
Archers Ct RH10 .... 201 D8
Archery Pl GU5 .... 133 C4
Archway Cl
Wallington SM6 .... 60 E7
Wimbledon SW19 .... 20 B4
Archway Mews 9 RH4 .... 136 A8
Archway Pl RH4 .... 136 A8
Archway St SW13,SW14 .... 7 E4
Arcturus Rd RH11 .... 200 E3
Arcus Rd BR1 .... 24 E2
Arden 17 SW19 .... 19 D7
Arden Cl Bracknell RG12 .... 28 A7
Reigate RH2 .... 139 B5
Arden Mead Cotts RH7 .... 164 A8
Arden Rd RH10 .... 201 F4
Ardenrun RH7 .... 164 B8
Ardenrun Cotts RH7 .... 164 A7
Ardent Cl SE25 .... 42 E6
Ardesley Wood KT13 .... 53 E6
Ardfern Ave SW16 .... 42 A6
Ardfillan Rd SE6 .... 24 D6
Ardgowan Rd SE6 .... 24 E7
Ardingly RG12 .... 27 A4
Ardingly Cl
Crawley RH11 .... 201 B8
South Croydon CR0 .... 62 D7
Ardingly Ct KT18 .... 76 D5
Ardleigh Gdns SM3 .... 40 A2
Ardley Cl SE23,SE6 .... 23 E5
Ardlui Rd SE27 .... 22 C6
Ardmay Gdns KT6 .... 37 E4
Ardmore Ave GU2 .... 109 B3
Ardmore Ho GU2 .... 109 B3
Ardmore Way GU2 .... 109 B3
Ardoch Rd SE6 .... 24 D6
Ardrossan Ave GU15 .... 66 A5
Ardrossan Gdns KT4 .... 58 A7
Ardshiel Dr RH1 .... 139 E7
Ardwell Rd SW2 .... 21 E6
Arena La GU11 .... 104 E5
Arena Sta SE25 .... 43 C4
Arena The RG12 .... 27 A7
Arenal Dr RG45 .... 45 C3
Arethusa Way GU24 .... 67 F3
Arford Comm GU35 .... 187 A6
Argent Cl TW20 .... 12 C2
Argent Terr GU47 .... 64 E8
Argonaut Pk SL3 .... 1 F6
Argosy Gdns TW18 .... 12 F2
Argosy La TW19 .... 13 D8
Argus Wlk RH11 .... 201 A3
Argyle Ave TW2,TW3 .... 5 A1
Argyle Ho SM2 .... 59 C4
Argyle Rd TW3 .... 5 B2
Argyle St GU24 .... 87 A6
Argyll Ct 15 SW2 .... 21 E8
Ariel Way TW4 .... 4 B4
Arkell Gr SE19 .... 22 B1
Arkendale RH19 .... 185 A4
Arkindale Rd SE6 .... 24 C5
Arklow Mews 3 KT6 .... 56 E8
Arkwright Dr RG42 .... 26 D7
Arkwright Ho 23 SW2 .... 21 E8
Arkwright Rd Poyle SL3 .... 1 E5
South Croydon CR2 .... 61 F2
Arlington Cl
Bracknell RG42 .... 27 A8
Sutton SM1 .... 59 A8
Twickenham TW1 .... 6 C1
Arlington Ct Reigate RH2 .... 118 A3
4 Twickenham TW1 .... 6 C1
Arlington Dr SM5 .... 59 F8
Arlington Lodge KT13 .... 53 B6
Arlington Rd
Ashford TW15 .... 13 F3
Richmond TW10 .... 17 D6
Surbiton KT6 .... 37 D3
Teddington TW11 .... 16 F4
Twickenham TW1 .... 6 C1
Arlington Sq RG12 .... 27 A7
Arlington Terr GU11 .... 104 F2
Armadale Rd Feltham TW14 .... 4 A2
Woking GU21 .... 69 A2
Armeston KT3 .... 38 D2
Armfield Cl KT8 .... 35 F4
Armfield Cres CR4 .... 40 F7
Armistice Gdns SE25 .... 43 A6
Armitage Ct SL5 .... 29 C3
Armitage Dr GU16 .... 65 F1
Armstrong Cl KT12 .... 35 A3
Armstrong Mall GU14 .... 84 D4
Armstrong Rd
Englefield Green TW20 .... 11 C2
Feltham TW13 .... 15 E3
Armstrong Way GU14 .... 84 B1
Armytage Rd TW5 .... 4 D7
Arnal Cres SW18 .... 19 E8
Arncliffe RG12 .... 27 A4
Arndale Way TW20 .... 12 A3
Arndell Ho 3 SM1 .... 59 C6
Arne Cl RH11 .... 200 F3
Arne Gr RH6 .... 160 E5
Arnella Ct 2 GU14 .... 105 D8
Arnewood Cl
Oxshott KT22 .... 74 B5
Roehampton SW15 .... 19 A7
Arney's La CR4 .... 41 A3
Arnfield Cl RH11 .... 200 E5
Arngask Rd SE6 .... 24 D8
Arnhem Cl GU11 .... 105 B2
Arnhem Dr CR0 .... 82 D8
Arnison Rd KT8 .... 36 D5
Arnold Cres TW7 .... 5 D2
Arnold Dr KT9 .... 56 D4
Arnold Rd Mitcham SW17 .... 20 F1
Sheerwater GU21 .... 70 B4
Staines TW18 .... 13 C1
Arnulf St SE6 .... 24 B4
Arnull's Rd SW16 .... 22 B2
Arosa Rd 3 TW1 .... 6 D1
Arragon Gdns
Streatham SW16 .... 21 E1
West Wickham BR4 .... 63 B7
Arragon Rd
Twickenham TW1 .... 17 A8
Wandsworth SW18 .... 20 A7
Arragon Wlk KT14 .... 71 F6
Arran Cl Crawley RH11 .... 201 B3
Wallington SM6 .... 60 C6
Arran Rd SE6 .... 24 C6
Arran Way KT10 .... 55 B8
Arrancourt RH12 .... 217 B2
Arras Ave SM4 .... 40 C4
Arreton Mead GU21 .... 69 F5
Arrivals Rd RH6 .... 181 F8
Arrol Rd BR3 .... 43 D6
Arrow Ind Est GU14 .... 84 F2
Arrow Rd GU14 .... 84 F2
Artel Croft RH10 .... 202 A6
Arterberry Rd SW20,
SW19 .... 39 D8
Arthur Cl Bagshot GU19 .... 47 E1
Farnham GU9 .... 125 B1
Arthur Ct CR0 .... 61 D7
Arthur Rd Biggin Hill TN16 .... 83 C3
Crawley RH11 .... 200 E6
Farnham GU9 .... 125 C1
Horsham RH13 .... 217 D1
6 Kingston u T KT2 .... 18 A1
West Barnes KT3 .... 39 B4
Wimbledon SW19 .... 20 A5
Wokingham RG41 .... 25 A6
Arthur St GU11 .... 105 B2
Arthur's Bridge Rd GU21 .... 69 D2
Artillery Rd
1 Aldershot GU11 .... 105 B2
Farnborough GU11,GU14 .... 105 D8
7 Guildford GU1 .... 109 D1
Artillery Terr GU1 .... 109 D1
Artington Wlk GU2 .... 130 C6
Arun Ho 7 KT2 .... 37 D8
Arun Way RH13 .... 217 E1
Arundale KT1 .... 37 D5
Arundel Ave Ewell KT17 .... 58 B1
Merton SM4 .... 39 F5
South Croydon CR2 .... 62 A1
Arundel Cl Crawley RH10 .... 202 C6
Croydon CR0,CR9 .... 61 B7
Hampton TW12 .... 16 B3
Arundel Ct 4 BR2 .... 44 E7
Arundel Ho Croydon CR0 .... 61 D5
Guildford GU1 .... 130 D8
Reigate RH2 .... 139 B5
Arundel Rd Belmont SM2 .... 58 F3
Dorking RH4 .... 136 A7
Frimley GU15 .... 66 C4
Hounslow TW4 .... 4 C4
Kingston u T KT1 .... 38 C7
Thornton Heath CR0 .... 42 D3
Arundell Pl 12 GU9 .... 125 B2
Arunside RH12 .... 217 A1
Arunside Sch RH12 .... 217 A2
Ascalon Ct 19 SW2 .... 21 F8
Aschurch Rd CR0 .... 42 F2
Ascot Ct GU11 .... 105 A1
Ascot Heath CE Jun Sch
SL5 .... 8 E1
Ascot Heath Inf Sch SL5 .... 8 E1
Ascot Ho 8 Egham TW20 .... 12 A3
Penge SE26 .... 23 B2
Ascot Mews SM6 .... 60 C2
Ascot Race Course SL5 .... 28 F6
Ascot Rd
East Bedfont TW14,TW15 .... 14 B6
Mitcham SW17 .... 21 A2
Ascot Sta SL5 .... 29 A5
Ascot Twrs SL5 .... 28 F7
Ascot Wood SL5 .... 29 A6
Asford Gdns KT11 .... 73 D3
Ash Bridge Cvn Pk
GU12 .... 126 E8
Ash Church Mews GU12 .... 106 A2
Ash Church Rd GU12 .... 106 B2
Ash Cl Ash GU12 .... 106 B3
Blackwater GU17 .... 64 C5
Box Hill KT20 .... 116 C4
Carshalton SM5 .... 59 F8
Crawley Down RH10 .... 204 C8
Kingston u T KT3 .... 38 D7
Lingfield RH7 .... 164 E5
Merstham RH1 .... 119 C5
Penge SE20 .... 43 C7
Pyrford GU22 .... 71 A4
Woking GU22 .... 89 E7
Ash Combe GU8 .... 191 A4
Ash Ct
East Grinstead RH19 .... 185 E3
Ottershaw KT16 .... 51 C5
West Ewell KT19 .... 57 C6
3 West Norwood SW16 .... 22 A3
Ash Dr RH1 .... 140 B7
Ash Gr East Bedfont TW14 .... 14 E7
Guildford GU2 .... 109 A2
Heston TW5 .... 4 D7
Penge SE20 .... 43 C7
Staines TW18 .... 13 C2
West Wickham BR4 .... 44 C1
Ash Grange Prim Sch
GU12 .... 106 B2
Ash Green La E GU12 .... 127 C8
Ash Green La W
Ash GU12 .... 126 F8
Ash,Ash Green GU12 .... 127 C8
Ash Green Rd GU12 .... 106 C1
Ash Hill Rd GU12 .... 106 B3
Ash Keys RH10 .... 201 E5
Ash La GU8 .... 148 C2
Ash Lodge 2 TW16 .... 14 F1
Ash Lodge Cl GU12 .... 106 A1
Ash Lodge Dr GU12 .... 106 A1
Ash Manor Sch GU12 .... 126 F8
Ash Mews KT18 .... 76 E6
Ash Rd Aldershot GU12 .... 126 D8
Cheam SM3,SM4 .... 39 F1
Crawley RH10 .... 202 A8
Croydon CR0 .... 63 A8
Littleton TW17 .... 34 A5
Pirbright GU24 .... 88 A1
Woking GU22 .... 89 E7
Ash St GU12 .... 106 A1
Ash Sta GU12 .... 106 B2
Ash Tree Cl
Croydon BR3,CR0 .... 43 E3
Farnborough GU14 .... 84 C3
Grayswood GU27 .... 189 F1
1 Surbiton KT6 .... 37 E1
Ash Tree Way CR0 .... 43 E3
Ash Vale GU8 .... 191 A5
Ash Vale Sta GU12 .... 106 A7
Ashbourne RG12 .... 26 F3
Ashbourne Cl Ash GU12 .... 106 C3
Coulsdon CR5 .... 79 C1
Ashbourne Rd CR4,SW17 .... 21 A1
Ashbourne Terr 1 SW19 .... 20 A1
Ashbrook Rd SL4 .... 11 B8
Ashburnham Pk KT10 .... 55 C6
Ashburnham Rd
Crawley RH10 .... 202 A4
Richmond TW10 .... 17 B5
Ashburton Ave CR0 .... 43 B1
Ashburton Cl CR0 .... 43 A1
Ashburton Com Sch CR0 .... 43 B2
Ashburton Gdns CR0 .... 62 A8
Ashburton Jun & Inf Sch
CR0 .... 43 B3
Ashburton Rd CR0,CR9 .... 62 A8
Ashbury Cres GU4 .... 110 C3
Ashbury Dr GU17 .... 65 A1
Ashbury Pl SW19 .... 20 C2
Ashby Ave KT19,KT9 .... 57 A4
Ashby Ct RH13 .... 217 E1
Ashby Grange 7 SM6 .... 60 C4
Ashby Way UB7 .... 3 A7
Ashby Wlk CR0 .... 42 C3
Ashcombe Ave KT6 .... 37 D2
Ashcombe Par GU22 .... 90 A7
Ashcombe Rd
Dorking RH4 .... 115 A1
Merstham RH1 .... 119 C8
Wallington SM5 .... 60 A4
Wimbledon SW19 .... 20 A3
Ashcombe Sch The RH4 .... 115 B1
Ashcombe Sq KT3 .... 38 C6
Ashcombe Terr KT20 .... 97 B7
Ashcroft GU4 .... 130 E2
Ashcroft Pk KT11 .... 73 E6
Ashcroft Rd KT9 .... 56 F7
Ashcroft Rise CR5 .... 79 E3
Ashdale KT23 .... 94 C1
Ashdale Cl Stanwell TW19 .... 13 E6
Twickenham TW2 .... 16 C8
Ashdale Way TW2 .... 16 B8
Ashdene Cl TW15 .... 14 C1
Ashdene Cres GU12 .... 106 A3
Ashdene Ho TW20 .... 11 C2
Ashdene Rd GU12 .... 106 A2
Ashdown Ave GU14 .... 85 E2
Ashdown Cl
13 Beckenham BR3 .... 44 B7
Bracknell RG12 .... 28 A7
Reigate RH2 .... 139 B5
7 Woking GU22 .... 89 E8
Ashdown Ct
Crawley RH10 .... 201 F3
Horsham RH13 .... 217 F4
11 Sutton SM2 .... 59 C4
Ashdown Dr RH10 .... 201 E3
Ashdown Gate RH19 .... 185 D2
Ashdown Gdns CR2 .... 81 B4
Ashdown Pl KT7 .... 37 A2
Ashdown Rd Ewell KT17 .... 77 A6
Forest Row RH18 .... 206 F2
Kingston u T KT1 .... 37 E7
Reigate RH2 .... 139 B5
Ashdown View RH19 .... 205 E7
Ashdown Way SW17 .... 21 A6
Ashely Cotts KT21 .... 95 F8
Ashen Gr SW19 .... 20 A6
Ashen Vale CR2 .... 62 D2
Ashenden Rd GU2 .... 108 F1
Ashfield RH14 .... 211 E2
Ashfield Ave TW13 .... 15 B7
Ashfield Cl
Beckenham BR3 .... 24 A1
Richmond TW10 .... 17 E7
Ashfields RH2 .... 118 B3
Ashford Ave TW15 .... 14 B2
Ashford CE Prim Sch
TW15 .... 14 B2
Ashford Cl TW15 .... 13 E4
Ashford Cres TW15 .... 13 E5
Ashford High Sch The
TW15 .... 13 E5
Ashford Hospl TW15 .... 13 E6
Ashford Ind Est TW15 .... 14 C4
Ashford Park Prim Sch
TW15 .... 13 D4
Ashford Rd
Feltham TW13,TW15 .... 14 E4
Littleton TW15,TW17 .... 14 C1
Staines TW18 .... 33 D8
Ashford Sta TW15 .... 13 F5
Ashgrove Rd
Ashford TW15 .... 14 D3
Catford BR1 .... 24 D2
Ashlake Rd SW16 .... 21 E4
Ashlea Ct CR6 .... 81 A1
Ashleigh Ave TW20 .... 12 C1
Ashleigh Cl RH6 .... 160 F3
Ashleigh Cotts RH5 .... 157 B7
Ashleigh Ct SE26 .... 23 B2
Ashleigh Gdns SM1 .... 59 B8
Ashleigh Ho 1 SW14 .... 7 E4
Ashleigh Point 8 SE26 .... 23 D5
Ashleigh Rd
Horsham RH12 .... 217 C4
Mortlake SW14 .... 7 E4
Penge SE20 .... 43 B6
Ashley Ave Epsom KT18 .... 76 D6
Morden SM4 .... 40 A4
Ashley CE Prim Sch
KT12 .... 35 A1
Ashley Cl Frimley GU16 .... 86 A6
Little Bookham KT23 .... 93 F2
Oatlands Park KT12,KT13 .... 34 F1
Ashley Ct 5 Epsom KT18 .... 76 D6
Knaphill GU21 .... 68 F1
Ashley Ctr KT18 .... 76 D6
Ashley Dr Banstead SM7 .... 78 A5
Blackwater GU17 .... 64 C4
Hounslow TW7 .... 5 E8
Twickenham TW2 .... 16 B7
Walton-on-T KT12 .... 54 A7
Ashley Gdns
Richmond TW10 .... 17 D6
Shalford GU4 .... 130 F2
Ashley Ho GU7 .... 150 E8
Ashley La CR0 .... 61 B6
Ashley Park Ave KT12 .... 53 F8
Ashley Park Cres KT12 .... 35 A1
Ashley Park Rd KT12 .... 54 A7
Ashley Rd Epsom KT18 .... 76 E4
Farnborough GU14 .... 85 D4
Hampton TW12 .... 36 A8
Knaphill GU21 .... 68 F1
Richmond TW9 .... 6 E4
Thames Ditton KT7 .... 36 F3
Thornton Heath CR7 .... 41 F5
Walton-on-T KT12 .... 54 A8
Westcott RH4 .... 135 C6
Wimbledon SW19 .... 20 B2
Ashley Rise KT12 .... 54 A7
Ashley Way GU24 .... 67 D6
Ashling Rd CR0,CR9 .... 43 A1
Ashlyn's Pk KT11 .... 73 E6
Ashlyns Way KT9 .... 56 D4
Ashmead Rd TW14 .... 15 A7
Ashmere Ave BR3 .... 44 D7
Ashmere Cl SM3 .... 58 D5
Ashmill Ct CR0 .... 42 C3
Ashmore Ct TW5 .... 5 A8
Ashmore Ho RH11 .... 181 D1
Ashmore La
Biggin Hill BR2 .... 83 C8
Rusper RH12 .... 199 C6
Ashridge GU14 .... 84 F7
Ashridge Gn 2 RG42 .... 27 B8
Ashridge Rd RG40 .... 25 D8
Ashridge Way
Ashford TW16 .... 15 A2
Merton SM4,SW20 .... 39 F5
Ashstead La GU7 .... 150 C2
Ashstead Sta KT21 .... 75 E3
Ashtead Ct 15 SW19 .... 19 D7
Ashtead Hospl The KT21 .... 95 E8
Ashtead La GU7 .... 150 D2
Ashtead Woods Rd KT21 .... 75 C3
Ashton Cl Cheam SM1 .... 59 A6
Hersham KT12 .... 54 B4
Ashton Ct BR3 .... 43 F8
Ashton Gdns TW4 .... 4 F3
Ashton Ho SW15 .... 19 B8
Ashton Rd 2 GU21 .... 68 F2
Ashtree Ave CR4 .... 40 D7
Ashtree Ct TW15 .... 14 B3
Ashtrees GU6 .... 174 E1
Ashtrees The GU12 .... 106 B2
Ashurst 3 KT18 .... 76 D6
Ashurst Cl
Horsham RH12 .... 218 A5
Kenley CR8 .... 80 D4
Penge SE20 .... 43 B8
Ashurst Dr Box Hill KT20 .... 116 B5
Crawley RH10 .... 202 D6
Littleton TW17 .... 33 E5
Ashurst Rd
Ash Vale GU12 .... 105 F4
Tadworth KT20 .... 97 C6
Ashurst Wlk CR0 .... 62 B8
Ashurst Wood Prim Sch
RH19 .... 206 E6
Ashurstwood Abbey
RH19 .... 206 F6
Ashvale Rd SW17 .... 20 F3
Ashview Cl TW15 .... 13 E3
Ashview Gdns TW15 .... 13 E3
Ashville Pk RG41 .... 25 B5
Ashville Way RG41 .... 25 A5
Ashway Ctr 5 KT2 .... 37 E8
Ashwell Ave GU15 .... 65 F6
Ashwell Ct TW15 .... 13 E6
Ashwick Cl CR3 .... 101 A3
Ashwood
5 Crawley RH11 .... 201 D5
Warlingham CR6 .... 101 C7
Ashwood Gdns CR0 .... 63 C4
Ashwood Pk
11 Belmont SM2 .... 59 A3
Fetcham KT22 .... 94 C4
Woking GU22 .... 70 A1
Ashwood Pl GU22 .... 70 A1
Ashwood Rd
Englefield Green TW20 .... 11 B2
Woking GU22 .... 70 A1
Ashworth Pl GU2 .... 108 F1
Aslett St SW18 .... 20 C8
Asmar Cl CR5 .... 79 E4
Aspen Cl Guildford GU4 .... 110 D4
Staines TW18 .... 12 F5
Stoke D'Abernon KT11 .... 73 E3
Aspen Ct Richmond TW9 .... 7 A7
Thorpe GU25 .... 31 E5
Aspen Gdns Ashford TW15 .... 14 C3
Mitcham CR4 .... 41 A4
Aspen Gr GU12 .... 126 E8
Aspen Ho CR6 .... 82 B4
Aspen House Sch SW2 .... 21 F8
Aspen Sq KT13 .... 53 D7
Aspen Vale CR3 .... 80 F1
Aspen Way Banstead KT17 .... 77 D5
Feltham TW13 .... 15 B5
Horsham RH12 .... 217 E4
Aspin Way GU17 .... 64 B5
Aspinall Ho SW12 .... 21 E7
Asprey Gr CR3 .... 101 A3
Asquith Ho SM7 .... 77 F4
Assembly Wlk SM5 .... 40 E2
Assher Rd KT12 .... 54 E7
Assheton-Bennett Ho 15
KT6 .... 37 E4
Astede Pl KT21 .... 75 F1
Astleham Rd TW17 .... 33 E6
Astley Ho 8 SE27 .... 22 C4
Astolat Ind Est The GU3 .... 130 C1
Aston Cl KT21 .... 75 C1
Aston Ct RH11 .... 201 B1
Aston Gn TW5 .... 4 C5
Aston Pl SW16 .... 22 B2
Aston Rd Claygate KT10 .... 55 E5
Merton SW20 .... 39 C7
Aston Way KT18 .... 76 F3
Astonville St SW18 .... 20 A7
Astor Cl Addlestone KT15 .... 52 D6
Kingston u T KT2 .... 18 B2
Astoria Ct 10 CR8 .... 80 A8
Astoria Mans 13 SW16 .... 21 E5
Astoria Par SW16 .... 21 E5
Astra Bsns Ctr RH1 .... 161 A7
Astra Mead RG42 .... 8 B2
Astwood Pl RH1 .... 118 E1
Asylum Arch Rd RH1 .... 139 F6
Atalanta Cl CR8 .... 61 A1
Atbara Ct TW11 .... 17 B2
Atbara Rd TW11 .... 17 B2

Atcham Rd TW3 ....5 C3
Atfield Gr GU20 ......48 D4
Atheldene Rd SW18 ...20 C7
Athelney Prim Sch SE6 .24 A5
Athelney St SE6 ......24 A5
Athelstan Cl RH10 ...202 E6
Athelstan Ho KT1 ....37 F5
Athelstan House Sch
  TW12 ....36 A8
Athelstan Rd KT1 ....37 F5
Athena Cl KT1 ....37 F6
Atherfield Ho RH2 ..139 C6
Atherfield Rd RH2 ..139 C6
Atherley Way TW4 ...15 F8
Atherton Cl Shalford GU4 130 E3
  Stanwell TW19 ....2 D1
Atherton Dr SW19 ....19 D4
Atherton Rd CR2 .....61 E4
Atherton Ho CR2 .....61 E4
Athlone KT10 ....55 E4
Athlone Rd SW2 ......22 A8
Atholl Ho ⑪ RH1 ...118 F1
Atkins Cl GU21 ......69 A1
Atkins Dr BR4 ....63 D8
Atkins Rd SW4,SW12 .21 D8
Atkinson Ct RH6 ....161 B2
Atkinson Morley's Hospl
  SW20 ....19 B1
Atkinson Rd RH10 ...202 C4
Atlanta Ct CR7 ......42 C6
Atrebatti Rd GU47 ...45 C1
Attebrouche Ct RG12 .27 D2
Attfield Cl GU12 ...105 F1
Attleborough Ct SE21 .23 B6
Attlee Cl CR7 ....42 C4
Attlee Ho ⑤ RH11 ..201 B2
Attwood Cl CR2 ......81 B5
Atwater Cl SW2 ......22 A7
Atwell Pl KT7 ....37 A1
Atwood KT23 ....93 E3
Atwood Ave TW9 ......7 A5
Atwood Ho SE21 .....22 E5
Atwood Prim Sch CR2 .81 A6
Aubyn Hill SE27 .....22 D4
Auchinleck Ct RH10 .204 B7
Auchinleck Way GU11 .104 E2
Auckland Cl
  Crawley RH11 ......181 D1
  South Norwood SE19 .42 F8
Auckland Ct SE27 ....22 C4
Auckland Gdns SE19 .42 C4
Auckland Hill SE27 ..22 C4
Auckland Rd
  Caterham CR3 ......100 E5
  Kingston u T KT1 ...37 F5
  South Norwood SE19,SE25 .42 F8
Auckland Rise SE19 .42 E8
Audley Cl KT15 ......52 B5
Audley Ct Surbiton KT5 .37 F3
  Twickenham TW2 .....16 D5
Audley Dr CR6 ....81 C4
Audley Firs KT12 ....54 C6
Audley Ho KT15 ......52 B5
Audley Pl SM2 ....59 B3
Audley Prim Sch CR3 .100 F6
Audley Rd TW10 ....6 F2
Audley Way SL5 .....28 D6
Audrey Cl BR3 ....44 B3
Audric Cl KT2 ....38 A8
Augur Cl TW18 ....12 F3
August La GU5 ......153 D7
Augusta Cl KT8 ......35 F6
Augusta Rd TW2 .....16 C6
Augustine Cl SL3 .....1 E4
Augustus Cl TW8 .....6 D7
Augustus Ct
  Feltham TW15 ....15 F4
  Hounslow TW3 ....5 C3
  ⑧ Putney SW19 ....19 E7
  South Norwood SE19 .22 E1
  Streatham SW16 .....21 D6
Augustus Gdns GU15 .66 C5
Augustus Rd SW19 ...19 E7
Aultone Way
  Carshalton SM5 .....59 F7
  Sutton SM5 ....59 C8
Aurelia Gdns CR7 ....41 F3
Aurelia Rd CR0,CR7,CR9 .41 F3
Auriol Cl KT19 ......57 E7
Auriol Jun Sch KT19 .57 F6
Auriol Park Rd KT19,KT4 .57 E7
Aurum Cl RH6 ......161 B2
Austen Cl RH19 ....185 B1
Austen Rd
  Farnborough GU14 ..85 A6
  Guildford GU1 .....130 F8
Austin Cl Coulsdon CR8 .80 B1
  Forest Hill SE23,SE6 .23 F8
  Twickenham TW1 .....6 C2
Austin Ho ⑲ KT6 ....37 E4
Austin's Cotts ⑦ GU9 .125 B2
Austyn Gdns KT5 ....38 B1
Autumn Cl SW19 .....20 C2
Autumn Dr SM2 ......59 B2
Avalon Cl SW20 .....39 E7
Avalon Ct CR0 ......42 F2
Avarn Rd SW17 ......20 F2
Avebury RG12 ....27 A3
Avebury Cl RH12 ...218 A2
Avebury Rd SW19 ...39 F8
Aveley La GU9 .....146 C7
Aveling Cl Crawley RH10 .202 C4
  Purley CR8 ....79 F6
Aven Cl GU6 ....174 E2
Avening Rd SW18 ....20 A8
Avening Terr SW18 ..20 A8

Avenue C KT15 ......52 E7
Avenue Cl Cranford TW5 ..4 B8
  Tadworth KT20 .....97 B5
Avenue Cres TW5 ....4 B7
Avenue Ct Penge SE20 .43 C8
  Tadworth KT20 .....97 B4
Avenue De Cagny GU24 .87 F5
Avenue Elmers KT6 ..37 E4
Avenue Gdns Cranford TW5 .4 B7
  Horley RH6 ....161 C2
  Mortlake SW14 ......7 E4
  South Norwood SE25 .43 A7
  Teddington TW11 ...16 F2
Avenue One KT15 ....52 E6
Avenue Par TW16 ....35 B6
Avenue Park Rd SE21,
  SE27 ....22 B6
Avenue Prim Sch The
  SM2 ....59 A1
Avenue Rd Banstead SM7 .78 B4
  Belmont SM2 ....59 A1
  Caterham CR3 .....100 E5
  Cobham KT11 ....73 D3
  Cranleigh GU6 .....174 F1
  Egham TW18 ....12 D3
  Epsom KT18 ....76 D5
  Farnborough GU14 ..85 D3
  Feltham TW13 ......14 F5
  Grayshott GU26 ...188 C3
  Hampton TW12 ......36 B8
  Hounslow TW7 ....5 F6
  Kingston u T KT1 ...37 E6
  Mitcham SW16 ......41 D7
  New Malden KT3 ....38 E5
  South Norwood, Annerley
    SE25 ....43 A7
  South Norwood, Elmers End
    BR3,SE20 ....43 D8
  Tatsfield TN16 ....103 E7
  Teddington TW11 ...17 A2
  Wallington SM6 ....60 C3
  Wimbledon SW20 ....39 B7
Avenue Row GU8 ....148 D4
Avenue S KT5 ....38 A2
Avenue Sucy GU15 ..65 B4
Avenue Terr KT3 ....38 C6
Avenue The
  Aldershot GU12 ...126 C7
  Beckenham BR3 ....44 C8
  Belmont SM2 ......58 F2
  Biggin Hill TN16 ..103 F5
  Brockham RH3 .....116 A1
  Camberley GU15 ...65 B5
  Chobham GU24 .....50 A3
  Claygate KT10 .....55 E5
  Compton GU3,GU7 .129 C5
  Coulsdon CR5 .....79 D4
  Cranford TW5 ......4 A6
  Crowthorne RG45 ..45 B5
  Dormansland RH19 .186 B6
  Egham TW20 ....12 B4
  Ewhurst GU6 ......175 E6
  Godalming GU7 ....150 F2
  Grayshott GU26 ...188 D3
  Hampton TW12 .....15 F2
  Haslemere GU27 ...207 F7
  Horley RH6 ....160 F2
  Hounslow TW3 ......5 B2
  Isleworth TW1 .....6 C2
  Lightwater GU18 ...48 A1
  ④ New Malden KT4 .39 A1
  North Ascot SL5 ...8 F1
  Oxshott KT22 .....74 F8
  Richmond TW9 ......6 F5
  Rowledge GU10 ...145 F3
  South Croydon CR0 .61 E7
  South Nutfield RH1 .140 E6
  Staines TW18 ......33 B8
  Stoneleigh KT17,SM3 .58 C3
  Sunbury TW16 .....35 B7
  Surbiton KT5 ......37 F3
  Tadworth KT20 ....97 B5
  Twickenham TW1 ....6 B2
  West Wickham BR4 ..44 E2
  Whyteleafe CR3 ...101 A8
  Woodham KT15 ....52 A1
  Worcester Park KT4 .57 F8
  Worplesdon GU3 ...88 E1
Avenue Three KT15 ..52 E7
Avenue Two KT15 ....52 E6
Averil Gr SW16 .....22 B2
Avern Gdns KT8 .....36 B5
Avern Rd KT8 ....36 B5
Avery Ct
  ⑥ Aldershot GU11 .105 B2
  Penge SE20 ....23 B1
Aviary Rd GU22 .....71 A3
Aviary Way RH10 ...184 C1
Aviemore Cl BR3 ...43 F4
Aviemore Way BR3 ..43 E4
Avington Cl GU1 ...109 E1
Avington Gr SE20 ...23 C1
Avoca Rd SW17 .....21 A4
Avocet Cres GU47 ..64 E8
Avon Cl Addlestone KT15 .52 A4
  Ash GU12 ....105 F1
  Farnborough GU14 ..84 E7
  Sutton SM1 ....59 C6
  Worcester Park KT4 .58 A8
Avon Ct Farnham GU9 .125 C1
  Guildford GU1 ....110 A1
Avon Ho ⑨ Redhill RH1 .118 F2
  ⑤ Teddington KT2 .37 D8
Avon Wlk RH11 ....200 F5
Avondale
  Aldershot GU12 ...105 F7

Avondale Ave
  Hinchley Wood KT10 .56 A7
  New Malden KT4 ....38 F1
  Staines TW18 ......12 F1
Avondale Cl
  Hersham KT12 .....54 C5
  Horley RH6 ....161 A5
Avondale Ct ⑨ SM2 .59 C3
Avondale Gdns TW4 ..4 F2
Avondale High CR3 .101 A6
Avondale Ho ⑥ SW14 .7 D4
Avondale Rd
  Aldershot GU11 ...126 B8
  Ashford TW15,TW19 .13 D5
  Bromley BR1 ....24 F2
  Mortlake SW14 .....7 D4
  South Croydon CR2 .61 C4
  Wimbledon SW19 ...20 B3
Avonmead GU21 ....69 C1
Avonmore Ave GU1 .109 F2
Avonwick Rd TW3 ...5 B5
Avro Way Byfleet KT13 .52 E1
  Wallington SM6 ....60 E3
Axbridge RG12 .....27 E4
Axes La RH1 ....140 D2
Axford Ho SW2 .....22 B7
Axwood KT18 ....76 C4
Aycliffe Ct KT1 ....38 A7
Ayebridges Ave TW20 .12 C1
Ayjay Cl GU11 ....126 A7
Aylesford St SM1 ..59 C7
Aylesford Rd BR3 ..43 E4
Aylesworth Spur SL4 .11 B8
Aylett Rd Croydon SE25 .43 B5
  Isleworth TW7 .....5 E5
Ayling Ct GU9 ....125 F7
Ayling Hill GU11 .104 F1
Ayling La GU11 ...125 F8
Aylward Rd
  Forest Hill SE23 ..23 D6
  Merton SW19 ......39 F6
Aylwin Ct RH12 ...217 A1
Aymer Cl TW18 .....32 E8
Aymer Dr TW18 ....32 E8
Aysgarth RG12 ....27 A3
Aysgarth Ct SM1 ..59 B7
Aysgarth Rd SE21 ..22 E8
Ayshe Court Dr RH13 .217 E3
Azalea Cl Purley CR8 .80 B8
  Woking GU22 ......89 D8
Azalea Ct GU27 ...207 F8
Azalea Way GU15 ..66 B6

B

Babbacombe Cl KT9 .56 D5
Babbage Way RG12 ..27 A3
Babbs Mead GU9 ...125 A1
Baber Dr TW14 ......4 C1
Babington Ct SW16 .21 D3
Babington Rd SW16 .21 D3
Babylon La KT20,RH2 .118 B8
Bachelor's La GU23 .92 A3
Back Gn KT12 ......54 C4
Back La Binstead GU10 .166 B8
  Brentford TW8 .....6 B8
  Crawley RH10 .....203 D1
  East Clandon GU4 .111 D4
  Elstead GU8 ......148 D4
  Plaistow RH14 ....211 E2
  Richmond TW10 ....17 C6
Back Path RH1 ....120 D2
Back Rd TW11 .....16 E2
Bacon Cl GU47 ....64 D6
Bacon La GU10 ...167 C3
Badajos Rd GU11 .104 F3
Baden Cl TW18 ....13 B1
Baden Dr RH6 ....160 E4
Baden Powell Cl KT6 .56 F8
Baden Rd GU2 ....109 B3
Bader Cl CR8 .....80 D4
Bader Ct GU14 ....84 F8
Badger Cl Feltham TW13 .15 B5
  Guildford GU2 ...109 B4
  Hounslow TW4 ......4 C4
Badger Ct GU10 ..146 A5
Badger Dr GU18 ...48 A1
Badger Way GU10 .124 D8
Badger's Mount CR8 .61 B1
Badgers Cl Ashford TW15 .13 F3
  Farncombe GU7 ...150 D8
  Horsham RH12 ....217 F6
  Woking GU21 .....69 C1
Badgers Copse
  Frimley GU15 .....65 E4
  Worcester Park KT4 .57 E8
Badgers Cross GU8 .149 E1
Badgers Ct ④ KT17 .76 E6
Badgers Hill GU25 .31 C4
Badgers Hollow GU7 .150 D6
Badgers Lodge ⑤ KT17 .76 E6
Badgers Way
  Bracknell RG12 ....27 F7
  East Grinstead RH19 .185 F2
  Loxwood RH14 ....213 A4
Badgers Wlk
  Kingston u T KT3 ..38 E7
  Purley CR8 ....79 C8
  Whyteleafe CR3 ...80 F1
Badgers Wood CR3 .100 D2
Badgerwood Dr GU16 .65 D2
Badingham Dr KT22 .94 E4
Badminton Rd SW12 .21 A8
Badshot Lea Inf Sch
  GU9 ....126 A6

Badshot Lea Rd GU11,
  GU9 ....126 A6
Badshot Pk GU9 ...126 A6
Bagden Hill KT23 .114 D5
Bagot Cl KT21 ....75 F3
Bagshot Gn GU19 ..47 E3
Bagshot Inf Sch GU19 .47 E2
Bagshot Rd Ascot SL5 .29 C2
  Bracknell RG12 ...27 C4
  Brookwood GU21,GU22,
    GU24,GU3 ....88 C5
  Englefield Green TW20 .11 C2
  West End GU24 ....68 B8
Bagshot Sta GU19 .47 E3
Bahram Rd KT19 ...57 D1
Baigents La GU20 ..48 D4
Bailes La GU3 ....107 D3
Bailey Cl Frimley GU16 .85 D8
  Horsham RH12 ....217 F1
Bailey Cres KT9 ...56 D3
Bailey Mews W4 ...7 B8
Bailey Pl SE26 ....23 D2
Bailey Rd RH4 ...135 C6
Baileys Cl GU17 ..64 C4
Bailing Hill RH12 .216 E7
Baillie Rd GU1 ...130 F8
Bain Ave GU15 ....65 B2
Bainbridge cl KT2 .17 E3
Baines Cl CR0 ....61 D5
Bainton Mead GU21 .69 A2
Baird Cl RH10 ...182 A1
Baird Dr GU3 ....108 B2
Baird Gdns SE19 ..22 E4
Baird Rd GU14 ...85 C6
Bakeham La TW20 .11 D1
Bakehouse Barn Cl
  RH12 ....217 F6
Bakehouse Rd RH6 .161 A5
Baker Cl RH10 ...201 D4
Baker La CR4 .....41 A7
Baker St SW13 ...53 B6
Baker's Cl RH7 ..164 E5
Baker's La RH7 ..164 E4
Bakers Cl CR8 ....80 C5
Bakers Ct SE25 ...42 E6
Bakers End SW20 .39 E8
Bakers Gdns SM5 ..59 E8
Bakers Mead RH9 .121 C5
Bakers Way RH5 ..178 C5
Bakery Mews KT6 ..38 A1
Bakewell Dr KT3 ..38 E7
Balaam Ho SM1 ...59 A6
Balaclava Rd KT6 .37 C2
Balchins La RH4 .135 B6
Balcombe Ct RH10 .202 D5
Balcombe Gdns RH6 .161 C2
Balcombe Ho ❸ SW2 .21 F7
Balcombe Rd
  Crawley, Tinsley Green
    RH6,RH10 ....182 D5
  Crawley, Worth RH10 .202 D5
  Horley RH6 ....161 B2
Baldreys GU9 ....146 A8
Baldry Gdns SW16 .21 F2
Baldwin Cl RH10 .202 C3
Baldwin Cres GU4 .110 C3
Baldwin Gdns TW3 .5 C6
Baldwin Ho ⑮ SW2 .22 A7
Baldwins Field RH19 .185 C4
Baldwins Hill Prim Sch
  RH19 ....185 D3
Balfont Cl CR2 ...81 A6
Balfour Ave GU22 .89 F5
Balfour Cres RG12 .27 B4
Balfour Gdns RH18 .206 E1
Balfour Rd Croydon CR0 .43 A5
  Hounslow TW3 .....5 B4
  Merton SW19 ......20 B1
  Wallington SM5 ...59 F3
  Weybridge KT13 ...53 A6
Balgowan Cl KT3 ..38 E5
Balgowan Prim Sch BR3 .43 E7
Balgowan Rd BR3 .43 F7
Balham Gr SW12 ..21 A8
Balham High Rd SW12,
  SW17 ....21 A7
Balham Hill SW12 .21 B8
Balham New Rd SW12 .21 B8
Balham Park Mans SW12 20 F7
Balham Park Rd SW12,
  SW17 ....21 A7
Balham Sta SW12 .21 B7
Balham Station Rd SW12 21 B7
Balintore Ct ⑧ GU47 .64 D8
Ball & Wicket La GU9 .125 C7
Ballands N The GU22 .94 E5
Ballands' S The KT22 .94 E5
Ballantine Dr KT20 .97 F6
Ballantyne Rd GU14 .85 A6
Ballard Cl KT2 ....18 D1
Ballard Ct GU15 ..66 A8
Ballard Rd GU15 ..66 A8
Ballards Farm Rd CR0,
  CR2 ....62 A4
Ballards Gn KT20 .97 E8
Ballards La RH8 ..123 C6
Ballards Rise CR2 .62 A4
Ballards Way CR0,CR2 .62 C4
Ballater Cl GU17 ..64 F5
Ballencrieff Rd SL5 .29 F2
Ballfield Rd GU7 .150 E6
Ballina St SE23 ..23 D8
Ballindune GU27 .208 C8
Balliol Cl RH10 ..182 D1
Balliol Way GU47 .45 E1
Balloch Rd SE6 ...24 D6
Ballsdown GU8 ...191 A3

Balmain Ct TW3 ....5 B6
Balmoral RH19 ...206 A8
Balmoral Ave BR3 .43 E5
Balmoral Cres
  East Molesey KT8 .36 A6
  Hale GU9 ....125 B6
Balmoral Ct Belmont SM2 .59 A3
  ⑥ Crawley RH11 ..201 B2
  North Cheam KT4 ..58 B8
  West Norwood SE27 .22 C4
Balmoral Dr Frimley GU16 .85 F8
  Woking GU22 ......70 C3
Balmoral Gdns CR2 .61 D1
Balmoral Grange TW18 .33 B7
Balmoral Ho ❸ GU12 .105 F5
Balmoral Rd Ash GU12 .106 B4
  Kingston u T KT1 ..37 F5
  North Cheam KT4 ..58 B8
Balmoral Way SM2 .59 A1
Balquhain Cl KT21 .75 D2
Baltic Cl SW19 ...20 D1
Baltimore Ho SW19 .20 D1
Balvernie Gr SW18 .20 A8
Bamford Rd BR1 ..24 D3
Bampfylde Cl SM6 .60 C7
Bampton Rd SE23 .23 D5
Bampton Way GU21 .69 A2
Banavie Gdns BR3 .44 C8
Banbury RG12 ....27 E2
Banbury Cl Frimley GU16 .86 A7
  Wokingham RG41 ..25 A6
Banbury Ct ⑱ SM2 .59 A3
Bancroft Cl TW15 .14 A3
Bancroft Ct RH2 .118 B1
Bancroft Rd
  Crawley RH10 ....202 D5
  Reigate RH2 ......118 B1
Band La ❶ TW20 ..12 A3
Banders Rise GU1 .110 C2
Bandon Hill Prim Sch
  SM6 ....60 D4
Bandon Rise SM6 .60 D4
Banfor Ct SM6 ...60 C4
Bank Ave CR4 ....40 D7
Bank Ho Addlestone KT15 .52 B6
  ❶ Sutton SM1 ....59 C4
Bank La Crawley RH10 .201 D6
  Kingston u T KT2 .17 E1
  Roehampton SW15 .7 E2
Bank Mews SM1 ..59 C4
Bank Rd GU11 ...105 D5
Bank Willow TW10 .17 B5
Bank's La KT24 ...93 B5
Bankfoot Rd BR1 .24 E4
Bankhurst Rd SE4,SE6 .23 F8
Banks Ho TW7 ....5 E5
Banks Rd RH10 ..202 C5
Bankside Heath End GU9 .125 F7
  South Croydon CR2 .61 F4
  Woking GU21 .....69 B1
Bankside Cl
  Biggin Hill TN16 ..83 C1
  Carshalton SM5 ...59 E4
  Elstead GU8 ......148 D3
  Isleworth TW7 ....5 F3
Bankside Dr KT7 ..56 B8
Bankside Way ❼ SE19 .22 E2
Banning Ho ❹ SW19 .19 D7
Bannister Cl
  Streatham SW2 ...22 A7
  Witley GU8 ....170 F6
Bannister's Rd GU2 .129 C3
Banstead Inf Sch SM7 .77 F4
Banstead Jun Sch SM7 .77 F4
Banstead Rd
  Banstead SM7 ....77 D7
  Belmont SM7 .....77 D7
  Caterham CR3 ....100 C6
  East Ewell KT17 ..77 D7
  Purley CR8 ....80 A8
  Sutton SM5 ....59 E3
Banstead Rd S SM2 .59 D1
Banstead Sta SM7 .77 F5
Banstead Way SM6 .60 E5
Barbara Cl TW17 ..34 B4
Barber Cl RH10 ...202 C2
Barber Dr GU6 ...174 E4
Barberry Way GU17 .64 F2
Barbon Cl GU15 ..66 D3
Barclay Cl KT23 ..94 B4
Barclay Rd CR0,CR9 .61 D7
Barcombe Ave SW2 .21 F6
Bardney Rd SM4 ..40 B5
Bardolph Ave CR0 .62 F2
Bardolph Rd TW9 .6 F4
Bardon Wlk GU21 .69 B2
Bardsley Cl CR0 ..61 F7
Bardsley Dr GU9 .146 A2
Barfield Ct ❾ RH1 .119 A3
Barfield Sch GU10 .126 B3
Barfields RH1 ....120 C2
Barfreston Way SE20 .43 B8
Bargate Cl KT3 ...39 A2
Bargate Ct
  Godalming GU7 ...150 C4
  ❷ Guildford GU1 .108 E1
Bargate Ho GU21 .69 F3
Bargate Rise GU7 .150 C4
Barge Cl GU11 ...105 E5
Barge Wlk KT1,KT6,KT7 .37 D5
Bargery Rd SE6 ..24 B7
Bargrove Cl SE20 .23 A1
Bargrove Cres SE6 .23 F6
Barham Cl KT13 ..53 C6
Barham Rd
  Croydon CR0,CR2 .61 C5
  Wimbledon SW20 ..19 A1

Barhatch La GU6 ......174 F6
Barhatch Rd GU6 ......174 F4
Baring Rd CR0,CR9 ....43 A1
Barker Cl KT3 ....38 B5
Barker Gn RG12 ....27 B4
Barker Ho SE21 ....22 E5
Barker Rd KT16 ....32 F2
Barker Wlk SW16 ......21 D5
Barkham Rd RG41 .....25 A5
Barkhart Dr RG40 .....25 C7
Barkhart Gdns RG40 ..25 C7
Barkis Mead GU47 ....45 E2
Barley Cl RH10 ......201 D5
Barley Mow Cl GU21 ..68 D2
Barley Mow Ct RH3 ...116 C1
Barley Mow Hill GU35 .187 A6
Barley Mow La GU21 ..68 D3
Barley Mow Rd TW20 ..11 C3
Barley Mow Way TW17 .34 A5
Barleymead RH6 ......161 B4
Barlow Cl SM6 ....60 B8
Barlow Rd Crawley RH11 200 E3
  Hampton TW12 ....16 A1
Barmeston Rd SE6 ....24 B6
Barmouth Rd GU10 ....62 D8
Barn Cl Ashford TW15 .14 B3
  Bracknell RG12 ......27 D7
  Camberley GU15 .....65 E6
  Epsom KT18 ....76 C4
  Woodmansterne SM7 ..78 D4
Barn Cres CR8 ....80 D6
Barn Ct GU8 ....148 E4
Barn Field SM7 ....78 B5
Barn Meadow La KT23 .93 F3
Barn Rd KT15 ....52 B2
Barnard Cl Frimley GU16 .85 F8
  Sunbury TW16 ....15 B1
  Wallington SM6 .....60 D3
Barnard Ct
  1 Knaphill GU21 ..68 E1
  Streatham SW16 ....21 F5
Barnard Gdns KT3 ....39 A5
Barnard Ho RH1 ......139 F4
Barnard Rd
  Chelsham CR6 ......102 B8
  Mitcham CR4 ....41 A4
Barnard Way GU11 ...104 F3
Barnards Pl CR2 ......61 B2
Barnato Cl KT14 ......71 E7
Barnby Rd GU21 ......68 D2
Barncroft GU9 ....125 C1
Barnes Bridge Sta SW13 .7 E5
Barnes Cl GU14 ....85 D4
Barnes Ct CR7 ....42 C6
Barnes End KT3 ......39 A4
Barnes High St SW13 ..7 F5
Barnes Hospl SW14 ...7 E4
Barnes Prim Sch SW13 .7 F4
Barnes Rd
  Farncombe GU7 .....150 E8
  Frimley GU16 ....85 E8
Barnes Wallis Dr KT14,
  KT14 ....71 E8
Barnett Cl
  Leatherhead KT22 ...95 B8
  Wonersh GU5 ....152 C8
Barnett Ct RG12 ......27 C7
Barnett Gn RG12 ....27 B3
Barnett La
  Lightwater GU18 ....66 F7
  Wonersh GU5 ....152 C7
Barnett Row GU4 ....109 D6
Barnett Wood Cty Inf Sch
  KT21 ....75 D2
Barnett Wood La
  Ashstead KT21,KT22 .75 D1
  Leatherhead KT22 ...95 B8
Barnett's Shaw RH8 .122 D8
Barnfield Cranleigh GU6 .174 E3
  New Malden KT3 .....38 E3
Barnfield Ave
  Croydon CR0 ....62 C8
  Kingston u T KT2 ....17 E3
  Mitcham CR4 ....41 B6
Barnfield Cl
  Coulsdon CR5 ......100 C8
  Wandsworth SW17 ..20 C5
Barnfield Cotts RH7 .165 A1
Barnfield Gdns KT2 ..17 E3
Barnfield Rd
  Crawley RH10 ......201 E7
  South Croydon CR2 .61 E2
  Tatsfield TN16 .....103 D6
Barnfield Way RH8 ..123 A2
Barnfield Wood Cl BR3 .44 F4
Barnfield Wood Rd BR3 .44 D3
Barnhill Ave BR2 ....44 F4
Barnlea Cl TW13 .....15 E6
Barnmead GU24 .....49 F1
Barnmead Rd BR3 ...43 E8
Barns The GU8 ......149 C8
Barnsbury Cl KT3 ...38 C5
Barnsbury Cres KT5 .38 C1
Barnsbury Jun & Inf Sch
  GU22 ....89 D6
Barnsbury La KT5 ...38 C1
Barnscroft SW20 ....39 B6
Barnsfold La RH12 ..213 E6
Barnsford Cres GU24 .68 A6
Barnsley Cl GU12 ....86 B2
Barnsnap Cl RH12 ..217 D6
Barnway TW20 ......11 C3
Barnwood Cl
  Crawley RH10 ......202 C7
  Guildford GU3 ......108 E3
Barnwood Ct GU2,GU3 .108 E3
Barnwood Rd GU2,GU3 .108 E3
Barnyard The KT20 ...97 A3

Baron Cl SM2 ....59 B1
Baron Ct CR4 ....40 E5
Baron Gr CR4 ....40 E5
Baron's Hurst KT18 ..76 C3
Baron's Way RH2 ...139 A5
Baron's Wlk CR0 ....43 E3
Barons Ct SM6 ......60 D7
Barons The TW1 .....6 B1
Barons Way TW20 ...12 D2
Baronsfield Rd TW1 ..6 B1
Barossa Rd GU15 ....65 D7
Barr Beacon SE23 ...23 C8
Barr's La GU21 ......68 D3
Barracane Dr RG45 ..45 B5
Barrack Path **8** GU21 .68 F1
Barrack Rd
  Aldershot GU11 .....105 A2
  Guildford GU1 ......109 A4
  Hounslow TW4 ....4 E3
Barrards Hall CR2 ...80 D8
Barrens Brae GU22 ..70 A1
Barrens Cl GU22 ....90 A8
Barrens Pk GU22 ....90 A8
Barrett Cres RG40 ...25 D7
Barrett Rd KT22 .....94 D3
Barrihill Rd SW2 ....21 E6
Barricane GU21 ......89 B8
Barrie Cl CR5 ....79 C3
Barrie Rd GU9 ......125 A7
Barrihurst La GU6 ..173 D2
Barringer Sq SW17 ..21 A4
Barrington Ct
  Dorking RH4 ....136 A6
  Staines TW18 ......12 F2
Barrington Gate RH12 .217 D2
Barrington Lodge KT13 .53 C5
Barrington Rd
  Cheam SM3 ....40 A1
  Crawley RH10 ......201 D3
  Dorking RH4 ....136 A6
  Horsham RH13 .....217 E2
  Purley CR8 ....79 C7
Barrington Wlk **10** SE19 .22 E2
Barrow Ave SM5 ....59 F3
Barrow Ct SE6 ......24 F7
Barrow Green Rd RH8 .122 C6
Barrow Hedges Cl SM5 .59 E3
Barrow Hedges Prim Sch
  SM5 ....59 E3
Barrow Hedges Way SM5 59 E3
Barrow Hill KT4 .....57 E8
Barrow Hill Cl KT4 ..57 E8
Barrow Hills Sch GU8 .170 E4
Barrow Rd Croydon CR0 .61 A5
  Streatham SW16 ....21 D2
Barrowsfield CR2 ....81 A7
Barry Cl RH10 ....201 E3
Barry Sq RG12 ......27 D2
Barry Terr TW15 .....13 F6
Bars The GU1 ....130 D8
Barsons Cl SE20 ....23 C1
Barston Rd SE27 ....22 C5
Barstow Cres SW2 ..21 F7
Bartholomew Cl GU27 .208 D8
Bartholomew Ct RH4 .136 A6
Bartholomew Way
  RH12 ....218 A2
Bartlett Pl GU16 ....85 F5
Bartlett St CR0,CR2 ..61 D5
Barton Cl Addlestone KT15 .52 A4
  Aldershot GU11 .....104 E1
  Knaphill GU21 ......68 C1
  Shepperton TW17 ...34 B3
Barton Cres RH1 ....206 A8
Barton Ct Beckenham BR2 .44 D6
  Farnborough GU14 ..85 C1
Barton Gn KT3 ......38 D7
Barton Pl GU1 ......110 A4
Barton Rd GU5 ......152 A7
Barton The KT11 ....73 D7
Barton Wlk RH10 ...202 B4
Barts Cl BR3 ....44 A4
Barttelot Rd RH12 ..217 D2
Barwell Bsns Pk KT9 .56 D2
Barwood Ave BR4 ...44 B1
Basden Gr TW13 ....16 A6
Basemoors RG12 ....27 E7
Bashford Way RH10 .202 D8
Basil Gdns Croydon CR0 .43 D1
  West Norwood SE27 .22 C4
Basildene Rd TW4,TW5 .4 D4
Basildon Cl SM2 .....59 B2
Basildon Way RH11 .200 E3
Basing Cl KT7 ....36 F2
Basing Dr GU11 .....126 B2
Basing Ho SE6 ......24 A4
Basing Rd SM7 .....77 F4
Basing Way KT7 ....36 F2
Basingfield Rd KT7 ..36 F2
Basinghall Gdns SM2 .59 B2
Baskerville Ct SW18 .20 E8
Baskerville Rd SW18 .20 E8
Basset Cl KT15 ......52 C1
Bassett Cl Belmont SM2 .59 B2
  Frimley GU16 ....85 E8
Bassett Dr RH2 .....118 A2
Bassett Gdns TW7 ...5 C7
Bassett Rd Crawley RH10 202 D3
  Woking GU22 ....70 C3
Bassetts Hill RH7 ...165 A2
Bassingham Rd SW18 .20 C8
Bat & Ball La
  Rowledge GU10 ....146 A5
  Wrecclesham GU10 .146 A6
Batavia Cl TW16 .....35 C8
Batavia Rd TW16 ....35 B8
Batcombe Mead RG12 .27 E2

Bateman Gr GU12 ...126 F8
Batemans St RH19 ..205 F8
Bates Cres Croydon CR0 .61 A5
  Streatham SW16 ....21 C1
Bates Wlk KT15 .....52 C4
Bateson Way GU21 ..70 C5
Bath Ct **3** SE26 ...23 A4
Bath House Rd CR0 ..41 E1
Bath Pas KT1 ....37 D7
Bath Rd Camberley GU15 .65 D6
  Cranford,Hounslow TW3,TW4,
   TW5 ....4 E5
  Harlington TW6,UB7,TW5 .3 D6
  Harmondsworth TW6,UB7 .2 E6
  Poyle SL3,UB7,TW6 ..1 E6
Bathgate Rd SW19 ..19 D5
Bathurst Ave SW19 .40 B8
Batsworth Rd CR4 ..40 D6
Batten Ave GU21 ....88 E8
Battenberg Wlk **10** SE19 .22 E3
Battersby Rd SE6 ...24 D5
Battersea Ct GU2 ...109 B1
Battle Cl SW19 ......20 C2
Battlebridge La RH1 .119 B5
Batts Hill RH2 ......118 E3
Batty's Barn Cl RG40 .25 D5
Baty Ho SW2 ....21 F7
Baudwin Rd SE6 ....24 E6
Bavant Rd SW16 ....41 F7
Baveno Ho GU14 ....85 C1
Bawtree Cl SM2 .....59 C1
Bax Cl GU6 ....174 E2
Baxter Ave RH1 .....118 F1
Baxter Cl RH10 .....202 B4
Bay Cl RH6 ....160 E6
Bay Dr RG12 ....27 E7
Bay Tree Ave KT22 ..95 A7
Bayards CR6 ....81 C1
Baydon Ct BR2 .....44 F6
Bayeux KT20 ....97 D5
Bayfield Ave GU16 ..65 E2
Bayfield Rd RH6 ....160 E4
Bayford Cl GU17 ....65 A1
Bayham Rd SM4 ....40 C5
Bayhorne La RH6 ...161 C1
Bayleaf Cl TW12 ....16 D3
Baylis Mews TW1 ...17 A8
Baylis Wlk RH11 ....201 B1
Bayliss Ct **2** GU1 .130 C8
Baynards Rd RH12 ..195 A2
Bays Cl SE26 ....23 C3
Baysfarm Ct UB7 ....2 C6
Baywood Cl GU14 ..84 C5
Bazalgette Cl KT3 ...38 D4
Bazalgette Gdns KT3 .38 D4
Beach's Ho **2** TW18 .13 A3
Beachborough Rd BR1 .24 C4
Beachy Rd RH11 ....201 A1
Beacon Cl Banstead SM7 .77 D3
  Rowledge GU10 ....146 A5
Beacon Ct Colnbrook SW3 .1 C7
  Horsham RH13 .....218 A4
Beacon Gr SM5 .....60 A6
Beacon Hill
  Dormansland RH7 ..186 B8
  Woking GU21 ....89 C8
Beacon Hill Com Prim Sch
  GU26 ....188 C6
Beacon Hill Ct GU26 .188 D6
Beacon Hill Rd
  Beacon Hill GU26 ...188 D6
  Crondall GU10 .....124 C8
Beacon Rd **10** SE26 .23 B3
Beacon Rd
  Farnborough GU14 .105 B8
  Harlington TW19,TW6 .3 A1
Beacon Rdbt TW6 ...3 A1
Beacon Sch The KT20 .77 E2
Beacon View Ho GU26 .188 C3
Beacon View Rd GU8 .148 C2
Beacon Way SM7 ...77 E3
Beaconsfield Gdns KT10 .55 E3
Beaconsfield Pl KT17 .76 E7
Beaconsfield Rd
  Claygate KT10 ......55 E3
  Kingston u T KT3 ...38 D7
  Langley Vale KT18 ..96 E8
  Old Woking GU22 ...89 F7
  Surbiton KT5 ....37 F2
  Thornton Heath CR0 .42 D3
  Twickenham TW1 ...6 B1
Beaconshaw BR1 ...24 E1
Beadle Ct CR4 ......40 E6
Beadles La RH8 ....122 D4
Beadlow Cl SM4 ...40 D3
Beadman Pl SE27 ..22 B4
Beadman St SE27 ..22 B4
Beadnell Rd SE23 ..23 D7
Beaford Gr SW20 ..39 F6
Beagle Ct TW13 ....15 B4
Beale Cl RG40 .....25 B7
Beale Ct RH11 .....201 A3
Beale's La KT13 ....53 B7
Beales La RH2 .....118 A2
Beales Rd KT23 ....94 B1
Bealeswood La GU10 .166 F6
Beam Hollow GU9 .125 C3
Bean Oak Rd RG40 .25 E6
Bear Cl GU9 ....125 C3
Bear Rd TW13 .....15 D4
Beard Rd TW10 ....17 F3
Beard's Hill TW12 .36 A8
Beard's Hill Cl TW12 .36 A8
Beardell St SE19 ...22 F2
Beards Hill Cl TW12 .36 A8

Beare Green Cotts RH5 157 D2
Beare Green Ct RH5 .157 D4
Bearfield Rd KT2 ...17 E1
Bears Den KT20 ....97 F5
Bears Rail Pk SL4 ..10 D1
Bearsden Way RH12 .216 D3
Bearwood Cl KT15 ..52 A4
Bearwood Cotts GU10 .145 F7
Beasley's Ait La TW16,
  TW17 ....34 F3
Beatrice Ave SW16 .41 F7
Beatrice Rd Oxted RH8 .122 E6
  1 Richmond TW10 .6 E2
Beatrix Potter Prim Sch
  SW18 ....20 C7
Beattie Cl
  East Bedfont TW14 .14 E7
  Little Bookham KT23 .93 F3
Beatty Ave GU1 ....110 A2
Beauchamp Rd
  East Molesey KT8 ..36 C4
  South Norwood CR7,SE25 .42 D8
  Sutton SM1 ....59 A6
  Twickenham TW1 ...17 A8
Beauchamp Villas KT2 .17 F1
Beauclare Ct KT21 ..95 D6
Beauclerc Inf Sch TW16 .35 C3
Beauclere Ho **1** SM2 .59 C3
Beauclerk Cl TW13 .15 B7
Beauclerk Ho **6** SW16 .21 E5
Beaufield Gate GU27 .208 D7
Beaufort Cl
  Reigate RH2 ....117 C2
  Woking GU22 ....70 C3
Beaufort Com Prim Sch
  GU21 ....68 F3
Beaufort Ct TW10 ..17 C2
Beaufort Gdns Heston TW5 .4 E6
  North Ascot SL5 ....28 E8
  South Norwood SW16 .21 F1
Beaufort Ho SE6 ...39 D8
Beaufort Mews GU21 .69 D2
Beaufort Rd
  Ash Vale GU12 .....105 F6
  Farnham GU9 ......125 C3
  Kingston u T KT1,KT5,KT6 .37 E5
  Reigate RH2 ....117 F2
  Richmond TW10 ...17 C4
  Twickenham TW1 ..17 C8
  Woking GU22 ......70 C3
Beaufort Way KT17 ..58 A3
Beauforts TW20 ....11 C3
Beaufoy Ho **3** SE27 .22 B5
Beaufront Cl GU15 .66 A4
Beaufront Rd GU15 .66 B7
Beaulieu Ave SE26 .23 B4
Beaulieu Cl
  Bracknell RG12 .....28 A6
  Hounslow TW4 .....4 F2
  Mitcham CR4 ......41 A8
  4 Twickenham TW1 .6 D1
Beaulieu Gdns GU17 .64 C5
Beaumaris Par GU16 .85 E8
Beaumont Ave TW9 .6 F4
Beaumont Cl **3** RH11 .200 E5
  Mitcham CR4 ......41 A7
Beaumont Ct Ascot SL5 .28 F5
Beaumont Dr TW15 .14 D3
Beaumont Gdns RG12 .27 E4
Beaumont Gr GU11 .104 E2
Beaumont Ho
  1 Streatham SW2 .21 E7
  Wimbledon SW19 ..20 A5
Beaumont Jun Sch
  GU11 ....104 F2
Beaumont Pl TW7 ...5 F2
Beaumont Prim Sch CR8 80 A6
Beaumont Rd Purley CR8 .80 A6
  Putney SW15,SW19 .19 E8
  South Norwood SE19 .22 C2
Beaumont Sq GU6 ..174 F3
Beaumont Terr **1** SE13 .24 E8
Beaumonts RH1 ....139 F1
Beaver Cl Hampton TW12 .36 B8
  Horsham RH12 .....217 F6
  8 Penge SE20 ...23 A1
  Wokingham RG41 ..25 B3
Beaver Zoological Gdns★
  TN16 ....103 B5
Beavers Com Prim Sch
  TW4 ....4 C4
Beavers Cres TW4 ...4 D3
Beavers Hill GU9 ..124 F2
Beavers La TW4 ....4 C4
Beavers Rd GU9 ...125 A2
Beck Ct BR3 ....43 D6
Beck Gdns GU9 ....125 A6
Beck Ind Est The GU12 .126 D8
Beck La BR3 ....43 D6
Beck Rd CR4 ....40 F3
Beck River Pk **4** BR3 .44 A8
Beck Way BR3 .....44 A6
Beckenham Bsns Ctr
  BR3 ....23 E2
Beckenham Ct BR3 .44 A8
Beckenham Gr BR2 .44 D7
Beckenham Hill Rd BR3,
  SE6 ....24 C3
Beckenham Hill Sta SE6 24 C3
Beckenham Hospl BR3 .43 F7
Beckenham Junction Sta
  BR3 ....44 A8
Beckenham La BR2 .44 F7
Beckenham Place Pk
  BR3 ....24 B1

Beckenham Rd
  Beckenham BR3 ....43 E8
  Penge BR3 ....43 E8
  West Wickham BR4 .44 C2
Beckenshaw Gdns SM7 .78 E6
Becket Cl Croydon SE25 .43 A3
  2 Merton SW19 ..40 B8
Becket Wood RH5 ..158 C4
Beckett Ave CR8 ...80 B4
Beckett Cl
  Streatham SW16 ...21 D6
  Wokingham RG40 ..25 E6
Beckett La RH11 ...181 D1
Beckett Wlk **11** RH19 .205 F8
Beckett Wlk BR3 ...23 E2
Becketts Cl TW14 ...4 B1
Becketts Pl KT1 ....37 D8
Beckford Ave RG12 .27 B3
Beckford Rd CR0,SE25 .42 F3
Beckford Way RH10 .202 B2
Beckingham Rd GU2 .109 A2
Beckley Cotts KT23 .94 C1
Beckmead Sch BR3 .44 A1
Beckway Rd SW16 .41 D7
Beckworth Pl KT13 .53 E8
Beclands Rd SW17 .21 A2
Becmead Ave SW16 .21 D4
Becondale Rd SE19 .22 E3
Bedale Cl RH11 ....201 C4
Beddington Cross CR0 .41 E1
Beddington Farm Rd
  Croydon CR0 ......60 F8
  Wallington CR0,CR9 .41 E1
Beddington Gdns SM5,
  SM6 ....60 A4
Beddington Gr SM6 .60 C6
Beddington Inf Sch SM6 60 C6
Beddington La CR0 .60 E8
Beddington Manor SM2 .59 D4
Beddington Park Cotts
  SM6 ....60 D7
Beddington Park Prim Sch
  CR0 ....60 D7
Beddlestead La CR6 .103 A6
Bedelsford Sch KT1 .37 E6
Bedfont Cl
  East Bedfont TW14 .3 C1
  Mitcham CR4 ......41 A7
Bedfont Court Est TW19 .2 B4
Bedfont Ct TW19 ...2 B4
Bedfont Green Cl TW14 .14 C7
Bedfont Ind Pk TW15 .14 D5
Bedfont Ind Pk N TW15 .14 C5
Bedfont Inf Sch TW14 .3 E1
Bedfont Jun Sch TW14 .3 E1
Bedfont La TW14,TW13 .14 D7
Bedfont Lakes Ctry Pk★
  TW14 ....14 C6
Bedfont Rd
  East Bedfont TW14,TW13 .14 D6
  Feltham TW14,TW13 .14 D6
  Stanwell TW19 ....2 F1
Bedford Ave GU16 ..85 E5
Bedford Cl **13** Chiswick W4 .7 E8
  Woking GU22 ......89 C4
Bedford Cres GU16 .85 F6
Bedford Ct
  6 Richmond TW9 .6 F3
  South Norwood SE19 .22 E1
Bedford Hill SW12,SW16,
  SW17 ....21 B6
Bedford Ho **3** GU1 .130 C8
Bedford La Frimley GU16 .85 F6
  Sunningdale SL5 ...30 B3
Bedford Pk CR0 ....42 C1
Bedford Pl CR0 ....42 C1
Bedford Rd
  Guildford GU1 .....130 C8
  Horsham RH13 ....217 D1
  North Cheam KT4 ..58 C8
  Twickenham TW2 ..16 D5
Bedford Terr **12** SM2 .59 C4
Bedgebury Gdns SW19 .19 E6
Bedlow Cotts GU6 ..174 F3
Bedlow Way CR0 ...60 F6
Bedser Cl
  South Norwood CR7 .42 C6
  Woking GU21 ......70 A3
Bedster Gdns KT8 ..36 B6
Bedwardine Rd SE19 .22 E1
Beech Ave Brentford TW8 .6 B7
  Camberley GU15 ...65 D4
  Effingham KT24 ...113 D6
  Farnham GU9 .....146 C5
  South Croydon CR2 .61 D1
  Tatsfield TN16 ....103 D8
Beech Cl Aldershot GU12 .126 E8
  Ashford TW15 ......14 D3
  Blindley Heath RH7 .163 E8
  Byfleet KT14 ......71 E7
  Carshalton SM5 ...59 F8
  Chiddingfold GU8 .191 C4
  Cobham KT11 .....73 B4
  Dorking RH4 ....136 A8
  2 East Grinstead RH19 .185 D2
  Effingham KT24 ...113 D7
  Hersham KT12 .....54 C5
  Putney SW15 ......19 A8
  Stanwell TW19 ....13 D1
  Sunbury TW16 ....35 D7
  Wimbledon SW19 .19 C2
Beech Close Ct KT11 .73 E8
Beech Copse CR2 ..61 E5
Beech Cres KT20 ..116 C5
Beech Ct Beckenham BR3 .23 F1

Beech Ct *continued*
Chipstead CR5 ... 78 F1
East Grinstead RH19 ... 185 D2
4 Guildford GU1 ... 130 F8
Haslemere GU27 ... 208 D7
Teddington TW11 ... 17 C2
5 West Norwood SW16 ... 22 A3
Beech Dr Blackwater GU17 64 D4
Kingswood KT20 ... 97 F5
Reigate RH2 ... 118 D1
Send Marsh GU23 ... 91 A3
Beech Farm Rd CR6 ... 102 D8
Beech Gdns
Crawley Down RH10 ... 204 A8
Woking GU21 ... 69 E4
Beech Glen RG12 ... 27 B5
Beech Gr Addlestone KT15 . 52 B6
Burgh Heath KT18 ... 77 B2
Caterham CR3 ... 100 E1
Great Bookham KT23 ... 114 A8
Guildford GU2 ... 108 F1
Kingston u T KT3 ... 38 D6
Mitcham CR4 ... 41 D5
Pirbright GU24 ... 87 D7
Beech Hall KT16 ... 51 C3
Beech Hanger End
GU26 ... 188 B3
Beech Hill
Bowlhead Green GU8 ... 189 F8
Headley Down GU35 ... 187 B5
Woking GU22 ... 89 D4
Beech Hill Rd
Headley Down GU35 ... 187 A5
Sunningdale SL5 ... 29 F3
Beech Ho Heston TW5 ... 4 E7
New Addington CR0 ... 63 B4
Beech Holme RH10 ... 204 B8
Beech Holt KT22 ... 95 C5
Beech House Rd CR0,CR9 61 D7
Beech La Flexford GU3 .. 107 A1
Grayshott GU26 ... 188 B4
Guildford GU2 ... 130 C6
Beech Lodge TW18 ... 12 E3
Beech Rd Biggin Hill TN16 . 83 C2
East Bedfont TW14 ... 14 E8
Epsom KT18 ... 76 F4
Farnborough GU14 ... 85 A7
Frimley GU16 ... 85 F6
Haslemere GU27 ... 208 D8
Horsham RH12 ... 218 B5
Merstham RH1 ... 99 C1
Oatlands Park KT13 ... 53 D6
Reigate RH2 ... 118 A4
Thornton Heath SW16 ... 41 F6
Beech Ride GU47 ... 45 B1
Beech Tree Cl RH10 ... 201 D7
Beech Tree Dr GU9 ... 126 A5
Beech Tree La TW18 ... 33 B7
Beech Tree Pl SM1 ... 59 B5
Beech Way Epsom KT17 .. 76 F4
Godalming GU7 ... 150 D3
Selsdon CR2 ... 81 D7
Twickenham TW2 ... 16 A5
Beech Wlk KT17 ... 77 A8
Beech Wood CR3 ... 100 F3
Beechcroft Ashstead KT21 . 95 F8
Kingston u T KT2 ... 38 B8
Beechcroft Ave
Kenley CR8 ... 80 D4
Kingston u T KT1,KT3 ... 38 C7
Beechcroft Cl Ascot SL5 .. 29 D5
Heston TW5 ... 4 E7
Streatham SW16 ... 21 F3
Beechcroft Ct RG12 ... 27 B6
Beechcroft Dr GU2 ... 129 D6
Beechcroft Lodge 12
SM2 ... 59 C3
Beechcroft Manor KT13 . 53 D7
Beechcroft Mans SW16 .. 21 F3
Beechcroft Rd
Chessington KT9 ... 56 F7
Mortlake SW14 ... 7 C4
Upper Tooting SW17 ... 20 E6
Beechcroft Sch SW17 ... 20 E6
Beechdene KT20 ... 97 B5
Beechen Cliff Way TW7 ... 5 F5
Beechen La KT20 ... 97 F2
Beechen Pl SE23 ... 23 C6
Beeches Ave The SM5 ... 59 E3
Beeches Cl
Kingswood KT20 ... 98 A4
Penge SE20 ... 43 C8
Beeches Cres RH10 ... 201 E4
Beeches La RH19 ... 206 D6
Beeches Mead RH19 ... 186 F5
Beeches Rd Cheam SM3 .. 39 E1
Upper Tooting SW17 ... 20 F5
Beeches The
Ash Vale GU12 ... 85 F1
Banstead SM7 ... 78 B3
Bramley GU5 ... 151 F6
Fetcham KT22 ... 94 E3
Hounslow TW3 ... 5 B6
Mitcham CR4 ... 40 E4
Staines TW18 ... 13 A3
Beeches Wlk SM2,SM5 ... 59 E2
Beeches Wood KT20 ... 98 A5
Beechey Cl RH10 ... 183 B3
Beechey Way RH10 ... 183 B3
Beechfield SM7 ... 78 B6
Beechfield Ct 7 CR0 ... 61 C6
Beechfield Rd SE6 ... 23 F7
Beechfields RH19 ... 185 F3
Beeching Cl GU12 ... 106 B3
Beeching Way RH19 ... 185 E1
Beechland Cotts KT20 .. 117 F7
Beechlawn GU1 ... 130 F8
Beechmeads KT11 ... 73 D6
Beechmont Ave GU25 ... 31 D4
Beechmont Cl BR1 ... 24 E3
Beechmore Gdns SM3 ... 58 D8
Beechnut Dr GU17 ... 64 B6
Beechnut Ind Est 9
GU12 ... 105 B1
Beechnut Rd 8 GU12 .. 105 B1
Beecholme KT17 ... 77 E5
Beecholme Ave CR4 ... 41 B8
Beecholme Fst Sch CR4 . 41 B8
Beechrow KT2 ... 17 E4
Beechside RH10 ... 201 E5
Beechtree Ave TW20 ... 11 B2
Beechvale 3 GU22 ... 69 F1
Beechway GU1 ... 110 B2
Beechwood Ave
Ashford TW16 ... 15 A2
Kingswood KT20 ... 98 A6
Oatlands Park KT13 ... 53 E6
Richmond TW9 ... 7 A6
Staines TW18 ... 13 B2
Thornton Heath CR7 ... 42 B5
Wallington CR5 ... 79 B4
Beechwood Cl
Knaphill GU21 ... 68 E2
Long Ditton KT6 ... 37 D2
North Ascot SL5 ... 8 F1
Oatlands Park KT13 ... 53 E6
Beechwood Ct
Carshalton SM5 ... 59 F6
Chiswick W4 ... 7 D8
Sutton SM1 ... 59 A5
Walton-on-T KT12 ... 54 A7
Beechwood Dr KT11 ... 74 A8
Beechwood Gdns CR3 .. 101 A5
Beechwood La CR6 ... 101 D8
Beechwood Manor KT13 . 53 E6
Beechwood Pk KT22 ... 95 C5
Beechwood Rd
Caterham CR3 ... 101 A5
Knaphill GU21 ... 68 D2
South Croydon CR2 ... 61 E2
Wentworth GU25 ... 31 B1
Beechwood Villas RH1 . 161 A7
Beechwoods Ct SE19 ... 22 F3
Beecot La KT12 ... 54 C8
Beeding Cl RH12 ... 218 A5
Beedingwood Dr RH12 . 218 F6
Beedon Dr RG12 ... 26 E3
Beehive La RG12 ... 26 C7
Beehive Rd
Bracknell RG12,RG42 ... 26 D7
Staines TW18 ... 12 F3
Beehive Ring Rd RH6 .. 182 B4
Beehive Way RH2 ... 139 B5
Beeleigh Rd SM4 ... 40 B5
Beeston Way TW14 ... 4 C1
Beeton's Ave GU12 ... 106 A4
Beggar's Roost La SM1 .. 59 A4
Beggars La
Chobham GU24 ... 68 C8
Gomshall RH5 ... 133 E4
Beggarshouse La RH6 .. 180 C8
Begonia Pl 1 TW12 ... 16 A2
Behenna Cl RH11 ... 200 E5
Beira St SW12 ... 21 B8
Bel La 2 TW13 ... 15 F5
Belcroft Cl BR1 ... 24 F1
Beldam Bridge Rd GU24 . 68 A6
Beldham Gdns KT8 ... 36 B6
Beldham Rd GU9 ... 145 F7
Belenoyd Ct SW16 ... 21 F5
Belfast Rd SE25 ... 43 B5
Belfield Rd KT19 ... 57 E3
Belfry The RH1 ... 118 F2
Belgrade Rd TW12 ... 36 B8
Belgrave Cl KT12 ... 54 B6
Belgrave Cres TW16 ... 35 B8
Belgrave Ct GU17 ... 64 D3
Belgrave Manor GU22 ... 89 E8
Belgrave Rd Barnes SW13 .. 7 F7
Hounslow TW4 ... 4 F4
Mitcham CR4 ... 40 D6
South Norwood SE25 ... 42 F5
Sunbury TW16 ... 35 B8
Belgrave Wlk CR4 ... 40 D6
Belgravia Ct RH6 ... 161 B3
Belgravia Gdns BR1 ... 24 E2
Belgravia Ho 1 TW11 ... 17 C1
Belgravia Mews KT1 ... 37 D5
Bell Bridge Rd KT16 ... 32 F1
Bell Cl GU14 ... 85 C6
Bell Cnr KT16 ... 32 F2
Bell Cres CR5 ... 99 B6
Bell Ct Tolworth KT5 ... 57 B8
13 Woking GU22 ... 69 F1
Bell Ctr RH10 ... 181 F2
Bell Dr SW18 ... 19 E8
Bell Farm Jun Sch KT12 . 54 C6
Bell Foundry La RG40 ... 25 C8
Bell Gn SE6 ... 23 F4
Bell Green La BR3,SE26,
SE6 ... 23 F4
Bell Hammer RH19 ... 205 E8
Bell Ho 15 SW2 ... 22 A8
Bell House Gdns RG41 ... 25 B6
Bell La Blackwater GU17 ... 64 C5
Fetcham KT22 ... 94 D4
Rowledge GU10 ... 145 E3
Twickenham TW1 ... 17 A7
Bell Lane Cl KT22 ... 94 D4
Bell Mdw Dulwich SE19 ... 22 E4
Godstone RH9 ... 121 C3
Bell Pl GU19 ... 47 F3
Bell Rd East Molesey KT8 .. 36 D4
Bell Rd *continued*
Hounslow TW3 ... 5 B3
Kingsley Green GU27 ... 208 B3
Warnham RH12 ... 217 A8
Bell St RH2 ... 139 B8
Bell Vale La GU27 ... 208 C4
Bell View BR3 ... 23 F1
Bell Weir Cl TW19 ... 12 B6
Bellamy Ho Heston TW5 ... 5 A8
Upper Tooting SW17 ... 20 D4
Bellamy Rd RH10 ... 202 C2
Bellamy St SW12 ... 21 B8
Belland Dr GU11 ... 104 E1
Bellasis Ave SW2 ... 21 E6
Belle Vue Cl
Aldershot GU12 ... 105 D2
Staines TW18 ... 33 A8
Belle Vue Ent Ctr GU12 . 105 E2
Belle Vue Inf Sch GU12 . 105 D2
Belle Vue Rd GU12 ... 105 D2
Bellerby Ct GU2 ... 129 E8
Bellever Hill GU15 ... 65 E5
Bellevue Pk CR7 ... 42 C5
Bellevue Rd
Kingston u T KT1 ... 37 E6
Upper Tooting SW17 ... 20 F7
Bellew Rd GU16 ... 86 B7
Bellew St SW17 ... 20 C5
Bellfield CR0 ... 62 F3
Bellfields Ct GU1 ... 109 C5
Bellfields Rd GU1 ... 109 D3
Bellingham Cl GU15 ... 66 C4
Bellingham Gn SE6 ... 24 A5
Bellingham Rd SE6 ... 24 C5
Bellingham Sta SE6 ... 24 B5
Bellingham Trad Est SE6 . 24 B6
Bellmarsh Rd KT15 ... 52 B6
Bellmore Ct 5 CR0 ... 42 F1
Bello Cl SE24 ... 22 B7
Belloc Cl RH10 ... 202 C7
Belloc Ct RH13 ... 218 A3
Bells La SL3 ... 1 B4
Belltrees Gr 1 SW16 ... 22 A3
Bellwether La RH1 ... 162 B7
Belmont KT13 ... 53 C4
Belmont Ave
Guildford GU2 ... 108 F4
West Barnes KT3 ... 39 A5
Belmont Cl GU14 ... 84 F7
Belmont Ho GU9 ... 146 A8
Belmont Mews
Camberley GU15 ... 65 C3
Putney SW19 ... 19 D6
Belmont Rd
Beckenham BR3 ... 43 F7
Belmont SM2 ... 59 A1
Camberley GU15 ... 65 C4
Crowthorne RG45 ... 45 B6
Croydon SE25 ... 43 B4
Leatherhead KT22 ... 95 A5
Reigate RH2 ... 139 C8
Twickenham TW2 ... 16 D6
Wallington SM6 ... 60 C5
Belmont Rise SM1,SM2 ... 58 F3
Belmont Sch RH5 ... 155 D6
Belmont Sta SM2 ... 59 B1
Belmore Ave GU22 ... 70 D3
Belsize Gdns SM1 ... 59 B6
Belsize Grange KT16 ... 33 C2
Belstone Mews GU14 ... 85 A7
Beltane Dr SW19 ... 19 D5
Belthorn Cres SW12 ... 21 C8
Belton Rd GU15 ... 65 E5
Belvedere Ave SW19 ... 19 E3
Belvedere Cl Esher KT10 .. 55 B5
Guildford GU2 ... 109 B3
Teddington TW11 ... 16 E3
Weybridge KT13 ... 53 A5
Belvedere Ct
Blackwater GU17 ... 64 D3
Crawley RH10 ... 202 B7
8 Kingston u T KT2 ... 18 A1
Redhill RH1 ... 119 A5
Belvedere Dr SW19 ... 19 E3
Belvedere Gdns KT8 ... 36 A4
Belvedere Gr SW19 ... 19 E3
Belvedere Grange SL5 ... 30 A1
Belvedere Ho
Feltham TW13 ... 15 A7
Weybridge KT13 ... 53 B5
Belvedere Rd
Biggin Hill TN16 ... 83 F1
Farnborough GU14 ... 85 C2
Penge SE19 ... 22 F1
Belvedere Sq SW19 ... 19 E3
Belvoir Cl GU16 ... 65 F1
Belvoir Lodge SE22 ... 23 A8
Belvoir Rd SE22 ... 23 A8
Bembridge Ct 4 GU12 . 105 C1
Benbow La GU8 ... 193 C4
Benbrick Rd GU2 ... 130 A8
Benbury Cl BR1 ... 24 C3
Bence The TW20 ... 32 B6
Bench Field CR2 ... 61 F5
Benchfield Cl RH19 ... 186 B1
Bencombe Rd CR8 ... 80 A5
Bencroft Rd SW16 ... 21 C1
Bencurtis Pk BR4 ... 63 D8
Bendon Valley SW18 ... 20 B8
Benedict Dr TW14 ... 14 D8
Benedict Fst Sch CR4 ... 40 D6
Benedict Rd CR4 ... 40 D6
Benedict Wharf CR4 ... 40 E6
Benen-Stock Rd TW19 ... 2 A2
Benett Gdns SW16 ... 41 E7
Benfleet Cl Cobham KT11 . 73 E7
Sutton SM1 ... 59 C7
Benham Cl
Chessington KT9 ... 56 C4
Coulsdon CR5 ... 80 B1
Benham Gdns TW3,TW4 ... 4 F2
Benhams Cl RH6 ... 161 A5
Benhams Dr RH6 ... 161 A5
Benhill Ave SM1 ... 59 C6
Benhill Ct SM1 ... 59 D6
Benhill Rd SM1 ... 59 D6
Benhill Wood Rd SM1 ... 59 C6
Benhilton Gdns SM1 ... 59 B7
Benhurst Cl CR2 ... 62 D1
Benhurst Ct
13 Penge SE20 ... 43 B8
Streatham SW16 ... 22 A3
Benhurst Gdns CR2 ... 62 C1
Benhurst La SW16 ... 22 A3
Benin St SE13 ... 24 D8
Benjamin Ct TW15 ... 14 C1
Benjamin Rd RH10 ... 202 D4
Benn Cl RH8 ... 123 A1
Benner La GU24 ... 68 A7
Bennet Cl KT1 ... 37 C8
Bennett Cl Cobham KT11 .. 73 A6
Crawley RH10 ... 202 B2
Bennett Ct GU15 ... 65 C5
Bennett Ho 2 SW4 ... 21 D8
Bennett St 2 W4 ... 7 E8
Bennett Way GU4 ... 111 B6
Bennetts Ave CR0 ... 62 E8
Bennetts Cl CR4,SW16 ... 41 B8
Bennetts Farm Pl KT23 .. 93 F2
Bennetts Rd RH13 ... 217 E1
Bennetts Rise GU11 ... 126 C8
Bennetts Way CR0 ... 62 F8
Bennetts Wood RH5 ... 178 C5
Benning Way RG40 ... 25 D8
Bens Acre RH13 ... 218 A2
Bensbury Cl SW15 ... 19 C8
Bensham Cl CR7 ... 42 C5
Bensham Gr CR7 ... 42 C7
Bensham La CR0,CR7 ... 42 B3
Bensham Manor Rd CR0,
CR7 ... 42 C5
Bensham Manor Sch
CR7 ... 42 C4
Bensington Ct TW14 ... 3 D1
Benson Cl TW3 ... 5 A3
Benson Prim sch CR0 ... 62 E7
Benson Rd
Croydon CR0,CR9 ... 61 A7
Forest Hill SE23 ... 23 C7
Benson's La RH12 ... 199 C1
Bentall Sh Ctr The 10
KT2 ... 37 E7
Benthall Gdns CR8 ... 80 C2
Bentham Ave GU21 ... 70 C4
Bentley Cl SW19 ... 20 A5
Bentley Copse GU15 ... 66 B4
Bentley Dr KT13 ... 53 A2
Benton's La SE27 ... 22 C4
Benton's Rise SE27 ... 22 D3
Bentsbrook Cl RH5 ... 136 B3
Bentsbrook Cotts RH5 .. 136 B3
Bentsbrook Pk RH5 ... 136 B3
Bentsbrook Rd RH5 ... 136 B3
Benwell Ct TW16 ... 35 A8
Benwell Rd GU24 ... 88 A8
Benwick Ct SE20 ... 43 C8
Benwood Ct SM1 ... 59 C7
Beomonds KT16 ... 33 A2
Beomonds Row KT16 ... 33 A2
Berberis Cl GU1 ... 109 C3
Bere Rd RG12 ... 27 E3
Beresford Ave
Tolworth KT5 ... 38 C2
Twickenham TW1 ... 6 C1
Beresford Cl GU16 ... 85 F6
Beresford Ct
Farnborough GU14 ... 85 C1
11 Twickenham TW1 ... 6 C1
Beresford Gdns TW4 ... 4 F2
Beresford Ho SE21 ... 22 E5
Beresford Rd
Belmont SM2 ... 58 F3
Dorking RH4 ... 136 B7
Kingston u T KT2 ... 37 F8
Kingston u T, Norbiton KT3 . 38 C5
Bergenia Ct GU24 ... 67 E6
Berkeley Ave TW4 ... 4 A5
Berkeley Cl
Crawley RH11 ... 200 E2
Kingston u T KT2 ... 17 E1
Stanwell TW19 ... 12 D6
Berkeley Cres GU16 ... 86 A8
Berkeley Ct Ashstead KT21 75 F1
Oatlands Park KT13 ... 53 E8
16 Streatham SW2 ... 22 A7
Wallington SM6 ... 60 C6
Berkeley Dr
East Molesey KT8 ... 36 A6
Winkfield SL4 ... 9 B7
Berkeley Gdns
Claygate KT10 ... 56 A4
Pyrford KT14 ... 70 F5
Walton-on-T KT12 ... 34 F2
Berkeley Ho 11 TW8 ... 6 D8
Berkeley Lodge KT21 ... 95 D8
Berkeley Pl Epsom KT18 .. 76 D4
Wimbledon SW19 ... 19 D2
Berkeley Prim Sch TW5 ... 4 D7
Berkeley Waye TW5 ... 4 D7
Berkeleys The KT22 ... 94 E3
Berkley Cl TW2 ... 16 E5
Berkley Ct Guildford GU1 109 E1
7 Twickenham TW1 ... 17 A8
Berkley Mews TW16 ... 35 C6
Berkshire Cl CR3 ... 100 D5
Berkshire Copse Rd
GU11 ... 104 E7
Berkshire Ho SE6 ... 24 A4
Berkshire Rd GU15 ... 65 F8
Berkshire Sq CR4 ... 41 E5
Berkshire Way
Bracknell RG12 ... 26 D6
Mitcham CR4 ... 41 E5
Bernard Ct GU15 ... 65 B4
Bernard Gdns SW19 ... 19 F3
Bernard Rd SM6 ... 60 B6
Berne Rd CR7 ... 42 C4
Bernel Dr CR0 ... 62 F7
Bernersh Cl GU47 ... 45 C1
Berney Ho BR3 ... 43 E4
Berney Rd CR0 ... 42 D2
Berridge Rd SE19 ... 22 E3
Berrington Dr KT24 ... 92 F3
Berry Ct TW4 ... 4 F2
Berry La Hersham KT12 ... 54 D5
Pirbright GU3 ... 88 C2
West Norwood SE21, SE27 . 22 D4
Woking GU22,GU3 ... 88 D4
Berry Meade KT21 ... 75 F2
Berry Wlk KT21 ... 95 F8
Berry's La KT14 ... 71 D8
Berrybank GU47 ... 64 E6
Berrycroft RG12 ... 27 D8
Berrylands Surbiton KT5 .. 37 F3
West Barnes SW20 ... 39 C5
Berrylands Ct 6 SM2 ... 59 B3
Berrylands Rd KT5 ... 37 F3
Berrylands Sta KT5 ... 38 B5
Berryman's La SE26 ... 23 D4
Berrymeade Wlk 6
RH11 ... 200 E5
Berryscourt KT14 ... 71 D8
Berryscroft Ct TW18 ... 13 C1
Berryscroft Rd TW18 ... 13 C1
Berstead Wlk 1 RH11 .. 200 F3
Bert Rd CR7 ... 42 C4
Bertal Rd SW17 ... 20 D4
Bertie Rd SE26 ... 23 D2
Bertram Cotts SW19 ... 20 A1
Bertram Rd KT2 ... 18 A1
Bertrand Ho 11 SW16 ... 21 E5
Bertrum House Sch
SW17 ... 21 A6
Berwyn Ave TW3 ... 5 B6
Berwyn Rd
Mortlake SW14,TW10 ... 7 B3
Streatham SE24 ... 22 B7
Beryl Harding Ho 3
SW19 ... 19 D1
Berystede KT2 ... 18 B1
Besley St SW16 ... 21 C2
Bessant Dr TW9 ... 7 B6
Bessborough Rd SW15 .. 19 A7
Bessborough Wks KT8 .. 35 F4
Beswick Gdns RG12 ... 27 F8
Beta Rd Chobham GU24 ... 49 F1
Farnborough GU14 ... 85 A5
Woking GU22 ... 70 B3
Beta Way TW20 ... 32 C8
Betchets Green Rd RH5 157 C6
Betchley Cl RH19 ... 185 E3
Betchworth Cl SM1 ... 59 D5
Betchworth Sta RH3 .. 116 E3
Betchworth The RH4 .. 116 A1
Betchworth Way CR0 ... 63 C2
Betchworth Works RH6 180 D6
Bethany Waye TW14 ... 14 E8
Bethel Cl GU9 ... 125 D6
Bethel La GU9 ... 125 D6
Bethersden Cl BR3 ... 23 F1
Bethesda Ct 6 SE20 ... 23 C1
Bethlem Royal Hospl The
BR3 ... 44 A2
Bethune Cl RH10 ... 202 D5
Bethune Rd RH13 ... 217 E1
Betjeman Cl CR5 ... 79 F2
Betley Ct KT12 ... 54 B7
Betony Cl CR0 ... 43 D1
Betts Cl BR3 ... 43 E7
Betts Way Crawley RH10 . 181 D2
Long Ditton KT6 ... 37 B1
Penge SE20 ... 43 B8
Bettswood Ct 16 SE20 ... 43 B8
Betula Cl CR8 ... 80 D4
Between Streets KT11 ... 73 A5
Beulah Ave CR7 ... 42 C7
Beulah Cres CR7 ... 42 C7
Beulah Gr CR0 ... 42 C3
Beulah Hill SE19,SW16 ... 22 C1
Beulah Inf Sch CR7 ... 42 C6
Beulah Jun Sch CR7 ... 42 C6
Beulah Rd Merton SW19 .. 19 F1
South Norwood CR7 ... 42 C6
Sutton SM1 ... 59 A6
Beulah Wlk CR3 ... 101 E7
Bevan Ct Crawley RH11 .. 201 B1
Croydon CR0 ... 61 A5
Bevan Gate RG42 ... 27 A8
Bevan Pk KT17 ... 57 F1
Beverley Ave
Hounslow TW4 ... 4 F3
Wimbledon SW20 ... 38 F8
Beverley Cl
Addlestone KT15 ... 52 D5
Ash GU12 ... 105 F1
Chessington KT9 ... 56 C6
East Ewell KT17 ... 77 C8
Frimley GU15 ... 66 D6
Oatlands Park KT13 ... 53 E8
Beverley Cotts SW15 ... 18 E5
Beverley Cres GU14 ... 84 F2
Beverley Ct Hounslow TW4 . 4 F3
Kingston u T SW20 ... 38 F8

Beverley Gdns
Barnes SW13 . . . . .7 F4
2 North Cheam KT4 . . . . . .39 A1
Beverley Ho BR1 . . . . .24 D3
Beverley Hts RH2 . . . . . .118 B3
Beverley Hyrst 7 CR0 . . .61 F8
Beverley La KT2 . . . . .18 E1
Beverley Lodge 6 TW10 . .6 E2
Beverley Mans TW4 . . . . . .4 F3
Beverley Mews RH10 . . . .202 A5
Beverley Rd Barnes SW13 . .7 F4
Kenley CR3 . . . . .80 F2
Mitcham CR4 . . . . .41 D5
New Malden KT3 . . . . . . .39 A5
North Cheam KT4 . . . . . .58 C8
Penge SE20 . . . . .43 B7
Sunbury TW16 . . . . .34 F8
Teddington KT1 . . . . .37 C8
Beverley Sch KT3 . . . . . . .39 A4
Beverley Trad Est SM4 . . .39 D2
Beverley Way
Kingston u T KT3,SW20,KT2 .38 F8
Wimbledon KT3,SW20 . . . .39 A6
**Beverley Way (Kingston By
Pass)** KT3,SW20 . . . . . . .39 A6
**Beverley Way Kingston
Bypass** KT3 . . . . .38 F8
Beverstone Rd CR7 . . . . .42 B5
Bevill Allen Cl SW17 . . . .20 F3
Bevill Cl SE25 . . . . .43 A6
Bevin Sq SW17 . . . . .20 F5
Bevington Rd BR3 . . . . . .44 B7
Bew Ct SE21 . . . . .23 A8
Bewbush Com Mid Sch
RH11 . . . . .200 F3
Bewbush Dr RH11 . . . . . .200 F3
Bewbush Fst Sch RH11 . .200 F3
Bewbush Manor RH11 . .200 E2
Bewley St SW19 . . . . .20 C2
Bewlys Rd SE27 . . . . .22 B3
Bexhill Cl TW13 . . . . .15 E6
Bexhill Rd Forest Hill SE4 . .23 F8
Mortlake SW14 . . . . .7 C4
Beynon Rd SM5 . . . . .59 F5
Bicester Rd TW9 . . . . .7 B4
Bickersteth Rd SW17 . . . .20 F2
Bickley Ct RH11 . . . . .201 A3
Bickley St SW17 . . . . .20 F3
Bicknell Rd GU16 . . . . . . .65 E2
Bickney Way GU22 . . . . . .94 C5
Bicknoller Cl SM2 . . . . . . .59 B1
Bidborough Cl 5 BR2 . . . .44 F4
Biddulph Rd CR2 . . . . .61 C2
Bideford Cl
Farnborough GU14 . . . . . .85 A7
Feltham TW13 . . . . .15 F5
Bideford Rd BR1 . . . . .24 F5
Bidmead Ct KT6 . . . . .56 E7
Bield The RH2 . . . . .139 A7
Bietigheim Way GU15 . . . .65 C6
Big Common La RH1 . . . .120 B3
Biggin Ave CR4 . . . . .40 F8
Biggin Cl RH11 . . . . .201 C4
Biggin Hill SE19 . . . . .22 B1
Biggin Hill Airport TN16 . .83 D5
Biggin Hill Bsns Pk TN16 .83 D4
Biggin Hill Cl KT2 . . . . . . .17 C3
Biggin Hill Jun & Inf Schs
TN16 . . . . .83 E3
Biggin Way SW19 . . . . . . .22 C1
Bignor Cl RH12 . . . . .218 A7
Bigginwood Rd SW16 . . . .42 B8
Bignor Cl RH12 . . . . .218 A7
Bilberry Cl RH11 . . . . . . .201 B3
Bilbets RH12 . . . . .217 C3
Billesden Rd GU24 . . . . . .87 D7
Billet Rd TW18,TW19 . . . . .13 C4
Billhurst Cotts RH7 . . . . .164 D4
Billingshurst Rd RH12 . .216 D3
Billington Ct 1 RH19 . . .185 F2
Billinton Dr RH10 . . . . . .202 B5
Billockby Cl KT9 . . . . .56 F4
Billsley Ct SE25 . . . . .42 E5
Bilton Ind Est RG12 . . . . .26 E5
Binbury Row TW18 . . . . . .12 E4
Binfield Rd
Bracknell, Dowlesgreen
RG40 . . . . .25 F7
Bracknell,Priestwood RG42 .27 A8
Byfleet KT14 . . . . .71 E7
South Croydon CR2 . . . . . .61 F5
Binfields GU9 . . . . .125 C3
Bingham Cnr CR0 . . . . . . .43 A1
Bingham Dr Knaphill GU21 .68 F1
Staines TW18 . . . . .13 D1
Bingham Rd CR0,CR9 . . . .43 B1
Bingley Rd TW16 . . . . .15 A1
Binhams Lea GU8 . . . . . .192 F5
Binhams Mdw GU8 . . . . .192 F5
Binley Ho SW15 . . . . .7 F1
Binney Ct RH10 . . . . .182 E1
Binscombe Cres GU7 . . .150 E8
Binscombe Jun Sch
GU7 . . . . .129 E1
Binscombe La GU7 . . . . .150 E7
Binstead Rd RH11 . . . . . .201 B8
Binsted Dr GU17 . . . . .64 D5
Binton La GU10 . . . . .146 A6
Birch Ave Caterham CR3 . .100 D3
Leatherhead KT22 . . . . . . .94 F7
Birch Circ GU7 . . . . .150 F8
Birch Cl Brentford TW8 . . . .6 B7
Camberley GU15 . . . . .65 E8
Crawley Down RH10 . . . . .204 C8
Hounslow TW3 . . . . .5 D5
New Haw KT15 . . . . .52 D2
Rowledge GU10 . . . . .146 A4
Send Marsh GU23 . . . . . . .90 F2

Birch Cl *continued*
Teddington TW11 . . . . .17 A3
Woking GU22 . . . . .89 C8
Birch Ct Ashstead KT21 . . .75 D2
Chipstead CR5 . . . . .78 F1
Sutton SM1 . . . . .59 C6
9 Wallington SM6 . . . . . .60 B6
Birch Dr GU17 . . . . .64 D3
Birch Gr Bracknell RG12 . . .27 C5
Guildford GU1 . . . . .109 C4
Kingswood KT20 . . . . .97 F3
Lewisham SE12 . . . . .24 F8
Upper Halliford TW17 . . . . .34 E7
Woking GU22 . . . . .70 D4
Birch Hill CR0 . . . . .62 D5
Birch Hill Prim Sch RG12 .27 B1
Birch Hill Rd RG12 . . . . . .27 B2
Birch Ho
Farnborough GU14 . . . . . .85 A7
Teddington TW11 . . . . . . .17 C1
Birch La Purley CR8 . . . . . .79 E5
West End GU24 . . . . .67 D7
Winkfield RG12,SL5 . . . . . .28 B8
Birch Lea RH10 . . . . .182 A1
Birch Platt GU24 . . . . .67 D6
Birch Rd Farncombe GU7 . .151 A8
Feltham TW13 . . . . .15 D3
Headley Down GU35 . . . . .187 B6
Windlesham GU20 . . . . . . .48 E4
Birch Side RG45 . . . . .45 A6
Birch Tree Ave BR4 . . . . .63 F6
Birch Tree View GU18 . . . .48 A1
Birch Tree Way CR0 . . . . .62 B8
Birch Vale KT11 . . . . .74 A6
Birch Way Ash Vale GU12 .106 A7
Warlingham CR6 . . . . .81 E1
5 Bromley BR2 . . . . .44 F5
Crawley RH10 . . . . .202 A7
Crawley RH10 . . . . .202 A8
East Horsley KT24 . . . . . . .92 E1
Farnborough GU14 . . . . . .84 D4
South Norwood SE25 . . . . .42 F7
Twickenham TW4 . . . . .15 F4
Woking GU22 . . . . .69 F1
Birchett Rd
Aldershot GU11 . . . . .105 A2
Farnborough GU14 . . . . . .84 E5
Birchetts Cl 1 RG42 . . . . .27 B8
Birchfield Cl
Addlestone KT15 . . . . .52 B6
Coulsdon CR5 . . . . .79 F3
Birchfield Gr KT17 . . . . . .58 C1
Birchfields GU15 . . . . . . .65 C4
Birchgrove KT11 . . . . .73 D5
Birchington Rd KT5 . . . . .37 F2
Birchlands Ave SW12 . . . .20 F8
Birchlands Ct GU47 . . . . .45 E2
Birchway RH1 . . . . .140 B7
Birchwood Ave
Beckenham BR3 . . . . .43 F5
Hackbridge SM6 . . . . .60 B7
Birchwood Cl
Crawley RH10 . . . . .202 C3
Horley RH6 . . . . .161 B4
Ifold RH14 . . . . .212 D3
Morden SM4 . . . . .40 B5
Birchwood Dr
Lightwater GU18 . . . . .48 C1
West Byfleet KT14 . . . . . . .71 A7
Birchwood Gr TW12 . . . . .16 A2
Birchwood La
Caterham CR3 . . . . .100 B2
Oxshott KT10,KT22 . . . . . . .55 E1
Birchwood Rd
Streatham SW17 . . . . .21 B3
West Byfleet KT14 . . . . . . .71 A7
Bird Mews RG40 . . . . . . .25 B6
Bird Wlk TW2 . . . . .15 F7
Bird-In-Hand Pas SE23 . . .23 C6
Birdham Cl RH11 . . . . . . .201 B8
Birdhaven GU10 . . . . .146 A6
Birdhurst CR3 . . . . .100 F7
Birdhurst Ave CR2 . . . . . .61 D6
Birdhurst Ct SM6 . . . . . . .60 C3
Birdhurst Gdns CR2 . . . . .61 D6
Birdhurst Rd
Mitcham SW19 . . . . .20 E2
South Croydon CR2 . . . . . .61 E5
Birdhurst Rise CR2 . . . . . .61 E5
Birds Hill Dr KT22 . . . . . .74 D6
Birds Hill Rd KT22 . . . . . .74 D6
Birds Hill Rise KT22 . . . . .74 D6
Birdsgrove GU21 . . . . . . .68 B1
Birdswood Dr GU21 . . . . .88 E7
Birdwood Cl Selsdon CR2 . .81 D8
Teddington TW11 . . . . . . .16 E4
Birdwood Rd GU15 . . . . . .64 F6
**Birdworld & Underwater
World✱** GU10 . . . . .145 B3
Birkbeck Hill SE21 . . . . . .22 B7
Birkbeck Pl
Sandhurst GU47 . . . . .45 E1
West Norwood SE21 . . . . . .22 C6
Birkbeck Rd Penge BR3 . . .43 D7
Wimbledon SW19 . . . . . . .20 B2

Birkbeck Sta SE20 . . . . . .43 C6
Birkdale RG12 . . . . .26 E2
Birkdale Cl SL5 . . . . .29 C4
Birkdale Dr RH11 . . . . . . .200 D5
Birkdale Gdns CR0 . . . . . .62 D6
Birkenhead Ave KT2 . . . . .37 F8
Birkenholme Cl GU35 . . .187 C4
Birkhall Rd SE6 . . . . .24 D6
Birkheads Rd RH2 . . . . . .118 A2
Birkwood Cl SW12 . . . . . .21 D8
Birnam Cl GU23 . . . . .91 A3
Birtley Ctyd GU5 . . . . . . .152 B3
Birtley Rd GU5 . . . . .152 B4
Birtley Rise GU5 . . . . . . .152 A5
Birtway Ct 15 SM1 . . . . . .59 C6
Biscoe Cl TW5 . . . . .5 A8
Bisenden Rd CR0 . . . . . . .61 E8
Bisham Cl Carshalton CR4 . .40 F1
Crawley RH10 . . . . .202 D3
Bishams Ct CR3 . . . . .100 F3
Bishop Bell Sch RH10 . . .201 F3
Bishop Challoner Sch
BR2 . . . . .44 D7
Bishop David Brown Sch The
GU21 . . . . .70 D6
Bishop Duppa's Almshouses
7 TW10 . . . . .6 E3
Bishop Duppas Pk TW17 . .34 E2
Bishop Fox Way KT8 . . . . .35 F5
Bishop Gilpin CE Prim Sch
SW19 . . . . .19 F3
Bishop Parkhurst GU1 . . .110 B3
Bishop Perrin CE Prim Sch
TW2 . . . . .16 B7
Bishop Reindorp CE Sch
GU1 . . . . .109 C4
Bishop Sumner Dr GU9 .125 C6
**Bishop Thomas Grant RC Sec
Sch** SW16 . . . . .21 F3
Bishop Wand CE Sec Sch The
TW16 . . . . .34 F7
Bishop's Cl CR5 . . . . .80 A1
Bishop's Cotts RH3 . . . . .116 B2
Bishop's Hall KT1 . . . . . . .37 D7
Bishop's La SL4 . . . . .8 B7
Bishop's Mead GU9 . . . . .125 B2
Bishop's Pl SM1 . . . . .59 C5
Bishop's Rd CR0 . . . . .42 B2
Bishopdale RG12 . . . . . . .27 A5
Bishopric RH12 . . . . .217 B2
Bishopric Ct RH12 . . . . . .217 B2
Bishops Cl SM1 . . . . .59 A7
Bishops Ct
1 Ashford TW16 . . . . .14 F1
Guildford GU1 . . . . .130 C7
Bishops Dr
East Bedfont TW14 . . . . . . .3 D1
Wokingham RG40 . . . . . . .25 C7
Bishops Gr Hampton TW12 .15 F4
Windlesham GU20 . . . . . . .48 C4
Bishops Hill KT17 . . . . . . .35 A2
Bishops Ho 3 GU7 . . . . .150 D4
Bishops Park Rd SW16 . . .41 E8
Bishops Rd GU9 . . . . .125 B7
Bishops Sq GU6 . . . . .174 F3
Bishops Way SW20 . . . . . .12 D2
Bishops Wlk CR0,CR9 . . . .62 E5
Bishops Wood GU21 . . . . .68 F2
Bishopscourt 6 CR0 . . . . .61 F8
Bishopsford Rd SM4 . . . . .40 D3
Bishopsgate Rd TW20 . . . .11 B5
Bishopsgate Sch SW20 . . .11 A5
Bishopsmead Cl
East Horsley KT24 . . . . . . .112 E7
Epsom KT19 . . . . .57 D1
Bishopsmead Ct KT19 . . . .57 E1
Bishopsmead Dr KT24 . . .112 F6
Bishopsmead Par KT24 . .112 F6
Bishopsthorpe Rd SE26 . . .23 D4
Bishopstone Wlk RH11 . .201 C1

Blackcap Cl RH11 . . . . . .201 C4
Blackcap Pl GU47 . . . . . . .64 E8
Blackdown Ave GU22 . . . .70 E4
Blackdown Cl GU22 . . . . . .70 D3
Blackdown Prim Sch
GU16 . . . . .86 E8
Blackdown Rd GU16 . . . . .86 C8
Blackenham Rd SW17 . . . .20 F4
Blackett Cl TW18 . . . . .32 F7
Blackett Rd RH10 . . . . . .202 C5
Blackfold Rd RH10 . . . . . .202 A5
Blackford Cl CR2 . . . . .61 B2
Blackham Ho SW19 . . . . . .19 E2
Blackheath RH10 . . . . . . .202 D8
Blackheath Gr GU5 . . . . . .152 B8
Blackheath La
Albury GU5 . . . . .132 B3
Wonersh GU5,GU4 . . . . . .152 C8
Blackheath Rd GU9 . . . . .125 A7
Blackhills KT10 . . . . .55 A2
Blackhorse La
Croydon CR0 . . . . .43 A2
Lower Kingswood KT20,
RH2 . . . . .118 C7
Blackhorse Lane Sta CR0 .43 A2
Blackhorse Rd GU21,
GU22 . . . . .88 E6
Blacklands Cres RH18 . . .206 F2
Blacklands Mdw RH1 . . . .119 E2
Blacklands Rd SE6 . . . . . .24 C4
Blackman Gdns GU11 . . .126 B8
Blackmeadows RG12 . . . .27 C3
Blackmoor Cl SL5 . . . . . . .28 D7
Blackmoor Wood SL5 . . . .28 D7
Blackmore Cres GU21 . . . .70 C5
Blackmore Ho SE23 . . . . .23 F7
Blackmore's Gr TW11 . . . .17 A2
Blackness La GU22 . . . . . .89 E8
Blacknest Cotts GU8 . . . .192 E3
Blacknest Gate Rd SL5 . . .30 B6
Blacknest Rd GU25,SL5 . . .30 E6
Blackshaw Rd SW17 . . . . .20 D3
Blacksmith Cl KT21 . . . . . .95 F8
Blacksmith La GU4 . . . . . .131 D3
Blacksmiths Hill CR2 . . . . .81 B6
Blacksmiths La KT16 . . . . .33 A2
Blackstone Cl
Farnborough GU14 . . . . . .84 D6
Reigate RH1 . . . . .139 E8
Blackstone Hill RH1,RH2 . .118 E1
Blackstone Ho SE21 . . . . .22 E5
Blackstroud La E GU18,
GU24 . . . . .67 D8
Blackstroud La W GU18 . .67 D8
Blackthorn Cl
Crawley RH11 . . . . .181 C1
Horsham RH13 . . . . .218 A2
Reigate RH2 . . . . .139 C7
Blackthorn Cres GU14 . . .84 F8
Blackthorn Ct Heston TW5 . .4 E7
7 West Norwood SW16 . . .22 A3
Blackthorn Dr GU18 . . . . .67 B7
Blackthorn Pl GU1 . . . . . .109 C4
Blackthorn Rd
Biggin Hill TN16 . . . . .83 E3
Reigate RH2 . . . . .139 C7
Blackthorne Ave CR0 . . . .43 C1
Blackthorne Cres SL3 . . . . .1 E5
Blackthorne Rd
Great Bookham KT23 . . . . .94 C1
Poyle SL3 . . . . .1 E4
Blackwater Cl GU12 . . . .106 A1
Blackwater La RH10 . . . . .202 D6
Blackwater Pk GU12 . . . .105 E1
Blackwater Sta GU17 . . . .64 E4
Blackwater Way GU12 . . .126 D8
Blackwell Ave GU2 . . . . .108 D1
Blackwell Farm Cotts
GU3 . . . . .129 C8
Blackwell Farm Rd
RH19 . . . . .185 F3
Blackwell Hollow RH19 . .185 F2
Blackwell Prim Sch
RH19 . . . . .185 E3
Blackwell Rd RH19 . . . . .185 F2
Blackwood Cl KT14 . . . . . .71 C7
Bladen Cl KT13 . . . . .53 E4
Blades Cl KT22 . . . . .95 D7
Bladon Cl GU1 . . . . .110 A2
Bladon Ct Beckenham BR2 .44 E7
Streatham SW16 . . . . .21 E2
Blagdon Rd KT3 . . . . .38 F5
Blagdon Wlk TW11 . . . . . .17 C2
Blair Cl GU16 . . . . .55 C8
Blair Ct Beckenham BR3 . . .44 B8
Catford SE6 . . . . .24 F7
Blairderry Rd SW2 . . . . . .21 E6
Blaise Cl GU14 . . . . .85 D3
Blake Cl Carshalton SM5 . . .40 E1
Crawley RH10 . . . . .201 F2
Crowthorne RG45 . . . . . . .45 C4
Wokingham RG40 . . . . . . .25 B8
Blake Ho BR3 . . . . .24 B2
Blake Mews 4 TW9 . . . . . .7 A6
Blake Rd Croydon CR0 . . . .61 E8
Mitcham CR4 . . . . .40 E6
Blake's Gn BR4 . . . . .44 C1
Blake's La GU4 . . . . .111 F3
Blakeden Dr KT10 . . . . . . .55 F5
Blakehall Rd SM5 . . . . . . .59 F4
Blakemore Rd
Streatham SW16 . . . . .21 E5
Thornton Heath CR7 . . . . . .41 F4
Blakeney Ave BR3 . . . . . . .43 F8
Blakeney Cl KT19 . . . . . . .76 D8
Blakeney Rd BR3 . . . . . . .43 F8

Blakes Ave KT3 . . . . .38 F3
Blakes La KT3 . . . . .38 F4
Blakes Terr KT3 . . . . .39 A4
Blakewood Cl TW13 . . . . . .15 C4
Blanchards Hill GU4 . . . .109 E8
Blanchland Rd SM4 . . . . . .40 B4
Blanchman's Rd CR6 . . . . .81 C5
Blandfield Rd SW12 . . . . . .21 A8
Blandford Ave Penge BR3 . .43 E7
Twickenham TW2 . . . . .16 B7
Blandford Cl
Wallington CR0 . . . . .60 E7
Woking GU22 . . . . .70 B2
Blandford Rd Penge BR3 . . .43 D7
Teddington TW11 . . . . . . .16 E3
Blane's La SL5 . . . . .28 C3
Blanford Rd RH2 . . . . . . .139 C8
Blanks La RH5,RH6 . . . . .159 B2
Blashford St SE13 . . . . . . .24 D8
Blatchford Cl RH13 . . . . .217 F3
Blatchford Ct KT12 . . . . . .35 A1
Blatchford Rd RH13 . . . . .217 F3
Blay's La TW20 . . . . .11 B2
Blays Cl TW20 . . . . .11 C2
Blean Gr SE20 . . . . .23 C1
Blegborough Rd SW16 . . .21 C2
Blencarn Cl GU21 . . . . . . .68 F3
Blendworth Point 4
SW15 . . . . .19 B7
Blenheim 26 SW19 . . . . . .19 D7
Blenheim Bsns Ctr CR4 . . .40 F7
Blenheim Cl
Crawley RH10 . . . . .182 D1
East Grinstead RH19 . . . . .186 A3
Tongham GU10 . . . . .126 E7
Wallington SM6 . . . . .60 C3
West Barnes SW20 . . . . . . .39 C6
West Byfleet KT14 . . . . . . .70 F6
Blenheim Cres Hale GU9 .125 A5
South Croydon CR2 . . . . . .61 C3
Blenheim Ct Bromley BR2 . .44 F5
Egham TW18 . . . . .12 D4
Farnborough GU14 . . . . . .85 D2
Richmond TW9 . . . . .6 F4
South Norwood SE19 . . . . .42 E8
Sutton SM2 . . . . .59 C4
Blenheim Fields RH18 . . .206 E3
Blenheim Gdns
Kingston u T KT2 . . . . .18 B1
Sanderstead CR2 . . . . .81 A7
Wallington SM6 . . . . .60 C3
Woking GU22 . . . . .89 B8
Blenheim High Sch KT19 .57 D1
Blenheim Ho TW3 . . . . .5 A4
Blenheim Park Rd CR2 . . .61 C2
Blenheim Pk GU11 . . . . . .105 C2
Blenheim Pl TW11 . . . . . . .16 F3
Blenheim Rd Epsom KT19 . .76 B8
Farnborough GU14 . . . . . .105 B7
Horsham RH12 . . . . .217 D4
Penge SE20 . . . . .23 C1
Sutton SM1 . . . . .59 B7
West Barnes SW20 . . . . . . .39 C6
Blenheim Way TW7 . . . . . .6 A6
Bleriot Rd TW5 . . . . .4 C7
Bletchingley Cl RH1 . . . . .119 C6
Bletchingley Rd
Godstone RH9 . . . . .121 B4
Merstham RH1 . . . . .119 E6
Nutfield RH1 . . . . .120 A2
Bletchingly Ct CR7 . . . . . .42 B5
Bletchmore Cl UB3 . . . . . . .3 D8
Blewburton Wlk RG12 . . . .27 E5
Blewfield GU7 . . . . .150 F2
Bligh Cl RH10 . . . . .201 F4
Bligh Ho 5 SE27 . . . . .22 C4
Blighton La GU10 . . . . . . .126 E3
Blincoe Cl SW19 . . . . .19 D6
Blind Cnr SE25 . . . . .43 B5
Blindley Ct RH7 . . . . .163 E8
Blindley Rd RH10 . . . . . . .182 D1
Bloggs Way GU6 . . . . . . .174 D3
Blomfield Dale RG42 . . . . .26 D7
Blondell Cl UB7 . . . . .2 D8
Bloom Gr SE27 . . . . .22 B5
Bloomfield Cl GU21 . . . . . .68 E1
Bloomfield Rd KT1 . . . . . .37 E6
Bloomhall Rd SE19 . . . . . .22 D3
Bloomsbury Cl KT19 . . . . .57 D1
Bloomsbury Ct
Cranford TW5 . . . . .4 B6
Guildford GU1 . . . . .130 F7
Bloomsbury Way GU17 . . .64 D3
Bloor Cl RH12 . . . . .217 D7
Blossom Cl CR2 . . . . .61 F5
Blossom Waye TW5 . . . . . .4 E7
Blount Ave RH19 . . . . . . .185 C1
Bloxham Cres TW12 . . . . .35 F8
Bloxham Rd GU6 . . . . . . .175 A3
Bloxworth Cl
9 Bracknell RG12 . . . . . .27 F5
Wallington SM6 . . . . .60 C7
Blue Anchor Alley 3 TW9 . .6 E3
Blue Ball La TW20 . . . . . . .11 F3
Blue Barn Way KT13 . . . . .72 A8
Blue Cedars SM7 . . . . . . .77 D5
Blue Cedars Pl KT11 . . . . .73 D7
Blue Coat Wlk GU22 . . . . .27 D4
Blue Leaves Ave CR5 . . . . .99 C6
Blue Ridges Pk RH5 . . . . .178 A3
Blue Sch CE Prim The
TW7 . . . . .6 A4
Bluebell Cl Crawley RH11 .201 B3
East Grinstead RH19 . . . . .185 B1

Bluebell Cl *continued*
Forest Hill SE26 22 F4
Horsham RH12 217 E5
Wallington CR4 41 B1
Bluebell Ct GU22 89 D8
Bluebell Hill RG12 27 E8
Bluebell La KT24 112 E6
Bluebell Mews GU15 65 D7
Bluebell Rise GU18 67 B8
Blueberry Gdns CR5 79 F3
Bluebird Ho RH6 160 D1
Bluefield Cl TW12 16 A3
Bluegates Stoneleigh KT17 58 A3
Wimbledon SW19 19 E3
Bluehouse Gdns RH8 123 A7
Bluehouse La RH8 122 F7
Bluethroat Cl GU47 64 E8
Bluff Cove GU11 105 C3
Blundel La KT11 74 B4
Blundell Ave RH6 160 F4
Blunden Rd GU14 84 F5
Blunt Rd CR0 61 D5
Blunts Ave UB7 3 A7
Blunts Way RH12 217 C3
Blyth Cl TW1 5 F1
Blyth Rd BR1 44 F8
Blythe Cl SE23 23 F8
Blythe Hill SE23,SE6 23 F8
Blythe Hill La SE23,SE6 23 F7
Blythe Vale SE23,SE6 23 F8
Blythewood La SL5 28 E7
Blythwood Dr GU16 65 D2
Blythwood Pk 12 BR1 44 F8
Blytons The RH19 185 B1
Boar Hill RH5 135 E1
Board School Rd GU21 69 F3
Bocketts Farm Pk* KT22 94 F2
Bockhampton Rd KT2 17 F1
Boddicott Cl SW19 19 E6
Bodens Ride SL5 28 F1
Bodiam Cl RH10 202 C6
Bodiam Ct Carshalton SM1 59 D6
Hayes BR2 44 F5
Bodiam Rd SW16 21 D1
Bodicea Mews TW4 5 A1
Bodley Cl KT3 38 E4
Bodley Manor Way SE24 22 A8
Bodley Rd KT3 38 E4
Bodmin Gr SM4 40 B4
Bodmin St SW18 20 A7
Bodnant Gdns SW20 39 B6
Bog La RG12 28 A5
Bognor Rd
Beare Green RH5 157 B2
Warnham RH12,RH5 197 D4
Bois Hall Rd KT15 52 D5
Bolderwood Way BR4 63 B8
Bolding House La GU24 67 F7
Boleyn Ave KT17 58 B1
Boleyn Cl Crawley RH10 202 D3
Egham TW18 12 E3
Boleyn Ct
East Molesey KT8 36 D5
11 Redhill RH1 119 A2
Boleyn Dr KT8 35 F6
Boleyn Gdns BR4 63 B8
Boleyn Wlk KT22 94 F7
Bolingbroke Gr SW11 20 F8
Bolingbroke Ho BR3 24 B3
Bolney Ct Crawley RH11 200 F3
Kingston u T KT6 37 C4
Bolsover Gr RH1 119 E6
Bolstead Rd CR4 41 B8
Bolters La SM7 78 A4
Bolters Rd RH6 161 A5
Bolters Rd S RH6 160 F6
Bolton Cl Chessington KT9 56 E4
Penge SE20 43 A7
Bolton Gdns Bromley BR1 24 F2
Teddington TW11 17 A2
Bolton Rd Chessington KT9 56 E4
Chiswick W4 7 C7
Crawley RH10 202 C2
Bolton's La
Harlington TW6,UB7 3 B7
Pyrford GU22 71 A3
Boltons Cl GU22 71 A3
Bomer Cl UB7 3 A7
Bonchurch Cl SM2 59 B3
Bond Fst Sch CR4 40 F7
Bond Gdns SM6 60 C6
Bond Rd Mitcham CR4 40 F7
Surbiton KT6 56 F8
Warlingham CR6 81 E1
Bond St TW20 11 C3
Bond Way RG12 27 B8
Bond's La RH5 136 B1
Bone Mill La RH9 121 E1
Bonehurst Rd RH1,RH6 161 A7
Bones La RH6,RH7 163 B2
Bonner Hill Rd KT1 38 A6
Bonners Cl GU22 89 F5
Bonnetts La RH11 181 A3
Bonnys Rd RH2 138 D8
Bonser Rd TW1 16 F6
Bonsey Cl GU22 89 E6
Bonsey La GU22 89 E6
Bonsey's La GU24,KT16 50 F2
Bonsor Dr KT20 97 E5
Bonus Pastor RC Sch
BR1 24 E4
Bonville Rd BR1 24 F3
Bookham Ct Mitcham CR4 40 D6
Little Bookham KT23 93 F4
Bookham Gr 2 KT23 94 B1
Bookham Grove Ho 3
KT23 94 B1
Bookham Ind Est KT23 93 F3
Bookham Ind Pk KT23 93 F4
Bookham Rd KT11 93 D7
Bookham Sta KT23 93 F4
Bookhurst Hill GU6 175 A4
Bookhurst Rd GU6 175 B4
Boole Hts RG12 27 A4
Booth Dr TW18 13 D2
Booth Rd Crawley RH11 200 E3
Croydon CR0,CR9 61 B8
Booth Way RH13 217 E3
Boothby Ho 2 SW16 21 C3
Boothroyd Ho TW7 5 F4
Borage Cl RH11 201 A2
Border Chase RH10 183 A2
Border Cres SE26 23 B3
Border Ct RH19 185 F4
Border End GU27 207 D6
Border Gate CR4 40 F8
Border Gdns CR0 63 B6
Border Rd Forest Hill SE26 23 B3
Haslemere GU27 207 D6
Bordesley Rd SM4 40 B5
Bordon Wlk 6 SW15 19 A8
Boreen The GU35 187 B5
Borelli Mews GU9 125 C2
Borelli Yd GU9 125 C2
Borers Arms Rd RH10 183 C3
Borers Yard Ind Est
RH10 183 C3
Borland Rd TW11 17 B1
Borough Grange CR2 81 A7
Borough Hill CR0,CR9 61 B7
Borough Rd
Godalming GU7 150 D5
Hounslow TW7 5 F6
7 Kingston u T KT2 18 A1
Mitcham CR4 40 E7
Tatsfield TN16 103 D6
Borough The
Brockham RH3 137 A8
Farnham GU9 125 B2
Borrowdale Cl
Crawley RH11 201 B4
Sanderstead CR2 80 F6
Thorpe Lea TW20 12 B1
Borrowdale Dr CR2 80 F7
Borrowdale Gdns GU15 66 D4
Bosbury Rd SE6 24 C5
Boscombe Cl TW20 32 C8
Boscombe Gdns SW16 21 E2
Boscombe Ho CR0 42 D1
Boscombe Rd
Merton SW19 40 B8
Mitcham SW17 21 A2
North Cheam KT4 39 D1
Bosham Rd RH10 202 C3
Boshers Gdns TW20 11 F2
Bosman Dr GU20 48 B6
Bostock Ave RH12 218 A5
Bostock Ho TW5 5 A8
Boston Ct
South Norwood SE25 42 F5
Sutton SM2 59 C3
Boston Gdns W4 7 E8
Boston Manor Rd TW8 6 C8
Boston Rd CR0 42 A3
Boswell Ho 5 SW16 21 C3
Boswell Rd
Crawley RH10 201 E3
Thornton Heath CR7 42 C5
Boswood Ct TW4 4 F4
Botany Hill GU10 126 D1
Botery's Cross RH1 120 B2
Bothwell Rd CR0 63 C1
Bothy The GU22 70 F2
Botsford Rd SW20 39 E7
Boucher Cl TW11 16 F3
Boughton Ave BR2 44 F2
Boughton Hall Ave GU23 90 F3
Bouldish Farm Rd SL5 29 A5
Boulevard The
Crawley RH10 201 E6
4 Upper Tooting SW17 21 A6
Boullen Ct SM1 59 C6
Boulogne Rd CR0 42 C3
Boulters Ho RG12 27 E5
Boulters Rd 2 GU11 105 B1
Boulthurst Way RH8 123 B3
Boundaries Mans 3
SW12 21 A7
Boundaries Rd
Feltham TW13 15 C7
Upper Tooting SW12,SW17 21 A7
Boundary Bsns Ct CR4 40 D6
Boundary Bsns Ctr GU21 70 A4
Boundary Cl
Crawley RH10 201 E7
Kingston u T KT1 38 B6
Penge SE20 43 A7
Boundary Cotts GU4 132 A4
Boundary Ho TW1 6 B2
Boundary Rd
Binstead GU10 145 E2
Crawley RH10 201 E7
Dockenfield GU10 166 D7
Farnborough GU14 85 C2
Grayshott GU26 188 D3
Mitcham SW19 20 D2
Staines TW15 13 C3
Wallington SM5,SM6 60 A3
Woking GU21 70 A4
Boundary Rd E KT15 52 B2
Boundary Rd N KT15 52 B2
Boundary Rd W KT15 52 B2
Boundary Way
Addington CR0 63 A5
Woking GU21 70 A4
Boundfield Rd SE6 24 E6
Boundstone Cl GU10 146 B5
Boundstone Rd GU10 146 A4
Bourbon Ho SE6 24 C4
Bourdon Rd SE20 43 C7
Bourg-de-Peage Ave
RH19 186 A1
Bourke Hill CR5 78 F1
Bourley La GU10 104 A2
Bourley Rd
Aldershot GU11 104 C2
Crondall GU10 104 C2
Bourne Ave KT16 33 A6
Bourne Bsns Pk KT15 52 E6
Bourne Cl Chilworth GU4 131 B3
Hinchley Wood KT7 55 F8
West Byfleet KT14 71 B6
Bourne Ct
Aldershot GU11 126 A8
Caterham CR3 101 A4
Chiswick W4 7 C8
1 Purley CR8 80 A8
West Byfleet KT14 71 E6
Bourne Dene GU10 146 A5
Bourne Dr CR4 40 D7
Bourne Firs GU10 146 D5
Bourne Gr Ashstead KT21 95 D8
Farnham GU10 146 E7
Bourne Grove Cl GU10 146 E7
Bourne Grove Dr GU10 146 E7
Bourne Hall Mus* KT17 57 F2
Bourne Ho TW15 14 A3
Bourne Hts GU9 146 C8
Bourne Inf Sch The
GU10 146 D6
Bourne La CR3 100 D6
Bourne Mdw TW20 32 B5
Bourne Mill Bsns Pk
GU9 125 E3
Bourne Park Cl CR8 80 E3
Bourne Rd
Farncombe GU7 150 F7
Merstham RH1 119 C5
Wentworth GU25 31 D4
Woodham KT15 52 B2
Bourne St CR0,CR9 61 B8
Bourne Vale BR2 44 F1
Bourne View CR8 80 D4
Bourne Way
Addlestone KT15 52 C5
Cheam SM1 58 F5
Coney Hall BR2,BR4 63 F8
West Ewell KT19 57 C6
Woking GU22 89 D5
Bournefield Rd CR3 81 A1
Bournemouth Rd SW19 40 A8
Bourneside GU25 31 A2
Bourneside Gdns SE6 24 C3
Bourneside Rd KT15 52 D5
Bournevale Rd SW16 21 E4
Bournewood Pk GU10 146 E7
Bourns Ct RH13 217 E3
Bournville Rd SE13,SE6 24 A8
Bousley Rise KT16 51 D4
Bouverie Ct SW16 21 E3
Bouverie Gdns CR8 79 F5
Bouverie Rd CR5 79 A1
Boveney Ho RG12 27 E5
Boveney Rd SE23 23 D8
Bovey Ho 3 RH1 119 A3
Bovill Rd SE23 23 D8
Bovingdon Sq CR4 41 E5
Bowater Gdns TW16 35 C7
Bowater Rd RH10 202 C3
Bowater Ridge KT13 53 D1
Bowden Cl TW14 14 E7
Bowden Rd SL5 29 D4
Bowen Dr SE21 22 E5
Bower Ct GU22 70 B3
Bower Hill Cl RH1 140 E6
Bower Hill La RH1 140 D7
Bower Rd GU10 146 A5
Bowerland La RH7 164 E7
Bowers Cl GU4 110 A5
Bowers Farm Dr GU4 110 B5
Bowers La GU4 110 A6
Bowers Pl RH10 204 B8
Bowes Cl RH13 217 E3
Bowes Rd Egham TW18 12 E2
Walton-on-T KT12 54 B8
Bowie Cl SW4 21 D8
Bowland Dr RG12 27 E2
Bowley Cl SE19 22 F2
Bowley La SE19 22 F3
Bowlhead Green Rd
GU8 170 B1
Bowling Green Cl SW19 19 B8
Bowling Green Ct GU16 85 E7
Bowling Green La RH12 217 D3
Bowling Green Rd GU24 49 E2
Bowlings The GU15 65 C6
Bowman Ct RH10 201 D7
Bowman Mews SW18 19 F7
Bowman's Mdw SM6 60 B7
Bowmans Lea SE23 23 C8
Bowness Cl 7 RH11 200 D5
Bowness Cres SW15 18 E3
Bowness Dr TW4 4 E3
Bowness Rd SE6 24 B8
Bowring Ho GU7 150 F6
Bowsley Ct TW13 15 A6
Bowsprit The KT11 73 C4
Bowyer Cres RG40 25 C8
Bowyer Wlk SL5 28 E8
Bowyers Cl KT21 75 F1
Box Cl RH11 201 C1
Box Hill Ctry Pk* RH4 115 D3
Box Hill Sch RH5 115 B8
Box La RH19 206 E6
Box Ridge Ave CR8 79 F7
Box Tree Wlk RH1 139 C7
Boxall Rd SE21 22 E8
Boxall Wlk RH13 217 D1
Boxall's Gr GU11 126 A8
Boxall's La GU11 126 B7
Boxford Cl CR2 81 D7
Boxford Ridge RG12 27 B6
Boxgrove Ave GU1 110 A3
Boxgrove La GU1 110 B2
Boxgrove Prim Sch
GU1 110 B2
Boxgrove Rd GU1 110 A2
Boxhill & Westhumble Sta
RH5 115 B4
Boxhill Farm Barns RH4 115 E2
Boxhill Rd RH4 115 E3
Boxhill Way RH3 137 B5
Boxhurst RH4 115 E3
Boxley Rd SM4,SW19 40 C5
Boxwood Way CR6 81 D2
Boyce Ho SW16 21 C3
Boyd Cl KT2 18 A1
Boyd Ct RG42 27 A8
Boyd Rd SW19 20 D2
Boyland Rd BR1 24 F3
Boyle Farm Rd KT7 37 A3
Brabazon Ave SM6 60 E3
Brabazon Rd TW5 4 D7
Brabham Ct KT4 58 B8
Braboeuf Manor (Coll of
Law) GU2 130 C5
Brabon Rd GU14 84 F5
Brabourne Cl 7 SE19 22 E3
Brabourne Rise BR3 44 D4
Brabrook Ct SM6 60 B5
Bracebridge GU15 65 A5
Bracewood Gdns CR0 61 F7
Bracken Ave
Balham SW12 21 A8
West Wickham CR0 63 B7
Bracken Bank SL5 28 C8
Bracken Cl Ashford TW16 14 F2
Copthorne RH10 183 B2
Crawley RH10 201 F8
Little Bookham KT23 93 F3
Twickenham TW2 16 A8
Woking GU22 69 F1
Wonersh GU5 152 B6
Bracken End TW7 5 D2
Bracken Gr RH12 218 B5
Bracken Hill Cl 7 BR1 44 F8
Bracken Hill La BR1 44 F8
Bracken Path KT18 76 B6
Bracken Way
Chobham GU24 49 F1
Guildford GU3 108 E3
Brackendale KT1 38 B7
Brackendale Cl
Frimley GU15 65 E3
Hounslow TW5 5 B6
Brackendale Ct 2 BR3 24 A1
Brackendale Rd GU15 65 D4
Brackendene GU12 106 C3
Brackendene Cl GU21 70 A4
Brackenhale Sch The
RG12 27 B5
Brackenhill KT11 74 B7
Brackenlea GU7 150 D7
Brackens BR3 24 A1
Brackens The RG45 45 A7
Brackenside RH6 161 B4
Brackenwood
Cranleigh GU6 174 B3
Frimley GU15 66 D5
Sunbury TW16 35 A8
Brackenwood Rd GU21 88 D8
Bracklesham Cl GU14 85 A7
Brackley KT13 53 D5
Brackley Cl SM6 60 E3
Brackley Rd BR3 24 A1
Bracknell Beeches RG12 27 B6
Bracknell Bsns Ctr The
RG12 26 F7
Bracknell Cl GU15 46 F1
Bracknell Coll
Bracknell RG12 27 C7
Bracknell,Wick Hill RG12 27 C8
Bracknell Enterprise Ctr
RG12 27 A7
Bracknell Rd
Bracknell GU19 47 E5
Camberley GU15 47 A1
Crowthorne RG45 45 D6
Winkfield RG42 8 A5
Bracknell Sta RG12 27 B6
Bracknell Wlk RH11 200 E3
Bracondale KT10 55 C5
Bradbury Rd RH10 202 C3
Braddon Rd TW9 6 F4
Bradenhurst Cl CR3 100 F2
Bradfield Cl
Guildford GU4 110 A4
Woking GU22 69 E1
Bradfields RG12 27 D4
Bradford Cl SE26 23 B4
Bradford Dr KT19 57 F4
Brading Rd
Streatham SW2 21 F8
Thornton Heath CR0 41 F3
Bradley Cl SM2 59 B1
Bradley Ct CR0 61 A6
Bradley Dr RG40 25 A2
Bradley La RH4,RH5 115 B3
Bradley Mews SW12 20 F7
Bradley Rd SE19 22 C2
Bradlord Ho SE21 22 E5
Bradmore Way CR5 79 F1
Bradshaw Cl SW19 20 A2
Bradshaws Cl SE25 43 A6
Bradsole Ho 13 BR3 24 A1
Bradstock Rd KT17 58 B5
Brae Ct
2 Kingston u T KT2 38 A8
South Norwood SE25 42 E8
Braemar Ave
South Croydon CR2 61 C2
Thornton Heath CR7 42 B6
Wimbledon SW18,SW19 20 A6
Braemar Cl Frimley GU16 85 F8
Godalming GU7 150 D3
Braemar Ct
5 Brentford TW8 6 D8
Catford SE6 24 F7
Braemar Gdns BR4 44 C1
Braemar Ho TW11 17 B3
Braemar Rd Brentford TW8 6 D8
North Cheam KT4 58 B7
Braes Mead RH1 140 E8
Braeside Beckenham BR3 24 B3
Horley RH6 161 A3
Woodham KT15 71 B8
Braeside Ave SW19 39 E8
Braeside Cl GU27 207 F8
Braeside Rd SW16 21 C1
Brafferton Rd CR0 61 C6
Braganza Ct GU1 109 F2
Bragg Rd TW11 16 F2
Braid Cl TW13 15 F6
Braidwood Rd SE6 24 D7
Brailsford Cl SW19 20 E1
Brainton Ave TW14 15 C8
Brake Rd GU14 84 E1
Brakey Hill RH1 120 E1
Bramber Cl
Crawley RH10 201 E8
Horsham RH12 218 B5
Bramble Acres Cl SM2 59 A3
Bramble Bank GU16 86 A6
Bramble Banks SM5 60 A2
Bramble Cl
Beckenham BR3 44 C4
Copthorne RH10 183 B3
Croydon CR0 63 B6
Guildford GU3 108 E3
Redhill RH1 140 A7
Upper Halliford TW17 34 D6
Bramble Ct GU6 175 E6
Bramble Hedge Farm (Ind
Est) KT11 72 C5
Bramble La TW12 15 F2
Bramble Rise KT11 73 C5
Bramble Twitten RH19 186 A1
Bramble Way GU23 90 F3
Bramble Wlk KT18 76 B6
Brambledene Cl GU21 69 C1
Brambledown
Hindhead GU26 188 E4
Staines TW18 33 B8
Brambledown Cl BR2,BR4 44 E4
Brambledown Rd
South Croydon CR2 61 E3
Wallington SM5,SM6 60 B3
Bramblegate RG45 45 A6
Brambles Cl Ash GU12 106 B1
Brentford TW7,TW8 6 B7
Caterham CR3 100 E5
Brambles Pk GU5 151 F6
Brambles The
Farncombe GU7 150 D7
8 Wimbledon SW19 19 F3
Brambleton Ave GU9 146 B7
Brambletye Jun Sch
RH1 140 A7
Brambletye La RH18 206 D4
Brambletye Park Rd
RH1 140 A7
Brambletye Prep Sch
RH19 206 C5
Brambletye Rd RH10 202 A5
Bramblewood RH2 119 B6
Bramblewood Cl SM5 40 E1
Brambling Cl RH13 218 A1
Brambling Rd RH13 218 A1
Bramcote Frimley GU15 66 C5
Weybridge KT13 53 C6
Bramcote Ave CR4 40 F5
Bramcote Ct CR4 40 F5
Bramerton Rd BR3 43 F6
Bramham Gdns KT9 56 D6
Bramley Ave
Coulsdon CR5 79 C4
Sunbury TW17 34 E6
Bramley CE Inf Sch
GU5 152 A5
Bramley Cl Chertsey KT16 33 B1
Crawley RH10 201 F6
Croydon CR2 61 C5
Redhill RH1 139 E7
Staines TW18 13 C2
Twickenham TW2 5 C1
Bramley Croft GU26 188 E4
Bramley Ct Mitcham CR4 40 D7
Redhill RH1 118 E3
Wallington SM6 60 C5
Bramley Gr KT21 95 E8
Bramley Grange GU5 151 F6
Bramley Hill CR0,CR2 61 C6
Bramley Ho Hounslow TW3 4 F3
1 Kingston u T KT2 18 B1
Redhill RH1 140 A8
Roehampton SW15 7 F1

Bramley La GU17 .64 B5
Bramley Park Ct GU5 .151 F6
Bramley Prep Sch KT20 .97 A2
Bramley Rd
Camberley GU15 .65 B2
Carshalton SM1 .59 D5
East Ewell SM2 .58 D2
Bramley Way
Ashstead KT21 .75 F2
Hounslow TW4 .4 F2
West Wickham BR4 .63 B8
Bramley Wlk RH6 .161 C3
Bramleyhyrst CR2 .61 C5
Brampton Gdns KT12 .54 C5
Brampton Ho RH1 .139 F5
Brampton Rd CR0 .42 F3
Bramshaw Rise KT3 .38 E3
Bramshot La
Blackwater GU51,GU14 .84 A5
Farnborough GU14 .84 C6
Bramshot Rd GU14 .84 A2
Bramshott Ct 3 KT6 .37 E3
Bramston Rd SW17 .20 C5
Bramswell Rd GU7 .150 F6
Bramwell Cl TW16 .35 D7
Brancaster La CR8 .80 C8
Brancaster Rd SW16 .21 E5
Brancker Cl SM6 .60 E3
Brandon Cl
Crawley RH10 .202 D4
Frimley GU15 .66 D4
Brandon Ho BR3 .24 B3
Brandon Rd SM1 .59 B6
Brandreth Rd SW17 .21 B6
Brandries The SM6 .60 D7
Brands Rd SL3 .1 B8
Brandsland RH2 .139 B6
Brandy Way SM2 .59 A3
Brangbourne Rd BR1 .24 C3
Brangwyn Cres SW19 .40 D7
Branksome Cl
Camberley GU15 .65 E6
Walton-on-T KT12 .54 D8
Branksome Hill Rd GU47 .64 E8
Branksome Park Rd
GU15 .65 E6
Branksome Rd SW19 .40 A8
Branksome Way KT3 .38 D8
Bransby Rd KT9 .56 E4
Branscombe Ct BR2 .44 E4
Branstone Ct 9 TW9 .6 F6
Branstone Rd TW9 .6 F6
Brantridge Rd RH10 .201 F4
Brants Bridge RG12 .27 E7
Brantwood Ave TW7 .6 A3
Brantwood Cl 1 KT14 .71 A6
Brantwood Ct KT14 .70 F6
Brantwood Dr KT14 .70 F6
Brantwood Gdns 2 KT14 71 A6
Brantwood Rd CR2 .61 D2
Brassey Cl
East Bedfont TW14 .15 A7
Limpsfield RH8 .123 A6
Brassey Hill RH8 .123 A6
Brassey Rd RH8 .123 A6
Brasted Cl Belmont SM2 .59 A1
Forest Hill SE26 .23 C4
Brasted Lodge 11 BR3 .24 A1
Brathway Rd SW18 .20 A8
Bratten Ct CR0 .42 D3
Bravington Cl TW17 .33 F4
Braxted Pk SW16 .21 F2
Bray Cl RH10 .202 D4
Bray Ct KT9 .56 F5
Bray Gdns GU22 .70 E3
Bray Rd Guildford GU2 .130 B8
Stoke D'Abernon KT11 .73 E3
Braybourne Dr TW7 .5 F7
Braybrooke Gdns SE19 .22 E1
Braycourt Ave KT12 .35 C2
Braye Cl GU47 .45 C1
Braywick Ct 9 KT2 .18 A1
Braywood Ave TW20 .12 A2
Braziers La RG42,SL4 .8 D4
Brazil Cl CR0 .41 E2
Breakfield CR5 .79 E3
Breakspeare SE21 .22 F5
Breamore Cl SW15 .19 A7
Breamwater Gdns TW10 .17 B5
Brecon Cl
Farnborough GU14 .84 D7
Mitcham CR4 .41 E6
North Cheam KT4 .58 C8
Brecon Ho SW18 .20 A8
Bredhurst Cl SE20 .23 C2
Bredinghurst SE22 .23 A8
Bredon Rd CR0 .42 F2
Bredune CR8 .80 D4
Breech La KT20 .97 A2
Breech The GU47 .64 E7
Breezehurst Dr RH11 .200 F3
Bregsells Dr RH5 .157 D4
Bregsells La RH5 .157 D4
Bremans Row SW18 .20 C6
Bremer Rd TW18,TW19 .13 A5
Bremner Ave RH6 .160 F4
Brenchley Cl BR2 .44 F3
Brenda Rd SW17 .20 F6
Brende Gdns KT8 .36 B5
Brendon Cl Esher KT10 .55 C4
Harlington UB7 .3 C7
Brendon Dr KT10 .55 C4
Brendon Ho SM2 .59 C4
Brendon Rd GU14 .84 D7
Brenley Cl CR4 .41 A6
Brent Ho BR1 .24 D3
Brent Knoll Spec Sch
SE26 .23 D5
Brent Lea TW8 .6 C7
Brent Rd Brentford TW8 .6 C8
South Croydon CR2 .62 B2
Brent Way TW8 .6 D7
Brentford Bsns Ctr TW8 .6 C7
Brentford High St TW8 .6 C8
Brentford Ho 7 TW1 .17 B8
Brentford Sch for Girls
TW8 .6 D8
Brentford Sta TW8 .6 C8
Brentmoor Rd GU24 .67 D6
Brentside TW8 .6 C8
Brentside Executive Ctr
TW8 .6 B8
Brentwaters Bsns Pk TW8 6 C7
Brentwood Ct KT15 .52 B6
Brereton Ho 3 SW2 .22 A8
Bret Harte Rd GU16 .65 E1
Bretherton Ct CR2 .61 E4
Bretlands Rd KT16 .51 E8
Brett Ho 1 SW15 .19 D8
Brett House Cl 2 SW15 .19 D8
Brettgrave KT19 .57 C1
Brettingham Cl RH11 .200 E3
Bretts RH4 .136 C4
Brew House Rd RH3 .137 B5
Brewer Rd RH10 .201 E4
Brewer St RH1 .120 C4
Brewers Cl GU14 .85 A5
Brewers La 11 TW9 .6 D2
Brewery La KT14 .71 E6
Brewery Mews Bsns Ctr 1
TW7 .6 A4
Brewery Rd GU21 .69 E2
Brewhurst La RH14 .213 A2
Breydon Wlk RH10 .202 B4
Brian Ave CR2 .80 E7
Briane Rd KT19 .57 C1
Briar Ave Lightwater GU18 67 A8
South Norwood SW16 .21 F1
Briar Banks SM5 .60 A2
Briar Cl Chelsham CR6 .82 A3
Crawley RH11 .181 C1
Hampton TW12 .15 F3
Isleworth TW7 .5 F2
West Byfleet KT14 .71 C8
Briar Ct Cheam SM3 .58 C6
Hampton TW12 .16 B3
Briar Gdns BR2 .44 F1
Briar Gr CR2 .81 A6
Briar Hill CR8 .79 E8
Briar La Croydon CR0 .63 B6
Wallington SM5 .60 A2
Briar Patch GU7 .150 D6
Briar Rd Littleton TW17 .34 A4
Send GU23 .90 B4
Thornton Heath SW16 .41 F6
Twickenham TW2 .16 E7
Briar Way GU4 .110 B5
Briar Wlk KT14 .71 A7
Briardale SW19 .19 F7
Briarleas Ct GU14 .105 D8
Briars Cl GU14 .84 D3
Briars Cross RH8 .123 D5
Briars Ct KT22 .74 D5
Briars The GU12 .106 B1
Briars Wood RH6 .161 C4
Briarswood Cl RH10 .202 D8
Briarwood SM7 .78 A4
Briarwood Cl TW13 .14 E5
Briarwood Ct 5 KT4 .39 A1
Briarwood Rd
Knaphill GU21 .88 D8
Stoneleigh KT17 .58 A4
Briary Lodge BR3 .44 C8
Briavels Ct KT18 .76 E4
Brick Farm Cl TW9 .7 B6
Brick Kiln La RH8 .123 C5
Brickersbury Ho GU14 .84 F8
Brickfield Cl TW8 .6 C7
Brickfield La
Harlington UB3 .3 D8
Hookwood RH6 .160 D1
Brickfield Rd
Outwood RH1 .162 C8
South Norwood CR7,SW16 .42 B8
Wimbledon SW19 .20 B4
Brickfields Ind Pk RG12 .27 A7
Brickhouse La RH7,RH9 .163 C4
Bricklands RH10 .204 B7
Bricksbury Hill GU9 .125 C7
Brickwood Cl SE26 .23 B5
Brickwood Rd CR0 .61 E8
Brickyard Copse RH5 .177 C4
Brickyard La
Crawley Down RH10 .204 B8
Wotton RH5 .134 D2
Brideake Cl RH11 .201 A3
Bridge Barn La GU21 .69 D1
Bridge Cl Byfleet KT14 .71 F7
Lower Halliford KT12 .34 F1
Staines TW18 .12 E4
Teddington TW1 .16 F4
Woking GU21 .69 C2
Bridge Cotts GU6 .174 B3
Bridge Ct
Leatherhead KT22 .95 A5
5 Weybridge KT13 .53 B6
Woking GU21 .69 D2
Bridge End GU15 .65 B4
Bridge Gdns
East Molesey KT8 .36 D5
Littleton TW15 .14 C1
Bridge Ho SM2 .59 B4
Bridge Ind Est RH6 .161 B3
Bridge La GU25 .31 F3
Bridge Mead GU24 .87 F1
Bridge Mews
Godalming GU7 .150 E4
Tongham GU10 .126 F7
Woking GU21 .69 D2
Bridge Par CR8 .80 A7
Bridge Pk GU4 .110 C4
Bridge Pl CR0 .42 D1
Bridge Rd
Aldershot GU11 .126 A8
Ascot SL5 .29 D4
Bagshot GU19 .47 E3
Camberley GU15 .65 B3
Chertsey KT16 .33 B2
Chessington KT9 .56 E5
Cobham KT11 .73 B4
Cranleigh GU6 .174 E3
East Molesey KT8 .36 E5
Epsom KT17 .76 F7
Farnborough GU14 .84 F4
Farncombe GU7 .150 E5
Haslemere GU27 .208 C7
Isleworth TW3,TW7 .5 D4
Penge BR3 .23 F1
Rudgwick RH12 .214 D7
Sutton SM2 .59 B4
Twickenham TW1 .6 B1
Wallington SM6 .60 C5
Weybridge KT13 .52 F6
Bridge Ret Pk RG40 .25 B5
Bridge Row CR0 .42 D1
Bridge Sq GU9 .125 C2
Bridge St Colnbrook SL3 .1 D7
Godalming GU7 .150 E4
Guildford GU1 .130 C8
Leatherhead KT22 .95 A5
Richmond TW10 .6 D2
Staines TW18 .12 E4
Walton-on-T KT12 .34 F2
Bridge View SL5 .30 B2
Bridge Way Chipstead CR5 98 E8
Twickenham TW2 .16 C8
Bridge Works
Camberley GU15 .65 B3
Leatherhead KT22 .95 A8
Bridgefield GU9 .125 D2
Bridgefield Cl SM7 .77 C4
Bridgefield Rd SM1 .59 A4
Bridgeham Cl KT13 .53 A5
Bridgeham Way RH6 .162 B2
Bridgehill Cl GU2 .109 A3
Bridgelands RH10 .183 A3
Bridgeman Rd TW11 .17 A2
Bridgemead GU16 .85 D8
Bridges Cl RH6 .161 D3
Bridges Ct RH12 .218 A5
Bridges La CR0 .60 E6
Bridges Rd SW19 .20 B2
Bridges Road Mews
SW19 .20 B2
Bridgetown Cl 5 SE19 .22 E3
Bridgewater Rd KT13 .53 D4
Bridgewood Cl SE20 .23 B1
Bridgewood Rd
North Cheam KT17,KT4 .58 A6
Streatham SW16 .21 D1
Bridgford St SW17,SW18 .20 C5
Bridle Cl Grayshott GU26 188 A3
Kingston u T KT1 .37 D5
Sunbury TW16 .35 A6
West Ewell KT19 .57 D5
Bridle Ct GU11 .104 E2
Bridle La
Oxshott KT11,KT22 .74 B4
Twickenham TW1 .6 B1
Bridle Path CR0 .60 E7
Bridle Path The KT17 .58 C1
Bridle Rd Addington CR0 .63 A6
Claygate KT10 .56 B4
Croydon CR0 .63 A7
Epsom KT17 .76 F6
Bridle Rd The CR8 .60 E1
Bridle Way
Crawley RH10 .202 D7
Croydon CR0 .63 A6
Bridle Way The SM6 .60 C5
Bridlepath Way TW14 .14 E8
Bridleway Cl KT17 .58 C1
Bridlington Cl TN16 .103 B8
Bridport Rd CR7 .42 B6
Brier Lea KT20 .97 F1
Brier Rd KT20 .97 B8
Brierley CR0 .63 B4
Brierley Cl SE25 .43 A5
Brierley Rd SW12 .21 C6
Brierly Cl GU2 .109 A3
Brigade Pl CR3 .100 C5
Briggs Cl CR4 .41 B8
Bright Hill GU1 .130 E7
Brightlands Rd RH2 .118 C3
Brightman Rd SW18 .20 D7
Brighton Cl KT15 .52 C5
Brighton Rd
Addlestone KT15 .52 C5
Aldershot GU11 .126 C8
Banstead SM2 .78 A7
Belmont SM2 .59 B2
Burgh Heath KT20,SM2,SM7 77 F3
Coulsdon CR5,CR8 .79 D4
Crawley RH11 .201 D4
Croydon CR2,CR8 .61 C3
Godalming GU7,GU8 .151 A1
Hooley CR5,RH1 .99 B6
Horley RH6 .160 F2
Horsham RH13 .217 E1
Kingston u T KT6 .37 D3
Kingswood KT20 .97 E5
Lower Kingswood KT20 .117 F8
Purley CR8 .80 B8
Brighton Rd *continued*
Redhill RH1 .139 F8
Salfords RH1 .140 A2
South Croydon CR2 .61 C3
Brighton Terr 6 RH1 .139 F8
Brightside Ave TW18 .13 C1
Brightwell Cl CR0 .42 A1
Brightwell Cres SW17 .20 F3
Brightwells Rd GU9 .125 C2
Brigstock Rd
Coulsdon CR5 .79 B3
Thornton Heath CR7 .42 B5
Brimshot La GU24 .49 E2
Brindle Cl GU11 .126 B7
Brindles The SM7 .77 F2
Brindley Ho
Carshalton SM1 .59 E5
22 Streatham SW12 .21 E8
Brine Ct KT6 .37 D4
Brinkley Rd KT4 .58 B8
Brinkworth Pl SL4 .11 B8
Brinn's La GU17 .64 C5
Brinsworth Cl TW2 .16 D6
Brisbane Ave SW19 .40 B8
Brisbane Cl RH11 .181 D1
Briscoe Rd SW19 .20 D2
Brisson Cl KT10 .54 F4
Bristol Cl Crawley RH10 .182 D1
Stanwell TW19 .2 E1
Wallington SM6 .60 E3
Bristol Ct 10 TW19 .2 E1
Bristol Rd SM4 .40 C4
Bristow Inf Sch GU15 .65 B2
Bristow Rd
Camberley GU15 .65 B3
Hounslow TW3 .5 C4
Wallington CR0 .60 E6
West Norwood SE19 .22 E3
Britannia Ind Est SL3 .1 E5
Britannia Rd KT5 .37 F2
Britannia Way TW19 .13 D8
British Home & Hospl for
Incurables SE27 .22 B3
British Wildlife Ctr*
RH7 .163 E3
Briton Cl CR2 .80 E8
Briton Cres CR2 .80 E8
Briton Hill Rd CR2 .61 F1
Brittain Ct GU47 .64 C7
Brittain Rd KT12 .54 D5
Britten Cl Ash GU12 .106 B2
Crawley RH11 .200 F3
Horsham RH13 .218 B4
Brittens Cl GU2,GU3 .109 A6
Brittingham Ho RH11 .201 D6
Britton Cl SE6 .24 D8
Brixton Hill SW2 .21 E8
Brixton Hill Pl SW2 .21 E8
Broad Acres GU7 .150 E8
Broad Cl KT12 .54 E7
Broad Green Ave CR0 .42 B2
Broad Ha'penny GU10 .146 A5
Broad Highway KT11 .73 D5
Broad La Bracknell RG12 .27 D6
Hampton TW12 .16 A2
Parkgate RH2,RH5 .158 E6
Broad Oak TW16 .14 F2
Broad Oaks KT6 .57 B8
Broad Oaks Way BR2 .44 F4
Broad St Guildford GU3 .108 D3
Teddington TW11 .16 F2
West End GU24 .67 D6
Wokingham RG40 .25 C6
Broad St Wlk RG40 .25 C6
Broad Wlk
Burgh Heath KT18 .97 D8
Caterham CR3 .100 F5
Cranleigh GU6 .174 F1
Crawley RH10 .201 D6
Frimley GU16 .65 E2
Heston TW5 .4 E6
Lower Kingswood CR5 .99 A4
Richmond TW9 .6 F7
Broadacre TW18 .13 A3
Broadacres GU3 .108 E2
Broadbridge Heath Rd
RH12 .216 D4
Broadbridge La
Burstow RH6 .183 B8
Smallfield RH6 .162 A2
Broadbridge Ret Pk
RH12 .216 E3
Broadcoombe CR2 .62 D3
Broadeaves Cl CR2 .61 E5
Broadfield Barton 4
RH11 .201 B2
Broadfield Cl
Burgh Heath KT20 .97 C7
Croydon CR0 .60 F8
Broadfield Dr RH11 .201 B3
Broadfield East Fst & Mid
Sch RH11 .201 C2
Broadfield Pl RH11 .201 B2
Broadfield Rd Catford SE6 24 E7
Peaslake GU5 .154 D8
Broadfields KT8 .36 E3
Broadford La GU24 .68 E7
Broadford Pk GU4 .130 D2
Broadford Rd GU4 .130 D2
Broadgates Rd SW18 .20 D7
Broadham Green Rd
RH8 .122 D2
Broadham Pl RH8 .122 D4
Broadhurst Ashstead KT21 75 E3
Farnborough GU14 .84 C5
Broadhurst Cl 8 TW10 .6 F2
Broadhurst Gdns RH2 .139 B6
Broadlands
Farnborough GU14 .85 E2
Feltham TW13 .16 A5
Frimley GU16 .85 F8
Horley RH6 .161 C4
Broadlands Ave
Shepperton TW17 .34 C3
Streatham SW16 .21 E6
Broadlands Bsns Pk
RH12 .198 C4
Broadlands Cl SW16 .21 E6
Broadlands Ct
Bracknell RG42 .26 E8
Richmond TW9 .7 A7
Broadlands Dr
Sunningdale SL5 .29 D2
Warlingham CR6 .101 C8
Broadlands Mans 2
SW16 .21 E6
Broadlands Way KT3 .38 F3
Broadley Gn GU20 .48 D4
Broadmead Ashstead KT21 75 F2
Catford SE6 .24 A5
Farnborough GU14 .84 D3
Horley RH6 .161 C4
Merstham RH1 .119 C7
Broadmead Ave KT4 .39 A2
Broadmead Cl TW12 .16 A2
Broadmead Inf Sch CR0 .42 D2
Broadmead Jun Sch CR0 42 D3
Broadmead Rd GU23 .90 B5
Broadmeads GU23 .90 B5
Broadmere Com Prim Sch
GU21 .70 D6
Broadmoor Cott RH5 .156 A8
Broadmoor Est RG45 .45 D4
Broadmoor Hospl RG45 .45 E5
Broadmoor Prim Sch
RG45 .45 D4
Broadoaks Cres KT14 .71 B6
Broadpool Cotts SL5 .9 A1
Broadview Est TW19 .14 A8
Broadview Rd SW16 .21 D1
Broadwater Cl
Hersham KT12 .54 A5
Sheerwater GU21 .70 D7
Wraysbury TW19 .11 E8
Broadwater Ho 1 KT13 .53 B7
Broadwater La GU7 .150 F6
Broadwater Pl KT13 .53 E8
Broadwater Prim Sch
SW17 .20 E4
Broadwater Rd SW17 .20 E4
Broadwater Rd N KT12 .54 A5
Broadwater Rd S KT12 .54 A5
Broadwater Rise GU1 .131 A8
Broadwater Sch GU7 .151 A8
Broadway Bracknell RG12 .27 C7
Knaphill GU21 .68 C1
Limpsfield RH8 .123 B5
Tolworth KT6 .38 B1
Winkfield SL4 .9 B7
Broadway Ave
Thornton Heath CR0 .42 D4
Twickenham TW1 .6 B1
Broadway Centre Adult Coll
SW17 .20 E4
Broadway Cl CR2 .81 B5
Broadway Ct
Beckenham BR3 .44 C6
Wimbledon SW19 .19 F2
Broadway Gdns CR4 .40 E5
Broadway Ho GU21 .68 C1
Broadway Mkt SW17 .20 F4
Broadway Pl SW19 .19 F2
Broadway Rd
Lightwater GU18 .48 C2
Windlesham GU18,GU20 .48 C2
Broadway The
Cheam SM3 .58 E4
Crawley RH10 .201 D6
Laleham TW18 .33 C7
Mortlake SW13 .7 E5
Sandhurst GU47 .64 B8
Sutton SM1 .59 C6
Thames Ditton KT10 .36 E1
Tolworth KT6 .38 A1
Wallington CR0 .60 E6
Wimbledon SW19 .19 F2
Woking GU21 .69 F2
Woodham KT15 .52 A1
Broadwell Ct TW5 .4 D6
Broadwell Rd GU10 .145 F6
Broadwood Cl RH12 .218 A5
Broadwood Cotts RH5 .178 E6
Broadwood Rise RH11 .201 A2
Brock Fst Sch The
RH10 .202 C3
Brock Rd RH11 .181 B1
Brock Way GU25 .31 C5
Brock's Cl GU7 .151 A5
Brockbridge Ho SW15 .7 F1
Brockenhurst KT8 .35 F3
Brockenhurst Ave KT4 .38 E1
Brockenhurst Cl GU21 .69 F5
Brockenhurst Rd
Aldershot GU11 .126 B8
Ascot SL5 .29 B3
Bracknell RG12 .28 A6
Croydon CR0 .43 B2
Brockenhurst Way SW16 41 D7
Brockham Cl SW19 .19 F3
Brockham Cres CR0 .63 D3
Brockham Ct 5 SM2 .59 B3
Brockham Dr SW2 .21 F8

Brockham Hill Pk KT20 116 C4
Brockham Ho 14 SW2 21 F8
Brockham Keep RH6 161 C4
Brockham La RH3 116 A1
Brockham Park Ho RH3 137 C4
Brockham Prim Sch RH3 137 B7
Brockham Row RH3 137 C5
Brockham Warren KT20 116 A3
Brockhamhurst Rd RH3 137 B2
Brockholes Cross KT24 113 A6
Brockhurst Cl RH12 216 F1
Brockhurst Cotts GU6 193 F4
Brockhurst Lodge GU9 146 B7
Brocklebank Ct CR6 81 A1
Brocklebank Rd SW18 20 C8
Brocklesby Rd SE25 43 B5
Brockley Combe KT13 53 D6
Brockley Pk SE23 23 E8
Brockley Rise SE23 23 E8
Brockley View SE23 23 E8
Brockman Rise BR1 24 D4
Brocks Dr Cheam SM3 58 E7
Fairlands GU3 108 C5
Brockshot Cl 1 TW8 6 D8
Brockton GU7 150 E5
Brockway Cl GU1 110 B2
Brockwell Park Gdns SE24 22 B8
Brockwell Park Row 9 SW2 22 A8
Brockworth KT2 38 B8
Broderick Ho SE21 22 E5
Brodie Ho 7 SM6 60 B6
Brodie Rd GU1 130 E8
Brodrick Gr KT23 94 A1
Brodrick Rd SW17 20 E6
Brograve Gdns BR3 44 B7
Broke Ct GU4 110 C4
Brokes Cres RH2 118 A3
Brokes Rd RH2 118 A3
Bromford Cl RH8 123 A2
Bromleigh Ct SE21,SE22 23 B6
Bromley Ave BR1 24 E1
Bromley Cres BR2 44 F6
Bromley Ct BR1 24 F1
Bromley Gdns BR2 44 F6
Bromley Gr BR2 44 D7
Bromley Hill BR1 24 E2
Bromley Pk 13 BR1 44 F8
Bromley Rd
Beckenham BR3 44 B8
Bromley BR2,BR3 44 D7
Catford SE6,BR1 24 B5
Bromley Road Inf Sch BR3 44 B8
Bromley Road Ret Pk SE6 24 B6
Brompton Cl Hounslow TW4 4 F2
Penge SE20 43 A7
Bromwich Ho 3 TW10 6 E1
Bronson Rd SW20 39 E7
Bronte Ct 14 RH1 119 A2
Brontes The RH19 185 D1
Brook Ave GU9 125 F7
Brook Cl Ash GU12 106 B3
Dorking RH4 115 C1
East Grinstead RH19 186 B1
Epsom KT19 57 E2
Sandhurst GU47 45 E1
Stanwell TW19 13 F8
Upper Tooting SW17 21 A6
West Barnes SW20 39 B6
Wokingham RG41 25 A8
Brook Ct Beckenham BR3 43 F8
6 Brentford TW8 6 D8
Cheam SM3 58 C6
7 Mortlake SW14 7 E4
Brook Dr Ashford TW16 14 E2
Bracknell RG12 27 E5
Brook Farm Rd KT11 73 D4
Brook Gdns Barnes SW13 7 F4
Farnborough GU14 84 F2
Kingston u T KT2 38 C8
Brook Gn Bracknell RG42 26 F8
Chobham GU24 49 F1
Brook Hill
Farley Green GU5 153 D8
Oxted RH8 122 C5
Brook Ho Cranleigh GU6 174 F4
Heath End GU9 125 D6
4 Twickenham TW1 17 A8
Brook La Chobham GU24 68 D8
Farley Green GU5 132 E1
Faygate RH12 218 C8
Send GU23 90 E5
Brook La Bns Ctr 4 TW8 6 D8
Brook La N 3 TW8 6 D8
Brook Manor RH19 205 D7
Brook Mdw GU8 191 C3
Brook Mead Milford GU8 170 F8
West Ewell KT19 57 E4
Brook Rd Bagshot GU19 47 E2
Brook GU8 190 D8
Camberley GU15 65 B4
Chilworth GU4 131 C3
Horsham RH12 217 E6
Merstham RH1 119 C7
Redhill RH1 139 F8
Surbiton KT6 56 E8
Thornton Heath CR7 42 C5
Twickenham TW1 6 A1
Wormley GU8 170 E1
Brook Rd S TW8 6 D8
Brook St KT1 37 E7
Brook The RH10 201 D7
Brook Trad Est The GU12 105 E2
Brook Valley RH5 136 B1
Brook View Lodge KT4 39 A1
Brook Way KT22 75 A1
Brookdale Rd SE6 24 B8
Brooke Ct Frimley GU16 85 F6
7 Kingston u T KT2 17 D4
Brooke Forest GU3 108 C5
Brookehowse Rd SE6 24 B5
Brookers Cl KT21 75 D2
Brookers Cnr RG45 45 C5
Brookers Ho KT21 75 D2
Brookers Row RG45 45 C6
Brookfield
Farncombe GU7 151 A8
Woking GU21 69 B3
Brookfield Ave SM1 59 E7
Brookfield Cl
Ottershaw KT16 51 D4
Redhill RH1 140 A3
Brookfield Gdns KT10 55 F4
Brookfield Prim Sch SM3 39 E1
Brookfield Rd GU12 105 F3
Brookfields Ave CR4 40 E4
Brookhill Cl RH10 183 A3
Brookhill Rd RH10 183 A3
Brookhouse 2 SW19 20 A2
Brookhouse Rd GU14 84 F3
Brookhurst Rd KT15 52 B4
Brooklands GU11 104 E1
Brooklands Ave SW18 20 B6
Brooklands Cl
Charlton TW16 34 E8
Cobham KT11 73 E4
Heath End GU9 125 D7
Brooklands Coll KT13 52 F4
Brooklands Ct
Kingston u T KT1 37 D5
Mitcham CR4 40 D7
New Haw KT15 52 D1
Reigate RH2 118 B3
Brooklands Ind Est
Byfleet KT13 52 E1
West Byfleet KT13 71 E8
Brooklands La KT13 52 F4
Brooklands Mus* KT13 53 A2
Brooklands Rd
Crawley RH11 201 C1
Heath End GU9 125 F7
Thames Ditton KT7 37 A1
Weybridge KT13 53 B3
Brooklands Sch RH2 118 B3
Brooklands Terr TW16 35 A5
Brooklands The TW7 5 D6
Brooklands Way
East Grinstead RH19 205 D8
Heath End GU9 125 E7
Redhill RH1 118 E3
Brookley Cl GU10 126 C3
Brookleys GU24 49 F1
Brooklyn 9 SE20 23 A1
Brooklyn Ave SE25 43 B5
Brooklyn Cl
Carshalton SM5 59 E8
Woking GU22 89 E8
Brooklyn Ct 2 GU22 89 E8
Brooklyn Gr SE25 43 B5
Brooklyn Rd Croydon SE25 43 B5
Woking GU22 89 E8
Brookmead CR4 41 C3
Brookmead Ct
Cranleigh GU6 174 E2
Farnham GU9 125 B1
Brookmead Rd CR0 41 C3
Brooks Cl KT13 53 A1
Brooks Ho 6 SW2 22 A7
Brooks La W4 7 A8
Brooks Rd W4 7 A8
Brooksby Cl GU17 64 B5
Brookscroft CR0 62 E1
Brookside
Beare Green RH5 157 F6
Chertsey KT16 32 E2
Colnbrook SL3 1 C7
Copthorne RH10 183 A3
Cranleigh GU6 174 E1
Cranleigh GU6 174 E3
Crawley RH10 201 F7
Guildford GU4 109 D6
Hale GU9 125 D6
Sandhurst GU47 64 C8
South Godstone RH9 142 D5
Wallington SM5 60 A5
Brookside Ave TW15 13 D3
Brookside Cl TW13 15 A5
Brookside Cres 1 KT4 39 A1
Brookside Ct SW16 21 C1
Brookside Way CR0 43 D3
Brookswood GU4 131 C3
Brookview RH10 183 A3
Brookview Rd SW16, SW17 21 C3
Brookwell La GU5 152 B2
Brookwood RH6 161 B4
Brookwood Ave SW13 7 F5
Brookwood Cl BR2 44 F5
Brookwood Ho RH6 161 B6
Brookwood Lye Rd GU21, GU24 88 C7
Brookwood Pk RH6 161 B2
Brookwood Prim Sch GU24 88 A7
Brookwood Rd
Farnborough GU14 85 D4
Hounslow TW3 5 B6
Brookwood Rd *continued*
Wandsworth SW18 20 A7
Brookwood Sta GU24 88 A6
Broom Acres GU47 45 B1
Broom Bank CR6 102 C8
Broom Cl Blackwater GU17 64 E4
Esher KT10 55 B5
Teddington TW11 17 D1
Broom Field GU18 67 A7
Broom Gdns CR0 63 A7
Broom Hall KT22 74 D5
Broom La GU24 49 E3
Broom Lock TW11 17 C2
Broom Pk KT1 17 D1
Broom Rd Croydon CR0 63 A7
Richmond TW11 17 C3
Broom Squires GU26 188 F4
Broom Water TW11 17 C3
Broom Water W TW11 17 C3
Broom Way KT13 53 E6
Broomcroft Cl GU22 70 D3
Broomcroft Dr GU22 70 D3
Broomdashers Rd RH10 201 F7
Broome Cl RH12 217 D5
Broome Ct 3 TW9 7 A6
Broome Hall RH5 156 D2
Broome Lodge TW18 13 B3
Broome Rd TW12 35 F8
Broome St KT18 96 C1
Broomehall Rd
Coldharbour RH5 156 D2
Ockley RH5 177 E8
Broomers La GU6 175 E5
Broomfield Elstead GU8 148 E4
Guildford GU2 108 E2
Staines TW18 13 A2
Sunbury TW16 35 A8
Broomfield Cl
Guildford GU3 108 E3
Sunningdale SL5 30 B2
Broomfield Cotts KT20 97 E8
Broomfield Ct KT13 53 B4
Broomfield La GU10 146 A1
Broomfield Pk
Sunningdale SL5 30 B2
Westcott RH4 135 C6
Broomfield Rd
Beckenham BR3 43 F6
Richmond TW9 6 F6
Surbiton KT5 37 F1
Teddington TW11 17 C2
Woodham KT15 71 B8
Broomfield Ride KT22 74 D7
Broomfields KT10 55 C5
Broomhall Bldgs 1 SL5 30 B2
Broomhall End GU21 69 E3
Broomhall La
Sunningdale SL5 30 A3
Woking GU21 69 E3
Broomhall Rd
South Croydon CR2 61 D2
Woking GU21 69 E3
Broomhill GU10 124 D8
Broomhill Rd GU14 84 D5
Broomhurst Ct RH4 136 B5
Broomlands La RH8 123 E8
Broomleaf Cnr GU9 125 D2
Broomleaf Rd GU9 125 E2
Broomleigh Bsns Pk SE6 23 F3
Broomloan La SM1 59 A8
Broomsquires Rd GU19 47 F2
Broomwood Cl CR0 43 D4
Broomwood Way GU10 146 C6
Broseley Gr SE26 23 E3
Broster Gdns SE25 42 F6
Brough Cl KT2 17 D3
Brougham Pl GU9 125 B7
Broughton Ave TW10 17 C4
Broughton Mews GU16 65 F1
Broughton Rd CR7 42 A3
Brow The RH1 140 A4
Browell Ho GU4 110 D2
Browells La TW13 15 B6
Brown Bear Ct TW13 15 D4
Brown Cl SM6 60 E3
Brown's Hill RH1 141 D2
Brown's Rd KT5,KT6 37 F2
Browne Ho 9 SE26 23 B3
Browngraves Rd UB7 3 C7
Brownhill Rd SE6 24 C8
Browning Ave
Carshalton SM1 59 E6
North Cheam KT4 39 B1
Browning Cl
Crawley RH10 202 C7
Frimley GU15 66 C4
Hampton TW12 15 F4
Browning Rd KT22 94 D2
Browning Way TW5 4 D6
Brownings The 1 RH19 185 C1
Brownjohn Ct RH10 202 A7
Brownlow Rd
Redhill RH1 118 E1
South Croydon CR0 61 F6
Brownrigg Cres RG12 27 E8
Brownrigg Rd TW15 14 A4
Browns La KT24 113 D8
Browns Wlk GU10 145 F5
Browns Wood RH19 185 E4
Brownsover Rd GU14 84 C4
Brox La KT15, KT16 51 D2
Brox Rd KT16 51 D4
Broxholm Rd SE27,SW16 22 A5
Broxted Rd SE23,SE6 23 F6
Bruce Ave TW17 34 C3
Bruce Cl KT14 71 E6
Bruce Dr CR2 62 D2
Bruce Hall Mews SW17 21 A4
Bruce Lawns SW17 21 A4
Bruce Rd Mitcham CR4 21 A1
South Norwood SE25 42 D5
Brudenell Rd SW17 21 A4
Brumana Cl KT13 53 B4
Brumfield Rd KT19 57 C5
Brunel Cl Cranford TW5 4 B7
South Norwood SE19 22 F2
Brunel Ct SW13 7 F5
Brunel Ctr RH10 181 F2
Brunel Dr RG45 45 C8
Brunel Ho 25 SW2 21 E8
Brunel Pl RH10 201 E5
Brunel Univ (Runnymede Campus) TW20 11 C5
Brunel Univ Coll (Twickenham Campus) TW1 6 B3
Brunel Univ Coll Osterley Campus TW7 5 F7
Brunel Wlk TW2 16 A8
Brunner Ct KT16 51 C5
Brunner Ho SE6 24 C4
Brunswick RG12 27 A2
Brunswick Cl
Crawley RH10 202 A4
Thames Ditton KT7 36 F1
Twickenham TW2 16 D5
Walton-on-T KT12 54 C8
Brunswick Ct
Crawley RH10 202 A4
Kingston u T KT2 17 D2
2 Penge SE19 23 A1
Brunswick Dr GU24 87 D7
Brunswick Gr KT11 73 C6
Brunswick Manor SM1 59 C6
Brunswick Mews SW16 21 D2
Brunswick Pl SE19 23 A1
Brunswick Rd
Kingston u T KT2 38 A8
Pirbright, Alexander Barracks GU24 87 C6
Pirbright,Blackdown Barracks GU16,GU24 86 E6
Sutton SM1 59 B6
Bruntile Cl GU14 85 D1
Brushfield Way GU21 68 C1
Brushwood Rd RH12 218 B6
Bruton Rd SM4 40 C5
Bruton Way RG12 27 E2
Bryan Cl TW16 15 A1
Bryanston Ave TW2 16 B7
Bryanstone Ave GU2 109 A4
Bryanstone Cl GU2 108 F4
Bryanstone Ct SM1 59 C7
Bryanstone Gr GU2 108 F5
Bryce Cl RH12 218 A5
Bryce Gdns GU11 126 C7
Bryden Cl SE26 23 E3
Brympton Cl RH4 136 A5
Bryn Rd GU10 145 F7
Brynford Cl GU21 69 E4
Bryony Ho RG42 26 E8
Bryony Rd GU1 110 B4
Bryony Way TW16 15 A2
Buccanear Way GU14 104 B8
Buchan Cty Pk* RH11 200 E1
Buchan The GU15 66 A8
Buchanan Ho
Dulwich SE21 22 E5
Wandsworth SW18 20 A8
Buchans Lawn RH11 201 B2
Bucharest Rd SW18 20 C8
Buckfast Rd SM4 40 B5
Buckhurst Ave CR4,SM5 40 F1
Buckhurst Cl
East Grinstead RH19 185 C3
Redhill RH1 118 F3
Buckhurst Cotts RH12 214 D8
Buckhurst Gr RG40 25 F5
Buckhurst Hill RG12 27 F5
Buckhurst La SL5 30 A6
Buckhurst Mead RH19 185 C4
Buckhurst Moors RG12 26 C6
Buckhurst Rd Ascot SL5 29 F7
Frimley GU16 85 F6
Buckhurst Way RH19 185 C3
Buckingham Ave
East Molesey KT8 36 B7
Feltham TW14 4 B1
South Norwood CR7 42 A8
Buckingham Cl
Guildford GU1 109 F2
Hampton TW12 15 F3
Buckingham Ct
Belmont SM2 59 A2
Crawley RH11 201 B2
Staines TW18 13 A4
Wokingham RG40 25 C6
Buckingham Dr RH19 206 A8
Buckingham Gate RH6 182 C7
Buckingham Gdns
Hampton KT8 36 B7
South Norwood CR7 42 A7
Buckingham La SE23 23 E8
Buckingham Prim Sch TW12 15 F3
Buckingham Rd
Hampton TW12 15 F3
Kingston u T KT1 37 F5
Mitcham CR4 41 E4
Richmond TW10 17 D6
South Holmwood RH5 157 C6
Buckingham Way SM6 60 C2
Buckland Cl GU14 85 C7
Buckland Cnr RH2 117 D2
Buckland Ct RH3 117 A2
Buckland Inf Sch KT9 56 F6
Buckland Jun & Inf Sch TW18 13 C1
Buckland Rd
Chessington KT9 56 F5
East Ewell SM2 58 D2
Lower Kingswood KT20 117 F7
Reigate RH2 117 D2
Buckland Way KT4 39 C1
Buckland Wlk SM4 40 C5
Bucklands Rd TW11 17 C2
Bucklebury RG12 27 A2
Buckleigh Ave SW20 39 F6
Buckleigh Ho SW19 20 D3
Buckleigh Rd SW16 21 E1
Buckleigh Way SE19 22 F1
Bucklers' Way SM5 59 F7
Buckles Way SM7 77 E3
Buckley Cl SE23 23 B8
Buckley Pl RH10 204 A8
Buckmans Rd RH11 201 D6
Bucknall Way BR3 44 C4
Bucknills Cl KT18 76 C5
Bucks Cl KT14 71 B5
Buckswood Dr RH11 201 A4
Buckthorn Cl RG40 25 E7
Buddhapadipa Temple The SW19 19 D4
Budebury Rd TW18 13 A3
Budge La CR4 40 F2
Budge's Cotts RG40 25 E8
Budge's Gdns RG40 25 E7
Budge's Rd RG40 25 D7
Budgen Cl RH10 182 D1
Budgen Dr RH1 119 A3
Budgwick Keep RH6 161 C4
Budham Way RG12 27 B3
Buff Ave SM7 78 B4
Buffbeards La GU27 207 E6
Buffers La KT22 95 A8
Bug Hill CR3,CR6 101 D7
Bugkingham Way GU16 65 F1
Bulbrook Row RG12 27 E7
Bulganak Rd CR7 42 C5
Bulkeley Cl TW20 11 C3
Bull Hill KT22 95 A6
Bull La Bracknell RG42 27 B8
Woking GU4 89 F1
Bullard Rd TW11 16 F2
Bullbeggars La
Godstone RH9 121 C3
Woking GU21 69 B3
Bullbrook Dr RG12 27 F8
Buller Ct GU14 85 C1
Buller Rd CR7 42 D6
Bullers Rd GU9 125 E6
Bullfinch Cl Horley RH6 160 E4
Horsham RH12 217 C7
Sandhurst GU47 64 E8
Bullfinch Ct 4 SE21 22 D6
Bullfinch Rd CR2 62 D1
Bullrush Cl
Carshalton SM5 59 E8
Thornton Heath CR0 42 E3
Bulls Alley SW14 7 D5
Bullswater Common Rd GU24,GU3 88 A2
Bullswater La GU24 88 A2
Bulstrode Ave TW3 5 A4
Bulstrode Gdns TW3 5 A4
Bulstrode Rd TW3 5 A4
Bunbury Way KT17 77 B4
Bunce Common Rd RH2 137 E2
Bunce Dr CR3 100 D4
Bunch La GU27 208 B8
Bunch Way GU27 208 A6
Bundy's Way TW18 12 F2
Bungalow Rd SE25 42 E5
Bungalows The
Caterham CR3 100 D4
Mitcham SW16 21 B1
Bunting Cl
Horsham RH13 217 F3
Mitcham CR4 40 F4
Buntings The GU9 145 F8
Bunyan Cl RH11 200 E3
Bunyard Dr GU21 70 C5
Burbage Gn RG12 27 F4
Burbage Rd SE21, SE24 22 D8
Burbeach Cl RH11 201 B3
Burberry Cl KT3 38 E7
Burbidge Rd TW17 34 A5
Burbury Woods GU15 65 E6
Burchets Hollow GU5 154 D7
Burchetts Way TW17 34 B3
Burcote 6 KT13 53 D4
Burcote Rd SW18 20 D8
Burcott Gdns KT15 52 D4
Burcott Rd CR8 80 A5
Burden Way GU2 109 A5
Burdenshot Hill GU3 89 B3
Burdenshott Ave TW10 7 B3
Burdenshott Rd
Guildford GU4 109 C8
Woking GU22,GU3,GU4 89 A2
Burdett Ave SW20 39 A8
Burdett Cl RH10 202 D5
Burdett Rd Richmond TW9 6 F4
Thornton Heath CR0 42 D3
Burdock Cl
Crawley RH11 201 A2
Croydon CR0 43 D1
Lightwater GU18 67 B8
Burdon La SM2 58 F2
Burdon Pk SM2 58 F2
Burfield Cl SW17 20 D4
Burfield Dr CR6 101 C8
Burfield Rd SL4 11 B8
Burford Cnr RH5 115 C4

Burford Ct RG40 . . . .25 E5
Burford La KT17 . . . . .77 C8
Burford Lea GU8 . . . .148 E4
Burford Lodge RH5 . . .115 C4
Burford Rd
  Camberley GU15 . . . .65 B4
  Forest Hill SE6 . . . . .23 F6
  Horsham RH13 . . . . .217 E2
  New Malden KT4 . . . .39 A2
  Sutton SM1 . . . . . . .59 A8
Burford Way CR0 . . . .63 C4
Burges Way TW18 . . . .13 A3
Burgess CI TW13 . . . . .15 E4
Burgess Mews SW19 . .20 B2
Burgess Rd SM1 . . . . .59 B6
Burgh CI RH10 . . . . .182 D1
Burgh Heath Rd KT17,
  KT18 . . . . .76 F4
Burgh Mount SM7 . . . .77 F4
Burgh Wood SM7 . . . .77 F4
Burghead CI GU47 . . . .64 D7
Burghfield KT17 . . . . .76 F4
Burghill Rd SE26 . . . . .23 E4
Burghley Ave KT3 . . . .38 D8
Burghley Ho SW19 . . . .19 E5
Burghley PI CR4 . . . . .40 F5
Burghley Rd SW19 . . . .19 E4
Burgos CI CR0 . . . . . .61 A4
Burgoyne Rd
  Ashford TW16 . . . . . .14 F2
  Camberley GU15 . . . .66 A6
  South Norwood SE25 . .42 F5
Burham CI SE20 . . . . .23 C1
Burhill Inf Sch KT12 . .54 D4
Burhill Rd KT12 . . . . .54 C3
Buriton CI SW15 . . . . . .7 E3
Burke CI SW15 . . . . . . .7 E3
Burlands RH11 . . . . .181 A1
Burlea CI KT12 . . . . . .54 B5
Burleigh Ave SM6 . . . .60 B7
Burleigh CI
  Addlestone KT15 . . . .52 B5
  Crawley Down RH10 . .204 B8
Burleigh Ct [1] KT22 . .95 A5
Burleigh Cty Inf Sch
  RH10 . . . . .204 B8
Burleigh Gdns
  Ashford TW15 . . . . . .14 C3
  Woking GU21 . . . . . .69 F2
Burleigh La
  Crawley Down RH10 . .204 C7
  North Ascot SL5 . . . . .28 E8
Burleigh Pk KT11 . . . .73 E7
Burleigh Rd
  Addlestone KT15 . . . .52 B5
  Cheam SM3,SM4 . . . .39 E1
  Frimley GU16 . . . . . .85 D8
  North Ascot SL5 . . . . .28 E7
Burleigh Way RH10 . .204 B8
Burleigh Wlk SE6 . . . .24 C7
Burley CI Loxwood RH14 .213 A4
  Mitcham SW16 . . . . . .41 D7
Burley Orch KT16 . . . .33 A3
Burley Way GU17 . . . .64 C6
Burleys Rd RH10 . . . .202 C6
Burlingham CI GU4 . . .110 D3
Burlington Ave TW9 . . . .7 A6
Burlington CI TW14 . . .14 D8
Burlington Ct
  [7] Aldershot GU11 . .105 A1
  Blackwater GU17 . . . .64 D3
  Chiswick W4 . . . . .7 C7
Burlington Jun Sch KT3 .38 F5
Burlington La W4 . . . . . .7 E8
Burlington PI RH2 . . . .118 A2
Burlington Rd
  Hounslow TW7 . . . . . .5 D6
  New Malden KT3 . . . .38 F5
  South Norwood CR7 . . .42 D7
Burlsdon Way RG12 . . .27 E8
Burma Rd GU24,KT16 . .49 F8
Burma Terr [11] SE19 . .22 E3
Burmarsh Ct SE20 . . . .43 C8
Burmester Ho SW17 . . .20 C5
Burmester Rd SW17 . . .20 C5
Burn CI Addlestone KT15 .52 D6
  Oxshott KT22 . . . . . .74 D4
Burn Moor Chase RG12 .27 E2
Burnaby Cres W4 . . . . . .7 C8
Burnaby Gdns W4 . . . . .7 B8
Burnbury Rd SW12 . . . .21 C7
Burne-Jones Dr GU47 . .64 D6
Burnell Ave TW10 . . . .17 C3
Burnell Ho [19] SW2 . .22 A7
Burnell Rd SM1 . . . . . .59 B6
Burnet Ave GU1 . . . . .110 B4
Burnet CI GU24 . . . . . .67 E6
Burnet Gr KT19 . . . . . .76 C6
Burney Ave KT5 . . . . . .37 F4
Burney CI KT23 . . . . . .94 C2
Burney Ct [5] RH11 . . .201 A3
Burney Ho [4] SW16 . . .21 C3
Burney Rd RH5 . . . . . .115 A4
Burnham CI GU21 . . . . .68 D1
Burnham Dr
  North Cheam KT4 . . . .58 D8
  Reigate RH2 . . . . . . .118 A2
Burnham Gates GU1 . .109 D1
Burnham Gdns
  Cranford TW5 . . . . . . .4 B6
  Croydon CR0 . . . . . . .42 F2
Burnham Manor GU15 . .66 A8
Burnham PI RH13 . . . .217 D1
Burnham Rd
  Knaphill GU21 . . . . . .68 D1
  Morden SM4 . . . . . . .40 B5
Burnham St KT2 . . . . . .38 A8
Burnham Way SE26 . . . .23 F3

Burnhams Rd KT23 . . . .93 E3
Burnhill Rd BR3 . . . . . .44 A7
Burns Ave TW14 . . . . . .4 A1
Burns CI
  Farnborough GU14 . . .84 F6
  Horsham RH12 . . . . .217 E1
  Mitcham SW17 . . . . . .20 D2
  Wallington SM5 . . . . .60 A2
Burns Ct SM6 . . . . . . .60 B3
Burns Dr SM7 . . . . . . .77 E5
Burns Rd RH10 . . . . . .202 C8
Burnsall CI GU14 . . . . .85 B6
Burnside KT21 . . . . . . .75 F1
Burnside CI TW1 . . . . . .6 A1
Burnside Ct SM6 . . . . .60 A2
Burnt Ash Prim Sch BR1 .24 F3
Burnt Hill Rd GU10 . . .146 B6
Burnt Hill Way GU10 . .146 B5
Burnt House La RH12 . .200 A7
Burnt Oak La RH5 . . . .179 F1
Burnt Pollard La GU24 . .48 E1
Burntcommon CI GU23 . .90 F2
Burntcommon La GU23 . .91 A2
Burntwood CI
  Caterham CR3 . . . . .101 A4
  Wandsworth SW18 . . .20 E7
Burntwood Ct SW17 . . .20 C5
Burntwood Grange Rd
  SW18 . . . . .20 E7
Burntwood La
  Caterham CR3 . . . . .101 A6
  Wandsworth SW17 . . .20 D6
Burntwood Sch SW17 . .20 D6
Burntwood View SE19 . .22 F3
Burnwood Park Rd KT12 .54 B6
Burpham Court Farm Pk★
  GU4 . . . . .110 A5
Burpham La GU4 . . . .110 A5
Burpham Prim Sch GU4 .110 A5
Burr Hill La GU24 . . . . .49 F2
Burr Rd SW18 . . . . . . .20 A8
Burrell CI CR0 . . . . . . .43 E3
Burrell Ct RH11 . . . . .200 F4
Burrell Ho [5] TW1 . . . .17 B8
Burrell Rd GU16 . . . . . .85 C8
Burrell Row BR3 . . . . . .44 A7
Burrell The RH4 . . . . .135 C6
Burrells [9] BR3 . . . . . .44 B7
Burritt Rd KT1 . . . . . . .38 A7
Burrow Hill Gn GU24 . . .49 E2
Burrow Wlk SE21 . . . . .22 C8
Burrows CI Guildford GU2 .108 F2
  Little Bookham KT23 . .93 F3
Burrows Cross GU5 . . .133 C2
Burrows Hill CI TW6,TW19 .2 C3
Burrows Hill La TW6,TW19 .2 C3
Burrows La GU5 . . . . .133 C3
Burrwood Gdns GU12 . .106 A3
Burstead CI KT11 . . . . .73 D7
Burston Gdns RH19 . . .185 D4
Burstow CI RH6 . . . . .160 F1
Burstow Ho RH6 . . . . .161 B6
Burstow Prim Sch RH6 .162 B3
Burstow Rd SW20 . . . . .39 E8
Burtenshaw Rd KT7 . . .37 A3
Burton CI Chessington KT9 .56 D3
  Horley RH6 . . . . . . .161 A2
  South Norwood CR7 . . .42 D6
  Windlesham GU20 . . . .48 D4
Burton Ct KT7 . . . . . . .37 A3
Burton Dr GU3 . . . . . .108 A6
Burton Gdns TW5 . . . . . .4 E6
Burton Ho SE26 . . . . . .23 B3
Burton Rd KT2 . . . . . . .17 E1
Burton's Rd TW12 . . . .16 C4
Burtons CI RH12 . . . . .217 C2
Burtwell La SE21,SE27 . .22 D4
Burwash Rd RH10 . . . .202 A5
Burway Cres KT16 . . . . .33 A5
Burwood Ave CR8 . . . . .80 B5
Burwood CI
  Guildford GU1 . . . . .110 D2
  Hersham KT12 . . . . . .54 C4
  Reigate RH2 . . . . . . .118 D1
  Tolworth KT6 . . . . . . .38 A1
Burwood Ct SE23 . . . . .23 C8
Burwood Ho RH8 . . . .122 E5
Burwood Rd
  Hersham KT12 . . . . . .54 B4
  Hersham KT12 . . . . . .54 C5
Bury CI GU21 . . . . .69 D3
Bury Fields GU2 . . . . .130 C7
Bury Gr SM4 . . . . .40 B4
Bury La GU21 . . . . .69 C3
Bury St GU2 . . . . .130 C7
Burys Court Sch RH2 . .138 C3
Burys The GU7 . . . . . .150 E5
Burywood Hill RH5 . . .177 E7
Busbridge CE Jun Sch
  GU7 . . . . .150 F2
Busbridge Inf Sch GU7 .150 F2
Busbridge La GU7 . . . .150 E3
Busby Ho SW16 . . . . . .21 C4
Busch CI TW7 . . . . .6 B6
Busch Cnr TW7 . . . . . . .6 B6
Busdens CI GU8 . . . . .170 F8
Busdens La GU8 . . . . .170 F8
Busdens Way GU8 . . . .170 F8
Bush CI KT15 . . . . .52 C5
Bush La GU23 . . . . . . .90 D3
Bush Rd Littleton TW17 . .33 F4
  Richmond TW9 . . . . . . .6 F8
Bush Wlk SW20 . . . . . .25 C6
Bushbury La RH3 . . . .137 A5
Bushell CI SW2 . . . . . .21 F6

Bushell Ho [3] SE27 . . .22 C4
Bushetts Gr RH1,RH2 . .119 B6
Bushey CI CR3 . . . . . . .80 F3
Bushey Croft RH8 . . . .122 C5
Bushey Ct SW20 . . . . . .39 B7
Bushey Down SW12 . . . .21 B6
Bushey La SM1 . . . . . . .59 A6
Bushey Rd Croydon CR0 . .63 A8
  Merton SW20 . . . . . . .39 D7
  Sutton SM1 . . . . .59 A6
  Sutton SM1 . . . . .59 B6
Bushey Way BR3 . . . . . .44 D4
Bushfield RH14 . . . . . .211 F2
Bushfield Dr RH1 . . . . .140 A4
Bushnell Rd SW17 . . . . .21 B5
Bushwood Rd TW9 . . . . .7 A8
Bushy Ct KT1 . . . . .37 C8
Bushy Hill Dr GU1 . . . .110 C3
Bushy Hill Jun Sch GU1 .110 D2
Bushy Park Gdns TW11 . .16 D3
Bushy Park Rd TW11 . . .17 B1
Bushy Rd Fetcham KT22 . .94 B5
  Teddington TW11 . . . .16 F1
Bushy Shaw KT21 . . . . .75 C2
Business Ctr The RG41 . .25 B4
Busk Cres GU14 . . . . . .84 F3
Bute Ave TW10 . . . . . . .17 E6
Bute Ct SM6 . . . . .60 C5
Bute Gdns SM6 . . . . . .60 C5
Bute Gdns W SM6 . . . .60 C5
Bute Rd
  Thornton Heath CR0 . . .42 A1
  Wallington SM6 . . . . .60 C6
Butler Rd Bagshot GU19 . .47 F2
  Crowthorne RG45 . . . .45 B6
Butlers Dene Rd CR3 . .102 A7
Butlers Hill SW15 . . . . . .7 F1
Butlers Rd RH13 . . . . .218 B4
Butt CI GU6 . . . . .174 E4
Butter Hill
  [5] Dorking RH4 . . . .136 A7
  Hackbridge SM5,SM6 . .60 A6
Buttercup CI RG40 . . . .26 A6
Buttercup Sq TW19 . . . .13 D7
Butterfield
  Camberley GU15 . . . . .65 B4
  East Grinstead RH19 . .185 B3
Butterfield CI TW1 . . . . .5 F1
Butterfield [1] KT23 . . .94 A1
Butterfly Wlk CR6 . . . .101 C7
Buttermer CI GU10 . . .145 F7
Buttermere CI
  East Bedfont TW14 . . . .14 F7
  Farnborough GU14 . . .84 E4
  Horsham RH12 . . . . .218 B6
  West Barnes SM4 . . . .39 D3
Buttermere Ct GU12 . . .105 F4
Buttermere Dr GU15 . . .66 D4
Buttermere Gdns
  Bracknell RG12 . . . . . .27 C6
  Sanderstead CR8 . . . . .80 D6
Buttermere Way TW20 . .12 B1
Buttersteep Rise GU20,
  SL5 . . . . .28 C1
Butterworth Ct SW16 . . .21 E5
Butts CI RH11 . . . . . . .201 B7
Butts Cotts
  [3] Feltham TW13 . . . .15 F5
  [4] Woking GU21 . . . . .69 A1
Butts Cres TW13 . . . . . .16 A5
Butts Ho TW13 . . . . . . .16 A5
Butts The TW8 . . . . .6 D8
Buxton Ave CR3 . . . . .100 E6
Buxton Cres SM3 . . . . .58 E6
Buxton Dr KT3 . . . . . . .38 D7
Buxton La CR3 . . . . . .100 E6
Buxton Rd Ashford TW15 .13 D3
  [4] Mortlake SW14 . . . .7 E4
  Thornton Heath CR7 . . .42 B4
Byards Croft SW16 . . . .41 D8
Byatt Wlk TW12 . . . . . .15 E2
Bychurch End [10] TW11 .16 F3
Bycroft St SE20 . . . . . .23 D1
Bycroft Way RH10 . . . .202 B8
Bye Ways TW2 . . . . . . .16 B5
Byerley Way RH10 . . . .202 E7
Byers La RH9 . . . . . . .142 C1
Byeway The SW14 . . . . .7 C4
Byeways The KT5 . . . . .38 B4
Byfield CI SW13 . . . . . . .7 F6
Byfield Rd TW7 . . . . . . .6 A4
Byfleet & New Haw Sta
  KT15 . . . . .52 D1
Byfleet Cnr KT14 . . . . .71 A6
Byfleet Ind Est KT14 . . .71 D8
Byfleet Prim Sch KT14 . .71 D8
Byfleet Rd
  New Haw KT14,KT15 . . .52 D2
  Weybridge KT11,KT13 . .72 C7
Byfleet Tech Ctr The
  KT14 . . . . .71 D8
Byfleets La RH12 . . . . .216 D6
Byfrons The GU14 . . . . .85 D2
Bygrove CR0 . . . . .63 B3
Bygrove Ct SW19 . . . . .20 D2
Bygrove Rd SW19 . . . . .20 D2
Bylands GU22 . . . . .70 A1
Byne Rd Carshalton SM5 . .59 E8
  Penge SE20,SE26 . . . .23 C3
Bynes Rd CR2 . . . . . . .61 D3
Byrd Rd RH11 . . . . . . .200 F3
Byrefield Rd GU2 . . . . .108 F4
Byrne Ct [4] CR8 . . . . . .80 A7
Byrne Rd SW12 . . . . . .21 B7
Byron Ave Carshalton SM1 .59 D6
  Coulsdon CR5 . . . . . . .79 F3

Byron Ave continued
  Cranford TW4 . . . . . . .4 B5
  Frimley GU15 . . . . . . .66 B3
  West Barnes KT3 . . . . .39 A4
Byron Ave E SM1 . . . . .59 D6
Byron CI Crawley RH10 . .202 B7
  Forest Hill SE26 . . . . .23 A4
  Hampton TW12 . . . . . .15 F4
  Horsham RH12 . . . . .217 E6
  Knaphill GU21 . . . . . .68 E2
  Streatham SW16 . . . . .21 E2
  Walton-on-T KT12 . . . .35 E1
Byron Ct Dulwich SE21 . .23 A7
  [1] Richmond TW10 . . .17 D4
  South Norwood CR7 . . .42 C7
Byron Dr RG45 . . . . . . .45 B3
Byron Gdns SM1 . . . . . .59 D6
Byron Gr [2] RH19 . . . .185 C1
Byron Ho BR3 . . . . . . .24 B2
Byron PI KT22 . . . . . . .95 B5
Byron Prim Sch CR5 . . .79 F2
Byron Rd Addlestone KT15 .52 E6
  South Croydon CR2 . . .62 B1
Byton Rd SW17 . . . . . .20 F2
Byttom Hill RH5 . . . . .115 C8
Byward Ave TW14 . . . . .4 C1
Byway The SM2 . . . . . .59 D2
Byways The
  Ashstead KT21 . . . . . .75 D1
  Worcester Park KT19 . .57 F6
Bywater Park RG12 . . . .27 A2
Bywood Ave CR0 . . . . .43 D3
Bywood CI CR8 . . . . . .80 B4
Bywood Terr CR0 . . . . .43 C3
Byworth CI GU9 . . . . .124 F2
Byworth Rd GU9 . . . . .124 F2

C

Cabbell PI KT15 . . . . . .52 C6
Cabell Rd GU2 . . . . . .108 E2
Cabin Moss RG12 . . . . .27 E2
Cable House Sch GU21 . .69 E4
Cabrera Ave GU25 . . . . .31 D3
Cabrera CI GU25 . . . . .31 D3
Cabrol Rd GU14 . . . . . .85 A5
Caburn Ct RH11 . . . . .201 C4
Caburn Hts RH11 . . . .201 C4
Cackstones The RH10 . .202 D7
Cadbury CI
  Ashford TW16 . . . . . .14 E1
  Isleworth TW7 . . . . . . .6 A6
Cadbury Rd TW16 . . . . .14 E2
Caddy CI [10] TW20 . . .12 A3
Cadley Terr SE23 . . . . .23 C6
Cadmer CI KT3 . . . . . . .38 E5
Cadnam CI GU11 . . . . .126 C6
Cadnam Point [14] SW15 .19 B7
Cadogan CI
  Beckenham BR3 . . . . .44 D7
  Teddington TW11 . . . .16 E3
Cadogan Ct Frimley GU15 .65 E3
  Sutton SM2 . . . . .59 B4
Cadogan Ho [11] GU1 . .130 F8
Cadogan Rd GU11 . . . .105 D7
Caen Wood Rd KT21 . . .75 C1
Caenshill Rd KT13 . . . . .53 A3
Caenswood Hill KT13 . . .53 A1
Caenwood CI KT13 . . . .53 A4
Caerleon CI
  Beacon Hill GU26 . . . .188 C6
  Claygate KT10 . . . . . .56 B3
Caernarvon GU16 . . . . .85 F8
Caernarvon CI CR4 . . . .41 E6
Caernarvon Ct [3] KT5 . .37 F4
Caesar Ct GU11 . . . . .104 E2
Caesar's Camp Rd GU15 .66 A8
Caesar's Way TW17 . . . .34 D3
Caesars Ct GU9 . . . . . .125 C7
Caesars Wlk CR4 . . . . .40 F4
Caffins CI RH10 . . . . . .201 E8
Caillard Rd KT14 . . . . .71 E8
Cain Rd RG12 . . . . . . .26 D7
Cain's La TW14 . . . . . . .3 E1
Cairn CI GU15 . . . . . . .66 B3
Cairndale CI BR1 . . . . .24 F1
Cairngorm CI [4] TW11 . .17 A3
Cairngorm PI GU14 . . . .84 E7
Cairo New Rd CR0,CR9 . .61 B8
Caister Ho [11] SW12 . .21 B8
Caister Mews SW12 . . .21 B8
Caistor Rd SW12 . . . . .21 B8
Caithness Dr KT18 . . . .76 D5
Caithness Rd CR4 . . . . .21 B1
Calbourne Rd SW12 . . .21 A8
Caldbeck Ave KT4 . . . . .39 B1
Caldbeck Ho [7] RH11 . .200 F3
Calder Rd SM4 . . . . . . .40 C4
Calder Way SL3 . . . . . . .1 E4
Calderdale CI RH11 . . .201 B4
Caldwell Rd GU20 . . . . .48 D5
Caledon PI GU4 . . . . . .110 A4
Caledon Rd SM6 . . . . . .60 A6
Caledonia Rd TW19 . . . .13 E7
Caledonian Ho RH10 . .201 D8
Caledonian Way RH6 . .182 B7
Calfridus Way RG12 . . .27 F6
California Ct SM2 . . . . .59 B1
California Rd KT3 . . . . .38 C6
Calley Down Cres CR0 . .63 D1
Callis Farm CI TW19 . . . .2 E1
Callisto CI RH11 . . . . .200 E4
Callow Field CR8 . . . . .80 A6
Callow Hill GU25 . . . . .31 C7
Calluna Ct GU22 . . . . . .69 F1

Calluna Dr RH10 . . . . .183 A3
Calmont Rd BR1 . . . . . .24 E2
Calonne Rd SW19 . . . . .19 D4
Calshot Rd TW6 . . . . . . .3 B5
Calshot Way Frimley GU16 .86 A7
  Harlington TW6 . . . . . .3 A5
Calthorpe Gdns SM1 . . .59 C7
Calton Gdns GU11 . . . .126 C7
Calverley Ct BR3 . . . . . .24 B2
Calverley Rd KT17 . . . . .58 A4
Calvert Ct GU12 . . . . .105 D1
Calvert Cres RH4 . . . . .115 B1
Calvert Ct
  [5] Leatherhead KT22 . .95 B5
  [5] Richmond TW9 . . . . .6 F3
Calvert Rd Dorking RH4 . .115 B2
  Effingham KT24 . . . . .113 B7
Calvin CI GU15 . . . . . . .66 B4
Calvin Wlk RH11 . . . . .200 E3
Camac Rd TW2 . . . . . . .16 D7
Camargue PI GU7 . . . .150 F4
Camber CI RH10 . . . . .202 C6
Camberley Ave SW20 . . .39 B7
Camberley CI SM3 . . . . .58 D7
Camberley Ct [7] SM2 . .59 B3
Camberley Inf Sch GU15 .65 C5
Camberley Rd TW6 . . . . .3 A4
Camberley Sta GU15 . . .65 D5
Camberley Twrs [1] GU15 .65 D5
Cambisgate SW19 . . . . .19 E3
Camborne CI TW6 . . . . .3 A4
Camborne Cres TW6 . . . .3 A4
Camborne Ho [9] SM2 . .59 B3
Camborne Rd
  Belmont SM2 . . . . . . .59 B3
  Croydon CR0 . . . . . . .43 A2
  Wandsworth SW18 . . . .20 A8
  West Barnes SM4 . . . .39 D4
Camborne Rd S TW6 . . . .3 A4
Camborne Way
  Harmondsworth TW6 . . .3 A4
  Heston TW5 . . . . .5 A6
Cambray Rd SW12 . . . . .21 C7
Cambria [6] BR3 . . . . . .44 B7
Cambria CI TW3 . . . . . . .5 A3
Cambria Ct Feltham TW14 .15 B8
  Staines TW18 . . . . . . .12 E4
Cambria Gdns TW19 . . .13 E8
Cambria Ho SE26 . . . . .23 A4
Cambrian CI
  Camberley GU15 . . . . .65 B5
  West Norwood SE27 . . .22 B5
Cambrian Rd
  Farnborough GU14 . . .84 D7
  Richmond TW10 . . . . . .6 F1
Cambridge Ave KT3,SW20 .38 F7
Cambridge CI
  Harmondsworth UB7 . . .2 D8
  Hounslow TW4 . . . . . . .4 E3
  Knaphill GU21 . . . . . .68 F1
  Wimbledon SW20 . . . .39 B8
Cambridge Cotts TW9 . . .7 A8
Cambridge Cres TW11 . .17 A3
Cambridge Ct
  Farnborough GU14 . . .85 C1
  Wimbledon SW20 . . . .39 B8
Cambridge Gdns KT1 . . .38 A7
Cambridge Gr SE20 . . . .43 B8
Cambridge Grove Rd
  Kingston u T KT1 . . . . .38 A6
  [5] Kingston u T KT1 . .38 A7
Cambridge Ho [2] TW11 . .17 A3
Cambridge Park Ct TW1 .17 D8
Cambridge PI GU9 . . . .125 C2
Cambridge Rd
  Aldershot GU11 . . . . .104 F2
  Barnes SW13 . . . . .7 F5
  Carshalton SM5 . . . . .59 E5
  Crowthorne RG45 . . . .45 C4
  Croydon SE20,SE25 . . .43 B6
  East Molesey KT8 . . . . .35 F5
  Hampton TW12 . . . . . .15 F1
  Horsham RH13 . . . . .217 D2
  Hounslow TW4 . . . . . . .4 E3
  Kingston u T KT1 . . . . .38 A7
  Littleton TW15,TW17 . . .14 C1
  Mitcham CR4 . . . . . . .41 C6
  New Malden KT3 . . . . .38 E5
  Richmond TW9 . . . . . . .7 A7
  Sandhurst GU47 . . . . .45 E1
  Teddington TW11 . . . .17 A3
  Walton-on-T KT12 . . . .35 B3
  Wimbledon SW20 . . . .39 B8
Cambridge Rd E GU14 . .85 D1
Cambridge Rd W GU14 . .85 C1
Cambridge Sq
  Camberley GU15 . . . . .65 C6
  Redhill RH1 . . . . . . .140 A6
Cambridge Wlk GU15 . . .65 C6
Camden Ave TW13 . . . . .15 C7
Camden Cotts KT13 . . . .53 B8
Camden Gdns
  South Norwood CR7 . . .42 B6
  Sutton SM1 . . . . .59 B5
Camden Hill Rd SE19 . . .22 E2
Camden Jun Sch SM5 . .59 F6
Camden Rd
  Carshalton SM5 . . . . .59 F6
  Lingfield RH7 . . . . . .164 D4
  Sutton SM1 . . . . .59 B5
Camden Way CR7 . . . . .42 B6
Cameford Ct [20] SW12 .21 D8
Camel CI KT2 . . . . .17 D3

Camellia Ct
21 Beckenham BR3 ....24 A1
West End GU24 ....67 F6
Camellia Pl TW2 ....16 B8
Camelot Cl
Biggin Hill TN16 ....83 C3
Wimbledon SW19 ....20 A4
Camelot Ct RH11 ......200 E6
Camelsdale Fst Sch
GU27 ....207 F5
Camelsdale Rd GU27 ...207 F5
Cameron Cl GU6 ....174 E1
Cameron Ct 3 SW19 ....19 E7
Cameron Ho 10 BR1 .....44 F8
Cameron Lodge TW3 .....5 C3
Cameron Rd
Farnborough GU11 ......105 D7
Forest Hill SE6 ....23 F6
Thornton Heath CR0 ......42 B3
Cameron Sq CR4 ....40 E8
Camilla Cl Ashford TW16 ..14 F2
Great Bookham KT23 .....94 B2
Camilla Ct 9 SM2 ......59 A3
Camilla Dr RH5 ....115 A5
Camille Cl SE25 ....43 A6
Camino Pk RH10 ....182 A4
Camlan Rd BR1 ....24 F4
Camm Gdns
6 Kingston u T KT1 ......37 F7
Thames Ditton KT7 ....36 F2
Camomile Ave CR4 ......40 F8
Camp End Rd KT11,KT13 .72 C8
Camp Farm Rd GU11 ...105 D5
Camp Hill GU10 ....147 C8
Camp Rd
Farnborough GU14 ......105 C8
Wimbledon SW19 ....19 C3
Woldingham CR3 ....101 E6
Camp View SW19 ....19 B3
Campbell Ave GU22 .....89 F6
Campbell Cl
Aldershot GU11 ....126 C7
Streatham SW16 ....21 D4
Twickenham TW2 ....16 D7
West Byfleet KT14 ....71 D7
Campbell Cres RH19 ...185 B1
Campbell Ct Dulwich SE21 23 A7
Leatherhead KT22 ....95 B5
Campbell Ho 6 SM6 ....60 B6
Campbell Pl GU16 ....65 F3
Campbell Rd
Aldershot GU11 ....105 A3
Caterham CR3 ....100 D6
Crawley RH10 ....202 C5
Thornton Heath CR0 ......42 B3
Twickenham TW2 ....16 D6
Weybridge KT13 ....53 A3
Campden Rd CR0,CR2 ...61 E5
Campen Cl SW19 ....19 E6
Camphill Ct KT14 ....71 A7
Camphill Ind Est KT14 ...71 B8
Camphill Rd KT14,KT15 ...71 B7
Campion Cl
Blackwater GU17 ....64 F3
South Croydon CR2 ....61 E6
Campion Dr KT20 ....97 B7
Campion Ho
Bracknell RG42 ....26 E8
6 Redhill RH1 ....119 A4
Campion House (Seminary)
TW7 ....5 D6
Campion Rd
Horsham RH12 ....217 E5
Hounslow TW7 ....5 F6
Campion Way RG40 .....25 E7
Camrose Ave TW13 ......15 C4
Camrose Cl Croydon CR0 ..43 E2
Morden SM4 ....40 A5
Can Hatch KT20 ....77 E1
Canada Ave RH1 ....140 A5
Canada Dr RH1 ....140 A5
Canada Ho RH1 ....140 A5
Canada Rd Byfleet KT14 ..71 D8
Cobham KT11 ....73 C6
Frimley GU16 ....86 E8
Canadian Ave SE6 ....24 B7
Canal Bank GU21 ....88 F8
Canal Bank Mews GU21 .69 E2
Canal Cl GU11 ....105 D5
Canal Cotts GU12 ......106 A4
Canal Wlk Croydon CR0 ...42 F3
Forest Hill SE26 ....23 C3
Canberra Cl
Crawley RH11 ....181 D1
Horsham RH12 ....217 F4
Canberra Pl RH12 ......217 F5
Canberra Rd TW6 ....3 A4
Canbury Ave KT2 ....37 F8
Canbury Bsns Pk 3 KT2 .37 E8
Canbury Ct KT2 ....17 E1
Canbury Mews SE26 ....23 A5
Canbury Park Rd KT2 ....37 F8
Candler Mews TW1 .....17 A8
Candlerush Cl GU22 .....70 B2
Candover Cl UB7 ....2 D7
Candy Croft KT23 ....94 B2
Canewdon Cl GU22 .....89 E8
Canfold Cotts GU6 .....175 B4
Canford Dr KT15 ....52 B8
Canford Gdns KT3 ....38 E3
Canham Rd SE25 ....42 E6
Canhams KT20 ....97 B6
Canmore Gdns SW16 ....21 C1
Canning Rd
Aldershot GU12 ....105 D2
Canning Rd *continued*
Croydon CR0,CR9 ....61 F8
Cannizaro Rd SW19 .....19 D3
Cannon Cl Hampton TW12 .16 B2
Sandhurst GU47 ....64 F8
West Barnes SW20 ....39 C6
Cannon Cres GU24 ......68 E8
Cannon Gr KT22 ....94 E6
Cannon Hill RG12 ....27 C3
Cannon Hill La KT3,SM4,
SW20 ....39 E5
Cannon Ho SE26 ....23 B2
Cannon Side KT22 ......94 E5
Cannon Way
East Molesey KT8 ....36 B5
Fetcham KT22 ....94 E6
Cannon (W End of General
Roy's Base Line)* TW6 ..3 B6
Canon's Hill CR5 ....80 A1
Canon's Wlk CR0 ....62 D7
Canonbie Rd SE23 ......23 C8
Canonbury Cotts RH12 .199 F6
Canons Cl RH2 ....117 F2
Canons La KT20 ....97 F8
Canopus Way TW19 .....13 E8
Cansiron La RH19 ......206 F6
Cantelupe Ho 1 RH19 ..185 F1
Cantelupe Mews 4
RH19 ....185 E1
Cantelupe Rd RH19 ....185 F1
Canter The RH10 ....202 E7
Canterbury Cl BR3 ......44 B8
Canterbury Ct
Ashford TW15 ....13 F4
3 Dorking RH4 ....136 A8
South Croydon CR2 ....61 C3
Canterbury Gr
West Norwood SE27 ......22 B5
West Norwood SE27,SW16 .22 A5
Canterbury Ho KT19 .....76 A8
Canterbury Mews KT22 ..74 C6
Canterbury Rd
Ash GU12 ....106 A3
Crawley RH10 ....201 E2
Farnborough GU14 ....85 D2
Feltham TW13 ....15 E6
Guildford GU2 ....108 F3
Morden SM4 ....40 C3
Thornton Heath CR0,CR7 ..42 A2
Cantley Cres RG41 ......25 A8
Cantley Gdns SE19 ......42 F8
Canute Ct SW16 ....22 A5
Canvey Cl RH11 ....201 C3
Capatus Ho SW14 ....7 D5
Cape Copse RH12 ......214 D7
Capel KT5 ....37 F2
Capel Ave SM6 ....60 F5
Capel Ct 7 Mortlake SW14 .7 D4
Penge SE20 ....43 C8
Capel La RH11 ....200 F5
Capel Lodge
5 Richmond TW9 ....6 F6
15 Streatham SW2 ....21 F8
Capel Rd RH12 ....199 A8
Capella Ho RH5 ....178 C5
Capern Rd SW18 ....20 C7
Capital Ind Est CR4 .....40 F4
Capital Pk GU22 ....90 B6
Caplan Est CR4 ....41 C8
Capper Rd GU15 ....65 A7
Capri Rd CR0 ....42 F2
Capricorn Cl RH11 .....200 E4
Capsey Rd RH11 ....200 E6
Capstans Wharf 7 GU21 .68 F1
Capstone Rd BR1 ....24 F4
Caradon Cl GU21 ....69 B1
Caradon Ct 7 TW1 ....6 C1
Caraway Cl RH11 ......201 B2
Caraway Pl
Guildford GU2 ....109 A6
Hackbridge SM6 ....60 B7
Carberry Rd 13 SE19 ....22 E2
Carbery La SL5 ....29 B6
Card Hill RH18 ....206 F1
Cardamom Cl GU2 .....109 A5
Cardigan Cl GU21 ......68 F1
Cardigan Rd
Richmond TW10 ....6 E1
Wimbledon SW19 ....20 C2
Cardinal Ave
Kingston u T KT2 ....17 E2
West Barnes SM4 ....39 E3
Cardinal Cl
West Barnes SM4 ....39 E3
Worcester Park KT19,KT4 ..58 A6
Cardinal Cl CR2 ....81 A6
Cardinal Cres KT3 ......38 C7
Cardinal Ct KT8 ....36 D5
Cardinal Dr KT12 ....35 D1
Cardinal Newman RC Sch
KT12 ....54 D7
Cardinal Rd TW13 ....15 B7
Cardinal Road Inf Sch
TW13 ....15 B7
Cardinal's Wlk
Ashford TW16 ....14 E2
Hampton TW12 ....16 C1
Cardingham GU21 ......69 B2
Cardington Sq TW4 ......4 D3
Cardwell Cres SL5 ......29 C4
Cardwells Keep GU2 ...109 A4
Carew Cl CR5 ....100 B8
Carew Ct SM2 ....59 B2
Carew Ho SW16 ....22 A5
Carew Manor Sch SM6 ..60 D7
Carew Rd Ashford TW15 ..14 C2
Mitcham CR4 ....41 A7
Thornton Heath CR7 ......42 B5
Carew Rd *continued*
Wallington SM6 ....60 C4
Carey Ho RH11 ....201 C6
Carey Rd RG40 ....25 C5
Carey's Wood RH6 .....162 B3
Carfax RH12 ....217 C2
Carfax Ave GU10 ......126 F8
Carfax Est GU10 ....126 F8
Cargate Ave GU11 .....105 A1
Cargate Gr GU11 ......105 A1
Cargate Hill GU11 .....104 F1
Cargate Terr GU11 .....104 F1
Cargill Rd SW18 ....20 C7
Cargo Forecourt Rd
RH6 ....181 D7
Cargo Rd RH6 ....181 D7
Cargreen Rd SE25 ......42 F5
Carholme Rd SE23 .....23 F7
Carisbrook Ct 1 SW16 ..21 F5
Carisbrooke GU16 ......85 F8
Carisbrooke Ct SM2 ....58 F3
Carisbrooke Rd CR4 ....41 E5
Carleton Ave SM6 ....60 D2
Carleton Cl KT10 ....36 D1
Carlingford Gdns CR4 ...21 A1
Carlingford Rd SM4 .....39 D3
Carlinwark Dr GU15 ....65 F7
Carlisle Cl KT2 ....38 A8
Carlisle Inf Sch TW12 ...16 B2
Carlisle Rd Cheam SM1 ...58 F4
Hampton TW12 ....16 B1
Rushmoor GU10 ....168 C6
Carlisle Way SW17 .....21 A3
Carlos St GU7 ....150 E4
Carlton Ave Feltham TW14 .4 C1
South Croydon CR2 ....61 E3
Carlton Cl
Chessington KT9 ....56 D4
Crawley RH10 ....201 E5
Frimley GU15 ....66 B3
Woking GU21 ....70 A5
Carlton Cres SM3 ......58 E6
Carlton Ct Horley RH6 ..161 A5
12 Penge SE20 ....43 B8
South Norwood SE19 ......42 F8
Staines TW18 ....13 A3
Carlton Gn RH1 ....118 E4
Carlton Ho Cheam SM1 ...58 F4
Hounslow TW4 ....5 A1
Carlton Park Ave SW20 ..39 D7
Carlton Pl 2 KT13 ......53 B6
Carlton Rd Ashford TW16 .14 F1
Blindley Heath RH9 ......142 C2
Headley Down GU35 .....187 C5
Kingston u T KT3 ....38 E7
Mortlake SW14 ....7 C3
Redhill RH1,RH2 ....118 E4
South Croydon CR2 ....61 D3
Walton-on-T KT12 ....35 B2
Woking GU21 ....70 A5
Carlton Terr SE26 ......23 C5
Carlton Tye RH6 ......161 C3
Carlwell St SW17 ....20 E3
Carlyle Cl KT8 ....36 B7
Carlyle Ct RG45 ....45 C5
Carlyle Rd Croydon CR0 ...62 A8
Staines TW18 ....13 A1
Carlyon Cl
Farnborough GU14 ....85 C4
Mytchett GU16 ....85 F4
Carlys Cl BR3 ....43 D7
Carmalt Gdns KT12 .....54 C5
Carman Wlk RH11 .....201 B1
Carmarthen Cl GU14 ....85 A7
Carmel Cl 9 GU22 .....69 E1
Carmela Ct TW15 ....14 D1
Carmichael Ct SW13 .....7 F5
Carmichael Ho 17 SE21 ..22 E4
Carmichael Mews SW18 .20 D8
Carmichael Rd SE25 ....43 A5
Carminia Rd SW17 ......21 B6
Carnac St SE21, SE27 ....22 D5
Carnation Cl RG45 ......45 B8
Carnation Dr RG42 ....8 B2
Carnegie Cl KT6 ....56 F8
Carnegie Pl SW19 ......19 D5
Carnforth Cl KT19 ......57 B4
Carnforth Rd SW16 .....21 D1
Carnoustie RG12 ....26 E2
Carole Ho 14 SE20 ......43 B8
Carolina Rd CR7 ....42 C8
Caroline Cl Hounslow TW7 ..5 E7
South Croydon CR0 ....61 E6
Streatham SW16 ....21 F5
Caroline Ct Ashford TW15 .14 B2
Catford SE6 ....24 D4
Crawley RH11 ....201 D4
17 Surbiton KT6 ....37 D2
Caroline Dr RG41 ....25 A7
Caroline Pl UB3 ....3 E7
Caroline Rd SW19 ......19 F1
Carolyn Cl GU21 ....88 F8
Carpenter Cl KT17 ......57 F2
Carpenters Ct TW2 .....16 E6
Carrara Villas KT1 ......37 F6
Carrick Cl TW7 ....6 A4
Carrick Gate KT10 ......55 C7
Carrigshaun KT13 ......53 D4
Carrington Ave TW3 ......5 B2
Carrington Cl
Croydon CR0 ....43 E2
Redhill RH1 ....118 F2
Carrington Ho SW19 .....20 A1
Carrington La GU12 ...106 A8
Carrington Lodge 3
TW10 ....6 E2
Carrington Pl KT10 .....55 C6
Carrington Rd TW10 ......7 A3
Carroll Ave GU1 ....110 B1
Carroll Cres SL5 ....28 F5
Carrow Rd KT12 ....54 D7
Carshalton Beeches Sta
SM5 ....59 F4
Carshalton Coll SM5 ....59 F7
Carshalton Gr SM1 .....59 D5
Carshalton High Sch for Boys
SM5 ....59 E8
Carshalton High Sch for Girls
SM5 ....59 E7
Carshalton Lodge KT13 ..53 E7
Carshalton Park Rd SM5 .59 F5
Carshalton Pl SM5 ......60 A5
Carshalton Rd
Camberley GU15 ....47 A1
Carshalton SM1,SM5 ......59 D5
Mitcham CR4 ....41 A4
Wallington SM7 ....78 F6
Woodmansterne SM7 .....78 F6
Carshalton Sta SM5 .....59 F6
Carson Rd SE21 ....22 D6
Carstairs Rd SE6 ....24 C5
Carswell Rd SE6 ....24 C8
Cartbridge Cl GU23 .....90 B4
Carter Cl SM6 ....60 D3
Carter Rd Crawley RH10 .202 D3
Mitcham SW19 ....20 D2
Carter's Cotts RH1 .....139 E7
Carter's Rd KT17 ....76 F4
Carterdale Cotts RH5 ..178 C5
Carters Cl Guildford GU1 .109 E5
North Cheam KT4 ....39 D1
Carters La GU22 ....90 D7
Carters Wlk GU9 ......125 D8
Cartersmead Cl RH6 ....161 B4
Carthouse Cotts GU4 ...110 C4
Carthouse La GU21 .....68 E5
Cartmel Cl RH2 ....118 E3
Cartmel Ct BR2 ....44 E7
Cartmel Gdns SM4 ......40 C4
Carwarden House Sch
GU15 ....66 A3
Caryl Ho 6 SW19 ....19 D7
Carylls Cotts RH12 .....199 F1
Cascades CR0 ....62 F1
Cascades Ct SW19 ......19 F1
Caselden Cl KT15 ....52 C5
Casewick Rd SE27 ......22 B4
Casher Rd RH10 ....202 C3
Cassel Hospl The TW10 ..17 D4
Cassilis Rd TW1 ....6 B1
Cassino Cl GU11 ......105 B2
Cassiobury Ave TW14 ....14 F8
Cassland Rd CR7 ....42 D5
Casslee Rd SE6 ....23 F8
Cassocks Sq TW17 ......34 D2
Castillon Rd SE6 ....24 E6
Castlands Rd SE6 ......23 F6
Castle Ave KT17 ....58 B2
Castle Cl Beckenham BR2 ..44 E6
Bletchingley RH1 ....120 C2
3 Charlton TW16 ....14 E1
Frimley GU15 ....65 F4
Reigate RH2 ....139 B5
Wimbledon SW19 ....19 D5
Castle Ct Belmont SM2 ...59 A4
Forest Hill SE26 ....23 E4
Morden SM4 ....40 D4
Castle Dr Horley RH6 ...161 C2
Reigate RH2 ....139 B4
Castle Field GU9 ......125 B3
Castle Gdns RH4 ......115 F1
Castle Gn KT13 ....53 E7
Castle Grove Rd GU24 ...68 E7
Castle Hill Farnham GU9 .125 B3
Guildford GU1 ....130 D7
Castle Hill Ave CR0 .....63 C2
Castle Hill Prim Sch CR0 63 C4
Castle Hill Rd TW20 .....11 C5
Castle Ho 3 SM2 ....59 A3
Castle Keep RH2 ......118 A1
Castle Of Mey Ho GU27 .207 F6
Castle Par KT17 ....58 A3
Castle Rd Aldershot GU11 104 E4
Broadbridge Heath RH12 .216 D3
Camberley GU15 ....65 F4
Epsom KT18 ....76 B4
Isleworth TW7 ....5 F5
Kingswood CR5 ....98 E6
Oatlands Park KT13 ....53 E7
Woking GU21 ....69 F5
Castle Sq
Bletchingley RH1 ....120 C2
Guildford GU1 ....130 D7
Castle St
Bletchingley RH1 ....120 C2
Farnham GU9 ....125 B3
Guildford GU1 ....130 D7
Kingston u T KT2 ....37 E7
Castle The RH12 ......217 E7
Castle View KT18 ....76 B5
Castle Way Ewell KT17 ...58 A2
Feltham TW13 ....15 C4
Wimbledon SW19 ....19 D5
Castle Wlk TW16 ....35 C6
Castle Yd 17 TW10 ......6 D2
Castlecombe Dr SW19 ..19 D8
Castlecraig Ct GU47 ....64 D7
Castledine Rd SE20 .....23 B1
Castlefield Ct RH2 .....118 B1
Castlefield Rd RH2 .....118 A1
Castlegate TW9 ....6 F4
Castlemaine Ave
Ewell KT17 ....58 B2
South Croydon CR0,CR2 ...61 F5
Castleman Ho SL5 ......29 D4
Castleton Cl
Banstead SM7 ....78 A4
Croydon CR0 ....43 E3
Castleton Ct KT5 ....37 F4
Castleton Dr SM7 ......78 A5
Castleton Rd CR4 ......41 D5
Castleview Rd KT13 .....53 B6
Caswell Cl GU14 ....84 F6
Catalina Rd TW6 ....3 B5
Catalpa Cl GU1 ....109 C3
Catena Rise GU18 ......48 B1
Cater Gdns GU3 ......108 F3
Caterfield La
Crowhurst RH7 ....143 F3
Oxted RH7,RH8 ....144 A5
Caterham By-Pass CR3 .101 B4
Caterham Cl GU24 ......87 E6
Caterham Dene Hospl
CR3 ....100 F4
Caterham Dr CR5 ......100 C8
Caterham Prep Sch
CR3 ....100 F1
Caterham Sta CR3 .....101 A3
Caterways RH12 ....217 A3
Catford Bridge Sta SE6 ..24 A8
Catford Broadway SE6 ...24 B8
Catford Cty Sch SE6 .....24 C5
Catford Cty Sch (Annexe)
BR1 ....24 E4
Catford Hill SE6 ....24 A7
Catford Rd SE6 ....24 A8
Catford Sta SE6 ....24 A8
Catharine Ct GU11 .....104 F1
Cathedral Cl GU2 ......130 B8
Cathedral Ct GU2 ......109 A1
Cathedral Hill GU2 ....109 A2
Cathedral Hill Ind Est
GU2 ....109 A2
Cathedral View GU2 ...108 F1
Catherine Baird Ct 13
SW12 ....21 B8
Catherine Cl KT14 ....71 F5
Catherine Ct 3 SW19 ...19 F3
Catherine Dr
Ashford TW16 ....14 F2
Richmond TW9 ....6 E3
Catherine Gdns TW3 .....5 D3
Catherine Ho TW7 ....6 B6
Catherine Howard Ct 8
KT13 ....53 B7
Catherine Rd KT6 ....37 D4
Catherine Villas GU27 ..208 B6
Catherine Wheel Rd TW8 .6 D7
Catherington Sch RH11 181 D2
Cathill La RH5 ....177 C3
Cathles Rd SW12 ....21 C8
Catlin Cres TW17 ....34 D4
Catlin Gdns RH9 ......121 B5
Catling Cl SE23 ....23 D5
Caton Ct BR2 ....44 E7
Cator Cl CR0 ....82 E8
Cator Cres CR0 ....82 E8
Cator La BR3 ....43 F8
Cator Park Girls Sch BR3 23 E1
Cator Rd Penge SE20,SE26 23 D2
Wallington SM5 ....59 F5
Catteshall Hatch GU7 ..151 A6
Catteshall La GU7 .....150 F4
Catteshall Rd GU7 .....151 A5
Catteshall Terr GU7 ....151 A5
Catteshall Wks GU7 ....151 A6
Causeway
Feltham TW14,TW4 ....4 B3
Horsham RH12 ....217 C1
Causeway Ct 1 GU21 ....68 F1
Causeway Est TW20 .....12 C4
Causeway The
Carshalton SM5 ....60 A8
Claygate KT10 ....55 F3
Egham TW18,TW20 ....12 D4
Sutton SM2 ....59 C2
Teddington TW11 ....16 F2
Wimbledon SW19 ....19 C3
Causewayside GU27 ....208 D6
Cavalier Ct TW15 ....14 D1
Cavalier Way RH19 ....205 F7
Cavalry Cres TW4 ....4 D3
Cavalry Ct GU11 ......104 E2
Cavans Rd GU11 ......105 C6
Cave Rd TW10 ....17 C4
Cavell Way
Crawley RH10 ....202 C5
Epsom KT19 ....76 A8
Knaphill GU21 ....88 C8
Cavendish Ave KT3 .....39 B5
Cavendish Cl
Ashford TW16 ....14 F2
Horsham RH12 ....217 D7
Cavendish Ct
Ashford TW16 ....14 F2
Blackwater GU17 ....64 D3
Poyle SL3 ....1 E6
Cavendish Dr KT10 .....55 E5
Cavendish Gdns RH1 ..119 A2
Cavendish Ho TW1 ....6 A1
Cavendish Meads SL5 ...29 D3
Cavendish Mews GU11 .105 A1
Cavendish Prim Sch W4 ..7 E7
Cavendish Rd
Aldershot GU11 ....105 A1
Ashford TW16 ....14 F2
Balham SW12 ....21 B8
Chiswick W4 ....7 C6
Mitcham SW19 ....20 E1
New Malden KT3 ....38 F5
Redhill RH1 ....119 A2
Sutton SM2 ....59 C3
Thornton Heath CR0 ......42 B1

Cedars The *continued*
Milford GU8 ....170 E8
Reigate RH2 ....118 D1
Teddington TW11 ....16 F2
Wallington SM6 ....60 C6
Cedarville Gdns SW16 ...21 F2
Cedarways GU9 ....146 B7
Cedric Ct RH12 ....217 A1
Celandine Cl
1 Crawley RH11 ....201 B2
Crowthorne RG45 ....45 C6
Celandine Rd KT12 .....54 E6
Celia Cres TW15 ....13 D2
Celia Ct Ewell KT17 ....57 F2
7 Richmond TW9 ......6 F6
Celtic Ave BR2 ....44 E6
Celtic Rd KT14 ....71 F5
Cemetery La TW17 ....34 B2
Cemetery Pales
Brookwood GU24 ......88 A6
Pirbright GU24 ....87 F5
Centaurs Bsns Pk TW7 ..6 A8
Central Ave
East Molesey KT8 .....35 F4
Isleworth TW3,TW7 ....5 C3
Wallington SM6 ....60 E5
Central Blgs 2 GU21 ..69 F2
Central Ct KT15 ....52 B6
Central Hill SE19 ......22 D2
Central La SL4 ....9 B7
Central Par Feltham TW14 15 C8
Heston TW5 ....5 A7
Kingston u T KT6 ......37 E3
New Addington CR0 ....63 C1
Penge SE20 ....23 D1
Central Pk Est TW4 ....4 D3
Central Rd Morden SM4 .40 B4
North Cheam KT4 ......58 A8
Central Sq KT8 ....35 F5
Central Terr BR3 ......43 D6
Central Veterinary
  Laboratory KT15 ......52 B2
Central Way Feltham TW14 .4 B2
Oxted RH8 ....122 D8
Sutton SM5 ....59 E3
Winkfield SL4 ....9 B7
Central Wlk RG40 .....25 C6
Centre The Feltham TW13 .15 B7
Walton-on-T KT12 .....34 F1
Centurion Ct 4 GU47 ..64 D8
Centurion Ct SM6 .....60 B8
Century Ct
Teddington TW11 ......17 A4
Woking GU21 ....69 F2
Century Rd TW18,TW20 ..12 C3
Century Way GU24 .....87 D8
Century Yd SE23 ......23 C6
Cerne Rd SM4 ....40 C3
Cerotus Pl KT16 ......32 F2
Chadacre Rd KT17 .....58 B5
Chadhurst Cl RH5 .....136 D4
Chadwick Ave SW19 ...20 A2
Chadwick Cl
Crawley RH11 ....201 B1
Roehampton SW15 .....18 F8
Teddington TW11 ......17 A2
Chadwick Rd KT6 .....37 C3
Chadworth Way KT10 ..55 D5
Chaffers Mead KT21 ...75 F3
Chaffinch Ave CR0 ....43 D3
Chaffinch Cl
Crawley RH11 ....201 B1
Croydon CR0 ....43 D3
Horsham RH12 ....217 D7
5 Sandhurst GU47 ....64 D8
Tolworth KT6 ....57 A7
Chaffinch Rd BR3 .....43 E8
Chaffinch Way RH6 ...160 E4
Chagford Ct SW19 ....20 E1
Chailey Cl
2 Crawley RH11 .....201 A3
Heston TW5 ....4 D6
Chailey Pl KT12 ......54 E6
Chalcot Cl SM2 ....59 A3
Chalcot Mews SW16 ...21 E5
Chalcott Gdns KT6 ....37 C1
Chaldon Cl RH1 ......139 E7
Chaldon Common Rd
CR3 ....100 C2
Chaldon Rd
Caterham CR3 ....100 D4
Crawley RH11 ....201 C1
Chaldon Way CR5 ....79 E1
Chale Wlk SM2 ....59 B2
Chalet Ct CR7 ....42 B4
Chalfont Dr GU14 .....85 C2
Chalfont Rd SE25 .....42 F6
Chalford Cl KT8 ......36 A5
Chalford Ct KT6 ......37 F2
Chalford Rd SE21 .....22 D4
Chalgrove Ave SM4 ...40 A4
Chalgrove Rd SM2 ....59 D3
Chalice Cl SM6 ....60 D4
Chalk La Ashstead KT21 ..96 A8
East Horsley KT24 ....112 F4
Epsom KT18 ....76 E3
Shackleford GU8 .....149 D8
Chalk Paddock KT18 ...76 D4
Chalk Pit La KT23 ....113 F8
Chalk Pit Rd
Banstead SM7 ....78 A2
Langley Vale KT18 ....96 C6
Chalk Rd Farncombe GU7 150 E5
Ifold RH14 ....212 C3
Sutton SM1 ....59 C4
Chalkenden Cl SE20 ...23 B1
Chalkers Cnr SW14 ....7 B4
Chalkley Cl CR4 ......41 A7

Cedar La GU16 ....85 D8
Cedar Lodge
Crawley RH11 ....201 D4
Milford GU8 ....149 F2
Weybridge KT13 ....53 A7
Cedar Mount GU8 ....148 D4
Cedar Pk CR3 ....100 E6
Cedar Rd Cobham KT11 ..73 B5
Cranford TW5 ....4 C5
Croydon CR0,CR9 .....61 E8
East Bedfont TW14 ....14 D7
East Molesey KT8 .....36 E5
Farnborough GU14 ....85 C3
Sutton SM2 ....59 C4
Teddington TW11 ......17 A3
Weybridge KT13 ....53 A6
Woking GU22 ....89 C7
Cedar Terr TW9 ....6 E3
Cedar Tree Gr SE27 ...22 B3
Cedar Way Charlton TW16 14 E1
Guildford GU1 ....109 C4
Kenley CR8 ....80 C3
Kingswood KT20 ......97 E7
Cedarcroft Rd KT9 ....56 F6
Cedars 2 Bracknell RG12 27 F3
Woodmansterne SM7 ..78 F5
Cedars Ave CR4 ......41 A6
Cedars Ct GU1 ....110 A4
Cedars Ho 5 SW2 ....21 F8
Cedars Prim Sch TW5 ..4 A7
Cedars Rd Barnes SW13 ..7 F5
Beckenham BR3 ....43 F7
Morden SM4 ....40 A5
Teddington KT8 ....37 C8
Wallington CR0 ....60 E6
Cedars The Ashstead KT22 95 D6
Brockham RH3 ....116 A1
Byfleet KT14 ....71 F7
Guildford GU1 ....110 A4

Chalkpit La
Brockham RH3 ....116 B2
Dorking RH4 ....136 A8
Oxted RH8 ....102 C1
Woldingham CR3,CR8 ..102 C1
Chalkpit Terr RH4 .....115 A1
Chalkpit Wood RH8 ...122 D8
Chalky La KT9 ....56 D1
Challen Ct RH12 .....217 B3
Challenge Ct KT22 ....95 B8
Challenge Rd TW15 ...14 B8
Challice Way SW2 .....21 F7
Challin St SE20 ....43 C8
Challis Pl RG42 ....26 E8
Challock Cl TN16 .....83 C3
Challoner Ct BR2 .....44 D7
Challoners Cl KT8 .....36 D5
Chalmers Cl RH6 .....180 E6
Chalmers Rd
Ashford TW15 ....14 B3
Banstead SM7 ....78 C4
Chalmers Rd E TW15 ..14 C3
Chalmers Way TW14 ...4 B2
Chalner Ho 21 SW2 ...22 A7
Chamber La GU10 ....145 C7
Chamberlain Cres BR4 ..44 B2
Chamberlain Gdns TW3 ..5 C6
Chamberlain Way KT6 ..37 E2
Chamberlain Wlk 1 TW13 ..15 E4
Chambers Ho 2 SW16 ..21 C4
Chambers Rd GU12 ...106 B6
Chamomile Gdns GU14 ..84 C5
Champion Cres SE26 ..23 E4
Champion Rd SE26 ....23 E4
Champness Cl 9 SE27 ..22 D4
Champney Cl SL3 .....1 A4
Champneys Cl SM2 ...58 F3
Chancellor Gdns CR2 ..61 B2
Chancellor Gr SE21 ...22 C5
Chancery La BR3 .....44 B7
Chancery Mews SW17 ..20 E6
Chanctonbury Chase
RH1 ....119 A1
Chanctonbury Dr SL5 ..29 E1
Chanctonbury Gdns SM2 59 B3
Chanctonbury Way
RH11 ....201 C4
Chandler CE Jun Sch The
GU8 ....170 F5
Chandler Cl
Crawley RH10 ....201 D4
Hampton TW12 ....36 A8
Chandler Ct
2 Tolworth KT5 ......38 B1
8 Wallington SM6 ....60 B4
Chandlers KT20 ....97 B6
Chandlers Cl TW14 ...14 F8
Chandlers Rd GU12 ...106 B4
Chandlers Way 11 SW2 ..22 A8
Chandon Lodge SM2 ..59 C3
Chandos Rd TW18 ....12 D3
Channel Cl TW5 ....5 A6
Channings GU21 ......69 E4
Channon Ct 3 KT6 ....37 E4
Chantlers Cl RH19 ....185 C2
Chanton Dr SM2 ......58 C1
Chantrey Cl KT21 .....95 C8
Chantrey Rd RH10 ....201 E3
Chantry Cl RH6 ......160 F4
Chantry Cotts GU4 ...131 B3
Chantry Ct Carshalton SM5 59 E7
Frimley GU16 ....33 C2
Chantry Hurst KT18 ...76 D4
Chantry La GU5 ......132 F4
Chantry Pl 5 GU1 ....130 E8
Chantry Rd Bagshot GU19 47 C2
Chertsey KT16 ....33 C2
Chessington KT9 .....57 A5
Chilworth GU4 ....131 B3
Chantry View Rd GU1 .130 E6
Chantry Way CR4 .....40 D6
Chantry Wood Nature Trail ★
GU1 ....130 E5
Chantrys Ct GU9 .....125 A2
Chantrys The GU9 ....125 A1
Chapel Ave
Addlestone KT15 .....52 B6
Brookwood GU24 ......88 B6
Chapel Cl Bracknell RG12 27 D6
Milford GU8 ....149 F2
Chapel Ct
10 Dorking RH4 .....136 A7
10 Dorking RH4 .....136 A8
Chapel Fields GU7 ....150 D7
Chapel Gdns GU8 ....80 A6
Chapel Gr Addlestone KT15 52 B6
Burgh Heath KT18 ....97 C8
Chapel Hill Dunsfold GU8 192 F1
Effingham KT24 ......113 D8
Chapel La
Ashurst Wood RH19 ..206 D6
Bagshot GU19 ....47 D2
Copthorne RH10 .....183 F4
Farnborough GU14 ....84 F8
Forest Row RH18 ....206 F2
Milford GU8 ....149 F2
Pirbright GU24 ....88 A4
Westcott RH4 ....135 C6
Westhumble RH5 .....114 D5
Chapel Lane Ind Est
RH4 ....135 C6
Chapel Park Rd KT15 ..52 B6
Chapel Rd
Camberley GU15 ......65 B5
Charlwood RH6 ......180 F7
Hounslow TW3 ....5 B4

Chapel Rd *continued*
Limpsfield RH8 ......123 C5
Redhill RH1 ....118 F1
Rowledge GU10 .....145 E3
Smallfield RH6 ......162 B4
Tadworth KT20 ......97 D4
Twickenham TW1 .....17 B8
Warlingham CR6 ......81 D1
West Norwood SE27 ..22 B4
Chapel Sq Sandhurst GU15 64 F6
Thorpe GU25 ....31 E5
Chapel St
Farnborough GU14 ....85 D6
Guildford GU1 ....130 D7
11 Woking GU21 ......69 F2
Chapel View CR2 .....62 C3
Chapel Way KT18,KT20 .77 C1
Chapelhouse Cl GU2 ..108 E1
Chaplain's Hill RG45 ..45 D4
Chaplin Cres TW16 ...14 E2
Chapman Ho 2 SE27 ..22 B5
Chapman Rd
Crawley RH10 ....202 C2
Thornton Heath CR0 ..42 A1
Chapman Sq SW19 ...19 D6
Chapman's La
East Grinstead RH19 ..185 D1
East Grinstead RH19 ..185 D1
Chapter Way TW12 ....16 A4
Chara Pl W4 ....7 D8
Charcot Ho SW15 .....7 F1
Chargate Cl KT12 ....54 A4
Charing Ct BR2 ....44 E7
Charlbury Cl 7 RG12 ..27 F5
Charlecombe Ct TW18 .13 A3
Charlecote Cl GU14 ...85 D3
Charlecote Gr SE26 ...23 B5
Charles Babbage Cl KT9 56 D3
Charles Cobb Gdns CR0 60 E6
Charles Ct 5 TW11 ...16 E3
Charles Darwin Sch
TN16 ....83 F3
Charles Dickens Ct SE25 43 A5
Charles Haller St 8 SW2 22 A8
Charles Hill GU10 ....147 E6
Charles Mills Ct SW16 ..21 E2
Charles Rd Merton SW19 40 A8
Staines TW18 ....13 D2
Charles Sq RG12 .....27 C7
Charles St Chertsey KT16 32 F1
Croydon CR0,CR9 .....61 C7
Hounslow TW3 ....4 F5
Mortlake SW13,SW14 ..7 E5
Charles Staunton Ho 3
SE27 ....22 D4
Charlesfield Rd RH6 ..160 F4
Charleston Cl TW13 ...15 A5
Charleston Rd RH10 ..202 B3
Charleville Cir SE19,SE26 23 A3
Charlmont Rd SW17 ..20 F2
Charlock Cl RH11 ....201 A2
Charlock Way GU1 ...109 B4
Charlotte Broadwood Flats
RH5 ....178 D6
Charlotte Cl GU9 ....125 D8
Charlotte Ct
Crawley RH11 ....201 C6
Esher KT10 ....55 C5
Charlotte Ho KT21 ....95 E8
Charlotte Mews 4 KT10 55 B6
Charlotte Rd Barnes SW13 7 F6
Wallington SM6 ......60 C4
Charlotte Sq 5 TW10 ..6 F1
Charlton Ave KT12 ....54 B6
Charlton Ct GU47 .....45 D1
Charlton Dr TN16 .....83 D2
Charlton Gdns CR5 ...79 C1
Charlton Ho 5 TW8 ....6 E8
Charlton Kings KT13 ..53 E7
Charlton La TW17 ....34 D5
Charlton Rd TW17 ....34 C7
Charlwood CR0 ....62 F2
Charlwood Cl
Copthorne RH10 .....183 B4
Little Bookham KT23 ..94 B3
Charlwood Dr KT22 ...74 D4
Charlwood Ho 1 SW2 ..21 F7
Charlwood La RH5 ....180 A5
Charlwood Rd
Crawley RH6,RH11 ...181 C4
Hookwood RH6,RH11 ..181 C8
Rusper RH11,RH6 ....180 E2
Charlwood Village Inf Sch
RH6 ....180 F7
Charlwood Wlk RH11 .181 B1
Charlwoods Bsns Ctr
RH19 ....185 D2
Charlwoods Pl RH19 ..185 E3
Charlwoods Rd RH19 .185 E3
Charm Cl RH6 ....160 E4
Charman Rd RH1 .....118 E1
Charmans Cl RH12 ...218 B5
Charmile Ct TW16 ....14 E1
Charminster Ave SW19 40 B7
Charminster Ct 3 KT6 ..37 D2
Charminster Rd KT4 ..39 D1
Charmouth Ct TW10 ..6 F2
Charnwood SL5 ....29 F3
Charnwood Ave SW19 .40 B7
Charnwood Cl KT3 ....38 E5
Charnwood Rd SE25 ..42 D5
Charrington Rd 2 CR0,
CR9 ....61 C8
Charrington Way RH12 216 C3
Charsley Rd SE6 .....24 B6
Chart Cl Bromley BR2 ..44 E8
Croydon CR0 ....43 C4

Cav – Cha **235**

Chart Cl *continued*
Dorking RH5 ....136 D5
Mitcham CR4 ....40 F5
Chart Downs RH5 ....136 D4
Chart Gdns RH5 .....136 C4
Chart Ho 1 CR4 ......40 F4
Chart House Rd GU12 ..106 A7
Chart La Dorking RH4 ..136 C7
Reigate RH2 ....139 C8
Chart La S RH5 ......136 D5
Charta Rd E TW20 ....12 C2
Charta Rd E TW20 ....12 C2
Charta Rd S TW20 ....12 C2
Charta Rd W TW20 ....12 C3
Charter Cres TW4 ....4 E3
Charter Ct KT3 ....38 E6
Charter Ho SM2 ......59 B4
Charter Pl TW18 .....13 A3
Charter Rd KT1 ......38 B6
Charter Sq KT1 ......38 B7
Charterhouse GU7 ...150 C7
Charterhouse Cl RG12 ..27 E4
Charterhouse Rd GU7 150 D6
Charters Cl Ascot SL5 ..29 D4
West Norwood SE19 ..22 B4
Charters Ct GU12 ....126 C8
Charters La SL5 ......29 D4
Charters Rd SL5 .....29 E2
Charters Sch SL5 ....29 D2
Charters Way SL5 ....29 F2
Chartfield Pl KT13 ...53 B5
Chartfield Rd RH2 ...139 C8
Chartham Gr SE27 ...22 B5
Chartham Rd SE25 ...43 B6
Charts Cl GU6 ....174 E2
Chartway RH2 ....118 B3
Chartwell Frimley GU16 ..85 F6
25 Putney SW19 .....19 D7
5 Woking GU22 .....69 E1
Wrecclesham GU9 ...145 F6
Chartwell Cl 2 CR0 ..42 D1
Chartwell Court Grange
RH4 ....136 B4
Chartwell Gdns
Cheam SM3 ....58 E6
Farnborough GU11 ...105 C7
Chartwell Lodge 5 BR3 24 A1
Chartwell Pl Cheam SM3 ..58 F6
Epsom KT18 ....76 E5
Chartwell Way 4 SE20 43 B8
Chartwood Pl 7 RH4 ..136 A7
Charwood SW16 ......22 A4
Charwood Rd RG40 ..25 F7
Chase Bridge Prim Sch
TW2 ....5 E1
Chase Ct Isleworth TW7 ..6 A5
Merton SW20 ....39 E7
Chase End KT19 .....76 D7
Chase Gdns TW2 .....16 D8
Chase La GU27 ......208 D2
Chase Plain GU26 ...188 C1
Chase Rd KT17,KT19 ..76 D7
Chase The Ashstead KT21 75 C1
Coulsdon CR5 ....79 D5
Crawley RH10 ....202 A5
Crowthorne RG45 .....45 A6
East Horsley KT24 ....92 F1
Farnborough GU14 ...85 D6
Guildford GU2 ....130 A8
Kingswood KT20 .....98 B6
Oxshott KT22 ....74 C4
Reigate RH2 ....139 D8
South Norwood SW16 .22 A1
Sunbury TW16 ....35 B8
Wallington SM6 ......60 F5
Chasefield Cl GU4 ...110 A4
Chasefield Rd SW17 ..20 F4
Chaseley Ct KT13 ....34 F1
Chasemore Cl CR4 ...40 F2
Chasemore Gdns CR0 .61 A5
Chaseside Ave SW20 .39 E7
Chaseside Gdns KT16 .33 B2
Chasewater Ct 8 GU11 105 A1
Chatelet Cl RH6 .....161 B4
Chatfield Cl GU14 ....85 C2
Chatfield Ct 3 CR3 ...100 D5
Chatfield Dr GU4 ....110 C3
Chatfield Rd CR0 ....42 B1
Chatfields RH11 .....201 B4
Chatham Ave BR2 ....44 F2
Chatham Cl SM3 .....39 F2
Chatham Rd KT1,KT2 ..38 A7
Chathill RH8 ....143 B6
Chatley Heath Semaphore
Twr ★ KT11 ....72 D1
Chatsfield KT17 ......58 A1
Chatsworth Ave
Haslemere GU27 .....208 C8
Merton SW20 ....39 E7
Chatsworth Cl BR2,BR4 ..63 F8
Chatsworth Cres TW3,TW7 5 D4
Chatsworth Gdns KT3 ..38 F4
Chatsworth Gr GU9 ..125 B6
Chatsworth Ho KT6 ..37 D4
Chatsworth Hts GU15 ..66 B7
Chatsworth Inf Sch TW3 ..5 D4
Chatsworth Jun Sch TW3 5 C4
Chatsworth Lodge BR4 63 C8
Chatsworth Pl
Mitcham CR4 ....40 F6
Oxshott KT22 ....74 D6
Teddington TW11 .....17 A4
Chatsworth Rd
Cheam SM3 ....58 E6
Chiswick W4 ....7 C8

Chatsworth Rd *continued*
Croydon CR0,CR9 . . . . . .61 D7
Farnborough GU14 . . . . . .85 E3
Chatsworth Way SE27 . . . .22 C5
Chattern Hill TW15 . . . . .14 B4
Chattern Rd TW15 . . . . . .14 C4
Chatterton Ct TW9 . . . . . .6 F5
Chatton Row GU24 . . . . . .68 A2
Chaucer Ave Cranford TW4 . .4 B5
3 East Grinstead RH19 . .185 C1
Richmond TW9 . . . . .7 A5
Weybridge KT13 . . . . .53 A3
Chaucer Cl Banstead SM7 . .77 E5
Wokingham RG40 . . . . . . .25 F6
Chaucer Ct
Guildford GU2 . . . . .130 C7
Redhill RH1 . . . . .119 A4
Chaucer Gdns SM1 . . . . . .59 A7
Chaucer Gn CR0 . . . . .43 C2
Chaucer Gr GU15 . . . . . . .65 D5
Chaucer Ho Sutton SM1 . . . .59 A7
2 West Norwood SE27 . . . .22 C4
Chaucer Rd Ashford TW15 . .13 F4
Crawley RH10 . . . . .202 C8
Crowthorne RG45 . . . . . . .45 B4
Farnborough GU14 . . . . . .84 F6
Sutton SM1 . . . . .59 A6
Chaucer Way
Addlestone KT15 . . . . .52 A4
Mitcham SW19 . . . . .20 D2
Chavasse Way GU14 . . . . . .84 D5
Chave Croft KT18 . . . . . . .97 C8
Chave Croft Terr KT18 . . . .97 C8
Chavey Down Rd RG42 . . . . .8 B2
Chaworth Cl KT16 . . . . . . .51 C4
Chaworth Rd KT16 . . . . . . .51 C4
Chawridge La SL4 . . . . .8 C7
Cheam Bracknell RG12 . .27 D4
Burgh Heath KT20 . . . . . .97 B6
Cheam Common Inf Sch
KT4 . . . . .58 B8
Cheam Common Jun Sch
KT4 . . . . .58 B8
Cheam Common Rd KT4 .58 C7
Cheam Court Flats SM3 . .58 E4
Cheam Fields Prim Sch
SM3 . . . . .58 E4
Cheam High Sch SM3 . . .58 E6
Cheam Mans SM3 . . . . . .58 E3
Cheam Park Farm Inf Sch
SM3 . . . . .58 E7
Cheam Park Farm Jun Sch
SM3 . . . . .58 E7
Cheam Park Way SM3 . . .58 E4
Cheam Rd Cheam SM1 . . . .59 A4
East Ewell KT17,SM2 . . . . .58 C1
Cheam Sta SM2 . . . . .58 E3
Cheapside GU21 . . . . .69 D5
Cheapside CE Prim Sch
SL5 . . . . .29 E8
Cheapside Rd SL5 . . . . . . .29 D7
Cheddar Rd TW6 . . . . .3 B5
Cheeseman Cl
Hampton TW12 . . . . .15 E2
Wokingham RG40 . . . . . . .25 D7
Cheetah Rd GU14 . . . . . . .85 B2
Chelford Rd BR1,E6 . . . . . .24 D3
Chellows La RH7 . . . . .143 F2
Chelmsford Cl SM2 . . . . . . .59 A2
Chelsea Cl Hampton TW12 .16 C3
New Malden KT4 . . . . .39 A4
Chelsea Fields SW19 . . . .40 D8
Chelsea Gdns SM3 . . . . . .58 E6
Chelsfield Gdns SE26 . . . .23 C5
Chelsham Common Rd
CR6 . . . . .82 A2
Chelsham Court Rd CR6 .82 E2
Chelsham Rd
Croydon CR2 . . . . .61 D4
Warlingham CR6 . . . . .81 F2
Chelsham Terr CR6 . . . . . .81 F1
Cheltenham Ave TW1 . .17 A8
Cheltenham Cl KT3 . . . . . .38 C6
Cheltenham Villas CR7 . .42 A3
Chelwood Cl
Crawley RH10 . . . . .201 F4
Ewell KT17 . . . . .76 F7
Chelwood Gdns TW9 . . . . . .7 A5
Cheney Cl
Crowthorne RG45 . . . . . . .45 C5
Forest Hill SE23 . . . . .23 D7
Cheniston Cl KT14 . . . . . . .71 A6
Cheniston Ct SL5 . . . . .30 A2
Chennells Way RH12 . . . . .217 A3
Chennestone Com Prim Sch
TW16 . . . . .35 B7
Chepstow Cl RH10 . . . . . .202 E6
Chepstow Rd CR0 . . . . .61 F8
Chequer Grange RH18 . .206 E1
Chequer Rd RH19 . . . . . . .185 F1
Chequer Tree Cl GU21 . . .68 E3
Chequers Cl Horley RH6 . .161 A4
Walton on the Hill KT20 . . . .97 A2
Chequers Ct
7 Croydon CR0 . . . . . . .42 F1
Horsham RH13 . . . . .217 E2
Walton on the Hill KT20 . . .97 A2
Chequers La KT20 . . . . . . .97 A2
Chequers Pl RH4 . . . . . . .136 B7
Cherbury Ct RG12 . . . . .27 E5
Cherimoya Gdns KT8 . . . . .36 A6
Cherington Way SL5 . . . . . .28 E7
Cheriton Ave 3 BR2 . . . .44 F4

Cheriton Ct
South Norwood SE25 . . . . .42 E4
Walton-on-T KT12 . . . . . . .35 C1
Cheriton Sq SW17 . . . . . . .21 A6
Cheriton Way GU17 . . . . . .64 D5
Cherkley Hill KT22,RH5 . . .95 D1
Cherrimans Orch GU27 .207 F6
Cherry Cl Banstead KT17 . .77 D5
Carshalton SM5 . . . . .59 F8
Merton SM4 . . . . .39 E5
5 Streatham SW2 . . . . . .22 A8
Cherry Cres TW8 . . . . .6 B7
Cherry Ct RH13 . . . . .217 D1
Cherry Green Cl RH1 . . . .140 B7
Cherry Hill Gdns CR0 . . . .60 F6
Cherry La RH11 . . . . .181 C1
Cherry Lodge
7 Aldershot GU12 . . . . . .105 B1
Horley RH6 . . . . .161 B2
Cherry Mdws RH11 . . . . . .201 C5
Cherry Orch
Ashstead KT21 . . . . .76 B1
Staines TW18 . . . . .13 A3
Cherry Orchard Gdns
6 Croydon CR0 . . . . . . .61 D8
East Molesey KT8 . . . . . . .35 F6
Cherry Orchard Rd
Croydon CR0 . . . . .42 E1
East Molesey KT8 . . . . . . .36 A6
Cherry St GU21 . . . . .69 E1
Cherry Tree Ave
Guildford GU2 . . . . .108 F1
Haslemere GU27 . . . . . .207 F7
Staines TW18 . . . . .13 B2
Cherry Tree Cl
Crawley RH10 . . . . .202 D8
Farnborough GU14 . . . . . .84 C5
Farnham GU9 . . . . .125 C3
Sandhurst GU47 . . . . .45 D1
Cherry Tree Ct CR5 . . . . . .79 F1
Cherry Tree Dr
Bracknell RG12 . . . . .27 D6
Streatham SW16 . . . . .21 E5
Cherry Tree Gn CR2 . . . . . .81 B5
Cherry Tree La GU7 . . . . .150 D8
Cherry Tree Rd
Milford GU8 . . . . .149 E1
Rowledge GU10 . . . . .145 E3
Cherry Tree Wlk
Beckenham BR3 . . . . .43 F5
Coney Hall BR4 . . . . .63 F6
Horsham RH12 . . . . .218 B6
Rowledge GU10 . . . . .145 E3
Cherry Way Horton SL3 . . . .1 C4
Upper Halliford TW17 . . . . .34 E5
West Ewell KT19 . . . . .57 D4
Cherrydale Rd GU15 . . . . . .66 D5
Cherryhill Gr GU11 . . . . . .104 F1
Cherryhurst GU8 . . . . . . .171 B1
Cherrywood Ave TW20 . . . .11 B1
Cherrywood Cl KT2 . . . . . . .18 A1
Cherrywood Com Prim Sch
GU14 . . . . .85 A6
Cherrywood Ct 1 KT1 . . .17 A3
Cherrywood La SM4,
SW20 . . . . .39 E5
Cherrywood Rd GU14 . . . . .85 B7
Chertsey Bridge Rd KT16,
TW18 . . . . .33 D2
Chertsey Bvd KT16 . . . . . . .32 F1
Chertsey Cl CR8 . . . . .80 B4
Chertsey Cres CR0 . . . . . . .63 C1
Chertsey Ct SW14 . . . . .7 B4
Chertsey Dr SM3 . . . . .58 E8
Chertsey Ho TW13 . . . . . . .16 A5
Chertsey La Egham TW18 . .12 F2
Epsom KT19 . . . . .76 A7
Chertsey Mus ★ KT15 . . . .33 A3
Chertsey Rd
Addlestone KT15 . . . . .52 B8
Ashford TW15 ,TW16 . . . . .14 D2
Burrowhill GU20,GU24 . . . .49 C6
Byfleet KT14 . . . . .71 D8
Chobham GU24,KT16,GU21 .50 D1
Feltham TW13,TW16 . . . . . .14 E4
Feltham,Ashford Common
TW13,TW16 . . . . .14 D2
Lower Halliford TW17 . . . . .34 A2
Shepperton TW17 . . . . . . .33 F2
Twickenham TW2 . . . . .16 D7
Windlesham GU20 . . . . . . .48 E5
Woking GU21 . . . . .69 F3
Chertsey St
Guildford GU1 . . . . .130 D8
Upper Tooting SW17 . . . . . .21 A3
Chertsey Sta KT16 . . . . . . .32 F1
Chervil Cl TW13 . . . . .15 A5
Cherwell Cl SL3 . . . . .1 B8
Cherwell Ct
Teddington KT1 . . . . .17 D1
West Ewell KT19 . . . . .57 C6
Cherwell Wlk RH11 . . . . . .200 F5
Cheselden Rd GU1 . . . . . .130 E8
Cheseman St SE26 . . . . . . .23 B5
Chesfield Rd KT2 . . . . .17 E1
Chesham Cl SM2 . . . . .58 E1
Chesham Cres SE20 . . . . . .43 C8
Chesham Ct
Kingston u T KT6 . . . . .37 D3
Wandsworth SW18 . . . . . . .20 D8
Chesham Mews 14 GU1 .130 F8
Chesham Rd
Guildford GU1 . . . . .130 F8
Kingston u T KT1,KT2 . . . . .38 A7
Penge SE20 . . . . .43 C8
Cheshire Cl
Mitcham CR4,SW16 . . . . . .41 E6

Cheshire Cl *continued*
Ottershaw KT16 . . . . .51 D4
Cheshire Gdns KT9 . . . . . .56 D4
Cheshire Ho Cheam SM4 . .40 B2
Ottershaw KT16 . . . . .51 D4
Chesney Cres CR0 . . . . . . .63 C3
Chessholme Ct TW16 . . . . .14 E1
Chessholme Rd TW15 . . . .14 C2
Chessington Cl KT19 . . . . .57 C4
Chessington Com Coll
KT9 . . . . .56 D3
Chessington Hall Gdns
KT9 . . . . .56 D4
Chessington Hill Pk KT9 .57 A5
Chessington North Sta
KT9 . . . . .56 E5
Chessington Par KT9 . . . .56 D4
Chessington Pk KT9 . . . . .57 A6
Chessington Rd KT19 . . . .57 D3
Chessington South Sta
KT9 . . . . .56 D3
Chessington Way BR4 . . .63 B8
Chessington World of
Adventures ★ KT9 . . . . .56 C1
Chester Ave
Richmond TW10 . . . . .6 F1
Twickenham TW2 . . . . .15 F7
Chester Cl Ash GU12 . . . .106 B2
Ashford TW15 . . . . .14 D3
Dorking RH4 . . . . .115 C1
Guildford GU2 . . . . .108 F3
1 Richmond TW10 . . . . . . .6 F1
Sutton SM1 . . . . .59 A8
Chester Ct 2 Bromley BR2 .44 F5
Dorking RH4 . . . . .115 C1
Chester Gdns SM4 . . . . . . .40 C3
Chester Ho KT1 . . . . .38 B7
Chester Rd Ash GU12 . . . .106 B2
Effingham KT24 . . . . .113 B7
Harlington TW6 . . . . .3 A4
Hounslow TW4 . . . . .4 A4
Wimbledon SW19,SW20 . . .19 C2
Chester Way GU10 . . . . . .126 F6
Chesterblade La RG12 . . . .27 E2
Chesterfield Cl RH19 . . . .184 C4
Chesterfield Ct KT6 . . . . . .37 E4
Chesterfield Dr KT10 . . . . .56 A8
Chesterfield Ho 6 SW16 .21 C3
Chesterfield Rd
Ashford TW15 . . . . .13 E3
Chiswick W4 . . . . .7 C8
West Ewell KT19 . . . . .57 D3
Chesterman Ct 8 W4 . . . . .7 E7
Chesters RH6 . . . . .160 E5
Chesters Rd GU15 . . . . . . .66 B5
Chesters The KT3 . . . . .38 E4
Chesterton Cl RH19 . . . . .205 F7
Chesterton Ct RH13 . . . . .218 A4
Chesterton Dr
Merstham RH1 . . . . .119 E7
Stanwell TW19 . . . . .13 F7
Chesterton Ho 6 SM1 . . .59 C6
Chesterton Terr KT1 . . . . .38 A7
Chestnut Ave
Aldershot GU12 . . . . .126 E8
Camberley GU15 . . . . .66 A6
Coney Hall BR4 . . . . .63 E6
Farnham GU9 . . . . .146 A8
Guildford GU2 . . . . .130 C5
Hampton TW12 . . . . .16 A1
Hampton,Hampton Ct KT8,
KT11 . . . . .36 F7
Haslemere GU27 . . . . . . .208 C2
12 Mortlake SW14 . . . . . . .7 D4
Tatsfield TN16 . . . . .103 E5
Thames Ditton KT10 . . . . . .36 D1
Wentworth GU25 . . . . .30 F5
Weybridge KT13 . . . . .53 C3
Whiteley Village KT12 . . . . .53 E2
Worcester Park KT4 . . . . . .57 E6
Chestnut Cl
Addlestone KT15 . . . . .52 D5
Ashford,Chattern Hill TW15 .14 B4
Ashford,Felthamhill TW16 . .14 C7
Blackwater GU17 . . . . .64 E4
Carshalton SM5 . . . . .40 F1
Catford SE6 . . . . .24 C4
East Grinstead RH19 . . . .186 A1
Englefield Green TW20 . . . .11 C1
Grayshott GU26 . . . . .188 C3
Harlington UB7 . . . . .3 B7
Kingswood KT20 . . . . .98 A4
Redhill RH1 . . . . .140 B7
Send Marsh GU23 . . . . . . .91 A3
West Norwood SW16 . . . . .22 A4
Chestnut Copse RH8 . . . .123 B2
Chestnut Cres KT12 . . . . .53 E2
Chestnut Dr
Aldershot GU12 . . . . .105 D2
Beckenham BR3 . . . . .24 A1
5 Croydon CR0 . . . . . . .61 C6
Farnham GU9 . . . . .125 A2
Feltham TW13 . . . . .15 D3
Horsham RH13 . . . . .217 E2
Hounslow TW3 . . . . .5 A4
Kingston u T KT3 . . . . .38 E6
Chestnut Dr TW20 . . . . . . .11 D2
Chestnut End GU35 . . . . .187 A4
Chestnut Gdns RH12 . . . .217 C5
Chestnut Gr Balham SW12 .21 A7
Isleworth TW7 . . . . .6 A3
Kingston u T KT3 . . . . .38 D6
Mitcham CR4 . . . . .41 D5
Penge SE20 . . . . .23 B1
South Croydon CR2 . . . . . .62 C1
Staines TW18 . . . . .13 C2
Woking GU22 . . . . .89 E7

Chestnut Grove Sch
SW12 . . . . .21 A7
Chestnut Ho
Crowthorne RG45 . . . . . . .45 C5
West Norwood SE27 . . . . . .22 C5
Chestnut La
Chobham GU24 . . . . .49 C4
Weybridge KT13 . . . . .53 B5
Chestnut Manor Cl TW18 13 B4
Chestnut Mead RH1 . . . . .118 E2
Chestnut Pl Dulwich SE26 .22 F4
Ewell KT17 . . . . .77 A8
Ashtead Kt21 . . . . .95 E8
Chestnut Rd
Ashford TW15 . . . . .14 B4
Farnborough GU14 . . . . . .85 A4
Guildford GU1 . . . . .109 D1
Horley RH6 . . . . .161 B5
Kingston u T KT2 . . . . .17 E1
Merton SM20 . . . . .39 D7
Twickenham TW2 . . . . .16 E6
West Norwood SE27 . . . . . .22 C5
Chestnut Way
Bramley GU5 . . . . .152 A4
Feltham TW13 . . . . .15 B5
Godalming GU7 . . . . .150 F2
Chestnut Wlk
Crawley RH11 . . . . .181 C1
Felcourt RH19 . . . . .185 C8
Upper Halliford TW17 . . . . .34 E5
West Byfleet KT14 . . . . . . .71 E7
Whiteley Village KT12 . . . . .53 E2
Chestnuts The
Dulwich SE21 . . . . .22 E7
Horley RH6 . . . . .161 A5
Penge BR3 . . . . .43 D6
Walton-on-T KT12 . . . . . . .54 A8
Cheston Ave CR0 . . . . .43 F1
Chesworth Cl RH13 . . . . .217 C1
Chesworth Cres RH13 . . .217 C1
Chesworth Cty Jun Sch
RH13 . . . . .217 E3
Chesworth Gdns RH13 . . .217 C1
Chesworth La RH12,
RH13 . . . . .217 C1
Chetwode Cl RG40 . . . . . . .25 E6
Chetwode Dr KT20 . . . . . . .77 D1
Chetwode Pl GU11 . . . . . .126 C7
Chetwode Rd
Burgh Heath KT18,KT20 . . .97 C8
Upper Tooting SW17 . . . . . .20 F5
Chetwode Terr GU11 . . . .104 E1
Chevening Cl RH11 . . . . . .201 C1
Chevening Rd SE19 . . . . . .22 D2
Chevington Villas RH1 . . .120 F3
Cheviot Cl Banstead SM7 . .78 B4
Farnborough GU14 . . . . . .84 E7
Frimley GU15 . . . . .66 C4
Harlington UB3 . . . . .3 D7
Sutton SM2 . . . . .59 D2
Cheviot Gdns SE27 . . . . . .22 B4
Cheviot Rd SE27 . . . . .22 B3
Cheviot Wlk RH11 . . . . . . .201 B6
Chevremont GU1 . . . . . . .130 E8
Chewter Cl GU19 . . . . .47 F3
Chewter La GU20 . . . . .48 B6
Cheyham Gdns SM2 . . . . . .58 D1
Cheyham Way SM2 . . . . . . .58 E1
Cheyne Ave TW2 . . . . .15 F7
Cheyne Ct Banstead SM7 . .78 B4
4 Wallington SM6 . . . . . .60 B4
Cheyne Hill KT5 . . . . .37 F5
Cheyne Rd TW15 . . . . .14 D2
Cheyne Way GU14 . . . . . . .84 F8
Cheyne Wlk Croydon CR0 . .62 A8
Horley RH6 . . . . .161 A1
Cheynell Wlk RH11 . . . . . .200 F4
Chichele Gdns CR0 . . . . . .61 E6
Chichele Rd RH8 . . . . .122 E7
Chichely Ct GU14 . . . . .85 B6
Chichester Cl
Crawley RH10 . . . . .201 E2
Dorking RH4 . . . . .115 B1
Hampton TW12 . . . . .15 F2
Witley GU8 . . . . .170 E5
Chichester Ct Ewell KT17 . .57 F2
Stanwell TW19 . . . . .13 E7
Chichester Dr CR8 . . . . . . .79 F7
Chichester Ho KT19 . . . . . .76 A8
Chichester Mews SE27 . . .22 A4
Chichester Rd Ash GU12 106 A3
Dorking RH4 . . . . .115 B2
South Croydon CR0 . . . . . .61 E7
Chichester Terr RH12 . . . .217 D2
Chichester Way TW14 . . . .15 C8
Chiddingfold Rd GU8 . . . .192 C3
Chiddingly Cl RH10 . . . . . .202 B5
Chiddingstone Cl SM2 . . . .59 A1
Chieveley Mews SL5 . . . . .30 A2
Chilberton Dr RH1 . . . . . .119 C5
Chilbolton TW20 . . . . .11 E3
Chilbrook Rd KT11 . . . . . . .73 A1
Chilchester Ct BR3 . . . . . . .44 B6
Chilcombe Ho 7 SW15 . . .19 A8
Chilcroft La GU27 . . . . . . .208 B1
Chilcroft Rd GU27 . . . . . . .207 F7
Chilcrofts Rd GU27 . . . . . .208 A1
Child Cl RG40 . . . . .25 D8
Childebert Rd SW17 . . . . . .21 B6
Childerly KT1 . . . . .38 A6
Childrens Trust (Tadworth
Court) The KT20 . . . . . .97 D6
Childs Hall Cl KT23 . . . . . .93 F2
Childs Hall Dr KT23 . . . . . .93 F2
Childs Hall Rd KT23 . . . . . .93 F2
Childs La 12 SE19 . . . . . . .22 E2

Chilham Cl GU16 . . . . .85 F8
Chillerton Rd SW17 . . . . . .21 A3
Chillingford Ho SW17 . . . . .20 C4
Chillingham Way GU15 . . . .65 C3
Chillingworth Gdns TW1 .16 F5
Chilmark Gdns
Merstham RH1 . . . . .119 E6
New Malden KT3 . . . . .39 A3
Chilmark Rd SW16 . . . . . . .41 D8
Chilmead 1 RH1 . . . . . . .118 E3
Chilmead La RH1 . . . . . . .119 D3
Chilsey Green Rd KT16 . . .32 E2
Chiltern GU22 . . . . .89 C5
Chiltern Ave
Farnborough GU14 . . . . . .84 D4
Twickenham TW2 . . . . .16 A7
Chiltern Cl Crawley RH11 .201 B6
Farnborough GU14 . . . . . .84 D4
Haslemere GU27 . . . . . . .208 B5
North Cheam KT4 . . . . . . .58 C8
South Croydon CR0 . . . . . .61 E7
Staines TW18 . . . . .13 A3
Chiltern Dr KT5 . . . . .38 B4
Chiltern Gdns BR2 . . . . . . .44 F5
Chiltern Rd
Sandhurst GU47 . . . . .45 A1
Sutton SM2 . . . . .59 C1
Chilterns The SM2 . . . . . . .59 B2
Chilthorne Cl SE6 . . . . .23 F8
Chiltington Ct RH12 . . . . .217 D4
Chilton Cl GU6 . . . . .193 C2
Chilton Ct KT12 . . . . .54 A6
Chilton Farm Pk GU14 . . .84 C4
Chilton Rd TW9 . . . . .7 A4
Chiltons Cl SM7 . . . . .78 B4
Chilworth CE Inf Sch
GU4 . . . . .131 D3
Chilworth Ct
8 Putney SW19 . . . . . . .19 D7
13 Redhill RH1 . . . . .118 F2
Chilworth Gdns SM1 . . . . .59 C7
Chilworth Rd GU4,GU5 . .132 A4
Chilworth Sta GU4 . . . . . .131 D3
Chimneys CT SW19 . . . . . .19 C1
China Mews SW2 . . . . .21 F8
Chinchilla Dr TW4 . . . . .4 C5
Chine The GU10 . . . . .145 F5
Chingford Ave GU14 . . . . . .85 D5
Chingley Cl BR1 . . . . .24 E2
Chinthurst La
Shalford GU4, GU5 . . . . . .130 F2
Wonersh GU5 . . . . .152 A7
Chinthurst Pk GU4 . . . . . .130 E1
Chinthurst Sch KT20 . . . . .97 C4
Chippendale Cl GU17 . . . .64 E4
Chippendale Rd RH11 . . . .201 B1
Chippenham 5 KT1 . . . . . .37 F7
Chipstead Ave CR7 . . . . . .42 B5
Chipstead Cl Belmont SM2 59 B2
Coulsdon CR5 . . . . .79 A3
Penge SE19 . . . . .22 F1
Redhill RH1 . . . . .140 A7
Chipstead Ct GU21 . . . . . . .68 E2
Chipstead Ho 4 SW2 . . . . .21 E7
Chipstead La CR5,KT20 . . .98 B3
Chipstead Rd SM7 . . . . . . .78 A2
Chipstead Sta CR5 . . . . . . .78 F1
Chipstead Station Par
CR5 . . . . .78 F1
Chipstead Valley Prim Sch
CR5 . . . . .79 A3
Chipstead Valley Rd CR5 .79 B3
Chipstead Way CR5,SM7 . .78 F3
Chirton Wlk GU21 . . . . .69 A1
Chisbury Cl RG12 . . . . .27 E3
Chisholm Rd Croydon CR0 .61 E8
13 Richmond TW10 . . . . . . .6 F1
Chislehurst Rd TW10 . . . . . .6 E2
Chislet Cl BR3 . . . . .24 A1
Chiswick Cl CR0 . . . . .60 F7
Chiswick Comm Sch W4 . .7 D7
Chiswick Ho ★ W4 . . . . .7 E7
Chiswick La W4 . . . . .7 F8
Chiswick Mall W4 . . . . .7 F8
Chiswick Quay W4 . . . . .7 C6
Chiswick Sq 10 W4 . . . . . . .7 E8
Chiswick Sta W4 . . . . .7 C7
Chiswick Staithe W4 . . . . . .7 C6
Chiswick Village W4 . . . . . . .7 E8
Chiswick Wharf 3 W4 . . . . .7 F8
Chithurst La RH6,RH7 . . .162 F2
Chittenden Cotts GU23 . . .71 E3
Chitterfield Gate UB7 . . . . .3 A7
Chitty's Wlk GU3 . . . . .108 F5
Chive Ct GU14 . . . . .84 C4
Chivelston 27 SW19 . . . . . .19 D7
Chivenor Gr KT2 . . . . .17 D3
Chobham Cl KT16 . . . . .51 B4
Chobham Common (Nature
Reserve) ★ KT16 . . . . . .49 F6
Chobham Gdns SW19 . . . . .19 D6
Chobham La KT16,GU24 . . .50 A8
Chobham Park La GU24 . . .50 B2
Chobham Rd
Chobham GU21 . . . . .69 D7
Frimley GU16 . . . . .66 A2
Knaphill GU21 . . . . .68 D3
Ottershaw KT16 . . . . .51 B4
3 Woking GU21 . . . . .69 F2
Woking,Horsell Common
GU21,GU24 . . . . .69 D5
Chobham St Lawrence CE
Prim Sch GU24 . . . . . . .68 E8
Choir Gn GU21 . . . . .68 E2
Cholmley Rd KT7 . . . . .37 B3
Cholmondeley Wlk TW9 . . .6 C2
Chrislaine Cl TW19 . . . . . . .2 D1

Chr – Cla 237

Chrismas Ave GU12 105 C1
Chrismas Pl GU12 105 C1
Christ Church CE Inf Sch
Kingston u T KT3 38 E6
Virginia Water GU25 31 B6
Christ Church CE Jun Sch
Kingston u T KT3 38 D6
Ottershaw KT16 51 D4
Christ Church CE Prim Sch
Forest Hill SE23 23 D6
Purley CR8 61 B1
Surbiton KT5 38 A3
Christ Church Mount
KT19 76 B7
Christ Church Rd
1 Beckenham BR3 44 A7
Epsom KT18 76 A6
Surbiton KT5 37 F3
Christ Church Streatham CE Prim Sch SW2 21 F7
Christ the King RC Prim Sch
TW19 2 E1
Christ's Sch (East Side)
TW10 7 A2
Christ's Sch (West Side)
TW10 6 F2
Christabel Cl TW7 5 E4
Christchurch Ave 5
TW11 17 A3
Christchurch Cl SW19 20 D1
Christchurch Cotts GU25 31 B6
Christchurch Dr GU47 64 D6
Christchurch Gdns KT19 76 B8
Christchurch Ho 2 SW2 21 E7
Christchurch Hts 9
RH2 118 F1
Christchurch Pk SM2 59 C3
Christchurch Pl KT19 76 B8
Christchurch Rd
Harlington TW6 3 A4
Mitcham SW19 20 D1
Mortlake SW14 7 C2
Purley CR8 80 B8
Streatham SW2 21 F7
Virginia Water GU25 31 C5
Christchurch Way 5
GU21 69 F2
Christian Fields SW16 22 A1
Christie Cl Guildford GU1 109 D4
Lightwater GU18 48 C1
Little Bookham KT23 93 F3
Christie Dr SE25 43 A4
Christie Ho 4 BR4 44 B1
Christie Wlk 4 CR3 100 D5
Christies RH19 205 D8
Christine Cl GU12 105 F1
Christmas Hill GU4 130 F2
Christmaspie Ave GU3 107 B1
Christopher Ct
Ashford TW15 13 E3
6 Croydon CR0 43 A1
Tadworth KT20 97 C4
Christopher Rd RH19 185 E1
Christy Est GU12 105 E2
Christy Rd TN16 83 C4
Chrystie La KT23 94 B1
Chuck's La KT20 97 B3
Chudleigh Ct 4 GU14 85 B4
Chudleigh Gdns SM1 59 C7
Chudleigh Rd TW2 16 F8
Chulsa Rd SE26 23 B3
Chumleigh Wlk KT5 37 F5
Church Almshouses 8
TW9 6 F3
Church App Dulwich SE21 22 D5
Thorpe TW20 32 C6
Church Ave
Beckenham BR3 44 A8
Farnborough GU14 85 C3
Mortlake SW14 7 D4
Church Circ GU14 85 C1
Church Cl Addlestone KT15 52 B6
6 Epsom KT17 76 E6
Fetcham KT22 94 D3
Grayswood GU27 189 F2
Hounslow TW4 4 F5
Laleham TW18 33 C6
Lower Kingswood KT20 117 F8
Milford GU8 149 F1
Pirbright GU24 87 F6
Woking GU21 69 E3
Church Cotts
Aldershot GU9 126 B6
Effingham KT24 113 D8
Church Ct Forest Hill SE26 23 E3
Great Bookham KT23 94 A2
Reigate RH2 118 B1
Church Dr BR4 63 E7
Church Farm La SM3 58 E4
Church Field Ho KT11 73 B5
Church Gdns
Dorking RH4 136 B8
Leatherhead KT22 95 B7
Church Gn Dunsfold GU8 192 D5
Elstead GU8 148 C3
Hersham KT12 54 C4
Church Gr KT1 37 C7
Church Hill
Aldershot GU11,GU12 126 C8
Camberley GU15 65 E5
Caterham CR3 100 F3
Merstham RH1 99 B1
Nutfield RH1 119 F2
Purley CR8 60 E1
Shamley Green GU5 152 E4
Shere GU5 133 A4
Tatsfield TN16 103 D5
Wallington SM5 59 F5
Church Hill *continued*
Wimbledon SW19 19 F3
Woking GU21 69 D3
Church Hill Rd
Cheam SM1,SM3 58 E6
Kingston u T KT6 37 E4
Church Ho KT23 94 A2
Church La Albury GU5 132 C4
Ascot SL5 29 D5
Ash GU12 106 B2
Binstead GU10 145 E3
Bisley GU21,GU24 68 A4
Bletchingley RH1 120 D3
Broadbridge Heath RH12 216 D3
Brook GU8 190 C8
Burgh Heath KT18,SM7 77 E2
Burstow RH6 182 F7
Caterham CR3 100 A3
Chelsham CR6 82 C3
Chessington KT9 56 F4
Copthorne RH10 183 B3
Cranleigh GU6 174 E3
Crawley RH10 201 F6
Crondall GU10 124 D8
East Grinstead RH19 185 F1
Farnborough GU14 84 E4
Godstone RH9 121 D3
Grayshott GU26 188 C3
Hambledon GU8 171 D2
Haslemere GU27 208 D7
Headley KT18 96 C2
Hooley CR5 99 B5
Merton SW19 39 F8
Newdigate RH5 158 C1
Oxted RH8 122 E6
Pirbright GU24 87 D4
Send GU23 90 C1
Shere GU5 133 A4
Sunningdale SL5 30 B4
Teddington TW11 16 F3
Thames Ditton KT7 37 A3
Twickenham TW1 17 A7
Upper Tooting SW17 21 A3
Upper Tooting,Furzedown
SW17 21 B4
Wallington SM6 60 D7
Wallis Wood RH5 176 F1
Warlingham CR6 81 D2
Weybridge KT13 53 A6
Witley GU8 170 E2
Worplesdon GU3 108 E8
Wrecclesham GU10 145 F7
Church La E GU11 126 B8
Church La W GU11 105 A1
Church Lane Ave CR5 99 B5
Church Lane Dr CR5 99 B5
Church Mdw KT6 56 C8
Church Mews KT15 52 C6
Church Paddock Ct SM6 60 D7
Church Par TW15 13 F4
Church Pas 16 GU9 125 B2
Church Path Ash GU12 106 A3
Farnborough GU14 105 C8
Merton SW19 40 A7
Mitcham CR4 40 E6
9 Woking GU21 69 F2
Church Pk RH11 181 E5
Church Pl CR4 40 E6
Church Rd
Addlestone KT15 52 B5
Aldershot GU11 126 C8
Ascot SL5 29 A5
Ashford TW15 13 F4
Ashstead KT21 75 D1
Bagshot GU19 47 D3
Barnes SW13 7 F5
Beckenham BR2 44 E6
Biggin Hill TN16 83 E2
Bracknell RG12 27 C7
Broadbridge Heath RH12 216 D3
Burstow RH6 183 A7
Byfleet KT14 71 E6
Caterham CR3 100 F3
Cheam SM3 58 E4
Claygate KT10 55 F3
Copthorne RH10 183 B3
Cranford TW5 4 B8
Crawley, Lowfield Heath
RH11 181 E5
Crawley, Worth RH10 202 E6
Croydon CR0,CR9 61 C7
Dunsfold GU8 192 D5
East Molesey KT8 36 D6
Egham TW20 12 A3
Epsom KT17 76 E6
Feltham TW13 15 D3
Fetcham KT23 94 A3
Frimley GU16 65 D1
Guildford GU1 130 D8
Hascombe GU8 172 E4
Haslemere GU27 208 C7
Haslemere,Shottermill
GU27 207 F6
Heston TW5 5 A7
Horley RH6 160 F2
Horley RH6 161 A3
Horne RH6 162 F5
Horsham RH12 218 B5
Hounslow TW7 5 E7
Kenley CR8 80 D4
Kingston u T KT1 37 F7
Leatherhead KT22 95 B5
Leigh RH2 138 A2
Lingfield RH7 164 D4
Little Bookham KT23 93 F4
Long Ditton KT6 37 C1
Lower Halliford TW17 34 B2
Milford GU8 149 F1
Church Rd *continued*
Mitcham CR4,SW19 40 D7
New Malden KT4 38 E1
Newdigate RH5 158 B1
Purley CR8 60 E1
Redhill RH1 139 E7
Richmond TW10,TW9 6 E2
Richmond, Ham Common
TW10 17 E4
Sandhurst GU15 64 F7
Sandhurst,Owlsmoor GU47 45 E1
South Norwood SE19 22 E1
Sunningdale SL5 30 A3
Teddington TW11 16 F3
Turners Hill RH10 204 A3
Wallington SM6 60 D7
Warlingham CR6 81 D2
West End GU24 67 F7
West Ewell KT19 57 D3
Whyteleafe CR3 100 F8
Wimbledon SW19 19 E4
Windlesham GU20 48 C4
Winkfield SL4 8 C5
Winkfield,Chavey Down SL5 28 B8
Woking,Horsell GU21 69 E4
Woking,St John's GU21 89 A8
Woldingham CR3 101 E4
Church Rd E
Crowthorne RG45 45 B5
Farnborough GU14 85 D2
Church Rd W GU14 85 C1
Church Rise
Chessington KT9 56 F4
Forest Hill SE23 23 D6
Church Row GU23 91 C6
Church Side Epsom KT18 76 B6
Gatton RH2 118 F6
Church Sq TW17 34 B2
Church St
Aldershot GU11 104 F2
Betchworth RH3 137 E8
Chiswick W4 7 F8
Cobham KT11 73 B4
Crawley RH11 201 C6
Crowthorne RG45 45 B4
Croydon CR0,CR9 61 C8
Dorking RH4 136 A7
Effingham KT24 113 D8
Epsom KT17,KT18 76 E6
Esher KT10 55 B6
Ewell KT17 58 A2
Godalming GU7 150 D4
Hampton TW12 36 C8
Isleworth TW7 6 B5
Kingston u T KT1 37 D7
Leatherhead KT22 95 B5
Old Woking GU22 90 C6
Reigate RH2 118 B1
Rudgwick RH12 214 E8
Rudgwick,Cox Green RH12 195 E1
Staines TW18 12 E4
Sunbury TW16 35 B6
Twickenham TW1 17 A7
Walton-on-T KT12 35 A2
Warnham RH12 216 F8
Weybridge KT13 53 A6
Church St E GU21 69 F2
Church St W GU21 69 E2
Church Street Sta CR0,
CR9 61 C8
Church Stretton Rd TW3 5 C2
Church Terr
20 Richmond TW10 6 D2
South Holmwood RH5 157 C6
Church Vale SE23 23 D6
Church View GU12 106 A2
Church View Cl RH6 160 F2
Church Villa TW16 35 B6
Church Way Oxted RH8 122 F3
South Croydon CR2 81 A8
Church Wlk
Bletchingley RH1 120 D2
Brentford TW8 6 C8
Caterham CR3 101 A3
Chertsey KT16 33 A3
Crawley RH10 201 D6
Horley RH6 160 F2
Leatherhead KT22 95 B5
Mitcham SW16 41 C7
Reigate RH2 118 C1
15 Richmond TW10 6 D2
Thames Ditton KT7 36 F3
Walton-on-T KT12 35 A1
West Barnes SW20 39 C6
Weybridge KT13 53 B8
Churchcroft Cl SW12 21 A8
Churchdale GU12 105 B1
Churchdown BR1 24 E4
Churchfield Rd
Reigate RH2 117 F2
Walton-on-T KT12 35 A1
Weybridge KT13 53 A6
Churchfields
East Molesey KT8 36 A6
Guildford GU4 110 A6
Witley GU8 170 E4
Woking GU21 69 E3
Churchfields Ave
Feltham TW13 16 A5
Weybridge KT13 53 B6
Churchfields Prim Sch
BR3 43 D6
Churchfields Rd BR3 43 E7
Churchill Ave
Aldershot GU12 126 C8
Horsham RH12 217 B3
Churchill Cl
East Bedfont TW14 14 F7
Churchill Cl *continued*
Farnborough GU14 85 B8
Fetcham KT22 94 E4
Warlingham CR6 81 D2
Churchill Cres GU14 85 B8
Churchill Ct
Crawley RH10 182 A1
Staines TW18 13 C2
Churchill Dr KT13 53 C6
Churchill Ho SM7 77 F4
Churchill Rd Epsom KT19 76 A8
Guildford GU1 130 F8
North Ascot SL5 28 F7
Smallfield RH6 162 B3
South Croydon CR2 61 C3
Churchill Way
Ashford TW16 15 A2
Biggin Hill TN16 83 D4
Churchley Rd SE26 23 B4
Churchley Villas SE26 23 B4
Churchmore Rd SW16 41 D8
Churchside Cl TN16 83 C2
Churchview Rd TW2 16 D6
Churston Cl 17 SW2 22 A7
Churston Dr SM4 39 E4
Churstonville Ct BR3 44 B6
Churt Rd
Beacon Hill GU26 188 C6
Headley Down GU10,GU35 187 C8
Churt Wynde GU26 188 D7
Churton Pl W4 7 B8
Chuters Cl KT14 71 F7
Chuters Gr KT17 76 F7
Cibber Rd SE23 23 D6
Cinder Path GU22 89 C8
Cinderford Way BR1 24 E4
Cinnamon Cl CR0 41 E2
Cinnamon Gdns GU2 109 A6
Cintra Ct SE19 22 F2
Cintra Pk SE19 22 F1
Circle Gdns Byfleet KT14 71 F6
Merton SW19 40 A7
Circle Hill Rd RG45 45 C5
Circle Rd KT12 53 E2
Circle The GU7 150 F6
Circuit Ctr KT13 71 E8
Circus The KT22 95 B7
Cissbury Cl RH12 218 A6
Cissbury Hill RH11 201 C4
Cissbury Ho 6 SE26 23 A5
City Bsns Ctr RH13 217 D1
City of London Freemen's Sch KT21 96 A8
City Prospect 6 SE19 22 E2
City Wharf Ho KT7 37 B3
Clacket La TN16 103 E2
Claire Ct Beckenham BR3 44 B6
Walton-on-T KT12 54 C7
Clairvale Rd TW5 4 E6
Clairview Rd SW16,SW17 21 B4
Clairville Ct 1 RH2 118 D1
Clairville Point 12 SE23 23 D5
Clammer Hill GU27 189 F1
Clandon Ave TW20 12 C1
Clandon CE Inf Sch
GU4 111 A4
Clandon Cl KT17 58 A4
Clandon Ct GU14 85 D3
Clandon Ho
Guildford GU1 130 F7
12 Kingston u T KT2 18 B2
Clandon Mews RH4 136 B4
Clandon Pk★ GU4 111 A3
Clandon Rd
Guildford GU1 130 E8
Send Marsh GU4,GU23 91 A1
West Clandon GU4,GU23 111 A8
Clanfield Ho 12 SW15 19 A7
Clanfield Ride GU17 64 D5
Clappers Gate RH10 201 D7
Clappers La GU24 68 D8
Clappers Mdw GU6 194 A3
Clare Ave RG40 25 C7
Clare Cl Crawley RH10 182 C1
West Byfleet KT14 71 A6
Clare Cotts RH1 120 B3
Clare Cres KT22 75 B1
Clare Ct Wimbledon SW19 19 E2
Wokingham RG40 25 C7
Woldingham CR3 102 A4
Clare Gdns TW20 12 A3
Clare Hill KT10 55 B5
Clare Hill (No 1) KT10 55 B5
Clare Hill (No 2) KT10 55 B5
Clare House Prim Sch
BR3 44 C7
Clare Lawn Ave SW14 7 D2
Clare Mead GU10 145 F4
Clare Park Hospl GU10 124 B4
Clare Rd Hounslow TW4 4 F4
Stanwell TW19 13 E8
Clare Wood KT22 75 B1
Claredale GU22 89 E8
Claredale Ct SM2 59 C3
Clarefield Ct SL5 30 A2
Claremont TW17 34 B3
Claremont Ave
Camberley GU15 65 F5
Esher KT10 54 F4
Hersham KT12 54 D6
Sunbury TW16 35 B8
West Barnes KT3 39 B4
Woking GU22 89 E8
Claremont Cl
Hamsey Green CR2 81 B4
Hersham KT12 54 D5
4 Streatham SW2 21 F7
Claremont Ct
Dorking RH4 136 B6
11 Kingston u T KT6 37 E3
Claremont Dr Esher KT10 55 B4
Shepperton TW17 34 B3
Woking GU22 89 E8
Claremont End KT10 55 B4
Claremont Fan Court Sch
KT10 55 A3
Claremont Gdns KT6 37 E4
Claremont Gr 10 W4 7 E7
Claremont Ho 7 SM2 59 A3
Claremont La KT10 55 B5
Claremont Landscape Gdn★
KT10 54 F3
Claremont Park Rd KT10 55 B4
Claremont Rd
Claygate KT10 55 E3
Croydon CR0 43 A1
Egham TW18 12 D3
Kingston u T KT6 37 E4
Redhill RH1 119 A4
Teddington TW11 16 F4
Twickenham TW1 6 C1
West Byfleet KT14 71 A7
Claremont Terr KT7 37 B2
Claremount Cl KT18 77 C2
Claremount Gdns KT18 77 D2
Clarence Ave
Kingston u T KT3 38 D7
Streatham SW4 21 D8
Clarence Cl
Aldershot GU12 105 D2
Hersham KT12 54 B6
Clarence Ct RH6 161 D4
Clarence Dr
Camberley GU15 66 B7
2 East Grinstead RH19 205 F7
Englefield Green TW20 11 C4
Clarence Ho KT12 54 B5
Clarence La SW15 7 F1
Clarence Mews 1 SW12 21 B8
Clarence Rd
Biggin Hill TN16 83 F1
Hersham KT12 54 B6
Horsham RH13 217 E1
Reigate RH1 139 D6
Richmond TW9 7 A6
Sutton SM1 59 B5
Teddington TW11 17 A2
Thornton Heath CR0 42 D2
Wallington SM6 60 B5
Wimbledon SW19 20 B2
Clarence St Egham TW20 11 F2
Kingston u T KT1,KT2 37 E7
4 Richmond TW9 6 E3
Staines TW18 12 E4
Clarence Terr TW3 5 B3
Clarence Way RH6 161 D4
Clarence Wlk RH1 139 D6
Clarendon Cres TW2 16 D5
Clarendon Ct
Blackwater GU17 64 D3
1 Richmond TW9 7 A6
Clarendon Gate KT16 51 D4
Clarendon Gr CR4 40 F6
Clarendon Mews KT21 95 F8
Clarendon Prim Sch
TW15 13 F4
Clarendon Rd
Ashford TW15 13 F4
Croydon CR0,CR9 61 B8
Mitcham SW19 20 E1
Redhill RH1 118 F2
Wallington SM6 60 C4
Clarendon Sch TW12 16 B2
Clarens St SE6 23 F6
Clares The CR3 101 A3
Claret Gdns SE25 42 E5
Clareville Rd CR3 101 A3
Clarewood Dr GU15 65 E6
Clarice Way SM6 60 E2
Claridge Gdns RH7 165 A2
Claridges Mead RH7 165 A2
Clark Rd RH11 201 A1
Clark Way TW5 4 D7
Clarke Cres GU15 64 E7
Clarke Pl GU6 173 F2
Clarke's Ave KT4,SM3 58 D8
Clarks Hill GU10 124 D1
Clarks La CR6,RH8,TN16 103 C4
Claudia Pl SW19 19 E7
Claver Dr SL5 29 D5
Claverdale Rd SW2 22 A8
Claverdon RG12 27 A2
Clavering Cl TW1 17 A4
Claverton KT21 75 E2
Clay Ave CR4 41 B7
Clay Cnr KT15 33 B1
Clay Hall La RH10 183 C4
Clay Hill Ho GU27 208 A6
Clay La
Guildford, Jacobswell GU4 109 E7
Guildford,Burpham GU4 110 A5
Headley KT18 96 B3
Horne RH7 163 D3
South Nutfield RH1 140 D7
Wokingham RG40 25 F5
Claycart Rd
Aldershot GU11 104 D4
Aldershot GU11 104 E3
Claydon Ct TW18 13 A4
Claydon Dr CR0 60 E6
Claydon Gdns GU17 65 A1
Claydon Rd GU21 69 A3

Clayford RH7 ....165 B2
Claygate Cl SM1 ....59 C7
Claygate Cres CR0 .....63 D4
Claygate La
  Hinchley Wood KT10 ....56 A8
  Thames Ditton KT7 ......37 A1
Claygate Lodge Cl KT10 .55 E3
Claygate Prim Sch KT10 .55 E3
Claygate Sta KT10 .....55 E4
Clayhall Ho 3 RH2 ...118 A2
Clayhall La RH2 ....138 E4
Clayhanger GU4 ....110 C3
Clayhill Cl Bracknell RG12 .28 A6
  Leigh RH2 ....138 A2
Clayhill Rd RH2 ....137 F1
Claylands Cl SE19 .....22 D3
Claymore Cl SM3,SM4 ...40 C2
Claypole Dr TW5 ....4 C6
Clays Cl RH19 ....205 E8
Clayton Dr GU2 ....108 F4
Clayton Gr RG12 ....27 E8
Clayton Hill RH11 .....201 C4
Clayton Ho KT7 ....37 B1
Clayton Mead RH9 .....121 B4
Clayton Rd
  Chessington KT10,KT9 ...56 D6
  Ewell KT17 ....76 E6
  Farnborough GU14 ....64 F1
  Isleworth TW7 ....5 E4
Clear Water Pl KT6 .....37 C3
Cleardene RH4 ....136 B7
Cleardown GU22 ....70 B1
Clears Cotts RH2 ......117 E3
Clears The RH2 ....117 E3
Clearsprings GU18 ......67 A8
Cleave Prior CR5 ....98 E8
Cleave's Almshouses 1
  KT2 ....37 E7
Cleaveland Rd KT6 ......37 D4
Cleaverholme Cl SE25 ...43 B3
Cleeve Ct TW14 ....14 E7
Cleeve Hill SE23 ....23 B7
Cleeve Ho RG12 ....27 E5
Cleeve Rd KT22 ....95 A7
Cleeve The GU1 ....110 A1
Cleeve Way SW15 ....18 F8
Cleeves Ct 6 RH1 .....119 A2
Clement Cl CR8 ....80 B3
Clement Rd Penge BR3 ...43 D7
  Wimbledon SW19 ....19 E3
Clements Ct TW4 ....4 D3
Clements Ho KT22 ....95 A8
Clements Mead KT22 ....95 A8
Clements Rd KT12 ....54 B8
Clensham Ct SM3 ....59 A8
Clensham La SM1 ....59 A8
Clerics Wlk TW17 ....34 D3
Clerks Croft RH1 ......120 D2
Cleve Ct GU21 ....68 D2
Clevedon KT13 ....53 D5
Clevedon Ct
  Farnborough GU14 ....85 D3
  Frimley GU16 ....86 A8
  West Norwood SE21 .....22 D5
Clevedon Gdns TW5 ......4 B6
Clevedon Ho 7 SM1 .....59 C6
Clevedon Rd
  Kingston u T KT1 ....38 A7
  Penge SE20 ....43 D8
  Twickenham TW1 ....6 D1
Clevehurst KT13 ....53 D5
Cleveland Ave
  Hampton TW12 ....15 F1
  Merton SW20 ....39 F7
Cleveland Cl KT12 ......54 B7
Cleveland Dr TW18 ......33 B8
Cleveland Gdns
  Barnes SW13 ....7 F5
  Worcester Park KT4 .....57 F8
Cleveland Pk TW19 ......2 E1
Cleveland Pl GU7 ......150 E2
Cleveland Rd Barnes SW13 .7 F5
  Isleworth TW7 ....6 A3
  New Malden KT3 ....38 E5
  Worcester Park KT4 .....57 E8
Cleveland Rise SM4 .....39 D2
Cleves Ave KT17 ....58 B2
Cleves Cl KT11 ....73 B5
Cleves Cres CR0 ....82 C8
Cleves Ct Epsom KT17 ...76 F7
  Kingston u T KT6 ....37 E3
Cleves Rd TW10 ....17 C5
Cleves Sch KT13 ....53 F6
Cleves Way Ashford TW16 .14 F2
  Hampton TW12 ....15 F1
Cleves Wood KT13 ......53 E6
Clewborough Dr GU15 ...66 B6
Clewborough House Prep
  Sch GU16 ....65 F1
Clewborough House Sch
  GU16 ....86 B5
Clews La GU24 ....68 B3
Clifden Centre (Richmond
  Adult & Community Coll)
  TW1 ....16 F7
Clifden Ho 7 TW8 ....6 D8
Clifden Rd Brentford TW8 .6 D8
  Twickenham TW1 ....16 F7
Cliff End CR8 ....80 B7
Cliffe Rd Croydon CR2 ...61 D5
  Godalming GU7 ....150 C2
Cliffe Rise GU7 ....150 C3
Cliffe Wlk 2 SM1 ......59 C5

Clifford Ave
  Mortlake SW14,TW10,TW9 ..7 B4
  Wallington SM6 ....60 C6
Clifford Ct SW18 ....20 D8
Clifford Gr TW15 ....14 A4
Clifford Ho BR3 ....24 B2
Clifford Manor Rd GU4 .130 E5
Clifford Rd Croydon SE25 .43 A5
  Hounslow TW4 ....4 D4
  Richmond TW10 ....17 D6
  Sutton SM2 ....78 B8
Clifton Ave Feltham TW13 .15 C5
Clifton Cl Caterham CR3 .100 D4
  Chertsey KT15 ....52 B8
  Horley RH6 ....161 D3
  Rowledge GU10 ....146 A4
Clifton Ct
  2 Beckenham BR3 ....44 B8
  South Norwood SE25 ....42 E4
  8 Stanwell TW19 ....2 E1
Clifton Gdns GU16 ......85 F6
Clifton Hill Sch CR3 ..100 D4
Clifton Lodge (Brunel Univ
  Coll Twickenham Campus)
  TW1 ....6 B2
Clifton Mews SE25 ......42 E5
Clifton Par TW13 ....15 C4
Clifton Park Ave SW20 ..39 C7
Clifton Pl SM7 ....78 A4
Clifton Rd Coulsdon CR5 .79 C4
  Crawley RH10 ....202 C5
  Crawley RH10 ....202 C5
  Harlington TW6 ....3 B4
  Hounslow TW7 ....5 E5
  Kingston u T KT2 ....37 F8
  South Norwood SE25 ....42 E5
  Teddington TW11 ....16 E4
  Wallington SM6 ....60 B5
  Wimbledon SW19 ....19 D2
  Wokingham RG41 ....25 A8
Clifton Terr RH4 ......136 B6
Cliftons La RH2 ....117 D2
Cliftonville RH4 ......136 B6
Climping Rd RH11 ......201 B8
Cline Rd GU1 ....130 F7
Clinton Ave KT8 ....36 C5
Clinton Cl Knaphill GU21 .68 D1
  Weybridge KT13 ....53 B8
Clinton Hill RH7 ......186 A8
Clinton Ho
  New Malden KT3 ....38 D1
  6 Surbiton KT6 ....37 D2
Clinton Rd KT22 ....95 C4
Clinton Terr SM1 ....59 C6
Clintons Gn RG42 ....27 A8
Clippesby Cl KT9 ....56 F4
Clipstone Rd TW3 ....5 A4
Clitherow Gdns RH10 ...201 E5
Clive Ct Streatham SW16 .21 D3
  Tolworth KT6 ....57 A8
Clive Gn RG12 ....27 B4
Clive Ho 3 Croydon CR0 .42 F1
  Redhill RH1 ....118 E3
Clive Rd Aldershot GU12 .105 C1
  Esher KT10 ....55 B6
  Feltham TW14 ....4 A1
  Mitcham SW19 ....20 E2
  Teddington TW11 ....17 A4
  West Norwood SE21, SE27 .22 D5
Clive Way RH10 ....202 C6
Cliveden Pl TW17 ....34 C3
Cliveden Rd SW19 ....39 F8
Clivedon Ho KT4 ....58 A8
Clock Barn La GU8 .....171 F6
Clock House Apartments
  GU8 ....171 B3
Clock House Cl KT14 ....71 F7
Clock House Cotts
  Capel RH5 ....178 C2
  Enton Green GU8 ......171 B3
Clock House Ct BR3 .....43 E7
Clock House Mead KT11 .74 B5
Clock House Rd BR3 .....43 E7
Clock House Sta BR3 ....43 E8
Clock Tower Rd TW7 ......5 F4
Clockhouse Cl SW19 .....19 C6
Clockhouse Ct GU1 .....109 C5
Clockhouse La
  Ashford TW14,TW15 .....14 B5
  Bramley GU5 ....151 F2
  East Bedfont TW14,TW15 .14 B5
Clockhouse La E TW20 ...12 B1
Clockhouse La W TW20 ...12 A1
Clockhouse Rd GU14 .....85 B4
Clodhouse Hill GU22 ....88 D5
Cloister Cl TW11 ....17 B3
Cloister Gdns SE25 .....43 B3
Cloisters The
  Frimley GU16 ....65 D1
  Old Woking GU22 ....90 B6
Clone The 5 KT2 ....18 B1
Clonmel Rd TW11 ....16 D4
Clonmore St SW18 ....19 F7
Close The Beckenham BR3 .43 E5
  Bracknell RG12 ....27 C5
  Brockham RH3 ....137 B5
  Cheam SM3 ....39 F2
  Croydon SE25 ....43 A3
  East Grinstead RH19 ..205 D8
  Esher KT10 ....55 B3
  Farnham GU9 ....125 D1
  Godalming GU7 ....150 F3
  Horley RH6 ....161 D1
  Hounslow TW7 ....5 D5
  Ifold RH14 ....212 D3
  Kingston u T KT3 ....38 C7

Close The continued
  Lightwater GU18 ....48 A1
  Mitcham CR4 ....40 F5
  Mortlake TW9 ....7 B4
  North Ascot SL5 ....28 D7
  Purley CR8 ....61 B1
  Purley, Russell Hill CR8 .60 F1
  Reigate RH2 ....139 B8
  Sandhurst GU47 ....64 E8
  Surbiton KT6 ....37 E3
  Virginia Water GU25 ...31 A4
  Wallington SM5 ....59 E2
  West Byfleet KT14 .....71 A6
  Woking GU22 ....70 B2
  Wonersh GU5 ....152 B7
Closeworth Rd GU14 ...105 E8
Cloudesdale Rd SW17 ....21 B6
Clouston Cl SM6 ....60 E5
Clouston Rd GU14 ....84 F5
Clovelly Ave CR6 ......101 B8
Clovelly Ct KT17 ....76 F6
Clovelly Dr GU26 ......188 D7
Clovelly Pk GU26 ......188 C7
Clovelly Rd
  Beacon Hill GU26 .....188 C7
  Hounslow TW3 ....5 B5
Clover Cl RG40 ....25 E7
Clover Ct GU22 ....89 D8
Clover Field RH12 .....215 D3
Clover Hill CR5 ....99 B6
Clover Ho TW3 ....5 C6
Clover Lea GU7 ....150 E8
Clover Rd GU2 ....108 E2
Clover Way
  Carshalton CR4 ....41 A1
  Smallfield RH6 ....162 C3
Cloverfields RH6 ......161 B4
Cloverlands RH10 ......201 F8
Clovers Cotts RH12 ....199 F1
Clovers End RH12 ......218 A5
Clovers Way RH12 ......218 D7
Clowders Rd SE6 ....23 F5
Clowser Cl 6 SM1 ......59 C5
Club La RG45 ....45 D5
Club Row GU24 ....87 D8
Clubhouse Rd GU11 ....104 F5
Clump Ave KT20 ....116 C4
Clumps Rd GU10 ....146 E4
Clumps The TW15 ....14 D4
Clyde Ave CR2 ....81 B4
Clyde Cl RH1 ....119 A2
Clyde Ct Aldershot GU12 .126 E8
  Redhill RH1 ....119 A2
Clyde Ho 3 KT2 ....37 D8
Clyde Rd Croydon CR0 ...61 F8
  Stanwell TW19 ....13 E7
  Sutton SM1 ....59 A5
  Wallington SM6 ....60 C4
Clyde Terr SE23 ....23 C6
Clyde Vale SE23 ....23 C6
Clydesdale Cl TW7 ....5 F4
Clydesdale Gdns TW10 ...7 B3
Clymping Dene TW14 ....15 B8
Clytha SE27 ....22 C4
Clyve Way TW18 ....32 E8
Coach House Cl GU16 ....65 E3
Coach House La SW19 ...19 D5
Coach House Mews
  RH1 ....139 F8
Coach Rd Brockham RH3 .137 A7
  Brockham,Pixham RH4 ..115 E1
  Crawley, North Terminal
  RH6 ....181 F8
  Crawley, South Terminal
  RH6 ....182 B7
  North Ascot SL5 ....8 E1
  Ottershaw KT16 ....51 C4
Coachlads Ave 3 GU2 ..108 F1
Coachmans Dr
  Crawley RH11 ....201 B2
  Sandhurst GU47 ....64 B7
Coalbrook Mans 4
  SW12 ....21 B7
Coaldale Wlk SE21 ......22 C8
Coast Hill RH4,RH5 ....134 F4
Coast Hill La RH4 .....135 A5
Coates Wlk 15 TW8 ......6 E8
Coatham Pl GU6 ....174 F3
Cob Cl RH10 ....204 C8
Cob Wlk RH11 ....201 A6
Cobb's Rd TW4 ....4 F3
Cobbets Ridge GU10 ...147 C8
Cobbett Cl RH10 ....202 C8
Cobbett Hill Rd GU3 ...107 E7
Cobbett Rd
  Guildford GU2 ....108 F2
  Twickenham TW2 ....16 A7
Cobbetts Cl GU21 ....69 B2
Cobbetts Farm GU24 ....68 A8
Cobbetts Hill KT13 .....53 B3
Cobbetts Mews 11 GU9 .125 B2
Cobbetts Way GU9 .....145 F6
Cobbetts Wlk GU24 .....68 A4
Cobbler's The RH12 ....215 D3
Cobbles Cres RH10 .....201 E7
Cobbsthorpe Villas SE26 .23 D4
Cobden La GU27 ....208 D7
Cobden Mews SE26 ......23 B3
Cobden Rd SE25 ....43 A4
Cobham Ave KT3 ....39 A4
Cobham Bus Mus * KT11 .72 B7
Cobham Cl SM6 ....60 E4
Cobham Cottage Hospl
  KT11 ....73 B6
Cobham Ct CR4 ....40 D7

Cobham Gate KT11 ......73 B5
Cobham Park Rd KT11 ...73 C2
Cobham Rd
  Fetcham KT11,KT22 .....94 C6
  Heston TW5 ....4 C7
  Kingston u T KT1,KT2 ...38 A7
Cobham Way
  Crawley RH10 ....182 B4
  East Horsley KT24 .....92 E1
Cobnor Cl RH11 ....200 F4
Cobs Way KT15 ....52 C1
Cochrane Ct KT23 ....94 A2
Cochrane Pl GU20 ....48 D5
Cochrane Rd SW19 ......19 F1
Cock La KT22 ....94 C5
Cock's La RG42 ....8 A6
Cock-A-Dobby GU47 .....45 A1
Cocks Cres KT3 ....38 F5
Cockshot Hill RH2 .....139 B7
Cockshot Rd RH2 ....139 C8
Codrington Ct GU21 .....68 F1
Codrington Hill SE23,SE4 .23 E8
Cody Cl Ash Vale GU12 ..105 F5
  Wallington SM6 ....60 D3
Cody Rd GU14 ....84 B1
Cody Tech Pk GU14 ......84 B1
Coe Ave SE25 ....43 A3
Coe Cl GU11 ....105 A1
Cogman's La RH6 ......162 D4
Cokenor Wood GU10 ....145 F6
Cokers La SE21 ....22 C7
Colborne Way KT4 ....58 C8
Colburn Ave CR3 ....100 F3
Colburn Cres GU4 ......110 A4
Colburn Way SM1 ....59 D7
Colby Rd Dulwich SE19 ..22 E3
  Walton-on-T KT12 ......35 A1
Colchester Vale RH18 ..206 E2
Colchester Villas CR7 ..42 A3
Colcokes Rd SM7 ....78 A3
Cold Harbour La GU14 ...84 F8
Coldharbour Cl TW20 ....32 C6
Coldharbour La
  Bletchingley RH1 .....120 F1
  Dorking RH4,RH5 ......135 F3
  Egham TW20 ....32 D6
  Purley CR8 ....61 A1
  Pyrford GU22 ....70 A4
  South Holmwood RH5 ...156 F6
  West End GU24 ....67 F8
Coldharbour Rd
  Croydon CR0 ....61 A5
  Pyrford CR0,KT14 ......70 F4
Coldharbour Way CR0 ....61 A5
Coldshott RH8 ....123 A2
Coldstream Rd CR3 .....100 C5
Cole Ave GU11 ....104 F3
Cole Cl RH11 ....201 B1
Cole Court Lodge 8
  TW1 ....17 A8
Cole Gdns TW5 ....3 D1
Cole Park Gdns TW1 ......6 A1
Cole Park Rd TW1 ....6 A1
Cole Park View 2 TW1 ....6 A1
Cole Rd TW1 ....6 A1
Cole's La RH5 ....178 B5
Colebrook KT16 ....51 D4
Colebrook Cl SW19 ......19 D8
Colebrook Rd SW16 ......41 E8
Colebrook Rise BR2 .....44 E7
Colebrooke Pl KT16 .....51 C3
Colebrooke Rd RH1 .....118 E3
Coleford Bridge Rd GU16 .85 E4
Coleford Cl GU16 ....85 E3
Coleford Paddocks GU16 .85 F4
Colekitchen La GU5 ....133 D6
Coleman Cl SE25 ....43 A7
Coleman Ct SW18 ....20 A8
Coleman Rd GU12 ......105 D1
Coleridge Ave SM1 ......59 E6
Coleridge Cl
  Crowthorne RG45 ....45 C4
  Horsham RH12 ....217 E6
Coleridge Cres SL3 ......1 E7
Coleridge Ct 2 TW10 ...17 D4
Coleridge Rd
  Ashford TW15 ....13 F4
  Croydon CR0 ....43 C2
  Coles La RH5 ....178 C5
Colesburg Rd BR3 ....43 F7
Colescroft Hill CR8 ....80 A4
Coleshill Rd TW11 ......16 E2
Colesmead Rd RH1 ......118 F4
Coleson Hill Rd GU10 ..145 F5
Colet Rd RH10 ....201 D3
Coleville Rd GU14 ......84 F5
Coley Ave GU22 ....70 A2
Colfe Rd SE23 ....23 E7
Colgate Cl RH11 ....201 B8
Colin Cl Coney Hall BR4 .63 F7
  Croydon CR0 ....62 F7
Colin Ct SW16 ....21 D6
Colin Rd CR3 ....101 A4
Coliston Rd SW18 ....20 A8
Coll of Liberal Arts SM1 .59 B4
Coll of St Barnabas
  RH7 ....185 F8
Coll of Tech Three Bridges
  Outpost RH10 ....202 A7
Collamore Ave SW18 .....20 E7
Collards La GU27 ......208 D6
College Ave Egham TW20 .12 B2
  Epsom KT17 ....76 F5
College Cl
  Addlestone KT15 ....52 D7
  Camberley GU15 ....65 D7
  East Grinstead RH19 ..185 F1

College Cl continued
  Lingfield RH7 ....164 D4
  Twickenham TW2 ....16 D7
College Cres Redhill RH1 .119 A4
  Sandhurst GU47 ....64 E8
College Ct CR0 ....62 A8
College Dr KT7 ....36 E2
College Fields Bsns Ctr
  SW19 ....40 E8
College Gdns
  Dulwich SE21 ....22 E7
  Farnham GU9 ....125 B2
  New Malden KT3 ....38 F4
  Upper Tooting SW17 ....20 E6
College Gn SE19 ....22 E1
College Hill
  Godalming GU7 ....150 C2
  Haslemere GU27 ....208 C6
College Hill Terr GU27 .208 C6
College La
  East Grinstead RH19 ..185 F1
  Woking GU22 ....89 C8
College Pl GU9 ....125 C1
College Rd Ash GU12 ...106 B3
  Bracknell RG12 ....27 D5
  Crawley RH10 ....201 E6
  Croydon CR0,CR9 ....61 D8
  Dulwich SE19, SE21 ....22 E6
  Epsom KT17 ....76 F5
  Ewell KT17 ....77 B5
  Guildford GU1 ....130 D8
  Hounslow TW7 ....5 F6
  Mitcham SW19 ....20 D2
  Sandhurst GU47 ....64 E8
  Woking GU22 ....70 B3
College Rdbt 1 KT1 .....37 E6
College Ride
  Bagshot GU19 ....47 C2
  Camberley GU15 ....65 D7
College Town Inf Sch
  GU47 ....64 E8
College Town Jun Sch
  GU47 ....64 E8
College Way TW15 ....13 F4
College Wlk KT1 ....37 E6
Collendean La RH6 .....159 F4
Collens Field GU24 .....87 E4
Collette Ct SE25 ....42 E4
Colley La RH2 ....117 C3
Colley Manor Dr RH2 ...117 D2
Colley Way RH2 ....117 E4
Collier Cl
  Farnborough GU14 ......84 D5
  West Ewell KT19 ....57 B4
Collier Row RH10 ......201 D4
Collier Way GU4 ....110 D3
Collier's Wood Sta SW19 .20 D1
Colliers RH10 ....101 A2
Colliers Cl GU21 ....69 B3
Colliers Water La CR7 ...42 A4
Collingdon GU6 ....174 F1
Collingsbourne KT15 ....52 B6
Collingtree Rd SE26 ....23 C4
Collingwood GU6 ....85 D2
Collingwood Ave KT5 ....38 C1
Collingwood Cl
  4 East Grinstead RH19 .205 F2
  Horley RH6 ....161 B4
  Horsham RH12 ....217 C4
  3 Penge SE20 ....43 B8
  Twickenham TW2 ....16 A8
Collingwood Coll GU15 ..66 A8
Collingwood Cres GU1 ..110 A2
Collingwood Ct SM1 .....59 B6
Collingwood Grange Cl
  GU15 ....66 B8
Collingwood Mount
  GU15 ....66 A7
Collingwood Pl
  Camberley GU15 ....66 B8
  Walton-on-T KT12 ......54 B7
Collingwood Rd
  Crawley RH10 ....202 C5
  Horsham RH12 ....217 B3
  Mitcham CR4 ....40 E6
  Sutton SM1 ....59 A6
Collingwood Rise GU15 ..66 C6
Collins Gdns GU12 .....106 B2
Collins Rd RH11 ....200 E4
Collis Prim Sch TW11 ...17 B2
Collyer Ave CR0 ....60 E6
Collyer Rd CR0 ....60 E6
Collyer's Sixth Form Coll
  RH12 ....217 D4
Colman Cl KT18 ....77 C2
Colman Ho RH1 ....118 F1
Colman Way RH1 ....118 E4
Colmans Hill GU5 ......154 E1
Colmer Rd SW16 ....21 E1
Coln Trad Est SL3 ....1 F6
Colnbrook By-Pass
  Colnbrook SL3,UB7 ......1 D5
  Harmondsworth UB7 .....2 C1
Colnbrook CE Prim Sch
  SL3 ....1 D7
Colnbrook Ct Poyle SL3 ...1 F6
  Upper Tooting SW17 ....20 D6
Colndale Rd SL3 ....1 E5
Colne Bank SL3,TW19 .....1 C4
Colne Ct KT19 ....57 C6
Colne Dr KT12 ....54 D7
Colne Ho 2 RH1 ....118 F2
Colne Lodge KT12 ....54 D7
Colne Rd TW2 ....16 E7
Colne Reach TW19 ....1 F2
Colne Way Ash GU12 ....106 A1
  Wraysbury TW19 ....12 B6
Colne Wlk RH11 ....200 F5

Colnebridge Cl TW18 ....12 E3
Coloma Convent RC Sch
  CR9 ....62 D7
Colonel's La KT16 ....33 A3
Colonial Ave TW2 ....5 C1
Colonial Rd TW14 .....14 E8
Colonsay Rd RH11 ....201 B3
Colony Gate GU16 .....66 D2
Colson Rd CR0,CR9 ....61 E8
Colson Way SW16 .....21 C4
Colston Ave SM5 ......59 E6
Colston Ct SM5 ....59 F6
Colston Rd SW14 ....7 C3
Coltash Rd RH10 .....202 A5
Coltsfoot Dr
  Guildford GU4 ....110 B8
  Horsham RH12 ....217 E5
Coltsfoot La RH8 .....123 A2
Columbia Ave KT4 .....38 F2
Columbia Ct KT3 ......38 F2
Columbine Ave CR2 ....61 B3
Columbus Dr GU14 ....84 C4
Colville Gdns GU18 ...67 C8
Colvin Cl SE26 ....23 C3
Colvin Rd CR7 ....42 A4
Colwood Gdns SW19 ...20 D1
Colworth Rd CR0 ......43 A1
Colwyn Cl Crawley RH11 ..200 F4
  Streatham SW16 ......21 C3
Colwyn Cres TW3 ....5 C6
Colyton Cl GU21 ......69 C1
Colyton La 2 SW16 ...22 A3
Combe Ho SW14 ....7 C5
Combe Hurst KT2 ......18 C3
Combe La Bramley GU5 .151 D2
  Chiddingfold GU8 ....191 A7
  Farnborough GU14 ....85 A6
  Shere KT24,GU4 ......133 B8
  Whiteley Village KT12 ...53 F2
  Wormley GU8 ....170 F1
Combe Martin Coll KT2 ..18 C3
Combe Rd GU7 ....150 E8
Combe Rise GU4 ......191 A5
Combe View GU8 ......191 A5
Combemartin Rd SW18 .19 E7
Combermere Rd SM4 ...40 B4
Comeragh Cl GU22 ....89 A7
Comet Cl GU12 ....105 F5
Comet Rd
  Farnborough GU14 ....84 C1
  Stanwell TW19 ....13 D8
Comforts Farm Ave
  RH8 ....123 A3
Comfrey Cl
  Farnborough GU14 ....84 C5
  Wokingham RG40 .....25 E8
Commerce Rd TW8 ......6 C7
Commerce Way CR0 ....60 F8
Commercial Rd
  Aldershot GU12 .....126 C8
  Guildford GU1 ......130 D8
  Staines TW18 ....13 A2
Commercial Way GU21 .69 F2
Commodore Ct GU14 ..105 B8
Common Cl GU21 ......69 D5
Common La Claygate KT10 56 A3
  New Haw KT15 ....52 C2
Common Rd
  Claygate KT10 ....56 A3
  Redhill RH1 ....139 F7
Common Side KT18 ....76 A4
Common The
  Cranleigh GU6 ......174 C3
  Wonersh GU5 ....152 B8
Commonfield Rd SM7 ..78 B6
Commonfields GU24 ...67 F6
Commonside
  Great Bookham KT23 ..94 A5
  Redhill RH1 ....139 F7
Commonside Cl
  Coulsdon CR5 ....100 B7
  Sutton SM2 ....78 B8
Commonside Ct SW16 ..21 E2
Commonside E CR4 ....41 B6
Commonwealth Lodge Sch
  CR8 ....79 D7
Commonwealth Rd CR3 101 A4
Community Cl TW5 ......4 B6
Como Rd SE23 ....23 E6
Compass Hill TW10 .....6 D1
Compasses Mobile Home Pk
  GU6 ....193 F5
Compassion Cl RH11 ..200 E4
Comper Cl RH11 ......200 E4
Comport Gn CR0 ....82 E7
Compound Rd GU14 ....85 A2
Compton Cl
  Bracknell RG12 ......26 E3
  Esher KT10 ....55 D5
  Sandhurst GU47 ......45 C1
Compton Cres
  Chessington KT9 .....56 E4
  Chiswick W4 ....7 C8
Compton Ct
  7 Guildford GU1 ....130 F8
  Sutton SM1 ....59 C6
  9 West Norwood SE19 ..22 E3
Compton Hts GU3 ....129 D6
Compton Place Bsns Ctr
  GU15 ....65 A4
Compton Rd Croydon CR0 ..61 A8
  Wimbledon SW19 .....19 F2
Compton Way GU10 ...126 B1
Comptons Brow La
  RH13 ....218 A3
Comptons Ct 4 RH13 .217 F3
Comptons La RH13 ...217 F3
Comsaye Wlk RG12 ....27 C4

Conal Ct SW16 ....21 D3
Conaways Cl KT17 ....58 A1
Concord Ho KT3 ......38 E6
Concorde Bsns Pk TN16 83 D4
Concorde Ct TW3 ......5 B5
Concorde Ho
  Addlestone KT15 ....52 B6
  Crawley RH6 ....182 B7
Concorde Rd GU14 ....84 C1
Condor Ct GU2 ....130 C2
Condor Rd TW18 ......33 C6
Conduit La CR0 ....62 A5
Conduit The RH1 .....120 D6
Coney Acre SE21 ......22 C7
Coney Cl RH11 ....201 B8
Coney Croft RH12 ....218 B5
Coney Hall Par BR4 ...63 E8
Coney Hill Rd BR4 ....63 F8
Coney Hill Sch BR2 ...63 F7
Coneyberry RH2 ......139 D5
Coneyberry RH2 ......120 E1
Coneybury RH2 ....139 D5
Coneybury Cl CR6 ....101 B8
Coneyhurst La GU6 ...175 D7
Conford Dr GU4 ......130 E2
Coniers Way GU4 .....110 B4
Conifer Cl RH2 ......118 A3
Conifer Ct 2 SW19 ...19 D7
Conifer Dr GU15 ......66 A6
Conifer Gdns
  Streatham SW16 ......21 F5
  Sutton SM1 ....59 B8
Conifer La TW20 ......12 C3
Conifers KT13 ....53 F6
Conifers Cl
  Horsham RH13 ......218 B6
  Teddington TW11 .....17 C1
Conifers The RG45 ....45 A7
Coningham RG12 ......27 C5
Coningsby Ct CR4 ....41 A7
Coningsby Rd CR2 ....61 C3
Conisborough Cres SE6 24 C5
Conista Ct GU21 .....68 F3
Coniston Cl Barnes SW13 ..7 F7
  Chiswick W4 ....7 C7
  Crawley RH11 ....200 D4
  Farnborough GU14 ....84 E3
  Frimley GU15 ....66 C3
  Horsham RH12 ......218 B6
  West Barnes SM4 .....39 D3
Coniston Ct
  Beckenham BR3 ......44 C8
  Chessington KT9 .....56 E1
  Lightwater GU18 .....48 B1
  Penge SE26 ....23 B2
  3 Wallington SM6 ....60 B6
  Weybridge KT13 ......53 B4
Coniston Dr GU9 ....125 A6
Coniston Gdns SM2 ...59 D4
Coniston Rd Catford BR1 .24 E2
  Coulsdon CR5 ....79 C3
  Croydon CR0 ....43 A2
  Old Woking GU22 .....90 B7
  Twickenham TW2 ......5 B1
Coniston Way
  Chessington KT9 .....56 E7
  Redhill RH2 ....118 E2
  Thorpe Lea TW20 .....12 B1
Connaught Ave
  Ashford TW15 ....13 E4
  Hounslow TW4 ....4 E3
  Mortlake SW14 ....7 C3
Connaught Bsns Ctr
  Mitcham CR4 ....40 F4
  Wallington SM6 ......60 F4
Connaught Cl SM1 ....59 D8
Connaught Cres GU24 .87 F7
Connaught Gdns
  Crawley RH10 ....201 D8
  Morden SM4 ....40 C5
Connaught Ho KT6 ....37 D7
Connaught Jun Sch
  GU19 ....47 E2
Connaught Rd
  Aldershot GU12 .....105 D2
  Bagshot GU19 ....47 C3
  Brookwood GU24 .....87 F7
  Camberley GU15 ......65 F5
  Carshalton SM1 ......59 D8
  New Malden KT3 .....38 E5
  4 Richmond TW10 .....6 F2
  Teddington TW11 .....16 D3
Connaught Sch The
  GU12 ....126 E7
Connell Ho 6 SM6 ....60 C4
Connington 2 KT1 ....38 A7
Connolly Ct GU25 ....31 E5
Connolly Ho Epsom KT19 ..57 B2
  Wimbledon SW19 .....20 C2
Connop Way GU16 .....65 F3
Conquest Rd KT15 ....52 A5
Conrad Dr KT4 ....39 D1
Conservatory Ct SE19 .22 E1
Consfield Ave KT3 ....39 A4
Consort Cl 1 GU22 ...69 E1
Consort Dr GU15 .....66 C7
Consort Mews TW7 .....5 D2
Consort Way RH6 ....161 A3
Consort Way E RH6 ..161 B2
Constable Gdns TW7 ...5 D2
Constable Rd RH10 ..201 D4
Constable Way GU47 ..64 E6
Constable Wlk SE21 ..22 E5
Constance Cres BR2 ..44 F1
Constance Rd Sutton SM1 59 C6
  Thornton Heath CR0 ..42 B2
  Twickenham TW2 .....16 B8
Constant Rd GU14 ....84 A1
Constantine Ho SW2 ..22 B7

Constitution Hill GU22 .89 E8
Control Tower Rd
  Crawley RH6 ....181 D6
  Harlington TW6 ....3 B4
Convent Cl BR3 ......24 C1
Convent Hill SE19 ....22 C2
Convent of the Sacred Heart
  Digby-Stuart Coll SW15 .7 F2
Convent Rd TW15 .....14 B3
Conway Cl GU16 ......65 F1
Conway Dr Ashford TW15 .14 C2
  Farnborough GU14 ....84 D4
  Sutton SM2 ....59 B4
Conway Gdns CR4 ....41 E5
Conway Ho Reigate RH2 139 A4
  6 Streatham SW2 ....21 F7
Conway Rd Feltham TW13 .15 D3
  Harlington TW6 ....3 B4
  Twickenham TW4 ......16 A8
  Wimbledon SW20 .....39 C8
Conway Wlk TW12 .....15 F2
Conyer's Rd SW16 ....21 D3
Conyers Ct KT1 ......54 D5
Cook Rd Crawley RH10 .201 B4
  Horsham RH12 ......217 D6
Cook Way GU2 ....108 D2
Cookes La SM3 ....58 E4
Cookham Cl GU47 ....45 C1
Cookham Rd RG12 ....26 E7
Cooks Hill RH12 .....214 A8
Cooks Mdw RH12 ....199 D7
Cooks Mead RH12 ...199 D7
Coolarne Rise GU15 ..66 A6
Coolgardie Rd TW15 ..14 C3
Coolham Ct RH11 ....200 F6
Coolhurst La RH13 ..218 A1
Coombe Ave CR0 ......61 E6
Coombe Bank KT2,KT3 .38 C8
Coombe Cl
  Crawley RH11 ....181 D1
  Frimley GU16 ....85 D8
  Hounslow TW3 ....5 A3
Coombe Cotts RH3 ...116 D4
Coombe Cres TW12 ...15 E1
Coombe Ct
  Beckenham BR3 ......43 F8
  Tadworth KT20 ....97 C4
Coombe Dene 8 BR2 ..44 F1
Coombe Dr KT15 .....51 F4
Coombe End KT2 ......18 D1
Coombe Gdns
  New Malden KT3 .....38 F5
  Wimbledon SW20 .....39 A8
Coombe Girls Sch KT3 .38 D7
Coombe Hill Glade KT2 .38 E7
Coombe Hill Inf Sch KT3 38 D8
Coombe Hill Jun Sch
  KT3 ....38 D8
Coombe Hill Rd
  East Grinstead RH19 .205 D6
  Kingston u T KT2 .....18 E1
Coombe House Chase
  KT3 ....38 D8
Coombe La
  South Croydon CR0 ...62 B5
  Wimbledon SW20 .....39 B7
  Worplesdon GU3 ....108 D7
Coombe La W KT2 ....18 E1
Coombe Lane Flyover
  SW20 ....38 F8
Coombe Lane Sta CR0 .62 C4
Coombe Manor GU24 ..68 B4
Coombe Neville KT2 ..18 D1
Coombe Pine RG12 ...27 D3
Coombe Pk KT2 ....18 D3
Coombe Rd Croydon CR0 .61 E6
  Forest Hill SE26 .....23 B4
  Hampton TW12 ....15 F2
  Kingston u T KT3 ....38 E6
  Kingston u T, Norbiton KT2 38 A8
  South Croydon CR0,CR2 61 E6
Coombe Ridings KT2 ..18 C3
Coombe Rise KT2 .....38 C8
Coombe The RH3 .....116 D4
Coombe Way KT14 ....71 F7
Coombe Wlk SM1 .....59 B7
Coombe Wood Hill CR8 .80 C6
Coombe Wood Rd KT2 .18 C3
Coombefield Cl KT3 ..38 E4
Coombelands La KT15 .52 A4
Coomber Way CR0,CR4 .41 D2
Coombes The GU5 ...152 A5
Cooper Cl RH6 ......162 A3
Cooper Cres SM5 .....59 F7
Cooper Ct GU14 ......85 C4
Cooper Ho Hounslow TW4 .4 F4
  7 West Norwood SW27 .22 B3
Cooper Rd
  Croydon CR0,CR9 .....61 B6
  Guildford GU1 ......130 F8
  Windlesham GU20 .....48 D4
Cooper Row RH10 ....182 A1
Cooper's Hill La TW20 .11 D4
Cooper's Hill Rd
  Nutfield RH1 ....120 A1
  South Nutfield RH1 ..141 B5
Cooper's Terr GU9 ...125 C3
Cooper's Yd SE19 ....22 E2
Coopers Cl TW18 .....13 B1
Coopers Hill Dr GU24 .87 C7
Coopers Rise GU7 ...150 C3
Cootes Ave RH12 ....217 A3
Copeland Ho SW17 ...20 D4
Copelands BR3 ....23 F1
Copelands Cl GU15 ...66 D4
Copeman Cl SE26 ....23 C3
Copenhagen Way KT12 .54 B7
Copenhagen Wlk RG45 .45 B4

Copers Cope Rd BR3 ..23 F1
Copgate Path SW16 ...22 A2
Copleigh Dr KT20 ....97 E7
Copley Cl Knaphill GU21 .88 E7
  Redhill RH1 ....118 E3
Copley Pk SW16 ......21 F2
Copley Way KT20 .....97 D7
Copnall Way RH12 ...217 C2
Coppard Gdns KT9 ...56 C4
Copped Hall Dr GU15 .66 C6
Copped Hall Way GU15 66 C6
Coppedhall 2 SE21 ...22 D6
Copper Beech Cl GU22 89 B6
Copper Beeches TW7 ..5 D6
Copper Cl SE19 ......22 F1
Copper Mill Dr TW7 ...5 F5
Copper Mill La SW17 .20 C4
Copperfield Ave GU47 .45 E2
Copperfield Cl CR2 ...80 C8
Copperfield Ct SM1 ..95 A6
Copperfield Pl RH12 .217 A3
Copperfield Rise KT15 51 F4
Copperfields
  Beckenham BR3 ......44 C8
  Fetcham KT22 ....94 C5
Coppermill Rd TW19 ...1 B2
Coppice Cl
  Beckenham BR3 ......44 B5
  Guildford GU2 ......108 D2
  Heath End GU9 ......125 E6
  West Barnes SW20 ...39 C6
Coppice Dr TW19 .....11 D8
Coppice End GU22 ....70 E3
Coppice La RH2 .....117 F3
Coppice Pl GU8 .....190 F8
Coppice Rd RH12 ....218 A5
Coppice The
  Ashford TW15 ....14 B2
  Crawley Down RH10 .204 B8
Coppice Wlk RH10 ...202 A7
Coppin Ho 2 SW2 ....22 B7
Copping Cl CR0 ......61 E6
Coppins The CR0 .....63 B4
Coppsfield 8 ....36 A6
Copse Ave
  Heath End GU9 .....125 E6
  West Wickham BR4 ...63 B7
Copse Cl Camberley GU15 66 A6
  Chilworth GU4 ......131 C3
  Crawley Down RH10 .204 B8
  East Grinstead RH19 .186 A3
  Horsham RH12 ......217 F6
Copse Cres RH11 ....201 C7
Copse Dr RG41 ....25 A7
Copse Edge
  Cranleigh GU6 ......174 F4
  Elstead GU8 ....148 C3
Copse Edge Ave KT17 .76 F6
Copse End GU15 ......66 A6
Copse Glade KT6 .....37 D1
Copse Hill Belmont SM2 59 B3
  Purley CR8 ....79 E6
  Wimbledon SW20 .....19 B1
Copse La RH6 ....161 C4
Copse Rd Cobham KT11 .73 B6
  Haslemere GU27 ....207 D5
  Knaphill GU21 ....68 F1
  Reigate RH1 ....139 D7
Copse Side GU7 .....129 D1
Copse The Caterham CR3 101 A1
  Farnborough GU14 ....84 D3
  Fetcham KT22 ....94 B4
  Rowledge GU10 .....145 F4
  South Nutfield RH1 ..140 E7
Copse View CR2 ......62 E2
Copse Way GU10 ....145 F6
Copse Wood Ct RH1 ..118 C3
Copsem Dr KT10 .....55 B4
Copsem La Esher KT10 .55 C1
  Oxshott KT22 ....55 C1
Copsem Way KT10 ....55 C4
Copsen Wood KT22 ...74 C8
Copsleigh Ave RH1 ..140 A3
Copsleigh Cl RH1 ...140 A3
Copsleigh Way RH1 ..140 A3
Copt Hill La KT20 ....97 F7
Copthall Gdns TW1 ..16 F7
Copthall Way KT15 ...52 A1
Copthorne Ave SW12 .21 D8
Copthorne Bank RH10,
  RH6 ....183 C4
Copthorne CE Prim Sch
  RH10 ....183 B3
Copthorne Chase TW15 13 E4
Copthorne Cl RH17 ...34 C3
Copthorne Common Rd
  RH10 ....183 C3
Copthorne Ct SM1 ....59 C7
Copthorne Dr GU18 ..48 B1
Copthorne Ho
  Crawley RH10 ......182 A1
  Kingswood KT20 .....97 D7
Copthorne Prep Sch
  RH10 ....183 E3
Copthorne Rd
  Copthorne RH10 ....182 F1
  Crawley RH10 ......202 E8
  Domewood RH19 ....184 D4
  Leatherhead KT22 ....95 B7
Copthorne Rise CR8 ..80 C6
Copthorne Way RH10 .182 F2
Copyhold Rd RH19 ..205 D4
Corban Rd TW3 ....5 A4
Corbet Cl SM6 ....60 A8
Corbet Rd KT17 ......57 E1
Corbett Cl CR0 ....82 D7
Corbett Ct 3 SE6 ....23 F4
Corbett Dr GU18 .....66 F7

Corbiere Ct SW19 ....19 D2
Corby Cl RH11 ......200 E3
Corby Dr TW20 ....11 C2
Cordelia Croft RG42 ..27 E8
Cordelia Gdns
  Ash Vale GU12 ....85 F1
  Stanwell TW19 ....13 E8
Cordelia Rd TW19 ....13 E8
Corderoy Pl KT16 ....32 F3
Cordrey Gdns CR5 ....79 E4
Cordrey Ho KT15 .....52 B8
Cordwalles Jun Sch
  GU15 ....65 F8
Cordwalles Rd GU15 .65 F8
Coresbrook Way GU21 88 B8
Corfe Cl KT21 ....75 C5
Corfe Gdns GU16 .....65 F1
Corfe Lodge 15 SE21 .22 D6
Corfe Way GU15 ......85 E1
Coriander Cl GU14 ...84 C4
Coriander Cres GU2 .109 A6
Corium Ho CR7 ......150 F5
Cork Tree Ho 3 SW27 22 B3
Corkran Rd KT6 ......37 E2
Corkscrew Hill BR4 ..63 D8
Cormongers La RH1 ..119 D2
Cormorant Ct 13 SE21 22 D6
Cormorant Pl Cheam SM1 58 F5
  Sandhurst GU47 ......64 E7
Cornbunting Cl GU47 .64 D8
Cornelia Cl GU14 ....84 D3
Corner Farm Cl KT20 .97 C5
Corner Fielde SW2 ...21 F7
Cornerstone Sch The
  KT19 ....76 C6
Corney Rd W4 ....7 E8
Corney Reach Way W4 .7 E7
Cornfield Rd RH2 ...139 C4
Cornfields GU7 .....151 A8
Cornflower La CR0 ...43 D1
Cornford Gr SW12 ...21 B6
Cornhill Cl KT15 .....52 B8
Cornish Gr SE20 .....43 B8
Cornwall Ave Byfleet KT14 71 F5
  Claygate KT10 ....55 F3
Cornwall Cl GU15 ....65 F7
Cornwall Gdns 6 RH19 205 F8
Cornwall Rd Belmont SM2 59 A2
  Thornton Heath CR0,CR9 .61 B8
  Twickenham TW1 .....17 A7
Cornwall Way TW18 ..12 E2
Cornwallis Cl CR3 ..100 C3
Coronation Cotts GU8 191 C5
Coronation Rd
  Aldershot GU11 .....126 B7
  Ascot SL5 ....29 A2
  East Grinstead RH19 .205 E7
Coronation Sq RG40 .25 D7
Coronet Cl RH10 ....202 E7
Coronet The RH6 ....161 C1
Corporation Ave TW4 ..4 E3
Corpus Christi RC Prim Sch
  KT3 ....38 C6
Corrib Dr SM1 ....59 E5
Corrie Gdns GU25 ....31 C2
Corrie Rd Addlestone KT15 52 D6
  Old Woking GU22 .....90 C7
Corrigan Ave CR5 ....79 A5
Corsair Cl TW19 .....13 E8
Corsair Rd TW19 .....13 E8
Corscombe Cl KT2 ...18 E3
Corsehill St SW16 ...21 C2
Corsham Way RG45 ..45 B5
Corsletts Ave RH12 .216 D3
Corsten Hollow 7 RH1 139 F8
Corunna Dr RH13 ...217 F2
Cosdach Ave SM6 ....60 D3
Cosedge Cres CR0,CR9 .61 B5
Cosford Rd GU8 .....169 C4
Cotelands CR0 ....61 E7
Cotesbach Rd E5 .....35 A8
Cotford Rd CR7 ......42 C5
Cotherstone KT19 ....57 D2
Cotherstone Rd SW2 .21 F7
Cotland Acres RH1 ..139 D7
Cotsford KT3 ....38 D7
Cotswold Cl
  Crawley RH11 ......201 B6
  Farnborough GU14 ...84 E7
  Hinchley Wood KT10 .55 F8
  Kingston u T KT2 ....18 C2
  Staines TW18 ....13 A3
Cotswold Ct RH13 ..217 E2
Cotswold Rd Belmont SM2 59 B1
  Hampton TW12 ....16 A2
Cotswold St SE27 ....22 B4
Cotswold Way KT4 ...58 C8
Cottage Cl
  Horsham RH12 ......218 B6
  Ottershaw KT16 ......51 D4
Cottage Farm Way TW20 32 C6
Cottage Gdns GU14 ..84 E4
Cottage Gr KT6 ......37 D3
Cottage Pl RH10 ....183 E3
Cottage Rd KT19 ....57 D3
Cottenham Dr SW20 ..19 B1
Cottenham Par SW20 .39 B7
Cottenham Park Rd
  SW20 ....39 B8
Cottenham Pl SW20 ..19 B1
Cottenhams RH7 ....163 E8
Cotterill Rd KT6 .....37 F1
Cottesbrooke Cl SL3 ..1 D6

Cottesloe Cl GU24 67 F3
Cottesmore RG12 27 A2
Cottimore Ave KT12 35 B1
Cottimore Cres KT12 35 B2
Cottimore La
Walton-on-T KT12 35 B2
Walton-on-T KT12 35 D1
Cottimore Terr KT12 35 B2
Cottingham Ave RH12 217 D7
Cottingham Rd SE20 23 D1
Cottington Rd TW13 15 D4
Cotton Cl GU11 104 F3
Cotton Hill BR1 24 D4
Cotton Ho 18 SW12 21 E8
Cotton Row RH5 176 C8
Cotton Wlk RH11 201 A1
Cottongrass Cl CR0 43 D1
Cottrell Flats GU14 105 D8
Cotts Wood Dr GU4 110 A6
Couchmore Ave KT10 55 E8
Coulsdon CE Prim Sch CR5 79 F1
Coulsdon Coll CR5 100 A8
Coulsdon Court Rd CR5 79 F3
Coulsdon High Sch CR5 100 B7
Coulsdon Ho 5 SW2 21 E7
Coulsdon La CR5 99 A8
Coulsdon Pl CR3 100 D5
Coulsdon Rd CR3,CR5 100 B7
Coulsdon Rise CR5 79 E2
Coulsdon South Sta CR5 79 D3
Coulthurst Ct SW16 21 E1
Council Cotts
Betchworth RH3 116 D1
Charlwood RH6 180 C6
Loxwood RH14 213 A2
Plaistow RH14 211 D3
West End GU24 67 F7
Countisbury Gdns KT15 52 B5
Countisbury Ho SE26 23 A5
Country Way TW13,TW16 15 C3
County Bsns Ctr RH11 181 D2
County Mall RH10 201 E5
County Oak Ind Est RH10 181 D2
County Oak La RH11 181 D3
County Oak Ret Pk RH11 181 D2
County Oak Way RH10, RH11 181 D2
County Rd CR7 42 B7
Courier Ho 17 SW2 22 A8
Courland Rd KT15 52 B7
Course Rd SL5 29 A6
Court Ave CR5 100 A8
Court Bushes Rd CR3 101 B7
Court Cl
East Grinstead RH19 185 F1
Twickenham TW2 16 B5
Wallington SM6 60 D3
Court Close Ave TW2 16 B5
Court Cres
Chessington KT9 56 D4
East Grinstead RH19 185 F1
Court Downs Rd BR3 44 B7
Court Dr Carshalton SM1 59 E6
Croydon CR0 60 F6
Court Farm Ave KT19 57 D5
Court Farm Cvn Pk CR6 81 A3
Court Farm Gdns KT19 76 C8
Court Farm Ind Est TW19 2 F1
Court Farm Rd CR6 81 A2
Court Gdns GU15 65 D5
Court Green Hts GU22 89 C7
Court Haw SM7 78 E4
Court Hill Sanderstead CR2 80 E7
Woodmansterne CR5 78 F2
Court House Mans KT19 76 D7
Court La Dulwich SE21 22 F8
Epsom KT19 76 C6
Court Lane Gdns SE21 22 E8
Court Lodge Inf Sch RH6 160 F3
Court Lodge Rd RH6 160 F3
Court One TW15 14 C5
Court Rd
10 Aldershot GU11 105 A2
Banstead SM7 78 A4
Caterham CR3 100 E4
South Norwood SE25 42 F6
Tyler's Green RH9 121 C4
Court The
Dockenfield GU10 166 D3
Guildford GU2 130 C7
Warlingham CR6 81 E1
Court Three TW15 14 C5
Court Two TW15 14 C5
Court Way TW2 16 F8
Court Wood La CR0 62 F1
Courtenay Ave SM2 59 A2
Courtenay Dr BR3 44 D7
Courtenay Mews GU21 70 A3
Courtenay Rd
Heath End GU9 125 E7
North Cheam KT4,SM3 58 C7
Penge BR3,SE20 23 D2
Woking GU21 70 A3
Courtfield Rd TW15 14 B2
Courtfield Rise BR4 63 D7
Courthope Rd SW19 19 E3
Courthope Villas SW19 19 E1
Courtland Ave SW16 21 F1
Courtlands
11 Beckenham BR3 44 B7
10 Belmont SM2 59 B3
Courtlands *continued*
Richmond TW10 7 A2
Walton-on-T KT12 35 A2
Courtlands Ave
Esher KT10 55 A4
Hampton TW12 15 F2
Richmond TW9 7 B5
West Wickham BR2 44 F1
Courtlands Cl CR2 62 A1
Courtlands Cres SM7 78 A3
Courtlands Dr KT19 57 F4
Courtlands Rd KT5 38 A2
Courtleas KT11 74 A6
Courtleigh Manor SL5 30 A2
Courtney Cl SE19 22 E2
Courtney Cres SM5 59 F2
Courtney Pl Cobham KT11 73 F7
Croydon CR0 61 A7
Dorking RH4 115 D1
Courtney Rd
Croydon CR0,CR9 61 A7
Harlington TW6 3 A4
Mitcham SW19 20 E1
Courtney Way TW6 3 A5
Courts Hill Rd GU27 208 B6
Courts Mount Rd GU27 208 B6
Courts The SW16 21 E1
Courtside SE23 23 C5
Courtwood Prim Sch CR0 62 F1
Courtyard The
Addlestone KT15 52 C6
Cranleigh GU6 153 E1
1 Crawley RH10 201 D5
Crawley, Whitevane Hill RH12 218 E4
East Grinstead RH19 186 B1
Kingswood KT20 98 C4
Oxted RH8 122 E6
West Byfleet KT14 71 A7
Whyteleafe CR3 80 F1
Coutts Ave KT9 56 E5
Coval Gdns SW14 7 B3
Coval La SW14 7 B3
Coval Rd SW14 7 C3
Cove Inf Sch GU14 84 E6
Cove Jun Sch GU14 84 E5
Cove Rd GU14 84 F4
Cove Sch GU14 84 E5
Coveham Cres KT11 73 A6
Coventry Hall SW16 21 E3
Coventry Rd SE25 43 A5
Coverack Cl CR0 43 E2
Coverdale Ct RH19 185 C3
Coverdale Gdns CR0 61 F7
Covers La GU27 207 C6
Covert Cl RH10 201 E7
Covert La RG12 27 C5
Covert The Ascot SL5 29 B2
Farnborough GU14 84 E8
South Norwood SE19 22 F1
Coverton Rd SW17 20 E3
Coverts Cl GU9 125 E4
Coverts Rd KT10 55 F3
Coves Farm Wood RG42 26 D7
Covey Cl
Farnborough GU14 85 A8
Merton SW19 40 B7
Covey The RH10 202 E8
Covington Gdns SW16 22 B1
Covington Way
South Norwood SW16 22 A1
South Norwood SW16 22 B1
Streatham SW16 21 F2
Cow La GU7 150 D4
Cowden St SE6 24 A4
Cowdray Cl RH10 202 C5
Cowdrey Rd SW19 20 C3
Cowfold Cl RH11 200 F3
Cowick Rd SW17 20 F4
Cowleaze Rd KT2 37 E8
Cowley Ave KT16 32 F2
Cowley Cl CR2 62 C2
Cowley Cres KT12 54 C6
Cowley La KT16 32 F2
Cowley Rd SW14 7 E4
Coworth Cl SL5 30 B4
Coworth Park Sch GU24 49 B6
Coworth Rd SL5 30 A4
Cowper Ave SM1 59 D6
Cowper Cl KT16 32 F3
Cowper Gdns SM6 60 C4
Cowper Rd
Richmond TW10 17 F3
Wimbledon SW19 20 C2
Cowshot Cres GU24 87 D7
Cowslip La RH5 115 B7
Cox Cnr RH5 177 A7
Cox Green Rd RH12 195 C2
Cox Ho RH12 217 B2
Cox La Chessington KT9 56 F6
West Ewell KT19 57 C5
Coxbridge GU9 124 F1
Coxbridge Rdbt GU9 145 F8
Coxcomb Wlk RH11 201 A4
Coxcombe La GU8 191 B4
Coxdean KT18 97 C8
Coxgreen GU47 64 D6
Coxley Rise CR8 80 C6
Coxs Ave TW17 34 E6
Coxwell Rd SE19 22 E1
Coxwold Path KT9 56 E3
Crab Hill BR3 24 D1
Crab Hill La RH1 140 F4
Crabbet Rd RH10 202 B7
Crabtree Cl KT23 94 C1
Crabtree Cnr TW20 32 B8
Crabtree Dr KT22 95 C2
Crabtree La Churt GU10 168 A2
Great Bookham KT23 94 C1
Headley KT18 96 C1
Westhumble RH5 115 A5
Crabtree Office Village TW20 32 C7
Crabtree Rd
Camberley GU15 65 B2
Crawley RH11 201 C7
Thorpe TW20 32 C7
Crabwood RH8 122 E7
Craddocks Ave KT21 75 F3
Craddocks Cl KT21 76 A3
Craddocks Par KT21 75 E2
Cradhurst Cl RH4 135 C6
Craig Rd TW10 17 C4
Craigans RH11 201 A5
Craigen Ave CR0 43 B1
Craigmore Twr 11 GU22 89 E8
Craignair Rd SW2 22 A8
Craignish Ave SW16 41 F7
Craigside Kingston u T KT2 38 B8
Purley CR8 79 F5
Craigwell Ave TW13 15 A5
Craigwell Cl TW18 32 E8
Crail Cl RG41 25 A3
Crake Pl GU47 64 D8
Crakell Rd RH2 139 C8
Cramhurst Ho 3 SM1 59 D5
Cramhurst La GU8 170 E6
Cramond Ct TW14 14 E7
Crampshaw La KT21 95 F7
Crampton Rd SE20 23 C2
Cranberry Wlk GU17 64 F3
Cranborne Ave KT6,KT9 57 A7
Cranborne Wlk RH10 201 F4
Cranbourne Cl
Horley RH6 161 B5
Thornton Heath SW16 41 E6
Cranbourne Cotts SL4 9 B5
Cranbourne Prim Sch SL5 9 A4
Cranbrook Ct 9 TW8 6 D8
Cranbrook Dr
Thames Ditton KT10 36 C1
Twickenham TW2 16 B7
Cranbrook Ho SE19 42 D8
Cranbrook Rd
Hounslow TW4 4 F3
South Norwood CR7 42 C7
Wimbledon SW19 19 E1
Cranbrook Terr GU6 174 F3
Crane Ave TW7 6 A2
Crane Ct Sandhurst GU47 64 D8
West Ewell KT19 57 C6
Crane Ho Catford BR1 24 D3
Feltham TW13 16 A5
Crane Lodge Rd TW5 4 B8
Crane Mead Ct TW1 16 F8
Crane Park Prim Sch TW13 15 F6
Crane Park Rd TW2 16 B6
Crane Rd Stanwell TW19 3 A1
Twickenham TW2 16 E7
Crane Way TW2 16 C8
Cranebank TW4 4 A4
Cranebrook TW2 16 C6
Craneford Cl TW2 16 F8
Craneford Way TW2 16 F8
Cranes Dr KT5 37 F5
Cranes Park Ave KT5,KT6 37 F5
Cranes Park Cres KT5 37 F5
Cranes Pk KT5,KT6 37 E4
Craneswater TW6 3 F7
Cranfield Ct 6 GU21 68 F1
Cranfield Rd E SM5 60 A2
Cranfield Rd W SM5 60 A2
Cranford Ave TW19 13 F8
Cranford Cl Purley CR8 80 C6
Stanwell TW19 13 E8
Wimbledon SW20 19 B1
Cranford Com Coll TW5 4 B8
Cranford Ct SM1 59 C6
Cranford Jun & Inf Schs TW4 4 B5
Cranford La Cranford UB3 4 A7
Harlington UB3 3 E7
Hatton TW6 3 F6
Hatton Cross TW6 3 F6
Heston TW5 4 D7
Cranford Lodge SW19 19 E6
Cranford Rise KT10 55 C5
Cranleigh Cl Penge SE20 43 B7
Sanderstead CR2 81 A7
Cranleigh Ct
Farnborough GU14 84 F4
Mitcham CR4 40 D6
Richmond TW9 7 A4
Cranleigh Gdns
Kingston u T KT2 17 F2
Sanderstead CR2 81 A7
South Norwood SE25 42 E6
Sutton SM1 59 B8
Cranleigh Ho SW20 39 B7
Cranleigh Inf Sch GU6 174 E3
Cranleigh Mead GU6 174 F2
Cranleigh Rd
Ewhurst GU6 175 D4
Feltham TW13 14 F4
Merton SW19 40 A6
Thames Ditton KT10 36 C1
Wonersh GU5 152 C7
Cranleigh Sch GU6 174 C5
Cranleigh Village Hospl GU6 174 D3
Cranley Cl GU1 110 A1
Cranley Dene GU1 110 A1
Cranley Gdns SM6 60 C3
Cranley Manor 4 GU1 110 A1
Cranley Pl GU21 68 D1
Cranley Rd Guildford GU1 109 F1
Hersham KT12 53 F5
Cranmer Cl
Warlingham CR6 81 E2
West Barnes SM4 39 E3
Weybridge KT13 53 A3
Cranmer Ct
Hampton TW12 16 B3
Kingston u T KT2 17 D4
Cranmer Farm Cl CR4 40 F5
Cranmer Gdns CR6 81 E2
Cranmer Prim Sch CR4 40 F5
Cranmer Rd
Croydon CR0,CR9 61 C7
Hampton TW12 16 B3
Kingston u T KT2 17 E3
Mitcham CR4 40 F5
Cranmer Terr SW17 20 D3
Cranmer Wlk RH10 202 C5
Cranmere Prim Sch KT10 36 C1
Cranmore Ave TW7 5 C7
Cranmore Cl GU11 104 E1
Cranmore Ct GU16 85 F4
Cranmore Gdns GU11 104 E1
Cranmore La
Aldershot GU11 104 E1
West Horsley KT24 112 C6
Cranmore Prep Sch KT24 112 C6
Cranmore Rd Catford BR1 24 F5
Mytchett GU16 86 A4
Cranston Cl
Hounslow TW3,TW4 4 E5
Reigate RH2 139 B8
Cranston Rd
East Grinstead RH19 185 F2
Forest Hill SE23 23 E6
Cranston Way RH10 204 C8
Cranstoun Cl GU3 108 F5
Crantock Rd SE6 24 C6
Cranwell Ct CR0 62 D8
Cranwell Gr
Lightwater GU18 66 F8
Littleton TW17 33 F5
Cranwell Rd TW6 3 B5
Craster Rd SW2 21 F8
Cravan Ave TW13 15 A6
Craven Cl GU10 146 C6
Craven Ct GU15 64 F4
Craven Gdns SW19 20 B3
Craven Ho 2 SW14 7 D4
Craven Rd Crawley RH10 202 B5
Croydon CR0 43 B1
Kingston u T KT2 37 F8
Cravens The RH6 162 A3
Crawford Cl TW7 5 E5
Crawford Gdns
Camberley GU15 65 B5
Horsham RH13 217 E4
Crawfurd Way RH19 185 F3
Crawley Ave
Crawley RH10 182 C1
Crawley, Ifield RH10,RH11 201 A6
Crawley Bsns Ctr RH10 181 E2
Crawley Chase RG42 8 B2
Crawley Coll RH10 201 E6
Crawley Coll (West Green Annexe) RH11 201 C7
Crawley Down CE Sch RH10 204 B8
Crawley Down Rd RH19 184 F4
Crawley Dr GU15 65 F6
Crawley Hill GU15 65 F5
Crawley Hospl RH11 201 C6
Crawley La RH10 202 C7
Crawley Mus Ctr★ RH11 201 C5
Crawley Rd
Crawley RH12 200 B1
Faygate RH12 218 D7
Horsham RH12 218 B5
Crawley Ridge GU15 65 F6
Crawley Ridge Inf Sch GU15 65 F6
Crawley Ridge Jun Sch GU15 65 F7
Crawley Sta RH10 201 E5
Crawley Wood Cl GU15 65 F5
Crawshaw Rd KT16 51 D4
Crawters Cl RH10 201 F7
Cray Ave KT21 75 F2
Crayke Hill KT9 56 E3
Crayonne Cl TW16 34 E8
Crealock St SW18 20 B8
Creasys Dr RH11 201 A1
Credenhill St SW16 21 C2
Crediton Way KT10 56 A5
Credon Cl GU14 84 F5
Cree's Mdw GU20 48 D3
Creek Rd KT8 36 E5
Creek The TW16 35 A4
Creeland Gr SE6 23 F7
Cremorne Gdns KT19 57 D2
Crerar Cl GU14 84 D3
Crescent Ct KT6 37 D4
Crescent Day Hospl CR0 63 C1
Crescent Gdns SW19 20 A5
Crescent Gr CR4 40 E5
Crescent La GU12 106 B5
Crescent Rd
Beckenham BR3 44 B7
Bletchingley RH1 120 C2
Caterham CR3 101 A3
East Grinstead RH19 185 D1
Kingston u T KT2 18 B1
Reigate RH2 139 A7
Shepperton TW17 34 C4
Wimbledon SW20 39 D8
Crescent Rd *continued*
Wokingham RG40 25 C5
Crescent The
Ashford TW15 13 F3
Barnes SW13 7 F5
Beckenham BR3 44 A8
Belmont SM2 78 A8
Bracknell RG12 27 C5
Carshalton SM1 59 D5
Chertsey KT16 33 A6
East Molesey KT8 36 A5
Egham TW20 11 F2
Epsom KT18 76 A4
Farnborough GU14 85 C3
Felcourt RH19 185 C8
Guildford GU2 109 A3
Harlington UB7 3 D7
Heath End GU9 125 D8
Horley RH6 182 B8
Horsham RH12 217 A2
Kingston u T KT6 37 E4
Kingston u T, Norbiton KT3 38 C7
Leatherhead KT22 95 B5
Lower Halliford TW17 34 F2
Reigate RH2 118 B1
Reigate,Mead Vale RH1 139 D6
Thornton Heath CR0,SE25 42 D3
West Wickham BR4 44 E3
Weybridge KT13 53 A7
Wimbledon SW19 20 A5
Woldingham CR3 102 A4
Crescent Way
Horley RH6 161 A1
South Norwood SW16 22 A1
Crescent Wood Rd SE21, SE26 23 A5
Cressage Ho 9 TW8 6 E8
Cressall Cl KT22 95 B7
Cressall Mead KT22 95 B7
Cressingham Gr SM1 59 C6
Cressinghams The KT18 76 D6
Cresswell Rd
Croydon SE25 43 A5
Feltham TW13 15 E4
Twickenham TW1 6 D1
Crest Hill GU5 133 E1
Crest Rd
South Croydon CR2 62 B3
West Wickham BR2 44 F2
Crest The Surbiton KT5 38 A4
10 West Norwood SW27 22 B3
Cresta Dr KT15 51 F1
Creston Ave GU21 68 E3
Creston Way KT4 39 D1
Crestwood Way TW4 4 E2
Creswell GU21 68 D2
Creswell Cnr GU21 68 D2
Crewdson Rd RH6 161 B3
Crewe's Ave CR6 81 C3
Crewe's Cl CR6 81 C2
Crewe's Farm La CR6 81 E2
Crewe's La CR6 81 D3
Crichton Ave SM6 60 D6
Crichton Rd SM5 59 F3
Cricket Cl GU26 188 D6
Cricket Ct RH19 185 E3
Cricket Field Gr RG45 45 D4
Cricket Field Rd RH12 217 B1
Cricket Gn
Hambledon GU8 171 C1
Mitcham CR4 40 F5
Cricket Green Sch CR4 40 E6
Cricket Hill RH1 140 F7
Cricket La
Farnham GU10 146 D6
Penge BR3 23 E3
Cricket View KT13 53 B5
Cricket Way KT13 53 E8
Cricketers Cl
Chessington KT9 56 D6
Ockley RH5 177 C4
Cricketers La
Windlesham GU20 48 D4
Winkfield RG42 8 A3
Cricketers Wlk SE26 23 C3
Cricklade Ave SW2 21 F6
Crieff Ct 3 TW11 17 C1
Criffel Ave SW2 21 D7
Criketers Terr 2 SM5 59 E7
Crimea Rd GU11 105 B2
Crimp Hill SL4,TW20 11 A6
Cripley Rd GU14 84 D6
Cripplecrutch Hill GU27 209 F5
Cripps Ho RH11 201 B2
Crispen Rd TW13 15 E4
Crispin Cl Ashstead KT21 75 F1
Wallington SM6 60 E8
Crispin Cres CR0 60 D8
Critchmere Hill GU27 207 E7
Critchmere La GU27 207 E6
Critchmere Vale GU27 207 E6
Critten La KT24,RH5 113 D2
Crittenden Lodge BR4 44 A1
Crocker Cl SL5 28 F8
Crockers La RH7 163 D4
Crockerton Rd SW17 20 F6
Crockford Cl KT15 52 C6
Crockford Park Rd KT15 52 C5
Crockham Cl RH11 201 C4
Crocknorth Rd KT24 113 A2
Crocus Cl CR0 43 D1
Croffets KT20 97 D6
Croft Ave Dorking RH4 115 B1
West Wickham BR4 44 C1
Croft Cl Harlington UB7 3 C7
Wokingham RG41 25 A2
Croft Ct SM1 59 D8
Croft Rd Aldershot GU11 126 B8

Croft Rd *continued*
Carshalton SM1 . . . .**59** E5
Godalming GU7 . . . .**150** E4
Merton SW19 . . . .**20** C1
South Norwood SW16 . . . . .**22** A1
Witley GU8 . . . .**170** E5
Wokingham RG40 . . . .**25** A1
Woldingham CR3 . . . .**102** A5
Croft The Crawley RH11 . . .**201** A6
Epsom KT17 . . . .**76** F5
Heston TW5 . . . .**4** E7
Croft Way Frimley GU16 . . .**65** F2
Horsham RH12 . . . .**217** A3
Richmond TW10 . . . .**17** B5
Crofter's Cl GU47 . . . .**64** A8
Crofters Cl TW7 . . . .**5** D2
Crofters Mead CR0 . . . .**62** F2
Croftleigh Ave SE8 . . . .**80** B3
Crofton Ashstead KT21 . . . . .**75** E1
Haslemere GU27 . . . .**207** F7
Crofton Ave Chiswick W4 . . . .**7** D7
Walton-on-T KT12 . . . .**54** C7
Crofton Cl Bracknell RG12 . .**27** E4
Ottershaw KT16 . . . .**51** C3
Crofton Terr TW9 . . . .**6** F3
Crofts Cl GU8 . . . .**191** B5
Crofts The TW17 . . . .**34** E5
Croftside The SE25 . . . .**43** A6
Croham Cl CR2 . . . .**61** E4
Croham Hurst Sch CR2 . . . .**61** E4
Croham Manor Rd CR2 . . . .**61** E4
Croham Mount CR2 . . . .**61** E3
Croham Park Ave CR0,
CR2 . . . .**61** F5
Croham Rd
Croydon CR0,CR2 . . . .**61** E5
South Croydon CR2 . . . .**61** E5
Croham Valley Rd CR2 . . . . .**62** B3
Croindene Rd SW16 . . . .**41** E8
Cromar Ct GU21 . . . .**69** C3
Cromer Ct SW16 . . . .**21** E5
Cromer Rd Croydon SE25 . .**43** B6
Harlington TW6 . . . .**3** A5
Mitcham SW17 . . . .**21** A2
Cromford Way KT3 . . . .**38** D8
Crompton Fields RH10 . . . .**181** E1
Crompton Way RH10 . . . . . .**181** E1
Cromwell Ave KT3 . . . .**38** F4
Cromwell Cl KT12 . . . .**35** B1
Cromwell Ct 15 KT2 . . . .**18** A1
Cromwell Gr CR3 . . . .**100** C6
Cromwell Ho CR0 . . . .**61** B7
Cromwell Pl
Cranleigh GU6 . . . .**174** F1
1 East Grinstead RH19 . . .**205** F7
Mortlake SW14 . . . .**7** C4
14 Redhill RH1 . . . .**118** F2
Cromwell Rd Ascot SL5 . . . .**29** B4
Beckenham BR3 . . . .**43** E6
Camberley GU15 . . . .**65** D7
Caterham CR3 . . . .**100** C6
Feltham TW13 . . . .**15** B7
Hounslow TW3 . . . .**5** A3
Kingston u T KT2 . . . .**37** E8
Redhill RH1 . . . .**118** F1
Teddington TW11 . . . .**17** A2
Thornton Heath CR0 . . . .**42** D2
Walton-on-T KT12 . . . .**35** C1
Wimbledon SW19 . . . .**20** B2
Worcester Park KT19,KT4 . . .**57** E7
Cromwell St TW3 . . . .**5** A3
Cromwell Way GU14 . . . .**85** C7
Cromwell Wlk 1 RH1 . . . . .**118** F1
Crondall Cl GU6 . . . .**65** B4
Crondall Ho SW15 . . . .**19** A7
Crondall La GU10,GU9 . . . .**124** D2
Crondall Rd GU10 . . . .**145** A6
Cronks Hill RH1,RH2 . . . . .**139** D7
Cronks Hill Cl RH1 . . . .**139** D7
Cronks Hill Rd RH1 . . . . . .**139** D7
Crooksbury Rd
Farnham GU10 . . . .**126** C2
Tilford GU10 . . . .**147** D8
Crosby Cl TW13 . . . .**15** E4
Crosby Hill Dr GU15 . . . .**65** F7
Crosby Way
Farnham GU9 . . . .**125** A1
Streatham SW2 . . . .**22** A8
Crosby Wlk SW2 . . . .**22** A8
Cross Deep TW1 . . . .**17** A6
Cross Deep Gdns TW1 . . . . .**16** F6
Cross Farm Inf Sch GU16 .**85** E6
Cross Fell RG12 . . . .**27** A5
Cross Gates Cl RG12 . . . . . .**27** F6
Cross Gdns GU16 . . . .**85** F6
Cross Keys RH10 . . . .**201** D6
Cross La Burstow RH6 . . . .**162** C1
Frimley GU16 . . . .**85** F6
Ottershaw KT16 . . . .**51** C4
Cross Lances Rd TW3 . . . . . .**5** B3
Cross Lanes GU1 . . . .**130** F8
Cross Oak La RH1 . . . .**161** C7
Cross Rd Ash GU12 . . . . . .**106** B3
Belmont SM2 . . . .**59** A1
Carshalton SM1 . . . .**59** D5
Croydon CR0 . . . .**42** D1
Farnborough GU14 . . . .**84** E1
Feltham TW13 . . . .**15** E4
Kingston u T KT2 . . . .**17** F1
Merton SW19 . . . .**20** A1
Oatlands Park KT13 . . . .**53** D7
Purley CR8 . . . .**80** B6
Tadworth KT20 . . . .**97** C5
Wentworth SL5 . . . .**30** A1
Cross St
6 Aldershot GU11 . . . . . .**105** A2
Farnborough GU14 . . . .**105** C8
Hampton TW12 . . . .**16** C3

Cross St *continued*
Mortlake SW13 . . . .**7** E4
Wokingham RG40 . . . .**25** C6
Crossacres GU22 . . . .**70** E4
Crossfield Pl KT13 . . . .**53** B3
Crossland Ho GU25 . . . .**31** E5
Crossland Rd
Redhill RH1 . . . .**119** A1
Thornton Heath CR7 . . . .**42** B3
Crosslands KT16 . . . .**51** E6
Crosslands Rd KT19 . . . .**57** D4
Crossley Cl TN16 . . . .**83** D4
Crossman Ct RH11 . . . .**201** B1
Crossman Hos 18 SW12 . . . .**21** B8
Crossness Ho KT19 . . . .**57** A1
Crosspath RH10 . . . .**201** E7
Crossroads The KT24 . . . . .**113** D7
Crosswater La GU10 . . . . . .**167** F4
Crossway Bracknell RG12 . .**27** C7
Crawley RH6 . . . .**181** F8
Walton-on-T KT12 . . . .**54** B8
West Barnes KT3,SW20 . . . .**39** C5
Crossways
Aldershot GU12 . . . .**105** C1
Charlton TW16 . . . .**14** F1
Churt GU10 . . . .**167** F1
Crawley RH10 . . . .**202** A7
Effingham KT24 . . . .**113** D6
Egham TW20 . . . .**12** D2
South Croydon CR0,CR2 . . . .**62** F3
Sutton SM2 . . . .**59** D2
Tatsfield TN16 . . . .**103** C7
Crossways Ave RH19 . . . . . .**185** C1
Crossways Cl Churt GU10 .**167** F1
Crawley RH10 . . . .**201** F7
Crossways Cotts GU6 . . . . .**194** A3
Crossways Ct TN16 . . . .**103** C7
Crossways La RH2 . . . .**118** D2
Crossways The
Beckenham BR3 . . . .**44** A5
Grayshott GU26 . . . .**188** D3
Mitcham CR4 . . . .**41** B6
Crossways The
Abinger Hammer RH5 . . . . .**134** B3
Coulsdon CR5 . . . .**100** A8
Guildford GU2 . . . .**129** F7
Heston TW5 . . . .**4** F7
Lower Kingswood RH2 . . . . .**118** C7
Merstham RH1 . . . .**119** C6
Crosswell Cl TW17 . . . .**34** C7
Crouch Cl BR3 . . . .**24** A2
Crouch Ind Est KT22 . . . . . .**95** B8
Crouch La SL4 . . . .**8** F7
Crouch Oak La KT15 . . . . . .**52** C6
Crouchfield RH4 . . . .**136** C4
Crouchmans Cl SE21,
SE26 . . . .**23** A5
Crowberry Cl RH11 . . . .**201** A2
Crowborough Cl CR6 . . . . . .**81** E1
Crowborough Dr CR6 . . . . . .**81** E1
Crowborough Rd SW17 . . . . .**21** A3
Crowholt SE25 . . . .**145** F5
Crowhurst SE25 . . . .**43** A6
Crowhurst Cl RH10 . . . .**202** E6
Crowhurst Keep RH10 . . . . .**202** E6
Crowhurst La RH7,RH8 . . . .**143** D4
Crowhurst Mead RH9 . . . . .**121** C5
Crowhurst Rd RH7 . . . .**164** D7
Crowhurst Village Rd
RH7 . . . .**143** E2
Crowland Rd CR7 . . . .**42** D5
Crowland Wlk SM4 . . . .**40** C3
Crowley Cres CR0 . . . .**61** A5
Crowmarsh Gdns SE23 . . . . .**23** C8
Crown Arc KT1 . . . .**37** D7
Crown Cl Colnbrook SW3 . . . .**1** C7
Walton-on-T KT12 . . . .**35** C2
Crown Cotts Bracknell SL5 .**28** C4
Englefield Green TW20 . . . . .**11** A1
Crown Ct Godalming GU7 . .**150** E4
4 Twickenham TW1 . . . .**17** B8
Crown Dale SE19, SE27 . . . .**22** C3
Crown Dr GU9 . . . .**126** A5
Crown Hill Ct SL5 . . . .**29** B4
Crown Hts GU1 . . . .**130** E6
Crown La Farnham GU9 . . .**126** A5
Merton SM4,SW19 . . . .**40** A5
South Norwood SW16 . . . . . .**22** A3
Wentworth GU25 . . . .**31** D3
Crown Lane Gdns SE27 . . . .**22** C4
Crown Lane Prim Sch
SE27 . . . .**22** C4
Crown Mdw SL3 . . . .**1** B7
Crown Par SM4 . . . .**40** A5
Crown Pas KT1 . . . .**37** D7
Crown Pl GU47 . . . .**45** E1
Crown Point Par SE19 . . . . .**22** B2
Crown Rd Kingston u T KT3 .**38** C8
Morden SM4,SW19 . . . .**40** B5
Sutton SM1 . . . .**59** B6
Twickenham TW1 . . . .**6** B1
Wentworth GU25 . . . .**31** C3
Crown Rise KT16 . . . .**32** F1
Crown Row RG12 . . . .**27** D3
Crown St TW20 . . . .**12** A4
Crown Terr TW9 . . . .**6** F3
Crown Wood Prim Sch
RG12 . . . .**27** E3
Crown Yd TW3 . . . .**5** C4
Crownbourne Ct SM1 . . . . . .**59** B6
Crownpits La GU7 . . . .**150** E3
Crowntree La TW7 . . . .**5** F4
Crowther Rd SE25 . . . .**43** A5
Crowthorne Bsns Est The
RG45 . . . .**45** D7
Crowthorne CE Sch
RG45 . . . .**45** C5
Crowthorne Cl SW18 . . . .**19** F7

Crowthorne Lodge RG12 . .**27** B5
Crowthorne Rd
Bracknell RG40,RG12 . . . . . .**26** F2
Bracknell,Easthampstead
RG12 . . . .**27** A5
Sandhurst GU47 . . . .**45** B2
Crowthorne Rd N RG12 . . . .**27** B6
Croxall Ho KT12 . . . .**35** C3
Croxden Wlk SM4 . . . .**40** C3
Croxted Cl SE21 . . . .**22** C8
Croyde Cl GU14 . . . .**85** A7
Croydon Airport Ind Est
CR9 . . . .**60** F4
Croydon Coll CR9 . . . .**61** D8
Croydon Coll (Selhurst
Tertiary Ctr) SE25 . . . .**42** C4
Croydon Coll Annexe
CR0 . . . .**42** D1
Croydon Flyover The
CR0,CR9 . . . .**61** C7
Croydon Gr CR0 . . . .**42** B1
Croydon High Sch CR2 . . . .**62** C1
Croydon La Banstead SM7 . .**78** D6
Wallington SM7 . . . .**78** D6
Croydon La S SM7 . . . .**78** B5
Croydon Rd
Beckenham BR3 . . . .**43** E6
Caterham CR3 . . . .**101** A5
Coney Hall BR2,BR4 . . . .**63** F7
Croydon CR0,SM6 . . . .**60** D7
Harlington TW6 . . . .**3** B4
Mitcham CR0,CR4,CR9 . . . . .**41** C4
Penge SE20 . . . .**43** C8
Reigate RH2 . . . .**118** C2
Tatsfield TN16 . . . .**103** F3
Titsey CR6 . . . .**102** D5
Croydon Rd Ind Est BR3 .**43** D5
Croydonbarn La RH6,
RH9 . . . .**163** B4
Croylands Dr KT6 . . . .**37** E2
Croysdale Ave TW16 . . . .**35** A6
Crozier Dr CR2 . . . .**62** B1
Cruikshank Lea GU47 . . . . . .**64** B8
Crunden Rd CR2 . . . .**61** D3
Crundwell Ct GU9 . . . .**125** D3
Crusader Gdns CR0 . . . .**61** E7
Crusoe Rd CR4 . . . .**20** F1
Crutchfield La
Sidlow RH6 . . . .**160** B5
Walton-on-T KT12 . . . .**54** B6
Crutchley Rd Catford SE6 . . .**24** E6
Wokingham RG40 . . . .**25** D7
Crystal Ct SE19 . . . .**22** F3
Crystal Palace National
Sports Ctr SE19 . . . .**23** A2
Crystal Palace Par SE19 . .**22** F3
Crystal Palace Park Rd
SE19,SE26 . . . .**23** B3
Crystal Palace Sta SE19 . .**23** A2
Crystal Palace Station Rd
SE19 . . . .**23** A2
Crystal Terr SE19 . . . .**22** D2
Crystal View Ct BR1 . . . .**24** D4
Cubitt Way GU21 . . . .**68** D1
Cuckfield Cl RH11 . . . .**200** F3
Cuckmere Cres RH11 . . . . .**200** F5
Cuckoo La GU24 . . . .**67** D6
Cuckoo Vale GU24 . . . .**67** D6
Cuda's Cl KT19 . . . .**57** F6
Cuddington Ave KT19,KT4 . .**57** F7
Cuddington Cl KT20 . . . .**97** D7
Cuddington Com Prim Sch
KT4 . . . .**57** F7
Cuddington Croft Prim Sch
SM2 . . . .**58** D2
Cuddington Glade KT19 . . . .**76** A7
Cuddington Park Cl SM7 . . .**77** F6
Cuddington Way SM2,
SM7 . . . .**77** D8
Cudham Dr CR0 . . . .**82** C8
Cudham Rd TN16 . . . .**103** E8
Cudham St SE6 . . . .**24** C8
Cudworth La RH5 . . . .**179** E8
Cuffs Hill RH10 . . . .**202** E2
Culham Ho RG12 . . . .**27** E5
Cull's Rd GU3 . . . .**107** C1
Cullens Mews 5 GU11 . . . .**105** A1
Cullerne Cl KT17 . . . .**57** F1
Cullesden Rd CR8 . . . .**80** B4
Culmer Hill GU8 . . . .**170** F2
Culmer La GU8 . . . .**171** A2
Culmington Rd CR2 . . . .**61** C2
Culsac Rd 1 KT6 . . . .**56** E8
Culver Dr RH8 . . . .**122** E5
Culver Ho GU1 . . . .**110** A1
Culver Rd GU47 . . . .**45** D1
Culverden Ct 5 KT13 . . . . . .**53** D7
Culverden Rd SW12 . . . .**21** C6
Culverden Terr KT13 . . . .**53** D7
Culverhay KT21 . . . .**75** E3
Culverhouse Gdns SW16 . . .**21** F5
Culverlands Cres GU12 . . .**106** A3
Culverley Rd SE6 . . . .**24** C7
Culvers Ave SM5 . . . .**59** F8
Culvers House Prim Sch
CR4 . . . .**41** A1
Culvers Retreat SM5 . . . .**59** F8
Culvers Way SM5 . . . .**59** F8
Culverstone Cl BR2 . . . .**44** F4
Culworth Ho GU1 . . . .**130** E8
Cumber Ho SW18 . . . .**20** A7
Cumberland Ave GU2,
GU3 . . . .**109** A6
Cumberland Cl
Epsom KT19 . . . .**57** E1
2 Twickenham TW1 . . . .**6** B2
6 Wimbledon SW20 . . . . . .**19** D1
Cumberland Ct 4 CR0 . . . . .**42** D1

Cumberland Dr
Bracknell RG12 . . . .**27** E8
Chessington KT9 . . . .**56** F7
Hinchley Wood KT10 . . . .**56** A8
Cumberland Ho KT2 . . . .**18** B1
Cumberland Lodge SL4 . . . .**10** D4
Cumberland Pl
Catford SE6 . . . .**24** F7
Sunbury TW16 . . . .**35** A5
Cumberland Rd
Ashford TW15 . . . .**13** D5
Barnes SW13 . . . .**7** F6
Beckenham BR2 . . . .**44** F6
Croydon SE25 . . . .**43** B3
Frimley GU15 . . . .**66** C4
Richmond TW9 . . . .**7** A7
Cumberland St TW18 . . . .**12** D3
Cumberlands CR8 . . . .**80** D4
Cumberlow Ave SE25 . . . . . .**43** A6
Cumbernauld Gdns KT6 . . . .**56** D8
Cumbernauld Wlk RH11 . . .**200** E2
Cumbrae Gdns KT6 . . . .**56** D8
Cumbria Ct GU14 . . . .**85** C1
Cumnor Gdns KT17 . . . .**58** A4
Cumnor House Sch CR2 . . . .**61** B2
Cumnor Rd SM2 . . . .**59** C4
Cumnor Rise CR8 . . . .**80** C2
Cumnor Way RG12 . . . .**27** E5
Cunard Mews GU6 . . . .**193** C2
Cunliffe Cl KT18 . . . .**96** B3
Cunliffe Rd KT19 . . . .**57** F6
Cunliffe St SW16 . . . .**21** C2
Cunningham Ave GU1 . . . . .**110** B2
Cunningham Cl BR4 . . . .**63** B8
Cunningham Rd SM7 . . . . . .**78** D4
Cunnington Rd GU14 . . . .**85** C2
Cunworth Ct RG12 . . . .**26** F3
Curfew Bell Rd KT16 . . . .**32** F2
Curl Way RG41 . . . .**25** A5
Curlew Ct CR2 . . . .**81** D8
Curlew Ct
Aldershot GU11 . . . .**126** A7
Tolworth KT6 . . . .**57** A7
Curlew Gdns GU4 . . . .**110** D3
Curley Hill Rd GU18 . . . .**66** F7
Curling Cl CR5 . . . .**100** A7
Curling Vale GU2 . . . .**130** A7
Curly Bridge Cl GU14 . . . . . .**84** F8
Curnick's La SE27 . . . .**22** C4
Curran Ave SM6 . . . .**60** A7
Currie Hill Cl SW19 . . . .**19** F4
Currie Ho 13 SW12 . . . .**21** D8
Curteys Wlk RH11 . . . .**201** A3
Curtis Cl GU15 . . . .**66** C7
Curtis Field Rd SW16 . . . . . .**22** A4
Curtis Gdns 2 RH4 . . . .**136** A8
Curtis Rd Dorking RH4 . . . .**136** A8
Twickenham TW4 . . . .**15** F8
West Ewell KT19 . . . .**57** C6
Curvan Cl KT17 . . . .**57** F1
Curzon Ave RH12 . . . .**217** B3
Curzon Cl KT13 . . . .**53** A6
Curzon Rd
Thornton Heath CR7 . . . .**42** A3
Weybridge KT13 . . . .**53** A5
Cusack Cl TW1 . . . .**16** F4
Cuthbert Gdns SE25 . . . .**42** E6
Cuthbert Rd Ash GU12 . . . .**106** B6
Thornton Heath CR0,CR9 . . . .**61** B8
Cuttinglye La RH10 . . . .**184** A1
Cuttinglye Rd RH10 . . . .**184** C2
Cutts Rd GU11 . . . .**105** D7
Cyclamen Cl 4 TW12 . . . . . .**16** A2
Cyclamen Way KT19 . . . .**57** C5
Cygnet Ave TW14 . . . .**15** D8
Cygnet Cl GU21 . . . .**69** B3
Cygnets Cl RH1 . . . .**119** A3
Cygnets The
Feltham TW13 . . . .**15** E4
Staines TW18 . . . .**12** F3
Cypress Ave TW2 . . . .**16** C8
Cypress Ct Sutton SM1 . . . . .**59** A4
Thorpe GU25 . . . .**31** F5
8 West Norwood SW16 . . . .**22** A3
Cypress Gr GU12 . . . .**105** F7
Cypress Hill Ct GU14 . . . . . .**64** F1
Cypress Inf Sch SE25 . . . . . .**42** E7
Cypress Jun Sch SE25 . . . . .**42** E7
Cypress Lodge SE25 . . . .**42** E7
Cypress Rd
Guildford GU1 . . . .**109** C4
South Norwood SE25 . . . .**42** E7
Cypress Way
Banstead KT17 . . . .**77** D5
Blackwater GU17 . . . .**64** B5
Grayshott GU26 . . . .**188** D2
Cypress Wlk TW20 . . . .**11** B2
Cyprian Ave GU24 . . . .**88** B6
Cyprus Rd GU16 . . . .**86** D8
Cyrillian Ho SM2 . . . .**59** B4

D

D'abernon Cl KT10 . . . .**55** A6
D'Abernon Dr KT11 . . . .**73** E3
D'arcy Rd SM3 . . . .**58** D6
Dacre Rd CR0 . . . .**41** E2
Dacres Rd SE23 . . . .**23** D5
Daffodil Cl Croydon CR0 . . . .**43** D1
7 Hampton TW12 . . . .**16** A2
Daffodil Dr GU24 . . . .**68** A3
Dafforne Rd SW17 . . . .**21** A5
Dagden Rd GU4 . . . .**130** E6
Dagley La GU4 . . . .**130** D6

Dagnall Pk CR0,SE25 . . . . . .**42** E4
Dagnall Rd SE25 . . . .**42** E4
Dagnan Rd SW12 . . . .**21** C8
Dahlia Gdns CR4 . . . .**41** D5
Dahomey Rd SW16 . . . .**21** C2
Daimler Way SM6 . . . .**60** E3
Dainford Cl BR1 . . . .**24** D3
Dairy Cl CR7 . . . .**42** C7
Dairy Cl SW17 . . . .**42** C7
Dairyfields RH11 . . . .**201** A5
Dairymans Wlk GU4 . . . .**110** B6
Daisy Cl CR0 . . . .**43** D1
Daisy Mdw TW20 . . . .**12** A3
Dakin Ho RH10 . . . .**202** C2
Dakins The RH19 . . . .**205** E8
Dakota Cl SM6 . . . .**60** F3
Dalcross RG12 . . . .**27** E3
Dalcross Rd TW4,TW5 . . . .**4** E5
Dale Ave TW4 . . . .**4** E4
Dale Cl Addlestone KT15 . . . .**52** B5
Horsham RH12 . . . .**217** F5
Sunningdale SL5 . . . .**30** A4
Wrecclesham GU10 . . . .**145** F7
Dale Ct 3 KT2 . . . .**17** F1
Dale Gdns GU47 . . . .**64** A8
Dale Lodge Rd SL5 . . . .**30** A4
Dale Park Ave SM5 . . . .**59** F8
Dale Park Rd SE19 . . . .**42** D8
Dale Rd Ashford TW16 . . . . . .**14** F1
Cheam SM1 . . . .**58** F6
Forest Row RH18 . . . .**206** F1
Purley CR8 . . . .**80** B7
Walton-on-T KT12 . . . .**34** F2
Dale View
Haslemere GU27 . . . .**207** F5
Headley KT18 . . . .**96** B4
Woking GU21 . . . .**69** B1
Dalebury Rd SW17 . . . .**20** F6
Daledene RH10 . . . .**205** F8
Dalegarth Gdns CR8 . . . .**80** D6
Daleham Ave TW20 . . . .**12** A2
Daleside Rd
Streatham SW17 . . . .**21** B3
West Ewell KT19 . . . .**57** D4
Dalewood Gdns
Crawley RH10 . . . .**201** F8
North Cheam KT4 . . . .**58** B8
Dalkeith Rd SE21 . . . .**22** C8
Dallas Rd Cheam SM3 . . . . . .**58** E4
Forest Hill SE26 . . . .**23** B5
Dallaway Gdns RH19 . . . . . .**185** E1
Dalley Ct GU47 . . . .**64** D7
Dallington Cl KT12 . . . .**54** C4
Dalmain Prim Sch SE23 . . . .**23** E7
Dalmain Rd SE23 . . . .**23** D7
Dalmally Rd CR0 . . . .**43** A2
Dalmeny Ave SW16 . . . .**42** A7
Dalmeny Cres TW3 . . . .**5** D3
Dalmeny Rd
North Cheam KT4 . . . .**58** B7
Wallington SM5 . . . .**60** A3
Dalmore Ave KT10 . . . .**55** F4
Dalmore Rd SE21 . . . .**22** C6
Dalston Cl GU15 . . . .**66** D3
Dalton Ave CR4 . . . .**40** F7
Dalton Cl Crawley RH11 . . . .**201** B1
Purley CR8 . . . .**80** C7
Dalton Ho 8 SW12 . . . .**21** B8
Dalton St SE27 . . . .**22** B5
Damascene Wlk SE21 . . . . . .**22** C7
Damask Cl GU24 . . . .**67** E6
Damer Ho 9 TW10 . . . .**6** F1
Dampier Wlk RH11 . . . .**201** B1
Damson Way SM5 . . . .**59** F2
Dan Bryant Ho 5 SW12 . . . . .**21** D8
Danbrook Rd SW16 . . . .**21** E1
Danbury Mews SM6 . . . .**60** B6
Danby Ct RH6 . . . .**161** B5
Dancer Rd TW9 . . . .**7** A4
Dane Ct GU22 . . . .**70** F4
Dane Ho SW17 . . . .**20** C4
Dane Rd Ashford TW15 . . . . .**14** D2
Merton SW19 . . . .**40** C8
Warlingham CR6 . . . .**81** D2
Danebury CR0 . . . .**63** B4
Danebury Ave SW15 . . . .**7** E1
Danebury Wlk GU16 . . . .**85** F8
Daneby Rd SE6 . . . .**24** C6
Danecourt Gdns CR0 . . . .**61** F7
Danehurst TW8 . . . .**6** C7
Danehurst Cl TW20 . . . .**11** B2
Danehurst Cres RH13 . . . . .**217** F2
Danehurst St SW17 . . . .**76** F6
Danemore La RH9 . . . .**142** F2
Danes Cl KT22 . . . .**74** C5
Danes Hill GU22 . . . .**70** B1
Danes Hill Prep Sch
KT22 . . . .**74** D6
Danes Way KT22 . . . .**74** D5
Danesbury Rd TW13 . . . .**15** B7
Danescourt Cres SM1 . . . . . .**59** C8
Danesfield GU23 . . . .**90** F4
Danesfield Cl KT12 . . . .**54** B8
Danesfield Sch KT12 . . . .**54** C8
Daneshill RH1 . . . .**118** E2
Daneshill Cl RH1 . . . .**118** E2
Danesmead KT11 . . . .**74** A8
Danesrood GU1 . . . .**130** F8
Daneswood Ave SE6 . . . .**24** C5
Danetree Cl KT19 . . . .**57** C3
Danetree Jun Sch KT19 . . . .**57** C4
Danetree Rd KT19 . . . .**57** D3
Daniel Cl SW17,SW19 . . . . . .**20** E2
Daniel Ct 3 BR3 . . . .**24** A1
Daniel Way SM7 . . . .**78** B5

242 Dan – Dew

Daniell Way CR0,CR9 .....41 F1
Daniels La CR6 ....81 F4
Danley La GU27 ....207 A3
Danses Cl GU4 ....110 D3
Danvers Way CR3 ......100 C4
Dapdune Ct GU1 ....109 C1
Dapdune Rd GU1 ....109 D1
Dapdune Wharf* GU1 .109 C1
Daphne Ct KT4 ....57 E8
Daphne St SW18 ....20 C8
Darby Cl CR3 ....100 C5
Darby Cres TW16 ....35 C7
Darby Gdns TW16 ....35 C7
Darby Green La GU17 ...64 B6
Darby Green Rd GU17 ...64 B5
Darcy Ave SM6 ....60 C6
Darcy Cl CR5 ....100 B8
Darcy Pl KT21 ....75 F2
Darcy Rd Ashstead KT21 ..75 F2
Isleworth TW7 ....6 A6
Thornton Heath SW16 ......41 E7
Darell Prim Sch TW9 .....7 A4
Darell Rd TW9 ....7 A4
Darent Ho BR1 ....24 D3
Darenth Way RH6 ......160 F6
Darfield Rd GU4 ....110 A4
Dargate Cl SE19 ....22 F1
Dark La GU3 ....128 B4
Darlaston Rd SW19 .....19 E1
Darley Cl Addlestone KT15 .52 C5
Croydon CR0 ....43 E3
Darley Dene Ct KT15 ....52 C6
Darley Dene Inf Sch
KT15 ....52 C5
Darley Dr KT3 ....38 D7
Darley Gdns SM4 ....40 B3
Darleydale RH11 ....201 C3
Darleydale Cl GU47 .....45 D2
Darlington Ct SE6 ....24 F7
Darlington Ho 2 KT6 ...37 D2
Darlington Rd SE27 .....22 B3
Darmaine Cl CR2 ....61 C3
Darnley Pk KT13 ....53 B7
Darracott Cl GU15 ......66 B8
Darrell Ct BR2 ....44 E6
Darsena Ho 6 SM2 .....59 C3
Dart Cl SL3 ....1 B8
Dart Ct RH19 ....186 A3
Dart Rd GU14 ....84 D6
Dartmouth Ave GU21 ....70 D5
Dartmouth Cl RG12 .....27 E6
Dartmouth Gn GU21 .....70 D5
Dartmouth Ho CR0 ......42 B2
Dartmouth Path GU21 ...70 D5
Dartmouth Pl
Chiswick W4 ....7 E8
Forest Hill SE23 ....23 C6
Dartmouth Rd
SE23,SE26 ....23 C5
Dartnell Ave KT14 ....71 C7
Dartnell Cl KT14 ....71 B7
Dartnell Cres KT14 ......71 B7
Dartnell Ct KT14 ....71 C7
Dartnell Park Rd KT14 ...71 C8
Dartnell Pl KT14 ....71 B7
Dartnell Rd CR0 ....42 F2
Darvel Cl GU21 ....69 A3
Darvills La GU9 ....125 C2
Darwall Dr SL5 ....28 D7
Darwin Cl RH12 ....217 F4
Darwin Ct GU15 ....65 E6
Darwin Gr GU11 ....105 C3
Daryngton Dr GU1 .....110 B1
Dashwood Cl
Bracknell RG12 ....27 D8
West Byfleet KT14 ....71 C7
Dashwood Ct TW3 ....5 C3
Dashwood Ho SE21 .....22 F5
Dashwood Lang Rd KT15 52 E6
Dassett Rd SE27 ....22 B3
Datchet Rd Forest Hill SE6 23 F6
Horton SL3 ....1 A4
Daux Hill RH12 ....217 B6
Davenant Rd CR0,CR9 ....61 B6
Davenport Cl TW11 .....17 A2
Davenport Lodge TW5 ....4 E7
Davenport Rd RG12 .....27 E8
Daventry Cl SL3 ....1 F6
Daventry Ct RG42 ....27 B8
David Cl UB3 ....3 E7
David Ho SE25 ....43 A6
David Livingstone Prim Sch
CR7 ....42 C8
David Rd SL3 ....1 F5
David's Rd SE23 ....23 C7
Davidson Inf Sch CR0 ...42 F2
Davidson Jun Sch CR0 ..42 F2
Davidson Lodge CR0 ....42 E2
Davidson Rd CR0,SE25 ...42 F3
Davies Cl
Croydon CR0,SE25 ....43 A3
Farncombe GU7 ....150 D7
Davies Wlk TW7 ....5 D6
Davis Cl RH11 ....201 A1
Davis Gdns GU47 ....64 E7
Davis Rd
Chessington KT9 ....57 A6
Weybridge KT13 ....52 F1
Davos Cl GU22 ....89 E8
Davy Cl RG40 ....25 C5
Dawell Dr TN16 ....83 C2
Dawes Ave TW7 ....6 A3
Dawes Ct KT10 ....55 B6
Dawes Green Cotts
RH2 ....138 A3
Dawley Ride SL3 ....1 E6
Dawlish Ave SW18 ......20 B6
Dawn Cl TW4 ....4 E4
Dawn Ct GU15 ....65 F7
Dawn Redwood Cl SL3 ...1 A4
Dawn Wlk BR2 ....44 D7
Dawnay Cl SL5 ....28 F8
Dawnay Gdns SW18 .....20 D6
Dawnay Prim Sch The
KT23 ....94 A1
Dawnay Rd
Camberley GU15 ....65 B7
Great Bookham KT23 .....94 C1
Wandsworth SW17,SW18 ..20 D6
Dawney Hill GU24 ....87 F5
Dawneys Rd GU24 ....87 E5
Dawsmere Cl GU15 ......66 C5
Dawson Rd Byfleet KT14 ..71 E8
Kingston u T KT1 ....37 F6
Dax Ct TW16 ....35 C6
Day Ct GU6 ....173 F2
Day's Acre CR2 ....61 F1
Daybrook Rd SW19 ......40 B6
Daymerslea Ridge KT22 .95 C6
Daysbrook Rd SW2 ......21 F7
Dayseys Hill RH1 ......162 A8
Dayspring GU2 ....109 B5
Daytone Ho SW20 ....39 D8
De Broome Rd TW13 ....15 C7
De Burgh Gdns KT20 ....97 D8
De Burgh Ho 10 SW19 ...20 C1
De Burgh Pk SM7 ....78 B4
De Frene Rd SE23,SE26 ..23 E5
De Havilland Dr KT13 ...71 E8
De Havilland Rd TW5 .....4 C7
De Havilland Way TW19 ..2 E1
De La Warr Rd RH19 ...185 F1
De Lara Way GU21 ....69 D1
De Mel Cl KT19 ....76 B7
De Montfort Par 1
SW16 ....21 E5
De Montfort Rd SW16 ...21 E6
De Ros Pl TW20 ....12 A2
de Stafford Coll CR3 ...100 F6
De'arn Gdns CR4 ....40 E6
De-Vitre Gn RG40 ....25 F7
Deacon Cl Downside KT11 .93 B8
Wallington CR8 ....60 E2
Wokingham RG40 ....25 C8
Deacon Ct RH7 ....164 C4
Deacon Field GU2 ......109 A2
Deacon Rd KT2 ....37 F8
Deacons Wlk TW12 ......16 A4
Deadbrook La GU12 ....105 E3
Deal Rd SW17 ....21 A2
Dean Cl GU22 ....70 E3
Dean Ct
Farncombe GU7 ....150 D6
10 Kingston u T KT2 ......18 A1
Dean Gr RG40 ....25 C7
Dean La RH1 ....99 C3
Dean Par GU15 ....65 F8
Dean Rd Croydon CR0 ....61 D6
Farncombe GU7 ....150 D6
Hampton TW12 ....16 A3
Isleworth TW3 ....5 B2
Dean Shaw Cotts RH8 ..122 A2
Dean Wlk KT23 ....94 B1
Deanery Pl 1 GU7 .....150 D4
Deanery Rd GU7 ....150 E6
Deanfield Gdns CR0 .....61 D6
Deanhill Ct SW14 ....7 B3
Deanhill Rd SW14 ....7 B3
Deanoak La RH2 ....159 D8
Deans Cl Chiswick W4 .....7 B8
South Croydon CR0 ....61 F7
Walton on the Hill KT20 ....97 B3
Deans Ct GU20 ....48 D4
Deans Gate Cl SE23 .....23 D5
Deans La Nutfield RH1 ...120 A2
Walton on the Hill KT20 ....97 B2
Deans Rd
Merstham RH1 ....119 C5
Sutton SM1 ....59 B7
Deans Wlk CR5 ....80 A1
Deansfield CR3 ....100 F2
Deansgate RG12 ....27 B2
Dearmer Ho 2 SW2 .....22 A8
Debden Cl KT2 ....17 D3
Deborah Cl TW7 ....5 E6
Deburgh Rd SW19 ....20 C1
Decon Pl CR3 ....100 C4
Dedham Ho SE6 ....24 C4
Dedisham Cl RH10 .....202 A5
Dedswell Dr GU4 ....111 A6
Dee Rd TW9 ....6 F3
Dee Way KT19 ....57 E1
Deedman Cl GU12 ......106 A2
Deep Pool La GU24 ......69 B6
Deep Well Dr GU15 ......65 E5
Deepcut Bridge Rd GU16 86 C7
Deepdale Bracknell RG12 .27 A5
Horley RH6 ....161 B2
Wimbledon SW19 ....19 D4
Deepdale Ave BR2 ....44 F5
Deepdene
Farnham GU10 ....146 D7
Haslemere GU27 ....207 E6
Deepdene Ave
Dorking RH4,RH5 ....136 C6
South Croydon CR0 ....61 F7
Deepdene Avenue Rd
RH4 ....115 C1
Deepdene Ct BR2 ....44 E6
Deepdene Dr RH4 ......136 C7
Deepdene Gdns
Dorking RH4 ....136 C8
Streatham SW2 ....21 F8
Deepdene Lodge 8 SW2 .21 F8
Deepdene Park Rd RH5 136 D8
Deepdene Point 9 SE26 .23 D5
Deepdene Rdbt RH4 ...136 C8
Deepdene Vale RH4 ....115 C1
Deepdene Wood RH5 ..136 D7
Deepfield Rd RG12 ......27 D7
Deepfield Way CR5 ......79 E3
Deepfields RH6 ....160 F5
Deeprose Cl GU3 ....109 B5
Deepwell Cl TW7 ....6 A6
Deer Leap GU18 ....67 A8
Deer Park Cl KT2 ....18 B1
Deer Park Gdns CR4 ....40 D5
Deer Park Rd SW19 .....40 C7
Deer Park Way BR4 ......63 F8
Deer Rock Hill RG12 ....27 C3
Deer Rock Rd GU15 .....65 F8
Deerbarn Rd GU2 ....109 B2
Deerbrook Rd SE24 ......22 B7
Deerhurst KT2 ....38 B8
Deerhurst Cl TW13 ....15 B4
Deerhurst Rd SW16 ......21 F3
Deerings Rd RH2 ....118 C1
Deerleap GU35 ....187 C4
Deerleap Cotts RH5 ....134 C4
Deerleap Rd RH4 ......135 B6
Deers Farm GU23 ....71 E3
Deerswood Cl
Caterham CR3 ....101 A3
Crawley RH11 ....201 B7
Deerswood Ct RH11 ....201 A7
Deerswood Lower Sch
RH11 ....201 A8
Deerswood Rd RH11 ...201 B7
Deerswood Upper Sch
RH11 ....201 A8
Deeside Rd SW17 ....20 D5
Defence Evaluation &
Research Agency
GU14 ....84 C1
Defiant Way SM6 ....60 E3
Defoe Ave TW9 ....7 A7
Defoe Cl SW17,SW19 ....20 E2
Defoe Pl SW17 ....20 F4
Delabole Rd RH1 ....119 E6
Delamare Cres CR0 .....43 C3
Delamere Rd
Reigate RH2 ....139 C5
Wimbledon SW20 ....39 D8
Delancey Ct RH12 ......217 C4
Delaporte Cl KT17 ....76 E7
Delcombe Ave KT4 ......39 C1
Delderfield KT21 ....95 D6
Delfont Cl RH10 ....202 D4
Delft Ho KT2 ....37 F8
Delia St SW18 ....20 B8
Delius Gdns RH12 .....218 B4
Dell Cl Fetcham KT22 ....94 E4
Haslemere GU27 ....208 A7
Mickleham RH5 ....115 C8
Wallington SM6 ....60 D6
Dell Close Cotts RH5 ..115 C8
Dell Gr GU16 ....65 F2
Dell Ho CR2 ....61 C2
Dell La KT17 ....58 A5
Dell Rd KT17 ....58 A4
Dell The Brentford TW8 ....6 C8
Burgh Heath KT20 ....97 C6
East Grinstead RH19 .....186 B1
Englefield Green SL4 .....11 A5
Feltham TW14 ....15 B8
Heath End GU9 ....125 D7
Horley RH6 ....161 B4
Reigate RH2 ....118 A2
Sidlow RH6 ....160 C5
South Norwood SE19 .....42 F8
Woking GU21 ....69 C1
Dell Wlk KT3 ....38 E7
Dellbow Rd TW14 ....4 B2
Dellfield Cl BR3 ....44 C8
Delliffe Cl CR4 ....40 E7
Dells Cl TW11 ....16 F2
Delmey Cl CR0 ....61 F7
Delphian Ct 5 SW16 ....22 A4
Delta Bglws RH6 ....161 A1
Delta Cl
Chobham GU24 ....49 F1
Worcester Park KT4 .....57 F7
Delta Dr RH6 ....161 A1
Delta Ho RH6 ....161 A1
Delta Rd
Chobham GU24 ....49 F1
Woking GU21 ....70 A3
Worcester Park KT19,KT4 ..57 E7
Delta Way TW20 ....32 C8
Delves KT20 ....97 D6
Delville Cl GU14 ....84 D3
Demesne Rd SM6 ....60 D6
Dempster Cl KT6 ....37 C1
Dempster Ho GU9 ......125 D8
Den Cl BR3 ....44 D6
Den Rd BR2 ....44 D6
Denbies Wine Est*
RH5 ....115 B3
Denbigh Cl SM1 ....58 F5
Denbigh Gdns TW10 ......6 F2
Denbigh Rd
Haslemere GU27 ....208 D5
Hounslow TW3 ....5 B5
Denby Ct GU14 ....85 C1
Denby Dene GU12 ......106 B2
Denby Rd KT11 ....73 C7
Denchers Plat RH11 ....181 D1
Dencliffe TW15 ....14 A3
Dendy St SW12 ....21 A7
Dene Ave TW3 ....4 F4
Dene Cl Ash GU12 ......106 C3
Dene Cl *continued*
Chipstead CR5 ....98 E8
Farnham GU10 ....146 E6
Haslemere GU27 ....208 C6
Hayes BR2 ....44 F1
Horley RH6 ....160 E5
Worcester Park KT4 ......57 F8
Dene Ct GU1 ....110 B3
Dene Gdns KT7 ....56 A8
Dene La GU10 ....146 E6
Dene La W GU10 ....146 E5
Dene Pl GU21 ....69 C1
Dene Rd Ashstead KT21 ...95 F8
Farnborough GU14 ....84 F3
Guildford GU1 ....130 E8
Dene St RH4 ....136 B7
Dene Street Gdns RH4 .136 B7
Dene The
Abinger Hammer RH5 ....134 B3
Belmont SM2 ....77 F8
East Molesey KT12,KT8 ....35 F4
South Croydon CR0 ....62 D6
Dene Tye RH10 ....202 D7
Dene Wlk GU10 ....146 E6
Denefield Dr CR8 ....80 D4
Denehurst Gdns
Mortlake TW10 ....7 A3
Twickenham TW2 ....16 D8
Denehyrst Ct 2 GU1 ...130 E8
Denewood 8 KT17 ....76 E6
Denewood Ho 10 SM1 ...59 C6
Denfield RH4 ....136 C5
Denham Cres CR4 ....40 F5
Denham Ct SE26 ....23 B5
Denham Gr RG12 ....27 C3
Denham Rd Egham TW20 .12 A4
Ewell KT17 ....76 F7
Feltham TW14 ....15 C8
Denholm Gdns GU4 ....110 A4
Denison Rd
Feltham,Lower Feltham
TW13 ....14 F4
Mitcham SW19 ....20 D2
Denleigh Gdns KT7 ......36 E3
Denly Way GU18 ....48 C1
Denman Dr Ashford TW15 .14 B2
Claygate KT10 ....56 A5
Denmans RH10 ....202 D7
Denmark Ave SW19 ......19 E1
Denmark Ct Morden SM4 .40 A4
2 Weybridge KT13 ....53 B7
Denmark Gdns SM5 .....59 F7
Denmark Rd
Carshalton SM5 ....59 F7
Croydon SE25 ....43 B4
Guildford GU1 ....130 E8
Kingston u T KT1 ....37 E6
Twickenham TW2 ....16 D5
Wimbledon SW19 ....19 D2
Denmark Sq GU12 ......105 E2
Denmark St
Aldershot GU12 ....105 D2
Wokingham RG40 ....25 C5
Denmead Ct RG12 ....27 E3
Denmead Ho SW15 ....7 F1
Denmead Rd CR0 ....42 B1
Denmead Sch TW12 ......16 B1
Denmore Ct SM6 ....60 B5
Dennan Rd KT6 ....37 F1
Denne Par RH12,RH13 ..217 C1
Denne Rd Crawley RH11 .201 D5
Horsham RH12 ....217 C1
Dennett Rd CR0 ....42 A2
Denning Ave CR0 ....61 A5
Denning Cl TW12 ....15 F3
Denningtons The KT4 ....57 E8
Dennis Cl Ashford TW15 ..14 D1
Redhill RH1 ....118 E3
Dennis Ho SM1 ....59 A6
Dennis Park Cres SW20 .39 E8
Dennis Rd KT8 ....36 C5
Dennis Reeve Cl CR4 ....40 F8
Dennis Way GU1 ....109 E6
Dennistoun Cl GU15 .....65 D5
Densham Dr CR8 ....80 A5
Densole Cl BR3 ....43 E8
Denton Cl RH1 ....140 A4
Denton Gr KT12 ....54 E8
Denton Rd
Twickenham TW1 ....6 D1
Wokingham RG40 ....25 C6
Denton Way Frimley GU16 65 D2
Woking GU21 ....69 A2
Dents Gr KT20 ....117 F7
Denvale Trad Pk
Crawley RH10 ....201 E5
Mitcham CR4 ....40 D5
Denvale Wlk GU21 ....69 A1
Denvegan Ho 7 SM2 ....59 C3
Denwood SE23 ....23 D5
Denzil Rd GU2 ....130 B8
Departures Rd RH6 .....181 F8
Depot Rd Crawley RH11 .181 D1
Epsom KT17 ....76 E6
Horsham RH13 ....217 E2
Hounslow TW3,TW7 ....5 D4
Derby Arms Rd KT18 ....76 F2
Derby Cl KT18 ....97 B8
Derby Hill SE23 ....23 C6
Derby Hill Cres SE23 ....23 C6
Derby Rd Cheam SM1,SM2 .58 F4
Guildford GU2 ....108 F1
Haslemere GU27 ....208 B7
Hounslow TW3 ....5 B3
Merton SW19 ....20 A1
Mortlake SW14 ....7 B3
Surbiton KT5,KT6 ....38 A1
Thornton Heath CR0 ......42 B1
Derby Sq The 10 KT19 ...76 D6
Derby Stables Rd KT18 ..76 F2
Derek Ave Hackbridge SM6 60 B6
West Ewell KT19 ....57 B5
Derek Cl KT19 ....57 B5
Derek Horn Ct GU15 .....65 B6
Deri Dene Cl 2 TW19 ....2 E1
Dering Pl CR0 ....61 C6
Dering Rd CR0,CR9 .....61 C6
Derinton Rd SW17 ......21 A4
Deronda Rd SE24,SW2 ...22 B7
Deroy Ct SM5 ....59 F4
Derrick Ave CR2 ....61 C1
Derrick Ho 13 SW2 ......22 A7
Derrick Rd BR3 ....43 F5
Derry Cl GU12 ....105 F5
Derry Rd
Farnborough GU14 ....84 F8
Wallington CR0 ....60 E7
Derrydown GU22 ....89 C6
Derryswood Ho GU5 ...152 E7
Derwent Ave
Ash Vale GU12 ....105 F4
Kingston u T SW15 ....18 E4
Derwent Cl
Addlestone KT15 ....52 D5
Claygate KT10 ....55 F4
Crawley RH11 ....200 F5
East Bedfont TW14 ....14 F7
Farnborough GU14 ....84 E4
Hale GU9 ....125 A6
Horsham RH12 ....218 B6
Derwent Dr CR8 ....80 E6
Derwent Ho Penge SE20 ..43 B7
Reigate RH2 ....139 A7
Derwent Lodge KT4 .....58 B8
Derwent Rd
Lightwater GU18 ....67 B8
Penge SE20 ....43 B7
Thorpe Lea TW20 ....12 B1
Twickenham TW2 ....5 B1
West Barnes SM4 ....39 D3
Derwent Wlk SM6 ....60 B3
Desborough Cl TW17 ....34 A2
Desborough Ct SE25 .....43 B5
Desford Way TW15 ......13 F6
Desmond Anderson Fst &
Mid Sch RH10 ....201 E2
Despard Ho SW2 ....22 A6
Detherick Ct TW3 ....5 C3
Detillens La RH8 ....123 A6
Detling Rd RH11 ....201 C1
Dettingen Cres GU16 ....86 D8
Dettingen Rd GU16 ......86 E8
Deutsche Schule TW10 ..17 D7
Devana End SM5 ....59 F7
Devas Rd SW20 ....39 C8
Devenish La GU20,SL5 ...29 D1
Devenish Rd GU20,SL5 ..29 D2
Deverill Ct SE20 ....43 C8
Devey Cl KT2 ....18 E1
Devil's La TW20 ....12 C2
Devitt Cl KT21 ....76 A3
Devoil Cl GU4 ....110 B5
Devoke Way KT12 ....54 D8
Devon Ave TW2 ....16 C7
Devon Bank GU2 ....130 C6
Devon Cl Kenley CR8 ....80 E3
Sandhurst GU47 ....64 D7
Devon Cres RH1,RH2 ...118 D1
Devon Ho Caterham CR3 .100 F3
Knaphill GU21 ....68 D2
Penge SE20 ....23 B1
Devon Rd Belmont SM2 ...58 E2
Hersham KT12 ....54 C6
Merstham RH1 ....119 C5
Devon Way
Chessington KT9 ....56 C6
West Ewell KT19 ....57 B5
Devon Waye TW5 ....4 F7
Devoncroft Gdns TW1 ...17 A8
Devonshire Ave
Box Hill KT20 ....116 C4
Sheerwater GU21 ....70 D6
Sutton SM2 ....59 C3
Devonshire Ct
Croydon CR0 ....44 A1
Feltham TW13 ....15 B6
6 Richmond TW9 ....6 F6
Devonshire Dr
Camberley GU15 ....65 F7
Long Ditton KT6 ....56 D8
Devonshire Gdns W4 .....7 C7
Devonshire Ho
16 Balham SW12 ....21 B8
Hounslow TW3 ....5 C4
14 Sutton SM2 ....59 C3
Devonshire Pl GU11 ....104 F1
Devonshire Prim Sch
SM2 ....59 C3
Devonshire Rd
6 Chiswick W4 ....7 E8
Feltham TW13 ....15 E4
Forest Hill SE23 ....23 C8
Hackbridge SM5,SM6 .....60 A6
Horsham RH13 ....217 D2
Mitcham SW17,SW19 .....20 E1
Sutton SM2 ....59 C3
Thornton Heath CR0 ......42 D2
Weybridge KT13 ....53 A6
Devonshire St 1 W4 .....7 E8
Devonshire Way CR0,CR9 .62 F8
Devonshires The KT18 ...76 F5
Dewar Cl 2 RH11 ....200 E5
Dewar Ho SW17 ....20 E3
Dewey St SW17 ....20 F3
Dewlands RH9 ....121 C4
Dewlands Cl GU6 ......174 E3

Dewlands La GU6 ...... .174 E3
Dewsbury Gdns KT4 ... .58 A7
Dexter Dr RH19 .... .205 E3
Diamedes Ave TW19 .....13 D7
Diamond Cotts GU5 ... .152 B6
Diamond Ct 4 RH1 .....119 A2
Diamond Est SW17 ....20 E5
Diamond Hill GU15 ......65 E6
Diamond Ridge GU15 ....65 E7
Diamond Way GU14 ......84 E5
Diana Gdns KT6 .... .56 F8
Dianthus Cl KT16 ....32 E2
Dianthus Ct GU22 ....69 D1
Dianthus Pl RG42 ....8 B2
Dibdin Cl SM1 .... .59 A7
Dibdin Rd SM1 .... .59 A8
Diceland Lodge SM7 ....77 F3
Diceland Rd SM7 ....77 F3
Dick Turpin Way TW14 ...3 E1
Dickens Cl
 East Grinstead RH19 ..185 C1
 Richmond TW10 ....17 E6
Dickens Dr KT15 .... .51 F4
Dickens Pl SL3 ....1 E6
Dickens Rd RH10 ...... .201 E3
Dickens Wood Cl SE19 ..22 B1
Dickenson's La SE25 ....43 A3
Dickenson's Pl SE25 ....43 A3
Dickerage Hill KT3 ......38 C6
Dickerage La KT3 ....38 C6
Dickerage Rd KT1,KT2,
 KT3 ....38 C7
Dickins Way RH13 .....217 F1
Dickinson Rd TW13 .....15 D3
Digby Cl CR0 ....61 F7
Digby Way KT14 ....71 F7
Digdens Rise KT18 ......76 C4
Dillwyn Cl SE26 ....23 E4
Dilston Rd KT22 ....95 A8
Dilton Gdns SW15 ......19 B7
Dingle Cl RH11 .... .201 B7
Dingle Rd TW15 ....14 B3
Dingle The RH11 ...... .201 B6
Dingley La SW16 ....21 D6
Dingley Way GU14 .....105 A8
Dingwall Ave CR0,CR9 ..61 C8
Dingwall Rd
 Croydon CR0,CR9 ......61 D8
 Wallington SM5 ....59 F2
 Wandsworth SW18 .....20 C8
Dinsdale Cl GU22 ....70 A1
Dinsdale Gdns SE25 ....42 E4
Dinsmore Rd SW12 .....21 B8
Dinton Rd Kingston u T KT2 17 F1
 Mitcham SW17,SW19 ...20 D2
Dione Wlk RH11 ...... .200 E4
Dippenhall Rd GU10 ...124 C2
Dippenhall St GU10 ...124 A5
Dirdene Cl KT17 ....76 F7
Dirdene Gdns KT17 .....76 F7
Dirdene Gr KT17 ....76 F7
Dirtham La KT24 ......113 B6
Dirty La RH19 ....206 F2
Discovery Pk RH10 ....182 A2
Disraeli Ct SL3 ....1 B8
Distillery Wlk 14 TW8 ...6 E8
Ditches La CR3,CR5 .....99 E6
Ditchling RG12 ....27 A2
Ditchling Hill RH11 ....201 C4
Ditton Cl KT7 ....37 A2
Ditton Grange Cl KT6 ...37 D1
Ditton Grange Dr KT6 ..37 D1
Ditton Hill KT6 ....56 D8
Ditton Hill Rd KT6 .....37 C1
Ditton Lawn KT7 ....37 A1
Ditton Pl 7 SE20 ....43 B8
Ditton Rd KT6 ....37 E1
Ditton Reach KT7 ....37 B3
Dittoncroft CR0 ....61 E6
Dixon Dr KT13 ....52 F1
Dixon Pl BR4 ....44 B1
Dixon Rd SE25 .... .42 F6
Dobbins Pl RH11 ......200 E5
Doble Ct CR2 ....81 A8
Dobson Rd RH11 ......181 D1
Dock Rd TW8 ....6 D7
Dockenfield St GU10 ..166 C6
Dockett Eddy La TW17 ..33 F1
Dockett Moorings KT16 .33 F1
Dockwell Cl TW14 ....4 A3
Dockwell's Ind Est TW14 .4 C2
Doctors Cl SE26 ....23 C3
Doctors La CR3 ....100 A3
Dodbrooke Rd SE27 ....22 A5
Dodd's La KT14 ....71 A5
Dodds Cres KT14 ....71 B5
Dodds Pk RH3 .... .137 B7
Doel Cl SW19 ....20 C1
Dogflud Way GU9 .....125 C3
Doggett Rd SE6 ....24 A8
Doghurst Ave UB7 ....3 B7
Doghurst Dr UB7 ....3 B7
Doghurst La CR5 ....98 F7
Doland St SW17 ....20 F2
Dollis Cl RH10 .... .202 C5
Dollis Ct GU9 ....125 D3
Dollis Dr GU9 ....125 D3
Dolphin Cl
 Haslemere GU27 ......207 E6
 Kingston u T KT6 ......37 D4
Dolphin Ct Bracknell RG12 27 C5
 Merton SW19 ....20 A1
 Stanwell TW19 ....13 A5
 2 Wallington SM6 .....60 B4
Dolphin Ct N TW19 .....13 A5
Dolphin Rd TW16 ....34 E8
Dolphin Rd N TW16 ....34 E8
Dolphin Rd S TW16 ....34 E8

Dolphin Rd W TW16 ....34 E8
Dolphin Sq 2 W4 ....7 E7
Dolphin Sq KT2 ....37 E8
Doman Rd GU15 ....65 A4
Dome Hill CR3 ....120 E1
Dome Hill Peak CR3 ...100 E1
Dome Hill Pk SE26 .....22 F4
Dome The RH1 .... .118 F2
Dome Way RH1 .... .118 F2
Dominion Rd CR0 ....42 F2
Donald Lynch Ho CR4 ..40 F7
Donald Rd CR0,CR9 ....41 F2
Donald Woods Gdns KT5 57 C8
Doncaster Wlk RH10 ..202 A4
Doncastle Rd RG12 .....26 E6
Donkey La
 Abinger Common RH5 .155 D8
 Crawley RH6 ....182 D7
Donnafields GU24 ....68 A3
Donne Cl RH10 .... .202 B8
Donne Gdns GU22 ......70 E4
Donne Pl CR4 ....41 B5
Donnington Cl GU15 ....65 B4
Donnington Ct 2 RH11 200 F4
Donnybrook RG12 ......27 A2
Donnybrook Rd SW16 ..21 D1
Donovan Ct KT19 ....57 D1
Donyngs Place Recn Ctr
 RH1 ....118 E2
Doods Brow Sch RH1 ..119 F2
Doods Park Rd RH2 ...118 C1
Doods Pl RH2 ....118 D2
Doods Rd RH2 .... .118 D2
Doods Way RH2 ....118 D2
Doomsday Gdn RH13 ..218 A1
Dora Rd SW19 ....20 A4
Dora's Green La GU10 .124 D5
Doradus Ct 20 SW19 ...19 D7
Doral Way SM5 ....59 F5
Doran Dr RH2 ....118 D1
Doran Gdns RH2 ......118 D1
Dorcas Ct GU15 ....65 B3
Dorchester Ct
 Reigate RH2 ....118 C2
 Staines TW18 ....13 A4
 5 Streatham SW16 ....21 E6
 Woking GU22 ....70 E3
Dorchester Dr TW14 .....3 E1
Dorchester Gr 8 W4 .....7 E8
Dorchester Mews
 New Malden KT3 ....38 D5
 Twickenham TW1 ....6 C1
Dorchester Prim Sch
 KT4 ....39 C1
Dorchester Rd
 Morden CR4 ....40 C2
 North Cheam KT4 ......39 C1
 Weybridge KT13 ......53 B7
Dore Gdns SM4 ....40 B2
Doreen Cl GU14 ....84 E7
Dorian Dr SL5 ....29 E8
Doric Dr KT20 ....97 F7
Dorien Rd SW20 ....39 D7
Dorin Ct Pyrford GU22 ..70 E4
Doris Rd TW15 ....14 D2
Dorking (Deepdene) Sta
 RH4 ....115 C1
Dorking Bsns Pk RH4 ..136 A8
Dorking General Hospl
 RH4 ....136 B6
Dorking Mus* RH4 ....136 A7
Dorking Rd
 Chilworth GU4 ....131 E3
 Epsom KT18 ....76 B4
 Gomshall GU5 ....133 D4
 Great Bookham KT23 .114 C8
 Kingsfold RH1,RH5 ...198 B4
 Leatherhead KT22 .....95 B3
 Lower Kingswood KT20 .97 C3
 Walton on the Hill KT20 .97 C3
Dorking Sta RH4 ......115 C1
Dorking West Sta RH4 .136 A8
Dorlcote GU8 ....170 E5
Dorlcote Rd SW18 ......20 E8
Dorling Dr KT17 ....76 F7
Dorly Cl TW17 ....34 E4
Dorman's Cl RH7 .....186 A8
Dormans RH11 ....201 A5
Dormans Ave RH7 .....165 A2
Dormans Gdns RH19 ..185 E6
Dormans High St RH7 .186 A8
Dormans Park Rd
 Dormans Park RH19 ..185 E6
 East Grinstead RH19 ..185 D3
Dormans Rd RH7 .....165 A2
Dormans Sta RH7 .....185 F8
Dormans Station Rd
 RH7 ....185 F7
Dormansland Prim Sch
 RH7 ....165 B1
Dormer Cl RG45 ....45 A5
Dormers Cl GU7 ......150 D7
Dormy Ho The GU25 ...30 F3
Dorney Gr KT13 ....53 B8
Dorney Way TW4 ....4 E2
Dornford Gdns CR5 ...100 C8
Dornton Rd
 South Croydon CR2 ....61 D5
 Upper Tooting SW12,SW17 .21 C6
Dorrien Wlk SW16 .....21 D6
Dorrington Ct SE25 ....42 E7
Dorrit Cres GU3 ......108 E3
Dorryn Ct SE26 ....23 D3
Dorset Ave RH19 .....185 C3

Dorset Ct Camberley GU15 .65 F8
 Epsom KT17 ....76 F7
Dorset Dr GU22 ....70 B2
Dorset Gdns
 East Grinstead RH19 ..185 C3
 Thornton Heath SW16 .41 F5
Dorset Ho 2 SE20 .....43 B8
Dorset Rd Ash GU12 ..106 B5
 Ashford TW15 ....13 D5
 Belmont SM2 ....59 A1
 Merton SW19 ....40 A7
 Mitcham CR4 ....40 E7
 Penge BR3 ....43 D6
Dorset Sq KT19 ....57 D1
Dorset Way Byfleet KT14 .52 D1
 Twickenham TW2 ......16 D7
Dorset Waye TW5 ....4 F7
Dorsten Sq RH11 .....200 F3
Dorton Villas UB7 ....3 A6
Dorton Way GU23 ......91 B6
Douai Cl GU14 ....85 C4
Douai Gr TW12 ....36 C8
Douglas Ave KT3 ....39 B5
Douglas Cl
 Guildford GU4 ....109 D6
 Wallington SM6 ....60 E4
Douglas Ct
 Biggin Hill TN16 ....83 E2
 Caterham CR3 ....100 D5
Douglas Dr Croydon CR0 .63 A7
 Godalming GU7 ......150 F5
Douglas Gr GU10 .....146 C5
Douglas Ho
 Little Bookham KT23 ...94 A3
 Twickenham TW1 ....6 B2
Douglas Houghton Ho 11
 RH1 ....118 F2
Douglas Mews SM7 ....77 F3
Douglas Pl GU14 ....85 A5
Douglas Rd
 Addlestone KT15 ......52 B7
 Hounslow TW3 ....5 B4
 Kingston u T KT1 ......38 B7
 Reigate RH2 ....118 B2
 Stanwell TW19 ....2 D1
 Surbiton KT6 ....37 F1
 Thames Ditton KT10 ...55 B8
Douglas Robinson Ct
 SW16 ....21 E1
Douglas Sq SM4 ....40 A3
Doultons The TW18 ....13 A2
Dounesforth Gdns SW18 20 B7
Dove Cl Crawley RH11 .201 D8
 Selsdon CR2 ....81 D8
 Wallington SM6 ....60 F3
Dove Ct TW19 ....13 E8
Dovecote Cl KT13 ......53 B7
Dovecote 9 SW14 ......7 D4
Dovedale Cl
 Guildford GU4 ....110 A4
 Sandhurst GU47 ....45 D2
Dovedale Cres RH11 ..201 B4
Dovedale Rise CR4 .....40 F8
Dovehouse Grn 1 KT13 .53 D6
Dover Ct Carshalton SM1 .59 D6
 Cranleigh GU6 ....175 A3
Dover Gdns SM5 ....59 F7
Dover Ho
 7 Beckenham BR3 .....24 A1
 15 Penge SE20 ....43 B8
Dover House Rd SW15 .19 B8
Dover Rd SE19 ....22 D2
Dover Terr TW9 ....7 A5
Dovercourt Ave CR7 ...42 A5
Dovercourt La SM1 ....59 C7
Dovercourt Rd SE21, SE22 22 E8
Doverfield Rd
 Guildford GU4 ....110 A4
 Streatham SW2 ....21 E8
Dovers Green Rd RH2 .139 B4
Dovers Green Sch RH2 .139 C5
Doversmead GU21 .....68 E3
Doveton Rd CR2 ....61 D5
Dowanhill Rd SE6 ......24 D7
Dowdeswell Cl SW15 ...7 E3
Dowding Ct RG45 ......45 C6
Dowding Rd TN16 ......83 D4
Dowell Ho SE21 ....22 F5
Dower Ave SM6 ....60 B2
Dower Cotts GU8 .....170 F8
Dower Ho GU8 ....170 F8
Dower Wlk RH11 .....201 A5
Dowes Ho 13 SW16 ...21 E5
Dowgate Rd RH10,RH6 .183 D7
Dowlans Cl KT23 .....114 A8
Dowlans Rd KT23 ....114 B8
Dowler Ct 2 KT2 ....37 F8
Dowman Ct 2 SW19 ...20 B1
Down Hall Rd KT2 .....37 D8
Down La GU3 ....129 B4
Down Lodge Ct KT18 ...76 E5
Down Rd Guildford GU1 .110 B1
 Teddington TW11 ......17 B2
Down St KT8 ....36 A4
Down Yhonda GU8 ....148 C6
Downderry Prim Sch
 BR1 ....24 E4
Downderry Rd BR1 .....24 E4
Downe Cl RH6 ....160 E5
Downe Rd CR4 ....40 F7
Downer Mdw GU7 ....150 D6
Downes Ct TW1 ....16 F7
Downfield 7 KT4 ....39 A1
Downfield Ho RH1 ......38 D1
Downham Enterprise Ctr
 SE6 ....24 F6

Downham La BR1 ....24 D3
Downham Way BR1 ....24 E4
Downhurst Rd GU6 ...175 D3
Downing Ave GU2 .....129 F8
Downing Ho 3 SW19 ..20 A1
Downing St GU9 ......125 B2
Downland Cl
 Burgh Heath KT18 .....77 B1
 Wallington CR5 ....79 B5
Downland Ct RH11 ...201 C4
Downland Dr RH11 ...201 C3
Downland Gdns KT18 ..77 B1
Downland Pl RH11 ...201 C4
Downland Way KT18 ...77 B1
Downlands Rd CR8 .....79 F6
Downmill Rd RG12 .....26 F7
Downs Ave KT18 ....76 F4
Downs Bridge Rd BR3 ..44 D8
Downs Cl GU14 ....84 E7
Downs Court Rd CR8 ..80 B6
Downs Ct Purley CR8 ...61 B1
 2 Redhill RH1 ....119 A4
 10 Wimbledon SW19 ..19 D1
Downs Hill BR2,BR3 ....44 D8
Downs Hill Rd KT18 ....76 E5
Downs La KT22 ....95 B3
Downs Rd Ashstead KT18 .96 C7
 Beckenham BR3 ....44 B7
 Coulsdon CR5 ....79 D1
 Epsom KT17,KT18 .....76 E3
 Mickleham RH5 ......115 C7
 Purley CR8 ....80 B8
 South Norwood CR7 ...42 C8
 Sutton SM2 ....78 C8
Downs Side SM2 ....77 F8
Downs The
 Leatherhead KT22 .....95 C2
 Wimbledon SW19,SW20 .19 D1
Downs View
 Dorking RH4 ....115 D1
 Hounslow TW7 ....6 A6
 Tadworth KT20 ....97 B6
Downs View Lodge 9
 KT6 ....37 E3
Downs View Rd KT23 .114 C8
Downs Way Epsom KT18 .76 F3
 Great Bookham KT23 ..94 C1
 Oxted RH8 ....122 E8
 Tadworth KT20 ....97 B6
Downs Way Sch RH8 ..122 E7
Downs Wood KT18 .....77 B2
Downsend Sch KT22 ...95 D7
Downsend Sch (Epsom
 Lodge) KT17 ....76 F7
Downshire Way
 Bracknell RG12 ....27 B6
 Bracknell RG12,RG42 ..27 A7
Downside
 Beacon Hill GU26 ....188 D7
 Epsom KT18 ....76 E5
 Twickenham TW1 ......16 F5
Downside Bridge Rd
 KT11 ....73 B4
Downside Cl SW19 .....20 C2
Downside Common Rd
 KT11 ....73 C1
Downside Ct RH1 .....119 C6
Downside Orch GU22 ..70 A2
Downside Rd
 Downside KT11 ....73 B2
 Guildford GU4 ....131 B8
 Carshalton SM2 ......59 E4
Downsman Ct RH10 ..201 D3
Downsview Ave GU22 ..89 F6
Downsview Cl KT11 ....93 B8
Downsview Ct GU1 ...109 C5
Downsview Gdns
 Dorking RH4 ....136 B6
 South Norwood SE19 ..22 C1
Downsview Prim Sch
 SE19 ....22 C1
Downsview Rd
 Headley Down GU35 ..187 C5
 Horsham RH12 ....218 B6
 South Norwood SE19 ..22 C1
Downsway Guildford GU1 110 E1
 South Croydon CR2 ....80 E8
 Whyteleafe CR3 ....80 F2
Downsway Cl KT20 .....97 A6
Downsway The SM2 ....59 C2
Downswood RH2 .....118 D4
Downton Ave SW2 .....21 F6
Downview Cl GU26 ...188 D6
Doyle Rd SE25 ....43 A5
Dr Johnson Ave SW17 .21 B5
Dragon La KT13 ....53 A1
Dragoon Ct GU11 .....104 E2
Drake Ave Caterham CR3 100 C5
 Mytchett GU16 ....86 A1
 Staines TW18 ....12 F3
Drake Cl Bracknell RG12 .27 B4
 Horsham RH12 ......217 E6
Drake Ct Dulwich SE19 .22 F3
 Kingston u T KT5 ......37 F5
Drake Rd Chessington KT9 57 A5
 Crawley RH10 ....201 E3
 Horley RH6 ....160 E3
 Mitcham CR4 ....41 A3
Drake's Cl KT10 ....55 A6
Drakefield Rd SW17 ...21 A5
Drakes Cl GU6 ....174 E3
Drakes Ct SE23 ....23 C7
Drakes Way GU22 ......89 D5
Drakewood Rd SW16 ..21 D1
Draper Cl TW7 ....5 D5
Drax Ave SW20 ....19 A1
Draxmont SW19 ....19 E2

Dray Ct GU2 ....130 B8
Draycot Rd KT6 ....38 A1
Draycott RG12 ....27 E4
Drayhorse Dr GU19 ....47 E2
Drayton Cl Bracknell RG12 27 D7
 Fetcham KT22 ....94 E3
 Hounslow TW4 ....4 F2
Drayton Ct Tolworth KT5 .57 B8
 West Byfleet KT14 .....71 A6
Drayton Rd CR0,CR9 ...61 B8
Dresden Way KT13 .....53 C5
Drew Ho 12 SW16 .....21 E5
Drew Pl CR3 ....100 D4
Drewstead Rd SW16 ...21 D6
Drift The KT24 ....92 E3
Drift Way SL3 ....1 C7
Drifters Dr GU16 ....66 D1
Driftway (Worple Road) The
 KT22 ....95 B4
Driftway The
 Banstead SM7 ....77 C4
 Leatherhead KT22 .....95 C4
 Mitcham CR4 ....41 A8
Driftwood Dr CR8 ......80 C2
Drill Hall Rd KT16 ......33 A2
Drive Rd CR5 ....99 F7
Drive Spur KT20 ....98 B6
Drive The Artington GU3 .130 B5
 Ashford TW15 ....14 D1
 Banstead SM7 ....77 E3
 Beckenham BR3 ....44 A8
 Belmont SM2 ....77 E3
 Cobham KT11 ....73 F5
 Copthorne RH10 .....183 C3
 Coulsdon CR5,CR8 ....79 E5
 Cranleigh GU6 ....174 F2
 Farnham GU9 ....146 B7
 Feltham TW14 ....15 C8
 Fetcham KT22 ....94 E5
 Godalming GU7 ......150 F2
 Guildford GU2 ....130 A7
 Guildford,Park Barn GU2 .108 F1
 Headley KT18,KT22 ...96 A3
 Horley RH6 ....161 B1
 Hounslow TW3,TW7 ....5 D5
 Ifold RH14 ....212 D2
 Kingston u T KT2 ......18 C1
 Leatherhead KT22,KT18 .95 F4
 Morden SM4 ....40 D4
 Shackleford GU7,GU8 .149 E4
 South Norwood CR7 ...42 D5
 Thames Ditton KT10 ...36 C1
 Thorpe GU25 ....31 F4
 Wallington CR8,SM6 ...60 D1
 West Ewell KT19 ....57 F4
 West Wickham BR4 ....44 D2
 Wimbledon SW19,SW20 .19 C1
 Woking GU22 ....89 B7
Drivers Mead RH7 ....164 D3
Drodges Cl GU5 ......151 F8
Droitwich Cl
 Bracknell RG12 ....27 E6
 Forest Hill SE26 ....23 A5
Drove Rd GU4 ....132 A2
Drovers Ct 3 KT1 ......37 E7
Drovers Rd CR2 ....61 D5
Drovers Way Ash GU12 .106 C1
 Bracknell RG12 ....27 F6
 Hale GU9 ....125 A6
Druce Wood SL5 ....28 E8
Druid's Cl KT21 ....95 F7
Druids Way BR2 ....44 D5
Drumaline Ridge KT4 ..57 E8
Drummond Cl RG12 ...27 F8
Drummond Cl 4 GU1 .109 D1
Drummond Ctr CR9 ....61 C8
Drummond Gdns KT19 .76 B8
Drummond Rd
 Crawley RH11 ....200 E5
 Croydon CR0,CR9 .....61 C8
 Guildford GU1 ....109 D1
Drummonds Pl TW9 .....6 E3
Drungewick La RH14 .213 D2
Drury Cl RH10 ....202 D4
Drury Cres CR0,CR9 ...61 A8
Drury Lo 7 RH19 .....185 F1
Dry Arch Rd SL5 ....29 F3
Dryden RG12 ....27 A2
Dryden Ct 11 TW10 ...17 D4
Dryden Rd
 Farnborough GU14 ....84 F6
 Wimbledon SW19 .....20 C2
Drynham Pk KT13 .....53 E7
Du Cane Ct SW12 .....21 A7
Ducavel Ho SW2 ....21 F7
Duchess Cl
 Crowthorne RG45 .....45 B7
 Sutton SM1 ....59 C6
Duck's Wlk TW1 ....6 C2
Dudley Cl KT15 ....52 C7
Dudley Dr SM4 ....39 E2
Dudley Gr KT18 ....76 C5
Dudley Ho RG12 ....27 C7
Dudley Rd Ashford TW15 .13 F4
 East Bedfont TW14 ....14 D7
 Kingston u T KT1 ......37 F6
 Richmond TW9 ....7 A5
 Walton-on-T KT12 .....35 A2
 Wimbledon SW19 .....20 A2
Dudset La TW5 ....4 A6
Duffield Rd KT20 ....97 B3
Duffins Orch KT16 .....51 C3
Duke Cl RH10 ....202 C2

Duke Of Cambridge CI
TW2 ....5 D1
Duke of Connaughts Rd
GU11 ....105 D5
Duke Of Cornwall Ave
GU15 ....46 D1
Duke Of Edinburgh Rd
SM1 ....59 D8
Duke of Kent Sch GU6 .154 D2
Duke St Carshalton SM1 .59 D6
Richmond TW10,TW9 ....6 D2
Woking GU21 ....69 F2
Duke's Ave W4 ....7 D8
Duke's Dr GU7 ....150 B7
Duke's Hill GU19 ......47 E5
Duke's La
Old Windsor SL4,SL5 ....10 B3
Winkfield SL5 ....9 F1
Duke's Rd RH5 ....179 D6
Duke's Ride RG45 ......45 B5
Dukes Ave Hounslow TW4 .4 E3
New Malden KT3 ....38 F6
Richmond KT2,TW10 ....17 D4
Dukes CI Ashford TW15 ..14 C4
Cranleigh GU6 ....175 A2
Hale GU9 ....125 A6
Hampton TW12 ....15 F3
Dukes Covert GU19 .....47 E6
Dukes Ct Addlestone KT15 .52 C6
Beckenham BR3 ....43 E6
Dulwich SE22 ....23 A2
Dukes Green Ave TW14 ..4 A2
Dukes Hill CR3 ....101 C1
Dukes Pk GU11 ....105 D6
Dukes Rd KT12 ....54 D5
Dukes Ride RH5 ....136 D4
Dukes Way BR4 ....63 E7
Dukes Wlk GU9 ....125 A6
Dukes Wood RG45 ....45 B5
Dukeshill Rd RG42 ......27 B8
Dukesthorpe Rd SE26 ...23 D4
Dulverton Ct [12] KT6 ...37 E4
Dulverton Rd CR2 ....62 C1
Dulwich Bsns Ctr SE23 ..23 D7
Dulwich Coll SE21 ......22 E6
Dulwich Coll Inf Sch
SE21 ....22 F5
Dulwich Coll Picture Gall★
SE21 ....22 E8
Dulwich Coll Prep Sch
SE21 ....22 E5
Dulwich Comm SE21 .....22 E7
Dulwich Ct SE22 ....23 B7
Dulwich Oaks The SE21 ..22 F5
Dulwich Village SE21 ....22 F6
Dulwich Wood Ave SE19 .22 E3
Dulwich Wood Pk SE19,
SE21 ....22 E4
Dumbarton Ct [16] SW2 ..21 E8
Dumbleton CI KT2 ....38 B8
Dump Rd GU14 ....84 E1
Dumphreys Ho [5] SW4 ..21 D8
Dumville Dr RH9 ....121 B4
Dunally Pk TW17 ....34 D2
Dunbar Ave
Beckenham BR3 ....43 E5
Thornton Heath CR7,SW16 .42 A7
Carshalton SM1 ....59 D5
Walton-on-T KT12 ......35 C1
Dunbar Ct [3] Bromley BR2 44 F5
Carshalton SM1 ....59 D5
Walton-on-T KT12 ......35 C1
Dunbar Rd Frimley GU16 ..85 F7
Kingston u T KT3 ....38 C5
Dunbar St SE27 ....22 C5
Dunboe PI TW17 ....34 C2
Dunbridge Ho SW15 .....7 F1
Duncan Dr Guildford GU1 110 A2
Wokingham RG40 ......25 E5
Duncan Gdns TW18 .....13 A2
Duncan Rd
Burgh Heath KT20 ......97 E8
Richmond TW9 ....6 E3
Duncombe Ct TW18 .....12 F1
Duncombe Hill SE23 .....23 E8
Duncombe Ho [7] SW19 ..19 D7
Duncombe Rd GU7 .....150 D2
Duncroft CI RH2 ....117 F1
Duncroft Manor TW18 ...12 E4
Duncton CI RH11 ......201 B8
Dundaff CI GU15 ....66 A5
Dundas CI RG12 ....27 B5
Dundas Gdns KT8 ......36 B6
Dundee Rd SE25 ....43 B4
Dundela Gdns KT17,KT4 .58 B6
Dundonald Prim Sch
SW19 ....19 F1
Dundrey Cres RH1 ......119 E6
Dundry Ho [8] SE26 .....23 A5
Dunedin Dr CR3 ....100 E2
Dunfee Way TW14 ....71 E7
Dunfield Gdns SE6 ......24 B3
Dunfield Rd SE6 ....24 B3
Dungates La RH3 ......117 A2
Dunheved CI CR7 ....42 A3
Dunheved Rd N CR7 .....42 A3
Dunheved Rd S CR7 .....42 A3
Dunheved Rd W CR7 .....42 A3
Dunhill Point [12] SW15 ..19 B7
Dunkeld Rd SE25 ....42 D5
Dunkirk St [12] SE27 ....22 C4
Dunleary CI TW4 ....15 F8
Dunley Dr CR0 ....63 C4
Dunlin CI RH1 ....139 F4
Dunlin Ct [12] SE21 .....22 D6

Dunlin Rise GU4 ....110 D3
Dunmail Dr CR2,CR8 .....80 E6
Dunmore GU2 ....108 D2
Dunmore Rd SW20 ......39 D8
Dunmow CI TW13 ....15 E4
Dunning's Rd RH19 ....205 F2
Dunnings Mill L Complex
RH19 ....205 E6
Dunnock Ct [11] SE21 ....22 D6
Dunnymans Rd SM7 ......77 F4
Dunoon Gdns SE23 ......23 D8
Dunoon Rd SE23 ....23 C8
Dunottar CI RH1 ....139 D7
Dunraven Ave RH1 .....140 B2
Dunraven Ho [11] TW9 ....6 F6
Dunraven Lower Sch
SW16 ....21 E5
Dunraven Upper Sch
SW16 ....21 E5
Dunsborough Cotts
GU23 ....91 C7
Dunsbury CI SM2 ....59 B2
Dunsdon Ave GU2 ......130 B8
Dunsfold Aerodrome
GU6,GU8 ....193 D5
Dunsfold CI RH11 ......201 A5
Dunsfold Common Rd
GU8 ....192 F6
Dunsfold Ct [3] SM2 .....59 B3
Dunsfold Ho
[10] Kingston u T KT2 ....18 B2
[7] Streatham SW2 ......21 F8
Dunsfold Rd Alfold GU6 .193 E3
Bramley GU6 ....173 C1
Dunsfold GU8 ....193 B8
Plaistow GU8,RH14 ....211 D4
Dunsfold Rise CR5 ......79 D6
Dunsfold Way CR0 ......63 C3
Dunsmore Rd KT12 ......35 B3
Dunstable Rd
East Molesey KT8 ......35 F5
Richmond TW10,TW9 ....6 E3
Dunstall Pk GU14 ....85 A7
Dunstall Rd SW19,SW20 .19 C2
Dunstall Way KT8 ....36 B6
Dunstan CI TW18 ....13 A4
Dunstan Rd CR5 ....79 D2
Dunstan's Rd SE22 ......23 A8
Dunster Ave SM4 ....39 D1
Dunster Ho [6] SE6 .....24 B5
Dunster Way SM6 ....41 A1
Dunton CI KT6 ....37 E1
Dunton Ct SE26 ....23 B6
Dunton Ho [14] SW16 ....21 E5
Dunsthill Rd SW18 ......20 B7
Dunvegan CI KT8 ....36 B5
Dunvegan Ho [12] RH1 ..118 F1
Dupont Rd SW20 ....39 D7
Duppas Ave CR0 ....61 B6
Duppas CI TW17 ....34 C4
Duppas Ct CR0 ....61 B7
Duppas Hill La CR0 ......61 B6
Duppas Hill Rd CR0 ......61 B6
Duppas Hill Terr CR0,CR9 .61 B7
Duppas Jun Sch CR0 .....61 B5
Duppas Rd CR0,CR9 .....61 B7
Dura Den CI BR3 ....24 B1
Durand CI SM5 ....40 F1
Durban Rd Beckenham BR3 43 F7
West Norwood SE27 .....22 D4
Durbin Rd KT9 ....56 F6
Durfold Dr RH2 ....118 C1
Durfold Rd RH12 ......217 D7
Durfold Wood RH14 ....211 D5
Durfold Wood Woodlands
Wlks★ GU8 ....211 C6
Durford Cres SW15 ......19 B7
Durham Ave BR2 ....44 F5
Durham CI Crawley RH10 201 E2
Guildford GU2 ....108 F3
Wimbledon SW20 ......39 B8
Durham Ct
[2] Leatherhead KT22 ....95 A5
Teddington TW11 ......16 E4
Durham Dr GU16 ....66 D1
Durham Hill BR1 ....24 F4
Durham Ho BR2 ....44 E5
Durham Rd
Beckenham BR2 ....44 F6
Feltham TW14 ....15 C8
Sandhurst GU47 ....45 E2
Wimbledon SW20 ......39 B8
Durkins Rd RH19 ......185 D3
Durleston Park Dr KT23 ..94 C2
Durley Mead RG12 ......27 F4
Durlston Rd KT2 ....17 E2
Durnford Ho SE6 ....24 B5
Durning Rd SE19 ....22 D3
Durnsford Ave SW18,
SW19 ....20 A6
Durnsford Rd SW18,SW19 20 B5
Durnsford Way GU6 ....175 A2
Durrell Way TW17 ......34 D3
Durrington Ave SW20 ...19 C1
Durrington Park Rd
SW20 ....39 C8
Dutch Barn CI TW19 .....2 D1
Dutch Gdns KT2 ....18 B2
Dutchells Copse RH12 ..217 E7
Dutton Ho SW2 ....22 B7
Duval PI GU19 ....47 E3
Duxford [10] KT1 ....38 A7
Duxhurst La RH2 ....160 B7
Dwelly La Haxted TN8 ...165 D8
Limpsfield TN8 ....144 D3
Dyehouse Rd GU8 ......169 C4
Dyer Ho TW12 ....36 B8

Dyer Rd RG40 ....25 E7
Dyer's Field RH6 ....162 B3
Dyers Almshouses
RH10 ....201 D7
Dykes Ct [11] SW2 ....21 F7
Dykes Path GU22 ....70 C4
Dykes Way BR2 ....44 F6
Dymes Path SW19 ......19 D6
Dynevor PI GU3 ....108 C5
Dynevor Rd TW10 ....6 E2
Dysart Ave KT2,TW10 ...17 C4
Dysart Sch
Kingston u T KT2 ....17 D4
Surbiton KT6 ....37 F2
Dyson Ct [8] RH4 ......136 A7
Dyson Wlk RH11 ......201 B1

E

Eady CI RH13 ....217 F2
Eagle CI Crowthorne RG45 .45 A7
Wallington SM6 ....60 E4
Eagle Ct [10] SE21 ......22 D6
Eagle Hill SE19 ....22 D2
Eagle Rd GU1 ....109 D1
Eagle Trad Est CR4 ......40 F3
Eagles Dr TN16 ....83 D1
Eagles Nest GU47 ....45 A1
Ealing Rd TW8 ....6 E8
Eardley Rd SW16 ....21 C2
Eardley Sch SW16 ......21 C2
Earl Rd SW14 ....7 C3
Earle Gdns KT2 ....17 E1
Earle Ho [3] RH19 .....185 F1
Earles Mdw RH12 ......218 B6
Earlswood GU1 ....65 F4
Earleydene SL5 ....29 B1
Earls Gr GU15 ....65 C6
Earlsbrook Rd RH1 .....139 F7
Earlsfield Prim Sch
SW18 ....20 C6
Earlsfield Rd SW18 .....20 C8
Earlsfield Sta SW18 .....20 C7
Earlsthorpe Rd SE26 ....23 D4
Earlswood RG12 ....27 B2
Earlswood Ave CR7 .....42 A4
Earlswood CI RH13 .....218 A4
Earlswood Ct RH1 ......139 F7
Earlswood Ho [2] SW2 ...21 F7
Earlswood Inf Sch RH1 .140 A8
Earlswood Rd RH1 .....139 F7
Earlswood Sta RH1 .....139 F7
Early Commons RH10 ..201 F7
Easby Cres SM4 ....40 B3
Easedale Ho TW7 ....5 F2
Eashing La
Godalming GU7,GU8 ...150 A3
Shackleford GU7,GU8 ..149 F3
Eashing Point [5] SW15 ..19 B7
Easington PI GU1 ......130 F8
East Ave Heath End GU9 .125 D6
Wallington SM6 ....60 F5
Whiteley Village KT12 ...53 F1
East Croydon Sta CR9 ...61 D8
East Dr Wallington SM5 ..59 F2
Wentworth GU25 ....31 B3
East Gdns
Mitcham SW17,SW19 ...20 E2
Woking GU22 ....70 C2
East Gn GU17 ....64 C4
East Grinstead Rd RH7 .164 D3
East Grinstead Sta
RH19 ....185 D1
East Grinstead Town Mus★
RH19 ....185 F2
East Hill Biggin Hill TN16 ..83 B1
Dormans Park RH19 ...185 E6
Oxted RH8 ....122 F6
South Croydon CR2 .....61 E1
Woking GU22 ....70 C2
East Hill Ct RH8 ....122 E5
East Hill La RH10 ......183 D5
East Hill Rd RH8 ......122 E6
East India Way CR0 .....42 F1
East La Kingston u T KT1 .37 D6
West Horsley KT24 .....92 D2
East Lodge [4] KT22 ....95 C6
East Meads GU2 ....130 A8
East Parkside CR6 ....82 B4
East Pk RH10 ....201 D5
East PI SE27 ....22 C4
East Ramp TW6 ....3 B6
East Rd East Bedfont TW14 14 D8
Kingston u T KT2 ....37 E8
Merton SW19 ....20 C2
Reigate RH2 ....117 F2
Weybridge KT13 ....53 D4
East Resr (Nature Reserve)★
RH9 ....121 B5
East Ring GU10 ....127 A7
East Shalford La GU4 ...131 A3
East Sheen Ave SW14 ....7 D3
East Sheen Prim Sch
SW14 ....7 E3
East St Brentford TW8 ....6 C7
Ewell KT17 ....76 E7
Farnham GU9 ....125 C3
Great Bookham KT23 ...94 B2
Horsham RH12 ....217 C1
Rusper RH12 ....199 E7
Turners Hill RH10,RH19 .204 C5
East Station Rd GU12 ...105 B1
East Stratton CI RG12 ...27 E4
East Surrey Coll RH1 ...119 A4

East Surrey Hospl The
RH1 ....140 A5
East Surrey Mus★ CR3 .101 A3
East View Cotts GU6 ...174 C3
East View La GU6 ......174 C3
East Way CR0 ....62 E7
East Whipley La GU5 ...173 F1
East Wlk RH2 ....118 B1
Eastbank Rd TW12 ......16 C3
Eastbourne Gdns SW14 ..7 C4
Eastbourne Rd
Chiswick W4 ....7 C8
Felbridge RH7 ....184 E8
Feltham TW13 ....15 D6
Godstone RH9 ....121 D2
Mitcham SW17 ....21 A2
Newchapel RH7 ......163 F5
South Godstone RH9 ..142 E4
Eastbrook CI GU21 ......70 A3
Eastbury Gr [7] W4 ......7 E8
Eastbury La GU3 ....129 A3
Eastbury Rd KT2 ....17 E1
Eastchurch Rd TW6 ......3 E4
Eastchurch Road Rdbt
TW6 ....3 E4
Eastcote Ave KT8 ....36 A4
Eastcourt Villas [4]
RH19 ....185 F1
Eastcroft Ct GU1 ......131 A8
Eastcroft Mews RH12 ..216 F1
Eastcroft Rd KT19 ......57 E3
Eastdean Ave KT18 ......76 B6
Easter Way RH9 ....142 F5
Eastern Ave KT16 ......33 A6
Eastern Bsns Pk TW6 .....3 F5
Eastern La RG45 ....45 F4
Eastern Perimeter Rd
TW14 ....3 F5
Eastern Rd
Aldershot GU12 ......105 E2
Bracknell RG12 ....27 D7
Eastern View TN16 ......83 C2
Eastfield Rd RH1 ......140 C8
Eastfields GU8 ....170 F5
Eastfields Rd CR4 ......41 A7
Eastgate SM7 ....77 F5
Eastgate Gdns GU1 ....130 E8
Eastgate Ho [3] GU1 ...130 E8
Easthampstead Park Sch
RG12 ....26 D3
Easthampstead Rd
Bracknell RG12 ....27 A7
Wokingham RG40 ......25 E4
Eastheath Ave RG41 .....25 A4
Eastheath Gdns RG41 ...25 B3
Eastlands CI RH8 ......122 D8
Eastlands Way RH8 ....122 D8
Eastleigh CI SM2 ....59 B3
Eastleigh Rd TW6 ....3 E4
Eastleigh Way TW14 .....15 A7
Eastleigh Wlk [10] SW15 .19 A8
Eastmead
Farnborough GU14 .....85 B3
Woking GU21 ....69 C1
Eastmearn Rd SE21,SE27 .22 C6
Eastmont Rd KT10 ......55 F8
Eastney Rd CR0 ....42 B1
Eastnor CI RH2 ....138 F6
Eastnor Rd RH2 ....139 A6
Easton Ho [4] SE27 .....22 B5
Eastry Ave BR2 ....44 F3
Eastway Crawley RH6 ...182 B7
Epsom KT19 ....76 D8
Guildford GU2 ....108 F1
Merton SM4,SW20 .....39 E5
Wallington SM6 ....60 C6
Eastway E RH6 ....182 C7
Eastwell CI BR3 ....23 E1
Eastwick CI [2] SW19 ...19 D7
Eastwick Dr KT23 ....94 B4
Eastwick Inf Sch KT23 ...94 B3
Eastwick Mid Sch KT23 ..94 B3
Eastwick Park Ave KT23 .94 B3
Eastwick Rd
Great Bookham KT23 ...94 B2
Hersham KT12 ....54 B5
Eastwood Crawley RH10 .201 F6
[3] Weybridge KT13 .....53 D4
Eastwood Lodge GU5 ...151 F7
Eastwood Rd GU5 ......151 F7
Eastwood St SW16 ......21 C2
Eastworth Rd KT15,KT16 .33 A1
Eaton Dr KT2 ....18 A1
Eaton Ho GU1 ....130 F7
Eaton Park Rd KT11 .....73 F5
Eaton Pk KT11 ....73 E5
Eaton Rd Camberley GU15 .65 B4
Isleworth TW3,TW7 .....5 D3
Sutton SM2 ....59 D4
Eatonville Rd SW17 .....20 F6
Eatonville Villas SW17 ..20 F6
Ebba's Way KT18 ....76 B4
Ebbisham CI RH4 ......136 A7
Felbridge RH19 ....185 A4
Ebbisham La KT20 ......97 A4
Ebbisham Rd KT18 ......76 B5
North Cheam KT4 ......58 C4
Ebenezer Wlk CR4 ......41 C8
Ebor Cotts SW15 ....18 E5
Ebury Mews SE27 ......22 B5
Ecclesbourne Inf Sch
CR7 ....42 C4

Ecclesbourne Jun Sch
CR7 ....42 C4
Ecclesbourne Rd CR7 ...42 C4
Eccleshill [6] Bromley BR2 .44 F5
Eccleshill RH5 ....136 C3
Echelford Prim Sch The
TW15 ....14 B3
Echelforde Dr TW15 .....14 A4
Echo Barn La GU10 ....145 F5
Echo Pit Rd GU1,GU4 ...130 E6
Eclipse Est KT19 ....76 C6
Ecob CI GU3 ....108 C5
Ecton Rd KT15 ....52 B6
Ector Rd SE6 ....24 E6
Eddeys CI GU35 ....187 B6
Eddeys La GU35 ....187 B6
Eddington Hill RH11 ....201 B1
Eddington Rd RG12 .....26 E3
Eddisbury Ho [7] SE26 ..23 A5
Eddy Rd GU12 ....105 C1
Eddystone Ct GU10 ....167 F1
Eddystone Wlk TW19 ....13 E8
Ede CI TW4 ....4 F4
Ede Ct KT17 ....76 F7
Ede's Cotts KT21 ....95 D8
Eden CI KT15 ....52 B5
Eden Grove Rd KT14 ....71 E6
Eden Park Ave BR3 ......44 A4
Eden Park Sch BR3 ......43 F4
Eden Park Sta BR3 ......44 A4
Eden Rd Crawley RH11 ..200 F4
Croydon CR0 ....61 D6
Penge BR3 ....43 E6
West Norwood SE27 ....22 B3
Eden St KT1,KT2 ....37 E7
Eden Vale
Dormans Park RH19 ...185 F5
East Grinstead RH19 ...185 D4
Eden Way Beckenham BR3 44 A3
Warlingham CR6 ....81 C1
Eden Wlk [5] KT1 ....37 E7
Edenbrook RH7 ....164 E4
Edencourt Rd SW16 .....21 B2
Edencroft GU5 ....151 F7
Edenfield Gdns KT4 .....57 F7
Edenham High Sch CR0 ..43 E3
Edenside Rd KT23 ....93 F3
Edensor Gdns W4 ....7 E7
Edensor Rd W4 ....7 E7
Edenvale CI CR4 ....21 A1
Edenvale Rd CR4 ....21 A1
Ederline Ave SW16 ......42 A7
Edgar CI RH10 ....202 E5
Edgar Ct KT3 ....38 E6
Edgar Rd
South Croydon CR2 .....61 D2
Tatsfield TN16 ....103 D6
Twickenham TW4 ......15 F8
Edgbarrow Rise GU47 ...45 A3
Edgbarrow Sch RG45 ...45 C3
Edgbarrowhill Star RG45 45 A3
Edgcumbe Park Dr RG45 45 A5
Edge CI KT13 ....53 A3
Edge Hill SW19 ....19 D1
Edge Hill Ct SW19 ......19 D1
Edge Point CI SE27 ......22 B3
Edgeborough Ct [6] GU1 130 F8
Edgeborough Sch GU10 146 E3
Edgecombe CI KT2 ......18 D1
Edgecombe Ho SW19 ....19 E8
Edgecoombe CR2 ....62 D2
Edgecumbe Ct [2] CR0 ..43 A1
Edgedale CI RG45 ....45 B4
Edgefield CI
Cranleigh GU6 ....174 C4
Redhill RH1 ....140 A4
Edgehill Ct KT12 ....35 C1
Edgehill Ho [2] RH1 ....118 F1
Edgehill Rd Mitcham CR4 .41 B8
Purley CR2,CR8 ....61 B1
Edgeley KT23 ....93 E3
Edgell CI GU25 ....31 F6
Edgell Rd TW18 ....12 F3
Edgemoor Rd GU16 .....66 C3
Edgewood CI RG45 ......45 A7
Edgewood Gn CR0 ......43 D1
Edgeworth CI CR3 ......81 A1
Edgington Rd SW16 .....21 D2
Edgington Way DA14 ....44 F7 *(?)*
Edinburgh CI GU12 ....106 A5
Edinburgh Ct Catford SE6 .24 F7
[2] Kingston u T KT1 .....37 E6
West Barnes SM4 ......39 E4
Edinburgh Dr TW15,TW18 13 D1
Edinburgh Ho SM1 ......59 D8
Edinburgh Rd SM1 ......59 D8
Edinburgh Way RH19 ..205 F7
Edith Gdns KT5 ....38 B2
Edith Rd
Thornton Heath SE25 ...42 D4
Wimbledon SW19 ......20 B2
Edmonds Ct RG12 ......27 C8
Edmund Gr TW13 ....15 F6
Edmund Rd CR4 ....40 E6
Edmunds Gate [4] GU7 ..150 D4
Edna Rd SW20 ....39 D7
Edrich Rd RH11 ....201 A1
Edridge Ho [9] SE27 .....22 B5
Edridge Rd CR0,CR9 .....61 D7
Edward Alleyn Ho SE21 ..22 E8
Edward Ave
Camberley GU15 ......65 A5
Morden CR4,SM4 ......40 D4
Edward CI TW12 ....16 C3
Edward Ct
Farnborough GU14 .....85 B4
Staines TW18 ....13 C2
Edward Ho RH1 ....140 A6
Edward II Ave KT14 .....71 F6

Edward Pauling Ho
  TW14 . . . . .14 F8
Edward Pauling Prim Sch
  TW13 . . . . .14 E6
Edward Pinner Ct **5** KT6 56 E8
Edward Rd
  Biggin Hill TN16 . . . . .83 E1
  Coulsdon CR5 . . . . .79 D4
  Croydon CR0 . . . . .42 E2
  Farnham GU9 . . . . .146 C7
  Hampton TW12 . . . . .16 C3
  Hatton TW14 . . . . .3 E2
  Penge SE20 . . . . .23 D2
  Windlesham GU20 . . . . . . .48 D4
Edward St **2** GU11 . . . .105 A2
Edward Way TW15 . . . . . .13 F6
Edwards Cl KT4 . . . . .58 D8
Edwin Cl KT24 . . . . .92 D2
Edwin Rd
  Twickenham TW2 . . . . . . .16 E7
  West Horsley KT24 . . . . . .92 D2
Edwina Ct SM1 . . . . .59 B6
Eelmoor Plain Rd GU11 104 D5
Eelmoor Rd
  Aldershot GU11 . . . . .104 D5
  Farnborough GU14 . . . . . .84 F2
Eelmoor Rd Trad Est
  GU14 . . . . .84 F2
Effingham Cl SM2 . . . . . .59 B3
Effingham Common Rd
  KT24 . . . . .93 C2
Effingham Ct
  Mitcham SW19 . . . . .20 E1
  13 Woking GU22 . . . . . .89 E8
Effingham Ho **9** KT2 . .18 B2
Effingham Junction Sta
  KT24 . . . . .93 A4
Effingham La RH10 . . . . .183 E4
Effingham Lodge **1** KT6 .37 E4
Effingham Pl KT24 . . . . .113 D8
Effingham Rd
  Copthorne RH10,RH6 . . . .183 D6
  Reigate RH2 . . . . .139 B8
  Thames Ditton KT6,KT7 . . .37 C2
  Thornton Heath CR0 . . . . .41 F2
Effort St SW17 . . . . .20 E3
Effra Ct SE19 . . . . .22 E1
Effra Rd SW19 . . . . .20 B2
Egbury Ho SW15 . . . . .7 F1
Egerton Ct
  7 Guildford GU2 . . . . .108 E1
  5 Richmond TW10 . . . . . .6 E2
Egerton Ho W4 . . . . .7 C8
Egerton Pl KT13 . . . . . . .53 C4
Egerton Rd
  Guildford GU2 . . . . .129 F8
  New Malden KT3 . . . . . . .38 F5
  Sandhurst GU15 . . . . .64 F7
  Sandhurst GU15 . . . . .65 A7
  South Norwood SE25 . . . . .42 E6
  Twickenham TW2 . . . . . . .16 E8
  Weybridge KT13 . . . . . . .53 C4
Eggar's Ct GU12 . . . . . .105 B1
Eggar's Hill GU12 . . . . .126 A8
Egham Bsns Village
  TW20 . . . . .32 C7
Egham By-Pass TW20 . . .12 A4
Egham Cl Cheam SM3 . . . .58 E8
  Putney SW19 . . . . .19 E6
Egham Cres SM3 . . . . . . .58 D8
Egham Ct KT6 . . . . .37 D4
Egham Hill TW20 . . . . . . .11 D2
Egham Hill TW20 . . . . . . .11 F3
Egham Mus ★ TW20 . . . . .12 A3
Egham Sta TW20 . . . . . . .12 A3
Egleston Rd SM4 . . . . . . .40 B3
Egley Dr GU22 . . . . .89 D5
Egley Rd GU22 . . . . .89 D6
Eglinton Rd GU10 . . . . . .168 B7
Eglise Rd CR6 . . . . .81 E2
Egmont Ave KT6 . . . . . . .37 F1
Egmont Ho **18** SM2 . . . .59 C3
Egmont Park Rd KT20 . . .97 A2
Egmont Rd
  New Malden KT3 . . . . . . .38 F5
  Surbiton KT6 . . . . .38 A1
  Sutton SM2 . . . . .59 C3
  Walton-on-T KT12 . . . . . . .35 B2
Egmont Way KT20 . . . . . .97 E8
Egremont Rd SE27 . . . . . .22 A5
Egret Gdns GU11 . . . . . .126 A7
Eight Acres GU26 . . . . . .188 C7
Eighteenth Rd CR4 . . . . . .41 E5
Eileen Rd SE25 . . . . .42 D4
Eisenhower Ho KT8 . . . . .37 C8
Eland Pl CR9 . . . . .61 B7
Eland Rd Aldershot GU12 105 D1
  Croydon CR0,CR9 . . . . . . .61 B7
Elberon Ave CR0 . . . . . . .41 C3
Elborough Rd SE25 . . . . . .43 A4
Elborough St SW18 . . . . . .20 A7
Elbow Mdw SL3 . . . . .1 F6
Elcho Rd GU24 . . . . .87 D8
Elder Cl GU4 . . . . .110 A4
Elder Gdns **9** SE27 . . . .22 C4
Elder Oak Cl SE20 . . . . . .43 B8
Elder Rd Bisley GU24 . . . . .68 A4
  West Norwood SE27 . . . . .22 C3
Elder Way RH5 . . . . .136 C3
Elderberry Gr **10** SE27 . .22 C4
Elderfield Rd SW17 . . . . .21 B4
Eldergrove GU14 . . . . . . .85 E2
Eldersley Rd RH1 . . . . . .118 F3
Eldersley Gdns RH1 . . . .118 F3
Elderslie Cl BR3 . . . . .44 B3
Elderton Rd SE26 . . . . . . .23 E4
Eldertree Pl CR4 . . . . . . .41 C8

Eldertree Way CR4 . . . . . .41 C8
Elderwood Ct **7** 22 C3
Eldon Ave Croydon CR0 . . .62 C8
  Heston TW5 . . . . .5 A7
Eldon Ct KT13 . . . . .53 C5
Eldon Dr GU10 . . . . .146 D5
Eldon Pk SE25 . . . . .43 B5
Eldon Rd CR3 . . . . .100 D6
Eldrick Ct TW14 . . . . .14 D7
Eldridge Cl TW14 . . . . . . .15 A7
Eleanor Ave KT19 . . . . . . .57 D1
Eleanor Ct GU1 . . . . .130 D7
Eleanor Gr SW13,SW14 . . .7 E4
Eleanor Ho **6** SW19 . . . .40 B8
Electric Par KT6 . . . . .37 D3
Elenora Terr **5** SM1 . . . .59 C5
Elfin Gr TW11 . . . . .16 F3
Elfrida Cres SE6 . . . . .24 A4
Elfrida Prim Sch SE6 . . . .24 A4
Elgar Ave
  Crowthorne RG45 . . . . . . .45 B7
  Thornton Heath SW16 . . . .41 E6
  Tolworth KT5,KT6 . . . . . . .38 B2
Elgar Ho Kenley CR8 . . . . .80 C5
  Twickenham TW2 . . . . .5 D1
Elgar Way RH13 . . . . . . .218 B4
Elger Way RH10 . . . . . . .183 A4
Elgin Ave TW15 . . . . .14 C2
Elgin Cl RH13 . . . . .217 F3
Elgin Cres Caterham CR3 101 A5
  Harlington TW6 . . . . .3 E5
Elgin Ct **6** CR0 . . . . . . .61 C6
Elgin Gdns GU1 . . . . . . .110 A2
Elgin Rd Croydon CR0 . . . .61 F8
  Sutton SM1 . . . . .59 C7
  Wallington SM6 . . . . .60 C4
  Weybridge KT13 . . . . .53 B5
Elgin Way GU16 . . . . .85 F8
Eliot Bank SE23,SE26 . . . .23 B6
Eliot Bank Prim Sch
  SE23 . . . . .23 B6
Eliot Cl GU15 . . . . .66 B7
Eliot Dr GU27 . . . . .207 E6
Eliot Ho **10** TW10 . . . . . . .6 F1
Elixwood Cotts RH5 . . . .134 D1
Elizabeth Ave
  Bagshot GU19 . . . . .47 F2
  Staines TW18 . . . . .13 D2
Elizabeth Cl
  Bracknell RG12 . . . . .27 C5
  Cheam SM1 . . . . .58 F6
Elizabeth Cotts **6** TW9 . . .7 A6
Elizabeth Cres East Grinstead RH19 .185 F3
Elizabeth Ct Ewell KT17 . . .57 F2
  Farncombe GU7 . . . . . . .150 E7
  Horley RH6 . . . . .161 A3
  Kingston u T KT2 . . . . . . .37 E8
  2 Oatlands Park KT13 . .53 D6
  Sunbury TW16 . . . . .35 C6
  3 Teddington TW11 . . . .16 E3
  West Barnes SM4 . . . . . . .39 E2
  Whyteleafe CR3 . . . . .80 F1
Elizabeth Gdns Ascot SL5 .29 B4
  Sunbury TW16 . . . . .35 C6
Elizabeth Hart Ct KT13 . . .52 F5
Elizabeth Ho **6** CR3 . . .101 A3
Elizabeth Rd
  Farncombe GU7 . . . . . . .150 E7
  Wokingham RG40 . . . . . . .25 D6
Elizabeth Way
  Feltham TW13 . . . . .15 C4
  South Norwood SE19 . . . . .22 D1
Elizabethan Cl TW19 . . . .13 D8
Elizabethan Way
  Crawley RH10 . . . . .202 C5
  Stanwell TW19 . . . . .13 D8
Elkins Gdns GU4 . . . . . . .110 A4
Elkins Gr GU9 . . . . .124 F2
Ellacombe Ho **1** SW2 . . .22 A8
Elland Rd KT12 . . . . .54 D8
Ellenborough Cl RG12 . . . .27 D8
Ellenbridge Way CR2 . . . .61 E2
Ellenbridge Ct GU12 . . . .106 A5
Elleray Rd TW11 . . . . .16 F2
Ellerdine Rd TW3 . . . . .5 C3
Ellerker Gdns TW10 . . . . . .6 E1
Ellerman Ave TW2 . . . . . .15 F7
Ellerslie Ct **6** SM6 . . . .60 B4
Ellerton Rd Surbiton KT6 . .37 F1
  Wandsworth SW17,SW18 . .20 D7
  Wimbledon SW20 . . . . . . .19 A1
Ellery Cl GU6 . . . . .174 E1
Ellery Rd SE19 . . . . .22 D1
Elles Ave GU1 . . . . .110 C1
Elles Cl GU14 . . . . .85 B3
Elles Rd GU14 . . . . .84 F2
Ellesfield Ave RG12 . . . . . .26 E5
Ellesmere Ave BR3 . . . . . .44 B7
Ellesmere Ct Chiswick W4 . .7 D8
  Penge SE20 . . . . .43 B7
  Weybridge KT12 . . . . .53 E4
Ellesmere Dr CR2 . . . . . . .81 B5
Ellesmere Pl KT12 . . . . . .53 E5
Ellesmere Rd
  Twickenham TW1 . . . . .6 C1
  Weybridge KT13 . . . . .53 E4
Ellice Rd RH8 . . . . .122 F6
Ellies Mews TW15 . . . . . .13 E6
Ellingham GU22 . . . . .89 D7
Ellingham Prim Sch KT9 .56 D3
Ellingham Rd KT9 . . . . . . .56 D4
Ellington Rd
  Feltham TW13 . . . . .14 F4
  Hounslow TW3 . . . . .5 B5
Ellington Way KT18 . . . . . .77 B2
Elliot Cl RH10 . . . . .202 C4
Elliot Pk GU12 . . . . .105 E2
Elliot Rise SL5 . . . . .28 C7

Elliott Ct GU21 . . . . .70 A3
Elliott Gdns TW17 . . . . . . .34 A5
Elliott Rd CR7 . . . . .42 B5
Ellis Ave GU2 . . . . .129 F7
Ellis Cl CR5 . . . . .99 F7
Ellis Farm Cl GU22 . . . . . .89 D5
Ellisfield Dr SW15 . . . . . . .19 A8
Ellison Way
  Tongham GU10 . . . . .126 F7
  Wokingham RG40 . . . . . . .25 B6
Ellman Rd RH11 . . . . . . .200 F4
Ellora Rd SW16 . . . . .21 D3
Ellson Cl RH10 . . . . .202 C4
Ellsworth Ct **18** KT6 . . . .37 D2
Ellswood Ct **18** KT6 . . . .37 D2
Ellwood Ct **18** KT6 . . . . .37 D2
Elm Bank Gdns SW13 . . . . .7 E5
Elm Bank Mans SW13 . . . . .7 E5
Elm Cl Box Hill KT20 . . . .116 C5
  Carshalton SM5 . . . . .40 F1
  Leatherhead KT22 . . . . . . .95 B5
  Send Marsh GU23 . . . . . . .91 A3
  South Croydon CR2 . . . . . .61 E4
  Stanwell TW19 . . . . .13 D7
  Tolworth KT5 . . . . .38 C2
  Twickenham TW2 . . . . . . .16 B6
  Warlingham CR6 . . . . .81 D2
  West Barnes SW20 . . . . . .39 C5
  Woking GU21 . . . . .69 D4
Elm Cotts RH5 . . . . .115 C8
Elm Court Sch SE27 . . . . .22 C6
Elm Cres Heath End GU9 .125 D7
  Kingston u T KT2 . . . . . . .37 E8
Elm Ct Catford SE6 . . . . . .24 B7
  5 Charlton TW16 . . . . . .14 F1
  3 East Grinstead RH19 .185 D2
  Knaphill GU21 . . . . .68 D2
  Mitcham CR4 . . . . .40 F7
  Sandhurst GU47 . . . . .45 E2
  Walton-on-T KT12 . . . . . . .54 C8
Elm Dr Chobham GU24 . . . .49 F1
  East Grinstead RH19 . . . .186 A1
  Leatherhead KT22 . . . . . . .95 B4
  Sunbury TW16 . . . . .35 C7
  Winkfield SL4 . . . . .9 B7
Elm Gdns
  Burgh Heath KT18 . . . . . .97 C8
  Claygate KT10 . . . . .55 F4
  Mitcham CR4 . . . . .41 D5
Elm Gr Bisley GU24 . . . . . .68 A3
  Caterham CR3 . . . . .100 E5
  Cranleigh GU6 . . . . .174 A3
  Epsom KT18 . . . . .76 C5
  Heath End GU9 . . . . .125 C7
  Horsham RH13 . . . . .217 E1
  Kingston u T KT2 . . . . . . .37 E8
  Sutton SM1 . . . . .59 B6
  Wimbledon SW19 . . . . . . .19 E1
Elm Grove Par SM6 . . . . . .60 A7
Elm Grove Rd
  Cobham KT11 . . . . .73 D3
  Farnborough GU14 . . . . . .85 B4
Elm Hill Bglws GU3 . . . .106 E3
Elm Ho **2** KT2 . . . . .17 F1
Elm La Ash GU10 . . . . . . .126 F8
  Forest Hill SE6 . . . . .23 F6
  Ockham GU23 . . . . .92 A8
Elm Park Rd SE25 . . . . . . .42 F6
Elm Pk Streatham SW2 . . . .21 F8
  Sunningdale SL5 . . . . .29 E1
Elm Pl GU11 . . . . .126 B8
Elm Rd Beckenham BR3 . . .43 F7
  Carshalton CR4,SM6 . . . . .41 A1
  Chessington KT9 . . . . .56 E6
  Claygate KT10 . . . . .55 F4
  East Bedfont TW14 . . . . . .14 D8
  Farncombe GU7 . . . . . . .150 F6
  Heath End GU9 . . . . .125 D7
  Kingston u T KT2 . . . . . . .37 F8
  Leatherhead KT22 . . . . . . .95 B5
  Mortlake SW14 . . . . .7 C3
  New Malden KT3 . . . . . . .38 D6
  Purley CR8 . . . . .80 B6
  Redhill RH1 . . . . .118 E1
  South Norwood CR7 . . . . .42 D5
  Stoneleigh KT17 . . . . .57 F4
  Warlingham CR6 . . . . .81 D2
  Woking GU21 . . . . .69 D1
  Woking,Horsell GU21 . . . . .69 F4
Elm Rd W SM4 . . . . .39 F2
Elm Tree Ave KT10 . . . . . .36 E2
Elm Tree Cl
  Addlestone KT16 . . . . .51 E8
  Ashford TW15 . . . . .14 B3
Elm View GU12 . . . . .106 B3
Elm Way North Cheam KT4 58 C7
  West Ewell KT19 . . . . .57 D5
Elm Wlk SW20 . . . . .39 D5
Elm Wood Sch SE27 . . . . .22 D5
Elmbank Ave
  Englefield Green TW20 . . . .11 B2
  Guildford GU2 . . . . .130 A8
Elmbourne Rd SW17 . . . . .21 B5
Elmbridge Ave KT5 . . . . . .38 B4
Elmbridge Cotts GU6 . . . .174 B3
Elmbridge La GU22 . . . . . .89 F8
Elmbridge Lodge Hospl
  KT7 . . . . .36 F2
Elmbridge Rd GU6 . . . . . .173 F2
Elmbrook Cl TW16 . . . . . . .35 B8
Elmbrook Rd SM1 . . . . . . .58 F6
Elmcourt Rd SE21,SE27 . . .22 B6
Elmcroft
  Little Bookham KT23 . . . . .94 A3
  12 Woking GU22 . . . . . .69 E1

Elmcroft Cl
  Chessington KT9 . . . . .56 E7
  Feltham TW14 . . . . .3 F1
  Frimley GU16 . . . . .85 F7
Elmcroft Ct RH10 . . . . . .201 E6
Elmcroft Dr Ashford TW15 14 A3
  Chessington KT9 . . . . .56 E7
Elmdene KT5 . . . . .38 C1
Elmdene Cl BR3 . . . . .43 E5
Elmdon Rd Hatton TW6 . . . .3 F4
  Hounslow TW5 . . . . .4 E5
Elmer Cotts KT22 . . . . . . .95 A4
Elmer Gdns TW7 . . . . .5 D4
Elmer Mews KT22 . . . . . . .95 A5
Elmer Rd SE6 . . . . .24 C8
Elmer's Dr TW11 . . . . .17 B2
Elmers End Rd
  Beckenham BR3 . . . . .43 D5
  Penge BR3,SE20 . . . . .43 D5
Elmers End Sta BR3 . . . .43 D5
Elmers Rd
  Croydon CR0,SE25 . . . . . .43 A2
  Ockley RH5 . . . . .177 C4
Elmerside Rd BR3 . . . . . . .43 E5
Elmfield KT23 . . . . .94 A4
Elmfield Ave Mitcham CR4 41 A8
  Teddington TW11 . . . . . . .16 F3
Elmfield Cotts GU3 . . . . .108 A2
Elmfield Ho GU4 . . . . . . .110 C3
Elmfield Mans **5** SW17 . .21 A4
Elmfield Rd SW17 . . . . . . .21 B6
Elmfield Way CR2 . . . . . . .61 F2
Elmgate Ave TW13 . . . . . .15 C5
Elmgrove Cl GU21 . . . . . . .88 D8
Elmgrove Rd Croydon CR0 .43 A2
  Weybridge KT13 . . . . .53 A7
Elmhurst SM1 . . . . .59 D8
Elmhurst Ave CR4 . . . . . . .21 B1
Elmhurst Ballet Sch
  GU15 . . . . .65 D5
Elmhurst Ct Croydon CR0 . .61 D5
  Guildford GU1 . . . . .130 F8
Elmhurst Dr RH4 . . . . . . .136 B5
Elmhurst Lodge **5** SM2 . .59 C3
Elmhurst Sch CR2 . . . . . . .61 D5
Elmore Rd CR5 . . . . .99 A6
Elmpark Gdns CR2 . . . . . .62 C1
Elms Cotts CR4 . . . . .40 F7
Elms Ct SW19 . . . . .20 B1
Elms Rd Aldershot GU11 . .105 A2
  Wokingham RG40 . . . . . . .25 B5
Elms The Ash GU10 . . . . .126 F8
  Ashford TW15 . . . . .14 A3
  Blackwater GU17 . . . . .64 D4
  Claygate KT10 . . . . .55 F3
  Croydon CR0 . . . . .42 C1
  Farnham GU9 . . . . .125 C2
  Mortlake SW13 . . . . .7 F4
Elmscott Rd BR1 . . . . .24 F3
Elmshorn RH7 . . . . .77 C3
Elmside Guildford GU2 . . .130 A8
  Milford GU8 . . . . .149 F1
  New Addington CR0 . . . . . .63 B4
Elmsleigh Ct
  Farnborough GU14 . . . . . .84 F4
  1 Sutton SM1 . . . . .59 B7
Elmsleigh Ctr The TW18 . .12 F3
Elmsleigh Ho TW2 . . . . . .16 D6
Elmsleigh Rd
  Farnborough GU14 . . . . . .84 F4
  Staines TW18 . . . . .12 F3
  Twickenham TW2 . . . . . . .16 D6
Elmslie Cl KT18 . . . . .76 C5
Elmstead RH19 . . . . .205 E8
Elmstead Cl KT19 . . . . . . .57 E5
Elmstead Gdns KT4 . . . . . .58 A7
Elmstead Rd KT14 . . . . . . .71 A5
Elmsway TW15 . . . . .14 A3
Elmswood KT23 . . . . .93 F3
Elmsworth Ave TW3 . . . . . .5 B5
Elmtree Cl KT14 . . . . .71 E6
Elmtree Rd TW11 . . . . . . .16 E3
Elmwood Ave TW13 . . . . . .15 B5
Elmwood Cl
  Ashtead KT21 . . . . .75 D2
  Hackbridge SM6 . . . . .60 B8
  Stoneleigh SM17 . . . . .58 A3
Elmwood Ct KT21 . . . . . . .75 D2
Elmwood Dr KT17 . . . . . . .58 A3
Elmwood Inf Sch CR0 . . . .42 B2
Elmwood Jun Sch CR0 . . . .42 B2
Elmwood Rd Chiswick W4 . .7 C8
  Croydon CR0 . . . . .42 B2
  Mitcham CR4 . . . . .40 F6
  Redhill RH1 . . . . .119 B5
  Thornton Heath CR0 . . . . .42 B2
Elmworth Gr SE21 . . . . . . .22 D6
Elphinstone Cl GU24 . . . . .88 A6
Elphinstone Ct SW16 . . . . .21 E2
Elsdon Rd GU21 . . . . .69 A1
Elsenham St SW18,SW19 . .19 F6
Elsenwood Cres GU15 . . . .66 A6
Elsenwood Dr GU15 . . . . . .66 A7
Elsinore Ave TW19 . . . . . .13 E8
Elsinore Rd SE23 . . . . . . .23 E7
Elsinore Way TW9 . . . . .7 B4
Elsley Cl GU16 . . . . .85 F6
Elstan Way CR0 . . . . .43 E2
Elstead Ct SM4 . . . . .39 E1
Elstead Gn GU8 . . . . .148 D4
Elstead Ho **12** SW2 . . . . .21 F8
Elstead Rd Milford GU8 . . .149 C3
  Seale GU10 . . . . .148 F8
  Shackleford GU8 . . . . . . .149 E6
Elsted Cl RH11 . . . . .201 B8
Elston Pl GU12 . . . . .126 C8
Elston Rd GU12 . . . . .126 C8

Edw – Enn 245

Elstree Hill BR1 . . . . .24 E1
Elsworth Cl TW14 . . . . . . .14 E7
Elsworthy KT7 . . . . .36 E3
Elthorne Ct TW13 . . . . . . .15 C7
Elton Cl KT1 . . . . .17 C1
Elton Rd Kingston u T KT2 . .38 A8
  Purley CR8 . . . . .79 C7
Elveden Cl GU22 . . . . .71 B2
Elveden Ct **5** KT22 . . . . .95 C6
Elveden Rd KT11 . . . . .73 C8
Elvington Gn RH2 . . . . . . .44 F4
Elvington Lodge **5** RH2 118 A4
Elvino Rd SE26 . . . . .23 E3
Elwell Cl TW20 . . . . .12 A2
Elwill Way BR3 . . . . .44 D5
Ely Cl Crawley RH10 . . . . .201 C2
  Frimley GU16 . . . . .86 A7
  Kingston u T KT3 . . . . . . .38 F7
Ely Ho **7** RH1 . . . . .118 F1
Ely Rd Hatton TW6 . . . . . . .3 F5
  Hounslow TW4 . . . . .4 C4
  Thornton Heath CR0 . . . . .42 D4
Elystan Cl SM6 . . . . .60 C2
Embankment The
  Twickenham TW1 . . . . . . .17 A7
  Wraysbury TW19 . . . . .11 C7
Embassy Ct
  Kingston u T KT6 . . . . . . .37 D4
  7 Wallington SM6 . . . . . .60 B4
Embassy Gdns BR3 . . . . . .43 F8
Ember Cl KT15 . . . . .52 D5
Ember Ctr KT12 . . . . .54 E8
Ember Farm Ave KT8 . . . . .36 D3
Ember Farm Way KT8 . . . .36 D4
Ember Gdns KT10,KT8 . . . .36 E3
Ember Ho BR1 . . . . .24 D3
Ember La KT10,KT8 . . . . . .36 D2
Embercourt Rd KT10,KT7,
  KT8 . . . . .36 E3
Emberwood RH11 . . . . . .201 D8
Embleton Rd GU35 . . . . . .187 B6
Embleton Wlk TW12 . . . . . .15 F3
Emerton Rd KT22 . . . . . . .94 C6
Emery Down Cl RG12 . . . . .28 A6
Emily Davison Dr
  Banstead KT18 . . . . .77 B1
  Burgh Heath KT18 . . . . . .97 B8
Emley Rd KT15 . . . . .52 B6
Emlyn La KT22 . . . . .95 A5
Emlyn Rd Horley RH6 . . . .160 E4
  Redhill RH1 . . . . .140 A7
Emmanuel Cl GU2 . . . . . .109 A4
Emmanuel Ho SE21 . . . . . .22 D5
Emmanuel Rd SW12 . . . . .21 C7
Emmbrook Rd RG41 . . . . .25 A8
Emmbrook Sch The
  RG41 . . . . .25 A8
Emmeline Ct KT12 . . . . . . .35 C2
Emmetts Cl GU21 . . . . . . .69 D2
Empire Villas RH1 . . . . . .161 B7
Empress Ave GU14 . . . . . .85 B5
Emsworth Cl RH10 . . . . . .202 C3
1 Sutton SM1 . . . . .59 B7
Emsworth St SW2 . . . . . . .21 F6
Ena Rd SW16 . . . . .41 E6
Endale Cl SM5 . . . . .59 F8
Endeavour Way
  Wallington CR0 . . . . .41 F2
  Wimbledon SW19 . . . . . . .20 B4
Enderley Ho SE19 . . . . . . .42 F8
Endlesham Ct **4** SW12 . .21 A8
Endlesham Rd SW12 . . . . .21 A8
Endsleigh Cl CR2 . . . . . . .62 C1
Endsleigh Gdns
  Hersham KT12 . . . . .54 C5
  Kingston u T KT6 . . . . . . .37 C3
Endsleigh Mans **4** SW16 21 E5
Endsleigh Rd RH1 . . . . . .119 C6
Endway KT5 . . . . .38 B2
Enfield Rd Ash GU12 . . . .106 B5
  Crawley RH11 . . . . .201 C2
  Harlington TW6 . . . . .3 E5
Enfield Road Rdbt TW6 . . . .3 E5
Engadine Cl CR0 . . . . .61 F7
Engadine St SW18 . . . . . . .20 A7
Engalee RH19 . . . . .185 C2
England Way KT3 . . . . .38 B5
Englefield RH12 . . . . . . .216 F2
Englefield Cl
  Englefield Green TW20 . . . .11 C2
  Thornton Heath CR0 . . . . .42 C3
Englefield Green Inf Sch
  TW20 . . . . .11 C3
Englefield Rd GU21 . . . . . .68 D2
Engleheart Dr TW14 . . . . . .3 F1
Engleheart Rd SE6 . . . . . .24 C8
Englehurst TW20 . . . . .11 C2
Englemere Pk Ascot SL5 . .28 D5
  Oxshott KT22 . . . . .74 B6
Englemere Pond Nature
  Trail ★ SL5 . . . . .28 C6
Englesfield GU15 . . . . .66 D5
Engliff La GU22 . . . . .71 A3
English Cotts RH1 . . . . . .120 A6
Enid Wood Ho RG12 . . . . .27 C7
Enmore Ave SE25 . . . . . . .43 A4
Enmore Gdns SW14 . . . . . .7 D2
Enmore Rd SE25 . . . . .43 A4
Ennerdale RG12 . . . . .27 A5
Ennerdale Cl Cheam SM1 . .58 F6
  Crawley RH11 . . . . .201 B4
  East Bedfont TW14 . . . . . .14 F7
Ennerdale Gr GU9 . . . . . .125 A6
Ennerdale Rd TW9 . . . . . . .6 F5
Ennismore Ave GU1 . . . . .109 F1
Ennismore Gdns KT7 . . . . .36 E3

Ennor Ct KT4 . . . . .58 C6
Ensham Sch SW17 . . . . .20 E6
Ensign Cl Purley CR8 . . . .61 A1
Stanwell TW19 . . . . .13 D7
Ensign Way TW19 . . . . . .13 D7
Enterdent Cotts RH9 . . .121 D2
Enterdent Rd RH9 . . . . .121 D2
Enterprise Cl CR0 . . . . . .42 A1
Enterprise Ct
  Bracknell RG12 . . . . . . .26 F7
  Crawley RH10 . . . . . . .181 D2
Enterprise Ctr The
  RH10 . . . . .181 F2
Enterprise Est GU1 . . . .109 E5
Enterprise Ho
  2 Aldershot GU11 . . . . .105 B2
  Walton-on-T KT12 . . . . . .35 B2
Enterprise Ind Est GU12 105 F7
Enterprise Way TW11 . . .16 F2
Enton Hall GU8 . . . . . . .171 B3
Enton La GU8 . . . . .171 B3
Enversham Ct SE23 . . . . .23 E5
Envis Way GU3 . . . . . . .108 C4
Eothen Cl CR3 . . . . .101 A3
Epping Way RG12 . . . . . .27 F5
Epping Wlk RH10 . . . . .201 F4
Epsom & Ewell High Sch
  KT19 . . . . .57 C5
Epsom Bsns Pk KT17 . . . .76 E8
Epsom Coll GU15 . . . . . .65 C8
Epsom Coll KT17 . . . . . . .77 A5
Epsom Downs Metro Ctr
  KT20 . . . . .97 B7
Epsom Downs Sta KT17 . .77 B4
Epsom General Hospl
  KT18 . . . . .76 C4
Epsom La N KT18,KT20 . . .97 B7
Epsom La S KT20 . . . . . .97 C5
Epsom Pl GU6 . . . . .174 F3
Epsom Prim Sch KT19 . . .76 D8
Epsom Rd
  Ashtead KT18,KT21 . . . . .76 A2
  Crawley RH10 . . . . . . .202 A4
  Croydon CR0 . . . . .61 A6
  East Clandon GU4 . . . . .111 D3
  Ewell KT17 . . . . .76 F8
  Guildford GU4 . . . . . . .110 F2
  Guildford,Merrow GU1,
    GU4 . . . . .110 C1
  Leatherhead KT22 . . . . . .95 C6
  Morden SM4 . . . . .39 C4
  West Horsley KT24,KT24 .112 C5
Epsom Sq TW6 . . . . .3 F5
Epsom Sta KT19 . . . . . . .76 D6
Epworth Rd TW7,TW8 . . . .6 A7
Eresby Dr BR3 . . . . .44 A1
Erica Cl GU24 . . . . .67 E6
Erica Cotts GU26 . . . . . .188 C6
Erica Ct GU22 . . . . .69 D1
Erica Dr RG40 . . . . .25 D5
Erica Gdns CR0 . . . . .63 B7
Erica Way
  Copthorne RH10 . . . . . .183 A2
  Horsham RH12 . . . . . . .217 D5
Eridge Cl RH10 . . . . . . .202 C6
Erin Cl BR1 . . . . .24 E1
Erindale Ct 2 BR3 . . . . . .44 A8
Eriswell Cres KT12 . . . . . .53 F4
Eriswell Rd KT12 . . . . . . .53 F5
Erkenwald Cl KT16 . . . . . .32 E3
Ermine Cl TW4 . . . . .4 C5
Ermyn Cl KT21 . . . . .95 D6
Ermyn Cotts RH6 . . . . . .163 A6
Ermyn Way KT22 . . . . . . .95 D6
Erncroft Way TW1 . . . . . . .5 F1
Ernest Ave SE27 . . . . . . .22 B3
Ernest Bevin Coll SW17 . .20 E6
Ernest Cl Beckenham BR3 .44 A4
  Farnham GU10,GU9 . . . .146 B6
Ernest Cotts KT17 . . . . . .57 F3
Ernest Gdns W4 . . . . .7 B8
Ernest Gr BR3 . . . . .43 F4
Ernest Rd KT1 . . . . .38 B7
Ernest Sq KT1 . . . . .38 B7
Ernle Rd SW20 . . . . .19 C1
Erridge Rd SW19 . . . . . . .40 A7
Errol Gdns KT3 . . . . .39 A5
Erskine Cl Carshalton SM1 59 E7
  Crawley RH11 . . . . .200 E2
Erskine Rd SM1 . . . . .59 E7
Esam Way SE27,SW16 . . .22 A3
Escombe Dr GU2,GU3 . . .109 B6
Escot Rd TW16 . . . . .14 E1
Escott Pl KT16 . . . . .51 D4
Esher Ave Cheam SM3 . . .58 D7
  Walton-on-T KT12 . . . . . .35 A1
Esher CE High Sch KT10 . .55 A7
Esher CE Prim Sch KT10 . .55 C5
Esher Cl KT10 . . . . .55 B5
Esher Coll KT7 . . . . .36 E2
Esher Cres TW6 . . . . .3 F5
Esher Gdns SW19 . . . . . .19 D6
Esher Gn KT10 . . . . .55 B6
Esher Green Dr KT10 . . . .55 B6
Esher Mews 3 CR4 . . . . .40 F6
Esher Park Ave KT10 . . . .55 B5
Esher Place Ave KT10 . . .55 B6
Esher Rd Camberley GU15 .47 A1
  East Molesey KT8 . . . . . .36 D4
  Hersham KT10,KT12 . . . . .54 E6
Esher Sta KT10 . . . . .55 B6
Eskdale Gdns CR8 . . . . . .80 D5
Eskdale Way GU15 . . . . . .66 D4
Eskmont Ridge SE19 . . . .22 E1
Esme Ho SW15 . . . . .7 F3

Esparto St SW18 . . . . . . .20 B8
Essame Cl RG40 . . . . .25 D6
Essenden Ct CR2 . . . . . . .61 E3
Essendene Cl CR3 . . . . .100 E4
Essendene Lodge Sch
  CR3 . . . . .100 E4
Essendene Rd CR3 . . . .100 E4
Essex Ave TW7 . . . . .5 E4
Essex Cl Addlestone KT15 .52 C6
  Frimley GU16 . . . . .86 A7
  West Barnes SM4 . . . . . .39 D2
Essex Ct Barnes SW13 . . . .7 F5
  South Norwood SE19 . . . .22 D2
Essex Dr GU6 . . . . .173 F2
Essex Gr SE19 . . . . .22 D2
Essex Ho 5 CR0 . . . . .61 D8
Essex Twr 5 SE20 . . . . . .43 B8
Estcots Dr RH19 . . . . . . .186 A1
Estcots Prim Sch RH19 . .186 A1
Estcourt Rd CR0,SE25 . . . .43 B3
Estella Ave KT3,SW20 . . . .39 B5
Estreham Rd SW16 . . . . .21 D2
Estridge Cl TW3 . . . . .5 A3
Eswyn Rd SW17 . . . . . . .20 F3
Ethel Bailey Cl KT19 . . . . .76 A7
Ethel Rd TW15 . . . . .13 E3
Ethelbert Rd SW20 . . . . .39 D8
Ethelbert St SW12 . . . . . .21 B7
Ethelworth Ct 4 SW2 . . . .22 A7
Etherley Hill RH5 . . . . . .177 A7
Etherow St SE22 . . . . . . .23 A8
Etherstone Gn SW16 . . . .22 A4
Etherstone Rd SW16 . . . .22 A4
Eton Ave Heston TW5 . . . . .5 A8
  New Malden KT3 . . . . . . .38 D5
Eton Cl SW18 . . . . .20 B8
Eton Ct TW18 . . . . .12 F3
Eton Ho 7 TW20 . . . . . . .12 A3
Eton Pl GU9 . . . . .125 B7
Eton St TW10 . . . . .6 E2
Etps Rd GU14 . . . . .105 B8
Ettrick Ct GU14 . . . . . . .105 B8
Etwell Pl KT5 . . . . .37 F3
Eureka Rd KT1 . . . . .38 A7
Europa Park Rd GU1 . . . .109 C2
Eurythmy Sch RH19 . . . .205 E6
Eustace Cres RG40 . . . . . .25 D8
Eustace Rd GU4 . . . . . . .110 D3
Euston Rd CR0 . . . . .42 A1
Evans Cl RH10 . . . . .202 D5
Evans Gr TW13 . . . . .16 A6
Evans Rd SE6 . . . . .24 E6
Eve Rd Isleworth TW7 . . . . .6 A3
  Sheerwater GU21 . . . . . . .70 B4
Evedon RG12 . . . . .27 B2
Evelina Rd SE20 . . . . .23 D1
Eveline Rd CR4 . . . . .40 F8
Evelyn Ave GU11 . . . . . .126 B8
Evelyn Cl Felbridge RH19 .184 F4
  Twickenham TW2 . . . . . . .16 B8
  Woking GU22 . . . . .89 D7
Evelyn Cotts
  Abinger Common RH5 . . .155 D8
  South Godstone RH9 . . . .142 E6
Evelyn Cres TW16 . . . . . .34 F8
Evelyn Ct CR0 . . . . .43 A2
Evelyn Gdns Richmond TW9 . .6 E3
  Tyler's Green RH9 . . . . .121 C5
Evelyn Rd Richmond TW9 . . .6 E4
  Richmond,Ham TW10 . . . .17 C5
  Wimbledon SW19 . . . . . .20 B2
Evelyn Terr TW9 . . . . .6 E4
Evelyn Way Epsom KT19 . .76 A8
  Stoke D'Abernon KT11 . . . .73 F3
  Sunbury TW16 . . . . .34 F8
  Wallington SM6 . . . . .60 D6
Evelyn Wlk RH10 . . . . . .201 E3
Evelyn Woods Rd GU11 . .105 C7
Evendon's Cl RG41 . . . . . .25 A3
Evendon's La RG41 . . . . .25 A3
Evening Hill BR3 . . . . . . .24 C1
Evenlode Way GU47 . . . . .64 D8
Everard La CR3 . . . . .101 B5
Everest Ct
  South Norwood SE19 . . . .42 E8
  Woking GU21 . . . . .68 E3
Everest Rd
  Camberley GU15 . . . . . . .65 D8
  Crowthorne RG45 . . . . . .45 B6
  Stanwell TW19 . . . . .13 E8
Everglade TN16 . . . . .83 D1
Everglades BR2 . . . . .44 E6
Evergreen Cl SE20 . . . . . .23 C1
Evergreen Ct TW19 . . . . .13 D8
Evergreen Rd GU16 . . . . .66 A3
Evergreen Way TW19 . . . .13 D8
Evergreens The GU8 . . . .171 B1
Everlands Cl 6 GU22 . . . .69 E1
Eversfield Ct 2 RH2 . . . .118 C1
Eversfield Rd
  Horsham RH13 . . . . . . .217 E1
  Reigate RH2 . . . . .118 B1
  Richmond TW9 . . . . .6 F5
Eversley Cres TW7 . . . . . . .5 D6
Eversley Pk SW19 . . . . . .19 B3
Eversley Rd
  Kingston u T KT5 . . . . . . .37 F4
  South Norwood SE19 . . . .22 D1
Eversley Way Croydon CR0 63 A7
  Thorpe TW20 . . . . .32 C7
Everton Rd CR0 . . . . .43 A1
Evesham Cl Belmont SM2 .59 A3
  Reigate RH2 . . . . .117 F2
Evesham Ct GU1 . . . . . . .131 A8
Evesham Gn SM4 . . . . . . .40 B3
Evesham Rd Morden SM4 .40 B3

Evesham Rd continued
  Reigate RH2 . . . . .117 F2
Evesham Rd N RH3 . . . . .117 F2
Evesham Wlk GU47 . . . . .45 D1
Ewart Rd SE23 . . . . .23 D8
Ewelands RH6 . . . . .161 C4
Ewell By-Pass KT17 . . . . .58 A1
Ewell Castle Sch KT17 . . .58 A2
Ewell Court Ave KT19 . . . .57 E5
Ewell Downs Rd KT17 . . . .77 A3
Ewell East Sta KT17 . . . . .57 F2
Ewell Grove Inf Sch KT17 57 F1
Ewell Ho KT17 . . . . .57 F1
Ewell House Gr KT17 . . . .57 F1
Ewell Park Gdns KT17 . . .58 A3
Ewell Park Way KT17 . . . .58 A3
Ewell Rd Cheam SM2,SM3 .58 D4
  Surbiton KT5,KT6 . . . . . .37 E2
  Thames Ditton KT6,KT7 . . .37 B2
  Tolworth KT6 . . . . .38 B1
Ewell West Sta KT19 . . . . .57 E2
Ewelme Rd SE23 . . . . . . .23 C7
Ewen Cres SW2 . . . . .22 A8
Ewhurst Ave CR2 . . . . . . .61 E2
Ewhurst CE Inf Sch GU6 .175 C5
  East Ewell SM2 . . . . .58 C2
Ewhurst Cl CR4 . . . . .40 D6
Ewhurst Rd
  Cranleigh GU6 . . . . .174 E3
  Crawley RH11 . . . . .201 C7
  Ewhurst GU5,GU6 . . . . .154 E3
Ewins Cl GU12 . . . . .106 A2
Ewood La RH5 . . . . .158 C6
Ewshot Hill Cross GU10 .124 D7
Exbury Rd SE6 . . . . .24 A6
Excalibur Cl RH11 . . . . .200 E5
Excelsior Cl KT1 . . . . .38 A7
Exchange Rd Ascot SL5 . . .29 C4
  Crawley RH11 . . . . .201 E6
Exchange The 8 CR8 . . . .80 A8
Exeforde Ave TW15 . . . . .14 A4
Exeter Cl RH10 . . . . .201 E2
Exeter Ct Kingston u T KT6 .37 E4
  Mitcham SW19 . . . . .20 E1
Exeter Ho Feltham TW13 . .16 A6
  Woking GU21 . . . . .69 F3
Exeter Rd Ash GU12 . . . .106 A3
  Croydon CR0 . . . . .42 F2
  Feltham TW13 . . . . .15 F5
  Harlington TW6 . . . . .3 E5
Exeter Way TW6 . . . . .3 E5
Explorer Ave TW19 . . . . .13 E7
Eyebright Cl CR0 . . . . . . .43 D1
Eyhurst Cl KT20 . . . . .97 F3
Eyhurst Spur KT20 . . . . . .97 F3
Eyles Cl RH12 . . . . .217 B4
Eylewood Rd SE27 . . . . . .22 C3
Eyre Ct RG40 . . . . .25 B4
Eyston Dr KT13 . . . . .53 A1

F

Fabyc Ho TW9 . . . . .7 A7
Factory Cotts GU10 . . . .124 D2
Factory La CR0,CR9 . . . . .61 B8
Fagg's Rd TW14 . . . . .4 B1
Fair Green Ct 1 CR4 . . . . .40 F6
Fair La CR5,RH2 . . . . .98 D1
Fair Oak Cl KT22 . . . . . . .74 D7
Fair St TW3 . . . . .5 C4
Fair View RH12 . . . . .217 A3
Fairacre Hounslow TW7 . . .5 D6
  Kingston u T KT3 . . . . . . .38 E6
Fairacres
  Burgh Heath KT20 . . . . . .97 C6
  Cobham KT11 . . . . .73 E7
  New Addington CR0 . . . . .62 F2
  Salfords RH1 . . . . .140 C1
Fairbairn Cl CR8 . . . . .80 A6
Fairbourne KT11 . . . . . . .73 D6
Fairbourne Cl GU21 . . . . .69 A1
Fairbourne La CR3 . . . . .100 C4
Fairbourne Way GU2 . . . .109 A4
Fairbriar Ct 5 KT18 . . . . .76 E6
Fairchildes Ave CR0 . . . . .82 D7
Fairchildes Cotts CR6 . . . .82 F6
Fairchildes Prim Sch
  CR9 . . . . .82 E7
Fairchildes Rd CR6 . . . . . .82 E4
Faircroft SE26 . . . . .23 C4
Faircross RG12 . . . . .27 B6
Fairdene Rd CR5 . . . . .79 D3
Fairfax RG42 . . . . .27 A8
Fairfax Ave Ewell KT17 . . .58 A3
  Redhill RH1 . . . . .118 F2
Fairfax Cl KT12 . . . . .35 B1
Fairfax Ind Est GU12 . . . .105 E2
Fairfax Mews GU14 . . . . .85 D2
Fairfax Rd
  Farnborough GU14 . . . . . .85 C7
  Old Woking GU22 . . . . . .90 B7
  Teddington TW11 . . . . . . .17 B1
Fairfield App TW19 . . . . . .11 D8
Fairfield Ave Horley RH6 .161 A1
  Staines TW18 . . . . .12 F4
  Twickenham TW2 . . . . . . .16 B7
Fairfield Cl Dorking RH4 .115 C1
  Great Bookham KT23 . . . .94 B1
  Guildford GU2 . . . . .109 A2
  Mitcham SW19 . . . . .20 E1
  West Ewell KT19 . . . . . . .57 E5
Fairfield Cotts GU8 . . . . .191 C3
Fairfield Ct Dorking RH4 .115 B1
  Leatherhead KT22 . . . . . .95 B6
Fairfield Dr Dorking RH4 .136 B8
  Frimley GU16 . . . . .65 E3

Fairfield E KT1 . . . . .37 E7
Fairfield Ind Est KT1 . . . . .37 F6
Fairfield La GU24 . . . . . . .68 A7
Fairfield N KT1,KT2 . . . . . .37 E7
Fairfield Path CR0,CR9 . . .61 D7
Fairfield Pk KT11 . . . . . . .73 D5
Fairfield Pl KT1 . . . . .37 E6
Fairfield Rd
  Beckenham BR3 . . . . .44 A7
  East Grinstead RH19 . . . .205 F8
  Kingston u T KT1 . . . . . . .37 E7
  Leatherhead KT22 . . . . . .95 B6
  South Croydon CR0,CR9 . .61 E7
Fairfield Rise GU2 . . . . . .108 F2
Fairfield S KT1 . . . . .37 F7
Fairfield The GU9 . . . . . .125 C2
Fairfield W KT1 . . . . .37 E7
Fairfield Way
  Coulsdon CR5 . . . . .79 D5
  West Ewell KT19 . . . . . . .57 E5
Fairfields Chertsey KT15 . .33 B1
  Lewisham SE6 . . . . .24 B8
Fairfields Rd TW3 . . . . .5 C4
Fairford SE6 . . . . .24 A7
Fairford Ave CR0 . . . . . . .43 D4
Fairford Cl Croydon CR0 . .43 E4
  Pyrford KT14 . . . . .70 F5
  Reigate RH2 . . . . .118 C3
Fairford Ct SM2 . . . . .59 B3
Fairford Gdns KT4 . . . . . .57 F7
Fairgreen Rd CR7 . . . . . . .42 B4
Fairhall RH2 . . . . .117 E2
Fairhaven TW20 . . . . .11 F3
Fairhaven Ave CR0 . . . . . .43 D3
Fairhaven Ct Croydon CR2 61 C5
  1 Egham TW20 . . . . . . .11 F3
Fairhaven Rd RH1 . . . . . .119 A5
Fairhill GU7 . . . . .150 D6
Fairholme
  East Bedfont TW14 . . . . . .14 E8
  2 New Malden KT3 . . . . .38 E5
Fairholme Cres KT21 . . . .75 C2
Fairholme Gdns GU9 . . . .125 C1
Fairholme Prim Sch
  TW14 . . . . .14 D7
Fairholme Rd
  Ashford TW15 . . . . .13 F3
  Cheam SM1 . . . . .58 F4
  Thornton Heath CR0 . . . . .42 A2
Fairings The KT12 . . . . . .54 B6
Fairlands Ave
  Fairlands GU3 . . . . .108 C5
  Sutton SM1 . . . . .59 A8
  Thornton Heath CR7 . . . . .42 A4
Fairlands Ct GU3 . . . . . .108 C5
Fairlands Rd GU3 . . . . . .108 D5
Fairlawn Weybridge KT13 .53 E5
  Little Bookham KT23 . . . . .93 F3
Fairlawn Cl Claygate KT10 .55 F4
  Feltham TW13 . . . . .15 F4
  Kingston u T KT2 . . . . . . .18 C2
Fairlawn Cres RH19 . . . . .185 B2
Fairlawn Dr
  East Grinstead RH19 . . . .185 B2
  Reigate RH1 . . . . .139 E7
Fairlawn Gr SM7 . . . . . . .78 D6
Fairlawn Pk
  Forest Hill SE26 . . . . . . .23 E3
  Woking GU21 . . . . .69 E4
Fairlawn Prim Sch SE23 . .23 C8
Fairlawn Prim Sch Annexe
  SE23 . . . . .23 C7
Fairlawn Rd Merton SW19 19 F1
  Sutton SM2,SM5 . . . . . . .78 C8
Fairlawnes SM6 . . . . .60 B5
Fairlawns Addlestone KT15 52 B5
  Guildford GU1 . . . . .110 C1
  Horley RH6 . . . . .161 B2
  Sunbury TW16 . . . . .35 A6
  Twickenham TW1 . . . . .6 C1
  Woodham KT15 . . . . .70 F8
Fairlawns Cl TW18 . . . . . .13 B2
Fairleas BR3 . . . . .44 B7
Fairlight Hampton TW12 . .16 B3
Fairlight Cl KT4 . . . . .58 C6
Fairlight Rd SW17 . . . . . .20 D4
Fairline Ct BR3 . . . . .44 C7
Fairlop Wlk GU6 . . . . . . .173 F2
Fairmead
  Tolworth KT5,KT6 . . . . . .38 B1
  Woking GU21 . . . . .69 C1
Fairmead Cl Heston TW5 . . .4 D7
  Kingston u T KT3 . . . . . . .38 D6
  Sandhurst GU47 . . . . . . .64 E7
Fairmead Rd CR0 . . . . . . .42 A2
Fairmeads KT11 . . . . .73 F6
Fairmile Ave Cobham KT11 73 F6
  Streatham SW16 . . . . . . .21 D3
Fairmile Ho TW11 . . . . . .17 A4
Fairmile Hts KT11 . . . . . .74 A6
Fairmile La KT11 . . . . . . .73 F5
Fairmile Park Copse
  KT11 . . . . .73 F6
Fairmile Park Rd KT11 . . .73 F6
Fairoak Cl CR8 . . . . .80 B4
Fairoak La
  Chessington KT9,KT22,KT10 75 D4
  Oxshott KT22 . . . . .74 E8
Fairoaks Airport GU24 . . .50 E1
Fairoaks Ct KT15 . . . . . . .52 B5
Fairs Rd KT22 . . . . .95 A8
Fairstone Ct RH6 . . . . . .161 B4
Fairview KT17 . . . . .77 C8
Fairview Ave GU22 . . . . . .69 F1

Fairview Cl
  Forest Hill SE26 . . . . . . .23 E3
  Woking GU22 . . . . .69 F1
Fairview Cotts GU25 . . . . .31 D3
Fairview Ct Ashford TW15 .14 A3
  Kingston u T KT2 . . . . . . .38 B8
  Staines TW18 . . . . .13 A2
Fairview Dr TW17 . . . . . . .33 F4
Fairview Gdns GU9 . . . . .125 D6
Fairview Ho 17 SW2 . . . . .21 F8
Fairview Pl SW2 . . . . .21 F8
Fairview Rd Ash GU12 . . .106 A3
  Carshalton SM1 . . . . .59 E5
  Ewell KT17 . . . . .76 F8
  Headley Down GU35 . . . .187 C5
  Thornton Heath SW16 . . . .41 F8
  Wokingham RG40 . . . . . .25 C5
Fairview Terr GU35 . . . . .187 A6
Fairwater Dr KT15 . . . . . .52 D2
Fairwater Ho TW11 . . . . .17 A4
Fairway Chertsey KT16 . . .33 B1
  Copthorne RH10 . . . . . .183 B2
  Crawley RH11 . . . . .200 D4
  Guildford GU1 . . . . .110 C1
  Sutton SM5 . . . . .78 C8
  West Barnes SW20 . . . . . .39 C4
Fairway Cl
  Copthorne RH10 . . . . . .183 A2
  Croydon BR3,CR0 . . . . . .43 E4
  Hounslow TW4 . . . . .4 D2
  West Ewell KT19 . . . . . . .57 C6
  Woking GU23 . . . . .89 B7
Fairway Est TW4 . . . . .4 C2
Fairway Gdns BR3 . . . . . .44 D3
Fairway Hts GU15 . . . . . .66 B6
Fairway Inf Sch RH10 . . .183 B3
Fairway The
  East Molesey KT8 . . . . . .36 B6
  Farnborough GU14 . . . . .104 B8
  Farnborough GU14 . . . . . .84 A1
  Frimley GU15 . . . . .66 A3
  Godalming GU7 . . . . . . .150 F2
  Heath End GU9 . . . . . . .125 D7
  Kingston u T KT3 . . . . . . .38 D8
  Leatherhead KT22 . . . . . .75 A1
  Pirbright GU3 . . . . .88 C3
  Weybridge KT13 . . . . . . .72 A3
Fairways Ashford TW15 . . .14 B2
  Beacon Hill GU26 . . . . . .188 B6
  Hounslow TW7 . . . . .5 E6
  Kenley CR8 . . . . .80 C2
  Teddington TW11 . . . . . . .17 D1
Fairways The RH1 . . . . . .139 D6
Fairwell La KT24 . . . . . . .112 B7
Fairwyn Rd SE26 . . . . . . .23 E4
Fakenham Way GU47 . . . .45 D2
Falaise TW20 . . . . .11 F3
Falaise Cl GU11 . . . . . . .105 B3
Falcon Cl Chiswick W4 . . . .7 C8
  Crawley RH11 . . . . .201 D8
  Lightwater GU18 . . . . . . .66 F8
Falcon Ct Frimley GU16 . . .65 D1
  Sheerwater GU21 . . . . . . .70 C6
  9 West Norwood SE21 . . .22 D6
Falcon Dr TW19 . . . . .2 E1
Falcon Rd Guildford GU1 .109 D1
  Hampton TW12 . . . . .15 F1
Falcon Way Feltham TW14 . .4 B2
  Sunbury TW16 . . . . .34 E7
Falcon Wood KT22 . . . . . .94 F7
Falconhurst
  4 Kingston u T KT6 . . . . .37 E4
  Oxshott KT22 . . . . .74 D4
Falconry Ct KT1 . . . . .37 E6
Falcons Cl TN16 . . . . .83 D2
Falconwood
  East Horsley KT24 . . . . . .92 F3
  Englefield Green TW20 . . .11 E3
Falconwood Rd CR0 . . . . .63 A3
Falcourt Cl SM1 . . . . .59 B5
Falkland Ct GU14 . . . . . .105 E8
Falkland Gr RH4 . . . . . . .136 A6
Falkland Ho SE6 . . . . .24 C4
Falkland Park Ave SE25 . .42 E7
Falkland Rd RH4 . . . . . . .136 A6
Falklands Dr RH13 . . . . . .218 B4
Falkner Rd GU9 . . . . .125 B2
Fallow Deer Cl RH13 . . . .218 B4
Fallowfield Way RH6 . . . .161 B4
Fallsbrook Rd SW16 . . . . .21 C2
Falmer Cl RH11 . . . . .201 C4
Falmouth Cl GU15 . . . . . .66 A4
Falmouth Rd KT12 . . . . . .54 C6
Falstone GU21 . . . . .69 B1
Fambridge Cl SE26 . . . . . .23 F4
Famet Ave CR8 . . . . .80 C6
Famet Cl CR8 . . . . .80 C6
Famet Gdns CR8 . . . . . . .80 C5
Famet Wlk CR8 . . . . .80 C6
Fanchford Rd RH2 . . . . . .117 E1
Fanes Cl RG42 . . . . .26 F8
Fanfare The GU22 . . . . . . .70 C4
Fanshawe Rd TW10 . . . . .17 C4
Faraday Ave RH19 . . . . . .205 F6
Faraday Cl RH10 . . . . . . .181 F2
Faraday Ctr The RH10 . . .181 F1
Faraday Ho
  7 Balham SW12 . . . . . . .21 B8
  5 Hampton TW12 . . . . . .16 B2
Faraday Rd
  Crawley RH10 . . . . .181 F2
  East Molesey KT8 . . . . . .36 A5
  Farnborough GU14 . . . . . .85 C6
  Wimbledon SW19 . . . . . .20 B2
Faraday Way CR0,CR9 . . .41 F1
Farcrosse Ct GU47 . . . . . .64 C8
Fareham Ho 13 SW15 . . . .19 A7
Fareham Rd TW14 . . . . . .15 C8

Farewell Pl CR4 . . . . .40 E8
Farhalls Cres RH12 . . . .217 F6
Faringdon Cl GU47 . . . . .45 C1
Faringdon Dr RG12 . . . . .27 D4
Farington Acres KT13 . . .53 D7
Faris Barn Dr KT15 . . . . .70 F8
Faris La KT15 . . . . .70 F8
Farleigh Ave BR2 . . . . . .44 F2
Farleigh Court Rd CR6 . .82 B5
Farleigh Ct Croydon CR2 . .61 C5
 ₃ Guildford GU1 . . . . . .108 E1
Farleigh Dean Cres CR0 . .82 B8
Farleigh Ho ₇ KT2 . . . . .18 B2
Farleigh Prim Sch CR6 . .81 E2
Farleigh Rd
  Warlingham CR6 . . . . . .81 E2
  Woodham KT15 . . . . . . .71 A8
Farleton Cl KT13 . . . . . . .53 D4
Farley Copse RG42 . . . . .26 E8
Farley Croft BR2 . . . . . . .44 E7
Farley Ct GU14 . . . . .85 D2
Farley Heath Rd GU5 . . .153 C6
Farley Ho SE26 . . . . . . .23 B5
Farley Moor RG42 . . . . . .26 D8
Farley Pk RH8 . . . . .122 D5
Farley Pl SE25 . . . . .43 A5
Farley Rd Lewisham SE6 . .24 C8
  South Croydon CR2 . . . . .62 B2
Farleycroft ₁ CR0 . . . . . .43 A1
Farleys Cl KT24 . . . . .92 C1
Farlington Pl SW15 . . . . .19 B8
Farlington Sch RH12 . . .216 B6
Farlton Rd SW18 . . . . . . .20 B8
Farm App RH9 . . . . .163 C5
Farm Ave Horsham RH12 .217 B3
  Streatham SW16 . . . . . . .21 E4
Farm Cl Ascot SL5 . . . . . .29 C4
  Bracknell RG42 . . . . . . .26 F8
  Byfleet KT14 . . . . .71 F7
  Chertsey KT16 . . . . .32 A3
  Chipstead CR5 . . . . .98 F7
  Coney Hall BR4 . . . . . . .63 F7
  Crawley RH10 . . . . .202 A7
  Crowthorne RG45 . . . . . .45 C7
  East Grinstead RH19 . . .206 B8
  East Horsley KT24 . . . . .112 F7
  Egham TW18 . . . . .12 E3
  Fairlands GU3 . . . . .108 C6
  Fetcham KT22 . . . . .94 E3
  Guildford GU1 . . . . .109 D4
  Lower Halliford TW17 . . .34 A2
  Loxwood RH14 . . . . . . .213 A3
  Sutton SM2 . . . . .59 D3
  Wallington SM6 . . . . . . .60 C1
  Warnham RH12 . . . . . . .216 F7
Farm Dr Croydon CR0 . . .62 F8
  Purley CR8 . . . . .79 D8
Farm Fields CR2 . . . . . . .80 F8
Farm La Addlestone KT15 .52 A3
  Ashstead KT21,KT18 . . . .76 B2
  Croydon CR0 . . . . .62 F8
  East Horsley KT24 . . . . .112 F7
  Purley CR8 . . . . .60 C1
  Send GU23 . . . . .90 C3
Farm Pk ✸ RH5 . . . . . . .198 A8
Farm Rd Aldershot GU12 .105 E3
  Frimley GU16 . . . . .65 F2
  Morden SM4 . . . . .40 B4
  Old Woking GU22 . . . . . .90 B7
  Staines TW18 . . . . .13 B2
  Sutton SM2 . . . . .59 D3
  Thames Ditton KT10 . . . .55 B8
  Twickenham TW4 . . . . . .15 E7
  Warlingham CR6 . . . . . .101 E8
Farm View KT20 . . . . . .117 F8
Farm Way
  North Cheam KT4 . . . . . .58 C7
  Stanwell TW19 . . . . .1 F1
Farm Wlk Ash GU12 . . . .127 C8
  Guildford GU2 . . . . .129 F7
Farmdale Rd SM5 . . . . . .59 E3
Farmer's Rd TW18 . . . . .12 E4
Farmet Ct RH19 . . . . . . .185 C3
Farmfield Dr RH6 . . . . . .181 B8
Farmfield Hospl RH6 . . .160 B1
Farmfield Rd BR1 . . . . . .24 E8
Farmhouse Cl GU22 . . . .70 D4
Farmhouse Rd SW16 . . . .21 C1
Farmington Ave SM1 . . . .59 D7
Farmleigh Cl RH10 . . . . .202 C8
Farmleigh Gr KT12 . . . . .53 F5
Farmstead ✸ 57 A2
Farmstead Ct SM6 . . . . .60 B5
Farmstead Rd SE6 . . . . .24 B4
Farmview KT11 . . . . .73 D3
Farnaby Rd BR1 . . . . . . .44 E8
Farnan Rd SW16 . . . . . . .21 E3
Farnborough (Sixth Form)
  Coll GU14 . . . . .85 B6
Farnborough Ave CR2 . . .62 C4
Farnborough Bsns Ctr
  GU14 . . . . .84 F2
Farnborough Bsns Pk
  GU14 . . . . .85 B6
Farnborough Coll of Tech
  GU14 . . . . .85 C2
Farnborough Cres
 ₃ Coney Hall BR2 . . . . . .44 F1
  South Croydon CR2 . . . . .62 E2
Farnborough Gate Ret Pk
  GU14 . . . . .85 C7
Farnborough Grange Com Inf
  Sch GU14 . . . . .85 A8
Farnborough Hill Sch
  GU14 . . . . .85 C5
Farnborough Ho ₁
  SW15 . . . . .19 A7

Farnborough Ind Est
  GU14 . . . . .85 A3
Farnborough Main Sta
  GU14 . . . . .85 B5
Farnborough North Sta
  GU14 . . . . .85 D6
Farnborough Rd
  Aldershot GU11 . . . . . . .104 E3
  Farnborough GU14 . . . . .85 C5
  Heath End GU11,GU9 . . .125 D7
Farnborough St GU14 . . .85 D6
Farncombe CE Inf sch
  GU7 . . . . .150 E7
Farncombe Hill GU7 . . .150 E6
Farncombe St GU7 . . . .150 E7
Farncombe Sta GU7 . . .150 F7
Farnell Mews KT13 . . . . .53 B7
Farnell Rd Isleworth TW7 . .5 D4
  Stanwell TW18 . . . . .13 A5
Farnell's Almshouses TW7 .5 F5
Farnham Bsns Ctr GU9 .125 D2
Farnham Bsns Pk GU9 . .146 A8
Farnham By-Pass GU9 . .125 C2
Farnham Castle ✸ GU9 .125 E3
Farnham Cl RG12 . . . . . .27 D7
Farnham Coll GU9 . . . . .125 C1
Farnham Com Hospl
  GU9 . . . . .125 E4
Farnham Ct SM3 . . . . . . .58 E4
Farnham Gdns SW20 . . . .39 B7
Farnham Heath End Sch
  GU9 . . . . .125 E6
Farnham La GU27 . . . . . .208 A3
Farnham Mus ✸ GU9 . . .125 B2
Farnham Park Cl GU9 . . .125 B6
Farnham Park Dr GU9 . . .125 B6
Farnham Rd Elstead GU8 .148 C4
  Guildford, Guildford Park
  GU1, GU2, GU3 . . . . . .130 B7
  Guildford,Onslow Village
  GU2,GU3 . . . . .129 E6
Farnham Rd Hospl GU2 .130 B7
Farnham Sta GU9 . . . . .125 C2
Farnham Trad Est GU9 . .125 F4
Farnhurst La GU6 . . . . . .193 F4
Farningham RG12 . . . . . .27 E3
Farningham Cres CR3 . . .101 A4
Farningham Ct SW16 . . . .21 D1
Farningham Rd CR3 . . . .101 A4
Farnley GU21 . . . . .68 F2
Farnley Rd CR7,SE25 . . . .42 D5
Farnsworth Ho ₈ SW27 . .22 B3
Farquhar Rd Dulwich SE19 .22 F3
  Wimbledon SW19 . . . . . .20 A5
Farquharson Rd CR0 . . . .42 C1
Farrell Cl GU15 . . . . .65 C3
Farren Ho GU14 . . . . . . .85 C1
Farren Rd SE23 . . . . .23 E6
Farrer's Pl CR0 . . . . .62 D6
Farrier Pl GU47 . . . . .64 B7
Farriers KT18 . . . . .96 C3
Farriers Cl KT17 . . . . . . .76 E7
Farriers Ct Belmont SM2 . .58 E3
  Wimbledon SW19 . . . . . .19 E1
Farriers Rd KT17 . . . . . . .76 E8
Farriers The GU5 . . . . . .152 A5
Farthingfield Ho GU9 . . .125 C3
Farthingham La GU6 . . .175 E6
Farthings GU21 . . . . .68 E3
Farthings The ₁ KT2 . . . .38 A8
Farwig La BR1 . . . . .44 F8
Fassett Rd KT1 . . . . .37 E5
Fauconberg Ct W4 . . . . . .7 C8
Fauconberg Rd W4 . . . . . .7 C8
Faulkner Pl GU19 . . . . . . .47 F4
Faulkner's Rd KT12 . . . . .54 C5
Faversham Rd
  Beckenham BR3 . . . . . . .43 F7
  Forest Hill SE6 . . . . .23 F7
  Morden SM4 . . . . .40 B3
  Sandhurst GU47 . . . . . . .45 D1
Fawcett Cl SW16 . . . . . . .22 A4
Fawcett Rd CR0,CR9 . . . .61 C7
Fawcus Cl KT10 . . . . .55 E4
Fawler Mead RG12 . . . . .27 F5
Fawley Cl GU6 . . . . .174 F2
Fawns Manor Cl TW14 . . .14 C7
Fawns Manor Rd TW14 . .14 D7
Fawsley Cl SL3 . . . . .1 E7
Fay Rd RH12 . . . . .217 C5
Faygate Bsns Ctr RH12 . .199 F1
Faygate La
  Blindley Heath RH9 . . . .142 E3
  Faygate RH12 . . . . .199 E4
Faygate Rd SW2 . . . . . . .22 A6
Faygate Sta RH12 . . . . . .199 F1
Fayland Ave SW16 . . . . . .21 C3
Fearn Cl KT24 . . . . .112 E6
Fearnley Cres TW12 . . . . .15 F2
Featherbed La CR0,CR6 . .82 C7
Feathercombe La GU8 . .171 E4
Feathers La TW19 . . . . . .12 A6
Featherstone RH7 . . . . .142 D1
Featherstone Rd SE23 . . .23 C6
Fee Farm Rd KT10 . . . . . .55 F3
Felbridge Ave RH10 . . . .202 D7
Felbridge Cl Belmont SM2 .59 B2
  East Grinstead RH19 . . .185 C3
  Frimley GU16 . . . . .65 F1
  Streatham SW16 . . . . . . .22 A4
Felbridge Ct
  East Grinstead RH19 . . .185 A4
  Feltham TW13 . . . . .15 B7
  Harlington UB3 . . . . .3 D8
Felbridge Ctr The RH19 .185 A3

Felbridge Prim Sch
  RH19 . . . . .184 F4
Felbridge Rd RH19 . . . .184 D3
Felcot Rd RH19 . . . . . . .184 C4
Felcote Ho RH2 . . . . . . .138 F7
Felcott Cl KT12 . . . . .54 C7
Felcott Rd KT12 . . . . .54 C7
Feld The RH19 . . . . .185 A4
Felcourt Cotts RH19 . . . .185 C8
Felcourt La RH19 . . . . . .164 C1
Felcourt Rd RH19,RH7 . . .185 C7
Felday Glade RH5 . . . . .155 B5
Felday Hos RH5 . . . . . . .155 C7
Felday Rd RH5 . . . . .133 F3
Feldemore Cotts RH5 . . .155 C6
Felicia Ct GU7 . . . . .150 E4
Felix Dr GU4 . . . . .111 A7
Felix La TW17 . . . . .34 F3
Felix Rd KT12 . . . . .35 A3
Fell Rd CR0,CR9 . . . . . . .61 C7
Felland Way RH2 . . . . . .139 D5
Fellbrook TW10 . . . . .17 B5
Fellcott Way RH12 . . . . .216 F1
Fellow Gn GU24 . . . . . . .67 F6
Fellow Green Rd GU24 . . .67 F6
Fellowes Ct UB3 . . . . .3 D8
Fellowes Rd SM1,SM5 . . .59 E8
Fellows Rd GU14 . . . . . . .85 D1
Felmingham Rd SE20 . . . .43 C1
Felnex Trad Est SM6 . . . .60 A8
Felsberg Rd SW2 . . . . . . .21 E8
Felside Ct KT3 . . . . .53 A5
Felstead Rd KT19 . . . . . .76 B8
Feltham Arena TW14 . . . .15 A8
Feltham Ave KT8 . . . . . . .36 E5
Feltham Bsns Complex
  TW13 . . . . .15 B6
Feltham Com Coll TW13 . .15 C6
Feltham Corporate Ctr
  TW13 . . . . .15 B5
Feltham Hill Jun & Inf Schs
  TW13 . . . . .14 F5
Feltham Hill Rd
  Ashford TW15 . . . . .14 C2
  Feltham TW13 . . . . .15 B4
Feltham Rd Ashford TW15 .14 C4
  Mitcham CR4 . . . . .41 A7
  Redhill RH1 . . . . .139 F4
Feltham Sta TW13 . . . . . .15 B7
Feltham Wlk RH1 . . . . . .139 F4
Felthambrook Ind Est
  TW13 . . . . .15 B5
Felthambrook Way TW13 .15 B3
Feltonfleet Sch KT11 . . . .72 E6
Felwater Ct RH19 . . . . . .185 A3
Fenby Cl RH13 . . . . .218 C4
Fenchurch Rd RH10 . . . .202 B4
Fencote RG12 . . . . .27 D3
Fendall Rd KT19 . . . . . . .57 C5
Fender Ho RH12 . . . . . . .217 B2
Fengates Rd RH1 . . . . . .118 E1
Fenhurst Cl RH12 . . . . . .216 F1
Fenn's Way GU21 . . . . . .69 E4
Fennel Cl Croydon CR0 . . .43 D1
  Farnborough GU14 . . . . .84 B4
  Guildford GU1 . . . . .110 B4
Fennel Cres RH11 . . . . . .201 B2
Fennells Mead KT17 . . . .57 F2
Fenner Ho KT12 . . . . . . .54 A6
Fenning Ct CR4 . . . . .40 E5
Fenns La GU24 . . . . .67 E5
Fenns Yd GU9 . . . . .125 B2
Fennscombe Ct GU24 . . .67 F6
Fenstanton Prim Sch
  SW2 . . . . .22 A7
Fenton Ave TW18 . . . . . .13 C3
Fenton Cl RH1 . . . . .119 A1
Fenton Ho TW5 . . . . .5 A8
Fenton Rd RH1 . . . . .119 A1
Fentum Rd GU2 . . . . . . .109 A3
Fenwick Cl GU21 . . . . . . .69 B1
Ferguson Ave KT5 . . . . . .37 F4
Ferguson Cl BR2 . . . . . . .44 D6
Fermandy La RH10 . . . . .184 A1
Fermor Dr GU11 . . . . . . .104 F3
Fermor Rd SE23 . . . . . . .23 E7
Fern Ave CR4 . . . . .41 D5
Fern Cl Crowthorne RG45 . .45 A7
  Frimley GU16 . . . . .66 C3
  Warlingham CR6 . . . . . . .81 E1
Fern Cotts RH5 . . . . .133 E4
Fern Ct GU12 . . . . .105 F1
Fern Gr TW14 . . . . .15 B8
Fern Hill Prim Sch KT2 . . .17 E2
Fern Lodge ₁₄ SW16 . . . .22 A3
Fern Rd GU7 . . . . .150 F6
Fern Twrs CR3 . . . . .101 A2
Fern Way RH12 . . . . .217 D5
Fern Wlk TW15 . . . . .13 D3
Fernbank Ave KT12 . . . . .35 E2
Fernbank Cres SL5 . . . . . .28 D8
Fernbank Pl SL5 . . . . . . .28 D7
Fernbank Rd
  Addlestone KT15 . . . . . . .52 A5
  North Ascot SL5 . . . . . . .28 D8
Fernbrae Cl GU10 . . . . . .146 B3
Ferndale GU3 . . . . .108 E3
Ferndale Ave
  Addlestone KT16 . . . . . . .51 E7
  Hounslow TW4 . . . . .4 E4
Ferndale Rd
  Ashford TW15 . . . . .13 E3
  Banstead SM7 . . . . .77 F3
  Croydon SE25 . . . . .43 B4
  Woking GU21 . . . . .69 F3
Ferndell Ho GU27 . . . . . .208 C2
Ferndell Rise GU7 . . . . .150 E7
Ferndown Crawley RH10 .182 D2

Ferndown continued
  Horley RH6 . . . . .161 A5
 ₅ Kingston u T KT6 . . . .37 E4
Ferndown Cl
  Guildford GU1 . . . . .131 A8
  Sutton SM2 . . . . .59 D4
Ferndown Ct GU10 . . . . .146 D5
Ferndown Gdns
  Cobham KT11 . . . . .73 C6
  Farnborough GU14 . . . . .84 E4
Fernery The TW18 . . . . . .12 E3
Ferney Ct KT14 . . . . .71 D8
Ferney Meade Way TW7 . .6 A5
Ferney Rd KT14 . . . . .71 D7
Ferngrove Cl KT22 . . . . . .94 E4
Fernham Rd CR7 . . . . . . .42 C6
Fernhead ₈ SM1 . . . . . . .59 C6
Fernhill Cl RH22 . . . . . . .74 D5
Fernhill Cl
  Crawley Down RH10 . . . .184 B1
  Farnborough GU17 . . . . .64 F1
  Hale GU9 . . . . .125 B6
  Woking GU22 . . . . .89 D7
Fernhill Ct KT2 . . . . .17 D3
Fernhill Dr GU9 . . . . . . .125 B6
Fernhill Gdns KT2 . . . . . .17 E3
Fernhill Ho GU14 . . . . . .85 D2
Fernhill La
  Farnborough GU17 . . . . .64 F1
  Hale GU9 . . . . .125 B6
  Woking GU22 . . . . .89 C7
Fernhill Pk GU22 . . . . . . .89 D7
Fernhill Prim Sch GU14 . .64 F1
Fernhill Rd
  Blackwater GU14,GU17 . .64 E2
  Crawley RH6 . . . . .182 D7
  Farnborough,West Heath
  GU14 . . . . .84 E6
Fernhill Sch GU14 . . . . . .64 F1
Fernhill Wlk GU17 . . . . . .64 F1
Fernhurst Cl RH11 . . . . .201 B8
Fernhurst Rd
  Ashford TW15 . . . . .14 C4
  Croydon CR0 . . . . .43 B1
Ferniehurst GU15 . . . . . .65 F4
Fernihough Cl KT13 . . . . .72 A8
Fernlands Cl KT16 . . . . . .51 E7
Fernlea GU23 . . . . .94 B3
Fernlea Rd Balham SW12 . .21 B7
  Mitcham CR4 . . . . .41 A8
Fernleigh Cl Croydon CR0 .61 A6
  Walton-on-T KT12 . . . . . .54 B7
Fernleigh Ct GU14 . . . . . .85 B4
Fernleigh Rise GU16 . . . .86 C7
Fernley Ho GU7 . . . . . . .150 E8
Ferns Cl CR2 . . . . .62 B1
Ferns Mead GU9 . . . . . .125 B1
Fernside Ave TW13 . . . . .15 B4
Fernside Rd SW12 . . . . . .21 A8
Fernthorpe Rd SW16 . . . .21 C2
Fernwood
  New Addington CR0,CR2 . .62 E2
  Putney SW19 . . . . .19 F7
Fernwood Ave SW16 . . . .21 D4
Feroners Cl RH10 . . . . . .202 A4
Feroners Ct RH10 . . . . . .202 A4
Ferrard Cl SL5 . . . . .28 D8
Ferraro Cl TW5 . . . . .5 A8
Ferrers Ave SM6 . . . . . . .60 D6
Ferrers Rd SW16 . . . . . . .21 D3
Ferriby Ct RG12 . . . . .27 C3
Ferring Cl RH11 . . . . . . .201 B8
Ferrings SE21 . . . . .22 E5
Ferris Ave CR0 . . . . .62 F7
Ferroners Ct RH10 . . . . .202 A4
Ferry Ave TW18 . . . . .12 E1
Ferry La East Molesey KT8 . .7 F8
  Brentford TW8 . . . . .6 E8
  Chertsey KT16 . . . . .33 A3
  Guildford GU2, GU3 . . . .130 C3
  Laleham TW18 . . . . .33 C1
  Lower Halliford TW17 . . . .34 A1
  Richmond TW9 . . . . .6 F8
  Wraysbury TW19 . . . . . . .11 D8
Ferry Rd East Molesey KT8 .36 A6
  Richmond TW11 . . . . . . .17 B3
  Thames Ditton KT7 . . . . .37 B3
  Twickenham TW1 . . . . . .17 B7
Ferry Sq ₁ TW8 . . . . .6 E8
Ferry Wks TW17 . . . . . . .34 A1
Ferrymoor TW10 . . . . . . .17 B5
Festival RH10 . . . . .202 C4
Fetcham Common La
  KT22 . . . . .94 B6
Fetcham Grove Cotts
  KT22 . . . . .95 A5
Fetcham Lodge KT22 . . . .94 D5
Fetcham Park Dr KT22 . . .94 E4
Fetcham Village Inf Sch
  KT22 . . . . .94 D5
Fettes Rd GU6 . . . . .175 A3
Fiddicroft Ave SM7 . . . . .78 C5
Field Cl Chessington KT9 . .56 C5
  Cranford TW4 . . . . .4 B6
  East Molesey KT8 . . . . . .36 B4
  Guildford GU4 . . . . .110 D4
  Hamsey Green CR2 . . . . .81 B5
  Harlington UB7 . . . . .3 C7
Field Ct Oxted RH8 . . . . .122 E8
  Wimbledon SW19 . . . . . .20 A5
Field End Coulsdon CR5 . .79 D5
  Farnham GU9 . . . . .125 F4
  West End GU24 . . . . .67 F6
Field House Cl SL5 . . . . . .29 A1
Field La Brentford TW8 . . . .6 C7
  Frimley GU16 . . . . .65 E1
  Teddington TW11 . . . . . .17 A3
Field Pk RG12 . . . . .27 D8

Field Pl KT3 . . . . .38 F3
Field Rd Farnborough GU14 .64 F1
  Feltham TW14 . . . . .4 B1
Field Stores App GU11 . .105 A2
Field View Egham TW20 . .12 C3
  Feltham TW13 . . . . .14 D5
Field View Cotts GU7 . . .150 B4
Field Way
  Aldershot GU12 . . . . . . .105 E3
  New Addington CR0 . . . . .63 B4
  Send Marsh GU23 . . . . . .90 F2
  Tongham GU10 . . . . . . .126 F7
Field Wlk RH6 . . . . .162 C4
Fieldcommon La KT12 . . .35 F1
Fielden Pl RG12 . . . . . . .27 D7
Fieldend Horsham RH12 .218 B5
  Teddington TW11 . . . . . .16 F4
Fieldend Rd SW16 . . . . . .41 C8
Fielders Gn ₃ GU1 . . . . .110 A1
Fieldgate Ct KT11 . . . . . .73 A5
Fieldhouse Rd SW12 . . . .21 C7
Fieldhouse Villas SM7 . . .78 E5
Fieldhurst Cl KT15 . . . . . .52 B5
Fielding Ave TW2 . . . . . . .16 C5
Fielding Gdns RG45 . . . . .45 B4
Fielding Ho ₃ W4 . . . . . . .7 E8
Fielding Rd GU47 . . . . . . .64 E6
Fieldings The
  Burgh Heath SM7 . . . . . .77 F2
  Forest Hill SE23 . . . . . . .23 C7
  Horley RH6 . . . . .161 C4
  Woking GU21 . . . . .68 F3
Fieldsend Rd SM3 . . . . . .58 E5
Fieldside Rd BR1 . . . . . . .24 D3
Fieldview Horley RH6 . . .161 B4
  Wandsworth SW17,SW18 . .20 D7
Fieldway GU27 . . . . .208 C2
Fiennes Ct RH12 . . . . . .217 D6
Fife Rd Kingston u T KT2 . .37 E7
  Mortlake SW14 . . . . .7 C2
Fife Way KT23 . . . . .94 A2
Fifehead Cl TW15 . . . . . .13 E2
Fifield La GU10 . . . . .146 C2
Fifield Path SE23 . . . . . . .23 D5
Fifth Cross Rd TW2 . . . . .16 D6
Figge's Rd CR4 . . . . .21 A1
Filbert Cres RH11 . . . . . .201 A6
Filby Rd KT9 . . . . .56 F4
Filey Cl Biggin Hill TN16 .103 B8
  Crawley RH11 . . . . .200 F4
  Sutton SM2 . . . . .59 C3
Filmer Ct GU7 . . . . .150 E5
Filmer Gr GU7 . . . . .150 E5
Finborough Rd SW17 . . . .20 F2
Finch Ave SE27 . . . . .22 D4
Finch Cl GU21 . . . . .68 C2
Finch Cres RH10 . . . . . .204 C5
Finch Dr TW14 . . . . .15 D8
Finch Rd GU1 . . . . .109 D1
Finch's Cross RH8 . . . . .144 A8
Finchampstead Rd RG41,
  RG40 . . . . .25 B3
Finchdean Ho SW15 . . . .18 F8
Finches Rise GU1 . . . . . .110 C3
Findhorn Cl GU47 . . . . . .64 D7
Findings The GU14 . . . . .84 E8
Findlay Dr GU3 . . . . .108 F5
Findon Cl KT15 . . . . .51 F5
Findon Rd RH11 . . . . . . .201 B8
Findon Way RH12 . . . . . .216 D3
Fingley Gdns KT15 . . . . . .52 C6
Finlay Gdns KT15 . . . . . .52 C6
Finlays Cl KT9 . . . . .57 A5
Finmere RG12 . . . . .27 C2
Finnart Cl KT13 . . . . .53 C6
Finney Dr GU20 . . . . .48 D4
Finney La TW7 . . . . .6 A6
Finsbury Cl RH11 . . . . . .201 C2
Finstock Gn RG12 . . . . . .27 F5
Finton Sch SW17 . . . . . . .20 F6
Fintry Pl GU14 . . . . .84 E7
Fintry Wlk GU14 . . . . . . .84 E7
Finucane Ct TW9 . . . . .6 F4
Fiona Cl KT23 . . . . .94 A3
Fir Acre Rd GU12 . . . . . .106 A6
Fir Cl KT12 . . . . .35 A2
Fir Dr GU17 . . . . .64 D3
Fir Gr KT3 . . . . .38 F3
Fir Grange Ave KT13 . . . .53 B5
Fir Rd Cheam SM3 . . . . . .39 F1
  Feltham TW13 . . . . .15 D3
Fir Tree Alley ₁₄ GU11 . . .105 A2
Fir Tree Ave
  New Haw GU27 . . . . . . .207 D6
  Banstead KT17 . . . . .77 C4
  Crawley RH11 . . . . .181 B1
  Esher KT10 . . . . .55 C5
  Leatherhead KT22 . . . . . .95 C4
  Streatham SW16 . . . . . . .21 C3
  Worcester Park KT19 . . . .57 F4
Fir Tree Gdns CR0 . . . . . .63 A6
Fir Tree Gr SM5 . . . . .59 F3
Fir Tree Rd
  Banstead KT17,SM7 . . . .77 D5
  Guildford GU1 . . . . .109 D4
  Hounslow TW4 . . . . .4 E3
  Leatherhead KT22 . . . . . .95 C4
Fir Tree Wlk RH2 . . . . . .118 D1
Fir Wlk KT17,SM3 . . . . . .58 D4
Firbank Cl BR2 . . . . .44 D6
Firbank Dr GU21 . . . . . . .89 B8
Firbank La GU21 . . . . . . .89 B8
Firbank Pl TW20 . . . . . . .11 B2
Firbank Way RH19 . . . . .185 D1
Fircroft Cl GU22 . . . . . . .69 F1
Fircroft Ct ₁₀ GU22 . . . . .69 F1

Fircroft Prim Sch SW17 20 F5
Fircroft Rd
Chessington KT9 56 F6
Upper Tooting SW17 20 F5
Firdene KT5 38 C1
Fire Bell Alley KT6 37 E3
Fire Station Cotts CR8 79 F6
Fire Station Rd GU11 105 B3
Fireball Hill SL5 29 D2
Firefly Cl SM6 60 E3
Firfield Rd
Addlestone KT15 52 A6
Farnham GU9 146 A7
Firfields KT13 53 B4
Firgrove GU21 89 B8
Firgrove Ct
7 Farnborough GU14 85 B4
Farnham GU9 125 C1
Firgrove Hill GU9 125 C1
Firgrove Par 5 GU14 85 B4
Firgrove Rd 6 GU14 85 B4
Firhill Rd SE6 24 A5
Firlands Bracknell RG12 27 C4
Horley RH6 161 B4
Weybridge KT13 53 E4
Firlands Ave GU15 65 D5
Firle Cl RH10 201 E8
Firmston Ho 10 SW14 7 D4
Firs Ave Bramley GU5 152 A6
Mortlake SW14 7 C3
Firs Cl Claygate KT10 55 E4
Dorking RH4 136 A5
Farnborough GU14 85 C2
Forest Hill SE23 23 E8
Mitcham CR4 41 B8
Firs Dr TW5 4 B7
Firs La GU5 152 D4
Firs Rd CR8 80 B4
Firs The Artington GU3 130 B5
Belmont SM2 59 B3
Bisley GU24 68 A3
6 Bracknell RG12 27 F5
2 Caterham CR3 100 D5
Claygate KT10 55 E4
2 Forest Hill SE26 23 B3
Forest Hill SE26 23 C3
Great Bookham KT23 94 C3
Lower Kingswood KT20 97 F1
Wimbledon SW20 19 A1
Firsby Ave CR0 43 E1
Firsdene Cl KT16 51 D4
First Ave East Molesey KT8 36 A5
Mortlake SW14 7 E4
Walton-on-T KT12 35 B3
West Ewell KT19 57 E2
Woodham KT15 52 B2
First Cl KT8 36 C6
First Cross Rd TW2 16 E6
First Quarter Bsns Pk
KT19 76 E8
Firstway SW20 39 C7
Firsway GU2 109 A2
Firswood Ave KT19 57 F5
Firtree Ave CR4 41 A7
Firtree Ct BR2 44 F6
Firway GU26 187 E5
Firwood Cl GU21 88 E8
Firwood Ct GU15 65 C5
Firwood Dr GU15 65 C5
Firwood Rd GU25 30 E3
Fisher Cl Crawley RH10 201 E4
Croydon CR0 42 F1
Hersham KT12 54 B6
Fisher La
Chiddingfold GU8 210 E7
Dunsfold GU8 211 B7
Fisher Rowe Cl GU5 152 A6
Fisherdene KT10 56 A3
Fisherman Cl TW10 17 C4
Fishermen's Cl GU11 105 E5
Fishers Cl SW16 21 D5
Fishers Ct Horsham RH12 217 C4
4 Teddington TW11 16 F3
Fishers Wood SL5 30 C1
Fishing Temple Park Homes
TW18 32 F8
Fishponds Cl RG41 25 A4
Fishponds Est RG41 25 A4
Fishponds Rd
Upper Tooting SW17 20 F4
Wokingham RG41 25 A4
Fiske Ct 1 Merton SW19 20 C1
Sutton SM2 59 C3
Fitch Ct CR4 41 A7
Fitchet Cl RH11 201 B8
Fitz Wygram Cl TW12 16 C3
Fitzalan Rd Claygate KT10 55 E3
Horsham RH12,RH13 218 A4
Fitzgeorge Ave KT2,KT3 38 D8
Fitzgerald Ave SW14 7 E4
Fitzgerald Rd
Mortlake SW14 7 D4
Thames Ditton KT7 37 A3
Fitzherbert Ho 11 TW10 6 F1
Fitzjames Ave CR0 62 A8
Fitzjohn Cl GU4 110 C4
Fitzrobert Pl TW20 12 A2
Fitzroy Cl RG12 27 A3
Fitzroy Cres W4 7 D7
Fitzroy Gdns SE19 22 E1
Fitzwilliam Ave TW9 6 F5
Fitzwilliam Ho TW9 6 D3
Fitzwilliam Hts SE23 23 C6
Five Acres RH10 201 E8
Five Oaks Cl GU21 88 E8
Five Oaks Rd
Broadbridge Heath RH12,
RH13 216 B2
Slinfold RH12,RH13 216 B2
Fiveacre Cl CR7 42 A3
Flag Cl CR0 43 D1
Flambard Way GU7 150 D4
Flamborough Cl TN16 103 B8
Flamsteed Hts RH11 201 B1
Flanchford Ho 2 RH2 118 A2
Flanchford Rd RH2 138 D5
Flanders Cotts GU5 152 D5
Flanders Cres SW17,
SW19 20 F2
Flanders Ct TW20 12 C3
Flatford Ho SE6 24 C4
Flats The GU17 64 C4
Flaxley Rd SM4 40 B2
Flaxmore Ct CR7 42 D7
Fleece Rd KT6 37 C1
Fleet Cl KT8 35 F4
Fleet Rd Aldershot GU11 104 D6
Blackwater GU51 84 A4
Farnborough GU14 84 C4
Fleet GU11,GU14 104 D6
Fleet Terr SE6 24 C8
Fleetside KT8 36 A4
Fleetway TW20 32 C6
Fleetwood Cl
Chessington KT9 56 D3
South Croydon CR0 61 F7
Tadworth KT20 97 D7
Fleetwood Ct
7 Stanwell TW19 2 E1
3 West Byfleet KT14 71 A6
Fleetwood Rd KT3 38 B6
Fleetwood Sq KT3 38 B6
Fleming Cl GU14 85 D6
Fleming Ct CR0 61 A5
Fleming Ctr The RH10 181 E2
Fleming Mead CR4,SW19 20 F1
Fleming Way
Crawley RH10,RH11 181 F2
Isleworth TW7 5 F3
Fleming Wlk RH19 205 F6
Flemish Fields KT16 33 A2
Flemming Ho KT19 57 B2
Fletcher Cl
Crawley RH10 201 E4
Ottershaw KT16 51 E4
Fletcher Gdns RG42 26 D8
Fletcher Rd KT16 51 D4
Fletchers Cl RH13 217 E1
Fleur Gates 7 SW19 19 D8
Flexford Gn RG12 26 E3
Flexford Rd GU3 107 C1
Flexlands Sch GU24 68 F8
Flimwell Cl BR1 24 E3
Flint Cl Banstead SM7 78 B5
Crawley RH10 202 B3
Great Bookham KT23 94 C1
Redhill RH1 118 F2
Flint Hill RH4,RH5 136 B5
Flint Hill Cl RH4 136 B4
Flintgrove RG12 27 D8
Flintlock Cl TW19 2 A3
Flitwick Grange GU8 149 F1
Flock Mill Pl SW18 20 B7
Flood La 4 TW1 17 A7
Flora Gdns CR0 82 C8
Floral Ct KT21 75 C1
Floral Ho KT16 32 F1
Florence Ave Morden SM4 40 C4
Woodham KT15 71 A8
Florence Cl KT12 35 B2
Florence Cotts
Kingston u T SW15 18 E5
Winkfield SL4 8 C7
Florence Ct Knaphill GU21 68 C1
Wimbledon SW19 19 E2
Florence Gdns
Chiswick W4 7 C8
Staines TW18 13 B1
Florence Ho 5 KT2 17 F1
Florence Rd
Feltham TW13 15 B7
6 Kingston u T KT2 17 F1
Penge BR3 43 E7
Sandhurst GU47 64 E7
South Croydon CR2 61 D2
Walton-on-T KT12 35 B2
Wimbledon SW19 20 B2
Florence Terr SW15 18 E5
Florence Way
Knaphill GU21 68 C1
Upper Tooting SW12 20 F7
Florian Ave SM1 59 D6
Florida Ct Beckenham BR2 44 F5
Staines TW18 13 A3
Florida Rd Shalford GU4 130 E3
South Norwood CR7 42 B8
Florys Ct 7 SW19 19 E7
Flower Cres KT16 51 C4
Flower La RH9 121 D6
Flower Wlk GU2 130 C6
Flowersmead SW17 21 A6
Floyd's La GU22 71 A3
Foden Rd GU11 105 A1
Foley Mews KT10 55 E4
Foley Rd Biggin Hill TN16 83 D1
Claygate KT10 55 E3
Folly Hill GU9 125 A5
Folly Hill Inf Sch GU9 125 A6
Folly La RH5 157 B7
Folly La N GU9 125 B6
Folly La S GU9 125 A6
Follyfield Rd SM7 78 A5
Fontaine Ct BR3 43 F8
Fontaine Rd SW16 21 F1
Fontana Cl RH10 202 E5
Fontenoy Rd SW12,SW17 21 C6
Fonthill Cl SE20 43 A7
Fonthill Ct SE23 23 C8
Fonthill Lodge Sch
RH19 205 C6
Fontigarry Farm Bsns Pk
RH2 160 C8
Fontley Way SW15 19 A8
Fontmell Cl TW15 14 A3
Fontmell Pk TW15 14 A3
Fontwell Cl GU12 105 D2
Fontwell Rd RH10 202 A3
Forbench Cl GU23 91 B5
Forbes Chase GU47 64 D7
Forbes Cl RH10 202 B2
Forbes Ct SE19 22 E3
Forburys GU9 146 B8
Ford Cl Ashford TW15 13 E2
Littleton TW17 34 A4
Thornton Heath CR7 42 B4
Ford La GU10 146 B6
Ford Manor Cotts RH7 165 B1
Ford Manor Rd RH7 165 B2
Ford Rd Ashford TW15 13 F4
Bisley GU24 67 F4
Chertsey KT16 33 B1
Chobham GU24 49 C1
Old Woking GU22 90 B7
Fordbridge Ct TW15 13 E2
Fordbridge Rd
Ashford TW15 13 F3
Sunbury TW16 35 A5
Upper Halliford TW16,TW17 34 F3
Fordel Rd SE6 24 D7
Fordingbridge Cl
Chertsey KT16 33 B1
Horsham RH12 217 C1
Fordington Ho SE26 23 B5
Fordmill Rd SE6 24 A6
Fordwater Rd KT15,KT16 33 B1
Fordwater Trad Est KT16 33 C1
Fordwells Dr RG12 27 F5
Fordyce Ho 3 SW16 21 C4
Foreman Pk GU12 106 B2
Foreman Rd GU12 106 B1
Forest Cl Bracknell SL5 28 C6
Crawley Down RH10 204 B8
East Horsley KT24 92 F2
Horsham RH12 218 B4
Woking GU22 70 D4
Forest Cres KT21 76 A3
Forest Croft SE23 23 B6
Forest Ct RG41 25 A4
Forest Dene Ct 10 SM2 59 C4
Forest Dr Charlton TW16 14 F1
Farnham GU10 146 C4
Kingswood KT20 98 A6
Forest End Rd GU47 64 A8
Forest Glade GU10 145 D3
Forest Gn RG12 27 D7
Forest Hill Bsns Ctr SE23 23 C6
Forest Hill Ct SE26 23 B5
Forest Hill Ind Est SE23 23 C6
Forest Hill Rd SE23 23 C8
Forest Hill Sec Sch SE23 23 D5
Forest Hill Sta SE23 23 C6
Forest Hills GU15 65 B4
Forest La KT24 92 F3
Forest Lodge
2 East Grinstead RH19 205 F8
Forest Hill SE23 23 C5
Forest Oaks RH13 218 B4
Forest Rd Cheam SM3,SM4 40 A2
Crawley RH12,RH13 218 D5
Crowthorne RG45 45 C5
East Horsley KT24 92 F2
Feltham TW13 15 C6
Richmond TW9 7 A7
Windsor SL4 9 E7
Winkfield RG42,SL5 8 D2
Woking GU22 70 D4
Forest Ridge BR3 44 A6
Forest Row Bsns Pk
RH18 206 F3
Forest Row CE Prim Sch
RH18 206 F2
Forest Sch The RH13 217 F1
Forest Side KT4 38 F1
Forest View RH10 202 A3
Forest View Rd RH19 205 E6
Forest Way KT21 76 A3
Forest Wlk GU6 173 F2
Forestdale GU26 188 E3
Forestdale Ctr The CR0 62 F3
Forestdale Prim Sch CR0 62 F2
Forester Rd RH10 201 E4
Foresters Cl Knaphill GU21 68 F1
Wallington SM6 60 D3
Foresters Dr CR8,SM6 60 D2
Foresters Prim Sch SM6 60 D4
Foresters Sq RG12 27 E6
Foresters Way RG45 45 F1
Forestfield Crawley RH10 202 B3
Horsham RH13 218 A3
Forestholme Cl SE23 23 C6
Forge Ave CR5 100 B7
Forge Cl
Broadbridge Heath RH12 216 D4
Farnham GU9 125 D3
Forge Cotts KT23 93 F4
Forge Dr KT10 56 A3
Forge End GU21 69 E2
Forge La
Broadbridge Heath RH12 216 D4
Cheam SM2,SM3 58 E3
Crawley RH10 202 A7
Forge La *continued*
Farnborough GU11 105 A6
Feltham TW13 15 E3
Sunbury TW16 35 A6
Forge Lane Prim Sch
TW13 15 E3
Forge Mews
Addington CR0 63 A5
Sunbury TW16 35 A6
Forge Rd Crawley RH10 202 A7
Headley GU35 166 A1
Forge Steading SM7 78 B4
Forge The Harlington UB3 3 D8
Warnham RH12 216 E7
Forge Wood RH10 182 D3
Forge Wood Ind Est
RH10 182 B2
Forgefield TN16 83 D3
Forman Ct TW1 16 F7
Forrest Gdns SW16 41 F6
Forrester Path SE26 23 C4
Forster Ho SE6 24 D5
Forster Park Prim Sch
SE6 24 E5
Forster Rd Beckenham BR3 43 E6
Streatham SW2 21 E8
Thornton Heath CR0 42 C2
Forsyte Cres SE19 42 E8
Forsyte Ct KT2 38 B8
Forsyth Path GU21 70 D6
Forsyth Rd GU21 70 C5
Forsythe Shades BR3 44 C8
Forsythia Pl GU1 109 C3
Fort La RH2 118 B5
Fort Narrien GU15 64 F7
Fort Rd Box Hill KT20 116 B4
Guildford GU1 130 E6
Fortescue Ave TW2 16 C5
Fortescue Rd
Mitcham SW19 20 D1
Weybridge KT13 52 F6
Forth Cl GU14 84 D6
Fortrose Cl GU47 64 D7
Fortrose Gdns SW12,SW2 21 E7
Fortune Dr GU6 174 E1
Fortyfoot Rd KT22 95 C6
Forum The
East Molesey KT8 36 B5
Thorpe KT16 32 F1
Forval Cl CR4 40 F4
Foss Ave CR0,CR9 61 A5
Foss Rd SW17 20 D4
Fosse Way KT14 70 F6
Fosseway RG45 45 A5
Fossewood Dr GU15 65 D7
Fosterdown RH9 121 B6
Fosters Gr GU20 48 B6
Fosters La GU21 68 C2
Foulser Rd SW17 21 A5
Foulsham Rd CR7 42 D6
Foundation Units GU1 109 E5
Founders Gdns SE19 22 C1
Foundry Cl RH13 217 E4
Foundry Ct KT16 33 A2
Foundry La
Haslemere GU27 208 A6
Horsham RH13 217 E3
Horton SL3 1 B4
Foundry Mews KT16 33 A2
Foundry Pl SW18 20 B8
Fountain Ct
New Malden KT3 38 C5
Penge SE26 23 C2
Fountain Dr Dulwich SE19 22 F4
Wallington SM5 59 F2
Fountain Ho 3 CR4 40 F7
Fountain Rd Redhill RH1 139 E7
South Norwood CR7 42 C7
Upper Tooting SW17 20 D4
Fountain Sch SM5 59 F1
Fountains Ave TW13 15 F5
Fountains Cl
Crawley RH11 201 A4
Feltham TW13 15 F5
Fountains Garth RG12 27 A6
Four Acres Cobham KT11 73 E6
Guildford GU1 110 C3
Four Seasons Cres SM3 58 F8
Four Square Ct TW4 5 A1
Four Wents KT11 73 C5
Fourth Cross Rd TW2 16 D6
Fourth Dr CR5 79 D3
Fowler Ave GU14 85 B2
Fowler Cl RH10 202 C4
Fowler Rd
Farnborough GU14 84 F3
Mitcham CR4 41 A7
Fowlers La RG42 27 B8
Fowlers Mead GU24 49 E2
Fowlerscroft GU3 129 B2
Fox Cl Crawley RH11 181 B1
Weybridge KT13 53 D5
Woking GU22 70 D4
Fox Cnr GU3 88 C2
Fox Covert Fetcham KT22 94 D3
Lightwater GU18 67 A8
Fox Covert Cl SL5 29 C4
Fox Ct GU47 64 C8
Fox Dene GU7 150 C2
Fox Gr KT12 35 B2
Fox Heath GU14 84 C3
Fox Hill SE19 22 F1
Fox Hill Gdns SE19 22 F1
Fox Hill Prim Sch RG12 27 B4
Fox Hills La GU12 106 C3
Fox Hills Rd KT16 51 B5
Fox La Little Bookham KT23 93 F3
Reigate RH2 118 B4
Fox La N KT16 32 F1
Fox La S KT16 32 F1
Fox Rd Bracknell RG12 27 C5
Farnham GU10 146 C7
Haslemere GU27 207 E6
Fox Way GU10 124 D8
Fox Yd GU9 125 B2
Foxacre CR3 100 E5
Foxborough Hill GU5 151 D6
Foxborough Hill Rd
GU5 151 D6
Foxbourne Rd SW17 21 A6
Foxbridge La RH14 212 C1
Foxburrows Ave GU2 108 F2
Foxburrows Ct GU2 108 F2
Foxcombe CR0 63 B4
Foxcombe Rd 6 SW15 19 A7
Foxdown Cl GU15 65 C5
Foxearth Cl TN16 83 E1
Foxearth Rd CR2 62 C2
Foxearth Spur CR2 62 C2
Foxenden Rd GU1 109 E1
Foxes Dale BR2 44 D6
Foxes Path GU4 89 F1
Foxglove Ave
Beckenham BR3 24 B1
Horsham RH12 217 E6
Foxglove Cl
Stanwell TW19 13 D7
Winkfield RG42 8 A2
Foxglove Gdns
Guildford GU4 110 C3
Purley CR8 79 F8
Foxglove La KT9 57 A6
Foxglove Way CR4 41 B1
Foxglove Wlk RH11 201 B3
Foxgrove Dr GU21 70 A4
Foxgrove Rd BR3 24 C1
Foxhanger Gdns GU22 70 A3
Foxhaven Ct SL5 29 C4
Foxheath RG12 27 E4
Foxhill Cres GU15 66 B8
Foxhills GU21 69 C2
Foxhills Cl KT16 51 C4
Foxhills Mews KT16 51 B7
Foxholes Rudgwick RH12 214 D8
Weybridge KT13 53 D5
Foxhurst Rd GU12 106 A4
Foxlake Rd KT14 71 F7
Foxleigh Chase RH12 217 F5
Foxley Cl Blackwater GU17 64 C5
Redhill RH1 140 A4
Foxley Ct SM2 59 C3
Foxley Gdns CR8 80 B6
Foxley Hall CR8 80 A6
Foxley Hill Rd CR8 80 A7
Foxley La CR8 60 E1
Foxley Lodge 5 CR8 80 A7
Foxley Rd Purley CR8 80 B5
Thornton Heath CR7 42 B5
Foxoak Hill KT12 53 E1
Foxon Cl CR3 100 E6
Foxon La CR3 100 E6
Foxon Lane Gdns CR3 100 E6
Foxtail Ho TW3 5 C6
Foxton KT1 38 A6
Foxton Gr CR4 40 D7
Foxwarren KT10 55 F2
Foxwood RH12 198 B6
Foxwood Cl Feltham TW13 15 B5
Wormley GU8 190 F8
Frailey Cl GU22 70 B3
Frailey Hill GU22 70 B3
Framfield Cl RH11 201 A8
Framfield Rd CR4 21 A1
Frampton Cl SM2 59 A3
Frampton Rd TW4 4 E2
France Hill Dr GU15 65 C5
Frances Ct Ascot SL5 29 D5
South Norwood SE25 42 F7
Franche Court Rd SW17 20 C5
Francis Ave TW13 15 A5
Francis Barber Cl SW16 21 F4
Francis Chichester Cl
SL5 29 B4
Francis Cl Littleton TW17 34 A5
West Ewell KT19 57 D6
Francis Cnr KT24 133 B8
Francis Ct
Farnborough GU14 84 F4
Guildford GU2 109 B3
Kingston u T KT5 37 E5
Francis Edwards Way
RH11 200 E2
Francis Gr SW19 19 F2
Francis Harrison Ho
GU2 129 E8
Francis Rd
Caterham CR3 100 D5
Hounslow TW4 4 D5
Thornton Heath CR0 42 B2
Wallington SM6 60 C4
Francis Way GU15 66 C4
Franciscan Prim Sch
SW17 21 A3
Franciscan Rd SW17 21 A4
Frangate KT24 112 E8
Frank Dixon Cl SE21 22 E7
Frank Dixon Way SE21 22 E7
Frank Towell Ct TW14 15 A7
Frankland Ho 4 SW12 21 B8
Franklands Dr KT15 51 F3
Franklin Cl
Kingston u T KT1 38 A6
West Norwood SE27 22 B5
Franklin Cres CR4 41 C5
Franklin Ct 2 GU2 108 F1
Franklin Ho BR2 44 E7

Franklin Ind Est SE20 ...43 C8
Franklin Rd
Crawley RH10 ...202 C5
Penge SE20 ...43 C8
Walton-on-T KT12 ...35 A3
Franklin Way CR0,CR9 ...41 E2
Franklyn Rd
Godalming GU7 ...150 B3
Walton-on-T KT12 ...35 B3
Franks Ave KT3 ...38 C5
Franks Ho TW7 ...6 B3
Franks Rd GU2 ...109 A3
Franksfield GU5 ...154 E7
Fransfield Gr SE26 ...23 B5
Frant Cl SE20 ...23 C1
Frant Rd CR0,CR7 ...42 B4
Franthorne Way SE6 ...24 B5
Fraser Gdns RH4 ...136 A8
Fraser Mead GU47 ...64 E6
Fraser Rd RG42 ...27 B8
Frederick Cl SM1 ...58 F5
Frederick Gdns
Cheam SM1 ...58 F5
Thornton Heath CR0 ...42 B3
Frederick Pl RG41 ...25 A6
Frederick Rd SM1 ...58 F5
Frederick Sanger Rd GU2 ...129 D8
Frederick St GU11 ...105 A2
Free Prae Rd KT16 ...33 A1
Freeborn Way RG12 ...27 E7
Freedown La SM2 ...78 C6
Freehold Ind Ctr TW4 ...4 C2
Freelands Ave CR2 ...62 D2
Freelands Rd KT11 ...73 B5
Freeman Cl TW17 ...34 E5
Freeman Dr KT8 ...35 F5
Freeman Ho 13 SW2 ...21 E8
Freeman Rd
Morden CR4,SM4 ...40 D4
Warnham RH12 ...216 F8
Freemantle Rd GU19 ...47 F4
Freemantles Sch (Specl Sch) KT16 ...32 E2
Freemason's Rd CR0 ...42 E1
Freesia Dr GU24 ...68 A3
Freethorpe Cl SE19 ...42 E8
French Apartments The CR8 ...80 A7
French Gdns
Blackwater GU17 ...64 D4
Cobham KT11 ...73 C5
French La GU8 ...169 E3
French St TW16 ...35 C7
Frenchaye KT15 ...52 C5
Frenches Ct 4 RH1 ...119 A3
Frenches Rd RH1 ...119 B4
Frenches The RH1 ...119 A3
Frenchlands Hatch KT24 ...112 E8
Frensham RG12 ...27 D3
Frensham Ct Mitcham CR4 40 D6
Rowledge GU10 ...146 B4
Frensham Ctry Pk★ GU10 ...167 E5
Frensham Dr
New Addington CR0 ...63 C3
Roehampton SW15 ...19 A6
Frensham Heights Rd GU10 ...146 A2
Frensham Heights Sch GU10 ...146 A2
Frensham Ho 7 KT6 ...37 E4
Frensham La GU35,GU10 166 F2
Frensham Rd
Crowthorne RG45 ...45 B7
Farnham GU10,GU9 ...146 D6
Purley CR8 ...80 B5
Frensham Vale GU10 ...146 C4
Frensham Way KT17 ...77 C3
Frere Cotts KT23 ...94 C1
Fresham Ho BR2 ...44 F6
Freshborough Ct 1 GU1 ...130 F8
Freshfield KT20 ...117 F8
Freshfield Bank RH18 ...206 E2
Freshfield Cl RH10 ...202 A5
Freshfields CR0 ...43 F1
Freshford Ct 14 BR2 ...44 F5
Freshford St SW17,SW18 .20 C5
Freshmount Gdns KT19 ..76 B8
Freshwater Cl SW17 ...21 A2
Freshwater Rd SW17 ...21 A2
Freshwood Cl BR3 ...44 B8
Freshwood Way SM6 ...60 C2
Freshwoods RH12 ...214 D8
Frewin Rd SW18 ...20 D7
Friar Mews SE27 ...22 B5
Friar's Gate GU2 ...130 A7
Friars Ave SW15 ...18 F5
Friars Croft GU4 ...110 C4
Friars Ct Farnham GU9 ...125 D7
5 Wallington SM6 ...60 B6
Friars Field GU9 ...125 B3
Friars Keep RG12 ...27 B5
Friars La TW9 ...6 D2
Friars Orch KT22 ...94 D6
Friars Rd GU25 ...31 D5
Friars Rise GU22 ...70 A1
Friars Rookery RH10 ...201 F6
Friars Stile Pl 9 TW10 ...6 E1
Friars Stile Rd TW10 ...6 E1
Friars Way KT16 ...33 A3
Friars Wood CR0 ...62 E2
Friary Bridge GU1 ...130 C7
Friary Ct GU21 ...68 F1
Friary Ho 4 GU1 ...130 C8
Friary Pas GU1 ...130 C7
Friary Rd Ascot SL5 ...29 B3
Wraysbury TW19 ...11 C8
Friary St GU1 ...130 C7
Friary The 5 GU1 ...130 C8
Friary Way RH10 ...201 E5
Friday Rd CR4 ...20 F1
Friday St
Abinger Common RH5 ...155 F8
Faygate RH12 ...198 E6
Ockley RH5 ...177 E4
Warnham RH12 ...216 E7
Friend Ave GU12 ...105 D1
Friends Cl RH11 ...181 D1
Friends Rd CR8 ...80 B7
Friends' Rd CR0,CR9 ...61 D7
Friendship Way RG12 ...27 B6
Friern Rd SE22 ...23 A8
Frimley Ave SM6 ...60 F5
Frimley Bsns Pk GU16 ...85 B8
Frimley CE Jun Sch GU16 ...85 E7
Frimley Cl
New Addington CR0 ...63 C3
Putney SW19 ...19 E6
Frimley Cres CR0 ...63 C3
Frimley Gdns CR4 ...40 E6
Frimley Green Rd GU16 ..85 E7
Frimley Grove Gdns GU16 ...65 E1
Frimley Hall Dr GU15 ...65 F6
Frimley High St GU16 ...85 D8
Frimley Ho CR4 ...40 E6
Frimley Park Hospl GU16 65 D2
Frimley Rd
Ash Vale GU12 ...106 A8
Camberley GU15,GU16 ...65 B3
Chessington KT9 ...56 E5
Frimley Sq GU16 ...65 E1
Frinton Rd SW17 ...21 A2
Friston Wlk RH11 ...201 A7
Frith End Rd GU34,GU35 166 A6
Frith Hill Rd
Farncombe GU7 ...150 D6
Frimley GU16 ...66 B1
Frith Knowle KT12 ...54 B5
Frith Pk RH19 ...185 E3
Frith Rd CR0,CR9 ...61 C8
Fritham Cl KT3 ...38 E3
Friths Dr RH2 ...118 B4
Frithwald Rd KT16 ...32 F2
Frobisher RG12 ...27 C2
Frobisher Cl CR8 ...80 C2
Frobisher Cres TW19 ...13 E8
Frobisher Ct Belmont SM2 58 F3
Forest Hill SE23 ...23 B6
Frobisher Gdns
Guildford GU1 ...110 A2
Stanwell TW19 ...13 E8
Frodsham Way GU47 ...45 E2
Frog Grove La GU3 ...107 F4
Frog Hall RG40 ...25 F5
Frog Hall Dr RG40 ...25 E5
Frog La Bracknell RG12 ...27 A6
Woking GU4 ...89 E2
Froggetts La RH5 ...176 C1
Frogmore Cl SM3 ...58 E7
Frogmore Comm Coll GU46 ...64 A5
Frogmore Ct GU17 ...64 C4
Frogmore Gdns SM3 ...58 E6
Frogmore Gr GU17 ...64 C4
Frogmore Inf Sch GU17 .64 B5
Frogmore Jun Sch GU17 .64 B5
Frogmore Park Dr GU17 .64 D4
Frogmore Rd GU17 ...64 C5
Frome Cl GU14 ...84 D6
Fromondes Rd SM3 ...58 E5
Fromow Gdns GU20 ...48 D4
Froxfield Down 6 RG12 .27 F4
Fruen Rd TW14 ...14 F8
Fry Cl RH11 ...201 B1
Fry La GU19 ...47 D2
Fry's Cross GU8 ...193 A2
Fryern Wood CR3 ...100 C3
Frylands Ct CR0 ...82 C8
Fryston Ave Croydon CR0 .62 A8
Wallington CR5 ...79 B5
Fuchsia Way GU24 ...67 E6
Fuel Farm Rd RH6 ...181 E8
Fulbourn 4 KT1 ...38 A7
Fulbourne Cl RH1 ...118 E3
Fulbrook La GU8 ...148 C5
Fulford Rd
Caterham CR3 ...100 D6
West Ewell KT19 ...57 D3
Fulham Cl RH11 ...201 B2
Fullbrook Ave KT15 ...71 A8
Fullbrook Sch KT15 ...71 A8
Fullbrooks Ave KT4 ...38 F1
Fuller's Wood CR0 ...63 A6
Fullers Ave KT6 ...56 F8
Fullers Farm Rd KT24 ..112 B1
Fullers Rd GU10 ...145 D3
Fullers Vale GU35 ...187 A5
Fullers Way N KT6 ...56 F7
Fullers Way S KT9 ...56 E7
Fullers Wood La RH1 ..119 C1
Fullerton Cl KT14 ...71 F5
Fullerton Ct 9 TW11 ...17 A3
Fullerton Dr KT14 ...71 E5
Fullerton Rd Byfleet KT14 .71 F5
Croydon CR0 ...42 F2
Wallington SM5 ...59 E2
Fullerton Way KT14 ...71 E5
Fullmer Way KT15 ...51 F1
Fulmar Cl 1 RH11 ...200 D5
Fulmar Ct Surbiton KT5 ...37 F3
6 West Norwood SE21 ...22 D6
Fulmar Dr RH19 ...186 B3
Fulmer Cl TW12 ...15 E3
Fulstone Cl TW4 ...4 F3
Fulvens GU5 ...133 E1
Fulwell Park Ave TW2 ...16 C6
Fulwell Rd TW11 ...16 D4
Fulwell Sta TW11 ...16 D4
Fulwood Gdns TW1 ...6 A1
Fulwood Wlk SW19 ...19 E7
Furlong Cl CR4 ...41 B1
Furlong Rd RH4 ...135 C6
Furlong Way RH6 ...181 F8
Furlough The GU22 ...70 A2
Furmage St SW18 ...20 B8
Furnace Dr RH10 ...201 F4
Furnace Farm Rd RH10 .202 A4
Furnace Par RH10 ...202 A4
Furnace Pl RH10 ...202 A4
Furnace Rd or Furnance Farm Rd RH19 ...184 C3
Furneaux Ave SE27 ...22 B3
Furness Rd SM4 ...40 B3
Furniss Ct GU6 ...173 F2
Furnival Cl GU25 ...31 D3
Furrows Pl CR3 ...100 F4
Furrows The KT12 ...54 C8
Furse Cl GU15 ...66 C4
Further Green Rd SE6 ...24 E7
Furtherfield GU6 ...174 E4
Furtherfield Cl CR0 ...42 A3
Furze Cl Ash Vale GU12 ..106 A7
Horley RH6 ...161 D3
Redhill RH1 ...118 F2
Furze Ct CR0 ...62 A8
Furze Field KT22 ...74 E6
Furze Gr KT20 ...97 F6
Furze Hill Kingswood KT20 97 F6
Purley CR8 ...79 F8
Furze Hill Cres RG45 ...45 C4
Furze Hill Rd GU35 ...187 C4
Furze La
East Grinstead RH19 ...185 B4
Farncombe GU7,GU3 ...150 F8
Purley CR8 ...79 F8
Furze Rd Addlestone KT15 .51 F4
Rudgwick RH12 ...214 D8
South Norwood CR7 ...42 C6
Furze Vale Rd GU35 ...187 B4
Furzebank SL5 ...29 D5
Furzedown Cl TW20 ...11 E2
Furzedown Dr SW17 ...21 B3
Furzedown Prim Sch SW17 ...21 A2
Furzedown Rd
Streatham SW17 ...21 B3
Sutton SM2 ...78 C8
Furzefield RH11 ...201 C7
Furzefield Chase RH19 .185 E6
Furzefield Cres RH2 ...139 C7
Furzefield Prim Sch RH1 ...119 D7
Furzefield Rd
East Grinstead RH19 ...185 D4
Horsham RH12 ...218 B5
Reigate RH2 ...139 C7
Furzehill RH1 ...118 E2
Furzeland Ho 2 KT3 ...38 E2
Furzemoors RG12 ...27 B4
Furzen Cotts RH12 ...196 A3
Furzen La RH12,RH5 ...196 B4
Furzewood TW16 ...35 A8
Fydlers Cl SL4 ...9 B2
Fyfield Cl Beckenham BR2 .44 D5
Blackwater GU17 ...64 D5

G

Gable Ct Forest Hill SE26 .23 B4
9 Redhill RH1 ...119 A2
Gable End
Farnborough GU14 ...85 B4
5 Aldershot GU11 ...105 B2
Gable Lodge BR4 ...44 C1
Gables Ave TW15 ...13 F3
Gables Cl Ash Vale GU12 .106 A5
Farnborough GU14 ...85 A4
Old Woking GU22 ...89 F7
Gables Ct GU22 ...89 F7
Gables The Banstead SM7 .77 F2
Copthorne RH10 ...183 B3
Elstead GU8 ...148 C3
Grayshott GU26 ...188 D3
Horsham RH12 ...217 D4
Oxshott KT22 ...74 C7
Weybridge KT13 ...53 C5
Gables Way SM7 ...77 F3
Gabriel Cl TW13 ...15 D4
Gabriel Dr GU15 ...66 B4
Gabriel Rd RH10 ...202 C2
Gabriel St SE23 ...23 E8
Gadbridge La GU6 ...175 E4
Gadbrook Rd RH3 ...137 D4
Gadd Cl RG40 ...25 F7
Gadesden Rd KT19 ...57 C4
Gaffney Cl GU11 ...105 D7
Gage Cl RH10 ...184 C1
Gage Ridge RH18 ...206 E2
Gainsborough RG12 ...27 C3
Gainsborough Cl
Beckenham BR3 ...24 A1
Camberley GU15 ...65 F7
Farnborough GU14 ...85 D2
Thames Ditton KT10 ...36 E1
Gainsborough Ct
Dulwich SE21 ...22 E6
Farnborough GU12 ...105 C8
Walton-on-T KT12 ...54 A6
Gainsborough Dr
North Ascot SL5 ...28 D7
Sanderstead CR2 ...81 A6
Gainsborough Gdns TW7 .5 D2
Gainsborough Ho RH10 201 D6
Gainsborough Mews SE26 ...23 B5
Gainsborough Rd
Crawley RH10 ...201 F3
Epsom KT19 ...57 C1
New Malden KT3 ...38 D2
Richmond TW9 ...6 F4
Gaist Ave CR3 ...101 B5
Galahad Ho RH1 ...119 A2
Galahad Rd RH11 ...200 E6
Galba Ct 1 TW8 ...6 D7
Gale Cl Hampton TW12 ...15 E2
Mitcham CR4 ...40 D6
Gale Cres SM7 ...78 A2
Gale Dr GU18 ...48 A1
Galen Cl KT19 ...76 A8
Gales Cl GU4 ...110 D3
Gales Dr RH10 ...201 F6
Gales Pl RH10 ...201 F6
Galgate Cl 4 SW19 ...19 E7
Gallery Rd Dulwich SE21 ..22 D7
Pirbright GU24 ...87 D8
Galleymead Rd SL3 ...1 F6
Gallop The
South Croydon CR2 ...62 B3
Sutton SM2 ...59 D2
Galloway Path CR0 ...61 D6
Gallwey Rd GU11 ...105 C3
Galpin's Rd CR4,CR7 ...41 F5
Galsworthy Rd
Chertsey KT16 ...33 A2
Kingston u T KT2 ...38 B8
Galton Rd SL5 ...29 F3
Galvani Way CR0,CR9 ...41 F1
Galvins Cl GU2 ...109 A4
Gambles La GU23 ...91 C2
Gambole Rd SW17 ...20 E4
Gander Green Cres TW12 ...36 A8
Gander Green La KT4, SM1,SM3 ...58 F7
Gangers Hill RH9 ...121 F7
Ganghill GU1 ...110 A3
Gannet Ct 5 SE21 ...22 D6
Ganymede Ct RH11 ...200 E3
Gap Rd SW19 ...20 B3
Gapemouth Rd GU16, GU24 ...86 E5
Garbetts Way GU10 ...126 F6
Garbrand Wlk KT17 ...57 F2
Garden Ave CR4 ...21 B1
Garden Cl
Addlestone KT15 ...52 D6
Ashford TW15 ...14 C2
Banstead SM7 ...78 A4
East Grinstead RH19 ...205 F7
Farnborough GU14 ...84 E3
Hampton TW12 ...15 F3
Leatherhead KT22 ...95 C3
Putney SW15 ...19 B8
Shamley Green GU5 ...152 D4
Wallington SM6 ...60 E5
Garden Ct
10 Belmont SM2 ...59 A3
4 Richmond TW9 ...6 F6
South Croydon CR0 ...61 F7
Garden Flats SW16 ...21 E5
Garden House La RH19 .205 F7
Garden La SW2 ...21 F7
Garden Pl RH12 ...217 C4
Garden Rd Mortlake TW9 ...7 A4
Penge SE20 ...43 C8
Walton-on-T KT12 ...35 B2
Garden Wlk
Beckenham BR3 ...43 F8
Crawley RH11 ...201 C6
Hooley CR5 ...99 B4
Horsham RH12 ...217 C4
Garden Wood Rd RH19 .205 C8
Gardener's Hill Rd GU10 ...146 B4
Gardener's Wlk KT23 ...94 B1
Gardeners Cl RH12 ...216 E8
Gardeners Ct RH13 ...217 D1
Gardeners Gn RH12 ...199 C6
Gardeners Rd
Thornton Heath CR0 ...42 B1
Winkfield RG42 ...8 A2
Gardenfields KT20 ...97 E8
Gardenia Ct 1 BR3 ...24 A1
Gardenia Dr GU24 ...67 F6
Gardens The
Beckenham BR3 ...44 D7
Esher KT10 ...55 A6
Hatton TW14 ...3 D1
Pirbright GU24 ...87 F5
Tongham GU10 ...126 F7
Gardner Ho TW13 ...15 F6
Gardner Ind Est SE26 ...23 F3
Gardner La RH10 ...204 A8
Gardner Pl TW14 ...4 B1
Gardner Rd GU1 ...109 D1
Garendon Gdns SM4 ...40 B2
Garendon Rd SM4 ...40 B2
Gareth Cl KT4 ...58 D8
Gareth Ct SW16 ...21 D5
Garfield Prim Sch SW19 .20 C2
Garfield Rd
Addlestone KT15 ...52 C6
Camberley GU15 ...65 C5
2 Twickenham TW1 ...17 A7
Wimbledon SW19 ...20 C2
Garibaldi Rd RH1 ...139 F8
Garland Dr TW3 ...5 C5
Garland Rd RH19 ...185 D2
Garland Way CR3 ...100 D5
Garlands Rd
Leatherhead KT22 ...95 C6
Redhill RH1 ...118 F1
Garlichill Rd KT17,KT18 ..77 B2
Garlies Rd SE23 ...23 E5
Garnet Ho KT4 ...38 D1
Garnet Rd CR7 ...42 D5
Garrad's Rd SW16 ...21 D4
Garrard Rd SM7 ...78 A3
Garrat La SW17,SW18 ...20 C5
Garratt Cl CR0 ...60 E6
Garratt La SW17,SW18 ...20 C5
Garratt Park Sec Sch SW18 ...20 C5
Garratt Terr SW17 ...20 E4
Garratts La SM7 ...78 A3
Garraway Ho SE21 ...22 F5
Garrett Cl RH10 ...202 C4
Garrett Mews 9 GU11 .105 A1
Garrick Cl Hersham KT12 .54 B6
1 Richmond TW9 ...6 D2
Staines TW18 ...13 A1
Garrick Cres CR0 ...61 E8
Garrick Gdns KT8 ...36 A6
Garrick Ho 4 Chiswick W4 .7 E8
2 Kingston u T KT1 ...37 E5
7 Streatham SW16 ...21 C3
Garrick Rd TW9 ...7 A5
Garrick Way GU16 ...85 E7
Garrick Wlk RH10 ...201 E3
Garrick's Ait KT8 ...36 C7
Garricks ho KT1 ...37 D7
Garrison Cl TW4 ...4 F2
Garrison La KT9 ...56 E3
Garrones The RH10 ...202 E7
Garside Cl TW12 ...16 B2
Garson Cl KT10 ...54 F4
Garson La TW19 ...11 D8
Garson Rd KT10 ...54 F4
Garson's La SL4 ...8 A7
Garston Gdns CR8 ...80 D4
Garston La CR8 ...80 D4
Garstons The KT23 ...94 A2
Garswood RG12 ...27 D3
Garth Cl Farnham GU9 ...146 A7
Kingston u T KT2 ...17 F3
West Barnes SM4 ...39 D2
Garth Ct W4 ...7 D8
Garth Hill Coll RG12 ...27 C8
Garth Rd Chiswick W4 ...7 D8
Kingston u T KT2 ...17 F3
West Barnes SM4 ...39 D2
Garth The Ash GU12 ...105 F1
Cobham KT11 ...73 E6
Farnborough GU14 ...85 D4
Hampton TW12 ...16 B2
Garthorne Rd SE23 ...23 D8
Garthside TW10 ...17 E3
Gartmoor Gdns SW19 ...19 F7
Garton Cl RH11 ...200 E5
Garvens SE19 ...22 E3
Gascoigne Rd
New Addington CR0 ...63 C2
Weybridge KT13 ...53 B7
Gasden Copse GU8 ...170 D5
Gasden Dr GU8 ...170 D6
Gasden La GU8 ...170 D6
Gaskyns Cl RH12 ...214 D7
Gassiot Rd SW17 ...20 F4
Gassiot Way SM1 ...59 D7
Gasson Wood Rd RH11 .200 E4
Gaston Bell Cl TW9 ...6 F4
Gaston Bridge Rd
Shepperton TW17 ...34 D3
Upper Halliford TW17 ...34 E4
Gaston Rd CR4 ...41 A6
Gaston Way TW17 ...34 D4
Gatcombe Ct BR3 ...24 A1
Gate Ct 4 KT13 ...53 B7
Gate Ho 4 KT6 ...37 E1
Gate Way 7 KT13 ...53 B7
Gateford Dr RH12 ...217 F6
Gatehouse Cl KT2 ...18 C1
Gates Cl RH10 ...202 C2
Gates Green Rd BR4 ...63 F7
Gatesden Cl KT22 ...94 C4
Gatesden Rd KT22 ...94 C4
Gateside Rd SW17 ...20 F5
Gatestone Ct 11 SE19 ...22 E2
Gatestone Rd SE19 ...22 E2
Gateway The GU21 ...70 C5
Gateways Guildford GU1 .131 B8
Kingston u T KT6 ...37 E4
Gateways Ct SM6 ...60 B5
Gateways The TW9 ...6 D3
Gatfield Gr TW13 ...16 A6
Gatfield Ho TW13 ...16 A6
Gatley Ave KT19 ...57 B5
Gatley Dr GU1 ...109 F4
Gatton Bottom
Gatton RH2,RH1 ...118 E7
Merstham RH1,RH2 ...119 B8
Gatton Cl Belmont SM2 ...59 B2
Reigate RH2 ...118 C4
Gatton Park Ct RH1 ...118 F4
Gatton Park Rd RH1,RH2 118 E4
Gatton Point RH1 ...119 A5
Gatton Rd Reigate RH2 ..118 C4
Upper Tooting SW17 ...20 E4
Gatwick Airport Sta RH6 ...182 B7

Gatwick Airport-London
RH6 ....**181** F7
Gatwick Aviation Mus★
RH6 ....**180** F5
Gatwick Gate Est RH11 .**181** E5
Gatwick Ind Est RH6 .....**180** F6
Gatwick Metro Ctr RH6 .**161** B4
Gatwick Park Hospl
RH6 ....**160** E2
Gatwick Rd
Crawley RH6,RH10 .....**182** A3
Wandsworth SW18 ......**19** F8
Gatwick Way RH6 ......**181** F8
Gauntlet Cres CR8 ......**100** D7
Gauntlett Rd SM1 ......**59** D5
Gavell Rd KT11 ....**73** A6
Gaveston Cl KT14 ......**71** F6
Gaveston Rd KT22 ......**95** A7
Gavina Cl SM4 ....**40** E4
Gayfere Rd KT17 ....**58** A5
Gayhouse La RH1 ......**162** E8
Gayler Cl RH1 ....**120** F2
Gaynesford Rd
Forest Hill SE23 ....**23** D6
Wallington SM5 ....**59** F3
Gays Cotts RH7 ....**143** A2
Gayton Cl KT21 ....**75** E1
Gayton Ct New Malden KT3 **38** F4
Reigate RH2 ....**118** A2
Gaywood Cl SW2 ....**22** A7
Gaywood Rd KT21 ....**75** F1
Geary Cl RH6 ....**162** B1
Gedge Ct CR4 ....**40** E5
Geffers Ride SL5 ....**28** E7
Gemini Cl RH11 ....**200** E4
Gemma Ct BR3 ....**43** F7
Genesis Bsns Pk
Horsham RH13 ....**217** F3
Sheerwater GU21 ....**70** C4
Genesis Cl TW19 ....**13** F7
Geneva Cl TW17 ....**34** E7
Geneva Rd
Kingston u T KT1 ....**37** E5
Thornton Heath CR7 ......**42** C4
Genoa Rd SE20 ....**43** C8
Gentles La GU30,GU35 ..**187** A3
Genyn Rd GU2 ....**130** B8
Geoffrey Ct TW18 ....**13** A1
George Abbot Sch GU1 ..**110** A3
George Denyer Cl GU27 .**208** C7
George Eliot Cl GU8 ...**170** F4
George Gdns GU11 .....**126** C2
George Groves Rd SE20 ..**43** A8
George Ho Ⓐ SE26 .....**23** B3
George Horley Pl RH5 ..**158** B1
George Pinion Ct RH12 .**217** B3
George Rd
Farncombe GU7 ....**150** F7
Guildford GU1 ....**109** D1
Kingston u T KT2 ....**18** C1
Milford GU8 ....**149** F2
New Malden KT3 ....**38** F4
George Sq SW19 ....**40** A4
George St
Croydon CR0,CR9 ....**61** D8
Hounslow TW3,TW5 ......**4** F5
Pirbright GU24 ....**87** A6
Richmond TW10 ....**6** D2
Staines TW18 ....**12** F4
George Street Sta CR0,
CR9 ....**61** C8
George Wyver Cl SW18 ..**19** E8
George's Rd TN16 ......**103** D7
Georgeham Rd GU47 .....**45** D2
Georgelands GU23 ......**91** B6
Georges Terr CR3 ......**100** D5
Georgetown Ct Ⓐ SE19 .**22** E3
Georgia Rd
Kingston u T KT3 ....**38** C5
South Norwood CR7 ......**42** B8
Georgian Cl
Camberley GU15 ....**65** E7
Crawley RH10 ....**202** D5
Staines TW18 ....**13** B4
Georgian Ct CR0,CR9 ...**42** D1
Georgina Ct Ⓐ TW1 .....**6** C1
Gerald Ct RH13 ....**217** E2
Gerald's Gr SM7 ....**77** D5
Geraldine Rd W4 ....**7** A8
Geranium Cl RG45 ......**45** B8
Gerard Ave TW4 ....**16** A8
Gerard Rd SW13 ....**7** F6
Germander Dr GU24 .....**68** A4
Gerrards Mead SM7 ......**77** F3
Ghent St SE6 ....**24** A6
Ghyll Cres RH13 ......**217** F1
Gibb's Acre GU24 ....**87** F4
Gibbet La GU15 ....**66** A7
Gibbon Rd KT2 ....**17** F1
Gibbons Cl Crawley RH10 **202** C3
Sandhurst GU47 ....**64** C8
Gibbs Ave SE19 ....**22** D3
Gibbs Brook La RH7,
RH8 ....**143** D7
Gibbs Cl SE19 ....**22** D3
Gibbs Ho Ⓐ Balham SW12 **21** B8
Ⓐ Bromley BR1 ....**44** F8
Gibbs Sq SE19 ....**22** D3
Giblets La RH12 ....**217** F7
Giblets Way RH12 .....**217** F6
Gibraltar Cres KT19 ....**57** E1
Gibson Cl Chessington KT9 **56** C4
Isleworth TW7 ....**5** D4
Gibson Ct KT10 ....**55** F7
Gibson Ho SM1 ....**59** A6

Gibson Pl TW19 ....**2** C1
Gibson Rd SM1 ....**59** B5
Gibson's Hill
South Norwood SW16 ...**22** A1
South Norwood SW16 ...**22** A2
Gidd Hill CR5 ....**79** A3
Giffard Dr GU14 ....**84** F5
Giffard Way GU2 ......**109** A4
Giffards Cl RH19 ......**185** F1
Giffards Mdw GU9 .....**125** E1
Giggs Hill Rd KT7 ......**37** A2
Giggshill Gdns KT7 .....**37** A1
Gilbert Cl Ⓐ SW19 .....**40** B8
Gilbert Ct CR5 ....**79** D3
Gilbert Ct Frimley GU15 ..**65** C2
Merton SW19 ....**20** C1
Gilbert Scott Jun & Inf Com
Sch CR2 ....**62** E3
Gilbert St TW3 ....**5** C4
Gilbey Rd SW17 ....**20** E3
Gilders Rd KT9 ....**56** F4
Giles Coppice SE19 .....**22** F4
Giles Travers Cl TW20 ..**32** C6
Gilesmead RH18 ....**206** E2
Gilham La RH18 ....**206** E2
Gilham's Ave SM7 ......**77** E7
Gill Ave GU2 ....**129** E8
Gillespie Ho GU25 ......**31** E5
Gillett Cl RH13 ....**218** B4
Gillett Ho RH13 ......**218** B4
Gillett Rd CR7 ....**42** D5
Gillette Cnr TW7 ....**6** A7
Gillham La GU27 ......**207** A5
Gillian Ave GU11,GU12 .**126** D8
Gillian Cl GU12 ....**126** D8
Gillian Park Rd SM3 .....**39** F1
Gilliat Dr GU4 ....**110** D3
Gilligan Ct RH12 ......**217** B2
Gillray Ho Ⓐ SM1 ......**59** D5
Gilmais KT23 ....**94** C2
Gilmore Cres TW15 ......**14** A2
Gilpin Ave SW14 ....**7** D3
Gilpin Cl CR4 ....**40** E7
Gilpin Cres TW2 ....**16** B8
Gilpin Way UB3 ....**3** D7
Gilsland Rd CR7 ....**42** D5
Gimcrack Hill KT22 .....**95** B5
Gingers Cl GU6 ....**174** F2
Ginhams Rd RH11 .....**201** B6
Gipsy Hill SE19 ....**22** E3
Gipsy Hill Sta SE19 .....**22** E3
Gipsy La Bracknell RG12 .**27** D7
Wokingham RG40 ....**25** C4
Gipsy Rd SE21, SE27 ....**22** D4
Gipsy Road Gdns SE27 ..**22** C4
Girdwood Rd SW18,SW19 **19** E8
Girling Way TW14 ....**4** A4
Girton Cl GU47 ....**45** E1
Girton Gdns CR0 ....**63** A7
Girton Rd SE26 ....**23** D3
Gisbourne Cl SM6 ......**60** D7
Gittens Cl BR1 ....**24** F4
Giunevere Ho RH1 .....**119** A2
Glade Cl KT6 ....**56** D8
Glade Gdns CR0 ....**43** E2
Glade Ho SL5 ....**29** D4
Glade Spur KT20 ....**98** B6
Glade The Ascot SL5 ....**29** C4
Belmont SM2 ....**58** E2
Binstead GU10 ....**145** B1
Coulsdon CR5,CR8 .....**100** A8
Crawley RH10 ....**202** A4
Croydon CR0 ....**43** D3
Fetcham KT22 ....**94** B5
Heath End GU9 ....**125** D7
Horsham RH13 ....**218** A3
Kingswood KT20 ....**98** B6
Mytchett GU16 ....**86** A2
Sheerwater KT14 ....**70** E6
Staines TW18 ....**13** B2
Stoneleigh KT17 ....**58** A4
West Wickham BR4 ......**63** B7
Glades The RH19 ......**186** B1
Gladeside
Chessington KT9 ....**56** D3
Croydon CR0 ....**43** D3
Gladeside Ct CR6 .....**101** B7
Gladiator St SE23 ......**23** E8
Gladiator Way GU11,
GU12 ....**105** A8
Gladioli Cl Ⓐ TW12 ....**16** A2
Gladsmuir Cl KT12 .....**54** C8
Gladstone Ave
Feltham TW14 ....**4** B1
Twickenham TW2 ....**16** D8
Gladstone Ct Ⓐ SW19 ..**20** A1
Gladstone Gdns TW3 .....**5** C6
Gladstone Ho Ⓐ CR4 ...**40** F7
Gladstone Mews Ⓐ SE20 **23** C1
Gladstone Pl KT8 ....**36** E4
Gladstone Rd
Ashtead KT21 ....**75** D1
Croydon CR0 ....**42** D2
Horsham RH12 ....**217** D3
Kingston u T KT1 ....**38** A6
Merton SW19 ....**20** A1
Surbiton KT6 ....**56** E8
Glamis Cl GU16 ....**85** F7
Glamis Ho Ⓐ RH2 .....**118** F1
Glamorgan Cl CR4,SW16 .**41** E6
Glamorgan Rd KT1 ......**17** C1
Glanfield Rd BR3 ....**43** F5
Glanty The TW20 ....**12** B4
Glanville Ho Ⓐ SW12 ..**21** C8
Glanville Wlk Ⓐ RH11 .**201** A3
Glasbrook Ave TW2 .....**15** F7

Glasford St SW17 ......**20** F2
Glassmill La BR2 ......**44** F7
Glassonby Wlk GU15 ....**66** C5
Glastonbury Rd SM4 ....**40** A2
Glayshers Hill GU35 ...**187** B6
Glazebrook Cl SE21 ....**22** D6
Glazebrook Rd TW11 ....**16** F1
Glaziers La GU3 ....**107** C2
Gleave Cl RH19 ....**186** A2
Glebe Ave CR4 ....**40** F6
Glebe Cl Aldershot GU11 **126** A7
Crawley RH10 ....**201** E7
Great Bookham KT23 .....**94** A1
Lightwater GU18 ....**48** C1
Sanderstead CR2 ....**80** F8
Glebe Cotts Feltham TW13 **16** A5
West Clandon GU4 .....**111** B3
Glebe Ct Guildford GU1 .**109** F1
Mitcham CR4 ....**40** F6
Glebe Gdns Byfleet KT14 .**71** E5
New Malden KT3 ....**38** E2
Glebe Ho TW13 ....**16** A5
Glebe Hyrst CR2 ....**80** F7
Glebe La
Abinger Common RH5 ..**155** D8
Rushmoor GU10 ....**168** C5
Glebe Path CR4 ....**40** F6
Glebe Rd Ashtead KT21 ..**75** D1
Belmont SM2 ....**58** E2
Cranleigh GU6 ....**174** E4
Dorking RH4 ....**135** F7
Egham TW20 ....**12** C2
Farnborough GU14 ......**84** F5
Merstham CR5 ....**99** B3
Staines TW18 ....**13** B3
Wallington SM5 ....**59** F4
Warlingham CR6 ....**81** D2
Glebe Sch BR4 ....**63** D8
Glebe Side TW1 ....**5** F1
Glebe Sq CR4 ....**40** F6
Glebe The
Blackwater GU17 ....**64** E4
Copthorne RH10 ......**183** B3
Ewhurst GU6 ....**175** E6
Felbridge RH19 ....**185** A4
Horley RH6 ....**160** F3
Leigh RH2 ....**138** A2
New Malden KT4 ....**38** F1
Streatham SW16 ....**21** D4
Glebe Way Coney Hall BR4 **63** E7
Feltham TW13 ....**16** A5
Sanderstead CR2 ....**80** F8
West Wickham BR4 ......**63** D8
Glebehyrst SE19 ......**22** E4
Glebeland Ctr Ⓐ RH4 .**136** A7
Glebeland Gdns TW17 ..**34** C3
Glebeland Rd GU15 .....**64** F6
Glebelands Claygate KT10 **55** F2
Crawley Down RH10 ...**204** A7
East Molesey KT8 ....**36** B5
Loxwood RH14 ....**212** F4
Glebelands Rd
East Bedfont TW14 ......**15** A8
Wokingham RG40 ....**25** C7
Glebelands Sch GU6 ...**174** D3
Glebeworld RG12 ....**27** C4
Gledhow Wood KT20 ....**98** B5
Gleeson Mews KT15 ....**52** C6
Glen Albyn Rd SW19 ...**19** D6
Glen Ave TW15 ....**14** A4
Glen Cl Beacon Hill GU26 **188** C6
Kingswood KT20 ....**97** E4
Littleton TW17 ....**34** B5
Glen Ct Addlestone KT15 ..**51** F5
Beacon Hill GU26 ......**188** C6
Ⓐ Bromley BR1 ....**24** F1
Ⓐ Penge SE20 ....**43** B8
Staines TW18 ....**12** F1
Woking GU21 ....**89** A8
Glen Dale Mews BR3 ....**44** B8
Glen Gdns CR0,CR9 ....**61** A6
Glen Innes GU47 ....**45** E1
Glen Rd Beacon Hill GU26 **188** C6
Chessington KT9 ....**56** E7
Grayshott GU26 ....**188** D3
Glen Road End SM6 ....**60** B2
Glen The Addlestone KT15 **51** F5
Ascot SL5 ....**29** D5
Beckenham BR2 ....**44** E7
Croydon CR0 ....**62** D7
Heath End GU9 ....**125** C6
Ⓐ Redhill RH1 ....**139** F8
Glen Vue RH19 ....**185** E1
Glen Wlk TW7 ....**5** D2
Glena Mount SM1 ......**59** C6
Glenalmond Ho TW15 ..**13** E5
Glenavon Cl KT10 ......**56** A4
Glenavon Ct KT4 ....**58** B8
Glenbow Rd BR1 ....**24** E3
Glenbuck Ct Ⓐ KT6 ....**37** E3
Glenbuck Rd KT6 ....**37** E3
Glenburnie Rd SW17 ...**20** F5
Glencairn Rd SW16 ....**21** E1
Glencoe Cl GU16 ....**86** A8
Glencoe Rd KT13 ....**53** A7
Glendale Cl
Horsham RH12 ....**218** A6
Woking GU21 ....**69** C1
Wokingham RG41 ....**25** A3
Glendale Dr
Guildford GU4 ....**110** C5
Wimbledon SW19 ....**19** F3
Glendale Rise CR8 .....**80** B4
Glendene Ave KT24 .....**92** E1
Glendon Ho Ⓐ RH10 ..**201** D5
Glendower Gdns Ⓐ SW14 **7** D4
Glendower Rd SW14 .....**7** D4

Glendyne Cl RH19 .....**206** A8
Glendyne Way RH19 ...**206** A8
Gleneagle Lodge BR3 ...**44** A8
Gleneagle Mews SW16 ..**21** D3
Gleneagle Rd SW16 ....**21** D3
Gleneagles Cl TW19 .....**2** D1
Gleneagles Ct
Crawley RH10 ....**201** D5
Ⓐ Teddington TW11 ...**17** A3
Gleneagles Dr GU14 ....**84** C3
Gleneagles Ho RG12 ...**26** E3
Glenesk Sch KT24 ......**92** D3
Glenfarg Rd SE6 ....**24** D7
Glenfield Cl RH3 ......**137** B5
Glenfield Cotts RH6 ...**180** D7
Glenfield Rd
Ashford TW15 ....**14** C2
Banstead SM7 ....**78** B4
Brockham RH3 ....**137** B6
Streatham SW12 ....**21** C7
Glenhaven Dr TW19 ......**2** A2
Glenheadon Cl KT22 ....**95** D4
Glenheadon Rise KT22 ..**95** D4
Glenhurst Cl GU17 ......**64** E4
Glenhurst Ct SE19 .....**22** F3
Glenhurst Rd TW8 ....**6** C8
Glenhurst Rise SE19 ...**22** C1
Glenister Park Rd SW16 .**21** D1
Glenlea GU26 ....**188** E1
Glenlea Hollow GU26 ..**207** E8
Glenlee GU22 ....**89** D8
Glenlion Ct Ⓐ KT13 ....**53** D7
Glenmill TW12 ....**15** F3
Glenmore Cl KT15 ......**52** B7
Glenmore Ho Ⓐ TW10 ...**6** E1
Glenmount Rd GU16 ....**86** A2
Glenn Ave CR8 ....**80** B8
Glennie Ct SE21 ....**23** A7
Glennie Rd Ⓐ SE27,SW16 **22** A5
Glenrose Ho Ⓐ SM1 ....**59** C6
Glenside Ⓐ RH19 .....**185** E1
Glentanner Way SW17 ..**20** D5
Glenthorne Ave CR0,CR9 **43** C1
Glenthorne Cl SM3 .....**40** A1
Glenthorne Gdns SM3 ..**40** A1
Glenthorne High Sch
SM3 ....**40** A1
Glenthorne Rd KT1 ....**37** F5
Glenthorpe Rd SM4 ....**39** D4
Glenview Cl RH10 .....**201** E8
Glenville Gdns GU26 ..**188** F4
Glenville Mews SW18 ..**20** A8
Glenville Rd KT2 ....**18** A1
Glenwood Bracknell RG12 **27** C5
Dorking RH5 ....**136** C5
Heath End GU9 ....**125** C6
Virginia Water GU25 ....**31** C8
Glenwood Rd
Forest Hill SE6 ....**24** A7
Hounslow TW3 ....**5** D4
Stoneleigh KT17 ....**58** A4
Glenwood Way CR0 .....**43** D3
Globe Farm La GU17 ...**64** B5
Glorney Mead GU9 ....**126** A6
Glory Mead RH4 ......**136** C4
Glossop Rd CR2 ....**61** D2
Gloster Cl GU12 ......**105** F5
Gloster Ct GU21 ....**69** F3
Gloster Rd
New Malden KT3 ....**38** E4
Old Woking GU22 ....**90** A7
Gloucester Cl
East Grinstead RH19 ..**206** A8
Frimley GU16 ....**85** E6
Thames Ditton KT7 ......**37** A1
Gloucester Cres TW18 ..**13** D2
Gloucester Ct
Dulwich SE22 ....**23** A7
Richmond TW9 ....**7** A7
Ⓐ Surbiton KT6 ....**37** D2
Gloucester Dr TW18,
TW19 ....**12** D2
Gloucester Gdns
Bagshot GU19 ....**47** E3
Sutton SM1 ....**59** B8
Gloucester Lodge Ⓐ CR0 **61** F8
Gloucester Rd
Aldershot GU11 ....**126** C7
Bagshot GU19 ....**47** E3
Crawley RH10 ....**201** E2
Croydon CR0 ....**42** E2
Feltham TW13 ....**15** C7
Guildford GU2 ....**108** F3
Hampton TW12 ....**16** B1
Hounslow TW4 ....**4** E3
Kingston u T KT1,KT2 ...**38** B7
Redhill RH1 ....**118** F2
Richmond TW9 ....**7** A7
Teddington TW11 ....**16** E3
Twickenham TW2 ....**16** C7
Glover's Rd
Charlwood RH6 ....**180** D7
Reigate RH2 ....**139** B8
Glovers Field GU27 ...**207** F6
Glovers Rd GU27 .....**207** F5
Gloxinia Wlk TW12 .....**16** A2
Glyn Cl Ewell KT17 ....**58** A1
South Norwood SE19,SE25 **42** E8
Glyn Ct SE27 ....**22** A5
Glyn Rd KT4,SM3 ....**58** D8
Glyn Tech Sch KT17 ...**76** F8
Glyndale Grange SM2 ..**59** B4
Glynde Ho RH10 ......**201** D5
Glynde Pl RH12 ......**217** C2

Glynswood Frimley GU15 .**65** F3
Rowledge GU10 ....**146** A4
Glynwood Ct SE23 .....**23** C6
Goat Rd CR4 ....**40** F2
Goat Wharf TW8 ....**6** E8
Goaters Rd SL5 ....**28** D7
Goatsfield Rd TN16 ...**103** C7
Godalming Bsns Ctr
GU7 ....**150** F2
Godalming Coll GU7 ...**150** D2
Godalming Jun Sch
GU7 ....**150** F5
Godalming Mus★ GU7 .**150** D4
Godalming Rd
Dunsfold GU8 ....**193** A8
Hascombe GU8 ....**172** E3
Godalming Sta GU7 ...**150** D2
Goddard Cl
Crawley RH10 ....**202** B3
Littleton TW17 ....**33** F6
Goddard Ho SW19 ......**19** D6
Goddard Rd BR3 ....**43** D5
Goddards Ho SM7 ......**78** B5
Goddards La GU15 .....**65** B3
Goddens The RH19 ...**205** E7
Godfrey Ave TW2 ......**16** D8
Godfrey Cl GU47 ......**64** D7
Godfrey Way TW4 ......**15** F8
Godley Rd Byfleet KT14 .**71** F6
Wandsworth SW18 ......**20** D7
Godolphin Cl SM2 .....**77** B8
Godolphin Ct RH10 ...**201** D5
Godolphin Ho Ⓐ SW2 ..**22** A7
Godolphin Rd KT13 ....**53** D4
Godric Cres CR0 ....**63** D1
Godson Rd CR0,CR9 ...**61** A7
Godstone Farm★ RH9 .**121** C3
Godstone Green Rd
RH9 ....**121** B4
Godstone Hill RH9 ....**121** C5
Godstone Mount Ⓐ CR8 .**80** B7
Godstone Rd
Bletchingley RH1 .....**120** F2
Caterham CR3 ....**101** A3
Lingfield RH7 ....**164** C4
Oxted RH8,RH9 ......**122** C5
Purley CR8 ....**80** C4
Sutton SM1 ....**59** C6
Twickenham TW1 ....**6** B1
Godstone Sta RH9 ....**142** C5
Godstone Vineyards★
RH9 ....**121** C7
Godwin Cl KT19 ....**57** C4
Godwin Way RH13 ....**218** A4
Goffs Cl RH11 ....**201** C5
Goffs La RH11 ....**201** B6
Goffs Park Rd RH11 ..**201** C4
Goffs Rd TW15 ....**14** C2
Gogmore Farm Cl KT16 .**32** F2
Gogmore La KT16 ......**33** A2
Goidel Cl SM6 ....**60** D6
Gold Cup La SL5 ....**28** D8
Gold La GU11 ....**105** E4
Goldcliff Cl SM4 ....**40** A2
Goldcrest Cl RH6 ....**160** E4
Goldcrest Way
New Addington CR0 ....**63** D3
Wallington CR8 ....**60** C1
Golden Ct Ⓐ TW9 ......**6** D2
Golden Mews SE20 ....**43** C8
Golden Orb Wood RG42 **26** D8
Goldfinch Cl
Crawley RH11 ....**201** D8
Horsham RH12 ....**217** C7
Goldfinch Gdns GU4 ..**110** D2
Goldfinch Rd CR0,CR2 .**62** C5
Goldfort Wlk GU21 .....**68** E3
Goldhill GU10 ....**146** C6
Golding Cl
Chessington KT9 ....**56** C4
Crawley RH10 ....**202** C5
Goldings The GU21 .....**68** F3
Goldney Rd GU15 ......**66** C4
Goldrings Rd KT22 .....**74** C6
Goldsmith Way RG45 ..**45** B4
Goldsmiths Cl GU21 ...**69** C1
Goldstone Farm View
KT23 ....**114** A8
Goldsworth Orch Ⓐ
GU21 ....**69** A1
Goldsworth Park Ctr
GU21 ....**69** A2
Goldsworth Park Trad Est
GU21 ....**69** B3
Goldsworth Prim Sch
GU21 ....**69** C1
Goldsworth Rd GU21 ..**69** D2
Goldsworth Road Ind Est
GU21 ....**69** D2
Goldwell Rd CR7 ......**41** F5
Gole Rd GU24 ....**87** D6
Golf Cl Pyrford GU22 ...**70** E5
South Norwood SW16 ..**42** A8
Golf Club Dr KT2 ......**18** D1
Golf Club Rd
Weybridge KT13 ....**53** C1
Woking GU22 ....**89** B7
Golf Course Cotts KT20 .**98** A4
Golf Dr GU15 ....**65** F4
Golf Links Ave GU26 .**188** B6
Golf Rd CR8 ....**80** D1
Golf Side Belmont SM2 ..**77** F8
Twickenham TW2 ....**16** D5
Golf Side Cl KT3 ......**38** E7
Goliath Cl SM6 ....**60** E3

Gomer Gdns TW11 . . . . . . **17** A2
Gomer Pl TW11 . . . . **17** A2
Gomshall Ave SM6 . . . . . . **60** E5
Gomshall Gdns CR8 . . . . . **80** E4
Gomshall La GU5 . . . . . . **133** B4
Gomshall Rd KT17,SM2 . . . **58** C1
Gomshall Sta GU5 . . . . . **133** D4
Gong Hill Dr GU10 . . . . . **146** D4
Gong Hill Frensham Rd
GU10 . . . . **146** D4
Gonston Cl SW19 . . . . **19** E6
Gonville Prim Sch CR7 . . **41** F4
Gonville Rd CR7 . . . . **41** F4
Good Shepherd RC Prim Sch
Catford BR1 . . . . **24** F4
New Addington CR0 . . . . . . **63** B3
Goodbehere Ho 7 SE27 . **22** C4
Goodchild Rd RG40 . . . . . **25** D6
Goodden Cres GU14 . . . . . **84** F3
Goodenough Rd SW19 . . . **19** F1
Goodenough Way CR5 . . . **99** F7
Goodhart Way BR4 . . . . . **44** E3
Goodhew Rd CR0,SE25 . . . **43** A3
Gooding Cl KT3 . . . . **38** C4
Goodings Gn RG40 . . . . . . **25** F6
Goodland Ho 1 KT3 . . . . **38** E2
Goodman Cres SW2 . . . . . **21** D6
Goodman Pl TW18 . . . . . . **12** F4
Goodson Ho SM4 . . . . **40** C2
Goodways Dr RG12 . . . . . **27** D7
Goodwin Cl
Crawley RH11 . . . . **200** F3
Mitcham CR4 . . . . **40** D6
Goodwin Gdns CR0,CR2 . . **61** B4
Goodwin Rd CR0 . . . . **61** B5
Goodwins Cl RH19 . . . . . **185** D3
Goodwood Cl
Camberley GU15 . . . . **65** C8
Crawley RH10 . . . . **202** A3
Morden SM4 . . . . **40** A5
Goodwood Ct SE27 . . . . . . **22** C5
Goodwood Ho SE26 . . . . . . **23** B2
Goodwood Lodge SM6 . . **60** D7
Goodwood Par BR3 . . . . . **43** E5
Goodwood Pl GU14 . . . . . **85** E3
Goodwood Rd RH1 . . . . . **118** F3
Goodwyns Pl RH4 . . . . . **136** B5
Goodwyns Rd RH4 . . . . . **136** C4
Goose Gn GU5 . . . . **133** C4
Goose Green Cl RH12 . . **217** D5
Goose La GU22 . . . . **89** B5
Goose Rye Rd
Woking GU3 . . . . **89** A2
Worplesdon GU3 . . . . **88** E1
Goossens Cl 1 SM1 . . . . . **59** C5
Gordon Ave
Camberley GU15 . . . . **65** C4
Isleworth TW1 . . . . **6** B2
Mortlake SW14 . . . . **7** E3
South Croydon CR2,CR8 . . . **61** C1
Gordon Cl
Addlestone KT16 . . . . **51** E7
Staines TW18 . . . . **13** B2
Gordon Cres
Camberley GU15 . . . . **65** C4
Croydon CR0 . . . . **42** F1
Gordon Dr
Addlestone KT16 . . . . **51** E7
Shepperton TW17 . . . . **34** D2
Gordon Rd
Aldershot GU11 . . . . **105** A1
Ashford TW15 . . . . **13** E5
Beckenham BR3 . . . . **43** F6
Camberley GU15 . . . . **65** C5
Caterham CR3 . . . . **100** D6
Chiswick W4 . . . . **7** B8
Claygate KT10 . . . . **55** E3
Crowthorne RG45 . . . . **45** D3
Farnborough GU14 . . . . . . **105** D8
Horsham RH12 . . . . **217** D4
Hounslow TW3 . . . . **5** C3
Kingston u T KT2 . . . . **37** F8
Redhill RH1 . . . . **119** A4
Richmond TW9 . . . . **6** F5
Shepperton TW17 . . . . **34** D3
Surbiton KT5 . . . . **37** F2
Wallington SM5 . . . . **59** F4
Gordon's Sch GU24 . . . . . **67** E7
Gordondale Rd SW18,
SW19 . . . . **20** A6
Gordons Way RH8 . . . . . **122** D7
Gore Rd SW20 . . . . **39** C7
Goring Rd TW18 . . . . **12** E3
Goring's Mead RH13 . . . **217** D1
Goring's Sq TW18 . . . . **12** E4
Gorling Cl RH11 . . . . **200** E5
Gorrick Sq RG41 . . . . **25** B3
Gorringe Park Ave CR4,
SW17 . . . . **21** A1
Gorringe Park Mid Sch
CR4 . . . . **41** A8
Gorringes Brook RH12 . **217** D6
Gorse Bank GU18 . . . . **67** A8
Gorse Cl Burgh Heath KT20 **97** B7
Copthorne RH10 . . . . **183** B2
Crawley RH11 . . . . **201** B1
Wrecclesham GU10 . . . . . **146** B6
Gorse Cotts GU26 . . . . . . **207** C8
Gorse Ct GU4 . . . . **110** C3
Gorse Dr RH6 . . . . **162** C3
Gorse End RH12 . . . . **217** D5
Gorse Hill La GU25 . . . . . . **31** D5
Gorse Hill Rd GU25 . . . . . . **31** D5
Gorse La Chobham GU24 . . **49** E3
Wrecclesham GU10 . . . . . **146** B6
Gorse Pl RG42 . . . . **8** B1
Gorse Rd Croydon CR0 . . . . **63** A7
Frimley GU16 . . . . **65** E2
Gorse Rise SW17 . . . . **21** A3
Gorselands GU9 . . . . **125** C7
Gorselands Cl Ash GU12 **106** A5
Headley Down GU35 . . . . . **187** C4
West Byfleet KT14 . . . . **71** C8
Gorsewood Rd GU21 . . . . **88** E7
Gort Cl GU11 . . . . **105** E7
Gosberton Rd SW12 . . . . . **21** A7
Gosbury Hill KT9 . . . . **56** E6
Gosden Cl Crawley RH10 . **202** A5
Shalford GU5 . . . . **151** F8
Gosden Comm GU5 . . . . . **151** E8
Gosden Cotts GU5 . . . . . **151** F7
Gosden Hill Rd GU4 . . . . **110** C5
Gosden Rd GU24 . . . . **67** F6
Gosden Sch GU5 . . . . **151** E8
Gosfield Rd KT19 . . . . **76** D7
Gosnell Cl GU16 . . . . **66** D3
Gospatric Home Ho 3
SW14 . . . . **7** E4
Gosport Ho 9 SW15 . . . . **19** A7
Gossops Dr RH11 . . . . . . **201** A5
Gossops Green Jun & Inf Sch
RH11 . . . . **201** A5
Gossops Green La RH11 **201** A5
Gossops Par RH11 . . . . . **200** F5
Gostling Rd TW2 . . . . **16** A7
Goston Gdns CR7 . . . . **42** A6
Gostrode La GU8 . . . . . . **210** A6
Gothic Ct Harlington UB3 . . . **3** D8
Sandhurst GU47 . . . . **64** B7
Gothic Rd TW2 . . . . **16** D6
Goudhurst Cl RH10 . . . . . **202** E6
Goudhurst Ho 9 SE20 . . . **23** C1
Goudhurst Keep RH10 . . **202** E6
Goudhurst Rd BR1 . . . . **24** F3
Gough Ho 4 KT1 . . . . **37** E7
Gough's La RG12 . . . . **27** D8
Gough's Mdw GU47 . . . . . **64** B7
Gould Ct Dulwich SE19 . . . **22** E3
Guildford GU4 . . . . **110** D3
Gould Rd
East Bedfont TW14 . . . . **14** E8
Twickenham TW2 . . . . **16** E7
Goulding Gdns CR7 . . . . . **42** C7
Government House Rd
GU11,GU14 . . . . **105** B7
Government Rd GU11 . . . **105** E4
Governor's Rd GU15 . . . . . **64** F6
Govett Ave TW17 . . . . **34** C4
Govett Gr GU20 . . . . **48** D5
Gower Ho SW19 . . . . **20** D3
Gower Lodge KT13 . . . . . . **53** D4
Gower Pk GU47 . . . . **64** D7
Gower Rd Horley RH6 . . . **160** E3
Hounslow TW7 . . . . **5** F8
Weybridge KT13 . . . . **53** D4
Gower The TW20 . . . . **32** C6
Gowland Pl BR3 . . . . **43** F7
Gowrie Pl CR3 . . . . **100** C5
Graburn Way KT8 . . . . **36** D6
Grace Bennett Cl GU14 . . **85** A7
Grace Bsns Ctr CR4 . . . . . **40** F3
Grace Ho SE26 . . . . **23** B3
Grace Path SE26 . . . . **23** C4
Grace Rd Crawley RH11 . . **201** A1
Thornton Heath CR0 . . . . . . **42** C3
Grace Reynolds Wlk
GU15 . . . . **65** C6
Gracedale Rd SW16,SW17 **21** B3
Gracefield Gdns SW16 . . . **21** E5
Gracious Pond Rd GU24 . **50** B4
Gradient The SE26 . . . . **23** A4
Graemesdyke Ave SW14 . . **7** B3
Graffham Cl RH11 . . . . . . **201** B8
Grafton Cl
Twickenham TW4 . . . . **15** F7
West Byfleet KT14 . . . . **70** F6
Worcester Park KT4 . . . . **57** E7
Grafton Ct TW14 . . . . **14** D7
Grafton Park Rd KT4 . . . . **57** E8
Grafton Rd
Kingston u T KT3 . . . . **38** E6
Thornton Heath CR0 . . . . . . **42** A1
Worcester Park KT19,KT4 . . **57** E7
Grafton Way KT8 . . . . **35** F5
Graham Ave CR4 . . . . **41** A8
Graham Cl CR0 . . . . **63** A8
Graham Gdns KT6 . . . . **37** E1
Graham Ho
5 Balham SW12 . . . . **21** B8
Little Bookham KT23 . . . . . . **94** A3
Redhill RH1 . . . . **118** E3
Graham Rd
Hampton TW12 . . . . **16** A4
Merton SW19 . . . . **19** F1
Mitcham CR4 . . . . **41** A8
Purley CR8 . . . . **80** A6
Windlesham GU20 . . . . **48** C4
Grainford Ct RG40 . . . . **25** C5
Grainger Rd TW7 . . . . **5** F5
Grampian Cl
Harlington UB3 . . . . **3** D7
Sutton SM2 . . . . **59** C3
Grampian Rd GU47 . . . . . . **45** A2
Granada St SW17 . . . . **20** F3
Granard Rd SW11,SW12 . . **20** F8
Granary Cl RH6 . . . . **161** A5
Granary Way RH12 . . . . . **217** A1
Grand Ave
Camberley GU15 . . . . **65** C6
Tolworth KT5 . . . . **38** B3
Grand Avenue Prim Sch
KT5 . . . . **38** C3
**Grand Avenue Prim Sch
(Upper Sch)** KT5 . . . . **38** C3
Grand Dr KT3,SM4,SW20 . . **39** C5
Grand Par Crawley RH10 **201** D6
Grand Par *continued*
Mortlake SW14 . . . . **7** C3
Tolworth KT6 . . . . **38** A1
Grand Stand Rd KT17,
KT18 . . . . **77** A2
Grand View Ave TN16 . . . . **83** C3
Granden Rd SW16 . . . . **41** E7
Grandfield Ct W4 . . . . **7** D8
Grandis Cotts GU23 . . . . . . **91** B5
Grandison Rd KT4 . . . . **58** C7
Grange Ave
Crowthorne RG45 . . . . **45** B6
South Norwood SE25 . . . . . . **42** E7
Twickenham TW2 . . . . **16** E6
Grange Cl Ashstead KT22 . **95** D7
Bletchingley RH1 . . . . **120** D2
Crawley RH10 . . . . **202** A8
East Molesey KT8 . . . . **36** B5
Godalming GU7 . . . . **151** A5
Guildford GU2 . . . . **109** B5
Heston TW5 . . . . **4** F8
Merstham RH1,RH2 . . . . . **119** B7
Grange Com Inf Sch The
KT15 . . . . **52** A1
Grange Com Jun Sch
GU14 . . . . **85** A7
Grange Cres RH10 . . . . . . **204** B7
Grange Ct Belmont SM2 . . . **59** B3
Egham TW20 . . . . **11** F3
Hackbridge SM6 . . . . **60** B7
Littleton TW17 . . . . **34** A5
Merstham RH2 . . . . **119** B7
South Godstone RH9 . . . . . **142** E5
5 Staines TW18 . . . . **13** A3
Walton-on-T KT12 . . . . **54** A8
Grange Dr
Merstham RH1 . . . . **119** B7
Woking GU21 . . . . **69** E4
Grange End RH6 . . . . **162** A3
Grange Farm Rd GU12 . . **106** A3
Grange Gdns
Banstead SM7 . . . . **78** B6
South Norwood SE25 . . . . . . **42** E7
Grange Hill SE25 . . . . **42** E7
Grange La SE21 . . . . **22** F6
Grange Lodge SW19 . . . . . **19** D2
Grange Mans KT17 . . . . . . **57** F3
Grange Mdw SM7 . . . . **78** B6
Grange Mills SW12 . . . . . . **21** C7
Grange Park Pl SW20 . . . . **19** B1
Grange Park Rd CR7 . . . . **42** D6
Grange Pk Cranleigh GU6 **174** F3
Woking GU21 . . . . **69** F5
Grange Pl Laleham TW18 . . **33** C7
Walton-on-T KT12 . . . . **54** A8
Grange Rd Ash GU12 . . . . **106** B1
Ashstead KT21 . . . . **95** D7
Belmont SM2 . . . . **59** A3
Bracknell RG12 . . . . **27** C8
Camberley GU15 . . . . **65** E5
Caterham CR3 . . . . **101** A2
Chessington KT9 . . . . **56** E6
Crawley Down RH10 . . . . . **204** A7
East Molesey KT8 . . . . **36** B5
Egham TW20 . . . . **11** F3
Farnborough GU14 . . . . **85** B7
Guildford GU2,GU3 . . . . . . **109** B5
Hersham KT12 . . . . **54** E6
Kingston u T KT1 . . . . **37** E6
Pirbright GU24 . . . . **87** D5
Rushmoor GU10 . . . . **168** C7
South Croydon CR2 . . . . **61** C2
South Norwood SE19,SE25 . . **42** D7
Tongham GU10 . . . . **126** E6
Woking GU21 . . . . **69** E5
Woodham KT15 . . . . **52** B1
Grange The
Bletchingley RH1 . . . . **120** D2
Chobham GU24 . . . . **49** E1
Croydon CR0 . . . . **62** F8
Frensham GU10 . . . . **167** D7
Horley RH6 . . . . **161** A6
New Malden KT3 . . . . **39** A4
Thorpe GU25 . . . . **31** E5
Walton on the Hill KT20 . . . **97** A2
Walton-on-T KT12 . . . . **54** B8
Wimbledon SW19 . . . . **19** D2
Worcester Park KT19 . . . . . **57** D6
Grange Vale SM2 . . . . **59** B3
Grangecliffe Gdns SE25 . **42** E7
Grangefields Rd GU4 . . . **109** D6
Grangemill Rd SE6 . . . . . . **24** A6
Grangemill Way SE6 . . . . . **24** A6
Grangemount KT22 . . . . . . **95** D7
Grangeway RH6 . . . . **162** A3
Grangewood La BR3 . . . . . **23** F2
Gransden Cl GU6 . . . . **175** E5
Grant Cl TW17 . . . . **34** B3
Grant Pl 2 CR0 . . . . **42** F1
Grant Rd Crowthorne RG45 **45** C3
Croydon CR0 . . . . **42** F1
Grant Way TW7,TW8 . . . . . . **6** A8
Grant Wlk SL5 . . . . **29** E1
Grantchester 3 KT1 . . . . . **38** A7
Grantham Cl GU47 . . . . **45** E1
Grantham Ho 5 TW16 . . . **14** E1
Grantham Rd W4 . . . . **7** E7
Grantley Ave GU5 . . . . . . **152** B6
Grantley Cl GU4 . . . . **130** E2
Grantley Ct GU9 . . . . **145** F6
Grantley Ho SW19 . . . . . . **19** D7
Grantley Pl KT10 . . . . **55** C5
Grantley Rd
Cranford TW4,TW5 . . . . **4** C5
Guildford GU2 . . . . **109** A2
Granton Prim Sch SW16 . **21** C1
Granton Rd SW16 . . . . **41** C8
Grants Cotts KT10 . . . . . . **55** D8
Grants La TN8,RH8 . . . . . **144** C6
Grantwood Cl RH1 . . . . . **140** B4
Granville Ave
Feltham TW13 . . . . **15** A6
Hounslow TW3,TW4 . . . . **5** A2
Granville Cl Byfleet KT14 . . **71** F6
South Croydon CR0 . . . . **61** E8
Weybridge KT13 . . . . **53** C4
Granville Gdns SW16 . . . . **21** F1
Granville Rd
Limpsfield RH8 . . . . **123** A7
Merton SW19 . . . . **20** A1
Wandsworth SW18 . . . . **19** F8
Weybridge KT13 . . . . **53** C4
Woking GU22 . . . . **89** F7
Granwood Ct TW7 . . . . **5** E6
Grapsome Cl KT9 . . . . **56** C3
Grasmere Ave
Kingston u T SW15 . . . . **18** E4
Merton SW19 . . . . **40** A6
Twickenham TW3 . . . . **5** B1
Grasmere Cl
East Bedfont TW14 . . . . **14** F7
Guildford GU1 . . . . **110** B2
Thorpe Lea TW20 . . . . **12** B1
Grasmere Ct
Forest Hill SE26 . . . . **23** A3
14 Sutton SM2 . . . . **59** C4
Grasmere Gdns RH12 . . **218** B6
Grasmere Rd Bromley BR1 **24** F1
Croydon SE25 . . . . **43** B4
Farnborough GU14 . . . . **84** E4
Hale GU9 . . . . **125** A6
Lightwater GU18 . . . . **48** B1
Purley CR8 . . . . **80** B8
Streatham SW16 . . . . **21** F3
Grasmere Way KT14 . . . . . **71** F7
Grassfield Cl CR5 . . . . **99** C8
Grasslands RH6 . . . . **162** A3
Grassmere RH6 . . . . **161** C4
Grassmount
Forest Hill SE23 . . . . **23** B6
Wallington CR8 . . . . **60** C1
Grassway SM6 . . . . **60** C6
Grately Ho 10 SW15 . . . . . **19** B7
Grattons Dr RH10 . . . . . . **182** C1
Grattons The RH13 . . . . . **215** E3
Gravel Hill
Leatherhead KT22 . . . . **95** B6
South Croydon CR0,CR2 . . . **62** E4
Gravel Hill Rd GU10 . . . . **145** A3
Gravel Hill Sta CR0 . . . . . . **62** E4
Gravel Pits La GU5 . . . . . **133** C4
Gravel Rd
Farnborough GU14 . . . . . . **105** D8
Hale GU9 . . . . **125** B7
Twickenham TW2 . . . . **16** E7
Graveley 7 KT1 . . . . **38** A7
Gravelly Hill CR3 . . . . **120** F7
Gravelpits Cotts GU5 . . . **133** C4
Gravenel Gdns SW17 . . . . **20** E3
Graveney Gr SE20 . . . . **23** C1
Graveney Rd
Crawley RH10 . . . . **202** C5
Upper Tooting SW17 . . . . . . **20** E4
Graveney Sch SW17 . . . . . **21** B3
Gravetts La GU3 . . . . **108** E5
Gravetye Cl RH10 . . . . . . **202** A4
Gray Ct 8 KT2 . . . . **17** D4
Gray Pl KT16 . . . . **51** D4
Gray's La KT21 . . . . **95** F8
Grayham Cres KT3 . . . . . . **38** D5
Grayham Rd KT3 . . . . **38** D5
Graylands GU21 . . . . **69** E3
Graylands Cl GU21 . . . . **69** E3
Graylands Ct 5 GU1 . . . . **130** F8
Grays Cl GU27 . . . . **208** E8
Grays La TW15 . . . . **14** B4
Grays Rd GU7 . . . . **150** F7
Grays Wood RH6 . . . . **161** C3
Grayscroft Rd SW16 . . . . . **21** D1
Grayshot Dr GU17 . . . . **64** C5
Grayshott CE Prim Sch
GU26 . . . . **188** B3
Grayshott Rd GU26,GU35 **187** C5
Grayswood CE Inf Sch
GU27 . . . . **189** F2
Grayswood Dr GU16 . . . . . **86** A2
Grayswood Gdns SW20 . . **39** B7
Grayswood Pl GU27 . . . . **208** E8
Grayswood Point 14
SW15 . . . . **19** A7
Grayswood Rd GU27 . . . **189** F1
Grazeley Ct SE19 . . . . **22** E3
Great Austins GU9 . . . . . **146** D8
Great Austins Ho GU9 . . **146** D8
Great Brownings SE21 . . . **22** F4
Great Chertsey Rd
Chiswick SW14,W4 . . . . **7** D6
Feltham TW13,TW2 . . . . **16** A5
Great Elshams SM7 . . . . . **78** A3
Great George St GU7 . . . **150** E4
Great Goodwin Dr GU1 . **110** B3
Great Hollands Inf Sch
RG12 . . . . **26** F4
Great Hollands Jun Sch
RG12 . . . . **26** E4
Great Hollands Rd RG12 . **26** F3
Great Hollands Sq RG12 . **26** F3
Great House Ct 4 RH19 . **205** F8
Great Oaks Pk GU4 . . . . . **110** C5
Great Quarry GU1 . . . . . **130** D6
Great South-West Rd
East Bedfont TW14,TW6,TW4,
TW5 . . . . **3** D2
Hounslow TW5 . . . . **4** B4
Great Tattenhams KT18 . . **77** C1
Great West Rd
Brentford TW8 . . . . **6** B8
Cranford,Heston TW5 . . . . **4** F6
Hounslow TW5,TW7 . . . . **5** C6
Great West Road Cedars Rd
W4 . . . . **7** C8
Great West Road Chiswick 1
W4 . . . . **7** F8
**Great West Road Ellesmere
Rd** W4 . . . . **7** D8
Great West Road Hogarth La
W4 . . . . **7** E8
Great West Trad Est TW8 . . **6** B8
Great Woodcote Dr CR8 . **60** D1
Great Woodcote Pk CR8,
SM6 . . . . **60** E1
Greatfield Cl GU14 . . . . . . **85** B8
Greatfield Rd GU14 . . . . . . **85** B8
Greatford Dr GU1 . . . . . . **110** D1
Greatham Rd RH10 . . . . . **202** C3
Greatham Wlk 8 SW15 . . **19** A7
Greathed Manor* RH7 . . **165** C1
Greathurst End KT23 . . . . **93** F3
Greatlake Ct RH6 . . . . . . **161** B4
Greatstone Ho 12 SE20 . . **23** C1
Greatwood Cl KT16 . . . . . . **51** C2
Greaves Pl SW17 . . . . **20** E4
Grebe Cres RH13 . . . . . . **218** A1
Grebe Ct Cheam SM1 . . . . . **58** F5
Staines TW18 . . . . **13** B4
Grebe Terr 4 KT1 . . . . **37** E6
Grecian Cres SE19 . . . . . . **22** B2
Green Acre GU11 . . . . **104** F1
Green Acres CR0 . . . . **61** F7
Green Bsns Ctr The
TW20 . . . . **12** C4
Green Cl Beckenham BR2 . . **44** E6
Carshalton SM5 . . . . **59** F8
Feltham TW13 . . . . **15** E3
Green Cotts The GU6 . . . **175** E4
Green Court Ave CR0 . . . . **62** B8
Green Court Gdns CR0 . . . **62** B8
Green Croft RG40 . . . . **25** E8
Green Cross La GU10 . . . **168** A1
Green Ct TW16 . . . . **14** F2
Green Curve SM7 . . . . **77** F4
Green Dene KT24 . . . . **112** E3
Green Dr Send Marsh GU23 **90** F4
Wokingham RG40 . . . . **25** E4
Green Dragon Prim Sch
TW8 . . . . **6** E8
Green End KT9 . . . . **56** E6
Green Farm Rd GU19 . . . . **47** F3
Green Finch Cl RG45 . . . . **45** A6
Green Hedges 8 TW1 . . . . . **6** C1
Green Hedges Ave
RH19 . . . . **185** D2
Green Hedges Cl RH19 . **185** D2
Green Hill BR6 . . . . **83** F7
Green Hill Cl GU15 . . . . . . **66** C6
Green Hill Rd GU15 . . . . . . **66** C6
Green House The 5
SW19 . . . . **19** E7
Green La
Addlestone KT15,KT16 . . . . **51** E7
Alfold Crossways GU6 . . . . **193** F4
Ascot SL5 . . . . **29** E8
Ashford TW16 . . . . **14** F2
Ashstead KT22 . . . . **95** D6
Ashstead, Lower Ashstead
KT21 . . . . **75** D1
Bagshot GU19 . . . . **47** F2
Blackwater GU17 . . . . **64** B4
Blackwater,Hawley GU17 . . . **64** E4
Burstow RH6 . . . . **182** F6
Byfleet KT14 . . . . **71** F7
Caterham CR3 . . . . **100** C5
Chessington KT9 . . . . **56** E3
Chobham GU24 . . . . **49** F1
Churt GU10 . . . . **168** A1
Cobham KT11 . . . . **73** E7
Copthorne RH10 . . . . **183** F4
Crawley, Northgate RH10 . **201** E8
Crawley, Worth RH10 . . . . **202** D6
Cudworth RH5 . . . . **179** D8
Dockenfield GU10 . . . . **166** E6
East Molesey KT8 . . . . **36** B4
Egham TW18 . . . . **32** E8
Egham TW20 . . . . **12** B3
Farncombe GU7 . . . . **150** E8
Farnham GU9 . . . . **146** A7
Farnham, Weybourne GU9 . **125** F5
Faygate RH12 . . . . **198** F4
Feltham TW13 . . . . **15** E3
Guildford GU1 . . . . **110** B1
Hersham KT12 . . . . **54** B5
Hounslow TW4 . . . . **4** C3
Kingsley Green GU27 . . . . . **208** B4
Leatherhead KT22 . . . . **95** D6
Leigh RH2 . . . . **158** E8
Lingfield RH7 . . . . **164** C4
Lower Kingswood KT20 . . . . **97** F1
Milford GU8 . . . . **170** E8
Morden SM4 . . . . **40** B3
New Malden KT3 . . . . **38** C4
North Cheam KT4 . . . . **39** A1
Penge SE20 . . . . **23** D1
Purley CR8 . . . . **60** D1
Redhill RH1 . . . . **118** E3
Redhill,Whitebushes RH1 . **140** A4
Reigate RH2 . . . . **117** F1
Sandhurst GU47 . . . . **64** C7
Shamley Green GU5 . . . . . . **153** A7
Shepperton TW17 . . . . **34** C4
South Norwood CR7,SW16 . **42** B8

Green La *continued*
South Nutfield RH1 . . . . . .**140** F1
Streatham SW16 . . . .**21** F1
Tilford GU10 . . . .**147** E6
West Clandon GU4 . . . . . .**111** B8
West Horsley GU23 . . . .**92** B3
Wood St V GU3 . . . .**108** A3
Green La E GU3 . . . .**128** B8
Green La Mews SM4 . . . . .**40** E2
Green La W GU12 . . . . . .**127** E8
Green Lane Ave KT12 . . . .**54** C5
Green Lane Cl
Addlestone KT16 . . . .**51** E8
Byfleet KT14 . . . .**71** F7
Camberley GU15 . . . .**65** C7
Green Lane Cotts GU10 . .**167** F1
Green Lane Gdns CR7 . . . .**42** C7
Green Lane Inf Sch GU7 **129** E1
Green Lane Prim Sch
KT4 . . . .**39** B2
Green Lanes KT19 . . . . . .**57** E2
Green Leaf Ave SM6 . . . . .**60** D6
Green Leas Ashford TW16 .**14** F2
Kingston u T KT1 . . . .**37** E6
Green Leas Cl TW16 . . . . .**14** F2
Green Man La TW14 . . . . . .**4** A3
Green Mead KT10 . . . .**54** F4
Green Pk TW18 . . . .**12** E5
Green Rd TW20 . . . .**32** B5
Green Sch The TW7 . . . . . .**6** A6
Green St TW16 . . . .**35** A7
Green The Bracknell RG12 .**27** B5
Burgh Heath KT20 . . . .**97** E8
Carshalton SM6 . . . .**60** A8
Chiddingfold GU8 . . . .**191** C3
Claygate KT10 . . . .**55** F4
Copthorne RH10 . . . .**183** B3
Crawley RH11 . . . .**201** C7
Ewell KT17 . . . .**77** A4
Ewhurst GU6 . . . .**175** E4
Farnham GU9 . . . .**126** A6
Feltham TW13 . . . .**15** B6
Fetcham KT22 . . . .**94** D3
Frimley GU16 . . . .**85** F6
Hale GU9 . . . .**125** C6
Heston TW5 . . . .**5** A8
Kingston u T KT3 . . . .**38** C7
Merton SM4 . . . .**39** E6
New Addington CR0 . . . .**62** F2
7 Richmond TW9 . . . .**6** D2
Ripley GU23 . . . .**91** C6
Staines TW18 . . . .**13** D3
Sutton SM1 . . . .**59** B7
The Sands GU10 . . . .**126** E1
Twickenham TW2 . . . .**16** E6
Tyler's Green RH9 . . . .**121** C4
Upper Halliford TW17 . . . . .**34** E5
Warlingham CR6 . . . .**81** D1
Whiteley Village KT12 . . . . .**53** E1
Wimbledon SW19 . . . .**19** D3
Woldingham CR3 . . . .**102** A4
Green View
Chessington KT9 . . . .**56** F3
Godstone RH9 . . . .**121** B4
Green Way
Aldershot GU12 . . . .**105** E3
Redhill RH1 . . . .**118** E3
Sunbury TW16 . . . .**35** A5
Hampton TW12 . . . .**15** F2
Green Wood SL5 . . . .**28** C8
Green Wrythe Cres SM5 . .**40** E1
Green Wrythe La SM4,
SM5 . . . .**40** E2
Green Wrythe Prim Sch
SM5 . . . .**40** D3
Green's School La GU14 . .**85** A4
Greenacre Knaphill GU21 . .**68** E3
Whyteleafe CR3 . . . .**101** B7
Greenacre Ct TW20 . . . . . .**11** C2
Greenacre Pl SM6 . . . .**60** B8
Greenacre Sch for Girls
SM7 . . . .**78** B6
Greenacres
Crawley RH10 . . . .**202** A5
Farnham GU10 . . . .**126** C2
Great Bookham KT23 . . . . . .**94** A3
Horsham RH12 . . . .**217** D6
Oxted RH8 . . . .**122** E8
Greenaway Terr TW19 . . . .**13** E7
Greenbank Way GU15 . . . .**65** D2
Greenbush La GU6 . . . . . .**174** F1
Greencroft
2 Farnborough GU14 . . . . .**85** B4
Guildford GU1 . . . .**110** B1
Greencroft Rd TW5 . . . .**4** F6
Greene Fielde End TW18 **13** D1
Greenfield Ave KT5 . . . . . .**38** B3
Greenfield Ho 28 SW19 . .**19** D7
Greenfield Link CR5 . . . . .**79** E4
Greenfield Rd
Farnham GU9,GU10 . . . . . .**146** A7
Slinfold RH13 . . . .**215** D3
Wrecclesham GU9 . . . .**145** F7
Greenfield Sch GU22 . . . . .**89** E8
Greenfield Way RG45 . . . .**45** A7
Greenfields Cl
Horley RH6 . . . .**160** E5
Horsham RH12 . . . .**218** A6
Greenfields Pl RH5 . . . . .**157** D4
Greenfields Rd
Horley RH6 . . . .**160** F5
Horsham RH12 . . . .**218** A5
Greenfields Sch RH18 . .**206** C1
Greenfields Way RH12 . .**218** A6

Greenfinch Way RH12 . .**217** D7
Greenford Rd SM1 . . . .**59** B6
Greenham Ho TW7 . . . .**5** D4
Greenham Wlk GU21 . . . . .**69** C1
Greenham Wood RG12 . . . .**27** C3
Greenhanger GU10 . . . . . .**188** A8
Greenhayes Ave SM7 . . . . .**78** A4
Greenhayes Cl RH2 . . . . .**118** C1
Greenhayes Gdns SM7 . . . .**78** A4
Greenhayes Sch BR4 . . . . .**63** C8
Greenheys Pl GU22 . . . . . .**69** F1
Greenhill SM1 . . . .**59** C8
Greenhill Ave CR3 . . . . . .**101** B6
Greenhill Cl
Godalming GU7 . . . .**150** D3
Wrecclesham GU9 . . . .**146** A7
Greenhill Gdns GU4 . . . . .**110** C3
Greenhill La CR6 . . . .**81** F2
Greenhill Rd GU9 . . . .**146** B8
Greenhill Way GU9 . . . . . .**146** A7
Greenhills GU9 . . . .**146** B8
Greenholme GU15 . . . .**66** D5
Greenhow RG12 . . . .**27** A6
Greenhurst La RH8 . . . . . .**123** A3
Greenhurst Rd SE27 . . . . . .**22** A3
Greenlake Terr TW18 . . . . .**13** A1
Greenlands KT16 . . . .**51** C7
Greenlands Rd
Camberley GU15 . . . .**65** B1
Staines TW18 . . . .**13** A4
Weybridge KT13 . . . .**53** C7
Greenlaw Gdns KT3 . . . . . .**38** F2
Greenlea Pk SW19 . . . .**40** E8
Greenleaf Cl 6 SW2 . . . . .**22** A8
Greenleas GU16 . . . .**65** E2
Greenleaves Ct TW15 . . . . .**14** B2
Greenmead SE21 . . . .**43** A4
Greenmeads GU22 . . . .**89** E5
Greeno Cres TW17 . . . .**34** A4
Greenoak Rise TN16 . . . . . .**83** C1
Greenoak Way SW19 . . . . .**19** D4
Greenock Rd SW16 . . . .**41** D8
Greensand Cl RH1 . . . .**119** D7
Greensand Rd RH1 . . . . . .**119** A2
Greenshaw High Sch
SM1 . . . .**59** D8
Greenside Cl Catford SE6 . .**24** D6
Guildford GU4 . . . .**110** C3
Greenside Cotts GU23 . . . .**91** C6
Greenside Rd CR0 . . . .**42** A2
Greenside Wlk TN16 . . . . . .**83** B1
Greensleeves Manor
SM1 . . . .**59** B4
Greenstede Ave RH19 . . .**185** F2
Greenvale Prim Sch CR2 **81** D8
Greenvale Rd GU21 . . . . . .**68** D1
Greenvale Spec Sch
SE23 . . . .**23** E5
Greenview Ave CR0 . . . . . .**43** E3
Greenview Ct
Ashford TW15 . . . .**13** F4
Wandsworth SW18 . . . .**20** E8
Greenway
Great Bookham KT23 . . . . . .**94** B4
Horsham RH12 . . . .**217** B3
Tatsfield TN16 . . . .**103** C7
Wallington SM6 . . . .**60** C6
West Barnes SW20 . . . .**39** C5
Greenway Cl KT14 . . . .**71** A6
Greenway Dr TW18 . . . . . .**33** D8
Greenway Gdns CR0 . . . . . .**62** F7
Greenway Sch RH12 . . . . .**217** B3
Greenway The
Epsom KT18 . . . .**76** A5
Hounslow TW4 . . . .**4** F3
Oxted RH8 . . . .**123** B2
Greenways
Beckenham BR3 . . . .**44** A7
Egham TW20 . . . .**11** E3
Forest Hill SE26 . . . .**23** C4
Hinchley Wood KT10 . . . .**55** E6
Sandhurst GU47 . . . .**45** B1
Walton on the Hill KT20 . . . . .**97** B2
Greenways Dr SL5 . . . .**29** E1
Greenways The 1 TW1 . . . .**6** A1
Greenways Wlk RH11 . . . .**201** C1
Greenwell Cl RH9 . . . .**121** B5
Greenwich Cl RH11 . . . . .**201** C2
Greenwood
4 Bracknell RG12 . . . .**27** F5
1 Putney SW19 . . . .**19** D8
Greenwood Cl
Hinchley Wood KT7 . . . .**37** A1
Merton SM4 . . . .**39** E5
Woodham KT15 . . . .**70** F8
Greenwood Ct 2 RH11 . .**201** B1
Greenwood Dr RH1 . . . . .**140** A4
Greenwood Flats RH6 . . .**182** F6
Greenwood Gdns
Caterham CR3 . . . .**101** A2
Oxted RH8 . . . .**123** A4
Greenwood La TW12 . . . . .**16** B3
Greenwood Pk KT2 . . . . . .**18** E1
Greenwood The GU1 . . . .**110** A1
Gregan Ct GU11 . . . .**104** F1
Gregory Cl Crawley RH10 .**202** C2
Woking GU21 . . . .**69** C2
Gregory Ct
2 East Grinstead RH19 . . .**185** E1
Purley CR8 . . . .**80** B6

Gregsons RH12 . . . .**216** E8
Grena Gdns TW9 . . . .**6** F3
Grena Rd TW10,TW9 . . . . . .**6** F3
Grenaby Ave CR0 . . . .**42** D2
Grenaby Rd CR0 . . . .**42** D2
Grenadier Pl CR3 . . . .**100** C5
Grenadier Rd GU12 . . . . .**106** B4
Grenadiers Way GU14 . . . .**84** E3
Grendon Cl RH6 . . . .**160** F5
Grenehurst Pk RH5 . . . . . .**178** B4
Grenfell Rd CR4,SW17 . . . .**20** F2
Grennell Cl SM1 . . . .**59** D8
Grennell Rd SM1 . . . .**59** C8
Grenside Rd KT13 . . . .**53** B7
Grenville Cl Cobham KT11 . .**73** E6
Tolworth KT5 . . . .**38** C1
Grenville Ct SE19 . . . .**22** F3
Grenville Gdns GU16 . . . . .**85** E6
Grenville Mews TW12 . . . .**16** B3
Grenville Pl Ashtead KT21 . .**75** F1
Bracknell RG12 . . . .**27** C3
Grenville Rd
New Addington CR0 . . . .**63** C2
Shackleford GU8 . . . .**149** D7
Gresham Ave CR6 . . . .**81** E1
Gresham Cl RH8 . . . .**122** F7
Gresham Ct
Farnborough GU14 . . . .**105** C8
Hounslow TW3 . . . .**5** C6
3 Purley CR8 . . . .**80** A8
3 Staines TW18 . . . .**13** A3
Gresham Ho
2 Teddington TW11 . . . . . .**16** F3
3 Thames Ditton KT7 . . . . .**37** A2
Gresham Ind Est GU12 . .**105** E2
Gresham Prim Sch CR2 . .**81** A7
Gresham Rd Croydon SE25 **43** A5
Hampton TW12 . . . .**16** A2
Hounslow TW3,TW5 . . . .**5** C6
Limpsfield RH8 . . . .**122** F6
Penge BR3 . . . .**43** E7
Staines TW18 . . . .**13** A3
Gresham Way
Frimley GU16 . . . .**85** E6
Wimbledon SW19 . . . .**20** A5
Gresham Way West SW19 .**20** B5
Gresham Wlk RH10 . . . . . .**201** E3
Gressenhall Rd SW18 . . . . .**19** F8
Greta Bank KT24 . . . .**92** C1
Greville Ave CR2 . . . .**62** D1
Greville Cl
Aldershot GU11 . . . .**104** F3
Ashtead KT21 . . . .**95** E8
Guildford GU2 . . . .**108** E1
Twickenham TW1 . . . .**17** B8
Greville Ct Ashtead KT21 . .**75** E1
Fetcham KT23 . . . .**94** C2
Greville Cty Prim Sch The
KT21 . . . .**75** F2
Greville Park Ave KT21 . . .**75** E1
Greville Park Rd KT21 . . . .**75** E1
Greville Rd TW10 . . . .**6** F1
Grey Alders KT17 . . . .**77** C5
Grey Cl KT5 . . . .**52** B5
Grey Court Sch TW10 . . . . .**17** C5
Greycot Rd BR3 . . . .**24** A3
Greyfields Cl CR8 . . . .**80** B6
Greyfriars 16 SE26 . . . .**23** A5
Greyfriars Dr Ascot SL5 . . . .**29** B3
Bisley GU24 . . . .**68** A4
Greyfriars Rd GU23 . . . .**91** A3
Greyhound Cl GU12 . . . . .**105** F1
Greyhound La SW16 . . . . . .**21** D2
Greyhound Rd SM1 . . . .**59** C5
Greyhound Slip RH10 . . . .**202** D7
Greyhound Terr SW16 . . . . .**41** C8
Greylees GU7 . . . .**150** E5
Greys Ct GU11 . . . .**104** E2
Greystead Pk GU10 . . . . . .**145** E5
Greystead Rd SE23 . . . .**23** C8
Greystoke Ct RG45 . . . .**45** A4
Greystone Cl CR2 . . . .**81** C8
Greystones Cl RH1 . . . . . .**139** D7
Greystones Dr RH2 . . . . . .**118** C3
Greyswood St SW16 . . . . . .**21** B2
Greythorne Rd GU21 . . . . . .**69** A1
Greytiles TW11 . . . .**16** F2
Greywaters GU5 . . . .**152** A6
Grice Ave TN16 . . . .**83** C6
Grier Cl RH11 . . . .**200** E5
Grierson Ho SW16 . . . .**21** C4
Grierson Rd SE23 . . . .**23** D8
Grieve Cl GU10 . . . .**126** E7
Griffin Ct Ashtead KT21 . . . .**95** E8
8 Brentford TW8 . . . .**6** E8
Great Bookham KT23 . . . . . .**94** B1
Griffin Ctr The
Feltham TW14 . . . .**4** B1
Kingston u T KT1 . . . .**37** D7
Griffin Pk (Brentford FC)
TW8 . . . .**6** D8
Griffin Way
Great Bookham KT23 . . . . . .**94** A1
Sunbury TW16 . . . .**35** A7
Griffiths Cl KT4 . . . .**58** B8
Griffiths Rd SW19 . . . .**20** B1
Griffon Cl GU14 . . . .**84** D3
Griggs Mdw GU8 . . . .**192** F7
Grimwade Ave CR0 . . . .**62** A7
Grimwood Rd TW1 . . . .**16** F8
Grindall Cl CR0 . . . .**61** B6
Grindley Gdns CR0 . . . .**42** F3
Grindstone Cres GU21 . . . .**68** B1
Grindstone Handle Cnr
GU21 . . . .**68** A2
Grinstead La RH19 . . . . . .**205** B1
Grisedale Cl
Crawley RH11 . . . .**201** C4

Grisedale Cl *continued*
Sanderstead CR8 . . . .**80** E5
Grisedale Gdns CR8 . . . . . .**80** E5
Grizedale Terr SE23 . . . . . .**23** B6
Grobars Ave GU21 . . . .**69** C4
Groom Cres SW18 . . . .**20** D8
Groombridge Cl KT12 . . . . .**54** B5
Groombridge Ho SE20 . . . .**23** D1
Groombridge Way RH12 .**216** F1
Groomfield Cl SW17 . . . . . .**21** A4
Grooms The RH10 . . . .**202** D8
Grosslea SM4 . . . .**40** D4
Grosvenor Ave
Mortlake SW14 . . . .**7** E4
Richmond TW10 . . . .**6** F1
Wallington SM5 . . . .**60** A4
Grosvenor Ct
Blackwater GU17 . . . .**64** D3
Guildford GU4 . . . .**110** B4
7 Leatherhead KT22 . . . . .**95** C6
Morden SM4 . . . .**40** A5
Penge SE19 . . . .**22** F2
7 Sutton SM2 . . . .**59** C4
Teddington TW11 . . . .**17** A2
Wimbledon SW19 . . . .**19** E2
Grosvenor Gdns
Kingston u T KT2 . . . .**17** D2
Mortlake SW14 . . . .**7** E4
Wallington SM6 . . . .**60** C3
Grosvenor Hill SW19 . . . . .**19** E2
Grosvenor Ho
East Grinstead RH19 . . . . .**185** E3
1 Farnborough GU14 . . . .**105** D8
8 Guildford GU1 . . . .**130** F8
Grosvenor Mews RH2 . . .**139** B6
Grosvenor Pl
1 Oatlands Park KT13 . . . . .**53** D7
1 Woking GU21 . . . .**69** F2
Grosvenor Rd
Aldershot GU11 . . . .**105** A1
Brentford TW8 . . . .**6** D8
Croydon SE25 . . . .**43** A5
East Grinstead RH19 . . . . .**185** D1
Godalming GU7 . . . .**150** E3
Hounslow TW3,TW4 . . . .**4** F4
Langley Vale KT18 . . . .**96** E8
Richmond TW10 . . . .**6** E2
Staines TW18 . . . .**13** A1
Twickenham TW1 . . . .**17** A7
West End GU24 . . . .**68** D6
West Wickham BR4 . . . .**63** B8
Groton Rd SW18 . . . .**20** B6
Grotto Rd
Twickenham TW1 . . . .**16** F6
Weybridge KT13 . . . .**53** B7
Grove Ave Epsom KT17 . . . .**76** E6
Sutton SM1 . . . .**59** A4
Twickenham TW1 . . . .**16** F7
Grove Cl Cranleigh GU6 . . .**174** F1
Epsom KT19 . . . .**57** B1
Forest Hill SE23 . . . .**23** E7
Old Windsor SL4 . . . .**11** B8
8 Kingston u T KT1 . . . .**37** F5
Grove Cnr 1 KT23 . . . .**94** B1
Grove Cres Feltham TW13 . .**15** E4
Kingston u T KT1 . . . .**37** E6
Walton-on-T KT12 . . . .**35** B2
Grove Cross Rd GU16 . . . . .**65** D1
Grove Ct Dorking RH4 . . . .**136** A6
East Molesey KT8 . . . .**36** D4
Egham TW20 . . . .**12** A3
Forest Hill SE26 . . . .**23** E4
Hounslow TW3 . . . .**5** A3
8 Kingston u T KT1 . . . .**37** E6
New Malden KT3 . . . .**38** E6
Penge SE20 . . . .**23** B1
Sutton SM1 . . . .**59** B4
Grove End GU19 . . . . .47** F5
Grove End La KT10 . . . .**36** D1
Grove End Rd GU9 . . . . . .**146** B8
Grove Farm Ct CR4 . . . .**40** F4
Grove Gdns TW11 . . . .**17** A4
Grove Heath Ct GU23 . . . . .**91** C4
Grove Heath La GU23 . . . . .**91** D4
Grove Heath N GU23 . . . . . .**91** B5
Grove Heath Rd GU23 . . . . .**91** B4
Grove Ho 7 Epsom KT17 . . .**76** E6
Old Windsor SL4 . . . .**11** C8
6 Redhill RH1 . . . .**118** F1
Walton-on-T KT12 . . . .**35** B2
Grove House Froebel Ed Inst
SW15 . . . .**7** F1
Grove La Kingston u T KT1 . .**37** E5
Wallington SM6 . . . .**79** B5
Winkfield RG42 . . . .**8** C7
Grove Mill Pl SM5 . . . .**60** A7
Grove Park Bridge W4 . . . . .**7** C7
Grove Park Gdns W4 . . . . . .**7** C7
Grove Park Prim Sch W4 . . .**7** C8
Grove Park Rd W4 . . . .**7** C8
Grove Park Terr W4 . . . .**7** B8
Grove Pl KT13 . . . .**53** C5
Grove Pl (Caravan Pk)
SM7 . . . .**78** F7
Grove Prim Sch The
GU16 . . . .**65** E2
Grove Rd Ash GU12 . . . . . .**106** A3
Ashtead KT21 . . . .**95** F8
Barnes SW13 . . . .**7** F5
Beacon Hill GU26 . . . .**188** C6
Camberley GU15 . . . .**65** F5
Chertsey KT16 . . . .**32** F3
Cranleigh GU6 . . . .**174** F1
East Molesey KT8 . . . .**36** D5
Epsom KT17,KT18 . . . .**76** E6
Godalming GU7 . . . .**150** D3
Guildford GU1 . . . .**110** C1

Grove Rd *continued*
Horley RH6 . . . .**160** F4
Hounslow TW3 . . . .**5** A3
Hounslow,Spring Grove TW7 .**5** E6
Kingston u T KT1 . . . .**37** E5
Lingfield RH7 . . . .**164** E5
Merton SW19 . . . .**20** C1
Mitcham CR4 . . . .**41** B7
Richmond TW10 . . . .**6** F1
9 Richmond TW10 . . . .**6** F1
Shepperton TW17 . . . .**34** C3
Sutton SM1 . . . .**59** A4
Tatsfield TN16 . . . .**103** C7
Thornton Heath CR7 . . . .**42** A5
Twickenham TW2 . . . .**16** D5
Woking GU21 . . . .**69** F3
Grove Rd Prim Sch TW3 . . .**5** A3
Grove Shaw KT20 . . . .**97** E3
Grove Terr TW11 . . . .**17** A2
Grove The
Addlestone KT15 . . . .**52** B5
Aldershot GU11 . . . .**105** A1
Biggin Hill TN16 . . . .**83** E1
Caterham CR3 . . . .**100** C6
Coulsdon CR5 . . . .**79** D5
Crawley RH11 . . . .**201** C6
Egham TW20 . . . .**12** A3
Epsom KT17 . . . .**76** E6
Farnborough GU14 . . . .**85** D1
Frimley GU16 . . . .**65** D1
Horley RH6 . . . .**161** B2
Hounslow TW3 . . . .**5** E6
North Ascot SL5 . . . .**28** C8
Teddington TW11 . . . .**17** A4
1 Twickenham TW1 . . . .**6** B1
Walton-on-T KT12 . . . .**35** B2
West Wickham BR4 . . . .**63** C7
Woking GU21 . . . .**69** F3
Grove Way KT10 . . . .**36** C1
Grove Wood Hill CR5 . . . . .**79** D5
Grovebarns TW18 . . . .**13** A2
Grovebell Ind Est GU9 . . .**145** E2
Grovefields Ave GU16 . . . . .**65** D1
Grovehill Ct BR1 . . . .**24** F2
Grovehill Rd RH1 . . . .**118** F1
Groveland Ave SW16 . . . . . .**21** F1
Groveland Rd BR3 . . . .**43** F6
Groveland Way KT3 . . . .**38** D4
Grovelands
East Molesey KT8 . . . .**36** A5
Farnham GU10 . . . .**146** E7
Horley RH6 . . . .**161** B2
Kingston u T KT1 . . . .**37** D5
Grovelands Rd CR8 . . . .**79** F7
Grovelands Sch KT12 . . . . .**35** B3
Groveley Rd TW13,TW16 . . .**14** F3
Groveside KT23 . . . .**114** A8
Groveside Cl
Carshalton SM5 . . . .**59** E8
Great Bookham KT23 . . . . . .**114** A8
Grovestile Waye TW14 . . . .**14** D8
Grovewood 10 TW9 . . . .**7** A6
Grovewood Cl TW7 . . . .**5** E6
Grub St RH8 . . . .**123** C6
Guardian Ct GU8 . . . .**148** C3
Guards Ave CR3 . . . .**100** C5
Guards Ct SL5 . . . .**30** B2
Guerdon Pl RG12 . . . .**27** D2
Guernsey Cl
Crawley RH11 . . . .**201** A2
Guildford GU4 . . . .**110** A6
Heston TW5 . . . .**5** A7
Guernsey Farm Dr GU21 . . .**69** D4
Guernsey Gr SE24 . . . .**22** C8
Guildables La RH8,TN8 . .**144** F1
Guildcroft GU1 . . . .**110** A1
Guildersfield Rd SW16 . . . .**21** E1
Guildford & Godalming
By-Pass Rd
Guildford GU2,GU3 . . . .**129** E6
Shackleford GU7,GU8 . . . . .**149** F6
Guildford Ave TW13 . . . . . .**15** A6
Guildford Business Park Rd
GU2 . . . .**109** A3
Guildford Castle ★ GU1 .**130** D7
Guildford Cath ★ GU2 . .**109** B1
Guildford Coll of F Ed & H Ed
GU1 . . . .**109** C2
Guildford Cty Sch GU2 . .**130** B7
Guildford Grove Prim Sch
GU2 . . . .**108** E1
Guildford High Sch for Girls
GU1 . . . .**109** C1
Guildford Ind Est GU2 . .**109** A2
Guildford Lodge Dr
KT24 . . . .**112** F6
Guildford Mus ★ GU1 . .**130** D7
Guildford Park Ave GU2 .**130** B8
Guildford Park Rd GU2 . .**130** C8
Guildford Rd
Aldershot GU11,GU12 . . . .**126** D7
Ash GU12,GU3 . . . .**106** D3
Bagshot GU19 . . . .**47** E3
Bisley GU24 . . . .
Broadbridge Heath RH12 . .**216** B6
Chertsey KT16 . . . .**32** F1
Cranleigh GU6 . . . .**174** B6
East Horsley KT24 . . . .**112** F5
Farncombe GU7 . . . .**151** B7
Farnham GU10,GU9 . . . . . .**125** F4
Farnham, Runfold GU10 . . .**126** B4
Fetcham KT22 . . . .**94** F3
Frimley GU16 . . . .**85** F6
Great Bookham KT23,KT22 . .**94** A1
Horsham RH12 . . . .**217** A2
Lightwater GU18,GU19 . . . . .**48** B3
Loxwood RH14 . . . .**212** F4
Mytchett GU16 . . . .**86** B5

Guildford Rd *continued*
Normandy GU3 . . . . **107** B4
Ottershaw KT16 . . . . **51** C5
Pirbright GU3 . . . . **88** C2
Rowhook RH12,RH13 . . . . **215** C5
Rowly GU6 . . . . **174** B6
Rudgwick RH12 . . . . **214** C6
Shamley Green GU5 . . . . **153** A1
Slinfold RH12,RH13 . . . . . **215** C7
Thornton Heath CR0 . . . . . **42** D3
West End GU24 . . . . **67** F7
West End,Castle Green
GU21,GU24 . . . . **68** D6
Westcott RH4 . . . . **135** C6
Windlesham GU19 . . . . . . **47** F2
Woking GU22 . . . . **89** E8
Woking,Westfield GU22,
GU4 . . . . **89** D4
Wotton RH5 . . . . **134** C3
Pirbright GU24 . . . . **87** F4
Guildford Rd E GU14 . . . . **85** C1
Guildford Rd W GU14 . . **85** C1
Guildford Road Trad Est
GU9 . . . . **125** D3
Guildford Sch of Acting
GU2 . . . . **130** C7
Guildford St
Chertsey KT16 . . . . **33** A2
Staines TW18 . . . . **13** A2
Guildford Sta GU1 . . . . . **130** C8
Guildford Way SM6 . . . . . **60** E5
Guildown Ave GU2 . . . . . **130** B6
Guildown Rd GU2 . . . . . **130** C6
Guildway Hos GU7 . . . . . **150** D7
Guileshill La GU23 . . . . . **91** F5
Guilford Ave KT5 . . . . **37** F4
Guillemont Fields GU14 . **84** D5
Guillemont Jun Sch
GU14 . . . . **84** D7
Guillemont Pk GU14 . . . . **84** C6
Guillemot Path 2 RH11 **200** D5
Guinevere Rd RH11 . . . . **200** E6
Guinness Ct
Crawley RH11 . . . . **201** C2
4 Knaphill GU21 . . . . . . **68** F1
3 South Croydon CR0 . . **61** F8
Gull Cl SM6 . . . . **60** E3
Gulliver Ct CR2 . . . . **61** B3
Gumbrells Cl GU3 . . . . . **108** C5
Gumley Gdns TW7 . . . . . . **6** A4
Gumley House RC Convent
Sch TW7 . . . . **6** A4
Gun Hill GU11 . . . . **105** B3
Gun Pit Rd RH7 . . . . **164** D4
Gunnell Cl SE25 . . . . **43** A3
Gunnell Ct 8 CR4 . . . . . . **40** E8
Gunners Rd SW18 . . . . . . **20** D6
Gunning Cl RH11 . . . . . . **201** A3
Gunters Mead KT22 . . . . **74** C8
Gunton Rd SW17 . . . . **21** A2
Gurdon's La GU8 . . . . . **170** F2
Gurney Cres CR0 . . . . **41** F1
Gurney Rd SM5 . . . . **60** A6
Gurney's Cl 4 RH1 . . . . **139** F8
Guy Rd SM6 . . . . **60** D7
Guyatt Gdns CR4 . . . . **41** A7
Gwydor Rd BR3 . . . . **43** D6
Gwydyr Rd BR2 . . . . **44** F6
Gwynne Ave CR0 . . . . **43** D2
Gwynne Cl 4 W4 . . . . **7** E8
Gwynne Gdns RH19 . . . . **185** C2
Gwynne Ho 6 SW2 . . . . . **21** F7
Gwynne Rd CR3 . . . . . . **100** D4
Gwynne Vaughan Ave
GU2 . . . . **109** B5

H

H Jones Cres GU11 . . . . . **105** C3
Habershon Dr GU11 . . . . . **66** D2
Haccombe Rd SW19 . . . . . **20** C2
Hackbridge Park Gdns
SM5 . . . . **59** F8
Hackbridge Prim Sch
SM6 . . . . **41** A1
Hackbridge Rd SM6 . . . . . **60** A8
Hackbridge Sta SM6 . . . . **60** B8
Hackenden Cl RH19 . . . . **185** E3
Hackenden La RH19 . . . . **185** E3
Hacketts La GU22 . . . . . . **70** F4
Hackhurst La RH5 . . . . . **133** F4
Hackington Cres BR3 . . . . **24** A2
Haddington Rd BR1 . . . . . **24** D4
Haddon Cl
New Malden KT3 . . . . . . **38** F4
Oatlands Park KT13 . . . . **53** E6
Haddon Rd SM1 . . . . **59** B6
Hadfield Rd TW19 . . . . **2** D1
Hadleigh Cl SW20 . . . . . . **39** F7
Hadleigh Dr SM2 . . . . **59** B2
Hadleigh Gdns GU16 . . . . **85** E6
Hadley Cl SL3 . . . . **1** E6
Hadley Pl KT13 . . . . **53** A3
Hadley Rd CR4 . . . . **41** D5
Hadley Wood Rise CR8 . . **80** B5
Hadleys GU10 . . . . **145** E3
Hadlow Pl SE19 . . . . **23** A1
Hadmans Cl RH12 . . . . . **217** C1
Hadrian Ct TW19 . . . . **13** E8
Hadrian Ct 1 SM2 . . . . . . **59** B3
Hadrian Way
Stanwell TW19 . . . . **13** D8
Stanwell TW19 . . . . **13** E8
Hafer Rd SW11 . . . . **20** C2
Hafton Rd SE6 . . . . **24** E6
Haggard Rd TW1 . . . . **17** B8

Haig Pl SM4 . . . . **40** A3
Biggin Hill TN16 . . . . **83** E2
Sandhurst GU15 . . . . **64** F6
Haigh Cres RH1 . . . . **140** B7
Hailes Cl SW19 . . . . **20** C2
Hailey Pl GU6 . . . . **174** F4
Hailsham Ave SW2 . . . . . . **21** F6
Hailsham Cl
Sandhurst GU47 . . . . . . **45** D1
Surbiton KT6 . . . . **37** D2
Hailsham Rd SW17 . . . . . **21** A2
Haines Ct KT13 . . . . **53** D5
Haines Wlk SM4 . . . . **40** B2
Haining Gdns GU16 . . . . . **86** A3
Hainthorpe Rd SE27 . . . . . **22** B4
Halcyon Ct TW18 . . . . **33** B7
Haldane Pl SW18 . . . . **20** B7
Hale End RG12 . . . . **27** F5
Hale Ends GU22 . . . . **89** B6
Hale House La GU10 . . . **168** B2
Hale Pit Rd KT23 . . . . **94** C1
Hale Pl GU9 . . . . **125** E5
Hale Rd GU9 . . . . **125** D5
Hale Rdbt GU9 . . . . **125** E5
Hale Reeds GU9 . . . . . . **125** E6
Hale Sch GU9 . . . . **125** B7
Hale St TW18 . . . . **12** E4
Hale Way GU16 . . . . **85** D8
Halebourne La GU24 . . . . **49** A2
Hales Ct 6 TW11 . . . . **17** A3
Hales Field GU27 . . . . . . **208** C6
Hales Ho 3 SW12 . . . . . . **21** B8
Hales Oak KT23 . . . . **94** C1
Halesowen Rd SM4 . . . . . **40** B2
Haleswood RH12 . . . . . . **216** F3
Halesworth Rd SE6 . . . . . **24** F8
Half Acre TW8 . . . . **6** D8
Half Acre Mews TW8 . . . . . **6** D8
Half Moon Hill GU27 . . . **208** C6
Half Moon St GU19 . . . . . **47** E3
Half Way Cotts GU10 . . . **124** C3
Halfacres RH10 . . . . **201** E7
Halford Ct KT9 . . . . **56** E3
Halford Rd TW10 . . . . **6** E2
Halfpenny Cl GU4 . . . . . . **131** D3
Halfpenny Cross KT11 . . . **73** A2
Halfpenny Ct 2 SL5 . . . . . **30** B2
Halfpenny La
Guildford GU4 . . . . **131** C5
Sunningdale SL5 . . . . . . **30** A2
Halfway Gn KT12 . . . . **54** B7
Halfway La GU7 . . . . **150** B4
Haliburton Rd TW1,TW7 . . . **6** A3
Halifax Cl Crawley RH10 **182** E1
Farnborough GU14 . . . . . **84** F3
Teddington TW11 . . . . **16** E2
Halifax St SE26 . . . . **23** B5
Halimote Rd GU11 . . . . . **105** A1
Haling Down Pas CR8 . . . **61** F2
Haling Gr CR2 . . . . **61** C3
Haling Manor High Sch
CR2 . . . . **61** B3
Haling Manor High Sch
(Pannuells Wing) CR2 . . **61** B3
Haling Park Gdns CR2 . . . **61** B4
Haling Park Rd CR2 . . . . . **61** C4
Haling Rd CR2 . . . . **61** D4
Hall Cl Camberley GU15 . . **65** F6
Farncombe GU7 . . . . . . **150** E7
Hall Ct TW11 . . . . **16** F3
Hall Dene Cl GU1 . . . . . . **110** C2
Hall Dr SE26 . . . . **23** C3
Hall Farm Dr TW2 . . . . . . **16** D8
Hall Grove Sch GU19 . . . . **48** A5
Hall Hill RH8 . . . . **122** D4
Hall La UB3 . . . . **3** D7
Hall Pl GU21 . . . . **70** A3
Hall Place Dr KT13 . . . . . . **53** E5
Hall Rd Bramley GU5 . . . **151** F6
Farnborough GU14 . . . . . **85** B2
Isleworth TW7 . . . . **5** D2
Wallington SM6 . . . . **60** B2
Hall Sch Wimbledon
Roehampton SW15 . . . . . **19** A5
Wimbledon SW20 . . . . . . **39** D8
Hall Way CR8 . . . . **80** B6
Hallam Rd GU7 . . . . **150** F5
Halland Cl RH10 . . . . **202** A7
Hallane Ho SE27 . . . . **22** C3
Halley Cl RH11 . . . . **201** B1
Halley's App GU21 . . . . . . **69** A1
Halley's Ct 1 GU21 . . . . . **69** A1
Halley's Wlk KT15 . . . . . . **52** C2
Hallgrove Bottom GU19 . . **47** F5
Halliards The KT12 . . . . . . **35** A3
Halliford Cl TW17 . . . . **34** E6
Halliford Rd
Sunbury TW16 . . . . **35** A5
Upper Halliford TW16,TW17 **34** F5
Halliford Sch TW17 . . . . . **34** C2
Hallington Cl GU21 . . . . . . **69** B2
Hallmark Cl GU47 . . . . . . **64** E8
Hallmead Rd SM1 . . . . . . **59** B7
Hallowell Ave CR0 . . . . . . **60** E6
Hallowell Cl CR4 . . . . **41** A6
Hallowfield Way CR4 . . . . **40** E6
Halls Farm Cl GU21 . . . . . **68** D2
Hallsland RH10 . . . . **204** C8
Halnaker Wlk 9 RH11 . . **200** F3
Halsford Croft RH19 . . . . **185** B3
Halsford Gn RH19 . . . . . **185** B3
Halsford La RH19 . . . . . . **185** C3
Halsford Park Prim Sch
RH19 . . . . **185** C2
Halsford Park Rd RH19 . **185** C2

Halstead Cl CR0,CR9 . . . . **61** C7
Halstead Sch SE19 . . . . . . **70** A4
Halters End GU26 . . . . . . **188** A3
Ham Cl TW10 . . . . **17** C5
Ham Comm TW10 . . . . **17** D5
Ham Farm Rd KT2,TW10 . . **17** E4
Ham Gate Ave
Richmond TW10 . . . . **17** E4
Richmond, Richmond Park
TW10 . . . . **18** A4
Ham Ho ★ TW10 . . . . **17** D3
Ham La Elstead GU8 . . . **148** E4
Englefield Green TW20 . . . **11** B4
Ham Ridings TW10 . . . . . . **17** F3
Ham St TW10 . . . . **17** C5
Ham The TW8 . . . . **6** C7
Ham View CR0 . . . . **43** E3
Hamble Ave GU17 . . . . **64** D5
Hamble Cl GU21 . . . . **69** A2
Hamble Ct KT1 . . . . **17** D1
Hamble Wlk GU21 . . . . **69** A2
Hambledon Ct RG12 . . . . . **27** E5
Hambledon Ct 9 SM6 . . . . **60** B4
Hambledon Gdns SE25 . . . **42** F6
Hambledon Hill KT18 . . . . **76** C3
Hambledon Rd 2 KT2 . . . . **18** B2
Hambledon Pk GU8 . . . . **171** B1
Hambledon Pl
Dulwich SE21 . . . . **22** F7
Little Bookham KT23 . . . . **94** A4
Hambledon Rd
Caterham CR3 . . . . **100** D4
Hydestile GU8,GU7 . . . . **171** D5
Wandsworth SW18 . . . . . **19** F8
Hambledon Vale KT18 . . . **76** C3
Hambleton Cl
Frimley GU16 . . . . **66** B3
North Cheam KT4 . . . . . . **58** C8
Hambleton Ct RH11 . . . . **201** C4
Hambleton Hill RH11 . . . **201** C4
Hambridge Way SW2 . . . . **22** A8
Hambro Rd SW16 . . . . **21** D3
Hambrook Rd SE25 . . . . . . **43** B6
Hamers Ho 19 SW2 . . . . . . **22** A8
Hamesmoor Rd GU16 . . . . **85** F4
Hamesmoor Way GU16 . . . **85** F4
Hamfield Cl RH8 . . . . **122** C8
Hamhaugh Island TW17 . . **53** A8
Hamilton Ave Cheam SM3 . **58** E8
Cobham KT11 . . . . **73** A6
Pyrford GU22 . . . . **70** E3
Tolworth KT6,SM3 . . . . . **57** A8
Hamilton Cl Ashford TW13 **14** F3
Bagshot GU19 . . . . **47** E3
Chertsey KT16 . . . . **32** F1
Epsom KT19 . . . . **76** C7
Guildford GU2 . . . . **109** A6
Hamilton Cres TW3 . . . . **5** B2
Hamilton Ct Catford SE6 . . **24** F7
Cobham KT11 . . . . **73** A6
Croydon CR0 . . . . **43** A1
Farnborough GU17 . . . . . . **64** E1
Great Bookham KT23 . . . . **94** B2
Hamilton Dr
Guildford GU2 . . . . **109** A6
Sunningdale SL5 . . . . **29** E2
Hamilton Gordon Ct
GU1 . . . . **109** C2
Hamilton Ho
5 Chiswick W4 . . . . **7** E8
11 Richmond TW9 . . . . . . **7** A2
Hamilton Mews KT13 . . . . **53** A6
Hamilton Par TW13 . . . . . . **15** A4
Hamilton Pl
Aldershot GU11 . . . . **104** F1
Guildford GU2 . . . . **109** A6
Kingswood KT20 . . . . **97** F4
Sunbury TW16 . . . . **15** B1
Hamilton Rd Brentford TW8 **6** D8
Feltham TW13 . . . . **14** F4
Horsham RH12 . . . . **217** B3
Merton SW19 . . . . **20** B1
South Norwood CR7 . . . . . **42** D6
Twickenham TW2 . . . . **16** E7
West Norwood SE27 . . . . . **22** D4
Hamilton Road Ind Est
SE27 . . . . **22** D4
Hamilton Road Mews 1
SW19 . . . . **20** B1
Hamilton Way SM6 . . . . . . **60** D2
Hamlash Cotts GU10 . . . **146** C2
Hamlash La GU10 . . . . . . **146** C1
Hamlet Rd SE19 . . . . **23** A1
Hamlet St RG42 . . . . **27** E8
Hamley Gr GU17 . . . . **64** E2
Hamlyn Gdns SE19 . . . . . . **22** E1
Hamm Court Est KT13 . . . . **52** F8
Hamm Moor La KT15 . . . . **52** E6
Hammelton Ct 4 BR1 . . . . **44** F8
Hammelton Rd 5 BR1 . . . . **44** F8
Hammer Hill GU27 . . . . . **207** C4
Hammer La
Grayshott GU10,GU26 . . **187** E6
Haslemere GU27,GU30 . **207** A6
Haslemere,Hammer GU27 **207** C5
Haslemere,Nutcombe
GU26,GU27 . . . . **207** C8
Hammer Vale GU27 . . . . **207** B6
Hammerfield Dr RH5 . . . **133** F3
Hammerpond Rd RH13 . . **217** F1
Hammersley Rd GU11 . . . **105** C7
Hammerwood Copse
GU27 . . . . **207** D5
Hammerwood Rd RH19 . . **206** E6
Hammond Ave CR4 . . . . . . **41** B7
Hammond Cl
Beckenham BR3 . . . . **24** B2
Hampton TW12 . . . . **36** A8

Hammond Cl *continued*
Woking GU21 . . . . **69** C4
Hammond Com Jun Sch
GU18 . . . . **48** A1
Hammond Rd GU21 . . . . . . **69** C4
Hammond Way GU18 . . . . . **48** B1
Hamond Cl CR2 . . . . **61** B2
Hampden Ave BR3 . . . . . . **43** E7
Hampden Cl RH10 . . . . . **182** C1
Hampden Rd
Beckenham BR3 . . . . **43** E7
Kingston u T KT1 . . . . . . **38** A6
Hamper's La RH13 . . . . . **218** A2
Hampers Ct RH13 . . . . . **217** D2
Hampshire Cl GU12 . . . . **126** D7
Hampshire Ct
Addlestone KT15 . . . . **52** C5
Barnes SW13 . . . . **7** F5
Hampshire Rd GU15 . . . . . **65** F8
Hampstead La RH4 . . . . . **135** F6
Hampstead Rd RH4 . . . . . **136** A6
Hampton Cl SW20 . . . . **19** C1
Hampton Com Coll TW12 **16** A3
Hampton Court Ave KT8 . . **36** E3
Hampton Court Cres KT8 **36** E5
Hampton Court Pal ★
KT8 . . . . **36** F6
Hampton Court Par KT8 . . **36** E5
Hampton Court Rd KT1,
KT8 . . . . **37** B6
Hampton Court Sta KT8 . . **36** E5
Hampton Court Way
KT10,KT7,KT8 . . . . **36** E3
Hampton Farm Ind Est
TW13 . . . . **15** E3
Hampton Gr KT17 . . . . **76** F8
Hampton Hill Bsns Pk
TW12 . . . . **16** C3
Hampton Hill Jun Sch
TW12 . . . . **16** B3
Hampton Inf Sch TW12 . . . **16** A1
Hampton Jun Sch TW12 . . **36** A8
Hampton La TW13 . . . . **15** E4
Hampton Lodge RH6 . . . . **161** A2
Hampton Rd Hale GU9 . . **125** B6
North Cheam KT4 . . . . . . **58** B8
Redhill RH1 . . . . **139** F4
Teddington TW11,TW12 . . . **16** D3
Thornton Heath CR0 . . . . . **42** C3
Twickenham TW2 . . . . **16** D5
Hampton Rd E TW13 . . . . . **15** F5
Hampton Rd W TW13 . . . . **15** E5
Hampton Road Ind Pk
CR0 . . . . **42** C3
Hampton Sch TW12 . . . . . **16** A3
Hampton Sta TW12 . . . . . . **36** A8
Hampton Terr GU26 . . . . **188** C6
Hampton Way RH19 . . . . **205** F7
Hampton Wick Inf Sch
KT1 . . . . **17** D1
Hampton Wick Sta KT1 . . . **37** C8
Hamsey Green CR6 . . . . . . **81** C3
Hamsey Green Inf Sch
CR6 . . . . **81** B3
Hamsey Green Jun Sch
CR6 . . . . **81** B3
Hamsey Way CR2 . . . . **81** B4
Hanbury Dr TN16 . . . . **83** B6
Hanbury Path GU21 . . . . . . **70** D5
Hanbury Rd RH11 . . . . . . **200** B5
Hanbury Way GU15 . . . . . . **65** C3
Hancock Rd SE19 . . . . **22** D2
Hancocks Mount SL5 . . . . **29** D3
Hancombe Rd GU47 . . . . . **45** A1
Handcroft Rd CR0 . . . . **42** B1
Handel Ho TW2 . . . . **5** D1
Handley Page Rd SM6 . . . . **60** F3
Handpost Cnr RG40 . . . . . **25** A1
Handside Cl KT4 . . . . **39** D1
Handsworth Ho 8
RH10 . . . . **201** D5
Hanford Cl SW18 . . . . **20** A7
Hanger Hill KT13 . . . . **53** B5
Hanley Pl BR3 . . . . **24** A1
Hannah Cl BR3 . . . . **44** C6
Hannah Ct SW19 . . . . **19** D1
Hannah Peschar Gall & Gdn ★
RH5 . . . . **177** A2
Hannay Wlk SW16 . . . . **21** D6
Hannen Rd SE27 . . . . **22** B5
Hannibal Rd TW19 . . . . . . **13** E8
Hannibal Way CR0 . . . . . . **60** F4
Hanning Lodge TW3 . . . . . . **5** C3
Hanover Ave TW13 . . . . . . **15** A6
Hanover Cl Cheam SM3 . . **58** F6
Crawley RH10 . . . . **201** F3
Englefield Green TW20 . . . **11** B2
Frimley GU16 . . . . **65** E1
Merstham RH1 . . . . **119** C2
Richmond TW9 . . . . **7** A7
Hanover Ct Dorking RH4 . **135** F7
Guildford GU1 . . . . **109** D3
1 Horsham RH13 . . . . . **217** F3
2 Penge SE19 . . . . **23** A1
4 Woking GU22 . . . . **89** B4
Hanover Gdns
Bracknell RG12 . . . . **26** F2
Farnborough GU14 . . . . . **84** E6
Hanover Ho 6 KT6 . . . . . . **38** A1
Hanover Rd SW19 . . . . **20** C1
Hanover St CR0,CR9 . . . . . **61** B7
Hanover Terr TW7 . . . . **6** A6
Hanover Wlk KT13 . . . . . . **53** E7
Hansard Ct KT8 . . . . **97** D8
Hansler Gr KT8 . . . . **36** D5
Hanson Cl Balham SW12 . . **21** B8
Beckenham BR3 . . . . **24** B2
Camberley GU15 . . . . **66** B7

Hanson Cl *continued*
Guildford GU1 . . . . **109** F4
Mortlake SW14 . . . . **7** C4
Hanworth Cl RG12 . . . . . . **27** C5
Hanworth La KT16 . . . . **32** F1
Hanworth Rd
Bracknell RG12 . . . . **27** A2
Feltham TW13 . . . . **15** B7
Hampton TW12 . . . . **16** A3
Hounslow TW3,TW4 . . . . . . **5** B2
Redhill RH1 . . . . **139** F4
Sunbury TW16 . . . . **15** A1
Twickenham TW4 . . . . **15** F8
Hanworth Terr TW3 . . . . **5** B3
Hanworth Trad Est
Chertsey KT16 . . . . **32** F1
Feltham TW13 . . . . **15** E5
Harberson Rd SW12 . . . . . **21** B7
Harbin Ho 5 SW2 . . . . **22** A7
Harbledown Rd CR2 . . . . . **81** A8
Harborough Rd SW16 . . . . **21** F4
Harbour Cl GU14 . . . . **85** A8
Harbourfield Rd SM7 . . . . **78** B4
Harbridge Ave SW15 . . . . . **19** A8
Harbury Rd SM5 . . . . **59** E3
Harcourt Ave SM6 . . . . **60** B6
Harcourt Cl Egham TW20 . . **12** C2
Isleworth TW7 . . . . **6** A4
Harcourt Field SM6 . . . . . . **60** B6
Harcourt Lodge 2 SM6 . . **60** B6
Harcourt Rd
Bracknell RG12 . . . . **27** B4
Camberley GU15 . . . . **65** B5
Merton SW19 . . . . **20** A1
Thornton Heath CR7 . . . . . **42** A3
Wallington SM6 . . . . **60** B6
Harcourt Way RH9 . . . . . **142** E6
Hardcastle Cl SE25 . . . . . . **43** A3
Hardcourts Cl BR4 . . . . . . **63** B7
Hardel Rise SW2 . . . . **22** B7
Hardel Wlk SW2 . . . . **22** A8
Hardell Cl TW20 . . . . **12** A3
Harden Farm Cl CR5 . . . . . **99** C6
Hardham Cl RH11 . . . . . . **201** A4
Harding Cl
Kingston u T KT2 . . . . . . **37** F8
South Croydon CR0 . . . . . **61** F7
Harding Ct SE25 . . . . **42** F7
Harding Ho SM6 . . . . **60** C2
Harding Pl SE23 . . . . **23** E8
Harding Rd KT18 . . . . **96** E8
Hardings La SE20 . . . . **23** D2
Hardman Rd KT2 . . . . **37** E7
Hardwell Way RG12 . . . . . **27** E5
Hardwick Cl KT22 . . . . **74** C4
Hardwick La KT16 . . . . . . **32** D1
Hardwick Rd RH1 . . . . . . **139** D7
Hardwicke Ave TW5 . . . . . . **5** A6
Hardwicke Rd
Reigate RH2 . . . . **118** A2
Richmond TW10 . . . . **17** C4
Hardy Cl Crawley RH10 . . **202** C7
Dorking RH5 . . . . **136** B3
Horley RH6 . . . . **160** E3
Horsham RH12 . . . . **217** B4
Hardy Gn RG45 . . . . **45** B4
Hardy Rd SW19 . . . . **20** B1
Hardys Cl KT8 . . . . **36** E5
Hare Hill KT15 . . . . **51** F4
Hare Hill Cl GU22 . . . . **71** A4
Hare La Claygate KT10 . . . **55** E4
Crawley RH11 . . . . **201** B8
Farncombe GU7 . . . . **150** F6
Horne RH7 . . . . **163** D5
Harebell Hill KT11 . . . . **73** E5
Harecroft Dorking RH4 . . **136** C4
Fetcham KT23 . . . . **94** C3
Haredon Cl SE23 . . . . **23** D8
Harefield KT10 . . . . **55** E7
Harefield Ave SM2 . . . . . . **58** E2
Harefield Rd SW16 . . . . . . **21** F1
Harelands Cl GU21 . . . . . . **69** C2
Harelands La GU21 . . . . . . **69** C2
Harendon KT20 . . . . **97** D6
Hares Bank CR0 . . . . **63** D1
Harestone Dr CR3 . . . . . . **100** F2
Harestone Hill CR3 . . . . . **100** F2
Harestone La CR3 . . . . . . **100** E2
Harestone Valley Rd
CR3 . . . . **100** F2
Harewood Cl
Crawley RH10 . . . . **182** A1
Reigate RH2 . . . . **118** C4
Harewood Gdns CR2 . . . . . **81** C4
Harewood Rd
Guildford GU4 . . . . **110** C4
Hounslow TW7 . . . . **5** F6
Mitcham SW19 . . . . **20** E2
South Croydon CR0 . . . . . **61** E4
Harfield Rd TW16 . . . . **35** D7
Harkness Cl KT17 . . . . **77** C3
Harland Ave CR0 . . . . **62** A7
Harlech Ct 1 SE23 . . . . . . **23** C7
Harlech Gdns TW5 . . . . **4** C7
Harlech Rd GU17 . . . . **64** D4
Harlequin Ave TW8 . . . . **6** A8
Harlequin Cl TW7 . . . . **5** E2
Harlequin Rd TW11 . . . . . . **17** B1
Harlequins RFC TW2 . . . . **16** E8
Harlington Cl UB3 . . . . **3** D6
Harlington Cnr UB3 . . . . **3** D6
Harlington Rd E TW13,
TW14 . . . . **15** C7
Harlington Rd W TW14 . . . . **4** B1
Harlow Ct 4 RH2 . . . . **118** D1

Harman Pl CR8 80 B8
Harmans Dr RH19 186 B1
Harmans Mead RH19 186 B1
Harmans Water Prim Sch
RG12 27 E4
Harmans Water Rd RG12 27 D4
Harmar Cl RG40 25 E6
Harmes Way GU14 105 D7
Harmondsworth La UB7 2 E8
Harmondsworth Prim Sch
UB7 2 D8
Harmony Cl
Crawley RH11 200 E4
Wallington SM6 60 E2
Harms Gr GU4 110 C4
Harold Ct TW11 16 E3
Harold Rd Carshalton SM1 59 D6
Crawley RH10 202 E5
South Norwood SE19 22 D1
Haroldslea RH6 161 E2
Haroldslea Cl RH6 161 C1
Haroldslea Dr RH6 161 D1
Haron Ct 3 CR4 40 E8
Harpenden Rd SE27 22 B6
Harper Dr RH10 202 C2
Harper's Rd GU12 106 C2
Harpesford Ave GU25 31 C4
Harps Oak La RH1 99 A2
Harpurs KT20 97 D5
Harrier Cl GU6 174 E4
Harrier Ct RH10 182 D1
Harrier Ho 10 KT2 37 E8
Harrier Rd GU14 84 C1
Harriet Gdns CR0 62 A8
Harriet Tubman Cl SW2 22 A8
Harrington Cl Leigh RH2 138 A2
Wallington CR0 60 E8
Harrington Ct 7 CR0 61 D8
Harrington Rd SE25 43 B5
Harrington Road Sta
SE25 43 C6
Harriotts Cl KT22 95 C7
Harriotts La KT21,KT22 95 C8
Harris City Tech Coll
SE19 42 F8
Harris Cl Crawley RH11 201 B3
Hounslow TW5 5 A6
Harris Lodge SE6 24 C7
Harris Way TW16 34 E8
Harrison Cl RH2 139 B8
Harrison Ct TW17 34 B4
Harrison's Rise CR0,CR9 61 B7
Harrodian Sch SW13 7 F7
Harrogate Ct 2 SE26 23 A5
Harrow Bottom Rd GU25 31 F3
Harrow Cl Chertsey KT15 52 B8
Chessington KT9 56 D3
Dorking RH4 136 A6
Harrow Gate Gdns RH4 136 A5
Harrow Gdns CR6 81 F3
Harrow La GU7 150 E7
Harrow Lodge SM2 59 D4
Harrow Rd Ashford TW15 14 A6
Carshalton SM5 59 E4
Warlingham CR6 81 F3
Harrow Rd E RH4 136 B6
Harrow Rd W RH4 136 A6
Harrow Way TW17 34 C7
Harrowdene GU6 174 E4
Harrowdene Ct SW19 19 E3
Harrowdene Gdns TW11 17 A1
Harrowlands Pk RH4 136 B6
Harrowsley Ct RH6 161 B4
Hart Cl Bletchingley RH1 120 E2
Farnborough GU14 84 E8
Hart Dene Ct GU19 47 E3
Hart Dyke Cl RG41 25 B2
Hart Gdns RH4 136 B8
Hart Ho SW2 22 A7
Hart Rd Byfleet KT14 71 E6
Dorking RH4 136 B8
Hart Sq SM4 40 A3
Hart The GU9 125 B2
Hart's La RH9 142 D7
Harte Rd TW3 4 F5
Hartfield Cres SW19 19 F1
Hartfield Gr SE20 43 C8
Hartfield Rd
Chessington KT9 56 D5
Forest Row RH18 206 F2
Merton SW19 20 A1
Hartford Rd KT19 57 B4
Hartford Rise GU15 65 D6
Hartham Cl TW7 6 A6
Hartham Rd TW7 6 A6
Harting Ct RH11 200 F3
Hartington Ct W4 7 B7
Hartington Pl RH2 118 A3
Hartington Rd Chiswick W4 7 C6
Twickenham TW1 6 B1
Hartland Cl KT15 52 C2
Hartland Pl GU14 85 A7
Hartland Rd
Addlestone KT15 52 A3
Cheam SM4 40 B2
Hampton TW12 16 B4
Isleworth TW7 6 A4
Hartland Way
Croydon CR0 62 E8
Morden SM4 39 F2
Hartlands The TW5 4 B8
Hartley Cl GU17 64 B5
Hartley Ct 2 CR4 40 E8
Hartley Down CR5,CR8 79 F5
Hartley Farm CR8 79 F4
Hartley Hill CR8 79 F4
Hartley Old Rd CR8 79 F5
Hartley Rd CR0 42 C2
Hartley Way CR8 79 F4
Harts Gdns GU2 109 B4
Harts Leap Cl GU47 45 B1
Harts Leap Rd GU47 64 A8
Harts Yd
14 Farnham GU9 125 B2
Godalming GU7 150 E4
Hartscroft CR0 62 E2
Hartsgrove GU8 191 B5
Hartshill GU2 108 D2
Hartshill Wlk GU21 69 B3
Hartspiece Rd RH1 140 B7
Hartswood RH5 136 D4
Hartswood Ave RH2 139 A5
Hartswood Ho 10 SW2 21 E7
Harvard Hill W4 7 B8
Harvard Rd Hounslow TW7 5 E6
Sandhurst GU47 45 E1
Harvest Bank Rd BR4 63 F7
Harvest Ct Beckenham BR3 24 A1
Littleton TW17 34 A5
Harvest Hill
East Grinstead RH19 205 E8
Godalming GU7 150 D4
Harvest La KT7 37 A3
Harvest Rd
Crawley RH10 202 C4
Englefield Green TW20 11 D2
Feltham TW13 15 A5
Harvest Ride RG12,RG42,
SL5 28 A8
Harvester Rd KT19 57 D1
Harvesters RH12 217 D5
Harvesters Cl TW7 5 D2
Harvestside RH6 161 C4
Harvey Cl RH11 201 A1
Harvey Ct KT19 57 B2
Harvey Dr TW12 36 A8
Harvey Lodge 8 GU1 130 E8
Harvey Rd
Farnborough GU14 84 C5
Guildford GU1 130 E8
Twickenham TW4 15 F8
Walton-on-T KT12 35 A2
Harwarden Cl RH10 204 C8
Harwood Ave CR4 40 E6
Harwood Gdns SL4 11 B8
Harwood Pk RH1 161 A8
Harwood Rd RH12,RH13 218 A3
Harwoods Cl 3 RH19 205 F7
Harwoods La RH19 205 F7
Hascombe Ct RH11 201 A5
Hascombe Ho 11 SW15 19 B7
Haseley End SE23 23 C8
Haseltine Prim Sch SE6 23 F4
Haseltine Rd SE26 23 F4
Haslam Ave SM3,SM4 39 E1
Hasle Dr GU27 208 B6
Haslemere & District Hospl
GU27 208 D7
Haslemere & Heathrow Est
The TW4 4 B4
Haslemere Ave
Cranford TW5 4 C5
Mitcham CR4,SW19 40 D7
Wimbledon SW18 20 B6
Haslemere Cl
Frimley GU16 66 C3
Hampton TW12 15 F3
Wallington SM6 60 E5
Haslemere Educational
Mus★ GU27 208 D7
Haslemere Fst Sch CR4 40 D7
Haslemere Ind Est
Feltham TW14 4 A2
Wimbledon SW18 20 B6
Haslemere Prep Sch
GU27 208 D5
Haslemere Rd
Brook GU8 170 C5
Kingsley Green GU27 208 B1
Thornton Heath CR7 42 B4
Haslemere Sta GU27 208 B6
Haslett Ave E RH10 202 A6
Haslett Ave W RH10 201 D5
Haslett Rd TW17 34 E7
Hassall Ct GU22 90 A6
Hassocks Cl SE23,SE26 23 B5
Hassocks Ct 3 RH11 200 F3
Hassocks Rd SW16 41 D8
Haste Hill GU27 208 D5
Hastings Cl GU16 86 A7
Hastings Ct SM1 59 D6
Hastings Dr KT6 37 C3
Hastings Pl 1 CR0 42 F1
Hastings Rd
Crawley RH10 202 C6
Croydon CR0 42 F1
Hatch Cl Addlestone KT15 52 B7
Alfold Crossways GU6 194 A3
Hatch End
Forest Row RH18 206 F2
Windlesham GU20 48 C4
Hatch Gdns KT20 97 D7
Hatch Hill GU27 208 B1
Hatch La
Harmondsworth UB7 2 D7
Kingsley Green GU27 208 B2
Ockham GU23 72 B1
Ockham GU23 92 B7
South Nutfield RH1 140 F3
Wormley GU8 190 D8
Hatch Pl TW10 17 F3
Hatch Rd SW16 41 E7
Hatch Ride RG45 45 B7
Hatch Ride Prim Sch
RG45 45 B7
Hatches The
Farnham GU9 145 F8
Frimley GU16 85 F6
Hatchet La SL4,SL5 9 B5
Hatchett Rd TW14 14 C7
Hatchetts Dr GU27 207 D7
Hatchgate RH6 160 F2
Hatchgate Copse RG12 26 E3
Hatching The GU3 89 C1
Hatchlands Capel RH5 178 C5
Horsham RH12 218 A7
Hatchlands Pk★ GU4 111 F5
Hatchlands Rd RH1 118 E1
Hatfield Cl Belmont SM2 59 B2
Mitcham CR4 40 D5
West Byfleet KT14 71 B7
Hatfield Fst Sch SM4 39 E3
Hatfield Gdns GU14 85 E3
Hatfield Ho
4 Ash Vale GU12 105 F5
16 Kingston u T KT6 37 E4
Hatfield Mead SM4 40 A4
Hatfield Rd KT21 95 F8
Hatfield Wlk RH11 200 E2
Hathaway Ct 10 RH1 119 A2
Hathaway Rd CR0 42 B2
Hatherleigh Cl
Chessington KT9 56 D5
Morden SM4 40 A5
Hatherleigh Ho SM4 40 A5
Hatherley Rd TW9 6 F6
Hatherop Rd TW12 15 F1
Hathersham Cl RH6 162 A4
Hathersham La RH1,RH6 161 F6
Hatherwood KT21 95 E6
Hatton Cross Rdbt TW6 3 F4
Hatton Cross Sta TW6 3 F3
Hatton Gdns CR4 40 F4
Hatton Gn TW14 4 A3
Hatton Hill GU20 48 C5
Hatton Rd
East Bedfont TW14 14 D8
Hatton TW14,TW6 3 E2
Thornton Heath CR0 42 A1
Hatton Rd N TW6 3 D6
Haughton Ho GU27 208 B6
Havana Rd SW18,SW19 20 A6
Havelock Cotts GU22 89 D5
Havelock Hall 8 CR0 42 F1
Havelock Ho
4 Croydon CR0 42 F1
Farnborough GU14 105 C8
Forest Hill SE23 23 C7
Havelock Rd Croydon CR0 61 F8
Wimbledon SW19 20 C3
Wokingham RG41 25 A6
Havelock St RG41 25 A6
Havelock Wlk SE23 23 C6
Haven Cl SW19 19 D5
Haven Ct BR3 44 C7
Haven Gdns RH10 184 B1
Haven Rd Ashford TW15 14 B5
Rudgwick RH12,RH14 214 D3
Haven The Ashford TW16 15 A1
Richmond TW9 7 A4
Haven Way GU9 125 D4
Havenbury Est 1 RH4 136 A8
Havenbury Ind Est RH4 135 F8
Havengate RH12 217 F5
Haverfield Gdns TW9 7 A7
Haverhill Rd SW12 21 C7
Havers Ave KT12 54 D5
Haversham Cl
Crawley RH10 201 F6
Twickenham TW1 6 D1
Haversham Dr RG12 27 B3
Haversham Ho RH6 161 B5
Havisham Pl SW16 22 B1
Hawarden Gr SE24 22 C8
Hawarden Rd CR3 100 C6
Hawes Down Schs BR4 44 D1
Hawes La
West Wickham BR4 44 D1
West Wickham BR4 63 E8
Hawes Rd KT20 97 D7
Haweswater Ho TW1 5 F2
Hawk La RG12 27 D5
Hawk's Hill KT22 94 F4
Hawke Rd SE19 22 E2
Hawkedale Inf Sch TW16 34 F6
Hawker Ct 14 KT2 18 A1
Hawker Rd GU12 105 F5
Hawkes Cl RG41 25 A7
Hawkes Leap GU20 48 B6
Hawkes Rd
East Bedfont TW14 15 A8
Mitcham CR4 40 F8
Hawkes Worth Dr GU19 47 E1
Hawkesbourne Rd RH12 217 F5
Hawkesfield Rd SE23,SE6 23 F6
Hawkesley Cl TW1 17 A4
Hawkesmoor Rd RH11 200 E4
Hawkewood Rd TW16 35 A6
Hawkfield Ct TW7 5 E5
Hawkhirst Rd CR8 80 E3
Hawkhurst KT11 74 A5
Hawkhurst Gdns KT9 56 E6
Hawkhurst Rd SW16 41 D8
Hawkhurst Way
New Malden KT3 38 D4
West Wickham BR4 63 B8
Hawkhurst Wlk RH10 202 B4
Hawkins Cl RG12 28 A7
Hawkins Rd
Crawley RH10 201 E4
Teddington TW11 17 B2
Hawkins Way Catford SE6 24 A3
Wokingham RG40 25 E6
Hawkley Gdns SE27 22 B6
Hawkridge RH12 195 E1
Hawkridge Ct RG12 27 E6
Hawks Hill Cl KT22 94 F4
Hawks Hill Ct KT22 95 A4
Hawks Rd KT1 37 F7
Hawksbrook La BR3 44 C3
Hawkshead Cl BR1 24 E1
Hawkshill Cl KT10 55 A4
Hawkshill Way KT10 55 A4
Hawksmoore Dr RH5 157 C4
Hawksview KT11 73 F6
Hawksway TW18 12 F5
Hawkswell Cl GU21 68 F2
Hawkswell Wlk GU21 68 F3
Hawkswood Ave GU16 65 F2
Hawkswood Ho RG42 26 E8
Hawkwood Dell KT23 94 A1
Hawkwood Ho 3 KT23 94 A1
Hawkwood Rise KT23 94 A1
Hawley Cl TW12 15 F2
Hawley Ct GU14 84 E8
Hawley Garden Cotts
GU17 64 D4
Hawley Gn GU17 64 E3
Hawley La GU14 85 B8
Hawley Lodge GU14 64 F2
Hawley Place Sch GU17 64 E1
Hawley Prim Sch GU17 64 E3
Hawley Rd GU14,GU17 64 F3
Hawley Way TW15 14 B3
Hawmead RH10 204 C8
Haworth Rd RH10 202 C5
Hawth Ave RH10 201 F4
Hawth Cl RH10 201 E4
Hawthorn Ave CR7 42 B8
Hawthorn Cl
Banstead SM7 77 E5
Bracknell RG42 27 A8
Cranford TW5 4 B7
Crawley RH11 181 C1
Hampton TW12 16 A3
Horsham RH12 217 C4
Redhill RH1 140 A4
Woking GU22 89 E7
Hawthorn Cres
Selsdon CR2 81 C8
Upper Tooting SW17 21 A3
Hawthorn Ct
1 Farnborough GU14 105 C8
Richmond TW9 7 B6
9 West Norwood SW16 22 A3
Hawthorn Dr BR4 63 E6
Hawthorn Gr SE20 43 B8
Hawthorn Hatch TW8 6 B7
Hawthorn La
Newell Green SL4 8 A7
Rowledge GU10 145 F3
Hawthorn Pl GU4 110 D3
Hawthorn Rd
Brentford TW8 6 B7
Carshalton SM1 59 E4
Frimley GU16 65 F2
Godalming GU7 150 B2
Send Marsh GU23 91 A3
Wallington SM5,SM6 60 B3
Woking GU22 89 D7
Hawthorn Way
Bisley GU24 68 A3
Redhill RH1 140 B8
Upper Halliford TW17 34 D5
Woodham KT15 52 C1
Hawthorndene Cl BR2 63 F8
Hawthorndene Rd BR2 63 F8
Hawthorne Ave
Biggin Hill TN16 83 D4
Mitcham CR4 40 D7
Wallington SM5 60 A3
Winkfield SL4 9 B6
Hawthorne Cl
Aldershot GU12 126 E7
Sutton SM1 59 C8
Hawthorne Cres GU17 64 E4
Hawthorne Ct TW19 13 D8
Hawthorne Dr SL4 9 B7
Hawthorne Pl KT17 76 E7
Hawthorne Rd TW20 12 C4
Hawthorne Way
Guildford GU4 110 B5
Stanwell TW19 13 D8
Winkfield SL4 9 B7
Hawthorns Sch (Pendell
Court) The RH1 120 B4
Hawthorns The
Ewell KT17 58 A3
Oxted RH8 123 A2
Poyle SL3 1 F6
Haxted Rd RH7,TN8 165 C7
Haxted Watermill Mus★
TN8 165 D8
Haybarn Dr RH12 217 E7
Haycroft Cl CR8 80 B1
Haycroft Rd KT6 56 E7
Hayden Ct KT15 71 B8
Haydn Ave CR8 80 A4
Haydock Lodge SM6 60 D7
Haydon Ct 3 KT22 95 A5
Haydon Park Rd SW19 20 B3
Haydon Pl GU1 130 D8
Haydon's Rd SW19 20 C2
Haydons Road Sta SW19 20 C3
Hayes Barton GU22 70 D3
Hayes Chase BR4 44 E3
Hayes Cres SM3 58 D6
Hayes Ct Streatham SW12 21 E7
Wimbledon SW19 19 E2
Hayes Hill BR2 44 E1
Hayes Hill Rd BR2 44 F1
Hayes La
Beckenham BR2, BR3 44 D5
Purley CR8 80 B3
Slinfold RH13 215 D2
Hayes Mead Rd BR2 44 E1
Hayes Prim Sch The CR8 80 B3
Hayes Sta BR2 44 F1
Hayes The KT18 96 E8
Hayes Way BR3 44 D5
Hayes Wlk RH6 162 A4
Hayesend Ho SW17 20 C4
Hayesford Park Dr BR2 44 F4
Hayfields RH6 161 C4
Haygarth Pl SW19 19 D3
Haygreen Cl KT2 18 B2
Haylett Gdns KT1 37 D5
Hayling Ave TW13 15 A5
Hayling Ct Cheam SM3 58 C6
Crawley RH11 201 C3
Haymeads Dr KT10 55 C4
Haymer Gdns KT4 58 A7
Hayne Rd BR3 43 F8
Haynes Cl GU23 91 B5
Haynes La SE19 22 E2
Haynt Wlk SW20 39 E6
Hays Bridge Bsns Ctr
RH9 163 C6
Hays Bridge Hos RH9 163 B7
Hays Wlk SM2 58 D1
Haysleigh Gdns SE20 43 A7
Haysleigh Ho SE20 43 B7
Haywain The RH8 122 D5
Hayward Cl SW19 40 B8
Hayward Ct CR4 40 D7
Hayward Rd KT7 36 F1
Haywardens RH7 164 D5
Haywards RH10 182 D1
Haywood RG12 27 C2
Hazel Ave
Farnborough GU14 84 F3
Guildford GU1 109 C5
Hazel Bank Ewhurst GU6 175 E5
South Norwood SE25 42 E7
Tolworth KT5 38 C1
Hazel Cl Brentford TW8 6 B7
Crawley RH11 181 C1
Crawley Down RH10 204 C8
Croydon CR0 43 D1
Englefield Green TW20 11 B2
Mitcham CR4 41 D5
Reigate RH2 139 C7
Twickenham TW2 16 C8
Hazel Ct Guildford GU1 109 D5
Warlingham CR6 81 E1
10 West Norwood SW16 22 A3
Hazel Dr GU23 90 F2
Hazel Gr Feltham TW13 15 A7
Forest Hill SE26 23 D4
Haslemere GU26 188 E2
Staines TW18 13 C2
Hazel Mead KT17 58 A1
Hazel Par KT22 94 C5
Hazel Rd Ash GU12 127 C8
Mytchett GU16 86 A2
Reigate RH2 139 C7
Hazel Way Chipstead CR5 78 F1
Crawley Down RH10 204 C8
Fetcham KT22 94 C4
Hazel Wlk RH5 136 C4
Hazelbank Ct
Chertsey KT16 33 C1
Chessington KT9 56 F4
Hazelbank Rd Catford SE6 24 E6
Chertsey KT16 33 C2
Hazelbury Cl SW19 40 A7
Hazeldene KT15 52 C5
Hazeldene Ct Kenley CR8 80 D4
Woking GU21 69 C4
Hazelhurst
Beckenham BR3 44 D8
Horley RH6 161 C4
Hazelhurst Cl GU4 110 B6
Hazelhurst Cres RH12 216 F1
Hazelhurst Ct SE6 24 C3
Hazelhurst Dr RH10 202 E6
Hazelhurst Rd SW17 20 D4
Hazell Hill RG12 27 C6
Hazell Rd GU9 124 F1
Hazelmere Cl Hatton TW14 3 E1
Leatherhead KT22 95 B8
Hazelmere Ct 10 SW2 21 F7
Hazelwick Ave RH10 202 B8
Hazelwick Mill La RH10 202 A8
Hazelwick Rd RH10 202 A7
Hazelwick Sch RH10 202 A8
Hazelwood RH11 201 A5
Hazelwood Ave SM4 40 B5
Hazelwood Cl RH10 203 F8
Hazelwood Cotts
Cranleigh GU6 194 D4
5 Godalming GU7 150 D4
Hazelwood Ct KT6 37 E3
Hazelwood Gr CR2 81 B6
Hazelwood Ho BR2 44 E6
Hazelwood Hts RH8 123 A4
Hazelwood La CR5 98 F8
Hazelwood Lodge BR4 44 C2
Hazelwood Rd
Knaphill GU21 68 E1
Oxted RH8 123 B3
Hazelwood Sch RH8 123 A4
Hazledean Rd CR0,CR9 61 D8
Hazleden Cross RH19 205 B6
Hazledene Rd W4 7 C8
Hazlemere KT12 54 C8
Hazlemere Gdns KT4 39 A1

Hazlewood GU8 ....148 E4
Hazlitt Cl TW13 ....15 E4
Hazon Way KT19 ....76 C7
Headcorn Pl CR7 ....41 F5
Headcorn Rd Bromley BR1 24 F3
  Thornton Heath CR7 .....41 F5
Headington Cl RG40 ....25 D8
Headington Dr RG40 ....25 D8
Headington Rd SW18 ...20 C6
Headlam Rd SW4 ....21 D8
Headland Way RH7 ....164 D4
Headley Ave SM6 ....60 F5
Headley Cl
  Chessington KT19 ....57 A4
  Crawley RH10 ....182 D1
Headley Common Rd
  KT18,KT20 ....116 D7
Headley Ct SE26 ....23 C3
Headley Dr
  Burgh Heath KT18 .....97 B8
  New Addington CR0 ....63 C3
Headley Gr
  Burgh Heath KT20 .....97 C7
  Headley KT20 ....116 D7
Headley Heath App
  KT20 ....116 B4
Headley Hill Rd GU35 .187 A5
Headley Rd Ashstead KT18 96 C6
  Grayshott GU26 ....188 C3
  Headley KT18,KT22 ....96 A4
  Leatherhead KT18,KT22 .95 E4
  Mickleham RH5 ....115 E7
Headon Ct GU9 ....125 D1
Headway Cl TW10 ....17 C4
Headway The KT17 ......57 F2
Hearn Vale GU35 ......187 A7
Hearn Wlk RG12 ....27 E8
Hearne Rd W4 ....7 A8
Hearnville Rd SW12 ....21 A7
Hearsey Gdns GU17 ....64 C6
Heath Bsns Ctr RH1 ...161 B8
Heath Bsns Ctr The TW3 .5 C3
Heath Cl Banstead SM7 ..78 B5
  Beacon Hill GU26 .....188 C7
  Broadbridge Heath RH12 216 E3
  Croydon CR2 ....61 B4
  Harlington UB3 ....3 D7
  Heath End GU9 ....125 C7
  Stanwell TW19 ....2 C1
  Virginia Water GU25 ...31 D5
  Wokingham RG41 ....25 B4
Heath Cnr GU15 ....66 A3
Heath Cotts GU26 .....188 C6
Heath Ct SM1 ....59 D8
Heath Dr Brookwood GU24 88 A7
  Send GU23 ....90 B5
  Sutton SM2 ....59 C2
  Walton on the Hill KT18 .97 A2
  West Barnes SW20 .....39 C5
Heath End Cotts GU8 ..170 E7
Heath Gdns TW1 ....16 F6
Heath Gr Ashford TW16 .14 F1
  Penge SE20 ....23 C1
Heath Hill
  Dockenfield GU10 ....166 E3
  Dorking RH4 ....136 B7
Heath Hill Rd N RG45 ..45 B5
Heath Hill Rd S RG45 ..45 B4
Heath Ho Frimley GU16 .85 F6
  Thornton Heath CR7 ...42 A4
  Weybridge KT13 ....53 A6
Heath La Albury GU5 ..132 E2
  Crondall GU10 ....124 B7
  Godalming GU7 ....151 A4
  Heath End GU9 ....125 C7
Heath Mead GU19 ....19 D5
Heath Mill La GU3 .....88 C2
Heath Rd Bagshot GU19 .47 E3
  Caterham CR3 ....100 D3
  Haslemere GU27 .....207 D6
  Isleworth TW3,TW7 .....5 C3
  Oxshott KT22 ....74 C7
  South Norwood CR7 ....42 C6
  Twickenham TW1 ....16 F7
  Weybridge KT13 ....53 A5
  Woking GU21 ....69 F4
Heath Ridge Gn KT11 ..74 A6
Heath Rise
  Camberley GU15 ....65 D5
  Hayes BR2 ....44 F3
  Virginia Water GU25 ...31 D5
  Westcott RH4 ....135 C5
Heath The CR3 ....100 C3
Heath View KT24 ....92 F2
Heath Way RH12 ......217 D5
Heathacre SL3 ....1 E6
Heatham Pk TW2 ....16 F8
Heathbridge KT13 ......53 A4
Heathcote KT20 ....97 D5
Heathcote Cl GU12 ...106 A3
Heathcote Dr RH19 ...185 C2
Heathcote Rd Ash GU12 106 B3
  Camberley GU15 ....65 D5
  Epsom KT18 ....76 E6
  Twickenham TW1 ....6 B2
Heathcroft Ave TW16 ..14 F1
Heathdale Ave TW4 .....4 E4
Heathdene
  Burgh Heath KT20 .....77 E1
  Weybridge KT13 ....53 A5
Heathdene Rd
  Streatham SW16 ....21 F1
  Wallington SM5,SM6 ...60 B3
Heathdown Rd GU22 ....70 D4
Heathedge SE23,SE26 ..23 B6
Heather Cl
  Aldershot GU11 ....104 E1
  Ash GU12 ....106 B5

Heather Cl continued
  Copthorne RH10 ......183 B2
  Guildford GU2 ....109 B3
  Hampton TW12 ....35 F8
  Horsham RH12 ....217 D5
  Isleworth TW7 ....5 D2
  Kingswood KT20 ....97 E5
  2 Lewisham SE13 .....24 D8
  Redhill RH1 ....119 B5
  Woking GU21 ....69 C4
  Woodham KT15 ....52 B1
  Wrecclesham GU9 ....145 F6
Heather Cotts GU12 ..106 A8
Heather Ct
  11 Aldershot GU11 ....105 A1
  Hindhead GU26 ....188 F4
Heather Dr SL5 ....30 B2
Heather Gdns
  Belmont SM2 ....59 A4
  Farnborough GU14 .....84 E2
Heather Mead GU16 ....65 F2
Heather Mead Ct GU16 .65 F2
Heather Pl 5 KT10 ....55 B6
Heather Ridge Arc GU15 66 C4
Heather Ridge Inf Sch
  GU15 ....66 D4
Heather Way
  Chobham GU24 ....49 E3
  Hindhead GU26 ....188 F4
  South Croydon CR2 ....62 D2
Heather Wlk
  Crawley RH11 ....201 B3
  Pirbright GU24 ....87 D7
  Smallfield RH6 ....162 C3
  Twickenham TW2 ......16 A8
  Whiteley Village KT11 ..53 F1
Heatherbank GU26 ....188 E4
Heatherbank Cl KT11 ..73 D8
Heatherdale Cl KT2 ...18 B1
Heatherdale Rd GU15 ..65 D4
Heatherdeane KT24 ....92 D2
Heatherdene Cl CR4 ...40 E5
Heatherdene Mans 2
  TW1 ....6 D1
Heatherlands
  Ashford TW15 ....15 A2
  Horley RH6 ....161 B4
Heatherleigh Ct RH12 .217 C4
Heatherley Cl GU15 ...65 B5
Heatherley Rd GU15 ...65 B5
Heathermount
  Bracknell RG12 ....27 E5
  Guildford GU3 ....108 E3
Heathermount Dr RG45 .45 A6
Heathers Land RH4 ...136 C4
Heathers The TW19 ....13 F8
Heatherset Cl KT10 ....55 C5
Heatherset Gdns SW16 .21 F1
Heatherside Cl KT23 ..93 F2
Heatherside Cnr GU15 .66 D6
Heatherside Dr GU25 ..31 A3
Heatherside Rd KT19 ..57 E1
Heathervale Rd KT15 ..52 B1
Heathervale Way
  West Byfleet KT15 .....71 C8
  Weybridge KT15 ......52 C1
Heatherway
  Crowthorne RG45 ......45 A5
  Felbridge RH19 ......184 F7
Heatherwood Hospl SL5 28 E6
Heathfield Cobham KT11 74 A5
  Crawley RH10 ....202 D8
  Reigate RH2 ....138 D8
Heathfield Ave Ascot SL5 29 E4
  Wandsworth SW18 .....20 D8
Heathfield Cl
  Ashstead KT21 ....95 C8
  Godalming GU7 ....150 E2
  Woking GU22 ....70 A1
Heathfield Ct
  Ashford TW15 ....13 E5
  Penge SE20 ....23 C1
  Wandsworth SW18 .....20 D8
Heathfield Dr
  Mitcham SW19 ....20 E1
  Redhill RH1 ....139 E4
Heathfield Gdns CR0 ..61 D6
Heathfield Inf Sch TW2 16 A7
Heathfield Jun Sch TW2 16 A7
Heathfield N TW2 ......16 F8
Heathfield Rd
  Bromley BR1 ....24 F1
  Croydon CR0 ....61 D6
  Hersham KT12 ....54 E6
  Wandsworth SW18 .....20 D8
  Woking GU22 ....70 A1
Heathfield S TW2 ......16 F8
Heathfield Sch SL5 ....28 B7
Heathfield Sq SW18 ...20 D8
Heathfield Vale CR2 ...62 E2
Heathhurst Rd CR2 ....61 E2
Heathland Sch The TW4 .4 F1
Heathland St GU11 ...105 A2
Heathlands
  Tadworth KT20 ....97 D5
  Upper Tooting SW12 ...21 B6
  Weybridge KT13 ......53 C5
Heathlands Cl
  Sunbury TW16 ....35 A7
  Twickenham TW1 ....16 F7
  Woking GU21 ....69 E5
Heathlands Ct
  Hounslow TW4 ....4 E2
  Mitcham CR4 ....41 A6
Heathlands Rd RG40 ...25 E2
Heathlands Way TW4 ...4 E2
Heathmere Prim Sch
  SW15 ....19 A7

Heathmoors RG12 ......27 C4
Heathpark Dr GU20 ....48 E4
Heathrise GU23 ....91 B4
Heathrow GU5 ....133 C4
Heathrow Airport London
  TW6 ....3 A5
Heathrow Airport Visitor
  Ctr ★ TW6 ....3 C6
Heathrow Bvd UB7 ......2 F7
Heathrow Causeway Est
  TW4 ....4 B4
Heathrow Central Sta
  TW6 ....3 C1
Heathrow Cl TW6 ....2 B6
Heathrow International Trad
  Est TW4 ....4 B4
Heathrow Prim Sch UB7 .2 F8
Heathrow Terminal 4 Sta
  TW6 ....3 C1
Heathsholt 8 TW10 .....6 E1
Heathside
  Hinchley Wood KT10 ...55 E7
  Twickenham TW4 ....15 E7
  Weybridge KT13 ....53 B5
Heathside Cl GU10 ....55 E7
Heathside Cres GU22 ..69 F2
Heathside Ct TW20 ....97 C4
Heathside Gdns GU22 ..70 A2
Heathside La GU26 ...188 D6
Heathside Park Rd GU22 70 A1
Heathside Pk GU15 ....66 C7
Heathside Pl KT18 .....77 D1
Heathside Rd GU22 ....69 F1
Heathside Sch SW13 ...52 F4
Heathvale Bridge Rd
  GU12 ....106 A6
Heathview GU21 ....69 A6
Heathview Ct SW19 ....19 D6
Heathview Gdns SW15 .19 C8
Heathview Rd
  Thornton Heath CR7 ...42 A5
  Witley GU8 ....170 E7
Heathway Camberley GU15 65 D5
  Caterham CR3 ....100 D2
  Croydon CR0 ....62 F7
  East Horsley KT24 .....93 A3
  North Ascot SL5 ......28 E8
Heathway Cl GU15 .....65 D5
Heathwood KT20 ....97 C4
Heathwood Ct
  Hounslow TW3 ....5 B3
  Streatham SW12 ......21 C7
Heathwood Point 7
  SE26 ....23 D5
Heathyfields Rd GU9 .125 A6
Heaton Rd CR4 ....21 A1
Heavers Farm Prim Sch
  SE25 ....42 F4
Hebdon Rd SW17 ......20 F5
Hebe Ct SM1 ....59 C6
Hectors La RH19 .....206 C7
Heddon Cl TW7 ....6 A3
Heddon Wlk 1 GU14 ...85 A4
Hedge Cnr KT20 ....97 F8
Hedge Croft Cotts GU23 91 B6
Hedge Wlk SE6 ....24 B4
Hedgecourt Pl RH19 ..184 E4
Hedgehog La GU27 ...208 B5
Hedgerley Ct GU21 ....69 C2
Hedgers Almshouses
  GU1 ....110 D2
Hedgeside RH11 ......201 C1
Hedgeway GU2 ....130 A2
Hedingham Cl RH6 ...161 C4
Hedley Rd TW2 ....16 A8
Heelas Rd RG41 ....25 A5
Heenan Cl GU16 ....85 E7
Heighton Gdns CR0 ...61 A5
Heights Cl Banstead SM7 77 E3
  Wimbledon SW20 .....19 B1
Heights The BR3 ....24 C1
Helder Gr SE12 ....24 F8
Helder St CR2 ....61 D4
Heldmann Cl TW7 ......5 D3
Helen Ave TW14 ....15 B8
Helen Cl KT8 ....36 B5
Helen Ct GU14 ....85 B4
Helena Ho RH1 ....140 A6
Helford Wlk 3 GU21 ..69 A1
Helgiford Gdns TW16 ..14 E1
Helicon Ho RH11 .....201 C5
Helios Rd SM6 ....41 A1
Helix Bsns Pk GU15 ...65 B3
Helix Ho TW7 ....6 A5
Helksham Cl GU47 ....45 D1
Helm Cl KT19 ....76 A7
Helme Cl SW19 ....19 F3
Helmsdale Bracknell RG12 27 E4
  3 Woking GU21 ....69 B1
Helmsdale Rd SW16 ...21 D1
Helston Cl GU16 ....86 A7
Helvellyn Cl TW20 ....12 C1
Helvetia St SE6 ....23 F6
Hemingford Rd SM3 ...58 C6
Hemlock Cl KT20 ......97 A4
Hemming Cl 7 TW12 ...36 A8
Hempshaw Ave SM7 ...78 F3
Hemsby Rd KT9 ....56 F4
Hemsby Wlk RH10 ....202 B4
Henage Cnr GU24 .....49 E2
Henbane Ct 2 RH11 ..201 B2
Henbit Cl KT20 ....97 B8
Henchley Dene GU4 ..110 D4
Henderson Ave GU2 ..109 B5
Henderson Cl RH12 ...216 E3
Henderson Hospl SM2 .59 B2
Henderson Rd
  Biggin Hill TN16 ......83 C7

Henderson Rd continued
  Crawley RH11 ....201 B1
  Thornton Heath CR0 ...42 D3
  Wandsworth SW18 .....20 E8
Henderson Way RH12 ..216 F1
Hendfield Ct 5 SM6 ...60 B4
Hendham Rd SW17 .....20 F6
Hendon Gr KT19 ....57 A2
Hendon Terr TW15 .....14 D2
Hendon Way TW19 ......2 D1
Hendrick Ave SW12 ....20 F8
Heneage Cres CR0 .....63 C1
Henfield Rd SW19,SW20 39 F8
Henfold Cotts RH5 ...158 A4
Henfold Dr RH5 ......157 E3
Henfold La RH5 ......157 F3
Hengelo Gdns CR4 ....40 D5
Hengist Cl RH12 .....217 A1
Hengist Way BR2 ......44 E5
Hengrave Rd SE23 .....23 D8
Hengrove Cres TW15 ..13 D5
Henhurst Cross La RH5 157 A2
Henley Ave SM3 ....58 E7
Henley Bank GU2 ....130 A7
Henley Cl Crawley RH10 202 D3
  Farnborough GU14 .....84 E3
  Hounslow TW7 ....5 F6
Henley Ct Mitcham CR4 .41 A4
  Old Woking GU22 .....90 A7
Henley Dr Frimley GU16 .85 E7
  Kingston u T KT2 ......18 F1
Henley Gate GU4 .....107 C8
Henley Lodge SE25 ....42 F5
Henley Way TW13 .....15 D3
Henley Wood CR6 .....82 A2
Hennel Cl SE23 ....23 C5
Hennessy Ct GU21 ....70 C6
Henry Cavendish Prim Sch
  SW12 ....21 C7
Henry Doulton Dr SW17 21 B4
Henry Hatch Ct SM2 ...59 C3
Henry Peters Dr TW11 .16 E3
Henry Randell's Almshouses
  GU17 ....64 C3
Henry Tate Mews SW16 22 A3
Henry Tyndale Sch GU14 85 D6
Hensford Gdns SE26 ..23 B4
Henshaw Cl RH11 ....200 F4
Henslow Way GU21 ....70 D5
Henson Rd RH10 .....202 B7
Hensworth Rd TW15 ..13 D3
Henty Cl RH11 ....200 E3
Hepburn Gdns BR2 ....44 F1
Hepple Cl TW7 ....6 B5
Hepplewhite Cl RH11 .201 B1
Hepworth Croft GU47 .64 E6
Hepworth Ct SM3 .....40 A1
Hepworth Rd SW16 ....21 E1
Hepworth Way KT12 ...34 F1
Heracles Cl SM6 ......60 E5
Herald Ct
  5 Aldershot GU12 ....105 B1
  South Norwood SE19 ..22 F2
Herald Gdns SM6 .....60 B7
Herbert Cl RG12 ....27 B4
Herbert Cres GU21 ....68 E1
Herbert Ct KT5 ....37 F3
Herbert Gdns W4 ....7 B8
Herbert Rd
  Kingston u T KT1 ......37 F6
  Merton SW19 ....19 F1
Herbs End GU14 ....84 C5
Hereford Cl
  Crawley RH10 ....201 E2
  Epsom KT18 ....76 D6
  Guildford GU2 ....108 F3
  Staines TW18 ....33 B8
Hereford Copse GU22 .89 B8
Hereford Ct Belmont SM2 59 A3
  6 Croydon CR0 ....42 F1
Hereford Gdns TW2 ...16 C7
Hereford Ho 10 GU11 .105 A1
Hereford La GU9 .....125 B7
Hereford Rd TW13 .....15 C7
Hereford Way KT9 .....56 D5
Hereward Ave CR8 ....61 A1
Hereward Rd SW17 ....20 F4
Heriot Rd KT16 ....33 A2
Heritage Cotts GU3 ..107 B4
Heritage Ct 2 TW20 ..12 A3
Heritage Ho 22 SW19 .19 D7
Heritage Lawn RH6 ..161 C4
Herlwyn Gdns SW17 ...20 F4
Herm Cl Crawley RH11 .201 A2
  Hounslow TW7 ....5 C7
Hermes Ho BR3 ....43 E8
Hermes Way SM6 .....60 D3
Hermitage Cl
  Claygate KT10 ....56 A4
  Farnborough GU14 .....85 D1
  Frimley GU16 ....65 F1
  Littleton TW17 ....34 A5

Hermitage The
  Barnes SW13 ....7 F6
  Feltham TW13 ....14 F5
  Forest Hill SE23 ......23 C7
  Kingston u T KT1 ......37 D5
  Richmond TW10 ....6 E2
Hermitage Woods Cres
  GU21 ....88 E7
Hermitage Woods Est
  GU21 ....88 E8
Hermits Rd RH10 .....201 F7
Hermonger La RH12 ..195 F2
Herndon Cl TW20 .....12 A4
Herne Rd KT6 ....56 E8
Heron Cl Cheam SM1 ...58 F5
  Crawley RH11 ....201 C8
  Guildford GU2 ....109 B4
  Mytchett GU16 ....85 F4
  North Ascot SL5 ......28 D8
Heron Ct 8 Dorking RH4 136 A8
  5 Kingston u T KT1 ....37 E6
  Staines TW18 ....13 B4
  Stanwell TW19 ....13 B8
  7 West Norwood SE21 .22 D6
Heron Dale KT15 ......52 D5
Heron Ho KT1 ....37 C8
Heron Pl RH19 ....205 F8
Heron Rd Croydon CR0 .61 E7
  Isleworth TW1 ....6 B3
Heron Shaw GU6 .....174 E1
Heron Sq 25 TW10 .....6 D2
Heron Way RH13 .....218 A1
Heron Way Prim Sch
  RH13 ....218 A1
Heron Wlk GU21 ....70 C5
Heron Wood Rd GU12 .126 D7
Heron's Way RG40 .....25 E7
Herondale Bracknell RG12 27 C2
  Haslemere GU27 .....207 E6
  Selsdon CR2 ....62 D2
Herondale Ave SW18 ..20 E7
Heronfield TW20 ......11 C2
Heronry The KT12 .....54 A4
Herons Cl RH10 ......184 B5
Herons Croft KT13 ....53 D4
Herons L Ctr The GU27 207 F6
Herons Lea RH10 ....184 A4
Herons Pl TW7 ....6 B4
Herons Way GU24 .....87 D6
Herons Wood Ct RH6 .161 B4
Heronscourt GU18 ....67 C8
Herontye Dr RH19 ...206 A8
Herontye Ho RH19 ...205 F7
Herrett St GU12 .....126 D8
Herretts Gdns GU12 .105 D1
Herrick Cl Crawley RH10 202 C8
  Frimley GU16 ....66 C3
Herrick Ct 4 TW10 ....17 D4
Herrings La GU24 .....48 D4
Herron Ct 18 BR2 .....44 F5
Herschel Wlk 9 RH11 .201 B1
Herschel Rd SE23 .....23 E8
Hersham Cl SW15 .....19 A8
Hersham Ctr KT12 ....54 D5
Hersham Gdns KT12 ..54 C6
Hersham Rd
  Walton-on-T KT12 .....54 B7
  Hersham Sta KT12 ....54 D6
  Hersham Trad Est KT12 54 E8
Hershell Ct SW14 ......7 B3
Hertford Ave SW14 .....7 E3
Hertford Lodge 10 SW19 19 E7
Hertford Sq CR4 ......41 E5
Hertford Way CR4 ....41 E5
Hesiers Hill CR6 .....82 E2
Hesiers Rd CR6 ......82 F3
Hesketh Cl GU6 .....174 E3
Heslop Ct 1 SW12 ....21 A7
Heslop Rd SW12 ......20 F7
Hessle Gr KT17 ....76 F8
Hester Terr TW9 ....7 A4
Hesterman Way CR0,CR9 41 F1
Heston Ave TW5 ....4 E7
Heston Com Sch TW5 ..5 A7
Heston Grange TW5 ....4 F8
Heston Grange La TW5 .4 F8
Heston Ind Mall TW5 ...4 F7
Heston Inf Sch TW5 ....5 A7
Heston Phoenix Distribution
  Pk TW5 ....4 C8
Heston Rd Heston TW5 ..5 A7
  Redhill RH1 ....139 F4
Heston Wlk RH1 ......139 F4
Hetherington Rd TW17 .34 C7
Hethersett Cl RH2 ...118 C4
Hetley Gdns 1 SE19 ..22 F1
Heverfield Ct CR4 ....20 F1
Hevers Ave RH6 ......161 A4
Hewers Way KT20 .....97 C2
Hewitt Cl CR0 ....63 A7
Hewitts Ind Est GU6 .174 B3
Hewshott La GU30 ...207 A5
Hexal Rd SE6 ....24 E5
Hexham Cl Crawley RH10 202 E6
  Sandhurst GU47 ....45 D2
Hexham Gdns TW7 .....6 A7
Hexham Rd Cheam SM4 .40 B1
  West Norwood SE27 ..22 C6
Hextalls La RH1 .....120 E6
Heybridge Ave SW16 ..21 F2

Heydon Ct BR4 63 E8
Heyford Ave SW20 39 F6
Heyford Rd CR4 40 E7
Heymede KT22 95 C4
Heythorp St SW18 19 F6
Heythorpe Cl GU21 68 F2
Heyward Ct SM2 59 A4
Heywod Dr GU19 47 D3
Hibernia Gdns TW3 5 A2
Hibernia Rd TW3 5 A3
Hickey's Almshouses 7 TW9 6 F3
Hickling Wlk RH10 202 B4
Hickmans Cl RH9 121 C3
Hicks La GU17 64 B5
Hidaburn Ct 7 SW16 21 C4
Hidcote Cl GU22 70 B3
Hidcote Gdns SW20 39 B6
Hidcote Ho 15 SM2 59 C3
Hieover SE21 22 C6
Higgins Wlk TW12 15 E2
Higgs La GU19 47 D3
High Ashton 11 KT2 18 B1
High Barn Rd KT24,RH5 113 E3
High Beech
Bracknell RG12 27 F5
South Croydon CR2 61 E3
High Beeches
Banstead KT17,SM7 77 D5
Frimley GU16 65 D2
High Beeches Cl CR8 60 D1
High Broom Cres BR4 44 B2
High Cedar Dr SW20 19 B1
High Close Sch RG40 25 C7
High Coombe Pl KT2 18 D1
High Copse GU9 125 A6
High Down Rd SM2 78 B8
High Dr
Kingston u T KT2,KT3 38 C7
Oxshott KT22 74 D5
Woldingham CR3 102 A5
High Fields SL5 29 F4
High Foleys KT10 56 B3
High Gables BR2 44 E7
High Garth KT10 55 C4
High Gdns GU22 89 B8
High Hill Rd CR6 82 C5
High La Haslemere GU27 208 C8
Warlingham CR3,CR6 101 F8
High Level Dr SE26 23 A4
High Limes 2 SE19 22 E2
High Loxley Rd GU8 193 B7
High Mead
Farncombe GU7 150 F6
West Wickham BR4 63 E8
High Meadow Cl RH4 136 B6
High Meadow Ho RH4 136 B6
High Meadow Pl KT16 32 F3
High Oaks RH11 201 B4
High Par The SW16 21 E5
High Park Ave
East Horsley KT24 92 F1
Richmond TW9 7 A6
High Park Rd
Farnham GU9 125 C3
Richmond TW9 7 A6
High Path SW19 40 C8
High Path Rd GU1 110 C1
High Pewley GU1 130 E7
High Pine Cl KT13 53 C5
High Pines CR6 101 C8
High Pitfold GU26 188 D1
High Rd Byfleet KT14 71 E6
Chipstead CR5,RH2 98 F4
High Ridge GU7 150 D2
High St Addlestone KT15 52 B6
Aldershot GU11 105 A2
Aldershot GU11,GU12 105 B1
Ascot SL5 29 A6
Ascot,Sunninghill SL5 29 D4
Bagshot GU19 47 E3
Banstead SM7 78 B4
Beckenham BR3 44 A7
Bletchingley RH1 120 D2
Bracknell RG12 27 B7
Bracknell RG12 27 C7
Bramley GU5 151 F6
Brentford TW8 6 E8
Brentford,Brentford End TW8 6 D7
Camberley GU15 65 D6
Carshalton SM5 60 A6
Caterham CR3 100 E4
Cheam SM1,KT17 58 E4
Chobham GU24 68 E8
Claygate KT10 55 F4
Cobham KT11 73 B4
Colnbrook SL3 1 C7
Cranford,Heston TW5 4 B7
Cranleigh GU6 174 D3
Crawley RH10 201 D6
Crowthorne RG45 45 C4
Croydon CR0,CR9 61 C7
Croydon, Woodside SE25 43 A5
Dorking RH4 136 B8
East Grinstead RH19 205 F8
East Molesey KT8 36 A5
4 Egham TW20 11 F3
Epsom KT17,KT18 76 D6
Esher KT10 55 B6
Ewell KT17 58 A2
Farnborough GU14 105 D8
Feltham TW13 15 A6
Godalming GU7 150 D4
Godstone RH9 121 C4
Great Bookham KT23 94 B2
High St *continued*
Guildford GU1, GU2 130 D7
Harlington UB3 3 D8
Harmondsworth UB7 2 D8
Haslemere GU27 208 D7
Horley RH6 161 B3
Hounslow TW3 5 B4
Kingston u T KT1 37 D6
Knaphill GU21 68 C2
Leatherhead KT22 95 B5
Limpsfield RH8 123 B7
Lingfield RH7 164 D4
Loxwood RH14 212 F3
Merstham RH1 119 B7
New Malden KT3 38 E5
Nutfield RH1 119 F2
Old Woking GU22 90 B6
Oxshott KT22 74 D5
Oxted RH8 122 D5
Penge SE19,SE20,BR3 23 C1
Purley CR8 80 A8
Redhill RH1 118 F2
Reigate RH2 118 A1
Ripley GU23 91 C6
Rowledge GU10 145 E4
Rusper RH12 199 D7
Sandhurst GU47 64 A8
Sandhurst,Little Sandhurst GU47 45 A1
Shepperton TW17 34 C3
South Norwood CR7,SE25 42 D5
South Norwood,Woodside SE25 43 A6
Staines TW18 12 F4
Stanwell TW19 2 D1
Sunningdale SL5 30 A4
Sutton SM1 59 B5
Tadworth KT20 97 C4
Teddington TW11 17 A3
Teddington, Hampton Wick KT1 37 D8
Teddington,Hampton Hill TW12 16 C2
Thames Ditton KT7 37 A3
Twickenham TW2 16 C8
Walton-on-T KT12 35 A1
West End GU24 67 F7
West Wickham BR4 44 B1
Weybridge KT13 53 A6
Wimbledon SW19 19 D3
Woking GU21 69 F2
Woking,Horsell GU21 69 C3
High St Mews SW19 19 E3
High Standing CR3 100 C2
High Street Collier's Wood SW17,SW19 20 D2
High Street Gn GU8 191 F2
High Street Harlington TW6 3 D7
High Thicket Rd GU10 166 D5
High Tree Cl KT15 52 A5
High Trees Croydon CR0 43 E1
Streatham SW2 22 A7
High Trees Cl CR3 100 F5
High Trees Ct
Caterham CR3 100 F4
Sidlow RH6 160 A4
High Trees Rd RH2 139 D8
High View Belmont SM2 77 F8
Godalming GU7 150 E4
Gomshall GU5 133 C4
5 Penge SE19 22 F1
High View Ave SM6 60 F5
High View Cl
Farnborough GU14 85 A4
South Norwood SE19,SE25 42 F7
High View Lodge 18 GU11 105 A2
High View Rd
Farnborough GU14 85 A4
Guildford GU2 129 E6
Lightwater GU18 66 F8
South Norwood SE19 22 D2
Highacre RH4 136 B4
Highams Hill RH11 200 F5
Highams La GU20,GU24 49 A5
Highbarrow Rd CR0 43 A1
Highbirch Cl RH12 218 B5
Highbury Ave CR7 42 B7
Highbury Cl
New Malden KT3 38 C4
West Wickham BR4 63 B8
Highbury Cres GU15 66 A8
Highbury Gr GU27 208 C8
Highbury Rd SW19 19 E3
Highclere Ascot SL5 29 D4
Guildford GU1 110 A4
Highclere Cl
Bracknell RG12 27 E7
Kenley CR8 80 C4
Highclere Ct GU21 68 C2
Highclere Dr GU15 66 A7
Highclere Gdns GU21 68 D2
Highclere Rd
Aldershot GU12 126 D8
Kingston u T KT3 38 D6
Knaphill GU21 68 C2
Highclere St SE26 23 E4
Highcliffe BR3 44 B8
Highcliffe Dr SW15 7 F1
Highcotts La GU4,GU23 91 A1
Highcroft
Beacon Hill GU26 188 D6
Milford GU8 170 F8
Purley CR8 79 F5
Shamley Green GU5 152 E4
2 Surbiton KT5 37 F4
Highcroft Ct KT23 94 A4
Highcroft Dr RH12 195 E1
Highcross Way 4 SW15 19 A7
Highdaun Dr SW16 41 F5
Highdene 6 GU22 69 F1
Highdown KT4 57 F8
Highdown Ct RH10 202 B3
Highdown Way RH12 217 F6
Higher Alham RG12 27 E2
Higher Dr
Belmont KT17,SM7 77 D6
East Horsley KT24 112 E8
Purley CR8 80 A6
Higher Gn KT17 77 A6
Highercombe Rd GU27 208 E8
Highfield Bracknell RG12 26 F3
Shalford GU4 130 F1
Woodmansterne SM7 78 E2
Highfield Ave GU11 126 A8
Highfield Cl
Aldershot GU11 126 B8
Englefield Green TW20 11 C2
Farnborough GU14 84 F4
Farnham GU9 146 B7
Long Ditton KT6 37 C1
Oxshott KT22 74 D8
Wokingham RG40 25 B6
Highfield Cres GU26 188 F4
Highfield Ct
Englefield Green TW20 11 D2
Mitcham CR4 40 E5
Highfield Dr
Beckenham BR2 44 F5
West Ewell KT19 57 F4
West Wickham BR4 63 C7
Highfield Gdns GU11 126 B8
Highfield Hill SE19 22 E1
Highfield Ho RH11 201 D7
Highfield Inf Sch BR2 44 E5
Highfield Jun Sch BR2 44 E5
Highfield La
Puttenham GU3 128 A3
Thursley GU8 169 B2
Highfield Path GU14 84 F4
Highfield Rd
Biggin Hill TN16 83 C3
Carshalton SM1 59 E5
Caterham CR3 101 A5
Chertsey KT16 33 A1
East Grinstead RH19 185 D3
Farnborough GU14 84 F4
Feltham TW13 15 A6
Hounslow TW7 5 F6
Purley CR8 61 A1
Tolworth KT5 38 C2
Upper Halliford TW16 34 F4
Walton-on-T KT12 35 A1
West Byfleet KT14 71 A6
Highfield Sch SW18 20 E8
Highfields Ashstead KT21 95 D8
East Horsley KT24 112 F7
Fetcham KT22 94 D3
Forest Row RH18 206 F2
Sutton SM1 59 A8
Highgate Ct
Crawley RH11 201 C2
Farnborough GU14 85 C5
Highgate Ho 11 SE26 23 A5
Highgate La GU14 85 C5
Highgate Rd RH18 206 F1
Highgate Wlk SE23 23 C6
Highgrove 2 GU14 85 B7
Highgrove Ct BR3 24 A1
Highgrove Ho GU4 110 C3
Highland Cotts SM6 60 C6
Highland Croft BR3 24 B2
Highland Lodge 2 SE19 22 F1
Highland Pk TW13 14 F4
Highland Rd
Aldershot GU12 105 D2
Beare Green RH5 157 D3
Bromley BR1 44 F8
Camberley GU15 65 E8
Purley CR8 80 A5
West Norwood SE19 22 E2
Highland View GU6 174 C7
Highlands KT21 95 C8
Highlands Ave
Horsham RH13 217 E2
Leatherhead KT22 95 C5
Highlands Cl
Farnham GU9 146 B7
Hounslow TW3 5 B6
Leatherhead KT22 95 B5
Highlands Cres RH13 217 E2
Highlands Ct SE19 22 E2
Highlands Heath SW15 19 C8
Highlands La GU22 89 E5
Highlands Pk KT22 95 D4
Highlands Rd
Heath End GU9 125 C7
Horsham RH13 217 F2
Leatherhead KT22 95 C5
Reigate RH2 118 D2
Highlands The KT24 92 E2
Highmead GU7 150 F6
Highpoint KT13 53 A5
Highridge Cl KT18 76 E5
Highridge Ct KT18 76 E5
Highview CR3 100 E2
Highview Cres GU15 46 F1
Highview Ct
2 Putney SW19 19 E7
2 Reigate RH2 118 D1
Highview Prim Sch SM6 60 E5
Highway RG45 45 A5
Highway The SM2 59 C2
Highwayman's Ridge GU20 48 B6
Highwold CR5 79 A1
Highwood BR2 44 D6
Highwood Cl CR8 80 C2
Highwoods
Caterham CR3 100 E2
Leatherhead KT22 95 C6
Highwoods Ct RH12 216 D3
Hilary Ave CR4 41 A6
Hilary Dr RG45 45 B6
Hilbert Rd SM3 58 D7
Hilborough Cl SW19 20 C1
Hildenborough Gdns BR1 24 F2
Hildenbrough Ho BR3 23 F1
Hildenlea Pl BR2 44 E7
Hildenley Cl RH1 119 D7
Hildens The RH4 135 C5
Hilder Gdns GU14 85 D3
Hilders La TN8 144 F4
Hilders The KT21 76 B2
Hilditch Ho 7 TW10 6 F1
Hildreth St SW12 21 B7
Hildreth Street Mews 3 SW12 21 B7
Hilgay GU1 109 F1
Hilgay Cl GU1 109 F1
Hilgay Ct GU1 109 F1
Hill Cl Cobham KT22 74 A7
Purley CR8 80 C6
Woking GU21 69 D3
Wonersh GU5 152 B6
Hill Copse View RG12 27 E8
Hill Corner Farm Est GU14 84 D7
Hill Cres Kingston u T KT5 37 F4
North Cheam KT4 58 C8
Hill Crest
Dormans Park RH19 185 E6
Elstead GU8 148 D4
Hill Crest Dr GU10 145 F6
Hill Ct Farncombe GU7 150 E6
Haslemere GU27 208 B6
8 Kingston u T KT2 18 B1
14 Kingston u T KT6 37 E4
Hill Dr SW16 41 F6
Hill Farm Cl GU27 207 F5
Hill Field Rd TW12 35 F8
Hill Gr TW13 15 F6
Hill Ho GU26 188 C6
Hill House Cl RH10 204 A5
Hill House Dr
Hampton TW12 36 A8
Reigate RH2 139 B7
Weybridge KT13 72 A8
Hill House Rd SW16 21 F3
Hill La KT20 97 E6
Hill Mead RH12 217 B3
Hill Park Dr KT22 94 F8
Hill Pl RH11 201 C5
Hill Rd Beacon Hill GU26 188 C6
Carshalton SM5 59 E4
Fetcham KT23 94 B5
Grayshott GU26 188 C3
Haslemere GU27 208 C6
Heath End GU9 125 D7
Mitcham CR4 21 B1
Purley CR8 79 F7
Sutton SM1 59 B5
Hill Rise Dorking RH4 115 A1
Forest Hill SE23 23 B7
Hinchley Wood KT10 56 B8
Richmond TW10 6 D2
Hill St TW10 6 D2
Hill The CR3 100 F3
Hill Top SM3,SM4 39 F2
Hill View CR4 41 E5
Hill View Cl Purley CR8 80 B8
Tadworth KT20 97 C6
Hill View Cres GU2 108 F3
Hill View Ct 15 GU22 69 E1
Hill View Rd
Claygate KT10 56 A3
Farnham GU9 124 F2
Twickenham TW1 6 A1
Woking GU22 69 F1
Hillacre CR3 100 E2
Hillard Ct SM6 60 D4
Hillars Heath Rd CR5 79 E4
Hillary Cl
East Grinstead RH19 186 A3
Farnham GU9 146 B7
Hillary Cres KT12 35 C1
Hillary Ct TW19 13 E7
Hillary Dr TW7 5 F2
Hillary Ho 10 RH1 118 F2
Hillary Rd GU9 146 B7
Hillbarn CR2 80 E8
Hillberry RG12 27 C2
Hillbrook Gdns KT13 53 A3
Hillbrook Rd SW17 21 A4
Hillbrook Rise GU9 125 B6
Hillbrook Sch SW17 21 A4
Hillbrow New Malden KT3 38 F6
3 Reigate RH2 118 C1
7 Richmond TW10 6 E1
Hillbrow Cl GU3 108 B2
Hillbrow Cotts RH9 121 C3
Hillbrow Ct RH9 121 C3
Hillbrow Rd Catford BR1 24 E2
Esher KT10 55 C6
Hillbury Cl CR6 81 C1
Hillbury Gdns CR6 81 C1
Hillbury Rd
Upper Tooting SW17 21 B5
Warlingham CR3,CR6 81 B1
Hillcote Ave SW16 22 A1
Hillcrest Heath End GU9 125 D8
Oxted RH8 122 E6
Hillcrest *continued*
Weybridge KT13 53 B6
Hillcrest (Mobile Home Pk) KT20 116 B4
Hillcrest Ave KT16 51 E6
Hillcrest Cl
Beckenham BR3 43 F3
Crawley RH10 202 D6
Epsom KT18 76 F4
Forest Hill SE26 23 A4
Hillcrest Ct
3 Lewisham SE13 24 D8
Sutton SM2 59 D4
4 Weybridge KT13 53 B6
Hillcrest Gdns KT10 55 F7
Hillcrest Ho GU4 110 C3
Hillcrest Par CR5 79 B5
Hillcrest Rd
Biggin Hill TN16 83 D3
Camberley GU15 66 B7
Guildford GU2 108 F2
Kenley CR3 80 F2
Wallington CR8 60 F1
Hillcrest View BR3 43 F3
Hillcroft GU27 208 C6
Hillcroft Ave CR5,CR8 79 D6
Hillcroft Coll KT6 37 E3
Hillcroft Ct CR3 100 E4
Hillcroft Cty Prim Sch CR3 100 E4
Hillcroome Rd SM2 59 D4
Hillcross Ave SM4 39 E4
Hillcross Prim Sch SM4 39 F5
Hilldale Rd SM1 58 F6
Hilldeane Rd CR8 61 A1
Hilldown Ct SW16 21 E1
Hilldown Rd
Streatham SW16 21 F1
West Wickham BR2 44 F1
Hillers KT20 97 B6
Hilley Field La KT22 94 C6
Hillfield Ave SM4 40 E4
Hillfield Cl Guildford GU1 110 C3
Redhill RH1 119 A1
Hillfield Rd RH1 119 A1
Hillford Pl RH1 140 A3
Hillgarth GU26 188 D5
Hillgate Pl SW12 21 B8
Hillhampton SL5 29 F2
Hillhouse La RH12 194 F1
Hillhurst Gdns CR3 100 E7
Hillier Gdns CR0 61 A5
Hillier Ho Guildford GU1 110 A1
Guildford,Guildford Park GU2 130 B7
Hillier Lodge TW11 16 D3
Hillier Mews GU1 110 A1
Hillier Pl KT9 56 C4
Hillier Rd GU1 110 A1
Hillier's La CR0,SM6 60 E7
Hillingdale
Biggin Hill TN16 83 B1
Crawley RH11 201 C1
Hillingdon Ave TW19 13 E7
Hillmead RH11 200 F6
Hillmont Rd KT10 55 E7
Hillmore Gr SE26 23 E3
Hillmount 13 GU22 69 E1
Hillrise Brands Hill SL3 1 A8
Walton-on-T KT12 34 F2
Hills Farm La RH12 216 F1
Hills Manor RH12 217 A2
Hills Pl RH12 217 A2
Hillsborough Ct GU14 84 E8
Hillsborough Pk GU15 66 C5
Hillside Ascot SL5 29 C4
Banstead SM7 77 E4
Crawley Down RH10 204 B8
Forest Row RH18 206 F3
Horsham RH12 217 A2
Sandhurst GU15 64 F7
Wentworth GU25 31 C3
Wimbledon SW19 19 D2
Woking GU22 89 D7
Hillside Ave CR8 80 B6
Hillside Cl Banstead SM7 77 E3
Brockham RH3 137 A8
Crawley RH11 201 B4
East Grinstead RH19 185 E3
Headley Down GU35 187 A6
Knaphill GU21 68 D2
Merton SM4 39 E5
Hillside Cres GU16 85 F7
Hillside Ct
6 Guildford GU1 130 E8
7 Kingston u T KT2 18 B1
Hillside Gdns
Addlestone KT15 51 F5
Brockham RH3 116 A1
Streatham SW2 22 A6
Wallington SM6 60 C3
Hillside La Coney Hall BR2 63 F8
Heath End GU9 125 D8
Hillside Pk SL5 29 F1
Hillside Rd
Aldershot GU11 126 A8
Ash GU12 106 B3
Ashstead KT21 75 F2
Beckenham BR2 44 F6
Belmont SM2 58 F3
Coulsdon CR5 79 F1
Croydon CR0 61 B6
East Ewell KT17 58 C1
Farnham GU10 146 C3
Haslemere GU27 207 F5
Heath End GU9 125 E7
Kingston u T KT5 38 A4
Streatham SW2 22 A6

Hillside Rd *continued*
Tatsfield TN16 103 E8
Whyteleafe CR3 81 A1
Hillside Way GU7 150 D7
Hillsmead Way CR2 81 B6
Hillspur Cl GU2 108 F2
Hillspur Rd GU2 108 F2
Hillswood Dr KT16 51 C6
Hilltop Cl Ascot SL5 29 E7
Guildford GU3 108 F5
Leatherhead KT22 95 C4
Hilltop Cotts RH6 160 D2
Hilltop Ct SE19 42 D8
Hilltop La CR3,RH1 100 A1
Hilltop Rd Kenley CR3 80 F2
Reigate RH2 139 B7
Hilltop Rise KT23 94 C1
Hilltop Wlk CR3 101 E6
Hillview Whyteleafe CR3 80 F2
Wimbledon SW20 19 B1
Hillview Ct SE19 22 E4
Hillview Dr RH1 140 A8
Hillview Rd SM1 59 D7
Hillworth 7 BR3 44 B7
Hillworth Rd SW2 22 A8
Hilly Mead SW19 19 E1
Hillybarn Rd RH11 180 C1
Hilsea Point 7 SW15 19 B7
Hilton Ct RH6 161 C4
Hilton Way CR2 81 B4
Himley Rd SW17 20 F2
Hinchley Cl KT10 55 F7
Hinchley Dr KT10 55 F7
Hinchley Way KT10 56 A7
Hinchley Wood Prim Sch KT10 56 A8
Hinchley Wood Sch & Sixth Form Ctr KT10 56 A8
Hinchley Wood Sta KT10 55 F7
Hindell Cl GU14 85 A8
Hindhead Cl RH11 201 C4
Hindhead Comm★ GU8 189 A5
Hindhead Point 6 SW15 19 B7
Hindhead Rd GU26,GU27 188 F2
Hindhead Way SM6 60 E5
Hindhead YH★ GU8 189 A6
Hindsley's Pl SE23 23 C6
Hine Cl CR5 99 C5
Hinstock Cl GU14 85 A3
Hinton Ave TW4 4 D3
Hinton Cl RG45 45 B7
Hinton Dr RG45 45 B7
Hinton Rd SM6 60 C4
Hipley Ct GU1 131 A8
Hipley St GU22 90 B7
Hitchcock Cl TW17 33 F6
Hitchings Way RH2 139 A5
Hither Green La SE13 24 E8
Hitherbury Cl GU2 130 C6
Hitherfield Prim Sch SW2 22 A6
Hitherfield Rd SE27,SW16 22 A5
Hitherhooks Hill RG42 26 E8
Hithermoor Rd TW19 2 A2
Hitherwood GU6 174 E2
Hitherwood Cl RH2 118 E3
Hitherwood Ct SE19 22 F4
Hitherwood Dr SE19 22 F4
Hoadly Rd SW16 21 D6
Hobart Gdns CR7 42 D6
Hobart Pl 14 TW10 6 F1
Hobart Rd KT4 58 B7
Hobbs Cl KT14 71 B6
Hobbs Ind Est RH7 184 D7
Hobbs Rd Crawley RH11 201 A2
5 West Norwood SE27 22 C4
Hobill Wlk KT5 37 F3
Hocken Mead RH10 202 D8
Hockering Gdns GU22 70 B1
Hockering Rd GU22 70 B1
Hockford Cl GU24 88 B1
Hockley Ind Ctr RH1 139 F8
Hodge La SL5 9 A3
Hodges Cl GU19 47 E1
Hodgkin Cl RH10 202 C5
Hodgson Gdns GU4 110 A4
Hoe Bridge Sch GU22 90 B8
Hoe Cotts GU5 154 E8
Hoe La Hascombe GU8 172 D4
Peaslake GU5,RH5 154 F8
Hoebrook Cl GU22 89 E6
Hogarth Ave TW15 14 C2
Hogarth Bsns Pk W4 7 E8
Hogarth Cl GU47 64 E6
Hogarth Cres
Mitcham CR4,SW19 40 D8
Thornton Heath CR0 42 C2
Hogarth Ct Dulwich SE19 22 F4
Heston TW5 4 E7
Hogarth Gdns TW5 5 A7
Hogarth Ho
1 Carshalton SM1 59 D5
6 West Norwood SE27 22 C4
Hogarth La W4 7 E8
Hogarth Rd RH10 201 F3
Hogarth Rdbt 9 W4 7 C8
Hogarth Way TW12 36 C8
Hoghatch La GU9 125 A6
Hogoak La SL4 8 A8
Hogscross La CR5 98 F5
Hogshill La KT11 73 C5
Hogsmill Way KT19 57 C6
Hogspudding La RH5 158 C2
Hogtrough La
Nutfield RH1 140 D8
Oxted RH8 122 B6
Hogwood Rd RH14 212 C3
Holbeach Mews 2 SW12 21 B7
Holbeach Prim Sch SE6 24 A8
Holbeach Rd SE6 24 B8
Holbeck RG12 26 F3
Holbein Rd RH10 201 F3
Holberry Ho 5 SE21 22 E4
Holborn Way CR4 40 F7
Holbreck Pl GU22 69 F1
Holbrook Cl GU9 125 F8
Holbrook Ct TW20 12 C3
Holbrook Ho 5 SW2 21 F7
Holbrook Mdw TW20 12 C2
Holbrook Prim Sch RH12 217 E7
Holbrook School La RH12 217 E7
Holbrook Way GU11 126 B7
Holcon Ct RH1 119 A4
Holden Pl KT11 73 B5
Holder Rd
Aldershot GU12 105 E1
Crawley RH10 202 B3
Holderness Way SE27 22 B3
Holdernesse Rd
Isleworth TW7 6 A6
7 Upper Tooting SW17 21 A6
Holdfast La GU27 208 F7
Holdsworth Ho 4 SW2 22 A8
Hole Hill RH4 135 B7
Hole La TN8 144 F7
Holford Rd GU1 110 C1
Holland Ave Belmont SM2 59 A2
Wimbledon SW20 38 F8
Holland Cl Coney Hall BR2 63 F8
Farnham GU9 146 E8
Redhill RH1 118 F1
Holland Cres RH8 123 A2
Holland Dr SE23 23 E5
Holland Gdns
Brentford TW8 6 E8
Egham TW20 32 F7
Holland Jun Sch RH8 123 A1
Holland La RH8 123 A2
Holland Pines RG12 26 F2
Holland Rd Croydon SE25 43 A4
Oxted RH8 123 A1
Holland Way BR2 63 F8
Hollands Field RH13 216 E4
Hollands The
Feltham TW13 15 D4
New Malden KT4 38 F1
3 Woking GU22 69 E1
Hollands Way
East Grinstead RH19 186 A4
Warnham RH12 216 F8
Holles Cl TW12 16 A3
Hollies Ave KT14 70 F6
Hollies Cl
South Norwood SW16 22 A2
Twickenham TW1 16 F6
Hollies Ct KT15 52 C5
Hollies Way 3 SW12 21 A8
Hollin Ct RH10 181 E1
Hollingbourne Cres RH11 201 C1
Hollingsworth Rd CR0, CR2 62 B4
Hollington Cres KT3 39 A3
Hollingworth Cl KT8 35 F5
Hollingworth Ct 7 KT6 37 D2
Hollis Row RH1 139 F7
Hollis Wood Dr GU10 145 E5
Hollman Gdns SW16 22 B2
Hollow Cl GU2 130 B8
Hollow La
Dormansland RH19,RH7 186 D6
Virginia Water GU25 31 C6
Wotton RH5 134 D2
Hollow The
Crawley RH11 200 F5
Shackleford GU7 149 F4
Holloway Dr GU25 31 E5
Holloway Hill
Godalming GU7 150 D4
Lyne KT16 51 D8
Holloway La UB7 2 E8
Holloway St TW3 5 B4
Holly Acre GU22 89 C4
Holly Ave Frimley GU16 66 B3
Walton-on-T KT12 35 D1
Woodham KT15 52 A1
Holly Bank Rd GU22 89 B7
Holly Bush Ind Pk GU11 105 E5
Holly Bush La TW12 15 F1
Holly Cl Aldershot GU12 105 C2
Beckenham BR3 44 C5
Crawley RH10 202 A8
Englefield Green TW20 11 B2
Farnborough GU14 85 A4
Feltham TW13 15 E3
Headley Down GU35 187 C5
Horsham RH12 218 B5
Longcross KT16 50 A7
Woking GU21 89 B8
Holly Cott KT7 37 A1
Holly Cres BR3 43 F4
Holly Ct 4 Belmont SM2 59 A3
Leatherhead KT22 95 A5
Holly Gn KT13 53 D6
Holly Grove Cl TW3 4 F3
Holly Hedge Cl GU16 65 E2
Holly Hedge Rd
Cobham KT11 73 B5
Frimley GU16 65 E2
Holly Hill Dr SM7 78 A3
Holly Hill Pk SM7 78 A2
Holly Ho Bracknell RG12 27 B3
Brentford TW8 6 C8
Whyteleafe CR3 80 F2
Holly Hock GU24 68 A4
Holly Hough KT20 116 B5
Holly La Banstead SM7 78 C2
Godalming GU7 150 C4
Woodmansterne SM7 78 C2
Worplesdon GU3 108 D7
Holly La E SM7 78 B3
Holly La W SM7 78 B2
Holly Lea GU4 109 D7
Holly Lodge KT13 53 E7
Holly Lodge Prim Sch GU12 105 F8
Holly Rd Aldershot GU12 105 D1
Farnborough GU14 85 A4
Hampton TW12 16 C2
Hounslow TW3 5 B3
Reigate RH2 139 B7
Twickenham TW1 17 A7
Holly Ridge GU24 67 E6
Holly Spring Inf Sch RG12 27 E7
Holly Spring Jun Sch RG12 27 E7
Holly Spring La RG12 27 D8
Holly Tree Rd CR3 100 E5
Holly Way
Blackwater GU17 64 D4
Mitcham CR4 41 D6
Holly Wlk SL4 9 E4
Hollybank GU24 67 E6
Hollybank Cl TW12 16 A3
Hollybank Rd KT14 71 A5
Hollybush Cl RH10 201 E8
Hollybush La GU11 105 E6
Hollybush Rd
Crawley RH10 201 E8
Kingston u T KT2 17 E2
Hollybush Ride GU19, GU20 47 F6
Hollycombe TW20 11 D4
Hollycroft Cl
Harmondsworth UB7 3 A8
South Croydon CR2 61 E5
Hollycroft Gdns UB7 3 A8
Hollydene BR1 44 F8
Hollyfield Rd KT5 37 F2
Hollyfield Sch The KT6 37 E4
Hollyfields Cl GU15 65 B5
Hollymead SM5 59 F7
Hollymead Rd CR5 79 A1
Hollymeoak Rd CR5 79 B1
Hollymoor La KT19 57 D1
Hollymount Sch SW20 39 C8
Hollyridge GU27 208 B6
Hollytree Cl SW19 19 D7
Hollytree Gdns GU16 85 D8
Hollywoods CR0 62 F2
Holm Cl KT15 70 E7
Holm Ct Dorking RH4 136 B4
Farncombe GU7 150 D7
Holman Ct KT17 58 A2
Holman Rd KT19 57 C5
Holmbank Dr TW17 34 E5
Holmbrook Cl GU14 84 C4
Holmbrook Gdns GU14 84 C4
Holmbury Ave RG45 45 A7
Holmbury Cl RH11 201 C4
Holmbury Ct
Mitcham SW19 20 E1
Upper Tooting SW17 20 F5
Holmbury Dr RH5 136 C4
Holmbury Gr CR0 62 F3
Holmbury Hill Rd RH5 155 B3
Holmbury Keep RH6 161 C4
Holmbury Rd RH5 155 D1
Holmbush Cl RH12 217 D6
Holmbush Farm World★ RH12 200 B1
Holmcroft Crawley RH10 201 E5
Walton on the Hill KT20 97 B2
Holmdene Cl BR3 44 C7
Holme Chase KT13 53 C4
Holme Cl RG45 45 A7
Holme Lodge GU7 150 E6
Holmes Cl Ascot SL5 29 C3
Woking GU23 89 F6
Wokingham RG41 25 A4
Holmes Cres RG41 25 A4
Holmes Rd Merton SW19 20 C1
Twickenham TW1 16 F6
Holmesdale 2 KT13 53 D4
Holmesdale Ave SW14 7 B3
Holmesdale Cl
Guildford GU1 110 B2
South Norwood SE25 42 F6
Holmesdale Pk RH1 119 F1
Holmesdale Rd
Dorking RH5 136 C3
Reigate RH2 118 B2
Richmond TW9 6 F6
South Norwood SE25 42 E5
South Nutfield RH1 140 F7
Teddington TW11 17 C2
Thornton Heath CR0 42 D4
Holmesdale Villas RH5 136 B1
Holmethorpe Ave RH1 119 B4
Holmethorpe Ind Est RH1 119 B4
Holmewood Cl RG41 25 A2
Holmewood Gdns SW2 21 F8
Holmewood Rd
South Norwood SE25 42 E6
Streatham SW2 21 F8
Holmgrove Ho CR8 80 A7
Holming End RH12 218 B5
Holmoaks Ho BR3 44 C7
Holmsdale Com Inf Sch RH2 118 B3
Holmshaw Cl SE26,SE6 23 E4
Holmsley Cl KT3 38 F2
Holmsley Ho SW15 18 F8
Holmstoun KT15 70 E7
Holmwood 2 KT5 37 F3
Holmwood Ave CR2 80 F6
Holmwood Cl
Addlestone KT15 52 A5
Cheam SM2 58 D3
East Horsley KT24 112 E6
Holmwood Gdns SM6 60 B4
Holmwood Rd
Chessington KT9 56 E5
East Ewell KT17,SM2 58 C2
Holmwood Sta RH5 157 C4
Holmwood View Rd RH5 136 B1
Holne Chase SM4 40 A3
Holroyd Rd KT10 55 F2
Holsart Cl KT20 97 B5
Holstein Ave KT13 53 A6
Holsworthy Way KT9 56 C5
Holt Cl GU14 85 C7
Holt La RG41 25 B7
Holt Pound La GU10 145 C5
Holt Sch The RG41 25 B7
Holt The Morden SM4 40 A5
Wallington SM6 60 C6
Holt Wood CR6 82 A3
Holton Heath 8 RG12 27 F5
Holtwood Rd KT22 74 C6
Holtye Ave RH19 186 A3
Holtye Pl RH19 186 B3
Holtye Rd RH19 186 B3
Holtye Wlk RH10 202 A4
Holwood Cl KT12 54 C8
Holy Cross Catholic Prim Sch SE6 24 C7
Holy Cross Hospl GU27 207 F7
Holy Cross Prep Sch KT2 18 C1
Holy Cross RC Convent Sch KT3 38 E4
Holy Family RC Prim Sch The KT15 52 A5
Holy Ghost RC Prim Sch SW12 21 A8
Holy Trinity CE Jun Sch
Mortlake TW10 7 A3
Wallington SM6 60 C6
Holy Trinity CE Mid Sch GU1 130 F7
Holy Trinity CE Prim Sch
Forest Hill SE23 23 C6
Streatham SW2 21 F8
Sunningdale SL5 30 A3
Wimbledon SW19 20 B2
Holy Trinity CE Sch GU24 68 A7
Holy Trinity Sch RH11 201 A4
Holybourne Ave SW15 19 A8
Holyhead Ct KT1 37 D5
Holyhook Cl RG45 45 A6
Holyoake Ave GU21 69 C2
Holyoake Cres GU21 69 C2
Holyrood RH19 206 A8
Holywell GU22 89 B6
Holywell Cl
Farnborough GU14 85 A7
Stanwell TW19 13 E7
Holywell Way TW19 13 E7
Homan Ho 6 SW4 21 D8
Hombrook Dr RG42 26 E8
Hombrook Ho RG42 26 E8
Home Cl Carshalton SM5 59 F8
Crawley RH10 202 C8
Fetcham KT22 94 D6
Home Ct KT6 37 D4
Home Farm RH2 118 F6
Home Farm Cl
Betchworth RH3 137 E8
Burgh Heath KT18 77 D2
Esher KT10 55 B4
Farnborough GU14 85 D6
Ottershaw KT16 51 A3
Thames Ditton KT7 36 F8
Upper Halliford TW17 34 E5
Home Farm Cotts GU8 149 C5
Home Farm Gdns KT12 54 C8
Home Farm Rd GU7 150 F2
Home Mdw SM7 78 A3
Home Park Cl GU5 151 F6
Home Park Rd SW19 19 F4
Home Park Wlk KT1 37 D5
Home Pk RH8 123 A4
Homebeech Ho 7 GU22 69 E1
Homecoppice Ho 1 BR1 24 F1
Homecourt TW14 15 A7
Homecroft Rd SE26 23 C3
Homefield
Leatherhead KT22 95 C6
Morden SM4 40 A5
Thursley GU8 169 C3
Homefield Cl Horley RH6 161 B4
Leatherhead KT22 95 C6
Woodham KT15 70 E7
Homefield Gdns
Burgh Heath KT20 97 C7
Mitcham CR4,SW19 40 D7
Homefield Ho SE23 23 D5
Homefield Pk SM1 59 B4
Homefield Prep Sch SM1 59 A5
Homefield Rd
Coulsdon CR3,CR5 100 B7
Walton-on-T KT12 35 E2
Warlingham CR6 101 C8
Wimbledon SW19 19 E3
Homegreen Ho GU27 208 A6
Homeland Dr SM2 59 B2
Homelands KT22 95 C6
Homelands Dr SE19 22 E1
Homelea Cl GU14 85 B8
Homeleigh Cres GU12 106 A8
Homeleigh Ct 8 SW16 21 E5
Homemead SW12 21 B6
Homemead Rd CR0 41 C3
Homepark Ho GU9 125 C2
Homer Rd CR0 43 D3
Homersham Rd KT1 38 B7
Homesdale Rd CR3 100 D4
Homestall GU2 108 D2
Homestall Rd RH19 206 E8
Homestead GU6 174 F4
Homestead Cvn Pk GU3 107 E4
Homestead Gdns KT10 55 E5
Homestead Rd
Caterham CR3 100 D4
Staines TW18 13 B2
Homestead The GU1 130 F7
Homestead Way CR0 82 D7
Homesteads The BR3 24 B2
Homewalk Ho SE26 23 C4
Homewater Ho 1 KT17 76 E6
Homewaters Ave TW16 34 F8
Homewood GU6 175 A3
Homewood Cl TW12 15 F2
Homewood Gdns SE25 42 E4
Homewoods 2 SW12 21 C8
Homeworth Ho 8 GU22 69 E1
Homildon Ho 10 SE26 23 A5
Homington Ct KT2 17 E1
Homstead The RH6 162 B1
Hone Hill GU47 64 B8
Hones Yard Bsns Pk GU9 125 D2
Honey Hill RG40 26 A1
Honeybrook Rd SW12, SW4 21 C8
Honeycrock Ct RH1 140 A2
Honeycrock La RH1 140 B2
Honeyhill Rd RG42 27 A8
Honeypot La TN8 144 D4
Honeypots Rd GU22 89 D5
Honeysuckle Bottom KT24 112 E2
Honeysuckle Cl
Crowthorne RG45 45 A7
Horley RH6 161 C4
Honeysuckle Gdns CR0 43 D1
Honeysuckle La
Crawley RH11 181 C1
Dorking RH5 136 C4
Headley Down GU35 187 B5
Honeysuckle Wlk RH12 218 A5
Honeywood La RH5 196 F5
Honeywood Rd
Horsham RH13 218 A4
Isleworth TW7 6 A3
Honeywood Wlk SM5 59 F6
Honister Hts CR8 80 E5
Honister Wlk GU15 66 D4
Honley Rd SE6 24 B8
Honnor Gdns TW7 5 D5
Honnor Rd TW18 13 D1
Honor Oak Rd SE23 23 C8
Hood Ave SW14 7 C2
Hood Cl CR0,CR9 42 B1
Hood Rd SW20 18 F1
Hook Heath Ave GU22 89 C8
Hook Heath Farm GU22 89 A7
Hook Heath Gdns GU22 88 F6
Hook Heath Rd GU22 89 B6
Hook Hill CR2 61 E1
Hook Hill La GU22 89 C6
Hook Hill Pk GU22 89 B6
Hook Ho 9 SW27 22 B3
Hook La Gomshall GU5 133 C2
Puttenham GU3 128 D3
West End GU24 67 C6
Hook Mill La GU18 48 D2
Hook Rd Chessington KT6 56 E7
Epsom KT19,KT17 57 C2
Ewell KT19 76 D8
Surbiton KT6,KT9 56 E7
Hook Rise N Surbiton KT6 56 E7
Tolworth KT6,KT9 57 B8
Hook Rise S
Chessington KT6 56 E7
Tolworth KT6,KT9 57 B8
Hook Underpass KT6 56 E7
Hooke Rd KT24 92 F2
Hookfield KT18,KT19 76 C6
Hookfield Mews KT19 76 C6
Hookhouse Rd GU8 192 D6
Hookley Cl GU8 148 E3
Hookley La GU8 148 E3
Hookstile La GU9 125 C1
Hookstone La GU24 67 F8
Hookwood Bglws RH8 123 B7
Hookwood Cnr RH8 123 B7
Hookwood Cotts KT18 96 C3
Hooley La RH1 139 F8
Hoover Ho SE6 24 C4
Hop Kiln The GU9 146 B8
Hop Kilns The GU10 125 F3
Hope Ave RG12 27 E2
Hope Cl SM1 59 C5
Hope Ct RH11 201 B1
Hope Fountain GU15 65 F4
Hope Grant's Rd GU11 105 A4
Hope La GU9 125 B6
Hope Pk BR1 24 F1
Hope St GU8 148 D4
Hope Way GU11 104 F3

Hopeman Cl GU47 .....64 D7
Hopes Cl TW5 ....5 A8
Hopfield GU21 .....69 E3
Hopfield Ave KT14 .....71 E6
Hophurst Cl RH10 .....204 B8
Hophurst Dr RH10 .....204 B8
Hophurst Hill RH19 .....184 D2
Hophurst La RH10 .....184 B1
Hopkins Ct RH11 .....201 B1
Hopper Vale RG12 .....27 A3
Hoppety The KT20 .....97 D5
Hoppingwood Ave KT3 .38 E6
Hopton Cl **1** GU2 .....108 E1
Hopton Gdns KT3 .....39 A3
Hopton Rd SW16 .....21 E3
Hopwood Cl SW17 .....20 C5
Horace Rd KT1 .....37 F6
Horatio Ave RG42 .....27 E8
Horatius Way CR0 .....60 F4
Hordern Ho RH12 .....217 A1
Horewood Rd RG12 .....27 B3
Horley Inf Sch RH6 .....161 A3
Horley Lodge La RH1 .....161 A8
Horley Rd Hookwood RH6 181 B7
Redhill RH1 .....139 F5
Horley Row RH6 .....161 A4
Horley Sta RH6 .....161 B2
Hormer Cl GU47 .....45 D1
Horn Rd GU14 .....84 E5
Hornbeam Cl
Farnborough GU14 .....84 C5
Horsham RH13 .....217 F1
Sandhurst GU47 .....45 D1
Hornbeam Cres TW8 .....6 B7
Hornbeam Rd
Guildford GU1 .....109 C3
Reigate RH2 .....139 C6
Hornbeam Terr SM5 .....40 E1
Hornbeam Wlk KT12 .....53 F2
Hornby Ave RG12 .....27 D2
Hornchurch Cl KT2 .....17 D3
Hornchurch Hill CR3 .....80 F1
Horndean Cl
Crawley RH10 .....182 D2
3 Roehampton SW15 .....19 A7
Horndean Rd RG12 .....27 F3
Horne Rd TW17 .....34 A5
Hornecourt Hill RH6 .....162 F7
Horner La CR4 .....40 D7
Hornhatch GU4 .....131 B3
Hornhatch Cl GU4 .....131 B3
Hornhatch La GU4 .....131 B2
Horniman Dr SE23 .....23 C8
Horniman Grange **7**
SE23 .....23 C7
Horniman Mus & Gdns★
SE23 .....23 B7
Horniman Prim Sch SE23 23 B7
Hornsby House Sch
SW12 .....21 A7
Hornshill La RH12 .....213 F7
Horse Fair KT1 .....37 D7
Horse Gate Ride SL5 .....29 A3
Horse Hill RH6 .....160 B4
Horse Shoe Gn SM1 .....59 B8
Horsebrass Dr GU19 .....47 E2
Horsecroft SM7 .....77 F2
Horsecroft Mdws SM7 .....77 F3
Horsell Birch
Woking GU21 .....69 A4
Woking GU21 .....69 B4
Horsell CE Jun Sch GU21 69 C3
Horsell Common Rd
GU21 .....69 C5
Horsell Ct KT16 .....33 B2
Horsell Moor GU21 .....69 D2
Horsell Park Cl GU21 .....69 D3
Horsell Pk GU21 .....69 E3
Horsell Rise GU21 .....69 E4
Horsell Rise Cl GU21 .....69 D4
Horsell Vale GU21 .....69 E4
Horsell Village Sch GU21 69 D3
Horsell Way GU21 .....69 C3
Horseshoe Bend GU26 .188 B3
Horseshoe Cl
Camberley GU15 .....65 F8
Crawley RH10 .....202 D7
Horseshoe Cres GU15 .....65 F8
Horseshoe La
Ash Vale GU12 .....106 A7
Cranleigh GU6 .....174 D4
Horseshoe La E GU1 .....110 C2
Horseshoe La W GU1 .....110 B1
Horseshoe Ridge KT13 .72 C8
Horseshoe The
Banstead SM7 .....77 F4
Coulsdon CR5,CR8 .....79 D6
Godalming GU7 .....150 C3
Horsham Hospl RH12 .217 C3
Horsham Mus★ RH12 .217 C1
Horsham Rd Alfold GU6 .193 F8
Bramley GU5 .....151 E7
Capel RH5 .....178 C2
Capel RH5 .....178 D8
Cranleigh GU6 .....174 E1
Cranleigh GU6,RH12 .194 C1
Crawley RH11 .....201 B4
Crawley,Palmers Cross
GU5,GU6 .....173 D5
Dorking RH4 .....136 A6
Dorking, Mid Holmwood
RH5 .....136 B2
East Bedfont TW14 .....3 C1
Ellen's Green GU6 .....176 B1
Ewhurst GU6 .....175 F3

Horsham Rd continued
Holmbury St M RH5 .....155 C5
Rusper RH12 .....199 B5
Sandhurst GU47 .....45 D1
Shalford GU4 .....130 E3
South Holmwood RH5 .157 C6
Wallis Wood RH12,RH5 .196 D5
Wallis Wood,Mayes Green
RH5,GU6 .....176 E4
Horsham Sta RH13 .....217 D2
Horsley Cl KT19 .....76 D6
Horsley Ct KT24 .....92 E1
Horsley Dr
Kingston u T KT2 .....17 D3
New Addington CR0 .....63 C3
Horsley Rd KT11,KT24 .....93 B7
Horsley Sta KT24 .....92 E2
Horsneile La RG42 .....27 B8
Horton Ctry Pk KT19 .....57 A3
Horton Hill KT19 .....76 C8
Horton La KT19,KT18 .....57 B2
Horton Park Children's
Farm★ KT19 .....57 A1
Horton Rd Horton SL3 .....1 A6
Poyle SL3,TW19 .....1 E4
Stanwell TW19 .....2 A2
Horton Trad Est SL3 .....1 C4
Horton Way CR0 .....43 D4
Horvath Cl RH13 .....53 D6
Hosack Rd SW12,SW17 .21 A6
Hoskins Pl RH19 .....186 A4
Hoskins Place Ind Est
GU15 .....65 B3
Hoskins Rd RH8 .....122 E6
Hoskins The RH8 .....122 E6
Hoskins Wlk RH8 .....122 E6
Hospital Bridge Rd TW2 .16 B7
Hospital Hill GU11 .....105 A3
Hospital of the Holy Trinity
(Almshouses) **5** CR9 .....61 C8
Hospital Rd
Aldershot GU11 .....105 B3
Hounslow TW3 .....5 A4
Hospital Way **1** SE13 .....24 D8
Hostel Rd GU14 .....105 B8
Hotham Cl KT8 .....36 A6
Hotham Rd SW19 .....20 C1
Houblon Rd TW10 .....6 E2
Houghton Cl TW12 .....15 E2
Houghton Rd RH10 .....202 C3
Houlder Cres CR0 .....61 B4
Houlton Ct GU19 .....47 F2
Hound House Rd GU5 .154 A5
Hounslow Ave TW3 .....5 B2
Hounslow Bsns Pk TW3 .5 B3
Hounslow Central Sta
TW3 .....5 B2
Hounslow East Sta TW3 .5 C5
Hounslow Ed Ctr (Specl Sch)
The TW4 .....4 E4
Hounslow Gdns TW3 .....5 B2
Hounslow Heath Jun & Inf
Schs TW4 .....4 E4
Hounslow Heath Nature
Reserve★ TW4,TW14 .....4 E1
Hounslow Manor Sch
TW3 .....5 C4
Hounslow Rd
Feltham,Hanworth TW13 .15 D4
Feltham,North Feltham TW14 .4 B1
Twickenham TW2,TW3 .....5 C1
Hounslow Sta TW3 .....5 B2
Hounslow Town Prim Sch
TW3 .....5 D4
Hounslow West Sta TW3 .4 E5
Houseman Rd GU14 .....84 F6
Houston Ct **3** CR0 .....42 E1
Houston Rd
Forest Hill SE23,SE6 .....23 E5
Thames Ditton KT7 .....37 B3
Houstoun Ct TW5 .....4 F7
Hove Gdns SM1 .....40 B5
Hovenden Ho **6** SE21 .....22 E4
How La CR5 .....79 A1
Howard Ave KT17 .....58 A1
Howard Bldgs GU4 .....110 A5
Howard Cl Ashford TW16 .14 F2
Ashtead KT21 .....75 F1
Hampton TW12 .....16 C2
Leatherhead KT22 .....95 C4
Walton on the Hill KT20 .....97 A2
West Horsley KT24 .....92 D2
Howard Cole Way GU11 104 E2
Howard Ct
Beckenham BR3 .....44 C7
Effingham KT24 .....113 D8
Reigate RH2 .....118 B2
Howard Dr GU14 .....84 B4
Howard Gdns GU1 .....110 A2
Howard Ho Penge SE20 .....43 C8
Reigate RH2 .....118 B2
Howard of Effingham Sch
KT24 .....113 E8
Howard Pl RH1 .....118 A3
Howard Prim Sch CR0 .....61 C6
Howard Rd Coulsdon CR5 .79 D5
Crawley RH11 .....200 D2
Croydon SE25 .....43 A3
Dorking RH4 .....136 A7
Dorking, North Holmwood
RH5 .....136 C3
East Horsley KT24 .....93 A4
Great Bookham KT23 .114 C8
Horsham RH13 .....218 A4
Isleworth TW7 .....5 F4
New Malden KT3 .....38 F5
Penge SE20 .....43 C8
Reigate RH2 .....139 B8

Howard Rd continued
Surbiton KT5 .....37 F3
Wokingham RG40 .....25 C5
Howard Ridge GU4 .....110 A5
Howard St KT7 .....37 B3
Howards Cl GU22 .....90 A7
Howards Crest Cl BR3 .....44 C7
Howards La KT15 .....51 F3
Howards Rd GU22 .....89 F7
Howberry Rd CR7 .....42 D7
Howden Ct SE25 .....42 F7
Howden Rd SE25 .....42 F7
Howe Dr CR3 .....100 D5
Howe The GU14 .....84 B1
Howell Hill Cl KT17 .....77 C8
Howell Hill Gr KT17 .....58 C1
Howgate Rd SW14 .....7 D4
Howitts Cl KT10 .....55 A5
Howland Ho **9** SW16 .....21 E5
Howley Rd CR0,CR9 .....61 C7
Howmic Ct **1** TW1 .....6 C1
Howorth Ct RG12 .....27 E5
Howson Terr TW10 .....6 E1
Hoylake Cl RH11 .....200 D5
Hoylake Gdns CR4 .....41 C6
Hoyle Hill RH5 .....157 C1
Hoyle Rd SW17 .....20 F3
Hrmondsworth Moor Ctry Pk
UB7 .....2 B7
Hub Bldgs The **1** SW12 .21 B7
Hubbard Dr KT9 .....56 C4
Hubbard Rd SE27 .....22 C4
Hubberholme RG12 .....27 A6
Huddleston Cres RH1 .119 D7
Hudson Cl Croydon SE25 .43 A5
Guildford GU2 .....108 F1
4 Merton SW19 .....40 B8
Hudson Rd Crawley RH10 201 E4
Harlington UB7 .....3 D8
Hudsons KT20 .....97 D6
Huggins Pl SW2 .....21 F7
Hugh Herland KT1 .....37 E6
Hughenden Rd KT4 .....39 A2
Hughes Cl CR0 .....42 A1
Hughes Rd Ashford TW15 .14 C2
Wokingham RG40 .....25 E7
Hughes Wlk CR0 .....42 C2
Hullbrook La GU5 .....152 D4
Hullmead GU5 .....152 E4
Hulton Cl KT22 .....95 C4
Hulverston Cl SM2 .....59 B2
Humber Way GU47 .....64 D8
Humbolt Cl GU2 .....108 F1
Hummer Rd TW20 .....12 A4
Humphrey Cl KT22 .....94 C5
Humphries Yd RG12 .....27 C5
Hungerford Cl GU47 .....64 C8
Hungerford Sq **4** KT13 .53 D6
Hungry Hill La GU23 .....91 D3
Hunstanton Cl
Colnbrook SW3 .....1 C7
8 Crawley RH11 .....200 D5
Hunston Rd SM4 .....40 B1
Hunter Cl SW12 .....21 A7
Hunter Ct KT19 .....57 A1
Hunter Ho RH10 .....201 D3
Hunter Rd Crawley RH10 201 D4
Farnborough GU14 .....84 F3
Guildford GU1 .....130 E8
South Norwood CR7 .....42 D6
Wimbledon SW20 .....39 C8
Hunters Chase RH9 .142 F6
Hunters Cl KT19 .....76 C6
Hunters **5** TW9 .....6 D2
Hunters Mdw SE19 .....22 E4
Hunters Mews GU11 .....104 F2
Hunters Rd KT9 .....56 E6
Hunters The BR3 .....44 C8
Hunters Way CR0 .....61 E6
Huntersfield Cl RH2 .....118 B4
Hunting Cl KT10 .....55 A6
Hunting Gate Dr KT9 .....56 E3
Hunting Gate Mews
Sutton SM1 .....59 B7
Twickenham TW2 .....16 E7
Huntingdon Cl CR4,SW16 .41 E5
Huntingdon Ct SW14 .....7 C4
Huntingdon Gdns
Chiswick W4 .....7 C7
North Cheam KT4 .....58 C7
Huntingdon House Dr
GU26 .....188 E3
Huntingdon Rd
Redhill RH1 .....118 F1
Woking GU21 .....68 F2
Huntingfield CR0 .....62 F3
Huntingfield Way TW20 .12 D2
Huntingford Cl GU26 .188 C7
Huntley Ho **7** SE21 .....22 E4
Huntley Way SW20 .....39 A7
Huntly Rd SE25 .....42 E5
Hunts Cl GU2 .....108 D2
Hunts Hill Rd GU3 .....107 A4
Hunts Slip Rd SE21 .....22 E4
Huntsgreen Ct RG12 .....27 C7
Huntsman Cl TW13 .....15 B4
Huntsman's Mews GU16 .85 F3
Huntsmans Cl
Fetcham KT22 .....94 D3
Warlingham CR6 .....101 C8
Huntsmans Ct **2** CR3 .....100 C6
Huntsmans Mdw SL5 .....28 F8
Huntsmoor Rd KT19 .....57 B5
Huntspill St SW17 .....20 C5
Huntsworth Ct SE6 .....24 A7
Hurland La GU30,GU35 .187 A3
Hurlands Bsns Ctr GU9 .125 F4
Hurlands Cl GU9 .....125 F4

Hurlands La GU8 .....192 F2
Hurlands Pl GU9 .....125 F4
Hurley Cl KT12 .....54 B8
Hurley Ct RG12 .....27 E5
Hurley Gdns GU4 .....110 A4
Hurlford GU21 .....69 A2
Hurlstone Rd SE25 .....42 E4
Hurn Court Rd TW5 .....4 D5
Hurn Ct TW5 .....4 D5
Huron Rd SW17 .....21 A5
Hurricane Rd SM6 .....60 E3
Hursley Ct **11** KT6 .....37 D2
Hurst Ave RH12 .....217 D3
Hurst Cl Chessington KT9 .57 A5
Crawley RH11 .....200 F4
Hayes BR2 .....44 F1
Headley KT18 .....96 C3
Woking GU22 .....89 C7
Hurst Croft GU1 .....130 E6
Hurst Ct Beckenham BR3 .24 A1
Horsham RH12 .....217 D3
South Norwood SE25 .....42 F5
Hurst Dr KT20 .....97 A1
Hurst Farm Cl GU8 .....149 F2
Hurst Farm Rd RH19 .....205 D7
Hurst Gr KT12 .....34 F1
Hurst Green Cl RH8 .....123 A3
Hurst Green Rd RH8 .....122 F3
Hurst Green Sch RH8 .....123 A3
Hurst Green Sta RH8 .122 F4
Hurst Hill Cotts GU5 .....152 A4
Hurst Ho **7** SE26 .....23 B3
Hurst La East Molesey KT8 .36 D6
Headley KT18 .....96 D4
Thorpe TW20 .....32 A7
Hurst Lodge **4** KT13 .....53 D4
Hurst Park Prim Sch KT8 36 A6
Hurst Rd Aldershot GU11 .105 C4
Croydon CR0 .....61 D5
East Molesey KT8,KT12 .36 C6
Epsom KT19 .....76 D8
Farnborough GU14 .....85 B8
Headley KT18,KT20 .....96 E4
Horley RH6 .....160 E4
Horsham RH12 .....217 D3
Walton-on-T KT8,KT12 .....35 D5
Hurst View Rd CR2 .....61 E3
Hurst Way Pyrford GU22 .70 E5
South Croydon CR2 .....61 E4
Hurstbourne KT10 .....55 F4
Hurstbourne Ho SW15 .....7 F1
Hurstbourne Priors CR2 .61 E4
Hurstcourt Rd SE23 .....23 E7
Hurstcourt Rd SM1 .....59 B8
Hurstdene Ave Hayes BR2 44 F1
Staines TW18 .....13 B2
Hurstfield Rd KT8 .....36 A6
Hurstlands RH8 .....123 A3
Hurstleigh Cl RH1 .....118 F3
Hurstleigh Dr RH1 .....118 F3
Hurstmere Cl GU26 .....188 D3
Hurstmere Ho GU26 .....188 D3
Hurstview Grange CR2 .61 B3
Hurstwood SL5 .....29 A3
Hurtbank Cotts RH5 .....155 C6
Hurtmore Chase GU7 .150 B7
Hurtmore Rd GU7 .....150 B7
Hurtwood House Sch
(International Sixth Form
Coll) RH5 .....155 A2
Hurtwood Rd KT12 .....35 F2
Hussar Ct GU11 .....104 E2
Hussars Cl TW4 .....4 E4
Hutchinson's Rd CR0 .....82 C8
Hutchins Ho **8** SW4 .....21 D8
Hutchins Way RH6 .....160 F5
Hutsons Cl RG40 .....25 D8
Hutton Cl GU20 .....48 D3
Hutton Rd GU12 .....106 A6
Huxley Cl GU7 .....150 D7
Huxley Rd GU2 .....129 C8
Hyacinth Cl **3** TW12 .....16 A2
Hyacinth Rd SW15 .....19 A7
Hyde Cl TW16 .....14 E2
Hyde Ct TW4 .....4 F2
Hyde Dr RH11 .....200 E5
Hyde Farm Mews SW12 .21 D7
Hyde Heath Ct RH10 .202 D8
Hyde Ho **8** SM7 .....77 F5
Hyde La
Beacon Hill GU10,GU8 .168 E1
Thursley GU8 .....169 A2
Hyde Rd Richmond TW10 .....6 F2
Sanderstead CR2 .....80 E6
Hyde Terr TW15,TW16 .....14 E2
Hyde Wlk SM4 .....40 A2
Hydestile Cotts GU8 .....171 D5
Hydethorpe Rd SW12 .....21 C7
Hydons The GU8 .....171 E5
Hylands Cl Crawley RH10 202 A5
Epsom KT18 .....76 C4
Hylands Mews KT18 .....76 C4
Hylands Rd KT18 .....76 C4
Hylton Lodge KT12 .....54 C5
Hyndewood **14** SE23 .....23 D5
Hyperion Ct RH11 .....200 E4
Hyperion Ho **1** SW2 .....21 F8
Hyperion Pl KT19 .....57 D2
Hyperion Wlk RH6 .....161 B1
Hyrstdene CR0 .....61 B6
Hythe Cl RG12 .....27 E4
Hythe End Rd TW19 .....12 A5
Hythe Field Ave TW20 .....12 D2
Hythe Park Rd TW20 .....12 D2
Hythe Prim Sch TW18 .....12 D3
Hythe Rd Egham TW18 .....12 D3
South Norwood CR7,SE25 .42 D7

Hythe The TW18 ....12 E3

I

Ian Ct SE23 .....23 C6
Iberian Ave SM6 .....60 E5
Iberian Way GU15 .....66 B6
Ibis La W4 .....7 C6
Ibotson Ct SL3 .....1 E6
Ibsley Gdns SW15 .....19 A7
Ibstock Place Sch SW15 .7 E1
Icehouse Wood RH8 .122 F4
Icklesham Ho **9** RH11 .200 F3
Icklingham Gate KT11 .73 C7
Icklingham Rd KT11 .....73 D7
Iden Cl BR2 .....44 E6
Idlecombe Rd SW17 .....21 A2
Idmiston Rd
New Malden KT4 .....38 F2
West Norwood SE21,SE27 .22 C6
Idmiston Sq KT4 .....38 F2
Ifield Ave RH11 .....201 C2
Ifield Cl RH1 .....139 E7
Ifield Com Coll RH11 .201 A7
Ifield Fst Sch RH11 .....201 A8
Ifield Gn RH11 .....181 A1
Ifield Mid Sch RH11 .201 A6
Ifield Rd Charlwood RH6 .180 E5
Crawley, West Green
RH11 .....201 C6
Ifield St RH11 .....200 F8
Ifield Sta RH11 .....201 C6
Ifield Watermill★ RH11 .200 E5
Ifield Wood RH11 .....180 E1
Ifold Bridge La RH14 .212 D4
Ifold Rd RH1 .....140 A7
Ifoldhurst RH14 .....212 C2
Ightham Ho BR3 .....23 F1
Ikona Ct KT13 .....53 C5
Ildersly Gr SE21 .....22 D6
Ilex Cl
Englefield Green TW20 .....11 B1
Sunbury TW16 .....35 C7
Ilex Ho KT15 .....52 A1
Ilex Way SW16 .....22 A3
Ilford Ct GU6 .....173 F2
Ilfracombe Rd BR1 .....24 F5
Ilkley Rd SE19 .....22 D2
Illingworth Cl CR4 .....40 D6
Illingworth Gr RG12 .....27 F5
Imber Cl KT7 .....36 D1
Imber Court Trad Est
KT8 .....36 D3
Imber Cross KT7 .....36 F3
Imber Gr KT10 .....36 D2
Imber Park Rd KT10 .....36 D1
Imberhorne Bsns Ctr
RH19 .....185 B3
Imberhorne La RH19 .....185 B2
Imberhorne Lower Sch
RH19 .....185 D3
Imberhorne Sch RH19 .185 C3
Imberhorne Way RH19 .185 B3
Imjin Cl GU11 .....105 B3
Immanuel & St Andrew CE
Prim Sch SW16 .....21 E2
Impact Ct SE20 .....43 B7
Imperial Ctr RH10 .....182 A3
Imperial Gdns CR4 .....41 B6
Imperial Ho GU25 .....31 E4
Imperial Pk KT22 .....95 A7
Imperial Rd TW14 .....14 E8
Imperial Way CR0,CR9 .....61 A4
Impington **8** KT1 .....38 A7
Imran Ct GU12 .....126 C8
Ince Rd KT12 .....53 E4
Inchmery Rd SE6 .....24 C7
Inchwood Bracknell RG12 .27 C1
Croydon BR4,CR0 .....63 B6
Independent Bsns Pk The
RH19 .....185 A3
Ingatestone Rd SE25 .....43 B5
Ingham Cl CR2 .....62 D2
Ingham Rd CR2 .....62 D2
Ingle Dell GU15 .....65 D4
Ingle Ho SW12 .....21 D7
Ingleboro Dr CR8 .....80 D6
Ingleby Way SM6 .....60 D3
Inglemere Ct CR4,SW17 .20 C1
Inglemere Rd
Forest Hill SE23 .....23 D5
Mitcham CR4,SW17 .....20 C1
Ingleside SL3 .....1 F6
Ingleside Cl BR3 .....24 A1
Ingleton RG12 .....27 A6
Ingleton Rd SM5 .....59 E2
Inglewood
Addlestone KT16 .....51 F7
New Addington CR0 .....62 E2
Woking GU21 .....69 B1
Inglewood Ave GU15 .....66 D5
Inglewood Ct **3** BR1 .....24 F1
Inglis Rd CR0 .....42 F1
Ingram Cl RH12 .....217 A2
Ingram High Sch for Boys
CR7 .....42 C8
Ingram Ho KT8 .....37 D8
Ingram Rd CR7 .....42 C8
Ingrams Cl KT12 .....54 C5
Ingrebourne Ho BR1 .....24 D3
Inholms La RH5 .....136 C3
Inkerman Rd GU21 .....68 E1
Inkerman Way GU21 .....68 E1
Inkpen La RH18 .....206 F1
Inman Rd SW18 .....20 C8
Inner Park Rd SW19 .....19 D6

Inner Ring E TW6 ....3 B4
Inner Ring W TW6 ....3 A4
Innes Cl SW20 ....39 E7
Innes Lodge SE23 ......23 D5
Innes Rd RH12 ....217 F4
Innes Yd CR9 ....61 C7
Innings La RG12 ....27 E8
Innisfail Gdns GU11 ...125 F8
Inst of Oceanographic
  Sciences GU8 ....170 F1
Institute Rd
  Aldershot GU12 ......105 D1
  Westcott RH4 ....135 C6
Institute Wlk 3 RH19 .185 E1
Instow Gdns GU14 ......85 A7
Inval Hill GU27 ....208 C8
Inveresk Gdns KT4 .....58 A7
Inverness Ct SE6 ....24 F7
Inverness Rd
  Hounslow TW3 ....5 A3
  North Cheam KT4 .....39 D1
Inverness Way GU47 ....64 D7
Invicta Cl TW14 ....14 F7
Invicta Ct KT9 ....56 F5
Invincible Rd GU14 .....85 A3
Inwood Ave
  Coulsdon CR5 ....100 A7
  Hounslow TW3 ....5 C4
Inwood Bsns Pk TW3 .....5 B3
Inwood Cl CR0 ....62 E8
Inwood Ct 1 KT12 ......54 C8
Inwood Rd TW3 ....5 C3
Iona Cl Crawley RH11 ..201 B3
  Forest Hill SE13,SE4,SE6 ..24 A8
  Morden SM4 ....40 B2
Ipsley Lodge GU10 ....126 E5
Ipswich Rd SW17 ....21 A2
Irene Rd KT11 ....74 B5
Ireton Ave KT13 ....53 F8
Iris Cl Croydon CR0 ....43 D1
  Surbiton KT6 ....37 F2
Iris Rd Bisley GU24 ....68 A4
  West Ewell KT19 ......57 B5
Iron La GU5 ....151 D5
Ironsbottom RH2 ......159 F8
Irvine Cl CR7 ....42 A3
Irvine Dr GU14 ....84 E8
Irvine Pl GU25 ....31 E4
Irving Wlk RH10 ......201 E3
Irwin Dr RH12 ....217 A2
Irwin Rd GU2 ....130 A7
Isabel Cotts KT18 .....76 B5
Isabella Ct 8 TW10 .....6 F1
Isham Rd SW16 ....41 E7
Isis Ct W4 ....7 B7
Isis St SW18 ....20 C6
Isis Way GU47 ....64 D8
Island Cl TW18 ....12 E4
Island Cotts GU23 .....91 D6
Island Farm Ave KT8 ...35 F4
Island Farm Rd KT8 ....36 A4
Island Ho SW19 ....40 C5
Island Rd CR4,SW19 ....20 F1
Island The KT11 ....73 B1
Islay Gdns TW4 ....4 D2
Isleworth & Syon Sch for
  Boys TW7 ....5 E7
Isleworth Bsns Complex
  TW7 ....5 F5
Isleworth Sta TW7 ......5 F5
Isleworth Town Prim Sch
  TW7 ....6 A5
Islington Ho 1 RH11 ...201 B2
Itchingwood Common Rd
  RH8 ....123 E2
Ivanhoe Cl RH11 ......181 D1
Ivanhoe Ho 12 SW12 ....21 B8
Ivanhoe Rd TW4 ....4 D4
Iveagh Cl RH11 ....201 C1
Iveagh Ct Beckenham BR3 ..44 B6
  Bracknell RG12 ......27 C4
Iveagh Rd GU2 ....130 B7
Ively Rd GU14 ....84 D1
Ively Rdbt GU14 ....84 E2
Iverna Gdns TW14 ....3 D2
Ivers Way CR0 ....63 B3
Ivestor Terr SE23 .....23 C8
Ivies The 2 RH1 ......139 F8
Ivor Cl GU1 ....131 A8
Ivory Ct TW13 ....15 A7
Ivory Wlk RH11 ....200 E3
Ivy Cl TW16 ....35 C7
Ivy Dene La RH19 .....206 D6
Ivy Dr GU18 ....67 A7
Ivy Gdns CR4 ....41 D6
Ivy Hall Bglw GU6 ....174 D3
Ivy Hatch Ct 2 BR3 ....24 F1
Ivy Ho CR0 ....43 D1
Ivy La Farnham GU9 ...125 B2
  Hounslow TW4 ....4 F3
  Woking GU22 ....70 B1
Ivy Mill Cl RH9 ......121 D3
Ivy Mill La RH9,RH19 ..121 B3
Ivy Rd Aldershot GU12 .105 E2
  Hounslow TW3 ....5 B4
  Tolworth KT6 ....38 A1
  Upper Tooting SW17 ...20 E3
Ivybank GU7 ....150 E6
Ivybridge Cl 3 TW1 ....17 A8
Ivybridge Prim Sch TW1 ..6 E1
Ivychurch Cl SE20 .....23 C1
Ivydale Rd SM5 ....59 F8
Ivyday Gr SW16 ....21 F5
Ivydene
  East Molesey KT12,KT8 ..35 F4
  Knaphill GU21 ....68 B1
Ivydene Cl Redhill RH1 .140 B4

Ivydene Cl continued
  Sutton SM1 ....59 C6
Ivymount Rd SE27 ......22 A5

J

Jacaranda Cl KT3 ......38 E6
Jack Goodchild Way KT1 38 B6
Jackass La RH9 ....121 F4
Jackdaw Cl RH11 ......201 C8
Jackdaw La RH12 ......217 E6
Jackman's La GU21 ....89 A8
Jackson Cl Bracknell RG12 27 B4
  Crawley GU6 ....173 F2
  Epsom KT18 ....76 D5
Jackson Way KT19 ......57 A2
Jackson's Pl CR0 ......42 E1
Jackson's Way CR0 .....63 B7
Jacob Cl RG42 ....26 D7
Jacob Rd GU15 ....65 A7
Jacobean Cl RH10 .....202 C5
Jacobs Well Rd GU4 ...109 D6
Jaggard Way SW12 ......20 F8
Jaguar Rd GU14 ....85 B2
Jail La TN16 ....83 E3
Jamaica Rd CR7 ....42 A3
James Boswell 1 SW16 .22 A4
James Dixon Prim Sch
  SE20 ....23 B1
James Est CR4 ....40 F7
James Rd Camberley GU15 65 B2
  Shalford GU3 ....130 C1
James S Searle Ind Est
  RH12 ....217 E4
James St TW3 ....5 D4
James Watt Way RH10 .182 A4
James Way GU15 ....65 B2
Jameston RG12 ....27 C1
Jamieson Ho TW4 ....15 F4
Jamnagar Cl TW18 ......12 F2
Janoway Hill GU21 .....89 C8
Japonica Cl GU21 .....69 C1
Japonica Ct GU12 .....105 F3
Jarrett Cl SW2 ....22 B7
Jarrow Cl SM4 ....40 B4
Jarvis Rd CR2 ....61 D4
Jasmin Rd KT19 ....57 B5
Jasmine Cl Redhill RH1 140 A4
  Woking GU21 ....68 F3
Jasmine Ct
  Horsham RH12 ....217 C2
  11 Wallington SM6 ....60 B4
Jasmine Gdns CR0 ......63 B7
Jasmine Gr SE20 ....43 B8
Jasmine Way KT7 ....36 C5
Jason Cl Redhill RH1 ..139 E4
  Weybridge KT13 ......53 C5
Jasmine Ct
  Horsham RH12 ....217 C2
Jasons Dr GU4 ....110 C4
Jasper Ho KT4 ....38 D1
Jasper Rd SE19 ....22 F2
Javelin Ct RH10 ......182 D1
Jawahar Bagh SW16 ....22 B2
Jay Ave KT15 ....52 E7
Jay Wlk RH10 ....204 C5
Jay's La GU27 ....209 C3
Jays Cl SL5 ....29 D5
Jays Nest Cl GU17 .....64 D4
Jayson Ct 7 CR0 ....43 A1
Jeal Oakwood Ct KT18 ..76 E5
Jean Batten Cl SM6 ....60 F3
Jean Ho SW17 ....20 E3
Jean Humbert Ho 2
  SE27 ....22 D4
Jeans Ct 10 RH11 .....201 B5
Jeddere Cotts RH7 ....165 A2
Jeffries Pas GU1 .....130 D8
Jeffries Rd KT24 .....112 C5
Jeffs Cl TW12 ....16 B2
Jeffs Rd SM1 ....58 F6
Jefton Ct SM6 ....60 C4
Jemmett Cl KT2 ....38 B8
Jengar Cl SM1 ....59 B6
Jenkins Pl GU11 .....105 D8
Jenkins' Hill London Rd
  GU19 ....47 D2
Jenner Dr GU24 ....68 A6
Jenner Rd Crawley RH10 181 F3
  Guildford GU1 ......130 E8
Jenner Way KT19 ....57 A2
Jenners Cl RH7 ....164 D4
Jennett Rd CR0,CR9 ....61 A7
Jennifer Rd BR1 ....24 F5
Jennings Cl
  Long Ditton KT6 ......37 C2
  New Haw KT15 ....52 C2
Jennings Way RH6 ....161 D3
Jenny La RH7 ....164 C4
Jennys Way CR5 ....99 C5
Jenson Way SE19 ....22 F1
Jeppo's La CR4 ....40 F5
Jerome Cnr RG45 ......45 C3
Jersey Cl Addlestone KT16 .51 F7
  Guildford GU4 ......110 B6
Jersey Rd Crawley RH11 .201 A2
  Hounslow TW5,TW7 .....5 D7
  Mitcham CR4 ....21 B2
Jerviston Gdns SW16 ...22 A2
Jesmond Cl CR4 ....41 B6
Jesmond Rd CR0 ....42 F2
Jessamy Rd KT13 ....53 B8
Jesses La GU5 ....154 C8
Jessie's Hollow GU5 ..133 C1
Jessiman Terr TW17 ....34 A4
Jessops Way CR0,CR4 ...41 C3
Jeston Ho 9 SE27 ......22 B5
Jevington RG12 ....27 C1
Jewell Ho 3 SW12 .....21 C8

Jewels Hill TN16 ......83 A6
Jews Wlk SE26 ....23 B4
Jeypore Rd SW18 ....20 C8
Jig's La S RG42 ....27 E8
Jillian Cl TW12 ....16 A1
Jobson's La GU27 .....209 D2
Jocelyn Rd TW9 ....6 E4
Jock's La RG42 ....26 E8
Jockey Mead RH12 ....217 A1
Jodie Ct BR3 ....24 A2
Jodrell Cl TW7 ....6 A6
Joe Hunte Ct 2 SW27 ...22 B3
John Austin Cl KT2 ....37 F8
John Baird Ct SE26 ....23 D4
John Baird Ho 18 SE20 .23 C1
John Burns Cotts RH8 .123 E5
John Cl GU11 ....105 D8
John Cobb Rd KT13 .....53 A3
John Dee Ho 3 SW14 ....7 D4
John F Kennedy Meml★
  TW20 ....11 D6
John Fisher Sch The CR8 60 E1
John Gale Ct KT17 .....57 F2
John Kaye Ct TW17 .....34 A4
John Kirk Ho 5 SW16 ...21 E5
John Nike Way GU22 ....26 C7
John Pounds Ho RH11 ..201 D4
John Ruskin Coll CR2 ..62 E3
John Russell Cl GU2 ..109 A4
John St Croydon SE25 ..43 A5
  Hounslow TW3,TW5 .....4 E5
John Watkin Cl SW17 ...57 B2
John Wesley Ct 6 TW1 ..17 A7
John William Cl KT2 ...37 D8
John Wiskar Dr GU6 ...174 D2
John's Ct SM2 ....59 B4
John's Rd TN16 ....103 D7
John's Terr 42 E1
Johns La SM4 ....40 C4
Johns Wlk CR3 ....101 A8
Johnsdale RH8 ....122 F6
Johnson Rd Heston TW5 ..4 C7
  Thornton Heath CR0 ..42 D2
Johnson Wlk RH10 ....201 E3
Johnson's Cl SM5 .....59 F7
Johnsons Dr TW12 ......36 C8
Johnston Gr GU2 .....109 A5
Johnston Wlk GU2 ....109 A5
Joinville Pl KT15 .....52 D6
Jolesfield RH11 ......200 F3
Jolliffe Rd RH1 ....99 C1
Jones Cnr SL5 ....28 E8
Jones Wlk 6 TW10 ......6 F1
Jonquil Gdns 5 CR0 ....43 D1
Jonson Cl CR4 ....41 B6
Jordan Cl CR2 ....80 F8
Jordans Cl Crawley RH11 201 D8
  Guildford GU1 ......110 A2
  Redhill RH1 ....140 A4
  Stanwell TW19 ....13 C8
Jordans Cres RH11 ....181 D1
Jordans The RH11 .....205 E8
Josef Perrin Ho 1 SE27 22 D4
Joseph Hood Fst Sch
  SW20 ....39 E6
Joseph Locke Way KT10 .55 A8
Joseph's Rd GU1 ......109 D2
Josephine Ave KT20 ...117 F8
Josephine Cl KT20 ....117 F8
Joshua Cl CR2 ....61 B3
Joshua Oldfield Ho
  SW17 ....20 F3
Joviel Ho TW18 ....13 A1
Jubilee Ave
  North Ascot SL5 .....28 E8
  Twickenham TW2 ....16 B7
  Wokingham RG41 ......25 B7
Jubilee Cl
  Farnborough GU14 ....84 D4
  North Ascot SL5 .....28 E8
  Stanwell TW19 ....13 D8
  Teddington KT1 ......37 C8
Jubilee Cres KT15 .....52 D5
Jubilee Ct Bracknell RG12 27 C6
  Hounslow TW3 ....5 B4
  Staines TW18 ....13 A4
  Thornton Heath CR7 ..42 A5
Jubilee Dr GU12 ......106 A6
Jubilee Hall Rd GU14 ..85 C4
Jubilee High Sch KT15 .52 A5
Jubilee Ho 5 TW12 .....36 A8
Jubilee La
  Grayshott GU26 .....188 C3
  Rowledge GU10 ......146 A5
Jubilee Rd
  Aldershot GU11 .....126 B7
  Cheam SM3 ....58 D3
  Mytchett GU16 ....86 A2
  Rudgwick RH12 ......214 D8
Jubilee Terr
  Brockham RH3 ....137 C5
  Dorking RH4 ....136 B8
Jubilee Villas KT10 ...36 E1
Jubilee Way
  East Bedfont TW14 ...15 A7
  Merton SW19 ....40 B8
  Tolworth KT4,KT9 .....57 B7
Jubilee Wks SW19 ......40 C7
Jubilee Wlk RH10 .....202 A6
Judge Wlk KT10 ....55 E4
Judy's Terr RH19 .....205 E8
Julian Cl GU21 ....69 C1
Julian Hill KT13 ......53 B3
Julian Ho SE21 ....22 E2
Julian Taylor Path SE23 23 B6
Julian's Sch SW16 .....22 A4

Julien Rd CR5 ....79 D4
Juliet Gdns RG42 ......27 F8
Julius Ct TW8 ....6 E7
Julius Hill RG42 ......27 F8
Jumps Rd GU10 ....168 B3
Junction Pl GU27 ....207 F6
Junction Rd
  Ashford TW15 ....14 D3
  Croydon CR2 ....61 D4
  Dorking RH4 ....136 A7
  Lightwater GU18 .....48 B1
June Cl CR5 ....79 B5
June La RH1 ....140 B2
Junewood Cl KT15 ......70 F8
Juniper RG12 ....27 C1
Juniper Cl Biggin Hill TN16 83 E2
  Chessington KT9 .....56 F5
  Guildford GU1 ......109 C6
  Reigate RH2 ....139 C7
Juniper Ct TW3 ....5 B3
Juniper Dr GU24 ....68 A4
Juniper Gdns
  Ashford TW16 ....14 F2
  Mitcham CR4 ....41 C8
Juniper Hall (Field Study Ctr)
  RH5 ....115 C6
Juniper Pl GU4 ....130 D2
Juniper Rd
  Crawley RH11 ....181 C1
  Farnborough GU14 ....84 C5
  Reigate RH2 ....139 C7
Juniper Terr GU4 .....130 D2
Juniper Wlk RH3 ......137 C7
Jura Cl RH11 ....201 B3
Justin Cl TW8 ....6 D7
Jutland Gdns CR5 ......99 F7
Jutland Pl TW20 ....12 C3
Jutland Rd SE6 ....24 C8
Juxon Cl RH11 ....200 F4

K

Kaithewood Ho RH12 ..218 B5
Kangley Bridge Ctr SE26 23 F3
Kangley Bridge Rd SE26 23 F3
Karen Ct BR1 ....44 F8
Kashmir Cl KT15 ....52 D2
Kashmir Ct 3 GU14 ....85 C1
Katana GU22 ....89 E8
Katharine Rd 1 TW1 ...17 A7
Katharine St CR0,CR9 ..61 C7
Katherine Cl KT15 .....52 A4
Katherine Ct
  2 Camberley GU15 ....65 D5
  Forest Hill SE23 ....23 C7
Kathleen Moore Ct BR4 63 C8
Kay Ave KT15 ....52 E7
Kay Cres GU35 ....187 B6
Kaye Ct GU1 ....109 C5
Kaye Don Way KT13 .....53 A1
Kayemoor Rd SM2 ......59 E4
Kaynes Pk SL5 ....28 E8
Keable Rd GU10 ......145 E7
Kearton Cl CR8 ....80 C2
Keates Gn RG42 ....27 B8
Keats Ave RH1 ....119 B3
Keats Cl Horsham RH12 .217 F7
  Mitcham SW17,SW19 ...20 D2
Keats Ho BR3 ....24 B2
Keats Pl RH19 ....185 D1
Keats Way
  Crowthorne RG45 .....45 B6
  Croydon CR0 ....43 C3
  New Malden KT4 ......38 F1
Keble Cl Crawley RH10 .182 D1
  New Malden KT4 ......38 F1
Keble Ct 7 SW19 ......20 C4
Keble St SW17 ....20 C4
Keble Way GU47 ....45 E2
Kedeston Ct SM3 ......40 B1
Keeble Ho RG41 ....25 A6
Keedonwood Rd BR1 ....24 F3
Keeley Rd CR0,CR9 .....61 C8
Keeling Ho 2 TW11 ....16 E3
Keen's Rd CR0 ....61 C6
Keens Cl SW16 ....21 D3
Keens La GU2,GU3 ....108 F5
Keens Park Rd GU3 ...108 F5
Keep Hatch Prim Sch
  RG40 ....25 D7
Keep The Catford SE6 ..24 B7
  Kingston u T KT2 .....17 F1
Keepers Cl GU4 ......110 D4
Keepers Combe RG12 ...27 D3
Keepers Mews TW11 ....17 C2
Keepers Terr GU25 ....31 B4
Keepers Wlk GU25 .....31 D4
Keephatch Rd RG40 ....25 E7
Keevil Dr SW19 ....19 E8
Keir Hardie Ho 7 RH11 201 B1
Keith Lucas Rd GU14 ..84 E7
Keith Park Cres TN16 ..83 C7
Keldholme RG12 ....27 A6
Kelling Gdns CR0 .....42 B2
Kellino St SW17 ....20 F4
Kelly Cl TW17 ....34 E7
Kelmscott 5 SE23 .....23 D5
Kelsey Cl RH6 ....160 F3
Kelsey Ct BR3 ....44 B6
Kelsey Gate 8 BR3 ....44 B6
Kelsey Gdns BR3 ......44 A6
Kelsey La BR3 ....44 A6
Kelsey Park Ave BR3 ..44 B7
Kelsey Park Rd BR3 ...44 A7
Kelsey Park Sch BR3 ..44 A6
Kelsey Sq 2 BR3 ......44 A7
Kelsey Way BR3 ....44 A6
Kelso Cl RH10 ....202 E7

Kelso Ct SE20 ....23 B1
Kelso Rd SM5 ....40 C2
Kelvedon Ave KT12 .....53 F3
Kelvedon Cl KT2 ....18 A2
Kelvin Ave KT22 ....94 F8
Kelvin Bsns Ctr RH10 .181 F2
Kelvin Cl KT19 ....57 A4
Kelvin Ct Chiswick W4 ..7 C7
  Isleworth TW7 ....5 E5
  8 Penge SE20 ....43 B8
  8 Twickenham TW1 .....6 B1
Kelvin Dr TW1 ....6 B1
Kelvin Gdns CR0 ....41 E2
Kelvin Gr Chessington KT6 56 F7
  Forest Hill SE26 ....23 B5
Kelvin Grove Prim Sch
  SE26 ....23 B5
Kelvin Ho RH10 ......181 F2
Kelvin La RH10 ......181 F2
Kelvin Way RH10 .....181 F2
Kelvinbrook KT8 ......36 B6
Kelvington KT20 ......43 C2
Kelyway Ho 20 SW2 ....22 A8
Kemble Cl KT13 ....53 D6
Kemble Cotts KT15 ....52 A6
Kemble Rd
  Croydon CR0,CR9 .....61 B7
  Forest Hill SE23 ....23 D7
Kembleside Rd TN16 ...83 C1
Kemerton Rd
  Beckenham BR3 ....44 B7
  Croydon CR0 ....42 F2
Kemishford GU22 ......89 A4
Kemnal Pk GU27 ......208 D7
Kemp Ct GU19 ....47 F2
Kemp Gdns CR0 ....42 C3
Kempshott Rd
  Horsham RH12 ....217 B4
  Streatham SW16 ......21 D1
Kempston Ho SM2 ......59 B2
Kempton Ave TW16 .....35 B8
Kempton Ct
  Farnborough GU14 ....84 F2
  Sunbury TW16 ....35 B8
Kempton Ho RH10 .....97 C4
Kempton Lodge SM6 ....60 D7
Kempton Park Race Course
  TW16 ....15 C1
Kempton Park Sta TW16 15 B1
Kempton Wlk CR0 ......43 E3
Kemsing Cl Coney Hall BR2 63 F8
  Thornton Heath CR7 ..42 C5
Kemsley Rd TN16 .....103 D8
Kendal Cl
  East Bedfont TW14 ...14 F7
  Farnborough GU14 ....84 E4
  Redhill RH2 ....118 D2
Kendal Ct 7 CR0 ......42 E2
Kendal Gdns SM1 ......59 C8
Kendal Gr GU15 ....66 D4
Kendal Ho 5 Croydon CR0 42 E1
  Penge SE20 ....43 B7
Kendale Cl RH10 .....202 C2
Kendale Rd BR1 ....24 E3
Kendall Ave Penge BR3 .43 E7
  South Croydon CR2 ...61 D2
Kendall Ave S CR2 ....61 D1
Kendall Ct 4 SE19 ....22 E2
Kendall Ct Bsns Pk GU17 64 F4
  Penge BR3 ....43 E7
Kendor Ave KT19 ......76 C8
Kendra Hall Rd CR2 ...61 B3
Kendrey Gdns TW2 .....16 E8
Kendrick Cl RG40 .....25 C5
Kenilford Rd SW12 ....21 B8
Kenilworth Ave
  Bracknell RG12 ......27 D8
  Oxshott KT11 ....74 B5
  Wimbledon SW19 ......20 A4
Kenilworth Cl
  Banstead SM7 ....78 B3
  Crawley RH11 ....201 B2
Kenilworth Ct 7 TW2 ..16 E6
Kenilworth Dr KT12 ...54 D7
Kenilworth Gdns SW18 .13 C3
Kenilworth Rd
  Ashford TW15,TW19 ...13 D5
  Farnborough GU14 ....84 C5
  Penge SE20 ....43 D8
  Stoneleigh KT17 .....58 A5
Kenilworth Terr 5 SM2 59 A3
Kenley Cl CR3 ....100 E7
Kenley Gdns CR7 ......42 B5
Kenley Ho CR8 ....80 D3
Kenley La CR8 ....80 D3
Kenley Prim Sch CR3 ..80 E3
Kenley Rd
  Headley Down GU35 ..187 C5
  Kingston u T KT1,KT3 .38 B7
  Merton SW19 ....40 A6
  Twickenham TW1 ....6 B1
Kenley Sta CR8 ....80 C5
Kenley Wlk SM3 ....58 D6
Kenlor Rd SW17 ....20 D3
Kenmara Cl RH10 .....182 A1
Kenmara Ct RH10 .....182 A2
Kenmare Dr CR4 ....20 F1
Kenmare Rd CR7 ....42 A3
Kenmore Cl Frimley GU16 85 D3
  Richmond TW9 ....7 A7
Kenmore Rd CR8 ....80 B5
Kennard Ct RH18 .....206 E3
Kennedy Ave RH19 ....185 D3

Kennedy Cl CR4 . 41 A7
Kennedy Ct TW15 . 14 C3
Kennedy Rd RH13 . 217 D1
Kennel Ave SL5 . 28 F8
Kennel Cl Fetcham KT22 . 94 C3
North Ascot SL5 . 8 F2
Kennel Gn SL5 . 28 E8
Kennel La Fetcham KT22 . 94 C4
Frensham GU10 . 146 C2
Hookwood RH6 . 160 D2
Windlesham GU20 . 48 C5
Kennel Ride SL5 . 8 F1
Kennel Wood SL5 . 28 F8
Kennel Wood Cres CR0 . 82 D8
Kennels La GU14 . 84 C2
Kennet Cl Ash GU12 . 106 A1
Crawley RH11 . 200 F5
Farnborough GU14 . 84 E6
Kennet Ho 6 RH1 . 118 F2
Kennet Rd TW7 . 5 F4
Kennet Sq CR4 . 40 E8
Kenneth Rd SM7 . 78 D4
Kennoldes SE21 . 22 D6
Kenny Dr SM5 . 60 A2
Kenrick Sq RH1 . 120 E1
Kensington Ave CR7 . 42 A8
Kensington Avenue Inf Sch CR7 . 42 A8
Kensington Avenue Jun Sch CR7 . 42 A8
Kensington Rd RH11 . 201 C2
Kensington Terr CR2 . 61 D3
Kent Cl Mitcham CR4,SW16 41 E5
Staines TW18 . 13 D2
Kent Dr TW11 . 16 E3
Kent Gate Way
Addington CR0 . 63 B5
New Addington CR0,CR2 . 62 F4
Kent Hatch Rd RH8,TN8 . 123 D4
Kent House La BR3 . 23 E3
Kent House Rd SE26,BR3 . 23 E2
Kent House Sta BR3 . 43 E8
Kent House Station App BR3 . 43 D8
Kent Lodge 9 SW19 . 19 D7
Kent Rd East Molesey KT8 . 36 C5
Kingston u T KT1 . 37 D6
Richmond TW9 . 7 A7
West Wickham BR4 . 44 B1
Windlesham GU20 . 48 D5
Woking GU22 . 70 C3
Kent Way KT6 . 56 F8
Kentigern Dr RG45 . 45 E5
Kenton Ave TW16 . 35 E7
Kenton Cl Bracknell RG12 . 27 D7
Frimley GU16 . 65 F1
Kenton Ct SE26 . 23 E4
Kenton Way GU21 . 68 F2
Kentwyns Rise RH1 . 140 F8
Kenwood Cl UB7 . 3 A8
Kenwood Dr
Beckenham BR3 . 44 C6
Hersham KT12 . 54 B5
Kenwood Pk KT13 . 53 D4
Kenwood Ridge CR8 . 80 B2
Kenworth Gr GU18 . 48 A1
Kenwyn Rd SW20 . 39 C8
Kenya Ct RH6 . 160 F4
Kenyngton Dr TW16 . 15 A3
Kenyngton Manor Prim Sch TW16 . 15 A2
Kenyons KT24 . 112 B7
Keogh Barracks GU16 . 86 B1
Keogh Cl GU12 . 86 B2
Keppel Rd RH4 . 115 B1
Keppel Spur SL4 . 11 B8
Kepple Pl GU19 . 47 F3
Kerlin Ct 4 CR4 . 40 E8
Kerria Way GU24 . 67 F6
Kerrill Ave CR5 . 100 A8
Kerrsland Cotts GU7 . 149 F7
Kerry Terr GU21 . 70 B3
Kersey Dr CR2 . 81 D7
Kershaw Ho 7 SE27 . 22 B5
Keston Ave
Coulsdon CR5,CR8 . 100 B8
Woodham KT15 . 71 A8
Keston Avenue Jun & Inf Schs CR5 . 100 A8
Keston Rd CR7 . 42 A3
Kestrel Ave TW18 . 12 F5
Kestrel Cl Crawley RH11 . 201 C8
Crondall GU10 . 124 D7
Epsom KT19 . 76 B8
Guildford GU4 . 110 D3
Horsham RH12 . 217 E5
Kingston u T KT2 . 17 D4
Kestrel Ho GU9 . 146 A8
Kestrel Rd GU14 . 85 B2
Kestrel Way
New Addington CR0 . 63 D2
Woking GU21 . 69 B3
Kestrel Wlk RH10 . 204 C5
Keswick Ave
Kingston u T SW15 . 18 E3
Merton SW19 . 40 A7
Upper Halliford TW17 . 34 E6
Keswick Cl
Crawley RH11 . 200 D4
Frimley GU15 . 66 D4
Sutton SM1 . 59 C6
Keswick Ct
15 Bromley BR2 . 44 F5
Catford SE6 . 24 F7
Keswick Dr GU18 . 67 B8
Keswick Rd
Fetcham KT22,KT23 . 94 C2
Thorpe Lea TW20 . 12 B1
Twickenham TW2 . 5 C1
West Wickham BR4 . 63 E8
Witley GU8 . 170 D6
Kettering Ct CR7 . 42 C5
Kettering St SW16 . 21 C2
Kettlewell Cl GU21 . 69 E4
Kettlewell Dr GU21 . 69 E5
Kettlewell Hill GU21 . 69 E4
Ketton Gn RH1 . 119 D7
Kevan Dr GU23 . 90 E2
Kevin Cl TW4 . 4 D5
Kew Bridge Rd TW8 . 6 F8
Kew Cres SM3 . 58 F7
Kew Foot Rd TW9 . 6 E4
Kew Gardens Rd TW9 . 7 A6
Kew Gardens Sta TW9 . 7 A6
Kew Gn TW9 . 6 F8
Kew Lodge 10 TW9 . 6 F6
Kew Montessori Sch TW9 . 7 A6
Kew Obsy* TW9 . 6 C4
Kew Pal* TW9 . 6 E7
Kew Rd TW9,W4 . 6 F5
Kew Ret Pk TW9 . 7 B6
Key Cross GU10 . 147 D5
Keymer Cl TN16 . 83 D3
Keymer Rd
Crawley RH11 . 201 D4
Streatham SW2 . 21 F6
Keynsham Rd SM4 . 40 B1
Keynsham Way GU47 . 45 D2
Keynsham Wlk SM4 . 40 B1
Keysham Ave TW5 . 4 A6
Keywood Dr TW16 . 15 A2
Khama Rd SW17 . 20 E4
Khartoum Rd
Upper Tooting SW17 . 20 D4
Witley GU8 . 170 E6
Kibble Gn RG12 . 27 C3
Kidborough Down KT23 114 A8
Kidborough Rd RH11 . 200 F4
Kidbrooke Rise RH18 . 206 E2
Kidderminster Pl CR0 . 42 B1
Kidderminster Rd CR0 . 42 C2
Kidmans Cl RH12 . 217 F5
Kidworth Cl RH6 . 160 F5
Kielder Wlk GU15 . 66 C4
Kier Pk SL5 . 29 C6
Kilberry Cl TW7 . 5 D6
Kilcorral Cl KT17 . 77 A5
Killasser Ct KT20 . 97 C4
Killburns Mill Cl SM6 . 60 B8
Killearn Rd SE6 . 24 D7
Killester Gdns KT17,KT4 . 58 B6
Killick Ho SM1 . 59 B6
Killicks GU6 . 174 F4
Killieser Ave SW2 . 21 E6
Killigrew Ho 4 TW16 . 14 E1
Killinghurst La GU27, GU8 . 209 D8
Killross Rd TW14 . 14 D7
Kilmarnock Pk RH2 . 118 B2
Kilmartin Ave SW16 . 42 A6
Kilmartin Gdns GU16 . 65 F1
Kilmington Cl RG12 . 27 E2
Kilmiston Ave TW17 . 34 C3
Kilmiston Ho TW17 . 34 C3
Kilmore Dr GU15 . 66 B4
Kilmorey Gdns TW1 . 6 B3
Kilmorey Rd TW1 . 6 B3
Kilmorie Prim Sch SE23 . 23 E6
Kilmorie Rd SE23 . 23 E6
Kilmuir Cl GU47 . 64 D7
Kiln Cl UB3 . 3 D8
Kiln Copse GU6 . 174 E4
Kiln Fields GU27 . 208 C8
Kiln La Bracknell RG12 . 27 A7
Brockham RH3 . 116 C1
Ewell KT17 . 76 E8
Farnham GU10,GU9 . 146 C6
Horley RH6 . 161 A5
Ripley GU23 . 91 B3
Sunningdale SL5 . 30 A4
Winkfield SL4 . 9 B2
Kiln Mdws GU3 . 108 C5
Kiln Mews SW17 . 20 D3
Kiln Rd RH10 . 204 B7
Kiln Way Aldershot GU11 . 126 B7
Grayshott GU26 . 187 E5
Kiln Wlk RH1 . 140 A4
Kilnfield Rd RH12 . 214 D8
Kilnmead RH10 . 201 E7
Kilnmead Cl RH10 . 201 E7
Kilnside KT10 . 56 A3
Kilnwood La
Crawley RH12 . 200 B3
Faygate RH12 . 199 F3
Kilross Rd TW14 . 14 E7
Kilrue La KT12 . 53 F6
Kilrush Terr GU21 . 70 A3
Kilsha Rd KT12 . 35 C3
Kimber Ct GU4 . 110 D3
Kimber Ctr The SW18 . 20 A8
Kimber Rd SW18 . 20 B8
Kimberley RG12 . 27 C1
Kimberley Cl RH6 . 160 E3
Kimberley Pl 7 CR8 . 80 A8
Kimberley Rd
Crawley RH10 . 202 B7
Penge BR3 . 43 D7
Thornton Heath CR0,CR7 . 42 B3
Kimberley Ride KT11 . 74 B6
Kimberley Wlk KT12 . 35 B2
Kimbers La GU9 . 125 D3
Kimble Rd SW17 . 20 D2
Kimbolton Cl 1 SE12 . 24 F8
Kimmeridge RG12 . 27 E3
Kimpton Bsns Ctr SM3 . 58 F8
Kimpton Ho SW15 . 19 A8
Kimpton Ind Est SM3 . 58 F8
Kimpton Rd SM3 . 58 F8
Kinburn Dr TW20 . 11 E3
Kindell Ho 4 SW14 . 7 D4
Kindersley Cl RH19 . 186 B3
Kinfauns Rd SW2 . 22 A6
King Acre Ct TW18 . 12 E5
King Alfred Ave SE6 . 24 A4
King Athelstan Prim Sch KT1 . 37 F6
King Charles Cres KT5 . 37 F2
King Charles Wlk 6 SW19 . 19 E7
King Charles' Rd KT5,KT6 37 F3
King Edward Dr KT6 . 56 E7
King Edward's Gr TW11 . 17 C2
King Edward's Sch GU8 170 F1
King Edwards Cl SL5 . 28 E8
King Edwards Rd SL5 . 28 E8
King Edwards Rise SL5 . 28 E8
King Garth Mews SE23 . 23 C6
King Gdns CR0 . 61 B5
King George Ave
East Grinstead RH19 . 185 C3
Walton-on-T KT12 . 35 D1
King George Cl
Ashford TW16 . 14 E3
Farnborough GU14 . 85 D2
King George Sq TW10 . 6 F1
King George V1 Ave TN16 . 83 D3
King George VI Ave CR4 . 40 F5
King George's Cotts GU8 . 192 F6
King George's Dr KT15 . 52 A1
King George's Lodge GU2 . 109 A4
King George's Trad Est KT9 . 57 A6
King Henry's Dr CR0 . 82 E8
King Henry's Rd KT1,KT3 . 38 B6
King St Chertsey KT16 . 33 A1
East Grinstead RH19 . 185 E1
Richmond TW10,TW9 . 6 D2
Twickenham TW1 . 17 A7
King Street Par 6 TW1 . 17 A7
King William IV Gdns SE20 . 23 C2
King's Ave Ashford TW16 . 14 F2
Hounslow TW3,TW5 . 5 B6
King's Cl Staines TW18 . 13 D1
Thames Ditton KT7 . 37 A2
King's Coll Sch SW19 . 19 D2
King's Court First Sch SL4 . 11 B8
King's Ct
Aldershot GU10,GU12 . 126 E8
Beckenham BR3 . 44 B6
Wimbledon SW19 . 20 A2
King's Dr KT7 . 37 B2
King's Head La KT14 . 71 D8
King's House Jun Sch TW10 . 6 F2
King's House Sch TW10 . 6 F2
King's Keep
Beckenham BR2 . 44 E6
Sandhurst GU47 . 45 B1
King's La SM1 . 59 D5
King's Paddock TW12 . 36 C8
King's Pas KT2 . 37 D8
King's Rd Aldershot GU11 104 F1
Ascot SL5 . 29 D4
Cranleigh GU6 . 174 F2
Crowthorne RG45 . 45 C5
Croydon SE25 . 43 A6
Egham TW20 . 12 A4
Farncombe GU7 . 150 F6
Haslemere GU27 . 208 A6
Horsham RH13 . 217 E3
Kingston u T KT2 . 18 E1
Long Ditton KT6 . 37 C1
Mortlake SW14 . 7 D4
Teddington TW11 . 16 D3
Twickenham TW1 . 6 B1
Wimbledon SW19 . 20 A2
King's Ride Bracknell SL5 . 28 D5
Camberley GU15 . 65 D7
King's Ride Ho SL5 . 28 E5
King's Shade Wlk 1 KT18 . 76 D6
King's Terr 8 TW7 . 6 A4
King's Way GU24 . 87 D8
King's Wlk GU15 . 64 F6
King's Yd SL5 . 28 E5
Kingates Ct BR3 . 44 B6
Kingcup Cl CR0 . 43 D1
Kingcup Dr GU24 . 68 A4
Kingfield Cl GU22 . 89 F7
Kingfield Dr GU22 . 89 F7
Kingfield Gdns GU22 . 89 F7
Kingfield Rd GU22 . 89 F7
Kingfield Sch GU22 . 90 A7
Kingfisher Cl
Crawley RH10 . 182 A1
Farnborough GU14 . 84 D6
Hersham KT12 . 54 E5
Putney SW19 . 19 E6
Kingfisher Ct Cheam SM1 . 58 F5
4 Dorking RH4 . 136 A8
East Molesey KT8 . 36 E5
Guildford GU4 . 110 D3
Isleworth TW3 . 5 B2
Sheerwater GU21 . 70 C5
Woking GU21 . 69 E2
Kingfisher Dr
Guildford GU4 . 110 C3
Redhill RH1 . 119 A3
Staines TW18 . 12 F4
Teddington TW11 . 17 B4
Kingfisher Gdns CR2 . 62 D1
Kingfisher La RH10 . 204 C5
Kingfisher Lodge TW11 . 17 A4
Kingfisher Rise RH19 . 205 F8
Kingfisher Sports Ctr The 12 KT1 . 37 E7
Kingfisher Way
Beckenham CR0 . 43 D4
Horsham RH12 . 217 C5
Kingfisher Wlk GU12 . 105 F2
Kingham Cl SW18 . 20 C8
Kingham Pl GU9 . 125 B2
Kings Acre RH1 . 140 F6
Kings Apartments GU15 . 65 C4
Kings Ave Ash GU10 . 126 F8
Bromley BR1 . 24 F2
Byfleet KT14 . 71 D7
New Malden KT3 . 38 F5
Redhill RH1 . 139 E7
Streatham SW12,SW4 . 21 D8
Wallington SM5 . 59 F3
Kings Chase KT8 . 36 C6
Kings Cl KT12 . 35 B1
Kings Copse 9 RH19 . 205 F8
Kings Cres GU15 . 65 C8
Kings Cross La RH1 . 140 E6
Kings Ct Horsham RH13 . 217 E3
16 Kingston u T KT2 . 18 B1
Leatherhead KT22 . 95 A6
11 Roehampton SW15 . 19 A8
Tadworth KT20 . 97 C5
3 Wallington SM6 . 60 B4
Kings Dr KT5 . 38 A3
Kings Dr The KT12 . 53 F2
Kings Farm Ave TW10 . 7 A3
Kings Gate
Farncombe GU7 . 150 F6
Woking GU21 . 69 D1
Kings Hall Rd BR3 . 43 E8
Kings Ho 12 KT2 . 37 E8
Kings International Coll GU15 . 65 C2
Kings Keep KT6 . 37 E5
Kings La
Englefield Green TW20 . 11 A2
Windlesham GU20 . 48 E5
Wrecclesham GU10 . 145 F6
Kings Mead
Smallfield RH6 . 162 B3
South Nutfield RH1 . 140 E7
Kings Mead Pk KT10 . 55 E3
Kings Mill La RH1 . 140 D5
Kings Par 3 SM5 . 59 E7
Kings Rd Belmont SM2 . 59 A1
Biggin Hill TN16 . 83 C2
Feltham TW13 . 15 C7
Horley RH6 . 161 A3
Mitcham CR4 . 41 A6
Richmond TW10,TW9 . 6 F2
Rudgwick RH12 . 214 D7
Shalford GU4 . 130 E2
Walton-on-T KT12 . 35 B1
West End GU24 . 68 A6
Woking GU21 . 70 A3
Wonersh GU5 . 152 B8
Woodham KT15 . 71 B8
Kings Ride Gate TW10 . 7 A3
Kings Warren KT22 . 74 D8
Kings Way CR0 . 60 F5
Kings Wlk CR2 . 81 B5
Kings' Coll for the Arts & Technology GU2 . 108 E1
Kings's Rd 2 GU1 . 109 D1
Kingsbridge Ho 11 SE20 . 43 B8
Kingsbridge Rd
Walton-on-T KT12 . 35 B2
West Barnes SM4 . 39 D2
Kingsbrook KT22 . 75 A1
Kingsbury Cres TW18 . 12 D4
Kingsbury Dr SL4 . 11 B8
Kingsclear Pk GU15 . 65 D4
Kingsclere Cl SW15 . 19 A8
Kingscliffe Gdns SW19 . 19 F7
Kingscote Hill RH11 . 201 B4
Kingscote Rd
Croydon CR0,CR9 . 43 B2
Kingston u T KT3 . 38 D6
Kingscote Sta RH19 . 204 F4
Kingscourt Rd SW16 . 21 D5
Kingscroft Jun Sch TW18 . 13 A2
Kingscroft La RG42 . 8 A6
Kingscroft Rd
Leatherhead KT22 . 95 B7
Woodmansterne SM7 . 78 E4
Kingsdale Rd SE20 . 23 D1
Kingsdale Sec Sch SE21 . 22 E5
Kingsdene KT20 . 97 B5
Kingsdown 1 SW19 . 19 D1
Kingsdown Ave CR2,CR8 . 61 C2
Kingsdown Rd
Cheam SM3 . 58 E5
Ewell KT17 . 77 A6
Kingsdowne Rd KT6 . 37 F2
Kingsfield GU5 . 153 E7
Kingsfield Bsns Pk RH1 140 A8
Kingsfold Ct RH12 . 198 B5
Kingsgate Bsns Ctr KT2 . 37 E8
Kingsgate Rd KT2 . 37 E8
Kingsgrove Ind Est GU14 85 A3
Kingshill Ave KT4 . 39 B2
Kingslake Ct 2 GU21 . 68 E1
Kingsland RH5 . 158 A1
Kingsland Ct RH10 . 202 A6
Kingslea Horsham RH13 . 217 E3
Leatherhead KT22 . 95 A7
Kingslee Ct 12 SM2 . 59 B3
Kingsleigh Pl CR4 . 40 F6
Kingsleigh Wlk BR2 . 44 F5
Kingsley Ave
Banstead SM7 . 78 A4
Camberley GU15 . 65 D3
Carshalton SM1 . 59 D6
Englefield Green TW20 . 11 B2
Hounslow TW3 . 5 C5
Kingsley Cl
Crowthorne RG45 . 45 B3
Horley RH6 . 160 F5
Kingsley Ct
Walton-on-T KT12 . 54 A7
Worcester Park KT4 . 57 F8
Kingsley Dr KT4 . 57 F8
Kingsley Gr RH2 . 139 B5
Kingsley Ho 8 KT6 . 37 E4
Kingsley Rd
Crawley RH11 . 201 A3
Farnborough GU14 . 84 F6
Horley RH6 . 160 F5
Hounslow TW3 . 5 C5
Thornton Heath CR0 . 42 A1
Wimbledon SW19 . 20 B3
Kingslyn Cres SE19 . 42 E8
Kingsmead
Biggin Hill TN16 . 83 D3
Cranleigh GU6 . 174 E3
Farnborough GU14 . 85 B4
Frimley GU16 . 85 E7
Richmond TW10 . 6 F1
Weybridge KT13 . 53 D4
5 Woking GU21 . 70 A3
Kingsmead Ave
Mitcham CR4 . 41 C6
North Cheam KT4 . 58 B7
Sunbury TW16 . 35 C7
Tolworth KT6 . 57 A8
Kingsmead Cl
Horsham RH12 . 218 B6
Teddington TW11 . 17 B2
West Ewell KT19 . 57 D3
Kingsmead Ct BR1 . 24 F1
Kingsmead Lodge SM2 . 59 D4
Kingsmead Pl RH12 . 216 C3
Kingsmead Rd
Broadbridge Heath RH12 . 216 D3
Streatham SW2 . 22 A6
Kingsmead Sh Ctr GU14 . 85 B3
Kingsmere SE6 . 24 B7
Kingsmere Rd
Bracknell RG42 . 26 F8
Putney SW19 . 19 D6
Kingsmill Bsns Pk KT1 . 37 F6
Kingsmount Ct SM1 . 59 B6
Kingsnympton Pk KT2 . 18 B2
Kingsridge SW19 . 19 E6
Kingsthorpe Rd SE26 . 23 D4
Kingston Ave Cheam SM3 . 58 E7
East Horsley KT24 . 92 E1
Feltham TW14 . 3 F1
Leatherhead KT22 . 95 B6
Kingston Bsns Ctr KT9 . 56 F7
Kingston By - Pass KT6 . 57 B8
Kingston By-Pass KT6, KT7,KT9 . 56 C7
Kingston Cl TW11 . 17 B2
Kingston Coll KT1 . 37 D6
Kingston Coll of F Ed KT2 . 37 E8
Kingston Cres
Beckenham BR3 . 43 F8
Staines TW15 . 13 D2
Kingston Gdns CR0 . 60 E7
Kingston Gram Sch KT2 . 37 F7
Kingston Hall Rd KT1 . 37 D6
Kingston Hill KT2 . 18 C2
Kingston Hill Pl KT2 . 18 C4
Kingston Hospl KT2 . 38 B8
Kingston House Est KT6 . 37 B3
Kingston House Gdns KT22 . 95 B6
Kingston La
Teddington TW11 . 17 B2
West Horsley KT24 . 112 A8
Kingston Lodge 1 KT3 . 38 E5
Kingston Mus* KT1 . 37 E7
Kingston Poly (Gipsy Hill Ctr) KT2 . 18 D3
Kingston Rd
Ashford TW15,TW17 . 13 F2
Ashtead KT22, KT9 . 75 A3
Camberley GU15 . 47 A1
Kingston u T KT1,KT3 . 38 C5
Leatherhead KT22 . 75 A1
Merton SW19,SW20 . 39 E7
New Malden KT3 . 38 C5
Putney SW15,SW19 . 19 B7
Staines TW15,TW18 . 13 B2
Teddington TW11 . 17 B2
Worcester Park KT17,KT19, KT4,KT5,KT6 . 57 D6
Kingston Rise KT15 . 52 A1
Kingston Sq SE19 . 22 D3
Kingston Sta KT2 . 37 E8
Kingston Univ
Kingston u T KT1 . 37 E6
Kingston u T,Kingston Vale KT2 . 18 D3
Kingston Univ Annex KT1 37 F7
Kingston Univ Roehampton Vale Ctr SW15 . 18 F5
Kingston Vale SW15 . 18 E5
Kingstons Ind Est GU12 105 E2

Kingsway Aldershot GU11 . **104** E1
  Blackwater GU17 . . . . **64** E5
  Coney Hall BR4 . . . . **63** F7
  Mortlake SW14,TW9 . . . . . . **7** B4
  Stanwell TW19 . . . . **13** E7
  West Barnes KT3 . . . . **39** C4
  Woking GU21 . . . . **69** D1
Kingsway Ave
  Selsdon CR2 . . . . **62** D2
  Woking GU21 . . . . **69** D1
Kingsway Bsns Pk GU21 . **70** C5
Kingsway Bsns Pk The
  TW12 . . . . **35** F8
Kingsway Rd SM3 . . . . . . **58** E3
Kingsway Terr KT13 . . . . **53** A2
Kingsway The KT17 . . . . . **57** F1
Kingswear Ho SE23 . . . . . **23** C6
Kingswick CI SL5 . . . . **29** D5
Kingswick Dr SL5 . . . . **29** D5
Kingswood GU26 . . . . . . **188** D2
Kingswood Ave
  Beckenham BR2 . . . . **44** E5
  Hampton TW12 . . . . **16** B2
  Hamsey Green CR2 . . . . . . **81** C4
  Hounslow TW3,TW5 . . . . **4** F5
  Thornton Heath CR7 . . . . . . **42** A4
Kingswood CI
  Englefield Green TW20 . . . . **11** D4
  Guildford GU1 . . . . **110** C2
  New Malden KT3 . . . . **38** F3
  Surbiton KT6 . . . . **37** E2
  Weybridge KT13 . . . . **53** B3
Kingswood Ct
  6 Richmond TW10 . . . . **6** E1
  Woking GU21 . . . . **69** E3
Kingswood Dr
  Belmont SM2 . . . . **59** B2
  Carshalton SM5 . . . . **40** F1
  Dulwich SE19,SE21 . . . . . . **22** F4
Kingswood Firs GU26 . . **188** C2
Kingswood Hall of Residence
  TW20 . . . . **11** D4
Kingswood Ho 3 KT2 . . . **18** B2
Kingswood House Sch
  KT19 . . . . **76** C6
Kingswood La
  Grayshott GU26 . . . . **188** C2
  Warlingham BR4 . . . . **81** C1
Kingswood Mans 8 SM2 **59** A3
Kingswood Pk KT20 . . . . . **97** E6
Kingswood Prim Sch
  Lower Kingswood KT20 . . . **117** F7
  West Norwood SE27 . . . . . . **22** D3
Kingswood Rd
  Beckenham BR2 . . . . **44** E6
  Merton SW19 . . . . **39** F8
  Penge SE20 . . . . **23** C2
  Streatham SW2 . . . . **21** E8
  Tadworth KT20 . . . . **97** B6
Kingswood Rise TW20 . . . **11** D4
Kingswood Sta KT20 . . . . **97** F6
Kingswood Way
  Hamsey Green CR2 . . . . . . **81** C6
  Selsdon CR2 . . . . **81** D7
  Wallington SM6 . . . . **60** E5
Kingsworth CI BR3 . . . . . . **43** E4
Kingsworthy CI KT1 . . . . . **37** F6
Kinloss Rd SM5 . . . . **40** C2
Kinnaird Ave Bromley BR1 **24** F2
  Chiswick W4 . . . . **7** C7
Kinnaird CI BR1 . . . . **24** F2
Kinnear Ct SW20 . . . . **39** D8
Kinnersley Wlk RH2 . . . . **139** B4
Kinnibrugh Dr RH7 . . . . . **165** A1
Kinross Ave Ascot SL5 . . . **28** F4
  Worcester Park KT4 . . . . . . **58** A8
Kinross CI TW16 . . . . **14** F3
Kinross Ct Ascot SL5 . . . . **28** F4
  Catford SE6 . . . . **24** F6
Kinross Dr TW16 . . . . **14** F3
Kinsella Gdns SW19 . . . . . **19** B2
Kintyre CI SW16 . . . . **41** F6
Kintyre Ct 17 SW2 . . . . . . **21** E8
Kinver Rd SE26 . . . . **23** C4
Kipings KT20 . . . . **97** D5
Kipling CI RH10 . . . . **202** C8
Kipling Ct RH13 . . . . **218** A4
Kipling Dr SW17 . . . . **20** D2
Kipling Way RH19 . . . . . . **185** C1
Kirby CI KT19 . . . . **57** F5
Kirby Rd GU21 . . . . **69** D2
Kirby Way KT12 . . . . **35** C3
Kirdford CI RH11 . . . . **201** A8
Kirk Rise SM1 . . . . **59** B7
Kirkby Ct GU16 . . . . **65** E1
Kirkdale SE26 . . . . **23** B5
Kirkefields GU2 . . . . **109** A4
Kirkgate The 2 KT17 . . . . **76** E6
Kirkham CI GU47 . . . . **45** D2
Kirkland Ave GU21 . . . . . . **68** F3
Kirkleas Rd KT6 . . . . **37** E1
Kirklees Rd CR7 . . . . **42** A4
Kirkley Rd SW19 . . . . **40** A8
Kirkly CI CR2 . . . . **61** E2
Kirkstall RH4 . . . . **136** A6
Kirkstall Gdns SW2 . . . . . **21** E7
Kirkstall Rd SW2 . . . . **21** E7
Kirksted Rd SM4 . . . . **40** B1
Kirkstone CI GU15 . . . . **66** D4
Kirkstone Way BR1 . . . . . . **24** E1
Kirrane CI KT3 . . . . **38** F4
Kirriemuir Gdns GU12 . . . **106** D3
Kirtley Rd SE26 . . . . **23** E4
Kitchener Rd
  Farnborough GU11 . . . . . . **105** D6
  South Norwood CR7 . . . . . . **42** D6
Kitchenride Cnr KT16 . . . . **51** A6

Kites CI RH11 . . . . **201** C6
Kithurst CI RH11 . . . . **201** D4
Kitley Gdns SE19 . . . . **42** F8
Kitsmead RH10 . . . . **183** A2
Kitsmead La KT16 . . . . **50** D8
Kittiwake CI
  Crawley RH11 . . . . **200** D4
  Selsdon CR0,CR2 . . . . **62** C1
Kittiwake PI SM1 . . . . **58** F5
Klondyke Villas GU27 . . . **190** A1
Knaggs Ho 1 TW11 . . . . . . **16** E3
Knap Ct GU21 . . . . **68** D2
Knapdale CI SE23 . . . . **23** B6
Knaphill Lower Sch The
  GU21 . . . . **68** B1
Knaphill Sch GU21 . . . . . . **68** C1
Knapmill Rd SE6 . . . . **24** B6
Knapmill Way SE6 . . . . **24** B6
Knapp Rd TW15 . . . . **13** F4
Knapton Mews SW17 . . . . . **21** A2
Knaresborough Dr SW18 **20** B7
Kneller Gdns TW7 . . . . **5** D1
Kneller Rd
  New Malden KT3 . . . . **38** E2
  Twickenham TW2 . . . . **5** D1
Knepp CI RH10 . . . . **202** C6
Knight Ho KT1 . . . . **58** A8
Knight's Hill SE27 . . . . . . **22** B4
Knight's Hill Sq SE27 . . . . **22** B4
Knight's Pk KT1 . . . . **37** E6
Knighton CI
  Crawley RH10 . . . . **182** D2
  Croydon CR2 . . . . **61** B2
Knighton Lodge KT12 . . . . **54** C8
Knighton Park Rd SE26 . . **23** D3
Knighton Rd RH1 . . . . **140** A7
Knightons La GU8 . . . . . . **193** A2
Knights CI TW20 . . . . **12** D2
Knights Ct
  Kingston u T KT1 . . . . **37** E6
  Penge BR3 . . . . **43** E8
Knights PI RH1 . . . . **119** A2
Knights Rd GU9 . . . . **125** E7
Knights Way GU15 . . . . . . **66** C4
Knightsbridge Cres
  TW18 . . . . **13** B2
Knightsbridge Ho 10
  GU1 . . . . **130** F8
Knightsbridge Rd GU15 . . **65** E7
Knightswood
  Bracknell RG12 . . . . **27** B1
  Woking GU21 . . . . **68** F1
Knightwood CI RH2 . . . . . **139** A7
Knightwood Cres KT3 . . . . **38** E3
Knipp Hill KT11 . . . . **73** F6
Knob Hill RH12 . . . . **198** A1
Knobfield RH5 . . . . **154** F8
Knock The GU47 . . . . **64** D7
Knockhundred La GU26 . . **207** C8
Knole CI Crawley RH10 . . . **202** D7
  Croydon CR0 . . . . **43** C3
Knole Gr RH19 . . . . **185** C3
Knole Wood SL5 . . . . **29** E1
Knoll Ct SE19 . . . . **22** F3
Knoll Park Rd KT16 . . . . . . **32** F1
Knoll Quarry GU7 . . . . . . **150** E6
Knoll Rd Camberley GU15 . . **65** D6
  Dorking RH4 . . . . **136** A5
  Farncombe GU7 . . . . **150** E6
Knoll The Beckenham BR3 . . **44** B8
  Cobham KT11 . . . . **74** A6
  Leatherhead KT22 . . . . **95** C6
Knoll Wood GU7 . . . . **150** E6
Knollmead KT4,KT5 . . . . . . **38** B1
Knollmead Prim Sch KT4 **57** C8
Knolls CI KT4 . . . . **58** B7
Knolls The KT17 . . . . **77** C3
Knolly's CI SW16 . . . . **22** A5
Knolly's Rd SW16 . . . . **22** A5
Knollys Rd GU11 . . . . **104** F3
Knott Park Ho KT22 . . . . . **74** C4
Knowl Hill GU22 . . . . **70** B1
Knowl Hill Sch GU24 . . . . **87** E5
Knowle CI RH10 . . . . **183** C3
Knowle Dr RH10 . . . . **183** B3
Knowle Gdns KT14 . . . . . . **70** F6
Knowle Gn TW18 . . . . **13** A3
Knowle Gr GU25 . . . . **31** C2
Knowle Grove CI GU25 . . . **31** C2
Knowle Hill GU25 . . . . **31** C2
Knowle La GU6,RH12 . . . . **194** D4
Knowle Lodge CR3 . . . . . **101** A4
Knowle Park Ave TW18 . . **13** B3
Knowle Park Inf Sch
  TW18 . . . . **13** A3
Knowle Pk KT11 . . . . **73** E4
Knowle Rd TW2 . . . . **16** E7
Knowle The GU35 . . . . **187** B5
Knowlton Gn 2 BR2 . . . . . . **44** F4
Knox Rd GU2 . . . . **109** B6
Kohat Ct GU11 . . . . **104** F2
Kohat Rd SW19 . . . . **20** B3
Kohima CI GU11 . . . . **105** B3
Koonowla CI TN16 . . . . **83** D4
Kooringa CR6 . . . . **101** B8
Korda CI TW17 . . . . **33** F6
Kreisel Wlk TW9 . . . . **6** E4
Krooner Rd GU15 . . . . **65** B3
Kuala Gdns SW16 . . . . **41** F8
Kyle CI RG12 . . . . **27** B6
Kynaston Ave CR7 . . . . **42** C4
Kynaston Cres CR0,CR7 . . **42** C4
Kynaston Ct CR3 . . . . **100** E2
Kynaston Ho 7 SW2 . . . . . **21** F7
Kynaston Rd CR0,CR7 . . . . **42** C4
Kynersley CI SM5 . . . . **59** F7

L

La Retraite RC Girls Sch
  SW12 . . . . **21** C8
Laburnum Ct 13 SW16 . . . **22** A3
Laburnum Ave 6 SM1 . . . . **59** E7
Laburnum CI
  1 Aldershot GU11 . . . . . . **105** A1
  Guildford GU1 . . . . **109** C4
Laburnum Cres TW16 . . . . **35** B8
Laburnum Ct CR4 . . . . **41** A7
Laburnum Gdns CR0 . . . . . **43** D1
Laburnum Gr
  Brands Hill SL3 . . . . **1** B8
  Hounslow TW3 . . . . **4** F3
  Kingston u T KT3 . . . . **38** D7
Laburnum Pas 2 GU11 . . **105** A1
Laburnum PI TW20 . . . . . . **11** B2
Laburnum Rd
  Aldershot GU11 . . . . **105** A2
  Chertsey KT16 . . . . **33** A1
  Epsom KT18 . . . . **76** E6
  Heath End GU9 . . . . **125** E7
  Merton SW19 . . . . **20** C1
  Mitcham CR4 . . . . **41** A7
  Woking GU22 . . . . **89** D7
Laburnum Way TW19 . . . . **13** F7
Laburnums The GU17 . . . . **64** B5
Lacey Ave CR5 . . . . **100** A7
Lacey CI TW20 . . . . **12** D1
Lacey Dr Coulsdon CR5 . . . **100** B7
  Hampton TW12 . . . . **35** F8
Lackford Rd CR5 . . . . **78** F1
Lacock CI SW19 . . . . **20** C2
Lacrosse Way SW16 . . . . . . **41** D8
Lacy Gn CR5 . . . . **100** A7
Ladas Rd SE27 . . . . **22** C3
Ladbroke Cotts 2 RH1 . . **119** A2
Ladbroke Ct 7 RH1 . . . . . **119** A3
Ladbroke Gr RH1 . . . . **119** A2
Ladbroke Hurst RH7 . . . . **165** A1
Ladbroke Rd Epsom KT18 . . **76** D5
  Horley RH6 . . . . **161** B5
  Redhill RH1 . . . . **119** A3
Ladbrook Rd SE25 . . . . **42** D5
Ladderstile Ride KT2 . . . . . **18** B3
Ladlands SE22 . . . . **23** A8
Lady Booth Rd 7 KT1 . . . . **37** E7
Lady Eleanor Holles Sch The
  (Jun Girls) TW12 . . . . **16** B3
Lady Eleanor Holles Sch The
  (Senior Girls) TW12 . . . . . . **16** B3
Lady Elizabeth Ho SW14 . . . **7** C4
Lady Forsdyke Way KT19 **57** A2
Lady Harewood Way
  KT19 . . . . **57** A2
Lady Hay KT4 . . . . **57** F8
Lady Jane Ct KT2 . . . . **37** F7
Lady Margaret Rd
  Crawley RH11 . . . . **201** A7
  Sunningdale SL5 . . . . **29** F2
Lady Margaret Wlk
  RH11 . . . . **201** A7
Ladybank RG12 . . . . **27** B1
Ladycross GU8 . . . . **170** E8
Ladyegate CI RH5 . . . . **136** D8
Ladyegate Rd RH5 . . . . . . **136** D8
Ladygate Dr GU26 . . . . . . **188** A3
Ladygrove CR2 . . . . **62** D2
Ladygrove Dr GU4 . . . . . . **110** B6
Ladymead RG12 . . . . **27** B1
Ladymead CI RH10 . . . . . . **202** C3
Ladymead GU1 . . . . **109** C2
Ladymead Ret Ctr GU1 . . **109** C2
Ladymead Retail Ctr
  GU1 . . . . **109** E2
Ladymere PI GU7 . . . . **150** C3
Ladythorpe CI KT15 . . . . . . **52** B6
Ladywood Ave GU14 . . . . . **84** C4
Ladywood Rd KT6 . . . . **57** A8
Laffan's Rd GU11 . . . . **104** E6
Lafone Ave TW13 . . . . **15** C6
Lafone Ho 11 SW2 . . . . . . **21** E8
Lagham Pk RH9 . . . . **142** E6
Lagham Rd RH9 . . . . **142** F5
Laglands CI RH2 . . . . **118** C3
Laings Ave CR4 . . . . **40** F7
Laings Cnr CR4 . . . . **40** F8
Lainlock PI TW3 . . . . **5** B6
Lainson St SW18 . . . . **20** A8
Laird Ct GU19 . . . . **47** E1
Lairdale CI SE21 . . . . **22** C8
Laitwood Rd SW12 . . . . . . **21** B7
Lake CI Byfleet KT14 . . . . . . **71** D7
  6 Wimbledon SW19 . . . . . **19** F3
Lake Cotts GU8 . . . . **169** F4
Lake End Way RG45 . . . . . . **45** A4
Lake Gdns Hackbridge SM6 **60** B7
  Richmond TW10 . . . . **17** B6
Lake Ho 4 SW27 . . . . **22** B3
Lake La Dockenfield GU10 **166** E6
  Horley RH1,RH6 . . . . **161** C6
Lake Rd Croydon CR0 . . . . . **62** F8
  Frimley GU16 . . . . **86** B6
  Ockley RH5 . . . . **177** D6
  Virginia Water GU25 . . . . . . **31** B5
  Wimbledon SW19 . . . . **19** F3
Lake Side The GU17 . . . . . . **64** D4
Lake View RH5 . . . . **136** C4
Lake View Cotts RH4 . . . . **135** A6
Lake View Rd
  Copthorne RH19 . . . . **184** C4
  Dormans Park RH19 . . . . . **185** F5
Lakefield CI SE20 . . . . **23** B1
Lakehall Gdns CR7 . . . . . . **42** B4
Lakehall Rd CR7 . . . . **42** B4
Lakehurst Rd KT19 . . . . . . **57** E5
Lakeland Dr GU16 . . . . **65** E1

Lakeman Ct CR7 . . . . **42** C7
Laker Ct RH10 . . . . **202** A6
Lakers Lea RH14 . . . . **212** F1
Lakers Rise SM7 . . . . **78** E3
Lakes CI GU4 . . . . **131** B3
Lakeside Beckenham BR3 . . **44** B6
  Hackbridge SM6 . . . . **60** B6
  Horsham RH12 . . . . **217** C5
  10 Kingston u T KT2 . . . . . . **18** B1
  Knaphill GU21 . . . . **88** E8
  Oatlands Park KT13 . . . . . . **53** E8
  Redhill RH1 . . . . **119** A3
  West Ewell KT19 . . . . **57** E5
Lakeside Bsns Pk GU47 . . **64** A7
Lakeside CI
  Ash Vale GU12 . . . . **105** F4
  Knaphill GU21 . . . . **88** E8
  South Norwood SE25 . . . . . **43** A7
Lakeside Dr KT10 . . . . **55** C4
Lakeside Est SL3 . . . . **2** A8
Lakeside Gdns GU14 . . . . . **84** D7
Lakeside Grange KT13 . . . . **53** C7
Lakeside Pk KT16 . . . . **33** C1
Lakeside Prim Sch GU16 . . **65** F1
Lakeside Rd
  Ash Vale GU11,GU12 . . . . . **105** F4
  Colnbrook SL3 . . . . **1** F7
  Farnborough GU14 . . . . . . **105** A4
Lakeview Rd SE27 . . . . **22** B3
Laleham CE Prim Sch
  TW18 . . . . **33** C7
Laleham Ct GU21 . . . . **69** E3
Laleham Lea Prep Sch
  CR8 . . . . **80** C8
Laleham Rd Catford SE6 . . . **24** C8
  Littleton TW17 . . . . **34** A4
  Staines TW18 . . . . **12** F2
Lamb's Bsns Pk RH9 . . . . **142** C5
Lamberhurst Rd SE27 . . . . **22** A3
Lamberhurst Wlk RH10 . . **202** A5
Lambert Ave TW9 . . . . **7** B4
Lambert CI TN16 . . . . **83** D3
Lambert Cotts RH1 . . . . . . **120** E2
Lambert Cres GU17 . . . . . . **64** C4
Lambert Ho SM7 . . . . **78** B5
Lambert Rd SM7 . . . . **78** B5
Lambert's PI CR0 . . . . **42** D1
Lambert's Rd KT6 . . . . **37** F4
Lambeth CI RH11 . . . . **201** B2
Lambeth Prospect SE19 . . **22** D2
Lambeth Rd CR0 . . . . **42** B1
Lambeth Wlk
  Crawley RH11 . . . . **201** B2
  Crawley RH11 . . . . **201** B3
Lambly Hill GU25 . . . . **31** E6
Lamborne CI GU47 . . . . **45** A1
Lambourn CI Croydon CR2 **61** B2
  East Grinstead RH19 . . . . . **185** E3
Lambourne Ave SW19 . . . . **19** F4
Lambourne CI RH10 . . . . . **201** F4
Lambourne Cres GU21 . . . . **70** D6
Lambourne Dr
  Bagshot GU19 . . . . **47** D2
  Cobham KT11 . . . . **73** D4
Lambourne Gr
  Bracknell RG12 . . . . **27** E7
  Kingston u T KT1 . . . . **38** B7
Lambourne Way GU10 . . . **126** F7
Lambrook Haileybury Sch
  RG42 . . . . **8** A3
Lambs Cres RH12 . . . . **217** F5
Lambs Farm CI RH12 . . . . **218** A5
Lambs Farm Rd RH12 . . . **218** A6
Lambs Green Rd RH12 . . . **199** D1
Lambton Rd SW20 . . . . **39** C8
Lambyn Croft RH6 . . . . . . **161** C4
Lamerock Rd BR1 . . . . **24** F4
Lammas CI
  Godalming GU7 . . . . **151** A6
  Staines TW18 . . . . **12** E5
Lammas Ct
  Farncombe GU7 . . . . **150** E5
  Stanwell TW19 . . . . **12** D5
Lammas Dr TW18 . . . . **12** D4
Lammas Gate GU7 . . . . . . **150** F6
Lammas Gn SE26 . . . . **23** B5
Lammas Hill KT10 . . . . **55** A5
Lammas La KT10 . . . . **55** A6
Lammas Rd
  Godalming GU7 . . . . **151** A5
  Richmond TW10 . . . . **17** C1
Lammermoor Rd SW12 . . . **21** B8
Lampard La GU10 . . . . **167** E2
Lampeter CI GU22 . . . . **69** E1
Lampeter Ho 4 GU22 . . . . . **69** E1
Lampton Ave TW5 . . . . **5** B6
Lampton Ct TW5 . . . . **5** B6
Lampton House CI SW19 . . **19** D4
Lampton Park Rd TW3 . . . . . **5** B5
Lampton Rd TW3,TW5 . . . . . **5** B5
Lampton Sch TW5 . . . . **5** A6
Lanain Ct SE12 . . . . **24** F8
Lanark CI Frimley GU16 . . . . **65** F2
  Horsham RH13 . . . . **217** E2
Lancaster Ave
  Farnham GU9 . . . . **146** D8
  Guildford GU1 . . . . **130** F7
  Mitcham CR4 . . . . **41** E4
  West Norwood SE21,SE27 . . **22** C6
  Wimbledon SW19 . . . . **19** D3
Lancaster CI
  Ash Vale GU12 . . . . **105** F5
  Beckenham BR2 . . . . **44** F5
  Crawley RH10 . . . . **182** D1
  Englefield Green TW20 . . . . **11** D3
  Kingston u T KT2 . . . . **17** D3
  Stanwell TW19 . . . . **2** E1

Lancaster CI continued
  Woking GU21 . . . . **70** A3
Lancaster Cotts 1 TW10 . . . **6** E1
Lancaster Ct
  Banstead SM7 . . . . **77** F5
  1 Belmont SM2 . . . . **59** A3
  Crawley RH10 . . . . **201** F5
  Epsom KT19 . . . . **57** D1
  Stanwell TW19 . . . . **13** E7
  Walton-on-T KT12 . . . . **35** B2
  West Norwood SE27 . . . . . . **22** B6
Lancaster Dr
  Camberley GU15 . . . . **65** D6
  East Grinstead RH19 . . . . . **186** A3
Lancaster Gdns
  Blindley Heath RH7 . . . . . . **163** E8
  Kingston u T KT2 . . . . **17** D3
  Wimbledon SW19 . . . . **19** E3
Lancaster Ho
  Bracknell RG12 . . . . **27** B4
  Redhill RH1 . . . . **139** E6
  Wandsworth SW18 . . . . **20** B8
Lancaster Mews 2 TW10 . . . **6** E1
Lancaster Pk TW10 . . . . **6** E2
Lancaster PI Hounslow TW5 **4** D5
  Twickenham TW1 . . . . **17** A8
  Wimbledon SW19 . . . . **19** D3
Lancaster Rd
  South Norwood SE25 . . . . . **43** A6
  Wimbledon SW19 . . . . **19** E3
Lancaster Way GU14 . . . . . **85** C7
Lancastrian Rd SM6 . . . . . **60** E3
Lancelot CI RH11 . . . . **200** E6
Lancelot Ho RH1 . . . . **119** A2
Lancer Ct GU11 . . . . **104** E2
Lanchester Dr RG45 . . . . . . **45** C7
Lancing CI RH11 . . . . **201** A8
Lancing Ct RH12 . . . . **218** A4
Lancing Rd Feltham TW13 . . **14** F6
  Thornton Heath CR0 . . . . . . **41** F2
Landen Ct RG40 . . . . **25** B4
Landen Pk RH6 . . . . **160** E5
Landgrove Rd SW19 . . . . . . **20** A3
Landon Way TW15 . . . . **14** B2
Landscape Rd CR6 . . . . . . **101** B8
Landsdowne CI KT5 . . . . . . **57** B8
Landseer CI
  3 Mitcham SW19 . . . . **40** D8
  Sandhurst GU47 . . . . **64** E1
Landseer Rd Cheam SM1 . . **59** A4
  New Malden KT3 . . . . **38** D2
Lane CI KT15 . . . . **52** B5
Lane Ct SW11 . . . . **20** B5
Lane End Epsom KT18 . . . . **76** B5
  Hambledon GU8 . . . . **191** B8
Lane End Dr GU21 . . . . **68** C2
Lane Gdns KT10 . . . . **55** F3
Lane Ho RH13 . . . . **217** D2
Lane The Chertsey KT16 . . . **33** A6
  Ifold RH14 . . . . **212** C4
  Thorpe GU25 . . . . **31** E6
  Thursley GU8 . . . . **169** C4
Lanercost CI SW2 . . . . **22** A6
Lanercost Rd
  Crawley RH11 . . . . **201** C5
  Streatham SW2 . . . . **22** A6
Lanesborough Prep Sch
  GU1 . . . . **109** F1
Lang CI KT23 . . . . **94** B4
Langaller La KT22 . . . . **94** B6
Langborough Rd RG40 . . . . **25** C5
Langbourne Prim Sch
  SE21 . . . . **22** E5
Langbourne Way KT10 . . . . **56** A4
Langcroft CI SM5 . . . . **59** F7
Langdale Ave CR4 . . . . **40** F6
Langdale CI
  Farnborough GU14 . . . . . . **84** E4
  Mortlake SW14 . . . . **7** B3
  Woking GU21 . . . . **69** C3
Langdale Dr SL5 . . . . **28** E7
Langdale Rd
  Crawley RH11 . . . . **200** D4
  Thornton Heath CR7 . . . . . . **42** A5
Langdon CI GU15 . . . . **66** C4
Langdon Pk TW11 . . . . **17** C1
Langdon PI SW14 . . . . **7** C4
Langdon Rd SM4 . . . . **40** C4
Langdon Wlk SM4 . . . . **40** C4
Langham CI GU7 . . . . **150** F4
Langham Ct
  Farnham GU9 . . . . **146** C7
  12 Twickenham TW1 . . . . **6** C1
  Wimbledon SW20 . . . . **39** C7
Langham Dene CR8 . . . . . . **80** B4
Langham Gdns TW10 . . . . . **17** C4
Langham House CI TW10 **17** D4
Langham Park PI BR2 . . . . . **44** F5
Langham Pk GU7 . . . . **150** F4
Langham PI Chiswick W4 . . . **7** E8
  Egham TW20 . . . . **11** F3
Langham Rd
  Teddington TW11 . . . . **17** B2
  Wimbledon SW20 . . . . **39** C8
Langholm CI SW12 . . . . **21** D8
Langhorn Dr TW2 . . . . **16** E8
Langhurst CI RH12 . . . . . . **198** A4
Langhurst La RH12 . . . . . **200** A8
Langhurstwood Rd
  RH12 . . . . **198** D3
Langland Gdns CR0 . . . . . . **62** F8
Langland Ho 8 SW19 . . . . . **20** D3
Langlands Rise KT19 . . . . . **76** C6
Langley Ave
  North Cheam KT4,SM3 . . . . **58** D8

Langley Ave *continued*
Surbiton KT6 ....**37** E1
Langley Cl Guildford GU1 **109** D2
Langley Vale KT18 .....**96** D8
Langley Cres UB3 ....**3** F7
Langley Ct RH2 ....**118** B2
Langley Dr
Aldershot GU11 ....**126** A8
Camberley GU15 ......**65** D6
Crawley RH11 ....**201** D8
Langley Gr KT3 ....**38** E7
Langley Green Fst Sch
RH11 ....**181** D1
Langley Green Mid Sch
RH11 ....**201** C8
Langley La RH11 ....**201** A8
Langley Manor RH3 ....**44** C4
Langley Oaks Ave CR2 ..**62** A1
Langley Par RH11 ......**181** C1
Langley Park Rd SM1,
SM2 ....**59** C3
Langley Park Sch for Boys
BR3 ....**44** B3
Langley Park Sch for Girls
BR3 ....**44** C3
Langley Pl RH11 ....**181** C1
Langley Rd
Beckenham BR3 ......**43** E8
Isleworth TW7 ....**5** F5
Merton SW19 ....**40** A8
Selsdon CR2 ....**62** D2
Staines TW18 ....**12** F2
Surbiton KT6 ....**37** E2
Langley Vale Rd KT18,
KT21 ....**76** E1
Langley Way BR4 ....**44** E2
Langley Wlk
Crawley RH11 ....**181** B1
Woking GU22 ....**89** B8
Langmans Way GU21 ...**68** E3
Langmead St SE27 .....**22** C4
Langport Ct KT12 ......**35** C1
Langridge Dr RH19 ....**205** E8
Langridge Ho RH12 ....**217** B2
Langridge Mews TW12 ..**15** F2
Langroyd Rd SW17 .....**20** F6
Langshott RH6 ....**161** D4
Langshott KT15 ....**70** F8
Langshott Inf Sch RH6 ..**161** C3
Langshott La RH6 ......**161** C4
Langsmead RH7 ....**163** E8
Langstone Cl RH10 ....**202** C3
Langthorne St SE6 .....**24** C4
Langton Ave KT17 ......**76** F8
Langton Cl
Addlestone KT15 .....**52** B7
Woking GU21 ....**68** F2
Langton Dr GU35 ......**187** A7
Langton Ho SW16 ......**21** C4
Langton Pl SW18 ....**20** A7
Langton Rd KT8 ....**36** C5
Langton Rise SE22,SE23 .**23** B8
Langton Way
Egham TW20 ....**12** C2
South Croydon CR0 ....**61** E6
Langwood Chase TW11 ..**17** C2
Langwood Cl KT21 .....**76** A2
Lanherne Ho SW19 .....**19** D1
Lanigan Dr TW3 ....**5** B2
Lankton Cl BR3 ....**44** C8
Lansbury Ave TW14 ......**4** B1
Lansbury Est GU21 .....**88** D8
Lansbury Rd RH11 .....**201** B1
Lansdell Rd CR4 ....**41** A7
Lansdown GU1 ....**110** A1
Lansdown Cl
Horsham RH12 ......**218** B6
Knaphill GU21 ....**88** F8
Walton-on-T KT12 .....**35** C1
Lansdowne Cl
Twickenham TW1 ......**16** F7
Wimbledon SW20 .....**19** D1
Lansdowne Copse [1]
KT4 ....**58** A8
Lansdowne Ct Purley CR8 .**61** B1
[2] Worcester Park KT4 ..**58** A8
Lansdowne Hill SE27 ....**22** B5
Lansdowne Pl SE19 .....**22** F1
Lansdowne Rd
Aldershot GU11 ......**105** A1
Croydon CR0 ....**42** D1
Frimley GU16 ....**86** A8
Hounslow TW3 ....**5** B4
Purley CR8 ....**80** A7
Staines TW18 ....**13** B1
West Ewell KT19 ......**57** D3
Wimbledon SW19,SW20 .**19** C1
Lansdowne Wood Cl [1]
SE27 ....**22** B5
Lanswood Ct KT4 ......**58** A8
Lantern Ct SW20 ....**39** D8
Lanyon Cl RH12 ....**218** A6
Lanyon Mews RH12 ....**218** A6
Lapse Wood Wlk SE22 ..**23** B7
Lapwing Cl
Horsham RH13 ......**217** F3
Selsdon CR0,CR2 ......**62** E1
Lapwing Ct KT6 ....**57** A7
Lapwing Gr GU4 ....**110** D3
Lara Cl KT9 ....**56** E3
Larbert Rd SW16 ....**21** C1
Larby Pl KT17 ....**57** F1
Larch Ave
Ascot SL5 ....**29** C4
Guildford GU1 ....**109** C4
Wokingham RG41 .....**25** A7

Larch Cl Camberley GU15 ..**65** E8
Kingswood KT20 ......**98** C6
Reigate RH1 ....**139** C7
Upper Tooting SW12 ...**21** B6
Warlingham CR6 ......**101** E8
Larch Cres KT19 ....**57** B4
Larch End RH12 ....**217** B4
Larch Rd GU35 ....**187** B6
Larch Tree Way CR0 .....**63** A7
Larch Way GU14 ....**84** C3
Larches SW14 ....**7** D3
Larches Ho RH19 ......**186** B4
Larches The
East Grinstead RH19 ..**186** B4
Horsham RH12 ......**218** C6
Woking GU21 ....**69** E3
Larches Way
Blackwater GU17 ......**64** B5
Crawley Down RH10 ..**204** C8
Larchvale Ct SM2 ....**59** B3
Larchwood [5] RG12 .....**27** F5
Larchwood Cl SM7 ......**77** E4
Larchwood Dr TW20 ....**11** B2
Larchwood Glade GU15 ..**66** A7
Larchwood Rd GU21 ....**88** D8
Larcombe Cl CR0 ....**61** F6
Larges Bridge Dr RG12 ..**27** D6
Larges La RG12 ....**27** C7
Largewood Ave KT6 .....**57** A8
Lark Ave TW18 ....**12** F5
Lark Rise Crawley RH11 ..**201** C8
East Horsley KT24 ....**112** E4
Turners Hill RH10 ....**204** C5
Larkbere Rd SE26 ....**23** E4
Larkfield Cobham KT11 ..**73** A6
Ewhurst GU6 ....**175** E4
Larkfield Cl
Coney Hall BR2 ....**63** F8
Farnham GU9 ....**124** F2
Larkfield Ct RH6 ....**162** A3
Larkfield Rd
Farnham GU9 ....**124** F2
Richmond TW9 ....**6** E3
Larkhall Cl KT12 ....**54** C4
Larkham Cl TW13 ....**14** E5
Larkin Cl CR5 ....**79** F2
Larkins Rd RH6 ....**181** D7
Larks Way GU21 ....**68** C3
Larksfield
Englefield Green TW20 ..**11** C1
Horley RH6 ....**161** B4
Larkspur Cl GU11 ......**126** A7
Larkspur Ct SM6 ....**60** B3
Larkspur Way
Dorking RH5 ....**136** D4
West Ewell KT19 ......**57** C5
Larkswood Cl GU47 .....**45** A1
Larkswood Dr RG45 .....**45** B5
Lascombe La GU3 ......**128** B4
Lashmere
Copthorne RH10 .....**183** D3
Cranleigh GU6 ....**174** B3
Laski Ct RH11 ....**201** B1
Lasswade Ct KT16 ......**32** F2
Lasswade Rd KT16 ......**32** F2
Lastingham Ct TW18 ....**13** A2
Latchmere Cl KT2,TW10 ..**17** F3
Latchmere Jun & Inf Schs
KT2 ....**17** F2
Latchmere La KT2,TW10 ..**17** F3
Latchmere Rd KT2 ......**17** F2
Latchwood La GU10 ....**146** D5
Lateward Rd TW8 ....**6** D8
Latham Ave GU16 ....**65** E2
Latham Cl Biggin Hill TN16 .**83** C3
[5] Twickenham TW1 .....**17** A8
Latham Rd TW1 ....**16** F8
Latham's Way CR0 ......**60** F8
Lathwood Ho [6] SE26 ...**23** B3
Latimer RG12 ....**27** B1
Latimer Cl Crawley RH11 **181** D1
North Cheam KT4 ......**58** B6
Woking GU22 ....**70** B3
Latimer Ct [4] BR2 ......**44** F5
Latimer Ho GU7 ....**150** E3
Latimer Rd
Croydon CR0,CR9 .....**61** B7
Godalming GU7 ......**150** E4
Teddington TW11 ......**16** F3
Wimbledon SW19 .....**20** B2
Wokingham RG41 .....**25** B5
Lattimer Pl W4 ....**7** E7
Latton Cl Esher KT10 ....**55** B6
Walton-on-T KT12 .....**35** E2
Latymer Ct KT13 ....**53** C6
Laud Dr RH10 ....**202** D5
Laud St CR0,CR9 ....**61** C7
Laud Way RG40 ....**25** E6
Lauder Cl GU16 ....**65** E2
Lauderdale GU14 ....**84** D3
Lauderdale Dr TW10 ....**17** D5
Lauderdale Ho TW18 ....**12** F3
Laughton Rd RH12 .....**217** F5
Launceston Ct CR7 ......**42** A3
Laundry La GU47 ....**64** E5
Laundry Mews SE23 .....**23** E8
Laundry Rd GU1 ....**130** C8
Laundry Way RH5 ......**178** C5
Lauradale RG12 ....**27** A5
Laurel Ave
Englefield Green TW20 ..**11** B3
Twickenham TW1 ......**16** F7
Laurel Cl Camberley GU15 .**65** D4
Crawley RH10 ....**202** A3
Farnborough GU14 .....**84** C3
Poyle SL3 ....**1** E7
Upper Tooting SW17 ...**20** E3
Laurel Cres Croydon CR0 .**63** A7

Laurel Cres *continued*
Sheerwater GU21 ......**70** D6
Laurel Ct SE25 ....**42** E4
Laurel Dene RH19 .....**185** F1
Laurel Dr RH8 ....**122** F4
Laurel Gdns
Aldershot GU11 ......**126** A7
Hounslow TW4 ....**4** E3
Woodham KT15 ....**52** B1
Laurel Gr Forest Hill SE26 ..**23** E4
Penge SE20 ....**23** C1
Rowledge GU10 ......**145** F5
Wrecclesham GU10 ...**146** A5
Laurel Ho SM4 ....**40** B4
Laurel Manor SM2 ......**59** C3
Laurel Rd
Teddington TW12 ......**16** D3
Wimbledon SW20 .....**39** B8
Laurel Wlk RH13 ......**217** F1
Laureldene GU3 ....**107** B1
Laurels The Banstead SM7 **77** F2
Cobham KT11 ....**73** E4
Crawley RH10 ....**182** A1
Effingham KT24 .....**113** D8
Heath End GU9 ......**125** F7
[6] Oatlands Park KT13 ..**53** D7
Laurier Rd CR0 ....**42** F2
Lauriston Cl GU21 ......**68** D2
Lauriston Rd SW19 .....**19** D2
Lauser Rd TW19 ....**13** C8
Laustan Cl GU1 ....**110** C2
Lavant Cl RH11 ....**200** F5
Lavender Ave
Mitcham CR4 ....**40** F8
North Cheam KT4,SM3 .**58** C7
Lavender Cl
Caterham CR3 ....**100** C2
Coulsdon CR5 ....**99** C8
Leatherhead KT22 ....**95** C5
Redhill RH1 ....**140** B4
Wallington SM5 ......**60** B6
Lavender Cotts KT22 ....**95** C5
Lavender Ct KT8 ....**36** B6
Lavender Gate KT22 .....**74** B5
Lavender Gr CR4 ....**40** E8
Lavender La GU10 ......**145** E2
Lavender Lodge KT17 ...**57** F2
Lavender Park Rd [4]
KT14 ....**71** A6
Lavender Pk SL5 ....**28** C6
Lavender Rd
Carshalton SM1 ....**59** D6
Thornton Heath CR0 ...**41** F3
Wallington SM5 ......**60** A6
West Ewell KT19 ......**57** B4
Woking GU22 ....**70** B3
Lavender Vale SM6 ......**60** D4
Lavender Way CR0 ......**43** D3
Lavengro Rd SE27 ......**22** C6
Laverock Sch BR8 ......**122** E7
Laverstoke Gdns SW15 ..**19** A8
Lavington Cl RH11 .....**201** A7
Lavington Rd CR0 ....**60** F6
Lavinia Ct BR1 ....**24** E1
Lawbrook La GU5 ......**154** C7
Lawday Link GU9 ......**125** A7
Lawday Pl GU9 ....**125** A7
Lawday Place La GU9 ...**125** A7
Lawdon Gdns CR0 ....**61** B6
Lawford Cl SM6 ....**60** E2
Lawford Gdns CR8 ......**80** C3
Lawford Rd W4 ....**7** C7
Lawford's Hill Cl GU3 ....**88** C3
Lawford's Hill Rd GU3 ...**88** C3
Lawman Ct [2] TW9 ....**6** F6
Lawn Cl KT3 ....**38** E7
Lawn Cres TW9 ....**7** A5
Lawn Rd Beckenham BR3 ..**23** F1
Guildford GU2 ....**130** C6
Lawns Cotts RH12 .....**195** A3
Lawns Rd RH12 ....**195** A3
Lawns The Belmont SM2 ..**58** E3
Farnborough GU14 .....**84** E3
Milford GU8 ....**149** F1
North Ascot SL5 ......**28** D6
Purley CR8 ....**61** B1
South Norwood SE19 ..**42** D8
[1] Wimbledon SW19 ...**19** F3
Lawnsmead GU5 ....**152** B7
Lawnwood Ct GU7 .....**151** A5
Lawrence Ave KT3 ......**38** E2
Lawrence Cl
Guildford GU4 ....**110** B6
Wokingham RG40 .....**25** D6
Lawrence Cres GU20 ....**48** D4
Lawrence Ctr RG41 .....**25** A4
Lawrence Est TW4 ....**4** C3
Lawrence Gr RG42 ......**26** D8
Lawrence La RH3 ......**117** B3
Lawrence Lodge GU15 ...**65** D7
Lawrence Rd
Hampton TW12 ....**15** F1
Hounslow TW4 ....**4** C3
Richmond TW10 ......**17** C4
South Norwood SE25 ..**42** F5
Lawrence Way GU15 .....**64** F4
Lawrence Weaver Cl
SM4 ....**40** A3
Lawrie Park Ave SE26 ...**23** B3
Lawrie Park Cres SE26 ..**23** B3
Lawrie Park Gdns SE26 ..**23** B3
Lawrie Park Rd SE19,
SE26 ....**23** C3
Laws Cl Crawley RH11 ...**200** E5
South Norwood SE25 ..**42** D5
Laws Terr GU11 ....**105** C3
Lawson Cl SW19 ....**19** D5
Lawson Ct [13] KT6 ......**37** D2

Lawson Way SL5 ....**30** B3
Lawson Wlk SM5 ....**60** A2
Lawson-Hunt Ind Pk
RH12 ....**216** D4
Laxton Ct CR7 ....**42** C5
Laxton Gdns RH1 ......**119** D7
Layard Rd CR7 ....**42** D7
Layburn Cres SL3 ....**1** B8
Layhams Rd
Coney Hall BR2,BR4 ...**63** F5
West Wickham BR2 ....**63** F1
Layton Cres CR0 ....**61** B5
Layton Ct KT13 ....**53** B6
Layton Pl TW9 ....**7** A6
Layton Rd TW3 ....**5** B3
Layton's La TW16 ....**34** F7
Lazell Gdns RH3 ......**137** C3
Le Chateau CR0 ....**61** D7
Le Marchant Rd GU15,
GU16 ....**65** F3
Le May Cl RH6 ....**161** A4
Le Personne Rd [1] CR3 **100** D5
Lea Cl Ash GU12 ....**106** A1
Crawley RH11 ....**200** F5
Farnham GU9 ....**126** A6
Lea Croft RG45 ....**45** B6
Lea Ct GU9 ....**125** F7
Lea Rd [2] Beckenham BR3 .**44** A7
Camberley GU15 ......**65** B2
Lea The TW20 ....**12** C1
Lea Way GU11 ....**105** F3
Leach Gr KT22 ....**95** C5
Leacroft
East Grinstead RH19 ..**185** D2
Staines TW18 ....**13** B4
Sunningdale SL5 ......**30** A4
Leacroft Ave SW12 .....**20** F8
Leacroft Cl Kenley CR8 ..**80** C3
Staines TW18 ....**13** B4
Leaf Cl KT7,KT8 ....**36** E4
Leaf Gr SE27 ....**22** A3
Leafield Cl
South Norwood SW16 ..**22** B2
Woking GU21 ....**69** B1
Leafield Copse RG12 ....**27** F5
Leafield Rd
Merton SW19,SW20 ...**39** F6
Sutton SM1 ....**59** A8
Leafy Way CR0 ....**61** F8
Leamington Ave SM4 ....**39** F5
Leamington Cl SW2 .....**22** A8
Leamington Ct [4] SE26 ..**23** D5
Leander Ct [5] KT6 ......**37** D2
[4] Streatham SW2 .....**21** F8
Thornton Heath CR7 ...**41** F5
Leapale La GU1 ....**130** D8
Leapale Rd GU1 ....**130** D8
Leas Cl KT9 ....**56** F3
Leas La CR6 ....**81** D1
Leas Rd Guildford GU1 ..**130** C8
Warlingham CR6 ......**81** D1
Leaside KT23 ....**94** A4
Leather Cl CR4 ....**41** A7
Leather La GU5 ....**133** C4
Leatherhead By-Pass Rd
KT22 ....**95** D5
Leatherhead General Hospl
KT22 ....**95** C5
Leatherhead Ind Est
KT22 ....**95** A6
**Leatherhead Mus of Local
History** ★ KT22 ....**95** B5
Leatherhead Rd
Ashtead KT21,KT22 ...**95** E7
Chessington KT9 ......**75** C6
Great Bookham KT23 ..**94** C2
Oxshott KT22 ....**74** D4
Leatherhead Sta KT22 ...**95** A6
Leaveland Cl BR3 ....**44** A5
Leaves Gn RG12 ....**27** D3
Leaves Green Cres BR2 ..**83** C6
Leaves Green Rd BR2 ....**83** D8
Leavesden Rd KT13 .....**53** B5
Leazes Ave CR3 ....**100** A4
Lebanon Ave TW13 .....**15** D3
Lebanon Ct [11] TW1 ....**17** B1
Lebanon Dr KT11 ....**74** A6
Lebanon Gdns TN16 ....**83** D2
Lebanon Pk TW1 ....**17** B8
Lebanon Rd CR0 ....**42** E1
Lebanon Road Sta CR0 ..**61** E8
Lechford Rd RH6 ......**161** A1
Leckford Rd SW18 ......**20** C7
Leckhampton Pl SW2 ....**22** A8
Leconfield Ave SW13,SW15 **7** F4
Ledbury Pl CR0 ....**61** C6
Ledbury Rd
Croydon CR0,CR9 .....**61** D6
Reigate RH2 ....**118** A2
Ledger Cl GU1 ....**110** B3
Ledger Dr KT15 ....**51** F4
Ledgers Rd CR6 ....**82** B1
Ledrington Rd SE19 .....**23** A2
Lee Ct GU11 ....**126** C8
Lee Hollow GU5 ....**133** C1
Lee Rd Aldershot GU11 ..**104** C2
Merton SW19 ....**40** B8
Lee St RH6 ....**160** E4
Leech La KT18 ....**96** C1
Leechcroft Rd SM6 ......**60** A7
**Leechpool & Owlbeech
Woods Nature Reserve** ★
RH13 ....**218** C4
Leechpool La RH12,
RH13 ....**218** A4
Leechpool Prim Sch
RH13 ....**218** A4

Leeds Ct Carshalton SM5 ..**59** F7
Catford SE6 ....**24** B5
Leegate GU21 ....**69** D3
Leehurst GU8 ....**149** E1
Lees Farm Barn GU22 ...**71** B4
Lees The CR0 ....**62** F8
Leeson Ho [8] TW1 ......**17** B8
Leeward Gdns SW19 ....**19** F2
Legge Cres GU11 ......**104** E1
Legion Cl SM4 ....**40** A3
Legion Ho BR1 ....**24** D3
Legrace Ave TW4,TW5 ....**4** D5
Legsheath La RH19 ....**205** D1
Leicester RG12 ....**27** E2
Leicester Ave CR4 ......**41** E5
Leicester Cl KT4 ....**58** C6
Leicester Ct RH10 .....**202** D6
Leicester Ho [2] KT7 .....**37** A2
Leicester Rd CR0 ....**42** E2
Leigh Cl Addlestone KT15 ..**51** F3
New Malden KT3 ......**38** D5
Leigh Court Cl KT11 .....**73** C3
Leigh Cres CR0 ....**63** C3
Leigh Ct CR0 ....**82** E8
Leigh Hill Rd KT11 ......**73** D5
Leigh Ho [4] KT2 ....**18** B2
Leigh Jenkins Way RH6 **182** B7
Leigh La GU9 ....**146** E8
Leigh Orchard Cl SW16 ..**21** F5
Leigh Pl KT11 ....**73** C5
Leigh Place La RH9 ....**121** E1
Leigh Place Rd RH2 ....**138** A3
Leigh Rd Betchworth RH3 **137** C2
Cobham KT11 ....**73** C5
Isleworth TW3 ....**5** D3
Leigh The KT2 ....**18** E1
Leigham Ave SW16 .....**21** E5
Leigham Court Rd SE27,
SW16,SW21 ....**22** A4
Leigham Dr TW7 ....**5** E7
Leigham Hall [3] SW16 ..**21** E5
Leigham Hall Par [2]
SW16 ....**21** E5
Leigham Vale SW2,SW16 .**22** A6
Leighlands RH10 ......**202** C8
Leighton Gdns
Sanderstead CR2 ......**81** B6
Thornton Heath CR0 ...**42** B1
Leighton Ho [7] KT6 .....**37** E3
Leighton St CR0 ....**42** B1
Leighton Way KT18 .....**76** D5
Leinster Ave SW14 ....**7** C3
Leisure La KT14 ....**71** B7
Leith Cl RG45 ....**45** A7
Leith Dr GU11 ....**104** F3
Leith Gr RH5 ....**157** D4
Leith Hill Rd
Abinger Common RH5 **155** F5
Wotton RH5 ....**156** A3
Leith Hill Twr ★ RH5 ...**156** B3
Leith Ho Leatherhead KT22 **95** A6
Reigate RH2 ....**139** A4
[16] Streatham SW2 ....**21** F8
Leith Lea RH5 ....**157** D4
Leith Rd
Beare Green RH5 ....**157** D4
Ewell KT17 ....**76** F7
Leith Twrs SM2 ....**59** B3
Leith Vale Cotts RH5 ...**177** A2
Leith View RH5 ....**136** C3
Leith View Cotts RH12 ..**198** B6
Leith View Rd RH12 ....**218** A5
Leithcote Gdns SW16 ....**21** F4
Leithcote Path SW16 ....**21** F5
Lela Ave TW4,TW5 ....**4** C5
Lemington Gr RG12 .....**27** B3
Lemmington Way RH12 **218** A7
Lemon Gr TW13 ....**15** A7
Lemon's Farm Rd RH5 ..**155** F6
Lendore Rd GU16 ....**85** D8
Lenelby Rd KT6 ....**38** A1
Leney Cl RG40 ....**25** D8
Lenham Rd
South Norwood CR7 ...**42** D7
Sutton SM1 ....**59** C5
Lennard Ave BR4 ....**63** E8
Lennard Cl BR4 ....**63** E8
Lennard Rd
Penge BR3,SE20,SE26 ..**23** E2
Thornton Heath CR0 ...**42** D7
Lennox Ct [13] RH1 ....**119** A2
Lennox Gdns CR0 ....**61** B6
Lenten Cl GU5 ....**133** D1
Lentmead Rd BR1 ....**24** F5
Lenton Rise TW9 ....**6** E4
Leo Ct [4] TW8 ....**6** D7
Leof Cres SE6 ....**24** B3
Leominster Rd SM4 .....**40** C4
Leominster Wlk SM4 ....**40** C4
Leonard Ave SM4 ....**40** C4
Leonard Cl GU16 ....**85** D8
Leonard Rd CR4,SW16 ...**41** C8
Leonard Way RH13 ....**217** F2
Leonardslee Ct RH10 ..**202** B3
Leopardstown Ho RH7 .**142** E1
Leopold Ave
Farnborough GU14 .....**85** B5
Wimbledon SW19 .....**19** F3
Leopold Rd
Crawley RH11 ....**201** C6
Wimbledon SW19 .....**19** F4
Leopold Terr SW19 ......**20** A3
Leppington RG12 ......**27** B2
Leret Way KT22 ....**95** B6
Lesbourne Rd RH2 ....**139** B8
Lescombe Cl SE23 ......**23** E5
Lescombe Rd SE23,SE6 ..**23** E5

Lesley Ct **8** SM6 . . . .**60** B6
Leslie Gdns SM2 . . . . . .**59** A3
Leslie Gr CR0 . . . .**42** E1
Leslie Park Rd CR0 . . . . .**42** E1
Leslie Rd Chobham GU24 . .**49** E1
   Dorking RH4 . . . .**115** D1
Lessing St SE23 . . . .**23** E8
Lessingham Ave SW17 . .**21** A4
Lessness Rd SM4 . . . . . .**40** C4
Lestor Ct TW7 . . . .**5** F4
Letchworth Ave TW14 . .**14** F8
Letchworth Ct RH11 . . .**200** E3
Letchworth St SW17 . . . .**20** F4
Letcombe Sq RG12 . . . . .**27** F5
Levana Cl SW19 . . . .**19** E7
Levehurst Ho SE27 . . . . .**22** C3
Levendale Rd SE23,SE6 . .**23** F6
Leveret Cl CR0 . . . .**82** D8
Leveret La RH11 . . . . . .**201** B8
Leverkusen Rd RG12 . . . .**27** B6
Levern Dr GU1 . . . .**125** C6
Leverson St SW16 . . . . . .**21** C2
Levett Ho **8** SW16 . . . . .**21** C3
Levett Rd KT22 . . . .**95** B7
Levylsdene GU1 . . . . . .**110** D1
Levylsdene Ct GU1 . . . .**110** D1
Lewes Cl RH10 . . . .**202** C6
Lewes Ct **5** CR4 . . . . . .**40** F6
Lewes Ho RH2 . . . .**139** B5
Lewes Rd
   Ashurst Wood RH19 . . .**206** C6
   East Grinstead RH19 . . .**206** C6
   Forest Row RH18 . . . . .**206** E2
Lewesdon Cl **13** SW19 . .**19** D7
Lewin Ct SW16 . . . .**21** E2
Lewin Rd Mortlake SW14 . .**7** D4
   Streatham SW16 . . . .**21** D2
Lewins Rd KT18 . . . .**76** B5
Lewis Cl KT15 . . . .**52** C6
Lewis Rd Mitcham CR4 . . .**40** E7
   18 Richmond TW10 . . . . .**6** D2
   Sutton SM1 . . . .**59** B6
Lewisham Cl RH11 . . . .**201** C2
Lewisham Way GU47 . . . .**45** D2
Lexden Rd CR4 . . . .**41** D5
Lexington Ct CR8 . . . . . .**80** C8
Lexton Gdns SW12 . . . . .**21** D7
Ley Rd GU14 . . . .**85** A8
Leybourne Pk TW9 . . . . . .**7** A6
Leybourne Ave KT14 . . . .**71** F6
Leybourne Cl Byfleet KT14 **71** F6
   Crawley RH11 . . . .**201** C1
Leyburn Gdns CR0 . . . . .**61** E8
Leycester Cl GU20 . . . . . .**48** B6
Leyfield KT4 . . . .**38** F1
Leylands La TW19 . . . .**2** A2
Leylands Rd RH5 . . . . . .**156** A6
Leys Rd KT22 . . . .**74** D7
Leys The KT12 . . . .**54** E6
Leyside RG45 . . . .**45** A5
Leyton Rd SW19 . . . .**20** C1
Liberty Ave SW19 . . . . . .**40** D8
Liberty Ct RH2 . . . .**139** D8
Liberty Hall Rd KT15 . . . .**52** A5
Liberty La KT15 . . . .**52** B5
Liberty Mid Sch CR4 . . . .**40** E7
Liberty Rise KT15 . . . . . .**52** A4
Lichfield Ct
   Kingston u T KT6 . . . . . .**37** E4
   Richmond TW9 . . . .**6** E3
Lichfield Gdns TW10,TW9 . .**6** E2
Lichfield Rd Hounslow TW4 . .**4** F4
   Richmond TW9 . . . .**6** F6
Lichfield Terr **1** TW9 . . . .**6** E2
Lichfield Way CR2 . . . . . .**62** D2
Lichfields RG12 . . . .**27** E7
Lickfolds Rd GU10 . . . . .**145** E3
Liddel Way SL5 . . . .**28** F5
Liddell Ct **2** CR8 . . . . . .**80** A7
Liddington Hall Dr GU3 **108** E4
Liddington Hall Est GU3 **108** E4
Liddington New Rd GU3 **108** E4
Lidiard Rd SW18 . . . .**20** C6
Lido Rd GU1 . . . .**109** D2
Lidsey Cl RH10 . . . .**202** C4
Lidstone Cl GU22 . . . . . .**69** B2
Lightwater Ctry Pk GU18 . .**47** F1
Lightwater Mdw GU18 . . .**67** A8
Lightwater Rd GU18 . . . .**67** C8
Lightwater Village Inf Sch
   GU18 . . . .**48** A1
Lightwood RG12 . . . .**27** D3
Lilac Ave GU22 . . . .**89** D2
Lilac Cl GU1 . . . .**109** C5
Lilac Gdns CR0 . . . .**63** A7
Lilian Rd CR4,SW16 . . . . .**41** C8
Lilian Rolfe Ho **5** SE27 . .**22** D4
Lilleshall Rd SM4 . . . .**40** D4
Lilley Dr KT20 . . . .**98** B5
Lillie Rd TN16 . . . .**83** D1
Lily Hill Dr RG12 . . . .**27** E7
Lily Hill Rd RG12 . . . .**27** F7
Lilycourt RG41 . . . .**25** A6
Lilyfields Chase GU6 . . .**175** E4
Lime Ave Camberley GU15 .**66** A6
   Horsham RH12 . . . .**218** A4
   Winkfield SL4 . . . .**9** F5
Lime Cl Carshalton SM5 . . .**59** F8
   Copthorne RH10 . . . . . .**183** B3
   Crawley RH11 . . . .**181** C1
   Reigate RH2 . . . .**139** B6
   West Clandon GU4 . . . . .**111** B7
Lime Cres Ash GU12 . . . .**106** B2
   Sunbury TW16 . . . .**35** C7
Lime Ct Chipstead CR5 . . .**78** F1
   Kingston u T KT1 . . . . . .**38** B6
   Mitcham CR4 . . . .**40** D7
Lime Gr Addlestone KT15 . .**52** A6

Lime Gr continued
   Guildford GU1 . . . .**109** B5
   Kingston u T KT3 . . . . . .**38** E6
   Twickenham TW1 . . . .**6** A1
   Warlingham CR6 . . . .**81** E1
   West Clandon GU4 . . . . .**111** B7
   Woking GU22 . . . .**89** E6
Lime Ho TW11 . . . .**17** C2
Lime Lodge **3** TW16 . . . .**14** F1
Lime Meadow Ave CR2 . .**81** B6
Lime Mews TW20 . . . .**11** F3
Lime St GU11 . . . .**104** F2
Lime St Rdbt GU11 . . . .**104** F2
Lime Tree Ave KT10,KT7 . .**36** E1
Lime Tree Cl KT23 . . . . . .**94** A3
Lime Tree Ct KT21 . . . . . .**75** E1
Lime Tree Gr CR0 . . . . . .**62** F7
Lime Tree Rd TW5 . . . .**5** B6
Lime Tree Wlk
   Coney Hall BR4 . . . .**63** F6
   Thorpe GU25 . . . .**31** B5
Lime Wlk RG12 . . . .**27** C5
Limebush Cl KT15 . . . . . .**52** C2
Limecroft KT19 . . . .**57** D3
Limecroft Rd GU21 . . . . .**68** B2
Limekiln Pl SE19 . . . .**22** F1
Limerick Cl
   Bracknell RG42 . . . .**27** A8
   Streatham SW12 . . . .**21** C8
Limerick Ct **1** SW12 . . .**21** C8
Limerick Ho GU22 . . . . . .**70** A1
Limes Ave Barnes SW13 . . .**7** F5
   Carshalton SM5 . . . .**40** F1
   Croydon CR0,CR9 . . . . . .**61** A7
   Horley RH6 . . . .**161** B1
   Penge SE20 . . . .**23** B1
Limes Cl TW15 . . . .**14** A3
Limes Ct BR3 . . . .**44** B7
Limes Field Rd SW14 . . . . .**7** E4
Limes Rd Beckenham BR3 . .**44** B7
   Egham TW20 . . . .**11** F3
   Farnborough GU14 . . . . . .**84** C5
   Thornton Heath CR0 . . . . .**42** D2
   Weybridge KT13 . . . .**53** A6
Limes The
   Dormans Park RH19 . . . .**185** A5
   East Molesey KT8 . . . .**36** B5
   Haslemere GU27 . . . . . .**208** A6
   Leatherhead KT22 . . . . . .**95** B4
   4 Woking GU21 . . . .**70** A3
   Woking,Horsell GU21 . . . .**69** D4
Limetree Cl SW2 . . . .**21** F7
Limetree Pl CR4 . . . .**41** B8
Limetree Wlk **2** SW17 . .**21** A3
Limeway Terr RH4 . . . . .**115** A1
Limewood Cl
   Beckenham BR3 . . . .**44** C4
   Knaphill GU21 . . . .**88** D7
Limpsfield Ave
   Putney SW19 . . . .**19** D6
   Thornton Heath CR7 . . . . .**41** F4
Limpsfield CE Inf Sch
   RH8 . . . .**123** C4
Limpsfield Grange Sch
   RH8 . . . .**123** A8
Limpsfield Rd
   Chelsham CR6 . . . .**102** B8
   Hamsey Green CR2,CR6 . . .**81** C3
Linacre Dr GU6,RH12 . . .**195** C4
Lince La RH4 . . . .**135** D6
Linchmere Pl RH11 . . . .**201** A7
Linchmere Rd
   Haslemere GU27 . . . . . .**207** D5
   Lewisham SE12 . . . .**24** F8
   Linchmere GU27 . . . . . .**207** C4
Lincoln Ave
   Twickenham TW2 . . . .**16** C6
   Wimbledon SW19 . . . .**19** D5
Lincoln Cl Ash Vale GU12 **105** F5
   Crawley RH11 . . . .**201** E3
   Croydon SE25 . . . .**43** B3
   Frimley GU15 . . . .**66** B4
   Horley RH6 . . . .**161** A2
Lincoln Terr **6** SM2 . . . .**59** A3
Lincoln Way TW16 . . . . . .**34** E8
Lincoln Wlk KT19 . . . . . .**57** D1
Lincolns Mead RH7 . . . .**164** C3
Lincombe Rd BR1 . . . . . .**24** F5
Lind Rd SM1 . . . .**59** C5
Linda Ct KT9 . . . .**56** D6
Lindale SW19 . . . .**19** E6
Lindale Cl GU25 . . . .**30** F5
Lindbergh Rd SM6 . . . . . .**60** E3
Linden **3** RG12 . . . .**27** E4
Linden Ave Coulsdon CR5 . .**79** B3
   East Grinstead RH19 . . . .**185** C2
   Hounslow TW3 . . . .**5** C3
   Thornton Heath CR7 . . . . .**42** B5
Linden Bridge Specl Sch
   KT4 . . . .**57** E7
Linden Cl Crawley RH10 . .**202** A3
   Horsham RH12 . . . .**217** E4
   Tadworth KT20 . . . .**97** D7
   Thames Ditton KT7 . . . . . .**37** A2
   Woodham KT15 . . . .**71** A8
Linden Cres KT1 . . . .**37** F7
Linden Ct Beckenham BR3 . .**44** B6

Linden Ct continued
   Camberley GU15 . . . .**65** F7
   Englefield Green TW20 . . . .**11** B2
   Leatherhead KT22 . . . . . .**95** B6
   Penge SE20 . . . .**23** B1
Linden Dr CR3 . . . .**100** C3
Linden Gdns KT22 . . . . . .**95** C6
Linden Gr Kingston u T KT3 **38** E6
   Penge SE20 . . . .**23** C2
   Teddington TW11 . . . .**16** F3
   Walton-on-T KT12 . . . .**53** F8
   Warlingham CR6 . . . .**81** E1
Linden Lea BR4 . . . .**136** C5
Linden Leas BR4 . . . .**63** D8
Linden Lodge Sch SW19 . .**19** E7
Linden Pit Path KT12 . . . .**95** B6
Linden Pl Ewell KT17 . . . .**76** E7
   Mitcham CR4 . . . .**40** E5
   Staines TW18 . . . .**13** A4
Linden Rd Guildford GU1 **109** D1
   Hampton TW12 . . . .**36** A8
   Headley Down GU35 . . . .**187** C5
   Leatherhead KT22 . . . . . .**95** B6
   Weybridge KT13 . . . .**53** C2
Linden Way
   Send Marsh GU23 . . . .**90** F3
   Shepperton TW17 . . . .**34** C4
   Wallington CR8 . . . .**60** C1
   Woking GU22 . . . .**89** F6
Lindenhill Rd RG42 . . . . .**26** F8
Lindens Cl KT24 . . . .**113** E7
Lindens The Chiswick W4 . . .**7** D8
   Copthorne RH10 . . . .**183** B3
   Farnham GU9 . . . .**125** D1
   New Addington CR0 . . . . . .**63** C4
Lindfield Gdns GU1 . . . .**109** F2
Lindfield Rd CR0 . . . .**42** F3
Lindgren Wlk RH11 . . . .**201** B1
Lindisfarne Rd SW20 . . . .**19** A1
Lindley Ct KT1 . . . .**37** C8
Lindley Ho KT14 . . . .**71** B7
Lindley Pl TW9 . . . .**7** A6
Lindley Rd
   Tyler's Green RH9 . . . . . .**121** C5
   Walton-on-T KT12 . . . .**54** D7
Lindon Bennett Sch
   TW13 . . . .**15** D3
Lindores Rd SM5 . . . .**40** C1
Lindsay Cl
   Chessington KT9 . . . .**56** E3
   Epsom KT18 . . . .**76** C6
   Stanwell TW19 . . . .**2** D2
Lindsay Dr TW17 . . . .**34** D3
Lindsay Rd Hampton TW12 **16** B4
   North Cheam KT4 . . . .**58** B8
   Woodham KT15 . . . .**71** B8
Lindsey Cl CR4,SW16 . . . .**41** E5
Lindsey Gdns TW14 . . . . .**14** D8
Lindum Cl GU11 . . . .**105** A1
Lindum Dene GU11 . . . . .**105** A1
Lindum Rd TW11 . . . .**17** C1
Lindums The BR3 . . . .**23** F2
Lindvale GU21 . . . .**69** E4
Lindway SE27 . . . .**22** B3
Linersh Dr GU5 . . . .**152** A6
Linersh Wood Cl GU5 . . .**152** B5
Lines Rd GU11 . . . .**105** D7
Linford Ct **6** CR4 . . . . . .**40** E8
Ling Cres GU35 . . . .**187** B6
Ling Dr GU18 . . . .**67** A8
Ling's Coppice SE21 . . . .**22** D6
Lingfield Ave KT1,KT5 . . .**37** F5
Lingfield Common Rd
   RH7 . . . .**164** C6
Lingfield Ct SW19 . . . . . .**19** D2
Lingfield Dr RH10 . . . . .**202** E7
Lingfield Gdns CR5 . . . .**100** B8
Lingfield Ho
   Kingston u T KT1 . . . .**37** C8
   Penge SE26 . . . .**23** B2
   Tadworth KT20 . . . .**97** D4
Lingfield Notre Dame Sch
   RH7 . . . .**164** F3
Lingfield Park Race Course
   RH7 . . . .**164** E2
Lingfield Prim Sch RH7 **164** D4
Lingfield Rd
   East Grinstead RH19 . . . .**185** D3
   Edenbridge TN8 . . . .**165** F8
   Haxted TN8 . . . .**165** F8
   North Cheam KT4 . . . .**58** C7
   Wimbledon SW19 . . . .**19** D2
Lingfield Sta RH7 . . . . .**164** E4
Lingwell Rd SW17 . . . . . .**20** E5
Lingwood RG12 . . . .**27** C3
Lingwood Gdns TW7 . . . . .**5** E7
Link La SM6 . . . .**60** E4
Link Prim Day Sch The
   CR0 . . . .**60** E6
Link Rd Addlestone KT15 . . .**52** E6
   Carshalton CR4,SM6 . . . . .**41** A1
   East Bedfont TW14 . . . . . .**14** F8
   Farnborough GU14 . . . . . .**84** D1
Link Sec Day Sch The
   CR0 . . . .**60** F6
Link The Crawley RH11 . .**201** D6
   Teddington TW11 . . . .**16** F1
Link Way Richmond TW10 . .**17** B6
   Staines TW18 . . . .**13** B2
Link's Rd KT17 . . . .**77** A5
Linkfield KT8 . . . .**36** B6
Linkfield Cnr RH1 . . . . .**118** E2
Linkfield Gdns RH1 . . . .**118** E1
Linkfield Rd TW7 . . . .**5** F5
Linkfield St RH1 . . . .**118** E1

Linklater's Cotts GU14 . .**84** B6
Links Ave SM4 . . . .**40** A5
Links Brow KT22 . . . .**94** E4
Links Cl Ashstead KT21 . . .**75** C2
   Ewhurst GU6 . . . .**175** E6
Links Gdns SW16 . . . .**22** A1
Links Green Way KT11 . . .**74** A5
Links Ind Est TW13 . . . . .**15** E5
Links Pl KT21 . . . .**75** D2
Links Prim Sch The
   SW17 . . . .**21** A2
Links Rd Ashford TW15 . . .**13** E3
   Ashstead KT21 . . . .**75** C2
   Bramley GU5 . . . .**151** E3
   Mitcham SW16,SW17 . . . . .**21** A2
   West Wickham BR4 . . . . . .**44** C1
Links The North Ascot SL5 . .**28** C7
   Walton-on-T KT12 . . . .**54** A8
Links View Ave RH3 . . . .**116** A1
Links View Rd
   Croydon CR0 . . . .**63** A7
   Hampton TW12 . . . .**16** C4
Links Way Beckenham BR3 **44** A3
   Effingham KT24 . . . .**113** C2
   Farnborough GU14 . . . . . .**84** C3
   Mitcham SW17 . . . .**21** A2
Linkscroft Ave TW15 . . . .**14** B2
Linkside KT3 . . . .**38** E7
Linkside E GU26 . . . . . .**188** D7
Linkside N GU26 . . . . . .**188** B7
Linkside S GU26 . . . . . .**188** C6
Linkside W GU26 . . . . . .**188** B6
Linkway Camberley GU15 . .**65** C5
   Crawley RH10 . . . .**182** C7
   Crowthorne RG45 . . . .**45** A5
   Guildford GU2 . . . .**108** F2
   West Barnes KT3,SW20 . . . .**39** B6
   West Barnes SW20 . . . . . .**39** B5
   Woking GU22 . . . .**70** C2
Linkway The SM2 . . . .**59** C2
Linley Ct **1** Dulwich SE21 .**22** E4
   Sutton SM1 . . . .**59** C6
Linnell Rd RH1 . . . .**140** B8
Linnet Cl Selsdon CR2 . . . .**62** D1
   Turners Hill RH10 . . . . . .**204** C6
Linnet Ct **5** CR4 . . . . . .**40** E8
Linnet Gr GU4 . . . .**110** D3
Linnet Mews SW12 . . . . . .**21** A8
Linsford Bsns Pk GU16 . . .**85** F3
Linsford La GU16 . . . .**85** F3
Linslade TW4 . . . .**4** E2
Linstead Rd GU14 . . . . . .**84** E8
Linstead Way SW18,SW19 **19** E8
Linton Cl CR4,SM5 . . . . . .**40** F2
Linton Glade CR0 . . . .**62** E1
Linton Gr SE27 . . . .**22** C3
Linton's La KT17 . . . .**76** E7
Lintott Ct TW19 . . . .**2** D1
Lintott Gdns RH13 . . . . .**217** E3
Lion & Lamb Way **9**
   GU9 . . . .**125** B2
Lion & Lamb Yd **13** GU9 **125** B2
Lion Ave TW1 . . . .**16** F7
Lion Cl Haslemere GU27 . .**207** F7
   Littleton TW17 . . . .**33** E6
Lion Ctr The TW13 . . . . . .**15** E5
Lion Gate Gdns TW9 . . . . .**6** F4
Lion Gate Mews SW18 . . .**20** A8
Lion Gn GU27 . . . .**207** F6
Lion Green Rd CR5 . . . . . .**79** D3
Lion La Haslemere GU27 . .**207** F7
   Turners Hill RH10 . . . . . .**204** A4
Lion Mead GU27 . . . . . .**207** F6
Lion Park Ave KT9 . . . . . .**57** A6
Lion Rd Farnborough GU14 **85** B2
   Thornton Heath CR0 . . . . .**42** C4
   Twickenham TW1 . . . .**16** F7
Lion Way GU22 . . . .**70** B3
Lion Wharf Rd TW7 . . . . . .**6** B4
Liphook Cres SE23 . . . . . .**23** C8
Liphook Rd
   Haslemere GU27 . . . . . .**207** F6
   Linchmere GU27 . . . . . .**207** A6
Lipsham Cl SM7 . . . .**78** D6
Lisbon Ave TW2 . . . .**16** C6
Liscombe RG12 . . . .**27** B2
Liscombe Ho RG12 . . . . . .**27** B2
Liskeard Dr **2** GU14 . . . .**85** A6
Liskeard Lodge CR3 . . . .**101** A1
Lisle Cl SW17 . . . .**21** B4
Lismore **9** SW19 . . . . . .**19** F3
Lismore Cl TW7 . . . .**6** A5
Lismore Cres RH11 . . . .**201** B3
Lismore Rd CR2 . . . .**61** E4
Lissant Cl KT6 . . . .**37** D2
Lissoms Rd CR5 . . . .**79** A1
Lister Ave RH19 . . . .**205** F6
Lister Cl SW19 . . . .**40** E8
Lister Ct **1** CR8 . . . .**80** B7
Litchfield Ave SM4 . . . . . .**39** F4
Litchfield Rd SM1 . . . .**59** C6
Litchfield Way GU2 . . . .**129** F7
Lithgow's Rd TW14,TW6 . . .**3** F3
Little Acre BR3 . . . .**44** B4
Little Austins Rd GU9 . . .**146** D8
Little Birch Cl KT15 . . . . .**52** D2
Little Bookham St KT23 . . .**93** F2
Little Bornes SE21 . . . . . .**22** E4
Little Borough RH3 . . . .**137** A4
Little Brownings SE23 . . .**23** B6
Little Browns La TN8 . . .**144** F4
Little Collins RH1 . . . . . .**162** B7
Little Common La RH1 . .**120** C3
Little Comptons RH13 . .**217** E3
Little Crabtree RH11 . . .**201** C6
Little Cranmore La
   KT24 . . . .**112** C2

Little Ct BR4 . . . .**63** E8
Little Dimocks SW12 . . . .**21** B6
Little Elms UB3 . . . .**3** D7
Little Ferry Rd TW1 . . . . .**17** B7
Little Gn GU8 . . . .**148** D4
Little Grebe RH17 . . . . . .**217** C5
Little Green La
   Addlestone KT16 . . . .**51** E7
   Wrecclesham GU9 . . . . . .**146** A6
Little Halliards KT12 . . . . .**35** A3
Little Hatch RH12 . . . . . .**217** F5
Little Haven La RH12 . . .**217** F5
Little Heath La KT11 . . . . .**74** A5
Little Heath Rd GU24 . . . .**49** E2
Little Hide GU1 . . . .**110** B3
Little Kiln GU7 . . . .**150** E8
Little King St RH19 . . . .**185** E1
Little London Shere GU5 **132** F2
   Witley GU8 . . . .**170** E5
Little Lullenden RH7 . . . .**164** E5
Little Manor Gdns GU6 . .**174** E2
Little Mead GU7 . . . .**68** F3
Little Mead Ind Est GU6 **174** B3
Little Moor GU47 . . . .**45** C1
Little Moreton Cl KT14 . . .**71** B7
Little Oak Cl TW17 . . . . . .**33** F5
Little Orch Woking GU21 . .**70** A8
   Woodham KT15 . . . .**71** A8
Little Orchard Way GU4 **130** E1
Little Orchards KT18 . . . . .**76** E5
Little Paddock GU15 . . . . .**66** A8
Little Park Dr TW13 . . . . .**15** D4
Little Park Enterprises
   RH6 . . . .**180** E3
Little Platt GU2 . . . .**108** D2
Little Queens Rd TW11 . . .**16** F2
Little Ringdale RG12 . . . . .**27** E5
Little Roke Ave CR8 . . . . .**80** B5
Little Roke Rd CR8 . . . . . .**80** C5
Little St GU2 . . . .**109** B5
Little St Leonards SW14 . . .**7** C4
Little Sutton La SL3 . . . . . .**1** B8
Little Tangley Flats
   GU5 . . . .**131** C1
Little Thatch GU7 . . . . . .**150** F6
Little Thurbans Cl GU9 . .**146** A6
Little Tumners Ct GU7 . . .**150** E6
Little Warren Cl GU4 . . . .**131** B7
Little Wellington St **9**
   GU11 . . . .**105** A2
Little Woodcote La CR8,
   SM5,SM6 . . . .**79** B8
Littlebourne **2** SE13 . . . .**24** E8
Littlebrook Cl CR0 . . . . . .**43** D3
Littlecote Cl SW19 . . . . . .**19** E8
Littledale Cl RG12 . . . . . .**27** E6
Littlefield Cl Ash GU12 . .**106** A1
   9 Kingston u T KT1 . . . . .**37** E7
Littlefield Cotts GU3 . . .**108** B6
Littlefield Ct UB7 . . . .**2** D7
Littlefield Gdns GU12 . . .**106** A1
Littlefield Way GU3 . . . .**108** D5
Littleford La GU4,GU5 . . .**152** F7
Littlehaven Inf Sch
   RH12 . . . .**217** F5
Littlehaven Sta RH12 . . .**217** F5
Littleheath Rd CR2 . . . . . .**62** B2
Littlemead KT10 . . . .**55** D6
Littleridding GU22 . . . . . .**70** B3
Littlers Cl SW19 . . . .**40** D8
Littlestone Cl BR3 . . . . . .**24** A2
Littleton CE Inf Sch
   TW17 . . . .**34** A6
Littleton Cross GU3 . . . .**130** A3
Littleton Ho **4** RH2 . . . .**118** A2
Littleton La
   Artington GU3 . . . .**130** A3
   Littleton TW17,TW18 . . . . .**33** E4
   Reigate RH2 . . . .**138** E7
Littleton Rd TW15,TW17 . .**14** C1
Littleton St SW18 . . . .**20** C6
Littlewick Cotts GU21 . . .**68** F4
Littlewick Rd GU21 . . . . .**68** E3
Littlewood GU6 . . . .**174** F3
Littlewood Ho CR2 . . . . . .**81** B5
Littleworth Ave KT10 . . . .**55** D5
Littleworth Common Rd
   KT10 . . . .**55** D7
Littleworth La KT10 . . . . .**55** D6
Littleworth Pl KT10 . . . . .**55** D6
Littleworth Rd
   Hinchley Wood KT10 . . . . .**55** E6
   Puttenham GU10 . . . . . .**148** A3
   The Sands GU10 . . . .**126** F1
Liverpool Rd
   Kingston u T KT2 . . . .**18** A1
   South Norwood CR7 . . . . . .**42** C6
Livesey Cl KT1 . . . .**37** F6
Livingstone Ct TW19 . . . .**13** E7
Livingstone Rd
   Caterham CR3 . . . .**100** D5
   Crawley RH10 . . . .**201** E4
   Horsham RH13 . . . .**217** D1
   Hounslow TW3 . . . .**5** C3
   South Norwood CR7 . . . . . .**42** D7
Llanaway Cl GU7 . . . . . .**150** F6
Llanaway Ho GU7 . . . . . .**150** F6
Llanaway Rd GU7 . . . . . .**150** F6
Llangar Gr RG45 . . . .**45** A5
Llanthony Rd SM4 . . . . . .**40** D4
Llanvair Cl SL5 . . . .**29** A3
Llanvair Dr SL5 . . . .**28** F3
Llewellyn Ct SE20 . . . . . .**43** C8

Lloyd Ave
Thornton Heath SW16 . . . . . .41 E8
Wallington CR5 . . . . .79 B5
Lloyd Ct [6] SE27 . . . . .22 B5
Lloyd Ho BR3 . . . . .24 B2
Lloyd Park Ave CR0 . . . . .61 F6
Lloyd Pk CR0 . . . . .61 F6
Lloyd Rd KT4,SM3 . . . . . . .58 D7
Lloyds Ct RH10 . . . . .181 E1
Lloyds Way BR3 . . . . .43 F4
Lobelia Rd GU24 . . . . .68 A4
Lochinvar St SW12 . . . . . .21 B8
Lochinver RG12 . . . . .27 B2
Lock Cl KT15 . . . . .70 E7
Lock La GU22,GU23 . . . . . .71 C3
Lock Rd
Farnborough GU11 . . . . . .105 D5
Guildford GU1 . . . . .109 D4
Richmond TW10 . . . . .17 C4
Lock's La CR4 . . . . .41 A7
Locke King Cl KT13 . . . . . .53 A3
Locke King Rd KT13 . . . . .53 A3
Locke Way GU21 . . . . .69 F2
Lockesley Sq KT6 . . . . . . .37 D3
Lockfield Cotts GU21 . . . . .69 A1
Lockfield Dr GU21 . . . . . . .68 F2
Lockhart Rd KT11 . . . . .73 C6
Lockhursthatch La GU5 153 E6
Locks Mdw RH7 . . . . .165 A1
Locks Ride SL5 . . . . .8 C2
Locksmeade Rd TW10 . .17 C4
Lockswood GU24 . . . . .88 B7
Lockton Chase SL5 . . . . . .28 D6
Lockton Ho RG40 . . . . .25 C6
Lockwood Cl
Farnborough GU14 . . . . . . .84 E8
Forest Hill SE26 . . . . .23 D4
Horsham RH12 . . . . .218 A5
Lockwood Ct RH10 . . . . . .201 F8
Lockwood Path GU21 . . . .70 E6
Lockwood Way KT9 . . . . . .57 A5
Locomotive Dr TW14 . . . . .15 A7
Lodden Lodge [17] SM2 . . .59 C3
Loddon Cl GU15 . . . . .66 A6
Loddon Rd GU14 . . . . .84 D6
Loddon Way GU12 . . . . . .106 A1
Loder Cl GU21 . . . . .70 D6
Lodge Ave CR0,CR9 . . . . . .61 A7
Lodge Cl Aldershot GU11 126 C8
Brentford TW7 . . . . .6 B6
Carshalton CR4 . . . . .41 A1
Crawley RH11 . . . . .201 C6
Dorking RH5 . . . . .136 C3
E Ewell KT17 . . . . .58 C1
East Grinstead RH19 . . . . .185 D1
Englefield Green TW20 . . . .11 D3
Fetcham KT22 . . . . .94 D5
Stoke D'Abernon KT11 . . . .73 F3
Lodge Gdns BR3 . . . . .43 F4
Lodge Hill CR8 . . . . .80 A4
Lodge Hill Cl GU10 . . . . . .146 D6
Lodge Hill Rd GU10 . . . . .146 E7
Lodge La
New Addington CR0 . . . . . .63 B3
Salfords RH1 . . . . .139 F1
South Croydon CR0 . . . . . .63 A4
South Holmwood RH5 . . . .157 F8
Lodge Pl SM1 . . . . .59 B5
Lodge Rd Fetcham KT22 . . .94 D5
Sutton SM1 . . . . .59 B5
Thornton Heath CR0 . . . . . .42 B2
Wallington SM6 . . . . .60 B5
Lodge Sch SE18 . . . . .79 D8
Lodge The Farnham GU9 .125 E4
Newchapel RH7 . . . . .163 E1
Lodge Way Ashford TW15 .13 E6
Charlton TW17 . . . . .34 C7
Lodge Wlk CR6 . . . . .82 A3
Lodgebottom Rd KT18,
RH5 . . . . .116 A8
Lodsworth GU14 . . . . .84 D3
Lofthouse Pl KT9 . . . . .56 C4
Logan Cl TW4 . . . . .4 F4
Loggetts GU21 . . . . .22 E5
Logmore La RH4 . . . . .135 D3
Lois Dr TW17 . . . . .34 B4
Lollesworth La KT24 . . . . .112 C6
Loman Rd GU16 . . . . .86 A4
Lomas Cl CR0 . . . . .63 C3
Lombard Bsns Pk
Merton SW19 . . . . .40 B7
Thornton Heath CR9 . . . . . .41 F2
Lombard Rd SW19 . . . . . . .40 B7
Lombard St GU8 . . . . .149 B7
Lombardy Cl GU21 . . . . . . .68 F2
Lomond Gdns CR2 . . . . . . .62 E3
Loncin Mead Ave KT15 . . . .52 C2
London Butterfly Ho★
TW8 . . . . .6 B6
London Cross KT24 . . . . . .112 F4
London Fields Ho RH11 201 C2
London La Bromley BR1 . .24 F1
Shere GU5 . . . . .133 A4
London Rd Ascot SL5 . . . . .29 D5
Ashford TW15,TW18,TW19,
TW14 . . . . .13 D5
Bagshot GU15,GU19 . . . . . .47 D2
Blackwater GU15,GU17 . . . .64 E4
Bracknell RG12,SL5 . . . . . .28 C6
Brands Hill SL3 . . . . .1 B8
Brentford TW7,TW8 . . . . . . .6 B6
Bromley BR1 . . . . .24 F1
Camberley GU15 . . . . .65 C6
Caterham CR3 . . . . .100 D4

London Rd continued
Crawley RH10 . . . . .181 E3
Dorking RH4RH5 . . . . . . .115 C3
East Grinstead RH19 . . . . .185 C3
Englefield Green TW20 . . . .11 C1
Forest Hill SE22,SE23 . . . . .23 C7
Forest Row RH18 . . . . . . .206 E4
Guildford GU1 . . . . .109 F1
Guildford,Burpham GU1,
GU4 . . . . .110 B4
Hackbridge SM6 . . . . .60 B7
Hindhead GU26 . . . . .188 F4
Horsham RH12 . . . . .217 C2
Hounslow TW3,TW7,TW1 ,
TW8 . . . . .5 D5
Kingston u T KT1,KT2 . . . . .37 F7
Mitcham CR4,SW17 . . . . . .40 F6
Morden SM4 . . . . .40 A5
Redhill RH1 . . . . .119 A3
Reigate RH2 . . . . .118 A2
Send Marsh GU23 . . . . . . .90 E1
Stoneleigh KT17,KT4,SM3 . . .58 B5
Sunningdale,Blacknest SL5 . .30 B6
Sunningdale,Shrubs Hill SL5 30 C4
Thornton Heath CR0,CR7,
SW16 . . . . .42 A3
Twickenham TW1 . . . . .17 A7
Virginia Water GU25,TW20 . .31 B7
Wentworth SL5,GU25 . . . . .30 C4
Windlesham GU19,GU20,
SL5 . . . . .48 C2
Wokingham RG40 . . . . .25 E6
London Rd N RH1 . . . . .99 B2
London Rd S
Merstham RH1 . . . . .119 B6
Redhill RH1 . . . . .119 B6
London Road Sta GU1 . . .109 E1
London Sq GU1 . . . . .109 E1
London St KT16 . . . . .33 A2
Lone Oak RH6 . . . . .162 B1
Loneacre GU20 . . . . .48 E4
Lonesome Fst Sch CR4 . . .41 B7
Lonesome La RH1,RH2 . . .139 D3
Lonesome Way CR4 . . . . . .41 C8
Long Acre RH10 . . . . .204 A8
Long Ave GU24 . . . . .88 A6
Long Beech Dr GU14 . . . . .84 C3
Long Bridge GU9 . . . . . . .125 C2
Long Cl RH10 . . . . .202 D6
Long Copse Cl KT23 . . . . .94 B4
Long Ditton Inf Sch KT6 . .37 C1
Long Dyke GU1 . . . . .110 B3
Long Garden Mews [3]
GU9 . . . . .125 B2
Long Garden Way GU9 . .125 B2
Long Garden Wlk [4]
GU9 . . . . .125 B2
Long Garden Wlk E [2]
GU9 . . . . .125 B2
Long Garden Wlk W [1]
GU9 . . . . .125 B2
Long Gdn Pl GU9 . . . . . . .125 B3
Long Gore GU7 . . . . .150 E8
Long Grove Rd KT19 . . . . .57 B1
Long Hill The Sands GU10 126 E1
Woldingham CR3 . . . . .101 F6
Long Hill Rd RG12,SL5 . . . .28 A7
Long Houses GU24 . . . . . .87 D3
Long La Croydon CR0 . . . . .43 C3
Stanwell TW19,TW18 . . . . .13 F7
Long Lodge Dr KT12 . . . . . .54 C7
Long Meadow BR4 . . . . . . .44 C2
Long Mickle GU47 . . . . . . .45 B1
Long Rd The GU10 . . . . . .146 A2
Long Reach GU23,KT24 . . .92 B3
Long Shaw KT22 . . . . .95 A7
Long Wlk
Burgh Heath KT18 . . . . . . .97 D8
Kingston u T KT3 . . . . .38 C6
Long Wlk The SL4 . . . . . . .10 D7
Long's Way RG40 . . . . .25 E7
Longacre GU12 . . . . .106 A2
Longacre Pl SM5 . . . . .60 A4
Longacre Sch GU5 . . . . . .152 D4
Longbourne Gn GU7 . . . . .150 E7
Longbourne Way TW16 . . .32 F3
Longboyds KT11 . . . . .73 B4
Longbridge Gate RH6 . . . .181 E8
Longbridge Rd
Crawley RH6 . . . . .181 F8
Horley RH6 . . . . .160 F1
Longbridge Rdbt RH6 . . . .160 E2
Longbridge Wlk RH6 . . . . .160 F1
Longchamp Cl RH6 . . . . . .161 C3
Longcroft Ave SM7 . . . . . .78 C5
Longcross Rd
Longcross KT16 . . . . .50 C7
Longcross KT16 . . . . .51 B7
Longcross Sta GU25 . . . . .30 F1
Longdene Rd GU27 . . . . . .208 B6
Longdown Cl GU10 . . . . . .146 D6
Longdown La N KT17 . . . . . .77 A6
Longdown La S KT17,
KT18 . . . . .77 A4
Longdown Lodge GU47 . . .64 B8
Longdown Rd Catford SE6 24 A4
Ewell KT17 . . . . .77 A6
Farnham GU10 . . . . .146 C5
Guildford GU4 . . . . .131 B6
Sandhurst GU47 . . . . .45 B1
Longfellow Cl RH12 . . . . .217 E7
Longfellow Rd KT4 . . . . . . .39 E1
Longfield [3] BR1 . . . . .44 F8
Longfield Ave CR4,SM6 . . . .41 A1
Longfield Cl GU14 . . . . . . .85 B8
Longfield Cres
Burgh Heath KT20 . . . . . . .97 C7
Forest Hill SE23,SE26 . . . . .23 C5

Longfield Dr
Mitcham SW19 . . . . .40 E8
Mortlake SW14 . . . . .7 B2
Longfield Rd Ash GU12 . . .106 A2
Dorking RH4 . . . . .135 F6
Horsham RH12 . . . . .217 A1
Longfield St SW18 . . . . .20 A8
Longford Ave
Feltham TW14 . . . . .3 F1
Stanwell TW19 . . . . .13 E7
Longford Cl Camberley GU15 . . . .65 D4
Feltham TW13 . . . . .15 E5
Hampton TW12 . . . . .16 A4
Longford Com Sch TW14 14 F8
Longford Ct KT19 . . . . .57 C6
Longford Gdns SM1 . . . . . .59 C8
Longford Ho Catford BR1 . .24 D3
Hampton TW12 . . . . .16 A4
Longford Ind Est TW12 . . .16 B2
Longford Rdbt UB7 . . . . .2 B6
Longford Way TW19 . . . . . .13 E7
Longford Wlk [10] SW2 . . . .22 A8
Longheath Dr KT23 . . . . . . .93 E3
Longheath Gdns CR0 . . . . .43 C4
Longhill Rd SE6 . . . . .24 D5
Longhope Dr GU10 . . . . . .146 A6
Longhurst Rd
Crawley RH11 . . . . .201 A1
Croydon CR0 . . . . .43 B3
East Horsley KT24 . . . . . . .112 E6
Longlands Ave CR5 . . . . . .79 A5
Longlands Ct CR4 . . . . .41 A8
Longlands Way GU15 . . . . .66 D5
Longleat Sq GU14 . . . . . . .85 E3
Longleat Way TW14 . . . . . .14 D8
Longley Rd
Farnham GU9 . . . . .125 D1
Thornton Heath CR0 . . . . . .42 B2
Upper Tooting SW17 . . . . . .20 F2
Longmead GU1 . . . . .110 C1
Longmead Bsns Ctr KT19 76 D8
Longmead Cl CR3 . . . . . . .100 E5
Longmead Ho SE27 . . . . . .22 C3
Longmead Rd Epsom KT19 57 E1
Thames Ditton KT7 . . . . . .36 F2
Upper Tooting SW17 . . . . . .20 F3
Longmeadow
Frimley GU15,GU16 . . . . . .65 F3
Little Bookham KT23 . . . . . .93 F2
Longmere Gdns KT20 . . . . .97 C8
Longmere Rd RH10 . . . . . .201 D8
Longmoors RG42 . . . . .26 E8
Longmore Rd KT12 . . . . . . .54 E6
Longpoles Rd GU6 . . . . . .174 F2
Longridge Gr GU22 . . . . . .70 E5
Longs Cl GU22 . . . . .71 A3
Longs Ct [2] TW9 . . . . .6 F3
Longsdon Way CR3 . . . . . .101 A3
Longshot Ind Est RG12 . . .26 E7
Longside Cl TW20 . . . . . . .32 C8
Longstaff Cres SW18 . . . . .20 A8
Longstaff Rd SW18 . . . . . .20 A8
Longstone Rd SW17 . . . . . .21 B3
Longthorne Lodge [7]
SW2 . . . . .22 A8
Longthornton Rd SW16 . . .41 D7
Longton Ave SE26 . . . . . . .23 A4
Longton Gr SE26 . . . . .23 B4
Longwater Rd RG12 . . . . . .27 C3
Longwood Dr SW15 . . . . . .19 B8
Longwood Rd CR8 . . . . . . .80 D3
Longwood View RH10 . . . .202 A3
Longyard Ho RH6 . . . . .161 B5
Lonsdale Gdns CR7,SW16 .41 F5
Lonsdale Mews [5] TW9 . . . .7 A6
Lonsdale Rd Barnes SW13 . .7 F7
Croydon SE25 . . . . .43 B5
Dorking RH4 . . . . .136 B8
Weybridge KT13 . . . . .53 A3
Look Out Discovery Ctr The★
RG12 . . . . .27 D1
Loop Rd Epsom KT18 . . . . .76 D2
Old Woking GU22 . . . . .89 F7
Loppets Rd RH10 . . . . . . .201 F3
Lorac Ct SM2 . . . . .59 A3
Loraine Gdns KT21 . . . . . . .75 E2
Loraine Ho [1] SM6 . . . . . . .60 B6
Loraine Rd W4 . . . . .7 B8
Lord Chancellor Wlk KT2 38 C8
Lord Knyvett Cl TW19 . . . . .2 D1
Lordell Pl SW19 . . . . .19 C2
Lords Cl Feltham TW13 . . . .15 E6
West Norwood SE21 . . . . . .22 C7
Lords Wood Ho CR5 . . . . . .99 D5
Lordsbury Field SM6 . . . . .60 C1
Lordsgrove Cl KT20 . . . . . .97 B7
Lordshill Rd GU5 . . . . .152 C5
Lordship La SE21,SE22 . . .23 A8
Loretto Cl GU6 . . . . .175 A3
Lorian Dr RH2 . . . . .118 C2
Loriners RH10 . . . . .201 D3
Loriners Cl KT11 . . . . .73 A5
Loring Rd TW7 . . . . .5 F5
Lorne Ave CR0 . . . . .43 D2
Lorne Gdns Croydon CR0 . .43 D2
Knaphill GU21 . . . . .88 D8
Lorne Rd [2] TW10 . . . . .6 F2
Lorne The KT23 . . . . .94 A1
Lorraine Ct BR3 . . . . .44 C8
Lorraine Rd GU15 . . . . .65 F8
Lorraine Sch GU15 . . . . . .65 E8
Lory Ridge GU19 . . . . .47 E4
Loseberry Rd KT10 . . . . . . .55 D5

Loseley Ho★ GU3 . . . . . . .129 E3
Loseley Rd GU7 . . . . .150 E8
Lothian Rd GU24 . . . . .87 A6
Lothian Wood KT20 . . . . . .97 B5
Lotus Rd TN16 . . . . .83 F1
Loubet St SW17 . . . . .20 F2
Loudwater Cl TW16 . . . . . .35 A5
Loudwater Rd TW16 . . . . . .35 A5
Loughborough RG12 . . . . .27 E3
Louis Fields GU3 . . . . .108 C5
Louisa Ct TW2 . . . . .16 E6
Louisa Ho SW15 . . . . .7 F3
Louise Margaret Rd
GU11 . . . . .105 C3
Louisville Rd SW17 . . . . . . .21 A5
Lovat Wlk TW5 . . . . .4 E7
Lovatt Ct SW12 . . . . .21 B7
Love La Cheam SM3 . . . . . .58 E4
Croydon SE25 . . . . .43 B6
Godstone RH9 . . . . .121 C3
Long Ditton KT6 . . . . .56 D8
Mitcham CR4 . . . . .40 E6
Morden SM4 . . . . .40 B2
Walton on the Hill KT20 . . . .97 A1
Loveday Ho [2] SW2 . . . . . .22 A7
Lovedean Ct RG12 . . . . . . .27 E5
Lovekyn Cl KT2 . . . . .37 F7
Lovel La SL4 . . . . .9 B3
Lovel Rd SL4 . . . . .9 B3
Lovelace Cl KT24 . . . . .93 A4
Lovelace Cotts GU23 . . . . .91 B6
Lovelace Dr GU22 . . . . .70 F3
Lovelace Gdns
Hersham KT12 . . . . .54 C5
Surbiton KT6 . . . . .37 D2
Lovelace Prim Sch KT9 . . .56 C5
Lovelace Rd
Bracknell RG12 . . . . .26 E5
Surbiton KT6 . . . . .37 D2
West Norwood SE21 . . . . . .22 C7
Lovelands La
Lower Kingswood KT20 . . . .118 B8
West End GU24 . . . . .68 C6
Loveletts RH11 . . . . .201 A5
Lovell Cl RH19 . . . . .185 C4
Lovell Ho [4] SW19 . . . . . . .40 C8
Lovell Path [1] RH11 . . . . .200 E5
Lovell Rd TW10 . . . . .17 C5
Lovells Cl GU18 . . . . .48 B1
Lovelock Cl CR8 . . . . .80 C2
Lovers La GU10 . . . . .167 C7
Lovett Dr SM5 . . . . .40 D2
Lovett Ho [8] GU9 . . . . . . .125 B2
Lovett Rd TW18 . . . . .12 D3
Low Cross Wood La SE21 22 F5
Low La GU9 . . . . .126 B6
Lowbury RG12 . . . . .27 E5
Lowburys RH4 . . . . .136 B4
Lowdells Cl RH19 . . . . . . .185 C4
Lowdells Dr RH19 . . . . . . .185 C4
Lowdells La RH19 . . . . . . .185 C3
Lowe Cl GU11 . . . . .104 F3
Lower Addiscombe Rd
CR0 . . . . .42 E1
Lower Barn Cl RH12 . . . . .217 F5
Lower Barn Rd CR8 . . . . . .80 D6
Lower Breache Rd GU6 . .176 B4
Lower Bridge Rd RH1 . . . .118 F1
Lower Broadmoor Rd
RG45 . . . . .45 D4
Lower Charles St GU15 . . .65 C6
Lower Church La [20]
GU9 . . . . .125 B2
Lower Church St CR0,CR9 61 B8
Lower Coombe St CR0,
CR9 . . . . .61 C6
Lower Court Rd KT19 . . . . .76 C8
Lower Ct Epsom KT19 . . . . .76 D8
Sutton SM1 . . . . .59 C6
Lower Dene RH19 . . . . . . .186 A1
Lower Downs Rd SW20 . . .39 D8
Lower Dunnymans [4]
SM7 . . . . .77 F5
Lower Eashing GU7 . . . . . .149 F4
Lower Edgeborough Rd
GU1 . . . . .130 F8
Lower Farm Rd KT24 . . . . .93 C3
Lower Farnham Rd
GU11,GU12 . . . . .126 C7
Lower Forecourt RH6 . . . .182 B7
Lower George St [13] TW10 .6 D2
Lower Gn KT12 . . . . .54 D5
Lower Gn W CR4 . . . . .40 E6
Lower Green Gdns [8]
KT4 . . . . .39 A1
Lower Green Rd
Esher KT10 . . . . .55 C8
Thames Ditton KT10 . . . . . .55 C8
Lower Grove Rd TW10 . . . . .6 F2
Lower Guildford Rd
GU21 . . . . .68 D1
Lower Ham La GU8 . . . . . .148 E4
Lower Ham Rd KT2 . . . . . . .17 D2
Lower Hampton Rd
TW12,TW16 . . . . .35 D7
Lower Hanger GU27 . . . . .207 D6
Lower Hill Rd KT19 . . . . . . .76 B7
Lower House Rd GU8 . . . . .169 F2
Lower Kings Rd KT2 . . . . . .17 E1
Lower Manor Rd
Farncombe GU7 . . . . .150 F6
Milford GU8 . . . . .149 D1
Lower Marsh La KT1,KT5 . .38 A5
Lower Mere RH19 . . . . . . .205 F8
Lower Mill Field GU19 . . . .47 D2
Lower Morden La SM4 . . . .39 E3
Lower Mortlake Rd TW9 . . .6 F4
Lower Moushill La GU8 . . .149 D1

Lower Nelson St [4]
GU11 . . . . .105 A2
Lower Northfield [5] SM7 .77 F5
Lower Nursery SL5 . . . . . .30 A4
Lower Park Rd CR5 . . . . . .78 E1
Lower Peryers KT24 . . . . .112 F1
Lower Pillory Down SM5 . .79 B7
Lower Rd Effingham KT24 113 D8
Forest Row RH18 . . . . . . .206 F3
Grayswood GU27 . . . . . . .189 F2
Great Bookham KT22,KT23 . .94 C3
Purley CR8 . . . . .80 B6
Reigate RH1 . . . . .139 D7
Sutton SM1 . . . . .59 C6
Lower Richmond Rd SW14,
TW9 . . . . .7 B4
Lower Sand Hills KT6 . . . . .37 C2
Lower Sandfields GU23 . . .90 D1
Lower Sawleywood [2]
SM7 . . . . .77 F5
Lower Shott KT23 . . . . .94 B1
Lower South St [2] GU7 . .150 D4
Lower South View GU9 . . .125 C3
Lower Sq RH18 . . . . .206 A4
Lower St
Haslemere GU27 . . . . . . .208 C6
Shere GU5 . . . . .133 A4
Lower Sunbury Rd TW12 36 A7
Lower Sydenham Sta
SE6 . . . . .23 F3
Lower Tanbridge Way
RH12 . . . . .217 B2
Lower Teddington Rd
KT1 . . . . .37 D8
Lower Village Rd SL5 . . . . .29 C4
Lower Weybourne La
Farnham GU9 . . . . .126 A6
Heath End GU9 . . . . .125 F6
Lower Wood Rd KT10 . . . . .56 B4
Lowestoft Wlk RH10 . . . . .202 B4
Loweswater Wlk GU15 . . . .66 D4
Lowfield Cl GU18 . . . . .67 A8
Lowfield Heath Rd
Charlwood RH6 . . . . .180 F5
Crawley RH6 . . . . .180 F5
Lowfield Heath Windmill★
RH6 . . . . .180 C6
Lowfield Rd RH13 . . . . . . .215 D3
Lowfield Way RH11 . . . . . .181 E5
Lowicks Rd GU10 . . . . . . .168 C5
Lowland Heath Ind Est
RH11 . . . . .181 E5
Lowlands Rd
Blackwater GU17 . . . . .64 C4
Stanwell TW19 . . . . .2 D2
Lowndes Bldgs GU9 . . . . .125 B3
Lowood Ct SE19 . . . . .22 F3
Lowry Cl GU47 . . . . .64 D6
Lowry Cres CR4 . . . . .40 E7
Lowry Ct [3] W4 . . . . .7 E7
Lowther Hill SE23 . . . . . . .23 E8
Lowther Rd Barnes SW13 . . .7 F6
Kingston u T KT2 . . . . .37 F8
Lowthorpe [5] GU21 . . . . . .69 A1
Loxford Ct GU6 . . . . .173 F2
Loxford Rd CR3 . . . . .100 F2
Loxford Way CR3 . . . . . . .100 F2
Loxley Cl SE26 . . . . .23 D5
Loxley Rd Hampton TW12 . .15 F4
Wandsworth SW18 . . . . . . .20 D7
Loxton Rd SE23 . . . . .23 E7
Loxwood Cl TW14 . . . . .14 E7
Loxwood Place Farm
RH14 . . . . .212 F3
Loxwood Prim Sch
RH14 . . . . .213 A4
Loxwood Rd Alfold GU6 . . .193 F2
Loxwood RH12,RH14 . . . . .213 D4
Loxwood,Alfold Bars GU6,
RH14 . . . . .212 F3
Plaistow RH14 . . . . .212 A2
Rudgwick RH12 . . . . .214 A6
Loxwood Wlk RH11 . . . . . .201 A8
Lucan Dr TW18 . . . . .13 D1
Lucas Cl RH19 . . . . .186 A1
Lucas Ct SE26 . . . . .23 E3
Lucas Field GU27 . . . . . . .207 E6
Lucas Gn GU24 . . . . .67 D4
Lucas Green Rd GU24 . . . . .67 C5
Lucas Rd Penge SE20 . . . . .23 C2
Warnham RH12 . . . . .216 F8
Lucerne Cl GU22 . . . . .89 C3
Lucerne Ct [8] BR3 . . . . . . .24 A1
Lucerne Dr RH10 . . . . .202 D4
Lucerne Rd CR7 . . . . .42 C5
Lucie Ave TW15 . . . . .14 B2
Lucien Rd
Upper Tooting SW17 . . . . . .21 A4
Wimbledon SW18 . . . . .20 B6
Lucille Ho SE26 . . . . .23 B2
Luckley Oakfield Sch
RG40 . . . . .25 B3
Luckley Path RG40 . . . . . . .25 C6
Luckley Rd RG41 . . . . .25 B3
Luckley Wood RG41 . . . . . .25 B3
Lucraft Ho [12] SW2 . . . . . .21 E8
Luddington Ave GU25 . . . .31 F7
Ludford Cl CR0 . . . . .61 B6
Ludgrove Sch RG40 . . . . . .25 D3
Ludlow RG12 . . . . .27 B2
Ludlow Cl GU16 . . . . .86 A7
Ludlow Rd Feltham TW13 . .15 A4
Guildford GU2 . . . . .130 B8
Ludovick Wlk SW15 . . . . . . .7 E3
Ludshott Gr GU35 . . . . . . .187 B5
Luke Rd GU11 . . . . .125 E8
Luke Rd E GU11 . . . . .125 F8
Lullarook Cl TN16 . . . . .83 C3

Lullington Rd SE20 ... 23 A1
Lulworth Ave TW5,TW7 ... 5 C7
Lulworth Cl
Crawley RH11 ... 201 B3
Farnborough GU14 ... 85 A7
Lulworth Cres CR4 ... 40 E7
Lumiere Ct 6 SW17 ... 21 A6
Lumley Ct RH6 ... 161 A4
Lumley Gdns SM3 ... 58 E5
Lumley Ho KT3 ... 38 D1
Lumley Rd
Cheam SM1,SM3 ... 58 E5
Horley RH6 ... 161 A3
Luna Rd CR7 ... 42 C6
Lunar Cl TN16 ... 83 D3
Lundy Cl RH11 ... 201 C3
Lunghurst Rd CR3 ... 102 A5
Lunham Rd SE19 ... 22 E2
Lunn Cotts GU26 ... 188 F4
Lupin Cl Bagshot GU19 ... 47 C1
Croydon CR0 ... 43 D1
Streatham SW2 ... 22 B6
Lupin Ride RG45 ... 45 B7
Lupus Ct SE19 ... 42 D8
Luscombe Ct BR2 ... 44 E7
Lushington Dr KT11 ... 73 B5
Lushington Ho KT12 ... 35 C3
Lushington Rd SE6 ... 24 B3
Lusted Hall La TN16 ... 103 C7
Lusteds Cl RH4 ... 136 C4
Lutea Ho SM2 ... 59 C3
Luther Rd TW11 ... 16 F3
Lutwyche Rd SE23,SE6 ... 23 F6
Lutyens Cl RH11 ... 200 E4
Luxford Cl RH12 ... 217 F5
Luxford's La
Ashurst Wood RH19 ... 206 B6
Forest Row RH19 ... 206 B6
Lyall Ave SE21 ... 22 F4
Lyall Pl GU9 ... 125 B7
Lycett Ho 10 SW2 ... 21 E8
Lych Way GU21 ... 69 D3
Lyconby Gdns CR0 ... 43 E2
Lydbury RG12 ... 27 F6
Lydden Gr SW18 ... 20 B8
Lydden Rd SW18 ... 20 B8
Lydele Cl GU21 ... 69 F4
Lydford Cl
2 Farnborough GU14 ... 85 A7
Frimley GU16 ... 86 A7
Lydhurst Ave SW2 ... 21 F6
Lydia Cvn Pk GU6 ... 193 C8
Lydney RG12 ... 27 B2
Lydney Cl SW19 ... 19 E6
Lydon Ho RH11 ... 181 D1
Lye Copse Ave GU14 ... 85 B8
Lye The KT20 ... 97 C5
Lye View Cotts GU21 ... 89 A8
Lyefield La GU6,RH5 ... 176 C5
Lyfield KT22 ... 74 B5
Lyford Rd SW18 ... 20 E7
Lygon Ct SW19 ... 19 F1
Lyham Rd SW2 ... 21 E8
Lyle Cl CR4 ... 41 A2
Lymbourne Cl SM2 ... 59 A1
Lymden Gdns RH2 ... 139 B7
Lyme Regis Rd SM7 ... 77 F2
Lymer Ave SE19 ... 22 F3
Lymescote Gdns SM1 ... 59 A8
Lyminge Gdns SW17,
SW18 ... 20 E7
Lymington Cl SW16 ... 41 D7
Lymington Ct SM1 ... 59 C7
Lymington Gdns KT19 ... 57 F5
Lyn Ct GU1 ... 131 A8
Lynch Rd GU9 ... 125 E2
Lynchen Cl TW5 ... 4 B6
Lynchford La GU11,GU14 105 E8
Lynchford Rd GU14 ... 105 D8
Lyncroft Gdns Ewell KT17 57 F2
Isleworth TW3 ... 5 C2
Lyndale Ct
3 Redhill RH1 ... 119 A4
5 West Byfleet KT14 ... 71 A6
Lyndale Rd RH1 ... 119 A4
Lynde Ho KT12 ... 35 C3
Lynden Gate SW15 ... 19 B8
Lynden Hurst CR0 ... 61 F8
Lyndhurst Ave
Aldershot GU11 ... 126 C6
Blackwater GU17 ... 64 C6
Mitcham SW16 ... 41 D7
Sunbury TW16 ... 35 A6
Tolworth KT5 ... 38 B1
Twickenham TW2 ... 16 A7
Lyndhurst Cl
Bracknell RG12 ... 28 A6
Crawley RH11 ... 201 D5
South Croydon CR0 ... 61 F7
Woking GU21 ... 69 D4
Lyndhurst Ct 12 SM2 ... 59 A3
Lyndhurst Dr KT3 ... 38 F2
Lyndhurst Farm Cl
RH19 ... 184 D4
Lyndhurst Ho 2 SW15 ... 19 A8
Lyndhurst Rd Ascot SL5 ... 29 A5
Coulsdon CR5 ... 79 A3
Reigate RH2 ... 139 A6
Thornton Heath CR7 ... 42 A5
Lyndhurst Sch GU15 ... 65 B5
Lyndhurst Way
Addlestone KT16 ... 51 E8
Belmont SM2 ... 59 A2
Lyndon Ave SM6 ... 60 A7
Lyndon Yd SW17 ... 20 B4
Lyndsey Cl GU14 ... 84 B4
Lyne & Longcross CE Sch
KT16 ... 51 B8
Lyne Cl GU25 ... 31 F3
Lyne Crossing Rd KT16,
GU25 ... 32 B3
Lyne Ct GU25 ... 31 F2
Lyne Ho RH5 ... 179 A1
Lyne La
Chertsey KT16,TW20,GU25 32 A3
Lyne KT16 ... 32 A2
Lyne Place Manor GU25 ... 31 F2
Lyne Rd GU25 ... 31 E3
Lynegrove Ave TW15 ... 14 C3
Lyneham Rd RG45 ... 45 B5
Lynfield Ct SE23 ... 23 D8
Lynmouth Ave SM4 ... 39 D2
Lynmouth Gdns TW5 ... 4 D6
Lynn Cl TW15 ... 14 D3
Lynn Ct Streatham SW16 ... 21 D3
Whyteleafe CR3 ... 80 F1
Lynn Rd SW12 ... 21 B8
Lynn Way GU14 ... 84 F7
Lynn Wlk RH2 ... 139 B6
Lynne Cl CR2 ... 81 C8
Lynne Ct Forest Hill SE23 ... 23 F8
13 Guildford GU1 ... 130 F8
South Croydon CR2 ... 61 E6
Wimbledon SW20 ... 39 B8
Lynne Wlk KT10 ... 55 C5
Lynscott Way CR2 ... 61 B2
Lynsted Ct BR3 ... 43 E7
Lynton KT7 ... 37 A2
Lynton Cl Chessington KT9 56 E6
East Grinstead RH19 ... 186 A2
Farnham GU9 ... 146 A7
Isleworth TW7 ... 5 F3
Lynton Ct SM2 ... 59 C4
Lynton Park Ave RH19 ... 186 A2
Lynton Prep Sch KT17 ... 76 F8
Lynton Rd
New Malden KT3 ... 38 D4
Thornton Heath CR0,CR7 ... 42 A3
Lynwick St
Rudgwick RH12 ... 214 C8
Rudgwick,Cox Green RH12 195 D1
Lynwood GU2 ... 130 B8
Lynwood Ave
Egham TW20 ... 11 E2
Epsom KT17 ... 76 F5
Wallington CR5 ... 79 B4
Lynwood Cl GU21 ... 70 D6
Lynwood Cres SL5 ... 29 E3
Lynwood Ct
Horsham RH12 ... 217 C3
Kingston u T KT1 ... 38 B7
Lynwood Dr
Mytchett GU16 ... 86 A3
North Cheam KT4 ... 58 A8
Lynwood Flats SL5 ... 29 E4
Lynwood Gdns CR0 ... 60 F6
Lynwood Rd Epsom KT17 ... 76 F5
Hinchley Wood KT7 ... 55 F8
Redhill RH1 ... 119 A3
Thames Ditton KT7 ... 36 F1
Upper Tooting SW17 ... 20 F4
Lynx Hill KT24 ... 112 F8
Lyon Cl RH10 ... 202 C2
Lyon Ct RH13 ... 217 E2
Lyon Rd Crowthorne RG45 ... 45 C6
Merton SW19 ... 40 C8
Walton-on-T KT12 ... 54 E8
Lyon Way GU16 ... 65 C1
Lyon Way Ind Est GU16 ... 65 C1
Lyons Cl RH13 ... 215 D3
Lyons Ct RH4 ... 136 B7
Lyons Dr GU2 ... 109 A6
Lyons Rd RH13 ... 215 E3
Lyonsdene KT20 ... 117 F8
Lyric Cl RH10 ... 202 D4
Lyric Mews SE26 ... 23 D4
Lyric Rd SW13 ... 7 F6
Lysander Rd CR0 ... 60 F4
Lysias Rd SW12 ... 21 B8
Lysons Ave GU12 ... 105 F8
Lysons Rd GU11 ... 105 A1
Lysons Way GU12 ... 106 A7
Lyster Mews KT11 ... 73 C6
Lytchet Minster Cl 4
RG12 ... 27 F4
Lytchgate Cl CR2 ... 61 E3
Lytcott Dr KT8 ... 35 F6
Lytham Bracknell RG12 ... 26 E3
Horley RH6 ... 161 B2
Lytham Ct SL5 ... 29 C4
Lytton Dr RH10 ... 202 D7
Lytton Gdns SM6 ... 60 D6
Lytton Ho 3 TW12 ... 16 B2
Lytton Pk KT11 ... 73 F7
Lytton Rd GU22 ... 70 B3
Lyveden Rd SW17,SW19 ... 20 F2
Lywood Cl KT20 ... 97 C5

M

Mabbotts KT20 ... 97 D6
Mabel St GU21 ... 69 D2
Maberley Cres SE19 ... 23 A1
Maberley Ct SE19 ... 23 A1
Maberley Rd Penge SE19 ... 23 A1
Penge, Elmers End BR3 ... 43 D6
Mabley Ct RG12 ... 27 A3
Macadam Ave RG45 ... 45 C7
MacArthur Ho 4 SW2 ... 21 E8
Macaulay Ave KT10 ... 55 E8
Macaulay Ct CR3 ... 100 E6
Macaulay Rd CR3 ... 100 E6
Macbeth Ct RG42 ... 27 E8
Macclesfield Rd CR0,
SE25 ... 43 C4
Macdonald Ct TW3 ... 5 C3
Macdonald Rd
Heath End GU9 ... 125 B7
Lightwater GU18 ... 67 A8
Macfarlane La TW7 ... 6 A8
MacGregor Ho SW12 ... 21 D7
Mackenzie Ho RH19 ... 185 A4
Mackenzie Rd BR3 ... 43 D7
Mackie Ho 18 SW2 ... 22 A8
Mackie Rd SW2 ... 22 A8
Mackies Hill GU5 ... 154 D7
Macklin Ho SE23 ... 23 B6
Mackrells RH1 ... 139 C6
Macleod Rd RH13 ... 217 F1
Macmillan Ho SM7 ... 77 F4
Macmillan Way SW17 ... 21 B4
Macnaghton Woods
GU15 ... 65 E6
Macphail Cl RG40 ... 25 E8
Maddison Cl TW11 ... 16 F2
Maddox La KT23 ... 93 E3
Maddox Pk KT23 ... 93 E4
Madehurst Ct RH11 ... 200 F3
Madeira Ave Bromley BR1 ... 24 E1
Horsham RH12 ... 217 C2
Madeira Cl KT14 ... 71 A6
Madeira Cres KT14 ... 70 F6
Madeira Rd Mitcham CR4 ... 40 F5
Streatham SW16 ... 21 E3
West Byfleet KT14 ... 71 A6
Madeira Wlk RH2 ... 118 D2
Madeline Rd SE20 ... 23 A1
Madgehole La GU5 ... 153 B3
Madingley RG12 ... 27 B1
Madingley Ct TW1 ... 6 C2
Madison Gdns BR2 ... 44 F6
Madox Brown End GU47 ... 64 E6
Madrid Rd GU2 ... 130 B8
Maesmaur Rd TN16 ... 103 D6
Mafeking Ave TW8 ... 6 E8
Mafeking Rd TW19 ... 12 B6
Magazine Cotts GU4 ... 131 C3
Magazine Pl KT22 ... 95 B5
Magazine Rd CR3 ... 100 B5
Magdala Rd Isleworth TW7 ... 6 A4
South Croydon CR2 ... 61 D3
Magdalen Cl KT14 ... 71 E5
Magdalen Cres KT14 ... 71 E5
Magdalen Ct SE25 ... 43 A4
Magdalen Rd SW18 ... 20 D7
Magdalene Cl RH10 ... 182 C1
Magdalene Rd
Littleton TW17 ... 33 F6
Sandhurst GU47 ... 45 F2
Magellan Terr RH10 ... 182 A2
Magna Carta La TW19 ... 11 E7
Magna Carta Sch The
TW20 ... 12 D2
Magna Rd TW20 ... 11 B2
Magnolia Cl
Kingston u T KT2 ... 18 B2
Sandhurst GU47 ... 45 D1
Magnolia Ct
3 Belmont SM2 ... 59 B3
Horley RH6 ... 161 A3
Penge SE26 ... 23 C3
Richmond TW9 ... 7 B6
Wallington SM6 ... 60 B5
Magnolia Dr TN16 ... 83 E3
Magnolia Pl GU1 ... 109 C4
Magnolia Rd W4 ... 7 B8
Magnolia Way
Dorking RH5 ... 136 D4
West Ewell KT19 ... 57 C5
Magnolia Wharf W4 ... 7 B8
Magpie Cl Coulsdon CR5 ... 79 C1
Crondall GU10 ... 124 D8
Magpie Wlk RH10 ... 201 F8
Maguire Dr Frimley GU16 ... 66 C3
Richmond TW10 ... 17 C4
Mahonia Cl GU24 ... 67 F6
Maida Rd GU11 ... 105 B4
Maiden La RH11 ... 201 C8
Maiden's Gn SL4 ... 8 B6
Maidenbower Dr RH10 ... 202 D4
Maidenbower Fst & Mid Sch
RH10 ... 202 C4
Maidenbower La RH10 ... 202 C4
Maidenbower Pl RH10 ... 202 C4
Maidenbower Sq RH10 ... 202 C4
Maidenshaw Rd KT19 ... 76 D7
Maids of Honour Row 4
TW9 ... 6 D2
Main Dr Winkfield RG42 ... 8 A1
Winkfield RG42,SL5 ... 28 B8
Main Rd TN16 ... 83 C5
Main St Chertsey KT15 ... 52 E7
Feltham TW13 ... 15 D3
Mainprize Rd RG12 ... 27 E7
Mainstone Cl GU16 ... 86 C7
Mainstone Cres GU24 ... 87 D6
Mainstone Rd GU24 ... 67 F3
Mainwaring Ct CR4 ... 41 A7
Mais Ho SE26 ... 23 B6
Maise Webster Cl TW19 ... 13 D8
Maisonettes The SM1 ... 58 F5
Maitland Cl Hounslow TW4 ... 4 F4
Walton-on-T KT12 ... 54 E8
West Byfleet KT14 ... 71 A6
Maitland Rd
Farnborough GU14 ... 105 B8
Penge SE26 ... 23 D2
Maitlands Cl GU10 ... 126 F6
Maizecroft RH6 ... 161 C4
Majestic Way CR4 ... 40 F7
Major's Farm Rd SL3 ... 1 A8
Major's Hill RH10 ... 203 C5
Malacca Farm GU4 ... 111 B7
Malan Cl TN16 ... 83 E2
Malcolm Cl SE20 ... 23 C1
Malcolm Dr KT6 ... 37 E1
Malcolm Gdns RH6 ... 160 D1
Malcolm Prim Sch SE20 ... 23 C1
Malcolm Rd Coulsdon CR5 79 D4
Croydon CR0,SE25 ... 43 A3
Penge SE20 ... 23 C1
Wimbledon SW19 ... 19 E2
Malden Ave SE25 ... 43 B6
Malden Ct Carshalton SM5 59 F6
West Barnes KT3 ... 39 B6
Malden Golf Course KT3 ... 38 F7
Malden Green Ave KT4 ... 39 A1
Malden Hill KT3 ... 38 F6
Malden Hill Gdns KT3 ... 38 F6
Malden Manor Prim Sch
KT3 ... 38 E2
Malden Manor Sta KT3 ... 38 E2
Malden Parochial CE Prim
Sch KT4 ... 38 E1
Malden Pk KT3 ... 38 F3
Malden Rd
Cheam KT4,SM3 ... 58 D5
New Malden KT3,KT4 ... 38 F2
Malden Way KT3 ... 39 A5
Malden Way (Kingston By
Pass) KT3,KT5 ... 38 E4
Maldon Ct SM6 ... 60 C5
Maldon Rd SM6 ... 60 B5
Malet Cl TW20 ... 12 D2
Maley Ave SE27 ... 22 B6
Malham Cl RH10 ... 202 C3
Malham Fell RG12 ... 27 A5
Malham Rd SE23 ... 23 D7
Malham Road Ind Est
SE23 ... 23 D7
Mall The Brentford TW8 ... 6 D8
6 Guildford GU1 ... 130 C8
Hersham KT12 ... 54 D5
Kingston u T KT6 ... 37 D4
Mortlake SW14 ... 7 C2
Mall The (Prep Sch) TW2 16 D5
Mallard Cl Ash GU12 ... 105 F2
Haslemere GU27 ... 207 E6
Horley RH6 ... 161 A5
Horsham RH12 ... 217 C5
Redhill RH1 ... 119 A4
Twickenham TW2 ... 16 A8
Mallard Ct
Aldershot GU11 ... 126 A7
7 Dorking RH4 ... 136 A8
6 Richmond TW10 ... 6 D1
Mallard Pl
East Grinstead RH19 ... 205 F8
Twickenham TW1 ... 17 A5
Mallard Rd CR2 ... 62 D1
Mallard Way SM6 ... 60 C2
Mallard Wlk BR3,CR0 ... 43 D4
Mallard's Reach KT13 ... 53 D8
Mallards The
Frimley GU16 ... 65 F2
Laleham TW18 ... 33 B7
Mallards Way GU18 ... 67 A8
Malling Cl CR0 ... 43 C3
Malling Gdns SM4 ... 40 C3
Malling Ho 9 BR3 ... 24 A1
Malling Way BR2 ... 44 F2
Mallinson Rd CR0 ... 60 D7
Mallow Cl
Burgh Heath KT20 ... 97 B8
Croydon CR0 ... 43 D1
Horsham RH12 ... 217 E6
Mallow Cres GU4 ... 110 C4
Mallowdale Rd RG12 ... 27 E2
Malmains Cl BR3 ... 44 D5
Malmains Way BR3 ... 44 D5
Malmesbury Prim Sch
SM4 ... 40 C2
Malmesbury Rd SM4 ... 40 C3
Malmstone Ave RH1 ... 119 D6
Malt Hill TW20 ... 11 E3
Malt Ho SL4 ... 11 B8
Malt House Cl SL4 ... 11 B8
Malta Rd GU16 ... 86 E8
Maltby Rd KT9 ... 57 A4
Malthouse Ct GU4 ... 130 E4
Malthouse Dr Chiswick W4 ... 7 F8
Feltham TW13 ... 15 D3
Malthouse La
Pirbright GU3 ... 88 C2
West End GU24 ... 67 F7
Malthouse Mead GU8 ... 170 F5
Malthouse Rd RH10 ... 201 D4
Malthouses The GU6 ... 174 E3
Malting Way TW7 ... 5 F4
Maltings Cl SW13 ... 7 E5
Maltings Lodge 5 W4 ... 7 E7
Maltings The Byfleet KT14 ... 71 F6
Oxted RH8 ... 122 F4
Staines TW18 ... 12 E4
Maltlhouse La GU8 ... 171 C1
Malton Ho SE25 ... 42 E5
Malus Cl KT15 ... 51 F3
Malus Dr KT15 ... 51 F3
Malvern Cl Mitcham CR4 ... 41 C6
Ottershaw KT16 ... 51 C4
Penge SE20 ... 43 A7
Surbiton KT6 ... 37 E1
Malvern Ct Belmont SM2 ... 59 A3
Brands Hill SL3 ... 1 A8
Epsom KT18 ... 76 D5
3 Surbiton KT6 ... 37 E1
Malvern Dr TW13 ... 15 D3
Malvern Rd
Crawley RH11 ... 201 C5
Farnborough GU14 ... 84 D7
Hampton TW12 ... 16 A1
Malvern Rd *continued*
Harlington UB3 ... 3 E7
Surbiton KT6 ... 37 E1
Thornton Heath CR7 ... 42 A5
Malyons The TW17 ... 34 D3
Manatee Pl SM6 ... 60 D7
Manby Lodge Inf Sch
KT13 ... 53 C5
Manchester Rd CR7 ... 42 C6
Mandeville Cl
Guildford GU2 ... 109 A4
Merton SW19 ... 39 E8
Mandeville Ct TW20 ... 12 A4
Mandeville Dr KT6 ... 37 D1
Mandeville Rd
Isleworth TW7 ... 6 A5
Littleton TW17 ... 34 A4
Mandora Rd GU11 ... 105 B4
Mandrake Rd SW17 ... 20 F5
Manfield Pk GU6 ... 174 B5
Manfield Rd GU12 ... 106 A2
Mangles Ct 1 GU1 ... 130 C8
Mangles Rd GU1 ... 109 D3
Manley Bridge Rd GU10 145 E4
Mann Cl CR0,CR9 ... 61 C7
Mann's Cl TW7 ... 5 F2
Mannamead KT18 ... 96 E8
Mannamead Cl KT18 ... 96 E8
Manning Cl RH19 ... 185 D2
Manning Pl TW10 ... 6 F1
Mannings Cl RH10 ... 182 D1
Manningtree Cl SW19 ... 19 E7
Manoel Rd TW2 ... 16 C6
Manor Ave Caterham CR3 100 E3
Hounslow TW4 ... 4 D5
Manor Chase KT13 ... 53 B5
Manor Cl
East Horsley KT24 ... 112 E7
Haslemere GU27 ... 207 E6
Horley RH6 ... 160 F3
New Malden KT4 ... 38 E1
Pyrford GU22 ... 70 F3
South Godstone RH9 ... 142 F5
Tongham GU10 ... 126 F7
Warlingham CR6 ... 81 E2
Manor Cotts GU21 ... 68 E5
Manor Cres Byfleet KT14 ... 71 F6
Epsom KT19 ... 76 A7
Guildford GU2 ... 109 B3
Haslemere GU27 ... 207 E6
Pirbright GU24 ... 87 D7
Surbiton KT5 ... 38 A3
Manor Ct Horsham RH12 ... 218 A5
Kingston u T KT2 ... 38 A8
Streatham SW16 ... 21 E5
13 Sutton SM1 ... 59 C6
Twickenham TW2 ... 16 C6
Wallington SM6 ... 60 A7
Weybridge KT13 ... 53 B6
Manor Dr Feltham TW13 ... 15 D3
Hinchley Wood KT10 ... 56 A7
Horley RH6 ... 160 F3
Sunbury TW16 ... 35 A7
Surbiton KT5 ... 38 A3
West Ewell KT19 ... 57 E4
Woodham KT15 ... 52 A1
Manor Dr N KT3,KT4 ... 38 D2
Manor Dr The KT4 ... 38 F1
Manor Farm 9 TW20 ... 12 A3
Manor Farm Ave TW17 ... 34 B3
Manor Farm Bsns Ctr
GU10 ... 126 F5
Manor Farm Cl
Ash GU12 ... 105 F1
New Malden KT4 ... 38 E1
Manor Farm Ct TW20 ... 12 A3
Manor Farm La TW20 ... 12 A3
Manor Farm Rd CR7,
SW16 ... 42 A7
Manor Fields
Horsham RH12,RH13 ... 218 A4
Milford GU8 ... 149 E2
Seale GU10 ... 127 B4
Manor Gdns
Effingham KT24 ... 113 D7
Farncombe GU7 ... 150 E7
Farnham GU10 ... 146 D5
Guildford GU2 ... 109 B3
Hampton TW12 ... 16 C1
Merton SW19,SW20 ... 39 F7
Richmond TW10,TW9 ... 6 F3
South Croydon CR2 ... 61 F4
Sunbury TW16 ... 35 A7
Manor Gn GU8 ... 149 E1
Manor Gr Beckenham BR3 ... 44 B7
Richmond TW9 ... 7 A4
Manor Green Rd KT19 ... 76 C7
Manor Hill SM7 ... 78 F4
Manor Ho SM6 ... 60 B5
Manor Ho The
Kingswood KT20 ... 98 C4
Limpsfield RH8 ... 123 B7
Manor House Ct KT18 ... 76 C6
Manor House Dr Ascot SL5 9 A1
Hersham KT13 ... 53 F5
Manor House Flats
GU10 ... 126 F6
Manor House Sch KT23 ... 113 E8
Manor House The GU15 ... 65 D6
Manor House Way TW7 ... 6 B4
Manor Inf Sch GU14 ... 84 E6
Manor Jun Sch GU14 ... 84 F6
Manor La Feltham TW13 ... 15 A6
Harlington UB3 ... 3 D8
Lewisham SE12 ... 24 F8

Manor La *continued*
Lower Kingswood KT20 ..118 A6
Shamley Green GU5 ....152 E3
Sunbury TW16 ....35 B7
Sutton SM1 ....59 C5
Manor Lea GU27 ......207 E6
Manor Lea Cl GU8 .....149 E4
Manor Lea Rd GU8 ....149 E2
Manor Leaze TW20 ....12 B3
Manor Lodge GU2 .....109 B3
Manor Mount SE23 .....23 C7
Manor Park Cl BR4 .....44 B1
Manor Park Ind Est 2
GU12 ....105 C1
Manor Park Prim Sch
SM1 ....59 C5
Manor Park Rd
Sutton SM1 ....59 C5
West Wickham BR4 ....44 B1
Manor Pk Richmond TW9 ..6 F3
Staines TW18 ....12 D5
Manor Pl
East Bedfont TW14 ......15 A7
Great Bookham KT23 .....94 A1
Mitcham CR4 ....41 C6
Staines TW18 ....13 B3
Sutton SM1 ....59 B6
Walton-on-T KT12 ....35 A2
Manor Rd
Aldershot GU11,GU12 ...126 A8
Ash GU10,GU12 ....126 F8
Ashford TW15 ....14 A3
Beckenham BR3 ....44 B7
Belmont SM2 ....58 F2
Croydon SE25 ....43 A6
East Grinstead RH19 ...185 C2
East Molesey KT8 ....36 D5
Farnborough GU14 ....85 D3
Farnham GU9 ....125 E4
Guildford GU2 ....109 B3
Horsham RH12 ....218 A6
Merstham RH1 ....119 C6
Merton SW20 ....39 F7
Mitcham CR4,SW16 ....41 C6
Reigate RH2 ....117 F3
Richmond TW10,TW9 ....6 F3
Send Marsh GU23 ....90 F4
Tatsfield TN16 ....103 E7
Teddington TW11 ....17 B3
Twickenham TW2 ....16 D6
Wallington SM5,SM6 .....60 B5
Walton-on-T KT12 ....34 F2
West Wickham BR4 ....63 B8
Woking GU21 ....69 C3
Wokingham RG41 ....25 A2
Manor Rd N
Hackbridge SM6 ....60 B6
Hinchley Wood KT7 ......56 A8
Manor Rd S KT10 ......55 E6
Manor Royal RH10 ....181 E1
Manor Royal Ind Est
RH10 ....181 E2
Manor Sch The KT14 ...71 E5
Manor The GU8 ....149 F1
Manor Way Bagshot GU19 .47 F3
Beckenham BR3 ....44 A6
Egham TW20 ....11 F2
Guildford GU2 ....129 F6
Mitcham CR4,SW16 ....41 C6
New Malden KT4 ....38 F1
Old Woking GU22 ....90 B6
Oxshott KT22 ....74 C3
Purley CR8 ....79 E7
South Croydon CR2 ......61 F4
Woodmansterne SM7 ......78 F3
Manor Way The SM6 ...60 B6
Manor Wlk
1 Aldershot GU12 .....105 A1
Weybridge KT13 ....53 B5
Manor Wood Rd SE7 ....79 E6
Manorcroft Prim Sch
TW20 ....12 A2
Manorcrofts Rd TW20 ..12 A2
Manordene Cl KT7 .....37 A1
Manorfields RH11 ....200 D2
Manorgate Rd KT2 .....38 A8
Manorhouse La KT23 ..113 E8
Mansard Beeches SW17 .21 A3
Mansard Manor 8 SM2 .59 C3
Manse Cl UB3 ....3 D8
Mansel Cl GU2 ....109 B6
Mansel Rd SW19 ....19 F2
Mansell Way CR3 .....100 D5
Mansfield Cl SL5 ......28 D7
Mansfield Cres RG12 ...27 B3
Mansfield Dr RH1 .....119 D6
Mansfield Pl SL5 ......28 D8
Mansfield Rd
Chessington KT9 ....56 D5
South Croydon CR2 ......61 D4
Wokingham RG41 ....25 A5
Manship Rd CR4 ....41 A8
Mansion Apartments The
BR3 ....44 C5
Manston Cl SE20 ....43 C8
Manston Dr RG12 ....27 C3
Manston Gr KT2 ....17 D3
Manston Rd GU4 ......110 A5
Mantelmas Cotts RH10 .204 A4
Mantilla Rd SW17 ......21 A4
Mantlet Cl SW16 ....21 C1
Manville Ct GU4 ......130 E1
Manville Gdns SW17 ....21 B5
Manville Rd SW17 ......21 B5
Many Gates SW12 ......21 B6

Manygate La TW17 .....34 C3
Maori Rd GU1 ....130 E8
Mapel Ct 3 RG12 ......27 F5
Maple Cl Ash Vale GU12 .106 A7
Blackwater GU17 ....64 C5
Crawley RH11 ....181 C1
Hampton TW12 ....15 F2
Horsham RH12 ....218 A4
Mitcham CR4 ....41 B8
Whyteleafe CR3 ....80 F2
Maple Ct Carshalton SM1 .59 D6
Catford SE6 ....24 B7
2 Croydon CR0 ....61 C6
Englefield Green TW20 ...11 B2
Kingston u T KT3 ....38 D1
12 West Norwood SW16 ...22 A3
Woking GU21 ....69 C3
Maple Dr
Crowthorne RG45 ....45 C7
East Grinstead RH19 ...186 A1
Lightwater GU18 ....66 F8
Maple Gdns TW15,TW19 .13 E6
Maple Gr Brentford TW8 ..6 B7
Guildford GU1 ....109 D3
Woking GU21 ....89 E6
Maple Ho
2 Kingston u T KT6 ....37 E4
8 Reigate RH2 ....118 F1
Maple Ind Est TW13 ...15 B5
Maple Inf Sch KT6 .....37 D4
Maple Leaf Cl
Biggin Hill TN16 ....83 D3
Farnborough GU14 ....84 F3
Maple Mews SW16 ......21 F3
Maple Pl KT17 ....77 D5
Maple Rd Ashstead KT21 ..95 D8
Kingston u T KT6 ....37 D4
Penge SE20 ....43 C8
Redhill RH1 ....139 F5
Send Marsh GU23 ....91 A3
Whyteleafe CR3 ....80 F2
Maple Way Feltham TW13 .15 B5
Headley Down GU35 .....187 B6
Hooley CR5 ....99 B6
Maple Wlk
Aldershot GU12 ....126 D8
Belmont SM2 ....59 B1
Mapledale Ave CR0 .....62 B7
Mapledrakes Cl GU6 ...175 E5
Mapledrakes Rd GU6 ...175 E5
Maplegreen RH11 .....201 C6
Maplehatch Cl GU7 ....150 E2
Maplehurst
2 Beckenham BR2 ......44 E7
Fetcham KT22 ....94 D4
Maplehurst Cl KT1 .....37 E5
Mapleleaf Cl CR2 ......81 D8
Maples The Banstead SM7 .78 B5
Ottershaw KT16 ....51 C4
4 Teddington KT1 .....17 C1
Maplestead Rd SW2 .....21 F8
Maplethorpe Rd CR7 ....42 B5
Marble Hill TW1 ......17 C8
Marble Hill Cl TW1 ....17 B8
Marble Hill Gdns TW1 ..17 B8
Marbles Way KT20 ......97 D8
March Rd
6 Twickenham TW1 ....17 A8
Weybridge KT13 ....53 A5
Marcheria Cl RG12 .....27 B3
Marches Rd RH12 .....197 E4
Marches The RH12 ....198 B5
Marchmont Ho 10 SW16 .21 C3
Marchmont Rd
Richmond TW10 ....6 F2
Wallington SM6 ....60 C3
Marchside Cl TW5 ....4 D6
Marcus Ct Brentford TW8 ..6 E7
Woking GU22 ....69 F1
Marcuse Rd CR3 ....100 D4
Mardale GU15 ....66 C4
Mardell Rd CR0 ....43 D4
Marden Ave BR2 ....44 F3
Marden Cres CR0 ....41 F3
Marden Lodge Prim Sch
CR3 ....101 B6
Marden Rd CR0 ....41 F3
Mardens The RH11 ....201 B7
Mare Hill GU8 ....170 E5
Mare Hill Cotts GU8 ..170 D4
Mare La GU8 ....172 C4
Mareschal Rd GU2 .....130 C7
Maresfield CR0 ....61 E7
Maresfield Ho GU4 ....110 D2
Mareth Cl GU11 ....105 B2
Marfleet Cl SM5 ....59 E8
Margaret Cl TW18 ......13 D2
Margaret Lockwood Cl
KT1 ....37 F5
Margaret Rd GU1 ......130 C8
Margaret Roper RC Prim Sch
CR8 ....61 A1
Margaret Way CR8 .....100 B8
Margery Gr KT20 ......117 E6
Margery Hall RH2 .....118 B5
Margery La KT20,RH2 ..118 A6
Margin Dr SW19 ....19 D4
Marham Gdns
Morden SM4 ....40 C3
Wandsworth SW17,SW18 ..20 E7
Maria Theresa Cl KT3 ..38 D4
Marian Ct SM1 ....59 B5
Marian Rd CR4,SW16 ....41 C8
Marian Vian Prim Sch
BR3 ....43 E4
Mariette Way SM6 ......60 E2
Marigold Cl RG45 ......45 A6

Marigold Ct GU1 .....109 E4
Marigold Dr GU24 ......68 A4
Marigold Way CR0 ......43 D1
Marina Ave KT3 ....39 B4
Marina Cl KT16 ....33 C1
Marina Way TW11 ....17 D1
Mariner Gdns TW10 .....17 C5
Mariners Dr
Farnborough GU14 ....85 C6
Normandy GU3 ....107 B4
Marion Ave TW17 ....34 B4
Marion Ct SW17 ....20 E3
Marion Rd Crawley RH10 .202 B3
Thornton Heath CR0 .....42 D4
Marist RC Prim Sch The
KT14 ....70 F6
Marius Mans 3 SW17 ...21 A6
Marius Rd SW17 ....21 A6
Marjoram Cl
Farnborough GU14 ....84 B4
Guildford GU2 ....109 A5
Marjorie Fosters Way
GU24 ....87 D8
Marjory Kinnon Sch TW14 3 E2
Marjory Pease Cotts
RH8 ....123 E5
Mark Oak La KT22 ......94 A6
Mark St RH2 ....118 B2
Mark Way GU7 ....150 B8
Markedge La CR5,RH1,
RH2 ....98 F2
Markenfield Rd GU1 ...109 D1
Markenhorn GU7 ......150 D7
Market Field Rd 14 RH2 118 F1
Feltham TW13 ....15 E6
Market Par Croydon SE25 .43 A5
Market Pl Bracknell RG12 .27 B7
Brentford TW8 ....6 C7
Kingston u T KT1 ....37 D7
Wokingham RG40 ....25 C5
Market Rd TW9 ....7 A4
Market Sq
Horsham RH12 ....217 C1
Reigate RH2 ....118 A1
Staines TW18 ....12 E4
Market St Bracknell RG12 .27 B7
Guildford GU1 ....130 D8
Market The SM1,SM4,SM5 .40 C1
Marketfield Way RH1 ..119 A1
Markfield CR0 ....81 F8
Markfield Rd CR3 .....101 B2
Markham Ct
Beckenham BR3 ....44 B6
Camberley GU15 ....65 D6
Markham Ho 9 SE21 ...22 E4
Markham Mews RG40 ....25 C6
Markham Rd RH5 ......178 C5
Markhole Cl TW12 ......15 F1
Marks Rd Warlingham CR6 .81 E1
Wokingham RG41 ....25 A8
Marksbury Ave TW9 ......7 A4
Markville Gdns CR3 ...101 A2
Markway The TW16 ......35 C7
Markwell Cl SE26 ......23 B4
Markwick La GU8 ......172 C2
Marlang Ct BR3 ....44 D8
Marlborough Rd TW7,TW8 ..6 B7
Marlborough 11 SW19 ...19 D7
Marlborough Cl
Crawley RH11 ....201 C2
Hersham KT12 ....54 D7
Horsham RH12 ....217 D5
Mitcham SW19 ....20 E2
Marlborough Cres UB3 ...3 D7
Marlborough Ct
Dorking RH4 ....136 B7
Wallington SM6 ....60 C3
Wokingham RG40 ....25 D7
Marlborough Cty Inf Sch
GU11 ....105 C7
Marlborough Dr KT13 ...53 C7
Marlborough Gdns KT6 ..37 D2
Marlborough Hill RH4 ..136 B7
Marlborough Ho SW19 ...19 D5
Marlborough Mews SM7 .78 A4
Marlborough Prim Sch
TW7 ....6 A6
Marlborough Rd
Ashford TW15 ....13 E3
Dorking RH4 ....136 B7
Feltham TW13 ....15 D6
Hampton TW12 ....16 A2
Mitcham SW19 ....20 E2
Richmond TW10 ....6 F1
South Croydon CR2 ......61 C3
Sutton SM1 ....59 A8
Woking GU21 ....69 A1
Marlborough Rise GU15 .65 E6
Marlborough Trad Est
TW9 ....7 B6
Marld The KT21 ....75 F1
Marler Rd SE23 ....23 F7
Marles La RH14 ....214 C1
Marlesford Ct SM6 .....60 C6
Marley Cl KT15 ....51 F4
Marley Combe Rd GU27 207 F4
Marley Croft TW18 .....12 E5
Marley Hanger GU27 ...208 A3
Marley La GU27 ....207 F4
Marley Rise RH4 ......136 A4
Marlfield Cl KT4 ....39 A1
Marlfield Ct KT3 ....38 F2
Marlin Cl TW16 ....14 E2
Marling Ct TW12 ....15 F2
Marlingdene Cl TW12 ...16 A2
Marlings Cl CR3 ....80 E2
Marlins Cl 3 SM1 ......59 C5

Marlow Cl SE20 ....43 B6
Marlow Cres TW1 ....5 F1
Marlow Ct RH10 ......201 D2
Marlow Dr SM3 ....58 D7
Marlow Ho TW11 ....17 A4
Marlow Rd SE20,SE25 ...43 B7
Marlowe Ct Dulwich SE19 .22 E1
6 Kingston u T KT2 ...17 D4
Marlowe Ho KT1 ....37 D5
Marlowe Lodge CR0 .....62 E8
Marlowe Sq CR4 ....41 C5
Marlowe Way CR0 ....60 E8
Marlpit Ave CR5 ....79 E2
Marlpit Cl RH19 ......185 E4
Marlpit La CR5 ....79 E2
Marlyns Cl GU4 ....110 A4
Marlyns Dr GU4 ....110 A4
Marmion Ho 14 SW12 ...21 B8
Marmot Rd TW4 ....4 D4
Marncrest Ct KT12 .....54 B5
Marnell Way TW4 ....4 D4
Marneys Cl KT18 ....76 A4
Marnfield Cres SW2 ....21 F7
Maroons Way SE6 ....24 A3
Marquean Twrs SW16 ...21 F1
Marquis Cl 1 KT1 .....37 E5
Marriott Cl TW14 ....3 D1
Marriott Ho SE6 ....24 C4
Marriott Lodge Cl KT15 .52 C6
Marrowbrook Cl GU14 ...85 A4
Marrowbrook La GU14 ...85 A3
Marrowells KT13 ....53 F7
Marryat Pl SW19 ....19 E4
Marryat Rd SW19 ......19 E3
Marsh Ave Epsom KT19 ..57 E1
Mitcham CR4 ....41 A7
Marsh Ct Crawley RH11 ..201 B1
3 Merton SW19 ....40 C8
Marsh Farm Rd TW2 .....16 F7
Marsh La KT15 ....52 B6
Marsh View RH5 ....133 C2
Marshall Cl
Farnborough GU14 ....84 F7
Frimley GU16 ....66 D2
Hounslow TW4 ....4 F2
Sanderstead CR2 ....81 A6
Marshall Ho 3 KT3 .....38 E1
Marshall Par GU22 .....70 F4
Marshall Pl KT15 ......52 C2
Marshall Rd
Crawley RH10 ....202 C4
Farncombe GU7 ....150 E6
Sandhurst GU47 ....64 D6
Marshall's Rd SM1 .....59 B6
Marshalls GU9 ....146 B8
Marshalls Cl KT19 .....76 C6
Marsham Ct 19 SW19 ...19 D7
Marshfields CE Inf Sch
KT16 ....51 E4
Marshwood Rd GU18 ....67 D8
Marston KT19 ....76 C8
Marston Ave KT9 ....56 E4
Marston Ct KT12 ....35 C1
Marston Dr
Farnborough GU14 ....85 B7
Warlingham CR6 ....81 C1
Marston Ho RH1 ....118 F2
Marston Rd
Farnham GU9 ....124 F2
Richmond TW11 ....17 B3
Woking GU21 ....69 B2
Marston Way
North Ascot SL5 ....28 E7
South Norwood SE19 .....22 C1
Martel Cl GU15 ....66 C7
Martell Rd SE21 ....22 D5
Martens Pl GU7 ....150 E6
Martin Cl Crawley RH11 .201 D8
Selsdon CR2 ....62 D1
Warlingham CR6 ....81 B3
Martin Cres CR0 ....42 A1
Martin Ct SW19 ....20 A1
Martin Gr SM4,SW19 ....40 A6
Martin Ho 5 KT3 ....38 E5
Martin Rd GU2 ....109 A3
Martin Way Frimley GU16 .65 E2
Merton SW19 ,SW20,SM4 ..39 E6
Woking GU21 ....69 A1
Martin's Heron Sta RG12 27 F5
Martin's Rd BR2 ....44 F7
Martindale SW14 ....7 C2
Martindale Ave GU15 ...66 C4
Martindale Cl GU4 ....110 D3
Martindale Rd
Balham SW12 ....21 B8
Hounslow TW4 ....4 E4
Woking GU21 ....69 A1
Martineau Cl KT10 .....55 D6
Martineau Dr RH4 .....136 B5
Martingale Cl TW16 ....35 A5
Martingale Ct GU11 ...104 E2
Martingales Cl TW10 ...17 D5
Martins Cl
Blackwater GU17 ....64 D4
Guildford GU1 ....110 C2
West Wickham BR4 ....63 D8
Martins Dr RG41 ....25 B7
Martins La RG12 ....27 C6
Martins Pk GU14 ....84 D7
Martins The
Crawley Down RH10 .....204 C8
Forest Hill SE26 ....23 B3
Martins Wood GU8 .....170 E7
Martinsyde GU22 ....70 C2
Martland Ind Est GU22 .89 A4
Martlet Cnr RH12 .....214 D7
Martlets Cl RH12 .....217 C5
Martlets The RH10 ....201 E6

Marton Cl SE6 ....24 A5
Marts The RH12 ....214 D7
Martyns Pl RH19 ......206 A4
Martyr Rd GU1 ....130 D8
Martyrs Ave RH11 .....181 C1
Martyrs La GU21 ....70 A7
Marvell Cl RH10 ......202 C8
Marwell BR4 ....63 F8
Mary Adelaide Cl SW15 .18 E5
Mary Ct SM2 ....59 C3
Mary Rd GU1 ....130 C8
Mary Rose Cl TW12 .....36 A8
Mary Vale GU7 ....150 D2
Mary's Terr TW1 ....17 A8
Marygold Ho TW3 ....5 C4
Maryhill Cl CR8 ....80 C2
Maryland Ct KT1 ....38 E7
Maryland Rd CR7 ....42 B8
Maryland Way TW16 ....35 A7
Marylebone Ho 15 RH1 .118 F2
Marymount International Sch
KT2 ....18 C1
Masefield Ct 19 KT6 ...37 D2
Masefield Gdns RG45 ...45 B3
Masefield Rd
Crawley RH11 ....200 E3
Hampton TW13 ....15 F4
Masefield Way TW19 ....13 F7
Maskall Cl SW2 ....22 A4
Maskani Wlk SW16 ......21 C1
Maskell Rd SW17 ....20 C5
Maskell Way GU14 ......84 D3
Mason Cl
East Grinstead RH19 ...185 E2
Hampton TW12 ....35 F8
Wimbledon SW20 ....39 D8
Mason Ct 3 SE19 ....22 F1
Mason Rd Crawley RH10 .201 E6
Farnborough GU14 ....84 E6
Mason Way GU11 ......126 B8
Mason's Ave CR0,CR9 ...61 C7
Mason's Bridge Rd RH1 140 C3
Mason's Pl CR4 ....40 F4
Masonic Hall Rd KT16 ..32 F3
Masons Paddock RH4 ...115 A1
Massetts Rd RH6 ......161 A2
Massingberd Way SW17 .21 B4
Master Cl RH8 ....122 E6
Masters Cl SW16 ....21 C2
Mastin Ho SW18 ....20 A7
Maswell Park Cres TW3 ..5 C2
Maswell Park Rd TW3 ....5 C3
Matham Rd KT8 ....36 D4
Mathew Terr GU11 .....105 C2
Mathews Cl GU14 .....105 E8
Mathias Cl KT18 ....76 C6
Mathisen Way SL3 ....1 E6
Mathon Ct GU1 ....109 F1
Matilda Cl SE19 ....22 D1
Matlock Cres SM3 ......58 E6
Matlock Gdns SM1,SM3 .58 E6
Matlock Pl SM1,SM3 ....58 E6
Matlock Rd CR3 ....100 E6
Matlock Way KT3 ....38 D8
Matthew Arnold Cl
Cobham KT11 ....73 A5
Staines TW18 ....13 C2
Matthew Arnold Sch The
TW18 ....13 C2
Matthew Ct CR4 ....41 D4
Matthew Rd GU11 .....125 E8
Matthew's Gdns CR0 ....82 D8
Matthew's Cl SL5 ......29 D5
Matthews Dr RH10 ....202 C3
Matthews La TW18 ......12 F4
Matthews Rd GU15 .....65 C8
Matthewsgreen Rd RG41 25 A4
Matthey Pl RH10 .....182 D1
Matthias Ct 12 TW10 ....6 E1
Maultway Cl GU15 ......66 B8
Maultway Cres GU15 ....66 B8
Maultway N GU15 ....47 B1
Maultway The GU15,GU16 66 D6
Maunsell Pk RH10 ....202 B6
Maurice Ave CR3 ......100 D5
Maurice Ct 3 TW8 ......6 D7
Mauveine Gdns TW3 ......5 A3
Mavery Ct 4 BR1 ......24 F1
Mavins Rd GU9 ....146 D8
Mavis Ave KT19 ....57 E5
Mavis Cl KT19 ....57 E5
Mawbey Rd KT16 ....51 D4
Mawson Cl SW20 ....39 E7
Mawson La W4 ....7 F8
Maxdata Ctr The RG12 ..27 A7
Maxine Cl GU47 ....45 B1
Maxton Wlk RH10 .....201 B2
Maxwell Cl CR0 ....41 E1
Maxwell Ct SE21 ....23 A7
Maxwell Dr KT14 ....71 C8
Maxwell Rd TW15 ......14 C2
Maxwell Way RH10 ....182 A1
May Cl Chessington KT9 ..56 F4
Godalming GU7 ....150 B2
2 Sandhurst GU47 ....64 D8
May Cotts CR5 ....98 B2
May Cres GU12 ....105 E1
May Ct 2 SW19 ....40 C8
May Gate Ave KT2 ......37 D8
May Rd TW2 ....16 E7
May's Hill Rd BR2 .....44 E6
Maybelle Cl RH5 ......157 D3
Mayberry Pl KT5 ....37 F2
Maybourne Cl SE26 .....23 B3
Maybourne Grange CR0 ..61 E8
Maybourne Rise GU22 ...89 D3
Maybury Bsns Ctr GU22 .70 A2

Maybury Cl
　Burgh Heath KT20 . . . . .97 E8
　Frimley GU16 . . . . .85 D8
Maybury Ct GU22 . . . . .70 B2
Maybury Hill GU21,GU22 . .70 B2
Maybury Ho GU22 . . . . .70 B2
Maybury Inf Sch GU21 . . . . .70 A3
Maybury Rd GU21 . . . . .70 A3
Maybury Rough GU22 . . . .70 B2
Maybury St SW17 . . . . .20 E3
Maycroft
　❷ Coney Hall BR2 . . . . . . .44 F1
　Reigate RH2 . . . . .139 C7
Maycross Ave SM4 . . . . . . .40 A5
Mayday Hospl CR7 . . . . . . .42 B3
Mayday Rd CR0,CR7 . . . . . .42 B3
Maydwell Ave RH13 . . . . .215 C2
Mayefield Rd CR7 . . . . .41 F4
Mayell Cl KT22 . . . . .95 C4
Mayes Cl CR6 . . . . .81 D1
Mayes La RH12 . . . . .197 F3
Mayfair Ave
　New Malden KT4 . . . . .39 A1
　Twickenham TW2 . . . . . . .16 C4
Mayfair Ct Beckenham BR3 44 B8
　Surbiton KT6 . . . . .37 E1
Mayfair Ct
　❶ Beckenham BR3 . . . . . . .44 B8
　❹ South Croydon CR0 . . . .61 F8
Mayfield Crawley RH10 . .202 D6
　Dormansland RH7 . . . . . .165 A1
　Hersham KT12 . . . . .54 C6
　Rowledge GU10 . . . . .145 F3
Mayfield Ave KT15 . . . . . . .52 C5
Mayfield Cl Ashford TW15 . .14 B2
　Farnham GU9 . . . . .126 B6
　Hersham KT12 . . . . .54 A6
　Hinchley Wood KT7 . . . . . .37 B1
　Penge SE20 . . . . .43 B8
　Redhill RH1 . . . . .140 A3
　Weybridge KT15 . . . . .52 C1
Mayfield Cres CR7 . . . . . . .41 F5
Mayfield Ct
　❶❶ Bromley BR2 . . . . .44 F5
　Redhill RH1 . . . . .139 F4
　Sutton SM2 . . . . .59 C3
Mayfield Gdns
　Egham TW18 . . . . .12 F2
　Walton-on-T KT12 . . . . . . .54 A6
Mayfield Gn KT23 . . . . . . .114 A3
Mayfield Rd
　Camberley GU15 . . . . .65 B1
　Farnborough GU14 . . . . . .84 F7
　Hersham KT12 . . . . .54 A6
　Merton SW19 . . . . .39 F8
　South Croydon CR2 . . . . . .61 D2
　Sutton SM3 . . . . .59 D4
　Weybridge KT13 . . . . .52 F5
Mayflower Cl RH10 . . . . .202 D5
Mayford Cl Balham SW12 . .20 F8
　Penge BR3 . . . . .43 D6
　Woking GU22 . . . . .89 D5
Mayford Gn GU22 . . . . . . .89 C5
Mayford Rd SW12 . . . . . . .21 A8
Mayhurst Ave GU22 . . . . . .70 C3
Mayhurst Cl GU22 . . . . . . .70 C3
Mayhurst Cres GU22 . . . . .70 C3
Maynard Cl RH10 . . . . . . .183 C4
Maynard Ct TW18 . . . . .13 A4
Maynooth Gdns CR4 . . . . .40 F2
Mayo Rd
　Thornton Heath CR0 . . . . .42 D4
　Walton-on-T KT12 . . . . . . .35 A2
Mayow Rd SE23,SE26 . . . . .23 D4
Maypole Rd
　Ashurst Wood RH19 . . . .206 E6
　East Grinstead RH19 . . . .185 D2
Mayroyd Ave KT6 . . . . .57 A8
Mays Cl KT13 . . . . .52 F1
Mays Cnr GU23 . . . . .90 D3
Mays Gr GU23 . . . . .90 D4
Mays Rd Teddington TW11 . .16 D3
　Wokingham RG40 . . . . . . .25 A6
Maysfield Rd GU23 . . . . . .90 D4
Maytree Cl GU1 . . . . .109 C5
Maytree Ct CR4 . . . . .41 A6
Maytree Wlk SW2 . . . . . . .22 A6
Maytrees GU21 . . . . .68 C2
Maywater Cl CR2 . . . . .80 D8
Maywood Cl BR3 . . . . .24 B1
Maywood Dr GU15 . . . . . . .66 A7
Maze Rd TW9 . . . . .7 A7
McAlmont Ridge GU7 . .150 D7
McCarthy Rd TW13 . . . . . . .15 D3
McCormick Ho ❾ SW2 . .22 A7
McDonald Ho ❶ KT17 . . . . .17 F1
Mcdonald's Almshouses
　GU9 . . . . .125 A1
McDonough Cl KT9 . . . . . .56 E6
McDougall Ct TW9 . . . . .7 A5
McGechie Ho RH19 . . . . .185 D3
McIndoe Rd RH19 . . . . . .185 D3
McIntosh Cl SW16 . . . . . . .60 E3
McIver Cl RH19 . . . . .184 F4
McKay Cl GU11 . . . . .105 C3
McKay Rd SW20 . . . . .19 C2
McKay Trad Est SL3 . . . . . .1 E5
McKenzie Way KT19 . . . . . .57 A1
McKinlay Ct BR3 . . . . .43 F7
Mcleod Ct SE21 . . . . .23 A7
McLeod Ho SE23 . . . . .23 C6
McMillan Ct Catford SE6 . .24 F7
　Whyteleafe CR3 . . . . .80 F1
McNaughton Cl GU14 . . . .84 D3
McRae La CR4 . . . . .40 F2
Meachen Ct RG40 . . . . . . .25 C6
Mead Ave RH1 . . . . .140 A1

Mead Cl Cranleigh GU6 . .174 E2
　Farnham GU10 . . . . .146 C1
　Redhill RH1 . . . . .119 A4
Mead Cotts GU7 . . . . .151 A6
Mead Cres Carshalton SM1 59 E6
　Little Bookham KT23 . . . . .94 A2
Mead Ct Egham TW20 . . . . .12 C2
　Woking GU21 . . . . .68 E3
Mead Dr CR5 . . . . .79 E5
Mead End KT21 . . . . .75 F3
Mead Inf Sch The KT19 . . .57 F6
Mead La Chertsey KT16 . . .33 C1
　Farnham GU9 . . . . .125 B2
Mead Pl CR0 . . . . .42 C1
Mead Rd Caterham CR3 . .100 F4
　Cranleigh GU6 . . . . .174 E3
　Crawley RH10 . . . . .201 F7
　Hersham KT12 . . . . .54 E6
　Hindhead GU26 . . . . .188 F4
　Richmond TW10 . . . . .17 C5
Mead The Ashstead KT21 . .95 E8
　Beckenham BR3 . . . . .44 C8
　Dorking RH4 . . . . .136 C4
　Farnborough GU14 . . . . . .85 B3
　Wallington SM6 . . . . .60 D4
　West Wickham BR4 . . . . . .44 D1
Mead Way Coulsdon CR5 . .79 F1
　Croydon CR0 . . . . .62 E8
　Guildford GU4 . . . . .110 C6
　Hayes BR2 . . . . .44 F4
Meadcroft Ho ❹ KT3 . . . .38 E2
Meade Cl W4 . . . . .7 A8
Meade Ct Bagshot GU19 . . .47 F3
　Walton on the Hill KT20 . . .97 A2
Meades Cl RH7 . . . . .165 B1
Meades The RH7 . . . . . . .165 A1
Meadfoot Rd SW16 . . . . . .41 C8
Meadhurst Pk TW16 . . . . . .14 E2
Meadlands Dr TW10 . . . . . .17 D6
Meadlands Prim Sch
　TW10 . . . . .17 C4
Meadow App RH10 . . . . .183 A3
Meadow Ave CR0 . . . . .43 D3
Meadow Bank
　East Horsley KT24 . . . . . .112 E8
　Farnham GU9 . . . . .125 B1
　Guildford GU1 . . . . .109 C3
Meadow Bglws GU4 . . . .131 B3
Meadow Brook Ind Ctr
　RH10 . . . . .182 A1
Meadow Cl Ash Vale GU12 . 85 F1
　Blackwater GU17 . . . . .64 D4
　Catford SE6 . . . . .24 A4
　Copthorne RH10 . . . . . . .183 A3
　Farncombe GU7 . . . . .150 E7
　Hersham KT12 . . . . .54 F6
　Hinchley Wood KT10 . . . . .55 F7
　Horsham RH12 . . . . .218 A5
　Milford GU8 . . . . .150 A1
　Purley CR8 . . . . .79 D6
　Richmond TW10 . . . . .17 E7
　Sutton SM1 . . . . .59 C8
　Twickenham TW4 . . . . . . .16 A8
　West Barnes SW20 . . . . . .39 C5
Meadow Cotts GU24 . . . . .67 F7
Meadow Croft Ct RH6 . . .182 C8
Meadow Ct Epsom KT18 . . .76 C6
　Farnborough GU14 . . . . . .84 F4
　Staines TW18 . . . . .12 E5
Meadow Dr GU23 . . . . .90 F4
Meadow Farm La RH12 . .217 F7
Meadow Gate KT21 . . . . . .75 E2
Meadow Gate Ave GU14 .84 F1
Meadow Gdns TW18 . . . . . .12 D3
Meadow Hill
　New Malden KT3 . . . . .38 E3
　Purley CR5,CR8 . . . . .79 C6
Meadow La KT22 . . . . .94 C5
Meadow Pl ❶ W4 . . . . .7 E7
Meadow Rd Ashford TW15 14 D3
　Ashstead KT21 . . . . .75 E2
　Beckenham BR2 . . . . .44 E7
　Carshalton SM1 . . . . .59 E6
　Claygate KT10 . . . . .55 E4
　Farnborough GU14 . . . . . .85 B7
　Feltham TW13 . . . . .15 E6
　Guildford GU4 . . . . .110 A5
　Merton SW19 . . . . .20 C1
　Wentworth GU25 . . . . . . .30 E4
　Wokingham RG41 . . . . . . .25 A5
Meadow Rise
　Coulsdon CR5 . . . . .79 D6
　Knaphill GU21 . . . . .68 C2
Meadow Stile CR0,CR9 . . .61 C7
Meadow The RH10 . . . . . .183 A3
Meadow Vale GU27 . . . . .208 A6
Meadow Vale Prim Sch
　RG42 . . . . .26 F8
Meadow View
　Chertsey KT16 . . . . .33 C1
　Smallfield RH6 . . . . .162 C3
Meadow View Rd CR7 . . . .42 B4
Meadow Way
　Addlestone KT15 . . . . .52 B6
　Aldershot GU12 . . . . .105 F3
　Blackwater GU17 . . . . .64 C5
　Bracknell RG42 . . . . .27 A8
　Burgh Heath KT20 . . . . . . .77 E2
　Chessington KT9 . . . . .56 E5
　Great Bookham KT23 . . . . .94 B4
　Reigate RH2 . . . . .139 B5
　Rowledge GU10 . . . . .145 F3
　West End GU24 . . . . .67 F6
　West Horsley KT24 . . . . . .92 D1
　Wokingham RG41 . . . . . . .25 A5
Meadow Waye TW5 . . . . . . .4 E7

Meadow Wlk
　Hackbridge SM6 . . . . .60 B7
　Walton on the Hill KT20 . . .97 B3
　West Ewell KT17,KT19 . . . .57 F3
　Wokingham RG41 . . . . . . .25 A6
Meadowbank KT5 . . . . .37 F3
Meadowbank Gdns TW4,
　TW5 . . . . .4 B6
Meadowbank Rd GU18 . . .48 C1
Meadowbrook RH8 . . . . . .122 D5
Meadowbrook Cl SL3 . . . . .1 F6
Meadowbrook Rd RH4 . .136 A7
Meadowcroft Cl
　Crawley RH11 . . . . .200 F5
　East Grinstead RH19 . . . .185 C2
Meadowcroft Com Inf Sch
　KT16 . . . . .51 F7
Meadowfield Cl KT3 . . . . . .39 C5
Meadowlands
　Cobham KT11 . . . . .73 A6
　Crawley RH11 . . . . .201 C6
　Oxted RH8 . . . . .123 A1
　West Clandon GU4 . . . . . .111 B5
Meadowlea Cl UB7 . . . . .2 D8
Meadows Bsns Pk The
　GU17 . . . . .64 E4
Meadows End TW16 . . . . . .35 A8
Meadows Leigh Cl KT13 . .53 C7
Meadows The Ash GU12 .106 B2
　Churt GU10 . . . . .167 F1
　Guildford GU2 . . . . .130 C6
　Sandhurst GU47 . . . . .64 E5
　Warlingham CR6 . . . . .81 E2
Meadowside
　Great Bookham KT23 . . . . .94 A4
　Horley RH6 . . . . .161 B4
　Twickenham TW1 . . . . . . .17 D8
　Walton-on-T KT12 . . . . . . .54 C8
Meadowside Mobile Home
　Pk RH7 . . . . .164 C6
Meadowside Rd SM2 . . . . .58 E2
Meadowview TW19 . . . . .1 F2
Meadowview Rd
　Catford SE6 . . . . .24 A3
　West Ewell KT19 . . . . .57 E2
Meadrow GU7 . . . . .150 F6
Meadrow Ct GU7 . . . . . . .151 A6
Meadrow Lock GU7 . . . . .151 A6
Meads Prim Sch The
　RH19 . . . . .205 E7
Meads Rd GU1 . . . . .110 B1
Meads The Cheam SM3 . . .58 E7
　East Grinstead RH19 . . . .205 E7
　Haslemere GU27 . . . . . . .207 F6
　Weybridge KT13 . . . . .53 D4
Meadside ❹ Epsom KT18 .76 D6
　❼ Woking GU21 . . . . .69 F1
Meadside Cl BR3 . . . . .43 E8
Meadsview Ct ❸ GU14 . . .85 B4
Meadvale RH2 . . . . .216 F2
Meadvale Rd CR0 . . . . .43 A3
Meadway Ashford TW15 . . .14 A4
　Beckenham BR3 . . . . .44 C8
　Effingham KT24 . . . . .113 E7
　Epsom KT19 . . . . .76 C7
　Esher KT10 . . . . .55 B2
　Frimley GU16 . . . . .65 F2
　Haslemere GU27 . . . . . . .207 F6
　Oxshott KT22 . . . . .74 E5
　Staines TW18 . . . . .13 A1
　Tolworth KT5 . . . . .38 C1
　Twickenham TW2 . . . . . . .16 D7
　Warlingham CR6 . . . . .81 C3
　West Barnes SW20 . . . . . .39 C5
Meadway Cl TW18 . . . . . . .13 A1
Meadway Dr
　New Haw KT15 . . . . .52 C3
　Woking GU21 . . . . .69 D4
Meadway The RH6 . . . . . .161 C3
Meaford Way SE20 . . . . . . .23 B1
Meare Cl KT20 . . . . .97 D4
Meath Green Ave RH6 . . .160 F5
Meath Green Inf Sch
　RH6 . . . . .160 F5
Meath Green Jun Sch
　RH6 . . . . .160 F6
Meath Green La RH1,
　RH6 . . . . .160 E6
Meath Sch KT16 . . . . .51 D3
Medawar Rd GU2 . . . . . . .129 D8
Medcroft Gdns SW14 . . . . .7 C3
Mede Cl TW19 . . . . .11 D7
Mede Ct TW18 . . . . .12 E5
Medefield KT22 . . . . .94 D3
Medfield St SW15 . . . . . . .19 B8
Medhurst Cl GU24 . . . . . . .49 F2
Medina Ave KT10 . . . . .55 E7
Medina Sq KT19 . . . . .57 A2
Medlake Rd TW20 . . . . . . .12 C2
Medland Cl CR4 . . . . .41 A1
Medlar Cl Crawley RH11 . .181 C1
　Guildford GU1 . . . . .109 C3
Medlar Dr GU17 . . . . .64 F3
Medlars Ct RH5 . . . . .158 B1
Medora Rd SW2 . . . . .21 F8
Medway RH10 . . . . .204 A5
Medway Cl CR0 . . . . .43 C3
Medway Ct
　Horsham RH12 . . . . .218 B5
　South Norwood SE25 . . . . .42 E4
Medway Dr
　East Grinstead RH19 . . . .205 D6
　Farnborough GU14 . . . . . .84 E7
Medway Ho ❻ KT2 . . . . . . .37 D8
Medway Rd RH11 . . . . . . .200 F5
Medwin Wlk RH12 . . . . . .217 C2
Melbourne Cl SM6 . . . . . . .60 C5
Melbourne Ct Penge SE20 23 A1

Melbourne Ct continued
　Twickenham TW2 . . . . . . .16 D7
Melbourne Mews SE6 . . .24 C8
Melbourne Rd
　Merton SW19 . . . . .40 A8
　Teddington TW11 . . . . . . .17 C2
　Wallington SM6 . . . . .60 C5
Melbourne Way RH12 . . .217 F5
Melbury Cl Chertsey KT16 . .33 A2
　Claygate KT10 . . . . .56 B4
　West Byfleet KT14 . . . . . . .71 A5
Melbury Gdns SW20 . . . . .39 B8
Melbury Ho TW2 . . . . .16 D6
Meldone KT3 . . . . .38 D1
Meldone Cl KT5 . . . . .38 B3
Meldrum Cl RH8 . . . . .123 A3
Melfield Gdns SE6 . . . . . . .24 C3
Melfont Ave CR7 . . . . .42 B6
Melford Cl KT9 . . . . .56 F5
Melford Ct Dulwich SE22 . .23 A8
　❷ Sutton SM2 . . . . .59 C3
Melford Rd SE21,SE22 . . . .23 A7
Melfort Rd CR7,SW16 . . . . .42 B6
Meliot Rd SE6 . . . . .24 D6
Melksham Cl RH13 . . . . . .217 E1
Meller Cl CR0 . . . . .60 E7
Mellersh Hill Rd GU5 . . .152 C6
Mellish Ct KT6 . . . . .37 E3
Mellison Rd SW17 . . . . . . .20 E3
Melliss Ave TW9 . . . . .7 B6
Mellor Cl KT12 . . . . .35 F2
Mellor Ct ❸ SW19 . . . . . . .20 C1
Mellor Ho ❷ SE21 . . . . . . .22 E4
Mellow Cl SM7 . . . . .78 C5
Mellows Rd SM6 . . . . .60 D5
Melody Rd TN16 . . . . .83 C1
Melrose RG12 . . . . .27 B1
Melrose Ave
　Farnborough GU14 . . . . . .84 C5
　Mitcham CR4 . . . . .21 B1
　Thornton Heath SW16 . . . .42 A6
　Twickenham TW2 . . . . . . .16 B8
　Wimbledon SW19 . . . . . . .20 A5
Melrose Gdns
　Hersham KT12 . . . . .54 C5
　Kingston u T KT3 . . . . .38 D6
　New Malden KT3 . . . . .38 D6
Melrose Rd Barnes SW13 . .7 F5
　Biggin Hill TN16 . . . . .83 C3
　Coulsdon CR5 . . . . .79 B4
　Merton SW19 . . . . .40 A8
　Weybridge KT13 . . . . .53 A5
Melrose Sch CR4 . . . . .40 E6
Melrose Tudor SM6 . . . . . .60 E5
Melsa Rd SM4 . . . . .40 C3
Melton Ct ❽ Croydon CR0 .61 F8
　❷ Twickenham TW1 . . . . .17 B8
Melton Fields KT19 . . . . . .57 D2
Melton Pl KT19 . . . . .57 D2
Melton Rd RH1 . . . . .119 C5
Melville Ave Frimley GU16 .65 F1
　South Croydon CR0,CR2 . .61 F5
　Wimbledon SW20 . . . . . . .19 A1
Melville Ct KT14 . . . . .71 E7
Melvin Ct ❶❷ TW9 . . . . . . .7 A6
Melvin Rd SE20 . . . . .43 C8
Melvinshaw KT22 . . . . .95 C6
Membury Cl GU16 . . . . . . .86 A7
Membury Wlk RG12 . . . . . .27 F5
Memorial Cl TW5 . . . . .4 F8
Memory Cotts KT20 . . . . . .97 E8
Mendip Cl Forest Hill SE26 .23 C4
　Harlington UB3 . . . . .3 D7
　North Cheam KT4 . . . . . . .58 C8
Mendip Rd Bracknell RG12 27 E4
　Farnborough GU14 . . . . . .84 E7
Mendip Wlk RH11 . . . . . .201 B6
Menin Way GU9 . . . . .125 D1
Menlo Gdns SE19 . . . . .22 D1
Meon Cl
　Farnborough GU14 . . . . . .84 D6
　Tadworth KT20 . . . . .97 B5
Meon Ct TW7 . . . . .5 E5
Meopham Rd CR4,SW16 . .41 C8
Merantun Way SW19 . . . . .40 C8
Mercer Cl Crawley RH10 .202 C3
　Thames Ditton KT7 . . . . . .36 F2
Mercer Rd RH12 . . . . . . .217 C8
Mercers Park Ctry Pk*
　RH1 . . . . .119 E4
Merchants Cl
　Croydon SE25 . . . . .43 A5
　Knaphill GU21 . . . . .68 C2
Merchiston Rd SE6 . . . . . .24 D6
Mercia Wlk ❽ GU21 . . . . . .69 F2
Mercury Cl RH11 . . . . . . .200 E3
Mercury Ctr TW14 . . . . .4 B2
Mere Cl SW15,SW19 . . . . . .19 D8
Mere End CR0 . . . . .43 D2
Mere Rd
　Oatlands Park KT13 . . . . . .53 D7
　Shepperton TW17 . . . . . . .34 B3
　Walton on the Hill KT20 . . .97 B4
Merebank RH5 . . . . .157 D4
Merebank La CR0 . . . . .60 F5
Meredith Ct KT1 . . . . .37 F7
Merefield KT18 . . . . .97 D8
Merefield Gdns KT20 . . . . .97 D8
Mereside Pk TW15 . . . . . . .14 C4
Meretune Ct SM4 . . . . .39 F6
Merevale Cres SM4 . . . . . .40 C3
Mereway Industry TW2 . . .16 E7
Mereway Rd TW2 . . . . .16 E7
Mereworth Cl BR2 . . . . . . .44 F4
Mereworth Dr RH10 . . . . .202 D8
Meridian Cl RH11 . . . . . . .200 D5
Meridian Ct Catford SE6 . .24 F7
　Croydon CR0 . . . . .61 A6
　Sunningdale SL5 . . . . .29 B1

Meridian Gr RH6 . . . . . . .161 C4
Meridian Way RH19 . . . . .185 F3
Merland Cl KT20 . . . . .97 C7
Merland Gn KT20 . . . . .97 C7
Merland Rise KT18,KT20 . .97 C8
Merland Rise Prim Sch
　KT18 . . . . .97 C8
Merle Common Rd RH8 144 B7
Merlewood RG12 . . . . .27 D4
Merlewood Cl CR3 . . . . . .100 D7
Merlin Cl Brands Hill SL3 . .1 B8
　Crawley RH11 . . . . .200 E6
　Mitcham CR4 . . . . .40 E6
　South Croydon CR0 . . . . . .61 E6
　Wallington SM6 . . . . .60 F4
Merlin Clove RG42 . . . . .8 B2
Merlin Ct Beckenham BR2 .44 F5
　Frimley GU16 . . . . .65 D1
　Sheerwater GU21 . . . . . . .70 C5
Merlin Ctr RH11 . . . . .181 D2
Merlin Gr BR3 . . . . .44 A4
Merlin Rd GU14 . . . . .85 B2
Merlin Way
　East Grinstead RH19 . . . .186 A3
　Farnborough GU14 . . . . . .84 D3
Merling Cl KT9 . . . . .56 D5
Merlins Cl GU9 . . . . .125 C1
Merrick Ho RH2 . . . . .118 C1
Merricks Ct SW14 . . . . .7 B3
Merrilands Rd KT4 . . . . . . .39 C1
Merrilyn Cl KT10 . . . . .56 A4
Merritt Gdns KT9 . . . . .56 C4
Merrivale Gdns GU21 . . . . .69 C2
Merrow Bsns Ctr GU4 . . .110 D4
Merrow CE Inf Sch GU4 110 D3
Merrow Chase GU1 . . . . .110 D1
Merrow Common Rd
　GU4 . . . . .110 D4
Merrow Copse GU1 . . . . .110 C2
Merrow Croft GU1 . . . . . .110 C2
Merrow Ct Guildford GU1 110 D1
　Mitcham CR4 . . . . .40 D7
Merrow Grange GU1 . . . .110 C1
Merrow La GU4 . . . . .110 C5
Merrow Pl GU4 . . . . .110 D3
Merrow Rd SM2 . . . . .58 D2
Merrow St GU4 . . . . .110 C2
Merrow Way
　Guildford GU1 . . . . .110 D2
　New Addington CR0 . . . . . .63 C4
Merrow Woods GU1 . . . .110 B3
Merryacres GU8 . . . . .170 E6
Merryfield Dr RH12 . . . . .217 A3
Merryhill Rd RG42 . . . . . . .27 B8
Merryhills Cl TN16 . . . . . . .83 D3
Merryhills La RH14 . . . . . .213 A5
Merrylands KT16 . . . . .51 E7
Merrylands Ct KT23 . . . . . .93 F4
Merrylands Rd KT23 . . . . .93 F3
Merrylands Farm KT23 . . .94 A3
Merryman Dr RG45 . . . . . .45 A7
Merrymeet SM7 . . . . .78 F5
Merryweather Ct ❶ KT3 . .38 E7
Merrywood ❸ KT22 . . . . . .95 C6
Merrywood Gr KT20 . . . . .117 E5
Merrywood Pk
　Frimley GU15 . . . . .65 F4
　Reigate RH2 . . . . .118 B3
Merrywood Pk (Mobile Home
　Pk) KT20 . . . . .116 B5
Merryworth Cl GU12 . . . .105 F1
Mersham Pl Penge SE20 . .43 B8
　South Norwood CR7 . . . . . .42 D7
Mersham Rd CR7 . . . . .42 D7
Merstham Com Prim Sch
　RH1 . . . . .119 C6
Merstham Rd RH1 . . . . . .120 A5
Merstham Sta RH1 . . . . . .119 C7
Merton KT18 . . . . .97 D8
Merton Abbey Fst Sch
　SW19 . . . . .40 B8
Merton Cl GU47 . . . . .45 F2
Merton Coll SM4 . . . . .39 F4
Merton Gdns KT20 . . . . . . .97 E8
Merton Hall Gdns SW20 .39 E8
Merton Hall Rd SW19,
　SW20 . . . . .39 E8
Merton High St SW19 . . . .20 C1
Merton Ho SW18 . . . . .20 A7
Merton Ind Pk SW19 . . . . .40 C8
Merton Mans SW20 . . . . . .39 D7
Merton Park Fst Sch
　SW19 . . . . .40 A7
Merton Park Par SW19 . . .39 F8
Merton Pl ❾ SW19 . . . . . . .20 C1
Merton Rd Croydon SE25 . .43 A4
　Merton SW19 . . . . .20 B1
　Wandsworth SW18 . . . . . .20 A7
Merton Road Ind Est
　SW18 . . . . .20 A8
Merton Way
　East Molesey KT8 . . . . . . .36 B6
　Leatherhead KT22 . . . . . . .95 A8
Merton Wlk KT22 . . . . .75 A1
Mervyn Rd TW17 . . . . .34 C2
Metana Ho RH10 . . . . . . .182 A3
Metcalf Rd TW15 . . . . .14 B3
Metcalf Way RH11 . . . . . .181 D2
Metcalfe Wlk TW13 . . . . . .15 E4
Meteor Way SM6 . . . . .60 E3
Meteorological Off (HQ)
　RG12 . . . . .27 D7
Metro Bsns Ctr The SE26 23 F3
Metro Ctr SM4 . . . . .39 D2

Metro Ind Ctr TW7 ....5 E5
Meudon Ave GU14 ......85 B3
Meudon Ct KT6 ....37 D4
Meville Ct GU2 ....130 C6
Mews Ct RH19 ....205 F6
Mews The Banstead SM7 ..78 B4
Broadbridge Heath RH12 .216 D4
Dunsfold GU8 ....192 F5
6 Farnham GU9 ....125 B2
Guildford GU1 ....130 C8
Mewsend TN16 ....83 D1
Meyer Ho 2 SW12 ......21 B8
Meyrick Cl GU21 ....68 E3
Mezel Hill Cotts SL4 ....10 C3
Miall Wlk SE26 ....23 E4
Michael Cres RH6 ....161 A1
Michael Fields RH18 ...206 E2
Michael Hall Sch RH18 .206 D1
Michael Rd SE25 ....42 E6
Michaelmas Cl SW20 ....39 C6
Michaelson Ho 4 SE21 ..22 E4
Micham Vale High Sch (Acacia Rd Site) CR4 ...41 B7
Michel's Row 2 TW9 .....6 E3
Micheldever Way RG12 ..27 F4
Michelet Cl GU18 ....48 B1
Michelham Gdns
Burgh Heath KT20 ....97 C7
Twickenham TW1 ....16 F5
Michell Cl RH12 ....217 A2
Michels Almshouses 11 TW10 ...6 E2
Michelsdale Dr 3 TW9 ...6 E3
Mickle Hill GU47 ....45 A1
Micklefield Sch RH2 ...118 A2
Mickleham Downs RH5 ..95 D1
Mickleham Dr KT22 .....95 C1
Mickleham Gdns SM3 ...58 E4
Mickleham Hall RH5 ...115 C7
Mickleham Way CR0 ....63 D5
Mid Holmwood La RH5 .136 B1
Mid St Nutfield RH1 .....119 F1
South Nutfield RH1 .....140 F7
Middle Ave GU9 ....146 D8
Middle Bourne La GU10 146 C7
Middle Church La 19 GU9 ....125 B2
Middle Cl Coulsdon CR5 .100 A7
Ewell KT17 ....76 E7
Frimley GU15 ....66 C6
Middle Farm Cl KT24 ..113 D8
Middle Farm Pl KT24 ..113 D8
Middle Gn Brockham RH3 137 B7
Staines TW18 ....13 D1
Middle Gordon Rd GU15 .65 D5
Middle Green Cl 3 KT5 ..37 F3
Middle Hill
Aldershot GU11 ....105 A3
Englefield Green TW20 ...11 D3
Middle La Ewell KT17 ....76 E7
Teddington TW11 ....16 F2
Middle Mill KT5 ....37 F6
Middle Old Pk GU9 ....124 F4
Middle Rd
Leatherhead KT22 ....95 B6
Mitcham SW16 ....41 D7
Middle Row 1 RH19 ...205 F8
Middle St Brockham RH3 .137 C5
Croydon CR0,CR9 ....61 C7
Horsham RH12 ....217 C2
Shere GU5 ....133 A4
Middle Way SW16 ......41 D7
Middlefield
Farnham GU9 ....146 A7
Horley RH6 ....161 C4
Middlefield Cl GU9 ....146 A8
Middlefields CR0 ....62 E2
Middlemarch GU8 .....170 E5
Middlemead Cl KT23 ...94 A2
Middlemead Rd KT23 ...93 F2
Middlemoor Rd GU16 ...85 E8
Middlesex Ct KT15 ......52 C6
Middlesex Ho 4 SE20 ...23 C1
Middlesex Rd CR4 ......41 E4
Middleton Gdns GU14 ...84 E6
Middleton Rd
Camberley GU15 ....65 F7
Downside KT11 ....93 C8
Epsom KT19 ....57 D1
Horsham RH12 ....217 A2
Morden SM4,SM5 ....40 D2
Middleton Way RH11 ...200 E5
Midgarth Cl KT22 ....74 D6
Midgley Rd RH10 ......201 F8
Midholm Rd CR0 ....62 E8
Midhope Cl GU22 ....89 E8
Midhope Gdns 5 GU22 ..89 E8
Midhope Rd GU22 ....89 E8
Midhurst SE26 ....23 C2
Midhurst Ave CR0 ......42 A2
Midhurst Cl RH11 ......201 A7
Midhurst Rd GU27 ......208 B5
Midleton Cl GU8 ....149 F2
Midleton Industrial Estate Rd GU2 ....109 B2
Midleton Rd
Guildford GU2 ....109 A2
Guildford GU2 ....109 B2
Kingston u T KT3 ....38 C7
Midmoor Rd
Streatham SW12 ....21 C7
Wimbledon SW19 ....39 E8
Midsummer Apartments 14 SM2 ....59 A3
Midsummer Ave TW4 .....4 F3
Midsummer Wlk GU21 ..69 D3
Midway Cheam SM3,SM4 ..39 F2
Walton-on-T KT12 ....54 B8
Midway Ave
Chertsey KT16 ....33 A6
Thorpe TW20 ....32 B6
Midway Cl TW19 ....13 B5
Miena Way KT21 ....75 D2
Mike Hawthorn Dr GU9 125 C3
Milbanke Ct RG12 ....26 F7
Milbanke Way RG12 .....26 F7
Milborne Rd RH10 .....202 C2
Milborough Cres SE12 ...24 E8
Milbourne La KT10 ......55 C5
Milbourne Lodge Jun Sch KT10 ....55 C4
Milbourne Lodge Senior Sch KT10 ....55 D4
Milbrook KT10 ....55 C4
Milburn Ho SW20 ....39 B7
Milburn Wlk KT18 ....76 E4
Milcombe Cl 5 GU21 ...69 B1
Milden Cl GU16 ....86 A6
Milden Gdns GU16 ......85 F6
Mile Path GU22 ....89 B7
Mile Rd
Carshalton CR4,SM6 .....41 A1
Wallington CR0,CR4,CR9, SM6 ....41 C1
Miles Ct CR9 ....61 B8
Miles La Cobham KT11 ...73 E6
South Godstone RH9 ....142 F7
Tandridge RH8 ....143 A7
Miles Pl GU18 ....66 F7
Miles Rd Ash GU12 .....106 B3
Epsom KT19 ....76 D7
Mitcham CR4 ....40 E6
Miles's Hill RH5 ....155 C3
Milestone Cl Ripley GU23 .91 B5
Sutton SM2 ....59 D3
Milestone Ct TW7 ....6 A6
Milestone Rd SE19 .....22 F2
Milford By Pass Rd GU8 .....149 D2
Milford Gdns CR0 ....43 D4
Milford Gr SM1 ....59 C6
Milford Heath Rd GU8 ..170 E8
Milford Ho GU8 ....150 A1
Milford Hospl GU7 .....171 C8
Milford Lodge GU8 .....170 F8
Milford Mews SW16 .....21 F5
Milford Rd GU8 ....148 E4
Milford Sta GU8 ....171 A7
Milking La
Biggin Hill,Downe BR6 .....83 E7
Biggin Hill,Leaves Green BR2 ....83 D8
Mill Bay La RH12 ......217 B1
Mill Cl Bagshot GU19 ....47 D3
Carshalton SM5 ....60 A8
East Grinstead RH19 .....205 E7
Great Bookham KT23 .....94 A3
Haslemere GU27 ....207 E6
Horley RH6 ....160 E4
Mill Copse Rd GU27 ...208 B4
Mill Cotts
East Grinstead RH19 ....205 E7
Rudgwick RH12 ....214 D5
Mill Ct SE19 ....22 E1
Mill Farm Ave TW16 ....14 E1
Mill Farm Cres TW4 .....15 E7
Mill Farm Rd RH13 ....218 A4
Mill Field GU19 ....47 D3
Mill Gdns SE26 ....23 B5
Mill Gn CR4 ....41 A2
Mill Green Bsns Pk CR4 .41 A2
Mill Green Rd CR4 ......41 A2
Mill Hill RH3 ....137 B8
Mill Hill La RH3 ....116 B1
Mill House La KT16 .....32 B5
Mill La Ascot SL5 ....30 A7
Bracknell RG12 ....26 F5
Bramley GU5 ....151 F6
Byfleet KT14 ....71 F6
Carshalton SM5 ....60 A7
Chiddingfold GU8 ....191 B3
Chilworth GU4,GU5 .....131 F4
Copthorne RH10 ....183 E3
Crawley RH11 ....201 A8
Croydon CR0 ....61 A7
Dorking RH4 ....136 B8
Dunsfold GU8 ....192 F4
Ewell KT17 ....57 F2
Felbridge RH19 ....184 E5
Felcourt RH7 ....164 F2
Fetcham KT22 ....95 A5
Forest Green RH5 ....176 D7
Frensham GU10 ....167 B7
Godalming GU7 ....150 D4
Guildford GU1 ....130 D7
Hookwood RH6 ....160 D3
Horton SL3 ....1 C4
Kingsley Green GU27 ....208 C3
Merstham RH1 ....119 D4
Ockham GU23 ....91 D8
Oxted RH8 ....122 F2
Parkgate RH5 ....158 D5
Pirbright GU24 ....87 E3
Shalford GU3 ....130 C1
The Chart RH8 ....123 F4
Thorpe TW20 ....32 C5
Witley GU8 ....170 F5
Mill Lane Trad Est CR0 ...60 F7
Mill Mead TW18 ....12 F4
Mill Pl KT1 ....37 F6
Mill Plat Isleworth TW7 ....6 A5
Isleworth TW7 ....6 B4
Mill Plat Ave TW7 ....6 A5
Mill Pond Rd GU20 ......48 B6
Mill Pool Ho GU7 ......150 D4
Mill Rd Cobham KT11 .....73 C4
Crawley RH10 ....202 B7
Epsom KT17 ....76 F7
Ewell KT17 ....76 F7
Kingswood KT20 ....97 D4
Merton SW19 ....20 C1
South Holmwood RH5 ....157 D7
Thames Ditton KT10 .....55 A8
Twickenham TW2 ....16 C6
Mill Reach GU4 ....131 F5
Mill Ride SL5 ....28 D8
Mill Shaw RH8 ....122 F3
Mill St Colnbrook SL3 .....1 D7
Kingston u T KT1 ....37 E6
Redhill RH1 ....139 F8
Mill Stream GU9 ......125 E6
Mill Vale BR2 ....44 F7
Mill View Cl KT17 ....57 F3
Mill View Gdns CR0 .....62 D7
Mill Way
East Grinstead RH19 .....205 E7
Feltham TW14 ....4 B2
Headley KT22,KT18 ....96 A2
Millais RH13 ....218 A3
Millais Cl RH11 ....200 F2
Millais Ct RH13 ....218 A4
Millais Lower Sch RH13 217 F2
Millais Rd KT3 ....38 E2
Millais Sch RH13 ....217 F2
Millais Way KT19 ....57 C6
Millan Cl KT15 ....52 B1
Milland Ho 11 SW15 .....19 A7
Millbank SM6 ....60 D5
Millbank The RH11 .....200 F6
Millbottom La RH5 .....157 D7
Millbourne Rd TW13 ....15 E4
Millbrook Guildford GU1 .130 D7
Oatlands Park KT13 ......53 E6
Millbrook Way SL3 ......1 E5
Millcroft Ho SE6 ....24 B4
Millennium Ctr GU9 ...125 A1
Millennium Ho RH11 ...200 F3
Millennium Way RG12 ...27 C8
Miller Ho 5 Penge SE20 ..23 A1
9 Streatham SW2 ....21 E8
Miller Rd Guildford GU4 .110 C4
Mitcham SW19 ....20 D2
Thornton Heath CR0 ......42 A1
Miller's Ct TW20 ....12 D2
Miller's La RH1 ....162 C7
Millers Bsns Ctr RG41 ..25 A5
Millers Cl TW18 ....13 B3
Millers Copse
Langley Vale KT18 ....96 D8
Outwood RH1 ....162 B7
Millers Gate RH12 .....217 D6
Millers Mead Ct SW19 ..20 D1
Millfarm Bsns Pk TW4 ..15 E8
Millfield Charlton TW16 ...34 D8
Kingston u T KT1 ....37 F6
Millfield La KT20 ....98 A2
Millfield Rd TW4 ....15 F7
Millford GU21 ....69 B2
Millford Sch GU8 ......149 F1
Millgate Ct GU9 ....125 D3
Millhedge Cl KT11 ......73 E3
Millholme Wlk GU15 ....66 C4
Millhouse Pl SE27 ......22 B4
Millins Cl GU47 ....45 E1
Millmead Byfleet KT14 ...71 F7
Guildford GU2 ....130 C7
Wokingham RG41 ....25 A7
Millmead Terr GU2 .....130 C7
Millpond Cotts GU8 ....172 D4
Millpond Ct KT15 ....52 E5
Millpond Pl SM6 ....60 A7
Mills Ho GU12 ....105 D3
Mills Rd KT12 ....54 C5
Mills Spur SL4 ....11 B8
Millside SM5 ....59 F8
Millside Ct KT23 ....94 A2
Millside Pl TW7 ....6 B5
Millstead Cl KT20 ......97 B5
Millstream The GU27 ...207 E5
Millthorpe Rd RH12 ....217 F4
Millview Cl RH2 ....118 D3
Millway RH2 ....118 D1
Millwood RH10 ....204 E5
Millwood Rd TW3,TW7 ....5 C2
Milman Cl RG12 ....28 A7
Milne Cl RH11 ....200 E3
Milne Pk E CR0 ....82 D8
Milne Pk W CR0 ....82 D8
Milner App CR3 ....101 A6
Milner Cl CR3 ....101 A5
Milner Dr Cobham KT11 ...73 F7
Twickenham TW2 ....16 D8
Milner Rd Caterham CR3 .101 A6
Kingston u T KT1 ....37 D6
Merton SW19 ....40 B8
Morden CR4,SM4 ....40 D4
South Norwood CR7 .....42 D6
Milnthorpe Rd W4 ....7 D8
Milnwood Rd RH12 ....217 C3
Milton Ave Carshalton SM1 59 E6
Croydon CR0 ....42 D2
Westcott RH4 ....135 D6
Milton Cl Bracknell RG12 ..27 B3
Carshalton SM1 ....59 D7
Horton SL3 ....1 A4
Milton Cres RH19 ......205 C8
Milton Ct Kingston u T KT2 .17 E4
Twickenham TW2 ....16 E5
Wokingham RG40 ....25 B7
Milton Dr Littleton TW17 ..33 E5
Wokingham RG40 ....25 B7
Milton Gdns Epsom KT18 .76 E5
Stanwell TW19 ....13 F7
Wokingham RG40 ....25 B6
Milton Grange GU12 ...106 A5
Milton Ho
12 Beckenham BR3 ....24 A1
5 Kingston u T KT2 ......18 B2
Sutton SM1 ....59 A7
Milton Lodge TW1 ....16 F8
Milton Mount RH10 ....182 D1
Milton Mount Ave RH10 202 D8
Milton Mount Fst & Mid Sch RH10 ....202 C8
Milton Rd Addlestone KT15 52 A4
Caterham CR3 ....100 D6
Crawley RH10 ....202 C7
Croydon CR0 ....42 D2
Egham TW20 ....11 F3
Hampton TW12 ....36 B8
Horsham RH12 ....217 C3
Mitcham CR4 ....21 A1
Mortlake SW14 ....7 D4
Sutton SM1 ....59 A6
Wallington SM6 ....60 D4
Walton-on-T KT12 ....54 D7
Wimbledon SW19 ....20 C2
Wokingham RG40,RG41 ....25 B6
Milton St RH4 ....135 D6
Milton Way KT23 ....94 C2
Miltoncourt La RH4 ....135 E7
Miltons Cotts GU8 .....170 F5
Miltons Cres GU7 ......150 B2
Milverton Ho SE23 ......23 E5
Milward Gdns RG12 .....26 C7
Mina Rd SW19 ....40 A8
Minard Rd SE6 ....24 E7
Minchin Cl KT22 ....95 A5
Mincing La GU24 ....49 F2
Mindelheim Ave RH19 ..186 B2
Minden Rd Cheam SM3 ...58 F8
Penge SE20 ....43 B8
Minehead Rd SW16 .....21 F3
Minehurst Rd GU16 .....85 F4
Minerva Cl TW19 ....2 A2
Minerva Rd KT1 ....37 F7
Minimax Cl TW14 ....4 A1
Mink Ct TW4 ....4 C5
Minley Cl GU14 ....84 E4
Minley Ct RH2 ....118 A2
Minley Rd
Blackwater GU17,GU14 ....84 A7
Farnborough GU14 ....84 D5
Minniedale KT5 ....37 F4
Minorca Ave GU16 ......66 E2
Minorca Rd Frimley GU16 .66 E1
Weybridge KT13 ....53 A6
Minshull Pl 24 BR3 ......24 A1
Minstead Cl RG12 ....27 F6
Minstead Gdns SW15 ....18 F8
Minstead Way KT3 ......38 E3
Minster Ave SM1 ....59 A8
Minster Ct
Camberley GU15 ....65 D7
Camberley,York Town GU15 .64 F4
Minster Dr CR0 ....61 E6
Minster Gdns KT8 ....35 F5
Minster Rd GU7 ....150 E1
Minsterley Ave TW16, TW17 ....34 E5
Minstrel Gdns KT5 ......37 F5
Mint Gdns RH4 ....136 A8
Mint La KT20 ....118 A6
Mint Rd Wallington SM6 ..60 B6
Woodmansterne SM7 .....78 C3
Mint St GU7 ....150 D4
Mint The GU7 ....150 D4
Mint Wlk Croydon CR0,CR9 61 C7
Knaphill GU21 ....68 E2
Warlingham CR6 ....81 D2
Miranda Wlk RH11 .....200 E4
Mirfield Ct SE20 ....43 A7
Misbrooks Green Rd RH5 ....178 E8
Missenden Cl TW14 .....14 F7
Missenden Gdns SM4 ...40 C3
Mission Sq 18 TW8 ....6 E8
Mistletoe Cl CR0 ....43 D1
Mistley Ct 6 KT18 ......76 D6
Misty's Field KT12 ......35 C1
Mitcham Garden Village CR4 ....41 A4
Mitcham Ind Est CR4 ....41 A8
Mitcham Junc CR4 ......41 A5
Mitcham La SW16 ....21 C3
Mitcham Pk CR4 ....40 F5
Mitcham Rd
Camberley GU15 ....47 A1
Thornton Heath CR0,CR9 ..41 F3
Upper Tooting SW17 ......20 F3
Mitcham Vale High Sch (Rowan Rd Site) SW16 .41 C7
Mitchell Gdns RH13 ....215 E3
Mitchell's Row GU4 ....130 E2
Mitchells Cl GU4 ....130 E3
Mitchells Cotts GU4 ....131 E1
Mitchells Rd RH10 .....201 F6
Mitchley Ave CR2,CR8 ...80 D6
Mitchley Gr CR2 ....81 A6
Mitchley Hill CR2 ....80 F6
Mitchley View CR2 ....81 A6
Mitford Cl KT9 ....56 C4
Mitford Wlk 10 RH11 ...201 A3
Mitre Cl Shepperton TW17 .34 D3
Sutton SM2 ....59 D3
Mixbury Gr KT13 ....53 D4
Mixnams La KT16 ....33 A6
Mizen Cl KT11 ....73 D5
Mizen Way KT11 ....73 D4
Moat Ct Ashstead KT21 ...75 E2
Ottershaw KT16 ....51 C4
Moat Rd RH19 ....185 E2
Moat Side TW13 ....15 C4
Moat The KT3 ....38 E8
Moat Wlk RH10 ....202 C7
Moated Farm Dr KT15 ...52 C3
Moats La RH1 ....140 F3
Moberly Rd SW4 ....21 D8
Model Cotts Mortlake SW14 7 C4
Pirbright GU24 ....87 D6
Moffat Ct
Upper Tooting SW17 ......20 E4
Wimbledon SW19 ....20 A3
Moffat Rd
South Norwood CR7 ......42 D7
Upper Tooting SW17 ......20 F4
Moffatts Cl GU47 ....64 A8
Mogador Cotts KT20 ...117 D7
Mogador Rd KT20 ......117 E7
Mogden La TW7 ....5 F2
Moir Cl CR2 ....62 A2
Moira Ct SW17 ....21 A6
Mole Abbey Gdns KT8 ...36 B6
Mole Bsns Pk KT22 ......95 A6
Mole Cl Crawley RH11 ...201 B8
Farnborough GU14 ....84 D6
Mole Ct KT19 ....57 C6
Mole Ho KT12 ....54 E5
Mole Rd Fetcham KT22 ...94 D6
Hersham KT12 ....54 D5
Mole St RH5 ....177 B5
Mole Valley Pl KT21 .....95 D8
Molember Ct KT7 ....36 E5
Molember Rd KT8 ....36 E4
Moles Cl RG40 ....25 D5
Moles Hill KT22 ....74 D8
Molesey Ave KT12,KT8 ...35 F4
Molesey Cl KT12 ....54 E6
Molesey Dr SM3 ....58 E7
Molesey Hospl KT8 .....36 A4
Molesey Park Ave KT8 ...36 B4
Molesey Park Cl KT8 ....36 C4
Molesey Park Rd KT8 ...36 C4
Molesey Rd
East Molesey KT12 ....35 E2
Hersham KT12 ....54 D5
Molesham Cl KT8 ....36 B6
Molesham Way KT8 .....36 B6
Molesley Rd
Hersham KT12 ....54 E8
Walton-on-T KT12 ....54 E8
Molesworth Rd KT11 ....73 A6
Moliner Ct 4 BR3 ....24 A1
Molins Ct 4 RH11 ......201 A3
Mollie Davis Ct SE19 ...22 F2
Mollison Dr SM6 ....60 E3
Molloy Ct GU21 ....70 A3
Molly Huggins Cl SW12 ..21 C8
Molly Millar Bridge RG41 25 B4
Molly Millar's La RG41 ..25 A4
Molyneux Dr SW17 ......21 B4
Molyneux Rd
Farncombe GU7 ....150 F7
Weybridge KT13 ....53 A5
Windlesham GU20 ....48 D4
Monahan Ave CR8 ......79 F8
Monarch Cl
Coney Hall BR4 ....63 F6
Crawley RH11 ....201 A3
East Bedfont TW14 ......14 E8
Monarch Mews SW16 ...22 A3
Monarch Par CR4 ....40 F7
Monaveen Gdns KT8 ....36 B6
Mondial Way UB7 ....3 C7
Monet Ho 4 W4 ....7 E7
Money Ave CR3 ....100 E5
Money Rd CR3 ....100 D5
Monica Ct SW16 ....21 D2
Monivea Rd BR3 ....23 F1
Monk's Wlk
Farnham GU10,GU9 .....146 F8
Reigate RH2 ....118 B1
Monkey Puzzle Rdbt GU14 ....84 E3
Monkleigh Rd SM4,SW20 .39 E5
Monks Ave KT8 ....35 F4
Monks Cl Ascot SL5 .....29 B3
Farnborough GU14 ....85 C4
Monks Cres
Addlestone KT15 ....52 B5
Walton-on-T KT12 ....35 B1
Monks Ct RH2 ....118 B1
Monks Dr SL5 ....29 B3
Monks Gn KT22 ....94 D6
Monks La Limpsfield TN8 .144 E6
Rowhook RH5 ....196 F5
Monks Manor RH5 .....196 F5
Monks Orchard Rd
Beckenham BR3,CR0 ......44 A2
Croydon BR3,CR0 ....44 A1
Monks Orchard Sch CR0 .43 D4
Monks Rd Banstead SM7 ..78 A3
Virginia Water GU25 .....31 D5
Monks Way
Beckenham BR3 ....44 A3
Harmondsworth UB7 ......2 E8
Staines TW18 ....13 D1
Monks Wlk SL5 ....29 B3
Monks' Well GU10 .....147 C8
Monksdene Gdns SM1 ...59 B7
Monksfield RH10 ......201 F7
Monkshanger GU9 .....125 E2
Monkshood Cl RG40 .....25 E7
Monkswell La CR5 ......98 B2
Monkton La GU9 ....125 E5
Monkton Pk GU9 ....125 F4
Monmouth Ave KT1 .....17 C1

Monmouth Cl CR4,SW16 .41 E5
Mono La TW13 .15 B6
Monro Dr GU2 .109 B4
Monro Pl KT19 .57 A2
Monroe Dr SW14 .7 B2
Mons Cl GU11 .105 E7
Mons Wlk TW20 .12 C3
Monsell Gdns TW18 .12 E3
Monson Rd RH1 .118 F4
Montacute Cl GU14 .85 D4
Montacute Rd
Forest Hill SE23,SE6 .23 F8
Morden SM4 .40 D3
New Addington CR0 .63 C2
Montagu Gdns SM6 .60 C6
Montague Ave CR2 .80 E7
Montague Cl
Camberley GU15 .65 B5
Lightwater GU18 .48 A1
Walton-on-T KT12 .35 A2
Wokingham RG40 .25 E7
Montague Dr CR3 .100 C5
Montague House Coll RG40 .25 C6
Montague Rd
Hounslow TW3 .5 B4
Merton SW19 .20 B1
Richmond TW10 .6 E1
Thornton Heath CR0 .42 B1
Montague Terr 7 BR2 .44 F5
Montana Cl CR2 .61 D1
Montana Gdns
2 Beckenham SE6 .23 F3
7 Sutton SM1 .59 C5
Montana Rd
Upper Tooting SW17 .21 A5
Wimbledon SW20 .39 C8
Montem Rd
Forest Hill SE23 .23 F8
New Malden KT3 .38 E5
Montford Rd TW16 .35 A5
Montfort Pl SW19 .19 D7
Montfort Rise RH1 .139 F1
Montgomerie Dr GU2 .109 A6
Montgomery Ave KT10 .55 E8
Montgomery Cl
Mitcham CR4 .41 E5
Sandhurst GU47 .64 B8
Montgomery Ct
Chiswick W4 .7 C8
Leatherhead KT22 .95 C7
Montgomery Ho 5 SW14 .7 D4
Montgomery Rd
Farnborough GU14 .84 F3
2 Woking GU22 .69 E1
Montpelier Ct 10 BR2 .44 F5
Montpelier Rd
Purley CR2,CR8 .61 B1
South Croydon CR2,CR8 .61 B1
Sutton SM1 .59 C6
Montpelier Row TW1 .17 C8
Montrave Rd SE20 .23 C1
Montrell Rd SW2 .21 E7
Montreux Ct RH11 .201 B6
Montrose Ave TW2 .16 B8
Montrose Cl
Ashford TW15 .14 C3
Frimley GU16 .65 E2
Montrose Ct SE6 .24 F6
Montrose Gdns
Mitcham CR4 .40 F7
Oxshott KT22 .74 D7
Sutton SM1 .59 B8
Montrose Rd TW14 .3 D1
Montrose Way SE23 .23 D7
Montrose Wlk KT13 .53 B7
Montrouge Cres KT17 .77 C3
Montserrat Cl SE19 .22 D3
Montway Hts SW19 .20 B1
Monument Bridge Ind Est E GU21 .70 B4
Monument Bridge Ind Est W GU21 .70 A4
Monument Bsns Ctr GU21 .70 B4
Monument Gn KT13 .53 B6
Monument Hill KT13 .53 B6
Monument Rd
Sheerwater GU21 .70 B4
Weybridge KT13 .53 B7
Monument Way E GU21 .70 B4
Monument Way W GU21 .70 A4
Moon Ct KT22 .94 D6
Moon's La RH7 .186 E8
Moons Hill GU10 .146 C2
Moons La RH13 .217 E1
Moonsgate RH13 .217 E1
Moor Cl GU47 .45 E1
Moor House Sch RH8 .122 F3
Moor La Bracknell RG12 .26 C6
Chessington KT9 .56 E5
Harmondsworth UB7 .2 C8
Lingfield RH7,TN8 .165 D3
Staines TW18 .12 D6
Woking GU22 .89 F5
Moor Lane Jun Sch KT9 .56 F5
Moor Mead Rd TW1 .6 A1
Moor Park Cres RH11 .200 D5
Moor Park Gdns KT2 .18 E1
Moor Park Ho RG12 .26 E3
Moor Park La GU10,GU9 126 A2
Moor Park Way GU9 .125 F2
Moor Pk RH6 .161 B2
Moor Pl
East Grinstead RH19 .185 D2
Windlesham GU20 .48 B5
Moor Rd
Farnborough GU14 .85 A8
Moor Rd *continued*
Frimley GU16 .85 F8
Haslemere GU27 .207 C5
Moorcroft RH9 .121 C3
Moorcroft Cl RH11 .201 B7
Moorcroft Rd SW16 .21 E5
Moordale Ave RG42 .26 E8
Moore Cl Addlestone KT15 .52 B5
Mitcham CR4 .41 B7
Mortlake SW14 .7 C4
Wallington SM6 .60 E3
Ash GU10 .126 F8
Moore Ct RH12 .217 A1
Moore Grove Cres TW20 .11 F1
Moore Ho 1 SE27 .22 C4
Moore Rd Pirbright GU24 .87 B6
South Norwood SE19 .22 C2
Moore Way SM2 .59 A2
Moore's Rd RH4,RH5 .136 B8
Mooreland Rd 3 BR1 .24 F1
Moores Gn RG40 .25 E8
Moorfield
Haslemere GU27 .207 F5
South Holmwood RH5 .157 D7
Moorfield Ctr The GU1 .109 D5
Moorfield Rd
Chessington KT9 .56 E5
Guildford GU1 .109 E5
Moorfields Cl TW18 .32 E8
Moorfields Ct 6 SW16 .21 C4
Moorhayes Dr TW18 .33 C6
Moorhead Rd RH12 .218 B5
Moorholme GU22 .89 E8
Moorhouse Rd RH8 .123 F5
Moorhurst La RH5 .157 B4
Moorings The
East Grinstead RH19 .185 A3
Great Bookham KT23 .94 A2
Hindhead GU26 .188 E3
Moorland Cl
Crawley RH10 .202 C3
Twickenham TW2 .16 A8
Moorland Rd UB7 .2 C8
Moorlands KT12 .54 A7
Moorlands Cl GU26 .188 E4
Moorlands Pl GU15 .65 B5
Moorlands Rd GU15 .65 B4
Moorlands The GU22 .89 F6
Moormead Dr KT19 .57 E5
Moormede Cres TW18 .12 F4
Moors La GU8 .148 C3
Moors The GU10 .126 F7
Moorside Cl GU14 .65 A1
Moorside Rd BR1 .24 F4
Moorsom Way CR5 .79 D2
Moray Ave GU47 .64 D7
Moray Ho 11 KT6 .37 E4
Mordaunt Dr RG45 .45 B3
Morden Cl Bracknell RG12 .27 F5
Burgh Heath KT20 .97 D7
Morden Court Par SM4 .40 A5
Morden Ct SM4 .40 B5
Morden Gdns CR4 .40 D5
Morden Hall Park★ SW19 .40 C6
Morden Hall Rd SM4, SW19 .40 C5
Morden Ho SM4 .40 A5
Morden Park Sch Sports Ctr SM4 .39 F4
Morden Prim Sch SM4 .40 A4
Morden Rd Merton SW19 .40 B7
Mitcham CR4,SM4,SW19 .40 D5
Morden South Sta SM4 .40 A4
Morden Sta SW19 .40 B6
Morden Way SM3 .40 A2
Mordred Rd SE6 .24 E6
More Circ GU7 .150 E7
More Cl CR8 .80 A8
More House Sch GU10 .146 C2
More La KT10 .55 B7
More Rd GU7 .150 E7
Morecambe Cl RH11 .200 F4
Morecoombe Cl KT2 .18 B1
Morecote Cl GU4 .130 E2
Moreland Ave SL3 .1 C7
Moreland Cl SL3 .1 C7
Morella Cl GU25 .31 D5
Morella Rd SW11,SW12 .20 F8
Moremead Rd SE6 .24 A4
Morena St SE6 .24 B8
Moresby Ave KT5 .38 B2
Moreton Ave TW7 .5 E6
Moreton Cl GU10 .167 E1
Moreton Ho SW17 .20 D4
Moreton Rd
North Cheam KT4 .58 B8
South Croydon CR2 .61 D5
Morgan Ct TW15 .14 B3
Moring Rd SW17 .21 A4
Morkyns Wlk SE21 .22 E5
Morland Ave CR0 .42 E1
Morland Cl Hampton TW12 15 F3
Mitcham CR4 .40 E6
Morland Rd
Aldershot GU11 .126 C6
Croydon CR0 .42 F2
Penge SE20 .23 D2
Sutton SM1 .59 C5
Morland's Rd GU11 .105 D5
Morley Ct Bromley BR3 .44 D8
Fetcham KT22 .94 D6
Hayes BR2 .44 F5
Sunningdale SL5 .29 F3
Morley Ho SW2 .21 E8
Morley Rd Cheam SM3 .39 F1
Farnham GU9 .125 D1
South Croydon CR2 .61 F1
Morley Rd *continued*
Twickenham TW1 .6 D1
Morningside Rd KT4 .58 C8
Mornington Cl TN16 .83 D2
Mornington Cres TW5 .4 B6
Mornington Rd TW15 .14 C3
Mornington Wlk TW10 .17 C4
Morrell Ave
Horsham RH12 .217 F6
Horsham RH12 .218 A6
Morris Cl BR3,CR0 .43 E4
Morris Gdns SW18 .20 A8
Morris Rd
Farnborough GU14 .105 D8
Isleworth TW7 .5 F4
South Nutfield RH1 .140 E7
Morrish Rd SW2 .21 E8
Morrison Ct 5 RH11 .201 B1
Morrison Ho SW2 .22 A7
Morriss Ct 3 RH2 .118 F1
Morston Cl KT20 .97 B7
Mortaine Rd TW15 .13 D5
Mortimer Cl SW16 .21 D6
Mortimer Cres KT4 .57 D7
Mortimer Lodge 11 SW19 .19 E7
Mortimer Rd
Biggin Hill TN16 .83 C7
Capel RH5 .178 D6
Mitcham CR4 .40 F8
Mortlake Cl CR0 .60 E7
Mortlake Dr CR4 .40 E8
Mortlake High St SW14 .7 D4
Mortlake Rd SW14,TW9 .7 A6
Mortlake Sta SW14 .7 C4
Morton KT20 .97 D6
Morton Cl Frimley GU16 .85 F7
Wallington SM6 .60 F3
Woking GU21 .69 D4
Morton Gdns SM6 .60 C5
Morton Ho SE27 .22 D3
Morton Rd
East Grinstead RH19 .205 E7
Morden CR4,SM4 .40 D4
Woking GU21 .69 D4
Morval Cl GU14 .84 E4
Morven Rd SW17 .20 F5
Moselle Cl GU14 .84 D5
Moselle Rd TN16 .83 F1
Mosford Cl RH6 .160 F5
Mospey Cres KT17 .76 F4
Mosquito Way GU14 .84 F2
Moss Gdns Feltham TW13 .15 A6
South Croydon CR2 .62 D3
Moss La GU7 .150 D4
Moss Lane Sch GU7 .150 D4
Mossfield KT11 .73 A6
Mosslea Rd Kenley CR3 .80 F2
Penge SE20 .23 C2
Mossville Gdns SM4,SW20 39 F5
Mostyn Rd SW19 .39 F7
Mostyn Terr RH1 .140 A8
Moth Cl SM6 .60 E3
Motspur Park Sta KT3 .39 B4
Motspur Pk KT3 .39 A3
Motts Hill La KT20 .97 A4
Mouchotte Cl TN16 .83 C7
Moulton Ave TW3,TW5 .4 F5
Mount Adon Pk SE21, SE22 .23 A8
Mount Angelus Rd SW15 18 F8
Mount Ararat Rd TW10 .6 E2
Mount Arlington 3 BR2 .44 E7
Mount Ash Rd SE26 .23 B5
Mount Ave CR3 .100 C3
Mount Cl Crawley RH10 .202 D7
Ewhurst GU6 .175 E5
Fetcham KT22 .94 F4
Kenley CR8 .80 D3
Wallington SM5 .60 A2
Woking GU22 .89 C6
Mount Cl The GU25 .31 D3
Mount Ct Guildford GU2 .130 C7
6 Kingston u T KT2 .18 B1
West Norwood SE27 .22 B5
West Wickham BR4 .63 E8
Mount Dr The RH2 .118 D3
Mount Ephraim La SW16 21 D5
Mount Ephraim Rd SW16 21 D5
Mount Felix KT12 .34 F2
Mount Gdns SE26 .23 B5
Mount Hermon Cl GU22 .69 E1
Mount Hermon Rd GU22 .69 E1
Mount La Bracknell RG12 .27 C7
Turners Hill RH10 .204 A4
Mount Lee TW20 .11 F3
Mount Mews TW12 .36 B8
Mount Nod Rd SW16,SW2 21 F5
Mount Noddy RH10 .203 C2
Mount Park Ave CR2 .61 B2
Mount Pk SM5 .60 A2
Mount Pl GU1 .130 C7
Mount Pleasant
Biggin Hill TN16 .83 D2
Bracknell RG12 .27 C6
Effingham KT24 .113 E7
Ewell KT17 .57 F1
Farnham GU9 .125 A1
Guildford GU2 .130 C7
Sandhurst GU47 .45 A1
West Horsley KT24 .112 B6
West Norwood SE27 .22 C4
Weybridge KT13 .53 A7
Wokingham RG41 .25 A6
Mount Pleasant Cl GU18 .48 A1
Mount Pleasant Cotts TW20 .11 D2
Mount Pleasant Rd
Aldershot GU12 .105 C2
Caterham CR3 .101 A4
Kingston u T KT3 .38 C6
Lingfield RH7 .164 C4
Mount Prim Sch The KT3 38 C6
Mount Rd Chessington KT9 56 F5
Chobham GU24 .69 B7
Cranleigh GU6 .174 E2
Feltham TW13 .15 E5
Kingston u T KT3 .38 D6
Mitcham CR4 .40 E7
South Norwood SE19 .22 D2
Wimbledon SW18,SW19 .20 B6
Woking GU22 .89 B6
Mount Rise
Forest Hill SE23 .23 C6
Reigate RH1 .139 D7
Mount St RH4 .136 A7
Mount The
Cranleigh GU6 .174 E2
Esher KT10 .55 A4
Ewell KT17 .57 F1
Ewhurst GU6 .175 E5
Fetcham KT22 .94 E4
Grayswood GU27 .189 F1
Guildford GU2 .130 C7
Headley Down GU35 .187 A6
Lower Kingswood KT20 .97 F1
New Malden KT3 .38 F6
North Cheam KT4 .58 B6
Oatlands Park KT13 .53 E8
Rusper RH1,RH12 .180 B1
Rusper RH12 .200 B8
Wallington CR5 .79 B5
Warlingham CR6 .101 A8
Wentworth GU25 .31 D3
Witley GU8 .170 F3
Woking GU21,GU22 .69 D1
Mount View GU11 .105 A1
Mount View Rd KT10 .56 B3
Mount Villas SE27 .22 B5
Mount Way SM5 .60 A2
Mountacre Cl SE26 .23 A4
Mountbatten Cl
Crawley RH11 .201 C2
6 West Norwood SE19 .22 E3
Mountbatten Ct 15 GU11 .105 A2
Mountbatten Gdns BR3 .43 E5
Mountbatten Rise GU47 .45 A1
Mountcombe Cl KT6 .37 E2
Mountcombe Ho SW19 .20 D3
Mountearl Gdns SW16, SW2 .21 F5
Mountfield Cl SE6 .24 D8
Mounthurst Rd BR2 .44 F2
Mounts Hill SL4 .9 C3
Mountsfield Cl TW19 .2 A2
Mountside Caterham CR3 100 F3
Guildford GU2 .130 C7
Mountside Pl 1 GU22 .69 F1
Mountview 5 SW16 .21 F5
Mountview Dr RH1 .139 E7
Mountwood KT8 .36 B6
Mountwood Cl CR2 .62 B1
Moushill La GU8 .170 E8
Mowat Ct KT4 .57 F8
Mowatt Rd GU26 .188 D2
Mowbray Ave KT14 .71 E6
Mowbray Cres TW20 .12 A3
Mowbray Ct SE19 .42 F8
Mowbray Dr RH11 .200 F4
Mowbray Gdns RH4 .115 B1
Mowbray Rd
Richmond TW10 .17 C5
South Norwood SE19 .42 F8
Mower Cl RG40 .25 F7
Mower Pl GU6 .174 E4
Moyne Ct 3 GU21 .68 F1
Moyne Rd RH11 .201 C2
Moys Cl CR0 .41 E3
Moys Ho RH1 .118 F3
Moyser Rd SW16,SW17 .21 B3
Muchelney Rd SM4 .40 C3
Muckhatch La TW20 .32 B7
Mudie Ho 8 SW2 .21 E8
Muggeridge Cl CR2 .61 D5
Muggeridge's Hill RH12, RH5 .198 E8
Muirdown Ave SW14 .7 D3
Muirfield SL5 .30 A1
Muirfield Cl RH11 .200 D5
Muirfield Ho RG12 .26 E3
Muirfield Rd GU21 .69 A1
Muirkirk Rd SE6 .24 C7
Mulberries The GU9 .125 F4
Mulberry Ave TW19 .13 E7
Mulberry Bsns Pk RG41 .25 A4
Mulberry Cl Ash GU12 .106 A4
Crowthorne RG45 .45 C4
Horsham RH12 .217 C5
1 Sandhurst GU47 .64 D8
Streatham SW16 .21 C4
Weybridge KT13 .53 B7
Woking GU21 .69 E5
Mulberry Cres TW8 .6 C7
Mulberry Ct
Ashstead KT21 .75 D1
1 Bracknell RG12 .27 F4
Guildford GU4 .110 D3
4 Surbiton KT6 .37 D2
Twickenham TW1 .16 F5
Wokingham RG40 .25 C6
Mulberry Gate SM7 .77 F3
Mulberry La CR0 .42 F1
Mulberry Mews 2 SM6 .60 C4
Mulberry Rd RH11 .181 B1
Mulberry The CR3 .80 F2
Mulberry Trees TW17 .34 D2
Mulgrave Ct SM2 .59 B4
Mulgrave Hall SM2 .59 B4
Mulgrave Manor SM2 .59 B4
Mulgrave Rd
Croydon CR0,CR9 .61 D7
Frimley GU16 .65 F2
Sutton SM2 .59 B4
Mulgrave Way GU21 .68 E1
Mulholland Cl CR4 .41 B7
Mullards Cl CR4 .40 F1
Mullberry Pl RH5 .158 C2
Mullein Wlk RH11 .201 A2
Mullens Rd TW20 .12 C3
Mullins Path SW14 .7 D4
Mulroy Dr GU15 .66 A6
Multon Rd SW18 .20 D8
Muncaster Cl TW15 .14 A4
Muncaster Rd TW15 .14 B3
Muncies Mews SE6 .24 C6
Munday's Boro GU3 .128 A4
Munday's Boro Rd GU3 .128 B4
Munnings Dr GU47 .64 E6
Munnings Gdns TW7 .5 D2
Munro Way GU14 .105 D8
Munroe Ho RH2 .139 A6
Munslow Gdns SM1 .59 D6
Munstead Ct 16 SM2 .59 C3
Munstead Heath Rd GU8 .151 C3
Munstead Pk GU8 .151 C2
Munstead View GU3 .130 C4
Munstead View Rd GU5 151 D5
Munster Ave TW4 .4 E2
Munster Ct TW11 .17 C2
Munster Rd TW11 .17 C2
Murdoch Cl TW18 .13 A3
Murdoch Rd RG40 .25 D5
Murfett Cl SW19 .19 E6
Murray Ave TW3 .5 B2
Murray Ct Ascot SL5 .29 C3
Crawley RH11 .201 A1
Horsham RH13 .218 B4
Murray Gn GU21 .70 C5
Murray Ho
Ottershaw KT16 .51 D4
Wokingham RG41 .25 A6
Murray Rd
Farnborough GU14 .84 F3
Ottershaw KT15,KT16 .51 D5
Richmond TW10 .17 C6
Wimbledon SW19 .19 D2
Wokingham RG41 .25 A6
Murray's La KT14 .71 E5
Murrell Rd GU12 .106 A3
Murrellhill La RG42 .26 C8
Murrells La GU15 .65 B3
Murrells Wlk KT23 .94 A3
Murreys The KT21 .75 D1
Muschamp Prim Sch SM5 .59 E8
Muschamp Rd SM1,SM5 .59 E8
Museum Hill GU27 .208 D6
Museum of Richmond★ TW10 .6 D2
Museum of Rugby★ TW1 .5 E1
Musgrave Ave RH19 .205 E8
Musgrave Rd TW7 .5 F6
Mushroom Castle La RG42 8 B2
Musical Mus The★ TW8 .6 E8
Musquash Way TW4 .4 C5
Mustard Mill Rd TW18 .12 F4
Mutton Hill RH7 .186 B7
Mutton Oaks RG12 .26 D8
Muybridge Rd KT3 .38 C7
Mychell Ho 8 SW19 .20 C1
Mychett Prim Sch GU16 .85 F4
Myers Way GU16 .66 D2
Mylis Cl SE26 .23 B4
Mylne Sq RG40 .25 D6
Mylor Cl GU21 .69 E5
Mynn's Cl KT18 .76 B5
Mynterne Ct 16 SW19 .19 D7
Mynthurst Farm Cotts RH2 .159 B7
Myrna Cl SW19 .20 E1
Myrtle Ave TW14 .3 E2
Myrtle Cl Lightwater GU18 .67 B8
Poyle SL3 .1 E6
Myrtle Dr GU17 .64 D5
Myrtle Gr KT3 .38 C7
Myrtle Rd Croydon CR0 .63 A7
Dorking RH4 .136 A8
Hampton TW12 .16 C2
Hounslow TW3 .5 C5
Sutton SM1 .59 C5
Mytchett Heath GU16 .86 A3
Mytchett Lake Rd GU16 .86 A1
Mytchett Place Rd GU12, GU16 .86 C1
Mytchett Rd GU12,GU16 .85 F3
Myton Rd SE21 .22 D5

N

Naafi Rdbt GU11 .105 B2
Nadine Ct SM6 .60 C2
Nailsworth Cres RH1 .119 D6
Nairn Cl GU16 .65 E2
Nairn Ct
3 Wallington SM6 .60 C4
Wimbledon SW19 .20 B2
Naldrett Cl RH12 .217 F4

Naldretts La RH12 214 D5
Nallhead Rd TW13 15 C3
Namba Roy Cl SW16 21 F4
Namton Dr CR7,SW16 41 F5
Nanhurst Park Ho GU6 173 E2
Napier Cl
Crowthorne RG45 45 D5
Farnborough GU11 105 E7
Napier Ct Caterham CR3 100 E5
10 Croydon CR0 61 F8
1 Surbiton KT6 37 D2
Woking GU21 69 E3
Napier Dr GU15 66 A8
Napier Gdns GU1 110 B2
Napier La GU12 106 A4
Napier Lodge TW15 14 D2
Napier Rd Ashford TW15 14 D1
Crowthorne RG45 45 C4
Croydon SE25 43 B5
Harmondsworth TW6 2 D6
Isleworth TW7 6 A3
South Croydon CR2 61 D3
Napier Way RH10 182 A1
Napier Wlk TW15 14 D1
Napoleon Ave GU14 85 B6
Napoleon Rd TW1 17 B8
Napper Cl SL5 28 D7
Napper Pl GU6 174 E1
Narrow La CR6 101 B8
Naseby RG12 27 B1
Naseby Cl TW7 5 E6
Naseby Rd SE19 22 D2
Nash Cl Carshalton SM1 59 D7
Farnborough GU14 84 F4
Nash Dr 6 RH1 119 A3
Nash Gdns
North Ascot SL5 28 E7
Redhill RH1 118 F3
Nash Rd RH10 201 E3
Nassau Rd SW13 7 F6
Nasturtium Dr GU24 68 A4
Natal Rd
South Norwood CR7 42 D6
Streatham SW16 21 D2
Natalie Cl TW14 14 D8
Natalie Mews TW2 16 D5
National Physical Laboratory
TW11 16 E2
National Wks TW4 4 F4
Nayland Ho SE6 24 C4
Neald Ct SW19 20 A2
Neale Cl RH19 185 B3
Neath Gdns SM4 40 C3
Neb La RH8 122 D4
Needles Bank RH9 121 B4
Needles Cl RH12 217 B1
Neelem Ct 4 GU14 85 C1
Neil Cl TW15 14 C3
Neil Wates Cres 18 SW2 22 A7
Nelgarde Rd SE6 24 A8
Nell Ball RH14 211 E2
Nell Gwynn Ave TW17 34 D3
Nell Gwynne Ave SL5 29 D5
Nell Gwynne Cl Ascot SL5 29 D5
Epsom KT19 76 A8
Nello James Gdns SE27 22 D4
Nelson Cl
Aldershot GU12 105 D1
Biggin Hill TN16 83 E2
Bracknell RG12 27 E7
Crawley RH10 202 C5
East Bedfont TW14 14 F7
Heath End GU9 125 D8
Thornton Heath CR0 42 B1
Walton-on-T KT12 35 B1
Nelson Ct Carshalton SM5 59 F7
Chertsey KT16 33 A1
Nelson Gdns
Guildford GU1 110 A2
Twickenham TW3,TW4 5 A1
Nelson Grove Rd SW19 40 C8
Nelson Ho 19 GU11 105 A2
Nelson Hospl SW20 39 F7
Nelson Prim Sch TW2 5 B1
Nelson Rd Ashford TW15 13 E3
Caterham CR3 100 D4
Harmondsworth TW6 2 F6
Heath End GU9 125 D8
Horsham RH12 217 C3
Merton SW19 20 C1
New Malden KT3 38 D4
Twickenham TW2 16 B8
Nelson St 3 GU11 105 A2
Nelson Trad Est SW19 40 B8
Nelson Way GU15 64 F4
Nelson Wlk KT19 57 A2
Nene Gdns TW13 15 F6
Nene Rd TW6,UB7 3 B6
Nepean St 4 SW15 19 A8
Neptune Cl RH11 200 E4
Neptune Ct RH12 217 B4
Neptune Rd TW6 3 C6
Nero Ct TW8 6 D7
Nesbit Ct RH11 200 E3
Nesbitt Sq SE19 22 E1
NESCOT Epsom's Coll of FE &
HE KT17 77 A8
Nether Mount GU2 130 B7
Netheravon Rd S 2 W4 7 F8
Netherby Pk KT13 53 E5
Netherby Rd SE23 23 C8
Nethercote Ave GU21 68 F2
Netherfield BR2 44 D6
Netherfield Rd SW17 21 A5
Netherlands Ct 15 SM2 59 C4
Netherlands The CR5 99 C8
Netherleigh Pk RH1 140 E6
Nethern Court Rd CR3 102 A4
Netherne Dr CR5 99 C5
Netherne La Hooley CR5 99 C6
Hooley CR5 99 C6
Netherton RG12 27 A5
Netherton Rd TW1 6 B2
Netherwood RH11 201 B4
Netherwood Ct GU7 150 E5
Netley Cl Cheam SM3 58 D5
Gomshall GU5 133 C5
New Addington CR0 63 C3
Netley Dr KT12 35 F2
Netley Gdns SM4 40 C2
Netley Rd Brentford TW8 6 E8
Morden SM4 40 C2
Netley Rd (W) TW6 3 D6
Netley St GU14 105 C8
Nettlecombe RG12 27 D3
Nettlecombe Cl SM2 59 B2
Nettlefold Pl SE27 22 B5
Nettles Terr 3 GU1 109 D1
Nettlestead Cl BR3 23 F1
Nettleton Rd TW6 3 B6
Nettlewood Rd SW16 21 D1
Neuchatel Rd SE6 23 F6
Neuman Cres RG12 27 A3
Nevada Cl
Farnborough GU14 84 D3
Kingston u T KT3 38 C5
Nevelle Cl RG42 26 D8
Nevile Cl RH11 201 A3
Neville Ave KT3 38 D8
Neville Cl Banstead SM7 78 B5
Esher KT10 54 F4
Hounslow TW3 5 B5
Neville Ct 10 SW12 21 C8
Neville Duke Rd GU14 84 F8
Neville Rd Croydon CR0 42 D2
Kingston u T KT1 38 A7
Richmond TW10 17 C6
Neville Wlk SM5 40 E2
Nevis Rd SW17 21 A6
New Acres Cvn Pk GU6 193 C8
New Barn Cl SM6 60 F4
New Barn La Kenley CR3 80 E3
Wallis Wood RH5 177 A3
New Barns Ave CR4 41 D5
New Battlebridge La
RH1 119 B5
New Beckenham Sta BR3 23 F1
New Belmont Ho 4
SE23 23 C7
New Berry La KT12 54 D5
New Chapel Sq TW13 15 B7
New Church Ct 4 SE19 23 A1
New Cl Feltham TW13 15 E3
Mitcham SW19 40 C6
New Colebrooke Ct SM5 60 A3
New Coppice GU21 88 E8
New Cotts
Betchworth RH3 116 D4
Pirbright GU24 87 D5
Sidlow RH2 138 F1
Turners Hill RH10 204 A4
New Cross Rd GU2 109 B3
New Cswy RH2 139 C6
New Ct KT15 52 C7
New Dawn Cl GU14 84 D3
New England Trad Est
RH8 123 A2
New Epsom & Ewell Cottage
Hospl The KT19 75 E8
New Farthingdale RH7 186 B8
New Forest Cotts GU22 89 F7
New Forest Ride RG12 27 F4
New Green Pl SE19 22 E2
New Haw Com Jun Sch
KT15 52 A1
New Haw Rd KT15 52 C4
New Heston Rd TW5 4 F7
New House Farm La
GU3 108 C2
New House La RH1 161 E8
New Inn La GU4 110 B4
New Kelvin Ave TW11 16 E2
New La GU22,GU4 89 F3
New Life Sch RH19 185 D2
New Lodge Dr RH8 122 F7
New Malden Sta KT3 38 E6
New Mdw SL5 28 D8
New Mile Rd SL5 29 C7
New Monument Sch
GU22 70 C4
New Moorhead Dr
RH12 218 C6
New North Rd RH2 138 F6
New Par TW15 13 F4
New Park Ct 26 SW2 21 E8
New Park Par 14 SW2 21 E8
New Park Rd
Ashford TW15 14 C3
Cranleigh GU6 174 F2
Streatham SW2 21 E8
Streatham, Streatham Hill
SW12,SW2 21 E7
New Pl CR0 63 A4
New Place Gdns RH7 164 E4
New Pond Rd GU3,GU7 129 E1
New Poplars The GU12 106 A1
New Rd Albury GU5 132 D3
Bagshot GU19 47 F3
Blackwater GU17 64 E4
Bracknell RG12 27 D7
Brentford TW8 6 D8
Carshalton CR4 41 A1
Chilworth GU4 131 B3
New Rd *continued*
Crowthorne RG45 45 C5
East Bedfont TW14 3 D1
East Clandon GU4 111 E4
East Molesey KT8 36 A6
Egham TW18 12 C4
Esher KT10 55 C6
Feltham TW13 15 E3
Feltham TW14 15 B7
Forest Green RH5 176 E6
Gomshall GU5 133 C4
Harlington TW6,UB7 3 C7
Haslemere GU27 207 F5
Hounslow TW3 5 B3
Hydestile GU8 171 F5
Kingston u T KT2 18 A1
Limpsfield RH8 123 B5
Littleton TW17 34 B6
Milford GU8 170 E8
North Ascot SL5 8 F1
Oxshott KT22 74 F8
Richmond TW10 17 C4
Sandhurst GU47 64 A8
Smallfield RH6 162 B3
Tadworth KT20 97 C4
Tandridge RH8 143 A7
Tongham GU10 126 F6
Weybridge KT13 53 C5
Windlesham GU19,GU20 48 A4
Wonersh GU5 152 B8
Wormley GU8 191 A8
New Rd Units TW3 5 B3
New Residences KT16 51 C7
New Scotland Hill Prim Sch
GU47 45 A2
New Site KT15 52 E7
New Sq TW14 14 C7
New St Crawley RH10 202 A7
Horsham RH13 217 D2
Staines TW18 13 A4
New Town RH10 183 B3
New Victoria Hospl The
KT3 38 E8
New Way GU7 150 C4
New Wickham La TW20 12 B1
New Wokingham Rd
RG45 45 A6
New Woodlands Sch BR1 24 E4
New Zealand Ave KT12 34 F1
Newall Rd TW6 3 C6
Newark Cl Guildford GU4 110 B6
Ripley GU23 91 A6
Newark Ct KT12 35 C1
Newark La Ripley GU23 91 B6
Woking GU22 90 F8
Newark Rd Crawley RH10 201 F8
South Croydon CR2 61 D4
Windlesham GU20 48 B6
Newbolt Ave SM3 58 D5
Newborough Gn KT3 38 D5
Newborough Ho SW19 20 D1
Newbridge Cl RH12 216 C3
Newbridge Ct
Cranleigh GU6 174 B3
Upper Tooting SW17 20 C4
Newbridge Point 3
SE23 23 D5
Newbury Gdns KT19 57 F6
Newbury Rd
Crawley RH10 202 D6
Harmondsworth TW6 2 F6
Newchapel Rd
Lingfield RH7 164 B3
Newchapel RH7 163 F2
Newcome Gdns SW16 21 E4
Newcome Pl GU12 126 D7
Newcome Rd GU9 125 E6
Newdigate CE Inf Sch
RH5 158 B1
Newdigate Ho 6 KT2 18 B2
Newdigate Rd
Beare Green RH5 157 E2
Rusper RH12 199 C8
Newenham Rd KT23 94 A1
Newent Cl SM5 40 F1
Newfield Ave GU14 84 E6
Newfield Cl TW12 36 A8
Newfield Rd GU12 106 A6
Newfoundland Rd GU16 86 D8
Newgate CR0 42 C1
Newgate Cl TW13 15 E5
Newhache RH7 165 A1
Newhall Gdns KT12 54 C8
Newhaven Cres TW15 14 D3
Newhaven Rd SE25 42 D4
Newhouse 5 KT3 38 E2
Newhouse Cl KT3 38 E2
Newhouse Wlk SM4 40 C2
Newland House Sch TW1 16 F4
Newland House Sch Annex
TW1 16 F4
Newlands Ave
Thames Ditton KT7 36 E1
Woking GU22 89 F6
Newlands Cl
Hersham KT12 54 E6
Horley RH6 160 F5
Newlands Cnr GU4 132 A7
Newlands Cres
East Grinstead RH19 185 D2
Guildford GU1 130 F7
Newlands Croft SE20 23 D2
Newlands Ct
Addlestone KT15 52 B5
1 Caterham CR3 100 C6
Streatham SW16 21 E3
Newlands Dr Ash GU12 106 B4
Poyle SL3 1 E4
Newlands Est GU8 170 F5
Newlands Flats GU1 109 F2
Newlands Pk
Copthorne RH10 183 E3
Penge SE26 23 D3
Newlands Pl RH18 206 F3
Newlands Rd
Camberley GU15 65 B1
Crawley RH11 201 C5
Horsham RH12 217 C4
Thornton Heath SW16 41 E7
Newlands The
Thames Ditton KT7 36 E1
Wallington SM6 60 D3
Newlands Way KT9 56 C5
Newlands Wood CR0 62 F2
Newlyn Ho 11 SM1 59 C6
Newman Cl RH10 202 C4
Newman Rd CR0 41 F1
Newmans Ct GU9 125 A7
Newmans Pl SL5 30 B2
Newmarket Rd RH10 202 A4
Newminster Rd SM4 40 C3
Newnham Cl CR7 42 C7
Newnham Ho SE6 24 C5
Newport Jun Sch GU12 105 D1
Newport Rd
Aldershot GU12 105 D1
Harmondsworth TW6 3 A6
Newquay Rd SE6 24 C6
Newry Rd TW1 6 A2
Newsham Rd 1 GU21 68 F2
Newstead Cl GU7 150 D6
Newstead Hall RH6 161 D1
Newstead Ho CR3 101 B1
Newstead Rd SE12 24 F8
Newstead Rise CR3 101 B1
Newstead Way SW19 19 E4
Newstead Wlk SM4,SM5 40 C2
Newton Ave RH19 205 F6
Newton Rd Crawley RH10 181 F2
Farnborough GU14 85 D6
Isleworth TW7 5 F5
Merton SW19 19 E1
Purley CR8 79 C7
Newton Way GU10 126 F7
Newton Wood Rd KT21 75 F3
Newtown Ct RH13 217 E1
Newtown Rd GU47 64 B8
Nexus Pk GU12 105 F8
Nicholas Ct 7 W4 7 E7
Nicholas Gdns GU22 70 F3
Nicholas Ho SE26 23 B2
Nicholas Lodge KT10 55 A8
Nicholas Rd CR0 60 E6
Nicholass Ct 2 CR8 80 B7
Nicholes Rd TW3 5 A3
Nichols Cl KT9 56 C4
Nicholsfield RH14 212 F4
Nicholson Mews 4 KT1 37 E5
Nicholson Rd CR0 42 F1
Nicholson Wlk 3 TW20 12 A3
Nicol Cl 6 TW1 6 B1
Nicola Cl CR2 61 C4
Nicola Ct GU12 105 D2
Nicosia Rd SW18 20 E8
Niederwald Rd SE26 23 E4
Nigel Fisher Way KT9 56 D3
Nightingale Ave KT24 92 D2
Nightingale Cl
Biggin Hill TN16 83 C4
Carshalton SM5 60 A8
Chiswick W4 7 C8
Cobham KT11 73 D8
Crawley RH11 201 C8
East Grinstead RH19 205 D7
Epsom KT19 76 A8
Farnborough GU14 84 C6
Nightingale Cres
Bracknell RG12 27 D4
West Horsley KT24 92 C2
Nightingale Ct
2 Knaphill GU21 68 F1
Penge SE19 22 F2
8 Redhill RH1 119 A2
Sutton SM1 59 C5
Nightingale Dr
Mytchett GU16 86 A3
West Ewell KT19 57 B4
Nightingale Gdns GU47 64 B8
Nightingale Ind Est
RH12 217 D3
Nightingale La
Balham SW11,SW12 20 F8
Richmond TW10 17 E8
Turners Hill RH10 204 C5
Nightingale Rd
Ash GU12 106 C3
Carshalton SM5 60 A8
East Horsley KT24 92 F2
East Molesey KT8 36 B4
Esher KT10 54 F4
Farncombe GU7 150 E6
Guildford GU1 109 E1
Hampton TW12 16 A2
Horsham RH12 217 D3
Selsdon CR2 62 D1
Walton-on-T KT12 35 B2
Nightingale Shott TW20 11 F2
Nightingale Sq SW12 21 A8
Nightingale Way RH1 120 E2
Nightingales
Cranleigh GU6 174 E1
Kenley CR8 80 D4
Nightingales Cl RH13 217 F2
Nightingales The TW19 13 F7
Nightjar Cl GU10 124 D8
Nimbus Rd KT19 57 D1
Nimrod Ct RH10 182 D1
Nimrod Rd SW16,SW17 21 B3
Nine Elms Cl TW14 14 F7
Nine Mile Ride RG12,
RG40 26 F1
Nineacres Way CR5 79 E3
Ninehams Cl CR3 100 D7
Ninehams Gdns CR3 100 D7
Ninehams Rd
Caterham CR3 100 D6
Tatsfield TN16 103 D6
Nineteenth Rd CR4 41 E5
Ninfield Ct RH11 200 F2
Niton Rd TW9 7 A4
Niven Cl RH10 202 D5
Noahs Ct RH10 204 A4
Nobel Dr TW6 3 E7
Noble Cnr TW5 5 A6
Noble Ct CR4 40 D7
Noble St KT12 54 C7
Nobles Way TW20 11 E2
Noel Ct TW4 4 F4
Noel Terr SE23 23 C6
Noke Dr RH1 119 A2
Nonsuch Court Ave KT17 58 B1
Nonsuch Ct SM3 58 E4
Nonsuch High Sch for Girls
SM3 58 D3
Nonsuch Ind Est KT17 76 E8
Nonsuch Prim Sch KT17 58 B5
Nonsuch Wlk SM2 58 D1
Noons Corner Rd RH5 156 A8
Norbiton Ave KT1,KT2 38 A7
Norbiton Common Rd
KT1,KT3 38 B6
Norbiton Hall KT2 37 F7
Norbiton Sta KT1 38 A8
Norbury Ave Isleworth TW3 5 D3
South Norwood CR7,SW16 42 B7
Norbury Cl SW16 42 B8
Norbury Court Rd SW16 41 E7
Norbury Cres SW16 42 A7
Norbury Cross SW16 41 E6
Norbury Hill SW16 22 B1
Norbury Manor Girls High
Sch CR7 42 A8
Norbury Manor Prim Sch
SW16 41 E8
Norbury Rd Reigate RH2 117 F1
South Norwood CR7 42 C6
Norbury Rise SW16 41 E6
Norbury Sta SW16 41 F8
Norbury Trad Est SW16 41 F7
Norbury Way KT23 94 C2
Norcroft Gdns SE22 23 A8
Norcutt Rd TW2 16 E7
Noreen Ho SM1 59 A4
Norfolk Ave CR2 62 A1
Norfolk Cl Crawley RH11 200 E2
Horley RH6 161 A2
5 Twickenham TW1 6 B1
Norfolk Cotts RH1 140 E7
Norfolk Ct Dorking RH5 136 D3
Horsham RH12 218 B5
Surbiton KT5 37 F3
Norfolk Farm Cl GU22 70 D3
Norfolk Farm Rd GU22 70 D3
Norfolk Ho
2 Croydon CR0 61 D8
11 Merton SW19 20 C1
Penge SE20 43 C8
Norfolk House Rd SW16 21 D5
Norfolk La RH5 136 B1
Norfolk Mews 9 RH4 136 A7
Norfolk Rd Claygate KT10 55 E5
Dorking RH4 136 A7
Feltham TW13 15 C7
Horsham RH12 217 D2
Mitcham SW19 20 E2
South Holmwood RH5 157 C6
South Norwood CR7 42 C6
Norfolk Terr RH12 217 D2
Norgrove St SW12 21 A8
Norheads La TN16 83 B2
Norhyrst Ave SE25 42 F6
Nork Gdns SM7 77 E5
Nork Rise SM7 77 D3
Nork Way KT17,SM7 77 D4
Norlands La TW18,TW20 32 E7
Norley Vale SW15 19 A7
Norman Ave Ewell KT17 76 F7
Feltham TW13 15 F6
South Croydon CR2,CR8 61 C1
Twickenham TW1 17 C8
Norman Cl KT18 97 B8
Norman Colyer Ct KT19 57 D1
Norman Cres TW5 4 D7
Norman Ct Dulwich SE22 23 A8
Farnham GU9 125 C1
9 Hampton TW12 36 A8
Streatham SW16 22 A3
Norman Ho Feltham TW13 15 F6
Lower Halliford TW17 34 A2
Reigate RH2 138 F6
Norman Keep RG42 27 F8
Norman Rd Ashford TW15 14 D2
Merton SW19 20 C1
Sutton SM1 59 A5
Thornton Heath CR7 42 B4
Norman's Rd RH1,RH6 162 C5
Normande Ct SE21 22 D7
Normandy RH12 217 C1
Normandy Cl
Crawley RH10 202 C4
7 East Grinstead RH19 205 F8
Forest Hill SE26 23 E5
Frimley GU16 86 E8
Normandy Gdns RH12 217 C1

Normandy Wlk TW20 ....12 C3
Normanhurst TW15 ....14 A3
Normanhurst Cl RH10 .201 F6
Normanhurst Dr TW1 ...6 B2
Normanhurst Rd
 Streatham SW2 ....21 F6
 Walton-on-T KT12 .....54 D8
Normans La TN8 ....165 E7
Normansfield Ave KT1,
 TW11 ....17 C1
Normansfield Hospl KT1 .17 C1
Normanton RH2 ....117 D2
Normanton Ave SW18,
 SW19 ....20 A6
Normanton Rd CR2 .....61 E4
Normanton St SE23 ....23 D6
Normington Cl SW16 ...22 A3
Norrels Dr KT24 ....92 F1
Norrels Ride KT24 .....92 F2
Norreys Ave RG40 .....25 D7
Norris Hill Rd GU51,
 GU14 ....104 A8
Norris Rd TW18 ....12 F4
Norstead Pl SW15 .....19 A6
North Acre SM7 ....77 F3
North Ash RH12 ......217 C4
North Ave
 Heath End GU9 ....125 D7
 9 Richmond TW9 ......7 A6
 Wallington SM5 ....60 A3
 Whiteley Village KT12 ..53 E2
North Breache Rd GU6 .176 A6
North Camp Sta GU12 .105 F8
North Cl Ash Vale GU12 .105 E1
 Crawley RH10 ....201 F6
 Dorking RH5 ....136 C3
 East Bedfont TW14 .....3 D1
 Farnborough GU14 ....85 A8
 Merton SM4 ....39 E5
North Comm KT13 .....53 C6
North Crofts SE21 .....23 B7
North Dene TW5 ....5 B6
North Down CR2 ....80 E7
North Downs Cres CR0 .63 B1
North Downs Private Hospl
 CR3 ....101 A2
North Downs Rd CR0 ...63 C1
North Dr Beckenham BR3 ..44 B5
 Hounslow TW3,TW7 ....5 C5
 Pirbright GU24 ....87 C6
 Streatham SW16 ......21 C4
 Wentworth GU25 .....30 E4
North End CR0,CR9 ....61 C8
North End La SL5 ......30 B2
North Farm Rd GU14 ...84 F8
North Farnborough Inf Sch
 GU14 ....85 D5
North Feltham Trad Est
 TW14 ....4 B3
North Gate Rd GU14 ...85 C2
North Gdns SW19 .....20 D1
North Gn RG12 ....27 D8
North Gr KT16 ....32 F3
North Heath Cl RH12 ..217 D5
North Heath Com Prim Sch
 RH12 ....217 D5
North Heath Est RH12 .217 D5
North Heath La RH12 ..217 E6
North Holmes Cl RH12 .218 B5
North Hyde La TW5 .....4 F8
North Rd
 Aldershot GU11,GU12 .105 D2
 Teddington TW11 ......16 F2
North Lodge Dr SL5 ....28 C7
North Mead
 Crawley RH10 ....201 E8
 Redhill RH1 ....118 F4
North Minden Ho GU16 .86 D7
North Moors GU1 .....109 C6
North Munstead La
 GU8 ....151 A1
North Par Chessington KT9 .56 F5
 Horsham RH12 ....217 C3
North Park La RH9 ....121 A5
North Pl Mitcham SW19 .20 F1
 Teddington TW11 ......16 F2
North Pole La BR2 ....63 F4
North Rd Ash Vale GU12 .105 F4
 Brentford TW8 ....6 E8
 Crawley RH10 ....202 A7
 Crawley RH10 ....202 A8
 East Bedfont TW14 .....3 D1
 Guildford GU2 ....109 B4
 Hersham KT12 ....54 C5
 Heston TW5 ....4 C8
 Kingston u T KT6 .....37 D3
 Mitcham SW17,SW19 ..20 C2
 Reigate RH2 ....138 F6
 Richmond TW9 ....7 A5
 1 West Wickham BR4 ..44 B1
 Winkfield SL5 ....28 B8
 Woking GU21 ....70 A3
North Sheen Sta TW10 .7 A3
North Side GU10 ......126 F7
North St Carshalton SM5 .59 F6
 Dorking RH4 ....136 A7
 Egham TW20 ....11 F7
 Farncombe GU7 ......150 E7
 Guildford GU1 ....130 D8
 Horsham RH12,RH13 ..217 D3
 Isleworth TW7 ....6 A4
 Leatherhead KT22 ....95 A6
 Redhill RH1 ....118 F2
 Turners Hill RH10 ....204 A4
 Westcott RH4 ....135 C6
 Winkfield SL4 ....9 A6
North Station App RH1 .140 F7

North Terminal App
 RH6 ....181 F8
North View
 Bracknell RG12 ....26 C6
 Wimbledon SW19 .....19 C3
North View Cres KT18 ..77 C2
North Weald La KT2 ...17 D3
North Weylands Ind Est
 KT12 ....54 E8
North Wlk CR0 ....63 C5
North Worple Way SW14 .7 D4
Northampton Cl RG12 ..27 E6
Northampton Rd CR0,CR9 .62 A8
Northanger Rd SW16 ..21 E2
Northborough Rd SW16 .41 E7
Northbourne GU7 .....150 F8
Northbrook Coll of Design &
 Tech RH12 ....217 C4
Northbrook Copse RG12 .27 F3
Northbrook Rd
 Aldershot GU11 ......126 B8
 Thornton Heath CR0 ...42 A1
Northcliffe Cl KT4 .....57 E7
Northcote KT15 ....52 D6
Northcote Ave
 Isleworth TW7 ....6 A2
 Tolworth KT5 ....38 B2
Northcote Cl KT24 ....92 C2
Northcote Cres KT24 ..92 C2
Northcote La GU5 ....152 E6
Northcote Pk KT22 ....74 C4
Northcote Rd
 Ash Vale GU12 ....106 A7
 Farnborough GU14 ....84 F6
 Isleworth TW1,TW7 ....6 A2
 Kingston u T KT3 .....38 D6
 Thornton Heath CR0 ...42 D3
 West Horsley KT24 ....92 C2
Northcott RG12 ....27 A1
Northcroft Cl TW20 ...11 B3
Northcroft Gdns TW20 .11 B3
Northcroft Rd
 Englefield Green TW20 .11 B3
 West Ewell KT19 ......57 E3
Northcroft Villas TW20 .11 B3
Northdown Cl RH12 ...217 F4
Northdown Ct RH9 ....121 C5
Northdown La GU1 ....130 E6
Northdown Rd
 Belmont SM2 ....59 A1
 Woldingham CR3 .....102 A2
Northdown Terr RH19 .185 D3
Northdowns GU6 .....174 E1
Northend Ct KT23 .....94 C1
Northern Perimeter Rd
 TW6 ....3 E6
Northern Perimeter Road
 (W) TW6 ....2 D6
Northernhay Wlk SM4 .39 E5
Northey Ave SM2 .....58 E1
Northfield
 Lightwater GU18 ......67 B8
 Shalford GU4 ....130 E1
 Witley GU8 ....170 F4
Northfield Cl GU12 ...105 D1
Northfield Cres SM3 ...58 E6
Northfield Ct TW18 ....33 B8
Northfield Pl KT13 ....53 B3
Northfield Rd
 Cobham KT11 ....73 B6
 Heston TW5 ....4 D7
 Staines TW18 ....33 B8
Northfields KT21 ......95 E8
Northgate Ave RH10 ..201 F7
Northgate Dr GU15 ...66 A7
Northgate Fst & Mid Sch
 RH10 ....201 E7
Northgate Pl RH10 ....201 E7
Northgate Rd
 Crawley RH10 ....201 D6
 Crawley, North Terminal
 RH6 ....181 F8
Northington Cl RG12 ..27 F3
Northlands Bglws RH5 .158 B1
Northlands Bsns Pk
 RH12 ....197 C4
Northlands Cotts RH12 .197 D4
Northlands Rd
 Horsham RH12 ....217 E7
 Warnham RH12 ......197 D2
Northmead GU14 .....85 B4
Northmead Jun Sch
 GU2 ....109 B4
Northmoor 4 SE23 ...23 D5
Northolmes Jun Sch
 RH12 ....218 A4
Northolt Rd TW6 ......2 D6
Northover BR1 ....24 F5
Northrop Rd TW6 .....3 E6
Northspur Rd SM1 ....59 A7
Northstead Rd SW2 ...22 A6
Northtown Trad Est
 GU12 ....105 E1
Northumberland Ave TW7 .6 A7
Northumberland Ct TW19 .2 E1
Northumberland Cres
 TW14 ....3 E1
Northumberland Gdns
 Hounslow TW7 ....6 A7
 Mitcham CR4 ....41 D4
Northumberland Pl 26
 TW10 ....6 D2
Northway Crawley RH6 ..181 D8
 Farncombe GU7 ......150 B7
 Guildford GU2 ....109 A3
 Merton SM4,SW20 ....39 E5
 Wallington SM6 ......60 C6
Northway Rd CR0 .....42 F2

Northwood Ave
 Knaphill GU21 ....68 D1
 Purley CR8 ....80 B6
Northwood Pk RH10 ..182 A2
Northwood Rd
 Forest Hill SE23 ......23 F7
 Harmondsworth TW6 ...2 D6
 South Norwood CR7 ...42 C7
 Wallington SM5 ....60 A4
Northwood Way 1 SE19 .22 E2
Norton Ave KT5 ....38 B2
Norton Cl GU3 ....88 D1
Norton Ct SE19 ....43 F8
Norton Gdns SW16 ...41 E8
Norton Ho 4 KT3 .....38 E5
Norton Pk SL5 ....29 C4
Norton Rd Frimley GU15 .66 C4
 Wokingham RG40 .....25 C5
Norwegian Sch SW19 ..19 C1
Norwich Ave GU15 ....65 E3
Norwich Rd
 Crawley RH10 ....202 B5
 South Norwood CR7 ...42 C6
Norwood Cl
 Effingham KT24 ......113 E7
 Twickenham TW2 .....16 D6
Norwood Cres TW6 ....3 C2
Norwood Farm La KT11 .73 B8
Norwood High St SE27 .22 C4
Norwood Hill RH6 ....159 D3
Norwood Junction Sta
 SE25 ....43 A5
Norwood Park Rd SE27 .22 C3
Norwood Rd
 Effingham KT24 ......113 E7
 Streatham SE24,SE27 .22 B7
Norwood Sch SE27 ....22 C3
Norwoodhill Rd RH6 ..159 F2
Noseby Ct KT12 ....54 C8
Notley End TW20 .....11 C1
Notson Rd SE25 ....43 B5
Nottingham Cl GU21 ..68 F1
Nottingham Ct 5 GU21 .68 F1
Nottingham Rd
 Croydon CR2 ....61 C5
 Isleworth TW7 ....5 F5
 Upper Tooting SW17 ..20 F7
Nova Mews SM4 ......39 E2
Nova Rd CR0 ....42 C2
Nower Lodge Sch RH4 .136 A6
Nower Rd RH4 ....136 A6
Nowhurst La RH12 ...216 A5
Noyna Rd SW17 ....20 F5
Nubia Way SE6 ....24 E5
Nuffield Ctr TW5 ......4 F7
Nuffield Dr GU47 .....45 F1
Nuffield Hospl GU2 ...108 E1
Nugee Ct SE27 ....22 C4
Nugent Cl GU8 ....192 F6
Nugent Ct Guildford GU2 .109 B4
 Streatham SW16 ......21 C4
Nugent Rd Guildford GU2 129 D8
 South Norwood SE25 ..42 F6
Numa Ct TW8 ....6 D7
Nunappleton Way RH8 .123 A3
Nuneaton RG12 ....27 E3
Nuneham SW16 ....21 D4
Nunns Field RH5 .....178 D6
Nuns Wlk GU25 ....31 D4
Nuptown La SL4 ....8 A8
Nursery Ave CR0 ......62 D8
Nursery Cl Capel RH5 .178 C5
 Croydon CR0 ....62 D8
 Ewell KT17 ....57 E1
 Feltham TW14 ....15 B8
 Frimley GU16 ....85 F7
 Walton on the Hill KT20 .97 B2
 Woking GU21 ....69 C3
 Woodham KT15 ....51 F1
Nursery Cotts GU21 ...88 F8
Nursery Gdns
 Chilworth GU4 ....131 B3
 Feltham TW12 ....15 F4
 Hounslow TW4 ....4 F2
 Staines TW18 ....13 B1
 Sunbury TW16 ....34 F7
Nursery Hill GU5 ....152 D5
Nursery La
 Hookwood RH6 ......160 D2
 North Ascot SL5 ......28 E8
Nursery Rd
 Farncombe GU7 .....150 F7
 Knaphill GU21 ....68 D2
 Merton SW19 ....40 B7
 Mitcham CR4 ....40 E6
 South Norwood CR7,SE25 .42 D5
 Sunbury TW16 ....34 F7
 Sutton SM1 ....59 C6
 Walton on the Hill KT20 .97 B2
 Wimbledon SW19 .....19 E1
Nurserylands RH11 ...201 A6
Nutborne Ho SW19 ...19 D2
Nutbourne GU9 ......125 E7
Nutbourne Cotts GU8 .191 E7
Nutbourne Ct TW18 ...12 F1
Nutcombe Height GU26 188 F4
Nutcombe La
 Dorking RH4 ....135 F7
 Haslemere GU26,GU27 .188 D5
Nutcroft Gr KT22 .....94 E6
Nutfield Church Prim Sch
 RH1 ....140 F8
Nutfield Cl SM5 ....59 E7
Nutfield Ct
 Camberley GU15 ......65 D7
 Nutfield RH1 ....119 D7
Nutfield Marsh Rd RH1 .119 E4
Nutfield Rd Coulsdon CR5 .79 A3

Nutfield Rd continued
 Merstham RH1 ....119 C5
 Nutfield RH1 ....119 C1
 Redhill RH1 ....119 C1
 Thornton Heath CR7 ...42 B5
Nutfield Sta RH1 .....140 E2
Nuthatch Cl GU10 ....124 D7
Nuthatch Gdns RH2 ..139 C5
Nuthatch Way
 Horsham RH12 ....217 D7
 Turners Hill RH10 ....204 C5
Nuthurst RG12 ....27 E4
Nuthurst Ave
 Cranleigh GU6 ....174 E3
 Streatham SW2 ....21 F6
Nuthurst Cl RH11 ....201 A7
Nutley RG12 ....27 A1
Nutley Ct 6 RH2 .....118 A1
Nutley Dean Bsns Pk
 RH6 ....159 E6
Nutley La RH2 ....117 C2
Nutmeg Cl GU14 ......84 C5
Nutshell La GU9 ......125 C6
Nutty La TW17 ....34 C6
Nutwell St SW17 ......20 E3
Nutwood GU7 ....150 D6
Nutwood Ave RH3 ....137 C6
Nutwood Cl RH3 .....137 C6
Nyefield Pk GU20 .....97 A1
Nylands Ave TW9 ......7 A5
Nymans Ct RH12 .....218 A7
Nymans Ct RH10 .....202 B5
Nymans Gdns SW20 ..39 B6
Nyon Gr SE23,SE6 ....23 F6

O

O'Connor Rd GU11 ...105 E7
O'Gorman Ave GU14 ..85 B2
Oak Ave Brookwood GU24 .88 A6
 Croydon CR0 ....63 B8
 Egham TW20 ....12 D1
 Hampton TW12 ....15 E2
 Heston TW5 ....4 E7
 Sandhurst GU47 ......45 D1
Oak Bank CR0 ....63 C4
Oak Cl Box Hill KT20 ..116 B5
 Chiddingfold GU8 ....191 A4
 Copthorne RH10 .....183 A3
 Farncombe GU7 .....150 E8
 Oak Cnr RH5 ....157 C4
Oak Cottage Cl
 Catford SE6 ....24 F7
 Wood St V GU3 ......108 C2
Oak Cotts Compton GU3 .129 C2
 Haslemere GU27 .....207 E6
Oak Croft RH19 ......206 A8
Oak Ct Chipstead CR5 ..78 F1
 Crawley RH10 ....181 D2
 Farnborough GU14 ....85 E1
 Farnham GU9 ....125 B1
Oak Dell RH10 ....202 C7
Oak Dr KT20 ....116 B5
Oak End RH5 ....157 C3
Oak End Way KT15 ...70 F7
Oak Farm Cl GU17 ....64 C5
Oak Farm Com Sch GU14 84 F6
Oak Gdns CR0 ....63 A8
Oak Glade KT19 ......76 A9
Oak Gr Cranleigh GU6 .174 F1
 Loxwood RH14 ......213 A4
 Sunbury TW16 ....15 B1
 West Wickham BR4 ...44 C1
Oak Grange Rd GU4 ..111 B6
Oak Grove Cres GU15 .64 F6
Oak Grove Rd SE20 ...43 C7
Oak Hill Epsom KT18 ..76 D2
 Guildford GU4 ....110 C6
 Surbiton KT6 ....37 E2
 Wood St V GU3 ......108 A3
Oak Hill Cres KT6 .....37 E2
Oak Hill Gr KT6 ......37 E3
Oak Hill Rd KT6 ......37 E3
Oak Ho Farnborough GU14 .85 A7
 Grayshott GU26 .....188 D3
 Penge SE20 ....43 B7
Oak House Apartments
 GU8 ....171 B3
Oak La
 Broadbridge Heath RH12 .216 E3
 Englefield Green TW20 .11 C5
 Isleworth TW7 ....5 E3
 Twickenham TW1 .....17 A8
 Woking GU22 ....70 B3
Oak Leaf Cl Epsom KT19 .76 C7
 Guildford GU2 ....108 D2
Oak Lodge
 4 Charlton TW16 .....14 F1
 Cobham KT11 ....73 C4
 Crowthorne RG45 ....45 C5
 14 Sutton SM1 ....59 C6
 14 West Norwood SE21 .22 D6
Oak Lodge Cl KT12 ...54 C5
Oak Lodge Dr
 Salfords RH1 ....140 A1
 West Wickham BR4 ...44 B2
Oak Lodge Prim Sch BR4 44 B2
Oak Lodge Sch SW12 .21 A8
Oak Mead GU7 ......150 E8
Oak Park Gdns SW19 .19 D7
Oak Pk KT14 ....70 E6
Oak Rd Caterham CR3 .100 E5
 Cobham KT11 ....73 E4
 Crawley RH11 ....201 C5
 Farnborough GU14 ....85 C3
 Kingston u T KT3 .....38 D7
 Leatherhead KT22 ....95 A8

Oak Rd continued
 Reigate RH2 ....118 B2
Oak Ridge RH4 ....136 B4
Oak Row CR4 ....41 C7
Oak Tree Cl
 Aldershot GU12 ......126 E8
 Ash Vale GU12 ....85 F1
 East Grinstead RH19 .185 C3
 Guildford, Jacobswell GU4 109 C6
 Guildford,Burpham GU4 .110 C6
 Knaphill GU21 ....68 B1
 Wentworth GU25 .....31 D3
Oak Tree Dr
 Englefield Green TW20 .11 C3
 Guildford GU1 ....109 C5
Oak Tree La
 Dunsfold GU8 ....192 F5
 Haslemere GU27 .....207 D6
Oak Tree Rd
 Knaphill GU21 ....68 B1
 Milford GU8 ....149 F1
Oak Tree View GU9 ...125 E6
Oak Tree Way RH13 ..217 F4
Oak Way Ashstead KT21 .75 F2
 Crawley RH10 ....201 E8
 Croydon CR0 ....43 D3
 East Bedfont TW14 ...14 E7
 Reigate RH2 ....139 D8
Oak Wlk SM6 ....41 A1
Oak's Rd GU21 ....69 E2
Oakapple Cl
 Crawley RH11 ....201 B1
 Hamsey Green CR2 ...81 B5
Oakbank Fetcham KT22 .94 D4
 Woking GU22 ....89 E8
Oakbank Ave KT12 ...35 F2
Oakbraes GU7 ....150 D6
Oakbrook 3 BR3 .....44 B7
Oakcroft Bsns Ctr KT9 .56 F6
Oakcroft Cl KT14 .....70 F5
Oakcroft Ho 3 KT3 ...38 E2
Oakcroft Rd
 Chessington KT9 .....56 F6
 Pyrford KT14 ....70 F5
 Oakcroft Villas KT9 ...56 F6
Oakdale Beckenham BR3 ..44 F5
 Bracknell RG12 ......27 D3
Oakdale Rd Epsom KT19 .57 D2
 Streatham SW16 ......21 E3
 Weybridge KT13 ......53 A7
Oakdale Way CR4 ....41 A2
Oakdene Chobham GU24 .49 F1
 Kingswood KT20 .....97 E7
 Sunningdale SL5 .....29 F3
 1 West Norwood SE19 .22 E2
Oakdene Ave
 Thornton Heath CR7 ..42 A1
Oakdene Cl
 Brockham RH3 ......137 C7
 Great Bookham KT23 .114 C8
Oakdene Ct
 Streatham SW16 ......21 E3
 Walton-on-T KT12 ....54 B7
Oakdene Dr KT5 ......38 C4
Oakdene Lodge SE20 .23 B1
Oakdene Mews SM3 ..39 F1
Oakdene Par KT11 ....73 B5
Oakdene Pl GU3 .....130 C1
Oakdene Rd
 Brockham RH3 ......137 C7
 Cobham KT11 ....73 B5
 Godalming GU7 .....150 D3
 Little Bookham KT23 ..93 F3
 Redhill RH1 ....118 F1
 Shalford GU3 ....130 C1
Oaken Coppice KT21 .96 A8
Oaken Copse GU15 ...66 C7
Oaken Copse Cres GU14 .85 B7
Oaken Dr KT10 ....55 F4
Oaken La KT10 ....55 E5
Oakengates RG12 ....27 A1
Oakenshaw Cl KT6 ...37 E2
Oakey Dr RG40 ....25 B5
Oakfield Plaistow RH14 .211 E2
 Woking GU21 ....68 E3
Oakfield Cl
 New Malden KT3 .....38 F4
 Weybridge KT13 ......53 C6
Oakfield Ct Croydon CR2 .61 C4
 5 Weybridge KT13 ....53 C5
 Wokingham RG41 ....25 A5
Oakfield Dr RH2 .....118 B3
Oakfield Gdns
 Beckenham BR3 ......44 A4
 Carshalton SM5 ......40 F1
 3 Dulwich SE19 ......22 E3
Oakfield Glade KT13 .53 C6
Oakfield Jun Sch KT22 .94 D4
Oakfield Prep Sch SE21 .22 D7
Oakfield Rd Ashford TW15 .14 B3
 Ashstead KT21 ....75 E1
 Blackwater GU17 .....64 F3
 Cobham KT11 ....73 B5
 Penge SE20 ....23 B1
 Thornton Heath CR0 ..42 C1
 Wimbledon SW19 .....19 D5
Oakfield Sch GU22 ....70 F4
Oakfield Way RH19 ..185 F3
Oakfields Camberley GU15 .65 B5
 Crawley RH10 ....202 D7
 Guildford GU3 ....108 F3
 Wallis Wood RH5 ....196 D8
 Walton-on-T KT12 ....35 A1
 West Byfleet KT14 ....71 B5
Oakhall Ct TW16 ......14 F3

Oakhall Dr TW16 ....14 F3
Oakham Cl SE6 ....23 F6
Oakham Dr BR2 ....44 F5
Oakhaven RH10 ....201 D4
Oakhill KT10 ....56 A4
Oakhill Cl KT21 ....75 C1
Oakhill Ct 8 Surbiton KT6 37 E3
Wimbledon SW19 ....19 D1
Oakhill Gdns KT13 ......53 E8
Oakhill Lodge Purley CR8 .80 A6
3 Sutton SM1 ....59 B7
Oakhill Rd
Addlestone KT15 ....51 F4
Ashstead KT21 ....75 C1
Beckenham BR3 ....44 C7
Headley Down GU35 ....187 B5
Horsham RH13 ....217 E2
Reigate RH2 ....139 B8
Sutton SM1 ....59 C7
Thornton Heath SW16 ...41 F8
Oakhurst Chobham GU24 .49 E2
Grayshott GU26 ....188 D3
Oakhurst Cl 4 TW11 ....16 E3
Oakhurst Gdns RH19 ...185 C2
Oakhurst La RH14 ......212 E7
Oakhurst Mews RH12 ...218 A4
Oakhurst Rd KT19 ......57 D4
Oakhurst Rise SM5 .....59 E1
Oakhyrst Grange Sch
CR3 ....100 D1
Oakington 6 KT1 ....38 A7
Oakington Dr TW16 .....35 C7
Oakland Ave GU9 ......125 E7
Oakland Way KT19 ......57 E4
Oaklands Croydon CR0 ..61 B5
Fetcham KT22 ....94 D3
Haslemere GU27 ....208 C7
Horley RH6 ....161 C3
Horsham RH13 ....217 E2
Purley CR8 ....80 C5
South Godstone RH9 ...142 E5
Twickenham TW2 ....16 C8
Oaklands Ave
Hounslow TW7 ....5 F8
Thames Ditton KT10 ....36 D1
Thornton Heath CR7 ....42 A5
West Wickham BR4 .....63 B7
Oaklands Cl
Chessington KT9 ....56 C6
North Ascot SL5 ....8 F1
Shalford GU4 ....130 E1
Oaklands Ct KT15 ......52 B7
Oaklands Dr
North Ascot SL5 ....8 F1
Redhill RH1 ....140 B7
Wokingham RG41 ....25 A5
Oaklands Gdns CR8 .....80 C5
Oaklands Inf Sch
Biggin Hill TN16 ....83 C3
Crowthorne RG45 ......45 A6
Oaklands Jun Sch
Biggin Hill TN16 ....83 C3
Crowthorne RG45 ......45 A6
Oaklands La
Biggin Hill TN16 ....83 C5
Crowthorne RG45 ......45 B7
Oaklands Pk RG41 .....25 A4
Oaklands Rd Bromley BR1 .24 E1
Mortlake SW14 ....7 D4
Oaklands Sch TW3 .....5 D4
Oaklands Way
Tadworth KT20 ....97 C5
Wallington SM6 ....60 D3
Oaklawn GU21 ....70 A4
Oaklawn Rd KT22 ....74 E2
Oaklea GU12 ....106 A5
Oaklea Ct CR2 ....61 D2
Oakleigh Epsom KT18 ...76 E5
Lightwater GU18 ....67 C8
Oakleigh Ave KT16 .....57 B8
Oakleigh Ct Oxted RH8 .122 E6
Penge SE20 ....23 B1
Oakleigh Rd RH12 ....217 F4
Oakleigh Way
Mitcham CR4 ....41 B8
1 Tolworth KT6 ....38 B1
Oakley Ave CR0 ....60 E6
Oakley Cl Addlestone KT15 52 D6
East Grinstead RH19 ...206 B7
Hounslow TW7 ....5 D6
Oakley Cotts RH19 ....206 C7
Oakley Ct Carshalton CR4 .41 A2
15 Redhill RH1 ....119 A2
Oakley Dell GU4 ....110 C3
Oakley Gdns
Banstead SM7 ....78 B4
Brockham RH3 ....137 C3
Oakley Ho GU7 ....150 E8
Oakley Rd Camberley GU15 65 B4
Croydon SE25 ....43 B4
Whyteleafe CR6 ....81 A1
Oakman Ho 29 SW19 ...19 D7
Oakmead Gn KT18 .....76 C4
Oakmead Pl CR4 ....40 E8
Oakmead Rd
Upper Tooting SW12 ....21 B7
Wallington CR0 ....41 D3
Oakridge GU24 ....67 F6
Oakridge La BR1 ....24 D3
Oakridge Rd BR1 ......24 E3
Oaks Ave Feltham TW13 ..15 F6
North Cheam KT4 ......58 B6
West Norwood SE19,SE27 .22 E3
Oaks Cl Horsham RH12 .218 B6
Leatherhead KT22 ......95 A6

Oaks Ct KT22 ....95 A6
Oaks La South Croydon CR0 62 C7
South Holmwood RH5 ..157 B8
Oaks Rd Purley CR8 .....80 B5
Reigate RH2 ....118 D2
South Croydon CR0 .....62 C6
Stanwell TW19 ....2 D1
Oaks Sports Ctr SM5 ...78 E8
Oaks Sq The 9 KT19 ...76 D6
Oaks The Bracknell RG12 .27 D7
Dorking RH4 ....136 B4
East Grinstead RH19 ...206 B8
Epsom KT18 ....76 F5
Farnborough GU14 .....84 D3
Smallfield RH6 ....162 B3
Staines TW18 ....12 F4
Sutton SM1 ....59 A5
Tadworth KT20 ....97 C4
West Byfleet KT14 ......71 A5
Wimbledon SW19 ....19 E2
Oaks Tk SM5,SM6 ......60 B1
Oaks Way
Burgh Heath KT18 ......97 B8
Long Ditton KT6 ....37 D1
Purley CR8 ....80 C5
Send Marsh GU23 ......91 A3
Wallington SM5 ....59 F3
Oaksford Ave SE26 .....23 B5
Oakshade Rd Catford BR1 24 D4
Oxshott KT22 ....74 C5
Oakshaw RH8 ....122 B8
Oakshaw Rd SW18 .....20 B8
Oakside Ct RH6 ....161 C4
Oakside La RH6 ....161 C4
Oaktree Sch The GU22 ..88 B8
Oaktree Way GU47 .....45 A1
Oaktrees Ash GU12 ...105 F1
Hale GU9 ....125 B6
Oaktrees Ct GU12 ....105 F1
Oakview RG40 ....25 B4
Oakview Gr CR0 ....43 E1
Oakview Rd SE6 ....24 B3
Oakway Aldershot GU12 .126 E8
Beckenham BR2 ....44 D7
Knaphill GU21 ....88 E8
West Barnes SW20 .....39 C5
Oakway Dr GU16 ....65 E1
Oakwood Guildford GU2 .109 A6
Wallington SM6 ....60 B2
Oakwood Ave
Beckenham BR3 ....44 C7
Epsom KT19 ....57 B2
Mitcham CR4 ....40 D7
Purley CR8 ....80 C7
Oakwood Cl
East Horsley KT24 ....112 E8
Redhill RH1 ....119 A1
South Nutfield RH1 ....140 F7
Oakwood Ct
Beckenham BR3 ....44 C7
Bisley GU24 ....68 A3
1 Sutton SM1 ....59 C6
Oakwood Dr
East Horsley KT24 ....112 E8
West Norwood SE19 ....22 C2
Oakwood Gdns
Knaphill GU21 ....68 B1
Sutton SM1 ....59 A8
Oakwood Grange KT13 .53 E7
Oakwood Hall KT20 ....98 C4
Oakwood Ind Pk RH10 .182 A2
Oakwood Pk RH18 ....206 F2
Oakwood Pl CR0 ....42 A3
Oakwood Rd
Bletchingley RH1 ......120 A6
Bracknell RG12 ....27 E7
Horley RH6 ....161 B4
Knaphill GU21 ....88 E8
Thornton Heath CR0,CR7 .42 A3
Thorpe GU25 ....31 C4
Wimbledon SW20 ......39 A8
Windlesham GU20 ......48 E4
Oakwood Rise CR3 ....100 E2
Oakwood Sch
Horley RH6 ....161 C3
Purley CR8 ....80 B6
Oareborough RG12 .....27 E8
Oast House Cl TW19 ...11 E8
Oast House Cres GU9 .125 D6
Oast House La GU9 ...125 D6
Oast La GU11 ....126 B7
Oast Lodge 6 W4 ....7 E7
Oast Rd RH8 ....122 F4
Oates Cl BR2 ....44 D6
Oates Wlk RH10 ......201 F3
Oatfield Rd KT20 ......97 B6
Oatlands Crawley RH11 .201 A5
Horley RH6 ....161 C1
Horley RH6 ....161 C1
Oatlands Ave KT13 .....53 E6
Oatlands Chase KT12,
KT13 ....53 E7
Oatlands Cl KT13 ......53 D6
Oatlands Ct 3 SW19 ...19 D7
Oatlands Dr KT13,KT12 .53 D7
Oatlands Gn KT13 .....53 D7
Oatlands Inf Sch KT13 .53 D6
Oatlands Mere KT13 ...53 D7
Oatlands Rd KT20 .....97 E8
Oban Rd SE25 ....42 D5
Obelisk Way GU15 .....65 C6
Oberon Way
Crawley RH11 ....200 E3
Littleton TW17 ....33 E6
Oberursel Way GU11 ..104 F2
Observatory Rd SW14 ...7 C3
Observatory Wlk 4
RH1 ....118 F1

Occam Rd GU2 ....129 D8
Ockenden Cl 15 GU22 ..69 F1
Ockenden Gdns GU22 ..69 F1
Ockenden Rd GU22 ....69 F1
Ockfields GU8 ....149 F1
Ockford Ct GU7 ......150 D4
Ockford Dr GU7 ......150 C3
Ockford Rd GU7 ......150 D4
Ockford Ridge GU7 ...150 B2
Ockham Dr KT24 ....92 D3
Ockham La GU23,KT11 ..92 D7
Ockham Rd N GU23,KT24 .92 C5
Ockham Rd S KT24 ....112 E7
Ockley Cl Guildford GU4 .110 B6
2 Sutton SM1 ....59 C6
Ockley Ho 8 KT2 ......18 B2
Ockley Rd Ewhurst GU6 .175 F6
Forest Green GU6,RH5 .176 C7
Ockley RH5 ....177 B7
Streatham SW16 ....21 E4
Thornton Heath CR0,CR9 .41 F2
Ockley Sta RH5 ....178 A5
Ockleys Mead RH1 ....121 C5
Octagon Rd KT12 ......53 E1
Octavia RG12 ....27 A1
Octavia Cl CR4 ....40 E4
Octavia Rd TW7 ....5 F4
Octavia Way TW18 .....13 A2
October Ct BR2 ....44 F6
Odard Rd KT8 ....36 A5
Odette Ho 6 SE27 .....22 D4
Odiham Rd GU9,GU10 ..124 D7
Off Upper Manor Rd
GU7 ....150 E7
Offley Pl TW7 ....5 D5
Ogden Ho TW13 ....15 C4
Ogden Pk RG12 ....27 E6
Okeburn Rd SW17 .....21 A3
Okehurst Rd RH14 ....214 C1
Okingham Cl GU47 .....45 D1
Olaf Palme Ho TW13 ...15 B5
Old Acre KT14 ....71 A5
Old Ave Sheerwater KT14 .70 E6
Weybridge KT13 ....53 C3
Old Avenue Cl KT14 ...70 E6
Old Bakery Ct GU6 ....175 E5
Old Bakery Mews GU5 .132 B4
Old Barn Cl SM2 ....58 E3
Old Barn Dr RH5 ......178 D6
Old Barn La Churt GU10 .168 B1
Kenley CR3 ....80 F3
Old Barn Rd KT18 ......76 C2
Old Barn View GU7 ....150 C2
Old Bisley Rd GU16 ....66 C3
Old Bracknell Cl RG12 ..27 B6
Old Bracknell La E RG12 .27 B6
Old Bracknell La W RG12 27 B6
Old Brickfield Rd GU11 .126 B7
Old Bridge St KT1 ......37 D7
Old Brighton Rd S RH11 181 E5
Old Bromley Rd BR1 ...24 D3
Old Bury Hill Ho RH4 .135 E5
Old Chapel La GU12 ...106 A1
Old Charlton Rd TW17 .34 C4
Old Chertsey Rd GU24 ..50 C1
Old Chestnut Ave KT10 .55 B4
Old Chiswick Yd 12 W4 ..7 E8
Old Church La GU9 ....146 D7
Old Church Path KT10 ..55 B6
Old Claygate La KT10 ..56 A5
Old Common Rd KT11 ..73 B7
Old Compton La GU9 ..125 F2
Old Control Rd RH6 ...181 D6
Old Convent The RH19 .185 E2
Old Corn Mews GU7 ..150 F6
Old Cote Dr TW5 ....5 A8
Old Cotts GU2 ....130 C2
Old Court Rd GU2 ....130 A8
Old Crawley Rd RH12 .218 C7
Old Cross Tree Way
GU12 ....127 C8
Old Ct KT21 ....95 E8
Old Dairy Mews SW12 ..21 A7
Old Dean Rd GU15 .....65 D7
Old Deer Park Gdns TW9 .6 E4
Old Denne Gdns RH12 .217 C1
Old Devonshire Rd SW12 21 B8
Old Dock Cl TW9 ....7 A8
Old Dr GU5 ....133 C5
Old Elstead Rd GU8 ...149 E2
Old Esher Cl KT12 .....54 D5
Old Esher Rd KT12 ....54 E5
Old Farleigh Rd CR6,CR22 81 E6
Old Farm Cl TW4 ....4 F3
Old Farm Pl GU12 ....105 F5
Old Farm Rd
Guildford GU1 ....109 D4
Hampton TW12 ....15 F2
Old Farmhouse Dr KT22 .74 D4
Old Farnham La
Bentley GU10 ....124 A1
Farnham GU9 ....146 C8
Old Ford Ho CR0 ....60 E7
Old Forge Cres TW17 ..34 B3
Old Forge End GU47 ...64 B7
Old Fox Cl CR3 ....100 B6
Old Frensham Rd GU10 .146 E4
Old Green La GU15 .....65 C7
Old Guildford Rd
Mytchett GU16 ....86 C4
Warnham RH12 ....216 E4
Old Haslemere Rd
GU27 ....208 C5
Old Heath Way GU9 ...125 C7
Old Hill GU22 ....89 D7
Old Hollow RH10 .....202 F7
Old Horsham Rd
Beare Green RH5 .....157 C4

Old Horsham Rd continued
Crawley RH11 ....201 B4
Old Hospital Cl SW12,
SW17 ....20 F7
Old House Cl Ewell KT17 .57 F1
Wimbledon SW19 ......19 E3
Old House Gdns 9 SW1 ..6 C1
Old Kiln GU9 ....125 A2
Old Kiln Cl GU10 ......167 F2
Old Kiln Ctyd 15 GU9 .125 B2
Old Kiln La
Brockham RH3 ....137 C8
Churt GU10 ....167 F2
Old Kingston Rd KT4 ...57 C7
Old La Aldershot GU11 .126 A7
Aldershot, North Town
GU12 ....105 E3
Dockenfield GU10 ....166 F4
East Horsley KT11 .....93 A5
Martyr's Green KT11 ...92 E7
Ockham GU23,KT11 ....72 B1
Oxted RH8 ....122 F5
Tatsfield TN16 ....103 D6
Old Lands Hill RG12 ....27 D8
Old Lane Gdns KT11 ...93 A5
Old Lane The GU10 ...187 F8
Old Lodge Cl GU7 ....150 B3
Old Lodge La CR8 ......80 A3
Old Lodge Pl 7 TW1 ....6 B1
Old London Rd
Epsom KT17,KT18 ......77 A2
2 Kingston u T KT2 ...37 E7
Mickleham RH5 ....115 C8
Old Malden La KT4 .....57 E8
Old Malt Way GU21 ....69 D2
Old Manor Cl RH11 ...201 A8
Old Manor Ct RH11 ...201 A8
Old Manor Dr TW7 ......5 C1
Old Manor Gdns GU4 .131 C3
Old Martyrs RH11 .....181 D1
Old Merrow St GU4 ...110 D3
Old Mill La RH1 ......119 B7
Old Mill Pl
Haslemere GU27 .....207 F7
Horton TW19 ....1 B1
Old Millmeads RH12 ..217 C5
Old Mus Ct GU27 .....208 D6
Old Nursery Pl TW15 ...14 B3
Old Oak Ave CR5 ......98 E8
Old Oak Cl KT11 ....73 B6
Old Orch Byfleet KT14 ..71 F7
Sunbury TW16 ....35 C7
Old Orchard The GU9 .146 A8
Old Orchards RH10 ...202 E6
Old Palace La TW9 ......6 C2
Old Palace Rd
Croydon CR0,CR9 ......61 C7
Guildford GU2 ....130 A8
Weybridge KT13 ....53 B7
Old Palace Sch of John
Whitgift CR0 ....61 B7
Old Palace Terr 8 TW9 ..6 D2
Old Palace Yd 2 TW9 ...6 D2
Old Park Cl GU9 ......125 A6
Old Park La
Farnham GU9 ....125 A4
Hale GU9 ....124 F6
Old Park Mews TW5 ....4 F7
Old Parvis Rd KT14 ....71 C7
Old Pasture Rd GU16,
GU15 ....65 F3
Old Pharmacy Ct RG45 .45 C4
Old Pond Cl GU15 .....65 C1
Old Portsmouth Rd
Artington GU2, GU3, GU7 .130 C3
Frimley GU15 ....66 A5
Thursley GU8 ....169 D4
Old Pottery Cl RH2 ...139 B7
Old Pound Cl TW7 ......6 A6
Old Quarry The GU27 .207 F4
Old Rd Addlestone KT15 .51 F3
Buckland RH3 ....116 F1
East Grinstead RH19 ..185 F1
Old Rectory Cl
Bramley GU5 ....151 F6
Walton on the Hill KT20 .97 A3
Old Rectory Dr GU12 .106 B2
Old Rectory Gdns
Farnborough GU14 .....85 D4
Godalming GU7 ....150 F2
Old Rectory La KT24 ...92 E1
Old Redstone Dr RH1 .140 A8
Old Reigate Rd
Brockham RH3 ....116 C1
Dorking RH4 ....115 F2
Old Sawmill La RG45 ...45 C6
Old School Cl Ash GU12 .106 A3
Merton SW19 ....40 A7
Penge BR3 ....43 E7
Old School Ct
Leatherhead KT22 .....95 B5
Wraysbury TW19 ....11 E8
Old School La RH3 ...137 A7
Old School Mews
Egham TW20 ....12 D3
Oatlands Park KT13 ....53 D6
Old School Pl
Croydon CR0 ....61 A6
Lingfield RH7 ....164 D4
Woking GU22 ....89 F6
Old School Sq KT7 ....36 F3
Old Schools La KT17 ...57 F2
Old St Mary's KT24 ...112 B6
Old Station App KT22 ..95 A6
Old Station Cl RH10 ..204 B7
Old Station La TW20 ...12 E6
Old Station Way GU7 .150 E6

Old Surgery The 5
RH19 ....185 F1
Old Surrey Mews The
RH9 ....121 C5
Old Swan Yd SM5 ......59 F6
Old Town CR0,CR9 .....61 B7
Old Tye Ave TN16 ......83 E3
Old Vicarage The GU10 .145 E2
Old Water Yd RH4 ....136 A8
Old Westhall Cl CR6 ..101 C4
Old Wharf Way KT13 ...52 F6
Old Wickhurst La RH12 216 D2
Old Woking Rd
Pyrford GU22,KT14 .....70 D3
West Byfleet KT14 ......71 A6
Woking GU22 ....70 A2
Old Wokingham Rd RG45 45 C7
Oldacre GU24 ....67 F7
Oldbury RG12 ....26 C6
Oldbury Cl Frimley GU16 .85 F8
Horsham RH12 ....218 A2
Oldbury Rd KT16 ......32 C2
Olde Farm Dr GU17 ....64 B5
Olden La CR8 ....80 A7
Oldfield Cl RH6 ....160 F1
Oldfield Gdns KT21 ....95 D8
Oldfield Ho SW16 .....21 B4
Oldfield Rd
Hampton TW12 ....35 F8
Horley RH6 ....160 F1
Wimbledon SW19 ......19 E2
Oldfields Rd SM1,SM3 .59 A8
Oldfields Trad Est SM1 .59 A7
Oldfieldwood GU22 ....70 B2
Oldham 10 SE21 ....22 E4
Oldhouse La Bisley GU24 .68 A5
Windlesham GU18 .....48 C2
Olding Ho 6 SW12 .....21 C8
Oldridge Rd SW12 .....21 B8
Oldstead RG12 ....27 D4
Oldstead Rd BR1 ......24 D4
Oldwood Chase GU14 ..84 C3
Oleander Cl RG45 .....45 A4
Olive Rd 3 SW19 ......20 C1
Oliver Ave SE25 ....42 F6
Oliver Cl Addlestone KT15 .52 B6
Brentford W4 ....7 B8
Oliver Ct TW7 ....5 F4
Oliver Gr SE25 ....42 F5
Oliver Ho GU22 ....69 E1
Oliver Rd Ascot SL5 ....29 B5
Carshalton SM1 ....59 D6
Horsham RH12 ....217 A1
Kingston u T KT3 ......38 C7
Olivier Rd RH10 ......202 D5
Ollerton RG12 ....27 A1
Olley Cl SM6 ....60 E4
Olveston Wlk SM4,SM5 .40 D3
Olyffe Dr BR3 ....44 C8
Omega RG21 ....70 A3
Omega Way TW20 ......32 C8
One Tree Cnr GU1 ....131 B8
One Tree Hill Rd GU4 .131 B3
Ongar Cl KT15 ....51 F4
Ongar Hill KT15 ....52 A4
Ongar Par KT15 ....52 A4
Ongar Pl KT15 ....52 A4
Ongar Place Inf Sch
KT15 ....52 A4
Ongar Rd KT15 ....52 A4
Onslow Ave Belmont SM2 .77 F3
Richmond TW10 ....6 E2
Onslow Avenue Mans 10
TW10 ....6 E2
Onslow Cl
Thames Ditton KT7 ....36 E1
Woking GU22 ....70 A2
Onslow Cres GU22 .....70 A2
Onslow Ct RH10 ......182 A1
Onslow Dr SL5 ....9 A1
Onslow Gdns
Sanderstead CR2 ......81 A7
Thames Ditton KT7 ....36 E1
Wallington SM6 ....60 C3
Onslow Ho 1 KT2 ......37 E7
Onslow Inf Sch GU2 ..129 F7
Onslow Lodge
Staines TW18 ....12 F1
Streatham SW2 ....22 A8
Onslow Mews SW16 ...33 A3
Onslow Rd Guildford GU1 109 D1
Hersham KT12 ....54 A5
New Malden KT3 ....39 A5
Richmond TW10 ....6 E1
Sunningdale SL5 ....30 B2
Thornton Heath CR0 ...42 A1
Onslow St GU1 ....130 C8
Onslow Way Pyrford GU22 70 F4
Thames Ditton KT7 ....36 E1
Ontario Cl RH6 ....162 A2
Onyx Ho KT4 ....38 F1
Onyz The RG12 ....27 E6
Opal Ho KT4 ....38 F1
Openview SW17,SW18 ..20 D6
Opladen Way RG12 ....27 E4
Opossum Dr TW4 ....4 C4
Opus Pk GU1 ....109 D6
Orangery The TW10 ...17 C6
Orchard Ave
Ashford TW15 ....14 C2
Carshalton CR4 ....41 A1
Croydon CR0 ....43 E1
Hatton TW14 ....3 D2
Heston TW5 ....4 F7
Hinchley Wood KT7 ....56 A8
Kingston u T KT3 ......38 E6
Woodham KT15 ....70 F8
Orchard Bsns Ctr SE26 .23 F3

Orchard Bsns Ctr The
RH1 161 A8
Orchard Cl
Ash Vale GU12 106 A5
Ashford TW15 14 C2
Banstead SM7 78 B5
East Horsley KT24 92 F3
Egham TW20 12 B3
Elstead GU8 148 E4
Farnborough GU17 64 F1
Farnham GU9 126 A6
Fetcham KT22 94 D5
Flexford GU3 107 B1
Guildford GU1 110 B1
Haslemere GU27 207 F5
Horley RH6 160 F4
Leatherhead KT22 94 F8
Thames Ditton KT6 37 B2
Walton-on-T KT12 35 B2
West Barnes SW20 39 C5
West End GU24 67 D6
West Ewell KT19 57 B4
Woking GU22 70 B3
Wokingham RG40 25 D6
Orchard Cotts
Charlwood RH6 180 F7
Lingfield RH7 165 B3
Orchard Ct Barnes SW13 7 F4
Bracknell RG12 27 C7
Croydon CR0 44 A1
Harmondsworth UB7 2 C7
Hounslow TW7 5 D7
New Malden KT4 39 A1
Wallington SM6 60 B5
Walton-on-T KT12 34 F1
Orchard Dene KT14 71 A6
Orchard Dr Ashstead KT21 95 D7
Sunbury TW17 34 E6
Woking GU21 69 F4
Orchard End
Caterham CR3 100 E5
Fetcham KT22 94 C3
Oatlands Park KT13 53 E8
Rowledge GU10 145 F3
Orchard Gate
Sandhurst GU47 64 B8
Thames Ditton KT10 36 D1
Orchard Gdns
Aldershot GU11 126 C8
Chessington KT9 56 E6
Cranleigh GU6 174 F2
Effingham KT24 113 E7
Epsom KT18 76 C4
Sutton SM1 59 A5
Orchard Gr Croydon CR0 43 E2
Penge SE20 23 A1
Orchard Hill
Rudgwick RH12 214 C7
Wallington SM5 59 F5
Windlesham GU20 48 D3
Orchard Ho
Crawley RH10 181 D1
Guildford GU4 110 D2
Tongham GU10 126 F7
Orchard House Cheyne Ctr
(Hospl) BR4 63 C7
Orchard Jun & Inf Sch The
TW3 5 A3
Orchard La
Thames Ditton KT8 36 D3
Wimbledon SW20 39 B8
Orchard Lea Cl GU22 70 E4
Orchard Mains GU22 89 C8
Orchard Pl RG40 25 C6
Orchard Rd Brentford TW8 6 C8
Chessington KT9 56 E6
Dorking RH4 136 B6
Farnborough GU14 85 A4
Farnham GU9 126 A6
Guildford,Burpham GU4 110 B5
Guildford,Onslow Village
GU2 129 F7
Hampton TW12 15 F1
Hamsey Green CR2 81 B5
Horsham RH13 217 E2
Hounslow TW4 5 A2
Kingston u T KT1 37 E7
Mortlake TW9 7 A4
Reigate RH2 118 B1
Shalford GU4 130 E3
Shere GU5 133 A4
Smallfield RH6 162 C3
Sunbury TW16 15 B1
Sutton SM1 59 A6
Twickenham TW1 6 B2
Orchard Rise Croydon CR0 43 F1
Kingston u T KT2 38 C8
Mortlake TW10 7 B3
Orchard Sch The KT8 36 D5
Orchard School Sports Ctr
SE20 43 A8
Orchard St RH10,RH11 201 D6
Orchard The
Banstead SM7 78 A4
Dorking RH5 136 C3
Ewell KT17 57 F1
Ewell,West Ewell KT17 57 F3
Horley RH6 161 A3
Horsham RH12 218 B4
Hounslow TW3 5 C5
Lightwater GU18 67 B8
Thorpe GU25 31 E4
Weybridge KT13 53 B6
Woking GU21 69 B3
Woking GU22 89 E5
Orchard Way
Addlestone KT15 52 B4
Aldershot GU11,GU12 126 C8
Orchard Way *continued*
Ashford TW15 13 F6
Beckenham BR3,CR0 43 E3
Camberley GU15 65 B2
Carshalton SM1 59 D6
Croydon BR3,CR0 43 E3
Dorking RH4 136 B6
East Grinstead RH19 185 E1
Esher KT10 55 C4
Flexford GU3 107 B1
Lower Kingswood KT20 97 F1
Oxted RH8 123 A2
Reigate RH2 139 B6
Send GU23 90 C2
Orchard Way Prim Sch
CR0 43 E2
Orchardfield Rd GU7 150 F7
Orchardleigh KT22 95 B5
Orchards Cl KT14 71 A5
Orchards Sch RH2 139 A6
Orchards The
Ashford TW15 14 D3
4 Crawley RH11 200 D5
Horsham RH12 217 F5
14 Woking GU22 69 F1
Orchid Cl KT9 56 C3
Orchid Dr GU24 68 A4
Orchid Mead SM7 78 B5
Orde Cl RH10 182 D1
Ordnance Cl TW13 15 A6
Ordnance Rd GU11 105 C3
Ordnance Rdbt GU11 105 B2
Oregano Way GU2 109 A6
Oregon Cl KT3 38 C5
Orestan La KT24 113 C8
Orewell Gdns RH2 139 B7
Orford Ct Wallington SM6 60 C5
West Norwood SE27 22 B6
Orford Gdns TW1 16 F6
Orford Rd SE6 24 B5
Oriel Cl Crawley RH10 182 C1
Mitcham CR4 41 D6
Oriel Ct 6 CR0 42 D1
Oriel Hill GU15 65 D4
Oriel Prim Sch TW13 15 E5
Oriental Cl GU22 70 A2
Oriental Rd Ascot SL5 29 D5
Woking GU22 70 A3
Orion RG12 27 A1
Orion Ct Crawley RH11 200 D4
Horsham RH12 217 B3
Orion Ctr The CR0 60 E8
Orlando Gdns KT19 57 D1
Orlean Ct 5 KT12 54 C8
Orleans Cl KT10 55 D8
Orleans Ct 10 TW1 17 B8
Orleans Inf Sch TW1 17 B8
Orleans Park Sch TW1 17 B8
Orleans Rd
South Norwood SE19 22 D2
10 Twickenham TW1 17 C8
Orltons La RH12 179 F2
Ormanton Rd SE26 23 A4
Orme Ho RH9 142 D8
Orme Rd
Kingston u T KT1,KT3 38 B7
Sutton SM1 59 B4
Ormeley Rd SW12 21 B7
Ormerod Gdns CR4 41 A8
Ormesby Wlk RH10 202 B4
Ormond Ave
Hampton TW12 36 B8
22 Richmond TW10 6 D2
Ormond Cres TW12 36 B8
Ormond Dr TW12 16 B1
Ormond Rd TW10 6 D2
Ormonde Ave KT19 57 D1
Ormonde Rd
Farncombe GU7 150 E6
Mortlake SW14 7 C4
Woking GU21 69 C3
Wokingham RG41 25 A5
Ormsby SM2 59 B3
Ormside Way RH1 119 B4
Ormuz Cotts RH7 164 C4
Orpin Rd RH1 119 C5
Orpwood Cl TW12 15 F2
Orwell Cl GU14 84 E6
Orwell Ho 7 RH1 118 F2
Osborn La SE23 23 E8
Osborn Rd GU9 125 D4
Osborne Ave TW19 13 F7
Osborne Cl
Beckenham BR3 43 E5
Feltham TW13 15 D3
Frimley GU16 85 F8
Osborne Ct
Crawley RH11 201 B2
Farnborough GU14 105 C8
10 Surbiton KT6 37 E3
Osborne Dr GU18 67 A8
Osborne Gdns CR7 42 C7
Osborne Pl SM1 59 D5
Osborne Rd Egham TW20 11 F2
Farnborough GU14 105 C8
Hounslow TW3,TW4 4 F4
Kingston u T KT2 17 E1
Redhill RH1 119 A4
South Norwood CR7 42 C7
Walton-on-T KT12 35 A1
Wokingham RG40 25 C6
Osborne Way KT9 56 F5
Osbourne Terr 1 SW17 21 A3
Osgood Ct GU10 126 E8
Osier Mews 6 W4 7 F8
Osier Pl TW20 12 C2
Osier Way
Banstead KT17,SM7 77 E5
Osier Way *continued*
Mitcham CR4 40 F4
Oslac Rd SE6 24 B3
Oslo Ct SW19 20 D1
Osman's Cl RG42 8 B1
Osmond Gdns SM6 60 C5
Osmund Cl RH10 202 E6
Osmunda Bank RH19 185 E6
Osnaburgh Hill GU15 65 B5
Osney Cl RH11 201 C5
Osney Wlk SM4,SM5 40 D3
Osprey Cl Cheam SM1 58 F5
Fetcham KT22 94 C5
Osprey Ct SW16 41 F7
Osprey Gdns
Aldershot GU11 126 A7
Selsdon CR0,CR2 62 E1
Ospringe Cl 8 SE20 23 C1
Ostade Rd SW2 21 F8
Osterley Ave TW7 5 D7
Osterley Cl RG40 25 F5
Osterley Cres TW7 5 F6
Osterley Ct TW7 5 D6
Osterley Lodge TW7 5 E6
Osterley Rd TW7 5 E6
Osterley Sta TW7 5 D7
Osterly Gdns CR7 42 C7
Oswald Cl KT22 94 C5
Oswald Rd KT22 94 C5
Osward CR0 62 F1
Osward Rd SW12,SW17 20 F6
Otford Cl SE20 43 C8
Othello Gr RG42 27 E8
Otho Ct 5 TW8 6 D7
Otter Cl Crowthorne RG45 45 A7
Ottershaw KT16 51 B4
Otter Mdw KT22 94 F8
Otterbourne Pl RH19 185 B1
Otterbourne Rd 1 CR0,
CR9 61 C8
Otterburn Gdns TW7 6 A7
Otterburn St SW17 20 F2
Otterden St SE6 24 A4
Ottermead La KT16 51 C4
Ottershaw Pk KT16 51 A3
Ottways Ave KT21 95 D8
Ottways La KT22 95 D8
Otway Cl RH11 200 F4
Oulton Wlk RH10 202 B4
Our Lady & St Philip Neri
Prim Sch SE26 23 E4
Our Lady & St Philip Neri RC
Sch
Forest Hill SE23 23 D5
Forest Hill SE26 23 E4
Our Lady of the Rosary RC
Sch TW18 13 A2
Our Lady Queen Of Heaven
RC Sch
Crawley RH11 201 B8
Putney SW19 19 D8
Our Lady's Prep Sch
RG45 45 B5
Our Ladys RC First Sch
KT16 33 A1
Ouseley Rd
Upper Tooting SW12 20 F7
Wraysbury TW19 11 D8
Outdowns KT24 113 B5
Outram Pl KT13 53 C5
Outram Rd CR0 61 F8
Outwood Ho 6 SW2 21 F8
Outwood La
Bletchingley RH1 141 D7
Chipstead CR5,KT20 98 C6
Outwood RH1 141 D1
Outwood Post Mill*
RH1 162 D8
Oval Ct 6 TW11 16 F3
Oval Prim Sch CR0 42 E1
Oval Rd CR0 42 E1
Oval The Banstead SM7 78 A5
Farncombe GU7 150 F7
Guildford GU2 130 A8
Wood St V GU3 108 B2
Overbrae BR3 24 A3
Overbrook
Godalming GU7 151 A5
West Horsley KT24 112 B6
Overbury Ave BR3 44 C6
Overbury Cres CR0 63 C1
Overbury Ct BR3 44 C6
Overdale Ashstead KT21 75 E3
Bletchingley RH1 120 C2
Dorking RH5 136 D8
Overdale Ave KT3 38 D7
Overdale Rise GU16 65 E3
Overdene Dr RH11 201 A6
Overdown Rd SE6 24 B4
Overford Cl GU6 174 E2
Overford Dr GU6 174 E2
Overhill CR6 101 C8
Overhill Rd
Dulwich SE21,SE22 23 A8
Wallington CR8 61 A1
Overhill Way BR3 44 D4
Overlord Cl GU15 65 C8
Overslea Lodge 6 KT22 95 C6
Overstand Cl BR3 44 A4
Overstone Gdns CR0 43 F2
Overthorpe Cl GU21 68 E2
Overton Cl
Aldershot GU11 126 C6
Hounslow TW7 5 F6
Overton Ct SM2 59 A3
Overton Grange Sch SM2 59 B2
Overton Ho SW15 18 F8
Overton Rd SM2 59 A3
Overton Shaw RH19 185 E4
Overton Toft SM2 59 A4
Overton's Yd CR0,CR9 61 C7
Oveton Way KT23 94 B1
Ovett Cl SE19 22 E2
Ovington Ct GU21 68 F3
Owen Cl CR0 42 D3
Owen Ho Feltham TW14 15 A8
6 Twickenham TW1 17 B8
Owen Pl KT22 95 B5
Owen Rd Farncombe GU7 150 F6
Windlesham GU20 48 D5
Owen Wlk 10 SE20 23 A1
Owens Way SE23 23 E8
Owers Cl RH13 217 E2
Owl Cl CR2 62 D1
Owlbeech Ct RH13 218 B4
Owlbeech Pl RH13 218 B4
Owlbeech Way RH13 218 B4
Owletts RH10 202 D7
Owlscastle Cl RH12 217 D5
Owlsmoor Prim Sch
GU47 45 E1
Owlsmoor Rd GU47 45 D1
Ownstead Gdns CR2 80 F8
Ownsted Hill CR0 63 D1
Oxdowne Cl KT11 74 B5
Oxenden Ct GU10 126 E8
Oxenden Rd GU10,GU12 126 F8
Oxenhope RG12 27 A5
Oxford Ave Harlington TW6 3 F7
Merton SW20 39 E7
Oxford Cl
Littleton TW15,TW17 14 C1
Mitcham CR4 41 C6
Oxford Cres KT3 38 D3
Oxford Ct Epsom KT18 76 E5
17 Kingston u T KT6 37 E4
Oxford Gdns W4 7 A8
Oxford Ho RG41 25 A6
Oxford Rd Carshalton SM5 59 E5
Crawley RH10 201 F2
Farnborough GU14 85 C1
Guildford GU1 130 D7
Horsham RH13 217 E2
Redhill RH1 118 E2
Sandhurst GU47 45 E2
South Norwood SE19 22 D2
Teddington TW11 16 D3
Wallington SM6 60 C5
Wokingham RG41 25 A6
Oxford Terr GU1 130 D7
Oxford Way TW13 15 D4
Oxleigh Cl KT3 38 E4
Oxlip Cl CR0 43 D1
Oxshott Rd Ashstead KT22 74 F3
Leatherhead KT22 75 A2
Oxshott Rise KT11 73 E5
Oxshott Sta KT22 74 C6
Oxshott Way KT11 73 E4
Oxted & Limpsfield Hospl
RH8 122 D7
Oxted Cl CR4 40 D6
Oxted Gn GU8 170 E7
Oxted Rd RH9 121 D4
Oxted Sch RH8 122 F7
Oxted Sta RH8 122 E6
Oxtoby Way SW16 41 D8
Oyster La KT14 71 E7

P

Pacific Cl TW14 14 F7
Pacific Hts BR3 24 A1
Packer Cl RH19 186 A3
Packham Ct KT4 58 C7
Packway GU9 146 E7
Padbrook RH8 123 A6
Padbrook Cl RH8 123 B6
Padbury Cl TW14 14 D7
Padbury Oaks UB7 2 B6
Paddock Cl
Beare Green RH5 157 D4
Camberley GU15 66 A6
Cobham KT11 73 C5
Forest Hill SE26 23 D4
Hambledon GU8 171 C1
Lingfield RH7 164 C4
New Malden KT4 38 E1
Oxted RH8 122 F4
Paddock Ct SW20 39 C5
Paddock Gdns
East Grinstead RH19 205 E7
South Norwood SE19 22 E2
Paddock Gr RH5 157 D4
Paddock Ho GU4 110 D2
Paddock Sch SW15 7 F3
Paddock The
Addington CR0 63 A4
Bracknell RG12 27 C6
Cranleigh GU6 174 D3
Crawley RH10 202 D7
Crowthorne RG45 45 A6
Ewhurst GU6 175 E4
Godalming GU7 150 F3
Grayshott GU26 188 A4
Guildford GU1 110 D2
Haslemere GU27 208 A8
Westcott RH4 135 C6
Paddock Way
Grayswood GU27 190 A2
Oxted RH8 122 F4
Putney SW15 19 C8
Sheerwater GU21 70 B5
Paddock Wlk CR6 101 B8
Paddockhurst Rd
Crawley RH10 203 C2
Paddockhurst Rd *continued*
Crawley RH11 201 A5
Paddocks Cl KT21 75 E1
Paddocks Mead GU21 68 F3
Paddocks Rd GU4 110 A5
Paddocks The
Flexford GU3 107 C1
Great Bookham KT23 94 B1
Oatlands Park KT13 53 E7
Woodham KT15 52 B1
Paddocks Way
Ashstead KT21 75 E1
Chertsey KT16 33 B1
Padley Cl KT9 56 F6
Padstow Wlk
Crawley RH11 200 F4
East Bedfont TW14 14 F7
Padua Rd SE20 43 C8
Padwick Rd RH13 218 A2
Page Cl TW12 15 E2
Page Cres CR0 61 B5
Page Croft KT15 52 B8
Page Ct RH13 217 D1
Page Rd TW14 3 D1
Page's Croft RG40 25 D5
Page's Yd 11 W4 7 E8
Pageant Wlk CR0 61 E7
Pagehurst Rd CR0 43 B2
Paget Ave SM1 59 D7
Paget Cl Camberley GU15 66 B7
Hampton TW12 16 D4
Paget La TW7 5 E4
Paget Pl Kingston u T KT2 18 C2
Thames Ditton KT7 36 F1
Pagewood Cl RH10 202 D4
Pagoda Ave TW9 6 F4
Paice Gn RG40 25 D7
Pain's Cl CR4 41 B7
Pains Hill RH8 123 C4
Painshill Landscape Gdn*
KT11 72 E5
Paisley Rd SM5 40 D1
Pakenham Cl SW12 21 A7
Pakenham Dr GU11 104 F3
Pakenham Rd RG12 27 D2
Palace Ct
South Norwood CR7 42 D5
Streatham SW2 22 A6
3 Woking GU21 70 A3
Palace Dr KT13 53 B7
Palace Gn CR0 62 F3
Palace Gr SE19 22 F1
Palace Rd
East Molesey KT8 36 D6
Kingston u T KT1 37 D5
Penge SE19 22 F1
Streatham SW2 22 A6
Woodham KT15 52 B2
Palace Sq SE19 22 F1
Palace View CR0 62 F6
Palace Way 6 KT13 53 B7
Palestine Gr SW19 40 D8
Palewell Common Dr
SW14 7 D2
Palewell Pk SW14 7 D3
Palgrave Ho TW2 16 C8
Pallingham Dr RH10 202 C3
Palliser Ct GU26 188 C6
Palm Ct BR3 43 F6
Palm Gr GU1 109 C5
Palmer Ave KT4,SM3 58 C6
Palmer CE Jun Sch The
RG40 25 D7
Palmer Cl
Crowthorne RG40 45 A8
Heston TW5 5 A6
Horley RH6 160 F5
Redhill RH1 140 A8
West Wickham BR4 63 D8
Palmer Cres
Kingston u T KT1 37 E6
Ottershaw KT16 51 D4
Palmer Rd RH10 202 C3
Palmer School Rd RG40 25 C6
Palmer's Lodge GU2 130 B8
Palmers Gr KT8 36 A5
Palmers Rd Mortlake SW14 7 C4
Thornton Heath SW16 41 F7
Palmersfield Rd SM7 78 B5
Palmerston Cl
Farnborough GU14 84 D3
Woking GU21 70 A5
Palmerston Ct 9 KT6 37 D2
Palmerston Gr 4 SW19 20 A1
Palmerston Ho SM7 77 F4
Palmerston Rd
Carshalton SM5 60 A6
Hounslow TW3 5 C6
Merton SW19 20 A1
Mortlake SW14 7 C3
Sutton SM1 59 C5
Thornton Heath CR0 42 D4
Twickenham TW2 5 E1
Palmerstone Ct GU25 31 E4
Pampisford Rd
Croydon CR2,CR8 61 B2
Purley CR2,CR8 61 B2
Pams Way KT19 57 D5
Pan's Gdns GU15 65 F4
Pandora Ct 4 KT6 37 E3
Panells Ash RH14 212 C3
Pangbourne Ct SW17 20 C4
Pankhurst Cl TW7 5 F4
Pankhurst Ct 11 RH11 201 B1
Pankhurst Dr RG12 27 D4

Pankhurst Rd KT12 ......35 C2
Panmuir Rd SW20 ....39 B8
Panmure Rd SE26 ....23 B5
Pannell Cl RH19 ....185 D1
Pannells GU10 ....146 D5
Pannells Cl KT16 ....32 F1
Pannells Ct GU1 ....130 D8
Pantile Rd KT13 ....53 D6
Pantiles Cl GU21 ....69 B1
Panton Cl CR0 ....42 B1
Paper Mews RH4 ......136 B8
Papercourt La GU23 .....90 F6
Papermill Cl SM5 ....60 A6
Papplewick Sch SL5 ......29 A2
Papworth Way SW2 .....22 A8
Parade Cl GU23 ....90 C4
Parade Mews SE27,SW2 ..22 B6
Parade The Ash GU12 ...106 A4
Ashford TW16 ....14 F1
Burgh Heath KT20 ....77 E2
Burgh Heath KT20 ....97 E8
Claygate KT10 ....55 E4
Coulsdon CR5 ....80 A1
Crawley RH10 ....201 E7
Epsom KT18 ....76 D6
Epsom,The Wells KT18 ....76 A5
2 Kingston u T KT2 ......37 E7
Leatherhead KT22 ....95 B7
Loxwood RH14 ....212 F4
Wallington CR0 ....60 F5
Wentworth GU25 ....31 D3
Paradise Rd TW10 ....6 E2
Paragon Gr KT5 ....37 F3
Parbury Rise KT9 ....56 E4
Parc Ho 11 KT2 ....37 E8
Parchmore Rd CR7 ......42 C6
Parchmore Way CR7 .....42 B7
Pares Cl GU21 ....69 D3
Parfew Ct SE22 ....23 B6
Parfitts Cl GU9 ....125 A2
Parfour Dr CR8 ....80 C3
Parham Rd RH11 ....200 F7
Parish Church CE Inf & Jun Schs CR0 ....61 B7
Parish Cl Ash GU12 .....106 B1
Hale GU9 ....125 A6
Parish Ct KT6 ....37 E3
Parish Ho 6 RH11 .....201 D5
Parish La SE20,SE26 .....23 D1
Parish Rd GU14 ....105 B8
Park Ave Bromley BR1 ....24 F2
Camberley GU15 ....65 D4
Caterham CR3 ....100 E3
Egham TW20 ....12 C1
Isleworth TW3 ....5 B1
Mitcham CR4 ....21 B1
Mortlake SW14 ....7 D3
Peper Harow GU8 ....149 C5
Salfords RH1 ....139 F1
Staines TW18 ....13 A2
Upper Halliford TW17 .....34 E6
Wallington SM5 ....60 A4
West Wickham BR4 ....63 C8
Wokingham RG40 ....25 B6
Park Ave E KT17 ....58 A4
Park Ave W KT17 ....58 A4
Park Avenue Mews CR4 .21 B1
Park Barn Dr GU2 .....108 E2
Park Barn E GU2 ....108 F2
Park Chase
Godalming GU7 ....150 E2
Guildford GU1 ....109 E1
Park Cl Binstead GU10 ...145 A2
Brockham RH3 ....137 B4
Esher KT10 ....55 A4
Fetcham KT22 ....94 D3
Grayswood GU27 ....190 A1
Hampton TW12 ....36 C8
Isleworth TW3,TW7 ....5 C2
Kingston u T KT2 ....38 A8
Limpsfield RH8 ....122 F7
Oatlands Park KT13 ....53 F8
Wallington SM5 ....59 F4
Woodham KT15 ....52 C1
Park Close Cotts TW20 ..10 F3
Park Copse RH5 ....136 D7
Park Corner Dr KT24 ...112 E7
Park Cotts 10 TW1 ....6 B1
Park Cres Sunningdale SL5 29 F3
Twickenham TW2 ....16 D7
Park Ct Beckenham BR3 ...44 B6
Farnham GU9 ....125 D3
New Malden KT3 ....38 D5
Teddington KT1 ....37 C8
Upper Tooting SW12 ....21 A7
Wallington SM6 ....60 E5
West Norwood SE21 ....22 D5
Woking GU22 ....69 F1
Park Dr Bramley GU5 ....151 F6
Cranleigh GU6 ....174 F3
Mortlake SW14 ....7 D3
Sunningdale SL5 ....29 F3
Weybridge KT13 ....53 B5
Woking GU22 ....69 F1
Park End BR1 ....44 F8
Park Farm GU9 ....126 A5
Park Farm Cl RH12 ....217 D7
Park Farm Ct BR3 ....44 B6
Park Farm Ind Est GU15 .65 C1
Park Farm Rd
Horsham RH12 ....217 D7
Kingston u T KT2 ....17 E1
Park Gate Cotts GU6 ...174 C3
Park Gate Ct
Teddington TW12 ....16 C3
Park Gate Ct *continued*
11 Woking GU22 ....69 E1
Park Gdns KT2 ....17 F3
Park Gn KT23 ....94 A3
Park Hall Rd
Reigate RH2 ....118 A3
West Norwood SE21 ......22 D5
Park Hall Road Trad Est SE21 ....22 D5
Park Hill Forest Hill SE23 ..23 C7
Richmond TW10 ....6 F1
Wallington SM5 ....59 F4
Park Hill Cl SM5 ....59 E5
Park Hill Ct
South Croydon CR0 ....61 E8
Upper Tooting SW17 ....20 F5
Park Hill Inf Sch CR0 ....61 E7
Park Hill Jun Sch CR0 ...61 E7
Park Hill Rd
Beckenham BR2 ....44 E7
Ewell KT17 ....76 F8
South Croydon CR0,CR2 ...61 E7
Wallington SM6 ....60 B3
Park Hill Rise CR0 ......61 F7
Park Hill Sch KT2 ....18 A1
Park Ho
3 Aldershot GU11 ......105 A1
Penge SE26 ....23 A3
Reigate RH2 ....138 F7
Park Horsley KT24 .....113 A6
Park House Cotts GU6 ..174 F3
Park House Dr RH2 ....138 F7
Park House Gdns TW1 ....6 C2
Park La Ashstead KT21 ...96 A8
Ashurst Wood RH19 .....206 D6
Brook GU8 ....190 A8
Camberley GU15 ....65 C5
Cheam SM3 ....58 E4
Cranford TW5 ....4 A7
Croydon CR0,CR9 ....61 D7
Guildford GU4 ....110 D3
Hooley CR5 ....99 D6
Horton SL3 ....1 A4
Lingfield RH7 ....164 F5
Ockley RH5 ....177 F7
Reigate RH2 ....138 E8
Richmond TW9 ....6 D3
Teddington TW11 ....16 F2
Wallington SM5,SM6 ......60 A5
Winkfield SL4 ....9 B7
Park La E RH2 ....139 A7
Park Lawn CR7 ....42 C7
Park Lawn Rd KT13 .....53 C6
Park Ley Rd CR3 ....101 D6
Park Lodge KT23 ....94 A2
Park Manor 3 SM2 .....59 C3
Park Mans SE26 ....23 C5
Park Mead Inf Sch GU6 175 A3
Park Mead Jun Sch GU6 ....175 A3
Park Mews TW19 ....13 F8
Park Pl Blackwater GU17 ..64 F3
Hampton TW12 ....16 C2
Horsham RH12 ....217 C1
4 Woking GU22 ....69 F1
Park Prim Sch GU11 ....126 C7
Park Rd Albury GU5 .....132 E2
Aldershot GU11 ....126 B8
Ashford TW15 ....14 B3
Ashstead KT21 ....75 E1
Banstead SM7 ....78 C3
Beckenham BR3 ....23 F1
Bracknell RG12 ....27 D8
Burstow RH6 ....162 C1
Camberley GU15 ....65 C4
Caterham CR3 ....100 E4
Cheam SM3 ....58 E4
Chiswick W4 ....7 D8
Crowhurst RH7 ....143 E2
Dormans Park RH19 .....185 F6
East Grinstead RH19 ....185 D1
East Molesey KT8 ....36 C5
Egham TW20 ....12 A4
Esher KT10 ....55 B6
Farnborough GU11,GU14 .105 E8
Farnham GU9 ....125 D4
Faygate RH12 ....199 F1
Feltham TW13 ....15 D4
Fickleshole CR6 ....82 E5
Forest Row RH18 ....206 F2
Godalming GU7 ....150 E2
Guildford GU1 ....109 D1
Hackbridge SM6 ....60 B8
Hampton TW12 ....16 C3
Haslemere GU27 ....208 C5
Hounslow TW3,TW7 ....5 C2
Isleworth TW7 ....6 B5
Kenley CR8 ....80 C4
Kingston u T KT2 ....18 A1
Limpsfield RH8 ....122 F7
Lower Halliford TW17 .....34 A1
Mitcham SW19 ....20 E2
New Malden KT3 ....38 D5
Redhill RH1 ....118 F3
Richmond TW10 ....6 F1
Sandhurst GU47 ....64 C8
Slinfold RH13 ....215 D3
South Norwood SE25 ......42 E5
Stanwell TW19 ....2 C1
Sunbury TW16 ....15 B1
Surbiton KT5 ....37 C8
Teddington TW11 ....16 F2
Teddington, Hampton Wick KT1 ....37 C8
Twickenham TW1 ....6 C1
Wallington SM6 ....60 B5
Woking GU22 ....70 A2
Wokingham RG40 ....25 B6
Park Rd *continued*
Woodmansterne CR5,KT20, SM7 ....78 C3
Park Rise Forest Hill SE23 .23 E7
Horsham RH12 ....217 B4
Leatherhead KT22 ....95 B6
Park Rise Rd SE23 ....23 E7
Park Road Ho 3 KT2 ....18 A1
Park Row GU9 ....125 B3
Park Sch The GU22 ......70 A2
Park Sheen SW14 ....7 B3
Park Sq 2 KT10 ....55 B6
Park St Bagshot GU19 ....47 E3
Camberley GU15 ....65 C5
Croydon CR0,CR9 ....61 C8
Guildford GU1, GU2 .....130 C7
Horsham RH12 ....217 D2
Poyle SL3 ....1 D6
Slinfold RH13 ....215 C3
Teddington TW11 ....16 E2
Park Terr
1 Carshalton SM5 ....59 E7
New Malden KT4 ....39 A1
Park Terr E RH13 ......217 D1
Park Terr W RH13 ......217 D1
Park The Forest Hill SE23 ..23 C7
Great Bookham KT23 .....94 A3
Wallington SM5 ....59 F5
Park View
Addlestone KT15 ....52 C5
Bagshot GU19 ....47 D3
Crawley RH11 ....201 C5
Great Bookham KT23 .....94 A2
Horley RH6 ....161 A3
Morden CR4 ....40 D4
New Malden KT3 ....38 F6
Purley CR8 ....80 B8
Tandridge RH8 ....143 B5
Park View Ct GU22 ......89 F8
Park View Dr CR4 ....40 D7
Park View Rd
Salfords RH1 ....140 A1
Woldingham CR3 ....101 F5
Park Way Crawley RH10 .202 C7
East Molesey KT8 ....36 B6
Feltham TW14 ....15 B8
Great Bookham KT23 .....94 A4
Horsham RH12 ....217 C2
Park Wlk KT21 ....95 F8
Park Wood Cl SM7 ......77 D4
Park Wood Rd SM7 .....77 D4
Park Wood View SM7 ....77 D4
Park Works Rd RH1 .....119 E2
Parkcroft Rd SE12 ......24 F8
Parkdale Cres KT4 ......57 D7
Parke Rd TW16 ....35 A5
Parker Cl Crawley RH10 .202 D5
Wallington SM5 ....59 F4
Parker Ct SW19 ....19 E1
Parker Rd CR0,CR9 ......61 C6
Parker's Cl KT21 ....95 E8
Parker's Hill KT21 ....95 E8
Parker's La Ashstead KT21 95 F8
Winkfield RG42 ....8 B5
Parkers Ct GU19 ....47 F3
Parkfield Godalming GU7 .150 F2
Horsham RH12 ....217 C3
Hounslow TW7 ....5 E6
Parkfield Ave
Feltham TW13 ....15 A5
Mortlake SW14 ....7 E3
Parkfield Cl RH11 ......200 F6
Parkfield Cres TW13 .....15 A5
Parkfield Par TW13 .....15 A5
Parkfield Rd TW13 ......15 A5
Parkfields Croydon CR0 ..43 F1
Oxshott KT22 ....74 D8
Parkfields Ave SW20 ....39 B7
Parkfields Cl SM5 ....60 A6
Parkfields Rd TW10 .....17 F3
Parkgate Cl KT2 ....18 B2
Parkgate Gdns SW14 .....7 D2
Parkgate Rd
Newdigate RH5 ....158 C3
Reigate RH2 ....139 B8
Wallington SM5,SM6 ......60 B5
Parkham Ct BR2 ....44 E7
Parkhill Cl GU17 ....64 D4
Parkhill Rd GU17 ....64 D4
Parkhurst KT19 ....57 C1
Parkhurst Cotts GU10 ..187 F8
Parkhurst Fields GU10 .167 F1
Parkhurst Gr RH6 ......160 F4
Parkhurst Rd
Carshalton SM1 ....59 D6
Guildford GU2 ....109 B2
Horley RH6 ....160 E4
Parkin Ho SE20 ....23 D1
Parkland Dr RG12 ....27 E8
Parkland Gdns 12 SW19 .19 D7
Parkland Gr Ashford TW15 14 A4
Heath End GU9 ....125 F8
Hounslow TW7 ....5 F6
Parkland Rd TW15 ......14 A4
Parklands
Addlestone KT15 ....52 C5
Dorking RH5 ....136 B3
Great Bookham KT23 .....94 A4
Haslemere GU26 ....188 E1
Kingston u T KT5 ....37 F4
Oxted RH8 ....122 E4
Redhill RH1 ....119 A3
Parklands Cl SW14 ....7 C2
Parklands Ct TW5 ....4 D5
Parklands Pl GU1 ....110 B1
Parklands Rd SW16,SW17 21 B3
Parklands Way KT4 ......57 E8
Parklawn Ave Epsom KT18 76 B6
Parklawn Ave *continued*
Horley RH6 ....160 F5
Parkleigh Ct SW19 ......40 B7
Parkleigh Rd SW19 ......40 B7
Parkleys KT2,TW10 ......17 D4
Parkpale La RH3 ....137 A4
Parkrise Cl KT22 ....95 B6
Parkshot TW9 ....6 E3
Parkside
1 Beckenham BR3 ....44 B7
Cheam SM3 ....58 E4
Crawley RH10 ....201 E6
East Grinstead RH19 ....185 C1
Hale GU9 ....125 C6
Teddington TW12 ....16 D3
Wimbledon SW19 ....19 D4
Woodham KT15 ....52 C1
Parkside Ave SW19 .....19 D3
Parkside Cl
East Horsley KT24 ....92 F2
Penge SE20 ....23 C1
Parkside Cotts
Tatsfield TN16 ....103 E6
West Clandon GU4 ......111 A3
Parkside Cres KT5 ......38 C3
Parkside Ct KT13 ....53 A6
Parkside Gdns
Coulsdon CR5 ....79 B2
Wimbledon SW19 ....19 D4
Parkside Ho GU4 ....110 A5
Parkside Hospl SW19 ....19 D5
Parkside Mews
Chelsham CR6 ....82 A3
Horsham RH12 ....217 D2
Parkside Pl
East Horsley KT24 ....92 F2
Staines TW18 ....13 A2
Parkside Prep Sch KT11 .74 A1
Parkside Rd Hounslow TW3 .5 B2
Sunningdale SL5 ....30 A4
Parkstone Dr GU15 ......65 C4
Parkthorne Rd SW12 ....21 D8
Parkview Lodge BR3 ....44 B6
Parkview Rd CR0,CR9 ....43 A1
Parkview Vale GU4 .....110 C3
Parkway Camberley GU15 .65 C3
Crowthorne RG45 ....45 A5
Dorking RH4 ....136 A8
Guildford GU1 ....109 E2
Horley RH6 ....161 A3
New Addington CR0 ......63 C1
Oatlands Park KT13 ......53 D6
West Barnes SM4,SW20 ...39 D5
Parkway The TW5 ....4 B7
Parkway Trad Est TW5 ....4 C8
Parkwood BR3 ....24 A1
Parkwood Ave KT10 ......36 C1
Parkwood Gr TW16 ......35 A6
Parkwood Rd
Biggin Hill TN16 ....103 F6
Hounslow TW7 ....5 F6
Nutfield RH1 ....119 E2
Wimbledon SW19 ....19 F3
Parley Dr GU21 ....69 C1
Parliament Mews SW14 ..7 C5
Parliamentary Rd GU24 .87 A6
Parnall Ho 11 SE19 ......22 E4
Parnell Cl RH10 ....202 D4
Parnham Ave GU18 ......67 D8
Parr Ave KT17 ....58 B2
Parr Cl KT22 ....94 F7
Parr Ct TW13 ....15 C4
Parr's Pl TW12 ....16 A1
Parris Croft RH4 ....136 C4
Parrs Cl CR2 ....61 D2
Parry Cl Horsham RH13 ..218 C4
Stoneleigh KT17 ....58 A3
Parry Dr KT13 ....53 A1
Parry Rd SE25 ....42 E6
Parsley Gdns CR0 ....43 D1
Parson's Mead CR0 ......42 B1
Parson's Mead Sch KT21 95 E8
Parson's Pightle CR5 ...100 A7
Parsonage Bsns Pk RH12 ....217 E4
Parsonage Cl
Warlingham CR6 ....81 F3
Westcott RH4 ....135 C5
Parsonage Farm Inf Sch GU14 ....84 C5
Parsonage La RH4 .....135 C6
Parsonage Rd
Cranleigh GU6 ....174 D3
Englefield Green TW20 ....11 D3
Horsham RH12,RH13 ....217 E4
Parsonage Sq 3 RH4 ...136 A7
Parsonage Way
Frimley GU16 ....65 E1
Horsham RH12 ....217 E4
Parsons Cl
Haslemere GU27 ....208 C8
Horley RH6 ....160 E4
Parsons Field GU47 .....64 B8
Parsons Gn GU27 ......208 C8
Parsons Green Ct GU1 .109 D3
Parsons Ho 21 SW12 .....21 E8
Parsons La GU26 ....188 D6
Parsons Mead KT8 ......36 C6
Parsonsfield Cl SM7 .....77 D4
Parsonsfield Rd SM7 ....77 D4
Parthia Cl KT20 ....97 B8
Partridge Cl
Crondall GU10 ....124 D8
Frimley GU16 ....65 E1
Partridge Knoll CR8 .....80 B6
Partridge La
Parkgate RH5 ....158 E2
Newdigate RH5,RH12 ....179 F3
Partridge Mead SM7 ....77 C4
Partridge Pl RH10 .....204 C6
Partridge Rd 8 TW12 ...16 A2
Partridge Way GU4 ....110 D3
Parvis Rd KT14 ....71 D7
Paschal Rd GU15 ....65 F8
Passfields SE6 ....24 C5
Passingham Ho TW5 .....5 A8
Pastens Rd RH8 ....123 C4
Pasture Rd SE6 ....24 F7
Pasture The RH10 .....202 C6
Pasture Wood Rd RH5 .155 D6
Pat Williams Ho SE27 ...22 C5
Patching Cl RH11 ......200 F7
Patchings RH13 ....217 F3
Paterson Cl GU16 ....66 C3
Pates Manor Dr TW14 ...14 D8
Path Link RH10 ....201 E7
Path The SW19 ....40 B8
Pathfield GU8 ....191 B4
Pathfield Cl
Chiddingfold GU8 ....191 B4
Rudgwick RH12 ....214 D7
Pathfield Rd
Rudgwick RH12 ....214 D7
Streatham SW16 ....21 D2
Pathfields GU5 ....133 A4
Pathfields Cl GU27 .....208 D7
Pathfinders The GU14 ...84 C3
Pathway The GU23 ......90 F2
Patmore La KT12 ....53 F4
Patricia Gdns SM2 ......78 A8
Patrington Cl RH11 .....201 A3
Patten Ash Dr RG40 .....25 E7
Patten Rd SW18 ....20 E8
Pattenden Rd SE23,SE6 ..23 F7
Patterdale Cl Catford BR1 .24 E2
Crawley RH11 ....201 C4
Patterson Ct SE19 ....22 F2
Patterson Rd SE19 ......22 F2
Paul Cl GU11 ....125 E8
Paul Gdns CR0 ....61 F8
Paul Vanson Ct KT12 ....54 D4
Paul's Pl KT21 ....96 B8
Pauline Cres TW2 ....16 C7
Pauls Mead RH7 ....164 E5
Paved Ct 9 TW9 ....6 D2
Pavement The
Crawley RH10 ....201 E6
11 West Norwood SE27 ...22 C4
Pavilion Gdns TW18 .....13 B1
Pavilion Rd GU11 ......104 E1
Pavilion The KT20 ....98 C4
Pavilion Way RH19 .....205 E8
Pavilions End The GU15 .65 D3
Paviors GU9 ....125 C3
Pawley Cl GU10 ....126 F7
Pawleyne Cl SE20 ....23 C1
Pawson's Rd CR0 ....42 C4
Pax Cl RH11 ....200 E4
Paxton Cl Richmond TW9 ...6 F5
Walton-on-T KT12 ....35 C2
Paxton Ct Forest Hill SE26 .23 E4
Mitcham CR4 ....40 F7
Paxton Gdns GU21 ......70 E7
Paxton Pl SE27 ....22 E4
Paxton Prim Sch SE19 ...22 E2
Paxton Rd Chiswick W4 ....7 E8
Forest Hill SE23 ....23 E5
Payley Dr RG40 ....25 E8
Payne Cl RH10 ....202 D8
Paynesfield Ave SW14 ....7 D4
Paynesfield Rd
Tatsfield TN16 ....103 D7
Tatsfield TN16 ....103 D8
Peabody Est SE24 ....22 C8
Peabody Hill SE21 ....22 C7
Peabody Rd GU11,GU14 .105 D8
Peacemaker Cl RH11 ...200 E4
Peach Rd TW13 ....15 A7
Peach St RG40 ....25 C6
Peach Tree Cl GU14 .....85 A7
Peaches Cl SM2 ....58 E3
Peacock Ave TW14 ......14 D7
Peacock Cotts RG40 .....26 C5
Peacock Gdns CR0,CR2 ..62 E1
Peacock La RG12 ....26 D6
Peacock Wlk 8 RH11 ...201 A3
Peacocks Sh Ctr The 1 GU21 ....69 E2
Peak Hill SE26 ....23 C4
Peak Hill Ave SE26 ......23 C4
Peak Hill Gdns SE26 .....23 C4
Peak Rd GU2 ....109 A4
Peak The SE26 ....23 C5
Peakfield GU10 ....167 C7
Peaks Hill CR8 ....60 E1
Peaks Hill Rise CR8 .....60 E1
Peall Rd CR0 ....41 F3
Pear Ave TW17 ....34 E6
Pear Tree Cl
Addlestone KT15 ....52 A5
Mitcham CR4 ....40 E7
Pear Tree Ct GU15 ....66 B8
Pear Tree Hill RH1 .....161 A8
Pear Tree Ho 4 SE19 ....22 E2
Pear Tree La GU10 .....145 F3
Pear Tree Rd
Addlestone KT15 ....52 A5
Ashford TW15 ....14 C3
Pearce Cl CR4 ....41 A7
Pearce Ho 7 SW2 ....21 E8
Pearcefield Ave 5 SE23 .23 C7
Pearfield Rd SE23 ....23 E5
Pearl Ct GU21 ....68 E3
Pearmain Cl TW17 ......34 B4
Pears Rd TW3 ....5 C4
Pearson Cl CR8 ....80 B8

Pearson Ct SM4 . . . . .40 B4
Pearson Rd RH10 . . . . . . .202 C6
Peartree Ave SW17 . . . . . .20 C5
Peartree Cl CR2 . . . . .81 B5
Peary Cl RH12 . . . . .217 D6
Peaslake La GU5 . . . . . . .154 D6
Peaslake Sch GU5 . . . . . .154 E7
Peat Comm GU8 . . . . . . .148 C2
Peatmore Ave GU22 . . . . . .71 A3
Peatmore Cl GU22 . . . . . . .71 A3
Peatmore Dr GU24 . . . . . . .87 C6
Pebble Cl KT20 . . . . .116 E6
Pebble Hill KT20 . . . . . . .112 C2
Pebble Hill Cotts RH8 . . .123 B6
Pebblehill Rd KT20,RH8 . .116 E5
Pebworth Ct 8 RH1 . . . . .119 A3
Pebworth Lodge SE25 . . . .42 F5
Peckarmans Wood SE21,
SE26 . . . . .23 A5
Peek Cres SW19 . . . . .19 D3
Peeks Brook La
  Crawley RH6 . . . . .182 E7
  Horley RH6 . . . . .161 F2
Peel Ave GU16 . . . . .86 A7
Peel Cl GU14 . . . . .105 C8
Peel Ctr The RG12 . . . . . . .27 B7
Peel Ho TW20 . . . . .11 F2
Pegasus Ave GU12 . . . . . .105 E2
Pegasus Cl GU27 . . . . . . .207 D5
Pegasus Ct
  Caterham CR3 . . . . .101 A4
  Crawley RH11 . . . . .200 E4
  Farnborough GU14 . . . . . .85 E1
  Kingston u T KT1 . . . . . . .37 D6
  8 Leatherhead KT22 . . . .95 C6
Pegasus Pl RH10 . . . . . . .182 A1
Pegasus Rd
  Croydon CR0,CR9 . . . . . . .61 A4
  Farnborough GU14 . . . . . .84 F7
  Farnborough GU14 . . . . . .85 B2
Pegasus Way RH19 . . . . . .186 B3
Pegg Rd TW5 . . . . .4 D7
Peggotty Pl GU47 . . . . . . .45 E2
Pegler Way RH11 . . . . . . .201 D6
Pegwell Cl RH11 . . . . . . .200 F4
Peket Cl TW18 . . . . .32 E8
Peldon Ct TW10 . . . . .6 E2
Pelham Ct Crawley RH11 . .201 B2
  Great Bookham KT23 . . . . .94 C1
  Horsham RH12 . . . . .217 B2
  Staines TW18 . . . . .13 B3
Pelham Ct Bsns Ctr
  RH11 . . . . .201 B2
Pelham Dr RH11 . . . . .201 A2
Pelham Ho CR3 . . . . .100 F3
Pelham Pl Crawley RH11 . .201 B2
  Rowledge GU10 . . . . .146 A4
Pelham Prim Sch SW19 . . .20 A1
Pelham Rd Merton SW19 . . .20 A1
  Penge BR3,SE20 . . . . .43 C7
Pelham Way KT23 . . . . . . .94 C1
Pelhams Cl KT10 . . . . .55 A6
Pelhams Wlk KT10 . . . . . . .55 A6
Pelinore Rd SE6 . . . . .24 E6
Pelling Hill SL4 . . . . .11 B7
Pelton Ave SM2 . . . . .59 B1
Pelton Ct CR2 . . . . .61 C4
Pemberley Chase KT19 . . . .57 B5
Pemberley Cl KT19 . . . . . . .57 B5
Pemberton Ho SE26 . . . . . .23 A4
Pemberton Pl KT10 . . . . . . .55 C7
Pemberton Rd KT8 . . . . . . .36 C5
Pemberton Terr KT8 . . . . . .36 C5
Pembley Gn RH10 . . . . . . .183 E3
Pembridge Ave TW4 . . . . . .15 F7
Pembroke RG12 . . . . .27 A1
Pembroke Ave
  Hersham KT12 . . . . .54 D6
  Surbiton KT5 . . . . .38 B4
Pembroke Broadway
  GU15 . . . . .65 C5
Pembroke Cl Ascot SL5 . . . .29 D4
  Banstead SM7 . . . . .78 B2
Pembroke Ct
  Beckenham BR3 . . . . .44 B6
  Woking GU22 . . . . .70 B3
Pembroke Gdns GU22 . . . . .70 A1
Pembroke Ho SW19 . . . . . .20 D3
Pembroke Mews SL5 . . . . . .29 D4
Pembroke Pl TW7 . . . . .5 E5
Pembroke Rd
  Crawley RH11 . . . . .182 C1
  Mitcham CR4 . . . . .41 A7
  South Norwood SE25 . . . . .42 E5
  Woking GU22 . . . . .70 A2
Pembroke Villas TW9 . . . . . .6 D3
Pembrook Lodge 2
  SW16 . . . . .21 F5
Pembury Ave KT4 . . . . .39 A2
Pembury Cl Hayes BR2 . . . .44 F2
  Wallington CR5 . . . . .79 A5
Pembury Ct UB3 . . . . .3 D8
Pembury Pl 3 GU12 . . . . .105 C1
Pembury Rd SE25 . . . . .43 A5
Pemdevon Rd CR0 . . . . . . .42 A2
Penarth Ct SM2 . . . . .59 C3
Penates KT10 . . . . .55 D6
Penberth Rd SE6 . . . . .24 C7
Penceat Ct SE20 . . . . .43 C7
Pendarves Rd SW20 . . . . . .39 C8
Pendell Ave UB3 . . . . .3 F7
Pendell Rd RH1 . . . . .120 B4
Pendennis Cl KT14 . . . . . . .71 A5
Pendennis Rd SW16 . . . . . .21 E4
Penderel Rd TW3 . . . . .5 A2
Penderry Rise SE6 . . . . . . .24 D6
Pendine Pl RG12 . . . . .27 B4

Pendle Ho 13 SE26 . . . . . .23 A5
Pendle Rd SW16 . . . . .21 B3
Pendlebury RG12 . . . . .27 A2
Pendleton Cl RH1 . . . . . . .139 F7
Pendleton Rd RH1 . . . . . . .139 E6
Pendragon Rd BR1 . . . . . . .24 F5
Pendragon Way GU15 . . . . .66 D3
Penerley Rd SE6 . . . . .24 B7
Penfold Cl CR0,CR9 . . . . . . .61 A7
Penfold Croft GU9 . . . . . . .125 F4
Penfold Ct CR4 . . . . .41 A7
Penfold Rd RH10 . . . . .202 B2
Penge East Sta SE20 . . . . .23 D1
Penge La SE20 . . . . .23 D1
Penge Rd SE20,SE25 . . . . . .43 A6
Penge West Sta SE20 . . . . .23 B2
Pengilly Rd GU9 . . . . .110 C1
Pengilly Rd GU9 . . . . .125 B1
Penhurst GU21 . . . . .69 F5
Peninsula Cl GU15 . . . . . . .66 B7
Peninsular Cl TW14 . . . . .3 E1
Penistone Rd SW16 . . . . . .21 E1
Penlee Ho 10 GU22 . . . . . .89 E8
Penn Cl RH11 . . . . .181 D1
Pennards The SE1 . . . . .35 C6
Pennefather's Rd GU11 . . .104 F3
Penner Cl SW19 . . . . .19 E6
Penners Gdns KT6 . . . . . . .37 E2
Pennine Cl RH11 . . . . .201 B6
Pennine Way
  Farnborough GU14 . . . . . .84 E7
  Harlington UB7 . . . . .3 D7
Pennings Ave GU3 . . . . . . .108 F3
Pennington Cl 10 SE27 . . . .22 D4
Pennington Dr KT13 . . . . . .53 E7
Pennington Lodge 18
  KT5 . . . . .37 E4
Penns Wood GU14 . . . . . . .85 D1
Pennthorpe Sch RH12 . . . .214 C7
Penny Dr GU3 . . . . .108 B2
Penny La TW17 . . . . .34 E2
Penny Mews SW12 . . . . . . .21 B8
Penny Royal SM6 . . . . .60 D4
Pennycroft CR0 . . . . .62 E2
Pennyfield KT11 . . . . .73 A6
Pennymead Dr KT24 . . . . .112 F8
Pennymead Rise KT24 . . . .112 F8
Pennypot La GU24 . . . . . . .68 C7
Penrhyn Cl GU11 . . . . .105 B1
Penrhyn Cres SW14 . . . . . . .7 C3
Penrhyn Gdns KT1 . . . . . . .37 D5
Penrhyn Rd KT1 . . . . .37 E6
Penrith Cl Beckenham BR3 . .44 B8
  Redhill RH2 . . . . .118 E2
Penrith Pl SE27 . . . . .22 B6
Penrith Rd
  New Malden KT3 . . . . .38 D5
  South Norwood CR7 . . . . . .42 C7
Penrith St SW16 . . . . .21 C2
Penrose Ct TW20 . . . . .11 C2
Penrose Dr KT19 . . . . .76 A8
Penrose Rd KT22 . . . . .94 C5
Penryn Dr GU35 . . . . .187 C5
Penryn Ho 5 RH1 . . . . . . .119 A3
Pensfold La RH12 . . . . . . .214 E5
Pensford Ave TW9 . . . . .7 A5
Pensford Cl RG45 . . . . .45 B7
Penshurst Cl RH10 . . . . . .202 D7
Penshurst Gn BR2 . . . . . . .44 F4
Penshurst Rd CR7 . . . . . . .42 B4
Penshurst Rise GU16 . . . . .85 F8
Penshurst Way SM2 . . . . . .59 A3
Penshurst Wlk 6 BR2 . . . .44 F4
Pentelow Gdns TW14 . . . . . .4 A1
Pentland Ave TW17 . . . . . .34 A4
Pentland Pl GU14 . . . . .84 E7
Pentlands BR3 . . . . .44 C8
Pentlands Cl CR4 . . . . .41 B6
Pentney Rd
  Streatham SW12 . . . . .21 C7
  Wimbledon SW19,SW20 . . .39 E8
Penton Ave TW18 . . . . .32 F8
Penton Ct TW18 . . . . .12 F2
Penton Hall TW18 . . . . .33 A8
Penton Hall Dr TW18 . . . . . .33 A8
Penton Ho SM2 . . . . .59 C3
Penton Hook Marina
  KT16 . . . . .33 A6
Penton Hook Rd TW18 . . . .33 A8
Penton Rd TW18 . . . . .12 F1
Pentreath Ave GU2 . . . . . .129 F8
Penwerris Ave TW5,TW7 . . . .5 C7
Penwerris Ct TW7 . . . . .5 C7
Penwith Dr GU27 . . . . . . .207 E5
Penwith Rd SW18 . . . . .20 B6
Penwith Wlk GU22 . . . . . . .89 D8
Penwood End GU22 . . . . . .89 B6
Penwood Gdns RG12 . . . . .26 D3
Penwood Ho SW15 . . . . .7 F1
Penwortham Prim Sch
  SW17 . . . . .21 B2
Penwortham Rd
  South Croydon CR2 . . . . . .61 D1
  Streatham SW16 . . . . .21 C2
Peper Harow Ho GU8 . . . .149 D4
Peper Harow La GU8 . . . . .149 C6
Peperham Cotts GU27 . . . .208 C8
Peperham Ho GU27 . . . . . .208 C7
Peperham Rd GU27 . . . . . .208 C8
Peperharow Rd GU7 . . . . .150 C6
Peppard Rd RH10 . . . . . . .202 D3
Pepper Cl CR3 . . . . .100 E2
Pepperbox La GU5 . . . . . . .173 E4
Peppermint Cl CR0 . . . . . . .41 E2
Pepys Cl Ashstead KT21 . . . .76 A2
  Brands Hill SL3 . . . . .1 B8
Pepys Rd SW20 . . . . .39 C8
Perak Ct KT5 . . . . .38 C2

Percheron Cl TW7 . . . . .5 F4
Percheron Dr GU21 . . . . . . .88 C8
Percival Cl KT22 . . . . .74 B8
Percival Rd Feltham TW13 . .14 F6
  Mortlake SW14 . . . . .7 C3
Percival Way KT19 . . . . .57 D6
Percy Ave TW15 . . . . .14 A3
Percy Bilton Ct TW5 . . . . . . .5 B6
Percy Bryant Rd TW16 . . . .14 E1
Percy Ct 1 KT5 . . . . .37 F3
Percy Gdns
  3 Isleworth TW7 . . . . .6 A4
  New Malden KT3 . . . . .38 C1
Percy Ho 4 SW16 . . . . .21 C4
Percy Rd Carshalton CR4 . . .41 A2
  Croydon SE25 . . . . .43 A4
  Guildford GU2 . . . . .109 B3
  Hampton TW12 . . . . .16 A1
  Horsham RH12 . . . . .217 B3
  Isleworth TW7 . . . . .6 A3
  Penge SE20 . . . . .43 D8
  Twickenham TW2 . . . . .16 C7
Percy Way TW2 . . . . .16 C7
Peregrine Cl
  Bracknell RG12 . . . . .27 B4
  Cranleigh GU6 . . . . .174 E4
Peregrine Gdns CR0 . . . . . .62 E8
Peregrine Rd TW16 . . . . . . .34 F7
Peregrine Way SW19,
  SW20 . . . . .19 C1
Performing Arts & Tech Sch
  SE25 . . . . .42 D3
Perifield SE21 . . . . .22 C7
Perimeter Rd E RH6 . . . . .182 B6
Perimeter Rd N RH6 . . . . .181 D8
Perimeter Rd S RH6,
  RH11 . . . . .181 E5
Perkin Cl TW3 . . . . .5 B3
Perkins Cl TW15 . . . . .13 F3
Perkins Way RG41 . . . . .25 A5
Perkstead Ct 6 RH11 . . . .201 A3
Perleybrooke La GU21 . . . . .69 A2
Perowne St GU11 . . . . .104 F2
Perran Rd SE24, SW2 . . . . .22 B6
Perran Wlk 16 TW8 . . . . . . .6 E8
Perrin Cl TW15 . . . . .13 F3
Perrin Ct GU21 . . . . .70 B4
Perring Ave GU14 . . . . .84 F7
Perring Rd GU14 . . . . .85 A1
Perrior Rd GU7 . . . . .150 E7
Perry Ave RH19 . . . . .185 E3
Perry Cl GU7 . . . . .151 B5
Perry Hill SE23,SE6 . . . . . . .23 F5
Perry Ho 24 SW2 . . . . .21 E8
Perry How KT4 . . . . .38 F1
Perry Oaks RG12 . . . . .27 E7
Perry Oaks Dr TW6,UB7 . . . .2 C5
Perry Rise SE23,SE6 . . . . . .23 E5
Perry Vale SE23 . . . . .23 D6
Perry Way Bracknell RG12 . .27 E7
  Farnham GU9 . . . . .125 B7
  Lightwater GU18 . . . . .66 F7
Perryfield Ho 7 RH10 . . . .201 D5
Perryfield Rd RH11 . . . . . .201 D5
Perryfield Way RH10 . . . . . .17 B6
Perrylands RH6 . . . . .180 F7
Perrylands La RH6 . . . . . . .162 A2
Perrymount Prim Sch
  SE23 . . . . .23 D6
Perryn Ct 2 TW1 . . . . .17 A8
Perrywood Bsns Pk
  RH1 . . . . .140 B1
Persant Rd SE6 . . . . .24 E6
Perseverance Cotts
  GU23 . . . . .91 C6
Persfield Mews KT17 . . . . .57 F1
Persfield Rd KT17 . . . . .58 A1
Pershore Gr SM5 . . . . .40 D3
Perth Cl Crawley RH11 . . . .181 D1
  Wimbledon SW20 . . . . .39 A7
Perth Rd BR3 . . . . .44 C7
Perth Way RH12 . . . . .217 F4
Perystreete SE23 . . . . .23 C6
Petavel Rd TW11 . . . . .16 E2
Peter Ave RH8 . . . . .122 D6
Peter Kennedy Ct CR0 . . . . .43 F3
Peter's Path SE26 . . . . .23 B4
Peterborough Rd
  Carshalton CR4,SM4,SM5 . .40 E3
  Crawley RH10 . . . . .201 E2
  Guildford GU2 . . . . .108 F3
Peterhouse Cl GU47 . . . . . .45 F2
Peterhouse Par RH10 . . . .182 C1
Peterlee Wlk RH11 . . . . . .200 E3
Peters Wood RH5 . . . . . . .178 C5
Petersfield Ave TW15,
  TW18 . . . . .13 C2
Petersfield Cres CR5 . . . . . .79 E4
Petersfield Rd TW18 . . . . . .13 C3
Petersfield Rise SW15 . . . . .19 B7
Petersham Ave KT14 . . . . . .71 E7
Petersham Cl
  Byfleet KT14 . . . . .71 E7
  Cheam SM1 . . . . .59 A5
  Richmond TW10 . . . . .17 D6
Petersham Rd TW10 . . . . . .17 C7
Petersham Terr CR0 . . . . . .60 E7
Petersmead Cl KT20 . . . . . .97 B4
Peterstow Cl SW19 . . . . . . .19 E6
Peterwood Pk CR9 . . . . . . .60 F8
Peterwood Way CR0 . . . . . .60 F8
Petrel Ct 8 SE21 . . . . .22 D6
Petridge Rd RH1 . . . . .139 F4
Petts La TW17 . . . . .34 A5
Petworth Cl Coulsdon CR5 . .99 C8
  Frimley GU16 . . . . .85 F8

Petworth Ct
  Crawley RH11 . . . . .200 F3
  Frimley GU15 . . . . .65 F4
  Haslemere GU27 . . . . . . .208 D6
Petworth Dr RH12 . . . . . . .217 F7
Petworth Gdns SW20 . . . . .39 B6
Petworth Rd
  Chiddingfold GU8 . . . . . . .191 C4
  Chiddingfold, Ansteadbrook
  GU27 . . . . .209 B6
  Witley GU8 . . . . .170 F5
  Wormley GU8 . . . . .171 A1
Pevensey Cl
  Crawley RH10 . . . . .202 C5
  Hounslow TW7 . . . . .5 C7
Pevensey Ct SW16 . . . . . . .22 A5
Pevensey Ho RH2 . . . . . . .139 B5
Pevensey Rd
  Feltham TW13 . . . . .15 E7
  Upper Tooting SW17 . . . . . .20 D4
Pevensey Way GU16 . . . . . .86 A8
Peverel Rd RH11 . . . . .200 E5
Peveril Dr TW11 . . . . .16 D3
Pewley Bank GU1 . . . . . . .130 E7
Pewley Down Inf Sch
  GU1 . . . . .130 E7
Pewley Hill GU1 . . . . .130 E7
Pewley Point GU1 . . . . . . .130 E7
Pewley Way GU1 . . . . .130 E7
Pewsey Vale RG12 . . . . . . .27 F4
Peyton's Cotts RH1 . . . . . .119 F3
Pharaoh Cl CR4 . . . . .40 F7
Pheasant Cl CR8 . . . . .80 B6
Philanthropic Rd RH1 . . . .140 B8
Philip Gdns CR0 . . . . .62 F8
Philip Morris Ho TW13 . . . .15 B7
Philip Rd TW18 . . . . .13 D2
Philip Southcote Sch
  KT15 . . . . .52 C8
Philips Ho GU26 . . . . .188 B3
Phillips Cl
  Aldershot GU10 . . . . .126 E8
  Crawley RH10 . . . . .202 C2
  Godalming GU7 . . . . .150 D2
Phillips Cotts GU7 . . . . . . .150 B4
Phillips Hatch GU5 . . . . . .152 C8
Philpot La GU24 . . . . .69 C7
Phipp's Bridge Rd CR4,
  SW19 . . . . .40 D6
Phoenix Bsns Pk RG12 . . . .26 C7
  West Wickham BR4 . . . . . .63 E8
Phoenix Cl
  13 Aldershot GU11 . . . . . .105 A2
  Croydon SE25 . . . . .43 A4
  3 Epsom KT17 . . . . .76 E6
  Guildford GU1 . . . . .130 D7
Phoenix Ctr The KT20 . . . . .97 C7
Phoenix La RH19 . . . . .206 E6
Phoenix Pl TW18 . . . . .13 A3
Phoenix Rd SE20 . . . . .23 C2
Phoenix Way TW5 . . . . .4 D8
Phyllis Ave KT3 . . . . .39 B4
Phyllis Ho CR0 . . . . .61 B6
Piccards The GU2 . . . . . . .130 C5
Pickering RG12 . . . . .27 A5
Pickering Gdns SE25 . . . . .42 F3
Picket Post Cl RG12 . . . . . .27 F6
Pickets St SW12 . . . . .21 B8
Pickford St GU11 . . . . .105 B2
Pickhurst Gn BR2 . . . . .44 F2
Pickhurst Inf Sch BR3 . . . .44 F3
Pickhurst Jun Sch BR3 . . .44 F3
Pickhurst La BR2,BR3,BR4 .44 F3
Pickhurst Mead BR2 . . . . . .44 F2
Pickhurst Pk BR2 . . . . .44 F4
Pickhurst Rd GU8 . . . . . . .191 D2
Pickhurst Rise BR4 . . . . . . .44 D1
Pickins Piece SL3 . . . . .1 A5
Pickwick Cl TW4 . . . . .4 E2
Pickwick Gdns GU15 . . . . . .66 B4
Pickwick Rd SE21 . . . . .22 E8
Picquets Way KT20,SM7 . . . .77 F2
Picton Cl GU15 . . . . .66 B7
Picton Ho 1 SW4 . . . . .21 E8
Pier Five Rd E RH6 . . . . . .181 E8
Pier Four Rd N RH6 . . . . . .181 E8
Pier Rd TW14 . . . . .4 B2
Pierrefondes Ave GU14 . . . .85 B5
Pierrepoint SE25 . . . . .42 E6
Pierson Ho 12 SE19 . . . . . .22 E4
Pigbush La RH14 . . . . .213 A7
Pigeon La TW12 . . . . .16 A4
Pigeon Pass RH10 . . . . . . .204 C5
Pigeonhouse La
  Lower Kingswood CR5 . . . .98 C3
  Winkfield SL5 . . . . .8 E4
Piggott Ct RH13 . . . . .217 E1
Piggott Rd RG40 . . . . .25 D6
Pigott Rd RG40 . . . . .25 E8
Pike Cl GU11 . . . . .105 C2
Pikes Hill KT17 . . . . .76 E6
Pikes La RH7 . . . . .143 F5
Pikethorne SE23 . . . . .23 D6
Pilgrim Cl SM4 . . . . .40 B2
Pilgrim Ct GU8 . . . . .170 F8
Pilgrim Hill SE27 . . . . .22 C4
Pilgrim Ho GU1 . . . . .130 D7
Pilgrim's Way CR2 . . . . .61 F5
Pilgrims Cl Farnham GU9 . .146 A8
  Shere GU5 . . . . .133 A4
  Westhumble RH5 . . . . . . .115 B4
Pilgrims La
  Caterham CR3 . . . . .100 B1
  Titsey RH8 . . . . .103 D3
Pilgrims Pl 1 RH2 . . . . . . .118 A3

Pea – Pin 275

Pilgrims View GU12 . . . . . .127 C8
Pilgrims Way Bisley GU24 . .68 A3
  Shere GU5 . . . . .133 A4
  Westhumble RH5 . . . . . . .115 B4
Pilgrims Way Cotts
  RH3 . . . . .116 C2
Pilgrims Way Prim Sch The
  GU9 . . . . .146 B8
Pilgrims' Way
  Guildford GU4 . . . . .130 E5
  Reigate RH2 . . . . .118 A3
Pilsden Cl SW19 . . . . .19 D7
Pilton Est The CR9 . . . . . . .61 B8
Pimms Cl GU4 . . . . .110 A5
Pinckards GU8 . . . . .191 B5
Pincott La KT24 . . . . .112 B6
Pincott Rd SW19 . . . . .40 C8
Pine Ave Brookwood GU24 . .88 A6
  Camberley GU15 . . . . .65 D3
  West Wickham BR4 . . . . . .44 B1
Pine Bank GU26 . . . . .188 E4
Pine Cl Ash Vale GU12 . . . .106 A6
  Crawley RH11 . . . . .181 C1
  Kenley CR8 . . . . .80 D2
  Penge SE20 . . . . .43 C8
  Sandhurst GU15 . . . . .64 E7
  Woking GU21 . . . . .69 C3
Pine Coombe CR0 . . . . .62 D6
Pine Cres SM5 . . . . .78 D8
Pine Croft KT13 . . . . .53 D4
Pine Croft Rd RG41 . . . . . .25 A2
Pine Ct Bracknell RG12 . . . .27 E5
  Farnborough GU14 . . . . . .85 C1
  1 Guildford GU1 . . . . . . .110 A1
  3 Weybridge KT13 . . . . . .53 C5
Pine Dean KT23 . . . . .94 B2
Pine Dr GU17 . . . . .64 E3
Pine Gdns Horley RH6 . . . .161 A2
  Surbiton KT5 . . . . .38 A3
Pine Gr
  East Grinstead RH19 . . . .185 B3
  Farnham GU10 . . . . .146 E6
  Weybridge KT13 . . . . .53 C5
  Wimbledon SW19 . . . . . . .19 F3
  Windlesham GU20 . . . . . . .48 D4
Pine Grove Mews 2
  KT13 . . . . .53 C5
Pine Hill KT18 . . . . .76 D4
Pine Lodge KT11 . . . . .73 C4
Pine Mount Rd GU15 . . . . . .65 D5
Pine Pl KT17 . . . . .77 D5
Pine Rd GU22 . . . . .89 C7
Pine Ridge SM5 . . . . .60 A2
Pine Ridge Dr GU10 . . . . .146 C5
Pine Ridge Inf Sch GU15 . .47 A1
Pine Shaw RH10 . . . . .202 D7
Pine Tree Cl TW5 . . . . .4 B6
Pine Tree Hill GU22 . . . . . .70 D3
Pine Tree Lodge BR2 . . . . .44 F5
Pine Trees Bsns Pk
  TW18 . . . . .12 E3
Pine View Cl
  Chilworth GU4 . . . . .131 F3
  Farnham GU9 . . . . .126 A5
  Haslemere GU27 . . . . . . .208 C8
Pine Way TW20 . . . . .11 B2
Pine Way Cl RH19 . . . . . . .205 E7
Pine Wlk Caterham CR3 . . .100 F5
  Cobham KT11 . . . . .73 D5
  East Horsley KT24 . . . . . .112 F7
  Great Bookham KT23 . . . . .94 B2
  Surbiton KT5 . . . . .38 A3
  Sutton SM5,SM7 . . . . .59 D1
  Woodmansterne CR5,SM7 . .78 F2
Pine Wood TW16 . . . . .35 A8
Pineacre Cl GU22 . . . . .70 B2
Pinecote Dr SL5 . . . . .29 F2
Pinefields KT15 . . . . .52 B6
Pinefields Cl RG45 . . . . . . .45 B4
Pinehill Rd RG45 . . . . .45 C3
Pinehill Rise GU47 . . . . . . .64 C8
Pinehurst Ascot SL5 . . . . . .29 C4
  Horsham RH12 . . . . .217 C4
  8 Woking GU22 . . . . .69 F1
Pinehurst Ave GU14 . . . . . .85 B3
Pinehurst Cl KT20 . . . . .98 A5
Pinehurst Cotts GU14 . . . . .85 B2
Pinehurst Rd GU14 . . . . . . .85 A2
Pinel Cl GU25 . . . . .31 E5
Pines Cl 14 SW19 . . . . .19 D3
Pines Inf Sch The RG12 . . . .27 A2
Pines Jun Sch The RG12 . . .27 A2
Pines The Camberley GU15 . .65 F7
  Dorking RH4 . . . . .136 B6
  Horsham RH12 . . . . .218 C5
  Purley CR8 . . . . .80 C6
  South Norwood SE19 . . . . .22 B2
  Sunbury TW16 . . . . .35 A6
  Woking GU21 . . . . .69 F5
Pines Trad Est The GU3 . . .108 C3
Pinetrees RH10 . . . . .183 B3
Pineview GU14 . . . . .85 A4
Pinewood Ave
  Crowthorne RG45 . . . . . . .45 C6
  Woodham KT15 . . . . .52 C1
Pinewood Cl
  Broadbridge Heath RH12 . .216 D3
  South Croydon CR0 . . . . . .62 E7
  Woking GU21 . . . . .70 A4
Pinewood Cotts GU21 . . . . .70 B7
Pinewood Cres GU14 . . . . .84 C5
Pinewood Ct
  Addlestone KT15 . . . . .52 D6

Pinewood Ct continued
1 Woking GU21 . . . . .70 A3
Pinewood Dr TW18 . . . . . .13 A3
Pinewood Gdns GU19 . . .47 C3
Pinewood Gr KT15 . . . . . . .52 B1
Pinewood Inf GU14 . . .84 D7
Pinewood Mews TW19 . . . .2 D1
Pinewood Pk
  Farnborough GU14 . . . . . . .84 C7
  Woodham KT15 . . . . .71 B8
Pinewood PI KT19 . . . . . . .57 D6
Pinewood Rd
  Feltham TW13 . . . . .15 B5
  Normandy GU12 . . . . . .106 D3
  Wentworth GU25 . . . . . . .31 A5
Pinfold Rd SW16 . . . . . . .21 E4
Pinglestone CI UB7 . . . . . . .2 E7
Pinkcoat CI TW13 . . . . . . .15 B5
Pinkerton PI SW16 . . . . . .21 D4
Pinkhurst La RH13 . . . . .216 A2
Pinks Mews GU8 . . . . . .170 F8
Pioneers Ind Pk CR9 . . . . .41 E1
Piper Rd KT1 . . . . .38 A6
Piper's End GU25 . . . . . . .31 D6
Pipers CI KT11 . . . . .73 D3
Pipers End RH13 . . . . . .215 E3
Pipers Gdns CR0 . . . . . . .43 E2
Pipers Patch 1 GU14 . . . .85 B4
Pipewell Rd SM5 . . . . . . .40 E3
Pippbrook Gdns RH4 . . .136 B8
Pippin CI CR0 . . . . .43 F1
Pippins Ct TW15 . . . . . . .14 B2
Pippins Sch SL3 . . . . .1 F6
Piquet Rd BR3,SE20 . . . . .43 C7
Pirbright Cres CR0 . . . . . .63 C4
Pirbright Ho 1 KT2 . . . . .18 B2
Pirbright Prim Sch GU24 87 E5
Pirbright Rd
  Farnborough GU14 . . . . . . .85 C3
  Normandy GU3 . . . . . . .107 B6
  Wandsworth SW18 . . . . . .20 A7
Pirbright Terr GU24 . . . . . .87 F4
Piries PI RH12 . . . . .217 C2
Pisley La RH5 . . . . .177 A4
Pit Farm Rd GU1 . . . . . .110 A1
Pit Wood Gn KT20 . . . . . .97 C7
Pitcairn Rd CR4 . . . . .20 F1
Pitchfont La CR6,RH8 . . .102 F2
Pitfold CI GU27 . . . . . . .207 D6
Pitfold Rd GU27 . . . . . . .207 E6
Pitlake CR0,CR9 . . . . .61 B8
Pitland St RH5 . . . . .155 C5
Pitson CI KT15 . . . . .52 D6
Pitt Cres SW19 . . . . .20 B4
Pitt La GU10 . . . . .167 A6
Pitt PI KT17 . . . . .76 E5
Pitt Rd Epsom KT17 . . . . . .76 E5
  Thornton Heath CR0,CR7 . . .42 C4
Pitt Way GU14 . . . . .84 F5
Pitts Rd GU11 . . . . .105 B4
Pittville Gdns SE25 . . . . . .43 A6
Pixfield Ct BR2 . . . . .44 F7
Pixham Firs RH4 . . . . . . .115 C2
Pixham La RH4 . . . . .115 C2
Pixholme Ct RH4 . . . . . . .115 C2
Pixholme Gr RH4 . . . . . . .115 C1
Pixton Way CR0,CR2 . . . . .62 E2
Place Ct GU11 . . . . .126 C7
Place Farm Rd RH1 . . . . .120 D4
Placehouse La CR5 . . . .80 A1
Plaistow & Kirdford Prim Sch
  RH14 . . . . .211 F3
Plaistow Rd
  Chiddingfold GU8 . . . . . .210 D6
  Dunsfold GU8 . . . . .192 D2
  Ifold RH14 . . . . .212 D1
Plaistow St RH7 . . . . . . .164 D4
Plane St SE26 . . . . .23 B5
Plane Tree Cres TW13 . . .15 B5
Plane Tree Wlk 5 SE19 . .22 E2
Planes The KT16 . . . . . . .33 C2
Plantagenet CI KT19 . . . .57 D6
Plantagenet Pk RG42 . . . .27 F8
Plantain Cres RH11 . . . .201 A2
Plantation La CR6 . . . . . .101 E8
Plantation Row GU15 . . . .65 B5
Plassy Rd SE6 . . . . .24 B8
Plat The RH12 . . . . .217 A3
Platt Mdw GU4 . . . . .110 D3
Platt The RH7 . . . . .186 A8
Platt's Eyot TW12 . . . . . . .36 A7
Plaws Hill GU5 . . . . .154 D6
Playden Ct 3 RH11 . . . .201 A3
Playgreen Way SE6 . . . . . .24 A4
Playground CI BR3 . . . . . .43 D7
Pleasant Gr CR0 . . . . .62 F7
Pleasant PI KT12 . . . . . . .54 D4
Pleasure Pit Rd KT21 . . . .76 B1
Plesman Way SM6 . . . . . .60 E2
Plevna Rd TW12 . . . . . . .36 B8
Pleydell Ave SE19 . . . . . .22 F1
Plough CI RH11 . . . . . . .200 F8
Plough Ind Est KT22 . . . . .95 A7
Plough La Downside KT11 .73 A2
  Horsham RH12 . . . . .217 E5
  Purley CR8 . . . . .60 F1
  7 Teddington TW11 . . . . .17 A3
  Wallington, Bandonhill SM6 60 E5
  Wimbledon SW17,SW19 . . .20 C4
  Wokingham RG40 . . . . . . .25 F6
Plough Lane CI SM6 . . . . .60 E5
Plough Rd
  Dormansland RH7 . . . . . .165 A2
  Smallfield RH6 . . . . .162 C3
  West Ewell KT19 . . . . . . .57 D3

Ploughlands RG42 . . . . . .26 F8
Ploughmans End TW7 . . . .5 D2
Plover CI Crawley RH11 . .201 C8
  Staines TW18 . . . . .12 F5
Plovers Rd RH13 . . . . . .217 F3
Plovers Rise GU24 . . . . . .87 E7
Plowman Ho SW19 . . . . . .19 D6
Plum CI TW13 . . . . .15 A7
Plummer La CR4 . . . . .40 F7
Plummer Rd SW4 . . . . . . .21 D8
Plumpton Way SM5 . . . . .59 E7
Plumtree CI SM6 . . . . . . .60 D3
Plynlimmon Cotts GU6 . .174 A3
Pocket CI RG42 . . . . .26 D7
Pocklington Ct SW15 . . . .19 A7
Pockford Rd GU8 . . . . . .191 D4
Poels Ct RH19 . . . . .185 E2
Point Royal RG12 . . . . . . .27 B4
Pointers Hill RH4 . . . . . .135 C5
Pointers Rd KT11 . . . . . . .72 E2
Pointers The KT21 . . . . . .95 E7
Polden CI GU14 . . . . .84 E7
Polecat Hill GU26 . . . . . .188 F1
Polecroft La SE6 . . . . .23 F6
Poles La RH11 . . . . .181 C3
Polesden Gdns SW20 . . . .39 B7
Polesden La Ripley GU23 . .91 A6
  Send Marsh GU23 . . . . . . .90 F5
Polesden Lacey★ KT23 . .114 B5
Polesden Rd KT23,RH5 . .114 B6
Polesden View KT23 . . . .114 B8
Polesteeple Hill TN16 . . . .83 D2
Police Station Rd KT12 . . .54 C4
Pollard Gr GU15 . . . . . . .66 C4
Pollard Ho KT4 . . . . .58 C6
Pollard Rd Morden SM4 . . .40 D4
  Woking GU22 . . . . .70 B3
Pollardrow Ave RG42 . . . .26 F8
Pollards RH11 . . . . .201 A5
Pollards Cres SW16 . . . . .41 E6
Pollards Dr RH13 . . . . . .217 F2
Pollards Hill E SW16 . . . . .41 E6
Pollards Hill N SW16 . . . . .41 E6
Pollards Hill S SW16 . . . . .41 E6
Pollards Hill W SW16 . . . . .41 E6
Pollards Oak Cres RH8 . .123 A3
Pollards Oak Rd RH8 . . .123 A3
Pollards Wood Hill RH8 123 B5
Pollards Wood Rd
  Limpsfield RH8 . . . . .123 B4
  Thornton Heath SW16 . . . .41 E6
Polsted La GU3 . . . . .129 C3
Polsted Rd SE6 . . . . .23 F8
Poltimore Rd GU2 . . . . . .130 B7
Polworth Rd SW16 . . . . . .21 E3
Polyanthus Way RG45 . . .45 B8
Polygon Bsns Ctr SL3 . . . .1 F5
Pond CI Hersham KT12 . . .54 A4
  Loxwood RH14 . . . . .212 F5
Pond Copse La RH14 . . .212 F5
Pond Cottage La BR3,BR4 44 A1
Pond Cotts SE21 . . . . . . .22 E7
Pond Farm RH7 . . . . . . .164 B5
Pond Farm CI KT20 . . . . .97 B3
Pond Head La
  Forest Green RH5 . . . . . .176 E5
  Wallis Wood RH5 . . . . . .176 D3
Pond Hill Gdns SM3 . . . . .58 E4
Pond Ho Chertsey KT16 . . .33 B2
  Guildford GU4 . . . . .110 D3
Pond La Frensham GU10 . .167 C5
  Peaslake GU5 . . . . .154 D7
Pond Mdw GU2 . . . . . . .108 E2
Pond Meadow Sch GU2 . .108 E2
Pond Moor Rd RG12 . . . . .27 B4
Pond Piece KT11 . . . . . . .74 B6
Pond Rd Egham TW20 . . . .12 C2
  Farnborough GU14 . . . . . .85 B2
  Headley Down GU35 . . . .187 B4
  Woking GU22 . . . . .89 B7
Pond Way
  East Grinstead RH19 . . . .186 B1
  Teddington TW11 . . . . . . .17 C2
Pond Wood Rd RH10 . . . .202 A8
Pondfield Ho SE27 . . . . . .22 C3
Pondfield Rd
  Farncombe GU7 . . . . . . .150 F7
  Kenley CR8 . . . . .80 B3
  Rudgwick RH12 . . . . . . .214 D8
  West Wickham BR2 . . . . . .44 E1
Pondpenny La GU14 . . . . .84 A1
Ponds La GU5 . . . . .153 F7
Ponds The KT3 . . . . .53 E4
Pondside CI UB3 . . . . .3 D7
Pondtail CI RH12 . . . . . .217 D6
Pondtail Dr RH12 . . . . . .217 D7
Pondtail Rd RH12 . . . . . .217 D6
Ponsonby Rd SW15 . . . . . .19 B8
Pontefract Rd BR1 . . . . . .24 F3
Ponton Ho SW2 . . . . .22 A7
Pony Chase KT11 . . . . . . .73 F6
Pook Hill GU8 . . . . .190 F3
Pool CI BR3 . . . . .24 A3
Pool Ct SE6 . . . . .24 A6
Pool End CI TW17 . . . . . . .34 A4
Pool Rd Aldershot GU11 . .126 C7
  East Molesey KT12,KT8 . . .35 F4
Poole Court Rd TW5 . . . . . .4 E5
Poole Ct TW5 . . . . .4 E5
Poole Rd West Ewell KT19 .57 D4
  Woking GU21 . . . . .69 E1
Pooley Ave TW20 . . . . . . .12 B3
Pooley Green CI TW20 . . . .12 C3
Pooley Green Rd TW20 . . .12 C3
Pope CI East Bedfont TW14 14 F7
  Mitcham SW17,SW19 . . . . .20 D2
Pope Ct 10 KT2 . . . . .17 D4
Pope's Ave TW2 . . . . .16 E6

Pope's Gr TW1,TW2 . . . . .16 F5
Popes CI SL3 . . . . .1 C7
Popes Gr CR0 . . . . .62 F7
Popes La RH8 . . . . .143 F8
Popes Mead GU27 . . . . .208 C2
Popeswood Rd RG42 . . . .26 D8
Popham CI Bracknell RG12 27 F4
  Feltham TW13 . . . . .15 F5
Popham Gdns TW9 . . . . . .7 B4
Poplar Ave
  Leatherhead KT22 . . . . . . .95 C5
  Mitcham CR4 . . . . .40 F8
  Windlesham GU20 . . . . . . .48 B6
Poplar CI Bracknell RG12 . .27 D6
  Crawley RH11 . . . . .181 C1
  Mytchett GU16 . . . . .86 A3
  Poyle SL3 . . . . .1 E6
Poplar Cotts Frimley GU16 85 F6
  Guildford GU3 . . . . .108 E4
Poplar Cres KT19 . . . . . . .57 C4
Poplar Ct
  4 Streatham SW16 . . . . .21 F5
  13 Twickenham TW1 . . . . .6 C1
  Wimbledon SW19 . . . . . . .20 A3
Poplar Dr KT17,SM7 . . . . .77 D5
Poplar Farm CI KT19 . . . .57 C4
Poplar Fst Sch SW19 . . . .40 A6
Poplar Gdns KT3 . . . . . . .38 D7
Poplar Gr Kingston u T KT3 38 D6
  Woking GU22 . . . . .89 E8
Poplar La BR3 . . . . .44 B4
Poplar Rd Ashford TW15 . .14 C3
  Cheam SM3 . . . . .39 F1
  Leatherhead KT22 . . . . . . .95 C5
  Merton SW19 . . . . .40 A7
  Shalford GU4 . . . . .130 E2
Poplar Rd S SM4,SW19 . . .40 A6
Poplar Way TW13 . . . . . . .15 B5
Poplar Wlk
  Caterham CR3 . . . . .100 E4
  Croydon CR0 . . . . .42 C1
  Heath End GU9 . . . . .125 D7
Poplars CI GU14 . . . . .84 C5
Poplars The Ascot SL5 . . .29 A4
  Horsham RH13 . . . . .217 E3
Poppy CI SM6 . . . . .41 A1
Poppy La CR0,CR9 . . . . . .43 C1
Poppy Rd RG40 . . . . .25 B6
Poppyhills Rd GU15 . . . . .65 F8
Porchester SL5 . . . . .29 A5
Porchester Mead BR3 . . . .24 B2
Porchester Rd KT1 . . . . . .38 B7
Porchfield CI SM2 . . . . . . .59 B1
Porlock Ho 5 SE26 . . . . .23 A5
Porridge Pot Alley GU2 . .130 C7
Port Way GU24 . . . . .68 A3
Portal CI SE27 . . . . .22 A5
Porteridges RH4 . . . . . . .136 C4
Portesbery Hill Dr GU15 . .65 E6
Portesbery Rd GU15 . . . . .65 E6
Portesbery Sch GU15 . . . .65 D6
Porthcawe Rd SE26 . . . . .23 F4
Portia Gr RG42 . . . . .27 E8
Portland Ave KT3 . . . . . . .38 F2
Portland Cotts
  Feltham TW13 . . . . .15 E3
  Wallington CR0 . . . . .41 D7
Portland Cres TW13,
  TW15 . . . . .14 D4
Portland Dr RH1 . . . . . . .119 D6
Portland Ho
  5 East Grinstead RH19 . .205 F8
  Merstham RH1 . . . . .119 D6
  20 Streatham SW2 . . . . .22 A7
Portland House Mews
  KT18 . . . . .76 D5
Portland PI Croydon SE25 . .43 A5
  Ewell KT17 . . . . .76 E7
Portland Rd Ashford TW15 13 E5
  Croydon SE25 . . . . .43 B4
  Dorking RH4 . . . . .136 A8
  East Grinstead RH19 . . . .205 F8
  Kingston u T KT1 . . . . . . .37 F6
  Mitcham CR4 . . . . .40 E7
Portland Terr TW9 . . . . . . .6 D3
Portley Wood Rd CR3 . . .101 A7
Portman Ave SW14 . . . . . .7 D4
Portman CI 5 RG42 . . . . .27 A8
Portman Rd KT1 . . . . .37 F7
Portmore Park Rd KT13 . .53 C4
Portmore Quays KT13 . . . .52 F6
Portmore Way KT13 . . . . .53 A7
Portnall Dr GU25 . . . . . . .30 F4
Portnall Rd GU25 . . . . . . .30 F4
Portnall Rise GU25 . . . . . .30 F3
Portnalls CI CR5 . . . . .79 B3
Portnalls Rd CR5 . . . . . . .79 B2
Portnalls Rise CR5 . . . . . .79 C3
Portobello Ho 6 SW27 . . .22 B3
Porton Ct KT6 . . . . .37 C3
Portsea Ho 3 SW15 . . . . .19 B7
Portsmouth Ave KT7 . . . . .37 A2
Portsmouth Rd
  Camberley GU15 . . . . .66 A7
  Cobham KT10,KT11 . . . . . .73 C7
  Downside KT11 . . . . .72 F6
  Esher KT10 . . . . .55 A4
  Esher KT10 . . . . .55 D7
  Godalming GU7,GU8 . . . .150 B2
  Guildford GU2 . . . . .130 B8
  Hinchley Wood KT10,KT7 . .55 E8
  Hindhead GU26 . . . . . . .188 E2
  Kingston u T KT1,KT6 . . . . .37 C3
  Milford GU8 . . . . .149 E1
  Putney SW15 . . . . .19 C8
  Ripley GU23 . . . . .91 B4
  Thames Ditton KT6,KT7 . . .37 C3

Portsmouth Rd continued
  Thursley GU8 . . . . .169 D3
  Wisley GU23,KT11 . . . . . . .72 C3
  Witley GU8 . . . . .170 B6
Portswood PI SW15 . . . . . .7 F1
Portugal Gdns TW2 . . . . .16 C6
Portugal Rd GU21 . . . . . .69 F3
Portway KT17 . . . . .58 A2
Portway Cres KT17 . . . . . .58 A2
Post Boys Row KT11 . . . . .73 A5
Post House La KT23 . . . . .94 A2
Post La TW2 . . . . .16 D7
Postford Mill Cotts GU4 131 F5
Postmill CI CR0,CR9 . . . . .62 D7
Potley Hill Prim Sch
  GU46 . . . . .64 A5
Potley Hill Rd GU46 . . . . .64 A5
Potter CI CR4 . . . . .41 B7
Potter's La SW16 . . . . . . .21 D2
Potterhill Ct TW11 . . . . . .17 B1
Potteries La GU16 . . . . . . .85 F4
Potteries The
  Farnborough GU14 . . . . . . .84 D6
  Ottershaw KT16 . . . . .51 C4
  Ottershaw KT16 . . . . .51 E4
Potterne CI 5 SW15,
  SW19 . . . . .19 D8
Potters CI Croydon CR0 . . .43 E1
  Milford GU8 . . . . .149 F2
Potters Cres GU12 . . . . .106 B2
Potters Croft RH13 . . . . .217 E2
Potters Gate GU9 . . . . . .125 B2
Potters Gate CE Prim Sch
  GU9 . . . . .125 A2
Potters Gr KT3 . . . . .38 C5
Potters Hill GU8 . . . . . . .171 D4
Potters La GU23 . . . . .90 B2
Potters PI RH12 . . . . .217 C2
Potters Way RH2 . . . . . . .139 C5
Pottersfield RH10 . . . . . .201 D7
Pottery Ct GU10 . . . . . . .145 F6
Pottery La GU10 . . . . . . .145 F6
Pottery Rd TW8 . . . . .6 E8
Poulett Gdns TW1 . . . . . .17 A7
Poullett Ho SW2 . . . . .22 B7
Poulton Ave SM1 . . . . . . .59 D7
Pound CI Godalming GU7 150 E4
  Long Ditton KT6 . . . . .37 C1
  Loxwood RH14 . . . . .212 F5
Pound Cres KT22 . . . . . . .94 D6
Pound Ct Ashtead KT21 . . .75 F1
  Wood St V GU3 . . . . . . .108 B2
Pound Farm La
  Normandy GU12 . . . . . . .106 D1
  Thames Ditton KT10 . . . . .36 D1
Pound Field GU1 . . . . . . .109 D1
Pound Hill GU3 . . . . .108 B2
Pound Hill Fst & Mid Schs
  RH10 . . . . .202 C7
Pound Hill PI
  Crawley RH10 . . . . .202 C6
  Crawley RH10 . . . . .202 C6
Pound La Epsom KT19 . . . .76 D8
  Godalming GU7 . . . . . . .150 E4
  Windlesham GU20 . . . . . . .48 C4
  Wood St V GU3 . . . . . . .108 B2
Pound Lane Cvn Site
  GU3 . . . . .108 B2
Pound PI GU4 . . . . .130 F3
Pound Place CI GU4 . . . .130 F3
Pound Rd
  Aldershot GU12 . . . . . . .105 C1
  Banstead SM7 . . . . .78 A2
  Chertsey KT16 . . . . .33 B2
Pound St SM5 . . . . .59 F5
Poundfield Ct GU22 . . . . .90 C7
Poundfield Gdns GU22 . . .90 C7
Poundfield La RH14 . . . .212 B3
Povey Cross Rd RH6 . . . .160 E1
Powder Mill La TW2 . . . . .16 A7
Powderham Ct GU21 . . . . .68 E1
Powell CI Chessington KT9 56 D5
  Guildford GU2 . . . . .129 F7
  Horley RH6 . . . . .160 E3
  Wallington SM6 . . . . .60 E3
Powell Corderoy Prim Sch
  RH4 . . . . .135 F6
Powell Ct CR0 . . . . .61 C6
Powell's Wlk W4 . . . . .7 E8
Powells CI RH4 . . . . .136 C4
Powers Ct TW1 . . . . .17 D8
Pownall Gdns TW3 . . . . . . .5 B3
Pownall Rd TW3 . . . . .5 B3
Poyle 14 Trad Est SL3 . . . .1 E4
Poyle Gdns RG12 . . . . . . .27 D8
Poyle Ho GU4 . . . . .110 D2
Poyle New Cotts SL3 . . . . .1 F5
Poyle Rd Guildford GU1 . .130 E7
  Poyle SL3 . . . . .1 E5
  Tongham GU10 . . . . .127 B7
Poyle Tech Ctr The SL3 . . .1 E5
Poynder Lodge TW7 . . . . . .6 A6
Poynders Gdns SW12,SW4 .21 C8
Poynders Rd SW12,SW4 . .21 D8
Poynes Rd RH6 . . . . .160 E5
Poynings Rd RH11 . . . . . .200 E5
Prairie CI KT15 . . . . .52 B7
Prairie Rd KT15 . . . . .52 B7
Pratts Cnr GU8 . . . . .193 A8
Pratts La KT12 . . . . .54 D6
Precinct The
  Cranleigh GU6 . . . . .174 E4
  East Molesey KT8 . . . . . . .36 B6
  Egham TW20 . . . . .12 A3
Precincts The SM4 . . . . . .40 A3
Prendergast Ho 7 SW4 . . .21 D8
Prentice CI GU14 . . . . . . .85 B8
Prentice Ct 2 SW19 . . . . .19 F3

Prentis Rd SW16 . . . . . . .21 D4
Presburg Rd KT3 . . . . . . .38 E4
Presbury Ct GU21 . . . . . . .69 A1
Prescott RG12 . . . . .26 F2
Prescott Rd SL3 . . . . .1 E5
Presentation Mews SW2 . .21 F7
Prestbury Cres SM7 . . . . .78 F3
Preston CI TW2 . . . . .16 E5
Preston Cross KT23 . . . . .93 F1
Preston Dr KT19 . . . . .57 F4
Preston Gr KT21 . . . . .75 C2
Preston La KT20 . . . . .97 C7
Preston PI TW10 . . . . .6 F2
Preston Rd Littleton TW17 .34 A4
  South Norwood SE19 . . . . .22 B2
  Wimbledon SW20 . . . . . . .18 F1
Prestwick CI RH11 . . . . . .200 D5
Prestwick La GU8,GU27 . .190 C3
Prestwood CI RH11 . . . . .181 B1
Prestwood Gdns CR0 . . . .42 C2
Prestwood La RH11 . . . . .180 C3
Pretoria Rd Chertsey KT16 32 F1
  Streatham SW16 . . . . .21 C3
Pretty La CR5 . . . . .99 C6
Prey Heath CI GU22 . . . . .89 C3
Prey Heath Rd GU22 . . . . .89 B3
Preymead Ind Est GU9 . .126 B7
Price CI SW17 . . . . .20 F5
Price Rd CR0 . . . . .61 B5
Price Way TW12 . . . . .15 E2
Prices La RH2 . . . . .139 B6
Prickley Wood BR2 . . . . . .44 F1
Priddy's Yd 4 CR9 . . . . . .61 C8
Prideaux Gdns RH5 . . . . .177 D4
Prides Crossing SL5 . . . . . .9 A1
Pridham Rd CR7 . . . . .42 D5
Priest Ave RG40 . . . . .25 F5
Priest Croft CI RH11 . . . .201 A6
Priest Hill
  Englefield Green TW19,
    TW20 . . . . .11 C3
  Limpsfield RH8 . . . . .123 B6
Priest Hill Sch Sports Ctr
  KT17 . . . . .77 B8
Priest La GU24 . . . . .67 C5
Priestfield Rd SE23 . . . . . .23 E5
Priestley Gdns GU22 . . . . .90 A7
Priestley Rd
  Guildford GU2 . . . . .129 D8
  Mitcham CR4 . . . . .41 A7
Priestley Way RH10 . . . . .182 A3
Priests Bridge SW14,SW15 7 E4
Priestwood Ave RG42 . . . .26 E8
Priestwood Court Rd
  RG42 . . . . .27 A8
Priestwood Sq 4 RG42 . . .27 A8
Prim Sch of Our Lady
  Immaculate KT6 . . . . . .38 B1
Primrose Ave RH6 . . . . . .161 B1
Primrose CI
  Carshalton CR4 . . . . .41 B1
  Catford SE6 . . . . .24 C3
  Crawley RH11 . . . . .201 B3
Primrose Copse RH12 . . .217 E4
Primrose Ct
  New Malden KT4 . . . . .39 A4
  11 Streatham SW12 . . . .21 D8
Primrose Dr GU24 . . . . . . .68 A4
Primrose Gdns GU14 . . . .84 E3
Primrose Ho 1 TW9 . . . . . .6 F6
Primrose La CR0 . . . . .43 D1
Primrose Rd KT12 . . . . . . .54 C5
Primrose Ridge GU7 . . . .150 B2
Primrose Way
  Bramley GU5 . . . . .151 D5
  Sandhurst GU47 . . . . .45 B1
Primrose Wlk
  Bracknell RG12 . . . . .27 C4
  Ewell KT17 . . . . .76 E7
Prince Albert Ct 6 TW16 14 E1
Prince Albert Dr SL5 . . . . .28 D4
Prince Albert Sq RH1 . . . .140 A4
Prince Andrew Way SL5 . .28 D7
Prince Charles Cres
  GU14 . . . . .85 C8
Prince Charles Way SM6 60 B7
Prince Consort Dr SL5 . . .28 D5
Prince Consort's Dr SL4 . .10 A6
Prince Dr GU47 . . . . .45 A1
Prince George's Ave
  SW20 . . . . .39 C7
Prince Georges Rd SW19 40 D8
Prince Of Wales Rd
  RH1 . . . . .141 A2
Prince of Wales Wlk
  GU15 . . . . .65 C6
Prince Of Wales' Rd SM1 59 D8
Prince Rd SE25 . . . . .42 E4
Prince Regent Rd TW3 . . . .5 C4
Prince William Ct TW15 . .13 F3
Prince's Ave
  Farnborough GU11 . . . . . .105 C5
  Farncombe GU7 . . . . . . .150 C7
Prince's CI TW11 . . . . .16 E4
Prince's Dr KT22 . . . . .74 E7
Prince's Rd Mortlake SW14 7 C4
  Redhill RH1 . . . . .139 F7
  Teddington TW11 . . . . . . .16 E4
  Weybridge KT13 . . . . .53 C5
  Wimbledon SW19 . . . . . . .20 A2
Prince's St TW10,TW9 . . . .6 E2
Princes Ave
  Hamsey Green CR2 . . . . . .81 B4
  Tolworth KT6 . . . . .57 A8
  Wallington SM5 . . . . .59 F2
Princes CI Bagshot GU19 . .47 E1

Princes Cl *continued*
Hamsey Green CR2 . . . . .81 B4
Princes Ct
New Malden KT3 . . . . .38 F6
Weybridge KT13 . . . . .53 B5
Princes Gdns GU3 . . . . . . .108 E8
Princes Mead GU14 . . . . . .85 B4
Princes Mews TW3 . . . . . . .5 A3
Princes Rd Ashford TW15 . .13 F3
Egham TW20 . . . . .11 F2
Feltham TW13 . . . . .14 F5
Kingston u T KT2 . . . . .18 A1
Penge SE20 . . . . .23 D2
Richmond TW10 . . . . .6 F2
Richmond,Kew TW9 . . . . . . .6 F6
Princes St SM1 . . . . .59 D6
Princes Way
Aldershot GU11 . . . . .105 A2
Coney Hall BR4 . . . . .63 F7
Croydon CR0 . . . . .60 F5
Putney SW15,SW19 . . . . . . .19 E7
Princess Anne Rd RH12 214 D6
Princess Ct
3 Farnborough GU14 . . . . .105 C8
9 Wimbledon SW19 . . . . . .19 D1
Princess Gdns GU22 . . . . .70 B3
Princess Ho 1 RH1 . . . . .119 A2
Princess Margaret Rd
RH12 . . . . .214 D7
Princess Mary's Rd KT15 52 C6
Princess Rd
Crawley RH11 . . . . .201 C6
Thornton Heath CR0 . . . . . .42 C3
Woking GU22 . . . . .70 C3
Princess Sq RG12 . . . . . . .27 B7
Princess Way
Camberley GU15 . . . . .65 C5
Redhill RH1 . . . . .119 A2
Princethorpe Rd SE26 . . .23 D4
Princeton Mews 3 KT2 . .38 A4
Pringle Gdns Purley CR8 . .60 F1
Streatham SW16 . . . . .21 C4
Prins Willem-Alexander Sch
GU22 . . . . .70 C2
Prior Ave SM2 . . . . .59 E3
Prior Croft Cl GU15 . . . . . .66 A4
Prior End GU15 . . . . .66 A5
Prior Heath Inf Sch
GU15 . . . . .66 A5
Prior Place Cross Roads
GU15 . . . . .66 B4
Prior Rd GU15 . . . . .66 A5
Prior's La GU15 . . . . .64 A5
Prioress Rd SE27 . . . . .22 B5
Priors Cl GU14 . . . . .85 B8
Priors Croft GU22 . . . . . . .90 A7
Priors Ct Ash GU12 . . . . . .105 E1
Woking GU21 . . . . .69 A1
Priors Field Sch GU7 . . .129 A1
Priors Hatch La GU7 . . . .128 F1
Priors Lodge 4 TW10 . . . .6 F1
Priors Mead KT23 . . . . . . .94 C2
Priors The KT21 . . . . .95 D8
Priors Wlk RH10 . . . . .201 F6
Priors Wood GU27 . . . . . .207 F6
Priorsfield Rd GU7 . . . . . .129 F2
Priorswood GU3 . . . . .128 F2
Priory Ave SM3 . . . . .58 D6
Priory CE Mid Sch SW19 20 B3
Priory CE Sch The RH4 . .135 F6
Priory Cl Beckenham BR3 .43 E6
Dorking RH4 . . . . .136 A5
Hampton TW12 . . . . .35 F8
Horley RH6 . . . . .160 F4
3 Merton SW19 . . . . .40 B8
Sheerwater GU21 . . . . .70 D6
Sunbury TW16 . . . . .15 A1
Sunningdale SL5 . . . . .30 A2
Walton-on-T KT12 . . . . . . .54 A7
Priory Cres Cheam SM3 . . .58 D6
South Norwood SE19 . . . . . .22 C1
Priory Ct Camberley GU15 .64 F5
Cheam SM1 . . . . .58 F5
Cheam SM3 . . . . .58 E6
Dorking RH4 . . . . .136 B5
Egham TW20 . . . . .12 C2
Farnham GU9 . . . . .146 C8
Hounslow TW3 . . . . .5 A4
Reigate RH2 . . . . .117 F1
Roehampton SW15 . . . . .7 F2
Priory Dr RH2 . . . . .139 A7
Priory Gdns
Hampton TW12 . . . . .35 F8
Mortlake SW13 . . . . .7 F4
South Norwood SE25 . . . . . .42 F5
Priory Gn TW18 . . . . .13 B3
Priory Hospl The SW15 . . .7 F2
Priory House Ct SE6 . . . . .24 B7
Priory La East Molesey KT8 36 B5
Frensham GU10 . . . . .167 E8
Roehampton SW15 . . . . .7 F2
Priory Lodge BR4 . . . . . . .63 E7
Priory Mews TW18 . . . . . .13 B3
Priory Pl KT12 . . . . .54 A7
Priory Rd Cheam SM3 . . . .58 D6
Chessington KT9 . . . . .56 E7
Forest Row RH18 . . . . .206 D2
Hampton TW12 . . . . .16 A1
Isleworth TW3 . . . . .5 C2
Mitcham SW19 . . . . .20 D1
Reigate RH2 . . . . .139 A6
Richmond TW9 . . . . .7 A7
Sunningdale SL5 . . . . .30 A2
Thornton Heath CR0 . . . . . .42 A2
Winkfield SL5 . . . . .28 B7
Priory Sch SE25 . . . . .42 F5
Priory Sch The SM7 . . . . .78 A4
Priory St GU14 . . . . .85 D4

Priory The Croydon CR0 . .61 A7
Godstone RH9 . . . . .121 B3
21 Kingston u T KT6 . . . . .37 E4
Priory Way UB7 . . . . .2 E8
Priory Wlk RG12 . . . . .27 F5
Priscilla Ho 8 TW16 . . . . .14 F1
Probyn Rd SW2 . . . . .22 B6
Proctor Cl Crawley RH10 202 C4
Mitcham CR4 . . . . .41 A8
Proctor Gdns KT23 . . . . . .94 B2
Proctors Cl TW14 . . . . .15 A7
Proctors Rd RG40 . . . . . . .25 F6
Proffits Croft KT12 . . . . . .97 D5
Profumo Rd KT12 . . . . .54 D5
Progress Bsns Pk CR9 . . . .60 F8
Progress Way CR0 . . . . . . .60 F8
Prologis Pk TW4 . . . . .4 C4
Promenade Approach Rd
W4 . . . . .7 E7
Promenade De Verdun
CR8 . . . . .79 D8
Promenade The W4 . . . . . . .7 E6
Propeller Rd GU14 . . . . . . .85 B2
Prospect Ave GU14 . . . . . .85 B6
Prospect Cl
Forest Hill SE26 . . . . .23 B4
Hounslow TW5 . . . . .4 F6
Prospect Cott GU12 . . . . .106 A4
Prospect Cotts RG42 . . . . .26 D8
Prospect Cres TW2 . . . . . . .5 C1
Prospect Ct 4 GU1 . . . . .130 E8
Prospect Ho TW19 . . . . . . .57 B1
Prospect La TW20 . . . . . . .11 A3
Prospect Pl
Crawley RH11 . . . . .201 C6
Ewell KT17 . . . . .76 E6
Staines TW18 . . . . .12 F3
Wimbledon SW20 . . . . .19 B1
Prospect Rd Ash GU12 . . .106 A5
Farnborough GU14 . . . . . . .85 A5
Rowledge GU10 . . . . .145 E3
Thames Ditton KT6 . . . . . . .37 C3
Prossers KT20 . . . . .97 D6
Providence Cotts RH3 . . .137 B8
Providence Ho GU19 . . . . .47 E3
Providence La UB3 . . . . . . .3 D7
Providence Pl Ewell KT17 .76 E7
Farnham GU9 . . . . .125 C2
West Byfleet GU22 . . . . . . .71 A5
Provincial Terr SE20 . . . . .23 D1
Prune Hill TW20 . . . . .11 E1
Prunus Cl GU24 . . . . .67 E6
Public Record Office TW9 7 B7
Puckridge Hill Rd GU11 104 C4
Puckshill GU21 . . . . .68 D2
Puckshott Way GU27 . . . .208 D8
Puddenhole Cotts RH4 . .116 A2
Pudding La RH6 . . . . .180 E7
Puffin Cl BR3,CR0 . . . . .43 D4
Puffin Hill RH10 . . . . .204 C5
Puffin Rd RH11 . . . . .200 D5
Pulborough Rd SW18 . . . . .19 F8
Pulborough Way TW4 . . . . .4 C3
Pullman Cl SW2 . . . . .21 F7
Pullman La GU7 . . . . .150 C2
Pullmans Pl 4 TW18 . . . . .13 A3
Pulteney Cl TW7 . . . . .6 A4
Pump Alley 8 TW8 . . . . . . .6 D7
Pump La SL5 . . . . .29 E8
Pump Pail N CR0,CR9 . . . . .61 C7
Pump Pail S CR0,CR9 . . . . .61 C7
Pumping Station Rd W4 . . .7 E8
Punch Copse Rd RH10 . . .201 F7
Punchbowl La RH4,RH5 . .136 D6
Punnetts Ct RH11 . . . . . . .200 F2
Purbeck Ave KT3 . . . . .38 F3
Purbeck Cl RH1 . . . . .119 D7
Purbeck Ct 6 GU2 . . . . . .108 E1
Purbeck Dr GU21 . . . . .69 F5
Purberry Gr KT17 . . . . .57 F1
Purberry Shot KT17 . . . . . .57 F1
Purbrook RH4 . . . . .115 C2
Purbrook Ct RG12 . . . . . . .27 E3
Purbrook Ho 2 SW15 . . . .19 B7
Purcell Cl KT21 . . . . .75 F1
Purcell Rd Crawley RH11 200 F3
Crowthorne RG45 . . . . .45 B7
Purcell's Cl KT21 . . . . .75 F1
Purdey Ct 3 KT4 . . . . .39 A1
Purley & District War Meml
Hospl CR8 . . . . .80 A8
Purley Bury Ave CR8 . . . . .80 C8
Purley Bury Cl CR8 . . . . . .80 C8
Purley Cl RH10 . . . . .202 D3
Purley Ct CR8 . . . . .81 B1
Purley Downs Rd CR2 . . . .80 F4
Purley Hill CR8 . . . . .80 B7
Purley Knoll CR8 . . . . .80 A8
Purley Oaks Prim Sch
CR2 . . . . .61 D3
Purley Oaks Rd CR2 . . . . .61 D1
Purley Oaks Sta CR2 . . . . .61 D2
Purley Par 9 CR8 . . . . .80 A8
Purley Park Rd CR8 . . . . . .80 B1
Purley Rd Purley CR8 . . . . .80 A8
South Croydon CR2 . . . . . . .61 D3
Purley Rise CR8 . . . . .79 F7
Purley Sta CR8 . . . . .80 A7
Purley Vale CR8 . . . . .80 B6
Purley View Terr CR2 . . . . .61 D3
Purley Way
Croydon CR0,CR9 . . . . .61 A4
Frimley GU16 . . . . .85 E8
Purley CR8 . . . . .80 A8
Thornton Heath CR0,CR9 . . .41 F1
Purmerend Ct GU14 . . . . . .84 C5
Pursers Hollow GU5 . . . . .154 D8
Pursers La GU5 . . . . .154 D8

Purslane RG40 . . . . .25 D5
Purton Rd RH12 . . . . .217 B4
Purvis Ho CR0 . . . . .42 D2
Putney Heath SW15 . . . . . .19 B8
Putney Heath La SW15 . . .19 C8
Putney Hill SW15 . . . . .19 D8
Puttenham CE Sch GU3 128 C4
Puttenham Common Nature
Trails* GU3 . . . . .148 E8
Puttenham Heath Rd
GU3 . . . . .128 E3
Puttenham Hill GU3 . . . . .128 E3
Puttenham La GU3,GU8 . .128 C1
Puttenham Rd GU10 . . . . .127 C4
Puttock Cl GU27 . . . . .207 D5
Pye Cl CR3 . . . . .100 D4
Pyecombe Ct 4 RH11 . . . .200 F3
Pyegrove Chase RG12 . . . .27 E2
Pyestock Cres GU14 . . . . . .84 C4
Pyke Cl RG40 . . . . .25 D6
Pylbrook Rd SM1 . . . . .59 B7
Pyle Hill GU22 . . . . .89 D3
Pylon Way CR0 . . . . .41 E1
Pymers Mead SE21 . . . . . .22 C7
Pyne Rd KT6 . . . . .38 A1
Pyrcroft Ct KT16 . . . . .32 F2
Pyrcroft Grange Prim Sch
KT16 . . . . .32 E3
Pyrcroft La KT13 . . . . .53 B5
Pyrcroft Rd KT16 . . . . .32 E2
Pyrford CE Prim Sch
GU22 . . . . .71 A3
Pyrford Common Rd
GU22 . . . . .70 E2
Pyrford Heath GU22 . . . . . .70 F3
Pyrford Rd GU22,KT14 . . . .71 A4
Pyrford Woods GU22 . . . . .70 F4
Pyrford Woods Cl GU22 . . .70 F4
Pyrland Rd TW10 . . . . .6 F1
Pyrmont Gr SE27 . . . . .22 B5
Pyrmont Rd W4 . . . . .7 A8
Pytchley Cres SE19 . . . . . .22 C2

Q

Quadrangle Lodge SW19 20 A2
Quadrangle The GU2 . . .130 A8
Quadrant Ct RG12 . . . . . . .27 E6
Quadrant Rd
Richmond TW9 . . . . .6 D3
Thornton Heath CR7 . . . . . .42 B5
Quadrant The
Ash Vale GU12 . . . . .106 A4
Epsom KT17 . . . . .76 E6
Merton SW20 . . . . .39 E8
Richmond TW9 . . . . .6 E3
Sutton SM2 . . . . .59 C4
Quadrant Way KT13 . . . . . .53 A6
Quail Cl RH12 . . . . .217 D5
Quail Gdns CR0 . . . . .62 E1
Quakers Way GU3 . . . . . . .108 C5
Qualitas RG12 . . . . .26 F1
Quality St RH1 . . . . .119 B7
Quantock Cl
Crawley RH11 . . . . .201 B6
Harlington UB3 . . . . .3 D7
Quantock Dr KT4 . . . . .58 C8
Quarr Rd SM5 . . . . .40 E3
Quarry Bank GU18 . . . . . . .67 A8
Quarry Cl Horsham RH12 .217 F6
Leatherhead KT22 . . . . .95 D6
Oxted RH8 . . . . .122 E5
Quarry Cotts RH1 . . . . .99 C1
Quarry Gdns KT22 . . . . . . .95 D6
Quarry Hill GU7 . . . . .150 B3
Quarry Hill Pk RH2 . . . . .118 C4
Quarry Park Rd SM1 . . . . . .58 F4
Quarry Rd Oxted RH8 . . . .122 E5
Shackleford GU7 . . . . .150 A7
Woldingham RH9 . . . . .121 C7
Quarry Rise Cheam SM1 . .58 F4
East Grinstead RH19 . . . . .186 A3
Quarry St GU1 . . . . .130 D7
Quarry The RH3 . . . . .116 D3
Quarter Mile Rd GU7 . . . .150 E2
Quarterbrass Farm Rd
RH12 . . . . .217 D7
Quartermain Ho GU2 . . . . .89 F5
Quartermaine Ave GU22 . .89 F5
Quarters Rd GU14 . . . . . . .85 C2
Quay W W11 . . . . .17 B3
Quayside Wlk KT1 . . . . . . .37 D7
Quebec Cl RH6 . . . . .162 A3
Quebec Gdns GU17 . . . . . .64 D4
Queen Adelaide Ct SE20 .23 C2
Queen Adelaide Rd SE20 23 C1
Queen Alexandra's Ct 5
SW19 . . . . .19 F3
Queen Alexandra's Way
KT19 . . . . .76 A7
Queen Anne Ave BR2 . . . .44 F6
Queen Anne Dr KT10 . . . . .55 E3
Queen Anne's Cl SL4 . . . . .10 B5
Queen Anne's Gdns
Leatherhead KT22 . . . . .95 B6
4 Mitcham CR4 . . . . .41 A8
Queen Anne's Terr KT22 .95 B6
Queen Annes Cl TW2 . . . . .16 D5
Queen Annes Cl KT22 . . . .95 B6
Queen Annes Gate GU9 125 D7
Queen Eleanor's CE Jun Sch
GU2 . . . . .130 A4
Queen Eleanor's Rd
GU2 . . . . .129 F8
Queen Elizabeth Cl
GU12 . . . . .106 A2
Queen Elizabeth Dr
GU11 . . . . .104 F2

Queen Elizabeth Gdns
SM4 . . . . .40 A5
Queen Elizabeth Ho 2
SW12 . . . . .21 A8
Queen Elizabeth Hospl
SM7 . . . . .78 C1
Queen Elizabeth II Jubilee
Sch The RH13 . . . . .217 F1
Queen Elizabeth Rd
Camberley GU15 . . . . .46 D1
Kingston u T KT2 . . . . .37 F7
Rudgwick RH12 . . . . .214 D7
Queen Elizabeth Way
GU22 . . . . .90 A8
Queen Elizabeth's Dr
CR0 . . . . .63 D7
Queen Elizabeth's Foundation
Training Coll KT22 . . . . . .74 D2
Queen Elizabeth's Gdns
CR0 . . . . .63 D1
Queen Elizabeth's Wlk
SM6 . . . . .60 D6
Queen Mary Ave
Camberley GU15 . . . . .65 A5
West Barnes SM4,SW20 . . .39 D4
Queen Mary Cl
Tolworth KT9 . . . . .57 A8
Woking GU22 . . . . .70 C3
Queen Mary Rd
Charlton TW17 . . . . .34 C7
South Norwood SE19 . . . . . .22 B2
Queen Mary's Ave SM4 . . .59 F3
Queen Mary's Dr KT15 . . . .52 A1
Queen Mary's Hospital Sch
SM5 . . . . .59 F2
Queen St Aldershot GU12 105 D2
Chertsey KT16 . . . . .33 A1
Croydon CR0,CR9 . . . . .61 C6
Godalming GU7 . . . . .150 E4
Gomshall GU5 . . . . .133 C4
Horsham RH13 . . . . .217 D1
Queen Victoria Cross Roads
GU15 . . . . .65 A6
Queen Victoria Ct GU14 . .85 B5
Queen Victoria Hospl The
RH19 . . . . .185 F3
Queen Victoria Way
GU24 . . . . .87 D8
Queen's Ave GU11 . . . . . .105 B5
Queen's CE Prim Sch The
TW9 .7 A7
Queen's Cl 1 KT10 . . . . . .55 B6
Queen's Cl
Farnborough GU14 . . . . . .105 B8
North Ascot SL5 . . . . .28 E8
Wallington SM6 . . . . .60 B5
Queen's Cres RH4 . . . . . . .136 A6
Queen's Ct
Beckenham BR3 . . . . .44 A8
Croydon CR2 . . . . .61 C5
Farnborough GU14 . . . . . .105 C8
Horley RH6 . . . . .161 A3
1 Kingston u T KT2 . . . . .18 A1
3 Richmond TW10 . . . . . . .6 F1
Staines TW18 . . . . .13 D2
Thornton Heath CR7 . . . . . .42 A4
Queen's Dr
Farncombe GU7 . . . . .150 C7
Guildford GU2 . . . . .109 A4
Thames Ditton KT7 . . . . . . .37 A3
Queen's Gate Rd GU14 . .105 B8
Queen's Gdns TW5 . . . . . . .4 E6
Queen's Ho TW11 . . . . .16 F2
Queen's Mead GU8 . . . . . .191 B4
Queen's Mead Rd BR2 . . . .44 F7
Queen's Park Rd CR3 . . . .100 E4
Morden SM4 . . . . .40 A5
Queen's Pl Ascot SL5 . . . . .29 A6
Morden SM4 . . . . .40 A5
Queen's Rd Ascot SL5 . . . .29 A6
Beckenham BR3 . . . . .43 E7
East Grinstead RH19 . . . . .185 E1
Egham TW20 . . . . .11 F2
Feltham TW13 . . . . .15 B7
Guildford GU1 . . . . .109 D1
Hampton TW12 . . . . .16 B4
Horley RH6 . . . . .161 A3
Hounslow TW3 . . . . .5 B4
Kingston u T KT2 . . . . .18 A1
Knaphill GU21 . . . . .68 D1
Mitcham CR4 . . . . .40 D6
Mortlake SW14 . . . . .7 D4
New Malden KT3 . . . . .38 F4
Richmond TW10 . . . . .6 F1
Richmond, Richmond Park
KT2,TW10 . . . . .18 A3
Teddington TW11 . . . . .16 F4
Thames Ditton KT7 . . . . . . .36 F4
Thornton Heath CR0 . . . . . .42 C3
Wallington SM6 . . . . .60 B5
Wimbledon SW19 . . . . .20 A2
Queen's Rdbt GU11 . . . . .105 B7
Queen's Rise TW10 . . . . . . .6 F1
Queen's Terr TW7 . . . . .6 A3
Queen's Way GU24 . . . . . . .87 D8
Queendale Ct GU21 . . . . . .68 F3
Queenhill Rd CR2 . . . . .62 B1
Queenhythe Rd GU4 . . . .109 D7
Queens Acre SM2,SM3 . . . .58 E3
Queens Ave Byfleet KT14 . .71 E7
Feltham TW13 . . . . .15 C4
Queens Cl Bisley GU24 . . . .68 A3
Walton on the Hill KT20 . . . .97 A3
Queens Court Ride KT11 .73 A6
Queens Cres TW10 . . . . . . .6 F1
Queens Ct Beckenham BR3 24 B1
Queens Dr Guildford GU1 . .109 C1

Pri – Rac 277

Queens Ct *continued*
Weybridge KT13 . . . . .53 E4
9 Woking GU22 . . . . .69 F1
Queens Dr Oxshott KT22 . . .74 F2
Surbiton KT5 . . . . .38 A3
Queens Gate RH6 . . . . . . .182 A8
Queens Hill Rise SL5 . . . . .29 C6
Queens Keep
Camberley GU15 . . . . .65 D5
10 Twickenham TW1 . . . . . .6 C1
Queens La GU9 . . . . .125 B7
Queens Park Gdns TW13 .14 F5
Queens Pine RG12 . . . . . . .27 E3
Queens Pl KT12,KT13 . . . . .53 E5
Queens Rd
Aldershot GU11 . . . . .104 F2
Belmont SM2 . . . . .78 A8
Bisley GU24 . . . . .67 F1
Camberley GU15 . . . . .65 B4
Farnborough GU14 . . . . . .105 D8
Hale GU9 . . . . .125 C6
Hersham KT12 . . . . .54 A6
Morden SM4 . . . . .40 A5
Twickenham TW1 . . . . .17 A7
Weybridge KT13 . . . . .53 C5
Queens Reach KT8 . . . . . . .36 E5
Queens Ride RG45 . . . . . . .45 B7
Queens Sq RH10 . . . . .201 D6
Queens Way Croydon CR0 .60 F5
Feltham TW13 . . . . .15 C4
Queens Wlk
Ashford TW15 . . . . .13 D4
East Grinstead RH19 . . . . .185 E1
Queensberry Ho 6 TW9 . . .6 D2
Queensbridge Pk TW7 . . . .5 E2
Queensbury Ct CR7 . . . . . .42 C7
Queensbury Pl GU17 . . . . .64 C3
Queensfield Ct SM3 . . . . . .58 C6
Queensgate KT11 . . . . .73 D7
Queenshill Lodge SL5 . . . .29 B6
Queensland Ave SW19 . . . .40 B8
Queensmead
Camberley GU15 . . . . .66 B8
Farnborough GU14 . . . . . . .85 B3
Queensmead Ave KT17 . . .58 B1
Queensmere Cl SW19 . . . . .19 D6
Queensmere Rd SW19 . . . .19 D6
Queensthorpe Rd SE26 . . .23 D4
Queensville Rd SW12,
SW4 . . . . .21 D8
Queensway Coney Hall BR4 63 F6
Cranleigh GU6 . . . . .174 F2
Crawley RH10 . . . . .201 E6
East Grinstead RH19 . . . . .185 E1
Frimley GU16 . . . . .86 A7
Hersham KT12 . . . . .54 C6
Horsham RH13 . . . . .217 C1
Redhill RH1 . . . . .118 F2
Sunbury TW16 . . . . .35 B7
Queensway N KT12 . . . . . .54 C5
Queensway S KT12 . . . . . . .54 C5
Queenswood Ave
Hampton TW12 . . . . .16 B2
Hounslow TW3,TW5 . . . . . . .4 F5
Thornton Heath CR7 . . . . . .42 A4
Wallington CR0,SM6 . . . . . .60 D6
Queenswood Ct 11 SE27 .22 D4
Queenswood Rd
Forest Hill SE23 . . . . .23 E5
Knaphill GU21 . . . . .88 D8
Quennel Ho 7 SW12 . . . . .21 C8
Quennell Cl KT21 . . . . .95 F8
Quennells Hill GU10 . . . .145 E6
Quentin Way GU25 . . . . . . .31 B5
Quicks Rd SW19 . . . . .20 B1
Quiet Cl KT15 . . . . .52 A6
Quillot The KT12 . . . . .53 F5
Quince Cl SL5 . . . . .29 D5
Quince Dr GU24 . . . . .68 B4
Quincy Rd TW20 . . . . .12 A3
Quinnettes GU10 . . . . .167 F1
Quinneys GU14 . . . . .85 D1
Quintilis RG12 . . . . .26 F1
Quintin Ave SW20 . . . . . . .39 F8
Quintin Ct W4 . . . . .7 C7
Quintock Ho 2 TW9 . . . . . .7 A6
Quinton Cl
Beckenham BR3 . . . . .44 C6
Hackbridge SM6 . . . . .60 B6
Heston TW5 . . . . .4 B7
Quinton Rd KT7 . . . . .37 A1
Quinton St SW18 . . . . .20 C6
Quintrell Cl GU21 . . . . .69 B2

R

Rabbit La KT12 . . . . .54 B3
Rabies Heath Rd
Bletchingley RH1 . . . . .120 F2
Godstone RH1,RH9 . . . . . .121 B1
Raby Rd KT3 . . . . .38 D5
Raccoon Way TW4 . . . . .4 C5
Racecourse Rd
Crawley RH6 . . . . .181 F8
Crawley RH6 . . . . .182 A8
Dormansland RH7 . . . . . . .165 A2
Lingfield RH7 . . . . .164 F3
Racecourse Way RH6 . . . .181 F8
Rachel Ct SM2 . . . . .59 D3
Rackfield GU27 . . . . .207 D7
Rackham Cl RH11 . . . . . . .201 B3
Rackham Mews SW16 . . . .21 C2
Racks Ct GU1 . . . . .130 D7
Rackstraw Rd GU47 . . . . . .45 D2

Racquets Court Hill
GU7 ....150 C6
Rad La
Abinger Hammer RH5 ....133 E1
Peaslake GU5 ....133 D1
Radar Rd GU14 ....84 D1
Radbourne Rd SW12 ......21 D7
Radcliff Mews TW12 .....16 C3
Radcliffe Cl GU16 ....86 A7
Radcliffe Gdns SM5 ......59 E3
Radcliffe Rd CR0 ....61 F7
Radcliffe Way RG42 ......26 E8
Radcot Point 2 SE23 .....23 D5
Radford Cl GU9 ....125 E5
Radford Rd RH6,RH10 ...182 C4
Radius Pk TW6 ....3 F3
Radlet Ave SE23 ....23 B6
Radley Cl TW14 ....14 F7
Radley Ct RH2 ....24 C4
Radley Lodge 30 SW19 ...19 D7
Radnor Cl
6 Forest Hill SE23 ....23 D5
Redhill RH1 ....118 E1
Radnor Gdns TW1 ....16 F6
Radnor La
Abinger Common RH5 .....155 B7
Ewhurst RH5 ....155 A2
Peaslake GU5,GU6 ....154 E4
Twickenham TW1 ....16 F6
Weybridge KT13 ....53 A7
Radnor Wlk CR0 ....43 E3
Radolphs KT20 ....97 D5
Radstock Way RH1 ....119 E7
Radstone Ct 11 GU22 ......69 F1
Rae Rd GU14 ....85 B1
Raebarn Ct 6 SW16 ....21 E5
Raeburn Ave KT5 ....38 B3
Raeburn Cl KT1 ....17 D1
Raeburn Gr GU21 ....89 A8
Raeburn Way GU47 ....64 D6
RAF Staff Coll GU22 ....89 C8
Rafdene Copse GU22 ....89 C8
Rag Hill TN16 ....103 E6
Rag Hill Cl TN16 ....103 E6
Rag Hill Rd TN16 ....103 E6
Raglan Cl
Aldershot GU12 ....105 C1
Frimley GU16 ....86 A8
Hounslow TW4 ....4 F2
Reigate RH2 ....118 D3
Raglan Ct CR0,CR2 ....61 B5
Raglan Prec The CR3 ......100 E5
Raglan Rd Knaphill GU21 ...68 E1
Reigate RH2 ....118 C3
Raglans Bglws RH2 ....118 B4
Ragwort Ct 1 SE26 ....23 B3
Raikes La RH5 ....134 B2
Railey Rd RH10 ....201 E7
Railshead Rd TW1,TW7 .....6 B3
Railton Rd GU2 ....109 B5
Railway App
Chertsey KT16 ....32 F1
East Grinstead RH19 ......185 E1
10 Twickenham TW1 ....17 A8
Wallington SM6 ....60 B5
Railway Cotts
East Grinstead RH19 ......204 F3
Purley CR8 ....79 F6
Railway Rd TW11 ....16 F4
Railway Side SW13,SW14 ...7 E4
Railway Terr Egham TW18 .12 D3
Feltham TW13 ....15 A7
Rainbow Cl GU21 ....68 E3
Rainbow Ctr The KT7 ....76 F7
Rainbow Ind Est SW20 .....39 B7
Rake La Milford GU8 ....171 A7
Witley GU8 ....170 F7
Rakers Ridge RH12 ....217 D5
Raleigh Ave SM6 ....60 D6
Raleigh Ct Beckenham BR3 .44 B8
Crawley RH10 ....182 A3
Dulwich SE19 ....22 F3
Staines TW18 ....13 A4
Wallington SM6 ....60 B4
Raleigh Dr Esher KT10 .....55 D5
Smallfield RH6 ....162 A3
Tolworth KT5 ....38 C1
Raleigh Gdns CR4 ....40 F6
Raleigh Ho 1 KT7 ....37 A2
Raleigh Rd
Feltham TW14,TW13 ....14 F6
Penge SE20 ....23 D1
Richmond TW9 ....6 F4
Raleigh Sch The KT24 .....92 C2
Raleigh Way
Feltham TW13 ....15 C3
Frimley GU16 ....65 F3
Ralliwood Rd KT21 ....96 A8
Ralph Perring Ct BR3 ....44 A5
Ralphs Ride RG12 ....27 E6
Rama Cl SW16 ....21 E1
Rama La SE19 ....22 F1
Rambler Cl SW16 ....21 C4
Ramblers Ct RH12 ....216 E1
Ramblers Way 12 RH11 ....201 B1
Rame Cl SW17 ....21 A3
Ramillies Cl GU11 ....105 E2
Ramillies Rd GU11 ....105 D5
Ramin Ct GU1 ....109 C4
Ramones Terr CR4 ....41 E5
Rams La GU8 ....193 B3

Ramsay Rd GU20 ....48 E5
Ramsbury Cl RG12 ....26 E3
Ramsdale Rd SW17 ....21 A3
Ramsdean Ho 1 SW15 ......19 B7
Ramsden Rd
Balham SW12 ....21 A8
Godalming GU7 ....150 D3
Ramsey Cl
Camberley GU15 ....66 B8
Horley RH6 ....160 F3
Horsham RH12 ....217 D5
Ramsey Ct
18 Crawley RH11 ....201 B1
Croydon CR9 ....61 B8
Ramsey Ho SW19 ....40 B8
Ramsey Pl CR3 ....100 C5
Ramsey Rd CR7 ....41 F3
Ramslade Rd RG12 ....27 D5
Rances La RG40 ....25 E5
Randal Cres RH2 ....139 A7
Randall Schofield Ct
RH10 ....202 A7
Randalls Cotts RH11 ....73 B7
Randalls Cres KT22 ....95 A7
Randalls Park Ave KT22 ....95 A7
Randalls Park Dr KT22 ......95 A6
Randalls Rd KT22 ....94 E7
Randalls Way KT22 ....95 A7
Randell Cl GU17 ....64 E1
Randisbourne Gdns SE6 ....24 B5
Randle Rd TW10 ....17 C4
Randlesdown Rd SE6 ....24 B5
Randmore Ct 6 BR3 ....24 A1
Randolph Cl
Kingston u T KT2 ....18 C3
Knaphill GU21 ....68 E2
Oxshott KT11 ....74 A4
Randolph Dr GU14 ....84 C3
Randolph Rd KT1 ....76 F5
Ranelagh CE Sch RG12 .....27 C6
Ranelagh Cres SL5 ....28 D8
Ranelagh Dr
Bracknell RG12 ....27 C6
Isleworth TW1 ....6 B2
Ranelagh Gdns W4 ....7 C7
Ranelagh Pl KT3 ....38 E4
Ranelagh Rd RH1 ....118 E1
Ranfurly Rd SM1 ....59 A8
Range Rd GU14 ....84 D1
Range Ridge GU15 ....64 F7
Range The GU5 ....152 A4
Range View GU47 ....64 E8
Range Villas TW17 ....33 E2
Range Way TW17 ....34 A2
Rangefield Prim Sch
BR1 ....24 E3
Rangefield Rd BR1 ....24 F3
Ranger Mans SE19 ....22 F2
Ranger Wlk KT15 ....52 B5
Rankine Cl GU9 ....126 A6
Ranmere St SW12 ....21 B7
Ranmore Ave CR0 ....61 F7
Ranmore Cl RH1 ....119 A4
Ranmore Common Rd
RH5 ....114 D2
Ranmore Ct
Kingston u T KT6 ....37 D4
Wimbledon SW20 ....39 D8
Ranmore Pl KT13 ....53 C5
Ranmore Rd
Dorking RH4 ....136 A8
East Ewell SM2 ....58 D2
Wotton RH4,RH5 ....114 E1
Rann Ho 1 SW14 ....7 D4
Rannoch Ct 9 KT6 ....37 E4
Ransford Ho 16 SE21 ....22 E4
Ransome Ct RH11 ....200 E3
Ranyard Cl KT9 ....56 F7
Rapallo Cl GU14 ....85 C4
Raphael Dr KT7 ....36 F1
Raphel Dr KT7 ....37 A2
Rapley Cl GU15 ....65 E8
Rapley Gn RG12 ....27 C3
Rapley's Field GU24 ....87 E4
Rapsley La GU21 ....68 B1
Rastell Ave SW12 ....21 D7
Ratcliffe Rd GU14 ....85 A8
Rathbone Ho
Crawley RH11 ....201 B1
8 Wimbledon SW19 ....19 D1
Rathfern Prim Sch SE23 ....23 F7
Rathfern Rd SE23,SE6 ....23 F7
Rathgar Cl RH1 ....140 A4
Rathlin Rd RH11 ....201 B3
Rattray Ct SE6 ....24 F6
Raven Cl Horsham RH12 ...217 E6
Turners Hill RH10 ....204 C5
Raven La RH11 ....201 C8
Ravendale Rd TW16 ....34 F7
Ravendene Ct 3 RH10 ......201 D5
Ravenfield Rd SW17 ....20 F5
Ravens Cl Bromley BR2 ......44 F7
Kingston u T KT6 ....37 D3
Knaphill GU21 ....68 C3
Redhill RH1 ....118 F2
Ravens Ho KT1 ....90 D7
Ravens Wold CR8 ....80 C4
Ravensbourne 3 TW1 ....6 C1
Ravensbourne Ave
Bromley BR2 ....44 E8
Catford BR2 ....44 E8
Stanwell TW19 ....13 E7
Ravensbourne Ct SE6 ....24 A8
Ravensbourne Ho BR1 ....24 D3
Ravensbourne Park Cres
SE6 ....23 F8
Ravensbourne Pk SE4,
SE6 ....24 A8

Ravensbourne Rd
Forest Hill SE23 ....23 F7
Twickenham TW1 ....6 C1
Ravensbourne Sta BR3 ......24 D1
Ravensbury Ave SM4 ....40 C4
Ravensbury Ct
5 Carshalton SM1 ....59 D5
Mitcham CR4 ....40 D5
Ravensbury Gr CR4 ....40 D5
Ravensbury La CR4 ....40 D5
Ravensbury Rd SW18 ....20 B6
Ravensbury Terr SW18 ....20 B6
Ravenscar Lodge 11
SW19 ....19 D1
Ravenscar Rd Catford BR1 .24 E4
Surbiton KT6 ....56 F8
Ravenscote Jun Sch
GU16 ....66 A3
Ravenscourt TW16 ....34 F8
Ravenscroft Cl GU12 ....106 C3
Ravenscroft Ct RH12 ....217 C3
Ravenscroft Rd
Penge BR3 ....43 D7
Weybridge KT13 ....72 C8
Ravensdale Gdns
Hounslow TW4 ....4 E4
South Norwood SE19 ....22 D1
Ravensdale Mews TW18 ....13 B2
Ravensdale Rd Ascot SL5 ...29 A4
Hounslow TW4 ....4 E4
Ravensfield TW20 ....11 C2
Ravensfield Gdns KT19 ......57 E6
Ravenshead Cl CR2 ....81 C8
Ravenside GU15 ....37 D4
Ravenslea Rd SW11,SW12 ..20 F8
Ravensmead Rd BR2 ....24 D1
Ravensroost SE19 ....42 D8
Ravenstone Prim Sch
SW12 ....21 A6
Ravenstone Rd GU15 ....66 D5
Ravenstone St SW12 ....21 A7
Ravensview Ct KT6 ....37 D4
Ravenswood Ave
Tolworth KT6 ....57 A8
West Wickham BR4 ....44 C1
Ravenswood Cres BR4 ....44 C1
Ravenswood Ct
Dorking RH4 ....136 B6
Kingston u T KT2 ....18 B2
Woking GU22 ....69 F1
Ravenswood Dr GU15 ....66 A5
Ravenswood Gdns TW7 ....5 E6
Ravenswood Rd
Balham SW12 ....21 B8
Croydon CR0,CR9 ....61 B7
Rawlins Cl CR2 ....62 F3
Rawlinson Rd GU15 ....64 F6
Rawnsley Ave CR4 ....40 E4
Raworth Ct RH10 ....202 C4
Ray Cl Chessington KT9 .....56 C4
Lingfield RH7 ....164 C5
Ray Cnr RH7 ....164 B6
Ray La Blindley Heath RH7 163 F7
Lingfield RH7 ....164 B6
Ray Rd KT8 ....36 B4
Raybell Ct TW7 ....5 F5
Rayford Ave SE12 ....24 F8
Rayleigh Ave TW11 ....16 E2
Rayleigh Ct 3 KT1 ....37 F7
Rayleigh Rd SW19 ....39 F8
Rayleigh Rise CR2 ....61 E4
Raymead Ave CR7 ....42 A4
Raymead Cl KT22 ....94 F5
Raymead Way KT22 ....94 F5
Raymer Wlk RH6 ....161 C4
Raymond Cl
Forest Hill SE26 ....23 C3
Poyle SL3 ....1 E6
Raymond Cres GU2 ....129 E8
Raymond Ct SM2 ....59 B4
Raymond Rd
Beckenham BR3 ....43 E5
Wimbledon SW19 ....19 E2
Raymond Way KT10 ....56 A4
Raynald Ho 15 SW16 ....21 E5
Rayners Cl SL3 ....1 C7
Raynes Park High Sch
KT3 ....39 B6
Raynes Park Sta SW20 ......39 C7
Raynesfield SW20 ....39 C6
Rays Rd BR4 ....44 C2
Raywood Cl UB7 ....3 C7
Read Cl KT7 ....37 A2
Read Rd KT21 ....75 D2
Reading Arch Rd RH1 ....118 F1
Reading Rd
Blackwater GU17 ....64 B4
Farnborough GU14 ....85 D1
Sutton SM1 ....59 C5
Wokingham RG41 ....25 A7
Readman Ct 9 SE20 ....43 B8
Reads Rest La KT20 ....98 A7
Reapers Cl RH12 ....217 D5
Reapers Way TW7 ....5 D2
Rebecca Ct BR3 ....44 A8
Recovery St SW17 ....20 E3
Recreation Cl GU14 ....64 F7
Recreation Rd
Bromley BR2 ....44 F7
Forest Hill SE26 ....23 D4
Guildford GU1 ....109 D1
Rowledge GU10 ....145 E3
Recreation Way CR4,
SW16 ....41 E6
Rectory Cl Ashtead KT21 ....95 F8
Bracknell RG12 ....27 C5

Rectory Cl continued
Byfleet KT14 ....71 E6
Ewhurst GU6 ....175 E5
Godalming GU7 ....150 F2
Guildford GU4 ....110 A3
Littleton TW17 ....34 A6
Long Ditton KT6 ....37 C1
Ockley RH5 ....177 C3
West Barnes SW20 ....39 C6
Wokingham RG40 ....25 C6
Rectory Ct Cranford TW5 .....5 C4
Feltham TW13 ....15 C4
Sanderstead CR2 ....80 F7
Wallington SM6 ....60 C6
Rectory Gdns BR3 ....44 A8
Rectory Gn BR3 ....43 F7
Rectory Gr
Croydon CR0,CR9 ....61 B8
Hampton TW12 ....15 A4
Rectory La Ashtead KT21 ....95 F8
Bracknell RG12 ....27 B5
Buckland RH3 ....116 F3
Byfleet KT14 ....71 E6
Charlwood RH6 ....180 D7
Crawley RH11 ....200 F8
Great Bookham KT23 ....113 F8
Long Ditton KT6 ....37 C1
Shere GU5 ....133 A4
Streatham SW17 ....21 A3
Titsey TN16 ....103 E4
Wallington SM6 ....60 C6
Windlesham GU20 ....48 C4
Woodmansterne CR5,SM7 ...78 C3
Rectory Orch SW19 ....19 E1
Rectory Pk CR2 ....80 F7
Rectory Rd
Beckenham BR3 ....44 A8
Cranford TW5 ....4 C5
Farnborough GU14 ....85 D4
Lower Kingswood CR5 ....98 C2
Sutton SM1 ....59 B4
Wokingham RG40 ....25 C6
Rectory Row RG12 ....27 B5
Red Admiral St RH12 ....217 E5
Red Deer Cl RH13 ....218 B4
Red Gables Dr CR2 ....61 D1
Red Ho The RH8 ....123 C5
Red House La
Elstead GU8 ....148 C2
Walton-on-T KT12 ....54 A8
Red House Rd CR0,CR9 ......41 D3
Red La Claygate KT10 ....56 A4
Headley Down GU35 ....187 B7
Limpsfield RH8 ....144 B7
South Holmwood RH5,RH3 136 F1
Red Lion Bsns Ctr KT6 ......56 F7
Red Lion Cotts GU5 ....152 E4
Red Lion La
Chobham GU24 ....49 E2
Farnham GU9 ....125 B1
Red Lion Rd
Chobham GU24 ....49 E2
Surbiton KT6 ....57 A8
Red Lion St TW10 ....6 D2
Red Lodge BR4 ....44 C2
Red Lodge Rd BR3,BR4 ....44 D2
Red Rd GU18,GU24,GU15 ....67 C7
Red River Ct RH12 ....217 B5
Redan Gdns GU12 ....105 C2
Redan Hill Est GU12 ....105 C2
Redan Rd GU12 ....105 C2
Redbarn Ct CR8 ....80 B8
Redberry Gr SE23,SE26 ......23 C8
Redcar Ho SE26 ....23 B2
Redcliffe Gdns W4 ....7 B7
Redcliffe Missionary Training
Coll W4 ....7 B7
Redclose Ave SM4 ....40 A4
Redclyffe Terr 2 SM2 ....59 A3
Redcote Pl RH4 ....115 D7
Redcourt Pyrford GU22 ....70 E4
Woking GU22 ....70 D4
Redcrest Gdns GU15 ....65 F5
Redcroft Wlk GU6 ....174 E2
Redding Way GU21 ....68 C1
Reddington Cl CR2 ....61 D2
Redditch RG12 ....27 C2
Redditch Cl RH11 ....200 E2
Reddons Rd BR3 ....23 E1
Reddown Rd CR5 ....79 D2
Rede Ct Farnborough GU14 .85 C1
Weybridge KT13 ....53 B7
Redehall Prep Sch RH6 .....162 B2
Redehall Rd
Burstow RH6 ....183 C8
Smallfield RH6 ....162 B2
Redesdale Gdns TW7 ....6 A7
Redfern Ave TW4 ....16 A8
Redfern Rd SE6 ....24 C8
Redford Ave
Horsham RH12 ....217 B4
Thornton Heath CR7 ....41 F5
Wallington, Clock House
CR5 ....79 B4
Wallington, Roundshaw
SM6 ....60 E4
Redford Cl TW13 ....14 F6
Redgarth Ct RH19 ....185 B3
Redgrave Cl SE25 ....42 F3
Redgrave Dr RH10 ....202 D5
Redgrove Ct GU12 ....105 F2
Redhall Ct CR3 ....100 D4
Redhearne Fields GU10 .....167 E2
Redhill Aerodrome RH1 .....140 D4
Redhill Coll RH1 ....140 B8
Redhill Ct SW2 ....22 A6
Redhill Distribution Ctr
RH1 ....161 A8

Redhill Rd KT11 ....72 B5
Redhill Sta RH1 ....119 A2
Redhouse Rd TN16 ....103 C6
Redkiln Cl RH13 ....217 F3
Redkiln Way RH13 ....217 F3
Redknap Ho TW10 ....17 C5
Redlake La RG40 ....25 F2
Redland Gdns KT8 ....35 E5
Redlands Coulsdon CR5 ......79 E3
Teddington TW11 ....17 A2
Redlands CE Inf Sch The
RH4 ....136 B4
Redlands Cotts RH5 ....136 B1
Redlands Ct BR1 ....24 F1
Redlands Jun Sch The
RH4 ....136 B4
Redlands La Crondall GU10 124 B7
Dorking RH5 ....136 A1
Redlands The 5 BR3 ....44 B4
Redlands Way SW2 ....21 F8
Redlane Cotts RH8 ....123 B2
Redleaf Cl SL2 ....94 E3
Redleaves Ave TW15 ....14 B2
Redlees Cl TW7 ....6 A3
Redlin Ct RH1 ....118 F3
Redmayne GU15 ....66 C4
Redroofs Cl BR3 ....44 B8
Redruth Ho SM2 ....59 B3
Redshank Ct 5 RH11 ....200 D5
Redstart Cl CR0 ....63 D1
Redstone Hill RH1 ....119 A1
Redstone Hollow RH1 ....140 A8
Redstone Manor RH1 ....119 A1
Redstone Pk RH1 ....119 B1
Redstone Rd RH1 ....140 A8
Redvers Buller Rd
GU11 ....105 D7
Redvers Ct CR6 ....81 C1
Redvers Rd
Bracknell RG12 ....27 B4
Warlingham CR6 ....81 C1
Redway Dr TW2 ....16 C8
Redwing Ave GU7 ....150 E8
Redwing Cl
Horsham RH13 ....217 F1
Selsdon CR2 ....81 D8
Redwing Gdns KT14 ....71 B7
Redwing Rd SM6 ....60 E3
Redwing Rise GU4 ....110 D3
Redwood TW20 ....32 E7
Redwood Cl
Crawley RH10 ....201 E8
Kenley CR8 ....80 C5
Redwood Ct 10 KT6 ....37 D2
Redwood Dr Frimley GU15 ..66 D4
Sunningdale SL5 ....30 B3
Redwood Est TW5 ....4 B8
Redwood Gr GU4 ....131 C3
Redwood Manor GU27 ....208 C7
Redwood Mews TW15 ....14 D1
Redwood Mount RH2 ....118 A4
Redwood Wlk KT6 ....37 D1
Redwoods
Addlestone KT15 ....52 A4
Roehampton SW15 ....19 A7
Reed Cl GU11 ....105 D5
Reed Dr RH1 ....140 A6
Reed Pl GU21,KT14 ....70 E6
Reed Place Bsns Pk
TW7 ....33 F1
Reed's Hill RG12 ....27 B1
Reedham Dr CR8 ....80 A6
Reedham Park Ave CR8 ......80 A3
Reedham Sta CR8 ....79 F6
Reedings RH11 ....200 D4
Reeds Rd The
Frensham GU10 ....146 E2
Tilford GU10 ....147 A3
Reeds Sch RH11 ....74 A7
Reedsfield Cl TW15 ....14 B5
Reedsfield Rd TW15 ....14 B4
Rees Gdns CR0 ....42 F3
Reeve Ct GU2 ....109 A5
Reeve Rd RH2 ....139 C5
Reeves Cnr CR0,CR9 ....61 B8
Reeves Rd GU12 ....105 C1
Reeves Way RG41 ....25 A3
Regal Cres SM6 ....60 B7
Regal Ct
1 Guildford GU1 ....109 D1
2 Mitcham CR4 ....40 F6
Regal Dr 10 RH19 ....205 F8
Regalfield Cl GU2 ....109 A5
Regan Cl GU2 ....109 B6
Regatta Ho TW11 ....17 A4
Regency Cl
6 Penge SE19 ....23 A1
4 Surbiton KT5 ....37 F4
Sutton SM1 ....59 B6
Wimbledon SW19 ....19 F1
Regency Dr KT14 ....70 F6
Regency Gdns KT12 ....35 D1
Regency Lodge KT13 ....53 E7
Regency Mews
Beckenham BR3 ....44 C8
Isleworth TW7 ....5 E2
Regency Wlk Croydon CR0 ..43 E3
8 Richmond TW10 ....6 E2
Regent Cl Cranford TW5 ......5 A6
New Haw KT15 ....52 D2
Regent Cres RH1 ....118 F3
Regent Ct Bagshot GU19 .....47 F2
Guildford GU2 ....109 A3
South Norwood SE19 ....22 B2

Regent Ho **1** SM7 ....77 F5
Regent Lodge **9** SW2 .....21 F7
Regent Par **8** SM2 .....59 C4
Regent Pk KT22 ....75 A1
Regent Pl Croydon CR0 ....42 F1
Wimbledon SW19 ....20 C3
Regent Rd KT5 ....38 A4
Regent St W4 ....7 A8
Regent Way GU16 ......66 A1
Regents Cl Crawley RH11 201 C2
South Croydon CR2 ......61 E4
Whyteleafe CR3 ....80 F1
Regents Ct
23 Beckenham BR3 .....24 A1
Bromley BR1 ....24 F1
Staines TW18 ....13 B2
Weybridge KT13 ....53 B4
Regents Ho **4** TW20 ....12 A3
Regents Mews RH6 ....161 A3
Regents Pl
1 Kingston u T KT2 ....37 E8
Sandhurst GU47 ....64 C8
Regents Wlk SL5 ....29 C2
Regiment Cl GU14 .....84 C3
Regina Coeli RC Prim Sch
CR2 ....61 B3
Regina Rd SE25 ....43 A6
Reginald Ct BR3 ....44 C8
Regis Ct East Bedfont TW14 .3 D1
Mitcham SW19 ....40 E8
Regnolruf Ct KT12 .....35 A2
Reid Ave CR3 ....100 D6
Reid Cl CR5 ....79 B3
Reid Ct SW19 ....7 C5
Reidonhill Cotts GU21 ..68 B1
Reigate Ave SM3,SM4 ..40 B1
Reigate Cl RH10 ......182 D1
Reigate Coll RH2 ......118 C1
Reigate Gram Sch RH1 .118 C1
Reigate Heath Cotts
RH2 ....117 E1
Reigate Hill RH2 ......118 B4
Reigate Hill Cl RH2 ...118 B4
Reigate Parish Church Inf
Sch RH2 ....118 C1
Reigate Priory Com Jun Sch
RH2 ....118 A1
Reigate Rd Banstead KT17 77 C4
Betchworth RH3 ....116 D2
Burgh Heath KT18 .....77 C4
Catford BR1 ....24 F5
Dorking RH4 ....115 E1
Ewell KT17 ....77 C4
Hookwood RH2,RH6 ..160 C4
Leatherhead KT22 .....95 D4
Reigate RH2 ....118 C1
Reigate Sch RH1 ......139 C6
Reigate Sch of Art & Design
RH2 ....118 D1
Reigate St Mary's Prep Sch
RH2 ....118 B1
Reigate Sta RH2 ......118 A2
Reigate Way SM6 ......60 E5
Reindorp Cl GU2 ......130 A8
Relko Ct KT19 ....76 D8
Relko Gdns SM1 ....59 D5
Rembrandt Ct KT19 ....57 F4
Rembrandt Way KT12 ..54 B8
Rendle Cl CR0,SE25 ....43 A4
Renfree Way TW5 ....4 E5
Renfrew Ct TW5 ....4 E5
Renfrew Rd Hounslow TW5 .4 E5
Kingston u T KT2 ......18 C1
Renmans The KT21 .....75 F3
Renmuir St SW17 ......20 F2
Rennie Cl TW15 ....13 D5
Rennie Terr RH1 ......140 A8
Renown Ct CR0 ....42 B1
Renshaw Ho **11** SW27 ...22 B3
Replingham Rd SW18 ..20 A7
Repton Cl SM5 ....59 E5
Repton Ct BR3 ....44 B8
Reservoir Rd GU14 ....84 D1
Reservoir Cl CR7 ......42 D6
Restmor Way SM5,SM6 ..60 A8
Restormel Cl TW3 ......5 A2
Restwell Ave GU6 ....174 B6
Retreat Ho TW9 ....6 D2
Retreat The
Englefield Green TW20 ..11 E3
Loxwood RH14 ....212 F5
5 Mortlake SW14 ......7 E4
North Cheam KT4 .....58 B8
South Norwood CR7 ...42 D5
Surbiton KT5 ....37 F3
Revell Cl KT22 ....94 B5
Revell Dr KT22 ....94 B5
Revell Rd Cheam SM1 ..58 F4
Kingston u T KT1 ......38 B8
Revelstoke Ave GU14 ..85 B6
Revelstoke Rd SW18,
SW19 ....20 A6
Revesby Cl GU24 ......67 D6
Revesby Rd SM5 ......40 E3
Rewley Rd SM4 ....40 D3
Rex Ave TW15 ....14 A3
Rex Ct GU27 ....207 F6
Rex Ho TW15 ....15 E5
Reynard Cl RH12 .....218 B5
Reynard Dr SE19 ......22 F1
Reynolds Ave KT9 .....56 E3
Reynolds Cl
Carshalton SM4,SM5 ...40 F1
Mitcham CR4,SW19 ....40 D8
Reynolds Gn GU47 ....64 D6
Reynolds Pl
Crawley RH11 ....201 C7
12 Richmond TW10 .....6 F1

Reynolds Rd
Crawley RH11 ....201 C7
Farnborough GU14 ....104 B8
New Malden KT3 ......38 D2
Reynolds Way CR0 .....61 E6
Rheingold Way SM6 ...60 E2
Rhine Banks GU14 ....84 D5
Rhodes-Moorhouse Ct
SM4 ....40 A3
Rhododendron Cl SL5 ..8 E1
Rhododendron Rd GU16 .86 B8
Rhododendron Ride SL4,
TW20 ....10 F3
Rhododendron Wlk SL5 ..8 E1
Rhodrons Ave KT9 .....56 E5
Rialto Rd CR4 ....41 A7
Ribble Pl GU14 ....84 E7
Ribblesdale RH4 ......136 B5
Ribblesdale Rd SW16 ..21 B3
Ricardo Ct GU5 ......151 F5
Ricards Lodge Sch SW19 19 F3
Ricards Rd SW19 ......19 F3
Rice's Cnr GU4 ....131 A2
Rices Hill RH19 ......185 E1
Richard Atkins Prim Sch
SW2 ....21 E8
Richard Challoner Sch
KT3 ....38 D2
Richard Thornton Ho
SW19 ....40 A7
Richards Cl Ash GU12 .106 A5
Harlington UB3 ....3 D8
Richards Ct BR3 ......43 D8
Richards Field KT19 ..57 D2
Richards Rd KT11 .....74 B5
Richardson Ct **17** RH11 201 B1
Richardson Ho TW7 ....5 F4
Richardson's Lawn Cotts
SL4 ....10 B5
Richbell Cl KT21 ......75 D1
Richborough Ct RH11 .201 C6
Richens Cl TW3 ....5 D5
Richfield Ct BR3 ......43 F8
Richland Ave CR5 .....79 A5
Richlands Ave KT17 ...58 A6
Richmond Adult & Com Coll
TW9 ....6 D3
Richmond Ave
Feltham TW14 ....3 E1
Merton SW20 ....39 E8
Richmond Bridge TW1 ..6 D1
Richmond Bridge Mans **1**
TW1 ....6 D1
Richmond Cl
Biggin Hill TN16 .....103 B8
Crawley RH10 ....201 E5
Epsom KT18 ....76 E5
Farnborough GU14 ....84 D3
Fetcham KT23 ....94 C3
Frimley GU16 ....65 F1
Richmond Coll TW10 ..17 E8
Richmond Com Healthcare
Hamlet TW9 ....6 E4
Richmond Cres TW18 ..12 F3
Richmond Ct
12 Kingston u T KT2 ...18 A1
Mitcham CR4 ....40 D6
Wimbledon SW20 ......39 B7
Richmond Dr TW17 ....34 D3
Richmond Gn CR0 ......60 E7
Richmond Hill TW10 ....6 E1
Richmond Hill Ct **5** TW10 6 E1
Richmond Ho
12 Forest Hill SE26 .....23 A5
Sandhurst GU47 ......64 C7
Richmond International Bsns
Ctr TW9 ....6 E3
Richmond Mans **5** TW1 .6 E1
Richmond Park Rd
Kingston u T KT2 ......17 E1
Mortlake SW14 ....7 D3
Richmond Rd
Coulsdon CR5 ....79 B4
Farncombe GU7 ......150 E6
Horsham RH12 ....217 D4
Isleworth TW7 ....6 A4
Kingston u T KT2 ......17 E2
Sandhurst GU47 ....64 E8
Staines TW18 ....12 F3
Thornton Heath CR7 ...42 B5
Twickenham TW1 ......17 B8
Wallington CR0 ....60 E7
Wimbledon SW20 ......39 B8
Richmond Sq RH19 ...185 D2
Richmond Sta TW9 .....6 E3
Richmond Upon Thames Coll
TW2 ....16 E8
Richmond Way
East Grinstead RH19 ..205 F8
Fetcham KT23 ....94 C3
Richmondwood SL5 ....30 B1
Rickard Cl SW2 ....22 A7
Rickards Cl KT6 ....56 E8
Ricketts Hill Rd TN16 .103 E3
Rickfield RH11 ....201 A5
Rickford Hill GU3 .....88 D1
Rickman Cl RG12 ......27 C3
Rickman Cres KT15 ....52 B7
Rickman Ct KT15 ......52 B7
Rickman Hill CR5 .....79 B2
Rickman Hill Rd CR5 ..79 B1
Rickman's La RH14 ...211 F2
Ricksons La KT24 ....112 B8
Rickwood RH6 ....161 B4
Rickyard GU2 ....108 D1

Riddens The RH12 ....214 A6
Riddings The CR3 .....100 F2
Riddlesdown Ave CR8 ..80 C7
Riddlesdown High Sch
CR2 ....80 E5
Riddlesdown Rd CR8 ..80 D5
Riddlesdown Sta CR8 ..80 C6
Ride La GU5 ....153 D7
Ride The RH14 ....212 C2
Ride Way GU5,GU6 ...154 C1
Riders Way RH9 ......121 C4
Rideway Cl GU15 ......65 B4
Ridge Cl Brockham RH3 .137 B5
Woking GU22 ....89 B6
Ridge Ct CR6 ....81 A1
Ridge Gn RH1 ....140 E6
Ridge Green Cl RH1 ..140 E6
Ridge Ho **4** KT2 ......18 B1
Ridge Langley CR2 ....62 A2
Ridge Moor Cl GU26 ..188 E5
Ridge Mount Rd SL5 ..30 A1
Ridge Pk SM6 ....60 A7
Ridge Rd Cheam SM3,SM4 .39 F1
Mitcham CR4 ....21 B1
Ridge The Coulsdon CR5 .79 E5
Epsom KT18,KT21 ......76 C1
Fetcham KT23 ....94 D3
Rudgwick RH12 ......214 D8
Sunningdale SL5 ......30 A2
Surbiton KT5 ....38 A4
Twickenham TW2 ......16 D8
Wallington CR8 ....60 D1
Woking GU22 ....70 B2
Woldingham CR3,CR6 ..102 D2
Ridge View Cotts GU7 .150 F4
Ridge Way Feltham TW13 .15 E5
Thorpe GU25 ....31 E4
8 West Norwood SE19 ...22 E2
Ridge Way The GU2 ...61 E1
Ridgedale RH10 ......204 B8
Ridgegate Ct RH2 ....118 D3
Ridgehurst Dr RH12 ..216 F1
Ridgelands GU22 .....94 D3
Ridgemead Rd TW20 ..11 B5
Ridgemount
Guildford GU2 ....130 B8
Oatlands Park KT13 ...53 E8
Ridgemount Ave
Coulsdon CR5 ....79 B2
Croydon CR0 ....62 D8
Ridgemount Cl SE20 ..23 B1
Ridgemount Est GU16 ..86 C7
Ridgemount Way RH1 .139 D7
Ridges The GU3 ......130 C4
Ridgeside RH10 ......201 F6
Ridgeway
East Grinstead RH19 ..205 E7
Epsom KT19 ....76 C7
11 Richmond TW10 ....6 E1
Walton-on-T KT12 .....34 F1
Wimbledon SW19,SW20 .19 D2
Woking GU21 ....69 D4
Ridgeway Cl
Cranleigh GU6 ....175 A3
Dorking RH4 ....136 A5
Lightwater GU18 ......67 A8
Oxshott KT22 ....74 C5
Woking GU21 ....69 D4
Ridgeway Ct RH1 .....118 F1
Ridgeway Dr RH4 ....136 A4
Ridgeway Gdns GU21 ..69 D4
Ridgeway Ho RH6 ....161 A1
Ridgeway Prim Sch CR2 .61 E1
Ridgeway Rd
Dorking RH4 ....136 A5
Hounslow TW7 ....5 E6
Redhill RH1 ....118 F1
Ridgeway Rd N TW7 ....5 E7
Ridgeway Sch The GU9 .146 C7
Ridgeway The
Bracknell RG12 ....27 C6
Brookwood GU24 .....88 A7
Cranleigh GU6 ....174 F3
Croydon CR0 ....60 F7
Fetcham KT22 ....94 D3
Guildford GU1 ....131 A8
Horley RH6 ....161 A1
Horsham RH12 ....217 B4
Lightwater GU18 ......48 B1
Oxshott KT22 ....74 C5
Ridgewell Cl SE26 ....23 F4
Ridgewood Ctr (Hospl)
GU16 ....66 C3
Ridgewood Dr GU16 ..66 D3
Ridgley Rd GU8 ......191 B4
Ridgway GU22 ....71 A4
Ridgway Ct SW19 .....19 D2
Ridgway Gdns SW19 ..19 D1
Ridgway Hill Rd GU9 .146 C8
Ridgway Pl SW19 .....19 E2
Ridgway Rd
Farnham GU9 ....146 C8
Pyrford GU22 ....70 F4
Ridgway The SM2 .....59 D4
Riding Hill CR2 ....81 A6
Riding The
Cranleigh GU6 ....174 E4
Sheerwater GU21 ......70 B5
Ridings The
Addlestone KT15 ......51 E4
Ashstead KT21 ....75 D2
Biggin Hill TN16 ......83 E2
Cobham KT11 ....74 A7
Crawley RH10 ....202 D7
East Horsley KT24 .....92 F2
Epsom KT18 ....76 F4
Ewell KT17 ....57 F2
Frimley GU16 ....66 B3

Ridings The continued
Kingswood KT20 ......97 F7
Redhill RH2 ....118 D3
Send Marsh GU23 .....91 A4
Sunbury TW16 ....35 A8
Surbiton KT5 ....38 A4
Ridlands Gr RH8 .....123 E5
Ridlands La RH8 .....123 E5
Ridlands Rise RH8 ...123 E5
Ridley Ct SW16 ....21 E2
Ridley Rd Bromley BR2 .44 F6
Merton SW19 ....20 B1
Warlingham CR6 ......81 D1
Ridley's Ct RH10 ....202 D8
Ridsdale Rd Penge SE20 .43 B8
Woking GU21 ....69 B2
Riesco Dr CR0 ....62 C4
Rifle Way GU14 ....84 C3
Rigby Cl CR0,CR9 .....61 A7
Rigg Ho **2** SW4 ......21 E8
Riggindale Rd SW16 ..21 D4
Rikkyo Sch in England The
RH14 ....213 D8
Riley Ho **1** SW4 .....21 D8
Rill Wlk RH19 ....186 B1
Rillside RH10 ....202 A3
Rimbault Cl GU11 ....105 E7
Rinaldo Rd SW12 .....21 B8
Ring Rd N RH6 ....182 C8
Ring Rd S RH6 ....182 C7
Ring The GU22 ....27 C7
Ringley Ave RH6 .....161 A2
Ringley Oak RH12 ....217 F4
Ringley Park Ave RH2 .139 D8
Ringley Park Rd RH2 .118 C1
Ringley Rd RH12 ....217 F4
Ringmead
Bracknell, Great Hollands
RG12 ....26 E4
Bracknell,Hanworth RG12 .27 B2
Ringmore Dr GU4 ....110 C4
Ringmore Rd KT12 ....54 C7
Ringmore Rise SE23 ..23 B8
Ringstead Ct **4** SM1 .59 D5
Ringstead Rd
Carshalton SM1 ....59 D5
Lewisham SE6 ....24 B8
Ringwold Cl BR3 ......23 E1
Ringwood RG12 ....26 F2
Ringwood Ave
Redhill RH1 ....118 F4
Thornton Heath CR0,CR9 .41 L2
Ringwood Cl Ascot SL5 .29 B5
Crawley RH10 ....201 E4
Ringwood Gdns SW15 .19 A7
Ringwood Lodge **1**
RH1 ....119 A4
Ringwood Rd
Blackwater GU17 ......64 C5
Farnborough GU14 ....85 C7
Ringwood Way TW12 ..16 A4
Ripley Ave TW20 ......11 E2
Ripley By-Pass GU23 ..91 C4
Ripley CE Inf Sch GU23 .91 B6
Ripley Cl CR0 ....63 C4
Ripley Court Sch GU23 .91 C6
Ripley Ct RH4 ....40 D7
Ripley Gdns Mortlake SW14 7 A4
Sutton SM1 ....59 C6
Ripley Ho
13 Kingston u T KT2 ....18 B2
2 Mortlake SW14 ....7 A4
5 Penge SE26 ....23 B3
Ripley La Ripley GU23 ..91 F3
West Horsley KT24,GU23 .112 A1
Ripley Rd
East Clandon GU23,GU4 .111 D7
Hampton TW12 ....16 A1
Ripley Way KT19 ......76 A8
Riplington Ct SW18 ..19 B8
Ripon Cl Frimley GU15 ..66 D3
Guildford GU2 ....108 F3
Ripon Gdns KT9 ......56 D5
Ripon Rd GU14 ....84 A7
Ripplesmere RG12 ....27 D5
Ripplesmore Cl GU47 ..64 B8
Ripston Rd TW15 .....14 D3
Risborough Dr KT4 ...39 A2
Rise Rd SL5 ....29 F3
Rise The Crawley RH10 .202 D6
Crowthorne RG45 .....45 A5
East Grinstead RH19 ..205 F8
East Horsley KT24 .....92 E1
Ewell KT17 ....57 F1
South Croydon CR2 ...62 C2
Tadworth KT20 ....97 C6
Woking GU21 ....69 D1
Wokingham RG41 .....25 A7
Ritchie Cl RH10 .....202 C2
Ritchie Rd CR0 ....43 B3
Ritherdon Rd SW17 ..21 B6
River Ave KT7 ....37 A2
River Bank KT7 ....36 F4
River Crane Way TW13 .15 F6
River Ct Kingston u T KT6 .37 D4
Sheerwater GU21 ......70 C5
River Gdns
Carshalton SM5 ....60 A2
Feltham TW14 ....4 B2
River Gdns Bsns Ctr TW14 4 B3
River Grove Pk BR3 ..43 F8
River Hill KT11 ....73 B4
River Ho Forest Hill SE26 .23 B5
Mortlake SW13 ....7 F5
River Island Cl KT22 ..94 D7
River La Cobham KT11 ..73 E3
Fetcham KT22 ....94 D6
Leatherhead KT22 .....94 D6

River La continued
Richmond TW10 ....17 D7
Richmond GU10,GU9 ..145 E7
River Mead
Crawley RH11 ....181 A1
Horsham RH12 ....217 B1
River Meads Ave TW2 ..16 B5
River Mount KT12 .....34 F2
River Mount Gdns GU2 .130 C6
River Park Ave TW18 ..12 D4
River Rd TW18 ....32 F8
River Reach TW11 .....17 C3
River Row Cotts GU9 .145 F8
River View TW15 ......52 C5
River View Gdns TW1 ..16 F6
River Way
Twickenham TW2 .....16 B6
West Ewell KT19 ......57 E5
River Wlk KT12 ....35 A3
Riverbank
East Molesey KT8 .....36 E5
Staines TW18 ....12 F1
Westcott RH4 ....135 B7
Riverbank Way TW8 ....6 C8
Riverdale Dorking RH4 .115 C3
Wrecclesham GU10 ..145 E7
Riverdale Dr
Wandsworth SW18 ....20 B7
Woking GU22 ....89 D6
Riverdale Gdns TW1 ...6 C2
Riverdale Rd
Feltham TW13 ....15 F4
Twickenham TW1 ......6 C1
Riverdene Ct KT6 .....37 D4
Riverdene Ind Est KT12 .54 D5
Riverfield Rd TW18 ...12 F2
Riverhead Dr SM2 ....59 B1
Riverholme Dr TW19 ..57 E2
Rivermead Bylfeet KT14 .71 F6
East Molesey KT8 .....36 C6
Kingston u T KT6 ......37 D4
Rivermead Cl
New Haw KT15 ....52 C3
Richmond TW11 ....17 B3
Rivermead Ho TW16 ..35 C6
Rivermead Rd GU15 ..65 B2
Rivernook Cl KT12 ....35 C4
Riverpark Gdns BR2 ..24 C4
Rivers Cl GU14 ....85 E1
Riversdale Prim Sch
SW18 ....20 A7
Riversdale Rd KT7 ....37 A3
Riversdell Cl KT16 ....32 F2
Riverside **4** Catford SE6 .23 F4
Dorking RH4 ....115 C1
Egham TW20 ....12 A5
Forest Row RH18 ....206 E3
Guildford GU1 ....109 D3
Guildford GU1 ....130 D7
Horley RH6 ....161 A1
Horsham RH12 ....217 A2
Oatlands Park TW17 ..34 E2
Sunbury TW16 ....35 D7
Twickenham TW1 ......17 C2
Wraysbury TW19 ......11 C8
Riverside Ave
East Molesey KT8 .....36 D4
Lightwater GU18 ......67 C8
Riverside Bsns Ctr
Guildford GU1 ....109 C1
Wandsworth SW18 ....20 B7
Riverside Bsns Pk
Farnham GU9 ....125 D3
Merton SW19 ....40 C8
Riverside Cl
Brookwood GU24 .....87 F7
Farnborough GU14 ....84 F5
Hackbridge SM6 ......60 B7
Kingston u T KT1 ......37 D5
Staines TW18 ....32 F8
Riverside Ct
Dorking RH4 ....115 D1
Farnham GU9 ....125 D3
Teddington TW11 .....17 C3
Riverside Dr
Bramley GU5 ....152 A7
Chiswick W4 ....7 E6
Egham TW18 ....12 E3
Esher KT10 ....35 A6
Mitcham CR4 ....40 E4
Richmond TW10 ....17 B7
Staines TW18 ....32 F8
Riverside Gdns
Cobham KT11 ....73 A6
Old Woking GU22 .....90 B6
Riverside Ho SW19 ...40 C5
Riverside Ind Pk GU9 .125 C3
Riverside Pk
Addlestone KT13 ......52 E5
Poyle SL3 ....1 C5
Riverside Pl TW19 .....2 D1
Riverside Rd
Hersham KT12 ....54 E6
Staines TW18 ....12 F1
Stanwell TW19 ....2 E1
Wandsworth SW17,SW19 .20 C5
Riverside The KT8 ....36 D6
Riverside Way GU15 ..65 A3
Riverside Wlk
Isleworth TW7 ....5 E4
3 West Wickham BR4 ...44 B1
Riversmeet GU10 ....147 D4
Riverstone Ct KT2 ....37 F8
Riverview Guildford GU1 .109 C1
Shepperton TW17 .....34 D2

Riverview CE Prim Sch
KT19 . . . . .57 D6
Riverview Gr W4 . . . . .7 B8
Riverview Pk SE6 . . . . . . .24 A6
Riverview Rd Chiswick W4 .7 B8
West Ewell KT19 . . . . . . .57 D6
Riverway TW18 . . . . .33 B8
Riverway Est GU3 . . . . . .151 C8
Riverwood Ct GU1 . . . . . .109 C3
Rivett-Drake Rd GU2 . . .109 A5
Rivey Cl KT14 . . . . .70 F5
Road House Est GU22 . . . .90 A7
Roakes Ave KT15 . . . . .52 B8
Robert Cl KT12 . . . . .54 B5
Robert Gerard Ho 7
SE27 . . . . .22 D4
Robert May Cty Fst Sch
RH10 . . . . .201 F4
Robert St CR0,CR9 . . . . . .61 C7
Robert Way
Horsham RH12 . . . . .217 F7
Mytchett GU16 . . . . .85 F3
Roberts Cl Cheam SM3 . . . .58 D3
South Norwood CR7 . . . . .42 D6
Stanwell TW19 . . . . .2 C1
Roberts Ct SE20 . . . . .43 C8
Roberts Ho 5 SE27 . . . . .22 B5
Roberts Rd
Aldershot GU12 . . . . .105 D1
Sandhurst GU15 . . . . .65 A6
Roberts Way TW20 . . . . . .11 C1
Robertsbridge Rd SM5 . .40 D2
Robertson Ct 5 GU21 . . .68 E1
Robertson Ho SW17 . . . . .20 E1
Robertson Way GU21 . . .105 F1
Robin Cl Addlestone KT15 .52 D5
Ash Vale GU12 . . . . .106 A6
Crawley RH11 . . . . .201 C8
2 East Grinstead RH19 .185 F1
Hampton TW12 . . . . .15 E3
Robin Ct SM6 . . . . .60 C4
Robin Gdns RH1 . . . . . . .119 A3
Robin Gr TW8 . . . . .6 C8
Robin Hill GU7 . . . . .150 D7
Robin Hill Dr GU15 . . . . . .66 A3
Robin Hood Cl
Farnborough GU14 . . . . . . .85 A7
Knaphill GU21 . . . . .68 F1
Robin Hood Cres GU21 . . .68 E2
Robin Hood Inf Sch SM1 .59 A5
Robin Hood Jun Sch
SM1 . . . . .59 B5
Robin Hood La
Kingston u T SW15 . . . . . .18 E4
Sutton SM1 . . . . .59 B5
Warnham RH12 . . . . .216 F5
Woking GU4 . . . . .89 F3
Robin Hood Prim Sch
SW15 . . . . .18 E3
Robin Hood Rd
Knaphill GU21 . . . . .68 E2
Knaphill GU21 . . . . .68 F1
Robin Hood Rdbt SW15 . .18 E5
**Robin Hood Way (Kingston
By Pass)** KT2,SW15,SW20 18 E3
Robin Hood Works GU21 68 E2
Robin La GU47 . . . . .45 C1
Robin Row RH10 . . . . . .204 D8
Robin Way Guildford GU2 109 B5
Staines TW18 . . . . .12 F5
Robin's Bow GU15 . . . . . .65 B4
Robin's Ct BR3 . . . . .44 D7
Robinhood Cl CR4 . . . . . . .41 C6
Robinhood La CR4 . . . . . . .41 C6
Robinia Cl SE20 . . . . .43 E6
Robins Ct TW10 . . . . .6 E1
Robins Dale GU21 . . . . . . .68 C2
Robins Ho RG42 . . . . .26 F8
Robinson Ct GU22 . . . . . . .90 C7
Robinson Ct 4 TW9 . . . . . .6 F3
Robinson Rd
Crawley RH11 . . . . .201 D5
Mitcham SW19 . . . . .20 E2
Robinsway KT12 . . . . .54 C6
Robinswood Ct RH12 . . .217 F4
Robinwood Pl SW15 . . . . .18 D4
Robson Rd SE21,SE27 . . . .22 C5
Roby Dr RG12 . . . . .27 D2
Rochdale 9 SE19 . . . . .22 E2
Roche Rd SW16 . . . . .41 F8
Roche Wlk SM4,SM5 . . . . .40 D3
Rochelle Ct BR3 . . . . .24 B1
Rochester Ave TW13 . . . . .14 F6
Rochester Cl SW16 . . . . . .21 E1
Rochester Ct SE23 . . . . . . .43 A7
Rochester Gdns
Caterham CR3 . . . . .100 E5
South Croydon CR0 . . . . . .61 E7
Rochester Par TW13 . . . . .15 A5
Rochester Rd
Carshalton SM5 . . . . .59 F6
Egham TW20 . . . . .12 D2
Rochester Wlk RH2 . . . . .139 B5
Rochford Way CR0 . . . . . . .41 E3
Rock Ave 14 SW14 . . . . . . .7 D4
Rock Cl CR4 . . . . .40 D7
Rock Gdns GU11 . . . . . . .104 F1
Rock Hill SE26 . . . . .22 F4
Rock La GU10 . . . . .146 A5
Rockbourne Rd SE23 . . . .23 D7
Rockdale Dr GU26 . . . . . .188 D3
Rockery The GU14 . . . . . . .84 E3
Rocket Rd GU14 . . . . .84 D1
Rockfield Cl RH8 . . . . . . .122 F4

Rockfield Rd RH8 . . . . . .122 F5
Rockfield Way 7 GU47 . .64 D8
Rockhampton Cl 4 SE27 22 A4
Rockhampton Rd
South Croydon CR2 . . . . . .61 E4
West Norwood SE27,SW16 .22 A4
Rockingham Cl SW15 . . . . .7 F3
Rockingham Ct 20 BR3 . .24 A1
Rockmount Prim Sch
SE19 . . . . .22 D2
Rockmount Rd SE19 . . . . .22 D2
Rocks The RH19 . . . . .206 D6
Rockshaw Rd RH1 . . . . . .119 E8
Rockwell Gdns SE19 . . . . .22 E4
Rocky La RH1,RH2 . . . . . .119 A6
Rocombe Cres SE23 . . . . .23 C8
Rodborough Sch GU8 . . .170 F7
Rodd Est TW17 . . . . .34 D4
Roden Gdns CR0,SE25 . . . .42 E3
Rodenhurst Rd SW4 . . . . .21 C8
Rodgate La GU27 . . . . . . .209 E5
Rodgers Ho 4 SW4 . . . . . .21 D8
Rodmel Ct GU14 . . . . .85 E1
Rodmill La SW2 . . . . .21 E8
Rodney Cl
New Malden KT3 . . . . .38 E4
Thornton Heath CR0 . . . . .42 B1
Walton-on-T KT12 . . . . . . .35 C1
Rodney Gn 3 KT12 . . . . . .54 C8
Rodney Pl SW19 . . . . .40 C8
Rodney Rd Mitcham CR4 . .40 E4
New Malden KT3 . . . . .38 E4
Twickenham TW2 . . . . .16 A8
Walton-on-T KT12 . . . . . . .54 C8
Rodney Way
Guildford GU1 . . . . .110 A2
Poyle SL3 . . . . .1 E6
Rodona Rd KT13 . . . . .72 D8
Rodway Rd SW15 . . . . .19 A8
Rodwell Ct
Addlestone KT15 . . . . .52 C6
Walton-on-T KT12 . . . . . . .54 B7
Roe Way SM6 . . . . .60 E4
Roebuck Cl Ashstead KT21 95 E7
Feltham TW13 . . . . .15 B4
Horsham RH13 . . . . .218 B4
Reigate RH2 . . . . .118 A1
Roebuck Ct 2 KT3 . . . . . .38 E4
Roedean Cres SW15 . . . . . .7 E2
Roedeer Copse GU27 . . .207 E6
Roehampton CE Prim Sch
SW15 . . . . .19 B8
Roehampton Gate SW15 . .7 E1
Roehampton High St
SW15 . . . . .19 A8
Roehampton La SW15,
SW19 . . . . .19 A8
Roehampton Vale SW15 . .18 F5
Roffes La CR3 . . . . .100 D2
Roffey Cl Horley RH6 . . . .160 F3
Purley CR8 . . . . .80 B3
Roffey Cnr RH12 . . . . . . .218 B4
Roffey's Cl RH10 . . . . . . .183 A4
Roffords GU21 . . . . .69 B2
Roffye Ct RH12 . . . . .218 A4
Roger Simmons Ct KT23 .94 A3
Rogers Ct Caterham CR3 .101 B5
Coulsdon CR5 . . . . .80 B1
Rogers La CR6 . . . . .81 F1
Rogers Mead RH9 . . . . . .121 B3
Rogers Rd SW17 . . . . .20 E4
Rogosa Rd GU24 . . . . .67 E6
Rojack Rd SE23 . . . . .23 D7
Roke Cl Purley CR8 . . . . . . .80 C5
Witley GU8 . . . . .170 E5
Roke Ho GU1 . . . . .110 C1
Roke La GU8 . . . . .170 F5
Roke Lane Cotts GU8 . .170 F5
Roke Lodge Rd CR8 . . . . .80 B6
Roke Prim Sch CR8 . . . . . .80 C5
Roke Rd CR8 . . . . .80 C5
Rokeby Cl RG12 . . . . .27 E8
Rokeby Ct GU21 . . . . .68 F2
Rokeby Ho 10 SW12 . . . . .21 B8
Rokeby Pl SW20 . . . . .19 B1
Rokeby Sch KT2 . . . . .18 C1
Rokefield Ho RH4 . . . . . .135 B7
Rokers La GU8 . . . . .149 D7
Roland Ct SE19 . . . . .42 F8
Roland Way KT4 . . . . .57 F8
Rollesby Rd KT19,KT9 . . . .57 A4
Rolleston Rd CR2 . . . . .61 D3
Rollit Cres TW3 . . . . .5 A2
Rolston Ho GU27 . . . . . . .207 F6
Roman Cl TW14 . . . . .4 C2
Roman Farm Rd GU2 . . .108 D2
Roman Ho RH2 . . . . .138 F7
Roman Ind Est CR0 . . . . . .42 E2
Roman Rd RH4 . . . . .136 B5
Roman Rise SE19 . . . . . . .22 D2
Roman Way Croydon CR9 .61 B8
Farnham GU9 . . . . .125 E4
Thornton Heath CR9 . . . . .61 B8
Wallington SM5 . . . . .59 F2
Winkfield RG42 . . . . .27 D8
Romana Ct TW18 . . . . .13 A4
Romanby Ct 11 RH1 . . . .139 F8
Romanfield Rd SW2 . . . . .21 F8
Romanhurst Ave BR2 . . . .44 E5
Romanhurst Gdns BR2 . .44 E5
Romans Bsns Pk GU9 . .125 D3
Romans Ind Pk GU9 . . . .125 D3
Romans Way GU22 . . . . . .71 A4
Romany Gdns SM3 . . . . . .40 A2

Romany Prospect SE19 . .22 D2
Romany The GU14 . . . . . . .84 A1
Romayne Cl GU14 . . . . . . .85 A5
Romberg Rd SW17 . . . . . . .21 A5
Romeo Hill RG42 . . . . .27 F8
Romeyn Rd SW16 . . . . .21 F5
Romley Ct GU9 . . . . .125 D1
Rommany Ct SE27 . . . . . . .22 D4
Rommany Rd SE27 . . . . . . .22 D4
Romney Cl Ashford TW15 .14 C3
Chessington KT9 . . . . .56 E6
Romney Ho RG12 . . . . .27 E5
Romney Rd
Farnborough GU14 . . . . . . .84 E1
New Malden KT3 . . . . .38 D3
Romola Rd SE24 . . . . .22 B7
Romsey Cl
Aldershot GU11 . . . . .126 C6
Blackwater GU17 . . . . .64 C6
Romulus Ct 6 TW8 . . . . . . .6 D7
Rona Cl RH11 . . . . .201 B3
Ronald Cl BR3 . . . . .43 F4
Ronald Ross Prim Sch
SW19 . . . . .19 E8
Ronelean Rd KT6 . . . . .56 F7
Ronneby Cl KT13 . . . . .53 E7
Ronson Way KT22 . . . . . . .95 A6
Ronver Rd SE12 . . . . .24 F7
Rook La CR3 . . . . .100 B3
Rook Way RH12 . . . . .217 F6
Rookeries Cl TW13 . . . . . .15 C5
Rookery Cl KT22 . . . . .94 E3
Rookery Dr RH4 . . . . .135 A5
Rookery Hill
Ashstead KT21 . . . . .76 A1
Outwood RH1,RH6 . . . . . .162 B6
Rookery Rd TW18 . . . . .13 B3
Rookery The RH4 . . . . . . .135 A5
Rookery Way KT20 . . . . . .117 F8
Rookley Cl SM2 . . . . .59 B2
Rooks Hill GU5 . . . . .152 C2
Rooksmead Rd TW16 . . . .35 A7
Rookstone Rd SW17 . . . . .20 F3
Rookwood Ave
Sandhurst GU47 . . . . .45 C2
Wallington SM6 . . . . .60 D6
West Barnes KT3 . . . . .39 A5
Rookwood Cl RH1 . . . . . .119 B6
Rookwood Ct GU2 . . . . . .130 C6
Rookwood Pk RH12 . . . .216 F3
Roothill La RH3 . . . . .137 A3
Ropeland Way RH12 . . . .217 E7
Roper Ho 13 SE21 . . . . . . .22 E4
Roper Way CR4 . . . . .41 A7
Ropers Wlk 13 SE24 . . . . .22 A8
Rorkes Drift GU16 . . . . . . .86 A4
Rosa Ave TW15 . . . . .14 A4
Rosalind Franklin Cl
GU2 . . . . .129 E8
Rosamond St SE26 . . . . . .23 B5
Rosamund Cl CR2 . . . . . . .61 D6
Rosamund Rd RH10 . . . .202 B3
Rosary Cl TW3,TW5 . . . . . . .4 E5
Rosary Gdns TW15 . . . . . .14 B4
Rosary RC Inf Sch The
TW5 . . . . .5 A8
Rosary RC Jun Sch The
TW5 . . . . .5 A8
Rose Ave Mitcham CR4 . . .40 F8
Morden SM4 . . . . .40 C4
Rose Bank Cotts GU22 . . .89 E5
Rose Bushes KT17 . . . . . . .77 C3
Rose Cotts
Enton Green GU8 . . . . . . .171 A2
Esher KT10 . . . . .55 D5
Horsham RH12 . . . . .218 D7
Rose Ct
10 Wimbledon SW19 . . . .19 F3
Wokingham RG40 . . . . . . .25 C6
Rose End KT4 . . . . .39 D1
Rose Gdns
Farnborough GU14 . . . . . . .84 E3
Feltham TW13 . . . . .15 A6
Stanwell TW19 . . . . .13 D8
Rose Hill Dorking RH4 . . .136 B7
Sutton SM1,SM4 . . . . .40 B1
Rose Hill Pk W SM1 . . . . .59 C8
Rose La GU23 . . . . .91 D5
Rose St RG40 . . . . .25 C3
Rose View KT15 . . . . .52 C5
Rose Wlk Purley CR8 . . . . .79 D8
Surbiton KT5 . . . . .38 B4
West Wickham BR4 . . . . . .63 D8
Rose Wood GU22 . . . . .90 A8
Roseacre RH8 . . . . .123 A1
Roseacre Cl TW17 . . . . . . .34 A4
Roseacre Gdns GU4 . . . .131 F3
Rosebank Epsom KT18 . . . .76 C5
Penge SE20 . . . . .23 B1
Rosebank Cl TW11 . . . . . . .17 A2
Rosebay RG40 . . . . .25 E8
Rosebery Ave Epsom KT17 76 E5
Kingston u T KT3 . . . . .38 F6
South Norwood CR7 . . . . . .42 C7
Rosebery Cl SM4 . . . . .39 D3
Rosebery Cres GU22 . . . . .89 F7
Rosebery Gdns SM1 . . . . .59 B6
Rosebery Rd
Cheam SM1,SM2 . . . . .58 F4
Isleworth TW3,TW7 . . . . . . .5 C2
Kingston u T KT1 . . . . .38 B7
Langley Vale KT18 . . . . . . .96 E8
Rosebery Sch KT18 . . . . . .76 C5
Rosebery Sq KT1 . . . . .38 B7
Rosebine Ave TW2 . . . . . .16 D8
Rosebriar Cl GU22 . . . . . . .71 A3
Rosebriars Caterham CR3 100 E7
Esher KT10 . . . . .55 C5

Rosebury Dr GU24 . . . . . . .68 A4
Rosecourt Rd CR0 . . . . . . .41 F3
Rosecroft Cl TN16 . . . . . . .83 F1
Rosecroft Gdns TW2 . . . . .16 D7
Rosedale Aldershot GU12 105 C2
Ashstead KT21 . . . . .75 C1
Caterham CR3 . . . . .100 E4
Rosedale Cl RH11 . . . . . . .201 A4
Rosedale Gdns RG12 . . . .27 A4
Rosedale Rd Richmond TW9 6 E3
Stoneleigh KT17 . . . . .58 A5
Rosedene Ave
Morden SM4 . . . . .40 A4
Streatham SW16 . . . . .21 F5
Thornton Heath CR0 . . . . .41 E2
Rosedene La GU47 . . . . . . .64 D7
Rosefield Cl SM5 . . . . .59 E5
Rosefield Gdns KT16 . . . .51 D4
Rosefield Rd TW18 . . . . . . .13 A4
Roseheath Rd TW4 . . . . .4 F2
Rosehill Claygate KT10 . . . .56 A4
Hampton TW12 . . . . .36 A8
Rosehill Ave
Carshalton SM1,SM5 . . . . .40 C1
Woking GU21 . . . . .69 C1
Rosehill Farm Mdw SM7 .78 B4
Rosehill Gdns SM1 . . . . . .59 C8
Rosehill Rd TN16 . . . . .83 C2
Roseleigh Cl 3 TW1 . . . . . .6 D1
Rosemary Ave
Ash Vale GU12 . . . . .106 A8
East Molesey KT8 . . . . .36 A5
Hounslow TW4 . . . . .4 C5
Rosemary Cl
Farnborough GU14 . . . . . . .84 D7
Oxted RH8 . . . . .123 A2
Thornton Heath CR0 . . . . .41 E3
Rosemary Cotts SW19 . . .19 C1
Rosemary Cres GU2 . . . .109 A5
Rosemary Ct
Haslemere GU27 . . . . . . .208 C5
Horley RH6 . . . . .160 E4
Rosemary Gdns
Blackwater GU17 . . . . .64 D5
Chessington KT9 . . . . .56 E6
Mortlake SW14 . . . . .7 C4
Rosemary Ho RH10 . . . . .182 A1
Rosemary La Alfold GU6 .212 E8
Blackwater GU17 . . . . .64 D5
Charlwood RH6 . . . . .180 E7
Horley RH6 . . . . .161 B3
Mortlake SW14 . . . . .7 C4
Rowledge GU10 . . . . .145 E4
Thorpe TW20 . . . . .32 B6
Rosemary Rd SW17 . . . . . .20 C5
Rosemead KT16 . . . . .33 B2
Rosemead Ave
Feltham TW13 . . . . .14 F5
Mitcham CR4,SW16 . . . . . .41 C7
Rosemead Cl RH1 . . . . . . .139 D7
Rosemead Prep Sch
SE27 . . . . .22 C6
Rosemont Rd
Kingston u T KT3 . . . . .38 C6
Richmond TW10 . . . . .6 E1
Rosemount Ave KT14 . . . .71 A6
Rosemount Par KT14 . . . .71 A6
Rosemount Point 10
SE23 . . . . .23 D5
Rosemount Twrs 5 SM6 .60 C4
Rosendale Prim Sch
SE21 . . . . .22 C8
Rosendale Rd SE21,SE24 .22 C7
Roseneath Ct CR3 . . . . . .101 A2
Roseneath Dr GU8 . . . . . .191 B4
Rosery The CR0 . . . . .43 D3
Roses Cotts RH4 . . . . .136 A7
Rosethorn Cl SW12 . . . . . .21 D8
Rosetrees GU1 . . . . .131 A8
Rosetta Ct SE19 . . . . .22 E1
Roseville Ave TW3,TW4 . . .5 A2
Rosevine Rd SW20 . . . . . . .39 C8
Rosewarne Cl GU21 . . . . . .69 A1
Rosewell Cl SE20 . . . . .23 B1
Rosewood
Haslemere GU27 . . . . . . .208 C5
Mytchett GU16 . . . . .86 A4
Rosewood Ct
Kingston u T KT2 . . . . .18 A1
2 Woking GU21 . . . . .70 A3
Rosewood Dr TW17 . . . . . .33 F4
Rosewood Gr SM1 . . . . . . .59 C8
Rosewood Way GU24 . . . .67 E6
Rosina Ct SW17 . . . . .20 E3
Roskeen Ct SW19 . . . . . . .19 C1
Roslan Ct RH6 . . . . .161 B2
Roslyn Cl CR4 . . . . .40 D7
Roslyn Ct 8 GU21 . . . . . . .69 A1
Ross Cl RH10 . . . . .201 F3
Ross Ct Croydon CR2 . . . . .61 C4
4 Putney SW15 . . . . .19 D8
Ross Ho TW2 . . . . .16 B6
Ross Par SM6 . . . . .60 B4
Ross Rd Cobham KT11 . . . .73 F2
South Norwood SE25 . . . . .42 E6
Twickenham TW2 . . . . .16 B7
Wallington SM6 . . . . .60 C5
Rossal Ct SE20 . . . . .23 B1
Rossdale SM1 . . . . .59 E5
Rossendon Ct 1 SM6 . . . .60 C4
Rossett Cl RG12 . . . . .27 B5
Rossignol Gdns SM5 . . . . .60 A8
Rossindel Rd TW3 . . . . .5 A2
Rossiter Lodge GU1 . . . . .131 A8
Rossiter Rd SW12 . . . . .21 B7
Rosslea GU20 . . . . .48 A6
Rosslyn Ave Feltham TW14 .4 A1

Rosslyn Ave continued
Mortlake SW13,SW14 . . . . . . .7 F4
Rosslyn Cl Ashford TW16 . .14 E2
Coney Hall BR4 . . . . .63 F7
Rosslyn Ho 8 TW9 . . . . . . .6 F6
Rosslyn Pk KT13 . . . . .53 D6
Rosslyn Rd TW1 . . . . .6 C1
Rossmore Cl RH10 . . . . . .182 D2
Rossmore Gdns GU11 . . .104 F1
Rosswood Gdns SM6 . . . .60 C4
Rostella Rd SW17 . . . . .20 D4
Rostrevor Rd SW19 . . . . . .20 A3
Rothbury Gdns TW7 . . . . . .6 A7
Rothbury Wlk GU15 . . . . . .66 C4
Rother Cl GU47 . . . . .64 C8
Rother Cres RH11 . . . . . . .200 F5
Rother Ho 4 RH1 . . . . . . .118 F2
Rother Rd GU14 . . . . .84 E1
Rotherfield Ave RG41 . . . .25 A7
Rotherfield Rd SM5 . . . . . .60 A5
Rotherhill Ave SW16 . . . . .21 D2
Rothervale RH6 . . . . .160 F5
Rotherwick Ct GU14 . . . .105 C8
Rotherwood Cl SW19,
SW20 . . . . .39 E8
Rothes Rd RH4 . . . . .136 B8
Rothesay Ave
Merton SW20 . . . . .39 E7
Mortlake SW14,TW10 . . . . . .7 B3
Rothesay Ct SE6 . . . . .24 F6
Rothesay Rd SE25 . . . . . . .42 E5
Rothsay Ct KT13 . . . . .53 D4
Rothschild St SE27 . . . . . .22 C4
Rothwell Ho
Crowthorne RG45 . . . . . . .45 C4
Heston TW5 . . . . .5 A8
Rotunda Est The GU11 . .105 B2
Rougemont Ave SM4 . . . . .40 A3
Rough Field RH19 . . . . . . .185 D4
Rough Rd GU22 . . . . .88 C5
Rough Rew RH4 . . . . .136 B4
Rough Way RH12 . . . . .217 F5
Roughets La RH1 . . . . .120 E6
Roughlands GU22 . . . . .70 E4
Rounce La GU24 . . . . .67 D6
Round Gr CR0 . . . . .43 D2
Round Hill SE23 . . . . .23 C5
Round Oak Rd KT13 . . . . . .52 F6
Roundabout Cotts RH12 214 C5
Roundacre SW19 . . . . .19 D6
Roundals La GU8 . . . . .191 E8
Roundell Ho 14 SE21 . . . . .22 E4
Roundhay Ct SE23 . . . . . . .23 D6
Roundhill GU22 . . . . .90 B8
Roundhill Dr GU22 . . . . . . .70 B1
Roundhill Way
Guildford GU2 . . . . .108 F1
Oxshott KT11 . . . . .74 B7
Roundshaw Ctr SM6 . . . . .60 E3
Roundtable Rd BR1 . . . . . .24 F5
Roundthorn Way GU21 . . .68 F3
Roundway Biggin Hill TN16 83 D4
Egham TW20 . . . . .12 C3
Frimley GU15 . . . . .66 C6
Roundway Cl GU15 . . . . . . .66 C6
Roundway Ct RH10 . . . . . .201 D8
Roundway The KT10 . . . . . .55 A6
Roundway View SM7 . . . . .77 D4
Roundway SM7 . . . . .77 D4
Roundwood View SM7 . . . .77 D4
Roupell Ho 7 KT2 . . . . .17 F1
Roupell Rd SW2 . . . . .21 F7
Rouse Gdns SE21 . . . . .22 E4
Routh Ct TW14 . . . . .14 D7
Routh Rd SW18 . . . . .20 E8
Row Hill KT15 . . . . .51 F4
Row La GU5 . . . . .153 E5
Row The RH7 . . . . .164 D4
Row Town KT15 . . . . .51 F3
Rowallan Ct SE6 . . . . .24 F7
Rowan 2 RG12 . . . . .27 F4
Rowan Ave TW20 . . . . .12 C3
Rowan Chase GU10 . . . . .146 A5
Rowan Cl Camberley GU15 .65 F8
Crawley RH10 . . . . .201 F6
Guildford GU1 . . . . .109 C4
Horsham RH12 . . . . .218 B5
Kingston u T KT3 . . . . .38 E7
Mitcham SW16 . . . . .41 C8
Reigate RH2 . . . . .139 C7
Rowan Cres SW16 . . . . . . .41 C8
Rowan Ct Forest Hill SE26 .23 C4
11 Kingston u T KT2 . . . . .18 A1
Wimbledon SW20 . . . . . . .39 B7
Rowan Dr RG45 . . . . .45 C6
Rowan Gdns CR0 . . . . .61 F7
Rowan Gn KT13 . . . . .53 D6
Rowan Gr CR5 . . . . .99 B6
Rowan Mead KT20 . . . . . . .97 B8
Rowan Prep Sch KT10 . . . .55 F3
Rowan Rd Brentford TW8 . . .6 B7
Mitcham SW16 . . . . .41 C7
Rowan Way RH12 . . . . . . .218 C5
Rowan Wlk RH10 . . . . . . .204 C8
Rowans Cl GU14 . . . . .64 E1
Rowans The Ashford TW16 .14 F3
Grayshott GU26 . . . . .188 D2
Woking GU22 . . . . .69 E1
Rowanside Cl GU35 . . . .187 C4
Rowbarns Way KT24 . . . .112 F5
Rowbury GU7 . . . . .151 A7
Rowcroft Cl GU12 . . . . . . .106 A6
Rowden Rd Penge BR3 . . . .43 F8
West Ewell KT19 . . . . .57 C6
Rowdown Cres CR0 . . . . . .63 E2
Rowdown Prim Sch CR0 .63 D1
Rowe La GU24 . . . . .88 A3
Rowfant Bsns Ctr RH10 .203 E6
Rowfant Cl RH10 . . . . . . .202 E6

Rowfant Rd SW12,SW17 21 A6
Rowhill Ave GU11 125 F8
Rowhill Cres GU11 125 F8
Rowhill Nature Trail* GU9 125 D8
Rowhills GU9 125 E8
Rowhills Cl GU9 125 F7
Rowhook Hill RH12 215 F8
Rowhook Rd
Rowhook RH12 196 E1
Slinfold RH12 216 A8
Rowhurst Ave KT15 52 B4
Rowland Cl RH10 183 E5
Rowland Gr SE26 23 B5
Rowland Hill Almshouses TW15 14 A3
Rowland Ho GU6 174 D3
Rowland Rd GU6 174 D3
Rowland Way
Littleton TW15 14 D1
Merton SW19 40 B8
Rowlands Rd RH12 218 A6
Rowledge CE Prim Sch GU10 145 E3
Rowley Cl Bracknell RG12 27 E6
Pyrford GU22 71 B3
Rowley Ct CR3 100 C5
Rowlls Rd KT1 37 F6
Rowly Dr GU6 174 A6
Rowly Edge GU6 174 A6
Rowntree Rd TW2 16 E7
Rowplatt La RH19 184 E4
Roxbee Cox Rd GU14 84 A1
Roxborough Ave TW7 5 F7
Roxburgh Cl GU15 66 C4
Roxburgh Rd SE27 22 B3
Roxeth Ct TW15 14 A3
Roxford Cl TW17 34 E4
Roxton Gdns CR0 63 A5
Roy Gr TW12 16 B2
Royal Alexandra & Albert Sch RH2 118 E6
Royal Ave KT4 57 E8
Royal Botanic Gdns* TW9 6 E6
Royal Cir SE27 22 B5
Royal Cl KT4 57 E8
Royal Ct
9 Kingston u T KT2 18 B1
Knaphill GU21 68 C1
Royal Dr KT18 97 B8
Royal Duchess Mews 15 SW12 21 B8
Royal Earlswood Pk RH1 140 A6
Royal Fst Sch The SL4 10 C4
Royal Gram Sch GU1 130 D8
Royal Holloway Univ of London TW20 11 D2
Royal Horticultural Society Cotts GU23 71 E3
Royal Horticultural Society's Gdn* GU23 71 E1
Royal Hosp SW19 19 E8
Royal Hunt Ho SL5 28 D8
Royal Huts Ave GU26 188 F4
Royal Jun Sch The GU26 188 D1
Royal Kent CE Prim Sch The KT22 74 C5
Royal Logistic Corps Mus* GU16 86 D8
Royal Marsden Hospl (Surrey Branch) The SM2 59 C1
Royal Mews KT8 36 E6
Royal Military Acad GU15 64 F6
Royal Military Acad Hospl GU15 65 A8
Royal Military Sch of Music (Kneller Hall) TW2 5 D1
Royal Oak Ctr The CR2 61 C1
Royal Oak Dr RG45 45 B8
Royal Oak Ho RH10 204 B7
Royal Oak Rd GU21 69 D1
Royal Orchard Cl SW18 19 E8
Royal Par GU26 188 F4
Royal Rd TW11 16 D3
Royal Russell Sch CR9 62 B5
Royal Sch of Church Music RH5 115 B4
Royal Sch The GU27 189 A2
Royal Surrey County Hospl GU2 108 E1
Royal Victoria Gdns SL5 29 A4
Royal Way The GU16 86 D7
Royal Wlk SM6 60 B7
Royale Cl GU11 126 C8
Royals The GU1 130 E8
Royce Rd RH10 182 A3
Roycroft Cl SW2 22 A7
Roydon Ct KT12 54 A6
Roydon Lodge KT15 52 D7
Roymount Ct TW2 16 E5
Royston Ave Byfleet KT14 71 E7
Carshalton SM1 59 D7
Wallington SM6 60 D6
Royston Cl Cranford TW5 4 B6
Crawley RH10 182 A2
Walton-on-T KT12 35 A1
Royston Ct
Hinchley Wood KT10 55 F8
3 Richmond TW9 6 F6
Tolworth KT6 57 A8
Royston Prim Sch SE20 43 D8
Royston Rd Byfleet KT14 71 E7
Penge BR3,SE20 43 D8
Richmond TW10 6 E2
Roystons The KT5 38 B4
Rozeldene GU26 188 E3
Rubens Gdns SE22 23 A8
Rubens St SE6 23 F6
Rubus Cl GU24 67 E6
Ruckmans La RH5 197 B7
Rudd Hall Rise GU15 65 E4
Ruden Way KT17 77 B4
Rudge Rise KT15 51 F5
Rudgwick Prim Sch RH12 214 D7
Rudgwick Rd RH11 200 F7
Rudloe Rd SW12 21 C8
Rudolph Ct SE22 23 B8
Rudsworth Cl SL3 1 D7
Ruffets Cl CR2 62 B3
Ruffetts The CR2 62 B3
Ruffetts Way KT20 77 E1
Rufus Bsns Ctr SW18 20 B6
Rufwood RH10 204 A8
Rugby Cl GU47 45 E1
Rugby La SM2 58 D2
Rugby Rd TW1,TW2,TW7 5 E1
Ruggles-Brise Rd TW15 13 D3
Ruislip St SW17 20 F4
Rumsey Cl TW12 15 F2
Runcorn Cl RH11 200 E2
Runes Cl CR4 40 E5
Runnemede Rd TW20 12 A4
Running Horse Yd 12 TW8 6 E8
Runnymede* Egham TW20 11 F5
Mitcham SW19 40 D8
Runnymede Cl TW2 16 B8
Runnymede Cotts TW19 12 D7
Runnymede Cres SW16 41 E8
Runnymede Ct
Egham TW20 12 A4
Farnborough GU14 85 A7
1 Wallington SM6 60 B4
Runnymede Gdns TW2 16 B8
Runnymede Hospl The KT16 51 D7
Runnymede Rd TW2 5 B1
Runnymede Rdbt TW20 12 B4
Runshooke Ct 9 RH11 201 A3
Runtley Wood La GU4 89 F2
Runwick La GU10 124 C1
Rupert Rd GU2 130 C8
Rural Life Ctr* GU10 146 F3
Rural Way Mitcham SW16 21 B1
Redhill RH1 119 A1
Ruscoe Dr GU22 70 A2
Ruscoe Ho 12 SW27 22 B3
Ruscombe Way TW14 14 F8
Rush Common Mews SW2 21 F8
Rush Croft GU7 151 A8
Rush The SW20 39 F8
Rusham Park Ave TW20 12 A2
Rusham Rd Balham SW12 20 F8
Egham TW20 11 F2
Rushams Rd RH12 217 B3
Rushbury Ct 6 TW12 36 A8
Rushden Cl SE19 22 D1
Rushden Way GU9 125 D7
Rushdene Wlk TN16 83 D2
Rushen Wlk SM5 40 D1
Rushett Cl KT7 37 B1
Rushett Dr RH4 136 C4
Rushett La KT9 75 D7
Rushett Rd KT7 37 B2
Rushetts Pl RH11 181 C1
Rushetts Rd
Crawley RH11 181 B1
Reigate RH2 139 C5
Rushey Cl KT3 38 D5
Rushey Gn SE6 24 B8
Rushey Green Prim Sch SE6 24 B7
Rushfords RH7 164 E5
Rushmead TW10 17 B5
Rushmead Cl CR0 61 F6
Rushmere Ct KT4 58 A8
Rushmere Ho 2 SW15 19 A7
Rushmere Pl
Englefield Green TW20 11 E3
Wimbledon SW19 19 D3
Rushmon Gdns KT12 54 B7
Rushmon Pl SM3 58 E4
Rushmoor Cl GU2 108 F5
Rushmoor Ct GU14 105 C8
Rushmoor Rd GU11 104 E4
Rusholme Gr SE19 22 E3
Rushton Ave RH9 142 D5
Rushworth Rd RH2 118 B2
Rushy Ho RG12 27 E5
Rushy Meadow La SM5 59 E7
Rushy Meadow Prim Sch SM5 59 E7
Ruskin Ave Feltham TW14 3 F1
Richmond TW9 7 A7
Ruskin Cl RH10 182 C1
Ruskin Dr KT4 58 C8
Ruskin Par CR0 61 D5
Ruskin Rd
Croydon CR0,CR9 61 B8
Isleworth TW7 5 F4
Staines TW18 12 F2
Wallington SM5 60 A5
Ruskin Way SW19 40 D8
Rusper Ct CR5 79 D3
Rusper Prim Sch RH12 199 C7
Rusper Rd Capel RH5 178 D2
Crawley RH11 200 D7
Faygate RH12 199 A1
Horsham RH12 217 F6
Newdigate RH12,RH5 179 C4
Ruspers Keep RH11 200 F7
Russ Hill RH6 180 C5
Russel Cl Beckenham BR3 44 C6
Bracknell RG12 27 D2
Russell Cl 5 Chiswick W4 7 F8
Walton on the Hill KT20 97 A2
Woking GU21 69 C4
Russell Ct
Blackwater GU17 64 D5
Bromley BR1 24 F1
Guildford GU1 109 C4
Hindhead GU26 188 F4
Leatherhead KT22 95 B5
Streatham SW16 21 F3
Surbiton KT6 37 E2
Wallington SM6 60 C5
Russell Dr TW19 2 D1
Russell Gdns
Harmondsworth UB7 3 A8
Richmond TW10 17 C6
Russell Green Cl CR8 61 A1
Russell Hill CR8 60 F1
Russell Hill Par 6 CR8 80 A8
Russell Hill Pl CR8 80 A8
Russell Hill Rd CR8 80 A8
Russell Kerr Cl W4 7 C7
Russell Par 5 CR8 80 A8
Russell Prim Sch The TW10 17 D7
Russell Rd
Lower Halliford TW17 34 C2
Merton SW19 20 A1
Mitcham CR4 40 E6
Twickenham TW1,TW2 5 F1
Walton-on-T KT12 35 A3
Woking GU21 69 C4
Russell Sch The TW10 17 D6
Russell Way
Crawley RH10 202 A5
Sutton SM1 59 B5
Russell Wlk 4 TW10 6 F1
Russell's Yd GU22 89 F7
Russells KT20 97 D5
Russells Cres RH6 161 A2
Russet Ave TW17 34 E6
Russet Cl Hersham KT12 54 E7
Horley RH6 161 C3
Stanwell TW19 1 F1
Tongham GU10 126 E7
Russet Dr CR0 43 E1
Russet Gdns GU15 65 D3
Russet Glade GU11 125 E8
Russet Ho TW3 4 F3
Russet Way RH5 136 D4
Russets KT20 97 C4
Russett Ct Caterham CR3 101 A2
Horsham RH12 218 A4
Russetts Cl GU21 69 F4
Russington Rd TW17 34 D3
Russley Gn RG40 25 A1
Rusthall Cl CR0 43 C3
Rustic Ave SW16 21 B1
Rustic Villas RH9 121 B5
Rustington Wlk SM4 39 F2
Ruston Ave KT5 38 B2
Ruston Cl RH10 202 C3
Ruston Way SL5 28 E7
Rutford Rd SW16 21 E3
Ruth Cl GU14 84 C5
Ruthen Cl KT18 76 B5
Rutherford Cl SM2 59 D4
Rutherford Ho 11 TW11 16 F3
Rutherford Way RH10 182 A3
Rutherford Way Ind Est RH10 182 A3
Rutherwick Cl RH6 160 F3
Rutherwick Rise CR5 79 E3
Rutherwyk Rd KT16 32 E2
Rutherwyke Cl KT17 58 A4
Rutland Cl
Aldershot GU11 105 A3
Ashtead KT21 75 E2
Epsom KT19 57 D1
Mitcham SW19 20 E1
Mortlake SW14 7 C4
Redhill RH1 118 F2
Rutland Dr Morden SM4 40 A2
Richmond TW10 17 E7
Rutland Gate BR2 44 F5
Rutland Gdns CR0 61 E6
Rutland Lodge
Forest Hill SE6 23 F6
Teddington TW11 16 E3
Rutland Pk SE6 23 F6
Rutland Rd
Mitcham SW19 20 E1
Twickenham TW2 16 D6
Rutland Terr GU11 105 A3
Rutland Wlk SE6 23 F6
Rutlish Rd SW19 40 A8
Rutlish Sch (Boys) SW20 39 F7
Rutson Rd KT14 71 F5
Rutter Gdns CR4,SW19 40 D5
Rutton Hill Rd GU8 189 E8
Ruxbury Ct TW15 13 E5
Ruxbury Rd KT16 32 D3
Ruxley Cl KT19 57 B5
Ruxley Cres KT10 56 B3
Ruxley Ct West Ewell KT19 57 C5
Woking GU22 89 D8
Ruxley Gdns TW17 34 C4
Ruxley La KT19 57 C5
Ruxley Mews KT19 57 B5
Ruxley Ridge KT10 56 A3
Ruxton Cl CR5 79 C4
Ryan Ct SW16 21 E1
Ryan Dr TW8 6 A8
Ryan Mount GU47 64 A8
Rybrook Dr KT12 54 C8
Rycott Path SE22 23 A8
Rydal Cl Crawley RH11 200 D4
Farnborough GU14 84 D3
Frimley GU15 66 D5
Sanderstead CR8 80 D6
Rydal Dr BR4 63 E8
Rydal Gdns
Kingston u T SW15 18 E3
Twickenham TW2,TW3 5 B1
Rydal Mount 9 BR2 44 F5
Rydal Pl GU18 67 B8
Rydal Rd SW16 21 D4
Rydal Way TW20 12 B1
Ryde Cl GU23 91 C6
Ryde Ct GU12 105 C1
Ryde Heron GU21 68 E2
Ryde Lands GU6 174 F4
Ryde Pl TW1 6 D1
Ryde The TW18 33 B8
Ryde Vale Rd SW12 21 C6
Ryde's Hill Cres GU2 108 F5
Ryde's Hill Rd GU2 108 F4
Rydens Ave KT12 54 C8
Rydens Cl KT12 54 C8
Rydens Ct KT12 54 C7
Rydens Gr KT12 54 D6
Rydens Pk KT12 54 D8
Rydens Rd KT12 54 C8
Rydens Sch KT12 54 C6
Rydens Way GU22 90 A7
Ryder Ho 5 SW19 40 B8
Ryders Way RH12 217 F7
Rydes Ave GU2 108 F4
Rydes Cl GU22 90 C7
Rydeshill Prep Sch GU3 108 F3
Rydon Bsns Ctr KT22 95 B8
Rydon Mews SW19 19 C1
Rydon's La CR5 100 C7
Rydon's Wood Cl CR5 100 C7
Rye Ash RH10 202 A7
Rye Brook Rd KT22 75 A1
Rye Cl Farnborough GU14 84 E7
Guildford GU2 108 E3
Winkfield RG12 27 D8
Rye Ct BR3 43 F8
Rye Field KT21 75 D3
Rye Gr GU20,GU18 48 F2
Ryebridge Cl KT22 75 A1
Ryebrook Bsns Pk KT22 95 A7
Ryecotes Mead SE21 22 E7
Ryecroft Ave TW2 16 B7
Ryecroft Dr RH12 217 A3
Ryecroft Gdns GU17 64 E4
Ryecroft Rd SW16 22 A2
Ryedale Ct 8 TW12 36 A8
Ryefield Path 7 SW15 19 A7
Ryefield Rd SE19 22 C2
Ryehill Ct KT3 38 F2
Ryelands Crawley RH11 201 A5
Horley RH6 161 C4
Ryelands Cl CR3 100 E6
Ryelands Ct KT22 75 A1
Ryelands Pl KT13 53 E7
Ryelands Prim Sch SE25 43 B4
Ryemead La SL4 8 C5
Ryersh La RH5 178 C8
Ryfold Rd SW19 20 A5
Rykens La RH3 137 C4
Ryland Cl TW13 14 F4
Ryland Ho 11 SW16 21 C3
Rylandes Rd CR2 62 B1
Ryle Rd GU9 146 B8
Rylton Ho KT12 35 A1
Rymer Rd CR0 42 E2
Rythe Cl KT9 56 C3
Rythe Ct KT7 37 A2
Rythe Ho BR1 24 D3
Rythe Rd KT10 55 E5
Rythe The KT22 55 C1

S

Sabah Ct TW15 14 A4
Sabin Gates RG12 27 B6
Sable Cl TW4 4 C4
Sable Ct 3 KT3 38 E4
Sabre Ct GU11 104 E2
Sachel Court Dr GU6 193 F2
Sachel Court Rd GU6 193 D3
Sackville Cl RH19 185 C3
Sackville Coll* RH19 185 F1
Sackville Com Coll RH19 186 A1
Sackville Cotts RH1 120 D1
Sackville Ct 3 RH19 205 F8
Sackville Gdns RH19 185 C3
Sackville Ho 16 SW16 21 E5
Sackville La RH19 185 C3
Sackville Rd SM2 59 A3
Sacred Heart Catholic Prim Sch KT3 39 A5
Sacred Heart RC Prim Sch TW11 17 B1
Saddleback Rd GU15 65 E8
Saddlebrook Pk TW16 14 E1
Saddler Cnr GU47 64 B7
Saddler Row RH10 201 D3
Saddlers Mews KT1 37 C8
Saddlers Scarp GU26 188 A4
Saddlers Way KT18 96 D8
Saddlewood GU15 65 C4
Sadler Cl CR4 40 F7
Sadlers Cl GU4 110 D2
Sadlers Ride KT8 36 C7
Saffron Cl Crawley RH11 201 A3
Thornton Heath CR0 41 E3
Saffron Ct
East Bedfont TW14 14 C8
Saffron Ct *continued*
Farnborough GU14 84 C4
Saffron Platt GU2 109 A5
Saffron Rd RG12 27 B5
Saffron Way KT6 37 D1
Sage Ho RH10 182 A1
Sailors La GU8 169 A2
Sainfoin Rd SW17 21 A6
Sainsbury Ctr The KT16 33 A2
Sainsbury Rd SE19 22 E3
Saint Hill Manor* RH19 205 C4
Saint Hill Rd RH19 205 C5
Saints Cl SE27 22 B4
SS Peter & Paul's RC Prim Sch CR4 40 F5
St Agatha's Dr KT2 17 F2
St Agatha's Gr CR4,SM5 40 F1
St Agatha's RC Prim Sch KT2 17 F2
St Agatha's RC Sch KT2 17 F1
St Agnes Rd RH19 185 E2
St Aidan's RC Prim Sch CR5 79 C3
St Alban's Gdns TW11 17 A3
St Alban's Gr SM5 40 E2
St Alban's RC Prim Sch KT8 36 C4
St Alban's Rd RH2 118 A3
St Alban's Rdbt GU14 105 C7
St Albans Ave
Feltham TW13 15 D3
Weybridge KT13 53 A7
St Albans Cl GU3 108 B2
St Albans Ho 2 SW16 22 A4
St Albans Rd Cheam SM1 58 F6
Kingston u T KT2 17 E2
St Amunds Cl SE6 24 A4
St Andrew Ave GU24 88 B6
St Andrew's & St Mark's CE Jun Sch KT6 37 D4
St Andrew's CE Fst & Mid Sch RH10 202 A4
St Andrew's CE High Sch CR0 61 B6
St Andrew's CE Inf Sch GU9 125 B2
St Andrew's CE Prim Sch KT11 73 C6
St Andrew's Cl
Hounslow TW7 5 E6
Reigate RH2 139 B8
Upper Halliford TW17 34 D5
Wraysbury TW19 11 E8
St Andrew's Ct
5 Carshalton SM1 59 E7
Wandsworth SW18 20 C6
St Andrew's RC Prim Sch SW16 21 E3
St Andrew's RC Sch The Grange KT22 95 D7
St Andrew's RC Sec Sch KT22 95 D7
St Andrew's Rd
Coulsdon CR5 79 B4
3 Croydon CR0,CR9 61 C6
Kingston u T KT6 37 D3
St Andrew's Sch GU21 69 D3
St Andrew's Sq KT6 37 D3
St Andrew's Way GU16 85 F7
St Andrew's Wlk KT11 73 B4
St Andrews
Bracknell RG12 26 E3
Cranleigh GU6 174 B4
Horley RH6 161 B2
St Andrews Cl
Hinchley Wood KT7 37 B1
Woking GU21 69 C2
St Andrews Ct Ascot SL5 29 C4
Chiswick W4 7 C6
New Malden KT3 38 F6
St Andrews Gate 2 GU22 69 F1
St Andrews Gdns KT11 73 C6
St Andrews Mews SW12 21 D7
St Andrews Rd
Carshalton SM5 59 E7
Crawley RH11 200 D5
St Andrews Way RH8 123 F4
St Ann's Cl KT16 32 F3
St Ann's Heath Jun Sch GU25 31 E4
St Ann's Hill SW18 20 C8
St Ann's Hill Rd KT16 32 D3
St Ann's Rd KT16 32 F3
St Ann's Sch SM4 40 B4
St Ann's Way CR2 61 B4
St Anne's Ave TW19 13 D8
St Anne's Dr RH1 119 A2
St Anne's Prim Sch TW19 13 E8
St Anne's RC Prim Sch
Banstead SM7 78 A3
Chertsey KT16 33 A1
St Anne's Rd
Crawley RH10 182 C2
Godalming GU7 151 A5
St Annes Bvd RH1 119 B3
St Annes Dr RG40 26 A6
St Annes Dr N RH1 119 A3
St Annes Glade GU19 47 D3
St Annes Mount 7 RH1 119 A2
St Annes Rise RH1 119 A2
St Annes Way 5 RH1 119 A2
St Anns Rd SW13 7 F6
St Anselm's Ct SW16 21 E3

St Anselm's RC Prim Sch
SW17 . . . . .21 A5
St Anthony's Ct
1 Balham SW12 . . . . .21 A8
Upper Tooting SW17 . . . . . .21 A6
St Anthony's Hospl KT4 . .39 D1
St Anthony's RC Prim Sch
SE20 . . . . .43 B8
St Anthony's Way TW14 . .3 F3
St Anthonys Cl
Bracknell RG42 . . . . .27 A8
Upper Tooting SW19 . . . . . .20 E6
St Arvans Cl CR0 . . . . . . .61 E7
St Aubin Cl RH11 . . . . .200 F2
St Aubyn's Ave
Hounslow TW3,TW4 . . . . . . .5 A2
Wimbledon SW19 . . . . .19 F3
St Aubyn's Ct SW19 . . . .19 E2
St Aubyn's Rd SE19 . . . . .22 F2
St Augustine's Ave
Croydon CR2 . . . . .61 C3
South Croydon CR2 . . . . . .61 C3
St Augustine's Cl GU12 .105 D1
St Augustine's RC Prim Sch
GU16 . . . . .65 F2
St Augustines Ct BR3 . .43 E7
St Augustines RC Prim Sch
SE6 . . . . .24 C3
St Austells Pl RH5 . . . .157 C7
St Austins GU26 . . . . . . .188 D3
St Barnabas Cl BR3 . . . . .44 C7
St Barnabas Rd RH10 . .202 C7
St Barnabas Rd
Carshalton SM1 . . . . .59 D5
Mitcham CR4 . . . . .21 A1
St Barnabas' Gdns KT8 . .36 A4
St Bartholomew CE Prim Sch
GU27 . . . . .208 C7
St Bartholomew's CE Prim
Sch SE26 . . . . .23 C4
St Bartholomew's Cl
SE26 . . . . .23 C4
St Bartholomew's Ct
GU1 . . . . .130 F7
St Bede's CE Jun Sch
GU23 . . . . .90 D3
St Bede's RC Inf Sch
SW12 . . . . .21 D7
St Bede's Sch RH1 . . . .118 E4
St Benedict's Cl
Aldershot GU11 . . . . .105 A1
Upper Tooting SW17 . . . . . .21 A3
St Benet's Gr SM4,SM5 . .40 C2
St Benets Cl SW17 . . . . .20 E6
St Bernadette RC Jun Sch
SW12 . . . . .21 C8
St Bernadette RC Prim Sch
GU14 . . . . .85 A5
St Bernards CR0 . . . . . . .62 E7
St Bernards Cl 8 SE27 . .22 D4
St Boniface RC Prim Sch
SW17 . . . . .20 F3
St Brelades Cl RH4 . . . .136 A5
St Brelades Rd RH11 . . .200 F2
St Catherine's Cross
RH1 . . . . .120 E2
St Catherine's Dr GU2 . .130 B5
St Catherine's Hill GU2 .130 C5
St Catherine's Jun Sch
GU5 . . . . .151 F6
St Catherine's Pk GU1 . .130 F7
St Catherine's Sch
Bramley GU5 . . . . .151 F7
Camberley GU15 . . . . .65 C4
Twickenham TW1 . . . . .17 A6
St Catherines
Weybridge KT13 . . . . .53 B7
Woking GU22 . . . . .89 C8
St Catherines Ct
Chessington KT9 . . . . .56 D4
Upper Tooting SW17 . . . . . .20 E6
St Catherines Ct TW13 . .15 A7
St Catherines Pl TW20 . .12 A3
St Catherines Rd
Crawley RH10 . . . . .182 D1
Frimley GU16 . . . . .86 A8
St Catherines Sch RH1 . .120 E2
St Cecilia's RC Prim Sch
SM3 . . . . .58 D8
St Cecilias Cl SM3 . . . . . .39 E1
St Chad Ave GU22 . . . . . . .88 C5
St Chad's RC Prim Sch
SE25 . . . . .42 E4
St Chads Cl KT6 . . . . . . .37 C2
St Charles Borromeo RC
Prim Sch KT13 . . . . .53 A7
St Charles Ct KT13 . . . . .53 A5
St Charles Pl KT13 . . . . .53 A5
St Christopher's RH7 . .164 D4
St Christopher's Cl
Haslemere GU27 . . . . . . .208 A6
Hounslow TW7 . . . . .5 E6
St Christopher's Ct 4
KT12 . . . . .54 C8
St Christopher's Gn
GU27 . . . . .208 A6
St Christopher's Hospice
SE26 . . . . .23 C3
St Christopher's Mews
SM6 . . . . .60 C5
St Christopher's Rd
2 Farnborough GU14 . . . .85 A3
Haslemere GU27 . . . . . . .208 A6
St Christopher's Sch
Beckenham BR3 . . . . .44 C7

St Christopher's Sch *continued*
Epsom KT18 . . . . .76 E5
St Christophers Cl
Aldershot GU12 . . . . .105 D2
Horsham RH12 . . . . .217 D4
St Christophers Day Hospl
RH12 . . . . .217 D3
St Christophers Gdns
North Ascot SL5 . . . . .28 D8
Thornton Heath CR7 . . . . . .42 A6
St Christophers Pl 1
GU14 . . . . .85 A3
St Clair Cl Oxted RH8 . .122 C5
Reigate RH2 . . . . .118 C5
St Clair Dr KT4 . . . . .58 B6
St Clair's Rd CR0 . . . . . . .61 E8
St Clare Bsns Pk TW12 . .16 C2
St Clement Rd RH11 . . .200 F2
St Clements Ct SW14 . . . .85 B7
St Clements RC Prim Sch
KT17 . . . . .57 F2
St Cloud Rd SE27 . . . . . .22 D4
St Crispin's Sch RG40 . . . .25 E6
St Crispins Way KT16 . . .51 C2
St Cross Rd
Farnham GU9 . . . . .125 C3
Frimley GU16 . . . . .86 B7
St Cuthbert Mayne RC Prim
Sch GU6 . . . . .174 E3
St Cuthbert's Cl TW20 . .11 D2
St Cuthbert's RC Prim Sch
TW20 . . . . .11 C1
St Cyprian's Sch SW17 . .20 F4
St David's CR5 . . . . .79 F2
St David's Cl
Farnborough GU14 . . . . . . .84 F8
Heath End GU9 . . . . .125 E7
Reigate RH2 . . . . .118 C2
West Wickham BR4 . . . . . . .44 B2
St David's Coll BR4 . . . . . .44 B2
St David's Sch TW15 . . . .13 F5
St Davids Cl 4 GU12 . . .105 B1
St Davids Dr TW20 . . . . .11 C1
St Denis Rd SE27 . . . . . .22 D4
St Deny's Cl GU21 . . . . . .68 D1
St Dominic's Sch GU8 . . .171 C1
St Dunstan's Cheam CE Prim
Sch SM3 . . . . .58 E3
St Dunstan's Coll SE6 . . . .24 A7
St Dunstan's Hill SM1,
SM3 . . . . .58 E3
St Dunstan's La BR3 . . . .44 C4
St Dunstan's RC Prim Sch
GU22 . . . . .70 A2
St Dunstan's Rd
Cranford TW5 . . . . .4 B5
Feltham TW13 . . . . .14 F5
South Norwood SE25 . . . . .42 F5
St Ebba's Hospl KT19 . . . .57 C2
St Edith Cl KT18 . . . . . . .76 C5
St Edmund's La TW2 . . . .16 B8
St Edmund's RC Prim Sch
Godalming GU7 . . . . .150 F2
Twickenham TW2 . . . . .16 B8
St Edmunds Cl
Crawley RH11 . . . . .181 D1
Upper Tooting SW17 . . . . . .20 E6
St Edmunds Sch GU26 . .188 D3
St Edward's Cl RH19 . . .185 C1
St Edwards Cl CR0 . . . . . .82 D8
St Elizabeth Dr KT18 . . . .76 C5
St Elizabeth's RC Prim Sch
TW10 . . . . .6 F1
St Elphege's RC Prim Sch
SM6 . . . . .60 E4
St Faith's Rd SE24 . . . . . .22 B7
St Fillans GU22 . . . . .70 B3
St Fillans Rd SE6 . . . . . .24 C8
St Francis Gdns RH10 . .183 C4
St Francis of Assisi RC Prim
Sch RH10 . . . . .201 A4
St Francis RC Prim Sch
CR3 . . . . .100 F6
St Francis RC Sch SL5 . . .29 A3
St Francis Wlk RH11 . . .200 E4
St George Ave GU22 . . . . .88 B5
St George's Ave KT13 . . .53 C4
St George's Bsns Ctr
KT13 . . . . .53 A2
St George's Cl
Farnham GU9 . . . . .126 B6
Weybridge KT13 . . . . .53 C5
St George's Coll KT15 . . .52 D7
St George's Coll KT13 . . .53 B7
St George's Ct GU47 . . . .45 E2
St George's Gdns
Epsom KT17 . . . . .76 F5
Horsham RH13 . . . . .217 E4
Tolworth KT6 . . . . .57 B8
St George's Gr SW17 . . . .20 D5
St George's Hospl SW17 . .20 D3
St George's Ind Est KT2 . .17 D3
St George's La SL5 . . . . .29 B5
St George's Lodge KT13 . .53 D5
St George's Rd
6 Aldershot GU11,GU12 . .105 B1
Beckenham BR3 . . . . .44 B8
Camberley GU15 . . . . .65 D6
Farnham GU9 . . . . .125 D1
Feltham TW13 . . . . .15 D4
Isleworth TW1 . . . . .6 B2
2 Kingston u T KT2 . . . . .18 A1
Mitcham CR4 . . . . .41 B6
Richmond TW9 . . . . .6 F4
South Nutfield RH1 . . . . . .140 C1
Wallington SM6 . . . . .60 B5
Weybridge KT13 . . . . .53 D4

St George's Rd *continued*
Wimbledon SW19 . . . . .19 F2
St George's Rd E GU12 . .105 B1
St George's Sch SL5 . . . .29 B6
St George's Sq KT3 . . . . .38 E6
St George's Wlk CR0,CR9 .61 C7
St Georges RH6 . . . . . . .161 B2
St Georges Cl RH6 . . . . .161 B3
St Georges Coll Jun Sch
KT15 . . . . .52 D7
St Georges Cotts RH7 . .143 E4
St Georges Ct
Addlestone KT15 . . . . .52 C6
Crawley RH10 . . . . .201 D8
East Grinstead RH19 . . . .185 C3
Penge SE20 . . . . .43 B8
St Georges Ind Est GU15 .65 B3
St Georges Mews GU9 . .125 C3
St Georges Rd
Addlestone KT15 . . . . .52 C6
Farnham GU10 . . . . .126 B4
St Georges Wood GU27 .208 D8
St Georges Yd 5 GU9 . .125 B2
St German's Rd SE23 . . . .23 E7
St Giles CE Inf Sch KT21 .75 F1
St Giles' Sch CR2 . . . . . .61 B4
St Gothard Rd SE27 . . . . .22 D4
St Helen's Cres SW16 . . .41 F8
St Helen's Rd SW16 . . . . .41 F8
St Helena Terr 23 TW9 . . .6 D2
St Helens KT7 . . . . .36 F2
St Helens Cres GU47 . . . .64 B8
St Helier Ave SM4 . . . . . .40 C3
St Helier Cl
Crawley RH11 . . . . .201 A2
Wokingham RG41 . . . . .25 B3
St Helier Hospl SM5 . . . . .40 C1
St Helier Sta SM4 . . . . . . .40 A3
St Heliers Ave TW3,TW4 . .5 A2
St Hilary's Prep Sch
GU7 . . . . .150 D3
St Hilda's Ave TW15 . . . .13 E3
St Hilda's Cl
Crawley RH10 . . . . .182 C1
Horley RH6 . . . . .161 B3
Knaphill GU21 . . . . .68 D2
St Hildas Cl SW17 . . . . . .20 E6
St Hugh of Lincoln RC Prim
Sch GU21 . . . . .88 D8
St Hugh's Cl RH10 . . . . .182 C1
St Hugh's Rd SE20 . . . . . .23 B1
St Hughes Cl SW17 . . . . .20 E6
St Ignatius RC Prim Sch
TW16 . . . . .35 A8
St Ives RH10 . . . . .202 C7
St Ives Sch GU27 . . . . . .208 E8
St James Ave Ewell KT17 .77 A8
Sutton SM1 . . . . .59 A5
St James CE Prim Sch
Elstead GU8 . . . . .148 C3
Weybridge KT13 . . . . .53 C7
St James Cl Epsom KT18 . .76 E5
Woking GU21 . . . . .69 A1
St James Ct
Ashstead KT21 . . . . .75 D2
East Grinstead RH19 . . . .185 E1
Farnham GU9 . . . . .125 C3
Thornton Heath CR0 . . . . . .42 B2
St James Ho
7 Banstead SM7 . . . . . . .77 F5
Woking GU21 . . . . .69 B1
St James Mews KT13 . . . .53 B6
St James Rd
Carshalton SM5 . . . . .59 E7
Sutton SM1 . . . . .59 A5
St James The Great RC Prim
Sch CR7 . . . . .42 B7
St James Wlk RH11 . . . .201 C2
St James' Ave GU9 . . . . .125 D3
St James' Cl KT3 . . . . . . .38 F4
St James' Ct 7 KT1 . . . . .37 E6
St James' Ct 12 KT6 . . . . .37 E3
St James' Rd
Kingston u T KT6 . . . . .37 D3
Mitcham CR4 . . . . .21 A1
Purley CR8 . . . . .80 C6
St James' Terr GU9 . . . .125 C3
St James's Ave
Beckenham BR3 . . . . .43 E6
Hampton TW12 . . . . .16 C3
St James's Cl SW17 . . . . .20 F6
St James's Cotts 14 TW10 .6 D2
St James's Dr
Balham SW12,SW17 . . . . .20 F8
Upper Tooting SW17 . . . . . .20 F8
St James's Lodge 4 CR0 42 E1
St James's Pk CR0 . . . . . .42 C2
St James's Pl GU6 . . . . .174 C3
St James's RC Prim Sch
TW2 . . . . .16 E5
St James's Rd
East Grinstead RH19 . . . .185 D1
Hampton TW12 . . . . .16 B3
Kingston u T KT1 . . . . .37 D7
Thornton Heath CR0 . . . . . .42 D2
St James's Terr 2 SW12 .21 A7
St Joan Cl RH11 . . . . . . .181 D1
St John Baptist CE Prim Sch
BR1 . . . . .24 C4
St John Cl RH13 . . . . . . .217 E1
St John Fisher RC Prim Sch
SW20 . . . . .39 D4
St John Rigby Rc Coll
BR4 . . . . .63 D6
St John the Baptist CE Jun
Sch KT1 . . . . .17 D1
St John The Baptist Comp
Sch GU22 . . . . .90 A8

St John's RH5 . . . . .136 C3
St John's Ave KT22 . . . . . .95 B6
St John's Beaumont Sch
TW19 . . . . .11 B6
St John's CE Fst Sch
GU10 . . . . .167 E1
St John's CE Inf Sch
CR3 . . . . .101 B2
St John's CE Jun Sch
CR3 . . . . .101 B2
St John's CE Prim Sch
Croydon CR0 . . . . .62 D7
Kingston u T KT1 . . . . .37 E6
Penge SE20 . . . . .23 C1
St John's Cl
East Grinstead RH19 . . . .185 E2
Guildford GU2 . . . . .130 A8
Leatherhead KT22 . . . . . . .95 C7
St John's Cotts 2 SE20 . .23 C1
St John's Cres RH12 . . .216 E3
St John's Ct
Brookwood GU24 . . . . .87 F7
Farnborough GU14 . . . . . . .84 D5
Isleworth TW7 . . . . .5 F5
Kingston u T KT1 . . . . .37 E5
St John's Ct RH4 . . . . . .135 C6
St John's Dr SW18 . . . . . .20 B7
St John's Gr Barnes SW13 .7 F5
1 Richmond TW9 . . . . . . .6 E3
St John's Hill CR8 . . . . . .80 A2
St John's Hill Rd GU21 . .89 B8
St John's Hospl TW1 . . . . .17 A8
St John's Lye GU21 . . . . .88 F8
St John's Lye (Festival Path)
GU21 . . . . .88 F8
St John's Mdw RH7 . . . .163 E8
St John's Prim Sch GU21 68 E1
St John's RC Prim Sch
RH12 . . . . .217 A1
St John's Rd
Carshalton SM5 . . . . .59 E7
Crawley RH11 . . . . .201 C6
Croydon CR0,CR9 . . . . . . .61 B7
East Grinstead RH19 . . . .185 E2
East Molesey KT8 . . . . . . .36 D5
Farnborough GU14 . . . . . . .84 E5
Farnham GU9 . . . . .146 B8
Feltham TW13 . . . . .15 F4
Guildford GU2 . . . . .130 A8
Isleworth TW7 . . . . .5 F5
Leatherhead KT22 . . . . . . .95 C6
North Ascot SL5 . . . . .8 F1
Penge SE20 . . . . .23 C2
Redhill RH1 . . . . .139 F7
Richmond TW9 . . . . .6 E3
Sandhurst GU47 . . . . .64 C7
Sutton SM1 . . . . .59 B8
Teddington KT1 . . . . .37 C7
Westcott RH4 . . . . .135 C6
Wimbledon SW19 . . . . .19 E2
Woking GU21 . . . . .69 B2
St John's Rise GU21 . . . .89 B8
St John's St GU7 . . . . . .150 F6
St John's Terrace Rd
RH1 . . . . .139 F7
St Johns Ave KT17 . . . . . .77 A7
St Johns Church Rd
RH5 . . . . .134 F4
St Johns Ct Egham TW20 . .12 A3
South Godstone RH9 . . . .142 F5
Woking GU21 . . . . .89 A8
St Johns Dr KT12 . . . . . . .35 C1
St Johns Gdns GU21 . . . .69 A1
St Johns Gr GU9 . . . . . .146 B8
St Johns Mews GU21 . . . .89 A8
St Johns Prim Sch RH1 139 E7
St Johns Rd KT3 . . . . .38 C6
St Johns Rd RG45 . . . . . .45 B4
St Johns Way KT16 . . . . . .33 A1
St Joseph's Coll SW16 . . .22 B7
St Joseph's RC Inf Sch
SE19 . . . . .22 C2
St Joseph's RC Jun Sch
SE19 . . . . .22 C2
St Joseph's RC Prim Sch
Bracknell RG12 . . . . .27 D7
Dorking RH4 . . . . .136 A7
Epsom KT18 . . . . .76 C5
Guildford GU2 . . . . .108 F3
Kingston u T KT1 . . . . .37 E7
Redhill RH1 . . . . .118 E2
St Joseph's Rd GU12 . . .105 A1
St Joseph's Sch GU6 . . . .174 F6
St Josephs RC Prim Sch
GU11 . . . . .126 A8
St Jude's CE Sch SW20 . .11 C2
St Jude's Cl TW20 . . . . . .11 C3
St Jude's Cotts TW20 . . . .11 C3
St Jude's Rd TW20 . . . . . .11 C3
St Julian 6 RH19 . . . . . .185 F1
St Julian's Cl SW16 . . . . .22 A4
St Julian's Farm Rd SE27,
SW16 . . . . .22 B4
St Katharines Rd CR3 . . .101 A2
St Kitts Terr SE19 . . . . . .22 E3
St Lawrence CE Jun Sch
KT8 . . . . .36 D5
St Lawrence Ct GU24 . . . .68 A3
St Lawrence Prim Sch
KT24 . . . . .113 D8
St Lawrence RC Prim Sch
TW13 . . . . .15 B6
St Lawrence Way CR3 . .100 D4
St Lawrences Way RH2 . .118 A1
St Leonard's CE Prim Sch
SW16 . . . . .21 D3
St Leonard's Gdns TW5 . .4 E6

St Leonard's Park Ho
RH13 . . . . .218 C5
St Leonard's Rd
Claygate KT10 . . . . .55 F4
Croydon CR0,CR9 . . . . . . .61 B7
Kingston u T KT6 . . . . .37 D4
Thames Ditton KT7 . . . . . . .37 A2
Windsor SL4 . . . . .9 B8
St Leonard's Sq KT6 . . . .37 D4
St Leonard's Wlk SW16 . .21 F1
St Leonards Com Inf Sch
RH13 . . . . .217 E2
St Leonards Ct SW14 . . . .7 C4
St Leonards Dr RH10 . . .202 A4
St Leonards Pk RH19 . . .185 E1
St Leonards Rd
Burgh Heath KT18 . . . . . . .97 C8
Horsham RH13 . . . . .218 A1
Mortlake SW14 . . . . .7 C4
St Louis Cl SE27 . . . . . . .22 D4
St Louis Rd SE27 . . . . . . .22 D4
St Luke's CE Prim Sch
Kingston u T KT2 . . . . .37 E8
West Norwood SE27 . . . . .22 C3
St Luke's Cl SE25 . . . . . .43 B3
St Luke's Rd CR3 . . . . . .80 F1
St Luke's Sq 9 GU1 . . . .130 F8
St Lukes Cl GU21 . . . . . . .70 C5
St Lukes Mews CR3 . . . . .80 F1
St Margaret Clitherow RC
Prim Sch RG12 . . . . .26 F2
St Margaret's Ave GU1 . .109 F1
St Margaret's Ave
Cheam SM3 . . . . .58 E2
Dormans Park RH19 . . . .185 F6
St Margaret's CE Fst & Mid
Sch RH11 . . . . .201 B7
St Margaret's Ct 9 TW1 . .6 B1
St Margaret's Dr TW1 . . . .6 B2
St Margaret's Gr TW1 . . . .6 A1
St Margaret's Rd
East Grinstead RH19 . . . .185 F3
Hooley CR5 . . . . .99 B6
Isleworth TW1 . . . . .6 B2
St Margaret's Sta TW1 . . .6 B1
St Margarets Ave TW15 . .14 B3
St Margarets Bsns Ctr 11
TW1 . . . . .6 B1
St Margarets Ct RH12 . .216 F7
St Margarets Dr KT18 . . .76 C5
St Mark Ave GU22,GU24 . .88 B5
St Mark's CE Prim Sch
Beckenham BR2 . . . . .44 F6
Croydon SE25 . . . . .43 A6
Farnborough GU14 . . . . . .105 D8
Godalming GU7 . . . . .150 B3
St Mark's Ct 9 GU22 . . . .89 E8
St Mark's Hill KT6 . . . . . .37 E3
St Mark's La RH12 . . . . .217 E6
St Mark's Pl SW19 . . . . . .19 F2
St Mark's RC Sch TW3 . . .5 A4
St Mark's Rd
Bracknell RG42 . . . . .26 C8
Croydon SE25 . . . . .43 A5
Teddington TW11 . . . . .17 B1
St Marks Cl GU14 . . . . . .85 C1
St Marks Pl GU9 . . . . . . .125 B4
St Marks Rd KT18,KT20 . .77 C1
St Martha's Ave GU22 . . .89 F6
St Martha's Cotts GU5 . .154 E8
St Martha's Ct GU4 . . . . .131 B3
St Martin in the Fields High
Sch for Girls SW2 . . . . . .22 A7
St Martin's Ave KT18 . . . .76 E5
St Martin's C of E Prim Sch
RH4 . . . . .136 A8
St Martin's CE Inf Sch
KT18 . . . . .76 D4
St Martin's CE Jun Sch
KT18 . . . . .76 D4
St Martin's CE Sch (Pixham)
RH4 . . . . .115 C1
St Martin's Cl KT17 . . . . .76 E6
St Martin's Ct
Staines TW15 . . . . .13 C3
West Norwood SE27 . . . . .22 B6
St Martin's La BR3 . . . . . .44 B4
St Martin's Mews GU22 . .71 A3
St Martin's Sq RH4 . . . . .136 B8
St Martin's Way SW17 . . .20 C5
St Martin's Wlk RH4 . . . .136 B8
St Martins Cl KT24 . . . . .112 E6
St Martins Ct KT24 . . . . .112 E6
St Martins Dr KT12 . . . . .54 C7
St Martins Mews 4
RH4 . . . . .136 A7
St Mary Ave SM6 . . . . . . .60 B7
St Mary Magdalen's RC Prim
Sch SW14 . . . . .7 D4
St Mary's 4 KT13 . . . . . .53 D7
St Mary's & St Peter's CE
Prim Sch TW11 . . . . .16 F3
St Mary's Ave
Beckenham BR2 . . . . .44 E6
Stanwell TW19 . . . . .13 D8
Teddington TW11 . . . . .16 F2
St Mary's CE Inf Sch
Leatherhead KT22 . . . . . . .95 C5
Shackleford GU8 . . . . . . .149 E6
St Mary's CE Jun Sch
Oxted RH8 . . . . .122 E7
Stanwell TW19 . . . . .13 E8
St Mary's CE Prim Sch
Byfleet KT14 . . . . .71 E6
Chessington KT9 . . . . .56 F4
Horsham RH12 . . . . .217 C1
Long Ditton KT7 . . . . .37 B1

St Mary's CE Prim Sch *continued*
Twickenham TW1 17 A8
St Mary's CE Sch RH19 185 D2
St Mary's Cl
Chessington KT9 56 F3
Ewell KT17 57 F2
Fetcham KT22 94 D4
Oxted RH8 122 E6
Stanwell TW19 13 D8
Sunbury TW16 35 A5
St Mary's Cottage Hospl TW12 35 F8
St Mary's Cres
Hounslow TW7 5 E7
Stanwell TW19 13 D8
St Mary's Ct
Kingston u T KT3 38 E6
Wallington SM6 60 C6
West Byfleet KT14 71 E7
St Mary's Dr
Crawley RH10 202 B8
East Bedfont TW14 14 C8
St Mary's Gdns
Bagshot GU19 47 E3
Horsham RH12 217 C1
St Mary's Gn TN16 83 C1
St Mary's Gr
Biggin Hill TN16 83 C1
Chiswick W4 7 B8
Richmond TW10,TW9 6 F3
St Mary's High Sch CR0 42 C1
St Mary's Hill SL5 29 C4
St Mary's Ho RH12 217 C1
St Mary's Mill GU8 191 C3
St Mary's Mt CR3 100 F3
St Mary's Pl GU9 125 C3
St Mary's RC Inf Sch
Carshalton SM5 59 F6
Croydon CR0 42 D1
St Mary's RC Jun Sch
Croydon CR0 42 D1
Wallington SM5 59 F5
St Mary's RC Prim Sch
Beckenham BR3 24 C1
Chiswick W4 7 E8
Isleworth TW7 6 A4
Merton SW19 20 A1
St Mary's Rd Ascot SL5 29 B3
Ash Vale GU12 106 A5
Camberley GU15 65 C6
East Molesey KT8 36 D4
Kingston u T KT6 37 D3
Long Ditton KT6 37 C1
Oatlands Park KT13 53 D6
Reigate RH2 139 B8
South Croydon CR2 61 D2
South Norwood SE25 42 E6
Wimbledon SW19 19 F3
Woking GU21 69 C2
Worcester Park KT4 57 E8
St Mary's Sch SL5 29 B2
St Mary's Univ Coll TW1 16 F5
St Marys CE Prim Sch GU8 191 C4
St Marys Cl GU47 64 C8
St Marys Cotts GU10 167 C7
St Marys Homes RH9 121 D3
St Marys La SL4 8 D5
St Marys Rd KT22 95 B4
St Marys Way GU2 108 E3
St Marys Wlk RH1 120 D2
St Matthew's Ave KT6 37 F1
St Matthew's CE Prim Sch
Redhill RH1 118 F3
Surbiton KT6 37 E2
St Matthew's CE Prim Sch SW20 39 A8
St Matthew's Ct TW15 14 A3
St Matthew's Rd RH1 118 F2
St Matthews CE Inf Sch KT11 73 B1
St Merryn Ct BR3 24 A1
St Michael's & St Martin's RC Prim Sch TW4 4 F4
St Michael's Ave GU3 108 C6
St Michael's CE Fst Sch RH5 115 C8
St Michael's CE Prim Sch SW18 19 F8
St Michael's Cl KT12 54 C8
St Michael's Easthampstead CE Prim Sch RG12 27 A4
St Michael's Hall GU11 126 B8
St Michael's Prim Sch SE26 23 E4
St Michael's RC Prim Sch TW15 14 A3
St Michael's Rd
Aldershot GU11,GU12 105 B1
Croydon CR0 42 C1
Farnborough GU14 85 B6
Sheerwater GU21 70 D5
Wallington SM6 60 C4
St Michaels RH8 123 A5
St Michaels CE Inf Sch GU11 126 B8
St Michaels CE Jun Sch GU11 126 C8
St Michaels Cl KT4 57 F8
St Michaels Cotts RG40 45 C8
St Michaels Ct 4 KT13 53 C5
St Michaels Ho 1 SE26 23 F4
St Michaels Rd
Ashford TW15 14 A3
Camberley GU15 65 B5
Caterham CR3 100 D5
East Grinstead RH19 185 E2
St Micheal's CE Prim Sch SL5 29 D4
St Mildred's Rd GU1 109 F2
St Mildreds Rd SE12,SE6 24 F8
St Monica's Rd KT20 97 F6
St Nazaire Cl TW20 12 C3
St Nicholas Ave KT23 94 B2
St Nicholas CE Prim Federal Sch GU6 174 D3
St Nicholas CE Prim Sch TW17 34 B3
St Nicholas CE Prim Sch (Inf Annexe) GU8 192 F6
St Nicholas Cres GU22 71 A3
St Nicholas Ct RH10 202 C7
St Nicholas Ctr SM1 59 B5
St Nicholas Dr TW17 34 A2
St Nicholas Glebe SW17 21 A2
St Nicholas Hill KT22 95 B5
St Nicholas Mans SW17 20 F6
St Nicholas Rd
Sutton SM1 59 B5
Thames Ditton KT7 36 F3
St Nicholas Sch
Merstham RH1 119 D6
Purley CR8 80 A6
St Nicholas Way SM1 59 B5
St Nicolas Ave GU6 174 F3
St Nicolas CE Inf Sch GU2 130 C7
St Nicolas Cl GU6 174 E3
St Normans Way KT17 58 A1
St Olave's Cl TW18 12 F1
St Olave's Wlk SW16 41 D7
St Omer Rd GU1 131 A8
St Omer Ridge GU1 131 A8
St Osmund's RC Prim Sch SW13 7 F6
St Oswald's Rd SW16 42 B8
St Patrick's RC Prim Sch GU14 85 D4
St Paul's Catholic Coll TW16 35 A8
St Paul's CE Inf Sch GU10 127 A7
St Paul's CE Jun Sch KT2 18 A1
St Paul's CE Jun Sch RG41 25 A6
St Paul's CE Prim Sch
Addlestone KT15 52 A6
Chessington KT9 56 E6
Dorking RH4 136 B6
St Paul's Cl
Addlestone KT15 52 A5
Ashford TW15 14 C3
Carshalton SM5 40 E1
Chessington KT9 56 D6
Hounslow TW3,TW4 4 E5
St Paul's Ct TW4 4 E4
St Paul's Gate RG41 25 A6
St Paul's RC Prim Sch KT7 36 E2
St Paul's Rd Brentford TW8 6 D8
Egham TW18 12 D2
South Norwood CR7 42 C6
St Paul's Rd E RH4,RH5 136 B7
St Paul's Rd W RH4 136 B6
St Pauls CE Prim Sch TW8 6 D8
St Pauls Cl GU10 126 F7
St Pauls Rd Richmond TW9 6 F4
Woking GU22 70 B2
St Pauls' CE Inf Sch GU10 126 F6
St Peter & St Paul CE Inf Sch CR3 100 A2
St Peter's CE Jun Sch GU14 85 C4
St Peter's Cl
Old Woking GU22 90 C7
Staines TW18 12 F2
St Peter's Gdns
West Norwood SE27 22 A5
Wrecclesham GU10 145 F6
St Peter's Hospl KT16 51 D7
St Peter's Prim Sch CR2 61 E4
St Peter's RC Comp Sch GU1 110 C2
St Peter's RC Prim Sch KT22 95 C7
St Peter's RC Sch RH19 185 C1
St Peter's Rd
Crawley RH11 201 C6
Croydon CR0,CR2 61 D6
East Molesey KT8 36 A5
Isleworth TW1 6 B2
Old Woking GU22 90 B7
St Peter's St CR0,CR2 61 D5
St Peter's Way
Addlestone KT15,KT16 51 F6
Chertsey KT15 52 B8
Frimley GU16 85 F7
St Peters CE Inf Sch RH8 122 A1
St Peters CE Prim Sch GU9 146 A7
St Peters Cl SW17 20 E6
St Peters Ct
East Molesey KT8 36 A5
Epsom KT18 76 E5
Hampton TW12 36 B8
St Peters Mead GU12 106 B2
St Peters Pk GU11 125 E8
St Peters Rd KT1 38 A7
St Peters Way UB3 3 D8
St Philip's Ave KT4 58 B8
St Philip's Rd KT6 37 D3
St Philips Sch KT9 56 D4
St Philomena's Sch SM5 59 E5
St Pier's La RH7,TN8 165 B5
St Piers Hospital Sch RH7 165 A4
St Pinnock Ave TW18 33 A8
St Polycarp's RC Prim Sch GU9 125 D1
St Richard's with St Andrew's CE Prim Sch TW10 17 B5
St Richards Ct TW10 17 B5
St Robert Southwell RC Prim Sch RH12 218 A6
St Sampson Rd RH11 200 F2
St Saviour's Coll SE27 22 D4
St Saviour's Pl GU1 109 C1
St Saviour's Rd CR0 42 C3
St Stephen Cl RH11 181 D1
St Stephen's CE Jun Sch TW1 6 B1
St Stephen's CE Prim Sch RH9 142 F6
St Stephen's Cl GU27 207 F6
St Stephen's Cres CR7 42 A6
St Stephen's Gdns TW1 6 C1
St Stephen's Rd TW3,TW4 5 A2
St Stephens Ave KT21 75 E3
St Stephens Ct RH9 142 E5
St Swithun's Cl RH19 185 F1
St Teresa's Prep Sch (Grove House) KT24 113 D7
St Teresa's RC Prim Sch SM4 40 D3
St Theresa Cl KT18 76 C5
St Theresa's RC Prim Sch RG40 25 D5
St Theresa's Rd TW14 3 F3
St Thomas Becket Prim Sch SE25 43 A3
St Thomas Cl GU21 69 C2
St Thomas of Canterbury RC Prim Sch
Guildford GU1 110 B1
Mitcham CR4 41 A6
St Thomas Wlk SL3 1 D7
St Thomas' Cl KT6 37 F1
St Thomas' Rd W4 7 C8
St Thomas's Dr GU4 111 E4
St Thomas's Mews GU1 130 F7
St Vincent Cl
Crawley RH10 202 D5
West Norwood SE27 22 B3
St Vincent Rd
Twickenham TW2 5 C1
Walton-on-T KT12 54 B7
St Wilfrid's RC Comp Sch RH11 201 B5
St William of York RC Prim Sch SE23 23 E7
St Winifred's RC Jun Sch SE12 24 F8
St Winifred's Rd
Biggin Hill TN16 83 F1
Teddington TW11 17 B2
St Winifreds CR8 80 C4
Salamander Cl KT2 17 C3
Salamander Quay KT1 37 D8
Salbrook Rd RH1 140 A1
Salcombe Dr SM4 39 D1
Salcombe Ho SE23 23 C6
Salcombe Rd TW15 13 E5
Salcot Cres CR0 63 C1
Salcott Rd CR0 60 F6
Sale Garden Cotts RG40 25 C5
Salehurst Rd RH10 202 E6
Salem Pl CR0,CR9 61 C7
Salerno Cl GU11 105 A2
Sales Ct 6 GU11 105 A1
Salesian Coll GU14 85 D1
Salesian Gdns KT16 33 A1
Salesian RC Sch KT16 51 E8
Salesian Sch KT16 33 A1
Salesian View GU14 105 E8
Salford Rd SW12,SW2 21 D7
Salfords Prim Sch RH1 140 A3
Salfords Sta RH1 140 B1
Salisbury Ave SM1,SM2 58 F4
Salisbury Cl
Wokingham RG41 25 A2
Worcester Park KT4 57 F7
Salisbury Gdns SW19 19 E1
Salisbury Gr GU16 86 A3
Salisbury Ho SW19 19 D5
Salisbury Pl KT14 71 C8
Salisbury Rd Ash GU12 106 A3
Banstead SM7 78 B5
Blackwater GU17 64 C5
Crawley RH10 201 F2
Croydon CR0,SE25 43 A3
Farnborough GU14 85 C3
Feltham TW13 15 C7
Harlington TW6 3 C1
Hounslow TW4 4 C4
Kingston u T KT3 38 D6
Richmond TW9 6 E3
Tyler's Green RH9 121 C4
Wallington SM5 59 F4
Wimbledon SW19 19 E1
Woking GU22 89 E8
Worcester Park KT19,KT4 57 E7
Salisbury Terr GU16 86 A3
Salix Cl Fetcham KT22 94 B4
Sunbury TW16 15 B1
Salliesfield TW2 5 D1
Salmon Rd GU11 105 D5
Salmons La CR3 100 F7
Salmons La W CR3 100 E7
Salmons Rd
Chessington KT9 56 E4
Salmons Rd *continued*
Effingham KT24 113 C6
Salt Box Rd GU3,GU4 109 B6
Salt La GU8 171 E5
Saltash Cl SM1 58 F6
Saltbox Hill TN16 83 B6
Saltdean Cl RH10 201 D3
Salter Ho 8 SW16 21 C4
Salter's Hill SE19, SE27 22 D3
Salterford Rd SW17 21 A2
Salterns Rd RH10 202 C3
Saltire Gdns 2 RG42 27 A8
Saltram Rd GU14 85 E2
Salvador SW17 20 F3
Salvation Pl KT22 95 A3
Salvia Ct GU24 68 A4
Salvington Rd RH11 200 F3
Salwey Cl RG12 27 B3
Samaritan Cl RH11 200 E4
Samarkand Cl GU15 66 B4
Sambrook Mews SE6 24 B7
Samos Rd SE20 43 B7
Samphire Cl RH11 201 A3
Sampleoak La
Chilworth GU4 131 E2
Wonersh GU4 131 E2
Sampson Bsns Pk GU15 65 B3
Sampson Ct TW17 34 C4
Sampson Pk RG42 26 D8
Sampson's Almshouses GU9 125 A1
Samuel Cody Ho GU12 105 F7
Samuel Cody Sch The GU14 105 B7
Samuel Ct BR3 44 B6
Samuel Gray Gdns KT2 37 D8
Samuel Johnson Cl SW16 21 F4
San Carlos App GU11 105 C2
San Feliu Ct RH19 186 B2
Sanctuary Rd TW19,TW6 3 A1
Sanctuary The SM4 40 A3
Sand Hill GU14 85 B7
Sand Hill Ct GU14 85 B7
Sandal Rd KT3 38 E5
Sandalwood GU2 130 B8
Sandalwood Ave KT16 51 E7
Sandalwood Rd TW13 15 B5
Sandbourne Ave SW19 40 B7
Sandcross Jun Sch RH2 138 F6
Sandcross La RH2 139 A5
Sanders Cl TW12 16 C3
Sanders Ho SW16 21 E2
Sandersfield Gdns SM7 78 A4
Sandersfield Rd SM7 78 B5
Sanderstead Cl SW12 21 C8
Sanderstead Court Ave CR2 81 A6
Sanderstead Ct CR2 81 A7
Sanderstead Hill CR2 80 F8
Sanderstead Hts CR2 81 A8
Sanderstead Rd CR2 61 D2
Sanderstead Sta CR2 61 D2
Sandes Pl KT22 75 A1
Sandfield Ct GU1 130 D8
Sandfield Gdns CR7 42 B6
Sandfield Pl CR7 42 C6
Sandfield Prim Sch GU1 130 D8
Sandfield Rd CR7 42 B6
Sandfield Terr GU1 130 D8
Sandfields GU23 90 D3
Sandford Ct GU11 104 F1
Sandford Down RG12 27 F4
Sandford Rd
Aldershot GU11 104 F1
Heath End GU9 125 B7
Sandgate Ho 14 BR3 24 A1
Sandgate La SW17,SW18 20 E7
Sandhawes Hill RH19 186 A4
Sandheath Rd GU26 188 C7
Sandhill La RH10 204 B7
Sandhills
Wallington CR0,SM6 60 D6
Walton on the Hill KT20 97 A3
Sandhills Ct GU25 31 E4
Sandhills La GU25,TW20 31 F4
Sandhills Mdw TW17 34 C2
Sandhills Rd RH2 139 A7
Sandhurst Ave KT5 38 B2
Sandhurst Cl CR2 61 E2
Sandhurst La GU17 64 B6
Sandhurst Prim Sch SE6 24 E7
Sandhurst Rd Catford SE6 24 D7
Crowthorne RG45 45 B3
Wokingham RG40 25 A1
Sandhurst Sch GU47 45 D1
Sandhurst Sta GU47 64 A8
Sandhurst Way CR2 61 E3
Sandiford Ho CR3 100 E3
Sandiford Rd SM3 58 F8
Sandiland Cres BR2 63 F8
Sandilands Croydon CR0 61 F8
South Croydon CR0 62 A7
Sandlands Gr KT20 97 A4
Sandlands Rd KT20 97 A3
Sandmartin Way SM6 41 A1
Sandmore GU23 90 D3
Sandon Cl KT10 36 D1
Sandon Ho 5 SW2 21 E8
Sandown Ave KT10 55 C5
Sandown Cl
Blackwater GU17 64 D5
Cranford TW5 4 A6
Sandown Cres GU11 126 B7
Sandown Ct
2 Belmont SM2 59 B3
Crawley RH10 202 D6
Sandown Ct *continued*
Redhill RH1 118 E2
Sandown Dr Frimley GU16 65 E2
Wallington SM5 60 A2
Sandown Gate KT10 55 D7
Sandown Ho SE26 23 B2
Sandown Ind Pk KT10 55 A8
Sandown Lodge KT18 76 D5
Sandown Pk KT10 55 C8
Sandown Rd
Coulsdon CR5 79 A3
Croydon SE25 43 B4
Esher KT10 55 C6
Sandpiper Cl RH11 200 D4
Sandpiper Rd Cheam SM1 58 F5
Selsdon CR2 81 D8
Sandpit Hall Rd GU24 69 A7
Sandpit Heath GU3 108 D5
Sandpit Rd Catford BR1 24 E3
Redhill RH1 139 F8
Sandpits Rd
Richmond TW10 17 D6
South Croydon CR0 62 D6
Sandra Cl TW3 5 B2
Sandra Ho KT8 36 D4
Sandringham Ave SW20 39 E7
Sandringham Cl
East Grinstead RH19 206 A8
Farnborough GU14 105 B8
1 Putney SW19 19 D7
Pyrford GU22 71 A3
Sandringham Ct
Beckenham BR3 44 C8
Belmont SM2 59 A2
Sandringham Dr TW15 13 D4
Sandringham Gdns TW5 4 A6
Sandringham Pk KT11 74 A7
Sandringham Rd
Crawley RH11 201 B2
North Cheam KT4 58 A7
Stanwell TW6 2 E2
Thornton Heath CR0 42 C4
Sandringham Sch GU16 85 F7
Sandringham Way GU16 85 F8
Sandrock GU27 208 C6
Sandrock Hill Rd GU10 146 A5
Sandrock Ho GU7 150 D6
Sandrock Pl CR0 62 D6
Sandrock Rd RH4 135 B5
Sandroyd Way KT11 74 A6
Sands Cl GU10 126 D2
Sands Rd GU10 126 D2
Sandstone TW9 7 A7
Sandways 7 TW9 7 A6
Sandy Cl GU22 70 C2
Sandy Cotts RH10 204 A8
Sandy Croft KT17 58 C1
Sandy Cross GU10 126 F4
Sandy Ct KT11 73 F6
Sandy Dr Cobham KT11 74 A8
East Bedfont TW14 14 E7
Sandy Hill Rd
Heath End GU9 125 B7
Wallington SM6 60 C2
Sandy Holt KT11 73 F6
Sandy La Albury GU5 132 D2
Artington GU2, GU3 130 B5
Belmont SM2 58 E2
Betchworth RH3 116 E1
Bletchingley RH1 120 C3
Bracknell RG12 27 C8
Camberley GU15 65 E6
Chobham GU24 49 E2
Cobham KT11,KT22 74 B7
Crawley Down RH10 204 A8
East Grinstead RH19 185 F1
Farnborough GU14 84 D7
Farncombe GU7 150 D6
Frensham GU10 146 C1
Grayswood GU27 189 E1
Haslemere GU26,GU27 207 C7
Haslemere, Nutcombe GU26 188 F2
Kingswood KT20 98 A4
Limpsfield RH8 123 B7
Milford GU8 170 E8
Mitcham CR4 41 A8
Normandy GU3 107 D4
North Ascot SL5 28 C8
Nutfield RH1 119 E1
Oxted RH8 122 C6
Pyrford GU22 71 A3
Reigate RH2 138 B8
Richmond TW10 17 D6
Rushmoor GU10 168 B5
Sandhurst GU47 45 A2
Send GU23 90 C4
Shere GU5 133 A3
Sunningdale SL5 30 A4
Teddington KT8,TW11 17 B1
Thorpe GU25 31 E5
Walton-on-T KT12 35 C3
Woking GU22 70 C2
Sandy La N SM6 60 D5
Sandy La S SM6 60 C3
Sandy Lane Prim Sch RG12 27 C8
Sandy Mead KT19 57 A2
Sandy Rd KT15 52 A4
Sandy Ride SL5 29 E5
Sandy Way Cobham KT11 74 A7
Croydon CR0 62 F7
Walton-on-T KT12 34 F1
Woking GU22 70 C2

Sandycombe Rd
East Bedfont TW14 . . . . . .15 A7
Richmond TW9 . . . . .7 A5
Sandycoombe Rd TW1 . . . .6 C1
Sanger Ave KT9 . . . . .56 F6
Sanger Dr GU23 . . . . .90 C4
Sangers Dr RH6 . . . . . . .160 F3
Sangers Jun Sch RH6 . . .160 F3
Sangley Rd Catford SE6 . . .24 C7
South Norwood SE25 . . . . .42 E5
Santina Cl GU9 . . . . .125 D8
Sanway Cl KT14 . . . . .71 E5
Sanway Rd KT14 . . . . .71 E5
Sappho Ct GU21 . . . . .68 E3
Sapte Cl GU6 . . . . .175 A3
Saracen Cl CR0 . . . . .42 D3
Sarah Ho SW15 . . . . .7 F3
Sarah Way GU14 . . . . .85 B4
Sardeson Ho [13] SW27 . . . .22 B3
Sarel Way RH6 . . . . .161 B5
Sargent Cl RH10 . . . . . . .201 F2
Sarjant Path SW19 . . . . . .19 D6
Sark Cl Crawley RH11 . . . .201 A2
Heston TW5 . . . . .5 A7
Sarsby Dr TW19 . . . . .12 A6
Sarsen Ave TW3 . . . . .5 A5
Sarsfeld Rd SW12,SW17 . . .20 F7
Sarum RG12 . . . . .26 F1
Sarum Cres RG40 . . . . . . .25 D7
Sarum Gn KT13 . . . . .53 E6
Satellite Bsns Village The
RH10 . . . . .181 E2
Satis Ct KT17 . . . . .76 F8
Saturn Cl RH11 . . . . .200 E4
Saturn Croft RG42 . . . . . . .8 B2
Saunders Cl RH10 . . . . . .202 B7
Saunders Copse GU22 . . . .89 B5
Saunders Ho [11] SW2 . . . . .22 A7
Saunders La GU22 . . . . . . .89 B5
Saundersfield Ho SM7 . . . .78 B5
Saunton Ave UB3 . . . . .3 F7
Saunton Gdns [1] GU14 . . . .85 A6
Savernake Way RG12 . . . . .27 F4
Savernake Wlk RH10 . . . .201 F3
Savery Dr KT9 . . . . .56 C5
Savile Cl New Malden KT3 . .38 E4
Thames Ditton KT7 . . . . . . .37 A1
Savile Gdns CR0 . . . . .61 F8
Savill Gardens The★
TW20 . . . . .10 E2
Savill Gdns SW20 . . . . . . .39 A6
Saville Cres TW15 . . . . . . .14 D2
Saville Gdns GU15 . . . . . . .66 B5
Saville Ho [6] TW20 . . . . . .12 A3
Saville Rd TW1 . . . . .16 F7
Saville Row RG42 . . . . . . .44 F1
Savin Lodge [11] SM2 . . . . .59 C3
Savona Cl SW19 . . . . .19 D1
Savona Ct SW20 . . . . .39 D8
Savoy Gr GU17 . . . . .64 D3
Sawkins Cl SW19 . . . . . . .19 E6
Sawtry Cl SM5 . . . . .40 E2
Sawyer Ho [15] SE21 . . . . . .22 E4
Sawyer's Hill TW10 . . . . . .17 F8
Saxby Rd SW2 . . . . .21 F8
Saxby's La RH7 . . . . .164 D5
Saxley RH6 . . . . .161 C4
Saxley Ct RH6 . . . . .161 A3
Saxon Ave TW13 . . . . .15 F6
Saxon Bsns Ctr SW19 . . . .40 C8
Saxon Cl KT6 . . . . .37 D3
Saxon Cres RH12 . . . . . . .217 B4
Saxon Croft GU9 . . . . . . .125 C1
Saxon Dr RG42 . . . . .27 F8
Saxon Ho Feltham TW13 . . .15 F6
Reigate RH2 . . . . .138 F6
Saxon Prim Sch TW7 . . . . .34 A4
Saxon Rd Ashford TW15 . . .14 D2
Bromley BR1 . . . . .24 F1
Crawley RH10 . . . . .202 E5
Kingston u T KT2 . . . . .37 E8
Thornton Heath CR0,SE25 . .42 D4
Walton-on-T KT12 . . . . . . .54 D7
Saxon Way
Harmondsworth UB7 . . . . . .2 C8
Reigate RH2 . . . . .117 F2
Saxonbury Ave TW16 . . . . .35 B7
Saxonbury Cl CR4 . . . . . . .40 D6
Saxonbury Gdns KT6 . . . . .37 C1
Saxoncroft Ho SW16 . . . . .21 D5
Saxonfield Cl SW2 . . . . . . .21 F8
Saxons KT20 . . . . .97 D6
Sayer Ct [4] GU21 . . . . . . .68 E1
Sayer's Wlk TW10 . . . . . . .17 F8
Sayers Cl Fetcham KT22 . . .94 C4
Frimley GU16 . . . . .85 E7
Horsham RH13 . . . . .217 E2
Sayers The [5] RH19 . . . . .185 C1
Sayes Court Farm Dr
KT15 . . . . .52 B5
Sayes Court Jun Sch
KT15 . . . . .52 B5
Sayes Ct KT15 . . . . .52 C5
Scallows Cl RH10 . . . . . . .202 A4
Scallows Rd RH10 . . . . . . .202 A7
Scampton Rd TW6 . . . . .2 F1
Scania Wlk RG42 . . . . .8 B2
Scarborough Cl
Belmont SM2 . . . . .77 F8
Biggin Hill TN16 . . . . .83 C1
Scarborough Rd TW6 . . . . . .3 C1
Scarbrook Rd CR0,CR9 . . . .61 C7
Scarlet Oaks GU15 . . . . . .65 E3
Scarlet Rd SE6 . . . . .24 E5
Scarlett Cl GU21 . . . . .68 E1

Scarlett's Rd GU11 . . . . . .105 A3
Scarlette Manor Way
SW2 . . . . .22 A8
Scarth Rd SW13 . . . . .7 F4
Scawen Cl SM5 . . . . .60 A6
Schaffer Ho RH10 . . . . . . .202 C4
Scholars Cl RH10 . . . . . . .204 A8
Scholars Rd SW12 . . . . . . .21 C7
Scholars Wlk GU2 . . . . . . .130 B8
School Cl Bisley GU24 . . . . .68 A4
Guildford GU1 . . . . .109 D3
Horsham RH12 . . . . .218 A6
School Cotts GU22 . . . . . . .89 C5
School Hill
Crowthorne RG45 . . . . .45 D4
Merstham RH1 . . . . .119 C7
Sandhurst GU47 . . . . .45 A1
Seale GU10 . . . . .127 B4
Warnham RH12 . . . . .216 F8
Wrecclesham GU10 . . . . . .145 F6
School House La TW11 . . . .17 C1
School Houses GU8 . . . . . .172 E4
School La Addlestone KT15 52 A6
Ashurst Wood RH19 . . . . . .206 E6
Bagshot GU19 . . . . .47 E2
Chiddingfold GU8 . . . . . . .191 C4
Crondall GU10 . . . . .124 D8
East Clandon GU4 . . . . . . .111 E4
Egham TW20 . . . . .12 A3
Farnham GU10 . . . . .146 D6
Fetcham KT22 . . . . .94 D5
Forest Row RH18 . . . . . . .206 F2
Lower Halliford TW17 . . . . . .34 B2
Mickleham RH5 . . . . .115 C8
Normandy GU3 . . . . .106 A4
Ockham GU23 . . . . .92 B5
Pirbright GU24 . . . . .87 E5
Puttenham GU3 . . . . .128 C4
Shackleford GU8 . . . . .149 E6
Surbiton KT6 . . . . .38 A1
Teddington KT1 . . . . .17 C1
Walton on the Hill KT20 . . . .97 A2
West Horsley KT24 . . . . . . .112 B6
Westcott RH4 . . . . .135 D6
Windlesham GU20 . . . . .48 D4
School Pas [4] SW11 . . . . . .37 F7
School Rd Ascot SL5 . . . . . .29 D4
Ashford TW15 . . . . .14 B2
Binstead GU10 . . . . .145 E3
East Molesey KT8 . . . . .36 D5
Grayshott GU26 . . . . .188 B4
Hampton TW12 . . . . .16 C2
Harmondsworth UB7 . . . . . . .2 D8
Haslemere GU27 . . . . .207 F5
Hounslow TW3 . . . . .5 C4
Teddington KT1 . . . . .37 C8
Windlesham GU20 . . . . .48 D4
Wokingham RG40 . . . . .25 D6
School Road Ave TW12 . . . .16 C2
School Wlk TW16 . . . . .35 A6
Schroder Ct TW20 . . . . . . .11 B3
Scillonian Rd GU2 . . . . . . .130 B7
Scilly Isles KT10 . . . . .55 E8
Scizdons Climb GU7 . . . . .150 F4
Scoles Cres SW2 . . . . .22 A7
Scope Way [3] KT1 . . . . . . .37 E5
Scordy Ct RH11 . . . . .201 A3
Scoresdale SE19 . . . . .42 E8
Scotia Rd SW2 . . . . .22 A8
Scotland Bridge Rd KT15 71 A8
Scotland Cl GU12 . . . . .106 A5
Scotland Farm Rd GU12 106 A5
Scotland Hill GU47 . . . . . . .64 A8
Scotland La GU27 . . . . . . .208 C5
Scotlands Cl GU27 . . . . . .208 B5
Scotlands Dr GU27 . . . . . .208 C5
Scotney Ho RH1 . . . . .139 F4
Scots Cl TW19 . . . . .13 D7
Scotsdale Cl SM2 . . . . .58 E3
Scotshall La CR6 . . . . .82 C4
Scott Cl Guildford GU3 . . . .109 A3
Thornton Heath SW16 . . . . .41 F8
West Ewell KT19 . . . . .57 C5
Scott Farm Cl KT7 . . . . . . .37 B1
Scott Gdns TW5 . . . . .4 D7
Scott Ho TW10 . . . . .17 C6
Scott Rd RH10 . . . . .201 F3
Scott Terr RG12 . . . . .27 F7
Scott Trimmer Way TW3 . . . .4 E5
Scott's Ave Ashford TW16 . .14 E1
Beckenham BR2 . . . . .44 D7
Scott's Ct GU14 . . . . .85 B7
Scott's Grove Cl GU24 . . . .68 D6
Scott's Grove Rd GU24 . . . .68 C6
Scott's Hill RH1,RH6 . . . . .162 D5
Scott's La BR2 . . . . .44 D7
Scott-Broadwood CE Inf Sch
Capel RH5 . . . . .178 D6
Ockley RH5 . . . . .177 D4
Scotts Dr TW12 . . . . .16 B1
Scotts Farm Rd KT19 . . . . .57 C4
Scrooby St [3] SE6 . . . . . . .24 B8
Scrutton Cl SW12 . . . . .21 D8
Scylla Cres TW6,TW14 . . . . .14 B8
Scylla Pl GU21 . . . . .89 A8
Scylla Rd TW14,TW6 . . . . . .3 B1
Seabrook Dr BR4 . . . . .63 E8
Seaford Rd
Crawley RH11 . . . . .201 A2
Stanwell TW6 . . . . .2 D2
Wokingham RG40 . . . . .25 D6
Seaforth Ave KT3 . . . . .39 B5
Seaforth Gdns KT19 . . . . . .57 F5
Seaforth Lodge SW13 . . . . .7 F5
Sealand Rd TW6 . . . . .3 A2
Seale La GU10,GU3 . . . . . .126 E4
Seale Rd GU8,GU10 . . . . . .148 B7

Seaman's Gn RH5 . . . . . . .178 D8
Searchwood Rd CR6 . . . . . .81 B1
Searle Ct [7] CR4 . . . . .40 E8
Searle Hill RH2 . . . . .139 A7
Searle Rd GU9 . . . . .146 C8
Searle's View RH12 . . . . . .217 E5
Seath Ho [4] SE26 . . . . .23 B3
Seaton Cl Putney SW15 . . . .19 B8
Twickenham TW2 . . . . .5 D1
Seaton Dr TW15 . . . . .13 E6
Seaton House Sch for Girls
SM2 . . . . .59 D1
Seaton Rd
Camberley GU15 . . . . .65 B5
Mitcham CR4 . . . . .40 E7
Twickenham TW2 . . . . .5 D1
Sebastopol Rd [3] GU11 . .105 B2
Second Ave Mortlake SW14 . .7 E4
Walton-on-T KT12 . . . . .35 B3
Woodham KT15 . . . . .52 B2
Second Cl KT8 . . . . .36 C5
Second Cross Rd TW2 . . . . .16 E6
Seddon Ct RH11 . . . . .201 B1
Seddon Rd SM4 . . . . .40 D4
Sedgefield Cl RH10 . . . . . .202 E7
Sedgehill Rd SE6 . . . . .24 B3
Sedgehill Sch SE6 . . . . . . .24 B3
Sedgemoor GU14 . . . . .85 B7
Sedgeway SE6 . . . . .24 F7
Sedgewick Cl RH10 . . . . . .202 C6
Sedgewick Ho SW19 . . . . . .19 D6
Sedgewood Cl BR2 . . . . . . .44 F2
Sedley Ct SE26 . . . . .23 B6
Seebys Oak GU47 . . . . .64 E6
Seeley Dr SE21 . . . . .22 E4
Seely Rd SW17 . . . . .21 A2
Seething Wells Halls Of
Residence KT6 . . . . .37 C3
Seething Wells La KT6 . . . . .37 C3
Sefton Cl GU24 . . . . .67 F6
Sefton Ct TW5 . . . . .5 B6
Sefton Ho [16] GU11 . . . . . .105 A2
Sefton Lodge
Kingston u T KT2 . . . . .17 E2
[2] Twickenham TW1 . . . . . . .6 C1
Sefton Rd Croydon CR0 . . . .43 A1
Epsom KT19 . . . . .57 D1
Sefton Villas RH5 . . . . . . .136 B3
Segal Cl SE23 . . . . .23 E8
Segrave Cl KT13 . . . . .53 A3
Segsbury Gr RG12 . . . . . . .27 F5
Sekhon Terr TW13 . . . . . . .16 A5
Selborne RG12 . . . . .27 B6
Selborne Ave GU11 . . . . . .126 C6
Selborne Cl GU17 . . . . .64 C6
Selborne Gdns GU9 . . . . . .146 A7
Selborne Rd
Kingston u T KT3 . . . . .38 E7
South Croydon CR0 . . . . . . .61 F7
Selbourne Ave KT15 . . . . . .52 B2
Selbourne Cl
Crawley RH10 . . . . .182 D2
Woodham KT15 . . . . .52 B1
Selbourne Rd GU4 . . . . . . .110 A4
Selbourne Sq RH9 . . . . . . .121 C5
Selby Cl KT9 . . . . .56 E3
Selby Ct TW2 . . . . .16 D6
Selby Gn SM5 . . . . .40 E2
Selby Rd Ashford TW15 . . . .14 C2
Carshalton SM5 . . . . .40 E2
Penge SE20 . . . . .43 A7
Selby Wlk [1] GU21 . . . . . . .69 B1
Selbys RH7 . . . . .164 E5
Selcroft Rd CR8 . . . . .80 B7
Selham Cl RH11 . . . . .201 A7
Selhurst Cl Putney SW19 . . .19 D7
Woking GU21 . . . . .69 F4
Selhurst New Ct SE25 . . . . .42 E5
Selhurst New Rd SE25 . . . .42 E4
Selhurst Park (Crystal Palace
FC) SE25 . . . . .42 E5
Selhurst Pl CR0,SE25 . . . . .42 E4
Selhurst Rd CR0,SE25 . . . . .42 E4
Selhurst Sta SE25 . . . . .42 E4
Selkirk Rd
Twickenham TW2 . . . . .16 C7
Upper Tooting SW17 . . . . . .20 E4
Sellar's Hill GU7 . . . . .150 E6
Sellincourt Inf Sch SW17 20 E1
Sellincourt Prim Sch
SW17 . . . . .20 E2
Sellincourt Rd SW17 . . . . . .20 E2
Sellindge Cl BR3 . . . . .23 F1
Sells Cl GU1 . . . . .130 C7
Selsdon Ave CR2 . . . . .61 D4
Selsdon Cl KT6 . . . . .37 E4
Selsdon Cres CR2 . . . . .62 C1
Selsdon High Sch CR2 . . . .62 D3
Selsdon Park Rd CR0,CR2 62 C2
Selsdon Prim Sch CR2 . . . .62 C2
Selsdon Rd Croydon CR2 . . .61 D4
West Norwood SE27 . . . . . .22 B4
Woodham KT15 . . . . .71 A8
Selsdon Road Ind Est
CR2 . . . . .61 D4
Selsey Ct [3] RH11 . . . . . . .201 B2
Selsey Rd RH11 . . . . .201 A1
Selsfield Rd RH10,RH19 . . .204 A4
Seltops Cl GU6 . . . . .174 F2
Selwood Ct TW19 . . . . .2 C1
Selwood Gdns TW19 . . . . . .2 C1
Selwood Rd Cheam SM3 . . .39 F1
Chessington KT9 . . . . .56 D6
Croydon CR0 . . . . .43 B1
Old Woking GU22 . . . . .90 B7
Selworthy Rd SE6 . . . . .23 F5
Selwyn Ave TW9 . . . . .6 F4
Selwyn Cl Crawley RH10 . . .182 C1

Selwyn Cl continued
Hounslow TW4 . . . . .4 E3
Selwyn Ct [7] TW10 . . . . .6 F2
Selwyn Rd KT3 . . . . .38 D4
Semaphore Rd GU1 . . . . . .130 E7
Semley Rd SW16 . . . . .41 E7
Semper Cl GU21 . . . . .68 E2
Send Barns La GU23 . . . . . .90 E4
Send CE Fst Sch GU23 . . . .90 E3
Send Cl GU23 . . . . .90 C4
Send Hill GU23 . . . . .90 C3
Send Marsh Rd GU23 . . . . .90 E4
Send Rd GU23 . . . . .90 E6
Seneca Rd CR7 . . . . .42 C5
Senga Rd CR4 . . . . .41 A1
Senhouse Rd SM3 . . . . .58 D7
Sequoia Pk RH11 . . . . .201 D8
Sergeants Pl CR3 . . . . .100 C5
Serpentine Gn RH1 . . . . . .119 D6
Serrin Way RH12 . . . . .217 E5
Service Rd RH6 . . . . .181 F8
Servite Ho Beckenham BR3 43 F8
Dorking RH4 . . . . .136 A5
Knaphill GU21 . . . . .68 D2
Servius Ct [2] TW8 . . . . .6 D7
Sessions Terr CR4 . . . . . . .40 F8
Setley Way RG12 . . . . .27 F6
Seven Acres SM5 . . . . .59 E8
Seven Arches App KT13 . . .53 A4
Seven Hills Cl KT12,KT13 . .53 E2
Seven Hills Rd
Weybridge KT11 . . . . .72 E6
Weybridge KT12,KT13 . . . . .53 E3
Seven Kings Way KT2 . . . . .37 E8
Sevenoaks Cl SM2 . . . . . . .59 B1
Severn Cl GU47 . . . . .64 C8
Severn Cres SL3 . . . . .1 B8
Severn Dr
Hinchley Wood KT10 . . . . . .56 A8
Walton-on-T KT12 . . . . .54 D8
Severn Rd Crawley RH10 202 C5
Farnborough GU14 . . . . . . .84 E6
Seward Rd BR3 . . . . .43 D7
Sewell Ave RG41 . . . . .25 A8
Sewer's Farm Rd RH5 . . . .155 F6
Sewill Cl RH6 . . . . .180 F7
Seychelle Ct BR3 . . . . .24 B1
Seymour Ave
Caterham CR3 . . . . .100 C4
Ewell KT17 . . . . .58 D4
West Barnes SM4 . . . . .39 D2
Seymour Cl KT8 . . . . .36 C4
Seymour Dr GU15 . . . . .66 B7
Seymour Fst & Mid Sch
RH1 . . . . .201 B2
Seymour Gdns
Feltham TW13 . . . . .15 C4
Kingston u T KT1 . . . . .37 F4
Twickenham TW1 . . . . .17 B8
Seymour Ho SM2 . . . . .59 B4
Seymour Mews KT17 . . . . . .58 A1
Seymour Pl Croydon SE25 . .43 B5
Woking GU23 . . . . .89 B7
Seymour Rd
Carshalton CR4 . . . . .41 A2
Crawley RH11 . . . . .201 B2
East Molesey KT8 . . . . .36 C4
Godalming GU7 . . . . .150 B3
Hampton TW12 . . . . .16 C3
Headley Down GU35 . . . . .187 C4
Teddington KT1 . . . . .37 D8
Wallington SM5 . . . . .60 A5
Wandsworth SW18 . . . . . . .19 F8
Wimbledon SW19 . . . . .19 D5
Seymour Terr SE20 . . . . . . .43 B8
Seymour Villas SE20 . . . . . .43 A8
Seymour Way TW16 . . . . . .14 E1
Shabden Cotts CR5 . . . . . . .98 F6
Shabden Pk CR5 . . . . .98 E5
Shackleford Rd
Elstead GU8 . . . . .148 F3
Old Woking GU22 . . . . .90 A7
Shackleford GU8 . . . . .149 E6
Shacklegate La TW11 . . . . .16 E4
Shackleton Cl
[3] Dulwich SE21 . . . . .22 D6
[6] Stanwell TW19 . . . . .2 E1
Shackleton Rd RH10 . . . . . .201 F3
Shackleton Wlk [4] GU2 . . .108 E1
Shackstead La GU7 . . . . . .150 D3
Shackster La GU7 . . . . . . .150 D3
Shadbolt Cl KT4 . . . . .57 F8
Shady Nook GU9 . . . . .125 B6
Shadyhanger GU7 . . . . . . .150 E6
Shaef Way TW11 . . . . .17 A1
Shaftesbury Ave TW14 . . . . .4 A1
Shaftesbury Cl RG12 . . . . . .27 D4
Shaftesbury Cres TW18 . . . .13 D1
Shaftesbury Ho
[2] Farnborough GU14 . . . .105 C8
Wokingham RG40 . . . . .25 D7
Shaftesbury Mount GU17 64 D3
Shaftesbury Rd
Beckenham BR3 . . . . .43 F7
Bisley GU24 . . . . .67 F3
Carshalton SM5 . . . . .40 E2
Crawley RH10 . . . . .202 D4
Richmond TW9 . . . . .6 E4
Woking GU22 . . . . .70 B2
Shaftesbury Way TW2 . . . . .16 D5
Shagbrook RH2 . . . . .117 C2
Shakespeare Ave TW14 . . . . .4 A1
Shakespeare Gdns GU14 . .84 D5

Shakespeare Rd KT15 . . . . .52 D6
Shakespeare Way
Feltham TW13 . . . . .15 C3
Winkfield RG42 . . . . .27 E8
Shalbourne Rise GU15 . . . .65 D5
Shalden Ho SW15 . . . . .7 F1
Shalden Rd GU12 . . . . . . .126 D8
Shaldon Dr SM4 . . . . .39 E4
Shaldon Way KT12 . . . . . . .54 C7
Shale Gn RH1 . . . . .119 D6
Shalesbrook La RH18 . . . . .206 F1
Shalford Inf Sch GU4 . . . . .130 E3
Shalford La GU4 . . . . .130 E4
Shalford Mill★ GU4 . . . . .130 E4
Shalford Rd GU1,GU4 . . . .130 D5
Shalford Sta GU4 . . . . . . .130 E3
Shalston Villas KT5,KT6 . . .37 F3
Shalstone Rd SW14,TW9 . . .7 B4
Shambles The GU1 . . . . . . .130 D7
Shamrock Cl
Fetcham KT22 . . . . .94 C6
Frimley GU16 . . . . .85 D8
Shamrock Ho SE26 . . . . . . .23 A4
Shamrock Rd CR0 . . . . .41 F3
Shandys Cl RH12 . . . . .217 A1
Shanklin Ct GU12 . . . . . . .105 C1
Shannon Cnr KT3 . . . . .39 A5
Shannon Commercial Ctr
KT3 . . . . .39 A5
Shannon Ct CR0 . . . . .42 C1
Shannon Way BR3 . . . . . . .24 B2
Shanti Ct SW18 . . . . .20 A7
Shap Cres SM5 . . . . .40 F1
Sharland Cl CR7 . . . . .42 A3
Sharon Cl Crawley RH10 . . .202 A4
Epsom KT19 . . . . .76 C6
Great Bookham KT23 . . . . . .94 A3
Long Ditton KT6 . . . . .37 C1
Sharonelle Ct RG40 . . . . . . .25 B6
Sharpthorne Cl RH11 . . . . .200 E6
Shaw Cl Ewell KT17 . . . . . . .76 F8
Ottershaw KT16 . . . . .51 C4
Sanderstead CR2 . . . . .80 F7
Shaw Cres CR2 . . . . .80 F7
Shaw Ct CR3 . . . . .100 D6
Shaw Dr KT12 . . . . .35 C2
Shaw Path BR1 . . . . .24 F5
Shaw Pk RG45 . . . . .45 B3
Shaw Rd Catford BR1 . . . . .24 F5
Tatsfield TN16 . . . . .103 C7
Shaw Way SM6 . . . . .60 E3
Shawfield La GU12 . . . . . . .105 F2
Shawfield Prim Sch
GU12 . . . . .106 A3
Shawfield Rd GU12 . . . . . .106 A3
Shawfields [2] GU1 . . . . . .110 A1
Shawford Ct [9] SW15 . . . . .19 A8
Shawford Rd KT19 . . . . .57 D4
Shawley Com Prim Sch
KT18 . . . . .77 C1
Shawley Cres KT18 . . . . . . .77 C1
Shawley Way KT18 . . . . . . .77 C1
Shaws Cotts GU3 . . . . .108 F6
Shaws Rd RH10 . . . . .201 F7
Shaxton Cres CR0 . . . . .63 C2
Shearing Dr SM4 . . . . .40 C2
Shears Ct TW16 . . . . .14 E1
Shearwater Ct [6] RH11 . . .200 D5
Shearwater Rd SM1 . . . . . . .58 F5
Sheath La KT22 . . . . .74 C6
Sheen Common Dr SW14,
TW10 . . . . .7 A2
Sheen Court Rd TW10 . . . . . .7 A3
Sheen Gate Gdns SW14 . . . .7 C3
Sheen La SW14 . . . . .7 C3
Sheen Mount Prim Sch
SW14 . . . . .7 B2
Sheen Pk TW10,TW9 . . . . . .6 E3
Sheen Rd TW10,TW9 . . . . . .6 E3
Sheen Way SM6 . . . . .60 F5
Sheen Wood SW14 . . . . .7 C2
Sheendale Rd TW9 . . . . .6 F3
Sheenewood SE26 . . . . .23 B4
Sheep Leas (Forest Walk)★
KT24 . . . . .112 E2
Sheep Walk Mews SW19 . .19 E2
Sheep Wlk
Langley Vale KT18 . . . . . . .96 D6
Reigate RH2 . . . . .117 E4
Sheepbarn La CR6 . . . . .82 F7
Sheepcote Cl TW5 . . . . .4 A7
Sheepfold Rd GU2 . . . . . . .108 F4
Sheephatch La GU10 . . . . .147 C6
Sheephouse GU9 . . . . .146 C8
Sheephouse Gn RH5 . . . . .134 F3
Sheephouse La RH5 . . . . . .135 A2
Sheephouse Way KT3 . . . . .38 E2
Sheeplands Ave GU1 . . . . .110 C3
Sheeps Ditch Cl TW18 . . . . .13 A1
Sheepwalk Littleton TW17 . .34 A3
Shepperton TW17 . . . . .33 F3
Sheepwalk La RH5 . . . . . . .113 A1
Sheerwater Ave KT15 . . . . .70 F7
Sheerwater Bsns Ctr
GU21 . . . . .70 C4
Sheerwater Cotts KT14 . . . .70 F6
Sheerwater Rd KT14,KT15 70 F6
Sheet Street Rd SL4 . . . . . .10 A7
Sheet's Heath La GU24 . . . .88 C7
Sheffield
Crawley RH10 . . . . .202 B4
Farnborough GU14 . . . . . . .84 F4
Stanwell TW19 . . . . .2 A2
Sheffield Rd TW14,TW6 . . . .3 C2
Sheffield Way TW14,TW6 . . .3 D2
Shefford Cres RG40 . . . . . .25 D8
Shelburne Dr TW4 . . . . .5 A1
Shelburne Ho [9] SW16 . . . .21 C3

Sheldon Cl
Crawley RH10 . . . . .202 D5
Penge SE20 . . . . .43 B8
Reigate RH2 . . . . .139 B8
Sheldon Ct 3 GU1 . . . . .130 F8
Sheldon Ho TW11 . . . . . .17 A2
Sheldon St CR0,CR9 . . . . .61 C7
Shelford 9 KT1 . . . . .38 A7
Shelford Rise SE19 . . . . .22 F1
Shelley Ave RG12 . . . . . .27 E7
Shelley Cl Coulsdon CR5 . .79 F7
Crawley RH10 . . . . .202 C8
Shelley Cres TW5 . . . . . . .4 D6
Shelley Ct
Camberley GU15 . . . . . . .65 C5
9 Kingston u T KT2 . . . . .17 D4
West Barnes KT3 . . . . . . .39 A4
Shelley Dr RH12 . . . . . . .216 C3
Shelley Rd
East Grinstead RH19 . . . .185 D1
Horsham RH12 . . . . .217 B3
Shelley Rise GU14 . . . . . .84 F6
Shelley Way SW17 . . . . . .20 D2
Shellwood Dr RH5 . . . . . .136 C3
Shellwood Rd RH2 . . . . . .137 D1
Shelly Cl SM7 . . . . .77 E4
Shelly Prim Sch RH12 . . .216 E3
Shellys Ct RH13 . . . . .218 A3
Shelson Ave TW13 . . . . . .14 F4
Shelton Cl Guildford GU2 109 A6
Warlingham CR6 . . . . .81 C2
Shelton Rd SW19 . . . . . . .40 A8
Shelvers Gn KT20 . . . . . . .97 C6
Shelvers Hill KT20 . . . . . .97 B6
Shelvers Spur KT20 . . . . .97 C6
Shelvers Way KT20 . . . . . .97 D6
Shene International Sch
SW14 . . . . .7 E3
Shenfield Ct CR5 . . . . . . .99 C8
Shenley Rd TW5 . . . . .4 E6
Shenstone Ho SW16 . . . . .21 C3
Shenstone Pk SL5 . . . . . . .29 E5
Shepherd & Flock Rdbt
GU9 . . . . .125 E3
Shepherd Cl
Crawley RH10 . . . . .201 E3
Feltham TW13 . . . . .15 E4
Shepherd's Hill
Guildford GU2 . . . . .109 A3
Haslemere GU27 . . . . . .208 C6
Merstham RH1 . . . . .99 C1
Shepherd's Hill Bglws
GU27 . . . . .208 C6
Shepherd's La GU2 . . . . .108 F4
Shepherd's Way GU4 . . . .130 E4
Shepherds Chase GU19 . . .47 E2
Shepherds Cl TW17 . . . . . .34 B3
Shepherds Ct GU9 . . . . . .146 C8
Shepherds Hill RG12 . . . . .27 C8
Shepherds La GU20 . . . . . .49 A6
Shepherds Way
Horsham RH12 . . . . .218 A5
South Croydon CR2 . . . . . .62 D3
Tilford GU10 . . . . .147 D4
Shepherds Wlk GU14 . . . . .84 E7
Shepherds' Wlk KT18 . . . . .96 B7
Shepherdsgrove La
RH19 . . . . .186 F5
Shepley Cl SM5 . . . . .60 A7
Shepley Ct SW16 . . . . .21 C4
Shepley Dr SL5 . . . . .30 D3
Shepley End SL5 . . . . .30 D4
Sheppard Cl KT6 . . . . .37 E5
Sheppard Ho 8 SW2 . . . . .22 A7
Shepperton Bsns Pk
TW17 . . . . .34 C4
Shepperton Court Dr
TW17 . . . . .34 B4
Shepperton Ct TW17 . . . . .34 B3
Shepperton Rd TW17,
TW18 . . . . .33 D5
Shepperton Sta TW17 . . . .34 C4
Shepperton Studios
TW17 . . . . .33 F6
Sheppey Cl RH11 . . . . . . .201 C3
Sheraton Cl GU17 . . . . . . .64 E4
Sheraton Dr KT19 . . . . . . .76 C6
Sheraton The 22 KT6 . . . . .37 E4
Sheraton Wlk 13 RH11 . . .201 B1
Sherborne Cl
Burgh Heath KT18 . . . . . .77 C2
Poyle SL3 . . . . .1 E6
Sherborne Cres SM5 . . . . .40 E2
Sherborne Ct
Guildford GU2 . . . . .130 C7
Penge SE20 . . . . .43 C7
Sherborne Rd Cheam SM3 40 A1
Chessington KT9 . . . . .56 E5
East Bedfont TW14 . . . . . .14 D7
Farnborough GU14 . . . . . .85 D1
Sherborne Wlk 1 KT22 . . .95 C6
Sherbourne GU5 . . . . . . .132 D5
Sherbourne Ct
2 Hampton TW12 . . . . . .36 A8
18 Sutton SM2 . . . . .59 C4
Sherbourne Dr SL5 . . . . . .30 D4
Sherbourne Farm*
GU5 . . . . .132 E6
Sherbourne Gdns TW17 . .34 E2
Shere Ave KT17,SM2 . . . . .58 C1
Shere CE Inf Sch GU5 . . .133 A4
Shere Cl Chessington KT9 . .56 D5
Dorking RH5 . . . . .136 C3
Shere Ct GU5 . . . . .133 B2
Shere La GU5 . . . . .133 A4

Shere Mus* GU5 . . . . . .133 A4
Shere Rd Albury GU4,GU5 132 C6
Ewhurst GU6 . . . . .175 D7
Shere GU5 . . . . .133 B5
West Clandon GU4,KT24 .111 B1
West Horsley KT24 . . . . .112 C4
Sherfield Cl KT3 . . . . .38 B5
Sherfield Gdns SW15 . . . . .7 F1
Sheridan Cl
Aldershot GU11 . . . . . . .126 A8
East Grinstead RH19 . . . .185 C1
Sheridan Ct TW4 . . . . .4 E2
Sheridan Dr RH2 . . . . . . .118 B3
Sheridan Grange SL5 . . . .30 A3
Sheridan Pl
Hampton TW12 . . . . .36 C8
Mortlake SW13 . . . . .7 F4
Sheridan Rd Frimley GU16 85 D8
Merton SW19 . . . . .39 F8
Richmond TW10 . . . . .17 C5
Sheridan Way BR3 . . . . . .43 F8
Sheridan Wlk SM5 . . . . . .59 F5
Sheridans Rd KT23 . . . . . .94 C1
Sheringdale Prim Sch
SW18 . . . . .19 F7
Sheringham Ave TW2 . . . .16 A7
Sheringham Ct SW18 . . . . .20 C6
Sheringham Rd SE20 . . . . .43 C6
Sherington Cl GU14 . . . . . .85 B6
Sherland Rd TW1 . . . . . . .16 F7
Shermanbury Ct RH12 . .217 D4
Sherringham Ave TW13 . . .15 A5
Sherrydon GU6 . . . . .174 F4
Sherwin Cres GU14 . . . . . .85 C7
Sherwood KT6 . . . . .56 D8
Sherwood Ave SW16 . . . . .41 D8
Sherwood Cl
Bracknell RG12 . . . . .28 A7
Fetcham KT22 . . . . .94 C4
Sherwood Cres RH2 . . . . .139 B5
Sherwood Ct 5 BR4 . . . . .44 B1
Sherwood Fst Sch GU14 . .41 C5
Sherwood Park Rd
Mitcham CR4 . . . . .41 D5
Sutton SM1 . . . . .59 A5
Sherwood Park Sch SM6 60 D7
Sherwood Rd
Coulsdon CR5 . . . . .79 C3
Croydon CR0,CR9 . . . . . .43 B1
Hampton TW12 . . . . .16 C3
Knaphill GU21 . . . . .68 E2
Merton SW19 . . . . .19 F1
Sherwood Way BR4 . . . . . .63 C8
Sherwood Wlk RH10 . . . .201 F3
Shetland Cl
Crawley RH10 . . . . .202 E7
Guildford GU4 . . . . .110 B6
Shetland Rd TW6 . . . . .3 C1
Shewens Rd KT13 . . . . . . .53 D6
Shey Copse GU22 . . . . . . .70 C2
Shield Dr TW8 . . . . .6 A8
Shield Rd TW15 . . . . .14 D4
Shifford Path SE23 . . . . . .23 D5
Shilburn Way GU21 . . . . . .69 A1
Shildon Cl GU15 . . . . .66 D3
Shillinglee Rd RH14 . . . .211 B4
Shimmings The GU1 . . . .110 A2
Shinners Cl SE25 . . . . .43 A4
Shinwell Wlk 3 RH11 . . .201 B1
Ship Alley GU14 . . . . .85 C6
Ship Field Cl TN16 . . . . .103 C6
Ship Hill TN16 . . . . .103 C6
Ship La Farnborough GU14 .85 C6
Mortlake SW14 . . . . .7 C5
Ship St RH19 . . . . .205 E8
Ship Yd 1 KT13 . . . . .53 B7
Shipka Rd SW12 . . . . .21 B7
Shiplake Cl SW17 . . . . . . .20 D4
Shiplake Ho RG12 . . . . . . .27 F5
Shipley Bridge La RH10 183 A3
Shipley Ct SE20 . . . . .43 A7
Shipley Rd RH11 . . . . . . .201 A6
Shipleybridge La RH6,
RH10 . . . . .182 F4
Shipman Par SE23 . . . . . .23 E6
Shipman Rd SE23 . . . . . . .23 D6
Shirburn Cl SE23 . . . . . . .23 C8
Shire Cl GU19 . . . . .47 E2
Shire Ct Aldershot GU11 .104 E2
Ewell KT17 . . . . .57 F3
Shire Horse Way TW7 . . . . .5 F4
Shire Par RH10 . . . . .202 D7
Shire Pl Crawley RH10 . . .202 D7
Redhill RH1 . . . . .140 A7
Wandsworth SW18 . . . . . .20 B8
Shires Cl KT21 . . . . .95 D8
Shires Ho KT14 . . . . .71 E6
Shires The TW10 . . . . . . .17 E4
Shirley Ave Belmont SM2 . .58 F1
Carshalton SM1 . . . . .59 E6
Coulsdon CR5 . . . . .100 B8
Croydon CR0,CR9 . . . . . .43 C1
Redhill RH1 . . . . .139 F4
Shirley Church Rd CR0 . . .62 E7
Shirley Cl Crawley RH11 .200 E4
Isleworth TW3 . . . . .5 C2
Shirley Cres BR3 . . . . .43 E5
Shirley Ct Guildford GU1 .130 D8
Thornton Heath SW16 . . . .41 F6
Shirley Dr TW3 . . . . .5 C2
Shirley High Sch CR0 . . . .62 D7
Shirley Hills Rd CR0 . . . . .62 D5
Shirley Hts SM6 . . . . .60 C2
Shirley Hyrst KT13 . . . . . .53 D6
Shirley Lodge SE26 . . . . . .23 E4
Shirley Oaks Hospl CR0 . .43 C2
Shirley Oaks Rd CR0,CR9 .62 D8
Shirley Park Rd CR0 . . . . .43 C1

Shirley Pl GU21 . . . . .68 C2
Shirley Rd
Croydon CR0,CR9 . . . . . .43 B1
Wallington SM6 . . . . .60 C2
Shirley Way CR0 . . . . .62 F7
Shoe La GU11 . . . . .105 A6
Sholto Rd TW6 . . . . .3 A2
Shop Cl TW10 . . . . .17 D5
Shophouse La GU5 . . . . . .153 E7
Shord Hill CR8 . . . . .80 D3
Shore Cl Feltham TW14 . . .15 A8
Hampton TW12 . . . . .15 E3
Shore Gr TW13 . . . . .16 A6
Shore's Rd GU21 . . . . .69 F5
Shoreham Cl CR0 . . . . . . .43 C3
Shoreham Rd RH10 . . . . .202 C3
Shoreham Rd (E) TW6 . . . .2 E2
Shoreham Rd (W) TW6 . . .2 E2
Shorndean St SE6 . . . . . . .24 C7
Short Cl RH11 . . . . .201 D8
Short Gallop RH10 . . . . . .202 D7
Short La Limpsfield RH8 . .123 B3
Stanwell TW15,TW19 . . . .13 F7
Short Rd Chiswick W4 . . . . .7 E8
Stanwell TW19 . . . . .2 E1
Short St GU11 . . . . .105 A2
Short Way TW2 . . . . .16 C8
Shortacres RH1 . . . . .119 F2
Shortcroft Rd KT17 . . . . . .57 F2
Shortdale Rd GU11 . . . . . .126 C6
Shortfield Rd GU10 . . . . .146 C1
Shortheath Crest GU9 . . .145 F6
Shortheath Rd GU9,
GU10 . . . . .146 A7
Shortlands UB3 . . . . .3 D8
Shortlands Gdns BR2 . . . .44 E7
Shortlands Gr
Beckenham BR2 . . . . .44 D6
Bromley BR2 . . . . .44 D6
Shortlands Rd
Beckenham BR2 . . . . .44 E6
Kingston u T KT2 . . . . . . .17 F1
Shortlands Sta BR2 . . . . . .44 E7
Shorts Rd SM5 . . . . .59 E5
Shortsfield Cl RH12 . . . . .217 C5
Shortwood GU22 . . . . .70 C3
Shortwood Ave TW18 . . . .13 B5
Shortwood Inf Sch TW18 13 B5
Shotfield SM6 . . . . .60 B4
Shott Cl 4 SM1 . . . . .59 C5
Shottermill RH12 . . . . . . .218 A7
Shottermill Fst Sch
GU27 . . . . .207 F7
Shottermill Jun sch
GU27 . . . . .207 F7
Shottermill Pk GU27 . . . .207 E7
Shottermill Rd GU27 . . . .207 E5
Shottfield Ave SW14 . . . . .7 E3
Shovelstrode La RH19 . . .206 D8
Shrewsbury Ave SW14 . . . .7 D3
Shrewsbury Cl KT6 . . . . . .56 E8
Shrewsbury House Sch
KT6 . . . . .56 E8
Shrewsbury Rd
Beckenham BR3 . . . . .43 E6
Carshalton SM5 . . . . .40 E2
Harlington TW14,TW6 . . . .3 D1
Redhill RH1 . . . . .118 E1
Shrewsbury Wlk 7 TW7 . . .6 A4
Shrewton Rd SW17 . . . . . .20 F1
Shrivenham Cl 3 GU47 . . .64 D8
Shroffold Rd BR1 . . . . . . .24 E4
Shropshire Cl CR4 . . . . . . .41 E5
Shrubbery Rd SW16 . . . . .21 E4
Shrubbery The
Farnborough GU14 . . . . . .84 D3
2 Surbiton KT6 . . . . .37 E1
Shrubbs Hill GU24 . . . . . .49 C2
Shrubbs Hill La SL5 . . . . . .30 C3
Shrubbs La GU10 . . . . . . .145 F4
Shrubland Ct SM7 . . . . . . .77 F3
Shrubland Gr KT4 . . . . . . .58 C7
Shrubland Rd SM7 . . . . . .78 A3
Shrublands Ave CR0 . . . . .63 A6
Shrublands Cl SE26 . . . . . .23 C5
Shrublands Dr GU18 . . . . .67 B8
Shute End RG40,RG41 . . . .25 B6
Sibford Ct 6 CR4 . . . . .40 F6
Sibthorp Rd 4 CR4 . . . . . .40 F7
Sibton Rd SM5 . . . . .40 E2
Sickle Mill GU27 . . . . . . .207 F6
Sickle Rd GU27 . . . . .208 A5
Sidbury Cl SL5 . . . . .30 A4
Siddeley Dr TW4 . . . . .4 E5
Siddons Rd
Croydon CR0,CR9 . . . . . .61 B7
Forest Hill SE23 . . . . .23 E6
Sidestrand Rd GU11 . . . .104 E7
Sideways La RH6 . . . . . . .160 D2
Sidings The
Aldershot GU11 . . . . . . .105 C3
Rudgwick RH12 . . . . . . .214 D7
Staines TW18 . . . . .13 B4
Sidlaws Rd GU14 . . . . .84 D6
Sidmouth Ave TW7 . . . . . . .5 E5
Sidney Gdns TW8 . . . . .6 D8
Sidney Rd Croydon SE25 . .43 A4
Penge BR3 . . . . .43 E7
Staines TW18 . . . . .13 A4
Twickenham TW1 . . . . .6 B1
Walton-on-T KT12 . . . . . .35 B1
Sidney Wood Forest Wlks*
GU6 . . . . .193 C2
Signal Ct RH7 . . . . .164 E5
Sigrist Sq 4 KT2 . . . . .37 E8
Silbury Ave CR4 . . . . .40 E8
Silbury Ho 9 SE26 . . . . . . .23 A5
Silchester Ct CR7 . . . . . . .42 A5

Silchester Dr RH11 . . . . .201 B4
Silistria Cl GU21 . . . . .68 C1
Silkham Rd RH8 . . . . .122 E8
Silkin Wlk 8 RH11 . . . . . .201 B1
Silkmore La
West Horsley KT24 . . . . .112 B7
West Horsley KT24 . . . . . .92 A7
Silo Cl GU7 . . . . .150 F8
Silo Dr GU7 . . . . .150 F8
Silo Rd GU7 . . . . .150 F8
Silver Birch Cl
Forest Hill SE6 . . . . .23 F5
Woodham KT15 . . . . .70 E7
Silver Birch Cotts GU10 168 E1
Silver Birches Way GU8 148 E3
Silver Cl KT20 . . . . .97 E3
Silver Ct KT22 . . . . .95 B7
Silver Dr GU16 . . . . .66 C3
Silver Hill GU47 . . . . .64 E8
Silver Jubilee Way TW4 . . .4 B5
West Wickham BR4 . . . . . .63 D8
Silver Tree Cl KT12 . . . . . .54 A6
Silverdale Ave
Oxshott KT22 . . . . .74 C5
Walton-on-T KT12,KT13 . .53 F7
Silverdale Cl
Brockham RH3 . . . . .137 B5
Cheam SM1 . . . . .58 F6
Silverdale Dr TW16 . . . . . .35 B7
Silvergate KT19 . . . . .57 C5
Silverglade KT9 . . . . .75 C7
Silverhall St TW7 . . . . .6 A4
Silverlands Cl KT16 . . . . . .51 E3
Silverlea Gdns RH6 . . . . .161 C2
Silverleigh Rd CR7 . . . . . .42 A4
Silvermere Ct
Caterham CR3 . . . . .100 F3
1 Purley CR8 . . . . .80 A7
Silvermere Rd SE6 . . . . . .24 B8
Silversmiths Way GU21 . . .69 C1
Silverstone Cl RH1 . . . . . .118 F3
Silverton Lodge SE19 . . . .22 E1
Silverwood Cl
Beckenham BR3 . . . . .24 A1
New Addington CR0 . . . . .63 A2
Silverwood Dr GU15 . . . . .66 A7
Silwood RG12 . . . . .26 E1
Silwood Cl SL5 . . . . .29 D7
Silwood Park (Imperial Coll)
SL5 . . . . .29 F6
Silwood Rd SL5 . . . . .29 F5
Sim's Cotts KT10 . . . . .55 F4
Simkins Ct RG42 . . . . .8 B2
Simmil Rd KT10 . . . . .55 E5
Simmonds Cl RG42 . . . . . .26 E8
Simmonds Cotts GU7 . . . .150 B4
Simmondstone La GU10 167 D2
Simmons Cl KT9 . . . . .56 C4
Simmons Gate KT10 . . . . .55 C5
Simmons Pl TW18 . . . . . . .12 E3
Simms Cl SM5 . . . . .59 E8
Simon Lodge 31 SW19 . . . .19 D7
Simone Dr CR8 . . . . .80 C3
Simons Cl KT16 . . . . .51 C4
Simons Wlk TW20 . . . . . . .11 C1
Simplemarsh Ct KT15 . . . .52 B6
Simplemarsh Rd KT15 . . . .52 B6
Simpson Rd
Richmond TW10 . . . . .17 C4
Twickenham TW4 . . . . .4 F1
Simpson Way KT6 . . . . . . .37 C3
Sinclair Cl RH10 . . . . .202 C4
Sinclair Ct
Beckenham BR3 . . . . .24 A1
2 Croydon CR0 . . . . .61 F8
Sinclair Dr SM2 . . . . .59 B2
Sinclair Ho SW12 . . . . . . .21 D7
Sincots Rd RH1 . . . . .118 F1
Sine Cl GU14 . . . . .85 B8
Singlegate Prim Sch
SW19 . . . . .20 D1
Singleton Cl
Mitcham SW17,SW19 . . . .20 F1
Thornton Heath CR0 . . . . .42 C2
Singleton Rd RH12 . . . . . .216 D3
Sinhurst Rd GU15 . . . . . . .65 B4
Sion Ct TW1 . . . . .17 B7
Sion Rd TW1 . . . . .17 B7
Sipson Cl UB7 . . . . .3 A8
Sipson La UB7 . . . . .3 B8
Sipson Rd UB7 . . . . .3 A7
Sipson Way UB7 . . . . .3 A7
Sir Cyril Black Way 2
SW19 . . . . .20 A1
Sir William Perkin's Sch
KT16 . . . . .32 F1
Sirdar Rd CR4 . . . . .21 A2
Sirl Cotts SL5 . . . . .29 C5
Siskin Ave RH10 . . . . .204 C5
Siskin Cl RH12 . . . . .217 E5
Sissinghurst Cl
Catford BR1 . . . . .24 E3
Crawley RH10 . . . . .202 D7
Sissinghurst Rd CR0 . . . . .43 A2
Sistova Rd SW12 . . . . .21 B7
Siward Rd SW17 . . . . .20 C5
Six Acres RH13 . . . . .215 D2
Six Cross-Roads GU21 . . . .70 A5
Sixth Cross Rd TW2 . . . . . .16 C5
Skeena Hill SW18,SW19 . . .19 E8
Skelbrook St SW18 . . . . . .20 C8
Skelmersdale Wlk RH11 200 E4
Skerne Rd KT2 . . . . .37 D8
Skerne Wlk KT2 . . . . .37 D8
Skid Hill La CR6 . . . . .82 F5
Skiff La RH14 . . . . .213 A1

Skiffington Cl SW2 . . . . . .22 A7
Skimmington Cotts
RH2 . . . . .138 D8
Skimpedhill La RG12 . . . . .27 B7
Skinners La
Ashstead KT21 . . . . .75 D1
Chiddingfold GU8 . . . . . .191 D5
Heston TW5 . . . . .5 B6
Skipton Ct SE24 . . . . .22 B7
Skipton Way RH6 . . . . . . .161 B5
Sky Bsns Pk TW20 . . . . . . .32 C7
Skyes Dr TW18 . . . . .13 B3
Skylark View RH12 . . . . . .217 D5
Skyline Ct CR0 . . . . .61 D7
Skyport Dr UB7 . . . . .2 D7
Skyway 14 Trad Est SL3 . . .1 F4
Slade Ct KT16 . . . . .51 D4
Slade Ho TW4 . . . . .4 F1
Slade Rd Ottershaw KT16 . .51 D4
Pirbright GU24 . . . . .87 D7
Slaidburn Gn RG12 . . . . . .27 E2
Slattery Rd TW13 . . . . .15 C7
Slaugham Ct RH11 . . . . . .200 F3
Sledmere Ct TW14 . . . . . . .14 E7
Sleets Rd RH12 . . . . .216 E3
Slim Cl GU11 . . . . .105 E7
Slim Rd GU15 . . . . .65 C7
Slines New Rd CR3,CR6 . .101 E7
Slines Oak Rd CR3,CR6 . .102 B6
Slinfold CE Prim Sch
RH12 . . . . .215 D4
Slinfold Wlk RH11 . . . . . .201 A6
Slip Of Wood GU6 . . . . . .174 F4
Slipshatch Rd RH2 . . . . . .138 E5
Slipshoe St RH2 . . . . .118 A1
Sloane Hospl BR3 . . . . . . .44 D8
Sloane Wlk CR0 . . . . .43 F3
Slocock Hill GU21 . . . . . . .69 C2
Slough La Buckland RH3 . .117 A3
Headley KT18 . . . . .96 C2
Sloughbrook Cl RH12 . . . .217 F5
Slyfield Ct GU1 . . . . .109 E4
Slyfield Gn GU1 . . . . .109 E5
Slyfield Ind Est GU1 . . . . .109 E5
Small's La RH11 . . . . .201 C6
Smallberry Ave TW7 . . . . . .5 F5
Smallberry Green Prim Sch
The TW7 . . . . .6 A5
Smallfield Rd
Horley RH6 . . . . .161 D3
Horne RH6 . . . . .162 E3
Smallmead RH6 . . . . .161 B3
Smalls Hill Rd RH2,RH6 . .159 C6
Smalls Mead RH11 . . . . . .201 C6
Smallwood Prim Sch
SW17 . . . . .20 D4
Smallwood Rd SW17 . . . . .20 D4
Smart's Heath La GU22 . . .89 A4
Smart's Heath Rd GU22 . . .89 B5
Smeaton Cl KT9 . . . . .56 D4
Smeaton Rd SW18 . . . . . . .20 A8
Smith Cl RH10 . . . . .201 D3
Smith Ct GU21 . . . . .70 D6
Smith Rd RH2 . . . . .138 C6
Smith Sq RG12 . . . . .27 D7
Smith St KT5 . . . . .37 F3
Smith's Yd SW18 . . . . .20 C7
Smitham Bottom La CR5,
CR8 . . . . .79 D7
Smitham Downs Rd CR5,
CR8 . . . . .79 E6
Smitham Prim Sch CR5 . . .79 C3
Smitham Sta CR5 . . . . . . .79 E4
Smithbarn RH13 . . . . . . .218 A2
Smithbarn Cl RH6 . . . . . .161 B4
Smithbrook Cotts GU6 . . .173 D3
Smithers Cotts RH12 . . . .214 F7
Smithers Ho SE20 . . . . . . .23 D1
Smithers The RH3 . . . . . .137 B7
Smithfield La GU35,
GU10 . . . . .167 A1
Smithwood Ave GU6 . . . . .174 B7
Smithwood Cl SW19 . . . . .19 E6
Smithwood Common Rd
GU6 . . . . .174 D7
Smithy Cl KT20 . . . . .97 F1
Smithy La
Headley Down GU10 . . . .166 E2
Lower Kingswood KT20 . . .97 F1
Smithy's Gn GU20 . . . . . . .48 D4
Smock Wlk CR0 . . . . .42 C3
Smoke La RH2 . . . . .139 B7
Smokejack Hill RH5 . . . . .196 D7
Smolletts RH19 . . . . .205 C8
Smoothfield TW3 . . . . .5 A3
Smugglers' La RH5 . . . . . .197 E7
Smugglers' Way GU10 . . . .126 C1
Snailslynch GU9 . . . . . . .125 D2
Snatts Hill RH8 . . . . .122 F6
Snelgate Cotts GU4 . . . . .111 D4
Snell Hatch RH11 . . . . . . .201 B6
Snellings Rd KT12 . . . . . . .54 C5
Snera Lodge SW19 . . . . . .20 E1
Snipe La GU27 . . . . .208 A1
Snow Hill
Copthorne RH10 . . . . . . .183 F3
Domewood RH10 . . . . . . .183 F5
Snow Hill Bsns Ctr
RH10 . . . . .184 A4
Snowdenham La GU5 . . . .151 E5
Snowdenham Links Rd
GU5 . . . . .151 D6
Snowdon Rd
Farnborough GU14 . . . . . .84 E7
Harlington TW6 . . . . .3 C1

Snowdown Cl SE20 43 D8
Snowdrop Cl
Crawley RH11 201 A2
2 Hampton TW12 16 A2
Snowdrop Way GU24 68 A2
Snowe Ho SE27 22 B5
Snowerhill Rd RH3 137 F6
Snowhill La RH10 183 F5
Snows Paddock GU20 48 B7
Snows Ride GU20 48 B6
Snowy Fielder Waye TW7 6 B5
Snoxhall Field GU6 174 D2
Soames Wlk KT3 38 E8
Soane Cl RH11 200 E4
Soaphouse La TW8 6 E7
Soho Mills SM6 41 B1
Sol-y-vista GU7 150 D6
Solartron Rd GU14 85 B3
Sole Farm Ave KT23 93 F2
Sole Farm Cl KT23 93 F3
Sole Farm Rd KT23 93 F2
Solecote KT23 94 A2
Solent Ct SW16 41 F7
Solent Rd TW6 2 F1
Soloms Court Rd CR5,
SM7 78 E2
Solway Cl TW4 4 E4
Somborne Ho SW15 19 A8
Somerfield Cl KT20 97 E8
Somergate RH12 216 F2
Somers Cl RH2 118 A2
Somers Pl
1 Reigate RH2 118 A2
Streatham SW2 21 F8
Somers Rd Reigate RH2 118 A2
2 Streatham SW2 21 F8
Somersbury La GU6,
RH12 195 F7
Somersby Est SE20 23 C1
Somerset Ave
Chessington KT9 56 D6
Wimbledon SW20 39 B7
Somerset Cl Epsom KT19 57 E2
Hersham KT12 54 B5
New Malden KT3 38 E4
Somerset Ct
Farnborough GU14 85 C1
3 Hampton TW12 36 A8
Somerset Gdns
Teddington TW11 16 E3
Thornton Heath SW16 41 F6
Somerset Ho
Wimbledon SW19 19 E5
12 Woking GU22 69 F2
Somerset Rd
Brentford TW8 6 C8
Farnborough GU14 85 C1
Kingston u T KT1 37 F7
Reigate RH1 139 D7
Teddington TW11 16 E3
Wimbledon SW19 19 D5
Somerset Waye TW5 4 E7
Somerswey GU4 130 E1
Somerton Ave TW9 7 B4
Somerton Cl CR8 80 A3
Somertons Cl GU2 109 A4
Somerville Ct SW16 21 D2
Somerville Dr RH10 182 C1
Somerville Rd
Cobham KT11 74 A5
Penge BR3,SE20 23 D1
Sondes Farm RH4 135 F7
Sondes Place Dr RH4 135 F7
Sonia Gdns TW5 5 A7
Sonnet Wlk TN16 83 C1
Sonning Ct CR0 62 A8
Sonning Gdns TW12 15 E2
Sonning Rd CR0 43 A3
Sonninge Cl GU47 64 D8
Soper Cl SE23 23 D6
Soper Dr CR3 100 D4
Sopwith Ave KT9 56 E5
Sopwith Cl
Biggin Hill TN16 83 D3
Richmond TW10 17 F3
Sopwith Dr KT13 71 E8
Sopwith Rd TW5 4 C7
Sopwith Way KT2 37 E8
Sorbie Cl KT13 53 D4
Sorrel Bank CR0 62 E2
Sorrel Cl Crawley RH11 201 A2
Farnborough GU14 84 C5
Wokingham RG40 25 E8
Sorrel Dr GU18 66 F7
Sorrel Ho TW3 5 C6
Sorrel Rd RH12 217 E5
Sorrento Rd SM1 59 B7
South Albert Rd RH2 117 F2
South Atlantic Dr GU11 105 C3
South Ave Egham TW20 12 C2
Heath End GU9 125 D6
Richmond TW9 7 A5
Wallington SM5 60 A3
Whiteley Village KT12 53 E1
South Bank KT6 37 E3
South Bank Lodge 2
KT6 37 E3
South Bank Terr KT6 37 E3
South Bookham Sch
KT23 114 C8
South Border The CR8 79 E8
South Cl Crawley RH10 201 F7
Morden SM4 40 A3
Twickenham TW2 16 A5
Woking GU21 69 C3
South Cl *continued*
Wokingham RG40 25 D4
South Close Gn RH1,
RH2 119 B6
South Croxted Rd SE21 22 D4
South Croydon Sta CR2 61 D5
South Dr Banstead SM7 78 E6
Belmont SM2 58 E2
Coulsdon CR5 79 D4
Dorking RH4 136 C7
Pirbright GU24 87 C6
Wentworth GU25 31 A2
Wokingham RG40 25 C5
South Eden Park Rd
Beckenham BR3 44 B4
West Wickham BR3 44 B2
South End
Croydon CR0,CR9 61 C6
Great Bookham KT23 94 B1
South Farm La GU19 48 A2
South Farnborough Inf Sch
GU14 105 D8
South Farnborough Jun Sch
GU14 85 D2
South Farnham Com Jun Sch
GU9 125 D1
South Gate Ave TW13 14 D4
South Gdns SW19 20 D1
South Gr Chertsey KT16 32 F3
Horsham RH13 217 D1
South Hill Godalming GU7 150 F4
Guildford GU1 130 D7
South Hill Rd
Beckenham BR2 44 E5
Bracknell RG12 27 B3
South Holmes Rd RH13 218 B4
South La Ash GU12 106 B1
Kingston u T KT1 37 D6
New Malden KT3 38 D3
South La W KT3 38 D5
South Lawn Ct GU7 150 D6
South Lodge TW2 5 C1
South Lodge Ave CR4,
CR7,SW16 41 E5
South Lodge Ct RH2 159 F7
South Lodge Rd KT12 54 B2
South Lynn Cres RG12 27 B4
South Mdw RG45 45 D3
South Mead Redhill RH1 118 F4
West Ewell KT19 57 F3
South Mead Rd GU11 126 B8
South Merton Sta SW20 39 F6
South Munstead La
GU8 172 B7
South Norwood Ctry Pk*
SE25 43 C5
South Norwood High Sch
SE25 43 B4
South Norwood Hill SE19,
SE25 42 F7
South Norwood Prim Sch
SE25 43 A5
South Oak Rd SW16 21 F4
South Par RH6 160 F4
South Park Cres SE6 24 F7
South Park Ct 25 BR3 24 A1
South Park Gr KT3 38 C5
South Park Hill Rd CR2 61 D6
South Park La RH1 142 A7
South Park Rd SW19 20 B2
South Pier Rd RH6 182 B7
South Pl Surbiton KT5 37 F2
Wokingham RG40 25 C6
South Rd Ash Vale GU12 106 A4
Bisley GU24 67 F3
Bracknell RG40,RG12 26 E1
Cranford TW5 4 D8
Crowthorne RG45 45 E3
Englefield Green TW20 11 D2
Feltham TW13 15 D3
Forest Hill SE23 23 D6
Guildford GU2 109 B3
Hampton TW12 15 F2
Mitcham SW19 20 D2
Reigate RH2 139 B8
Twickenham TW2 16 D5
Weybridge KT13 53 B2
Weybridge KT13 53 C5
Woking GU21 69 C4
South Ridge KT13 72 B8
South Rise SM5 59 E2
South Side GU10 126 F7
South St Dorking RH4 136 A7
Epsom KT18 76 D5
Farnborough GU14 85 E1
Farnham GU9 125 C2
Godalming GU7 150 D4
Horsham RH12 217 C2
Isleworth TW7 6 A4
Staines TW18 12 F3
South Station App RH1 140 F7
South Terr Dorking RH4 136 B6
Surbiton KT6 37 E3
South Thames Coll SW17 20 E3
South Vale SE19 22 E2
South Vale Rd 4 KT6 56 E8
South View
Bracknell RG12 26 C6
Epsom KT19 57 A1
Oxted RH8 123 A2
Wimbledon SW19 19 D2
South View Cl RH10 183 E3
South View Cotts GU5 152 D4
South View Ct SE19 22 C1
South View Rd KT21 95 D8
South Way Croydon CR0 62 E7
Sutton SM5 59 D1
South Western Rd TW1 6 B1
South Wimbledon Sta
SW19 20 B1
South Wlk
Aldershot GU12 105 D2
Coney Hall BR4 63 E7
South Worple Way SW14 7 D4
Southall La TW5 4 B8
Southam Ho KT15 52 B5
Southampton Cl GU17 64 C6
Southampton Gdns CR4 41 E4
Southampton Rd TW6 2 F1
Southampton St GU14 105 B8
Southbank KT7 37 B2
Southborough Cl KT6 37 D1
Southborough Rd KT6 37 E1
Southborough Sch KT6 56 E7
Southbridge Pl CR0,CR9 61 C6
Southbridge Rd CR0,CR9 61 C6
Southbrook RH11 201 C1
Southbrook Rd SW16 41 E8
Southbury GU2 130 C7
Southcote GU21 69 D3
Southcote Ave
Feltham TW13 15 A6
Tolworth KT5 38 B2
Southcote Dr GU15 66 A5
Southcote Rd
Croydon SE25 43 B3
Merstham RH1 119 C6
South Croydon CR2 61 F1
Southcroft TW20 11 B3
Southcroft Ave BR4 63 C8
Southcroft Rd SW17 21 A2
Southdean Gdns SW19 19 F6
Southdown Cl RH12 218 A5
Southdown Dr SW20 19 D1
Southdown Rd
Hersham KT12 54 E6
Wallington SM5 60 A2
Wimbledon SW20 39 D8
Woldingham CR3 101 F5
Southend La Catford SE6 24 B4
Forest Hill SE26,SE6 23 F4
Southend Rd BR3 44 A8
Southerland Cl KT13 53 C6
Southern Ave
East Bedfont TW14 15 A7
Salfords RH1 140 A1
South Norwood SE25 42 F6
Southern Bglws GU4 131 B2
Southern Cotts TW19 2 A2
Southern Ind Area RG12 26 F6
Southern Perimeter Rd
East Bedfont TW6 3 B1
Harlington TW14,TW6 3 D2
Stanwell TW19,TW6 2 D2
Southern Rd GU15 65 C6
Southern Way
Farnborough GU14 84 E3
Farnham GU9 125 C1
Southerns La CR5 98 C3
Southey Ct KT23 94 B3
Southey Rd SW19 20 A1
Southey St SE20 23 D1
Southfield Gdns TW1 16 F4
Southfield Pl KT13 53 B3
Southfield Sch RG40 25 D5
Southfields KT8 36 E3
Southfields Ave TW15 14 B2
Southfields Com Coll
SW18 20 A7
Southfields Ct SM3 59 A8
Southfields Rd CR3 102 B3
Southfields Sta SW18 19 F7
Southgate Ave RH10 201 E4
Southgate Dr RH10 201 E4
Southgate Fst & Mid Sch
RH10 201 D4
Southgate Par RH10 201 D4
Southgate Rd RH10 201 D4
Southgate West Fst & Mid
Sch RH11 201 C4
Southholme Cl SE19 42 E8
Southland Way TW7 5 D2
Southlands
East Grinstead RH19 205 E7
Horley RH6 160 F3
Tandridge RH8 122 C2
Southlands Ave RH6 161 A4
Southlands Cl Ash GU12 106 A1
Coulsdon CR5 79 F2
Wokingham RG40 25 D5
Southlands Dr SW19 19 D6
Southlands La RH8 122 C1
Southlands Rd
Ash GU12 106 A1
Wokingham RG40 25 D4
Southmead Prim Sch
SW19 19 E7
Southmead Rd SW19 19 E7
Southmont Rd KT10 55 E7
Southpark Ct 4 SW19 20 A2
Southridge Pl SW20 19 D1
Southsea Rd KT1 37 E5
Southside Comm SW19 19 D3
Southview Cl SW17 21 A3
Southview Cotts GU10 146 D1
Southview Ct 14 GU22 69 E1
Southview Gdns SM6 60 C3
Southview Rd
Catford BR1 24 D4
Headley Down GU35 187 B5
Woldingham CR3 102 B3
Southviews CR2 62 D2
Southville Cl
East Bedfont TW14 14 E7
West Ewell KT19 57 D2
Southville Cres TW14 14 E7
Southville Jun & Inf Schs
TW14 14 F7
Southville Rd
East Bedfont TW14 14 E8
Thames Ditton KT7 37 B2
Southwark KT18 97 D8
Southwark Cl RH11 201 B2
Southwater Cl
Beckenham BR3 24 B1
Crawley RH11 201 A6
Southway Camberley GU15 65 B4
Guildford GU2 108 F1
Wallington SM6 60 C6
West Barnes SW20 39 D5
Southway Ct GU2 108 E1
Southway Pk GU2 109 A2
Southways Pk RH10 181 D3
Southwell Park Rd GU15 65 C5
Southwell Rd CR0,CR7 42 A3
Southwick GU19 47 E1
Southwick Cl RH19 185 D2
Southwick Ct RG12 27 E3
Southwick Ho RH19 185 D2
Southwold RG12 26 E1
Southwood RG40 25 D4
Southwood Ave
Coulsdon CR5 79 C4
Kingston u T KT2,KT3 38 C8
Knaphill GU21 68 D1
Ottershaw KT16 51 C3
Southwood Chase GU6 174 F1
Southwood Cl KT4 39 D1
Southwood Cres The
GU14 84 D3
Southwood Ct KT13 53 B5
Southwood Dr KT5 38 C1
Southwood Gdns KT10 56 A7
Southwood Inf Sch GU14 84 D3
Southwood La
Farnborough GU51 84 A3
Farnborough,Southwood
GU14 84 D3
Southwood Rd GU14 84 E4
Sovereign Ct
East Molesey KT8 35 F5
3 Richmond TW9 6 F3
4 Sunningdale SL5 30 B2
Sovereign Dr GU15 66 B7
Sovereign Ho
Ashford TW15 13 E4
Wimbledon SW19 19 E2
Spa Cl SE19 42 E8
Spa Ct SW16 21 F4
Spa Dr KT18 76 A5
Spa Hill CR7,SE19 42 D8
Spa View 6 SW16 21 F5
Space Waye TW14 4 B2
Spalding Rd SW17 21 B3
Sparks Cl TW12 15 E2
Sparrow Cl TW12 15 E2
Sparrow Farm Dr TW14 15 D8
Sparrow Farm Inf Sch
TW14 15 C8
Sparrow Farm Jun Sch
TW14 15 C8
Sparrow Farm Rd KT17,
KT4 58 B6
Sparrow Row GU24 49 B4
Sparrowhawk Cl GU10 124 D8
Sparrows Mead RH1 119 A4
Sparvell Rd GU21 88 B8
Sparvell Way GU15 65 C6
Spats La GU35 187 A8
Speaker's Ct 3 CR0 42 D1
Speart La TW5 4 E7
Speedbird Way UB7 2 C7
Speedwell Cl GU4 110 C4
Speedwell Ho 5 RH1 119 A4
Speedwell Way RH12 217 E5
Speer Rd KT7 36 F3
Speirs Cl KT3 38 F3
Speke Rd CR7 42 D7
Speldhurst Cl 4 BR2 44 F4
Spelthorne Coll TW15 13 F4
Spelthorne Gr TW16 14 F1
Spelthorne Inf Sch TW15 14 E2
Spelthorne Jun Sch
TW15 14 D2
Spelthorne La TW15,
TW17 34 C8
Spelthorne Mus* TW18 12 E3
Spence Ave KT14 71 F5
Spencer Cl Frimley GU16 85 E6
Langley Vale KT18 96 E8
Sheerwater GU21 70 D6
Spencer Ct
Leatherhead KT22 95 C4
Wimbledon SW20 39 B8
Spencer Gdns
Englefield Green TW20 11 D3
Mortlake SW14 7 C2
Spencer Hill SW19 19 E1
Spencer Hill Rd SW19 19 E1
Spencer Ho
24 Putney SW19 19 D7
Wimbledon SW19 19 D5
Spencer Pl CR0 42 D2
Spencer Rd
Bracknell RG42 26 F8
Bromley BR1 24 F1
Carshalton CR4 41 A2
Caterham CR3 100 D6
Chiswick W4 7 C7
Cobham KT11 73 B4
East Molesey KT8 36 C4
Hounslow TW3,TW5,TW7 5 C6
Mitcham CR4 41 A6
South Croydon CR2 61 E5
Spencer Rd *continued*
Twickenham TW2 16 E6
Wimbledon SW20 39 B8
Spencer Way RH1 140 A4
Spencer's Rd RH12 217 B3
Spencers La RH6 159 F2
Spencers Pl RH12 217 B4
Spencers Rd RH11 201 D5
Spenser Ave KT13 53 A2
Spenser Ct 5 TW10 17 D4
Spenser Mews SE21 22 D7
Spiceall GU3 129 B3
Spicer Cl KT12 35 C3
Spicers Field KT22 74 E6
Spices Yd CR0 61 C6
Spiers Way RH6 161 B1
Spindle Way RH10 201 F5
Spindlewood Gdns CR0,
CR2 61 E6
Spindlewoods KT20 97 B4
Spinis RG12 26 F1
Spinnaker Ct 2 KT1 37 D8
Spinner Gn RG12 27 B4
Spinney Cl
Beckenham BR3 44 B5
Cobham KT11 74 A8
Crawley Down RH10 204 C8
Horsham RH12 218 B6
New Malden KT3 38 E4
Worcester Park KT4 57 F8
Spinney Dr TW14 14 C8
Spinney Gdns SE19 22 F3
Spinney Hill KT15 51 F5
Spinney La SL4 9 B7
Spinney Oak KT16 51 D4
Spinney The Ascot SL5 29 E4
Burgh Heath KT18 97 B8
Cheam SM3 58 C6
Crawley RH11 201 B4
Frimley GU15 66 C6
Grayshott GU26 188 A4
Great Bookham KT23 94 B3
Haslemere GU27 208 C8
Horley RH6 161 A5
Oxshott KT22 74 C7
Purley CR8 80 B8
Ripley GU23 111 C8
Streatham SW16 21 D5
Sunbury TW16 35 A8
Spinneycroft KT22 74 D4
Spinning Wlk The GU5 133 A4
Spire Ct 10 TW10 6 E1
Spital Heath RH4 136 C8
Spitfire Rd SM6 60 F3
Spoil La GU10 126 F7
Spokane Cl GU11 125 F8
Spook Hill RH5 136 B3
Spooner Ho TW5 5 A8
Spooner Wlk SM6 60 D5
Spooners Rd RH12 218 A4
Sportsbank St SE6 24 C8
Spout Hill CR0 63 A5
Spout La TW19 2 A3
Spout La N TW19 2 B3
Spratts Alley KT16 51 E4
Spratts La KT16 51 E4
Spread Eagle Wlk 2
KT18 76 D6
Spreighton Rd KT8 36 B5
Spring Ave TW20 11 F2
Spring Bottom La RH1 120 C8
Spring Cnr TW13 14 F5
Spring Copse
Copthorne RH10 183 C3
East Grinstead RH19 185 D3
Spring Copse Bsns Pk
RH13 215 C3
Spring Cotts
Kingston u T KT6 37 D4
South Holmwood RH5 157 C6
Spring Ct Ewell KT17 57 F2
Guildford GU2 109 A5
Spring Gdns Ascot SL5 29 B5
Biggin Hill TN16 83 C1
Copthorne RH10 183 C3
Dorking RH4 136 A8
East Molesey KT8 36 C5
Farnborough GU14 85 A7
Frimley GU15 66 A5
Wallington SM6 60 C5
Spring Gr Brentford W4 7 A8
Farncombe GU7 150 E8
Fetcham KT22 94 B4
Hampton TW12 36 B8
Mitcham CR4 41 A8
Spring Grove Cres TW3,
TW5 5 C6
Spring Grove Prim Sch
TW7 5 D5
Spring Grove Rd
Hounslow TW3,TW5,TW7 5 C6
Richmond TW10 6 F2
Spring Hill SE26 23 C4
Spring Hill Wildfowl Pk*
RH18 206 A1
Spring Ho SW19 39 F8
Spring La
Croydon CR0,SE25 43 B3
Hale GU9 125 A7
Oxted RH8 122 D4
Slinfold RH13 215 C3
Spring La W GU9 125 A6
Spring Mdw
Bracknell RG12 27 D8
Forest Row RH18 206 F1
Spring Park Ave CR0 62 D8
Spring Park Prim Sch
CR0 63 A7

Spring Park Rd CR0 . . . . .62 D8
Spring Plat RH10 . . . . . .202 C6
Spring Plat Ct RH10 . . . .202 C6
Spring Rd TW13 . . . . .14 F5
Spring Rise TW20 . . . . .11 E2
Spring St KT17 . . . . .57 F2
Spring Terr TW10 . . . . .6 E2
Spring Way RH19 . . . . . .186 A4
Spring Woods
 Sandhurst GU47 . . . . . . .45 C1
 Virginia Water GU25 . . . .31 B5
Springbank Rd SE13 . . . . .24 E8
Springbourne Ct BR3 . . . .44 C8
Springclose La SM3 . . . . .58 E4
Springcopse Rd RH2 . . . .139 C7
Springcross Ave GU17 . . . .64 D4
Springfarm Rd GU27 . . . .207 E5
Springfield
 East Grinstead RH19 . . .185 D4
 Elstead GU8 . . . . .148 D3
 Lightwater GU18 . . . . . . .67 D8
 Oxted RH8 . . . . .122 D5
 South Norwood SE25 . . .43 A6
Springfield Ave
 Hampton TW12 . . . . .16 B2
 Merton SW20 . . . . .39 F6
Springfield Cl GU21 . . . . . .68 E1
Springfield Cres RH12 . . .217 B2
Springfield Ct
 Crawley RH11 . . . . .201 D5
 Horsham RH12 . . . . . . .217 C2
 9 Kingston u T KT1 . . . .37 E6
 Wallington SM6 . . . . .60 B5
Springfield Dr KT22 . . . . . .94 F8
Springfield Gdns BR4 . . . .63 B8
Springfield Gr TW16 . . . . .35 A8
Springfield Hospl SW17 . . .20 C5
Springfield La KT13 . . . . . .53 B6
Springfield Mdws KT13 . . .53 B6
Springfield Park Ho
 RH12 . . . . .217 C3
Springfield Park Rd
 RH12 . . . . .217 B2
Springfield Pl KT3 . . . . . . .38 C5
Springfield Prim Sch
 TW16 . . . . .34 F7
Springfield Rd
 Ash GU12 . . . . .106 A5
 Ashford TW15 . . . . .13 F4
 Bracknell RG12 . . . . .26 C8
 Brands Hill SL3 . . . . .1 B7
 Crawley RH11 . . . . .201 D5
 East Ewell KT17 . . . . . . .58 C1
 Frimley GU15 . . . . .66 B5
 Guildford GU1 . . . . .109 E1
 Horsham RH12 . . . . . . .217 C2
 Kingston u T KT1 . . . . . . .37 E6
 Penge SE26 . . . . .23 B3
 South Norwood CR7 . . . .42 C8
 8 Teddington TW11 . . . .17 A3
 Twickenham TW2 . . . . . .16 A7
 Wallington SM6 . . . . .60 B5
 Westcott RH4 . . . . .135 C6
 Wimbledon SW19 . . . . . .20 A3
Springfield Rise SE26 . . . .23 B5
Springfield Terr GU5 . . . .151 F6
Springfield Way GU8 . . . .148 E3
Springfields Cl KT16 . . . . .33 B1
Springhaven GU8 . . . . . . .148 E3
Springhaven Cl GU1 . . . .110 A1
Springhill GU8 . . . . .148 E3
Springhill Ct RG12 . . . . . . .27 B5
Springholm Cl
 Aldershot GU9 . . . . .126 B6
 Biggin Hill TN16 . . . . .83 C1
Springhurst Cl CR0 . . . . . .62 F6
Springlakes Est GU12 . . .105 E3
Springmead Ct
 Haslemere GU27 . . . . . .207 D5
 Sandhurst GU47 . . . . . . .45 E1
Springpark Dr BR3 . . . . . .44 C6
Springside Ct GU1 . . . . . .109 C2
Springvale Ct KT23 . . . . . .94 B1
Springwell Cl SW16 . . . . . .21 F4
Springwell Ct TW5 . . . . . . .4 D5
Springwell Jun & Inf Schs
 TW5 . . . . .4 E7
Springwell Rd
 Beare Green RH5 . . . . . .157 D3
 Heston TW5 . . . . .4 D6
 Streatham SW16 . . . . . . .22 A3
Springwood GU8 . . . . . . .150 A1
Springwood Ct CR2 . . . . . .61 E6
Sprint Ind Est KT14 . . . . . .71 D8
Spruce Cl RH1 . . . . .118 F2
Spruce Dr GU18 . . . . .67 A7
Spruce Pk BR2 . . . . .44 F5
Spruce Rd TN16 . . . . .83 D3
Sprucedale Gdns
 South Croydon CR0 . . . . .62 D6
 Wallington SM6 . . . . .60 E2
Sprucefield Ct RH11 . . . .201 B6
Spur Rd Brentford TW7 . . . .6 B7
 Feltham TW14 . . . . .4 B3
Spur The GU21 . . . . .68 B1
Spurfield KT8 . . . . .36 B6
Spurgeon Ave SE19 . . . . . .42 D8
Spurgeon Cl RH11 . . . . . .201 C7
Spurgeon Rd SE19 . . . . . .22 D1
Spurgeon's Coll SE25 . . . .42 E7
Spurs Ct GU11 . . . . .104 E2
Spy La RH14 . . . . .213 A4
Sq The GU26 . . . . .188 D3
Square Dr GU27 . . . . .208 B1
Square The Bagshot GU19 .47 E3
 Bracknell RG12 . . . . .27 E5
 Crawley RH10 . . . . .201 D6
 Elstead GU8 . . . . .148 D4

Square The continued
 Guildford GU2 . . . . .129 F7
 Harmondsworth TW6 . . . . .2 B6
 Lightwater GU18 . . . . . . .48 C1
 Lingfield RH7 . . . . .164 C4
 12 Richmond TW10 . . . . .6 D2
 Rowledge GU10 . . . . . . .145 E3
 Shere GU5 . . . . .133 A4
 Tatsfield TN16 . . . . .103 C7
 Wallington SM5 . . . . .60 A5
 Weybridge KT13 . . . . . . .53 C5
 Wisley GU23 . . . . .71 E3
Squarey St SW17 . . . . . . .20 C5
Squire Ct 2 CR0 . . . . .42 E1
Squire's Bridge Rd TW17 34 A5
Squires Bridge Rd KT17 . .33 F5
Squires Cl RH10 . . . . .204 A8
Squires Ct Chertsey KT16 .33 B1
 Wimbledon SW19 . . . . . .20 A4
Squires Hill La GU10 . . . .147 C4
Squires Wlk TW15 . . . . . . .14 D1
Squirrel Cl Crawley RH11 181 B1
 Hounslow TW4 . . . . .4 C4
 Sandhurst GU47 . . . . . . .64 B8
Squirrel Dr SL4 . . . . .9 B7
Squirrel La GU14 . . . . .85 A5
Squirrel Wood KT14 . . . . . .71 B7
Squirrel's Way KT18 . . . . .76 D4
Squirrels Cl GU7 . . . . .129 D1
Squirrels Ct KT4 . . . . .57 F8
Squirrels Gn
 Great Bookham KT23 . . . .94 A4
 12 Redhill RH1 . . . . .118 F2
 Worcester Park KT4 . . . . .58 A8
Stable Cl Crawley RH10 . .202 D3
 Langley Vale KT18 . . . . . .96 E8
Stable Croft GU19 . . . . . . .47 D2
Stable Ct Caterham CR3 . .101 A5
 Wallington SM6 . . . . .60 A7
Stable Mews
 Reigate RH2 . . . . .118 A1
 West Norwood SE27 . . . .22 C3
Stables The
 Bletchingley RH1 . . . . . .120 D4
 Cobham KT11 . . . . .73 F5
 Sunningdale SL5 . . . . . . .30 B1
Stace Way RH10 . . . . . . .202 E8
Stacey Ct RH1 . . . . .119 C6
Stacey's Farm Rd GU8 . . .148 D4
Stacey's Mdw GU8 . . . . . .148 C4
Stack Ho RH8 . . . . .122 E5
Stackfield Rd RH11 . . . . .200 E5
Staddon Ct BR3 . . . . .43 E5
Staff College Rd GU15 . . . .65 B6
Staff Rd GU12 . . . . .105 C2
Staffhurst Wood Rd
 TN8,RH8 . . . . .144 C6
Stafford Cl Caterham CR3 100 F4
 Cheam SM3 . . . . .58 E4
Stafford Gdns CR0 . . . . . . .60 F5
Stafford Lake GU21 . . . . . .68 A1
Stafford Pl TW10 . . . . .17 F8
Stafford Rd
 Caterham CR3 . . . . .101 A6
 Crawley RH11 . . . . .181 B1
 Croydon CR0 . . . . .61 A6
 Kingston u T KT3 . . . . . . .38 C6
 Wallington CR0,SM6 . . . .60 E4
Stafford Sq 4 KT13 . . . . . .53 D6
Staffords Pl RH6 . . . . .161 B2
Stag Hill GU2 . . . . .130 A8
Stag Hill Ct GU2 . . . . .109 B1
Stag La SW15 . . . . .18 F5
Stag Leys KT21 . . . . .95 E7
Stag Leys Cl SM7 . . . . .78 E4
Stagbury Ave CR5 . . . . . . .78 E1
Stagbury Cl CR5 . . . . .98 E8
Stagbury Ho CR5 . . . . .98 E8
Stagelands RH11 . . . . . . .201 C8
Stagelands Ct RH11 . . . . .201 C8
Stags Way TW7 . . . . .5 F8
Stainash Cres TW18 . . . . . .13 B3
Stainash Par TW18 . . . . . . .13 B3
Stainbank Rd CR4 . . . . . . .41 B6
Staines Ave SM3 . . . . . . .58 D8
Staines By-Pass TW18,
 TW18 . . . . .13 C3
Staines La KT16 . . . . .33 A3
Staines Lane Cl KT16 . . . . .32 F4
Staines Prep Sch TW18 . .13 A3
Staines Rd Chertsey KT16 .33 A5
 East Bedfont TW14 . . . . . .14 D8
 Feltham,Hounslow TW14,
 TW3,TW4 . . . . .4 D2
 Laleham TW18 . . . . .33 B7
 Twickenham TW2 . . . . . .16 C6
 Wraysbury TW19 . . . . . . .11 F7
Staines Rd E TW12,TW16 .35 C8
Staines Rd W TW15 . . . . . .14 D1
Staines Sta TW18 . . . . . . .13 A3
Stainford Cl TW15 . . . . . . .14 D1
Stainton Rd SE13 . . . . .24 D8
Stainton Wlk GU21 . . . . . . .69 C1
Staiths Way KT20 . . . . .97 B7
Stake La GU14 . . . . .85 A4
Stakescorner Rd GU3 . . .130 A2
Stambourne Way
 South Norwood SE19 . . . .22 F1
 West Wickham BR4 . . . . .63 C7
Stamford Ave GU16 . . . . . .65 F1
Stamford Dr BR2 . . . . .44 F5
Stamford Green Prim Sch
 KT19 . . . . .76 B7
Stamford Green Rd KT18 76 B6
Stamford Rd KT12 . . . . . . .54 D7

Stammerham Bsns Ctr
 RH12 . . . . .198 E8
Stan Hill RH6 . . . . .180 D8
Stan's Way RH12 . . . . . . .217 C2
Stanborough Cl TW12 . . . .15 F2
Stanborough Rd TW3,TW7 5 D4
Stanbridge Cl RH11 . . . . .200 E6
Stancliffe Ho 9 SM1 . . . . .59 C6
Standard Rd TW4 . . . . .4 E4
Standen Cl RH19 . . . . . . .185 A4
**Standen House (National
 Trust)★** RH19 . . . . .205 D4
Standen Pl RH12 . . . . . . .218 A7
Standen Rd SW18 . . . . . . .20 A8
Standinghall La RH10 . . . .203 A3
Standlake Point 1 SE23 .23 D5
Standon La RH5 . . . . .176 F2
Stane Cl SW19 . . . . .20 B1
Stane St Ockley RH5 . . . .177 D1
 Slinfold RH12,RH13 . . . .215 C4
Stane Way KT17 . . . . .58 A1
Stanedge Ct SW16 . . . . . . .21 E3
Stanford Cl SW12 . . . . . . .15 F2
Stanford Cotts GU24 . . . . .87 E1
Stanford Ct RH10 . . . . . . .202 C4
Stanford Orch RH12 . . . . .216 F8
Stanford Prim Sch SW16 41 D8
Stanford Rd SW16 . . . . . . .41 E7
Stanford Way
 Broadbridge Heath RH12 216 D3
 Mitcham SW16 . . . . .41 D7
Stanfords Pl RH7 . . . . . . .164 D3
Stanfords The KT17 . . . . . .76 F7
Stangate Mans TW1 . . . . .16 F5
Stanger Rd SE25 . . . . .43 A5
Stangrave Hall RH9 . . . . .121 B3
Stanhope Ave BR2 . . . . . . .44 F1
Stanhope Cotts RH7 . . . . .164 F3
Stanhope Gr BR3 . . . . .43 F5
Stanhope Heath TW19 . . . .2 C1
Stanhope Rd
 Camberley GU15 . . . . . . .64 F4
 South Croydon CR0 . . . . .61 E7
 Wallington SM5 . . . . .60 A3
Stanhope Way TW19 . . . . . .2 C1
Stanhopes RH8 . . . . .123 B7
Stanier Cl RH10 . . . . .202 B5
Staniland Dr KT13 . . . . . . .52 F1
Stanley Ave
 Beckenham BR2, BR3 . . .44 C6
 West Barnes KT3 . . . . . . .39 A4
Stanley Cl Coulsdon CR5 . .79 F2
 Crawley RH10 . . . . .201 E4
Stanley Cotts GU21 . . . . . .68 D2
Stanley Ct Belmont SM2 . .59 B3
 Wallington SM5 . . . . .60 A3
 3 Wimbledon SW19 . . . .20 A2
Stanley Ctr RH10 . . . . . . .181 F2
Stanley Dr GU14 . . . . .84 C3
Stanley Gardens Rd
 TW11 . . . . .16 E3
Stanley Gdns
 Hersham KT12 . . . . .54 C4
 Mitcham CR4 . . . . .21 A2
 Sanderstead CR2 . . . . . . .81 A7
 Wallington SM6 . . . . .60 C4
Stanley Gr CR0,CR7 . . . . .42 A3
Stanley Hill GU24 . . . . .87 C5
Stanley Inf Sch TW11 . . . .16 E4
Stanley Jun Sch TW11 . . .16 E4
Stanley Mans SW17 . . . . .20 F6
Stanley Park High Sch
 SM5 . . . . .60 A4
Stanley Park Inf Sch SM5 59 F3
Stanley Park Jun Sch
 SM5 . . . . .59 F3
Stanley Park Rd SM5,SM6 60 A3
Stanley Rd Ashford TW15 .13 E3
 Belmont SM2 . . . . .59 B3
 Hounslow TW3 . . . . .5 C3
 Mitcham CR4 . . . . .21 A1
 Morden SM4 . . . . .40 A5
 Mortlake SW14 . . . . .7 B3
 Teddington TW11 . . . . . .16 E3
 Thornton Heath CR0,CR7 .42 A3
 Twickenham TW2 . . . . . .16 D5
 Wallington SM5 . . . . .60 A3
 Wimbledon SW19 . . . . . .20 A2
 Woking GU21 . . . . .69 F2
 Wokingham RG40 . . . . . .25 E6
Stanley Sq SM5 . . . . .59 F2
Stanley St CR3 . . . . .100 E6
**Stanley Tech High Sch for
 Boys** SE25 . . . . .42 F6
Stanley Wlk RH13 . . . . . . .217 D2
Stanleycroft Cl TW7 . . . . . .5 E6
Stanmore Cl SL5 . . . . .29 A5
Stanmore Gdns
 Richmond TW9 . . . . .6 F4
 Sutton SM1 . . . . .59 C4
Stanmore Rd TW9 . . . . .6 F4
Stanmore Terr 3 BR3 . . . .44 A7
Stannet Way SM6 . . . . . . .60 C6
Stansfield Rd TW4,TW5 . . .4 B5
Stanstead Cl BR2 . . . . . . .44 F3
Stanstead Gr SE23 . . . . . .23 F7
Stanstead Manor SM1 . . . .59 A4
Stanstead Rd
 Caterham CR3,RH1 . . . .100 E2
 Forest Hill SE23,SE6 . . . .23 E7
Stansted Rd TW6 . . . . .2 F2
Stanthorpe Cl SW16 . . . . .21 E3
Stanthorpe Rd SW16 . . . .21 E3
Stanton Ave TW11 . . . . . . .16 E2
Stanton Cl Cranleigh GU6 174 A4
 North Cheam KT4 . . . . . . .39 D1
 West Ewell KT19 . . . . . . .57 B5
Stanton Rd Barnes SW13 . .7 F5

Stanton Rd continued
 Thornton Heath CR0 . . . .42 C2
 Wimbledon SW20 . . . . . .39 D8
Stanton Sq 2 SE6 . . . . . . .23 F4
Stanton Way SE26,SE6 . . .23 F4
Stantons Wharf GU5 . . . .152 A7
Stanwell Cl TW19 . . . . .2 D1
Stanwell Gdns TW19 . . . . .2 D1
Stanwell Moor Rd
 Harmondsworth TW19,TW6,
 UB7 . . . . .2 B4
 Stanwell TW19 . . . . .2 B4
Stanwell New Rd TW18,
 TW19 . . . . .13 B5
Stanwell Rd Ashford TW15 13 E4
 East Bedfont TW14,TW19,
 TW6 . . . . .14 B8
 Horton SL3,TW19 . . . . . . .1 C4
Stanworth Ct TW5 . . . . . . .5 B4
Stanyhurst SE23 . . . . .23 E7
Staple Hill GU24,KT16 . . .49 E6
Staple La
 East Clandon GU4,GU5 . .111 C3
 Shere GU4 . . . . .132 F8
Staplecross Ct 1 RH11 . .201 A3
Staplefield Cl 3 SW2 . . . .21 E7
Stapleford Cl
 Kingston u T KT1 . . . . . . .38 A6
 Putney SW19 . . . . .19 E8
Staplehurst RG12 . . . . . . .26 E2
Staplehurst Cl RH2 . . . . . .139 C5
Staplehurst Rd
 Reigate RH2 . . . . .139 C5
 Sutton SM5 . . . . .59 E3
Stapleton Gdns CR0 . . . . .61 A5
Stapleton Rd SW17 . . . . . .21 A5
Star & Garter Hill TW10 . .17 E8
Star Cl RH13 . . . . .218 A4
Star Hill GU10 . . . . .167 D2
Star Hill Dr GU10 . . . . . . .167 D2
Star La Ash GU12 . . . . . . .105 F2
 Hooley CR5 . . . . .99 A6
 Woking GU21 . . . . .89 C8
Star Post Rd GU15 . . . . . . .65 F8
Star Rd TW7 . . . . .5 D5
Starborough Cotts RH7 .185 F7
Starborough Rd TN8 . . . . .165 E5
Starhurst Sch RH5 . . . . . .136 C5
Starling Wlk TW12 . . . . . . .15 E3
Starmead Dr RG40 . . . . . . .25 E5
Starrett Ct KT12 . . . . .54 C8
Starrock La CR5 . . . . .99 A7
Starrock Rd CR5 . . . . .99 C8
Starwood Cl KT14 . . . . . . .71 C8
Staten Gdns TW1 . . . . .16 F7
Statham Ct RG42 . . . . .26 E8
Station App
 Ash Vale GU12 . . . . .106 A4
 Ashford TW15 . . . . .13 F4
 6 Beckenham BR3 . . . . .44 A8
 Beckenham, Lower Sydenham
 SE6 . . . . .23 F3
 Belmont SM2 . . . . .59 B1
 Belmont,Cheam SM2 . . . .58 E3
 Blackwater GU17 . . . . . . .64 C4
 Chipstead CR5 . . . . .78 F1
 Coulsdon CR5 . . . . .79 D4
 3 Croydon CR0 . . . . .61 D8
 Dorking RH4 . . . . .115 C1
 East Horsley KT24 . . . . . .92 E1
 Epsom KT17,KT19 . . . . . .76 D6
 Ewell KT17 . . . . .58 B1
 Faygate RH12 . . . . .199 F1
 Godalming GU7 . . . . .150 D4
 Guildford GU1 . . . . .130 E8
 Hampton TW12 . . . . .36 A8
 Haslemere GU27 . . . . . .208 B6
 Hinchley Wood KT10 . . . .55 F7
 Horley RH6 . . . . .161 B2
 4 Kingston u T KT1,KT2 .38 A8
 Leatherhead KT22 . . . . . .95 A6
 6 New Malden KT4 . . . . .39 A1
 Ockley RH5 . . . . .178 B5
 Oxted RH8 . . . . .122 E6
 Purley CR8 . . . . .80 A8
 Richmond TW9 . . . . .7 A6
 Shalford GU4 . . . . .130 E3
 Shepperton TW17 . . . . . .34 D4
 South Croydon CR2 . . . . .61 D2
 Staines TW18 . . . . .13 A3
 Streatham SW16 . . . . . . .21 D3
 Sunbury TW16 . . . . .35 A8
 1 Surbiton KT6 . . . . .37 E3
 Virginia Water GU25 . . . .31 D5
 West Byfleet KT14 . . . . . .71 A7
 Weybridge KT13 . . . . . . .53 A4
 Whyteleafe CR3 . . . . .81 A1
 Woking GU22 . . . . .69 F2
 Worcester Park KT19 . . . .58 A5
 Wormley GU8 . . . . .190 F8
Station App E RH1 . . . . . .139 F7
Station App Rd KT20 . . . . .97 C4
Station App W RH1 . . . . . .139 F7
Station Approach Rd
 Chiswick W4 . . . . .7 C7
 Coulsdon CR5 . . . . .79 D4
 Crawley RH6 . . . . .182 B7
Station Ave
 Caterham CR3 . . . . .101 A3
 Kingston u-T KT3 . . . . . . .38 E6
 Walton-on-T KT12 . . . . . .54 A6
 West Ewell KT19 . . . . . . .57 C2
Station Bldgs SW20 . . . . . .39 C7
Station Cl Hampton TW12 .36 B8
Station Cotts CR8 . . . . .80 C5
Station Cres TW15 . . . . . . .13 E4
Station Est BR3 . . . . .43 D5

Station Estate Rd TW14 . .15 B7
Station Flats 3 SL5 . . . . . .30 B2
Station Gdns W4 . . . . .7 C7
Station Hill Ascot SL5 . . . .29 B7
 Crawley RH10 . . . . .202 B7
 Farnham GU9 . . . . .125 C2
Station Ind Est RG40 . . . . .25 B6
Station La
 Enton Green GU8 . . . . . .171 A7
 Wormley GU8 . . . . .170 F1
Station Par Ashford TW15 .13 F4
 East Horsley KT24 . . . . . .92 E1
 Feltham TW14 . . . . .15 B8
 Richmond TW9 . . . . .7 A6
 Sunningdale SL5 . . . . . . .30 A2
 6 Sutton SM2 . . . . .59 C4
 4 Upper Tooting SW12 . .21 A7
 Virginia Water GU25 . . . .31 E4
Station Path TW18 . . . . . . .12 F4
Station Rd
 Addlestone KT15 . . . . . . .52 D6
 Aldershot GU11 . . . . . . .105 A2
 Ashford TW15 . . . . .13 F4
 Bagshot GU19 . . . . .47 E4
 Barnes SW13 . . . . .7 F5
 Beckenham BR2 . . . . . . .44 E7
 Belmont SM2 . . . . .59 A1
 Betchworth RH3 . . . . . . .116 E3
 Bracknell RG12 . . . . .27 B7
 Bramley GU5 . . . . .152 A7
 Carshalton SM5 . . . . .59 F6
 Chertsey KT16 . . . . .33 A1
 Chessington KT9 . . . . . . .56 E5
 Chobham GU24 . . . . .69 B6
 Claygate KT10 . . . . .55 E5
 Cranleigh RH12 . . . . . . .195 C3
 Crawley RH10,RH11 . . . .201 D5
 Crawley Down RH10 . . . .204 B8
 Croydon CR0 . . . . .42 C1
 Dorking RH4 . . . . .136 A8
 East Grinstead RH19 . . .185 D1
 Egham TW20 . . . . .12 A3
 Esher KT10 . . . . .55 D8
 Farnborough GU14 . . . . .85 B4
 Farncombe GU7 . . . . . . .150 F7
 Forest Row RH18 . . . . . .206 F3
 Godalming GU7 . . . . .150 D4
 Gomshall GU5 . . . . .133 D4
 Hampton TW12 . . . . .36 B8
 Horley RH6 . . . . .161 B3
 Horsham RH13 . . . . .217 D2
 Hounslow TW3 . . . . .5 B3
 Hydestile GU8 . . . . .171 D6
 Kenley CR8 . . . . .80 C5
 Kingston u T KT2 . . . . . . .38 A8
 Leatherhead KT22 . . . . . .95 A6
 Lingfield RH7 . . . . .164 E4
 Loxwood RH14 . . . . .213 A3
 Merstham RH1 . . . . .119 C7
 Merton SW19 . . . . .40 C8
 Penge SE20 . . . . .23 C2
 Redhill RH1 . . . . .118 F2
 Rudgwick RH12 . . . . . . .214 D7
 Shalford GU4 . . . . .130 E3
 Shepperton TW17 . . . . . .34 C4
 South Godstone RH9 . . .142 E5
 South Norwood SE25 . . .42 F5
 Stoke D'Abernon KT11 . . .73 E3
 Sunbury TW16 . . . . .15 A1
 Sunningdale SL5 . . . . . . .30 A4
 Teddington TW11 . . . . . .17 A2
 Teddington, Hampton Wick
 KT1 . . . . .37 D8
 Thames Ditton KT10 . . . .55 D8
 Thames Ditton,Weston Green
 KT7 . . . . .36 F2
 Twickenham TW1 . . . . . .16 F8
 Warnham RH12 . . . . . . .217 B8
 West Barnes KT3 . . . . . . .39 B4
 West Byfleet KT14 . . . . . .71 A7
 West Wickham BR4 . . . . .44 C1
 Whyteleafe CR3 . . . . .80 F1
 Wokingham RG40 . . . . . .25 B6
 Woldingham CR3 . . . . . .101 F5
 Wraysbury TW19 . . . . . . .1 A1
Station Rd E
 Ash Vale GU12 . . . . .106 A7
 Oxted RH8 . . . . .122 E6
Station Rd N
 5 Egham TW20 . . . . . . .11 F3
 Merstham RH1 . . . . .119 C7
Station Rd S RH1 . . . . . . .119 C7
Station Rd W
 Ash Vale GU12 . . . . .105 F8
 Oxted RH8 . . . . .122 E6
Station Rise SE27 . . . . . . .22 B6
Station Row GU4 . . . . .130 E3
Station Terr RH4 . . . . .136 A8
Station View GU12 . . . . . .106 A8
Station Way
 Bracknell RG12 . . . . .27 C7
 Cheam SM2,SM3 . . . . . .58 E3
 Crawley RH10,RH11 . . . .201 D5
Station Yd TW1 . . . . .17 A8
Staunton Rd KT2 . . . . .17 F1
Staveley Gdns W4 . . . . .7 D6
Staveley Rd Ashford TW15 14 D2
 Chiswick W4 . . . . .7 D7
Staveley Way GU21 . . . . . .68 E2
Staverton Cl RG40 . . . . . . .25 F6
Stavordale Rd SM4,SM5 . .40 C2
Stayne End GU25 . . . . .31 A5
Stayton Rd SM1 . . . . .59 A7
Steadfast Rd KT1 . . . . .37 D8
Steam Farm La TW14 . . . . .3 F3

Steel's La KT11, KT22 ... 74 C5
Steele Rd TW7 ... 6 A3
Steele's Rd GU11 ... 105 B4
Steep Hill Chobham GU24 . 49 C3
South Croydon CR0 ... 61 E6
Streatham SW16 ... 21 D5
Steeple Cl SW19 ... 19 E4
Steeple Heights Dr TN16 83 D2
Steepways GU26 ... 188 B6
Steeres Hill RH12 ... 199 C6
Steerforth Copse GU47 .. 45 E2
Steerforth St SW18 ... 20 C6
Steers La RH10 ... 182 C4
Steers Mead CR4 ... 40 F8
Steetley Ct 19 SM2 ... 59 C3
Steinman Ct TW7 ... 5 F4
Stella Rd SW17 ... 20 F2
Stembridge Rd SE20 ... 43 B7
Stenning Ct KT22 ... 95 B5
Stennings The RH19 ... 185 C3
Stepgates KT16 ... 33 B2
Stepgates Cl KT16 ... 33 B2
Stepgates Com Prim Sch KT16 ... 33 B2
Stephanie Chase Ct RG40 ... 25 D7
Stephen Cl TW20 ... 12 C2
Stephen Ct 18 SW19 ... 19 D7
Stephen Gould Ho GU14 ... 105 B8
Stephendale Rd GU9 .. 125 D4
Stephens Field GU8 ... 191 A4
Stephenson Ct
Belmont SM2 ... 58 F3
Farnham GU9 ... 146 A8
Stephenson Dr RH19 ... 205 F7
Stephenson Pl RH10 ... 202 B6
Stephenson Rd TW2 ... 16 A8
Stephenson Way RH10 . 202 B6
Stepney Cl RH10 ... 202 C4
Sterling Ave TW17 ... 34 E6
Sterling Bldgs RH12 ... 217 C2
Sterling Pk RH10 ... 182 B3
Sternhold Ave SW12,SW2 21 D6
Sterry Dr
Thames Ditton KT7 ... 36 E3
Worcester Park KT19 ... 57 E6
Steucers La SE23 ... 23 E7
Steve Biko La SE6 ... 24 A4
Steve Biko Way TW3 ... 5 A4
Stevenage Rd RH11 ... 200 E3
Stevens Cl
Beckenham BR3 ... 24 A2
Epsom KT17 ... 76 E6
Hampton TW12 ... 15 F2
Stevens Ct BR3 ... 24 A2
Stevens Ho KT1 ... 37 D7
Stevens Pl CR8 ... 80 B6
Stevens' La KT10 ... 56 A4
Stewards Rise GU10 ... 145 F7
Stewart KT20 ... 97 D6
Stewart Ave TW17 ... 34 A5
Stewart Cl Hampton TW12 . 15 E2
Woking GU21 ... 68 F2
Stewart Fleming Prim Sch SE20 ... 43 C6
Steyning Cl
Crawley RH10 ... 201 E8
Purley CR8 ... 80 B3
Steyning Way TW4 ... 4 C3
Sthrathbrook Rd SW16 .. 21 F1
Stickle Down GU16 ... 86 D8
Stile Gdns GU27 ... 207 F6
Stile Ho GU4 ... 110 D2
Stile Path TW16 ... 35 A6
Stilwell Ave SM6 ... 60 E3
Stirling Cl
1 Ash Vale GU12 ... 105 F5
Banstead SM7 ... 77 F2
Crawley RH10 ... 202 C5
Farnborough GU14 ... 85 A3
Frimley GU16 ... 65 E2
Mitcham SW16 ... 41 C8
Stirling Dr CR3 ... 100 C6
Stirling Gr TW3 ... 5 C5
Stirling Ho 18 RH1 ... 118 F1
Stirling Rd Guildford GU2 108 E1
Stanwell TW6 ... 2 F1
Twickenham TW2 ... 16 B8
Stirling Way
East Grinstead RH19 ... 186 B3
Horsham RH13 ... 217 E3
Thornton Heath CR0 ... 41 E2
Stirrup Way RH10 ... 202 D7
Stites Hill Rd CR3,CR5 .. 100 C7
Stoatley Ho 10 SW15 ... 19 A7
Stoatley Hollow GU27 .. 208 A8
Stoatley Rise GU27 ... 208 A8
Stoats Nest Rd CR5 ... 79 E5
Stoats Nest Village CR5 .. 79 E4
Stock Hill TN16 ... 83 D2
Stockbridge Dr GU11 .. 126 C6
Stockbury Rd CR0 ... 43 C3
Stockfield RH6 ... 161 B4
Stockfield Rd
Claygate KT10 ... 55 E5
Streatham SW16 ... 21 F5
Stockhams Cl CR2 ... 61 D1
Stocklund Sq GU6 ... 174 D3
Stockport Rd SW16 ... 41 D8
Stocks Cl RH6 ... 161 B2
Stockton Ho RH2 ... 139 A6
Stockton Rd RH2 ... 139 A6
Stockwell Ctr RH10 ... 202 A6
Stockwell Rd RH19 ... 205 E6
Stockwood Rise GU15 ... 65 F5
Stockwood Way GU9 ... 125 F7
Stocton Cl GU1 ... 109 C2
Stocton Rd GU1 ... 109 D2
Stodart Rd SE20 ... 43 C8
Stoford Cl SW19 ... 19 E8
Stoke Brunswick Sch RH19 ... 206 E7
Stoke Cl KT11 ... 73 F3
Stoke Fields 8 GU1 ... 109 D1
Stoke Gr GU1 ... 109 D1
Stoke Hills GU9 ... 125 C3
Stoke Hosp (Almshouses) 6 GU1 ... 109 D1
Stoke Park Ct 5 GU1 .. 109 D1
Stoke Rd Guildford GU1 .. 109 D1
Kingston u T KT2 ... 18 C1
Stoke D'Abernon KT11 ... 73 E3
Walton-on-T KT12 ... 54 C7
Stoke Rd Cotts KT22 ... 94 D6
Stokeford Cl 5 RG12 ... 27 F4
Stokers Cl RH6 ... 181 E7
Stokes Cl RH10 ... 202 C4
Stokes Rd CR0 ... 43 D3
Stokes Ridings KT20 ... 97 D4
Stokesby Rd KT9 ... 56 F4
Stokesheath Rd KT22 ... 74 C8
Stompond La KT12 ... 54 A8
Stoms Path SE6 ... 24 A3
Stonards Brow GU5 ... 152 D4
Stondon Pk SE23 ... 23 E8
Stone Cotts RH10 ... 203 B1
Stone Cres TW14 ... 14 F8
Stone Hatch GU6 ... 194 A3
Stone House Gdns CR3 . 100 E2
Stone Park Ave BR3 ... 44 B5
Stone Pl KT4 ... 58 A8
Stone Rd BR2 ... 44 F4
Stone St GU12 ... 126 D8
Stone's Rd KT17 ... 76 E7
Stonebanks KT12 ... 35 A2
Stonebridge Ct
Crawley RH11 ... 201 C2
Horsham RH12 ... 217 A2
Stonebridge Fields GU4 ... 130 D2
Stonebridge Wharf GU4 ... 130 D2
Stonecot Cl SM3,SM4 ... 39 E1
Stonecot Hill SM4 ... 39 E1
Stonecourt Cl RH6 ... 161 C3
Stonecroft Way CR0 ... 41 E2
Stonecrop Cl RH11 ... 201 B3
Stonecrop Rd GU4 ... 110 C3
Stonedene Cl GU35 ... 187 B4
Stonefield Cl RH10,RH11 201 D5
Stonegate GU15 ... 66 C6
Stonehaven BR3 ... 44 B7
Stonehill Cl
Little Bookham KT23 ... 94 A2
Mortlake SW14 ... 7 D2
Stonehill Cres KT16 ... 50 E4
Stonehill Pk GU35 ... 187 C4
Stonehill Rd
Chobham GU24,KT16 ... 50 D3
Headley Down GU35 ... 187 C4
Lightwater GU18 ... 48 A1
Mortlake SW14 ... 7 D2
Stonehill's Mans 3 SW16 ... 21 E6
Stonehills Ct SE21 ... 22 E5
Stonehouse Rise GU16 .. 65 E1
Stoneleigh Ave KT17,KT4 . 58 A7
Stoneleigh Broadway KT17 ... 58 A5
Stoneleigh Cl RH19 ... 185 F1
Stoneleigh Cres KT19 ... 57 F5
Stoneleigh Ct GU16 ... 65 F1
Stoneleigh Fst Sch KT4 .. 58 B6
Stoneleigh Lodge 12 TW9 .. 6 F6
Stoneleigh Park Ave CR0 43 D3
Stoneleigh Park Rd KT19, KT4 ... 58 A5
Stoneleigh Pk KT13 ... 53 C4
Stoneleigh Rd
Carshalton SM5 ... 40 E2
The Chart RH8 ... 123 E5
Stoneleigh Sta KT19 ... 58 A5
Stonepit Cl GU7 ... 150 C4
Stones La RH4 ... 135 C6
Stoneswood Rd RH8 ... 123 B5
Stoneworth Ct SE25 ... 43 A3
Stoney Bottom GU26 ... 188 C3
Stoney Brook GU2 ... 108 E2
Stoney Croft CR5 ... 99 C5
Stoney Deep TW11 ... 17 A4
Stoney La SE19 ... 22 F2
Stoney Rd RG42 ... 27 A8
Stoneybrook RH12 ... 216 F1
Stoneycroft GU11 ... 104 F1
Stoneycroft Cl SE12 ... 24 F8
Stoneycroft Wlk 3 RH11 ... 200 D5
Stoneyfield Rd CR5 ... 79 F2
Stoneyfields GU9 ... 125 E1
Stoneyland Ct 6 TW20 .. 11 F3
Stoneylands Rd TW20 .. 11 F3
Stonny Croft KT21 ... 75 F2
Stony Hill KT10 ... 54 F3
Stoop Ct KT14 ... 71 B7
Stoop Meml Ground TW2 ... 16 E8
Stopham Rd RH10 ... 202 C3
Stormont Way KT9 ... 56 C5
Storr's La GU3 ... 88 C3
Storrington Ct RH11 ... 201 A7
Storrington Rd CR0 ... 42 F1
Stoughton Ave SM3 ... 58 E5
Stoughton Cl SW15 ... 19 A7
Stoughton Inf Sch GU2 . 109 B4
Stoughton Rd GU1,GU2 . 109 B3
Stourhead Cl
Farnborough GU14 ... 85 D4
6 Putney SW19 ... 19 D8
Stourhead Gdns SW20 ... 39 A6
Stourton Ave TW13 ... 15 F4
Stovold's Way GU11 ... 125 F8
Stovolds Hill GU6,GU8 .. 193 D7
Stowell Ave CR0 ... 63 D2
Stowford Coll SM2 ... 59 C3
Strachan Pl SW19,SW20 .. 19 C2
Strachey Ct 1 RH11 ... 201 B1
Strafford Rd Hounslow TW3 4 F4
Twickenham TW1 ... 17 A8
Straight Rd SL4 ... 11 C8
Strand Cl Crawley RH10 . 202 D4
Langley Vale KT18 ... 96 D8
Strand-on-the-Green W4 7 A8
Strand-on-the-Green Inf Sch W4 ... 7 A8
Strand-on-the-Green Jun Sch W4 ... 7 A8
Stranraer Way 1 TW6 ... 2 E1
Stratfield RG12 ... 26 E1
Stratfield Ho 12 GU11 .. 105 A2
Stratford Ct
Farnborough GU14 ... 85 C4
Farnham GU9 ... 125 C1
New Malden KT3 ... 38 D5
Stratford Rd
Ash Vale GU12 ... 85 F1
Harlington TW6 ... 3 C2
Thornton Heath CR7 ... 42 B6
Strathavon Cl GU6 ... 174 B7
Strathcona Ave KT24 ... 113 E7
Strathcona Gdns
Knaphill GU21 ... 68 D1
Knaphill GU21 ... 88 C8
Strathdale SW16 ... 21 F3
Strathdon Dr SW17 ... 20 D5
Strathearn Ave
Harlington UB3 ... 3 F7
Twickenham TW2 ... 16 C7
Strathearn Rd Sutton SM1 59 A5
Wimbledon SW19 ... 20 A4
Strathmore Cl CR3 ... 100 E6
Strathmore Ct 3 GU15 .. 65 D5
Strathmore Rd
Crawley RH11 ... 181 A1
Teddington TW11 ... 16 E4
Thornton Heath CR0 ... 42 D2
Wimbledon SW19 ... 20 A5
Strathmore Sch TW10 ... 17 D6
Strathville Rd SW18 ... 20 B6
Strathyre Ave CR7,SW16 . 42 A6
Stratton Ave SM6 ... 60 D2
Stratton Cl Heston TW5 ... 5 A6
Merton SW19 ... 40 A7
Walton-on-T KT12 ... 35 C1
Stratton Ct 10 KT6 ... 37 E4
Stratton Rd Merton SW19 . 40 A7
Sunbury TW16 ... 34 F7
Stratton Wlk GU14 ... 85 A7
Straw Cl CR3 ... 100 C4
Strawberry Cl GU24 ... 87 D7
Strawberry Fields GU24 . 68 A4
Strawberry Hill Cl TW1 .. 16 F5
Strawberry Hill Rd TW1 . 16 F5
Strawberry Hill Sta TW2 . 16 F5
Strawberry La SM5 ... 60 A7
Strawberry Rise GU24 ... 68 A4
Strawberry Vale TW1 ... 17 A5
Stream Cl KT14 ... 71 E7
Stream Farm Cl GU10 .. 146 D7
Stream Pk RH19 ... 185 A3
Stream Valley Rd GU10 . 146 C6
Streamline Ct SE22 ... 23 A7
Streamline Mews SE22 ... 23 A7
Streatham & Clapham High Sch (Prep Dept) SW2 .. 21 F6
Streatham & Clapham High Sch (Senior Sch) SW16 . 21 D5
Streatham Cl SW16 ... 21 E6
Streatham Comm N SW16 ... 21 F3
Streatham Comm S SW16 ... 21 F2
Streatham Common Sta SW16 ... 21 D1
Streatham Ct SW16 ... 21 E5
Streatham High Rd SW16, SW2 ... 21 E3
Streatham Hill SW2 ... 21 E7
Streatham Hill Sta SW2 . 21 E6
Streatham Pl SW2 ... 21 E8
Streatham Rd CR4 ... 41 A8
Streatham Sta SW16 ... 21 D3
Streatham Vale SW16 ... 21 D1
Streatham Wells Prim Sch SW2 ... 22 A6
Streathbourne Rd SW17 . 21 A5
Streatleigh Par 4 SW16 . 21 E6
Street Hill RH10 ... 202 E5
Street The Albury GU5 .. 132 C4
Ashstead KT21 ... 75 F1
Betchworth RH3 ... 116 E1
Capel RH5 ... 178 D6
Charlwood RH6 ... 180 E7
Compton GU3 ... 129 B2
Dockenfield GU10 ... 166 E6
East Clandon GU4 ... 111 E4
Effingham KT24 ... 113 D8
Ewhurst GU6 ... 175 E5
Fetcham KT22 ... 94 D5
Frensham GU10 ... 167 C7
Plaistow RH14 ... 211 E2
Street The *continued*
Puttenham GU3 ... 128 C4
Shackleford GU8 ... 149 C8
Shalford GU4 ... 130 E3
Slinfold RH13 ... 215 D4
Thursley GU8 ... 169 C4
Tongham GU10 ... 126 F6
West Clandon GU4 ... 111 B5
West Horsley KT24 ... 112 B7
Wonersh GU5 ... 152 A7
Wrecclesham GU10 ... 145 F6
Streete Court Sch RH9 . 121 E5
Streeters Cl GU7 ... 151 A6
Streeters La SM6 ... 60 D7
Streetfield GU8 ... 169 C4
Streetfield Rd RH13 ... 215 E3
Streets Heath GU24 ... 67 F7
Stretton Rd Croydon CR0 . 42 E2
Richmond TW10 ... 17 C6
Strickland Cl 4 RH11 .. 200 E5
Strickland Row SW18 ... 20 D8
Strides Ct KT16 ... 51 C4
Stringer's Ave GU4 ... 109 D7
Stringhams Copse GU23 . 91 A3
Strode Ho 3 SW2 ... 22 A7
Strode St TW20 ... 12 A4
Strode's Coll TW20 ... 11 F3
Strode's Cres TW18 ... 13 C3
Strodes College La TW20 11 F3
Strood Ho 11 SE20 ... 23 C1
Strood La
Warnham RH12 ... 216 C7
Winkfield SL5 ... 9 C2
Stroud Cres SW15 ... 19 A5
Stroud Green Gdns CR0 . 43 C2
Stroud Green Way CR0 .. 43 C3
Stroud La
Shamley Green GU5 ... 153 A3
Yateley GU17 ... 64 A4
Stroud Rd Croydon SE25 .. 43 A3
Wimbledon SW19 ... 20 A5
Stroud Way TW15 ... 14 B2
Stroude Rd Egham TW20 .. 12 A1
Thorpe GU25,TW20 ... 31 E6
Stroudes Cl KT4 ... 38 F2
Stroudley Cl RH10 ... 202 B5
Stroudwater Pk KT13 ... 53 C4
Strudgate Cl RH10 ... 202 B4
Strudwicks Field GU6 .. 174 F4
Stuart Ave KT12 ... 35 C1
Stuart Cl Crawley RH10 . 202 D5
Farnborough GU14 ... 85 A5
Stuart Cres Croydon CR0 .. 62 F7
Reigate RH2 ... 139 A6
Stuart Ct Godalming GU7 . 150 E4
16 Redhill RH1 ... 119 A2
Stuart Gr TW11 ... 16 E3
Stuart Ho Bracknell RG42 . 26 F8
5 Horsham RH13 ... 217 F3
Stuart Lodge
7 Epsom KT18 ... 76 D6
South Norwood SE25 ... 42 E7
Stuart Pl CR4 ... 40 F8
Stuart Rd Reigate RH2 .. 139 A6
Richmond TW10 ... 17 B5
South Norwood CR7 ... 42 C5
Warlingham CR3,CR6 ... 101 C7
Wimbledon SW19 ... 20 A5
Stuart Way
East Grinstead RH19 ... 205 F7
Staines TW18 ... 13 B2
Virginia Water GU25 ... 31 A5
Stubbs Folly GU47 ... 64 D7
Stubbs Ho SE19 ... 22 D1
Stubbs La KT20 ... 118 A7
Stubbs Moor Rd GU14 ... 84 F5
Stubbs Way 4 SW19 ... 40 D8
Stubfield RH12 ... 217 A3
Stubs Cl RH4 ... 136 C5
Stubs Hill RH4 ... 136 C4
Stubs Ind Site GU11 ... 105 E5
Stucley Rd TW5,TW7 ... 5 C7
Studios Rd TW17 ... 33 F6
Studland Rd Byfleet KT14 . 71 F6
Kingston u T KT2 ... 17 E2
Penge SE26 ... 23 D3
Study Prep Sch The SW19 ... 19 C3
Stumblets RH10 ... 202 C7
Stumps Hill La BR3 ... 24 A2
Sturdee Cl GU16 ... 65 E1
Sturges Rd RG40 ... 25 D5
Sturt Ave GU27 ... 207 F5
Sturt Ct GU4 ... 110 B3
Sturt Rd Frimley GU16 ... 85 F5
Haslemere GU27 ... 207 F5
Heath End GU9 ... 125 B7
Sturt's La KT20 ... 117 A8
Stychens Cl RH1 ... 120 C2
Stychens La RH1 ... 120 C2
Styles End KT23 ... 114 B8
Styles Way BR3 ... 44 C5
Styventon Pl KT16 ... 32 F2
Subrosa Dr RH1 ... 119 B5
Succomb's Hill CR3,CR6 101 B7
Succombs Pl CR6 ... 101 B8
Sudbrook Gdns TW10 ... 17 E5
Sudbrook La TW10 ... 17 E6
Sudbury Gdns CR0 ... 61 E6
Suffield Cl CR2 ... 81 D7
Suffield La GU3 ... 128 B2
Suffield Rd SE20 ... 43 C7
Suffolk Cl Bagshot GU19 .. 47 E2
Horley RH6 ... 161 A2
Suffolk Ct 3 SW16 ... 22 A4
Suffolk Dr GU4 ... 110 B6
Suffolk Ho
4 Croydon CR0 ... 61 D8
Suffolk Ho *continued*
Penge SE20 ... 43 C8
Suffolk Rd Barnes SW13 ... 7 F7
South Norwood SE25 ... 42 F5
Worcester Park KT4 ... 57 F8
Sugden Rd KT7 ... 37 B1
Sulina Rd SW2 ... 21 E8
Sullington Hill RH11 ... 201 D4
Sullington Mead RH12 . 216 E3
Sullivan Cl
East Molesey KT8 ... 36 B6
Farnborough GU14 ... 85 A4
Sullivan Ct 4 CR0 ... 43 A1
Sullivan Dr RH11 ... 200 E3
Sullivan Ho Kenley CR8 .. 80 C5
Twickenham TW2 ... 5 D1
Sullivan Rd GU15 ... 65 A5
Sullivans Reach KT12 ... 35 A2
Sultan St BR3 ... 43 D7
Summer Ave KT8 ... 36 E4
Summer Gdns
Frimley GU15 ... 66 C5
Thames Ditton KT8 ... 36 E4
Summer Rd
East Molesey KT8 ... 36 D4
Thames Ditton KT7,KT8 ... 36 F4
Summer Trees TW16 ... 35 B8
Summer's Rd GU7 ... 151 A8
Summerene Cl SW16 ... 21 C1
Summerfield KT21 ... 95 D8
Summerfield La
Long Ditton KT6 ... 56 D8
Rowledge GU10 ... 146 B2
Summerfield Pl KT16 ... 51 D4
Summerfield St SE12 ... 24 F8
Summerfields Cl KT15 ... 51 F5
Summerhayes Cl GU21 .. 69 E5
Summerhays KT11 ... 73 D6
Summerhill GU7 ... 150 D6
Summerhill Way CR4 ... 41 A8
Summerhouse Ave TW5 .. 4 E6
Summerhouse Cl GU7 .. 150 D4
Summerhouse Ct GU26 . 188 D3
Summerhouse La UB7 ... 2 D8
Summerhouse Rd GU7 . 150 D3
Summerlands GU6 ... 174 E4
Summerlay Cl KT20 ... 97 E7
Summerleigh 5 KT13 ... 53 D4
Summerley St SW18 ... 20 B6
Summerly Ave RH2 ... 118 A2
Summers Cl Belmont SM2 59 A3
Weybridge KT13 ... 72 A8
Summers La GU7 ... 150 A8
Summersbury Dr GU4 .. 130 E1
Summersbury Hall GU4 130 E1
Summersby Cl GU7 ... 150 F7
Summersell Ho SE27 ... 22 D3
Summerstown SW17 ... 20 C4
Summersvere Cl RH10 . 182 A1
Summerswood Cl CR8 ... 80 D3
Summerville Gdns SM1 .. 58 F4
Summerwood Rd TW1, TW7 ... 5 F1
Summit Ave GU14 ... 84 C3
Summit Ctr
Farnborough GU14 ... 84 D4
Harmondsworth UB7 ... 2 D7
Summit Pl KT13 ... 53 A3
Summit The TW16 ... 15 A1
Summit Way SE19 ... 22 E1
Sumner Cl KT22 ... 94 D3
Sumner Ct GU9 ... 125 C3
Sumner Gdns CR0 ... 42 A1
Sumner Pl KT15 ... 52 A5
Sumner Rd Farnham GU9 125 C3
Thornton Heath CR0 ... 42 B1
Sumner Rd S CR0 ... 42 A1
Sun Alley 5 TW9 ... 6 E3
Sun Brow GU27 ... 208 A5
Sun Hill GU22 ... 89 A6
Sun Inn Rd GU8 ... 192 F5
Sun Life Trad Est TW14 ... 4 A4
Sun Ray Est GU47 ... 64 A8
Sunbury Ave SW14 ... 7 D3
Sunbury Cl KT12 ... 35 A3
Sunbury Court Island TW16 ... 35 D6
Sunbury Court Rd TW16 . 35 C7
Sunbury Cres TW13 ... 14 F4
Sunbury Cross Ctr 9 TW16 ... 14 F1
Sunbury Ct TW16 ... 35 D7
Sunbury Ct (Con Ctr) TW16 ... 35 D7
Sunbury Int Bsns Ctr TW16 ... 34 E8
Sunbury La KT12 ... 35 A3
Sunbury Manor Sch TW16 ... 34 F8
Sunbury Rd Cheam SM3 .. 58 E7
Feltham TW13 ... 14 F4
Sunbury Sta TW16 ... 35 A8
Sunbury Way TW13 ... 15 C3
Suncroft Pl SE26 ... 23 C5
Sundale Ave CR2 ... 62 C1
Sunderland Ct
Dulwich SE22 ... 23 A8
11 Stanwell TW19 ... 2 E1
Sunderland Mount SE23 . 23 D6
Sunderland Rd SE23 ... 23 D6
Sundew Cl Crawley RH11 201 A2
Lightwater GU18 ... 67 D8
Wokingham RG40 ... 25 E7
Sundial Ave SE25 ... 42 F6
Sundial Ct KT5 ... 57 B8
Sundon Cres GU25 ... 31 C4
Sundown Ave CR2 ... 80 F8
Sundown Rd TW15 ... 14 C3

Sundridge Rd
Croydon CR0,CR9 ....43 A1
Old Woking GU22 ......90 A7
Sunhill Ho RH9 ....142 E2
Sunkist Way SM6 ......60 E2
Sunlight Cl SW19 ......20 C2
Sunmead Cl KT22 ......94 F5
Sunmead Rd TW16 ......35 A6
Sunna Gdns TW16 ......35 B7
Sunniholme Ct CR2 ....61 C5
Sunning Ave SL5 ......29 E2
Sunning Ho Ascot SL5 .29 C5
Windlesham GU20 ......48 F8
Sunningdale RH6 ......161 B2
Sunningdale Ave TW13 .15 E6
Sunningdale Cl **2** KT6 .56 E8
Sunningdale Ct
Crawley RH10 ....201 D4
16 Kingston u T KT2 ...18 A1
Sunningdale Park (Civil
Service Coll) SL5 .....29 A4
Sunningdale Rd SM1 ...58 F6
Sunningdale Sch SL5 ..29 F3
Sunningdale Sta SL5 ..30 A2
Sunninghill Cl SL5 ....29 D5
Sunninghill Ct SL5 ....29 D5
Sunninghill Lodge
Ascot SL5 ....29 C7
Ascot SL5 ....29 D5
Sunninghill Rd Ascot SL5 .29 D5
Windlesham GU20 ......48 A7
Winkfield SL4,SL5 .....9 E2
Sunningvale Ave TN16 ..83 D3
Sunningvale Cl TN16 ...83 D3
Sunny Ave RH10 ......204 A8
Sunny Bank Croydon SE25 .43 A6
Epsom KT18 ....76 C3
Warlingham CR6 ....81 E2
Sunny Down GU8 .....170 E5
Sunny Hill Rd GU11 ..104 D2
Sunny Nook Gdns CR2 .61 D4
Sunny Rise CR3 ......100 D3
Sunny View Cl GU12 ..105 C1
Sunnybank SL5 ....29 A5
Sunnybank Mews GU22 .106 B3
Sunnybank Rd GU14 ...84 D6
Sunnybank Villas RH1 .120 F3
Sunnycroft Rd
Croydon SE25 ....43 A6
Hounslow TW3 ....5 B5
Sunnydell La GU10 ...146 A3
Sunnydene Rd CR8 ....80 B6
Sunnydene St SE26 ....23 E4
Sunnydown Sch CR3 ..100 F6
Sunnyhill GU8 ....170 E6
Sunnyhill Cl RH10 ...204 A8
Sunnyhill Prim Sch SW16 .21 E4
Sunnyhill Rd SW16 ....21 E4
Sunnyhurst Cl SM1 ....59 A7
Sunnymead RH11 .....201 D6
Sunnymead Ave CR4,
SW16 ....41 D6
Sunnymede Ave
Sutton SM5 ....78 D8
West Ewell KT19 ......57 E3
Sunnyside
Walton-on-T KT12 ......35 C4
Wimbledon SW19 ......19 E2
Sunnyside Pl SW19 ....19 E2
Sunnyside Rd
Headley Down GU35 ..187 C4
Teddington TW11 ......16 F4
Sunray Ave KT5 ....57 B8
Sunrise Cl TW13 ......15 F5
Sunset Gdns SE25 .....42 F7
Sunset Rd SW19 ......19 B3
Sunshine Way CR4 ....40 F7
Sunstone Gr RH1 .....119 E6
Sunvale Ave GU27 ....207 D6
Sunvale Cl GU27 .....207 D6
Surbiton Boys Prep Sch
KT6 ....37 E4
Surbiton Cres KT1,KT6 .37 E5
Surbiton Ct KT6 ......37 D3
Surbiton Hall Cl KT1 ..37 E5
Surbiton High Sch For Girls
KT1 ....37 E5
Surbiton Hill Pk KT5 ..38 A4
Surbiton Hill Rd KT6 ..37 E4
Surbiton Hospl KT6 ...37 E5
Surbiton Rd
Camberley GU15 ......47 A1
Kingston u T KT1 .....37 E5
Surbiton Sta KT6 .....37 E3
Surrey Ave GU15 ......65 A4
Surrey Bsns Pk KT17 ..76 E8
Surrey Cloisters GU7 .150 F6
Surrey Countryside Scheme
Vst Ctr★ GU4 ....132 A7
Surrey Ct SM6 ....60 C4
Surrey Gdns KT24 .....93 A4
Surrey Gr SM1 ....59 D7
Surrey Heath Mus★
GU15 ....65 D6
Surrey Hills Ave KT20 .116 C4
Surrey Hills Way KT20 .116 C5
Surrey Inst of Art & Design
The GU9 ....125 A2
Surrey Inst of Art & Design
Univ Coll
Epsom KT18 ....76 D5
Ewell KT17 ....76 E7
Surrey Lodge SE1 .....54 B5
Surrey Mews SE27 ....22 E4
Surrey Mount SE23 ...23 B7
Surrey Rd BR4 ....44 B1
Surrey Research Pk The
GU2 ....129 D8

Surrey St CR0,CR9 .....61 C7
Surrey Tech Ctr GU2 .129 D8
Surrey Twrs KT15 .....52 C5
Surridge Ct GU19 .....47 E2
Surridge Gdns SE19 ...22 D2
Sury Basin KT2 ....37 E8
Sussex Ave TW7 ....5 E4
Sussex Cl Knaphill GU21 .68 C1
New Malden KT3 ......38 E5
Reigate RH2 ....139 D8
4 Twickenham TW1 ....6 B1
Sussex Ct Addlestone KT15 .52 C5
Barnes SW13 ....7 F5
Horsham RH13 ....217 E1
Knaphill GU21 ....68 C2
Sussex Gdns KT9 .....56 D4
Sussex Lodge RH12 ..217 C4
Sussex Manor Bsns Pk
RH10 ....182 A2
Sussex Mews SE6 .....24 A7
Sussex Pl KT3 ....38 E5
Sussex Rd Croydon CR2 .61 D4
Knaphill GU21 ....68 C1
Mitcham CR4 ....41 E4
New Malden KT3 ......38 E5
South Croydon CR2 ...61 D4
Wallington SM5 ....59 F4
2 West Wickham BR4 ..44 B1
Sussex Terr **3** SE20 ...23 C1
Sutherland Ave
Biggin Hill TN16 ......83 E1
Guildford GU4 ....109 E7
Hounslow TW16 ....34 F7
Sutherland Chase SL5 .28 E7
Sutherland Dr
Mitcham SW19 ....40 D8
Guildford GU4 ....110 A4
Sutherland Gdns
Mortlake SW14 ....7 E4
North Cheam KT4 .....39 B1
Sunbury TW16 ....34 F7
Sutherland Gr
Putney SW18,SW19 ...19 F8
Teddington TW11 .....16 E3
Sutherland Ho
Guildford GU4 ....110 A5
Richmond TW10 ....17 C6
9 Sutton SM2 ....59 C4
Sutherland Rd Chiswick W4 .7 E8
Thornton Heath CR0 ..42 A2
Sutton Arc SM1 ....59 B5
Sutton Ave GU21 .....88 C6
Sutton Cl BR3 ....44 B8
Sutton Common Rd
Cheam SM3 ....40 A1
Sutton SM1,SM3 ......59 B8
Sutton Common Sta SM1 59 B8
Sutton Court Rd
Chiswick W4 ....7 C8
Sutton SM1 ....59 C4
Sutton Courtenay Ho
SW17 ....20 D4
Sutton Ct Chiswick W4 .7 C8
East Molesey KT8 .....35 F4
Penge SE19 ....22 F1
Sutton SM2 ....59 C4
Sutton Dene TW3 ......5 B6
Sutton Gdns
Croydon CR0,SE25 ....42 F4
Merstham RH1 ....119 D6
Sutton Gr SM1 ....59 D5
Sutton Gram Sch For Boys
SM1 ....59 C5
Sutton Green Rd GU4 .89 F1
Sutton Hall TW5 ....5 A7
Sutton High Sch For Girls
SM1 ....59 B4
Sutton Hospl SM2 ....59 B1
Sutton Hts SM2 ......59 D3
Sutton La
Abinger Common GU5 .155 C8
Banstead SM2,SM7 ...78 B6
Brands Hill SL3 ....1 B8
Hounslow TW3,TW4,TW5 ..4 F5
Sutton La S W4 ....7 C8
Sutton Lodge GU1 ...109 E1
Sutton Park Rd SM1 ..59 B4
Sutton Pl Brands Hill SL3 ..1 B8
Peaslake RH5 ....154 F8
Sutton Rd Camberley GU15 .47 A1
Heston TW5 ....5 A6
Sutton Sq TW5 ....4 F6
Sutton Sta SM2 ......59 C4
Sutton Way TW5 ....4 F6
Swaby Rd SW17,SW18 .20 C6
Swaffield Prim Sch
SW18 ....20 C8
Swaffield Rd SW18 ...20 C8
Swail Ho **8** KT18 ......76 D6
Swain Cl SW16,SW17 ..21 B2
Swain Rd CR7 ....42 C4
Swains Rd CR4,SW17,
SW19 ....20 F1
Swale Ho **2** RH1 .....119 A3
Swale Rd GU14 ....84 E6
Swaledale RG12 ......27 A4
Swaledale Cl RH11 ...201 C3
Swallands Rd SE6 ....24 A5
Swallow Cl Staines TW18 .12 F4
Witley GU8 ....170 F2
Swallow Gdns SW16 ..21 D3
Swallow La RH5 ......136 B1
Swallow Pk KT6 ....56 F7
Swallow Rd RH11 ....201 C8
Swallow Rise GU21 ...68 C2
Swallow St RH10 ....204 C5

Swallowdale
New Addington CR2 ...62 D2
Selsdon CR2 ....62 D2
Swallowfield
Dormansland RH7 ....165 A2
Englefield Green TW20 .11 B2
Swallows Ct SE20 .....23 D1
Swallowtail Rd RH12 ..217 E6
Swan Barn Rd GU27 .208 D6
Swan Cl Croydon CR0 .42 E2
Feltham TW13 ....15 E4
Swan Ct Feltham TW13 .15 E4
Guildford GU1 ....109 D3
Leatherhead KT22 ....95 B5
Swan Ctr SW17 ....20 C5
Swan Ho GU47 ....64 B7
Swan La Charlwood RH6 .180 F7
Guildford GU1 ....130 D7
Sandhurst GU47 ......64 B7
Swan Mill Gdns RH4 ..115 D1
Swan Pl SW13 ....7 F5
Swan Rd TW13 ....15 E4
Swan Sq RH12 ....217 C2
Swan St TW7 ....6 B4
Swan Wlk Horsham RH12 217 C2
Oatlands Park TW17 ...34 E2
Swancote Gn RG12 ....27 B4
Swandrift TW18 ....12 F1
Swann Ct **6** TW7 ....6 A4
Swann Way RH12 ....216 E3
Swanns Mdw KT23 ....94 A1
Swans Ghyll RH18 ...206 E3
Swansea Rd TW14,TW6 .3 D1
Swansmere Sch KT12 ..35 C1
Swanton Gdns SW19 ..19 D7
Swanwick Cl SW15 ...18 F8
Swanworth La RH5 ...115 B7
Swayne's La GU1 .....110 E1
Swaynesland Rd RH8 ..123 F1
Swaything Ho SW15 ....7 F8
Swedish Sch SW13 .....7 F8
Sweeps Ditch Cl TW18 .13 B1
Sweeps La TW20 ......11 F3
Sweet La GU5 ....154 E8
Sweetbriar RG45 ......45 A7
Sweetwater Cl GU5 ..152 D4
Sweetwater La
Enton Green GU8 ....171 B2
Shamley Green GU5 ..152 D4
Swievelands Rd TN16 ..83 C1
Swift Ct SM2 ....59 B3
Swift La Crawley RH11 .201 C8
Windlesham GU19 ....47 F3
Swift Rd Feltham TW13 .15 E4
Heath End GU9 ......125 C7
Swift's Cl GU10 .....126 B1
Swiftsden Way BR1 ...24 E2
Swinburne Cres CR0 ..43 C3
Swindon Rd Harlington TW6 .3 C2
Horsham RH12 ....217 B4
Swinfield Cl TW13 ....15 E4
Swingate Rd GU9 ....146 D8
Swinley Prim Sch SL5 .29 A4
Swinley Rd SL5 ....28 C4
Swiss Cl GU10 ....146 A4
Swissland Hill RH19,RH7 185 E7
Switchback La
Rowledge GU10 ......145 F4
Rowledge GU10 ......146 A3
Swordsman's Rd GU46 .86 D8
Sycamore Ave RH12 ..218 C4
Sycamore Cl
Carshalton SM5 ......59 F6
Crawley RH11 ....181 C1
Feltham TW13 ....15 A5
Fetcham KT22 ....94 F5
Frimley GU16 ....65 E1
Sandhurst GU47 ......64 B8
Sycamore Ct
Farncombe GU7 .....150 E8
Forest Hill SE26 ......23 C4
7 Guildford GU1 .....130 E8
Hounslow TW4 ....4 E3
Ottershaw KT16 ......51 C5
Oxted RH8 ....122 E6
Walton-on-T KT13 ....53 F7
11 West Norwood SW16 .22 A3
Sycamore Dr
Ash Vale GU12 ....106 A7
East Grinstead RH19 ..186 A1
Frimley GU16 ....65 E1
Wrecclesham GU10 ..146 A6
Sycamore Gdns CR4 ..40 D7
Sycamore Gr
Kingston u T KT3 .....38 E6
Penge SE19 ....43 A8
Sycamore Ho CR6 ....82 B4
Sycamore Lodge **7**
TW16 ....14 F1
Sycamore Rd
Farnborough GU14 ...85 D2
Guildford GU1 ....109 D1
Wimbledon SW19,SW20 .19 C2
Sycamore Rise
Banstead RH17,SM7 ..77 D5
Bracknell RG12 ......27 D6
Sycamore Way TW11 ..17 C2
Sycamore Wlk
Englefield Green TW20 .11 B2
Reigate RH2 ....139 C6
Sycamores The
Blackwater GU17 .....64 B5
Farnborough GU14 ...85 D3
Sydcote SE21 ....22 C7
Sydenham Ave SE26 ..23 B3
Sydenham High Sch For Girls
SE26 ....23 B3

Sydenham Hill SE21,SE22,
SE23, SE26,SE19 .....23 B5
Sydenham Hill Sta SE21 .22 F5
Sydenham Ho **16** KT6 .37 D2
Sydenham Ind Est SE26 .23 F3
Sydenham Park Mans
SE26 ....23 C5
Sydenham Park Rd SE23,
SE26 ....23 C5
Sydenham Pk SE26 ...23 C5
Sydenham Rd
Forest Hill SE26,SE6 .23 D3
Guildford GU1 ....130 E8
Thornton Heath CR0 ..42 D2
Sydenham Rise SE23 ..23 B6
Sydenham Sch SE26 ..23 B5
Sydenham Sta SE26 ..23 C4
Sydenham Station App
SE26 ....23 C3
Sydmons Ct SE23 .....79 F7
Sydney Cl RG45 ......45 C7
Sydney Cotts KT10 ...55 F4
Sydney Cres TW15 ...14 B2
Sydney Pl GU1 ......130 E7
Sydney Rd
East Bedfont TW14 ...15 A7
Guildford GU1 ....130 E8
Merton SW20 ....39 D7
Richmond TW10,TW9 ..6 E3
Sutton SM1 ....59 A6
Teddington TW11 .....16 F3
Sydney Terr KT10 ....55 F4
Sydney Villas GU12 ..106 A8
Sylva Ct **3** SW15 .....19 D8
Sylvan Cl Limpsfield RH8 .123 B6
South Croydon CR2 ...62 B1
Woking GU22 ....70 B2
Sylvan Gdns KT6 .....37 D2
Sylvan Hill SE19 ......42 E8
Sylvan Rd Crawley RH10 .202 A4
South Norwood SE19 ..42 F8
Sylvan Ridge GU47 ...45 A1
Sylvan Way
Coney Hall BR4 ....63 E6
Redhill RH1 ....140 A8
Sylvanus RG12 ....26 F2
Sylvaways Cl GU6 ...175 A3
Sylverdale Rd
Croydon CR0,CR9 ....61 B7
Purley CR8 ....80 B6
Syon Gate Way TW7,7 SW8 .6 A7
Syon House & Pk★ TW8 .6 C6
Syon La Brentford TW7 ..5 F8
Hounslow TW7 ....6 A7
Syon Lane Sta TW7 ...6 A7
Syon Park Cotts TW8 ..6 C6
Syon Park Gdns TW7 ..5 F7
Syon Park SW7 ....6 B6
Syon Pl GU14 ....85 D4
Sythwood GU21 ......69 B2
Sythwood Prim Sch
GU21 ....69 B3
Szabo Cres GU3 .....107 B1

T

Tabard Ho KT1 ....37 C8
Tabarin Way KT17 ....77 C3
Tabor Ct SM3 ....58 E4
Tabor Gdns SM2,SM3 .58 F3
Tabor Gr SW19 ....19 F1
Tachbrook Rd TW14 ..14 F8
Tadlow KT1 ....38 A6
Tadmor Cl TW16 ......34 F7
Tadorne Rd KT20 .....97 C5
Tadworth Ave KT3 ....38 F4
Tadworth Cl KT20 ....97 D5
Tadworth Prim Sch KT20 97 C5
Tadworth St KT20 ....97 C5
Tadworth Sta KT20 ...97 C5
Taffy's How CR4 .....40 E6
Taggs Ho KT1 ....37 D7
Tait Rd CR0,SE25 ....42 E2
Talavera Inf Sch GU11 .105 B3
Talavera Jun Sch GU11 .105 B3
Talbot Cl Mytchett GU16 .86 A4
Reigate RH2 ....139 B8
Talbot La RH12 ......217 C1
Talbot Lodge KT10 ...55 A5
Talbot Pl GU19 ....47 E4
Talbot Rd Ashford TW15 .13 E3
Farnham GU9 ....146 B8
Isleworth TW1,TW7 ....6 A3
Lingfield RH7 ....164 D4
South Norwood CR7 ..42 D5
Twickenham TW2 .....16 F7
Wallington SM5 ......60 A5
Talcott Path **12** SW2 ..22 A7
Taleworth Cl KT21 ...95 D7
Taleworth Pk KT21 ...95 D7
Taleworth Rd KT21 ...95 E7
Talfourd Way RH1 ...140 A6
Talgarth Dr GU14 ....85 D2
Taliesin Hts GU7 ....150 D6
Talisman Sq SE26 ....23 A4
Talisman Way KT17 ...77 C3
Tall Elms Cl BR2 .....44 F4
Tall Trees Poyle SL3 ....1 E6
Thornton Heath SW16 .41 E6
Tallis Cl RH11 ....200 F3
Tally Rd RH8 ....123 E4
Talma Gdns TW2 .....16 E8
Talmage Cl SE23 .....23 C8
Talman Cl RH11 .....200 E5
Tamar Cl RH10 ......202 C5
Tamarind Cl GU2 ....109 A6

Tamarind Ct **3** TW20 ..11 F3
Tamarisk Rise RG40 ..25 C7
Tamerton Sq **1** GU22 .89 E8
Tamesa Ho TW17 .....34 A2
Tamesis Gdns KT4 ...57 E8
Tamian Ind Est TW4 ...4 C3
Tamian Way TW4 ......4 C3
Tamworth RG12 ......27 D2
Tamworth La CR4 .....41 B6
Tamworth Manor High Sch
CR4 ....41 D6
Tamworth Pk CR4 ....41 B6
Tamworth Pl **3** CR0,CR9 .61 C8
Tamworth Rd CR0,CR9 .61 C8
Tanbridge Ho RH12 ..217 B1
Tanbridge House Sch
RH12 ....216 F2
Tanbridge Pk RH12 ..217 B1
Tanbridge Pl RH12 ..217 B1
Tandem Ctr SW19 ....40 D8
Tandridge Ct
Caterham CR3 ....101 A5
Sutton SM2 ....59 B4
Tandridge Gdns CR2 ..81 A6
Tandridge La RH7,RH8 .143 B4
Tandridge Rd CR6 ...101 D8
Tandridgehill La RH9 .121 F6
Tanfield Ct RH12 ....217 B2
Tanfield Rd CR0,CR9 ..61 C6
Tangier Ct GU11 ....104 F2
Tangier Rd
Guildford GU1 ....131 A8
Mortlake TW10 ....7 B4
Tangier Way KT20 ....77 E1
Tangier Wood KT20 ..77 E1
Tangle Oak RH19 ....184 E4
Tanglewood Cl
Longcross KT16 ......50 B7
South Croydon CR0 ..62 C7
Woking GU22 ....70 D3
Tanglewood Ride GU24 .67 A7
Tanglewood Way TW13 .15 B5
Tangley Dr RG41 .....25 B4
Tangley Gr SW15 .....18 F8
Tangley La GU3 .....108 F6
Tangley Park Rd TW12 .15 F3
Tanglyn Ave TW17 ...34 B4
Tangmere Gr KT2 .....17 D3
Tangmere Rd RH11 ..200 F6
Tanhouse La RG41 ...25 A5
Tanhouse Rd RH8 ...122 E3
Tanhurst Ho **27** SW2 ..21 E8
Tanhurst La RH5 .....155 E2
Tank Rd GU15 ....64 F5
Tankerton Rd KT6 ....56 F8
Tankerton Terr CR0 ..41 F3
Tankerville Rd SW16 ..21 E1
Tanner Ho **1** SW19 ...40 C8
Tanner's Ct RH3 ....137 C5
Tanner's Hill RH3 ...137 B8
Tanners Cl KT12 .....35 B3
Tanners Ct GU27 ....208 C2
Tanners Dean KT22 ..95 D5
Tanners La GU27 ....208 C2
Tanners Mdw RH3 ...137 B5
Tanners Yd GU19 .....47 E3
Tannery Cl
Beckenham BR3,CR0 .43 D4
Slinfold RH13 ....215 D3
Tannery La GU23 .....90 E5
Tannery The RH1 ....118 F1
Tannsfeld Rd SE26 ...23 D3
Tansy Cl GU4 ....110 C3
Tantallon Rd SW12 ...21 A7
Tanyard Ave RH19 ...202 A3
Tanyard Cl Crawley RH10 .202 C3
Horsham RH13 ....217 E1
Tanyard La GU5 .....151 F8
Tanyard Way RH6 ...161 B4
Tapestry Cl SM2 .....59 B3
Taplow Ct CR4 ....40 E5
Tapner's Rd RH2 ....137 F3
Tapping Cl **5** KT2 ....18 A1
Tara Ct **4** BR3 ....44 B7
Taragon Ct GU2 .....109 A5
Tarbat Ct **6** GU47 ....64 D8
Target Cl TW14 ....3 E1
Tarham Ct RH6 ......160 E5
Tarleton Gdns SE23 ..23 B7
Tarmac Way UB7 ......2 B7
Tarn Cl GU14 ....84 E2
Tarn Rd GU26 ......188 E3
Tarnbrook Way RG12 .27 E2
Tarquin Ho SE26 .....23 A4
Tarragon Cl GU14 ....84 C4
Tarragon Dr GU2 ....109 A5
Tarragon Gr SE26 ....23 D2
Tarrington Cl SW16 ..21 D5
Tartar Hill KT11 ......73 B6
Tartar Rd KT11 ....73 C6
Tasker Cl UB7 ....3 C7
Tasman Ct TW16 .....14 E1
Tatchbury Ho SW15 ...7 F1
Tate Cl KT22 ....95 C4
Tate Rd SM1 ....59 A5
Tate's Way RH12 ....214 D7
Tatham Ct RH11 .....201 B1
Tatsfield La TN16 ...103 F6
Tatsfield Prim Sch
TN16 ....103 D6
Tattenham Corner Rd
KT18 ....77 A1
Tattenham Corner Sta
KT18 ....77 B1

Tattenham Cres KT18 77 B1
Tattenham Gr KT18 97 B8
Tattenham Way KT18, KT20 77 E2
Tattersall Cl RG40 25 E5
Taunton Ave
Caterham CR3 100 F4
Hounslow TW3 5 C5
Wimbledon SW20 39 B7
Taunton Cl SM3 40 A1
Taunton La CR5 100 B8
Tavern Cl SM5 40 E2
Tavistock Cl TW18 13 D1
Tavistock Cres CR4 41 E5
Tavistock Ct 1 CR0 42 D1
Tavistock Gdns GU14 85 B7
Tavistock Gr CR0 42 D2
Tavistock Rd
Carshalton SM5 40 D1
Croydon CR0 42 D1
Tavistock Wlk SM5 40 D1
Tavy Ho 3 RH1 118 F2
Tawfield RG12 26 E2
Tawny Cl TW13 15 A5
Tay Cl GU14 84 E6
Tayben Ave TW2 5 E1
Tayles Hill Dr KT17 57 F1
Tayles Hill Ho KT17 57 F1
Taylor Ave TW9 7 B5
Taylor Cl Epsom KT19 76 A8
Hampton TW12 16 C3
Hounslow TW3 5 C6
Taylor Ct SE20 43 C7
Taylor Ho 10 SW2 22 A7
Taylor Rd Ashstead KT21 75 D2
Farnborough GU11 105 D7
Mitcham CR4,SW19 20 E1
Wallington SM6 60 B5
Taylor Wlk RH11 201 C6
Taylor's La SE26 23 B4
Taylors Cres GU6 174 F3
Taylors Ct TW13 15 A6
Taymount Grange SE23 23 C6
Taymount Rise SE23 23 C6
Taynton Dr RH1 119 D6
Teal Cl Horsham RH12 217 C5
Selsdon CR2 81 D8
Teal Ct 5 Dorking RH4 136 A8
Wallington SM6 60 C5
Teal Pl SM1 58 F5
Tealing Dr KT19 57 D6
Teasel Cl Crawley RH11 201 B3
Croydon CR0 43 D1
Teazlewood Pk KT22 75 A1
Tebbit Cl RG12 27 D7
Tebbs Ho 14 SW2 22 A8
Teck Cl TW7 6 A5
Tedder Cl KT9 56 C5
Tedder Rd CR2 62 D2
Teddington Cl KT19 57 D1
Teddington Meml Hospl TW11 16 E2
Teddington Park Rd TW11 16 F4
Teddington Pk TW11 16 F3
Teddington Sch TW11 17 C2
Teddington Sta TW11 17 A2
Tedham La RH9 163 B7
Tees Cl GU14 84 E6
Teesdale RH11 201 C3
Teesdale Ave TW7 6 A6
Teesdale Gdns
Isleworth TW7 6 A6
South Norwood SE25 42 E7
Teevan Cl CR0 43 A2
Teevan Rd CR0,CR9 43 A2
Tegg's La GU22 70 F3
Tekels Ave GU15 65 D4
Tekels Ct GU15 65 E4
Tekels Way GU15 65 F3
Telconia Cl GU35 187 C4
Telegraph La KT10 55 F5
Telegraph Rd SW15 19 C8
Telegraph Tk SM5,SM6 60 A1
Telfer Ho 8 SE21 22 E4
Telferscot Prim Sch SW12 21 D7
Telferscot Rd SW12 21 D7
Telford Ave
Crowthorne RG45 45 C8
Streatham SW12,SW2 21 E7
Telford Avenue Mans 7 SW2 21 E7
Telford Cl SE19 22 F2
Telford Ct 2 GU1 130 F8
Telford Dr KT12 35 C2
Telford Parade Mans 8 SW2 21 E7
Telford Pl RH10 201 E5
Telford Rd TW2 16 A8
Telham Ct 5 RH11 200 F3
Tellisford KT10 55 B6
Temperley Rd SW12 21 A8
Tempest Ho 9 KT2 37 E8
Tempest Rd TW20 12 C2
Templar Cl GU47 64 A8
Templar Ct CR0 62 E2
Templar Pl TW12 16 A1
Temple Ave CR0 62 F7
Temple Bar Rd GU21 88 F8
Temple Cl RH10 202 D5
Temple Ct 9 TW10 6 E2
Temple Field Cl KT15 52 B4
Temple Gdns TW18 32 F8
Temple La RH5 178 F5
Temple Market KT13 53 B6
Temple Rd
Biggin Hill TN16 83 D2
Croydon CR0 61 D6
Epsom KT19 76 D7
Hounslow TW3 5 C3
Richmond TW9 6 F4
Temple Sheen SW14 7 C2
Temple Sheen Rd SW14 7 C3
Temple Way
Bracknell RG42 26 E8
Carshalton SM1 59 D7
Temple Wood Dr RH1 118 F4
Temple's Cl GU10 126 C1
Templecombe Mews GU22 70 B3
Templecombe Way SM4 39 E4
Templecroft TW15 14 D2
Templedene BR2 44 D7
Templedene Ave TW18 13 C2
Templeman Cl CR8 80 B3
Templemere KT13 53 D7
Templer Ave GU14 85 A2
Templeton Cl CR7,SE19 42 D8
Templewood Ho RH1 118 F4
Ten Acre GU21 69 A1
Ten Acre La TW20 32 C7
Ten Acres KT22 94 D3
Ten Acres Cl KT22 94 D3
Tenbury Ct SW12 21 D7
Tenby Dr SL5 29 D4
Tenby Rd GU16 86 A8
Tenchley's La
Limpsfield RH8 123 D4
The Chart RH8 123 E2
Tenham Ave SW2 21 D6
Tenniel Cl GU2 109 B3
Tennison Cl CR5 100 B7
Tennison Rd SE25 42 F4
Tennyson Ave
Twickenham TW1 16 F7
West Barnes KT3 39 B4
Tennyson Cl
Crawley RH10 202 B8
Feltham TW14 4 A1
Horsham RH12 217 E6
Tennyson Ct 3 TW10 17 D4
Tennyson Rd
Addlestone KT15 52 E6
Ashford TW15 13 E3
Hounslow TW3 5 C5
Penge SE20 23 D1
Wimbledon SW19 20 C2
Tennyson Rise RH19 205 C8
Tennyson's La
Haslemere GU27 208 E4
Lurgashall GU27 209 A2
Tennysons GU27 208 E4
Tennysons Ridge GU27 208 E5
Tensing Ct TW19 13 E7
Tenterden Gdns CR0 43 A2
Tenterden Rd CR0 43 A2
Tern Rd RH11 200 D5
Terrace Gdns SW13 7 F5
Terrace La TW10 6 E1
Terrace Rd KT12 35 B3
Terrace The
Addlestone KT15 52 E5
Ascot SL5 29 D4
Barnes SW13, SW14 7 E5
Camberley GU15 65 A5
Crowthorne RG45 45 D5
Old Woking GU22 90 A6
Wokingham RG40 25 B6
Terracotta Rd RH9 142 C5
Terrapin Ct SW17 21 B5
Terrapin Rd SW17 21 B5
Terrapins KT6 37 D2
Terry Ho SW2 22 A7
Terry Rd RH11 201 B1
Tersha St TW9 6 E3
Testard Rd GU2 130 C7
Testers Cl RH8 123 B3
Teviot Cl GU2 109 A4
Tewkesbury Ave SE23 23 B8
Tewkesbury Cl KT14 71 D8
Tewkesbury Rd SM5 40 D1
Thackeray Cl
Isleworth TW7 6 A5
Wimbledon SW19 19 D1
Thackeray Manor SM1 59 C5
Thackery Lodge TW14 3 D1
Thakeham Cl SE26 23 B3
Thames Ave KT16 33 A6
Thames Bank SW14 7 C5
Thames Cl Chertsey KT16 33 C2
East Molesey TW12 36 B7
Farnborough GU14 84 E6
Thames Cotts KT7 37 B3
Thames Cres W4 7 E7
Thames Ct KT8 36 B7
Thames Ditton Inf Sch KT7 36 F3
Thames Ditton Island KT7 37 A4
Thames Ditton Jun Sch KT7 36 F2
Thames Ditton Sta KT7 36 F2
Thames Eyot 7 TW1 17 A7
Thames Haven KT6 37 D4
Thames Link Ho 6 TW9 6 E3
Thames Mdw
East Molesey KT8 36 A6
Lower Halliford KT12,TW17 34 E1
Thames Mead KT12 35 A2
Thames Rd W4 7 B8
Thames Side
Kingston u T KT1 37 D8
Thames Side *continued*
Laleham KT16,TW18 33 C4
Staines TW18 12 F2
Thames Ditton KT7 37 B3
Thames St
East Molesey TW12 36 B7
Kingston u T KT1,KT2 37 D7
Staines TW18 12 F3
Sunbury TW16 35 B6
Walton-on-T KT12 34 F2
Weybridge KT13 53 B7
Thames View Ho TW12 35 A3
Thames Village W4 7 C6
Thamesfield Ct TW17 34 C2
Thamesgate TW18 33 B8
Thamesgate Cl TW10 17 B4
Thameside TW11 17 D1
Thameside Ctr TW8 6 F8
Thamesmead Sch TW17 34 D3
Thamespoint TW11 17 D1
Thamesvale Cl TW3 5 A5
Thanescroft Ct CR0 61 F7
Thanescroft Gdns CR0 61 E7
Thanet Ho 1 SE27 22 B5
Thanet Pl CR0 61 C6
Tharp Rd SM6 60 D5
Thatcher Cl RH10 201 D3
Thatchers Cl Horley RH6 161 B5
Horsham RH12 217 E4
Thatchers La GU3 108 E8
Thatchers Way TW7 5 D2
Thaxted Pl 7 SW20 19 D1
Thayers Farm Rd BR3 43 E8
Theal Cl GU47 64 D8
Theatre Rd GU14 105 B8
Thelma Gr TW11 17 A2
Thelton Ave RH12 216 D3
Theobald Rd CR0,CR9 61 B8
Theobalds Way GU16 66 C3
Thepps Cl RH1 140 F6
Therapia La
Thornton Heath CR0 41 E3
Wallington CR0 41 D2
Wallington CR0 41 E2
Theresa's Wlk CR2 61 D2
Therfield Sch KT22 95 A8
Thesiger Rd BR3,SE20 23 D1
Thetford Ct SE21 23 B6
Thetford Rd Ashford TW15 13 E5
New Malden KT3 38 E4
Thetford Wlk RH11 200 E2
Thetis Terr TW9 7 A8
Theydon Cl RH10 202 A4
Thibet Rd GU47 64 C8
Thicket Cres SM1 59 C6
Thicket Ct 5 SM1 59 C6
Thicket Gr SE20 23 A1
Thicket Rd
Penge SE19,SE20 23 B1
Sutton SM1 59 C6
Thickthorne La TW18 13 C1
Third Cl KT8 36 C5
Third Cross Rd TW2 16 D6
Thirlestane Ct GU26 188 F5
Thirlmere Cl
Farnborough GU14 84 E4
Thorpe Lea TW20 12 B1
Thirlmere Ho TW1 5 F2
Thirlmere Rd
Crawley RH11 200 D4
Streatham SW16 21 D4
Thirlmere Rise BR1 24 F2
Thirlmere Wlk GU15 66 D4
Thirsk Ct GU12 105 D2
Thirsk Rd Mitcham CR4 21 A1
South Norwood SE25 42 D5
Thistle Way RH6 162 C3
Thistlecroft Rd KT12 54 C6
Thistledene
Thames Ditton KT7 36 E3
West Byfleet KT14 70 F6
Thistledown Vale RH14 212 D3
Thistlewood Cres CR0 82 D7
Thistleworth Cl TW7 5 D7
Thistley La GU6 174 E4
Thomas Ave CR3 100 C6
Thomas Bennett Com Coll RH10 201 D3
Thomas Dean Rd SE26 23 F4
Thomas Moore Ho RH2 118 C1
Thomas More Sch CR8 61 A1
Thomas Pooley Ct KT6 37 E2
Thomas Rd GU11 105 D7
Thomas Wall Cl SM1 59 B5
Thomas' La SE6 24 A8
Thompson Ave TW9 7 A4
Thompson Cl SM3 40 A1
Thompson Ct 16 RH11 201 B1
Thompson Rd TW3 5 B3
Thompson's La GU24 49 D2
Thompsons Cl GU24 87 D4
Thomson Cres CR0 42 A1
Thorburn Chase GU47 64 E6
Thorburn Way 2 SW19 40 D8
Thorfield GU8 169 C4
Thorkhill Gdns KT7 37 B1
Thorkhill Rd KT7 37 B2
Thorlands GU27 208 A7
Thorley Cl KT14 71 A5
Thorley Gdns KT14 71 A5
Thorn Bank GU2 130 A7
Thorn Cl GU10 145 F4
Thorn Rd GU10 146 A5
Thornash Cl GU21 69 C4
Thornash Rd GU21 69 C4
Thornash Way GU21 69 C4
Thornbank Cl TW19 2 A2
Thornbury Ave TW7 5 D7
Thornbury Cl RG45 45 B5
Thornbury Ct
Hounslow TW7 5 E7
Whyteleafe CR3 100 F7
Thornbury Rd TW7 5 D6
Thorncombe St GU5 151 E2
Thorncroft
Englefield Green TW20 11 C1
4 Leatherhead KT22 95 A5
Thorncroft Cl CR5 100 A8
Thorncroft Rd SM1 59 B6
Thorndean St SW18 20 C6
Thorndon Gdns KT19 57 E6
Thorndown La GU20 48 D3
Thorndyke Cl RH10 202 D5
Thorne Cl
Crowthorne RG45 45 A7
Littleton TW15 14 C1
Thorne St SW13,SW14 7 E4
Thorne's Cl BR3 44 C6
Thorneloe Gdns CR0,CR9 61 B5
Thorneycroft Cl KT12 35 C3
Thornfield Gn GU17 64 F3
Thornfield Rd SM7 78 A2
Thornhill Bracknell RG12 27 E5
Crawley RH11 201 B4
Thornhill Ave KT6 56 E8
Thornhill Cres GU11 105 C3
Thornhill Rd
Aldershot GU11 105 D4
Surbiton KT6 56 F8
Thornton Heath CR0 42 C2
Thornhill Way TW17 34 A4
Thornlaw Rd SE27 22 B4
Thornleas Pl KT24 92 E1
Thornsbeach Rd SE6 24 C6
Thornsett Pl SE20 43 B7
Thornsett Rd Penge SE20 43 B7
Wandsworth SW18 20 B7
Thornsett Terr SE20 43 B7
Thornton Ave
Streatham SW2 21 D7
Thornton Heath CR0 41 F3
Thornton Cl
Guildford GU2 109 A4
Horley RH6 160 E3
Thornton Cres CR5 100 A8
Thornton Ct SW20 39 D4
Thornton Dene BR3 44 A7
Thornton Gdns SW12 21 D7
Thornton Heath Sta CR7 42 C5
Thornton Hill SW19 19 E1
Thornton Pl RH6 160 F3
Thornton Rd
Carshalton SM5 40 D1
Mortlake SW14 7 D4
Streatham SW12,SW2 21 D7
Thornton Heath CR0,CR7, CR9 41 F3
Wimbledon SW19 19 D1
Thornton Rd E SW19 19 D2
Thornton Row CR7 42 A4
Thornville Gr CR4 40 D7
Thornycroft Ct TW9 6 F5
Thornyhurst Rd GU16 86 A4
Thorold Cl CR0,CR2 62 D1
Thorold Ho 6 SW2 21 E8
Thorold Rd GU9 125 C3
Thoroughfare The KT20 97 A3
Thorpe By-Pass TW20 32 B6
Thorpe CE Inf Sch TW20 32 B6
Thorpe Cl Forest Hill SE26 23 D4
New Addington CR0 82 C8
Wokingham RG41 25 A3
Thorpe Ind Est TW20 32 C7
Thorpe Ind Pk TW20 32 C8
Thorpe Lea Prim Sch TW20 12 D2
Thorpe Lea Rd TW20 12 C2
Thorpe Pk★ TW20 32 E5
Thorpe Rd Chertsey KT16 32 D4
Egham TW18,TW20 12 D3
Kingston u T KT2 17 E1
Thorpes Cl GU2 109 A4
Thorpeside Cl TW18, TW20 32 E7
Thorpewood Ave SE23, SE26 23 B6
Thorsden Cl GU22 89 E8
Thorsden Ct 10 GU22 69 E1
Thorsden Way 2 SE19 22 E3
Thrale Almhouses SW16 21 E3
Thrale Rd SW16 21 C3
Three Acres RH12 217 A1
Three Arch Rd RH1 140 A5
Three Bridges Fst Sch RH10 202 A7
Three Bridges Mid Sch RH10 201 F6
Three Bridges Rd RH10 202 A6
Three Bridges Sta RH10 202 B6
Three Gates GU1 110 C3
Three Gates La GU27 208 E8
Three Pears Rd GU1 110 E1
Three Stiles Rd GU9 124 F3
Three Ways GU10 166 D6
Threestile Rd RH12 197 F1
Threshfield RG12 27 A4
Thriffwood SE23,SE26 23 D5
Thrift Vale GU4 110 D4
Thrigby Rd KT9 56 F4
Throwley Rd SM1 59 B5
Throwley Way SM1 59 B5
Thrupp Cl CR4 41 B7
Thrupps Ave KT12 54 D5
Thrupps La KT12 54 D5
Thundery Hill GU10 126 F4
Thurbans Rd GU9 146 A7
Thurbarn Rd SE6 24 B3
Thurbarns Hill RH5 157 E1
Thurlby Rd SE27 22 A4
Thurleigh Rd SW11,SW12 20 F8
Thurleston Ave SM4 39 E4
Thurlestone Cl TW17 34 C3
Thurlestone Par TW17 34 C3
Thurlestone Rd SE27 22 A4
Thurlow Hill SE21 22 C6
Thurlow Ho 17 SW16 21 E5
Thurlow Park Rd SE21, SE24 22 C6
Thurlow Twrs SE27 22 A5
Thurlow Wlk GU6 174 E1
Thurlton Ct GU21 69 E3
Thurnby Ct TW2 16 E5
Thurne Way RH12 214 D7
Thurnham Way KT20 97 D7
Thursby Rd GU21 69 A1
Thursley Cres CR0 63 D3
Thursley Gdns SW19 19 D6
Thursley Ho
3 Kingston u T KT2 18 B1
13 Streatham SW2 21 F8
Thursley National Nature Reserve★ GU8 169 C5
Thursley Rd
Churt GU10,GU8 168 C3
Thursley GU8,GU10 169 B6
Thurso St SW17 20 D4
Thurstan Rd SW20 19 B1
Thurston Ho BR3 24 B2
Thurza Ct TW7 5 F5
Thyme Ct
Farnborough GU14 84 C5
Guildford GU4 110 B4
Thyme Ho RH10 182 A1
Tibbenham Pl SE6 24 A6
Tibbet's Cnr SW19 19 D8
Tibbet's Ride SW19 19 D8
Tibbets Cl SW19 19 D7
Ticehurst Cl RH10 202 E6
Ticehurst Rd SE23 23 E6
Tichborne Cl GU17 64 D5
Tichborne Pl GU12 126 D8
Tichbourne Cl GU16 65 F3
Tichmarsh KT19 57 C1
Tidenham Gdns CR0 61 E7
Tides End Ct GU15 65 F4
Tideswell Rd CR0 63 A7
Tideway Cl TW10 17 C4
Tideway Yd SW13 7 E5
Tidwells Lea RG12 27 E8
Tiepigs La BR2,BR4 44 F1
Tierney Ct 1 CR0 61 F8
Tierney Rd SW2 21 E7
Tierney Terr SW2 21 E7
Tiffin Girls' Sch The KT2 17 E2
Tiffin Sch KT2 37 F7
Tilburstow Cotts RH9 121 C3
Tilburstow Hill Rd RH9 142 D5
Tile Barn Cl GU14 85 A5
Tilehouse Rd GU4 130 E5
Tilehurst La
Betchworth RH3,RH5 136 F5
Dorking RH3,RH5 136 F5
Tilehurst Rd Cheam SM3 58 E5
Wandsworth SW17,SW18 20 D7
Tiler's Way RH2 139 C5
Tiler's Wlk RH2 139 C5
Tilford Ave CR0 63 C2
Tilford Gdns SW19 19 D7
Tilford Ho 11 SW2 21 F8
Tilford Rd
Beacon Hill GU10,GU26 188 D7
Farnham GU10,GU9 146 F7
Hindhead GU26 188 F4
Rushmoor GU10 168 C4
Tilford GU10 147 C4
Tilford St GU10 147 D5
Tilgate Comm RH1 120 C2
Tilgate Dr Crawley RH10 202 A2
Crawley RH10,RH11 201 E2
Tilgate Forest Bsns Ctr RH11 201 D1
Tilgate Mans RH10 201 F1
Tilgate Par RH10 201 E3
Tilgate Pk Ctry Pk★ RH10 201 F1
Tilgate Pl RH10 201 E3
Tilgate Way RH10 201 E3
Tilgates Cotts RH1 120 C3
Tilletts La RH12 216 E8
Tilley La KT18 96 C4
Tillingbourne Jun Sch GU4 131 B2
Tillingbourne Mews GU5 132 B4
Tillingbourne Rd GU4 130 E3
Tillingdown Hill CR3 101 A5
Tillingdown La
Caterham CR3 101 B2
Caterham CR3 101 B3
Tillman Ho 8 SW2 21 F7
Tillotson Cl RH10 202 D5
Tilly's La TW18 12 F4
Tilney Ct KT6 37 D4
Tilson Gdns SW2,SW4 21 E8
Tilson Ho SW2 21 E8
Tilt Cl KT11 73 E3
Tilt Mdw KT11 73 E3
Tilt Rd KT11 73 D3
Tilthams Corner Rd GU5,GU7 151 C8
Tilthams Gn GU7 151 B8
Tiltview KT11 73 C4
Tiltwood Dr RH10 204 C8
Timber Bank GU16 86 A6

Timber Cl Farnham GU9 ..125 B2
Great Bookham KT23 ...114 C8
Pyrford GU22 ....70 F5
Timber Ct RH12 ......217 C3
Timber Hill KT21 ......95 E8
Timber Hill Rd CR3 ..101 A3
Timber La CR3 ....101 A3
Timbercroft KT19 .....57 E6
Timberham Farm Rd
RH6 ....181 D8
Timberham Ho RH6 ..181 E8
Timberham Way RH6 .181 E8
Timberlands 14 RH11 .201 B1
Timberling Gdns CR2 .61 D1
Timbermill Ct GU27 ..207 F6
Timberslip Dr SM6 ....60 D2
Timbertop Rd TN16 ...83 C1
Times Sq SM1 ....59 B5
Timline Gn RG12 ......27 F7
Timperley Ct RH1 ....118 E3
Timperley Gdns RH1 .118 E3
Timsbury Wlk 5 SW15 .19 A7
Timsway TW18 ....12 F3
Tina Ct SW16 ....22 A5
Tindale Cl CR2 ....80 D8
Tinsey Cl TW20 ....12 B3
Tinsley Cl RH10 ......182 A1
Tinsley Gn RH10 .....182 B4
Tinsley La RH10 .....182 A1
Tinsley La N RH10 ...182 B3
Tinsley La S RH10 ...202 A8
Tintagel Cl KT17 ......76 F5
Tintagel Ct RH13 ....217 D1
Tintagel Dr KT22 ......65 F1
Tintagel Way GU22 ...70 A3
Tintells La KT24 .....112 B7
Tintern Cl SW19 ......20 C2
Tintern Rd
Carshalton SM5 ......40 D1
Crawley RH11 ....201 A4
Tippits Mead RG42 ...26 D8
Tipton Dr CR0 ....61 E6
Tiree Path RH11 .....201 B3
Tirlemont Rd CR2 .....61 C3
Tirrell Rd CR0 ....42 C3
Tisbury Rd SW16 .....41 E7
Titchfield Rd SM5 ....40 D1
Titchfield Wlk SM5 ...40 D2
Titchwell Rd SW18 ...20 D7
Tite Hill TW20 ....11 D3
Tithe Barn Cl KT2 ....37 F8
Tithe Barn The GU4 .111 D4
Tithe Cl GU25 ....31 D3
Tithe Ct RG40 ....25 C7
Tithe La TW19 ....1 A1
Tithe Orch RH19 ....184 E4
Tithepit Shaw La CR6 .81 B3
Titlarks Hill Rd SL5 ..30 B1
Titmus Dr RH10 .....201 F2
Titsey Cnr RH8 ......123 B7
Titsey Hill CR6,RH8 .103 B4
Titsey Pl★ RH8 ......123 B8
Titsey Rd Limpsfield RH8 .123 B8
Titsey RH8 ....103 B1
Tiverton Rd TW3 ......5 C5
Tiverton Way
Chessington KT9 .....56 D5
Frimley GU16 ....65 F1
Tivoli Rd Hounslow TW4 ..4 E3
West Norwood SE27 ..22 C3
Toad La GU17 ....64 E4
Tobias Sch of Art RH19 .205 E6
Toby Way KT5,KT6 ....57 B8
Todds Cl RH6 ....160 E5
Toftwood Cl RH10 ...202 C5
Toll Bar Ct SM2 ....59 B2
Toll Gdns RG12 ....27 E5
Tolldene Cl GU21 .....68 E2
Tollers Ct CR5 ....99 F8
Tollgate GU1 ....110 D1
Tollgate Ave RH1 ....139 F4
Tollgate Ct RH1 .....139 F4
Tollgate Dr SE21 ......22 E6
Tollgate Hill RH11 ..201 C1
Tollgate Prim Sch CR0 .43 C3
Tollgate Rd RH4 ....136 B4
Tollhouse La SM6 .....60 C2
Tolson Ho 2 TW7 ......6 A4
Tolson Rd TW7 ....6 A4
Tolvaddon GU21 ......69 A2
Tolverne Rd SW20 ....39 C8
Tolworth Cl KT6 ......57 B8
Tolworth Girls' Sch KT6 .56 F7
Tolworth Hospl KT6 ..57 A8
Tolworth Inf Sch KT6 .37 F1
Tolworth Jun Sch KT6 .37 F1
Tolworth Park Rd KT6 .56 F8
Tolworth Rd KT6 ......56 E8
Tolworth Rise N KT5 ..38 B1
Tolworth Rise S KT5 ..38 B1
Tolworth Sta KT5 .....57 B8
Tolworth Underpass KT5,
KT6 ....57 B8
Tomlin Cl KT19 ....76 D8
Tomlin Ct KT19 ....76 D8
Tomlins Ave KT6 ......56 E2
Tomlinscote Sch GU16 .66 A2
Tomlinscote Way GU16 .66 A2
Tompset's Bank RH18 .206 F1
Tomtit Cres RH10 ...204 C5
Tomtits La RH18 ....206 E1
Tonbridge Cl SM7 .....78 F5
Tonbridge Rd KT12,KT8 .35 F5
Tonfield Rd SM3 ......39 F1
Tonge Cl BR3 ....44 A4
Tongham Mdws GU10 .126 F7
Tongham Rd
Aldershot GU12 .....126 D8

Tongham Rd continued
Farnham GU10 ....126 C4
Tonstall Rd Epsom KT19 .76 D8
Mitcham CR4 ....41 A7
Tooting Bec Gdns SW16 .21 D4
Tooting Bec Rd
Streatham SW16 .....21 B4
Upper Tooting SW17 ..21 B4
Tooting Bec Sta SW17 .21 A4
Tooting Broadway SW17 .20 F3
Tooting Broadway Sta
SW17 ....20 E3
Tooting Gr SW17 ......20 E3
Tooting High St SW17,
SW19 ....20 E3
Tooting Mkt SW17 ....20 F3
Tooting Sta SW17 .....20 F2
Tootswood Rd BR2 ...44 E5
Top Pk BR3 ....44 E4
Topaz Ho KT4 ....38 D1
Topiary Sq TW9 ....6 F4
Topiary The
Ashtead KT21 ....95 E8
Farnborough GU14 ...84 E3
Toplady Pl GU9 ......125 C7
Topsham Rd SW17 ...21 A4
Tor La KT13 ....72 D8
Tor Rd GU9 ....124 F2
Torcross Dr SE23 .....23 C6
Torin Ct TW20 ....11 C3
Torland Dr KT22 ......74 D6
Tormead Cl SM1 ......59 A4
Tormead Rd GU1 ....109 F1
Tormead Sch GU1 ...109 F1
Toronto BR2 ....44 E6
Toronto Dr RH6 .....162 A3
Torr Rd SE20 ....23 D1
Torre Wlk SM5 ....40 E1
Torridge Rd Brands Hill SL3 ..1 B8
Thornton Heath CR7 ..42 B4
Torridon Cl GU21 .....69 B2
Torridon Inf Sch SE6 .24 D6
Torridon Jun Sch SE6 .24 D6
Torridon Rd SE13,SE6 .24 D7
Torrington Cl KT10 ...55 E4
Torrington Ct SE26 ...23 A3
Torrington Rd KT10 ..55 E4
Torrington Sq CR0 ...42 D2
Torrington Way SM4 .40 A3
Torwood La CR3 ....100 F8
Totford La GU10 ....127 E4
Totham Lodge SW20 .39 B8
Totland Cl GU14 ......85 A6
Tottenham Rd GU7 ..150 E6
Tottenham Wlk GU47 .45 D1
Totterdown St SW17 .20 F3
Totton Rd CR7 ....42 A6
Toulouse Cl GU1 .....66 B2
Tournai Cl GU11 .....105 E7
Toutley Rd RG41 .....25 A8
Tovil Cl SE20 ....43 B7
Tower Approach Rd
RH6 ....181 E6
Tower Cl
East Grinstead RH19 .185 E2
Hindhead GU26 .....188 E4
Horley RH6 ....160 F3
Penge SE20 ....23 B1
Woking GU21 ....69 D2
Tower Cotts KT10 .....54 F1
Tower Ct RH19 ......185 E2
Tower Gdns KT10 .....56 A3
Tower Gr KT13 ....53 E8
Tower Hill Dorking RH4 .136 B5
Farnborough GU14 ...85 A3
Tower Hill Com Prim Sch
GU14 ....84 F3
Tower Hill Rd RH4 ..136 B5
Tower Hill Rise GU5 .133 C3
Tower Pl CR6 ....82 A4
Tower Rd Crawley RH12 .218 F8
Hindhead GU26 .....188 E4
Tadworth KT20 ....97 C4
Twickenham TW1 .....16 F5
Tower Rise TW9 ....6 E4
Tower View CR0 ....43 E2
Towerhill GU5 ....133 C3
Towers Dr RG45 ......45 B4
Towers Pl TW10 ....6 E2
Towers The Kenley CR8 .80 C4
1 Richmond TW9 .....6 F3
Towers Wlk KT13 .....53 B4
Towfield Ct TW13 ....15 F6
Towfield Rd TW13 ...15 F6
Town Barn Rd RH11 .201 C2
Town End Cl
Caterham CR3 ....100 E5
Godalming GU7 .....150 E4
Town End St GU7 ...150 E4
Town Farm Prim Sch
TW19 ....13 D8
Town Farm Way TW19 .13 D8
Town Field Way TW7 ..6 A5
Town Hall (Mus)★ KT15 .33 A2
Town Hill RH7 ....164 E4
Town La TW19 ....13 D7
Town Mdw TW8 ....6 D7
Town Mead
Bletchingley RH1 ...120 D2
Crawley RH11 ....201 D2
Town Quay TW18 .....33 C6
Town Sq Bracknell RG12 .27 C4
Camberley GU15 .....65 C6
6 Woking GU21 ......69 F2
Town Tree Rd TW15 ..14 A3
Townend Ct 8 BR1 ...44 F8
Townfield Ct RH4 ...136 A6

Townfield Rd RH4 ...136 A6
Towngate KT11 ....73 E4
Townmead Rd TW9 ...7 B5
Townsend Cl RG12 ...27 E4
Townsend La GU22 ...90 B6
Townsend Rd TW15 ..13 E3
Townshend Rd TW9 ...6 F3
Townshend Terr TW9 ..6 F3
Townshott Cl KT23 ..94 A1
Townside Pl GU15 ....65 D6
Towpath Way CR0,SE25 ..42 F4
Towton Rd SE27 ......22 C6
Toynbee Rd SW19,SW20 .39 E8
Tracery The SM7 .....78 B4
Tracious Cl GU21 .....69 B3
Traemore Ct SW16 ...22 A5
Trafalgar Ave KT4,SM3,
SM4 ....39 D1
Trafalgar Com Inf Sch
RH12 ....217 B4
Trafalgar Ct Cobham KT11 .73 A6
Farnham GU9 ....125 C1
Hounslow TW3 ....4 F4
West Barnes KT3 .....39 B6
Trafalgar Inf Sch TW2 .16 D6
Trafalgar Jun Sch TW2 .16 D6
Trafalgar Rd
Horsham RH12 ......217 C4
Merton SW19 ....20 C1
Twickenham TW2 .....16 D6
Trafalgar Way
Camberley GU15 .....64 F4
Croydon CR0,CR9 ....60 F8
Trafford Rd Frimley GU16 .85 D8
Thornton Heath CR7 ..41 F4
Traherne Lodge 3 TW11 .16 F3
Tramsheds The CR0 ..41 D2
Tramway Path CR4 ...40 E5
Tranmere Rd
Twickenham TW2 .....16 B8
Wandsworth SW17,SW18 .20 C6
Tranquil Dale RH3 ..116 F3
Transport Ave TW8 ...6 B8
Transport Police Training Ctr
KT20 ....97 A4
Transport Rd GU14 ..85 B1
Trap La RH5 ....176 F2
Traps La KT2,KT3 .....38 E8
Trasher Mead RH4 ..136 C4
Travellers Way TW5 ..4 C5
Travis La GU47 ....64 C7
Treadcroft Dr RH12 .217 E5
Treadwell Rd KT18 ...76 F4
Treaty Ctr TW3 ....5 B4
Trebor Ave GU9 .....146 D8
Tredenham Cl GU14 .105 C8
Tredown Rd SE26 ....23 C3
Tredwell Cl SW2 ......21 F6
Tredwell Rd SE27 ....22 B4
Tree Cl TW10 ....17 D7
Tree Tops CR6 ....81 A1
Tree Tops Ave GU15 .66 B8
Tree View Cl SE19 ....42 E8
Treebourne Rd TN16 .83 C1
Treebys Ave GU4 ...109 D7
Treelands RH5 ......136 C4
Treemount Ct KT17 ..76 E6
Treen Ave SW13,SW14 ..7 F4
Treeside Dr GU9 ....125 E7
Treetops RH9 ....142 E6
Treetops Ct CR7 ......42 C4
Treeview RH11 ......201 C1
Treeview Ct 3 RH2 ..118 D1
Treeway RH2 ....118 B4
Trefoil Cl Horsham RH12 .217 E5
Wokingham RG40 ....25 E7
Trefoil Cres RH11 ...201 A2
Trefusis Ct TW5 ....4 B4
Tregaron Gdns KT3 ..38 E5
Tregarth Pl GU21 .....68 F2
Tregarthen Pl KT22 ..95 C6
Treglos Ct KT13 ......53 E8
Tregolls Dr GU14 ....85 D3
Trehaven Par RH2 ..139 B6
Trehern Rd 13 SW14 ..7 D4
Treherne Ct SW17 ...21 A4
Trelawn Cl KT16 ......51 C3
Trelawne Dr GU6 ...174 E2
Trelawney Gr KT13 ..53 A4
Treloar Gdns SE19 ...22 D2
Tremaine Rd SE20 ...43 B7
Trematon Pl TW11 ...17 C1
Tremayne Wlk GU15 .66 C4
Trenance GU21 ....69 A2
Trenchard Cl KT12 ...54 C5
Trenchard Ct SM4 ....40 A3
Trenear Cl RH13 ....217 E2
Trenham Dr CR6 ......81 C3
Trenholme Cl SE20 ..23 B1
Trenholme Ct CR3 ..101 A4
Trenholme Rd SE20 ..23 B1
Trenholme Terr SE20 .23 B1
Trent Cl Crawley RH11 .200 F4
Farnborough GU14 ...84 E6
Trent Ho 8 KT2 ....37 D8
Trent Rd SL3 ....1 B8
Trent Way KT4 ....58 C7
Trentham Cres GU22 .90 A6
Trentham Rd RH1 ...140 A7
Trentham St SW18 ...20 A7
Trenton Cl GU16 ......66 F1
Treport St SW18 .....20 B8
Treryn Hts GU7 .....150 D6
Tresco Cl BR1 ....24 E2
Tresidder Ho 10 SW4 .21 D8
Tresillian Way GU21 ..69 B2

Tresta Wlk GU21 ......69 A3
Trevanne Plat RH10 .202 D7
Trevelayan Rd SW17 .20 F2
Trevelgan RG12 ....26 E2
Trevelyan Ct KT3 .....38 F2
Trevelyan Ho 13 SE23 .23 D5
Trevelyan Rd SW17 ...20 F2
Trevenna Ho 13 SE23 .23 D5
Trevereux Hill RH8 .123 F4
Treversh Ct 9 BR1 ...44 F8
Treville St SW15 ......19 B8
Treviso Rd SE23 ......23 D6
Trevithick Cl TW14 ..14 F7
Trevor Cl Hayes BR2 .44 F2
Isleworth TW7 ....5 F2
Trevor Rd SW19 ......19 E1
Trevose Ave KT14 ....70 F5
Trewenna Dr KT9 .....56 D5
Trewince Rd SW20 ...39 C8
Trewint St SW18 .....20 C6
Trewsbury Rd SE26 ..23 D3
Treyford Cl RH11 ...200 F6
Triangle The
Kingston u T KT3 .....38 C7
Woking GU21 ....69 C1
Trickett Ho SM2 ......59 B2
Trident Ind Est SL3 ....1 E4
Trig St RH5 ....178 F8
Trigg's Cl GU22 ......89 D8
Trigg's La GU21,GU22 .89 D8
Trigo Ct KT19 ....76 D8
Trilby Rd SE23 ....23 D6
Trimmer Ct TW7 ....5 F4
Trimmer Wlk 11 TW8 ..6 E8
Trimmer's Almshouses
GU9 ....125 A1
Trimmers Cl GU9 ...125 C7
Trimmers Field GU9 .125 D1
Trimmers Wood GU26 .188 E6
Trindles Rd RH1 ....140 F7
Tring Ct TW1 ....17 A4
Tringham Cl
Knaphill GU21 ....68 C1
Ottershaw KT16 ......51 C5
Tringham Cotts GU24 .67 F7
Trinity GU1 ....45 E2
Trinity Cl Crawley RH10 .202 C8
Hounslow TW4 ....4 E3
South Croydon CR2 ..61 E2
Stanwell TW19 ....2 C1
Trinity Cotts TW9 ....6 F4
Trinity Cres
Sunningdale SL5 .....30 A4
Upper Tooting SW17 .21 A6
Trinity Ct Bracknell RG12 .26 F7
Forest Hill SE23 ......23 C5
Horsham RH12 ......217 C3
Thornton Heath SE25 .42 E3
Twickenham TW2 .....16 E6
1 Wimbledon SW19 ..20 A2
Trinity Fields GU9 ..125 A6
Trinity Hill GU9 .....125 A6
Trinity Mews Penge SE20 .43 B8
Wandsworth SW18 ...20 A7
Trinity Par 1 TW3 .....5 B4
Trinity Rd Knaphill GU21 .68 B1
Richmond TW9 ....7 A4
Upper Tooting SW17,SW18 .20 E7
Wimbledon SW19 ....20 A2
Trinity Rise SW2,SW2 .22 B8
Trinity Sch CR9 ......62 C8
Trinity Sq RH12 .....217 D2
Trinity St Mary's CE Prim Sch
SW12 ....21 A7
Tristram Rd BR1 ......24 F4
Tritton Ave CR0 ......60 E6
Tritton Rd SE21 ....22 C5
Trittons KT20 ....97 D6
Triumph Cl UB7 ....3 C6
Trodd's La GU1,GU4 .110 E1
Trojan Way CR0 ......60 F7
Troon RH6 ....161 B2
Troon Cl RH11 ......200 D5
Troon Ct SL5 ....29 C4
Troston Ct TW18 .....12 F3
Trotsworth Ave GU25 .31 E5
Trotsworth Ct GU25 ..31 D5
Trotter Way KT19 .....76 A7
Trotters La GU24 .....69 B7
Trotton Cl RH10 .....202 C3
Trotwood Cl GU47 ...45 E2
Trout Rd GU27 ......207 E6
Troutbeck Wlk GU15 .66 D3
Trowers Way RH1 ...119 B4
Trowlock Ave TW11 ..17 C2
Trowlock Way TW11 ..17 D2
Troy Cl KT20 ....97 B7
Troy La TN8 ....144 F4
Troy Rd SE19 ....22 D2
Trumpeters Inn TW9 ..6 C2
Trumpetshill Rd RH2 .138 D7
Trumps Green Cl GU25 .31 E4
Trumps Green Inf Sch
GU25 ....31 D3
Trumps Mill La GU25 .31 F4
Trumpsgreen Ave GU25 .31 E4
Trumpsgreen Rd GU25 .31 D3
Trundle Mead RH12 .217 C5
Trunk Rd GU14 ....84 C5
Trunley Heath Rd GU5 .151 C8
Truslove Rd SE27 ....22 B3
Truss Hill Rd SL5 .....29 C4
Trust Wlk SE21 ....22 B7
Trys Hill KT16 ....51 A8
Trystings Cl KT10 ....56 A4
Tucker Rd KT16 ......51 D4
Tuckers Dr GU6 .....174 B3
Tuckey Gr GU23 ......90 F3
Tudor Ave Hampton TW12 .16 A1

Tim – Tur 291

Tudor Ave continued
North Cheam KT4 .....58 B6
Tudor Circ GU7 .....150 E7
Tudor Cl Ashford TW15 .13 C8
Banstead SM7 ....77 E4
Cheam SM3 ....58 E4
Chessington KT9 .....56 E5
Cobham KT11 ....73 F6
Coulsdon CR5 ....80 A1
Crawley RH10 ....202 D5
East Grinstead RH19 .205 F8
Grayshott GU26 ....188 D2
Hampton TW12 ......16 C3
Hamsey Green CR2 ..81 B4
Little Bookham KT23 .94 A3
Smallfield RH6 ......162 B3
Wallington SM6 ......60 C3
Woking GU22 ....70 A2
Wokingham RG40 ....25 F5
Tudor Ct Biggin Hill TN16 .83 C7
Farncombe GU7 ....150 E5
Feltham TW13 ....15 C4
Haslemere GU27 ...208 C7
4 Purley CR8 ....80 A8
12 Redhill RH1 .....119 A2
3 Stanwell TW19 .....2 E1
5 Sutton SM2 ....59 C4
Teddington TW11 ....16 F2
Tudor Dr Kingston u T KT2 .17 E3
Walton-on-T KT12 ...35 D1
West Barnes SM4 ....39 E3
Tudor Gdns
6 Mortlake SW13,SW14 ..7 E4
Twickenham TW1 .....16 F7
West Wickham BR4 ..63 C7
Tudor Grange KT13 ..53 E8
Tudor Ho Bracknell RG12 .27 B4
Feltham TW13 ....15 C4
2 Horsham RH13 ...217 F3
Weybridge KT13 .....53 A4
Weybridge KT13 .....53 A4
Tudor La SL4 ....11 C8
Tudor Lodge KT20 ...97 F6
Tudor Pl SW19 ....20 E1
Tudor Rd Ashford TW15 .14 D2
Beckenham BR3 ......44 C6
Croydon CR0,SE25 ..43 B4
Farncombe GU7 ....150 E7
Hampton TW12 ......16 A1
Isleworth TW3 ....5 D3
Kingston u T KT2 .....18 A1
Penge SE19 ....22 F1
Tudor Wlk
Leatherhead KT22 ...94 F7
3 Weybridge KT13 ..53 B7
Tudors The 2 BR3 ....44 B7
Tuesley Cnr GU7 ...150 D3
Tuesley La
Godalming GU7,GU8 .150 D1
Milford GU7 ....171 C7
Tufton Gdns KT8 .....36 B7
Tugela Rd CR0 ....42 D3
Tugela St SE6 ....23 F6
Tuggles Plat RH12 ..216 E7
Tulip Cl Croydon CR0 ..43 D1
Hampton TW12 ......15 F2
Tulip Ct RH12 ......217 C4
Tulip Tree Ct SM2 ....78 A8
Tull St CR4 ....40 F2
Tullett Rd RH10 .....202 B2
Tulse Cl BR3 ....44 C6
Tulse Hill SW2,SE24 .22 A8
Tulse Hill Sta SE27 ..22 B6
Tulsemere Rd SE21,SE27 .22 C6
Tulyar Cl KT20 ....97 B7
Tumber Cl GU2 .....106 A2
Tumber St KT18 ......96 C2
Tumblewood Rd SM7 .77 E3
Tumbling Bay KT12 ..35 A3
Tummons Gdns SE25 .42 E7
Tunbridge Ct 1 SE26 .23 A5
Tunley Rd SW12,SW17 .21 A6
Tunnel Link Rd TW6 ..3 A2
Tunnel Rd GU14 ......84 E1
Tunnel Rd E TW6 .....3 B6
Tunnel Rd W TW6 ....3 B6
Tunnmeade 7 RH11 .200 E5
Tunsgate GU1 ....130 D7
Tunsgate Sq GU1 ...130 D7
Tunstall Ct 13 TW9 ...6 F6
Tunstall Rd CR0 ......42 E1
Tunstall Wlk 10 TW8 ..6 E8
Tunworth Cres SW15 ..7 A1
Tuppers Ct GU5 ....132 C4
Tupwood Ct CR3 ....101 A2
Tupwood La CR3 ...101 A1
Tupwood Scrubbs Rd
CR3 ....121 A8
Turf Hill Rd GU15 .....65 F8
Turfhouse La GU24 ..49 E2
Turing Dr RG12 ......27 A4
Turkey Oak Cl SE19 ..42 E8
Turle Rd SW16 ....41 E7
Turnberry Bracknell RG12 .26 E2
Sunningdale SL5 .....30 A1
Turner Ave Mitcham CR4 .40 F8
Twickenham TW2 ....16 C5
Turner Cl Biggin Hill TN16 .83 C7
Guildford GU1 ......109 F4
Turner Ct
East Grinstead RH19 .186 A3
Godalming GU7 ....150 D4
Turner Ho RH5 ......157 C4
Turner Lodge 10 SW19 .19 D7

Turner Pl GU47 ....64 D6
Turner Rd KT3 ....38 D2
Turner's Hill Rd RH19 ..205 B6
Turners Cl TW18 ....13 B3
Turners Hill CE Sch
RH10 ....204 A3
Turners Hill Pk RH10 ..204 C5
Turners Hill Rd
  Copthorne RH10 ....183 F2
  Crawley RH10 ....203 D3
  Crawley Down RH10 ....204 A7
  Turners Hill RH10 ....203 F5
Turners La KT12 ....54 B3
Turners Mead GU8 ..191 C3
Turners Meadow Way
BR3 ....43 F8
Turners Way CR0,CR9 ....61 A8
Turney Prim & Sec Specl Sch
SE21 ....22 C8
Turney Rd SE21 ....22 D8
Turnham Rd GU2 ..130 C5
Turnoak Ave GU22 ....89 E7
Turnoak Cnr GU22 ....89 E8
Turnoak La GU22 ....89 E8
Turnoak Rdbt GU22 ....89 E8
Turnpike La SM1 ....59 C5
Turnpike Link CR0 ....61 E8
Turnpike Pl RH11 ..201 D8
Turnpike Rd RG42 ....26 D7
Turnpike Way TW7 ......6 A6
Turnstone Cl CR0,CR2 ....62 E1
Turnville Cl GU18 ....48 A1
Turpin Rd TW14 ......3 F1
Turpin Way SM6 ....60 C5
Turpins Rise GU20 ....48 B6
Turret Ct RH19 ..185 C3
Turret Ho KT2 ....17 E2
Turtledove Ave RH10 ..204 C5
Turville Ct KT23 ....94 B2
Tuscam Way GU15 ....64 F4
Tuscany Gdns RH10 ..201 E8
Tushmore Ave RH10 ..181 E1
Tushmore Cres RH10 ..181 E1
Tushmore La RH10 ..201 E8
Tushmore Rdbt RH11 ..201 D8
Tussock Cl RH11 ..201 A4
Tuxford Cl RH10 ..202 C4
Tweed Cl GU14 ....84 E6
Tweed La Brockham RH3 ..137 B5
  Rusper RH11 ..180 F1
Tweed Rd SL3 ......1 B1
Tweeddale Prim Sch
SM5 ....40 D2
Tweeddale Rd SM5 ....40 D1
Tweedsmuir Cl GU14 ....84 D3
Tweedy Rd 6 BR1 ....44 F8
Twelve Acre Cl KT23 ....93 F3
Twelve Acre Cres GU14 ....84 E5
Twickenham Bridge TW9 ..6 C2
Twickenham Cl CR0 ....60 F7
Twickenham Pl KT7 ....55 F8
Twickenham Prep Sch
TW12 ....36 B8
Twickenham Rd
  Feltham TW13 ....15 F5
  Isleworth TW1,TW7 ......6 A4
  Richmond TW1,TW9 ......6 C3
  Teddington TW11 ....17 A4
Twickenham Rugby Football
Union Ground TW2 ......5 E1
Twickenham Sta TW1 ....17 A8
Twickenham Trad Ctr
TW1 ......5 F1
Twilley St SW18 ....20 B8
Twining Ave TW2 ....16 D5
Twinoaks KT11 ....74 A6
Twitten La RH19 ..184 E4
Twittens The RH11 ..201 C6
Two Oaks KT13 ....53 B6
Two Rivers Sh Ctr TW18 ..12 E4
Two Ways RH14 ..213 A4
Twycross Rd
  Farncombe GU7 ..150 D7
  Wokingham RG40 ....25 E7
Twyford La GU10 ..146 B6
Twyford Par KT6 ....38 A1
Twyford Rd
  Carshalton SM5 ....40 D1
  Wokingham RG40 ....25 B8
Twyhurst Ct RH19 ..185 D3
Twyne Cl RH11 ..200 F4
Twyner Cl RH6 ..161 C4
Twynersh Ave KT16 ....32 F3
Tybenham Rd SW19 ....40 A6
Tychbourne Dr GU4 ..110 C4
Tydcombe Rd CR6 ..101 D8
Tyers Ho 1 SW16 ....21 C3
Tylden Way RH12 ..217 F6
Tylecroft Rd SW16 ....41 E7
Tylehost GU2 ..109 A5
Tyler Gdns KT15 ....52 C6
Tyler Rd RH10 ..201 D3
Tylers Cl RH9 ..121 B5
Tylers Path SM5 ....59 F6
Tylney Ave SE19 ....22 F3
Tylney Ct KT22 ....95 C6
Tylney Wood GU10 ..187 F7
Tymperley Ct RH13 ..217 E3
Tynamara KT1 ....37 D5
Tynan Cl TW14 ....15 A7
Tyndalls GU26 ..188 F4
Tyne Cl Crawley RH10 ..202 C5
  Farnborough GU14 ....84 E6
Tyne Ho 4 KT2 ....37 D8
Tynedale Rd RH3 ..137 B5

Tynemouth Rd CR4 ....21 A1
Tynley Gr GU4 ..109 D7
Tynwald Ho 14 SE26 ....23 A5
Tyrell Ct SM5 ....59 F6
Tyrolean Ct SM7 ....78 B4
Tyrols Rd SE23 ....23 D7
Tyrrell Ho BR3 ....24 B3
Tyrrell Sq 9 CR4 ....40 E8
Tyrwhitt Ave GU2 ..109 B5
Tyson Rd SE23 ....23 C8
Tythe Cl KT12 ....35 B3
Tythebarn Cl GU4 ..110 B6
Tythebarns La GU23 ....91 B1
Tytherton RG12 ....27 C7

U

Uckfield Rd CR4 ....41 A8
Udney Park Rd TW11 ....17 A2
Uffington Dr RG12 ....27 E5
Uffington Rd SE27 ....22 A4
Ujima Ct SW16 ....21 E4
Ujima Ho SW16 ....21 E4
Ullathorne Rd SW16 ....21 C5
Ullswater GU22 ......26 F2
Ullswater Ave GU14 ....84 E3
Ullswater Cl
  Hale GU9 ..125 A6
  Kingston u T SW15 ....18 D4
  Lightwater GU18 ....48 B1
Ullswater Cres
  Coulsdon CR5 ....79 E3
  Kingston u T SW15 ....18 D4
Ullswater Rd
  Lightwater GU18 ....48 B1
  West Norwood SE27 ....22 B6
Ulstan Cl CR3 ..102 A4
Ulster Ct KT2 ....17 D2
Ulverstone Rd SE27 ....22 B6
Ulwyn Ave KT14 ....71 E5
Underhill Cl GU7 ..150 E3
Underhill La GU10 ..146 B7
Underhill Park Rd RH2 ..118 A4
Underhill Rd
  Dulwich SE21,SE22 ....23 B8
  Newdigate RH5 ..158 B1
Undershaw Rd BR1 ....24 F5
Underwood
  Bracknell RG12 ....26 E3
  New Addington CR0 ....63 C5
Underwood Ave GU12 ..105 F1
Underwood Cl RH10 ..204 B8
Underwood Ct CR3 ..100 F2
Underwood Rd
  Caterham CR3 ..100 E2
  Haslemere GU27 ..207 F7
Undine St SW17 ....20 F3
Unicorn Sch TW9 ......6 F6
Unicorn Trad Est The
GU27 ..208 B7
Union Cl GU47 ....45 E2
Union Ct 2 TW10 ......6 E2
Union Rd Farnham GU9 ..125 C2
  Frimley GU16 ....86 D8
  Thornton Heath CR0 ....42 C2
Union St Aldershot GU11 ..105 A2
  Farnborough GU14 ....85 B4
  Kingston u T KT1 ....37 D7
  Pirbright GU24 ....87 A6
Union Terr 7 GU11 ..105 A2
Unity Cl
  New Addington CR0 ....63 B2
  West Norwood SE19 ....22 C3
Univ of Greenwich The
SW15 ....19 A8
Univ of Surrey GU2 ..109 B1
University Ct GU2 ..109 B1
University Rd SW19 ....20 D2
Unstead La GU5 ..151 C7
Unstead Wood GU3 ..130 C1
Unwin Ave TW14 ......3 D2
Unwin Rd TW7 ......5 E4
Upavon Gdns RG12 ....27 F4
Upchurch Cl SE20 ....23 B1
Updown Hill GU20 ....48 D4
Upfield Horley RH6 ..161 A1
  South Croydon CR0,CR9 ....62 B7
Upfield Cl RH6 ..161 A1
Upfold Cl GU6 ..174 B5
Upfold La GU6 ..174 C5
Upfolds Gn GU4 ..110 C5
Upgrove Manor Way 12
SE24 ....22 A8
Upland Ct SE23 ....23 C6
Upland Rd
  Camberley GU15 ....65 D7
  Croydon CR2 ....61 D5
  Dulwich SE21,SE22 ....23 A8
  Sutton SM2 ....59 D3
  Woldingham CR3 ..102 B7
Upland Way KT18 ....77 C1
Uplands Ashtead KT21 ....95 D7
  Beckenham BR3 ....44 A7
  Warlingham CR6 ....81 F1
Uplands Cl
  Haslemere GU27 ..208 D8
  Mortlake SW14 ......7 B2
  Sandhurst GU47 ....64 B8
Uplands Dr KT22 ....74 D5
Uplands Prim Sch GU47 ..64 B8
Uplands Rd
  Farnham GU9 ..125 E1
  Kenley CR8 ....80 C2
Uppark Gdns RH12 ..217 F6
Upper Beulah Hill SE19 ..42 E8
Upper Bourne La GU10 ..146 B5

Upper Bourne Vale
GU10 ..146 A5
Upper Bridge Rd RH1 ..118 F1
Upper Brighton Rd KT6 ..37 E2
Upper Broadmoor Rd
RG45 ....45 D5
Upper Butts TW8 ......6 C8
Upper Charles St GU15 ..65 C6
Upper Chobham Rd
GU15 ....66 B4
Upper Church La 18
GU9 ..125 B2
Upper Cl RH18 ..206 F2
Upper College Ride
GU15 ....65 E6
Upper Court Rd
  Epsom KT19 ....76 C8
  Woldingham CR3 ..102 A3
Upper Dr TN16 ....83 C1
Upper Dunnymans 6
SM7 ....77 F5
Upper Edgeborough Rd
GU1 ..130 F8
Upper Elmers End Rd
BR3 ....43 E4
Upper Elms Rd GU11 ..105 A1
Upper Fairfield Rd KT22 ..95 B6
Upper Farm Rd KT8 ....35 F5
Upper Forecourt RH6 ..182 B7
Upper Gn E CR4 ....40 F7
Upper Gn W CR4 ....40 F7
Upper Gordon Rd GU15 ..65 D5
Upper Gr SE25 ....42 F5
Upper Grotto Rd TW1 ....16 F6
Upper Guildown Rd
GU2 ..130 C6
Upper Hale Rd GU9 ..125 C6
Upper Halliford Rd
  Upper Halliford TW17 ..34 E5
  Upper Halliford TW17 ..34 E6
Upper Halliford Sta
TW16 ....34 E7
Upper Ham Rd KT2,TW10 ..17 D4
Upper Harestone CR3 ..121 D4
Upper High St KT17 ....76 E6
Upper House La GU5 ..152 F1
Upper Manor Rd
  Farncombe GU7 ..150 E6
  Milford GU8 ..149 F1
Upper Mount GU27 ..189 F1
Upper Mulgrave Rd SM2 ..58 E3
Upper Nursery GU15 ....66 B4
Upper Old Park La GU9 ..125 A5
Upper Park Rd
  Camberley GU15 ....65 E6
  Kingston u T KT2 ....18 A2
Upper Pillory Down SM5 ..79 A7
Upper Pines SM7 ....78 F2
Upper Pinewood Rd
GU12 ..106 D3
Upper Queen St GU7 ..150 E4
Upper Rd SM6 ....60 E5
Upper Richmond Rd SW15 ..7 F3
Upper Richmond Rd W
TW10,SW14,SW15 ......7 C3
Upper Rose Hill RH4 ..136 B6
Upper Sawleywood 3
SM7 ....77 F5
Upper School Dr GU27 ..207 F5
Upper Selsdon Rd CR2 ..62 A2
Upper Shirley Rd CR0,
CR9 ....62 D7
Upper South View GU9 ..125 C3
Upper Springfield GU8 ..148 D3
Upper Sq
  Forest Row RH18 ..206 F3
  Isleworth TW7 ......6 A4
Upper St GU5 ..133 A4
Upper St Michael's Rd
GU11 ..105 A1
Upper Stanford Rd GU24 ..87 F1
Upper Sunbury Rd TW12 ..36 A8
Upper Sutton La TW5 ......5 A6
Upper Teddington Rd
KT1,KT8 ....37 C8
Upper Tooting Independent
High Sch SW17 ....20 F6
Upper Tooting Park Mans 1
SW17 ....21 A6
Upper Tooting Pk SW17 ..20 F6
Upper Tooting Rd SW17 ..20 F5
Upper Tulse Hill SW2 ....21 F8
Upper Union St 1
GU11 ..105 A2
Upper Union Terr 5
GU11 ..105 A2
Upper Vann La GU8 ..172 A1
Upper Vernon Rd SM1 ..59 D5
Upper Verran Rd GU15 ..65 D3
Upper Village Rd SL5 ..29 D4
Upper Warlingham Sta
CR6 ....81 A1
Upper Way GU9 ..146 B8
Upper West St RH2 ..117 F1
Upper Weybourne La
GU9 ..125 E7
Upper Wlk GU25 ....31 E5
Upper Woodcote Village
CR8 ....79 D7
Upperton Rd GU2 ..130 C7
Upshire Gdns RG12 ....27 F5
Upshott La GU22 ....70 F2
Upton GU21 ....69 B2
Upton Cl GU14 ....85 D3
Upton Ct 7 Penge SE20 ..23 C1
  4 Wimbledon SW19 ....19 D1
Upton Dene SM2 ....59 B3
Upton Rd Hounslow TW3 ..5 A4

Upton Rd *continued*
  South Norwood CR7 ....42 D7
Upwood Rd SW16 ....41 E8
Urmston Dr SW19 ....19 E7
Urquhart Ct BR3 ....23 F1
Ursuline Convent Prep Sch
SW19 ....19 D1
Ursuline High Sch
Wimbledon SW20 ....39 D8
Usherwood Cl KT20 ..116 C4
Uvedale Cl CR0 ....82 D8
Uvedale Cres CR0 ....82 E8
Uvedale Rd RH8 ..122 F5
Uxbridge Rd
  Feltham TW13 ....15 D6
  Hampton TW12 ....16 B3
  Kingston u T KT1,KT6 ....37 D4

V

Vachery La GU6 ..194 E7
Vaillant Rd KT13 ....53 C6
Valan Leas BR2 ....44 E6
Vale Cl Coulsdon CR5 ....79 E5
  Farnham GU9 ..146 C4
  Oatlands Park KT13 ....53 D7
  Twickenham TW1 ....17 A5
  Woking GU21 ....69 E3
Vale Cres SW15 ....18 E4
Vale Croft KT10 ....55 F2
Vale Ct Ash Vale GU12 ..106 A7
  Oatlands Park KT13 ....53 D7
Vale Dr RH12 ..217 B3
Vale Farm Rd GU21 ....69 E2
Vale Ho GU21 ....69 E2
Vale Lodge SE23 ....23 C6
Vale Prim Sch The KT18 ..96 E8
Vale Rd Ash Vale GU12 ..106 A5
  Camberley GU15 ....65 A4
  Claygate KT10 ....55 F3
  Mitcham CR4 ....41 D5
  Oatlands Park KT13 ....53 D7
  Sutton SM1 ....59 B6
  Worcester Park KT19,KT4 ..57 F7
Vale Rd N KT6 ....56 E8
Vale Rd S KT6 ....56 E8
Vale The Ashford TW16 ..15 A2
  Coulsdon CR5,CR8 ....79 E5
  Croydon CR0 ....62 D8
  Feltham TW14 ......4 B1
  Heston TW5 ......4 E8
Vale Wood Dr GU10 ..146 D4
Vale Wood La GU26 ..188 C4
Valens Ho 1 SW2 ....22 A7
Valentine Ct SE23 ....23 D6
Valentyne Cl CR0 ....82 E8
Valerie Ct SM2 ....59 B3
Valeswood Rd BR1 ....24 F3
Valewood Rd GU27 ..208 C4
Valley Cres RG41 ....25 A8
Valley Ct CR3 ..101 E3
Valley End CE Inf Sch
GU24 ....49 A4
Valley End Rd GU24 ....49 B4
Valley Gdns
  Mitcham SW19 ....20 D1
  ★ Virginia Water TW20 ....30 E7
Valley La GU10 ..146 C2
Valley Mews 1 TW1 ....17 A6
Valley Mushroom Farm
TN16 ....83 D1
Valley Pl KT6 ....37 E3
Valley Prim Sch BR2 ....44 F7
Valley Prospect 3 SE19 ..22 E2
Valley Rd Beckenham BR2 ..44 E2
  Frimley GU16 ....86 B8
  Kenley CR3,CR8 ....80 C4
  Streatham SW16 ....21 F4
Valley The GU2 ..130 C5
Valley View
  Biggin Hill TN16 ....83 D1
  Godalming GU7 ..150 D4
  Sandhurst GU47 ....64 A7
Valley View Gdns CR8 ....80 E4
Valley Wlk CR0 ....62 C8
Valleyfield Rd SW16 ....21 F3
Vallis Way KT9 ....56 D6
Valnay St SW17 ....20 F3
Valroy Cl GU15 ....65 D6
Van Dyck Ave KT3 ....38 D2
Van Gogh Cl TW7 ......6 A4
Vanborough Ct 3 SM2 ..59 C4
Vanbrugh Cl RH11 ..200 E3
Vanbrugh Dr KT12 ....35 C3
Vancouver Cl KT19 ....76 C8
Vancouver Ct RH6 ..162 A3
Vancouver Dr RH10,
RH11 ..181 D1
Vancouver Rd
  Forest Hill SE23 ....23 E6
  Richmond TW10 ....17 C4
Vanderbilt Rd SW18 ....20 C7
Vandyke RG12 ....26 E3
Vandyke Cl Putney SW15 ..19 D8
  Redhill RH1 ..118 F3
Vanfame Ct KT3 ....38 F6
Vanguard Cl CR0 ....42 B1
Vanguard Ho
  7 Merton SW19 ....20 C1
  5 Stanwell TW19 ......2 E1
Vanguard Way
  Harlington TW6 ......3 E5
  Wallington SM6 ....60 E3
Vann Farm Rd RH5 ..177 E4
Vann La Chiddingfold GU8 ..191 E4
  Hambledon GU8 ..171 D1
Vann Lake RH5 ..177 F4

Vann Lake Rd
  Ockley RH5 ..177 E5
  Ockley RH5 ..178 A4
Vanners RH10 ..201 E7
Vanners Par KT14 ....71 E5
Vant Rd SW17 ....20 F3
Vapery La GU24 ....87 D6
Varley Way CR4 ....40 D7
Varna Rd TW12 ....36 B8
Varney Cl GU14 ....84 E5
Varsity Dr TW1,TW7 ......5 F1
Varsity Row SW14 ......7 C5
Vaughan Almshouses
TW15 ....14 B3
Vaughan Rd KT7 ....37 B2
Vaughan Way RH4 ..136 A2
Vaux Cres KT12 ....54 B4
Vauxhall Gdns CR2 ....61 C4
Veals Mead CR4 ....40 E8
Vectis Gdns SW17 ....21 B2
Vectis Rd SW17 ....21 B2
Vegal Cres TW20 ....11 C3
Vellum Dr SM5 ....60 A7
Venner Rd SE20,SE26 ....23 C3
Ventnor Rd SM2 ....59 B3
Ventnor Terr GU12 ..105 C1
Venton Cl GU21 ....69 B2
Venture Ho TW18 ....13 A4
Verbania Way RH19 ..186 B1
Verdant Ct 3 SE6 ....24 E8
Verdant La SE6 ....24 E7
Verdayne Ave CR0,CR9 ..62 D8
Verdayne Gdns CR6 ....81 C3
Vere Bank SW19 ....19 F7
Vereker Dr TW16 ....35 A6
Verge Wlk GU11 ..126 A7
Vermont Rd
  South Norwood SE19 ....22 E2
  Sutton SM1 ....59 B7
Verney Ho TW3 ......5 C3
Vernon Ave SW20 ....39 D7
Vernon Cl Horsham RH12 ..218 A4
  Ottershaw KT16 ....51 D4
  West Ewell KT19 ....57 C4
Vernon Dr Caterham CR3 ..100 C3
  North Ascot SL5 ....28 E7
Vernon Rd Carshalton SM1 ..59 D5
  Feltham TW13 ....14 F6
  Mortlake SW14 ......7 D4
Vernon Way GU2 ..108 F2
Verona Dr KT6 ....56 E8
Veronica Gdns CR4,SW16 ..41 C8
Veronica Rd SW17 ....21 B6
Verralls 2 GU22 ....70 B2
Verran Rd Balham SW12 ..21 B8
  Camberley GU15 ....65 D3
Versailles Rd SE20 ....23 A1
Verulam Ave CR8 ....79 C7
Veryan GU21 ....69 A2
Vesey Cl GU14 ....85 A5
Vestris Rd SE23 ....23 D6
Vevers Rd RH2 ..139 C6
Vevey St SE23,SE6 ....23 F6
Vibart Gdns SW2 ....21 F8
Vibia Cl TW19 ....13 D8
Viburnum Ct GU24 ....67 E6
Vicarage Ave TW20 ....12 B3
Vicarage Cl
  Farnham GU9 ..146 D7
  Kingswood KT20 ....97 E3
  Lingfield RH7 ..164 D4
  Little Bookham KT23 ....94 A2
  New Malden KT4 ....38 E1
Vicarage Cres TW20 ....12 B3
Vicarage Ct
  Beckenham BR3 ....43 E6
  East Bedfont TW14 ....14 C8
  Egham TW20 ....12 B3
  8 Roehampton SW15 ....19 A8
Vicarage Dr
  Beckenham BR3 ....44 A8
  Mortlake SW14 ......7 D2
Vicarage Farm Ct TW5 ......4 F7
Vicarage Farm Rd TW3,
TW4,TW5 ......4 E6
Vicarage Fields KT12 ....35 C3
Vicarage Gate GU2 ..130 A7
Vicarage Gdns Ascot SL5 ..29 A4
  Grayshott GU26 ..188 C3
  Mitcham CR4 ....40 E6
  Mortlake SW14 ......7 D2
Vicarage Hill GU10,GU9 ..146 D7
Vicarage Ho 2 KT1 ....37 F7
Vicarage La Capel RH5 ..178 D6
  Farnham GU9 ..125 B2
  Farnham, Middle Bourne
  GU9 ..146 D7
  Haslemere GU27 ..207 F6
  Heath End GU9 ..125 C7
  Horley RH6 ..160 F4
  Laleham TW18 ....33 C6
  Leatherhead KT22 ....95 B5
  Send GU23 ....90 D1
  Wraysbury TW19 ....11 F7
Vicarage Rd Ashford TW16 ..14 F2
  Bagshot GU19 ....47 C3
  Blackwater GU17 ....64 E4
  Chobham GU24 ....68 E8
  Crawley Down RH10 ..204 A8
  Croydon CR0,CR9 ....61 A7
  Egham TW20 ....12 B3
  Kingston u T KT1,KT2 ....37 D7
  Lingfield RH7 ..164 D4
  Mortlake SW14 ......7 D2
  Staines TW18 ....12 E5

Vicarage Rd continued
Sutton SM1 . . . . .59 B7
Teddington TW11 . . . . .17 A3
Teddington, Hampton Wick
KT1,KT8 . . . . .37 C8
Twickenham TW2 . . . . .5 C1
Twickenham,Strawberry Hill
TW2 . . . . .16 E6
Woking GU22 . . . . .89 F6
Vicarage Way SL3 . . . . .1 D7
Vicars Oak Rd SE19 . . . . .22 E2
Viceroy Ct 5 CR0 . . . . .42 D1
Viceroy Lodge 6 KT6 . . . . .37 E4
Vickers Cl SM6 . . . . .60 F3
Vickers Ct 9 TW19 . . . . .2 E1
Vickers Dr N KT13 . . . . .52 E1
Vickers Dr S KT13 . . . . .71 E8
Vickers Rd GU12 . . . . .105 F5
Victor Ct RH10 . . . . .182 D1
Victor Rd Penge SE20 . . . . . .23 D1
Teddington TW11 . . . . .16 E4
Victor Seymour Inf Sch
SM5 .59 F6
Victoria Almshouses
4 Redhill RH1 . . . . .119 A4
1 Reigate RH2 . . . . .118 C1
Victoria Ave
Camberley GU15 . . . . .65 A5
East Molesey KT8 . . . . .36 B6
Hackbridge SM6 . . . . .60 A7
Hounslow TW3,TW4 . . . . .5 A2
Kingston u T KT6 . . . . .37 D3
South Croydon CR2 . . . . .61 C1
Victoria Cl
East Molesey KT8 . . . . .36 A6
Horley RH6 . . . . .161 A3
Oatlands Park KT13 . . . . .53 D7
Victoria Cotts 8 TW9 . . . . . . .7 A6
Victoria Cres
Merton SW19 . . . . .19 F1
West Norwood SE19 . . . . .22 E2
Victoria Ct Bagshot GU19 . . .47 E1
Guildford GU1 . . . . .130 D8
Horsham RH13 . . . . .217 D2
Penge SE26 . . . . .23 C2
Redhill RH1 . . . . .140 A6
Shalford GU4 . . . . .130 E3
Victoria Dr
Blackwater GU17 . . . . .64 C4
Putney SW15,SW19 . . . . .19 D7
Victoria Entertainments Ctr
The 2 GU21 . . . . .69 E2
Victoria Gdns
Biggin Hill TN16 . . . . .83 C4
Heston TW5 . . . . .4 E6
Victoria Jun Sch TW13 . . . . .15 B7
Victoria La UB7 . . . . .3 D8
Victoria Lodge SW19 . . . . . .19 C1
Victoria Mews
Wandsworth SW18 . . . . .20 C7
Weybridge KT13 . . . . .53 A6
Victoria Pl 6 Esher KT10 . . .55 B6
Ewell KT17 . . . . .76 E7
16 Richmond TW10 . . . . .6 D2
Victoria Rd
Addlestone KT15 . . . . .52 D6
Aldershot GU11 . . . . .105 A2
Ascot SL5 . . . . .29 A4
Carshalton SM1 . . . . .59 D5
Coulsdon CR5 . . . . .79 D4
Cranleigh GU6 . . . . .174 D3
Crawley RH11 . . . . .201 C6
Farnborough GU14 . . . . .85 B4
Farnham GU9 . . . . .125 C2
Feltham TW13 . . . . .15 B7
Godalming GU7 . . . . .150 E4
Guildford GU1 . . . . .109 E1
Horley RH6 . . . . .161 B2
Kingston u T KT1 . . . . .37 F7
Kingston u T, Seething Wells
KT6 .37 D3
Knaphill GU21 . . . . .68 E1
Mitcham CR4,SW19 . . . . .20 F1
Mortlake SW14 . . . . .7 D4
Oatlands Park KT13 . . . . .53 D7
Redhill RH1 . . . . .140 A8
Sandhurst GU47 . . . . .45 E1
Staines TW18 . . . . .12 E5
Teddington TW11 . . . . .17 A2
Twickenham TW1 . . . . .17 B8
Woking GU22 . . . . .69 F2
Victoria St
Englefield Green TW20 . . . . . .11 C2
Horsham RH13 . . . . .217 D2
Victoria Terr 6 RH4 . . . . . .136 A7
Victoria Villas TW9 . . . . .6 F3
Victoria Way
East Grinstead RH19 . . . . . . .205 F7
Oatlands Park KT13 . . . . .53 D7
Woking GU21,GU22 . . . . .69 E2
Victors Dr TW12 . . . . .15 E2
Victory Ave SM4 . . . . .40 C4
Victory Bsns Ctr The TW7 . . .5 F3
Victory Cotts KT24 . . . . .113 E7
Victory Park Rd KT15 . . . . . .52 C6
Victory Pl SE19 . . . . .22 E2
Victory Rd Chertsey KT16 . . .33 A1
Horsham RH12 . . . . .217 B3
Merton SW19 . . . . .20 C1
Victory Road Mews 5
SW19 . . . . .20 C1
Vidler Cl KT9 . . . . .56 C4
Vienna Ct GU14 . . . . .85 A6
View Cl TN16 . . . . .83 C3
View Terr RH7 . . . . .165 A1
Viewfield Rd SW18 . . . . .19 F8
Viggory La GU21 . . . . .69 C4
Vigilant Cl SE26 . . . . .23 A4

Viking RG12 . . . . .26 E4
Viking Ct TW12 . . . . .36 B8
Village Cl 3 KT13 . . . . .53 D7
Village Ct SL5 . . . . .29 C4
Village Gdns KT17 . . . . .57 F1
Village Gate TW17 . . . . .34 B4
Village Green Ave TN16 . . . . .83 E2
Village Green Way TN16 . . . .83 E2
Village Rd TW20 . . . . .32 C6
Village Row SM2 . . . . .59 A3
Village St RH5 . . . . .158 B1
Village The SL4 . . . . .10 B5
Village Way Ashford TW15 . . 14 A4
Beckenham BR3 . . . . .44 A6
Sanderstead CR2 . . . . .81 A6
Villas The RH7 . . . . .163 D1
Villiers Ave
Kingston u T KT5 . . . . .37 F5
Twickenham TW2 . . . . .15 F7
Villiers Cl KT5 . . . . .37 F5
Villiers Gr SM2 . . . . .58 D2
Villiers Mead RG41 . . . . .25 A6
Villiers Rd Hounslow TW7 . . . .5 E5
Kingston u T KT1 . . . . .37 F6
Penge BR3 . . . . .43 D7
Villiers The KT13 . . . . .53 D4
Vinall Gdns RH12 . . . . .216 D4
Vincam Cl TW2 . . . . .16 A8
Vincent Ave Sutton SM5 . . . . .78 D8
3 Tolworth KT5 . . . . .38 B1
Vincent Cl Chertsey KT16 . . .32 E2
Esher KT10 . . . . .55 B7
Fetcham KT23 . . . . .94 B4
Harmondsworth UB7 . . . . .3 A8
Horsham RH13 . . . . .217 F2
Vincent Dr Dorking RH4 . . . .136 A6
Upper Halliford TW17 . . . . . . .34 E6
Vincent Ho KT3 . . . . .38 F5
Vincent La RH4 . . . . .136 A7
Vincent Rd Chertsey KT16 . . .32 E2
Coulsdon CR5 . . . . .79 C3
Croydon CR0 . . . . .42 E2
Dorking RH4 . . . . .136 A7
Hounslow TW7 . . . . .5 D6
Hounslow,Hounslow West
TW4 . . . . .4 D4
Kingston u T KT1 . . . . .38 A6
Stoke D'Abernon KT11 . . . . . .73 E3
Vincent Rise RG12 . . . . .27 E6
Vincent Row TW12 . . . . .16 C3
Vincent Sq TN16 . . . . .83 C6
Vincent Wks RH4 . . . . .136 A7
Vincents Cl CR5 . . . . .98 F7
Vine Cl
Farnborough GU11 . . . . .105 A6
Rowledge GU10 . . . . .146 A4
Stanwell TW19 . . . . .2 A2
Surbiton KT5 . . . . .37 F3
Sutton SM1 . . . . .59 C7
Worplesdon GU3 . . . . .88 D3
Vine Cotts GU6 . . . . .174 B3
Vine Ct KT12 . . . . .54 C4
Vine House Cl GU16 . . . . .86 A3
Vine La GU10 . . . . .146 A5
Vine Pl TW3 . . . . .5 B3
Vine Rd Barnes SW13,SW15 . .7 F4
East Molesey KT8 . . . . .36 C5
Vine St GU11 . . . . .105 A1
Vine Way GU10 . . . . .146 A5
Vineries Cl UB7 . . . . .3 A8
Viners Cl KT12 . . . . .35 C3
Viney Bank CR0 . . . . .62 F2
Vineyard Cl Forest Hill SE6 . .24 A7
Kingston u T KT1 . . . . .37 F6
Vineyard Hill Rd SW19 . . . . .20 A4
Vineyard Path SW14 . . . . .7 D4
Vineyard Prim Sch The
TW10 .6 E1
Vineyard Rd TW13 . . . . .15 A5
Vineyard Row KT1,KT8 . . . . .37 C8
Vineyard The TW10 . . . . .6 E2
Vineyards The TW13 . . . . .15 A5
Vinter Ct TW17 . . . . .34 A4
Viola Ave Feltham TW14 . . . . .4 C1
Stanwell TW19 . . . . .13 E7
Viola Croft RG42 . . . . .27 F8
Violet Cl Carshalton CR4 . . . .41 A1
Cheam SM3 . . . . .39 E1
Violet Gdns CR0 . . . . .61 B5
Violet La CR0 . . . . .61 B5
Violette Szabo Ho 4
SE27 .22 D4
Virginia Ave GU25 . . . . .31 C4
Virginia Beeches GU25 . . . . .31 C6
Virginia Cl Ashstead KT21 . . .75 D1
Kingston u T KT3 . . . . .38 C5
Laleham TW18 . . . . .33 C6
Weybridge KT13 . . . . .53 C4
Virginia Ct GU25 . . . . .31 D5
Virginia Dr GU25 . . . . .31 C5
Virginia Gdns GU14 . . . . .85 C2
Virginia Ho TW11 . . . . .17 A3
Virginia Pl KT11 . . . . .73 A5
Virginia Rd CR7 . . . . .42 B8
Virginia Water★ SL5 . . . . . . .30 E6
Virginia Water Sta GU25 . . .31 E4
Viscount Cl GU15 . . . . .105 F5
Viscount Gdns KT14 . . . . .71 E7
Viscount Ind Est SL3 . . . . .1 E4
Viscount Rd TW19 . . . . .13 E7
Viscount Way TW6 . . . . .3 F4
Vivien Cl KT9 . . . . .56 E3
Vivienne Cl
Crawley RH11 . . . . .181 D1
Twickenham TW1 . . . . .6 D1
Vivienne Ho TW18 . . . . .13 A3
Voewood Cl KT3 . . . . .38 F3

Vogan Cl RH2 . . . . .139 B6
Volta Way CR0,CR9 . . . . .41 F1
Voltaire 14 TW9 . . . . .6 F6
Voltaire Way GU7 . . . . .150 E6
Voss Ct SW16 . . . . .21 E2
Vowels Forest Wlk★
RH19 . . . . .204 E3
Vowels La RH19 . . . . .204 E3
Vulcan Bsns Ctr CR0 . . . . . . .63 E2
Vulcan Cl Crawley RH11 . . . .201 C2
Sandhurst GU47 . . . . .64 A7
Vulcan Way
New Addington CR0 . . . . .63 E1
Sandhurst GU47 . . . . .64 B7
Vumba Ho 13 SM2 . . . . .59 C4
Vyne Ho SM5 . . . . .59 F4

W

Wadbrook St KT1 . . . . .37 D7
Waddington Ave CR5,
CR8 .100 B8
Waddington Cl
Coulsdon CR5 . . . . .100 B8
Crawley RH11 . . . . .201 A3
Waddington Way CR7,
SE19 .42 D8
Waddon Cl CR0,CR9 . . . . .61 A7
Waddon Court Rd CR0,
CR9 . . . . .61 A7
Waddon Inf Sch CR0 . . . . . . .61 A5
Waddon Marsh Sta CR0 . . . .61 A8
Waddon Marsh Way CR0,
CR9 . . . . .41 F1
Waddon New Rd CR0,CR9 . .61 B8
Waddon Park Ave CR0,
CR9 . . . . .61 A7
Waddon Rd CR0,CR9 . . . . . . .61 B7
Waddon Sta CR0 . . . . .61 A6
Waddon Way CR0,CR2,
CR9 . . . . .61 B4
Wade's La TW11 . . . . .17 A3
Wadham GU47 . . . . .45 F1
Wadham Cl
Crawley RH10 . . . . .182 C1
Shepperton TW17 . . . . .34 C2
Wadhurst Cl SE20 . . . . .43 B7
Wadlands Brook Rd
RH19 . . . . .185 D5
Wagbullock Rise RG12 . . . . . .27 C3
Wagg Ct KT13 . . . . .53 D6
Wagg Cl RH19 . . . . .186 A1
Waggon Cl GU2 . . . . .108 E2
Waggoners Hollow GU47 . . . .64 A7
Waggoners Way GU26 . . . . .188 A4
Waggoners Wells Rd
GU26 . . . . .188 A2
Wagner Mews 23 KT6 . . . . . .37 E4
Wagtail Cl RH12 . . . . .217 D7
Wagtail Gdns CR2 . . . . .62 E1
Wagtail Wlk BR3 . . . . .44 C4
Waights Ct KT2 . . . . .37 E8
Wain End RH12 . . . . .217 D5
Wainford Cl SW19 . . . . .19 D7
Wainwright Gr RG40 . . . . .26 A6
Wainwright Gr TW7 . . . . .5 D3
Wainwrights RH10 . . . . .201 D3
Waite Davies Rd SE12 . . . . . .24 F8
Wakefield Cl KT14 . . . . .71 E7
Wakefield Gdns SE19 . . . . . . .22 E1
Wakefield Ho SE22 . . . . .23 B7
Wakefield Rd 19 TW10 . . . . . .6 D2
Wakehams Green Dr
RH10 . . . . .182 D1
Wakehurst Dr RH10 . . . . .201 D3
Wakehurst Mews RH12 . . . . .216 F1
Wakehurst Path GU21 . . . . . . .70 C5
Wakelin Ho 8 SE27 . . . . .22 B5
Wakely Cl TN16 . . . . .83 C1
Walburton Rd CR8 . . . . .79 C7
Walbury RG12 . . . . .27 E5
Waldby Ct RH11 . . . . .201 A3
Waldeck Gr SE27 . . . . .22 B5
Waldeck Rd Brentford W4 . . . .7 A8
Mortlake SW14 . . . . .7 C4
Waldeck Terr SW14 . . . . .7 C4
Waldegrave Ct 1 TW11 . . . .16 F3
Waldegrave Gdns TW1 . . . . .16 F6
Waldegrave Pk TW1 . . . . .16 F4
Waldegrave Rd
Penge SE19 . . . . .22 F1
Teddington TW1,TW11 . . . . . .16 F4
Waldegrave Sch for Girls
TW2 .16 D5
Waldegrove CR0 . . . . .61 F7
Waldemar Rd SW19 . . . . .20 A3
Walden Cotts GU3 . . . . .108 B1
Walden Gdns CR7,SW16 . . . .41 F5
Waldens Park Rd GU21 . . . . .69 C3
Waldens Rd GU21 . . . . .69 C2
Waldenshaw Rd SE23 . . . . . . .23 C7
Waldo Pl SW19 . . . . .20 E1
Waldorf Cl CR2 . . . . .61 B2
Waldorf Sch of SW London
The SW16 . . . . .21 D6
Waldram Cres SE23 . . . . .23 C7
Waldram Park Rd SE23 . . . . .23 D7
Waldram Pl 6 SE23 . . . . .23 C7
Waldron Gdns BR2 . . . . .44 D6
Waldron Hill RG12 . . . . .27 F8
Waldronhyrst CR0,CR2 . . . . .61 B6
Waldrons The
Croydon CR0 . . . . .61 C6
Oxted RH8 . . . . .122 C4
Waldy Rise GU6 . . . . .174 E4
Wales Ave SM5 . . . . .59 E5

Walesbeech RH10 . . . . .202 A5
Waleton Acres SM6 . . . . .60 C4
Waley's La RH5 . . . . .177 C1
Walford Rd RH5 . . . . .136 C3
Walham Rise SW19 . . . . .19 E2
Walhatch Cl RH18 . . . . .206 F2
Walk The Ashford TW16 . . . . .14 F1
Tandridge RH8 . . . . .122 A2
**Walkden Hall (Hall of
Residence)** KT2 . . . . .18 D4
Walker Cl
East Bedfont TW14 . . . . .14 F8
Hampton TW12 . . . . .15 F2
Walker Rd RH10 . . . . .202 C4
Walker's Ridge GU15 . . . . . . .65 E5
Walkerscroft Mead SE21 . .22 C7
Walkfield Dr KT18 . . . . .77 B2
Walking Bottom GU5 . . . . . .154 C6
Wall Hill Rd RH18, RH19 . . . .206 E5
Wallace Cl Fairlands GU3 . . .108 C4
Upper Halliford TW17 . . . . . . .34 D5
Wallace Cres SM5 . . . . .59 F5
Wallace Fields KT17 . . . . .77 A6
Wallace Fields Com Jun Sch
KT17 .77 A7
Wallace Fields Inf Sch
KT17 .77 A6
Wallace Sq CR5 . . . . .99 D5
Wallace Way GU11 . . . . .104 F3
Wallage La RH10 . . . . .203 D6
Walled Garden Cl BR3 . . . . . .44 B5
Walled Gdn The
Betchworth RH3 . . . . .137 D8
Loxwood RH14 . . . . .212 F7
★ Sunbury TW16 . . . . .35 B6
Waller La CR3 . . . . .100 F4
Wallingford Cl RG12 . . . . .27 E5
Wallington Ct 10 SM6 . . . . . .60 B6
Wallington High Sch for Boys
SM6 .60 B2
Wallington High Sch for Girls
SM6 .60 B2
Wallington Rd GU15 . . . . .47 A1
Wallington Sq 4 SM6 . . . . . .60 C4
Wallington Sta SM6 . . . . .60 B4
Wallis Ct RH10 . . . . .181 F2
Wallis Ho RH19 . . . . .185 E1
Wallis Mews KT22 . . . . .95 A5
Wallis Way RH13 . . . . .218 A4
Wallner Way RG40 . . . . .25 E5
Wallorton Gdns SW14 . . . . . . .7 D3
Walmer Cl
Crowthorne RG45 . . . . .45 C5
Frimley GU16 . . . . .86 A7
Walmer Ho 10 SE20 . . . . .23 C1
Walmsley Ho 1 SW16 . . . . . .21 C4
Walnut Cl
Aldershot GU11 . . . . .126 A8
Epsom KT18 . . . . .76 F4
Wallington SM5 . . . . .59 F5
Wokingham RG40 . . . . .25 C6
Walnut Ct RH13 . . . . .217 E1
Walnut Dr KT20 . . . . .97 E3
Walnut Gr SM7 . . . . .77 D5
Walnut Ho RH2 . . . . .139 C7
Walnut La RH11 . . . . .181 B1
Walnut Mews
Bracknell RG42 . . . . .26 F8
Sutton SM2 . . . . .59 C3
Walnut Tree Ave CR4 . . . . . . .40 E6
Walnut Tree Cl
Barnes SW13 . . . . .7 F6
Belmont SM7 . . . . .77 E7
Guildford GU1 . . . . .130 C8
Walnut Tree Gdns GU7 . . . . .150 E7
Walnut Tree La KT14 . . . . . . .71 D7
Walnut Tree Pk GU1 . . . . . . .109 C1
Walnut Tree Rd
Brentford TW8 . . . . .6 E8
Charlton TW17 . . . . .34 C7
Heston TW5 . . . . .4 F8
Walpole Ave
Chipstead CR5 . . . . .98 F8
Richmond TW9 . . . . .6 F5
Walpole Cres 8 TW11 . . . . . .16 F3
Walpole Ct TW2 . . . . .16 E6
Walpole Gdns TW2 . . . . .16 E6
Walpole Pl 4 GU11 . . . . .105 B2
Walpole Pl 7 TW11 . . . . .16 F3
Walpole Rd
Croydon CR0,CR9 . . . . .61 D8
Mitcham SW19 . . . . .20 D2
Old Windsor SL4 . . . . .11 B8
Surbiton KT6 . . . . .37 E3
Teddington TW11 . . . . .16 F3
Twickenham TW2 . . . . .16 E6
Walsh CE Jun Sch
GU12 . . . . .106 A1
Walsh Cres CR0 . . . . .82 E7
Walsh Meml CE Inf Sch
GU12 . . . . .105 F1
Walsham Rd TW14 . . . . .15 B8
Walsingham Gdns KT19 . . . .57 F5
Walsingham Rd
Mitcham CR4 . . . . .40 F4
New Addington CR0 . . . . .63 C1
Walstead Ho 2 RH10 . . . . . .201 D5
Walter Inf Sch RG41 . . . . .25 A6
Walter St 2 KT2 . . . . .37 E8
Walter's Mead KT21 . . . . .75 E2
Walter's Rd SE25 . . . . .42 E5
Waltham Ave GU2 . . . . .109 B5
Waltham Cl GU47 . . . . .45 D1
Waltham Rd
Carshalton SM5 . . . . .40 E1

Waltham Rd continued
Caterham CR3 . . . . .101 B5
Walton Ave Cheam SM3 . . . . .58 F7
New Malden KT3 . . . . .38 F5
Walton Bridge Rd KT12,
TW17 . . . . .34 C2
Walton Comm Hospl
KT12 .54 B8
Walton Ct GU21 . . . . .70 A3
Walton Dr
Horsham RH13 . . . . .218 C4
North Ascot SL5 . . . . .28 F8
Walton Gdns TW13 . . . . .14 F4
Walton Gn CR0 . . . . .63 C3
Walton Heath RH10 . . . . .202 D6
Walton La
Lower Halliford TW17 . . . . . . .34 D2
Oatlands Park KT12 . . . . .34 E1
Weybridge KT12,KT13 . . . . . .53 C8
Walton Leigh Sch KT13 . . . . .53 F6
Walton on the Hill Prim Sch
KT20 .97 B3
Walton Park La KT12 . . . . . . .54 D8
Walton Pk KT12 . . . . .54 D8
Walton Rd Ashstead KT18 . . .96 C6
East Molesey KT8,KT12 . . . . .36 B5
Walton-on-T KT12,KT8 . . . . . .35 E4
Woking GU21 . . . . .70 A3
Walton St KT20 . . . . .97 B3
Walton Terr GU21 . . . . .70 B4
Walton Way CR4 . . . . .41 C5
Walton-on-thames Sta
KT12 .54 A6
Wanborough Dr SW15 . . . . . .19 B7
Wanborough Hill GU3 . . . . . .128 C6
Wanborough La GU6 . . . . . . .175 A3
Wanborough Sta GU3 . . . . . .107 C1
Wandle Bank
Merton SW19 . . . . .20 D1
Wallington CR0 . . . . .60 E7
Wandle Cl Ash GU12 . . . . . . .106 A1
Crawley RH10 . . . . .202 C5
Wandle Court Gdns CR0 . . . .60 E7
Wandle Ct Wallington CR0 . . .60 E7
West Ewell KT19 . . . . .57 C6
Wandle Ho Catford BR1 . . . . .24 D3
5 Redhill RH1 . . . . .118 F2
Wandsworth SW18 . . . . .20 B8
Wandle Lodge CR0 . . . . .60 E7
Wandle Pk Sta CR0 . . . . .61 A8
Wandle Prim Sch SW18 . . . . .20 B7
Wandle Rd
Croydon CR0,CR9 . . . . .61 C7
Hackbridge SM6 . . . . .60 B8
Morden CR4,SM4,SW19 . . . .40 D4
Upper Tooting SW17 . . . . .20 E6
Wallington CR0 . . . . .60 E7
Wandle Side Croydon CR0 . . .60 F7
Hackbridge SM6 . . . . .60 B7
Wandle Tech Pk CR4 . . . . . . .40 F2
Wandle Trad Est CR4 . . . . . . .40 F2
Wandle Valley Sch SM5 . . . . .40 F4
Wandle Way Mitcham CR4 . . .40 F4
Wandsworth SW18 . . . . .20 B7
Wandsdyke Cl GU16 . . . . .85 F8
Wandsworth Common Sta
SW12 . . . . .20 F8
Wansbeck Ho RH2 . . . . .139 A6
Wansford Gn 3 GU21 . . . . . .68 F2
Wanstraw Gr RG12 . . . . .27 E2
Wantage Cl
Bracknell RG12 . . . . .27 E4
Crawley RH10 . . . . .202 C3
Wantage Rd GU47 . . . . .64 D8
Waplings The KT20 . . . . .97 B3
Wapshott Rd TW18 . . . . .12 E3
War Coppice Rd CR3 . . . . . . .120 D7
War Meml Homes W4 . . . . .7 D7
War Meml Hospl SM5 . . . . . . .59 F4
Warbank Cl CR0 . . . . .63 E1
Warbank Cres CR0 . . . . .63 E1
Warbank La KT2 . . . . .18 F1
Warbeck Ho KT13 . . . . .53 D5
Warblers Gn KT11 . . . . .73 F5
Warbleton Ho 6 RH11 . . . . .200 F3
Warboys App KT2 . . . . .18 B2
Warboys Rd KT2 . . . . .18 B2
Warburton Cl RH19 . . . . .206 A8
Warburton Rd TW2 . . . . .16 B7
Warbury La GU21 . . . . .68 C3
Ward Cl RG40 . . . . .25 D8
Ward La CR6 . . . . .81 D4
Ward St GU1 . . . . .130 D8
Wardle Cl GU19 . . . . .47 E3
Wardley St SW18 . . . . .20 B8
Wardrobe The 3 TW9 . . . . . . .6 D2
Wards Stone Pk RG12 . . . . . .27 E2
Ware Ct SM1 . . . . .58 F6
Wareham Cl TW3 . . . . .5 B3
Wareham Rd RG12 . . . . .27 E3
Warenne Hts RH1 . . . . .139 D7
Warenne Rd KT22 . . . . .94 C5
Warfield Rd
Bracknell RG12 . . . . .27 C8
East Bedfont TW14 . . . . .14 E8
Hampton TW12 . . . . .36 B8
Wargrove Dr GU47 . . . . .64 D8
Warham Rd CR0,CR2 . . . . . . .61 C5
Waring St SE27 . . . . .22 C4
Warkworth Gdns TW7 . . . . . . .6 A7
Warlingham Park Sch
CR6 . . . . .82 A3
Warlingham Rd CR7 . . . . .42 B5
Warlingham Sec Sch
CR6 . . . . .81 B3

Warltersville Way RH6 .161 C1
Warminster Gdns SE25 .43 A7
Warminster Rd SE25 .43 A7
Warminster Sq SE25 .43 A7
Warminster Way CR4 .41 B7
Warner Ave SM3 .58 E8
Warner Cl Crawley RH10 .202 C2
  Feltham TW12 .15 F3
  Harlington UB3 .3 D7
Warner Ct Cheam SM3 .58 E8
  Sandhurst GU47 .64 E7
Warner Ho BR3 .24 B2
Warner Rd BR1 .24 F1
Warners La GU5 .132 E2
Warnford Ho SW15 .7 E1
Warnham CE Prim Sch
  RH12 .216 F8
Warnham Court Rd SM5 .59 F3
Warnham Ct RH12 .216 F7
Warnham Ho [9] SW2 .21 F8
Warnham Manor RH12 .216 C7
Warnham Nature Reserve*
  RH12 .217 B6
Warnham Rd
  Broadbridge Heath RH12 .216 D4
  Crawley RH10 .202 B4
  Horsham RH12 .217 B5
Warnham Sta RH12 .217 C8
Warpole Pk KT13 .53 A3
Warramill Rd GU7 .151 A5
Warren Ave Belmont SM2 .58 F1
  Bromley BR1 .24 E1
  Mortlake SW14,TW10 .7 B3
  South Croydon CR2 .62 D3
Warren Cl Esher KT10 .55 B6
  Felbridge RH19 .184 E3
  Sandhurst GU47 .64 A8
  West Norwood SE21 .22 C8
Warren Cnr GU10 .124 C7
Warren Ct
  [18] Beckenham BR3 .24 A1
  [6] Croydon CR0 .42 E1
Warren Cutting KT2 .18 D1
Warren Down RG42 .26 E8
Warren Dr Crawley RH11 201 A8
  Kingswood KT20 .98 A4
Warren Dr N KT5,KT6 .38 B1
Warren Dr S KT5 .38 C1
Warren Farm Cotts
  KT24 .113 C5
Warren Farm Mobile Home
  Pk GU23 .91 B8
Warren Hill KT18 .76 D3
Warren House Rd RG40 .25 D8
Warren La Oxshott KT22 .74 C7
  Oxted RH8 .123 A1
  Woking GU22 .71 B1
Warren Lodge KT20 .97 E3
Warren Lodge Dr KT20 .97 E3
Warren Mead SM7 .77 C4
Warren Mead Com Jun Sch
  SM7 .77 D4
Warren Mead Inf Sch
  SM7 .77 D4
Warren Park Rd SM1 .59 E4
Warren Pk
  Kingston u T KT2 .18 C2
  Warlingham CR6 .81 D1
Warren Rd Ashford TW15 .14 E1
  Banstead KT17,SM7 .77 D5
  Croydon CR0 .42 F1
  Farncombe GU7 .150 E7
  Guildford GU1 .131 A8
  Kingston u T KT2 .18 C2
  Mitcham SW19 .20 E2
  Purley CR8 .80 B8
  Reigate RH2 .118 B2
  Twickenham TW2 .5 D1
  Woodham KT15 .52 A1
Warren Rise Frimley GU16 65 F3
  Kingston u T KT3 .38 D8
Warren Row SL5 .28 D7
Warren The
  Aldershot GU11 .104 F1
  Ashstead KT21 .95 F7
  East Horsley KT24 .112 F5
  Heath End GU9 .125 E8
  Heston TW5 .4 F7
  Kingswood KT20 .97 E4
  Oxshott KT22 .74 D6
  Wallington SM5 .59 E2
  Weybridge KT13 .53 A5
  Worcester Park KT19,KT4 .57 D7
Warren Way KT13 .53 C4
Warren Wood Cl BR2 .63 F8
Warreners La KT13 .53 D3
Warrenhyrst GU1 .131 A8
Warrenne Rd RH3 .137 C7
Warrenne Way RH2 .118 A1
Warrington Cl RH11 .200 E2
Warrington Mews GU11 125 E8
Warrington Rd
  Croydon CR0,CR9 .61 B7
  [21] Richmond TW10 .6 D2
Warrington Spur SL4 .11 B8
Warwick RG12 .27 E3
Warwick Ave
  Staines TW18 .13 C2
  Thorpe Lea TW20 .32 C8
Warwick Cl
  Aldershot GU11 .126 C8
  Frimley GU15 .66 B3
  Hampton TW12 .16 B3
  South Holmwood RH5 .157 B7

Warwick Ct
  [1] Beckenham BR2 .44 E7
  Weybridge KT13 .53 A5
Warwick Deeping KT16 .51 C5
Warwick Gdns
  Ashtead KT21 .75 C2
  Thames Ditton KT7 .36 F4
  Thornton Heath CR7 .42 A5
Warwick Gr KT5 .37 F2
Warwick Ho
  Aldershot GU11 .126 C8
  [6] Kingston u T KT2 .37 E8
Warwick La GU21 .89 A8
Warwick Lodge SM1 .58 F6
Warwick Quadrant RH1 119 A2
Warwick Rd
  Ash Vale GU12 .106 A8
  Ashford TW15 .13 E3
  Coulsdon CR5 .79 D5
  Hounslow TW4 .4 B4
  Kingston u T KT3 .38 C6
  Penge SE20 .43 B6
  Redhill RH1 .119 A2
  South Holmwood RH5 .157 C7
  Sutton SM1 .59 C5
  Teddington KT1 .37 C8
  Thames Ditton KT7 .36 F4
  Thornton Heath CR7 .42 A6
  Twickenham TW2 .16 E7
Warwick Sch The RH1 .119 A2
Warwick Villas TW20 .32 C8
Warwick Wold Rd RH1 .120 A7
Warwick's Bench Rd
  GU1 .130 E6
Warwicks Bench GU1 .130 D6
Wasdale Cl GU47 .45 D2
Washington Cl RH2 .118 A3
Washington Ct SW17 .20 F2
Washington Rd
  Crawley RH11 .200 E3
  Kingston u T KT1 .38 A7
  North Cheam KT4 .39 B1
Washpond La CR6 .82 C1
Wasp Green La RH1 .162 C8
Wassand Cl RH10 .202 A6
Wasdale Gdns SE23 .23 D7
Watchetts Cty Jun Sch
  GU15 .65 B2
Watchetts Dr GU15 .65 C2
Watchetts Lake Cl GU15 .65 D3
Watchetts Rd GU15 .65 B4
Watchmoor Pk GU15 .65 B3
Watchmoor Rd GU15 .65 A4
Watchmoor Trade Ctr
  GU15 .65 A3
Watcombe Cotts TW9 .7 A8
Watcombe Rd SE25 .43 B4
Water La
  Abinger Common RH5 ..155 B8
  Albury GU5 .132 B5
  Bisley GU24 .87 E8
  Cobham KT11 .73 F5
  Enton Green GU8 .171 A2
  Farnborough GU14 .85 A7
  Farnham GU9 .125 F4
  Kingston u T KT1 .37 D8
  Limpsfield RH8 .123 A8
  Lingfield TN8 .165 D7
  Little Bookham KT23 .93 E1
  Richmond TW10,TW9 .6 D2
  South Godstone RH9 .142 D5
  Twickenham TW1 .17 A7
Water Lea RH10 .202 A5
Water Mead CR5 .78 F2
Water Mill Way TW13 .16 A6
Water Splash La SL5 .29 E8
Water View RH6 .161 C3
Waterbank Rd SE6 .24 C4
Watercress Pl RH13 .217 F3
Watercress Way GU21 ..69 B2
Waterden Cl GU1 .130 F8
Waterden Rd GU1 .130 E8
Waterer Gdns KT20 .77 E1
Waterer Ho SE6 .24 C4
Waterer Rise SM6 .60 D4
Waterers Rise GU21 .68 D2
Waterfall Cl GU25 .31 A6
Waterfall Cotts SW19 ..20 D2
Waterfall Rd SW19 .20 D2
Waterfall Terr SW17 .20 E2
Waterfield KT20 .97 B7
Waterfield Cl RH13 .217 E3
Waterfield Dr CR6 .101 C8
Waterfield Fst Sch
  RH11 .200 E4
Waterfield Gdns
  Crawley RH11 .200 E4
  South Norwood SE25 ..42 E4
Waterfield Gn KT20 .97 B7
Waterfields KT22 .95 B8
Waterford Cl KT11 .73 E8
Waterford Way RG40 ..25 C6
Watergardens The KT2 .18 C2
Watergate SE6 .24 B3
Waterham Rd RG12 .27 B3
Waterhouse Ct [5] TW11 .16 F3
Waterhouse La
  Bletchingley RH1,RH9 ..121 A3
  Coulsdon CR8 .100 C8
  Kingswood KT20 .97 E6
Waterhouse Mead GU47 .64 D7
Waterlands La RH13 .196 E1
Waterloo Cl
  Camberley GU15 .66 B7
  East Bedfont TW14 .14 F7
Waterloo Cotts [4] SM6 .59 E7
Waterloo Cres RG40 .25 E4
Waterloo Pl TW9 .7 A8

Waterloo Rd
  Aldershot GU12 .105 C1
  Carshalton SM1 .59 D5
  Crowthorne RG45 .45 B4
  Epsom KT17,KT19 .76 D6
  Wokingham RG40 .25 F5
Waterlow Rd RH2 .139 D8
Watermans Ct [12] TW8 .6 D8
Watermead
  East Bedfont TW14 .14 E7
  Tadworth KT20 .97 B6
  Woking GU21 .68 F3
Watermead Ho [2] SM1 .59 C4
Watermead La CR4 .40 F2
Watermead Rd SE6 .24 C4
Watermen's Sq [2] SE20 .23 C1
Watermill Cl TW10 .17 C5
Watermill Way SW19 ..40 C8
Waterperry La GU24 .49 F1
Waters Dr TW18 .12 F4
Waters Rd Catford SE6 ..24 E5
  Kingston u T KT1 .38 B7
Waters Sq KT1 .38 B6
Watersedge KT19 .57 C6
Waterside
  [5] Beckenham BR3 .44 A8
  East Grinstead RH19 ..186 B1
  Horley RH6 .161 A5
Waterside Cl
  Crawley RH11 .200 E4
  Godalming GU7 .151 A5
  Surbiton KT6 .56 E8
Waterside Ct SM6 .60 A7
Waterside Dr KT12 .35 B4
Waterside La GU7 .150 C5
Waterside Mews GU1 .109 C3
Waterside Rd GU1 .109 D4
Waterside Trad Est KT15 .52 E6
Waterside Way
  Wimbledon SW17 .20 C3
  [2] Woking GU21 .69 B1
Watersland Rd RH1 ..118 E1
Watersmeet Cl GU4 ..110 A6
Watersplash Cl KT1 .37 E6
Watersplash Rd TW17 .34 A5
Waterway Rd
  Fetcham KT22 .95 A5
  Leatherhead KT22 .95 A5
Watery La SW19,SW20 .39 F7
Wates Way CR4 .40 F3
Watford Cl GU1 .109 F1
Wathen Rd RH4 .136 B8
Watlings Cl CR0 .43 E3
Watlington Gr SE26 .23 E3
Watney Cotts SW14 ..7 C4
Watney Rd SW14 .7 C4
Watneys Rd CR4 .41 D4
Watson Ave SM3 .58 E8
Watson Cl Crawley RH10 .202 C3
  Mitcham SW19 .20 E1
Watson Ho [3] SW2 .21 E8
Watson Rd RH4 .115 C8
Watt's La Tadworth KT20 .97 D5
  Teddington TW11 .17 A3
Watt's Mead KT20 .97 D5
Wattenden Prim Sch The
  CR8 .80 B3
Wattendon Rd CR8 .80 B3
Watts Lea GU21 .69 A4
Watts Rd
  Farnborough GU14 .84 F5
  Thames Ditton KT7 .37 A2
Wavel Ct [7] SW16 .21 E5
Wavel Pl SE19,SE26 .22 F4
Wavendene Ave TW20 .12 C1
Waveney Ho [5] RH1 .118 F1
Waveney Wlk RH10 .202 B4
Waverleigh Rd GU6 .174 E1
Waverley RG12 .26 E4
Waverley Abbey* GU9 .147 B7
Waverley Abbey CE Jun Sch
  GU10 .147 D5
Waverley Ave Kenley CR8 .80 E3
  Sutton SM1 .59 C8
  Tolworth KT5 .38 C3
  Twickenham TW2 .16 A7
Waverley Cl
  Farnham GU9 .125 D2
  Frimley GU15 .65 F4
Waverley Ct
  Horsham RH12 .217 B2
  Woking GU22 .69 E1
Waverley Dr
  Addlestone KT16 .51 D7
  Ash Vale GU12 .106 A6
  Camberley GU15 .65 F5
  Virginia Water GU25 ..31 A5
Waverley Gdns GU12 .106 A6
Waverley La
  Farnham GU10,GU9 ..147 C8
  Farnham, Compton GU9 .125 E1
Waverley Pl KT22 .95 B5
Waverley Rd
  Bagshot GU19 .47 E3
  Croydon SE25 .43 B6
  Farnborough GU14 .85 D3
  Oxshott KT22 .74 B5
  Stoneleigh KT17,KT4 ..58 B5
  Weybridge KT13 .53 A5
Waverley Way SM2 .59 E4
Waverton Rd SW18 .20 C8
Wavertree Ct [9] SW2 .21 E7
Wavertree Rd SW2 .21 E7
Way The RH2 .118 D2
Waye Ave TW5 .4 A6
Wayland Cl RG12 .27 F5
Waylands Mead BR3 ..44 B8

Waylett Pl SE27 .22 B5
Wayman Rd GU14 .84 E8
Wayneflete Tower Ave
  KT10 .55 A7
Waynflete Ave CR0,CR9 .61 B7
Waynflete La GU9 .124 F2
Waynflete St SW18 .20 C6
Ways End GU15 .65 E4
Wayside Capel RH5 .178 D6
  Crawley RH11 .200 E4
  Mortlake SW14 .7 C2
  New Addington CR0 .63 B4
Wayside Cotts
  Ellen's Green GU6 .195 F4
  Holmbury St M RH5 .155 C6
Wayside Ct Hounslow TW7 .5 E5
  Twickenham TW1 .6 C1
  Woking GU21 .68 F3
WC Lee's Resthouses
  GU20 .48 D4
Weald CE Prim Sch The
  RH5 .157 D3
Weald Cl GU4 .130 E3
Weald Day Hospl The
  RH11 .201 C6
Weald Dr RH10 .202 A4
Weald The RH19 .185 F4
Weald View Cotts RH5 .156 D3
Weald Way
  Caterham CR3 .120 E8
  Reigate RH2 .139 C5
Wealdon Ct [1] GU2 .108 F1
Wealdstone Rd SM3 .58 F8
Weall Cl CR8 .79 F7
Weapon Rd GU14 .85 B2
Weare St Capel RH5 .178 B4
  Ockley RH5 .177 F1
Weasdale Ct GU21 .68 F3
Weather Way RG12 .27 C7
Weatherall Cl KT15 .52 B5
Weatherhill Cl RH6 .161 E3
Weatherhill Cotts RH6 .162 A4
Weatherhill Rd RH6 .162 A3
Weatherill Ct SE25 .43 B3
Weaver Cl [5] RH11 .200 E4
Weaver Moss GU47 .64 B7
Weaver Wlk SE27 .22 B4
Weavers Cl TW7 .5 E3
Weavers Gdns GU9 .145 F7
Weavers Yd [17] GU9 .125 B2
Webb Cl Bagshot GU19 .47 E1
  Crawley RH11 .201 B1
Webb Ct RG40 .25 E8
Webb Ho TW13 .15 E5
Webb Rd GU8 .170 C6
Webster Cl KT22 .74 B5
Websters Cl GU22 .89 B7
Weddell Rd RH10 .201 F3
Wedgewood Ct [1] BR2 .44 F5
Wedgwood Way SE19 ..22 C1
Wedgwoods TN16 .103 C6
Weeks Ho TW10 .17 C4
Weighbridge Rd KT15 ..52 B2
Weighton Rd SE20 .43 B7
Weihurst Ct SM1 .59 E5
Weihurst Gdns SM1 .59 D5
Weir Ave GU14 .85 A3
Weir Cl GU14 .85 A3
Weir Ho [8] SW12 .21 C8
Weir Pl TW18 .32 E8
Weir Rd Chertsey KT16 ..33 B2
  Farnborough GU14,GU51 .84 A2
  Streatham SW12 .21 C8
  Walton-on-T KT12 .35 A3
  Wimbledon SW18,SW19 .20 B5
Weir Wood Resr (Nature
  Reserve)* RH19 .205 E2
Weirbrook RH10 .202 A3
Welbeck RG12 .26 E4
Welbeck Cl Ewell KT17 ..58 A3
  Farnborough GU14 .84 F3
  New Malden KT3 .38 F4
Welbeck Rd SM1,SM5 ..59 D8
Welbeck Wlk SM5 .40 D1
Welcome Cotts CR3 .102 A4
Welcomes Rd CR8 .80 C3
Welcomes Terr CR3 .80 F3
Weldon Cl
  [7] Carshalton SM1 .59 D5
  Thornton Heath CR7 ..42 B4
Weldon Dr KT8 .35 F5
Weldon Way RH1 .119 D6
Welford Pl SW19 .19 E4
Welham Rd SW16,SW17 .21 B2
Welhouse Rd SM5 .59 E8
Well Cl Camberley GU15 .65 B4
  Streatham SW16 .21 F4
  Woking GU21 .69 C2
Well Ct KT6 .37 D2
Well Farm Rd CR3,CR6 .101 A8
Well Ho SM7 .78 B4
Well La Haslemere GU27 .208 D6
  Mortlake SW14 .7 C2
  Woking GU21 .69 C2
Well Path GU21 .69 C2
Well Way KT18 .76 A5
Welland Ct SL3 .1 B8
Wellburn Cl GU47 .64 B7
Welldon Ct [1] SE21 .22 D6
Weller Cl RH10 .202 D5
Weller Dr GU15 .65 C3
Wellers Ct GU5 .133 A4
Wellesford Cl SM7 .77 F2
Wellesley
  Ash Vale GU12 .105 F7
  Bagshot GU19 .47 C3
Wellesley Court Rd [1]
  CR0,CR9 .61 D8

Wellesley Cres TW2 .16 E5
Wellesley Ct Cheam SM3 .39 E1
  Twickenham TW2 .16 E5
Wellesley Gate [3] GU12 .105 B1
Wellesley Gdn GU9 .125 C7
Wellesley Gr CR0,CR9 .61 D8
Wellesley Rd
  Aldershot GU11 .104 E2
  Croydon CR0 .42 C1
  Rushmoor GU10 .168 C6
  Sutton SM2 .59 C4
  Twickenham TW2 .16 E5
Wellfield RH19 .206 C7
Wellfield Gdns SM5 .59 E2
Wellfield Rd SW16 .21 E4
Wellhouse La RH3 .137 D6
Wellhouse Rd BR3 .44 A5
Wellington Ave
  Aldershot GU11 .104 F1
  Hounslow TW3,TW4 .5 A1
  North Cheam KT4 .58 C7
  Virginia Water GU25 ..31 B4
Wellington Cl
  Crawley RH10 .182 E1
  Sandhurst GU47 .64 C8
  Walton-on-T KT12 .34 F1
Wellington Coll RG45 ..45 A3
Wellington Cotts KT24 .112 C6
Wellington Cres KT3 ..38 C6
Wellington Ct
  Stanwell TW19 .13 E8
  [5] Surbiton KT6 .37 E3
  Teddington TW11 .16 D3
Wellington Ctr The [20]
  GU11 .105 A2
Wellington Dr
  Bracknell RG12 .27 E4
  Wallington CR8 .60 F1
Wellington Gdns
  Aldershot GU11 .104 F1
  Teddington TW2 .16 D4
Wellington La GU9 .125 D7
Wellington Mews SW16 .21 D5
Wellington Pl
  Ash Vale GU12 .105 F4
  Cobham KT11 .73 C7
  Farncombe GU7 .150 E7
Wellington Prim Sch TW3 .4 F5
Wellington Rd
  Ashford TW15 .13 E3
  Caterham CR3 .100 C5
  Crowthorne RG45 .45 C4
  Hatton TW14 .3 E2
  Horsham RH12 .217 D2
  Sandhurst GU47 .64 C8
  Teddington TW12,TW2 .16 D4
  Thornton Heath CR0 .42 B2
  Wimbledon SW19 .20 A6
  Wokingham RG40 .25 B5
Wellington Rd N TW4 ..4 F4
Wellington Rd S TW4 ..4 F3
Wellington Rdbt GU11 .104 E2
Wellington St [8] GU11 .105 A2
Wellington Terr
  [6] Knaphill GU21 .68 E1
  Sandhurst GU47 .64 C8
Wellington Town Rd
  RH19 .185 D2
Wellington Way
  Byfleet KT13 .52 F1
  Horley RH6 .160 F5
Wellingtonia Ho KT15 ..52 A5
Wellmeadow Rd SE13,
  SE6 .24 E7
Wellow Wlk SM5 .40 D1
Wells Cl
  Great Bookham KT23 ..94 C3
  Horsham RH12 .216 F2
  South Croydon CR2 ..61 E5
Wells Cotts GU9 .146 A7
Wells Ct [1] CR4 .40 E8
Wells La Ascot SL5 .29 B5
  Normandy GU3 .107 C4
Wells Lea RH19 .185 D3
Wells Mdw RH19 .185 D3
Wells Park Ct SE26 .23 B4
Wells Park Rd SE21,SE26 .23 B4
Wells Pl RH1 .119 B6
Wells Rd Crawley RH10 .201 E2
  Epsom KT18 .76 B4
  Guildford GU4 .110 C4
Wells The GU27 .208 C6
Wellside Gdns SW14 ..7 C2
Wellwood Cl
  Coulsdon CR5,CR8 .79 E5
  Horsham RH13 .218 B4
Wellwynds Rd GU6 .174 E2
Welwyn Ave TW14 .3 F1
Welwyn Cl RH11 .200 E2
Wembley Rd TW12 .36 A8
Wembury Pk RH7 .163 E1
Wend The CR5 .79 D5
Wendela Cl GU22 .69 F1
Wendley Dr KT15 .51 F1
Wendling Rd SM1 .59 D8
Wendover Dr
  Frimley GU16 .66 C3
  New Malden KT3 .38 F3
Wendover Pl TW18 .12 D3
Wendover Rd TW18,TW20 12 D3
Wendron Cl [2] GU21 ..69 A1
Wendy Cres GU2 .109 A3
Wenlock Cl RH11 .201 A4
Wenlock Edge RH4 .136 C5
Wensleydale RH11 .201 C3
Wensleydale Dr GU15 ..66 D5
Wensleydale Gdns TW12 .16 B1
Wensleydale Rd TW12 .16 B1

Wentland Cl SE6 24 D6
Wentland Rd SE6 24 D6
Wentworth RH6 161 B2
Wentworth Ave SL5 28 C7
Wentworth Cl
Ash Vale GU12 106 A7
Ashford TW15 14 B4
Heath End GU9 125 F6
Long Ditton KT6 56 D8
Morden SM4 40 A2
Ripley GU23 91 B6
Wentworth Cres GU12 106 A6
Wentworth Ct
20 Kingston u T KT6 37 E4
Twickenham TW2 16 E5
Wentworth Dene KT13 53 B5
Wentworth Dr
Crawley RH10 202 D7
Wentworth GU25 30 F5
Wentworth Golf Club GU25 31 A4
Wentworth Ho KT15 52 B6
Wentworth Rd CR0 42 A2
Wentworth Way
Hamsey Green CR2 81 A4
North Ascot SL5 28 C7
Werndee Rd SE25 43 A5
Wesco Ct GU21 70 A3
Wescott Inf Sch RG40 25 D6
Wescott Rd RG40 25 D6
Wesley Ave TW3 4 F5
Wesley Cl Crawley RH11 200 E3
Horley RH6 161 A5
Reigate RH2 138 F8
Wesley Dr TW20 12 A2
Wesley Pl SL4 9 B6
Wessels KT20 97 D6
Wessex Ave SW19 40 A6
Wessex Cl
Hinchley Wood KT7 55 F8
Kingston u T KT1,KT2 38 B8
Wessex Ct 4 TW19 2 E1
Wessex Pl GU9 125 C1
Wessex Rd
Farnborough GU14 84 E1
Harmondsworth TW19,TW6 2 E4
Wesson Ho 3 CR0 43 A1
West Ashtead Prim Sch KT21 95 E7
West Ave Crawley RH10 202 A8
Heath End GU9 125 D7
Redhill RH1 140 A3
Wallington SM6 60 E5
Whiteley Village KT12,KT13 53 E2
West Bank RH4 136 A6
West Barnes La
West Barnes KT3 39 B5
West Barnes KT3,SW20 39 B4
West Barnes KT3,SW20 39 B6
West Byfleet Inf Sch KT14 71 B7
West Byfleet Jun Sch KT14 71 B7
West Byfleet Sta KT14 71 A7
West Cl Ashford TW15 13 E4
Heath End GU9 125 D7
West Clandon Sta GU4 111 B6
West Cotts GU26 188 C6
West Cross Ctr TW8 6 B8
West Cross Way TW8 6 B8
West Croydon Sta CR0 42 C1
West Ct Guildford GU4 110 B5
Hounslow TW7 5 C7
West Down KT23 114 B8
West Dr Belmont SM2 58 E2
Burgh Heath KT20 77 D1
Streatham SW16,SW17 21 C4
Sutton SM5 59 D1
Wentworth GU25,SL5 30 E2
Woodham KT15 52 B2
West Dulwich Sta SE21 22 D7
West End Cotts GU23 91 B5
West End Gdns KT10 54 F5
West End Gr GU9 125 A2
West End Inf Sch GU11 104 F2
West End La
Chiddingfold GU27 190 E1
Esher KT10 54 F4
Frensham GU10 146 B1
Harlington UB7 3 C7
West Ewell Inf Sch KT19 57 D5
West Farm Ave KT21 95 D8
West Farm Cl KT21 95 C8
West Farm Dr KT21 95 D8
West Flexford La GU3 128 E8
West Gdns Ewell KT17 57 F1
Mitcham SW19 20 E2
West Gr KT12 54 B6
West Green Dr RH11 201 C6
West Green Fst Sch RH11 201 C7
West Hall Rd TW9 7 B6
West Hanger Nature Trail* GU5 133 A7
West Heath GU24 87 D4
West Heath Rd GU14 84 F4
West Hill Biggin Hill BR6 83 F7
Dormans Park RH19 185 E6
East Grinstead RH19 205 D8
Elstead GU8 148 C3
Epsom KT18,KT19 76 C6
Oxted RH8 122 D5
Putney SW15 19 D8
South Croydon CR2 61 E2
Woking GU22 89 E8
West Hill Ave KT19 76 C7
West Hill Bank RH8 122 D5
West Hill Cl
Brookwood GU24 88 B7
Elstead GU8 148 C3
West Hill Rd
Wandsworth SW18 20 A8
Woking GU22 89 E8
West Hill Sch KT22 75 A1
West Ho Penge SE20 23 D1
9 Streatham SW12 21 C8
West Hoathly Rd RH19 205 D4
West House Cl SW19 19 E7
West La
East Grinstead RH19 205 D8
Wotton RH5 134 D4
West Leigh RH19 205 E7
West Mead KT19 57 E4
West Mead Sch RG40 25 E6
West Meads GU2 129 F8
West Middlesex Univ Hosp TW7 6 A5
West Mount GU2 130 C7
West Norwood Sta SE27 22 C4
West Oak BR3 44 D8
West Palace Gdns KT13 53 B7
West Par RH12 217 C4
West Park Ave TW9 7 B6
West Park Cl TW5 4 F8
West Park Hospl KT19 75 E7
West Park Rd
Domewood RH10,RH7 183 F5
Epsom KT19 75 F7
Horne RH7 184 B7
Richmond TW9 7 A6
West Parkside CR6 82 A3
West Pl SW19 19 C3
West Ramp TW6 3 A6
West Rd Bracknell RG40 26 D2
Camberley GU15 65 D5
Chessington KT9 75 C8
East Bedfont TW14 14 D8
Farnborough GU14 85 B8
Guildford GU1 130 E8
Kingston u T KT2,KT3 38 C8
Reigate RH2 139 B8
Weybridge KT13 53 B3
West Ring GU10 126 F7
West Sheen Vale TW9 6 F3
West Side Comm SW19 19 C3
West St Carshalton SM5 59 F6
Crawley RH11 201 D5
Croydon CR0,CR9 61 C6
Dorking RH4 136 A7
Dormansland RH7 165 A1
East Grinstead RH19 205 E8
Epsom KT18,KT19 76 C6
Ewell KT17 57 F1
Farnham GU9 125 A2
Haslemere GU27 208 C6
Horsham RH12 217 C2
Reigate RH2 117 F1
Sutton SM1 59 B5
Woking GU21 69 F2
West Street La SM5 59 F6
West Street Pl 1 CR0, CR9 61 C6
West Surrey Estates TW15 34 C8
West Sussex Ho GU2 129 E8
West Sutton Sta SM1 59 A6
West Temple Sheen SW14 7 B2
West Thames Coll TW7 5 E6
West Thornton Prim Sch CR0 41 F3
West View TW14 14 C8
West View Ave CR3 80 F1
West View Cotts RH8 122 A2
West View Gdns RH19 205 E8
West View Rd
Headley Down GU35 187 C4
Warlingham CR6 101 B8
West Way Crawley RH10 202 A7
Croydon CR0 62 E7
Heston TW5 4 F6
Shepperton TW17 34 D3
Slinfold RH13 215 D3
Sutton SM2,SM5 59 D1
West Wickham BR4 44 E3
West Way Gdns CR0 62 D8
West Wickham Sta BR4 44 C2
West Wimbledon Prim Sch SW20 39 B6
Westacres KT10 54 F3
Westbank Rd TW12 16 C2
Westborough Com Prim Sch GU2 108 F2
Westbourne RH4 136 C5
Westbourne Ave SM3 58 E8
Westbourne Dr SE23 23 D6
Westbourne Ho
Heston TW5 5 A8
9 Twickenham TW1 17 B8
Westbourne Prim Sch SM1 59 A7
Westbourne Rd
Croydon CR0 42 F3
Feltham TW13 14 F5
Penge SE26 23 D2
Sandhurst GU47 64 E7
Staines TW18 13 B1
Westbrook RH18 206 E3
Westbrook Ave TW12 15 F1
Westbrook Gdns RG12 27 D8
Westbrook Hill GU8 148 C3
Westbrook Rd
Godalming GU7 150 C5
Heston TW5 4 F7
South Norwood CR7 42 D7
Staines TW18 12 F3
Westbury Ave KT10 55 F4
Westbury Cl
Crowthorne RG45 45 B6
Shepperton TW17 34 B3
Whyteleafe CR3 80 F1
Westbury Ct BR3 44 B8
Westbury Gdns GU9 125 E4
Westbury House Sch KT3 38 D4
Westbury Pl 2 TW8 6 D8
Westbury Rd
Beckenham BR3 43 E6
Feltham TW13 15 D6
New Malden KT3 38 D4
Penge SE20 43 D8
Thornton Heath CR0 42 D3
Westbury Way GU12 105 D2
Westcar La KT12 54 B5
Westcombe Ave CR0 41 F2
Westcombe Cl RG12 27 E2
Westcoombe Ave SW20 38 F8
Westcote Rd SW16 21 C3
Westcott CE Fst Sch RH4 135 D5
Westcott Cl CR0 63 B2
Westcott Keep RH6 161 C4
Westcott Rd RH4 135 F7
Westcott St RH4 135 B6
Westcott Way SM2 58 C1
Westcroft Gdns SM4, SW20 39 F5
Westcroft Rd SM5,SM6 60 A6
Westdene GU7 150 E3
Westdene Mdws GU6 174 A3
Westdene Way KT13 53 E7
Westdown Rd SE13,SE6 24 A8
Westende RG40 25 D6
Westende Jun Sch RG40 25 D6
Westerdale Dr GU16 66 B3
Westerfolds Cl GU22 70 C2
Westerham 13 KT6 37 E4
Westerham Cl
Belmont SM2 59 A1
New Haw KT15 52 C4
Westerham Lodge 10 BR3 24 A1
Westerham Rd RH8, TN16 123 C6
Westerley Cres SE26,SE6 23 F3
Westermain KT15 52 C1
Western Ave
Brookwood GU24 88 A6
Chertsey KT16 33 A6
Thorpe TW20 32 B6
Western Cl KT16 33 A6
Western Ctr The RG12 26 F7
Western Dr TW17 34 D3
Western Ind Area RG12 26 F7
Western La SW12 21 A8
Western Par RH2 139 B6
Western Perimeter Rd TW19,TW6,UB7 2 B5
Western Perimeter Rd Rdbt TW19 2 C2
Western Rd
Aldershot GU11 104 E1
Bracknell RG12 26 F7
Mitcham CR4,SW19 40 E7
Sutton SM1 59 A5
Westfield Ashtead KT21 75 F1
Peaslake RH5 154 E8
Reigate RH2 118 B4
Westfield Ave
Sanderstead CR2 80 E6
Woking GU22 89 E7
Westfield Cl SM1 58 F6
Westfield Comm GU22 89 E5
Westfield Ct
Kingston u T KT6 37 D4
New Haw KT15 52 D1
Westfield Dr KT23 94 B5
Westfield Gdns 2 RH4 136 A7
Westfield Gr GU22 89 E7
Westfield La GU10 145 E6
Westfield Par KT15 52 D1
Westfield Prim Sch GU22 89 E6
Westfield Rd
Beckenham BR3 43 F7
Camberley GU15 65 B2
Cheam SM1 58 F6
Crawley RH11 201 B6
Guildford GU1 109 E5
Kingston u T KT6 37 D4
Mitcham CR4 40 F7
Thornton Heath CR0,CR9 61 B8
Walton-on-T KT12 35 E2
Woking GU22 89 E5
Westfield Way GU22 89 F5
Westfields Mortlake SW13 7 F4
Witley GU8 170 F5
Westfields Ave SW13,SW14 7 E4
Westgate Ho KT18 76 D4
Westgate Rd
Beckenham BR3 44 C8
Croydon SE25 43 B5
Westglade GU14 84 D4
Westhall Pk CR6 101 C8
Westhall Rd CR6 101 B8
Westhay Gdns SW14 7 B2
Westhumble St RH5 115 B4
Westland Cl TW19 2 E1
Westland Dr BR2,BR4 63 F8
Westlands RH13 217 E3
Westlands Ct
East Molesey KT8 36 E5
Epsom KT18 76 C4
Westlands Way RH8 122 D8
Westleas RH6 160 E5
Westlees Cl RH5 136 D4
Westleigh Ave CR5 79 B3
Westmacott Dr TW14 14 F7
Westmark Point 13 SW15 19 B7
Westmead
Farnborough GU14 85 B3
10 Farnham GU9 125 B2
Putney SW15 19 B8
Woking GU21 69 B2
Westmead Dr RH1 140 A1
Westmead Rd SM1 59 D6
Westmeads RH6 161 C3
Westminster Ave CR7 42 B7
Westminster Cl
East Bedfont TW14 15 A7
Teddington TW11 17 A3
Westminster Ct
Old Woking GU22 90 B6
South Norwood CR7 42 C7
Westminster Rd
Carshalton SM1 59 D8
Crawley RH10 202 C5
Westmoat Cl BR3 24 C1
Westmont Rd KT10 55 E8
Westmore Rd TN16 103 C7
Westmoreland Dr SM2 59 B2
Westmoreland Rd
Barnes SW13 7 F6
Beckenham BR2 44 F5
Westmoreland Terr SE20 23 B1
Westmorland Cl
Epsom KT19 57 E2
3 Twickenham TW1 6 B1
Westmorland Ct 12 KT6 37 D2
Westmorland Dr GU15 66 B3
Westmorland Sq CR4 41 E4
Westmorland Way CR4 41 E4
Weston Ave
Addlestone KT15 52 B6
East Molesey KT8 35 F5
Thames Ditton KT10,KT7 36 E2
Weston Cl Coulsdon CR5 99 F7
Farncombe GU7 150 E6
Weston Ct
Farncombe GU7 150 E6
3 Kingston u T KT1 37 E6
Weston Dr CR3 100 C6
Weston Farm Cotts GU5 132 B4
Weston Fields GU5 132 C4
Weston Gdns
Hounslow TW7 5 E6
Pyrford GU22 70 E3
Weston Gn KT7 36 E1
Weston Gr Bagshot GU19 47 F2
1 Bromley BR1 44 F8
Weston Green Prep Sch KT7 36 E1
Weston Green Rd KT7 36 E2
Weston Lea KT24 92 D2
Weston Park Cl KT7 36 E1
Weston Pk
Kingston u T KT1 37 E7
Thames Ditton KT10,KT7 36 E1
Weston Rd Bromley BR1 24 F1
Ewell KT17 76 E8
Guildford GU2 109 A2
Thames Ditton KT7 36 E1
Weston Way GU22 70 E3
Weston Yd GU5 132 C4
Westons Cl RH12 217 D7
Westover Cl SM2 59 B2
Westover Rd SW18 20 C8
Westow Hill SE19 22 F2
Westow St SE19 22 E2
Westpoint BR2 44 D6
Westside Ho RH1 140 B2
Westview 5 GU22 69 F1
Westview Cl RH1 139 E6
Westville Rd KT7 37 A2
Westward Ho GU1 109 F3
Westwates Cl RG12 27 D8
Westway Caterham CR3 100 D5
Copthorne RH10 183 A3
Crawley RH6 182 B7
Guildford GU2 108 F3
West Barnes KT3,SW20 39 C5
Wormley GU8 190 F8
Westway Cl SW20 39 B6
Westway Ct CR3 100 D4
Westway Gdns RH1 119 A4
Westways KT19 57 F6
Westwell Rd SW16 21 E2
Westwell Road App SW16 21 E2
Westwick Gdns TW4,TW5 4 B5
Westwood Ave
South Norwood SE19 42 C8
Woodham KT15 70 F7
Westwood Cl KT10 55 C7
Westwood Ct
3 Forest Hill SE23 23 C7
Guildford GU2 108 F2
7 Wimbledon SW19 19 F3
Westwood Gdns SW13 7 F4
Westwood Hill SE19,SE26 23 B4
Westwood La
Normandy GU3 107 A2
Wanborough GU3 128 B7
Westwood Language Coll for Girls SE19 22 D1
Westwood Pk SE23 23 B8
Westwood Pl SE26 23 A4
Westwood Rd
Coulsdon CR5 79 D1
Mortlake SW13,SW15 7 F4
Windlesham GU20 48 E6
Wetheral Ct SW17 20 D4
Wetherby Ct SE25 42 E7
Wetherby Gdns 2 GU14 85 C1
Wetherby Ho GU15 65 D7
Wetherby Way KT9 56 E3
Wettern Cl CR2 61 E1
Wetton Pl TW20 11 F3
Wexfenne Gdns GU22 71 B3
Wexford Rd SW12 20 F8
Wey Ave KT16 33 A6
Wey Cl Ash GU12 106 A1
Camberley GU15 65 B5
West Byfleet KT14 71 B6
Wey Ct Farncombe GU7 151 A6
7 Guildford GU1 130 C8
New Haw KT15 52 D2
West Ewell KT19 57 C6
Wey House Sch GU5 151 E8
Wey Manor Rd KT15 52 D2
Wey Rd Godalming GU7 151 A5
Weybridge KT13 52 F7
Wey Ret Pk KT14 71 E7
Wey View Ct GU1 130 C8
Weybank GU23 71 E3
Weybank Cl GU9 125 C3
Weybarton KT14 71 F6
Weybourne Inf Sch GU9 125 E6
Weybourne Pl CR2 61 D1
Weybourne Rd GU11, GU9 125 E6
Weybourne St SW18 20 C6
Weybridge Bsns Pk KT15 52 E6
Weybridge Ho KT13 53 D5
Weybridge Hospl KT13 53 A6
Weybridge Pk KT13 53 B5
Weybridge Rd
Addlestone KT15,KT13 52 E6
Thornton Heath CR7 42 A5
Weybridge Sta KT13 53 A4
Weybrook Dr GU4 110 B6
Weycombe Rd GU27 208 C8
Weydon Hill Cl GU9 146 B8
Weydon Hill Rd GU9 146 C8
Weydon La Farnham GU9 146 A8
Wrecclesham GU9 145 F8
Weydon Mill La GU9 125 B1
Weydon Sch GU9 145 F7
Weydown Cl
Guildford GU2 109 A6
Putney SW19 19 E7
Weydown Ct GU27 208 B7
Weydown Ind Est GU27 208 B7
Weydown La GU2 109 A6
Weydown Rd GU27 208 B7
Weyfield Prim Sch GU1 109 D4
Weyhill GU27 208 A6
Weylands Pk KT13 53 D4
Weylea Ave GU4 110 A4
Weymead Cl KT16 33 C1
Weymede KT14 71 F7
Weymouth Ct
Belmont SM2 59 A3
18 Streatham SW2 21 F8
Weyside Farnham GU9 125 C2
Weybridge KT13 53 B8
Weyside Cl KT14 71 F7
Weyside Gdns GU1 109 C3
Weyside Pk GU7 151 A5
Weyside Rd GU1 109 B3
Weysprings GU27 208 A6
Weyvern Pk GU3 130 B1
Weyview Cl GU1 109 C3
Weywood Cl GU9 125 F7
Weywood La GU9 125 E7
Whaley Rd RG40 25 D8
Wharf Bridge Rd TW7 6 B4
Wharf La Send GU23 90 C4
Twickenham TW1 17 A7
Wharf Rd Ash GU12 106 A4
Frimley GU16 86 A6
Guildford GU1 109 C1
Wraysbury TW19 11 D8
Wharf St GU7 150 E4
Wharf Way GU16 86 A6
Wharfedale Gdns CR7, SW16 41 F6
Wharfenden Way GU16 85 F6
Wharncliffe Gdns SE25 42 E7
Wharncliffe Rd SE25 42 E7
Whateley Rd
Guildford GU2 109 B5
Penge SE20 23 D1
Whatley Ave SW20 39 E6
Whatley Gn RG12 27 B3
Whatman Rd SE23 23 D8
Whatmore Cl TW19 2 A1
Wheat Knoll CR8 80 C3
Wheatash Rd KT15 52 B8
Wheatfield Way
Horley RH6 161 C4
Kingston u T KT1 37 E7
Wheathill Ho SE20 43 B7
Wheathill Rd SE20 43 B6
Wheatlands TW5 5 A8
Wheatlands Rd SW17 21 A5
Wheatley RG12 26 E4
Wheatley Ho 3 SW15 19 A8
Wheatley Rd
Aldershot GU11 104 F3
Isleworth TW7 5 F4
Wheatsheaf Cl
Horsham RH12 217 E5
Ottershaw KT16 51 D4
Woking GU21 69 F3
Wheatsheaf La TW18 12 F1

Wheatstone Cl
 Crawley RH10 . . . . .182 B3
 Mitcham SW19 . . . . .40 E8
Wheeler Ave RH8 . . . . .122 D6
Wheeler La GU8 . . . . .170 E6
Wheeler Rd RH10 . . . . .202 B4
Wheelers La
 Brockham RH3 . . . . .137 C7
 Epsom KT18 . . . . .76 C5
 Smallfield RH6 . . . . .162 B3
Wheelers Way RH19 . . . . . .184 E3
Wheelwrights La GU26 . . . .188 A4
Wheelwrights Pl SL3 . . . . . . .1 C7
Whelan Way SM6 . . . . .60 D7
Wherwell Lodge GU2 . . . . .130 C7
Wherwell Rd GU2 . . . . .130 C7
Whetstone Rd GU3 . . . . .84 C4
Whimbrel Cl CR2,CR8 . . . . . .80 D8
Whinfell Cl SW16 . . . . .21 D3
Whins Cl GU15 . . . . .65 B4
Whins Dr GU15 . . . . .65 B4
Whinshill Ct SL5 . . . . .30 A1
Whipley Cl GU4 . . . . .110 B6
Whistler Cl RH10 . . . . .201 F3
Whistler Gr GU47 . . . . .64 D6
Whistley Cl RG12 . . . . .27 E6
Whitby Cl Ash Vale GU12 . . . .85 F1
 Biggin Hill TN16 . . . . .83 B1
Whitby Gdns SM1 . . . . .59 D8
Whitby Rd SM1 . . . . .59 D8
Whitchurch Cl GU11 . . . . . .126 D6
Whitchurch Ct SW17 . . . . . . .20 D4
Whitchurch Ho SE6 . . . . .24 C5
Whitcome Mews TW9 . . . . . . .7 B6
White Acres Rd GU16 . . . . . .85 F4
White Beam Way KT20 . . . . .97 A6
White Bridge Ave CR4 . . . . . .40 D6
White Bridge Cl TW14 . . . . . . .3 F1
White Bushes RH1 . . . . . . .140 A4
White City RG45 . . . . .45 D5
White Cottage Cl GU9 . . . . .125 D6
White Ct GU2 . . . . .109 A4
White Hart Ct
 Horsham RH12 . . . . .217 C4
 Ripley GU23 . . . . .91 C6
White Hart Ind Est GU17 . . . .64 E4
White Hart La
 Mortlake SW14 . . . . .7 E4
 Wood St V GU3 . . . . .108 A2
White Hart Mdws GU23 . . . .91 C6
White Hart Row KT16 . . . . . .33 A2
White Heron Mews TW11 . . .16 F2
White Hill Kingswood CR5 . . .98 D4
 South Croydon CR2 . . . . . . .61 D1
 Windlesham GU20 . . . . .48 B6
White Ho **3** SW4 . . . . .21 D8
White Horse Dr KT18 . . . . . . .76 C5
White Horse La GU23 . . . . . . .91 C6
White House Ct BR3 . . . . . . .44 C8
White House La GU4 . . . . . .109 D6
White House Sch RG41 . . . . .25 A3
White House Wlk GU9 . . . . .125 D7
White Knights Rd KT13 . . . . .53 C3
White Knobs Way CR3 . . . . .101 A2
White La Guildford GU4 . . . .131 D7
 Titsey RH8,TN16 . . . . .103 B3
 Tongham GU10,GU12 . . . . .127 C7
White Lion Ct KT11 . . . . .73 A5
White Lion Wlk GU1 . . . . . .130 D7
White Lodge
 Ashstead KT21 . . . . .95 E7
 South Norwood SE19 . . . . . .22 B1
White Lodge Cl
 Isleworth TW7 . . . . .6 A5
 Sutton SM2 . . . . .59 C3
White Lodge Ct TW16 . . . . . .35 C8
White Lodge Gdns RH1 . . . .140 A1
White Lodge The Royal Ballet
 Sch TW10 . . . . .18 D7
White Oak Dr BR3 . . . . .44 D7
White Pillars GU23 . . . . .89 B7
White Post La GU10 . . . . . .146 A4
White Rd GU15 . . . . .64 F6
White Rose La
 Farnham GU9,GU10 . . . . . .146 B7
 Old Woking GU22 . . . . .90 A8
 Woking GU22 . . . . .69 F1
White Way KT23 . . . . .94 B1
Whitebeam Dr RH2 . . . . . . .139 B6
Whitebeam Gdns GU14 . . . . .84 C3
Whiteberry Rd RH5 . . . . . . .156 B7
Whitebines GU9 . . . . .125 D2
Whitecroft RH6 . . . . .161 B4
Whitecroft Cl BR3 . . . . .44 D5
Whitecroft Way BR3 . . . . . . .44 D5
Whitefield Ave CR8 . . . . .80 B3
Whitefield Ho CR8 . . . . .80 B3
Whitefoot La BR1,SE6 . . . . . .24 D5
Whitefoot Terr BR1 . . . . .24 F5
Whitegate Way KT20 . . . . . . .97 B7
Whitegates
 Old Woking GU22 . . . . .89 F7
 Whyteleafe CR3 . . . . .101 A8
Whitehall Cres KT9 . . . . .56 D5
Whitehall Dr RH11 . . . . .200 E6
Whitehall Farm La GU25 . . . .31 E4
Whitehall Gdns W4 . . . . .7 B8
Whitehall La Egham TW20 . . .11 F1
 Horton TW19 . . . . .1 A1
 Reigate RH2 . . . . .138 F6
Whitehall Park Rd W4 . . . . . . .7 B8
Whitehall Pl SM5 . . . . .60 B6
Whitehall Rd CR7 . . . . .42 A4
Whitehead Cl SW18 . . . . .20 C8
Whitehill Cl GU15 . . . . .65 D7

Whitehill La
 Bletchingley RH1 . . . . .120 D6
 Martyr's Green GU23 . . . . . .92 C4
Whitehill Pl GU25 . . . . .31 E4
Whitehorse La SE25 . . . . . . .42 E5
Whitehorse Manor Inf Sch
 CR7 . . . . .42 D5
Whitehorse Manor Jun Sch
 CR7 . . . . .42 D5
Whitehorse Rd
 Horsham RH12 . . . . .218 B6
 Thornton Heath CR0,CR7,
 SE25 . . . . .42 D3
Whitehouse Cl GU14 . . . . . . .85 B6
Whitehouse Dr GU1 . . . . . . .110 B1
Whitelands Coll,
 Roehampton Inst SW18 . . .19 E8
Whitelands Dr SL5 . . . . .28 D8
Whiteley Ct **1** TW13 . . . . . . .15 F5
Whiteley Ho **9** SW4 . . . . . . .21 D8
Whiteley House & Hospl
 KT12 . . . . .53 F2
Whiteley Rd SE19 . . . . .22 D3
Whiteleys Ho TW13 . . . . .16 A5
Whiteleys Way TW13 . . . . . . .16 A5
Whitelocke Inf Sch RG40 . . .25 D7
Whitely Hill RH10 . . . . .202 F1
Whitemore Rd GU1 . . . . . . .109 D5
Whiteoak Ho SE19 . . . . .22 C1
Whiteoaks SM7 . . . . .78 B6
Whitepost Hill RH1 . . . . . . .118 C4
Whitepost Ho RH1 . . . . .118 C4
Whites Dr BR2 . . . . .44 F2
Whites Rd GU14 . . . . .85 E1
Whitethorn Ave CR5 . . . . . . .79 B4
Whitethorn Cl GU12 . . . . . .106 B3
Whitethorn Cotts GU6 . . . . .174 B6
Whitethorn Gdns CR0 . . . . . .62 B8
Whiteways Ct TW18 . . . . .13 B1
Whiteways End GU10 . . . . . .126 D4
Whitewood Cotts
 Horne RH9 . . . . .163 B7
 Tatsfield TN16 . . . . .103 C7
Whitewood La RH9 . . . . . . .163 B7
Whitfield Cl
 Guildford GU2 . . . . .109 A4
 Haslemere GU27 . . . . .189 C1
Whitfield Ct **3** SE21 . . . . . . .22 E4
Whitfield Rd GU27 . . . . .189 C1
Whitford Gdns CR4 . . . . .40 F6
Whitgift Ave CR2 . . . . .61 C5
Whitgift Ctr CR9 . . . . .61 C8
Whitgift Ho CR2 . . . . .61 C5
Whitgift Sch CR2 . . . . .61 C5
Whitgift St CR0,CR9 . . . . . . .61 C7
Whitgift Wlk RH10 . . . . .201 D3
Whitland Rd SM5 . . . . .40 D1
Whitlet Cl GU9 . . . . .125 B1
Whitley Cl TW19 . . . . .2 E1
Whitley Ct **12** BR2 . . . . .44 F5
Whitlock Dr SW19 . . . . .19 E7
Whitmead Cl CR2 . . . . .61 E4
Whitmead La GU4 . . . . .147 E4
Whitmoor La GU4 . . . . .89 D1
Whitmoor Rd GU19 . . . . .47 F2
Whitmoor Vale Rd
 GU26 . . . . .188 A5
Whitmore Cl GU47 . . . . .45 D1
Whitmore Gn GU9 . . . . .125 E6
Whitmore Hill Cotts
 GU26 . . . . .188 C3
Whitmore La SL5 . . . . .30 A5
Whitmore Rd BR3 . . . . .43 F6
Whitmore Vale GU10,
 GU26 . . . . .187 F7
Whitmore Vale Rd
 Grayshott GU26 . . . . .188 A4
 Headley Down GU26 . . . . .187 F7
Whitmore Way RH6 . . . . . . .160 E3
Whitmores Cl KT18 . . . . .76 C4
Whitstable Cl BR3 . . . . .43 F8
Whittaker Ave TW10,TW9 . . . .6 D2
Whittaker Ct KT21 . . . . .75 D2
Whittaker Pl **24** TW10 . . . . . . .6 D2
Whittaker Rd SM3 . . . . .58 F7
Whittam Ho SE27 . . . . .22 C3
Whittell Gdns SE26 . . . . .23 C5
Whittingham Ct W4 . . . . .7 C7
Whittington Coll RH19 . . . . .185 A4
Whittington Ct SE20 . . . . . . .43 B7
Whittington Rd RH10 . . . . . .201 D3
Whittle Cl Ash Vale GU12 . . .105 F5
 Sandhurst GU47 . . . . .45 A1
Whittle Cres GU14 . . . . .84 F7
Whittle Rd TW5 . . . . .4 C7
Whittle Rdbt GU14 . . . . .84 C1
Whittle Way RH10 . . . . .182 A3
Whittlebury Cl SM5 . . . . .59 F3
Whitton Dene
 Isleworth TW2,TW3,TW7 . . . .5 D2
 Twickenham TW2,TW7 . . . . .5 D1
Whitton Manor Rd TW7 . . . . .5 C1
 Hounslow TW3 . . . . .5 B2
 Twickenham TW1 . . . . .17 A8
Whitton Sch TW2 . . . . .16 B6
Whitton Sta TW2 . . . . .16 C8
Whitton Waye TW2,TW3 . . . . .5 A1
Whitwell Hatch GU27 . . . . . .208 D5
Whitworth Rd
 Crawley RH11 . . . . .181 D2
 South Norwood SE25 . . . . . .42 F5
Whopshott Ave GU21 . . . . . . .69 C3
Whopshott Cl GU21 . . . . .69 C3
Whopshott Dr GU21 . . . . . . .69 C3
Whynstones Rd SL5 . . . . .29 A4
Whyte Ave GU12 . . . . .126 D7
Whyteacre CR3 . . . . .101 B7

Whytebeam View CR3 . . . . . .80 F1
Whytecliffe Rd N CR8 . . . . . .80 B8
Whytecliffe Rd S CR8 . . . . . .80 B8
Whytecroft TW5 . . . . .4 D7
Whyteleafe Bsns Village
 CR3 . . . . .80 F2
Whyteleafe Hill CR3 . . . . .80 F1
Whyteleafe Rd CR3 . . . . . . .100 F6
Whyteleafe Sch CR3 . . . . . . .80 F1
Whyteleafe South Sta
 CR3 . . . . .101 A8
Whyteleafe Sta CR3 . . . . .80 F2
Wick & Grove Ho RH4 . . . . .136 A6
Wick Ho **1** KT1 . . . . .37 D8
Wick La TW20 . . . . .10 F3
Wick Rd
 Englefield Green TW20 . . . . .11 B1
 Teddington TW11 . . . . .17 C1
Wickers Oake SE19 . . . . .22 F4
Wicket Hill GU10,GU9 . . . . .146 A6
Wicket The CR0 . . . . .63 A5
Wickets The TW15 . . . . .13 E4
Wickham Ave
 Cheam KT4,SM3 . . . . .58 C5
 Croydon CR0 . . . . .43 E1
Wickham Chase BR4 . . . . . . .44 E2
Wickham Cl Horley RH6 . . . .160 F4
 New Malden KT3 . . . . .38 F4
Wickham Court Rd BR4 . . . . .63 E8
Wickham Court Sch BR4 . . . .63 D6
Wickham Cres BR4 . . . . .63 C8
Wickham La TW20 . . . . .12 A1
Wickham Rd
 Beckenham BR3 . . . . .44 B6
 Camberley GU15 . . . . .65 E8
 Croydon CR0,CR9 . . . . .62 E8
Wickham Vale RG12 . . . . . . .26 E3
Wickham Way BR3 . . . . .44 C4
Wickhurst La RH12 . . . . .216 E3
Wickland Ct RH10 . . . . .201 D3
Wicklow Ct SE26 . . . . .23 C3
Wide Way CR4,SW16 . . . . . . .41 D6
Widgeon Way RH12 . . . . . . .217 C5
Widmer Ct TW5 . . . . .4 E5
Wiggie La RH1 . . . . .119 A3
Wighton Mews TW7 . . . . .5 E5
Wigley Rd TW13 . . . . .15 D7
Wigmore La RH5 . . . . .157 C1
Wigmore Rd SM5 . . . . .40 E1
Wigmore Wlk SM5 . . . . .59 D8
Wilberforce Ct KT18 . . . . . . .76 D5
Wilberforce Way
 Bracknell RG12 . . . . .27 D4
 Wimbledon SW19 . . . . .19 D2
Wilbury Ave SM2 . . . . .58 F1
Wilbury Rd GU21 . . . . .69 D2
Wilcot Cl GU24 . . . . .68 A3
Wilcot Gdns GU24 . . . . .68 A3
Wilcox Gdns TW17 . . . . .33 F6
Wilcox Rd Sutton SM1 . . . . . .59 B6
 Teddington TW11 . . . . .16 D4
Wild Acres KT14 . . . . .71 C8
Wildacre Cl RH14 . . . . .212 D3
Wildbank Ct **12** GU22 . . . . . .69 F1
Wildcroft Dr
 Dorking RH5 . . . . .136 D4
 Wokingham RG40 . . . . .25 A1
Wildcroft Manor SW15 . . . . .19 C8
Wildcroft Rd SW15 . . . . .19 C8
Wildcroft Wood GU8 . . . . . .170 D6
Wilde Pl SW18 . . . . .20 D8
Wilde Theatre RG12 . . . . . . .27 C2
Wilderness Ct GU2 . . . . .129 F7
Wilderness Rd
 Frimley GU16 . . . . .65 E2
 Guildford GU2 . . . . .129 F7
 Oxted RH8 . . . . .122 E5
Wilderness Rise RH19 . . . . .186 A6
Wilderness The
 East Molesey KT8 . . . . .36 C4
 Hampton TW12 . . . . .16 B4
Wilders Cl Frimley GU16 . . . . .65 F3
 Woking GU21 . . . . .69 C1
Wilderwick Rd RH19 . . . . . .186 A5
Wildfell Rd SE6 . . . . .24 B8
Wildfield Cl GU3 . . . . .108 B2
Wildgoose Dr RH12 . . . . . . .216 F3
Wildridings Prim Sch
 RG12 . . . . .27 A5
Wildridings Rd RG12 . . . . . . .27 A5
Wildridings Sq RG12 . . . . . . .27 A5
Wildwood Cl
 Cranleigh GU6 . . . . .174 F1
 East Horsley KT24 . . . . .92 F2
 Lewisham SE12 . . . . .24 F8
 Pyrford GU22 . . . . .70 F4
Wildwood Ct CR8 . . . . .80 D4
Wildwood La GU6 . . . . .194 C5
Wilford Rd CR0 . . . . .42 C2
Wilfred Owen Cl SW19 . . . . .20 C2
Wilfred St GU21 . . . . .69 D1
Wilhelmina Ave CR5 . . . . . . .99 C8
Wilkes Rd **3** TW8 . . . . .6 E8
Wilkins Cl CR4 . . . . .40 E8
Wilkinson Ct
 4 Crawley RH11 . . . . .201 B1
 Upper Tooting SW17 . . . . . .20 D4
Wilkinson Ho TW7 . . . . .5 F4
Wilks Gdns CR0 . . . . .43 E1
Will Miles Ct **6** SW19 . . . . . .20 C1
Willats Cl KT16 . . . . .33 A3
Willcocks Cl KT9 . . . . .56 E7
Willems Ave GU11 . . . . .104 F2
Willems Rdbt GU11 . . . . . . .104 F2
Willerton Lodge **1** KT13 . . .53 D4
Willett Pl CR7 . . . . .42 A4
Willett Rd CR7 . . . . .42 A4

Willetts RH4 . . . . .136 C4
Willetts Way RH14 . . . . .212 F3
Willey Broom La CR3 . . . . . .100 A2
Willey Farm La CR3 . . . . . . .100 C1
Willey La CR3 . . . . .100 C1
William Booth Rd SE20 . . . . .43 A8
William Brown Ct SE27 . . . . .22 B6
William Byrd Prim Sch
 UB7 . . . . .3 D8
William Cobbett Jun Sch
 GU9 . . . . .125 E6
William Ct
 Farnborough GU14 . . . . . . .85 B4
 South Norwood SE19 . . . . . .22 D1
William Dyce Mews
 SW16 . . . . .21 D4
William Evans Rd KT19 . . . . .76 A8
William Evelyn Ct RH5 . . . . .134 F4
William Farthing Cl **17**
 GU11 . . . . .105 A2
William Harvey Ho **1**
 SW19 . . . . .19 E7
William Hitchcock Ho
 GU14 . . . . .85 B7
William Lilly Ho **1** SW2 . . . .54 C5
William Morris Prim Sch
 CR4 . . . . .41 D6
William Rd
 Caterham CR3 . . . . .100 D5
 Guildford GU1 . . . . .109 C1
 Merton SW19 . . . . .19 E1
 Sutton SM1 . . . . .59 C5
William Russell Ct **3**
 GU21 . . . . .68 E1
William Sim Wood RG42 . . . . .8 B2
William St SM5 . . . . .59 F7
William Swayne Ho **1**
 GU1 . . . . .130 E8
William Winter Ct SW2 . . . . .22 A8
William Wood Ho SE26 . . . . .23 C5
Williams Cl
 Addlestone KT15 . . . . .52 B5
 Ewhurst GU6 . . . . .175 E5
Williams Dr TW3 . . . . .5 A3
Williams Gr KT6 . . . . .37 C3
Williams Ho **14** SW2 . . . . . . .22 A7
Williams La Morden SM4 . . . .40 C4
 Mortlake SW14 . . . . .7 C5
Williams Terr CR2 . . . . .61 A4
Williams Way RH10 . . . . . . .202 B5
Williamson Cl GU27 . . . . . . .189 F1
Willian Pl GU26 . . . . .188 E6
Willingham Way KT1 . . . . . . .38 A7
Willington Cl GU15 . . . . .65 B6
Willington Sch SW19 . . . . . . .19 F3
Willis Ave SM2 . . . . .59 E4
Willis Cl KT18 . . . . .76 B5
Willis Rd CR0 . . . . .42 C2
Willlows The CR0 . . . . .62 E8
Willmore End SW19 . . . . .40 B7
Willoughby Ave CR0 . . . . . . .60 F6
Willoughby Rd
 Bracknell RG12 . . . . .26 F6
 Kingston u T KT2 . . . . .37 F8
 Twickenham TW1 . . . . .6 C1
Willoughbys The **8** SW15 . . .7 E4
Willow Ave SW13 . . . . .7 F5
Willow Bank GU22 . . . . .89 F6
Willow Brean RH6 . . . . .160 E5
Willow Cl
 Beare Green RH5 . . . . .157 C4
 Brentford TW8 . . . . .6 C8
 Catford SE6 . . . . .24 C7
 Colnbrook SL3 . . . . .1 C7
 Crawley RH10 . . . . .201 E8
 East Grinstead RH19 . . . . .185 D3
 Mytchett GU16 . . . . .85 E4
 Woodham KT15 . . . . .70 F8
Willow Cnr RH6 . . . . .180 F7
Willow Cotts
 Carshalton CR4 . . . . .40 F2
 Dorking RH5 . . . . .136 D4
 Feltham TW13 . . . . .15 E5
 Richmond TW9 . . . . .7 A8
Willow Cres GU14 . . . . .85 B7
Willow Ct Ash Vale GU12 . . .106 A7
 2 Ashford TW16 . . . . .14 E1
 9 Chiswick W4 . . . . .7 E7
 Frimley GU16 . . . . .65 D1
 Horley RH6 . . . . .161 B6
 3 Streatham SW16 . . . . . . .21 F5
 Thornton Heath CR7 . . . . . .42 D4
 Wokingham RG41 . . . . .25 B6
Willow Ctr The CR4 . . . . .40 F3
Willow Dr Bracknell RG12 . . .27 C8
 Flexford GU3 . . . . .107 C1
 Send Marsh GU23 . . . . .91 A3
Willow End KT6 . . . . .37 E1
Willow Fields GU12 . . . . . . .106 B3
Willow Gdns TW5 . . . . .5 A6
Willow Glade RH2 . . . . .139 B6
Willow Gn GU24 . . . . .68 A6
Willow Ho Chelsham CR6 . . . .82 B3
 Feltham TW14 . . . . .4 B2
Willow La
 Blackwater GU17 . . . . .64 D4
 Guildford GU1 . . . . .110 A2
 Mitcham CR4 . . . . .40 F3
Willow Lodge **6** TW16 . . . . .14 F1
Willow Manor SM1 . . . . .58 F6
Willow Mead
 6 Dorking RH4 . . . . .136 A8
 8 East Grinstead RH19 . . .205 F8
 Witley GU8 . . . . .170 G5
Willow Mews GU8 . . . . .170 F5
Willow Mount CR0 . . . . .61 E7
Willow Pk GU12 . . . . .105 F2

Willow Rd
 Farncombe GU7 . . . . .150 F8
 Horsham RH12 . . . . .218 B5
 Kingston u T KT3 . . . . .38 C5
 Poyle SL3 . . . . .1 E5
 Reigate RH1 . . . . .139 C4
 Wallington SM6 . . . . .60 B3
Willow Ridge RH10 . . . . . . .204 E8
Willow Tree Cl SW18 . . . . . . .20 B7
Willow Vale KT23 . . . . .94 B4
Willow View SW19 . . . . .40 D8
Willow Way
 Aldershot GU12 . . . . .126 E8
 Forest Hill SE26 . . . . .23 C5
 Godstone RH9 . . . . .121 B3
 Guildford GU1 . . . . .109 B5
 Heath End GU9 . . . . .125 D6
 Sunbury TW16 . . . . .35 A5
 Twickenham TW2 . . . . .16 B6
 West Byfleet KT14 . . . . .71 C8
 West Ewell KT19 . . . . .57 D4
 Woking GU22 . . . . .89 E7
Willow Wlk Box Hill KT20 . . .116 B5
 Cheam SM1,SM3 . . . . .58 F7
 Chertsey KT16 . . . . .33 B2
 Englefield Green TW20 . . . . .11 C3
 Redhill RH1 . . . . .140 A1
 Shere GU5 . . . . .133 A4
Willow Wood Cres SE25 . . . .42 E3
Willowbank Gdns KT20 . . . . .97 B5
Willowbrook Rd TW19 . . . . . .13 E6
Willowdene Cl TW2 . . . . .16 C8
Willowfield **4** RH11 . . . . . .201 D5
Willowhayne Dr KT12 . . . . . .35 B2
Willowhayne Gdns KT4 . . . . .58 C6
Willowherb Cl RG40 . . . . . . .25 E7
Willowmead TW18 . . . . .33 B8
Willowmead Cl GU21 . . . . . . .69 A3
Willowmere KT10 . . . . .55 C6
Willows Ave SM4 . . . . .40 B4
Willows End GU47 . . . . .64 B8
Willows Path KT18 . . . . .76 B5
Willows The
 Beckenham BR3 . . . . .44 A8
 1 Bracknell RG12 . . . . .27 F5
 Byfleet KT14 . . . . .71 E8
 Chiddingfold GU8 . . . . . . .191 A4
 Claygate KT10 . . . . .55 E4
 Farnham GU10 . . . . .126 C4
 Guildford, Pitch Place GU2 .108 D3
 Guildford,Bushy Hill GU4 . .110 D3
 Horsham RH12 . . . . .217 D3
 Lightwater GU18 . . . . .48 C1
 3 Redhill RH1 . . . . .139 F8
 Weybridge KT13 . . . . .53 A7
Willowtree Way SW16 . . . . . .42 A8
Wills Cres TW3 . . . . .5 B1
Willson Rd TW20 . . . . .11 B3
Wilmar Gdns BR4 . . . . .44 B1
Wilmer Cl TW10 . . . . .17 F3
Wilmer Cres KT2,TW10 . . . . .17 F3
Wilmerhatch La KT18,
 KT21 . . . . .76 B2
Wilmington Ave W4 . . . . .7 D7
Wilmington Cl RH11 . . . . . . .201 C1
Wilmington Ct SW16 . . . . . . .21 D1
Wilmot Ho **17** SM2 . . . . .59 C4
Wilmot Rd Purley CR8 . . . . . .80 A7
 Wallington SM5 . . . . .59 F5
Wilmot Way
 Banstead SM7 . . . . .78 A5
 Frimley GU15 . . . . .65 F3
Wilmot's La RH1,RH6 . . . . . .162 E5
Wilmots Cl RH2 . . . . .118 C2
Wilna Rd SW18 . . . . .20 C8
Wilson Ave CR4,SW19 . . . . . .40 E8
Wilson Cl Crawley RH10 . . . .202 D3
 Croydon CR0 . . . . .61 C5
Wilson Dr KT16 . . . . .51 B5
Wilson Ho TW13 . . . . .15 A5
Wilson Rd
 Aldershot GU12 . . . . .105 D4
 Chessington KT9 . . . . .56 F4
 Farnborough GU14 . . . . . . .84 F3
Wilson Way GU21 . . . . .69 D3
Wilson's Sch SM6 . . . . .60 E4
Wilsons KT20 . . . . .97 C6
Wilsons Rd GU35 . . . . .187 B5
Wilton Cl UB7 . . . . .2 D8
Wilton Cres SW19 . . . . .39 F8
Wilton Ct
 Farnborough GU14 . . . . . . .85 D3
 4 Richmond TW10 . . . . .6 E2
Wilton Gdns
 East Molesey KT8 . . . . .36 A6
 Walton-on-T KT12 . . . . .35 D1
Wilton Gr Merton SW19 . . . . .39 F8
 New Malden KT3 . . . . .38 F3
Wilton Hill Ct **5** RH1 . . . . . .139 F8
Wilton Lodge KT12 . . . . .54 C8
Wilton Par TW13 . . . . .15 B6
Wilton Pl Beckenham BR3 . . .44 C6
 New Haw KT15 . . . . .52 D2
Wilton Rd Camberley GU15 . .65 B3
 Hounslow TW4 . . . . .4 D4
 Mitcham SW19 . . . . .20 E1
 Redhill RH1 . . . . .139 F8
Wilton Wlk TW13 . . . . .15 B7
Wiltshire Ave RG45 . . . . .45 B5
Wiltshire Dr RG40 . . . . .25 D7
Wiltshire Gdns TW2 . . . . .16 C7
Wiltshire Rd
 Thornton Heath CR7 . . . . . .42 A6
 Wokingham RG40 . . . . .25 C2
Wilverley Cres KT3 . . . . .38 E3
Wilwood Rd RG42 . . . . .26 E8
Wimbart Rd SW2 . . . . .21 F8
Wimbledon Bridge SW19 19 F2

Wimbledon Central
SW19 . . . . .19 F2
Wimbledon Chase Prim Sch
SW20 . . . . .39 E8
Wimbledon Chase Sta
SW20 . . . . .39 E7
Wimbledon Cl
Camberley GU15 . . . . .46 F1
2 Wimbledon SW20 . . . .19 D1
Wimbledon Coll
West Barnes SW20 . . . . . .39 C4
Wimbledon SW19 . . . . . . .19 D1
Wimbledon Common Prep
Sch SW19 . . . . .19 D1
Wimbledon High Sch
SW19 . . . . .19 E2
Wimbledon Hill Rd SW19 19 F2
Wimbledon House Sch
SW19 . . . . .40 A8
Wimbledon Lawn Tennis
Mus★ SW19 . . . . .19 E5
Wimbledon Park Ct
SW19 . . . . .19 F7
Wimbledon Park Prim Sch
SW19 . . . . .20 B6
Wimbledon Park Rd
SW18,SW19 . . . . .19 F7
Wimbledon Park Side
SW19 . . . . .19 D7
Wimbledon Park Sta
SW19 . . . . .20 A5
Wimbledon Rd
Camberley GU15 . . . . .46 F1
Wandsworth SW17 . . . . . .20 C4
Wimbledon Sch of Art
SW19 . . . . .39 E8
Wimbledon Sch of Art
Annexe SW19 . . . . .20 A1
Wimbledon Sta SW19 . . .19 F2
Wimbledon Stad SW17 . .20 C4
Wimbledon Stadium Bsns Ctr
SW17 . . . . .20 B5
Wimbledon Windmill★
SW19 . . . . .19 C5
Wimblehurst Ct RH12 . .217 C4
Wimblehurst Rd RH12 . .217 C4
Wimborne Ave RH1 . . . .140 A4
Wimborne Ct Epsom KT17 76 E6
North Cheam KT4 . . . . . . .39 C1
Wimborne Ho
Croydon CR0 . . . . .43 C4
Farnborough GU14 . . . . . .85 D2
South Norwood SE19 . . . .22 D2
Upper Tooting SW12 . . . . .21 C5
Wimborne Way BR3 . . . .43 E5
Wimbourne Ct
Mitcham SW19 . . . . .20 D1
South Croydon CR2 . . . . . .61 E4
Wimbourne Ho RH11 . .201 C6
Wimland Hill RH12 . . . .199 D2
Wimland Rd
Faygate RH12 . . . . .199 D1
Rusper RH12 . . . . .199 D1
Wimlands La RH12 . . . .199 E3
Wimpole Cl 1 KT1 . . . . .38 A7
Wimshurst Cl CR0 . . . . . .41 E1
Wincanton Cl RH10 . . . .202 D6
Wincanton Rd SW18 . . . .19 F8
Winchcombe Rd SM5 . . . .40 E1
Winchelsea Rise CR2 . . . .61 F4
Winchendon Rd TW11 . . .16 D4
Winchester Ave TW5 . . . . .4 F4
Winchester Cl
Beckenham BR2 . . . . .44 F6
Esher KT10 . . . . .55 A7
Kingston u T KT2 . . . . . . .18 B1
Poyle SL3 . . . . .1 E6
Winchester Ho KT19 . . . .76 A7
Winchester Pk BR2 . . . . .44 F6
Winchester Rd
Ash GU12 . . . . .106 A3
Beckenham BR2 . . . . .44 F6
Crawley RH10 . . . . .201 E2
Feltham TW13 . . . . .15 F5
Harlington UB3 . . . . .3 E7
Rushmoor GU10 . . . . . . .168 B7
Twickenham TW1 . . . . .6 B1
Walton-on-T KT12 . . . . . . .35 A1
Winchester St GU14 . . . .105 C8
Winchester Way GU17 . . .64 C6
Winchet Wlk CR0 . . . . . . .43 C3
Winchfield Ho SW15 . . . . .7 F1
Winchfield Rd SE26 . . . . .23 E4
Winchilsea Cres KT8 . . . .36 C7
Winchstone Cl TW17 . . . .33 F5
Windborough Rd SM5 . . . .60 A3
Windermere Ave SM4,
SW19 . . . . .40 B6
Windermere Cl
East Bedfont TW14 . . . . . .14 F7
Farnborough GU14 . . . . . .84 E3
Stanwell TW19 . . . . .13 D6
Thorpe Lea TW20 . . . . . . .12 B1
Windermere Ct
Barnes SW13 . . . . .7 F8
Purley CR8 . . . . .80 B4
Wallington SM5 . . . . .60 A4
9 Woking GU21 . . . . . . .69 A1
Windermere Ho TW1 . . . . .5 F2
Windermere Rd
Coulsdon CR5 . . . . .79 E4
Croydon CR0 . . . . .42 F1
Kingston u T SW15 . . . . . .18 E3
Lightwater GU18 . . . . .48 B1
Mitcham SW16 . . . . .41 D7
West Wickham BR4 . . . . . .63 E8
Windermere Way
Hale GU9 . . . . .125 A6

Windermere Way continued
Redhill RH2 . . . . .118 E2
Windermere Wlk GU15 . .66 D5
Windfield KT22 . . . . .95 B5
Windfield Cl SE26 . . . . . . .23 D4
Windgates GU4 . . . . .110 C4
Windham Ave CR0 . . . . . . .63 D1
Windham Rd TW9 . . . . .6 F4
Winding Wood Dr GU15 . .66 B3
Windings The CR2 . . . . . . .80 F8
Windle Cl GU20 . . . . .48 C6
Windlebrook Gn 3 RG42 27 A8
Windlesham Cl GU20 . . . .48 C6
Windlesham Gr SW19 . . . .19 D7
Windlesham Rd
Bracknell RG42 . . . . .26 F8
Chobham GU24 . . . . .49 C3
West End GU24 . . . . .67 F7
Windlesham Village Cty Sch
GU20 . . . . .48 B6
Windley Cl SE23 . . . . .23 C6
Windmill Ave KT17 . . . . . .76 F8
Windmill Bridge Ho 1
CR0 . . . . .42 E1
Windmill Bsns Village
TW16 . . . . .34 E8
Windmill Cl
Caterham CR3 . . . . .100 C6
Charlton TW16 . . . . .14 E1
Ewell KT17 . . . . .76 F7
Horley RH6 . . . . .161 B3
Horsham RH13 . . . . .218 A4
Long Ditton KT6 . . . . .37 C2
Windmill Ct
1 Aldershot GU12 . . . . .105 C1
Crawley RH10 . . . . .201 D8
Windmill Dr
Headley Down GU35 . . . .187 B6
Leatherhead KT22 . . . . . . .95 C4
Redhill RH2 . . . . .118 E3
Windmill End KT17 . . . . . .76 F7
Windmill Field GU20 . . . .48 D4
Windmill Gr CR0 . . . . .42 C3
Windmill La
Ashurst Wood RH19 . . . .206 C7
East Grinstead RH19 . . . .185 D3
Ewell KT17 . . . . .76 F7
Thames Ditton KT7 . . . . . .37 B2
Windmill Lodge TW16 . . .34 E8
Windmill Rd
Aldershot GU12 . . . . .105 C1
Bracknell RG42 . . . . .27 A8
Brentford TW8 . . . . .6 D8
Charlton TW16 . . . . .34 E8
Hampton TW12 . . . . .16 C3
Mitcham CR4 . . . . .41 C5
Roehampton SW19 . . . . . .19 B5
Thornton Heath CR0 . . . . .42 C2
Windmill Rd W TW16 . . . .34 E8
Windmill Rise KT2 . . . . . .18 B1
Windmill Shott TW20 . . . .11 F2
Windmill Terr TW17 . . . . .34 E8
Windmill Trad Est TW16 . .34 E8
Windmill Way RH2 . . . . .118 D3
Windrush Cl
Bramley GU5 . . . . .151 F6
Chiswick W4 . . . . .7 C7
Crawley RH11 . . . . .200 F4
Windrush Ho 8 RH1 . . . .118 F2
Windrush Hts GU47 . . . . . .64 B8
Windrush La SE23 . . . . . . .23 D5
Winds Ridge GU23 . . . . . .90 C2
Windsor Ave Cheam SM3 . .58 E7
East Molesey KT8 . . . . . . .36 A6
Merton SW19 . . . . .40 C8
New Malden KT3 . . . . .38 C4
Windsor Cl Brentford TW8 . .6 B8
Crawley RH11 . . . . .201 C4
Farnborough GU14 . . . . . .85 B4
Guildford GU2 . . . . .129 F7
West Norwood SE27 . . . . .22 C4
Windsor Cres GU5 . . . . . .151 F6
Windsor Ct Ashford TW16 .15 A1
Chobham GU24 . . . . .49 E2
3 Horsham RH13 . . . . . .217 F3
South Norwood SE19 . . . .42 E8
Whyteleafe CR3 . . . . .80 F1
Windsor Dr TW15 . . . . . . .13 D4
Windsor Gdns Ash GU12 105 F1
Wallington CR0 . . . . .60 E7
Windsor Gr 2 SE27 . . . . .22 C4
Windsor Great Pk★ SL4 . .10 C4
Windsor Ho
5 Egham TW20 . . . . . . .12 A3
Reigate RH2 . . . . .139 B4
Windsor Mews
Catford SE6 . . . . .24 C7
Forest Hill SE23 . . . . .23 E7
Windsor Park Rd UB3 . . . . .3 F7
Windsor Pk SW19 . . . . . . .40 C8
Windsor Pl Chertsey KT16 .33 A3
East Grinstead RH19 . . . .206 A8
Windsor Rd Ashford TW16 .14 A1
Chobham GU24 . . . . .49 D3
Cranford TW4,TW5 . . . . . . .4 C5
Englefield Green TW19,
TW20 . . . . .11 C6
Farnborough GU14 . . . . . .85 D1
Kingston u T KT2 . . . . . . .17 E1
North Ascot SL5 . . . . .29 A8
Richmond TW9 . . . . .6 F5
South Norwood CR7 . . . . .42 B7
Teddington TW11 . . . . . . .16 D3
Worcester Park KT4 . . . . . .58 A4
Windsor Ride
Bracknell SL5 . . . . .28 C4
Sandhurst GU15 . . . . .65 A8

Windsor St KT16 . . . . .33 A3
Windsor Way
Aldershot GU11 . . . . .105 B2
Frimley GU16 . . . . .85 F8
Woking GU22 . . . . .70 C3
Windsor Wlk
Walton-on-T KT12 . . . . . . .35 D1
Weybridge KT13 . . . . .53 B5
Windways GU8 . . . . .192 F7
Windy Ridge Cl SW19 . . . .19 D3
Windy Wood GU7 . . . . . .150 C3
Windycroft Cl CR5,CR8 . . .79 D6
Windyridge RH11 . . . . . .201 A5
Winern Glebe KT14 . . . . . .71 D6
Winery La KT1 . . . . .37 F6
Winey Cl KT9 . . . . .56 C3
Winfield Cl RH5 . . . . .158 B1
Winfield Gr RH5 . . . . . . .158 B1
Winfrith Rd SW18 . . . . . . .20 C7
Wingate Cres CR0 . . . . . . .41 E3
Wingate GU11 . . . . .104 F2
Wingfield Cl KT15 . . . . . . .52 B1
Wingfield Ct SM7 . . . . . . .78 A4
Wingfield Gdns GU16 . . . .66 D3
Wingfield Rd KT2 . . . . . . .18 A2
Wingham Ho 3 SE26 . . . .23 B3
Wingrove Rd SE6 . . . . . . .24 E6
Wings Cl Hale GU9 . . . . . .125 B6
Sutton SM1 . . . . .59 A6
Wings Rd GU9 . . . . .125 B6
Winifred Rd Coulsdon CR5 79 B4
Hampton TW12 . . . . .16 A4
Merton SW19 . . . . .40 A8
Winkfield Cl RG41 . . . . . . .25 B3
Winkfield La SL4 . . . . .8 D7
Winkfield Rd Ascot SL5 . . .29 B7
Windsor SL4 . . . . .9 C8
Winkfield Row RG42 . . . . . .8 B3
Winkfield St SL4 . . . . .8 C8
Winkfield St Mary's CE Prim
Sch RG42 . . . . .8 B3
Winkworth Arboretum★
GU8 . . . . .172 C7
Winkworth Pl SM7 . . . . . .78 A5
Winkworth Rd SM7 . . . . . .78 A5
Winlaton Rd BR1,SE6 . . . .24 C4
Winner Way RH6 . . . . . . .181 D6
Winnington Way GU21 . . . .69 C1
Winscombe RG12 . . . . . . .26 E4
Winsford Rd SE6 . . . . .23 F5
Winslade Way SE6 . . . . . .24 B8
Winslow Way
Feltham TW13 . . . . .15 E5
Walton-on-T KT12 . . . . . . .54 C7
Winstanley Cl KT11 . . . . . .73 B5
Winstanley Wlk KT11 . . . .73 B5
Winston Churchill Sch The
GU21 . . . . .68 F1
Winston Cl GU16 . . . . .85 F6
Winston Dr KT11 . . . . .73 E3
Winston Way GU22 . . . . . .90 B7
Winston Wlk GU10 . . . . .146 C6
Winter Box Wlk TW10 . . . . .6 F2
Winter Cl GU12 . . . . .106 A8
Winterbourne RH12 . . . . .217 F1
Winterbourne Ct RG12 . . .27 D7
Winterbourne Gr KT13 . . .53 C4
Winterbourne Inf Sch
CR7 . . . . .42 A5
Winterbourne Jun Boys' Sch
CR7 . . . . .42 A5
Winterbourne Jun Girls' Sch
CR7 . . . . .42 A5
Winterbourne Rd
Forest Hill SE23,SE6 . . . . .23 F7
Thornton Heath CR7 . . . . .42 A5
Winterbourne Wlk GU16 . .85 F8
Winterdown Gdns KT10 . .54 F4
Winterdown Rd KT10 . . . . .54 F4
Winterfold RH10 . . . . . . .202 A3
Winterfold Cl SW19 . . . . . .19 E6
Winterhill Way GU4 . . . . .110 B5
Winters Rd KT7 . . . . .37 B2
Wintersells Ind Est KT14 52 D1
Wintersells Rd KT14 . . . . .52 E1
Winterstoke Rd SE23,SE6 .23 F7
Winterton Ct
Horsham RH13 . . . . .217 D2
Teddington KT1 . . . . .37 D8
Winton Ct KT5 KT6 . . . . . .37 D2
Winton Rd
Aldershot GU11 . . . . .105 A1
Farnham GU9 . . . . .125 D4
Winton Way SW16 . . . . . .22 A3
Winward Ct 16 SM2 . . . . .59 C4
Wire Mill La RH7 . . . . . . .184 F8
Wireless Rd TN16 . . . . . . .83 D4
Wirrall Ho 15 SE26 . . . . .23 A5
Wisbeach Rd CR0 . . . . . . .42 D4
Wisborough Ct RH11 . . . .200 F3
Wisborough Rd CR2 . . . . .61 F2
Wisdom Ct 5 TW7 . . . . . . .6 A4
Wiseman Ct 12 SE19 . . . . .22 E3
Wiseton Rd SW17 . . . . . . .20 F7
Wishanger La GU10 . . . . .167 B2
Wishbone Way GU21 . . . . .68 F3
Wishford Ct KT21 . . . . . . .75 F1
Wishmoor Cl GU15 . . . . . .65 E8
Wishmoor Rd GU15 . . . . . .65 E8
Wishmore Cross Sch
GU24 . . . . .49 F1
Wisley Court Ho RH4 . . . .136 B4
Wisley Gdns GU14 . . . . . .84 D2
Wisley La GU23 . . . . .71 E3
Wispers Sch GU27 . . . . . .189 C1
Wiston Ct RH11 . . . . .200 F3
Witham Ct SW17 . . . . .20 F5
Witham Rd Hounslow TW7 . .5 D6

Witham Rd continued
Penge BR3,SE20 . . . . .43 C6
Wither Dale RH10 . . . . . .160 A4
Witherby Cl CR0,CR2 . . . . .61 E6
Withers Cl KT9 . . . . .56 C4
Withers Cl KT9 . . . . .56 C4
Witherslack Cl GU35 . . . .187 C4
Withey Brook RH6 . . . . . .160 D1
Withey Mdws RH6 . . . . . .160 D1
Witheygate Ave TW18 . . . .13 B2
Withies La GU3 . . . . .129 C2
Withies The Knaphill GU21 68 E2
Leatherhead KT22 . . . . . . .95 B6
Withy Cl GU18 . . . . .48 C1
Withybed Cnr KT20 . . . . . .97 B4
Withypitts RH10 . . . . .204 A3
Withypitts E RH10 . . . . . .204 A3
Witley & Milford Commons
Nature Reserve★ GU8 . .170 B6
Witley CE Inf Sch GU8 . . .170 C6
Witley Centre (Visitor Ctr)
The★ GU8 . . . . .170 C6
Witley Cres CR0 . . . . .63 C4
Witley Ho 5 SW2 . . . . . . .21 F8
Witley Point 13 SW15 . . . .19 B7
Witley Sta GU8 . . . . .190 F8
Witney Path SE23 . . . . . . .23 D5
Witten Ho KT3 . . . . .38 D1
Wittenham Rd RG12 . . . . .27 F8
Wittering Cl KT2 . . . . .17 D3
Wittersham Rd BR1 . . . . . .24 F3
Wittmead Rd GU16 . . . . . .85 F4
Wivenhoe Ct TW4 . . . . .4 F3
Wiverton Rd SE20,SE26 . . .23 C1
Wix Hill KT24 . . . . .112 B4
Woburn Ave
Farnborough GU14 . . . . . .85 D3
Purley CR8 . . . . .80 A8
Woburn Cl Frimley GU16 . .66 A1
Merton SW19 . . . . .20 C2
Woburn Ct Croydon CR0 . .42 C1
Richmond TW9 . . . . .6 F4
Woburn Hill KT15 . . . . . . .52 D8
Woburn Hill Pk KT15 . . . .52 D8
Woburn Rd
Carshalton SM5 . . . . .40 E1
Crawley RH11 . . . . .201 A4
Croydon CR0 . . . . .42 C1
Wodeland Ave GU2 . . . . .130 B7
Woffington Cl KT1,KT8 . . .37 C8
Woking Bsns Pk GU21 . . . .70 B4
Woking Cl SW15 . . . . .7 F3
Woking Coll GU22 . . . . . . .90 A7
Woking Com Hospl GU22 69 F1
Woking High Sch GU21 . . .69 D4
Woking Nuffield Hospl The
GU21 . . . . .69 E5
Woking Rd GU1,GU4 . . . .109 D5
Woking Sta GU22 . . . . . . .69 F2
Wokingham Hospl RG41 . .25 A6
Wokingham Rd RG42 . . . . .26 F8
Wokingham Sta RG40 . . . .25 B6
Wold Cl RH11 . . . . .200 F4
Wold The CR3 . . . . .102 A5
Woldhurstlea Cl RH11 . . .201 A4
Woldingham Rd CR3,
CR6 . . . . .101 C6
Woldingham Sch CR3 . . .101 D5
Woldingham Sta CR3 . . . .101 D5
Wolf's Cnr RH8 . . . . .123 B6
Wolf's Hill RH8 . . . . .123 A4
Wolf's Row RH8 . . . . .123 B5
Wolfe Rd GU12 . . . . .105 C1
Wolfington Rd SE27 . . . . .22 B4
Wolfs Wood RH8 . . . . . . .123 A3
Wolseley Ave SW18,SW19 20 A6
Wolseley Gdns W4 . . . . . . .7 B8
Wolseley Rd
4 Aldershot GU11 . . . . .105 A1
Carshalton CR4 . . . . .41 A2
Farncombe GU7 . . . . .150 F6
Wolsey Cl Isleworth TW3 . . .5 C3
Kingston u T KT2 . . . . . . .38 B8
Wimbledon SW20 . . . . . . .19 B1
Worcester Park KT19,KT4 . .58 A6
Wolsey Cres
New Addington CR0 . . . . . .63 C2
West Barnes SM4 . . . . . . .39 F2
Wolsey Ct BR1 . . . . .24 F1
Wolsey Dr
Kingston u T KT2 . . . . . . .17 E2
Walton-on-T KT12 . . . . . . .35 D1
Wolsey Gr 3 KT10 . . . . . . .55 B6
Wolsey Ho 2 TW12 . . . . . .16 B2
Wolsey Inf & Jun Schs
CR0 . . . . .63 C3
Wolsey Pl Sh Ctr 3
GU22 . . . . .69 E2
Wolsey Rd Ashford TW15 . .13 F4
Ashford, Felthamhill TW16 .14 F1
East Molesey KT8 . . . . . . .36 D5
Esher KT10 . . . . .55 B6
Hampton TW12 . . . . .16 C2
Wolsey Way KT9 . . . . .57 A5
Wolsey Wlk 7 GU21 . . . . .69 F2
Wolstonbury Cl RH11 . . . .201 C4
Wolvens La
Coldharbour RH5 . . . . . . .156 C5
Westcott RH4,RH5 . . . . . .135 B2
Wolverton Ave KT2 . . . . . .38 A8
Wolverton Cl RH6 . . . . . . .160 F1
Wolverton Gdns RH6 . . . .160 F2
Wolves Hill RH5 . . . . .178 C4
Wonersh & Shamley Green
CE Inf Sch GU5 . . . . . . .152 D5
Wonersh Way SM2 . . . . . .58 D2
Wonford Cl King T KT2,KT3 38 E8

Wonford Cl continued
Walton on the Hill KT20 . . .97 A1
Wonham La RH3 . . . . .137 F8
Wonham Way
Gomshall GU5 . . . . .133 D3
Peaslake GU5 . . . . .133 D1
Wontford Rd CR8 . . . . .80 B4
Wontner Rd SW12,SW17 . .20 F6
Wood Cl RH1 . . . . .161 A8
Wood Crest 4 SM2 . . . . . .59 C3
Wood Ct GU2 . . . . .109 B2
Wood End RH12 . . . . .218 C5
Wood End Cl GU22 . . . . . . .70 F3
Wood End The SM6 . . . . . .60 B2
Wood La Banstead KT20 . . .77 C2
Bracknell RG42 . . . . .26 E8
Caterham CR3 . . . . .100 D3
Farnborough GU14 . . . . . .85 A3
Hounslow TW7 . . . . .5 F7
Knaphill GU21 . . . . .68 D1
Seale GU10 . . . . .127 B5
Weybridge KT13 . . . . .53 C2
Wood Lodge La BR4 . . . . .63 C3
Wood Rd
Beacon Hill GU26 . . . . . . .188 D6
Biggin Hill TN16 . . . . .83 C1
Camberley GU15 . . . . .65 B1
Farncombe GU7 . . . . .150 F7
Heath End GU9 . . . . .125 C7
Littleton TW17 . . . . .34 A5
Wood Riding GU22 . . . . . .70 E4
Wood Rise GU3 . . . . .108 E3
Wood St Ash Vale GU12 . .106 A6
Carshalton CR4 . . . . .41 A2
East Grinstead RH19 . . . .185 D1
Kingston u T KT2 . . . . . . .37 E8
Merstham RH1 . . . . .119 C2
Wood Street Gn GU3 . . . .108 A2
Wood Street Inf Sch
GU3 . . . . .108 C3
Wood Vale SE22 . . . . .23 B8
Woodall Cl KT9 . . . . .56 D4
Woodall Ho TW7 . . . . .5 F4
Woodbank Rd BR1 . . . . . . .24 F5
Woodbarn The GU9 . . . . .125 C1
Woodbastwick Rd SE26 . .23 D4
Woodberry Cl
Ashford TW16 . . . . .15 A2
Chiddingfold GU8 . . . . . .191 A5
Woodbine Cl
Sandhurst GU47 . . . . .64 C7
Twickenham TW2 . . . . . . .16 D6
Woodbine Cotts
Egham TW20 . . . . .11 F2
Shalford GU4 . . . . .130 E2
Woodbine Gr SE20 . . . . . .23 B1
Woodbine La KT4 . . . . . . .58 C7
Woodbines Ave KT1 . . . . . .37 D6
Woodbourne Ave SW16 . . .21 D5
Woodbourne Cl SW16 . . . .21 E5
Woodbourne Dr KT10 . . . .55 F4
Woodbourne Gdns SM6 . .60 B5
Woodbridge Ave KT22 . . . .75 A1
Woodbridge Ct RH12 . . . .218 A5
Woodbridge Dr GU15 . . . .65 D7
Woodbridge Gr KT22 . . . . .75 A1
Woodbridge Hill GU2 . . . .109 B2
Woodbridge Hill Gdns
GU2 . . . . .109 A2
Woodbridge Manor
GU15 . . . . .65 D7
Woodbridge Mdws GU1 109 C2
Woodbridge Park Est
GU1 . . . . .109 C2
Woodbridge Rd
Blackwater GU17 . . . . .64 B5
Guildford GU1,GU2 . . . . .109 C2
Woodbrook Sch BR3 . . . . .43 F8
Woodbury Ave RH19 . . . .186 B1
Woodbury Cl
Biggin Hill TN16 . . . . .83 F1
East Grinstead RH19 . . . .206 B8
South Croydon CR0 . . . . . .61 F8
Woodbury Dr SM2 . . . . . . .59 C1
Woodbury Ho SE26 . . . . . .23 B5
Woodbury St SW17 . . . . . .20 E3
Woodby Dr SL5 . . . . .29 F2
Woodcock Dr GU24 . . . . . .49 C3
Woodcock Hill RH19 . . . .184 F6
Woodcock La GU24 . . . . . .49 B3
Woodcombe Cres SE23 . . .23 C7
Woodcot Gdns GU14 . . . . .84 D4
Woodcote Artington GU2 .130 B5
Cranleigh GU6 . . . . .174 B4
Farncombe GU7 . . . . .150 D6
Horley RH6 . . . . .161 C4
Woodcote Ave
Thornton Heath CR7 . . . . .42 B5
Wallington SM6 . . . . .60 B3
Woodcote Cl Epsom KT18 .76 D5
Kingston u T KT2 . . . . . . .17 F3
Woodcote Dr CR8 . . . . . . .60 D1
Woodcote End KT18 . . . . .76 D4
Woodcote Gn SM6 . . . . . . .60 C4
Woodcote Green Rd
KT18 . . . . .76 C4
Woodcote Grove Rd CR5 . .79 D5
Woodcote Hall
Epsom KT18 . . . . .76 D5
Wallington SM6 . . . . .60 B2
Woodcote High Sch CR5 . .79 D6
Woodcote Ho KT18 . . . . . .76 D4
Woodcote House Ct
KT18 . . . . .76 D4

Woodcote House Sch
GU20 ....48 B5
Woodcote Hurst KT18 ..76 C3
Woodcote Inf Sch CR5 ..79 D5
Woodcote Jun Sch CR5 ..79 D5
Woodcote La CR8 ......79 D7
Woodcote Mews
Epsom KT18 ....76 D4
Wallington SM6 ....60 B4
Woodcote Park Ave CR8 .76 C7
Woodcote Park Rd KT18 .76 C4
Woodcote Pl
North Ascot SL5 ....28 F8
1 West Norwood SE27 ..22 B3
Woodcote Rd Epsom KT18 76 D5
Forest Row RH18 ......206 F2
Wallington SM6 ....60 C2
Woodcote Side KT18 ...76 B4
Woodcote Valley Rd CR5,
CR8 ....79 E7
Woodcote Villas SE27 ..22 C3
Woodcott Ho 1 SW15 ..19 A8
Woodcott Terr GU12 ..126 D8
Woodcourt RH11 ....201 C1
Woodcrest Rd CR8 .....79 E6
Woodcrest Wlk RH2 ..118 E3
Woodcroft Rd
Crawley RH11 ....200 D4
Thornton Heath CR0,CR7 ..42 B3
Woodcut Rd GU10 ....145 F6
Woodend
Farnborough GU14 .....85 D3
Leatherhead KT22 ......95 C2
South Norwood SE19 ..22 C2
Sutton SM1 ....59 C8
Thames Ditton KT10 ...55 C8
Woodend Cl
Crawley RH10 ....202 A8
North Ascot SL5 ....28 F8
Woking GU21 ....89 A8
Woodend Dr SL5 ....29 B4
Woodend Pk KT11 .....73 C6
Woodend Rd GU16 .....86 C7
Woodenhill RG12 ......26 E1
Woodenhill Prim Sch
RG12 ....26 E2
Wooderson Cl SE25 ....42 E5
Woodfield KT21 ....75 D2
Woodfield Ave
Streatham SW16 ......21 D5
Wallington SM5 ....60 A3
Woodfield Cl
Ashstead KT21 ....75 D2
Coulsdon CR5 ....99 C8
Crawley RH10 ....201 E7
Redhill RH1 ....118 E3
South Norwood SE19 ..22 C1
Woodfield Gdns KT3 ..38 F4
Woodfield Gr SW16 ....21 D5
Woodfield Hill CR5 ....99 B8
Woodfield Ho
1 Forest Hill SE23 ....23 D5
Hinchley Wood KT7 ....55 F8
New Malden KT3 ....38 F4
Woodfield La KT21 ....75 E2
Woodfield Rd
Ashstead KT21 ....75 D2
Cranford TW4,TW5 .....4 B5
Crawley RH10 ....201 F7
Hinchley Wood KT7 ....55 F8
Rudgwick RH12 ....214 D7
Woodfield Sch RH1 ..119 E6
Woodfield Way RH1 ..118 E3
Woodfields Ct SM1 ....59 C7
Woodfields The CR2 ...80 F8
Woodford Gn RG12 ....27 F5
Woodgate Ave KT9 ....56 D5
Woodgate Dr SW16 ....21 D1
Woodgates Cl RH13 ..217 F3
Woodgavil SM7 ....77 F3
Woodger Cl GU4 ......110 C3
Woodgrange Ct 1 BR2 ..44 F1
Woodhall Ave SE21 ....22 F5
Woodhall Dr SE21 .....22 F5
Woodhall La SL5 ....48 E8
Woodham La
New Haw KT15 ....52 B1
Sheerwater GU21,KT15 ..70 D7
Woodham Park Rd KT15 .51 F1
Woodham Park Way
KT15 ....70 F8
Woking GU21 ....69 F4
Woodham Rise GU21 ..70 A4
Woodham Waye GU21 ..70 B5
Woodhatch Rd RH1,RH2 139 E5
Woodhatch Spinney CR5 .79 E5
Woodhaw TW20 ....12 B4
Woodhayes RH6 ......161 B4
Woodhayes Rd SW19,
SW20 ....19 C2
Woodhill GU23 ....90 D2
Woodhill Ct GU23 .....90 E2
Woodhill La GU5 .....152 F4
Woodhouse La RH5 ...155 A8
Woodhouse St RG42 ...26 E8
Woodhurst La RH8 ...122 E4
Woodhurst Pk RH8 ...122 E5
Woodhyrst Gdns CR8 ..80 B4
Wooding Gr 15 RH11 ..201 B1
Woodland Ave GU1 ...174 F3
Woodland Cl
East Horsley KT24 ....112 F8
Horsham RH13 ....218 B4
Oatlands Park KT13 ...53 D6

Woodland Cl continued
West Ewell KT19 ....57 E4
West Norwood SE19 ...22 E2
Woodland Cotts GU8 .190 B8
Woodland Cres GU14 ..85 C6
Woodland Ct Ewell KT17 ..76 F7
Oxted RH8 ....122 E7
Sutton SM1 ....59 A4
Woodland Dr
Crawley Down RH10 ..204 B8
East Horsley KT24 ....112 F8
Farnham GU10 ....146 B6
Ockley RH5 ....178 A5
Woodland Gdns
Isleworth TW7 ....5 E4
Selsdon CR2 ....81 C8
Woodland Gr KT13 ....53 D6
Woodland Hill SE19 ...22 F3
Woodland Mews SW16 ..21 E5
Woodland Rd
Thornton Heath CR7 ...42 A5
West Norwood SE19 ...22 F3
Woodland Rise GU8 ..122 C5
Woodland View GU7 ..129 E1
Woodland Way
Caterham CR3 ....120 E8
Croydon CR0,CR9 ......43 E1
Horsham RH13 ....218 B4
Kingswood KT20 ....97 E4
Merton SM4 ....39 F5
Mitcham CR4 ....21 A1
Purley CR8 ....80 A6
Tolworth KT5 ....57 B8
West Wickham BR4 ....63 C7
Weybridge KT13 ....53 D5
Woodlands
Beckenham BR3 ....24 B1
Bromley BR2 ....44 F5
Chertsey KT15 ....52 E7
Crawley RH10 ....202 D8
Horley RH6 ....161 D4
Send Marsh GU23 .....90 F2
West Barnes SW20 ....39 D5
14 Woking GU22 ....89 E8
Woodlands Ave
Heath End GU9 ......125 F7
Kingston u T KT3 ......38 D8
Redhill RH1 ....118 F1
West Byfleet KT14,KT15 ..70 F7
Worcester Park KT4 ...58 A8
Woodlands Cl Ascot SL5 ..28 F7
Ash GU12 ....106 A5
Claygate KT10 ....55 F3
Cranleigh GU6 ....174 F2
Crawley Down RH10 ..204 B7
Farnborough GU17 ....64 E1
Ottershaw KT16 ....51 B1
Woodlands Copse KT21 .75 D3
Woodlands Ct
11 Bromley BR1 ......44 F8
Dulwich SE22 ....23 B8
Sandhurst GU47 ......45 F1
7 Woking GU21 ....69 A1
12 Woking GU22 ......89 E8
Woodlands Dr
South Godstone RH9 ..142 E6
Sunbury TW16 ....35 C7
Woodlands Gdns KT18 ..77 C2
Woodlands Gr
Coulsdon CR5 ....79 B2
Isleworth TW7 ....5 E5
Woodlands Ho GU21 ..70 C5
Woodlands La
Haslemere GU27 .....207 F7
Stoke D'Abernon KT11 ..74 B2
Windlesham GU20,GU24 ..48 E3
Woodlands Par TW15 ..14 C2
Woodlands Pk
Addlestone KT15 ......51 F5
Box Hill KT20 ....116 B4
Guildford GU1 ....110 B2
Sheerwater GU21 .....70 C5
Woodlands Rd
Camberley GU15 ......65 B5
East Grinstead RH19 .186 A4
Effingham KT23 ......113 F6
Epsom KT18 ....76 A4
Farnborough GU14 ....84 D6
Guildford GU1 ....109 D5
Hambledon GU8 .....171 D1
Isleworth TW7 ....5 E5
Leatherhead KT22 .....74 D1
Mortlake SW13 ....7 F4
Pyrford KT14 ....70 F5
Redhill RH1 ....139 F7
Surbiton KT6 ....37 D2
Virginia Water GU25 ..31 C5
Woodlands Rd E GU25 ..31 C5
Woodlands Rd W GU25 ..31 C5
Woodlands Ride SL5 ...29 A3
Woodlands Sch SE12 ..24 D8
Woodlands St SE13 ...24 D8
Woodlands The
Isleworth TW7 ....5 E5
Lewisham SE13 ....24 D8
Mitcham CR4 ....41 A6
Smallfield RH6 ....162 B3
South Norwood SE19 ..22 C1
Thames Ditton KT10 ...55 C8
Wallington SM6 ....60 B2
Woodlands Way
Ashstead KT21 ....76 B2
Box Hill KT20 ....116 C5
Woodlands Wlk GU17 ..64 E1
Woodlark Glade GU15 ..65 D7
Woodlarks Camp Site
GU10 ....146 F7
Woodlawn Cres TW2 ..16 B6

Woodlawn Dr TW13 ...15 D6
Woodlawn Gr GU21 ...69 F4
Woodlea Cotts RH12 .215 F7
Woodlea Dr BR2 ....44 E4
Woodlea Prim Sch CR3 101 F5
Woodlee Cl GU25 ......31 C7
Woodleigh 1 KT5 .....37 F4
Woodleigh Gdns SW16 ..21 E5
Woodley Cl SW17 .....20 F1
Woodley Ho GU7 .....150 E8
Woodley La SM5 ......59 E6
Woodlodge Ashstead KT21 75 E2
4 Wimbledon SW19 ...19 F3
Woodman Rd CR5 .....79 D4
Woodmancote Ct RH12 217 D5
Woodmancote Gdns
KT14 ....71 A6
Woodmancott Cl RG12 ..27 F3
Woodmancourt GU7 ..150 C8
Woodmans Hill RH11 .201 C2
Woodmansterne La
Banstead SM7 ....78 D4
Wallington SM5,SM6 ...79 A7
Woodmansterne SM7 ..78 D4
Woodmansterne Prim Sch
Streatham SW16 ......41 D8
Woodmansterne SM7 ..78 F5
Woodmansterne Rd
Coulsdon CR5 ....79 C4
Streatham SW16 ......41 D8
Wallington SM5 ....59 E2
Woodmansterne Sta CR5 79 B3
Woodmere RG12 ......27 E5
Woodmere Ave CR0 ...43 D2
Woodmere Cl CR0 .....43 D2
Woodmere Gdns CR0 ..43 D2
Woodmere Way BR3 ..44 D4
Woodnook Rd SW16 ..21 B3
Woodpecker Cl
Cobham KT11 ....73 E7
Crondall GU10 ....124 D8
Woodpecker La RH5 .158 C2
Woodpecker Mount CR0 .62 F2
Woodpecker Way
Turners Hill RH10 ....204 C5
Woking GU22 ....89 D3
Woodpeckers
Bracknell RG12 ....27 B5
Witley GU8 ....170 E7
Woodplace Cl CR5 .....79 C1
Woodplace La CR5 .....99 C7
Woodridge Cl RG12 ...27 C6
Woodrising KT13 ......53 C4
Woodrough Copse GU5 152 A5
Woodrow Dr RG40 ....25 F6
Woodroyd Ave RH6 ..160 F2
Woodroyd Gdns RH6 .160 F1
Woodruff Ave GU1 ...110 B4
Woods Hill Cl RH19 ..206 D6
Woods Hill La RH19 .206 D6
Woodshore Cl GU25 ...31 B3
Woodside
Blackwater GU17 ......64 C3
1 Farnborough GU14 ..85 B7
Fetcham KT22 ....94 B5
Horsham RH13 ....218 B4
Lower Kingswood KT20 ..117 F7
Sandhurst GU15 ......64 F7
Walton-on-T KT12 .....35 A1
West Horsley KT24 ....92 C1
Weybridge KT13 ....53 A5
Wimbledon SW19 .....19 F3
Woodside Ave
Croydon SE25 ....43 B4
Hersham KT12 ....54 B6
Thames Ditton KT10 ...36 C2
Woodside Cl
Caterham CR3 ....100 E3
Chiddingfold GU8 ....191 B4
Knaphill GU21 ....68 D2
Tolworth KT5 ....38 C2
Woodside Cotts GU8 .148 C3
Woodside Court Rd CR0,
CR9 ....43 A2
Woodside Cres RH6 ..162 A3
Woodside Gn CR0,SE25 ..43 A3
Woodside Ho SW19 ...19 F2
Woodside Jun & Inf Schs
CR0 ....43 A2
Woodside La SL4 ......9 C3
Woodside Park Est GU7 150 F4
Woodside Pk SE25 ....43 B3
Woodside Rd
Beare Green RH5 ....157 D3
Chiddingfold GU8 ....191 B5
Cobham KT11 ....74 A6
Crawley RH10 ....201 F8
Croydon SE25 ....43 B3
Farnborough GU11 ...104 F7
Guildford GU2 ....108 F2
Heath End GU9 ......125 E7
Kingston u T KT2 .....17 E1
Kingston u T KT3 .....38 E7
Purley CR8 ....79 E6
Sutton SM1 ....59 C7
Winkfield SL4 ....9 B2
Woodside Sta SE25 ...43 B3
Woodside Way
Croydon CR0 ....43 C3
Redhill,Earlswood RH1 .140 A8
Redhill,South Earlswood
RH1 ....140 A3
Streatham CR4 ....41 C8
Virginia Water GU25 ..31 B6
Woodsome Lodge KT13 .53 C4
Woodspring Rd SW19 ..19 E6

Woodstock
East Grinstead RH19 .185 C2
West Clandon GU4 ...111 B7
Wokingham RG40 .....25 C6
Woodstock Ave
Cheam SM3,SM4 ......39 F2
Isleworth TW7 ....6 A2
Woodstock Cl
Cranleigh GU6 ....174 F1
Horsham RH12 ......217 D5
Woking GU21 ....69 E3
Woodstock Ct KT17 ...76 F7
Woodstock Gdns BR3 ..24 B1
Woodstock Gr GU7 ..150 E7
Woodstock La N KT6 ..56 C8
Woodstock La S KT10,
KT6 ....56 C6
Woodstock Rd
Coulsdon CR5 ....79 C4
Croydon CR0,CR9 .....61 D7
Wallington SM5 ....60 A5
Woodstock Rise SM3 ..39 F2
Woodstock Way CR4 ..41 C7
Woodstocks GU14 .....85 D6
Woodstone Ave KT17,KT4 58 A5
Woodsway KT22 ....74 E5
Woodsyre SE19,SE26 ..22 F4
Woodthorpe Rd
Ashford TW15 ....13 D4
Staines TW15 ....13 D4
Woodvale Ave SE25 ...42 F7
Woodvale Ct SE25 ....42 F6
Woodvale Wlk SE27 ..22 C3
Woodview KT9 ....75 C8
Woodview Cl
Hamsey Green CR2 ....81 B5
Kingston u T SW15 ...18 D4
Woodview Ct KT13 ....53 C5
Woodville Cl
Blackwater GU17 ......64 B5
Teddington TW11 .....17 A4
Woodville Gdns KT6 ..37 D2
Woodville Pl CR3 ....100 C5
Woodville Rd
Leatherhead KT22 .....95 B7
Merton SM4 ....40 A5
Richmond TW10 ......17 C5
South Norwood CR7 ..42 D6
Woodville Sch The KT22 .95 B7
Woodward Cl KT10 ...55 F4
Woodwards RH11 ....201 C1
Woodway Camberley GU15 65 B5
Guildford GU1 ....110 B2
Woodwicks GU6 .....174 F2
Woodyard La SE21 ....22 E8
Woodyers Cl GU5 ....152 B7
Wool Rd SW20 ....19 B2
Woolborough Cl RH10 ..201 E7
Woolborough La
Crawley RH10 ....181 F1
Crawley,Three Bridges
RH10 ....202 A8
South Nutfield RH1 ..161 F8
Woolborough Rd RH10 201 E7
Woolf Dr RG40 ....25 C7
Woolf Meml Cotts RG40 .25 C7
Wolford Cl RG42 ....8 C1
Woolfords La GU8 ...169 B7
Woolhampton Way RG12 27 D4
Woolhams CR3 ....101 A1
Woollards Rd GU12 ..106 B4
Woolmead Ct GU9 ...125 C3
Woolmead Rd GU9 ...125 C3
Woolmead The GU9 ..125 C3
Woolmer Hill Ho GU27 .207 C6
Woolmer Hill Rd GU27 207 D7
Woolmer Hill Sch GU27 207 D7
Woolmer View GU26 .188 D3
Woolsack Way GU7 ..150 F4
Woolstone Rd SE23,SE6 .23 E6
Wooshill La
Wokingham RG41 .....25 A5
Wokingham RG41 .....25 A6
Wootton KT10 ....55 C6
Wootton Cl KT18 ......76 F3
Wootton Grange 3 GU22 89 E8
Worbeck Rd SE20 .....43 C7
Worcester Cl Croydon CR0 63 A8
Farnborough GU14 ....85 B7
Mitcham CR4 ....41 A7
Worcester Ct
Ashford TW15 ....14 B3
Walton-on-T KT12 .....35 C1
2 Walton-on-T KT12 ..54 C8
Worcester Park KT4 ...57 E7
Worcester Dr TW15 ...14 B3
Worcester Gdns KT4 ..57 E7
Worcester Ho RH1 ...118 E3
Worcester Park Rd KT4 .57 D7
Worcester Park Sta KT4 .39 A1
Worcester Rd
Belmont SM2 ....59 B3
Crawley RH10 ....201 E2
Guildford GU2 ....108 F3
Reigate RH2 ....118 A2
11 Wimbledon SW19 ..19 F3
Wordsworth RG12 ....26 F4
Wordsworth Ave CR8 ..80 D4
Wordsworth Cl RH10 .202 B8
Wordsworth Dr KT4,SM3 .58 C6
Wordsworth Mead RH1 .119 B3
Wordsworth Pl RH12 .217 E7
Wordsworth Rd
Addlestone KT15 ......52 D6
Hampton TW12 ....15 F4
Penge SE20 ....23 D1
Wallington SM6 ......60 D4

Wordsworth Rise 6
RH19 ....185 C1
Works Rd KT15 ....52 B2
World Bsns Ctr TW6 ...3 C6
World's End KT11 .....73 A5
Worlds End Hill RG12 ..27 F3
Wormley La GU8 .....171 E1
Worple Ave Isleworth TW7 ..6 A2
Staines TW18 ....13 B2
Wimbledon SW19 .....19 D1
Worple Ct SW19 ......19 E2
Worple Prim Sch TW7 ..6 A3
Worple Rd Epsom KT18 ..76 D4
Epsom KT18 ....76 E5
Isleworth TW7 ....6 A3
Leatherhead KT22 .....95 B4
Staines TW18 ....13 B1
Wimbledon SW19,SW20 ..39 D8
Worple Road Mews
SW19 ....19 F2
Worple St SW14 ....7 D4
Worple Way TW10 .....6 E3
Worplesdon Hill Heath House
Rd GU22 ....88 D5
Worplesdon Prim Sch
GU3 ....108 D4
Worplesdon Rd GU2 .109 A4
Worplesdon Sta GU22 ..89 B3
Worsfold Cl GU23 .....90 B4
Worslade Rd SW17 ...20 D1
Worsley Bridge Jun Sch
BR3 ....24 A1
Worsley Bridge Rd
Beckenham BR3,SE6 ..24 A2
Catford SE6 ....23 F3
Worsley Ho SE23 .....23 B6
Worsley Rd GU16 .....85 F7
Worsted Gn RH1 .....119 D6
Worsted La RH19 ....206 B8
Worth Abbey* RH10 .203 B1
Worth Park Ave RH10 .202 C7
Worth Rd RH10 ......202 C6
Worth Sch RH10 .....203 B1
Worth Way RH10 ....202 E5
Worthfield Cl KT19 ...57 D3
Worthing Rd Heston TW5 ..4 F8
Horsham RH12 ......217 B1
Worthington Cl CR4 ..41 B6
Worthington Ho 16 SW2 .22 A7
Worthington Rd KT6 ..37 F1
Wortley Rd CR0 ......42 A2
Worton Ct TW7 ....5 E3
Worton Gdns TW7 .....5 D5
Worton Hall Est TW7 ..5 D3
Worton Rd TW7 ....5 E4
Worton Way TW3,TW7 ..5 D5
Wotton Dr RH5 ......134 E3
Wotton Way SM2 .....58 C1
Wr Twr Hill CR0,CR2 ..61 D6
Wrabness Way TW18 ..33 B8
Wray Cl RH19 ....206 D6
Wray Common Prim Sch
RH2 ....118 D2
Wray Common Rd RH2 .118 D2
Wray Ho 11 SW2 ......21 E7
Wray La RH2 ....118 D4
Wray Mill Ho RH2 ...118 E3
Wray Mill Pk RH2 ...118 E3
Wray Park Rd RH2 ..118 C2
Wray Rd SM2 ....58 F2
Wrayfield Ave RH2 ..118 C2
Wrayfield Rd SM3 ....58 D7
Wraylands Dr RH2 ..118 D3
Wraymead Pl RH2 ...118 B2
Wraymill Ct 4 RH2 ..118 D1
Wraysbury Cl TW4 .....4 E2
Wraysbury Gdns TW18 .12 E4
Wraysbury Rd TW18 ..12 C5
Wraysbury Sta TW19 ..11 C1
Wrecclesham Hill GU10 145 E5
Wrecclesham Rd GU10,
GU9 ....145 F8
Wrekin The GU14 .....85 E1
Wren Cl Horsham RH12 .217 D7
Selsdon CR2 ....62 D2
Wren Cres KT15 ....52 D5
Wren Ct Ash GU12 ...106 B3
Crawley RH10 ....201 E3
South Croydon CR0 ...61 D6
Wren Ho 4 TW12 .....16 B2
Wren St RH10 ....204 C5
Wren Way GU14 ....84 F7
Wren's Hill KT22 ......74 C4
Wrens Ave TW15 ......14 C4
Wrenthorpe Rd BR1 ..24 E4
Wright Cl RH10 ......202 C2
Wright Gdns TW17 ...34 A4
Wright Rd TW5 ....4 C7
Wright's Row SM5 ....60 B6
Wrighton Ct SM1 .....58 F4
Wrights Rd SE25 .....42 E6
Wriotsley Way KT15 ..52 A4
Wrotham Hill GU8 ...192 E3
Wrotham Ho BR3 .....23 F1
Wroxham RG12 ....26 F4
Wroxham Wlk RH10 .202 B4
Wrythe Gn SM5 ....59 F7
Wrythe Green Rd SM5 .59 F7
Wrythe La SM5 ....59 E7
Wyatt Cl TW13 ....15 D7
Wyatt Park Mans 1 SW2 21 E6
Wyatt Park Rd SW2 ..21 F6
Wyatt Rd TW18 ......13 A3
Wyatt's Almshouses
GU7 ....151 A6
Wyatt's Cl GU7 ......151 A6
Wych Elm Rise GU1 ..130 E6
Wych Hill GU22 ....89 C8

Wych Hill La GU22 ....89 E8
Wych Hill Pk GU22 ....89 D8
Wych Hill Rise GU22 ....89 D8
Wych Hill Way GU22 ....89 D8
Wyche Gr CR2 ....61 D2
Wychelm Rd GU18 ....67 C8
Wychwood RH14 ....212 D3
Wychwood Ave
  Bracknell RG12 ....27 F5
  South Norwood CR7 ....42 C6
Wychwood Cl Ash GU12 .105 F2
  Ashford TW16 ....15 A2
Wychwood Pl GU15 ....66 B8
Wychwood Way SE19 ....22 D2
Wycliffe Bldgs GU2 ..130 C2
Wycliffe Ct RH11 ....200 E3
Wycliffe Rd SW19 ....20 B2
Wydell Cl SM4 ....39 D3
Wydenhurst Rd CR0,CR9 .43 B2
Wye Cl TW15 ....14 B4
Wyecliffe Gdns RH1 ..119 C5
Wyeth's Mews KT17 ....76 F6
Wyeth's Rd KT17 ....76 F6
Wyke Ave GU12 ......106 E3
Wyke Bglws GU12 ....106 D3
Wyke Cl TW7 ....5 F8
Wyke La GU12 ......106 D2
Wyke Prim Sch GU3 ..106 F4
Wyke Rd SW20 ....39 C7
Wykeham Cl UB7 ......3 A8
Wykeham Ho
  Farnborough GU14 ....105 C8
  Merton SW19 ....40 A8
Wykeham Rd
  Farnham GU9 ......125 C3
  Guildford GU1 ......110 D2
Wykehurst Ho SW19 ....20 D3
Wylam RG12 ....26 F4
Wyldewood SL5 ....29 D3
Wyleu St SE23 ....23 E8
Wymering Ct GU14 ....85 D3
Wynash Gdns SM5 ....59 E5
Wynbourne Ct SE20 ....43 B7
Wyncliffe Ct BR2 ....44 E5
Wyncote Way CR2 ....62 D2
Wyndham Ave KT11 ....73 A6
Wyndham Cl SM2 ....59 A3
Wyndham Cres
  Cranleigh GU6 ......174 A3
  Twickenham TW4 ....5 A1

Wyndham Rd
  Kingston u T KT2 ....17 F1
  Woking GU21 ....69 B1
Wyndham St GU12 ....105 C1
Wyndhams GU22 ....70 B3
Wynell Rd SE23 ......23 D5
Wynfields GU16 ......85 F3
Wynlea Cl RH10 ....204 A8
Wynne Ct 4 TW7 ....6 A4
Wynnstow Pk RH8 ..122 F4
Wynsham Way GU20 ....48 B6
Wynton Gdns SE25 ....42 F4
Wynton Gr KT12 ......54 A7
Wyphurst Rd GU6 ....174 E4
Wyresdale RG12 ......27 F2
Wysemead RH6 ......161 C4
Wythegate TW18 ......12 F1
Wyvern Cl
  2 Ash Vale GU12 ....105 F5
  Bracknell RG12 ....27 A5
Wyvern Est The KT3 ....39 A5
Wyvern Pl KT15 ......52 B6
Wyvern Rd CR8 ......61 B1

Y

Yaffle Rd KT13 ......53 C1
Yale Cl Hounslow TW4 ....4 F2
  Sandhurst GU47 ......45 F2
Yarborough Rd 1 SW19 .40 D8
Yarbridge Cl SM2 ....59 B1
Yard Mead TW20 ......12 A5
Yardley RG12 ....26 F4
Yardley Cl RH2 ......118 B3
Yardley Ct SM3 ......58 C6
Yarm Cl KT22 ....95 C4
Yarm Court Rd KT22 ....95 C4
Yarm Way KT22 ......95 D4
Yarmouth Cl RH10 ....202 A4
Yarnold Cl RG40 ......25 F7
Yarrow Cl RH12 ....217 E5
Yateley Ct CR8 ......80 C5
Yatesbury Cl GU9 ....145 F7
Yattendon Jun Sch RH6 161 A4
Yattendon Rd RH6 ....161 B3
Yaverland Dr GU19 ....47 D2
Ye Market CR0 ....61 D5
Yeats Cl RH1 ......139 C6
Yeend Cl KT8 ....36 A5

Yehudi Menuhin Sch
  KT11 ....94 A8
Yellowcress Dr GU24 ...68 A3
Yelverton Ct 2 KT23 ...94 A1
Yelverton Lodge TW1 ....17 C8
Yenston Cl SM4 ......40 A3
Yeoman Cl SE27 ......22 B5
Yeoman Ct
  6 Carshalton SM1 ....59 D5
  Heston TW5 ....4 F7
Yeoman Way RH1 ....140 B4
Yeomanry Cl KT17 ....76 F7
Yeomans Cl Ash GU10 .126 F8
  Farnborough GU14 ....85 A5
Yeomans Croft KT23 ....94 A2
Yeomans Mews TW7 ....5 D2
Yeomans Way GU15 ....65 E5
Yeoveney Cl TW19 ....12 D6
Yeovil Cl GU14 ......85 D1
Yeovil Rd
  Farnborough GU14 ....85 E1
  Sandhurst GU47 ......45 E1
Yeovilton Pl KT2 ......17 C3
Yetminster Rd GU14 ....85 D1
Yew Cnr RG12 ....27 C6
Yew Ct Crawley RH11 ..201 D5
  1 East Grinstead RH19 .185 D2
Yew La RH19 ......185 B3
Yew Pl KT13 ....53 F7
Yew Tree Bottom Rd
  KT17,KT18 ....77 C2
Yew Tree Cl
  Chipstead CR5 ....98 F8
  Farnborough GU14 ....84 C3
  Horley RH6 ....161 A4
  New Malden KT4 ......38 E1
Yew Tree Cotts KT10 ....55 D8
Yew Tree Ct 10 SM2 ....59 C3
Yew Tree Dr
  Caterham CR3 ......100 F2
  Guildford GU1 ......109 C6
Yew Tree Gdns KT18 ....76 C4
Yew Tree Ho KT4 ......38 E1
Yew Tree La RH2 ....118 B4
Yew Tree Rd
  Charlwood RH6 ......180 E7
  Dorking RH4 ......115 A1
  Witley GU8 ....170 D6
Yew Tree Wlk
  Effingham KT24 ....113 D8

Yew Tree Wlk continued
  Frimley GU16 ....65 F1
  Hounslow TW4 ....4 F2
  South Croydon CR8 ....61 C1
Yew Trees TW17 ......33 F5
Yewbank Cl CR8 ......80 D4
Yewdale Cl BR1 ......24 E2
Yewens GU8 ....191 B5
Yewlands Cl SM7 ......78 C4
Yewlands Wlk RH11 ..200 D4
Yews The Ashford TW15 ..14 B4
  West Byfleet KT14 ....71 E7
Yewtree Rd BR3 ......43 F6
Yewtrees TW20 ......32 C6
Yockley Cl GU15 ......66 D3
Yolland Cl GU9 ......125 C7
York Ave
  East Grinstead RH19 ..206 A8
  Mortlake SW14 ....7 C2
York Cl Byfleet KT14 ....71 E7
  Horsham RH13 ......217 F3
  Morden SM4 ....40 B5
York Cres GU11 ....104 F1
York Ct Beckenham BR3 ..44 D8
  Epsom KT19 ....76 A7
  Kingston u T KT2 ....17 D2
  Wallington SM6 ......60 C4
York Gdns KT12 ......54 D8
York Hill SE27,SW16 ....22 B5
York Ho Bracknell RG42 ..26 F8
  Forest Hill SE26 ......23 C3
  4 Kingston u T KT2 ....17 F1
  Richmond TW9 ....7 A6
  South Norwood SE25 ...42 E5
York Rd Aldershot GU11 .104 F1
  Ash GU12 ....106 A3
  Belmont SM1,SM2 ....59 A3
  Biggin Hill TN16 ....103 B8
  Byfleet KT14 ....71 E7
  Camberley GU15 ......65 D7
  Crawley RH10 ......201 E2
  Farnborough GU14 ....84 F1
  Farnborough,South Farnborough
    GU14 ....85 C1
  Farnham GU9 ......125 C1
  Guildford GU1 ......130 D8
  Hounslow TW3 ....5 B4
  Kingston u T KT2 ....17 F1
  3 Richmond TW10 ......6 F2
  Selsdon CR2 ....62 D1

York Rd continued
  Teddington TW11 ......16 E4
  Thornton Heath CR0 ....42 A2
  Weybridge KT13 ......53 C6
  Wimbledon SW19 ......20 C2
  Woking GU22 ....69 E1
York St Carshalton CR4 ...41 A2
  Twickenham TW1 ......17 A7
York Town Ind Est GU15 .65 A5
York Way Chessington KT9 .56 E3
  Feltham TW13 ....15 F5
  Sandhurst GU47 ......64 B8
Yorke Gate CR3 ......100 D5
Yorke Gdns RH2 ....118 A2
Yorke Rd RH2 ......118 A2
Yorkshire Rd CR4 ....41 E5
Yorktown Rd
  Sandhurst GU47 ......64 C7
  Sandhurst GU47 ......64 E7
Youlden Cl GU15 ......66 A5
Youlden Dr GU15 ......66 B6
Young St Fetcham KT22 ...94 F3
  Leatherhead KT22 ....95 A3
Youngman RH7 ......165 B4
Youngs Dr GU12 ....105 F2
Youngstroat La GU24 ....50 E1
Yukon Rd SW12 ......21 B8

Z

Zealand Ave UB7 ......2 E7
Zenith Ct GU47 ......45 E1
Zennor Rd SW12 ......21 C7
Zermatt Rd CR7 ......42 C5
Zig Zag Rd Kenley CR8 ..80 C3
  Mickleham KT20,RH4,RH5 .115 D4
Zinnia Dr GU24 ......68 A3
Zion Pl CR7 ....42 D5
Zion Rd CR7, SE25 ....42 D5
Zodiac Ct CR0 ....42 B1

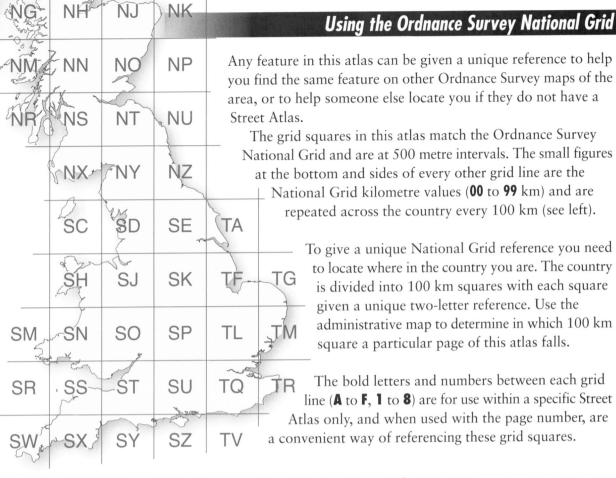

Any feature in this atlas can be given a unique reference to help you find the same feature on other Ordnance Survey maps of the area, or to help someone else locate you if they do not have a Street Atlas.

The grid squares in this atlas match the Ordnance Survey National Grid and are at 500 metre intervals. The small figures at the bottom and sides of every other grid line are the National Grid kilometre values (**00** to **99** km) and are repeated across the country every 100 km (see left).

To give a unique National Grid reference you need to locate where in the country you are. The country is divided into 100 km squares with each square given a unique two-letter reference. Use the administrative map to determine in which 100 km square a particular page of this atlas falls.

The bold letters and numbers between each grid line (**A** to **F**, **1** to **8**) are for use within a specific Street Atlas only, and when used with the page number, are a convenient way of referencing these grid squares.

Example *The railway bridge over DARLEY GREEN RD in grid square B1*

Step 1: Identify the two-letter reference, in this example the page is in **SP**

Step 2: Identify the 1 km square in which the railway bridge falls. Use the figures in the southwest corner of this square: Eastings **17**, Northings **74**. This gives a unique reference: **SP 17 74**, accurate to 1 km.

Step 3: To give a more precise reference accurate to 100 m you need to estimate how many tenths along and how many tenths up this 1 km square the feature is (to help with this the 1 km square is divided into four 500 m squares). This makes the bridge about **8** tenths along and about **1** tenth up from the southwest corner.

This gives a unique reference: **SP 178 741**, accurate to 100 m.

Eastings (read from left to right along the bottom) come before Northings (read from bottom to top). If you have trouble remembering say to yourself "Along the hall, THEN up the stairs"!

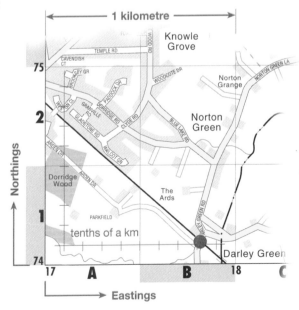

Addresses

Name and Address	Telephone	Page	Grid reference

Name and Address	Telephone	Page	Grid reference

PHILIP'S MAPS

the Gold Standard for serious driving

◆ Philip's street atlases cover every county in England and Wales, plus much of Scotland

◆ All our atlases use the same style of mapping, with the same colours and symbols, so you can move with confidence from one atlas to the next

◆ Widely used by the emergency services, transport companies and local authorities

◆ Created from the most up-to-date and detailed information available from Ordnance Survey

◆ Based on the National Grid

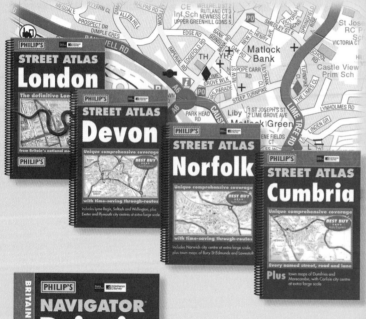

For national mapping, choose **Philip's Navigator Britain** – the most detailed road atlas available of England, Wales and Scotland. Hailed by Auto Express as 'the ultimate road atlas', this is the only one-volume atlas to show every road and lane in Britain.

Street atlases currently available

England

- Bedfordshire
- Berkshire
- Birmingham and West Midlands
- Bristol and Bath
- Buckinghamshire
- Cambridgeshire
- Cheshire
- Cornwall
- Cumbria
- Derbyshire
- Devon
- Dorset
- County Durham and Teesside
- Essex
- North Essex
- South Essex
- Gloucestershire
- North Hampshire
- South Hampshire
- Herefordshire Monmouthshire
- Hertfordshire
- Isle of Wight
- Kent
- East Kent
- West Kent
- Lancashire
- Leicestershire and Rutland
- Lincolnshire
- London
- Greater Manchester
- Merseyside
- Norfolk
- Northamptonshire
- Northumberland
- Nottinghamshire
- Oxfordshire
- Shropshire
- Somerset
- Staffordshire
- Suffolk
- Surrey
- East Sussex
- West Sussex
- Tyne and Wear
- Warwickshire
- Birmingham and West Midlands
- Wiltshire and Swindon
- Worcestershire
- East Yorkshire Northern Lincolnshire
- North Yorkshire
- South Yorkshire
- West Yorkshire

Wales

- Anglesey, Conwy and Gwynedd
- Cardiff, Swansea and The Valleys
- Carmarthenshire, Pembrokeshire and Swansea
- Ceredigion and South Gwynedd
- Denbighshire, Flintshire, Wrexham
- Herefordshire Monmouthshire
- Powys

Scotland

- Aberdeenshire
- Ayrshire
- Edinburgh and East Central Scotland
- Fife and Tayside
- Glasgow and West Central Scotland
- Inverness and Moray

All England and Wales coverage

How to order

Philip's maps and atlases are available from bookshops, motorway services and petrol stations. You can order direct from the publisher by phoning **01903 828503** or online at **www.philips-maps.co.uk**

For bulk orders only, phone 020 7644 6940